Leyton Orient

The Complete Record

breedonbooks

Leyton Orient

The Complete Record

Every game, every scorer, every player and every attendance. Memorable matches, complete history, pen pictures, manager profiles, appearance records

NEILSON N. KAUFMAN and ALAN E. RAVENHILL

First published in Great Britain in 2006 by
The Breedon Books Publishing Company Limited
Breedon House, 3 The Parker Centre, Derby, DE21 4SZ.

ISBN 1 85983 480 9

Printed and bound by Biddles Ltd, Hardwick Industrial Estate,
King's Lynn, Norfolk.

Contents

Foreword

It gives me immense pleasure to congratulate Leyton Orient Football Club on the publication of this excellent official history.

Clubs like Leyton Orient are at the heart of English football. Through many ups and downs and several name changes over the years, they have maintained the loyalty of their fans in East London and beyond.

Most of their history has, of course, been spent in the lower Divisions, but in their one season in the top Division, the old Football League Division One, they famously launched their campaign with a 1–0 win at Brisbane Road against Manchester United.

More recently, a mere 28 years go, they reached an FA Challenge Cup semi-final, beating Norwich City, Blackburn Rovers, Chelsea and Middlesbrough on the way.

For older O's supporters, these will be memorable achievements and moments they will never forget. Football produces such moments, that is why it is such a wonderful game.

Who knows what the next 100 years might produce?

We congratulate the O's on their 125th anniversary and on the achievement of gaining promotion under manager Martin Ling in 2005–06.

Geoff Thompson
Chairman
The Football Association
May 2006

Foreword

It gives me great pleasure to write the foreword for *Leyton Orient: The Complete Record* – particularly at this exciting time in the history of the club.

2006 is the club's anniversary year on two fronts: 125 years since formation and 100 years of Football League membership, and it also coincides with the major steps forward we are making both on and off the field. The promotion achieved by the side at the end of the 2005–06 season provided me with my best moment of 30 years in sport, and that's with all due respect to the great champions I've worked with. It was the culmination of so much hard work and effort by everyone at the club, and the manner in which it was achieved with literally seconds of the season remaining that must mark it down as one of the most dramatic footballing climaxes of all time.

It is to Martin Ling's eternal credit that he has turned the fortunes of our team around. We would have been bottom of the Football League had we lost his first game in charge – and here we are now celebrating a magnificent promotion-winning season.

Martin, his staff and the players have deservedly written their names in the history of the club, and now their challenge changes to taking on unchartered territory.

It was also highly appropriate that the first season of the magnificent new West Stand at the Matchroom Stadium was capped with promotion. The facilities, both for viewing the matches and for hospitality, are of the highest quality, and, therefore, deserving of a better stage.

Likewise, we are in the process of developing a new North Stand which will bring about a much-desired return to a four-sided stadium. The increased capacity and facilities that come with the whole redevelopment help to make the club more financially self-sufficient, and that is imperative for its long-term survival and growth. Leyton is in the middle of an area which will undergo enormous regeneration over the next few years as we approach the Olympic Games of 2012, and it is our aim to become an integral part of the new east London.

There is no doubt that we are a club on the up and that is being recognised by supporters, the media and the football world, which is something we can all be proud of.

This book is an essential companion for all Orient supporters – I hope you enjoy reading it.

Up the O's.

Barry Hearn
June 2006

Foreword

I'm delighted to welcome you to *Leyton Orient: The Complete Record*, a book I'm sure you'll enjoy reading.

Leyton Orient as a club has held a large place in my heart since I signed as a player in July 1996. During my near 200 appearances in four years as a player with the club we came close to promotion once, by reaching the Play-off Final at Wembley in 1999. That day ended in disappointment, as did the corresponding match two years later in Cardiff when I was youth-team manager.

I could tell how much it meant to everyone at the O's to achieve promotion, and when I was made manager in late September 2003 I made it my sole aim to lead the club out of the bottom Division.

Therefore, 6 May 2006 at the Kassam Stadium will stand alone in my memory bank as the highlight of my career so far. As a player, I will always remember winning the Man of the Match award at Wembley when Swindon gained a place in the Premiership and then playing against the best sides in the country the following season.

But for me, building and then working with a squad of players who wanted to win for themselves, each other and for the club so much was the biggest pleasure of all and the promotion was nothing more than anyone deserved.

As well as the players, there are two other teams that have helped me enormously, namely my family (wife Caroline and children Charlotte and Samuel) and my backroom staff, particularly Dean Smith, my good friend and assistant manager.

I have also been lucky to work for Barry Hearn, who has supported me unwaveringly throughout and been a model chairman to serve.

I could sense too (it wasn't difficult) the desire of the supporters to see success after 17 years without promotion, and I know that, if nothing else, you will always savour the memory of that season.

This is a club moving forward both in terms of its team and its other activities with the stadium taking shape and the local area undergoing mass regeneration.

It is long overdue and now we have a chance to move forward together, it is a chance we must take.

Enjoy the book and, as ever, up the O's.

Martin Ling
June 2006

On behalf of The Football League I would like to extend our congratulations and best wishes to Leyton Orient on celebrating your 125th anniversary.

This is a wonderful landmark and a historic achievement which is a testament to the dedication and hard work of all those involved with the club over the years. It is particularly poignant that Orient have enjoyed a successful season which is just reward to the club's loyal supporters.

Best wishes for continued success during the coming season as well as the next 125 years!

Andy Williamson
May 2006
Chief Operating Officer

Dedication

This book is dedicated to my mother, Millie Kaufman, and my father, Zalic 'Sid' Kaufman. It was he who first planted the seed about the O's, telling me about the former great players of Clapton Orient, whom he went to see as a young man, and then in 1957 taking me down to Brisbane Road to watch players like Phil Woosnam and Tommy Johnston, which led to my interest and an effort in searching out the facts about the early history and on the former players of the club.

Also, to my brother Alan Kaufman, who sadly died from cancer in October 2005. He took me to watch midweek matches, picking me up from school and then straight down to the Orient to cheer on the boys in royal blue in the days before floodlights, and in later years stood with me on the terracing in all sorts of weathers cheering on the O's.

Acknowledgements

First and foremost, I give thanks to All Mighty God for allowing me good health, happiness and trust and for being able to always look towards Him. I am grateful for the opportunity to complete this book, and also for the opportunity to make so many new, good friends, rekindling old friendships and working once again with Alan Ravenhill on this, possibly my final book on the O's.

I would like to thank my wife, Debbie, and our twin daughters, Amy and Samantha, for their patience, love, understanding and prayers over the past two years that I have been working on this particular book.

Being the only official Football League club historian based outside of the UK, in the past obtaining information from South Africa on the O's history had always proved to be difficult; however, with the advent of the internet and emails most of the barriers have now fallen away.

I feel a special mention should made of a few people who have been a tremendous help to me in the compilation of this book.

Alan E. Ravenhill, my very able assistant and joint author over many years on a number of books related to the club. Alan has a wonderful knowledge when it comes to the affairs of Leyton Orient and is a mine of information. I thank him for his accuracy and willingness to check everything I have sent to him without a murmur. It's been a real pleasure and honour working with him over these past 30-odd years, and I'm sure our friendship will continue over the years to follow, when, who knows, maybe we will write about the O's playing in the Premiership.

Gudrun Osborne formerly of the Leyton Orient Fans' Trust, who spent many hours at a number of local libraries and at Colindale Library in Brent for me, searching for attendance figures, match reports and doing research on the O's in the Southern League, without whom this particular section of the book would not have been possible to complete.

Shirley E. Kelly, an O's fan of nearly 60 years, from when her mother Alice Underwood started to work for the club, first went to Brisbane Road to watch Orient, and previously her family supported Leytonstone FC. With her daughter, Stella Fox, she undertook research on the internet and at Colindale Library for me. A special thank you to Shirley for also being the 'go-between' for Alan and myself, emailing me her items for the book for her to post on to Alan to save us valuable time and frustration with the airmail post.

Ian Nannestad, editor of the excellent publication *Soccer History Magazine*, for his great help in locating seasonal details on the O's in World War Two games and on former players.

Peter Holme, researcher at the National Football Museum in Preston, for his help on various matters, including details on players who appeared for the O's during World War Two from the Football League registers.

Andy Porter, historian of Tottenham Hotspur Football Club, for his outstanding help over many years on matters related to Orient and the players.

Russell Coburn, an O's fan, as always a big thank you for taking the time in tracking me down back in early 1999 via the fantastic O's email group to ask 'Where is Neil K? We want another Complete Record book. So, while I was recuperating over a few months after major eye surgery in December 1999, I started with some very 'low key' research for a book on the O's, the results being a further four books on the club and the players. Well, Russell, this update of the 1990 *Compete Record* book is dedicated to you.

Brian Blower, the former O's commercial manager, who first gave me the opportunity to write about the history of the club in the programme back in 1973.

The following have also given generously of their valuable time and knowledge:

Peter Allen, Stuart Allen, Anthony Ambrosen, Ian Anders, David Barber, Jorgen Bolin, Jim Blackstone, David Bloomfield, Clive M. Brown, Tony Brown, Alison Bull, Michael Burgess, Stephen Byrne, Tim Carder, Johnny Carey, Steve Cedar, Peter Chapman, Stan Charlton, Ian Christon, Bob Common, James Creasy, Bryan Daniels, Gareth M. Davies, Steve Dixon, David Dodd, Mark Eyres, Barrie Fairbrother, Terry Frost, Javier Garcia, David Godfrey, Michael Grade, Doug Harper, Mark Harris, Barry Hearn, Mary Holcroft, Ann Holman, Keith Howard, Terry Howard, Colin Hunt, Paul Joannou, Jean Johnston, Tommy Johnston, Stephen Jenkins, Trefor Jones, Colin Jose, Michael Joyce, Ian Juryeff, Jonathan Kaye, Ian King, Peter Kungler, Ron Lambert, Eddie Lewis, Tony McDonald, Gordon Macey, Nick Madden, Terry 'Henry' Mancini, Adrian Martin, Leonard Mitty, Ken Mortimer, Taylor Northrop, Kirstine Nicholson, Non-League website, Michael R. Ovenden, Richard J. Owen, Ian A. Page, P&O Shipping Group, Tony Paris, Simon Parker, Mike Peterson, Kevin Platt, Paul Plowman, James Pope, Matthew Porter, Peter Raath, Ian Rawlings, Jack Rollin, Matthew Roper, David Ross, Lloyd Scott, Andy Shalders, Keith Sharman, Phil Sherwin, Ray Simpson, Kenneth Smales, Dave Smith, Martin P. Smith, Karel Stokkermans, Jamie Stripe, Martin Strong, Nicola Struthers, Roger J. Triggs, Dave Twydell, Leo Tyrie, Keith Warsop, Mark S. Waters, Ian Watts, Julian Lloyd Webber, Roger Wedge, Paul West, Ros Wheeler, Alex White, Mark Wilson, Brian B. Winston, Gerry Wolstenholme, Phil Woosnam, Chris Zoricich and Delia Zussman.

Also, many thanks to Stephen Etberg, Greg Hochstadter, Ferdi Kruger and Paul Sandler, who have assisted me during my many computer crises.

Photographs

Also a big thank to those who, over the years, have allowed the reproduction of their photographs, namely *The Hackney Gazette, Ilford Recorder, Walthamstow Guardian,* and Mike Childs, Bryan Daniels for his great patience, George Flower, Tony Furby, Linda Mabbott, Mark Priddy, David Read, Tim Reder, Graham Smith, Chris Unwins, Mark Williams, and last but certainly not least a special thank you to David Winter (all the way from France) for allowing us to use his many excellent photographs, especially those from the O's two Play-off matches and two Play-off Finals at Wembley and the Millennium Stadium and photographs from the 2005–06 season.

The above names are listed in alphabetical order, and our sincere apologies for anyone who has mistakenly been left out.

The authors would like to thank the following football clubs and other organisations for supplying historical and player information and attendance figures for matches pertaining to the O's.

Aldershot Town, Arsenal, Aston Villa, Barnet, Barry Town, Barnsley, Blackpool, Blackburn Rovers, Bolton Wanderers, AFC Bournemouth, Bradford City, Bradford Park Avenue, Brentford, Brighton & Hove Albion, Bristol City, Bristol Rovers, Bromley, Burnley, Burton Albion, Cardiff City, Carlisle United, Celtic, Chelmsford City, Chelsea, Chesterfield, Colchester United, Coventry City, Crewe Alexandra, Crystal Palace, Dundee United, Dunfermline, East Fife, Enfield, Everton, Exeter City, Folkestone Invicta, Fulham, Gillingham, Glasgow Rangers, Gravesend & Northfleet, Grimsby Town, Halifax Town, Harlow Town, Hartlepool United, Harrow Borough, Heart of Midlothian, Hendon, Homerton College (Cambridge), Huddersfield Town, Hull City, Ipswich Town, Kings Lynn, Leeds United, Leicester City, Leyton, *Leyton Orientear* Fanzine, Lincoln City, Liverpool, London Maccabi

Lions, Luton Town, Maidstone United, Manchester City, Manchester United, Margate, MCC, Middlesbrough, Milton Keynes Dons, Montrose, Motherwell, Newcastle United, Newport School (Leyton), Northampton Town, Norwich City, Nottingham Forest, Notts County, Oldham Athletic, Oxford United, Paris St Germain, Partick Thistle, Peterborough United, Port Vale, Portsmouth, Preston North End, Queen's Park Rangers, Reading, Rhyl Athletic, Rochdale, Rotherham United, Scunthorpe United, Sheffield United, Sheffield Wednesday, Southampton, Southend Manor, Southend United, Southport, Stoke City, Sunderland, Surrey CCC, Swansea City, Swindon Town, Torquay United, Tottenham Hotspur, Walsall, Watford, West Bromwich Albion, West Ham United, Wingate & Finchley, Wolverhampton Wanderers, Wycombe Wanderers, Wrexham, Yeading and York City.

The design and layout of this book are largely the results of the efforts of Breedon Books, and a big thank you goes to owner Steve Caron, Susan Last and editor Michelle Grainger and the team for their assistance, co-operation and support in this, one of the first books in their re-launch of the complete record series, and we are happy that this book on Leyton Orient was one of the first on their list.

To all those who have played a part in this official history book, the authors are more than grateful than the above acknowledgment implies. And last, but not least, to all the players, managers, trainers, back-room staff, directors and, of course, the supporters, past, present and future, this book is dedicated to you all.

In our very first book on the club, published back in October 1974, the owner at that time, Brian Winston, wrote in his foreword to the book:

'At Orient, we read, we have been Cinderellas, poor relations, underdogs as well as many other descriptions, both complimentary and otherwise. Irrespective of whatever the experts may say, there are 4,000 regular supporters of the Orient to whom the word means so much more.'

In conclusion, we hope you enjoy reading the various chapters on the history of this grand old club as much as we have enjoyed putting it together.

As a loyal O's fan, I am sure that you will be proud of the fine beginning and history of the club and the great, new, modern Matchroom Stadium and also the wonderful achievement of promotion attained in May 2006. Developments at a football club happen so quickly, with our tight printing deadlines, but we are happy that we could make a brief mention of the club's record transfer of Gabriel Zakuani to Fulham for £1 million (with an extra £500,000 based on appearances and a sell-on clause).

Up the O's

Neilson N. Kaufman
June 2006

Introduction

The two authors first met during June 1974 when they got together to write the very first history on the club, and since those days they have collaborated together in writing a further four books on the club and players over the past 30 years.

It is quite remarkable that with Alan living in Walthamstow, London, and me in Johannesburg, South Africa, we have kept in contact with each other by letter over all those years on the history of this grand old club.

It's been 16 years since the last complete record book was published just after the O's had gained promotion in 1989 under manager Frank Clark. It is, therefore, an opportune time to update the book, especially as it's been 101 years since the O's played their very first match in the Football League, away at Leicester Fosse on 2 September 1905, and 102 years since they first entered the famous FA Cup competition, defeating Enfield 4–1 on 17 September 1904. This year the club celebrates their 125th anniversary since starting as the Glyn Cricket club back in 1881 and the opening of the new stand at Brisbane Road.

One of the gaps in the first complete record book was missing attendance figures between 1905 to 1924; however, after working on this for over one year and with the help of football statistician Brian Tabner, a number of club historians and various newspapers around the country, this will be the only football club history book to have every attendance figure, and we list them all for the O's 4,246 League, FA Cup and League Cup games played by between September 1904 (the O's first match in the FA Cup) up to and including the 2005–06 season.*

The authors have added some new and exciting chapters, including the O's record in the Southern League in 1904, and the record from both the World War One and World War Two years.

Neilson N. Kaufman
Johannesburg, South Africa
May 2005

*The total of 4,246 matches played by the O's excludes eight Play-off games and two Play-off Finals and the three abandoned games from the 1939–40 season.

Introduction to the seasonal grids – League attendance figures

All the League attendance figures noted in the seasonal grids that follow were obtained from match reports in local newspapers and from historians of a number of clubs.

From the 1925–26 season the Football League made it mandatory for club secretaries to supply the actual attendance figure for each home game played. The problem with season tickets meant that club secretaries had to apportion the value of these tickets across each game and adjust the attendance figure accordingly.

Therefore, the 'official' figure supplied to the Football League may not be the same as that supplied to the media on the day of the game.

Seasonal grids from 1991–92 onwards have been supplied by Tony Brown.

Substitutes

Playing substitutes' codes within the seasonal grids are identified as follows:
Substitute 12 = *, Substitute 13 = +, Substitute 14 = #.

Home matches are in capitals.

Leyton Orient Football Club

Year formed: 1881
Year turned professional: 1903
Year first entered FA Cup: 1904
Year joined Football League: 1905
Year became limited company: 1906

Club Names

Glyn Cricket Club: 1881–86
Eagle Cricket Club: 1886–88
Orient Football Club: 1888–98
Clapton Orient Football Club: 1898–1946
Leyton Orient Football Club: 1946–66
Orient Football Club: 1966–87
Leyton Orient Football Club: 1987–present day

O's in the Football League

First League match: 2 September 1905
1,000th League match: 10 March 1934
2,000th League match: 25 April 1964
3,000th League match: 1 May 1987
Record League victory: 9–2 v Aldershot, 1933–34
Most League goals (O's career): Tommy Johnston, 121 (180 games), 1956–58, 1959–61
Most League goals (season): Tommy Johnston, 35 (30 games), 1957–58

Most League appearances (O's career): Peter Allen, 424, 1965–78
Most games won (season): 29 (46 games), 1955–56
Fewest games won (season): 5 (42 games), 1965–66; 6 (46 games), 1994–95
Fewest home defeats (season): 0 (19 games, 14 wins, 5 draws), 1913–14
Most games lost (season): 32 (46 games) 1984–95; 27 (42 games), 1962–63
Most games drawn (season): 20 (12 goalless), 1974–75
Most away wins (season): 11, 1955–56, 1961–62, 2005–06

Record Attendances

Home grounds:
Millfields Road: 37,615 v Tottenham Hotspur, 1928–29
Lea Bridge Road: 20,288 v Millwall, 1936–37
Brisbane Road: 34,345 v West Ham United (FA Cup), 1963–64; 33,363 v Birmingham City (League), 1971–72

Lowest League Attendances (Brisbane Road)

1,443 v Halifax Town, 22 April 1986
1,668 v Preston North End, 17 December 1982
1,828 v Torquay United, 18 March 1986
1,846 v Doncaster Rovers, 2 October 1982
2,121 v Scarborough, 19 March 1996 (lowest home attendance of the 1990s)

Highest Away League /FA Cup Attendances

53,086 at Aston Villa, 4 January 1929, FA Cup
49,698 v Arsenal, 8 April 1978, FA Cup semi-final (at Chelsea)
48,141 at Newcastle United, 25 January 1930, FA Cup
41,200 at Manchester United, 17 December 1974, League
40,343 at Liverpool, 3 January 1960, FA Cup
40,260 at Tottenham Hotspur, 27 March 1963, League
39,467 at Aston Villa, 26 September 1959, League

Record Transfer Fees

Record transfer fee received: £1 million for Gabriel Zakuani from Fulham in 2006.
Record transfer fee paid: £175,000 to Wigan Athletic for Paul Beesley in 1989.

O's League Goals

1,000th League goal: Arthur Cropper v Torquay, 14 March 1931
2,000th League goal: Ken Facey (penalty) v Southend, 27 November 1954
3,000th League goal: Gordon Riddick v Middlesbrough, 20 March 1971
4,000th League goal: Mark Cooper v Wigan, 14 April 1990
(At the start of the 2006–07 season the O's were 68 short of their 5,000th League goal.)

Club Honours

Division Three South champions: 1955–56

Division Two runners-up (promoted): 1961–62
Division Three champions: 1969–70
Division Four promoted after Play-offs: 1988–89
League Two third (promoted): 2005–06
FA Cup semi-finalists: v Arsenal, 1977–78
Anglo-Scottish Cup finalists: v Nottingham Forest, 1976–77

Club Colours 1888–2006

1888–98	Red shirts with white 'O' on back, white shorts
1898–1901	Blue shirts with white 'O' on back, white shorts
1901–03	Red shirts, white shorts
1903–05	Red and green striped shirts, black shorts
1905–06	Red, white and green striped shirts, white shorts
1906–09	White shirts, black shorts (sometimes wore blue shorts)
1909–31	White shirts with a red chevron, black shorts
1931–44	Red and white hooped shirts, black shorts
1944–45	White shirts with a red chevron, black shorts
1945–47	White shirts with a blue chevron, black shorts
1947–65	Blue shirts, white shorts
1965 (Jul–Dec)	Blue shirts with thick white Sash, white shorts
1966 only	Blue shirts, white shorts
1966–67	Blue shirts, blue shorts
1967–73	Red shirts, red shorts
1973–76	Red shirts, white collar, white shorts
1977–82	White shirts and shorts with red side stripes
1982–88	Red shirts, red shorts
1988–91	Red shirts, white shorts
1991–93	Red shirts with black and white front bars, white shorts
1993–95	Red shirts with white pin stripes, white shorts
1995–96	Red shirts with white front, red shorts with white patch
1996–97	Red shirts with white flashes, black shorts
1997–98	Red shirts with white front band, white shorts
1998–99	Red and white check shirts, black shorts with white and red stripe
1999–2000	White shirts with a red chevron, black shorts with white stripe
2000–01	Red shirts, red shorts
2001–02	Red and white check shirts, black shorts
2002–03	Red shirts with thick white band, red shorts
2003–04	Red shirts with black sides, red shorts with black sides
2004–05	Red shirts with white shoulders and inner arm stripe, red shorts with white side flashes
2005–06	Red shirts with white shoulders and inner white stripe, red shorts with white side

The Orient Story

Over the years many different accounts have been written on how the present Leyton Orient Football Club was formed. Indeed even the year of its formation has been questioned.

In the 2004–05 *Sky Sports Football Yearbook* (formerly *Rothman's Football Yearbook*) it states: 'There is some doubt about the formation of Leyton Orient and, indeed, some confusion with other clubs like Leyton and Clapton over their early history'. The *Sky Yearbook* continues... 'As regards the foundation, the most favoured version is that Leyton Orient was formed originally by members of Homerton Theological College, who established the Glyn Cricket Club in 1881, and they carried on through the winter months playing football. Eventually many members of the Orient Shipping Line became involved so the name Orient was chosen in 1888.'

Other stories claim that Leyton Orient was started by members of the Clapton Park Cricket Club, another suggests it was by a football team called Star in 1883, who later became Trafalgar, and finally possibly by members of the Orient Steamship Company.

How it all began – The official version

Well, after more than 60 years of researching into the history of Leyton Orient Football Club, every available local newspaper of the period and every O's home programme from 1907, *Oriental Notes*, has been checked, and it soon becomes very clear that none of the above entries are quite correct. Although the Homerton Theological College and the Orient Steamship Company did play a part, nothing was ever found about the other clubs named above.

The various stories on the early days of the club located by the authors confirm that today's club owes its origins to former old boys of Homerton College, a theological teacher training college for Non-Conformists and Puritans. In 1881 they formed the Glyn Cricket Club, matches being played in Victoria Park. The college was situated on the north side of 75 Homerton High Street.

Meetings took place in the home of Rene Gronland, who was the first secretary. The joint captains were Jack Bartlett and Mr Steven Rolley, and these gentlemen took a great interest in the club during the early years up to entry into the Second Division of the Southern League in 1904.

From a playing point of view, the Glyn Cricket Club was not a great success, but in 1882 they signed on some good players including Harry Lavender and R.P. 'Pomp' Haines, and the latter was elected captain, his vice-captain was Gronland and the secretary was G.J. Galpin.

The following few seasons continued in unremarkable fashion against local clubs. In 1886, at the AGM at 'Pomp' Haines's House, the members decided to change the name of the club to Eagle Cricket Club, which also saw a change of fortune when an extremely good cricket season was had. In 1887 several good players joined the club including Teddy Wiggins – who was the chairman when the club entered the Football League in 1905 – and H.G. 'Tich' Woods.

In particular, Woods was a much sought after cricketer, and it was reported in the minutes of one of the club meetings that he possessed a prize bat and that he was happy to lend it to some of the better players as they went in to bat.

On 3 March 1888 the seventh annual meeting was held at 'Pomp' Haines's new home at 36 Dunlace Road, Hackney. At the meeting, two important resolutions were passed that would change the course of the club's history.

Committee member Jack R. Dearing suggested that a football section be started to keep the members together over the winter months. He further suggested that the club be renamed Clapton Orient because he worked for the Orient Steam Navigation Company (now the P&O Group). Dearing fondly remembered the launch of the company's first ship, the SS *Orient*, in 1879.

He stated at the meeting that the new name would also mean the 'east' end of London and would also bring mystique to the club.

Most of the members thought the name Orient to be a very clever move but did not like the idea of having Clapton in the title. Local people, they claimed, would associate them with a number of other clubs who already used the title Clapton and that confusion would reign in the area.

So the members voted and the name Orient Football Club was successfully adopted. The committee found a piece of waste ground in Glyn Road, Clapton, with a disused shed serving as dressing rooms. They played a number of friendly matches in the season with just one defeat. Their colours were red shirts with a large capital 'O' on their backs. Thus came about the club's nickname of the O's, when supporters would shout out 'Play up the O's' when they were winning or 'Buck up the O's' when losing.

The club moved to new headquarters at Gregory's on the corner of Millfields Road, and in 1891 the annual meeting was held there. The following seasons a number of matches against local rivals the Saracens were played, and one of the O's more notable players was Harry Edgar. He was tall, very well built and had a large, broad moustache. He appeared somewhat crude in the finer points of the game, and in a number of reports it was stated that he would 'hang around' the opponent's penalty area, and when the ball came to him he would punt it forward and push anyone who got in his way, then gallop after it in an ungainly fashion and smash the ball through the ropes. Edgar scored quite a few goals for the O's.

One report stated that he also had a way with the officials. He argued a referee into awarding his colleague Freddy Nesbitt a goal when there was doubt whether his shot went under the Saracens cross-rope, as there were no goal nets in those days.

During the 1893–94 season Orient were elected into the Clapton & District League and finished third out of eight teams. The following season they won the League with 19 points from 12 games, being two points clear of runners-up Spiders FC.

Clapton & District League (final table 1894–95)

	P	W	D	L	F	A	Pts
ORIENT	12	9	1	2	46	10	19
Spiders	12	8	1	3	29	16	17
Alamore R	12	7	2	3	23	28	16
Grove A	12	5	3	4	22	24	13
Grove Institute	12	3	1	8	9	13	7
Leymor	12	3	1	8	9	25	7
Stamford	12	2	1	9	10	32	5

In their ranks the O's had a fine goalkeeper in Jack – known as Jake – Turner. The story goes that he became a goalkeeper only because in his early days he was an outfield player who often made last-ditch clearances when the game did not include a specialist goalkeeper.

The club aroused considerable interest, and with crowds of up to 1,000 attending matches it was this support that lifted the players to become a title-winning side.

The 1895–96 season found the O's located in new headquarters at the Mermaid Inn in Mare Street, Hackney. At the annual meeting J.B. Bunch was elected president and a few top-class players joined the club, namely Harold Kier-Gibson and Ken Gibson from the Saracens club and W. Bradford from the Clapton Circle. Match details were very rarely reported in the local newspapers, and only the likely team line ups were printed in the Friday editions.

The O's played a few friendly matches that season, and they beat Paddington 4–0 (Ken Gibson (2), Haines and Gardner), Clapton Clifton 7–0 and Clifford Wall 4–0. The season ended with them in fourth position.

Clapton & District League (final table 1895–96)

	P	W	D	L	F	A	Pts
Grove A	13	11	2	0	36	12	24
Bow Avondale	13	6	3	4	23	14	15
Walth'stow Holborn	13	7	1	5	18	12	15
ORIENT	13	6	2	5	17	13	14
Leymor A	13	4	3	6	21	20	11
Archibald	13	3	2	8	10	27	8
Central Finsbury	13	2	3	8	9	19	7
St Matthias*	7	2	0	5	6	14	4

* dropped out mid-season, subsequent points awarded to opponents in table.

During the 1896–97 season Orient entered the Third Division of the London League and took a big step forward when securing their own private ground, the Whittle Athletic ground, in Millfields Road. Two railway carriages were purchased for use as dressing rooms, and the club obtained a short lease on the ground from the local council. A new, white wooden fence was erected around the pitch, and so the committee took the first step along the road to becoming a senior football club in Clapton and the surrounding areas. A number of new players were signed, including James Little from the Custom House club. The team responded by winning seven of their 12 games, gaining promotion into the Second Division of the London League as runners-up.

The had some good wins, including a 10–1 win over Guildhall (Haines (5), E. Wiggins (2), Rhyder, Nash and Barrow), Crouch End Vampires 2–1 (Rhyder (2)) and Walthamstow Holburn 2–1 (Gregory and Field). They were defeated by Clapton Ferncliffe 7–0, West Ham Garfield 4–0, Bow Avondale 2–0 and Thames Ironworks (today's West Ham United) 2–1 (Lambe). They also played the Royal Horse Artillery team, drawing 1–1 (Holehouse), with further drawn matches against Old St Lukes 2–2 (Hadler and Gage) and People Palace Old Boys 1–1 (Lambe).

When Orient left the local Clapton & District League to join the London League, it so incensed the editor of the local *North London Guardian* newspaper, who were instrumental in setting up that League in 1892, that he refused to write about the club for getting 'big ideas'.

This annoyed the Orient committee, and they forfeited a number of the O's reserve fixtures in the Clapton & District League when the team just did not arrive for matches.

For the start of the 1897–98 season, the club's headquarters had moved to the Britannia in Mare Street, Hackney, and the ever popular Teddy Wiggins took up the reins of secretary after the resignation of both Frederick Lamplough and Raymond Hodder. The team struggled on the field and finished in seventh position out of 10 clubs.

They started the season with a 1–0 win over Thames Ironworks (Hilsdon), followed up with wins over the Metropolitan Railway team 4–0 (Gardner (2), McGeorge (2)), the Queens Printer 3–0 (Summerville, Robinson and Nash) and the 2nd Grenadier Guards 6–1 (Rhyder (5) and Barrow). The biggest win of the season was against East Ham 10–1 (Hilsdon (3), McGeorge (3), Rhyder (2), Haines and an own goal by Lander). They suffered some heavy defeats as well, against Fulham 6–1 (Hilsdon) and Barnet 5–1 (Hitch).

Brighter days were imminent, and, despite the lowly position, they were elected into the First Division of the London League by the management committee.

Orient moved their headquarters to the Priory in Blurton Road, Hackney, a public house owned by a Mr Charles J. Lovelock. The first annual meeting in June 1898 was held there and some important decisions were made by the committee.

One of the matters on the agenda was that of changing the name of the club to 'The Clapton Orient AFC'. The motion for the new name was once again put forward by Jack Dearing, who had suggested the name change from Eagle to Orient 10 years earlier.

He addressed his fellow committee members by saying 'with Clapton now being considered a good district socially, the name of Clapton Orient would give the club more respectability and a wider support base'.

After a few murmurs, the vote was taken by a show of hands and it was unanimously passed by the committee, which comprised Teddy Wiggins, H. Robertson, J. Bunch, R. Robinson, H.G. 'Tich' Woods, A. Simpson and Messrs Alf Wallis, Roberts, Gill, Osborne and Dearing.

Chairman Wiggins told his fellow committee members 'The prospects of the club under its new title of Clapton Orient AFC looked very bright.'

The committee re-signed all of the previous season's players, as well as new men Dyke (Woolwich Arsenal), Marriott and Manniger (Eton Mission), Ginger Merritt (Walthamstow) and the Ratyer brothers (Bow club).

The O's trainer Alf Wallis had moulded what looked to be quite a good side, and the 1898–99 season opened in exceptional style under the new title.

Clapton Orient's first match was at the Whittles Athletic ground on 10 September 1898, a friendly against Lower Clapton FC, which was won 2–1. The first London League match occurred two weeks later against Barnet, and the O's forward Jack Hilsdon scored both goals to secure victory. The team that day was Stephens, Dyke, Marriott, Hodder, Manniger, J. Ratyer, Gibson, Hilsdon, Merritt, G. Ratyer, R. Haines.

Of the first 16 fixtures played in various competitions, the O's won 12 and drew two, and both their defeats came in the London League. They scored 49 goals and conceded 21. The O's defeated Thames Ironworks 6–0, in front of a record home crowd of over 2,500, the gate money reaching a whopping £25, and it was reported that the committee counted the money over a dozen times before they could accept that it was not a dream but a hard-cash reality. This victory was followed by a 3–0 win over Annerley with goals from Ken Gibson, Carr and Gardiner before 950 fans. They went to East Sheen and played before just 95 spectators, winning 3–2 (Carr (2) and Manniger), and then hammered Novocostians at home 7–1. As the 1898–99 season closed, the team had scored 115 goals with 62 against, 25 wins, 4 draws and 11 losses.

In the Middlesex Senior Cup the O's won away at Crouch End Vampires 3–1, Polytechnic 5–1 and Hanwell 1–0 and finished in a respectable fifth position in the London League. The reserve side won the Great Western League.

During February 1899 the O's held their annual dinner dance, at which chairman Wiggins informed the guests that 'The club had done wonderfully well since starting as the Glyn Cricket Club some 18 years earlier.' This social function was, he said, 'the most successful that we have held and was worthy of the great advances made by the club since its formation in 1881'.

The O's opened the 1899–1900 season with a visit from Kent side Bromley to the Whittles Athletic ground. Hills opened the scoring for Orient, but the visitors equalised when reserve goalkeeper Mason fumbled the ball into his own net.

An historic match, or should we say two, took place on 16 December 1899. Eighty-two minutes of the game against Hammersmith & Chiswick Athletic had been completed, with the O's leading 4–0, when fog descended. The referee decided to abandon the match and the remaining eight minutes were played on 24 March 1900, with the O's scoring one further goal to record a 5–0 victory.

In the same season, the O's met Thames Ironworks and also Millwall Athletic (later Millwall) in the London League. They finished the season in sixth spot in the London League out of 13 clubs on 13 points, scoring 40 goals.

During December 1899, at a meeting of the London Football Association, it was recorded the LFA's amateur status committee were satisfied with the books of the club, although the club's financial secretary, Mr A. Simpson, and the club itself would be suspended for one week in January 1900 for not producing certain figures required by the committee.

Further problems arose for the O's management committee, namely finding a new ground, and there was even a report in a local newspaper that the club may have to close. During March 1900 a local sports editor reported 'I am in a position to state that the ground now occupied by the O's and known as the Whittles Athletic ground will be closed down next season by the local council, it is to become an electric power station. Where will the O's deposit themselves now? The loss of such a convenient ground will be a big blow to the Orient committee, who have stated to the council, in no uncertain manner, that if no suitable ground can be found for the club, there is a serious doubt whether the club could continue into its 19th year of existence after the end of the present season.'

The council did come to the rescue with an offer for the club to move to a site in Millfields Road, and after viewing the ground the committee accepted the offer and the club was saved from closure.

The new ground was not far from the old Whittles Athletic venue and was considered to be an excellent stadium capable of holding up to 10,000 spectators.

The Clapton Orient club looked forward to the 1900–01 season in their new home competing in the First Division of the London League, and the reserve side, considered one of the strongest in London, entered the prestigious Middlesex League and the Second Division of the London League.

For the new season the committee re-signed all their star players, including the excellent goalkeeper Tommy Longstreeth, skipper Sid Carr, Jack Hills, Ken Gibson, centre-forward Jack Hilsdon, 'Pomp' Haines, Hugh McLelland and the famous Ainger brothers from Kent.

The first match of the new season against Queen's Park Rangers attracted 1,400 spectators to the new Millfields ground, with the O's winning 2–1. There was also the first ever meeting against Woolwich Arsenal, with a victory, and a win over West Ham United. The O's finished the season seventh out of 11 teams.

During 1901–02 the O's had a good season, finishing in fifth spot in the London League, and ended it in style by winning two major Cups for the first time in their history.

In April 1902 they defeated Clapton FC 1–0 at the Spotted Dog ground to win the West Ham

Charity Cup, and during the following month they beat Ealing 1–0 to take the Middlesex County Football Challenge Cup, the first season of that competition. The cup and the lid were both made of silver and presented to the County Association by a Mr C.S. Goldmann.

The first half of the match at Clapton was scoreless, although the home side did all the attacking. Late on in the second half, Jack Hills broke away down the left-wing, crossing the ball in for Gibson to shoot. The home goalkeeper, Smith, could only manage to push the ball into the path of the O's forward Robertson, who scored easily. The Mayor of West Ham, Alderman Spratt, presented the Cup and gold medals to the Clapton Orient players, which marked a triumphant end to a wonderful season.

This was to be Jack Hilsdon's last season at the club as he joined Luton Town after scoring more than 60 goals for Orient, including 21 goals in 1901–02. He joined the O's in August 1897 and was their very first prolific goalscorer. He is not to be confused with his more famous brother George Hilsdon of England, Chelsea and West Ham United fame.

During the summer of 1902 the committee decided to make improvements to the Millfields Road ground. The pitch was re-turfed and new seats placed in the grandstand, with new terracing laid. The previous season, the first at Millfields, the spectators had to stand ankle-deep in mud and water, so cinder ash was laid around the ground to make it more comfortable in the winter months.

The club strengthened their playing resources by taking over local amateur club Clapton Marlborough, which was a successful side in the Stoke Newington area. This side entered the strong Metropolitan Amateur League, playing as Clapton Orient reserves, and finished as runners-up.

Before the start of the new 1902–03 season the players assembled for a group photograph, proudly showing the two cups they had won at the end of the previous season.

Clapton Orient pictured in 1902. Back row (left to right): Mr A. Watson, Mr Osborne, Mr C. Howitt, Mr H.G. 'Tich' Woods (treasurer), Mr C.J. Lovelock (president), Mr E.A. 'Teddy' Wiggins (secretary, later chairman), Mr E.H. Roberts, Mr J.T. Robinson. Middle: Mr J. Westrop, Mr A. Thompson, Mr A.E. Simpson, Mr A. Wallis (trainer/coach), Billy Price, Ernie Ward, Bob Chalkley, Mr A. Unwin, Mr G. Jarvis, Mr Arthur Haynes, Mr Symons (groundsman, standing behind Haynes). Seated: Claude Berry, Ernie Bailey, Hugh McClelland. On ground: Ken Gibson, 'Pomp' Haynes, 'Ginger' Merritt, Jack Hills (captain), Bob McGeorge.

The first match of the 1902–03 season was at home against West Hampstead, who included in their ranks Herbert Kingaby, a man who later starred for the O's, and the match ended 0–0. The first victory came with a 3–0 win over Deptford before 1,700 spectators, who witnessed the new signing, Blunden from Brighton, score twice.

The O's put on some excellent displays at Millfields, and none more so than the 6–0 victory over top Essex side Ilford. Wallace, the new signing from West Ham United, opened the scoring and further goals were added by Gibson, Bailey, Hills (2) and Wallace, who netted a sixth. The O's side that day was: Ward, Chalkley, Price, Bailey, Haines, McLelland, Hills, Merritt, Wallace, McGeorge, Gibson.

In November 1902 a London League game against Millwall resulted in rowdy crowd scenes and two players being sent off. One local newspaper match report stated 'The match was extremely rough and the visitors quickly took the lead, but the O's were level after Gibson was crudely pulled down in the box, he slowly picked himself up and converted the spot-kick. Seven home players were seen to be limping near the end of the match, and when Robertson was hacked down by Millwall's Devine a fight broke out amongst the players and with a few of the fans, among the more than 3,000 crowd. After the two players were sent-off, the home fans swarmed onto the pitch to try and get hold of the Millwall players.

'It was a very dangerous situation and the referee decided to end the match five minutes early, and I [reporter] witnessed the Orient committee and players trying to get the visiting players and officials into the dressing room. It was the Orient players who returned to the pitch to persuade the incensed O's fans to disperse and go home.' After which, the police had to escort the Millwall fans out of the ground.

The O's had some interesting results that season. They defeated teams like Ilford Alliance 6–0 (Clancy (2), Gibson (2, 1 pen), Robertson and McGeorge), Chesham Town 4–1 (Gibson (2), McGeorge and Dwyer), London Welsh 5–2 (Hills (3) and Merritt (2)), Ilford 6–3 (Wallace (2), Gibson, Bailey and Hills (2)), Wandsworth 2–0 (Hills and Merritt) and Southall 5–1 (Gibson (3), Wallace and McGeorge). However, they lost to Tottenham Hotspur Reserves by 5–1 (Dwyer) and Woolwich Arsenal Reserves 2–1 (Hills).

For the start of the 1903–04 season the committee decided to introduce a new colourful playing strip. The shirts had two-inch vertical stripes of white, red and green and the shorts were blue. Indeed, the outlook of the club looked very bright, with home attendances averaging more than 2,000 people.

During October 1903 the committee were informed by the Middlesex Football Association (MFA) that they were being investigated regarding their amateur status. The problem was the apparent payment of player 'Ginger' Merritt, who helped re-turf the playing surface during the close season, and also they were looking into payments to certain players of gifts in kind.

Club president Charles Lovelock informed the MFA that the club would not take on Merritt again in the hope that they would deal lightly with them, although the club felt that the County Association were behaving rather foolishly and made this fact known through the local press, something that upset the governing body.

A commission was appointed to look into the affairs of the club and the following month reported back that, in their view, Clapton Orient Football Club had failed to satisfy them that it was a bona fide amateur club and, therefore, their membership of the Middlesex FA would cease.

The charge against the club, which was published in the local press from a statement made by the club, was that during the 1902–03 season Merritt made a number of first-team appearances with the amateur club of Clapton Orient, but during the summer months he put in two days' work at the ground re-laying the turf. Club secretary Mr T. Wiggins paid him the 'ordinary rates'. The Middlesex FA took exception to the payment, and, for this somewhat trivial matter, the club was punished and banned.

This newspaper report found its way to the Middlesex FA, and the club's management were worried that a total ban would be enforced on them.

After an emergency meeting of the Orient management committee during November 1903, it was decided that the only course of action was for the Clapton Orient Football Club to turn professional. A number of professional players were signed up, and admission charges were raised to meet the added expense. It would now cost 6d to enter the ground. Ladies were admitted for 3d, boys 2d and admission to the enclosure was an extra 2d.

The club's first match as a professional outfit was at Millfields Road on 14 November 1903 against Shepherds Bush. A crowd of over 1,300 were in attendance and were delighted to see their new heroes gain a record 11–0 victory. A reporter from the local newspaper, the *Hackney Spectator*, wrote 'While we are glad for the winners, let us shed a tear for the reputation of the losers', he said, 'who was mightily glad to the pencil worn out with marking down the Orient scorers in the most one sided game I have ever witnessed.' The scorers were Wallace (4), Bob McGeorge (3), Jones (2), Bush and Seeley. The O's team that historic day was Ward, Price, Chalkley, Berry, Simpson, McLelland, Bush, R. McGeorge, Wallace, Seeley, Jones. An 8–1 victory of Luton Clarence and a 3–1 win over Fulham Reserves soon followed. The best of the victories were Maidstone 2–0 (Wallace (2)), West Ham United Reserves 1–0 (Seeley), Reading Reserves 4–1 (Wallace (2, 1 pen) and Bush (2)), Grays 5–1 (Wallace, Bush, Seeley (2), Jones), and they also played the 1st Grenadier Guards, drawing 1–1 (Wallace). The heaviest defeats were against Woolwich Arsenal Reserves 10–2 (Seeley, R. McGeorge), Tottenham Hotspur Reserves 3–1 (Wallace) and New Brompton 2–0.

To mark the development of professionalism, Bristol City, members of the Football League's Second Division, were invited to Millfields Road to play a friendly match. City fielded their strongest team, who had just defeated Burnley 6–0 and Grimsby Town 4–0. More than 2,000 spectators were in attendance, even though heavy rain was falling, but the O's were defeated 2–1 with Alfred George Seeley scoring Orient's goal. (He was born in Risbridge in 1877, and he played in the Southern League with Southampton in 1896. He later played for QPR in 1901 and Southampton Wanderers in 1902, and after his spell with the O's he moved to Leyton FC.) The City manager Sam Hollis stated that he was impressed with the Londoners' play, and he thought that Clapton Orient had a bright future in the professional game. Little did he know that just two seasons later the O's would be playing in the Second Division of the Football League. The 1903–04 season saw them make a profit of £10. This was the last season for Hugh McLelland, who was born on 10 July 1880 in West Ham, having joined Orient in 1899, and always wore the number-six shirt. The following information was supplied by Ian McLelland about his grandfather. 'My grandfather lived in Stratford, he served in the Army during World War One and suffered a mustard gas attack. He died in 1945, aged 64.'

In the following season of 1904–05 the committee took a major step by applying for membership of the Second Division of the Southern League. In those days the First Division of the Southern League was the premier competition when the Football League was dominated by teams from the North and the Midlands, and the committee were overjoyed when their application was accepted.

Orient's seasonal record in the First Division of the London League up to entry into the Southern League:

Season	Div	P	W	D	L	F	A	Pts	Pos	Teams in Div
1896–97	3	12	7	2	3	27	22	16	2nd	7
1897–98	2	18	7	0	11	30	45	14	7th	10
1898–99*	1	16	7	2	7	29	32	16	5th	9
1899–1900	1	18	4	5	9	40	50	13	6th	10
1900–01	1	20	8	2	10	36	31	18	7th	11
1901–02	1	18	8	3	7	49	37	19	5th	10
1902–03	1	18	6	5	7	23	17	17	7th	10
1903–04	1	20	6	6	8	26	33	18	6th	11
1904–05	1	18	6	3	9	37	46	15	7th	10

* Orient were elected into Division One

Many improvements had to be made to the playing staff and to the Millfields Road ground as the prelude to a new chapter for Clapton Orient Football Club, for besides playing in the Southern League the team was also about to make their first appearance in the FA Cup.

The Orient committee, led by Teddy Wiggins, 'Tich' Woods, Ted Roberts and president Charles Lovelock, saw the move as a stepping stone to the First Division of the Southern League or even into the Second Division of the Football League.

O's in the Southern League

The players that were re-signed were goalkeeper Liles, Robertson, McGeorge, Berry and Hills. Among the new signings were Joseph Redding, a goalkeeper from the Amersham club, Herbert Kingaby, a fast-raiding winger from the West Hampstead club, Allan William Nicol, a forward from Grays Athletic FC, John Rance, a full-back from Queen's Park Rangers, Sidney William Cavendish, the former Southampton reserve – 22 goals in 1898–99 – Freemantle, an inside-forward, and Jack William 'Billy' Reynolds, the former Manchester City reserve and Burton United centre-forward.

It was the end for goalkeeper Ernie Ward after a number of seasons at the club, and he joined West Ham, and Jack Wallace had moved to Luton, having joined the O's in December 1902.

Once again the terracing around the ground had been much improved, the grandstand repainted, all the seats repaired and new drainage laid beneath the pitch. Season tickets were introduced at a cost of 5s and 7s 6d (25p and 37½p) and had sold very well.

The O's played their first historic home Southern League fixture on Saturday 8 October 1904 before nearly 3,000 spectators against Brighton & Hove Albion, and the hearts of the committee members were filled with joy as the money rolled in as the fans flocked on to the terracing and into the dressing carriages and stand. The toss was won by the O's captain, Reynolds, and he elected to play with a fairly stiff wind down the ground and the sun on his back, the team in their unusual shirts of red and green and black shorts and the visitors in blue and white shirts. The O's went on the attack from the start, and winger Hills beat the Brighton defence with some neat dribbling, and he crossed the ball in only for Berry's shot to be saved by Whitehurst, the Brighton goalie, and, with Kingaby giving the visiting burly defender Hume the run-around, a goal seemed inevitable, but half-time came with no goals scored. With Whitehurst in top form, the Orient forwards could not beat him and the match ended 0–0. As the local reporter stated, a little disappointedly, 'thus the O's gained their first point in Southern League football, in the Second Division of that League it is true, but everything has to have a start'. The O's team that day was: Redding, Rance, Archer, Berry, McGeorge, Lane, Kingaby, Nicol, Cavendish, Reynolds, Hills.

The journalist from the *Hackney Spectator* appeared more upset with the seller of programmes, fixture cards and chocolate bars at 1d, writing 'All throughout the match he was crying out trying to sell his items. It was enough to give one the blues. People want to watch the games sometimes and no shouting should take place during the play, he is the terror of Millfields Road.' (The club took heed, and he was stopped from selling his items during games.)

The first away match took place at Southampton on 22 October, and it was Sid Cavendish, returning to his former club, who netted a hat-trick to secure a 3–3 draw before over 4,000 fans. The Saints forward 36-year-old Harry Wood – father of Arthur Wood, later to become the O's greatest ever goalkeeper – netted twice.

The O's first victory in the Southern League, a 2–1 win, occurred at Brighton on 12 November before a crowd in excess of 2,000, with Nicol and Cavendish securing the points. The following week they maintained their fine start to the season with a 2–0 win over West Ham United to the delight of the 3,500-strong crowd, with goals from Kingaby and Cavendish.

By the turn of the year the O's had lost just once, a 4–1 reverse at Swindon Town. During January 1905 they were in a couple of remarkable games. On 14 January they entertained Watford and within 10 minutes held a 3–0 lead with goals from Reynolds, Hammond and McGeorge. By half-time they led 4–1 and things looked good for a comfortable win, to the delight of the 500-strong crowd. However, in the second half the O's seemed to go to sleep, and the visiting centre-forward Lees bagged four goals to see his side forge ahead 7–4. McGeorge scored a consolation goal, but they ended up losing 7–5.

The following week the O's went to Wycombe Wanderers, with T.C. Hills and Robertson coming into the defence and Reynolds and Nicol upfront. Once again they started off in bright fashion with Reynolds and Kingaby scoring by half-time, putting the O's 2–1 up. Then the Wycombe centre-forward Bryan came into the action and scored four goals to take the match 6–4 before 250 home fans. This was a rather surprising result because Wycombe had lost the previous week 10–1 to Grays United.

The O's picked up during February and early March with five points from four games. They were due to go by train from Waterloo Station for the match at Portsmouth on Wednesday 29 March, but two of the players, goalie Joe Redding and full-back John Rance, got confused and went to London Bridge. And so the O's only turned up with nine men and played without a goalkeeper and one less in defence. It was no wonder they got trounced 13–0 and, as reported in the local paper, 'Orient have a bad time at Portsmouth'. However, the team seemed to bounce back with a 3–0 win over Swindon, with Hammond and Cavendish (2) scoring, and in the following week a 7–1 win over Grays Athletic, with both Nicol and new signing George Nidd playing against their former club on a very wet afternoon, the scorers being Cavendish (2), Hammond (2), Reynolds (2) and Berry. George Frederick Nidd was born in Boston, Lincolnshire, in January 1869 and was a highly experienced full-back, having played for Everton, Preston North End, Bury, Lincoln City, Grimsby Town and Fulham.

After a 5–0 reverse at home to Southampton, the Southern League season ended with a 2–0 loss at Grays, with Nidd accidentally scoring twice through his own goal.

On 12 April 1905 the committee appointed the experienced former Manchester City, Accrington Stanley and Stockport County man Samuel Ormerod as manager, who was chosen from over 150 applicants.

After watching his new side, Ormerod informed the directors and new president Horatio Bottomley that the whole side had to be strengthened with more experienced Football League players; this was apparent after watching them throw away leads against both Watford and Wycombe Wanderers.

Even so, the committee were happy with the progress of the club, and at a meeting on 7 March 1905 it was unanimously agreed to form the club into a limited liability company with a share capital of £3,000. The first directors were Edward Alfred Wiggins (chairman), Charles James Lovelock, Arthur Harvey Haines, James Thomas Robertson and Henry George Woods. All the gentlemen had been involved with the club from the early days. Arthur Haines was the brother of R.P. 'Pomp' Haines, who had a major influence in the first years of the club.

The directors informed the fans through the local newspapers of their intention to apply for membership of the First Division of the Southern League, a body more powerful in those days than the Football League. It had a strong London and southern representation and only Woolwich Arsenal had gone against the stream by playing in the Football League, which they joined in 1893.

Their application was favourably received at first, but, unexpectedly, the management of Tottenham Hotspur officially objected by letter, saying 'we are not having them (Clapton Orient) on our doorsteps.' When the vote came in, their application was rejected, so attention was then turned to membership of the Football League.

The O's programme in 1908, looking back on the days of the application into the First Division of the Southern League, reported: (The article was written by director Mr D. McCarthy.)

'The torments of Balthazar are as nothing compared to the feelings of those member clubs of the Southern League who in 1905 permitted themselves to be cajoled into becoming parties to the subordination of the Southern League to the selfish interests of a few prominent clubs.

'In 1905, Clapton Orient applied for election into the First Division of the Southern League, having credentials of the highest order, a good manager, a fine secretary and a group of good players with experience. In anticipation of its acceptance a limited company had been formed with financial arrangements made. We know our application was never even considered, when the cry came up by a number of clubs [including Tottenham Hotspur] that our membership was inconvenient to them and the door was kept tightly shut against us!'

Mr S. Allen of Swindon Town wrote to the secretary stating 'The majority of the members wanted both Chelsea and Clapton Orient to join our ranks in the First Division of the Southern League. There was pressure brought to the members by a number of London clubs (Fulham against the entry of Chelsea, and Spurs against the entry of Clapton Orient) who predicted dire ruin to themselves if these clubs were admitted, so, not wishing to injure the existing members, the members voted loyally not to vote in both Chelsea and Clapton Orient.'

McCarthy concluded by saying 'The moment the Southern League Council Chamber let their integrity be tampered with, dignity departed from them and the bond which bound them together was severed, and so the writing is on the wall for these gentlemen.'

Manager Sam Ormerod and the directors held many meetings in and around Clapton to discuss the O's application to join the Second Division of the Football League. Mr Horatio Bottomley – in latter years to become MP for South Hackney – became a large shareholder of the club, and with influence among the top brass in the Football League the directors were confident of being elected.

At the Football League AGM the O's gained just a single vote; however, 30 minutes later a motion was passed to extend the Second Division to 20 clubs and a new vote was taken.

This time Clapton Orient gained 26 votes, six more than Doncaster Rovers. It was later reported that the directors of Chelsea canvassed quite a few votes to help Orient gain more than Doncaster, as they wanted another London-based club in the Second Division.

So, the O's, from such humble beginnings, had succeeded in gaining admission into the Second Division of the Football League along with Chelsea, Leeds City and Stockport County. For all his efforts, Bottomley was made president of the club.

Wiggins had stated that it had cost the club nearly £2,000 to gain entry, and they also had to agree to pay all visiting clubs their travel expenses for the first season, with Horatio Bottomley agreeing to pay all the funds required.

The Edwardian era saw a general movement of southern-based clubs into the Football League after Orient's and Chelsea's election, including Fulham (1907) and Tottenham Hotspur (1908).

During May 1905 manager Ormerod hired a hotel room in Manchester to receive applicants to pay for the club after placing adverts in the northern newspapers. The following players were signed: Joseph Butler, a goalkeeper with over 100 senior appearances for Stockport County, William Holmes, a defender from Manchester City with more than 150 appearances, Rowland Codling, an attacking left-half from Stockport County, John Boden, a centre-half with 90 appearances for Glossop North End, Isaac Evenson, with more than 100 appearances for both Glossop North End and Manchester City, and Peter Boyle, the Irish international full-back with Sunderland, Sheffield United and Motherwell.

Further players were signed on Ormerod's return to London in June. Richard Bourne, with more than 100 League appearances with Sheffield United, Barnsley and Preston North End, and who cost the O's a fee of £100, which was fixed by a League tribunal, from Preston, Peter Proudfoot, who joined from Millwall, Walter Leigh, a dashing centre-forward who had played for Aston Villa, Grimsby Town, Bristol City and New Brompton, James Wootten, who came with a good reputation from Leyton FC, and finally the Lamberton brothers, George (from Luton Town) and John (from Stalybridge Celtic). All the players were on a fixed wage of £4 per week.

The fans were questioning if Ormerod could mould the new squad of players into a decent Football League team. Well, time would tell.

A crowd of over 5,000 attended the first trial game, some of the proceeds of which were given to the North Eastern Hospital. The teams lined up as the Old Colours and the New Colours, with no goals being scored. The teams were: Old Colours: Redding, Butcher, Reason, McGeorge, Proudfoot, Poulton, Hudson, Evenson, Leigh, Lamberton and Bourne. New Colours: Butler, Lamberton, Boyle, Holmes, Boden, Codling, Robson, Wootten, Powell, Orton and Purdey.

The first League match was at Leicester Fosse on 2 September 1905, which the O's lost (see Matches to Remember section). On the following Monday they entertained First Division side Derby County in a friendly, and what an exciting match it turned out to be, before 2,500 spectators.

The O's played some bright football, but it was Derby's famous forward Steve Bloomer in his final season with the club before his move to Middlesbrough who opened the scoring with a fierce shot. But Leigh soon equalised from a Bourne centre, then outside-left Frank Middleton beat the whole of the home defence to score a goal. The visiting goalkeeper Henry Maskrey dropped an easy cross for Proudfoot to equalise, and Wootten scored with a great shot. Bloomer scored a fine third, and in the second half the Derby forwards gained the upper hand with goals from Bloomer and two from Ben Warren for a 6–3 win.

The O's first League victory came on 11 September 1905 when they defeated Glossop North End by 2–0, Walter Leigh netting both goals. Their first away victory came at Lincoln City on 16 September 3–2, with goals from Evenson, Leigh and Kingaby.

By November the team were third from bottom of Division Two, and by the following January the club was in financial crisis and rooted to the bottom of the League. Teddy Wiggins resigned as chairman, having been associated with the club since 1887.

A 20-man committee were elected under the chairmanship of Captain Henry Wells-Holland, and in March 1906 both Bert Kingaby and Rowland Codling were sold to Aston Villa for a joint-fee of £880, and Peter Proudfoot joined Chelsea for £120 to save the club from closure.

The committee decided that Clapton Orient FC should be voluntarily wound-up, and a reconstruction scheme was completed by the issue of a further £3,000-worth of shares, divided into 12,000 shares of five shillings (25p) each. The committee appointed William Holmes as player-manager after the departure of Ormerod.

In April Walter Leigh notched up all four goals against Bradford City to secure the O's best League win of the season by 4–0. The season ended with Orient at the bottom of Division Two, recording just seven wins and gaining 21 points, and the top League goalscorer was Walter Leigh with eight goals. It was a difficult situation for Henry Wells-Holland, having to face the Football League members to apply for re-election.

Wells-Holland was born on 8 June 1864. He worked for the Bank of England and had taken part in municipal affairs in Hackney, having been the mayor in 1902. He had served for many years as a captain with the First Tower Hamlets Rifle Brigade and with the 4th Royal Fusiliers.

Wells-Holland was invited by the official receiver Mr Charles Lovelock to chair the 20-man committee to handle the affairs of the club on a daily basis. His very first duty was to attend the League's annual meeting at the Tavistock Hotel, London, and he soon realised that his task would be formidable as the other main candidate, Oldham Athletic, had strong support with the northern clubs. Both Chesterfield and Burton United seemed certain to gain re-election. So other than the vote of Chelsea, the O's looked likely to lose their League status.

Wells-Holland, however, was not a man to give up the fight easily, and he and his fellow committee members worked hard lobbying for votes.

After Chesterfield, Burton and Wigan had put their case, it was the turn of Wells-Holland, who informed the League committee members 'I have come here as a novice in the League, being chairman of Clapton Orient for only a short period of a few months. I ask, I beg you to extend a little sympathy towards the Orient. We were unfortunate last season.

'I ask you not to refer to the many promises that have been made on behalf of this club in the past, but ask that you look, as we are, to the future.'

He continued 'The club has fulfilled all its liabilities to the League and the member clubs. Yet, in truth, it was a near thing whether the club would cease to exist between December 1905 and January 1906. I have taken control when money owed all around, yet we succeeded in finishing the season.

'I beg you to extend to us the benefit of the "first offenders act", after all, it has been our first year in the League. We will do infinitely better this forthcoming season.

'Although last year we had to sell some of our excellent players, bringing in over £1,000, some new, good players have been secured. We have succeeded, even though, not doing badly in securing the crowds, who have followed the fortunes of the club even more devoutly than ever. The O's are celebrating their Silver Jubilee this year, having started as a cricket club in 1881 that turned to the game of football in March 1888.

'The population of Hackney and Clapton is upwards of a quarter of a million people. Our ground at Millfields is nearly seven acres and is one of the largest in the South of England, and can easily be made capable of holding upwards of 60,000 people; therefore, I conclude, let us continue in the League so that all of East London can be proud of Clapton Orient Football Club. I thank you Sirs, for you close attention.'

Then it was the turn of the delegate from Oldham Athletic, a Mr Towne. He said 'Oldham was a great centre for rugby, but the local public are going more than ever for the game of football. We are a three penny fare from Manchester, and the city itself has a population of over 200,000.'

He concluded 'There are many factories employing thousands of people in the town, and we have the interest of several local businessmen in the club. We have a magnificent ground with every accommodation and a great deal of money is available to provide the finest players. Oldham were formed in 1894 and turned professional three years later. They deserve to be in the League.'

After a one-hour deliberation, the League members placed their votes by written, secret ballot. The voting was then made known.

Chesterfield gained 36 votes, Burton 32, Clapton Orient 21, Oldham Athletic 20 and Wigan five votes. So, the O's had scraped through by a single vote over the Lancashire club, who nevertheless were elected the following season after Burslem Port Vale resigned. Wells-Holland was informed that members wanted southern-based clubs in the League and this certainly helped Orient's case.

Wells-Holland had done it. His personality undoubtedly went a long way in securing the club's re-election. For the new 1906–07 season, manager Holmes secured some new players, and four of them most certainly played a major role in the O's finishing in a safe 17th position.

William Martin, the 23-year-old, golden-haired lad from Poplar, joined the club as a half-back from Hull City. He was tried as a centre-forward and hit 17 League goals from 30 appearances. In one spell during November and December he scored 11 goals from just six games. Thirty-three-year-old half-back, Scottish-born David Buchanan, who came from Plymouth Argyle and played in 31 matches, also joined. The third player, 26-year-old Edinburgh-born Mark Bell, who joined from Fulham, proved to be one of the most talented players to appear for the O's in the Edwardian era, having appeared for Scotland in 1901 while with Hearts. Buchanan or 'Buck', as he was known, was completely bald and was the only outfield player to have worn a skull-cap while on the field of play. He stood at just 5ft 7in but was a clever player and a real tower of strength in the side. Finally, there was 26-year-old Harry Lappin, the former Manchester United and Grimsby Town nippy little winger, who joined from non-League Rossendale United and was ever present throughout the season.

The O's ended the season with the visit of Chelsea, who had already been promoted along with Nottingham Forest, the match attracting the largest crowd seen at Millfields with over 21,000 spectators in attendance.

The O's attracted 151,810 spectators during the season, a vast improvement over the previous season, and they managed a net profit of £127 6s 10d, which would help pay the players' summer wage bill of £40. So, Wells-Holland's optimism at the League's annual meeting the previous May was well justified.

It was on 2 September 1907 that the club issued their first ever magazine-style matchday programme against Hull City, when Bill Martin scored the only goal of the game. The largest victory of the 1907–08 season was in November, a 5–1 win over Chesterfield before 5,000 fans, with goals from Greechan (2), Martin, Goffin and Parker, and they ended the season losing 6–1 at Stockport County. It was a few days after this match that County signed Bill Martin for £150, but after just 11 League appearances and three goals he moved on to Oldham Athletic.

Clapton Orient in 1907–08: Back row (left to right): Mr Robinson, Mr Arber, Captain Wells-Holland (chairman), Mr Goodger. Third row: Mr Holmes (manager), Reason, Henderson, Bower, W. Whittaker, Stewart, Bell, Mr Wilson (trainer). Second row: Liddell, Shelley, Gates, Buchanan (wearing his skull cap), Thacker, Howshall, Greechan. Front row: Parker, Leigh, Martin, Oliver, Pemberton.

So the O's ended the 1907–08 season in a respectable 14th position. The 1908–09 season started off in terrible fashion, with the first win only coming in the eighth League game, a 1–0 win over West Bromwich Albion through a 'Jumbo' Reason penalty.

The best performance came in the 1–0 victory over Tottenham Hotspur at White Hart Lane before a crowd of 32,821, George Scott scoring the goal – this was Scott's first season with club. Born in West Stanley on 29 September 1885, he proved to be one of the great pre-World War One O's players (see Matches to Remember). Three days later the O's took a point off Spurs, being one of three teams to take three points off them, and they were promoted as runners-up to Bolton Wanderers.

Two other players that caught the eye during the season were the England amateur international Lionel Arthur Louch, who gained three caps while with the O's, against Sweden (1909), France and Denmark (1910), to become the club's first international player, and also inside-forward George Gates, who came from Brentford and top scored with seven League goals. He was transferred to Grimsby Town in July 1909 and was converted to a centre-half.

The O's lost their last four League games but managed a 15th position finish and made a profit that season of £1,125. Only Tottenham Hotspur (£4,073) and Burnley (£1,831) made a larger profit out of all the Second Division clubs in the season, which saw a number of large clubs making a loss, like Birmingham City (£2,170), Fulham (£1,580) and West Bromwich Albion (£1,237). The total gross income for the O's that season was £6,554 and total wages paid were £3,252.

In 1909 there was suggestion that the club should change its name to London City Football Club and also change the colours. The club programme stated at the time that the proposed name had an impressive sound about it, with the ground being the nearest to the city. The directors of the club stated a week later that the present title would remain and a name change will not be considered.

There was not much to report during the following 1909–10 season when a 16th spot was secured. A couple of goods wins over promotion-chasing Leicester Fosse and Manchester City took place. On 13 November 1909, at Glossop North End, half-back Ned Liddell had to play in goal because the two goalkeepers on the books – Bower and Whittaker – were injured. The O's lost 3–1, but he performed well between the sticks. Burly 30-year-old centre-forward Fred Bevan was top scorer with seven goals (20 appearances), and left-winger Austin 'Tosher' Underwood had a fine season (37 appearances), proving to be a great goal provider.

It was during the season, on 10 January 1910, that centre-forward Jack Williams, the former Bury man, set up a club record when he scored all of the O's eight goals in the reserve clash with Leyton FC in the South Eastern Counties League in an 8–2 victory, but after just 12 first-team appearances he joined Leyton FC.

The 1910–11 season proved to be the best so far. By September they were top of Division Two, for the first time in their history, with four straight wins and nine goals scored. Although they lost just once at home all season, it was the away results which cost them a promotion place with 12 defeats. Yet, eventually they finished in fourth spot, winning 19 matches and scoring just 44 goals. Manager Holmes realised that new faces were needed, and he went to Fulham to sign one of their star players, Robert Dalrymple, for a record fee of £300. A few games later the exciting winger Joe Dix got injured at Bolton Wanderers in February and missed 12 games. Dix had joined the O's during the summer in unusual circumstances: he walked out of Portsmouth and signed for the Londoners. Pompey directors complained to the Football League, and after an enquiry the O's were fined and ordered to pay a transfer fee of £100.

The prospects for the O's seemed bright, and talk of First Division football was on the lips of officials and fans alike in 1911–12, if only they could improve that away form and score a few more goals. However, it was not to be, with 11 away defeats during the following campaign, finishing in fourth position again on 45 points, behind Derby County, Chelsea and Burnley.

One player who certainly caught the imagination was 21-year-old Scotsman Richard McFadden. He scored on his debut against Derby County on 2 September 1911 and went on to record 19 League goals (37 appearances) to break Bill Martin's record of 17 goals in 1906–07. He scored 66 League and two FA Cup goals from 142 appearances up to World War One.

During the season the O's defeated Millwall Athletic 3–0 in the Final of the London Challenge Cup, and in November 1911 the O's reserves set a club record with a 15–1 win over Catford. Their scorers were Prior (5), Scott (4), Cavanagh (4) and Dunn (2).

Everyone connected with the club was very encouraged towards the new 1912–13 season as the directors had spent money on the ground, enhancing the comfort of the spectators, and promotion to Division One was 'highly probable'. The promotion of Chelsea last season was a blow, with a loss of around £300 in gates receipts due to their promotion.

Following a very encouraging start to the 1912–13 campaign, in which the O's won five games and were defeated just once from the first eight games, they lost their form somewhat to finish in a disappointing 14th spot. Dickie McFadden topped the goals chart with 10 goals. The following season the O's home form was magnificent, being undefeated all season in both League and FA Cup (20 games), but, alas, that away form was again poor, with just two wins and 11 defeats.

The talking news in London before the following season commenced was the move of Woolwich Arsenal from their Plumstead ground to Gillespie Road, Highbury. Both the O's and Tottenham Hotspur objected to the Football League about the move, issuing a joint statement, saying it was a menace to their own interests. The Football League declined to intervene and gave their blessing to the move, saying there was ample population in the area for the three clubs.

The O's started the season considerably well with a home win over Fulham before 18,000 fans through a McFadden penalty, then they went to Glossop North End and won 3–0 (Hunter, Dalrymple and Parker). On 6 December, at Nottingham Forest, the O's goalie Jimmy Hugall was stretchered off the field injured and was replaced in goal by forward Willie Jonas, and it was McFadden with a late equaliser that earned the O's a credible 1–1 draw.

A week later McFadden was on target again with a 20-yarder, which flashed past the Arsenal goalie, Lievesley, in front of a record 26,580 crowd. The O's gained a wonderful 5–2 win on Christmas Day over Bristol City at Millfields Road. After trailing 2–1 with just 20 minutes to go, Robert Dalrymple netted a hat-trick, with further goals from Forrest and Jonas to secure the two points. It was over this period that McFadden turned down a £3,000 move to First Division Middlesbrough.

On 3 January 1914 the O's were leading Glossop North End by 4–1 when referee Mr J. Pearson blew his whistle seven minutes early. As the players were trooping off the Millfields Road pitch, he realised his mistake and called the players back to complete the match, with George Scott adding a fifth.

In February Orient signed the Belgium international centre-half Ike van den Eynden, who had won 17 caps for his country. He made his debut in the 3–0 win over Hull City before a big crowd of more than 18,000, with the O's running out easy winners by 3–0 (McFadden (2, 1 pen) and Jonas). The Belgian, who picked up the nickname of 'Vandy', received a huge ovation from the home crowd every time he touched the ball. However, trouble occurred when the visiting Hull fans kept calling the team 'slant eyes' in reference to the club's Chinaman mascot pictured on the front of the programme.

On Monday 2 March the Leeds City team arrived at Millfields early for a midweek fixture. At 2pm the officials from both clubs were haggling over the kick-off time: the O's officials wanted to start at

Clapton Orient in 1912–13. Back row (left to right): Billy Holmes (manager), Mawby (assistant trainer), Scott, Hind, Bower, Hugall, Johnson, Evans, Wilson (trainer), Ludford (director). Middle row: Griffiths, Holmes, Bartleman, Benson, Jonas, Liddell, Willis, Stonehouse, Johnson, A.E. Simpson (director), C.W.H. Dean (secretary). Front row: Parker, Dalrymple, Trenholm, McFadden, Dix.

4.30pm as advertised, and City wanted the match to start 20 minutes earlier, but the O's secretary forgot to inform the referee of the change of plans.

More confusion reigned when the referee ordered the Leeds goalkeeper to change his jersey because of a colour clash, which delayed the start to after 4.30pm. As half-time approached, with Leeds 1–0 up, the light was deteriorating so the referee restricted the break to just two minutes. The *Yorkshire Post* journalist covering the match thought it was now impossible to see the middle of the field from the main stand. The match restarted and the O's ran in three late goals, all long speculative shots, to secure a 3–1 win (Billy Hind (2) and Nolan Evans), and the match ended in near darkness.

The Leeds manager Herbert Chapman was an angry man as he left the stadium, and he complained bitterly to the referee that his goalkeeper could not see the ball and wanted the match to be replayed at a later date.

After studying the referee's report, the Football League ruled that the result should stand, but the O's were fined £25. At the end of the season Leeds missed out on promotion by only two points, having a better goal difference than Bradford Park Avenue who were eventually promoted.

The season ended in even more dramatic fashion with the O's first ever visit to Arsenal's new ground in Highbury. The Gunners needed a win to clinch promotion over the Bradford club, and with just five minutes remaining they looked safe with a 2–0 lead. Then, with a few minutes remaining, Fred Parker scored with a long shot, and in the dying seconds McFadden scored from a corner for a 2–2 draw (see Matches to Remember). So the Bradford club could thank the O's for helping them to the runners'-up spot. The O's finished in sixth spot with the best defensive record in the League, yet again the poor showing away from home let them down with just two wins and nine goals scored all season.

It was McFadden once again who stole the show in the 1914–15 season, with 21 League goals and his great striking partnership with his friend Jonas. The season ended with the outbreak of war. The final match of the season against Leicester Fosse, a 2–0 win, attracted a crowd of 21,000, who after the match watched the O's players in the official parade around the ground to say farewell before they went off to war.

Orient in World War One

The 1914–15 season was overshadowed by the start of the great war of the 20th century in August 1914. Orient ended the season in ninth position with Richard McFadden top scorer with 21 goals from 37 League starts. During that season the club had various collections at the ground on match days. It was reported that one donation made by a Mrs Arkell, who gave £2 and 40 pence, was distributed among Lord Kitchener's wounded soldiers in local hospitals.

As the season progressed, in 1915, with war still on everyone's mind, a campaign was begun by Lord Northcliffe to stop League football. He wrote in the press that football players and spectators attending matches were unpatriotic by attending them. He never got his will and the season was completed.

The Orient directors decided to bring wounded soldiers from the London Hospital to watch Orient play against Fulham on 2 January 1915, with McFadden bagging two goals. It was a long, hard season and everyone involved was relieved to see it finally over. The war sped into a worldwide conflict and League football was suspended between 1915 and 1919.

The war officially ended on 11 November 1918, with eight percent of Great Britain's population

Clapton Orient players parade around Millfields Road before going off to war, 24 April 1915.

Clapton Orient players take to the field against Leicester Fosse, 24 April 1915.

Fred Parker (left) tosses the coin with skipper Horace Burton of Leicester Fosse, 24 April 1915.

either killed or wounded. It was decided that a full League programme would restart in August 1919, five years after its suspension.

During the suspension all the London League teams plus Watford were to play in the London Combination League. Clubs were instructed not to pay their players more than one shilling (five pence) per month each.

The real seriousness of the war was brought home when an anti-aircraft gun was positioned on top of the Spion Kop hill at Millfields Road ground, presumably to attack German aircraft raiders as they flew over Clapton and Hackney.

The newspapers of the time were informing the general public of Clapton Orient's splendid lead in having the highest number of players and club officials from any football club in the country to volunteer for Kitchener's army.

At the beginning of the war only men 5ft 6in and over and with a chest measurement of 35 inches were considered for active duty, but by May 1915 this was changed and soldiers only had to be 5ft 3in and the age limit was raised to 40.

At the start of the campaign Britain only had 247,432 regular troops, so it was clear more troops were needed.

Some 40 Orient players and officials joined the Footballers (Service) Battalion of the 17th Middlesex Regiment. They were led by the O's 'keeper Jimmy Hugall, and skipper Fred Parker and Richard McFadden were the very first footballers to join.

After military training at the White City and then in Clipstone, the Battalion embarked for Flanders in France on 18 November 1915.

These were the Orient players who went off to fight for their country as reported in the O's programme on 2 December 1919:

The Roll of Honour:

Killed: Company Sergeant Major F/162 Richard McFadden, aged 27, on 24 October 1916. Private F/32 William Jonas, aged 26, killed in action, 23 July 1916 at Delville Wood. Private 1583 George Scott was killed on 16 August 1916 moving from La Chausee to Vignacourt.

Wounded: J. Hugall, R. Dalrymple, N. Evans, H. Gibson, T. Pearson, G. Saunders, N. Holmes, A. Spencer, H. Reason, W. Askew.

With the Forces: F. Parker, G. Beech, S. Morris, J. Ing, J. Lamb, E. Ferris, J. Spencer, A. Norris, A. Parsons, R. McCullough, J. Gasgoigne, J. Rutherford, W. Hampson, J. Reynolds, W. Mawbey, R. Evans, A. Tilley, D. Wilson, A. Crossley, C. Scatterthwaite, J. Carney, W. Ashurst, G. Jones, F. Dunn, J. Lee, R. Chapman, D. Upex.

The following month a few more names were listed as wounded: F.J.C. Blake, Joe Bailey and 'Gunner' Hull.

There were subsequent reports in various local newspapers concerning the deaths of two other players, Bob Dalrymple and Harry Gibson, but these were later proved to be untrue.

A moving account was published in an Orient programme during November 1616 from a letter received from McFadden. It read:

'On the morning of 27 July 1916, at the front line in Delville Wood, I, Richard McFadden, sadly report to you concerning my friend and fellow Orient player Willie Jonas.

We were both trapped in a trench near the front. Willie turned to me and said "Goodbye Mac, best of luck, love to my wife and best regards to the lads at the Orient." Before I could reply to him, he was up and over. No sooner had he jumped out of the trench, my best friend as a young boy and at the Orient was killed.'

Richard McFadden, Orient's pre-war goalscorer extraordinaire and a company sergeant major, had suffered serious wounds and died in hospital on 24 October 1916.

All the staff at the club were shattered by the loss of the three players. Captain Fred Parker reported that a splendid cross was made by the club and players for them, with a football and a badge of the club placed on top.

Many references to the players were published.

In the Arsenal programme the following was printed:

'Two things distinguished these players' careers as men and footballers. Their heroism and great playing ability.

'In civil life they were heroes (McFadden had saved a small boy from drowning in the River Lea, for which he received a medal) and they proved themselves heroes on the battlefield. Brave men and a very brave football club.

'We at Arsenal Football Club say… Thank you to Clapton Orient for taking the lead in the numbers you had joining up and showing the way.'

A special letter was delivered to the club from King George V, which stated:

'The whole Country, myself and the whole of the Royal family say thank you and good luck to CLAPTON ORIENT FOOTBALL CLUB, no club has paid a greater price to patriotism.'

The two young royal princes had a soft spot for the club, and it was in April 1921 that Edward, Prince of Wales, became the first member of the royal family to watch a Football League match (they had watched Cup Finals in previous years), and his brother, the Duke of York, came to Millfields in 1922.

The prince informed Orient chairman Gray-Robbins that his visit was in recognition and acknowledgement of what Clapton Orient did for their country during the war. (A fuller account of the visit of Edward, Prince of Wales, appears later in this section.)

Of the seasons in the London Combination, there was very little published in the local press or in the club programme.

The League authorities suspended all player contracts, and players were, therefore, at liberty to play for the clubs of their choice. So a club like Clapton Orient had little hope of attracting many decent players.

The O's did have a few outside players guesting for them during the period. Players like Sunderland-born goalkeeper John William Mew, who between 1912–25 made 186 League appearances for Manchester United, mostly after the war. He appeared in goal for the O's in November 1916. Mew also made an appearance for England against Ireland in 1920, and he also represented the Football League and toured South Africa with an FA Party in 1921.

There was James George William Harrold, born in Plaistow on 26 March 1892, a centre-half, noted for his fine heading ability, who started his career with Custom House before playing as an amateur with both Huddersfield Town and West Ham United in 1913. It was while with Leicester Fosse that he made 206 League and 12 FA Cup appearances between 1913–23. He moved to Millwall in 1924 for £1,000 but made just two League appearances. In August 1925 he joined Clapton Orient at the age of 33 but never got a look in and retired from football to concentrate on his cricket career with Essex CCC until 1929, playing 11 county matches for Essex with 19 innings, 88 runs at an average of 5.50; he also took three wickets for 123 runs from 180 balls. He died in Epsom, Surrey, on 7 October 1950.

There was 20-year-old Irishman Patrick O'Connell who joined the O's in April 1915 but had little chance to impress after the war interrupted his time at Millfields Road. Like a number of top-flight players of the time, he was exempt from combat duties, having played 34 games for Manchester United, and he also captained Ireland. After the war, he made quite a name for himself as a manager in Spanish football with Santander, spending seven seasons with the coastal club. He was then appointed manager of Real Betis in Seville, leading them to their first Championship in 1934. He then had a spell as boss of Barcelona; however, this was interrupted by the civil war in Spain. In 1942 he managed Seville. O'Connell died in London during 1959 a forgotten man, whose great times as the only Irish-born manager in Spanish football had never really been noted. Walter John Kimberley, a centre-half with Aston Villa, Coventry City and Walsall, also played a few games in January 1918 just before he left for the front, but sadly just four months later he died from wounds received in the battle of Marne. Terence Percival Hanney, a player with Manchester City in 1913–19, played for the O's, and after the war he joined Reading.

During the early part of the 1915–16 season, the O's attracted crowds of around 8,000. In September 1915 they signed three new players: Beech, Buckley and Wheelhouse.

Goalscorers 1915–16

Layton 12, Beech 7, Turnbull 3, Bailey 2, Lamb 2, Ashurst 1, Barber 1, Caldwell 1, Craddock 1, Dalrymple 1, Dunn 1, Jones 1, Odger 1, Taylor 1, Upex 1, Whalley 1, Williams 1.

London Combination (final table 1915–16)

	P	W	D	L	F	A	Pts
Chelsea	22	17	3	2	71	18	37
Millwall Ath	22	12	6	4	46	24	30
Arsenal	22	10	5	7	43	46	25
West Ham U	22	10	4	8	47	35	24
Fulham	22	10	4	8	45	37	24
Tottenham H	22	8	8	6	38	35	24
Brentford	22	6	8	8	36	40	20
Queen's Park R	22	8	3	11	27	41	19
Crystal Palace	22	8	3	11	35	55	19
Watford	22	8	1	13	37	46	17
CLAPTON ORIENT	22	4	6	12	22	44	14
Croydon Common	22	3	5	14	24	50	11

London Combination – 1915–16 Supplementary Tournament

	P	W	D	L	F	A	Pts
Chelsea	14	10	1	3	50	15	21
West Ham U	14	9	2	3	32	16	20
Tottenham Hotspur	14	8	3	3	32	22	19
Fulham	14	9	0	5	38	19	18
Millwall Athletic	14	8	2	4	30	22	18
Crystal Palace	14	8	2	4	41	29	18
Watford	14	5	3	6	22	20	13
Brentford	14	5	2	7	29	33	12
Croydon Common	14	4	3	7	28	27	11
CLAPTON ORIENT	14	3	4	7	17	27	10
Arsenal	14	3	4	7	19	31	10
Luton Town	14	4	1	9	31	44	9
Queen's Park R	14	2	5	7	14	37	9
Reading	14	3	2	9	23	64	8

The admission prices were 7d for the ground and 1s 2d for the enclosure, inclusive of tax, in the 1916–17 season. A few notes were located from the season, and the team that beat Millwall 3–0 on 2 September 1916 read: W. Bower, W. Hind, A. Goodman, E. King, H. Willis, J.C. Ing, G.S. Walden, D. Bailey, A. Layton, T. Simons, T. Kerr.

The O's programme editor reported that a letter had been received by the Orient manager Billy Holmes from our goalkeeper 2nd Lieutenant James Hugall of the Durham Light Infantry, which read:

'I was very grieved to hear of Billy Jonas' death. Same old Billy out there as he was on the football field, and was liked by everybody. I think he had a heart of a lion and was the life and soul of the football Battalion. If it were possible I would dearly love to turn out for you. I am expecting leave any day now. I hope you can get some men together and keep the name of the old club flying.'

For the match on 23 September at Millfields, the short match report stated that it was a rough game and indifferent play, and two of the visitors were sent off. Orient lost 3–0. On 4 November, for the visit of Chelsea, the O's gave a trial to local player J. Cheriton at right-back, who did fairly well, with over 4,000 in attendance. A week later they lost 4–0 at Arsenal before more than 6,000 spectators and lost again the following week at home to Luton Town by 7–1, with Geggus playing in goal. He became a regular over the following months. On 13 January 1917, after a 3–0 loss at Crystal Palace, the O's occupied the last position in the London Combination.

Orient had a rare away win 3–2 at Luton Town on 10 February. The match report stated that after a finely contested match they ran out worthy winners. However, owing to a railway mishap the Clapton boys arrived very late and the game started more than hour late. When Orient entered the field they received a polite round of applause from the 3,000 crowd, and they also found four inches of snow on the field. Blake opened the scoring for the O's after five minutes, but then Butcher and Leggett gave the Hatters the lead. Orient equalised when, after a fine run by Blake, his shot was saved by the Luton goalie, Mitchell, but Stevens dashed in and scored. It was Bailey who scored the winner for Orient. On 6 March they had one of their best wins during the war years (there were only 18 recorded during the four seasons of wartime football), a 6–1 victory against Portsmouth before 1,500

Millfields Road fans, with Blake (3), Cheriton (2) and Bailey being the scorers. It was reported that the Orient players were spurred on by the return of goalkeeper Hugull, who turned out for the club after an absence of three years, and also Harry Gibson, back from the front, played for the boys.

On 17 March 1917 Tottenham Hotspur were the visitors and the O's team read: E. Lilley, A. Goodman, H. Willis, A. Hicks, B.W.J. Ferris, W. Chilcott, J. Cheriton, F. Blake, J. Barclay, J. Bailey and G.S. Stevens. Spurs won 5–2 and the match report stated 'E. Lilley in goal was not a great success. The game was too much for him and his display was enough to make any of the backs rather nervy; I must admit I also shook in my boots every time the ball came near him. At the interval he was replaced and told to go and play as an outfield player. B.W. Ferris went in goal and, though lacking in style, he saved many good Spurs shots.'

In the home defeat by Millwall, 2–1, in March, H.S.C. Cushway, a full-back from Leytonstone, made his debut before 3,000 spectators.

In the last match of the season on 28 April 1917, the O's went down to the tune of 8–0, and the reporter, being so disgusted, tore up his notes on the match.

Goalscorers 1916–17

Layton 14, Bailey 9, Blake 5, Cheriton 5, Goodman 5, Stevens 3, Walden 2, Barlow 1, Chamberlain 1, Chapman 1, Little 1, Simon 1, Upex 1

London Combination 1916–17

	P	W	D	L	F	A	Pts
West Ham U	40	30	5	5	110	45	65
Millwall A	40	26	6	8	85	48	58
Chelsea	40	24	5	11	93	48	53
Tottenham Hotspur	40	24	5	11	112	64	53
Arsenal	40	19	10	11	62	47	48
Fulham	40	21	3	16	102	63	45
Luton T	39	20	3	16	101	82	43
Crystal Palace	38	14	7	17	68	72	35
Southampton	39	13	8	18	57	80	34
Queen's Park Rangers	39	10	9	20	48	86	29
Watford	39	8	9	22	69	115	25
Brentford	40	9	7	24	56	99	25
Portsmouth	40	9	4	27	58	117	22
CLAPTON ORIENT	40	6	7	27	49	104	19

In September of the 1917–18 season the O's lost at home to Fulham by 5–1 with barely 2,000 spectators at the ground. During the same month the local reporter wrote 'Orient lost 2–0 at Queen's Park Rangers. Orient gifted two own goals by Holmes and Chilcott who blasted the ball past his goalkeeper.'

In October came the visit of Tottenham Hotspur, with less than 3,000 in attendance, who run out winners by 2–1, Powell scoring the O's goal. The most surprising thing was that Spurs could only muster two goals.

The following week less than 1,000 people watched Brentford at Millfields. The visitors won 3–1 as Orient played their usual ineffective game. Hodgson scored the lone O's goal. The Orient defence were at times very poor, while the forwards lacked combination and they deserved yet another loss.

In November West Ham United were the Millfields visitors with more than 5,000 at the ground and their strong side won 4–1. Cruttenden had little chance, with Shea the best player on view. Stevens scored Orient's goal.

Goalscorers 1917–18

Fifield 9, Layton 4, Nisbitt 4, Powell 3, Goodwin 2, Stevens 2, Blake 1, Burke 1, Gibson 1, Goodman 1, Gray 1, Hodgson 1, Parkes 1, Smith 1, Tyler 1, White 1

London Combination 1917–18

	P	W	D	L	F	A	Pts
Chelsea	36	21	8	7	82	39	50
West Ham U	36	20	9	7	103	51	49
Fulham	36	20	7	9	75	60	47
Tottenham Hotspur	36	22	2	12	86	56	46
Arsenal	36	16	5	15	76	57	37
Brentford	36	16	3	17	81	94	35
Crystal Palace	36	13	4	19	54	83	30
Queen's Park Rangers	36	14	2	20	48	73	30
Millwall	36	12	4	20	52	74	28
CLAPTON ORIENT	36	2	4	30	34	104	8

In the 1918–19 season some of the players to appear for the club were goalkeepers Fisher and Moorwood, full-backs Page, Nicholls, Kimberley, Tonner, Pugh, halves Forrest, Lee, Shore, Hind, Gibson, Worboys, Wednot, and forwards Dalrymple, Smith, Moore, Dimmock, Bowyer, Flavell, Parker, Simms and Gray.

The O's finished bottom of the League on just 12 points, conceding 123 goals.

Goalscorers

Dimmock 8, Bowyer 4, Dalrymple 4, Moore 4, Nash 2, Nesbit 2, White 2, Blake 1, Brightwell 1, Chesney 1, Eves 1, Jones 1, Lee 1, Roe 1, Smith 1, Wiseman 1, Opponents own goals: 2 goals

London Combination 1918–19

	P	W	D	L	F	A	Pts
Brentford	36	20	9	7	94	46	49
Arsenal	36	20	5	11	85	56	45
West Ham U	36	17	7	12	65	51	41
Fulham	36	17	6	13	70	55	40
Queen's Park Rangers	36	16	7	13	69	60	39
Chelsea	36	13	11	12	70	53	37
Tottenham Hotspur	36	13	8	15	52	72	34
Crystal Palace	36	14	6	16	66	73	34
Millwall	36	10	9	17	50	67	29
CLAPTON ORIENT	36	3	6	27	35	123	12

After the war

In an effort to rebuild their side after the war, manager Billy Holmes made some astute signings for the start of the 1919–20 season, including the three Tonner brothers from Scotland, Jack, James and Samuel, John Townrow and Owen Williams and a few of the more familiar faces from before the war, including Dalrymple, Forrest, Hugall, 'Spider' Parker, Hind and Layton.

The season started with a 2–1 defeat at Huddersfield Town, and the highlights included a Ben Ives hat-trick in a 4–1 win over South Shields, a Millfields Road ground record of 32,644 spectators with receipts of £1,480 to see Tottenham Hotspur win 4–0, a huge 44,268 White Hart Lane crowd to see the O's go down 2–1 and a 1–0 'double' over West Ham United. The O's finished in 15th position in Division Two.

The following season, 1920–21, saw a marked improvement, seventh position. The season started with a 2–0 defeat at home to Leicester City before 18,000 fans. On Monday 30 August 1920 the O's introduced League football to Wales, playing Cardiff City at Ninian Park before 25,000 spectators. The Welsh club presented an inscribed memento on vellum to the Londoners, which read 'Presented to Clapton Orient FC by the directors of Cardiff City AFC as a memento of the first English League match in Wales.' Later it was inscribed with the names of the directors and the players who appeared in the goalless draw. On 28 October 1920 the O's beat Crystal Palace at Millfields by 2–1 before a crowd of 7,000 to win the London Professional Charity Fund, with goals from Jack Tonner and Owen Williams, but Palace got their revenge when defeating them the following May to win the London Challenge Cup Final, played at White Hart Lane before 10,000 spectators.

On 25 December 1920, for the home match with Hull City, the players wore black armbands and the 30,000-strong crowd stood for a minute's silence as a mark of respect of the death of amateur goalkeeper Guy Paul Dale, who died in a motorcar accident in Framington, Kent, on 14 December, having played just one League game against Bury the previous October. Dale, who was born in Barnsley in 1894, worked as the secretary and house governor of the Metropolitan Hospital.

The season closed on an historic note as the Prince of Wales visited Millfields Road for the match with Notts County.

Esteemed visitor, on Saturday 30 April 1921, to Clapton Orient was Edward, the Prince of Wales, who that day became the first member of the royal family ever to attend a Football League match. The previous evening was one of tense excitement for the local population, for it seemed the whole of Clapton, Hackney and Homerton had been painted for the royal visit. All roads seem to lead to the club's Millfields Road ground, the Prince travelling through the streets from the West End in an open-top car. By 2pm over 19,000 had assembled inside the ground and over 40,000 outside it. For the occasion they played a match against Notts County, and the directors had the ground repainted. The grandstand was decked with the flags of many nations, while the directors' box was decorated with flowers in the Prince's own colours. At 3.10pm the Prince finally arrived at the ground to loud cheers, his car escorted by three mounted policeman. His Highness was welcomed by Clapton Orient chairman Mr H. Gray-Robbins, who introduced the Prince to his fellow directors. Miss Elsie Marsden, daughter of Orient's managing director, presented the Prince with a souvenir match programme.

When the royal party appeared on the pitch, the crowd sang *God Bless the Prince of Wales*, accompanied by the bands of the Upton House School and the local United Services Club. Orient captain and goalkeeper Jimmy Hugall presented his players to the Prince. Two disappointed men

Clapton Orient in 1921–22. Back row (left to right): C.W.H. Dean (secretary), N. Mardall (director), A. Unwin (director), E.T. Wimms (director), Wood, S. Gough, Hugall, D. McCarthy (director), T.S. Ludford (director), P.H. Arber (director), H. Gray-Robbins (chairman). Third row: Billy Holmes (manager), F. Powell (trainer), Bradbury, Dixon, Townrow, Whipp, Cheriton, Forest, Nicholson, Nicholls, Worboys, Osmond, W. Hind (assistant trainer). F. Bevan (reserve-team coach). Front row: Smith, Leggett, T. Williams, Gillatt, Parker, Rennox, Bratby, Denton, O. Williams. On floor: S. Tonner, Kean, Nunn, J. Tonner.

were Orient's England international players John Townrow and Owen Williams, who were both injured.

Orient's team that day read Hugall, Sam Tonner, Osmond, Forrest, Worboys, Nicholson, Smith, Gillatt, Dixon, Parker and Nunn.

The Prince moved on to the visitors, and he joined in the laughter that was prompted when he was introduced to County's legendary and giant goalkeeper Albert Iremonger. He stood at 6ft 5in, and the Prince had to stretch up to exchange a few words with him.

Back in the directors' box, the Prince sat next to the Mayor of Hackney, Herbert Morrison, an Orient shareholder. Soon after the start of the match the Prince was applauding an Orient goal through Dixon. Orient followed up in the second half with further goals from Forrest and Gillatt for a 3–0 victory. The Prince told Gray-Robbins that he had enjoyed the O's victory very much and that he hoped the club would see him again next season. In fact it was the Prince's brother, the Duke of York, who was visiting them a year later.

It was just after the visit in May 1921 that manager Holmes signed the huge 27-year-old Arthur Wood from Southampton, and what a capture he turned to be, playing for the next 10 seasons with a record number of appearances, and a great custodian and folk-hero.

The plan for the visit of the Duke of York to Millfields Road was to be on 22 April 1922 for the match with Bristol City. However, just four days before the royal visit, manager Billy Holmes collapsed and died in Hackney from a heart attack after 16 years with the club. It was a great loss, but the directors decided, after consulting Buckingham Palace, to carry on with the Duke's visit, but the players, wearing black armbands, understandably never got going and lost the match 1–0. It was former player Peter Proudfoot who was appointed as manager in his place.

One other unique feature of the season was the appearance in the League of the three Tonner brothers – John, Samuel and James. They appeared together in 12 League games and in one FA Cup tie during the season.

Within the profiles on the three Tonner brothers (all of whom appeared for the O's in the 1920s) in other books by the authors, mention is made of seven other sets of three brothers to have appeared in the Football League or FA Cup together for the same team in the same season.

Many have requested names on these trios of brothers and there is a full list in the Star Players section under the Tonner brothers.

In the 1922–23 season the O's had three sets of brothers on their books, although they never all appeared in the same match together. They were: Jack and Robert Duffus, who played once together in a League match against Bury on 9 December 1922, Jack and Samuel Tonner, also in the same side, who appeared in 22 League games together, and the Williams brothers, Owen and Tom, who played twice with the Tonners in the Christmas and Boxing Day fixtures against Stockport County.

The O's only escaped relegation after two wins over Bradford City, the final two fixtures of the season, and it was Bertie Bliss who scored three in the two games to secure the four points, the last game at home a 1–0 win attracting 18,000 fans.

Towards the end of the decade the O's struggled in their League campaigns. The club was being crippled financially by having to pay rent of £2,500 per annum to the Clapton greyhound syndicate, who now owned the Millfields Road ground. There was also an economic recession and subsequent unemployment at the same time, which affected gates as the team battled to avoid relegation.

During the decade five O's players were awarded international caps. Winger Owen Williams became the first O's player to gain full international honours when he played for England against Ireland at West Bromwich on 22 October 1922, creating both goals in a 2–0 victory, and he gained one further cap against Wales in 1923. Centre-half John Townrow gained his first English cap against Scotland in 1925, and one further cap followed in 1926 against Wales. The following three players gained Welsh caps: Tom Evans won three caps against Scotland twice (1927, 1928) and England (1928), Ernie Morley won three caps against England, Scotland and

Richardson, Bury's goalkeeper, collects the ball from O's forward Tommy Green during Clapton Orient's 1–0 win in October 1923.

Clapton Orient players Bertie Bliss (heading) and John Townrow in action against Leeds United in October 1923. The O's played them twice during that month and lost both games 0–1.

Northern Ireland all in 1929, and Eddie Lawrence won one cap against Northern Ireland in 1930.

During the 1923–24 season the O's had 14 wins. One of the best was the 3–0 victory over League leaders South Shields on 20 October 1923 before 20,000 fans, with goals from Owen Williams, who tapped into the empty net after Rennox had barged the visiting goalkeeper Walker, who then dropped the ball, Clatworthy Rennox, who after dribbling past three defenders netted from 15 yards, and George Waite, who scored from a Rennox free-kick, all goals coming in the second half.

The story of Albert Arthur Pape, playing that season, makes remarkable reading. The big, bustling 28-year-old centre-forward made 24 League appearances and scored 11 goals for the O's, yet he still had time to write his name in football record books through his bizarre transfer to promotion-chasing Manchester United on 7 February 1925.

The Manchester United directors first approached Orient about the transfer of Pape in January 1925; they made a £1,000 offer which was rejected. Then late on Friday 6 February 1925 – the next day the teams were due to meet at Old Trafford – the United chairman George H. Lawton phoned his O's counterpart Mr Gray-Robbins to make an offer of £2,000, and after hours of deliberation by the O's board of directors they finally agreed terms. The player himself was only told on the train up to Manchester, and when informed about the possible move the O's players were amazed. The player himself did not like the idea of playing against his teammates.

On arrival in Manchester at 1pm, Pape was whisked away to meet the United officials and discuss the personal terms. At 2.15pm Pape still had not signed; in fact he was sitting in the visitors dressing room wearing his O's shirt waiting for the wire from the Football League to ratify the transfer, which eventually arrived. Pape took off his O's jersey and said his farewells to his former teammates. He quickly put pen to paper and changed dressing rooms. The 18,250 crowd and the press were stunned to hear of the transfer news on the loudspeaker, and Pape went on to score United's third in their 4–2 victory. He made 18 League appearances for United with five goals before his transfer to Fulham just nine months later. A man of many clubs, Pape scored 103 career League goals from 266 appearances.

By the end of the 1925–26 season, the O's were fighting for their Second Division survival. They

Some of the 24,600 crowd that watched the FA Cup sixth-round match against Manchester City on 6 March 1926. Orient lost 1–6.

were level with Stoke City on 31 points, Stockport County having already been relegated. They were away at Middlesbrough on 1 May 1926 and needed at least a point; City were at home to Southampton. The O's came up trumps with an excellent 2–1 victory at Ayresome Park, Cock and Broadbent being the scorers before 7,788 fans. City could only manage a 1–1 draw, so the O's were saved from relegation and finished in 20th spot.

The 1926–27 season was another battle, and once again they waited until the end of the season, with three wins coming in the last few games. A crowd of 25,329 witnessed one of the O's best performances of the season, a 3–0 home win over Chelsea, then followed a 1–0 win at Blackpool.

A victory on the final day of the season assured Second Division football for another season, winning 1–0 at Reading on 7 May 1927, thanks to a Gardner penalty.

It was in the 1926–27 season that veteran winger Jack Rutherford made nine League appearances. He became the oldest player to appear for the O's in a League fixture, and he played his match in the 4–5 home defeat by Portsmouth on 2 April 1927 at the age of 42 years and 172 days (this record is now held by goalkeeper Peter Shilton; his final League game for the O's was on 21 January 1997, aged 47 years and 124 days).

The 1927–28 season was no different, the O's escaped the drop into the Third Division South by gaining a 0–0 draw at home to Wolverhampton Wanderers before 12,891 fans, at the expense of Fulham. The Cottagers played away at Blackpool, trying to avoid the drop, but were thrashed 4–0 and were relegated along with South Shields.

After all the fixtures had been completed, there were grave allegations against the O's by Fulham about the conduct of the manager Peter Proudfoot. An FA commission decided that charges against Proudfoot that he had made proposals with the object of pre-arranging match results had proved unfounded. However, they found that he had acted irregularly in a number of matches and suspended him from his management duties for six months. The club was not docked any points, so remained in Division Two.

Division Two 1927–28 (bottom four places)

	P	W	D	L	F	A	Pts
Blackpool	42	13	8	21	83	101	34
Clapton Orient	42	11	12	19	55	85	34
Fulham	42	13	7	22	68	89	33
South Shields	42	7	9	26	56	111	23

After four seasons in which relegation was narrowly avoided, there were no last-minute heroics in 1929, losing their last four away fixtures, and it was no surprise that they were relegated for the first time in their 20-year League history, finishing bottom of the League on 32 points, two behind Port Vale, who were also relegated, and four points behind both Bristol City and Swansea Town.

For the first campaign in the Third Division South, with Proudfoot suspended, they appointed Arthur Grimsdell as player-manager. He was one of the finest half-backs of his era, with Tottenham Hotspur and England, and he was seen as the man to lead the O's back to Division Two. The best home crowd of the season, 18,054, was on the opening day, a 2–0 defeat by Plymouth Argyle.

Alas, Grimsdell ran into immediate problems – the club forgot to register him as a player with the FA, and his first appearance came in the eighth game, by which time the O's had only managed one victory. Things did not improve much with just two wins from 13 games.

The 1930s

From January 1930 results improved with 12 wins to secure a 12th spot. At the end of March 1930 Grimsdell had resigned, and Peter Proudfoot was back in charge. They had two impressive results, a 5–0 win at Torquay United (up to the end of the 2005–06 season, 1,939 League matches had been played away from home, and this has been the only 5–0 away victory) and a 6–1 home win over Luton Town, and ended the season with a 4–1 win over Brighton & Hove Albion. It was during this season that secretary Cornelius Dean retired after more than 24 years in office, having joined the club in March 1906.

After much pressure from the greyhound racing syndicate, the club was forced to leave the Millfields Road ground after more than 30 years. The directors chose a ground just a mile away down Lea Bridge Road, and the O's first League match there was on 4 September 1930, against Newport County, resulting in a 3–1 win before 5,055 fans, Jack Fowler scoring the opening goal.

On 8 November Torquay United were the visitors to Lea Bridge Road and, after their 4–0 defeat, they complained to the FA that the white fencing around the ground was too close to the pitch. Morton Cadman from the FA visited the ground and decided that the club must close it for alterations. The next two 'home' fixtures were to be played at the famous Wembley Stadium. On 22 November 1930 they defeated Brentford 3–1 (Cropper (2) and Tricker) before 8,319 fans. The next match at Wembley was played on a very wet and windy December day, which restricted the attendance to just 1,916. The O's won 3–1 (Fowler (2) and Tricker).

The season ended with just two wins from nine games, and Orient slid down the table, ending in 19th position, and a financial crisis appeared to looming.

On 18 April 1931, for the match against Luton Town, two significant events took place: the last home game of the legendary 34-year-old goalkeeper Arthur Wood, in all he made 373 League and 22 FA Cup appearances, including 225 consecutive appearances between 1921–26, and also the day saw the appointment of Jimmy Seed as the secretary-manager. Seed had been a wonderful player with both Tottenham Hotspur and Sheffield Wednesday.

His first decision was to change the club colours for the following season to white shirts with red hoops and black shorts, but Seed found the club in a massive fight for financial survival.

His first season in charge started off with a couple of defeats then a good 4–0 home win over Mansfield Town. In October the best crowd of the season, 17,072, saw Southend United run out winners 4–2 at Lea Bridge not long after. During January 1932 the O's went to Luton Town and won 5–1, but the following week they lost 4–3 at Mansfield. In the end 16th spot was the best they could obtain, with Charlie Fletcher bagging 20 League goals from 41 appearances followed by Reg Tricker on 19 goals.

The following season was another real battle both on and off the field, with just three wins from the first 21 games played. Yet games 24 and 25, both home games, saw the O's hit Crystal Palace 4–1 and Swindon Town 7–1, but from then on just two wins from the final 16 games saw them scrape in by the skin of their teeth to avoid having to apply for re-election as they had a better goal average.

Division Three South 1932–33 (bottom four places)

	P	W	D	L	F	A	Pts
Cardiff City	42	12	12	23	69	99	31
Clapton Orient	42	8	13	21	59	93	29
Newport County	42	11	7	24	61	105	29
Swindon Town	42	9	11	22	60	105	29

It was no real surprise that manager Jimmy Seed resigned and took charge of Charlton Athletic with the O's near to bankruptcy. They appointed the former Celtic and Liverpool player David Pratt to take charge; however, the first thing he had to do was to release the entire playing staff. There was talk of a move to the Hackney Wick Stadium and a merger with another financially-strapped club, Thames Association, but both of these never happened.

The club was near to closure, and between May and June 1933 the Football League suspended them for failing to meet a payment of £2,000. Orient were warned that unless the payment was made quickly they would cease to be a member of the League and their place would be taken by another club.

The chairman of the League, a Mr McKenna, wrote to the club stating 'Clapton Orient are a very lucky club, having a generous lot of gentlemen by allowing them to continue, but I will say clearly now that there will be no further sympathy with your club, unless you put your financial affairs in order by 22 June 1933.'

Supporters arranged a large number of fundraising meetings, in particular at the George public house in Glyn Road, owned by George Harris, a director of the club, 100 yards from Millfields and close by the fields where Orient first kicked a ball about. But even after all the efforts it seemed like the end.

Frank Snewin, the club chairman and former Mayor of Hackney, stated that the club's resources were depleted and it looked like the end of Clapton Orient, which had been around since 1881, as they could only muster £500.

Then out of the blue Snewin received a phone call from a Mr Arthur Phillips, a director of the Godfrey Phillips Company, who promised a cheque of £400. Snewin went to the factory to meet Phillips, who handed over the cheque. He informed Snewin that certain pool money raised in the factory, if not won, would go to the club. He said that he had supported the club since he was a young boy and did not want to see the club die.

A sympathetic letter arrived by hand on 21 June from the Prince of Wales with a cheque for £2,000. The letter stated that he (Prince of Wales) had followed the fortunes of the club for many seasons and was sorry to see them struggling financially, and he would like to give to the club a cheque for the full amount owed to the League and that would see them going forward. He wished much luck in their future endeavours.

A number of the London-based clubs donated money, and the Gliksten brothers, owners of Charlton Athletic, donated £50. Indeed, with the money flowing in the debt to the League was paid by the due date and there was even enough money for manager Pratt to sign some new players.

In fact, he made some astute captures and signed-up 26 new players during the season, including some old star veteran players, and his style of play was like a breath of fresh air at the club. There was Wynn Crompton a sturdy left-half from Wrexham (64 League appearances) with three Welsh caps, 30-year-old right-half William Fogg, with more than 65 appearances for Huddersfield Town, 30-year-old goalkeeper James Gill, with over 85 appearances for Bradford City, 37-year-old Thomas Lucas, who made a total of 366 appearances for Liverpool between 1919–32 and had won three England caps, 33-year-old left-winger Arthur Rigby, who had made over 320 League appearances with Bradford City, Blackburn Rovers, Everton and Middlesbrough, winning five England caps, 26-year-old left-half Eddie Ware, with more than 90 appearances for Brentford, and 30-year-old Tommy Yews, with more than 360 appearances for West Ham United. Two younger players he brought in were 24-year-old Jackie Mayson from Bolton Wanderers and 23-year-old Harold Taylor from Southport. Both gave good service to the club over the following seasons. Twenty-six-year-old centre-forward Edmund Crawford joined in July 1933 from Liverpool; he went on to have a wonderful career with the O's until his retirement from playing in May 1945.

In November 1933 Tommy Mills gained his first full cap for Wales and scored the winning goal against England at Newcastle.

In December 1933 an excellent signing was that of 36-year-old David Halliday for £1,500, a wonderful forward who had played for the likes of Dundee, Sunderland, Arsenal and Manchester City, scoring more than 300 goals, and during the season he netted a trio of hat-tricks, and from just 21 League appearances he scored a remarkable 19 goals. The team finished in 11th spot, the highest position in eight seasons. They recorded some excellent wins, but none more so than the record League victory – 9–2 over Aldershot on 10 February 1934 (see Matches to Remember).

By December 1934 Pratt had left the club to take the job at Notts County, and the O's appointed Sid White as a caretaker manager until the return of Peter Proudfoot the following January and finished in 14th spot. The best win of the season was the 6–0 drubbing of Brighton & Hove Albion in April.

The following seasons the O's maintained their mid-table position in Division Three South but without any major fireworks, with only the scoring feats of Ted Crawford to keep the fans happy. He broke Dickie McFadden's long-standing League goalscoring record (21 League goals in 1914–15) with 23 League goals from 41 appearances in 1935–36. The following season the O's had two players named Smith (Harold and Jack) and two named Taylor (Harold and John), but neither were brothers.

Clapton Orient pictured in 1936–37. Back row (left to right): E. Coakley, D. Murray, V. Farrell, F. Searle, B. Herod. Third row: P. Proudfoot (manager), T. Wells, G. Heinemann, A. Rossiter, J. Iceton, H. Watson, C. Hillam, D. Affleck, C. Brooks, T. Halsey (secretary). Second row: S. White (trainer), A. Banfield, F. Fisher, V. Hammond, R. Quinn, E. Crawford, J. Fletcher, H. Smith, H. Taylor, W. Wright (assistant trainer). Seated on ground: J. McCombe, A. Mulraney, I. Miles, A. Codling.

In 1937 the club was on its travels again, this time to a new home at Osborne Road, off Leyton High Road, previously the home of Leyton Amateurs. The name Leyton means 'Town on the River Ley', and since 1570 the Ley had become known as the River Lee or Lea.

Although the name Leyton had been around since the ninth century, in 1722 Daniel Defoe described Leyton as an expanding area, with new houses for the richest citizens.

The first League match was against Cardiff City on 28 August 1937, when 14,598 spectators witnessed a 1–1 draw, Fred Tully scoring the O's first League goal on the new ground.

This was not the first League match to be played in the Borough of Leyton: Woolwich Arsenal met Leicester Fosse at the Essex County Cricket ground in High Road, Leyton, on 9 March 1895.

The O's ended the 1938–39 season in a disappointing 20th position, only two points off the re-election zone on 35 points, with both Walsall and Bristol Rovers finishing on 33 points.

In the programme for the match with Reading on 4 March 1939 came an appeal for funds to be used for team building as an effort to retain the players on the books at that time. Also the editor wrote 'I really think that the 1939–40 season is going to be a real snorter. Cheerio, do your best won't you.' Perhaps lacking something in vision with what the forthcoming season was to yield.

In January 1939 Peter Proudfoot left the club due to ill health and was replaced by Thomas Halsey, who moved from the supporters' club official to club secretary and then acting manager. After just three League games in the 1939–40 season it was stopped due to the outbreak of World War Two and all records of those three matches were expunged.

Orient in the war years

(see later section on page 517 for details of the war years)

For the commencement of the 1939–40 season, manager Tom Halsey signed a number of new players to strengthen the squad. After just three League matches, the season was abandoned due to players going off to fight against Germany in World War Two.

In December 1939 Halsey stepped down and was replaced by William Peter Wright, who held the club throughout the war years, even playing in goal in emergencies. In September 1946 he was replaced by the former great Tottenham Hotspur and England inside-forward Willie Hall. Billy Wright remained at the club as trainer and later was the masseur. Within two months Hall had to leave the club due to ill health, having been struck down with thrombosis, and within 13 months he had lost both legs. On 1 January 1946 Orient appointed 61-year-old captain Charles Hewitt as secretary-manager, as he had achieved much success with both Chester and Millwall.

When war was declared on Germany on 3 September 1939, all Football League matches were cancelled. Once it was safe to commence outdoor activities, some sort of regional football was started in October 1939, and the O's began with a 2–1 win over Watford with Bob Shankly hitting the opener. They had the benefit of fielding some of the first-team players from the previous season and also a number of well-known guest players in later seasons like Dai Astley, Horace Cumner and the great Trevor Ford. However, they also had to field a number of unknown local amateurs in times of emergency and even a few supporters in the crowd to make up the numbers.

The only official records of appearances is that of team sheets supplied by the clubs, but unfortunately in many instances the clubs did not know who was turning up so they listed a position as A.N. OTHER (another player) or in some instances S.O. ELSE (someone else)!

Orient had to 'borrow' other teams' players when they just did not turn up for matches, hence the reason for a large number of players listed as making just a single wartime appearance for the O's. A number of supporters also made single appearances for them when the announcer would ask over the tannoy if any player of decent ability would like a game. In some instances they fielded less than 11 players in a match.

The team colours during the war years were red and white hooped shirts, black shorts and socks with red tops. For away games they sometimes changed to blue hooped shirts.

The first match the O's played in 1939 after the suspension of the Football League was a friendly against Finchley, a 6–1 win, with Bob Shankly bagging five goals.

In 1941 London clubs were unhappy about having to travel long distances and the high costs it involved, so they decided to form their own League called the London League and all, including Orient, were suspended by the Football League that year, although they kept their membership.

The Football Association decided to act as a peacemaker, and in 1942 the problem was resolved and all the London clubs were brought back into the fold.

This was a difficult time for most clubs with everybody's attention focused on the war against Germany, so crowds dwindled. Players were paid around 30 shillings a match.

Many clubs were ignoring the FA regulations on payment to amateur players and proper registration of players, and in fact the O's were actually suspended on 21 April 1941 for failure to meet certain obligations and ignoring the regulations of obtaining certain players and using supporters from the crowd as match officials (anything to gain a few much needed points), but they were reinstated just four days later.

In later seasons players were allowed to play for clubs stationed near their base and often played the odd game here and there for numerous clubs around the country. Some of the O's results were quite farcical, like a 16–1 defeat at Portsmouth on 28 February 1942, Pompey inside-forward Andy Black netting eight of their goals that day. Black was a guest player for Pompey and also played for them in the London War Cup Final, having been on the books of Heart of Midlothian. After the war, he was with Manchester City and recorded 52 goals from 146 senior appearances while at Maine Road, between 1946 and 1950.

A 15–2 defeat at Arsenal on 8 February 1941 (having drawn 3–3 at home a week earlier), in the match at Highbury, saw Leslie Compton (brother of Denis), who was normally a centre-half and was on leave from the army, chosen as centre-forward, and he scored a remarkable 10 goals, six through headers. He had played in 253 League games for the Gunners and managed just five goals between 1931–51. This was followed by a 10–3 defeat at West Ham United on 2 January 1943. During one period, 12 October 1940 to 25 April 1941, the O's conceded 115 goals from 20 matches, scoring just 18 goals themselves with a record of 19 defeats and one draw, 3–3 at home to Arsenal. One player who always seemed to play well against Orient was the Spurs centre-forward Jackie Gibbons, who scored a hat-trick against them in four consecutive games in the 1940–41 season. He notched another hat-trick against the O's in February 1942. After the war, he enjoyed a decent run with Brentford.

The highest of the O's victories during seven years of wartime matches were three 5–1 wins, all in the 1939–40 season against Southend United (twice) and Brighton & Hove Albion. They also recorded an exciting 5–4 win over Fulham on 25 March 1944. Seven different players recorded eight hat-tricks during the period – Robert Shankly (twice), Harold M. Smith, James McNeil, Matthew Armstrong, Trevor Ford, Alex Younger and Albert Robson, with one player, John Hewitt, bagging four goals versus Fulham in 1942.

League football returns in August 1946

League football returned to England almost seven years to the day after it ended, when on 31 August 1946 the O's entertained Ipswich Town in a 2–2 draw before 12,350 fans, with goals from George Willshaw and William Charles Brown.

There was only one familiar face from the 1938–39 squad: 26-year-old goalkeeper Stan Hall. Manager Hewitt had to sign a whole new squad and there were some interesting players like Arnold Seigel (sometimes also written as Siegel), a Jewish amateur player from the Hendon club, who was one of just four known players to have worn spectacles in the Football League. The other three were: Albert Cook, an amateur full-back or left-half with Burslem Port Vale, who made 32 League appearances with Vale, Stoke City and Stockport County between 1901 and 1907, James 'Jim' Frederick Mitchell, who kept goal for England against Ireland on 22 October 1924 and played in goal for Blackpool, Preston North End and Manchester City, and Alexander 'Alec' Galloway Raisbeck, a centre-half with eight caps for Scotland, who played for Hibernian, Stoke City, Liverpool, Partick Thistle and Hamilton Academicals. More recently, Edgar Davids, the current Dutch international star with Juventus, wears protective glasses during matches to protect his eyes, and research also shows that two other players wore spectacles: Jeff Jurion from Belgium, in the 1960s, and a Stanley Bourne, who was a West Ham United junior and reserve player between 1906–12.

Pictured in August 1947 are Stroud, Brown and Sales.

On 20 September 1946 manager Hewitt caused quite a stir when he walked out on the club because he felt he was not given the funds to buy new players, and it was first-team trainer William Bulloch Wright who was appointed manager and was in charge for three matches, all defeats, before Hewitt was reinstated as manager, so Wright's reign lasted just 19 days (two less that Paul Went some 30 years later). It was at this time that for home games the O's had a magician doing his tricks on the pitch before kick-off, and a supporter in the crowd once shouted at him, as he made his exit, 'Don't go, we might need you later.'

They battled throughout the season, finishing 19th in Division Three South, only a couple of away wins in May 1947 at Notts County 2–1 and at bottom place Mansfield Town 3–1 saving their bacon. The O's had not won a game in the previous eight. In fact, it was Cyril Bacon with his two goals at Mansfield that helped them in not having to apply for re-election.

In the next few seasons the team fared no better, and in May 1948 Hewitt was fired, and he returned to Millwall as manager. It was Scotsman Neil McBain (Hewitt's assistant manager) who took his place. He had been the manager of New Brighton, and at the age of 52 years and four months he became the oldest player to appear in the League. He appeared as an emergency goalkeeper for New Brighton against Hartlepools United on 15 March 1947.

Nothing really changed under his managership, with just 11 wins throughout the 1948–49 season, and the following July he went to Argentina to manage Estudianties De La Plata.

It was a very sad afternoon on 11 September 1948 when, against Northampton Town, the O's great full-back Ledger Ritson broke his leg and never played again, eventually having to have his leg amputated.

The 1949–50 season saw a number of changes at the club. Harry Zussman was appointed chairman after the death of George Harris, who held the position for 10 years, and the very first thing Zussman did was to appoint Alec Stock as manager, who had been most successful with non-League side Yeovil Town. There were no real fireworks with another lowly 18th spot attained.

The major talking points were a couple of heavy defeats during the season: in October a 7–1 loss at Notts County before a big crowd of 36,346 and a 7–2 reverse at Leyton at the hands of Aldershot in February, and there were the goals from Scotsman George Burns Sutherland, a player picked up from Partick Thistle in August. He became the first O's player to have scored hat-tricks against the same side in the same season (Ipswich Town), and he bagged 16 League goals from 29 appearances.

This was to be the last season of big centre-forward Frank Neary, who moved to Queen's Park Rangers in October for £7,000. Neary had scored 44 goals from 81 senior appearances with some powerful shooting, and few who saw it will ever forget his thunderous shot that KO'd the Torquay goalkeeper Archie McFeat in November 1948. The poor chap was never to be the same again as the experience took the wind out of his sails, and he was not seen again in English League football.

On 6 May 1950, in a game at home to Southend United, the O's needed a point to avoid the indignity of having to apply for re-election, and on the other hand the visitors needed a win to take them to the runners'-up position. The match came down to the final seconds with Orient down by 2–1, and the noise of the 13,197 crowd could be heard throughout Leyton. The O's great captain Arthur Banner, with his sleeves rolled-up, waved his men forward for one final fling. Banner floated up a free-kick into the penalty box.

Wally Pullen, only playing that day because of injury to top scorer George Sutherland, received the ball at his feet, but with his back to goal. Somehow he managed to swivel around and flick the ball into the corner of the net for the equaliser. Southend had only managed to kick-off again when the final whistle sounded.

In July 1950 manager Stock pulled off a coup with the capture of Welsh international forward Billy Rees from Tottenham Hotspur for a record £14,000, having outbid both Fulham and West Ham United for his services. Rees proved to be a wonderful servant with 66 goals from 198 senior appearances during his six seasons with the O's. It was the skilful Jimmy Blair who stole the show with 16 League appearances, and 17-year-old winger Brian Jackson looked an exciting prospect. 1951 saw the return of former player Jack Tonner as head groundsman, and Les Gore was appointed as trainer.

The highlight during the following season, other than the great FA Cup run, was the 7–0 demolition of Colchester United, their highest score in 18 years after the 9–2 defeat of Aldershot in 1933, having lost the previous week 6–1 at Exeter City. Tommy Brown opened the scoring on five minutes. The second came 20 minutes later when Brown crossed for Dennis Pacey, and he scored with a stinging drive. On 30 minutes Pacey made the third for Billy Rees to nod in. The fourth came on 35 minutes. Tommy Harris received a pass from Rees, he ran down the down the wing, beat a number of defenders and sent a piledriver into the back of the net.

The second half continued in similar fashion, with the O's on all-out attack, and Harris seized a loose ball and scored a brilliant fifth. The sixth goal came a couple of minutes later when Paddy Blatchford crossed for Pacey to score from a yard out. Blatchford himself ran in the seventh, netting with a ground shot from 20-yards. Tommy Brown was just magnificent, his passing, dribbling and general all-round play could hardly have been bettered.

The find of the season for the O's was that of youngster Dennis Pacey. But, as expected, in November 1951 Brian Jackson, another of the O's youngsters, was snapped up by Liverpool for £7,500 (plus winger Donald Woan).

Manager Alec Stock presenting Mrs Alice Underwood with a bouquet after their 3–1 victory against Everton in the 1951–52 FA Cup third-round tie. Mrs Underwood ironed and mended the playing kit and worked for Leyton Orient for over 25 years.

Leyton Orient 1951–52. Back row (left to right): Jimmy Richardson (assistant trainer), Les Blizzard, Stan Aldous, Pat Welton, Arthur Banner, Jackie Deverall, Les Gore (trainer). Front row: Des Woan, Dennis Pacey, Tommy Harris, Alec Stock (manager), Paddy Blatchford, Taffy Evans, unknown.

In the 1952–53 season the fans began to see an upturn in fortunes with both Pacey, Rees and Ken Facey, a 25-year-old from Walthamstow Avenue, firing in the goals, and the O's finished in 14th position in Division Three South. The improvement was maintained in 1953–54 with 18 wins, 79 goals scored and an 11th-spot finish.

In October 1952 came the visit of Millwall, and it was their debutant, 20-year-old centre-forward John Shepherd, who smashed in four goals. He was no one-match wonder as he notched 64 League goals from 150 appearances in a five-year career with the Lions.

There have been a number of astonishing goals down the years scored at Brisbane Road, but two came about early in the 1953–54 season. On 29 August 1953, in a match against Bournemouth, with the O's already leading by 4–0, striker Denis Pacey had the chance of a hat-trick in the final minute. He chased a long, hopeful ball up the left wing. Unmarked and not far from the corner flag, he looked up and, seeing the goalkeeper off the line, he smashed a tremendous shot into the goal from the narrowest of angles and from way out for his hat-trick, to the delight of the 18,366 fans.

Five days later Brighton & Hove Albion were the visitors to Leyton, and the Seagulls' burly Welsh-born full-back Des Tennent hit a free-kick from the halfway line that flashed like a rocket past the O's goalie Dave Groombridge and into the net. Tennent was no stranger to scoring such goals, and during his career with Brighton he scored 40 League goals from 400 appearances.

In the 1954–55 season the O's had a good start with 10 wins from 15 matches, and they had a wonderful spell between the end of October and December with six straight wins, which included a record 7–1 win at Exeter City (see Matches to Remember), a 5–1 win at home to Southend United and a 7–2 win at Torquay United, in which they tore the home team apart, the only question being how many would Orient score. The danger man was Vic Groves, who scored a hat-trick, with Ken Facey crashing home the seventh in the final minute of play. In the end they could not match the form of Bristol City, who finished nine points ahead of them in the table as champions (only one team was promoted in those days), but still what a wonderful season it was for the O's with 26 wins and 89 goals scored.

The fans could appreciate that Alec Stock and his great squad worked well together, and in 1955–56 they started in great fashion, unbeaten in seven games. In September came an 8–0 win over Colchester United, with 22-year-old Vic Groves having a blinder at centre-forward, watched by a number of scouts, including the Arsenal manager Tom Whittaker. Groves's second goal was a peach: he raced 20 yards to volley home a perfect pass from Phil Woosnam.

Then in November came the news that both Groves and Stan Charlton had both signed for Arsenal for a joint fee of £30,000, and the following week saw a drop in the attendance by more than 10,000 fans, but the team hit Crystal Palace for eight and the fans soon returned. The O's were 5–0 up by half-time. It should be noted that the visitors' goalkeeper Roy Bailey left the field having injured his shoulder, and when he returned he played at centre-forward with full-back Len Choules donning the green jersey.

Another shock occurred in February 1956 when manager Alec Stock moved to Arsenal as assistant manager to Tom Whittaker, this after just turning down a lucrative offer to manage Middlesbrough a few days earlier. At the end of that month Gore made the significant signing of Scotsman Tommy Johnston from Newport County. Meanwhile, the football world were shocked by the news that Stock had decided to quit his job at Highbury after just 53 days to return to Brisbane Road. He said 'Hard as I tried, I could never stop thinking about Orient. My mind said Arsenal, but my heart said Orient. I realised that friendship to me is more important, much more valuable than all the progress and

The Leyton Orient team that finished as runners-up in 1954–55. Only one team was promoted in those days.

prestige I might have had at Highbury.' Another factor, which only came out much later, was that the senior Arsenal players did not appear to listen much to Stock, and he felt that Tom Whittaker, the manager, did not give him his full backing.

The O's recorded 15 wins from 16 games, including some magnificent wins against Queen's Park Rangers 7–1, Aldershot 8–3 and, on Stock's return, Shrewsbury Town 5–2. Les Gore had a wonderful record when in charge, which read: played 10, won 9, lost one, goals for 32 and against 11, points 18.

In March 1956 the O's had a fantastic 8–3 win over Aldershot at Brisbane Road, yet it was the visitors who opened the scoring through Lacey. Tommy Johnston equalised on 19 minutes and Ron Heckman added another seven minutes later. Phil Woosnam got two quick goals and the first half ended 4–1. The second half opened with Johnston notching up two further goals to get a hat-trick. On 60 minutes Menzies pulled one back for the Shots, but Johnny Hartburn headed in the O's seventh, and then from a White cross Ron Heckman headed in the eighth. Menzies scored the Shots third to end the scoring. However, there was none better than the 2–1 win over struggling Millwall to secure the Third Division South Championship, witnessed by 22,377 people (see Matches to Remember). The post-match scenes were something to behold: the excitement, the joy and the tears. The loudest cheer of all came when the Championship shield was presented to chairman Harry Zussman after the match by the president of the Football League, Mr Arthur Oakley.

Johnston had a major impact with eight goals from 15 appearances, but it was the goalscoring of John Hartburn on 20 goals and Ronnie Heckman with 23 goals that secured promotion (Heckman in fact netted 29 League and Cup goals that season, a new record).

It was a grand season, the O's first success since entering the League in 1905, and they scored a record 106 League goals with 29 wins. The average home gate was 17,524 (the highest ever achieved in the club's League history), and they made a healthy profit of £17,965.

For the new season the O's dismantled the old grandstand and replaced it with one bought from the old Mitcham Stadium. Stock signed some experienced players for the return to the Second Division: Stan Willemse came from Chelsea, Alex Forbes from Arsenal, and Jimmy Andrews and Dave Sexton both from West Ham United.

Over 25,000 turned up for the opener against Nottingham Forest, but the visitors ran out easy winners 4–1, with Sexton scoring the O's lone goal. The first victory came in a 4–3 win over Bury on 1 September, with White, Hartburn, Willemse and Johnston scoring the goals, but on 22 September they went to Stoke City and were thrashed 7–1. The following couple of months saw a big improvement in results, with Johnston bagging 12 goals. At the end of the season the O's went to promoted Leicester City and won 4–1 and finished in 15th position, but the whole season was about one man – Tommy Johnston – who scored a club record 27 League goals.

With Stock leaving to join Roma, the 1957–58 season started poorly with a 7–2 defeat at Grimsby Town, but the talk during the season was once again that man Johnston, and by early January he was already sitting on 35 League goals, and Dixie Dean's record of 60 League goals in a season looked to be in danger.

Then Johnston became unsettled with talk of a transfer, and between 18 January and 8 March he failed to score one goal. Then came the news everyone was expecting, a £15,000 move to Blackburn Rovers in March. This proved to be one of Les Gore's last acts as manager; Alec Stock was returning from Italy. The season ended with the O's in a respectable 12th position.

In October 1958 the 'Welsh Wizard' Phil Woosnam won his first Welsh cap against Scotland, and a month later he was transferred to West Ham United for the third highest transfer fee ever paid for a player, £30,000. The money was used by manager Stock to bring in some experienced forwards like Eddie Baily, Eddie Brown, known as the 'brown bomber' for his remarkable speed, and, in February 1959, the welcome return of Tommy Johnston from Blackburn Rovers. The combined ages of the three totalled 93 years, yet their inspired play managed to get the O's off the bottom of Division Two and up to 17th position. Johnston scored 10 goals from 14 appearances. Also, that December saw the return of old favourite Stan Charlton from Arsenal in a swap deal with Len Julians.

The 1958–59 season saw the introduction of young Irishman Joe Elwood, and he bagged four goals in the 4–2 win over Bristol City. Another highlight was the demolition of Middlesbrough by 6–0 in March: history shows it was one of the O's better performances, and Brown scored four of them. In April they crushed Charlton Athletic 6–1, with Elwood leading the way with a hat-trick, but it was the trickery of Eddie Baily, playing his 'push and run' style of football, that meant in the end the boys from South London were humiliated. Stock left again that season to join Queen's Park Rangers, and Gore again took over as manager in February 1959.

The 1959–60 season saw the O's improve and move up to 10th spot, with Brown and Johnston firing on all cylinders. Johnston bagged another 25 League goals and Brown 12 goals. The season also saw the introduction of exciting 21-year-old winger Terry McDonald from West Ham United, and he weighed in with nine goals.

During November the O's were actually lying in sixth position, chasing leaders Aston Villa. They went to Anfield to play Liverpool and what a great match it turned out to be. Although the O's lost 4–3, they put on a scintillating performance, and Johnston scored two great headed goals, the first of which was his 200th League career goal before an appreciative 34,321 crowd.

The Swinging Sixties and the Seventies

On 31 August 1960 the O's played their first home fixture under floodlights against Brighton & Hove Albion and ended up winning 2–1 before a crowd of 12,937. With the signing of West Ham United's big centre-forward Dave Dunmore, swapped for youngster Alan Sealey in March, fans could see the end of the road for the legendary Tommy Johnston with Orient – and so it proved. He scored the vital goal against Norwich City on 22 April to secure the O's place in Division Two in 19th position.

In July 1961 came the appointment of Johnny Carey as manager, a man with vast experience both as a player with Manchester United and manager with both Blackburn Rovers and Everton. Johnston had a fall out with the new boss over training the reserves and taking a big wage cut, and in the end Johnston moved to Gillingham for £3,000, a sad end to a wonderful O's career. What a record Johnston had with the O's (as highlighted in the recently published biography – *The Happy Wanderer*). He scored a total of 123 League and FA Cup goals from 190 appearances, and today he is still considered by the fans as the greatest ever player to appear for the club.

The 1961–62 season, under manager Carey and trainers Les Gore and Eddie Baily, opened with a 0–0 draw at Newcastle and a 1–3 loss at home to Southampton, so already in the minds of most of the O's fans was that this was going to be another struggle to stay in the Second Division.

However, from then on the team's performances greatly improved, rattling up five wins from six games, including a 5–1 win at Walsall, a team unbeaten at home for 16 months, with Yorkshireman Malcolm Graham scoring a hat-trick. Between December and January they won nine games on the trot, with 10 goals from Dave Dunmore.

In the final run in they seemed to be faltering; however, on 23 April they went to Luton Town and won 3–1, Derek Gibbs playing in only his second League game and bagging two goals.

The final promotion place to follow the already crowned Champions Liverpool into the First Division was dependant, five days later, on the outcome of the final match of the season. The O's were level with Sunderland on 52 points and were at home to Bury, and Sunderland had to visit third from bottom Swansea Town. The tension at the Bury match was unbearable, and most of the 21,617 crowd were in the ground well before kick-off, cheering and singing to ease their tension. Their hopes were well rewarded when the late replacement for the injured Ron Foster, Malcolm Graham, gave the O's the lead with a great header – although the Wearsiders were leading 1–0 at Vetch Field.

Many spectators around the ground carried transistor radios to listen to what was happening down in Wales, and the Brisbane Road crowd erupted when the news was passed around that Swansea had equalised. Then, almost at the same time, Graham picked up a loose ball, beat a Bury defender and went round goalkeeper Chris Harker before driving low and hard into the empty net. Graham, tears of joy welling in his eyes, was mobbed by his fellow players and young supporters.

The final minutes were nerve-wracking, but the O's held their 2–0 lead and the final whistle went. The news was announced that Sunderland had dropped a point and those pocket radios were thrown into the air. Leyton Orient were in the First Division.

The scenes were just unforgettable. Thousands of exultant fans ran on to the pitch, and loyal skipper Stan Charlton was carried shoulder-high towards the tunnel. Dave Dunmore had a great season with 22 League goals, and the half-back line of Malcolm Lucas, Sid Bishop and Cyril Lea were just brilliant throughout, but all eyes that day were on the hero Malcolm Graham. In the dressing room the tears were flowing, and director Leslie Grade called over Graham saying 'Malcolm, thank you, my dreams have come true. If I can give you anything, anything, just tell me now.' To this Graham replied 'Yes, another drink of champagne.' As Graham informed the author a few years ago from his home in Barnsley, 'I was young, shy and naïve in those days. I should have said "Mr Grade – my bond." And you know what? He would have paid it, he was dead serious.'

Final top three positions in Division Two – 1961–62 were:

	P	W	D	L	F	A	Pts
Liverpool	42	27	8	7	99	43	62
Leyton Orient	42	22	10	10	69	40	54
Sunderland	42	22	9	11	85	50	53

Just before he died in 1995, Johnny Carey informed the authors that 'The promotion to the First Division was a tremendous achievement by all the players and staff; I cannot, however, accept all the credit.

'The foundation had already been made by chairman Harry Zussman and his board of directors and especially by the influence of acting manager Les Gore, whose astute work in assembling players of exceptional ability and experience was completed before I arrived.

'My contribution was not to seek changes in the team. The blend was perfect. I was delighted to see their efforts fully rewarded because they were a smashing bunch of lads.'

For the start of the first ever season in the First Division, money was spent to extend the main grandstand but surprisingly not on any new players. The season kicked-off with a 2–1 home defeat by Arsenal, Derek Gibbs scoring the O's goal before 26,300 spectators. The first point came in the 1–1 draw at Birmingham City, and the first victory came over local rivals West Ham United by 2–0 in front of 29,918 fans.

A great 1–0 win came against Manchester United, with Terry McDonald scoring a brilliant individual goal in the final minute (a goal he still talks about to this day), then came a brilliant 3–0 victory over Everton, with goals from Dunmore and Deeley and the first League goal for the young Gordon Bolland. After a 2–0 win at Fulham at the end of September, the remainder of the season was a downhill struggle.

The season ended with a game at Old Trafford, with United having to win to avoid the drop with the O's into Division Two. A crowd of 39,759 cheered United on to a 3–1 win. Dunmore put the O's ahead, but it was one of Bobby Charlton's 'specials' that secured the two points.

Within three seasons Orient had dropped into the Third Division, and only 2,286 fans turned up on a rainy evening with the pitch looking more like a swamp in a vital match against Middlesbrough, but the O's took a 2–0 lead with two goals from little winger Terry Price. Amazingly, the referee decided to continue the game in the second half. The O's were attacking the deep end, totally under water, so it was not surprising that the second half belonged to the visitors, who ran out winners 3–2 to seal the O's fate of Third Division football. The final match of the season was against promotion contenders Southampton, who needed a point for promotion, which they obtained from a 1–1 draw before 19,839 spectators. The Orient goal was scored by youngster Peter Allen, his first season with the club.

It was no real surprise that crowds had dropped from an average home attendance of 16,406 in 1962–63 down to 5,981 in 1966–67, a drop of 10,425 per game. Managers came and went – like Benny Fenton and Dave Sexton – therefore, it was no surprise that in 1966 the club announced they were losing £500 per week and were in debt to the tune of more than £100,000.

On 22 November 1966 the famous 'pass the bucket' meeting took place at Brisbane Road. There had been financial difficulties before, in 1906 and 1933, but this latest crisis seemed to be the end. There to lead the fight for survival were chairman Arthur Page and director Harry Zussman. After all the speeches, a bucket was passed around and sixpences, pennies and notes were thrown into the bucket, with over £1,000 being raised. Also there was a £5,000 donation from Leslie Grade, and young Paul Went was sold to Charlton Athletic for £24,250 to save the club from liquidation. Due to the required financial cut-backs at the club, Leslie Gore left after 15 years of loyal service, and he joined Charlton as a scout.

So Page and Zussman had saved the club. Sadly, Page died in July 1977 and Zussman in July 1981. On the field, the players, who offered to take pay cuts to help save the club, responded magnificently and the O's finished in 14th place. It was 36-year-old veteran Cliff Holton who weighed in with 17 League goals; he had one of the most powerful shots around, and he was a great inspiration to the younger players.

At the club's annual meeting in November 1966, it was decided that the club would be renamed Orient Football Club, and a new all-red strip was introduced to replace the royal blue. The change came about after Leyton had disappeared into the new Borough of Waltham Forest; the directors felt the Leyton title had become an anachronism and was dropped.

Orient played their first League game under their new title in an all-new red strip at Grimsby Town on 19 August 1967, and the match, a drab affair, ended goalless.

On 8 March 1968 manager Dick Graham had resigned and Jimmy Bloomfield was appointed as

Orient in 1966–67. Back row (left to right): Bradbury, Sneddon, Forsyth, Ferry, Rouse, Willis, Bowtell, Whitehouse, Went, unknown, Street, Wigg, Clarke (trainer). Middle row: Goodgame, Jenkins, Smith, O'Brien, Carter, Allen, Metchick, LeFlem, Jones, Bailey, Woodward, Sorrell, unknown. Front row: Rofe, Brisley, Price, Les Gore (trainer), Eddie Heath (youth manager), Dick Graham (manager), Mr C. Bent-Marshall (director), Arthur Page (chairman), George Hicks (secretary) Johnny Hartburn (pools organiser), Commons, Vancoeverden.

Orient in 1967–68. Back row (left to right): Barry Fry, Mick Jones, Ray Goddard, Ron Willis, Bert Howe, Terry Price. Middle row: Malcolm Slater, Peter Allen, Brian Wood, Tony Ackerman, John Snedden, Eddie Werge, Tom Anderson. Front row: Brian Whitehouse, George Hicks (secretary), Neville Ovenden (director), Arthur Page (chairman), Frank Harris (director), Reg Briggs (director), Dick Graham (manager), Cliff Holton.

player-manager. His first season in charge was a bit of a struggle with only a 4–0 victory over Shrewsbury Town helping to avoid the drop into the Fourth Division. Most of the 6,115 crowd went wild with delight, a few hundred doing a knees-up in the centre circle.

For the 1969–70 season Bloomfield decided to concentrate on his managerial duties, and what a great season it turned out to be. By the New Year the O's were top of the table, with their nearest rivals Luton Town faltering under the pressure.

A headed goal from Mickey Bullock at Bradford City on Wednesday 15 April guaranteed the O's promotion. They clinched the Championship 10 days later, when a Mark Lazarus headed goal secured the two points against Shrewsbury Town. The chairman Arthur Page called a celebration meeting on Sunday 26 April, which was well attended, in complete contrast to the meeting held that we have recalled previously.

Page and manager Bloomfield thanked everyone concerned in the revival of the club, and the following day the O's played out the season against Gillingham with 16,334 in attendance, and after the match skipper Mancini was handed the Third Division Cup by Charlton Athletic's chairman Mr Glikstein. It was a moving scene as thousands of fans all around the ground began to sing *You'll never walk alone.* In celebration of their promotion the O's played a friendly against Italian side Roma in

Champions of Division Three in 1969–70. Back row (left to right): Terry Brisley, Peter Allen, Dickie Plume, Mick Jones, Brian Scrimshaw. Middle row: Charlie Simpson (physiotherapist), Peter Angell (trainer), Terry Mancini, Steve Bowtell, Ray Goddard, Dave Harper, Peter Brabrook, Jimmy Bloomfield (manager). Front row: Mark Lazarus, Mick Bullock, Terry Parmenter, Barry Dyson, Dennis Rofe, Barrie Fairbrother.

Promotion celebrations in 1970 with author Neilson Kaufman (far right) and friend Ingrid Austin.

Skipper Terry Mancini holds aloft the Third Division trophy in May 1970.

May. Bloomfield was voted the Third Division manager of the season, so ably assisted by Peter Angell. Bullock top scored with 19 League goals, followed by youngster Barrie Fairbrother with 13 goals, his first season in the first team. Skipper Terry 'Henry' Mancini led brilliantly on the field.

Jimmy Bloomfield was quite happy with his squad and did not make one single signing, yet the O's kicked-off their first season back in Division Two after five years with a cracking 3–1 win over Sheffield United on 15 August 1970, with goals from Dave Harper and two from winger Mark Lazarus, who was a colourful character and always did a 'lap of honour' around the ground after a scoring a goal, so it was no wonder he was quite tired after the end of this particular game!

On 25 September the match between Orient and Sunderland had to be held-up for seven minutes due to torrential rain (on the same day a match at Millwall versus Sheffield United was abandoned), and the O's returned and won the game through a Terry Parmenter cross-come-shot, which found its way into the visitors' net.

However, from being in third spot in October, they slipped down to below halfway, and it was at this time that starlet Tommy Taylor was sold to West Ham United for £78,000, with Peter Bennett coming to Brisbane Road. On the same day Bloomfield paid £10,000 for Gordon Riddick from Charlton Athletic. They finished the season in 17th spot, scoring a paltry 29 League goals, the second lowest total in the club's entire League history, with Lazarus the top scorer on just six goals – another all-time low.

Anyway, the fans were happy having seen the O's come a long way from the shipwreck days of 1966. During the summer Bloomfield made a notable signing of young Ian Bowyer from Manchester City for £25,000, but at the end of June 1971 Bloomfield had gone to manage Leicester City. His departure had occurred while chairman Arthur Page was away on holiday, and on hearing the news he was not at all happy; he would have wanted more time to discuss compensation as Bloomfield was still under contract, but vice-chairman Neville Ovenden had passed the move, for which he resigned from the club on Page's return to London.

The man to replace Bloomfield was Crystal Palace coach George Petchey on 12 July, having got the job over former O's player Cyril Lea, a coach with Ipswich Town. Page stated 'I am sure we have picked the right man. He was chosen because of his fine record for Palace, and we feel sure he will do well at Orient.'

The new season did have a few memorable aspects: the Bowyer hat-trick on his home debut in a 4–1 win over Cardiff City in August and a terrible mauling 6–1 at Burnley in September, soon after Petchey signed Phil Hoadley from his old club Crystal Palace for £30,000. In the same month the O's went to Bristol City and by half-time they were leading 3–1, and the first away win of the season looked a good bet, but in the end they lost 5–3.

The best win of the season came in early January, a 5–0 win over Sunderland, with goals from Bowyer (2), Bullock (2) and Tom Walley before 6,966 fans. The season ended with a match against promotion-chasing Birmingham City at Brisbane Road, the Midlanders having to win to gain promotion over Millwall, and a record Brisbane Road League attendance of 33,363 saw the visitors win. So the season ended with the O's in 17th spot again, not really good enough! The following season saw little improvement in the club's standing. But for seven home wins between January and April, the O's could have been in danger of relegation.

Many felt that the 1973–74 season would be a 'dog-fight' for the O's to stay in Division Two, even a number of so-called football experts felt they were one of the favourites for relegation, even more so after the introduction of a new three-up and three-down system in all Divisions.

Surprisingly, the season saw the O's play some exciting 'push and run' football, and there was a fluency about their play that was exciting, the masterminds being Petchey, Peter Angell and the new football consultant Arthur Rowe, a great player and later manager with Tottenham Hotspur and assistant manager with Crystal Palace.

During the new season some new names emerged like Bobby Fisher and then came more experienced goalkeeper John Jackson and Bill Roffey for £30,000, but on the same day Ian Bowyer, who had been in dispute with the club, was sold to Nottingham Forest for £40,000. By Christmas they looked to be promotion material, and the team were holding second spot behind Middlesbrough.

However, things began to change in the new year, after a long FA Cup run and mounting injuries began to take their toll. Even the footballing fans were finding things a little difficult when Sunday games and early midweek kick-offs became the norm due to the country's industrial problems and the prohibition of floodlights during a power workers' dispute.

It was a ding-dong battle to see who would be promoted with Middlesbrough between Luton Town, Blackpool, Orient and Carlisle United. It all came down to the O's final League match of the season; a victory over Aston Villa would secure promotion back to the First Division after a gap of 11 years. The match was to be played on Friday 3 May after the original fixture back in February was postponed due to a waterlogged pitch. Any win would do as the goal average was better than Carlisle's.

The atmosphere was electric, with a crowd of 29,766, and one could see the O's players being very tense with much of the play in midfield. It ended goalless at half-time. In the second half a break down the left wing by Little ended with a late tackle by Hoadley, which sent the winger crashing down, resulting in a penalty, and Ray Graydon converted the kick. They began to fight for their lives, and, after a long throw by Roffey, Mickey Bullock scored with a lob. Fairbrother went close, then came the final chance from a move by Heppolette and Queen, and the ball came to Bullock, whose full-blooded drive was tipped over the bar by the Villa 'keeper, Coombes.

The 'Super O's', as they were called throughout the campaign, had failed, a single point would have done it, but it was not meant to be.

This was to be the last season as chairman for Arthur Page, who retired and was appointed Life President and replaced by new chairman Brian Winston.

Manager George Petchey during a team talk before the Aston Villa game in May 1974.

An Orient home win as Laurie Cunningham makes it 2–1.

It was very clear where the O's went wrong: it was between January and April 1974, winning just two of their 16 matches. The following season was another great disappointment, they finished in 12th spot and scored a record low of 28 League goals with 12 goalless draws. No wonder the average home crowd had dropped from 11,369 in 1973–74 to 7,605 the following season. Possee top scored with seven goals.

One highlight was the exciting play of youngster Laurie Cunningham, who scored his first senior goal against Southampton on 26 April 1975. In the final game of the season he turned up late for the pre-match meeting and was warned by Petchey that he would be heavily fined if he did not score a goal. Well, he duly obliged, when he ran on to a flick from Mickey Bullock, outpaced defender Peter Rodrigues, the Welsh international captain, and, as their 'keeper came out, he flicked it under his diving body to give the O's a 2–1 win, it was a delight to watch.

Not much to report during the following few seasons. In 1974–75 the O's finished in 12th spot, and Peter Allen broke Arthur Wood's League appearance total record of 373 games on 13 March 1976 against Sunderland. (In 2005 Allen was still the only O's player to have made more than 400 League appearances for them.)

In 1976 Tony Grealish won the first of his seven caps for Eire, while he was an Orient player, and in March 1977 Laurie Cunningham, one of the O's greatest ever players, was transferred to West Bromwich Albion for £110,000 plus Allan Glover and Joe Mayo. In the same year a new young star in the making was given his League debut, Nigerian-born John Chiedozie, and it was in the 1970s that the O's won both the London and national Five-a-Side Championships, beating Queen's Park Rangers 6–1 and Tottenham Hotspur 2–0 respectively.

In 1976 Orient reached the Final of the Anglo-Scottish Cup, losing to Nottingham Forest in the two-leg Final by 5–1 on aggregate (see Other Cup Games).

In May 1977 it was a Glover goal that earned a 1–1 draw against Hull City to secure the O's Second

Orient pictured in 1976–77. Back row (left to right): David Payne, Mike Everett, Glenn Roeder, Peter Bennett, John Jackson, Nigel Gray, Gerry Queen, Bill Roffey, Ricky Heppolette. Third row: Tony Grealish, Gary Hibbs, Bobby Fisher, Peter Allen, Bill Hurley, John Smeulders, John Holmes, Phil Hoadley, Doug Allder, Laurie Cunningham, Derek Possee, John Chiedozie. Second row: Peter Angell (coach), Robert Hunt (groundsman), Carol Stokes (office assistant), Mike Blake (assistant secretary), Peter Barnes (secretary), George Petchey (manager), Brian Winston (chairman), Harry Zussman (director), Adrian Harding (director), Max Page (director), Brian Blower (commercial manager), Arthur Rowe (youth advisor), Terry Long (coach). Front row: Chris Henney, Stephen Johnson, Terry Glynn, Tunji Banjo, Billy Porter, Colin Johnson, Henry Hughton, Kevin Godfrey, Terry Emanuel, Tony Scanes.

Divisions status. The crowd numbered 8,400, and at the final whistle one might have been forgiven for thinking the O's had gained promotion, as the champagne flowed and the fans danced and sang and the players applauded up to the directors' box.

A turning point in the club's history came in the summer of 1977 with the signing of striker Michael Peter Kitchen from Doncaster Rovers for £25,000. Peter, or 'Kitch' as he was known, was a great success, although a few weeks after he joined manager Petchey was fired by chairman Brian Winston, and Jimmy Bloomfield returned as manager. It was later during the season that Bloomfield was in and out of hospital suffering from cancer, and Peter Angell, who took charge, held regular meetings in the hospital with Bloomfield.

Of course everything in the season was overshadowed by the O's great FA Cup run (see The FA Cup). However, when the final League match of the season came in May 1978, the O's had to win at Cardiff City to secure their Second Division status. It was Kitchen who came up trumps with the only goal of the game, with more than 1,000 Orient fans at Ninian Park cheering on their team. Kitchen scored 21 League and seven FA Cup goals. Not since the heady days of Tommy Johnston back in the 1950s had the O's had such a prolific goalscorer.

It's not very often that the O's had a player near the top of the division goalscoring charts, but Kitchen was top of the pile in 1977–78.

The O's in 1977–78. Back row (left to right): Fisher, Terry Long (trainer), Alan Stephenson (trainer), Peter Angell (coach), Kitchen, Bennett, Gray, Jackson, Smeulders, Roffey, Grealish, Glower, Chiedozie, Allen, Hoadley, Roeder, Payne, Clarke.

Orient met Arsenal at Stamford Bridge in the FA Cup semi-finals in 1978. Malcolm MacDonald scored the second as the Gunners went on to win 3–0, and the O's Cup dream was over.

Division Two leading scorers 1977–78:

Player	*Club*	*League*	*FAC*	*FLC*	*Total*
Peter Kitchen	Orient	21	7	1	29
Bob Hatton	Blackpool	22	1	1	24
Paul Randall	Bristol Rovers	20	2	0	22
Mick Vinter	Notts County	18	4	0	22
Steve Taylor	Oldham Athletic	20	1	0	21
Neil Whatmore	Bolton Wanderers	19	1	1	21
John Duncan	Tottenham Hotspur	16	1	3	20
Garth Crooks	Stoke City	18	0	1	19
Phil Boyer	Southampton	17	1	1	19
Gary Rowell	Sunderland	17	1	1	19

In 1978–79 the O's started off with two wins then lost four in a row. They signed Ian Moores (£55,000) and Ralph Coates (on a free), both from Tottenham Hotspur, and both starred in the 2–0 victory at Charlton Athletic, in fact it was two goals from Moores that earned the two points.

On Boxing Day 1978 the O's gained two points with a rare win against West Ham United in front of the Hammers' second highest attendance of that season, 29,220. They went into the lead after 17 minutes with an easy goal. Ian Moores chipped the ball over the defence for big Joe Mayo to score. In the second half it was a constant barrage from the home forwards, with John Jackson playing splendidly in goal, but with five minutes remaining John Chiedozie ran half the length of the pitch to seal victory to the delight of their fans.

The 1979–80 season started in tragic fashion with the death of 47-year-old assistant manager Peter Angell, having been with the club for 11 years. During that season the O's staged the England B versus New Zealand international match, which England won 4–1 before a crowd of just under 10,000, and the O's £100,000 goalkeeper Mervyn Day was on the subs' bench that evening.

Orient's Margerrison misses from the spot during the 1–4 defeat by Newcastle United on 8 September 1979.

Celebrating the O's centenary at King David Suite, London, in May 1981 are Ted Croker and chairman Brian Winston.

The O's finished in 14th spot, and Billy Jennings and Joe Mayo were joint-top scorers on 11 goals each. The following season they had some great new players in their ranks. With Stanley Bowles signed from Nottingham Forest for £90,000 and Peter Taylor from Tottenham Hotspur for a then club record of £150,000, the future seemed bright, but yet again they struggled in the League.

Centenary celebrations

On 5 May 1981 the O's celebrated their centenary and chairman Brian Winston was presented with an illuminated address by FA secretary Ted Croker at a Centenary Ball, held at the King David Suite, Great Cumberland Hotel, London. In July that year director Harry Zussman died at his shoe factory in Shoreditch, London, after serving the club for more than 33 years.

The following August John Chiedozie was sold for a record outgoing fee of £600,000 – to be paid over four years. It was no surprise that top players had to be sold over the years, between 1966 and 1981, and the O's sold eight home-produced players for nearly £1.5 million, including David Webb, Paul Went, Laurie Cunningham, Glenn Roeder and Tony Grealish, as the club's survival depended on their ability to produce and sell local players.

In August 1981 boss Jimmy Bloomfield was so incensed at the sale of Chiedozie that he resigned, and reserve coach Paul Went was appointed in his place. Went lasted just 21 days in charge, and he was sacked on 12 October 1981, with the O's bottom of Division Two. (This is not the shortest reign by an O's manager, William Bulloch Wright holds that record, he was in charge for three games between September and October 1946, just 19 days.)

The man appointed to lead the fight in October was Ken Knighton, and the following month Frank Clark was appointed as his assistant. Their track record was good together, having taken Sunderland to promotion in 1979–80. The season ended quite dismally with relegation to the old Third Division and the average home attendance dropping to just 4,419.

In November 1982 Neville Ovenden took control of the club from Brian Winston and Adrian Harding. Ovenden's son Michael was made a director and Harding was chairman, with Winston leaving the club.

The O's battled in the 1982–83 season with some heavy defeats, like 6–0 at Huddersfield Town, 5–2 at Brentford, at home against Newport County 5–1, Bristol Rovers 5–1 and Oxford United 5–1, but at the end of April they defeated Exeter City 5–1. In the end they had to beat Sheffield United to avoid the drop into the Fourth Division. They won 4–1 before a 4,468 crowd, with goals from Houchen, Kitchen – who had returned from Hong Kong earlier in the season – Godfrey and Roffey, and they ended in 20th position.

The following season Ken Knighton resigned and Frank Clark was put in charge, and they began the season in promising style. By September, after a 1–0 win versus Rotherham United, they went top of Division Three. However, the success did not last, with some heavy defeats during mid-season, like 5–2 versus Oxford United and 6–2 at home to Wimbledon, with the O's defence leaking 81 League goals. So they finished in 11th position. The highlights of the season were a 4–3 win at Exeter City, with central-defender Tommy Cunningham scoring a hat-trick, and Peter Kitchen's four goals against

Peter Kitchen wheels away after completing his hat-trick against Millwall on 21 April 1984 at Brisbane Road. He went on to grab a fourth as the O's won 5–3.

The O's in 1983–84. Back row (left to right): Songhurst (physiotherapist), Banfield, Godfrey, Sussex, Wilmot, Foster, Corbett, McNeil, Holland (coach), Hallybone snr (trainer). Front row: Hales, Brooks, Stride, Cornwell, Clark (manager), Cunningham, Cadette, Castle, Silkman.

Millwall in a 5–3 victory in April, and 'Kitch' ended as top scorer on 12 goals. In the summer he was surprisingly released by manager Clark and left to join Dagenham & Redbridge.

The 1984–85 season opened brightly with a 1–0 win at Brentford, but then the O's suffered five consecutive defeats. During November at Brisbane Road they led Hull City 4–1 and looked like winners but somehow managed to lose 5–4. In April they defeated Bolton Wanderers 4–3, with Kevin Godfrey scoring a hat-trick, but once again they found themselves having to win at home on the final day of the season against Bournemouth to avoid relegation to Division Four. Sadly this time there were no last-ditch heroics, Burnley had won their game and the O's could only manage a 0–0 draw before a disappointed 3,570 crowd, and they went down to the Fourth Division for the first time in their history.

The fans were surprised that Frank Clark had kept his job for the first campaign in the lower reaches, and everyone expected to go up at the first attempt, but it never happened. Over the following three seasons the O's just missed out on the promotion Play-offs.

In 1985–86 they started off well with a 3–1 win over Tranmere Rovers but then got dumped 5–1 at Southend United, with former O's player Cadette bagging four goals. The season ended with Steve Castle scoring all four goals for the O's in a victory at Rochdale. Striker Paul Shinners ended up on 16 League goals. During that October Tony Wood, a coffee merchant in Rwanda, was appointed as a director having supported the club as a young boy.

On 16 August 1986 the O's fans were shocked to read the headlines in the local press: 'O's shocker, Nearly Went Bust'. The same story also appeared in the programme for the visit of Cambridge United in the Littlewoods Cup on 26 August, it read 'Yes, we were so close to having the receiver in…' revealed Brian Winston.

'An incredible amount has happened behind the scenes at Orient during the close season. The worrying news that Neville Ovenden had to resign due to ill health, coupled with the tremendous financial pressures that the club has faced, meant a massive reorganisation and restructuring.

'It is many years since I had the privilege of writing an article in the programme, and I am sad that the foregoing circumstances have led to this one.

'One usually finds that out of any problems comes forth some good, and on this occasion it is the appointment of Tony Wood as chairman of the club, and the willingness of Neville Ovenden to remain as a director.

'On 14 July the directors were faced with a real possibility of having to appoint a receiver to wind up the club's affairs, but because of their continued efforts and various connections and contacts they were able to put together a financial package to ensure Orient's survival and to be certain that they could honour the liabilities and commitments of the club.

'There is a tendency to forget that Orient Football Club is a limited company and has legal and moral obligations placed upon it by common-day law.'

In the local press Winston revealed details of the crisis, 'because the club are now safe and we want to let the fans know what exactly happened. We kept it quiet because we wanted to do things our way. We didn't want to wash our dirty linen in public.'

The report ran that the club was just hours away from going bust and folding up in July, but they were saved by a complex financial rescue deal the night before the receivers were due to be called in. It was chairman Ovenden who called in Brian Winston, a former chairman, who worked as a business consultant to study the books and assess the club's position. He discovered that the club was losing too much money, and, with a further £50,000 revenue disappearing the following season because of changes in the League-distributed TV revenue, things looked critical.

Juryeff and Comfort scored the goals in the 2–0 Brisbane Road victory over Hartlepool United on 27 September 1986. Here Comfort threatens the Hartlepool 'keeper.

Orient pictured in 1986–87: Back row (left to right): Chris Jones, Steve Castle, Alan Comfort, Stephen John, Ian Juryeff. Third row: Pat Holland (youth manager), Colin Foster, John Cornwell, Robert Quinnell, Peter Wells, Dean Greygoose, Peter Mountford, Kevin Godfrey, Andy Sussex, Bill Songhurst (physiotherapist). Second row: Tommy Cunningham, Shaun Brooks, John Sitton, Frank Clark (manager), Lee Harvey, Paul Shinners, Kevin Hales, Kevin Dickenson. Front row: Kevin Nugent, Darren Went, Chris Snell, Warren Barton, Richard Mason, Mark Gribble, Barry Shorter, Hakan Heyrettin, Michael Gilbert, Ian Rawlings.

The crunch came with the introduction of the new company insolvency laws, which made the Orient directors personally responsible for the club's debts.

So Winston, in his capacity as financial advisor, had no choice but to recommend that the club went into liquidation after a 105-year history. Receivers were due to be called in immediately after the board's annual meeting on 15 July 1986, when the club was to be officially wound-up.

But following four days of frantic negotiations, Winston and the directors managed to put together a rescue deal that saved the club literally hours before it was to go out of business.

Winston said 'It was literally an 11th-hour rescue. I was on the point of calling in the receiver.

'At 4pm, the evening of the annual meeting, I got the final telephone call from Africa that the club's financial position was OK until June 1987.'

The rescue deal involved the appointment of Leyton-born Tony Wood OBE as chairman. He provided most of the cash for the rescue deal and Winston returned to the club as deputy-chairman.

Manager Frank Clark was fully aware of the crisis but turned down a job with Southend United to remain at the club.

Another twist in the story was that other board members felt the story should not have been splashed all over the press as it would only serve to lower the morale of the players, supporters and staff. In November 1986 Winston resigned. Frank Clark was appointed as managing director and Ovenden returned as deputy chairman.

On the field, the O's missed out again on a Play-off place, finishing in seventh place. They lost the chance after going down 2–1 at Burnley before a crowd of 15,781, where the clarets had to win to avoid the drop into the Vauxhall Conference. On 1 May 1987, at Tranmere Rovers, the O's recorded their 3,000th Football League match, becoming the 33rd club to achieve that figure.

On 1 July 1987 the club reverted back to their former name of Leyton Orient Football Club, to the delight of the fans, and the sports writers predicted that this would be the O's season for promotion. The season started off with a bang, only one defeat from the first 12 matches, including their 1,000th League victory, a 4–1 win over Newport County on 29 September 1987, and soon after followed an 8–0 thrashing of Rochdale.

On 12 December 1987, after a 3–1 home win over Tranmere Rovers, the O's hit the top of Division Four after just four defeats from 21 games, but the following week they went to Wolverhampton Wanderers and lost 2–0 and also the top spot, a position they never regained during the season.

Even though they recorded 86 League goals, the best return for many a season, including 16 goals from just 23 appearances from Ian Juryeff, they still could not manage a Play-off place, and the final match of the season, a 2–0 defeat at home by the Division's Champions Wolverhampton Wanderers, condemned the O's to yet another season in the Fourth Division. The average home attendance for the season was 3,784.

Other records during the season were: in August 1987 the O's staged their 950th League match at Brisbane Road, on 30 April 1988 Kevin Godfrey scored their 3,900th Football League goal against Hereford United and their 200th FA Cup tie was recorded with a 2–0 win over Swansea City. Also, 50 years at their Brisbane Road ground was celebrated.

However, supporters were asking the questions, would Orient ever achieve promotion? Would Frank Clark be moved upstairs to make way for a new boss?

Well, Clark was still the man in charge for the 1988–89 season, and the team struggled early on, their first win only occurring in the sixth game. In the 10th game the O's thumped Colchester United

In the dressing room before the home game against Crewe on 16 January 1988 are Kevin Hales, Mark Smalley and Keith Day. Nugent scored the goal in the 1–1 draw.

8–0, with Alan Hull scoring his first hat-trick in League football; this was Colchester's record defeat since entering the Football League in 1950. In November they were dumped out of the FA Cup by non-League side Enfield and the following month were near the bottom of Division Four. It was during this time that Neville Ovenden and his son Michael both resigned from the board, but they retained their seven percent shareholding in the club and stated 'I'll support them from the heart.'

The turning point of the season came early in 1989 when Clark signed young Arsenal striker Kevin Campbell in January on a three-month loan, and with the signing of another striker Mark Cooper from Gillingham for £21,500, as both players proved to be inspirational.

On 24 December the *Daily Mirror* reported that cellist and supporter of Orient Julian Lloyd Webber (brother of Andrew) wanted to buy the club for £1 million from Tony Wood, but both parties denied the story.

The team had a better look about it with Steve Castle, Terry Howard and the irrepressible Alan Comfort showing some fine form. In April they put on a most memorable display, beating Grimsby Town 5–0.

In the run-in the O's lost just twice from 16 matches, and a Castle goal at Lincoln City on 6 May assured a Play-off place. To end the season, Cooper scored a hat-trick in a 4–1 home win over Scunthorpe United, which placed them in sixth position. So at last they had made it into the Play-offs, and they were paired with Scarborough, while Scunthorpe United (fourth) were paired with Wrexham (seventh). On Sunday 21 May a Brisbane Road crowd of 9,289 witnessed a solid O's display in a 2–0 win, with hero Mark Cooper scoring with two fine headers, the vital second goal coming with just eight minutes remaining. In the second leg the Seasiders threw everything at the O's but could only manage a 1–0 win. The defence was superb, with John Sitton having an outstanding game, so it was a happy band of O's fans that travelled home that Wednesday evening with a two-leg Final against Wrexham to come, who had rather surprisingly knocked out Scunthorpe United. It was the men from North Wales who would be the barrier to the O's gaining promotion back to the Third Division.

The first leg took place in Wales on Tuesday 30 May, with the O's having much more of the play, and on just

Steve Baker signs for Orient in March 1988 for £50,000 from Southampton. Frank Clark is the manager as well as managing director.

Prior to the Play-off Final Orient went to Wrexham and won 1–0 on 8 April 1989. Here Comfort grabs the winner.

eight minutes a Cooper header came back off the crossbar. They were rarely troubled and the match ended goalless.

The second leg of the Final took place on Sunday 3 June. The midday start was delayed by 20 minutes and the attendance eventually numbered 13,355, and there was an electric atmosphere as the game commenced. (See Matches to Remember.) In the end the O's won 2–1 to gain promotion.

One player who missed out on all the celebrations was winger Alan Comfort, who was due to be married in Ireland at 5.30pm that same afternoon. It meant a dash to Hackney Marshes to board a helicopter to Heathrow then a flight to Ireland. He made it with half an hour to spare.

This was to be Comfort's last season with the O's, and what a season he had, scoring a remarkable 18 League goals from the left wing. He was signed by Middlesbrough for £175,000 plus a further £25,000 on his 40th first-team appearance.

A couple of milestones took place in the 1989–90 season: in September the win over Preston North End took the O's past the 3,000 points mark in the Football League, and two weeks later Mark Cooper scored their 4,000th League goal in the 1–0 win over Wigan Athletic. On 14 April 1990, when Bury won 3–2 at Brisbane Road, it was the 1,000th League game played at the stadium.

The club announced that consideration was being given to an all-seater stadium, but the final decade before entering the 21st century was a difficult time for many lower Division clubs, and none more so than Leyton Orient Football Club. It was made increasingly difficult by the advent of the Premier League in 1992.

The decisive goal as Cooper hits the winner against Wrexham in the 1989 Play-off Final.

The crowd celebrate the Play-off victory over Wrexham in June 1989.

A New Decade in Division Two

On the field the O's had entered the new decade having gained promotion into the old Division Three via the Play-offs in 1989. The team had consolidated the following season under the leadership of Frank Clark and Peter Eustace and things were looking bright.

So to the new season in Division Three. The O's gained their first victory in the new campaign in

Dressing room celebrations after the Play-off win against Wrexham in 1989, with manager Frank Clark and the two-goal hero.

September, 3–1 over Preston North End. The following month they beat Reading 4–1, with a fine display by Carl Hoddle – younger brother of Glenn – and the debut of record £175,000 signing Paul Beesley, a defender from Wigan Athletic. They entered the 1990s just above the relegation zone but had a problem scoring goals, and Andy Sayer was signed from Fulham for £70,000 in February to solve this issue, but he scored only once, and the O's finished in 14th position, winning their last four away games and conceding only four goals in their last 10 away trips.

However, things over the next few years only got worse, and the club struggled both on and off the field.

The new decade (1990–91) started with the club in the old Division Three and the appointment of Peter Eustace (replacing Brian Eastick) as assistant to manager Frank Clark. Clark himself had been with the club since 1981.

The appointment of Eustace certainly raised a few eyebrows. Although a top player in his day with both Sheffield Wednesday and West Ham United, he was manager of Sheffield Wednesday during 1989 when they won just two of their 19 League games under his leadership. They were beaten in the League Cup by Third Division Blackpool and went out to Blackburn Rovers in the FA Cup, who at that time were a struggling Second Division side. His stay as manager at Hillsborough proved to be an unmitigated disaster, and he was fired. It was the shortest reign of any manager with Sheffield Wednesday.

Eustace said of his new appointment, 'I've already introduced some new ideas and I have been delighted with the reaction.'

He admitted that he did not know a great deal about the Third Division. 'I don't think it's a problem for me, at the moment I don't know too much about the players in this Division, but football is football and I will soon catch on.'

Having lost 0–2 at Brisbane Road in the first leg of the League Cup tie against Everton, Orient went to Goodison Park in October 1989. The game ended with a credible 2–2 draw.

Leyton Orient in 1989–90. Back row (left to right): Brian Eastick (assistant manager), Greg Berry, Michael Marks, John Sitton, Paul Ward, Terry Howard, Paul Heald, Lee Harvey, Mark Smalley, Mark Cooper, Carl Hoddle, Kevin Nugent, Bill Songhurst (physiotherapist). Front row: Jeremy Gill, Alan Hull, Steve Castle, Keith Day, Frank Clark (manager), Steve Baker, Kevin Dickenson, Kevin Hales, Danny Carter.

It appeared Orient were to stay at their Brisbane Road ground when plans for a new ground to be shared with near neighbours West Ham United on Eton Manor's grounds, owned by the Lee Valley Regional Park Authority, were shelved.

The season looked distinctly promising, and by Christmas Orient had reasonable hopes of gaining at least a Play-off position as they were lying in fourth spot. However, as the season's events unfolded, they were badly affected by injuries to a number of key players, and only managed to finish in 13th position. Steve Castle top scored with 12 League goals.

The 1991–92 season was not dissimilar to the previous season. Peter Eustace was installed as manager with Frank Clark handling the administrative side of the club as managing director. The club said goodbye to long-serving physiotherapist Bill Songhurst, who stepped down after 16 years' service with the club to devote more of his time to his private clinic.

Clark's first job was to find a large amount of money, with the shock announcement that the club must sell one or two of their players and obtain £150,000 to be sure of saving the Brisbane Road ground from closure. They had to spend a large amount of money in order to obtain a safety certificate and to balance the books. The stadium was a big liability to the club, having fallen into decay.

There were a number of possibilities: Terry Howard – Clark had already turned down two offers for him – Kevin Nugent, Steve Castle or 17-year-old Chris Bart-Williams. In fact, it was Bart-Williams who eventually left the club, joining Sheffield Wednesday for £350,000 in November 1991. This was enough to save the ground and put the books in order, and for the time being there was even money left over to strengthen the squad.

Welcoming new signing Andy Jones is manager Peter Eustace (left) in October 1991. The other players are: Achampong, Nugent, Harvey, Zoricich, Dickenson and Carter.

Leyton Orient in 1991–92. Back row (left to right): Whitbread, Howard, Cooper, Heald, Newell, Nugent, Taylor, Roeder. Middle row: Dixon (scout), Jones, Berry, Burnett, Turner, Hackett, Day, Otto, Songhurst (physiotherapist). Bottom row: Dickenson, Carter, Achampong, Eustace (manager), Clark (managing director), Castle, Harvey, Hales.

Andy Jones, an experienced Welsh International forward, was signed from AFC Bournemouth for £90,000, and a large part of the money for Jones had come from the Leyton Link Fund. Goalkeeper Chris Turner joined from Sheffield Wednesday for £75,000 (as part of the Bart-Williams deal), while Glenn Roeder returned to the club later in the season for a short spell from Watford. Orient went out to First Division Sheffield Wednesday in the Rumbelows League Cup, losing 4–1 over the two legs.

On 3 March came a brilliant win at West Brom 3–1, goals from Howard, Berry and Nugent inside the first 20 minutes of the match sparking feelings of euphoric optimism at Brisbane Road, with the O's moving up to seventh spot.

Playing against Real Valladolid during a pre-season friendly in September 1991, this photograph features Terry Howard and the famous Carlos Valderrama.

However, Nugent was surprisingly sold on 23 March 1992 to Plymouth Argyle for £200,000, having netted 16 League and Cup goals. Some fans were disgusted. How could the club sell their top marksman with a Play-off spot in sight?

The fact of the matter was that two directors had previously loaned money to the club, but during the recession they had to call the loan in. Nugent went quickly, against Eustace's wishes, as he knew it would upset the fans and also hinder the O's push for promotion. But the club just had to cover the debts, and the two directors were then paid out.

Nugent had been with the club for almost 10 years, and in the last 18 months he really began to fulfil his potential as a striker.

Being so geographically close to West Ham, Arsenal and Tottenham, never having a comparatively large following and losing money, is it any wonder that players like Nugent had to be sold to balance the books?

The O's fans are a loyal bunch, and they seem to revel in adversity.

Just hours after Nugent's sale, Orient recorded their biggest win of the season, 4–0 over Bury. It was 21-year-old striker Greg Berry who did the damage, scoring his first hat-trick in professional football. In fact, it nearly never happened. The O's boss revealed that he almost took Berry off, but was reminded he was on for a hat-trick.

The team followed up with some abysmal performances, missing the goal power of Nugent, and after a home defeat by Stoke City, which ended their nine-month unbeaten home run, their Play-off dreams had gone when six defeats followed on the trot. They finished in a disappointing 10th position.

However, one always has it in the back of one's mind that had Nugent stayed, would they have been promoted to Division One?

Terry Howard and Darren Bradley of West Bromwich Albion on 7 November 1992.

FA Cup fourth-round action at Fratton Park, 4 January 1992, with Steve Castle (centre) battling for possession with Portsmouth's Martin Kuhl. Orient lost 2-0.

Lee Harvey's back-post header against Bradford City on 1 May 1993.

Ludden and Hackett are impressed by Mark Cooper's overhead kick in 1993.

Peter Eustace reflected on the 1991–92 season saying 'We sold some players, had two decent Cup runs and we were a bit unfortunate with injuries.' In the League Orient had had a tough match against Brentford in December 1991, which resulted in six goals, five yellow cards, a sending-off and a 16-player brawl on the field (see Matches to Remember). Eustace also stated in frustration, concerning the O's away form that season, 'I find the whole team have a collective lack of confidence away from home, and how frustrating it is to keep telling them they can win away, I've tried to build up each player's confidence and self-belief and tell them to become more aggressive, they are so timid away from home. But on the day most of their League performances were "pathetic" and so frustrating to watch.'

Could 1992–93 be Orient's season?

Very few additions were made to Orient's squad, but they won six of their first seven matches, going to the top of Division Two on 17 October 1992 when Ricky Otto gave them a 1–0 win over AFC Bournemouth. This is the only time the club have been top of their respective League during the decade (up to the 2003–04 season). Otto struck in the 76th minute with Orient well on top in the match: Chris Zoricich threw a long ball from the right, substitute Mark Cooper headed on, and the ball bounced over Otto's head before he turned quickly, beat a defender to the loose ball and fired home from close range.

Eustace stated 'It's a nice feeling to lead the Division, and the lads have earned it. They've worked hard in training, and we must keep it going – then we may have something come the end of the season.

'There are people who have been at the club a lot longer than me, like Frank Clark, Tony Wood and their fellow directors and backroom staff – they deserve it.'

How they stood in Barclays League Division Two (Top Four)

	P	W	D	L	F	A	Pts
Leyton Orient	12	7	2	3	18	12	23
West Brom	12	7	1	4	21	11	22
Swansea	12	6	4	2	18	8	22
Hartlepool	12	6	4	2	14	8	22

However, seeing the O's on top of a League table was short lived; they went to Bradford City and lost 1–0, losing the top position, which they did not see again.

It was during October 1992 that 34-year-old Chris Turner was appointed assistant player-manager under Peter Eustace. The boss said 'Chris is highly respected by everyone and has some good ideas to give to the players.' On 7 November 1992 the O's attracted their biggest League gate, 8,640, for 11 years (excluding Play-off matches) for the visit of West Bromwich Albion. Eustace played his new 'Diamond shape' midfield with four players, and it polished off Albion 2–0 with goals from Robert Taylor and defender Sam Kitchen.

During December 1992 Orient hit Mansfield Town for five, with midfielder Terry Howard scoring his first ever hat-trick, yet just three days earlier Howard had been banished to the reserves for some poor displays. After that win, they had scored more League goals and taken more League points at home than any other club in the country.

Brisbane Road also held an England Under-21 UEFA Championship game during the season against Turkey, which saw the return of former favourite Chris Bart-Williams, but there was little joy for England as they lost 1–0. A crowd of 7,879 turned up and Frank Clark stated 'It was a marvellous turn out, the only thing that spoilt it was the result.'

During the campaign there were times when the O's looked as though reaching the Play-offs was very much on the cards. Unfortunately, they picked up injuries and failed to win a League game throughout March, thus leaving themselves a mountain to climb, and it proved too much.

They did manage to win four of the remaining five matches, including an excellent 4–1 win at Preston on their plastic pitch in April. There was nothing artificial about this win, but it came at a heavy price with two players – 'keeper Heald and defender Benstock – being stretchered off. Substitute striker Andy Jones went into goal for the final 21 minutes. The game started well for the O's, with two goals inside the first three minutes through Harvey and Lakin. It was ace marksman Robert Taylor who sealed victory with two further goals.

In the last match of the season Orient needed to win by a large score, and though they won 1–0 at Swansea to finish level with the last Play-off placed team – Stockport County – they were still 11 goals behind the Cheshire side's goal total. There were some positive aspects to the campaign, including Robert Taylor's 18 League goals, he looked a dangerous striker, and several players showed consistent form, among them Kevin Hales, Keith Day, Adrian Whitbread, Gary Bellamy, stalwart Terry Howard and not forgetting the trickery and electric pace of Ricky Otto, who will never forget his brilliant hat-trick at Brighton in February 1993.

It was the third season in a row that the East Londoners had gone close to a top-six finish, but, alas, it was their away form that let them down badly again – promotion was just a dream.

Eustace said 'It is obviously a big disappointment to have come so close again, our away form was again the problem.' Terry Howard said 'We had high hopes, but it just wasn't to be, we've missed the boat yet again.' A choked Frank Clark could only say 'It has all gone horribly wrong.'

A number of influential players left the club in the summer of 1993. These included Adrian Whitbread, to Swindon Town for £500,000, Ricky Otto, to Southend United for £100,000, Lee Harvey, Kenny Achampong, who went off to France for a trial, and both Keith Day and Kevin Hales were sadly lost to non-League football. The unfortunate Andy Jones had to retire through injury.

This was not the only loss, the shock announcement came of the departure of 49-year-old Frank Clark after a marvellous 11 years with Orient. There was more than a tear at the club as the departing former manager and managing director packed his bags to take up his new appointment as manager of First Division Nottingham Forest, replacing the retiring Brian Clough.

Clark said 'I'm still sorting out my emotions. It really hit me as I walked through my office door for the final time to begin clearing out my desk.'

'I've had many wonderful times and, despite difficult financial periods, I am leaving with many lovely memories. I've thoroughly enjoyed working for the club and knowing the people, the whole experience has been great. There are few jobs I would leave Leyton Orient for, but the Forest job was one of them for personal reasons.' He added 'I would like to thank everybody connected with the club and the fans for the way they have supported me over the years, I will be retaining many fond memories.'

Clark joined Orient in November 1981 as assistant to Ken Knighton, and during May 1993 he was appointed as the club's 15th manager since World War Two. As a manager, he took the O's to promotion in May 1989, but it was as managing director that he proved to be a brilliant administrator and balanced the books like few others could, keeping the club afloat during many difficult times.

Clark always tried to play an attacking 4–4–2 formation with two wingers, one reason why his team scored over 80 goals in a couple of seasons when he was in charge. When he took over as manager the average crowds were 3,212, and this jumped in his final season to 5,372, and he made profits in the transfer market in excess of £1 million, money that was used to keep the club going. He left the club in much better shape than when he joined.

Supporters might not have known of Clark's wicked sense of humour and his love of music. He wanted to be a rock guitarist, but instead he pulled the strings at Brisbane Road for a decade, and it was only after he left that the club began to come off the rails. It was quite remarkable that he returned to the club a week after leaving to attend a board meeting to discuss the appointment of a new manager. Chairman and owner Tony Wood stated 'I always thought the day would come when Frank would move on. He has been a solid anchor for me and shouldered most of the negotiations with the authorities. He has left a big, big hole to fill.'

Peter Eustace, the assistant to Clark, was appointed as manager, and he paid tribute to Clark by saying, 'Frank had a wonderful relationship with chairman and owner Tony Wood, the playing staff and all at the club.'

Eustace added 'I hope everyone realises all the hard work he put into the club day and night and what a marvellous manager and administrator he was.' Now it was up to Eustace to continue where Clark left off, and his contract was extended up to June 1995.

Tony Wood stated that Clark's administrative position would not be filled; members of the board would handle the duties. Frank Woolf was made non-executive commercial director.

Another appointment was that of former skipper John Sitton as youth-team manager, replacing Geoff Pike, whose contract was not renewed. Sitton was one of 71 applicants for the job, including Tommy Taylor (later to become manager in 1996). Sitton had turned down a coaching job with Charlton to rejoin Orient.

Pulling the score back to 2–3 against Port Vale, Mark Cooper is congratulated by Vaughan Ryan and Martin Thomas on 2 April 1994.

The 1993–94 season started in a disappointing fashion as the O's went out of the Coca-Cola League Cup to Wycombe Wanderers by a 3–0 aggregate. It was Wycombe's 'keeper Paul Hyde who pulled off a string of wonderful saves. Eustace said 'We could have scored five or six goals over the two matches if not for Hyde's heroics.' Some years later Hyde joined Orient.

The O's had lost five of the first six matches played, and people were already asking, was Eustace the right man for the job? Things did not get any better as the season progressed. In April 1994 Eustace was sacked and assistant manager Chris Turner, with youth coach John Sitton, took over the reins of the club for the remainder of the season. The O's finished in a lowly 18th position, with Colin West top scoring on 14 League goals.

The club issued a statement concerning the departure of Eustace, which read as follows:

> 'With all the recent upheaval at the club the board of directors feel it is only right that we should take some time to explain the events that have taken place in the last 10 days here at Brisbane Road.
>
> 'The situation regarding the departure of Peter Eustace as manager is currently in the hands of the solicitors and we cannot elaborate on specific details. But suffice to say serious differences in opinion had developed between Mr Eustace and the board, and the two legal parties are still discussing the situation. We are confident that an amicable financial settlement can be reached, and we would not want to jeopardise that procedure. Therefore, we are not prepared to comment much further at this moment in time.
>
> 'However, it is fair to say, as regards team affairs, that everybody at the football club has been extremely disappointed with the way the season has progressed.
>
> 'Back in August we started the season confident of making a serious assault on winning promotion up to Division One. We honestly thought we had assembled a squad that was good enough to finish near the top of the table, and, contrary to what supporters may wish to believe, the club was gearing up for Division One football next season.
>
> 'There were handsome bonuses on offer to players – in the region of 200,000 pounds if they secured promotion – and it cost the club around 50,000 pounds to insure against that bonus being won. That was quite a heavy investment for a club of our size, but it proved just how much we all wanted to see the club move forward.
>
> 'The planned redevelopment of Brisbane Road – that continues to progress extremely well – would also have benefitted greatly from promotion. The grant we would have received from the Football Trust as a Division One club would have been far greater than what we will be now getting.
>
> 'All in all, the club had been very ambitious but, sadly, even accounting for the terrible crop of injuries that we have suffered, the season has been a big disappointment to everyone. But now it is time to look forward and not back.
>
> 'And that is why, in principle, we have appointed Chris Turner and John Sitton as the club's joint coaches until the end of the season. We were very impressed by their positive attitude in what was a very difficult situation leading up to last week's game at Huddersfield. That positive outlook was reflected in the way the team played in that game – in difficult windy conditions – and the general atmosphere among the players during the whole trip was refreshing. Sitton himself praised Eustace; he took the trouble to phone both myself and Chris to wish us luck. Peter told us to get stuck in and get some sort of response from the players. He proved just what a big man he was.'

Mark Warren celebrates an Orient goal from Darren Purse against Birmingham City in August 1994.

The club had received over 50 applications for the manager's job; some of those interested were Mervyn Day, Steve Wicks, Alvin Martin and Alan Mullery, but it was Turner and Sitton who got the job on a temporary basis.

Turner stated 'We don't feel under any real pressure, we can't change what has happened at the club this season, we can't suddenly make players fit again.'

Vice-chairman Derek Weinrabe said the new management team has the complete support of the board. Peter Eustace's four-year spell at Orient, if measured by results, was a successful period, each season the club had flirted with a Play-off position, but he failed to win over the fans with his brand of dour football.

The supporters had voted with their feet after touching a 10-year high during the season; the season's gates had plummeted to an average of 4,282 and the absence of over 1,000 people a game started the club on its financial downturn.

The players often failed to come to terms with Eustace's many changes in shape and style as team members often played in unfamiliar positions, which was difficult to digest from the uncomplicated decade of Frank Clark's 4–4–2 formation.

In February 1994 it was announced that former chairman and owner of the club Neville Ovenden had died after a long illness. He had played his part as one of those men who had saved Orient from financial disaster over the years.

If anyone had thought the club had been dogged by ill fortune in 1993–94, the following campaign was to be 10 times worse…

It came as no surprise that both Sitton and Turner were appointed as joint managers, after all who from outside would want the job knowing there was no money to spend on new players.

Chairman Tony Wood said 'The two will be in charge until the end of the season and then the situation will be reviewed.'

Sitton stated 'We are delighted to be given the opportunity and are excited at the challenge. I firmly think we can bring success to Leyton Orient.'

The players seem to have been in support of their appointment.

Terry Howard, the club's longest serving professional, said 'I'm sure that all the players will welcome the appointment.'

He continued 'The players were impressed by the duo's methods, we got used to their style and what they wanted from the players, and I know everyone will work really hard for them.

'John knows all there is to know about Leyton Orient as a player and youth coach, and Chris has been at the club for three years, both as player and assistant manager. Therefore, they don't have to go through the learning process, they know all about the players and that must be a bonus.'

As, prior to the start of the 1994–95 season, the O's chairman Tony Wood had much of his Rwandan coffee business ravaged by the war in that trouble-torn region, it became very clear that Wood could not keep on bailing out the club financially, as he had done in the past.

There were delays in paying the players' wages, and money owing did not arrive from Rwanda in time. It appeared no one else could tide them over, so the club was forced to go to the Professional Footballers Association (PFA) for financial assistance to pay the players, and they were temporarily blocked from signing any new players. In this environment it was hardly an ideal situation for both Chris Turner and John Sitton to be in charge.

Orient's youth development officer and chief scout Bernie Dixson, who had spent nine years with the club, was questioned by the new management team about his youth policy, and he was given little option but to resign.

Dixson stated 'The youth policy and scouting system had produced 2.5 million pounds worth of players and four of the team that opened the season against Birmingham City, I cannot understand their motives.'

'I'm proud of the youngsters I've produced such as Chris Bart-Williams, Wayne Burnett, Greg Berry and Adrian Whitbread. I'm very sad to be leaving.'

The first match of the new season saw Orient triumph against Birmingham City against all the odds. Youngster Darren Purse, with a 20-yard effort, scored the opening goal after seven minutes. Steve Claridge equalised for the Blues. Then star of the match Barry Lakin went on a great run and passed to Ian Bogie, who finished in style for a 2–1 win. But this turned out to be just one of only six League wins during the whole season.

It shouldn't have been a real surprise to the fans that the team would struggle throughout the season. As the financial problems worsened, the team slipped to second from bottom of Division Two, but worse was to follow.

The club's very existence was now under threat – as always the Orient supporters' club gave every possible financial assistance it could. However, the club needed a very large cash injection to overcome these problems.

A number of individuals showed interest in the club, including Ron Noades and pop star Rod Stewart, via agent and former Orient player Barry Silkman, and local businessman David Baker, but local businessman Philip Wallace seemed the most likely to save the club. Wallace came to the club to stop it going into liquidation and to view the books and meet with supporters, and he was funding Orient during this period out of his own pocket. He had given himself two months to make a decision about taking over the club.

'I have been talking to the club for a few months, but every time I looked at the books things were worse than I thought,' said Wallace. Chairman-elect Wallace paid tribute to the joint management team of Sitton and Turner, 'They are doing a really hard job in very difficult circumstances.' He said 'They cannot buy or loan players, they should not be judged on what's happening this season.

'It's no consolation for the fans that the last manager spent over £400,000 in the transfer market and the supporters have not seen any dividend.'

Wallace placed nine players on the transfer list to help reduce costs, and the team travelled to away matches on the same day to avoid hotel bills. After the two-month period was over, Wallace declared that the financial situation of the club was far too severe for him to take over, and he pulled out.

This financial crisis seemed much worse than the financial crisis of previous years, as if they weren't bad enough.

The club was in debt to the tune of over £500,000, losing £10,000 each week, and could not even pay the players' wages. Now, the one real potential buyer had shied away due to the severity of the club's financial position.

Could this be the final chapter in the club's 114-year history?

Just when it seemed all was lost, an announcement was released that Barry Hearn, the famous snooker and boxing impresario, had moved into his third sport by taking over Leyton Orient Football Club and becoming owner and chairman of the club. Hearn took over control of the club from Tony Wood, and it was reported that Hearn would take care of all the debts. The club was saved by Mr Hearn and the chapters in the history of our grand old club would continue.

Wood stated 'I really feel sorry for our two managers because I have not been able to give them any money as I would have liked.'

Hearn said 'Tony Wood, who has been on the board for eight years, is a smashing man and will stay on at the club as a director.'

The club at this stage was still unable to buy any new players under the PFA embargo, and their League position was almost hopeless.

Sitton said 'I hope Hearn will not rock the boat at the club and pay off the PFA and allow us to buy some new players, our shoestring squad are wilting under the pressure, some of the young players need a rest, but we just can't do it at the moment unless we get some new faces.'

The supporters displayed their gratitude when Mr Hearn took his seat in the directors' box for the vital Auto Windscreens Shield second-leg semi-final against Birmingham City at Brisbane Road on 14 March 1995. The crowd broke out into long, spontaneous applause.

Hearn said 'The supporters were something special – it was fantastic.' Hearn, who went for a drink in the supporters' club with the fans, added, 'I've had a blinding night. It's something you can't buy, a soap opera of dreams – the fans even bought me a drink.'

'There are a few clubs one could buy at the moment – but I would not go anywhere else, there is a certain feel about the place.'

Speaking at a packed Leyton Assembly during a meeting with supporters, Hearn informed those present that he now owned 94 percent of the club's shares.

Orient's management duo of Sitton and Turner warned Barry Hearn that without any investment it would be virtually impossible to achieve any short-term success.

Sitton stated 'Barry is seen as the saviour of the club, but short term Chris and myself believe we have been the saviours because the money we have saved on wages, the money we have brought in on transfers and the money generated from the Auto Windshields Shield comes to around £425,000. And if we had not agreed to let our best players go, there would not be a Leyton Orient Football Club.'

With Ian Hendon and Ian Bogie both sold on deadline day, Sitton added 'It appears supporters can't seem to grasp there is no money being made available – all we ask from them is a level of understanding. We would love to be able to unveil new signings, but we don't want to give the fans false hope. Everyone has got to understand that we have no money available at all. We tried to sign striker Sean Devine last week for £8,000 from Fisher Athletic, but we received a fax from the owner saying there was no money available for him, it appears we were outbid by Gravesend. Yet the money we saved on players' wages between deadline day and end of the season would have paid for Devine's transfer fee plus his wages for the year,' added Sitton. 'It's a shame, he was the best player we had on trial in 12 months,' added Turner.

The duo wondered where the players would come from next season if no money was available, as only five players of the current squad were still under contract. 'What side are we going to have here next season? They could get rid of us and employ a celebrity manager – but a celebrity manager would not be able to work with free transfers,' concluded Turner. While Sitton added 'I've been forthright, candid, open and honest. Possibly too much, and a lot of what I have said in the past has been taken out of context. I've said the club have been pillaged for the past 12 years – I know I upset Bernie Dixson, Frank Clark and Bill Songhurst. The last thing I wanted to do was upset those particular three people. If the club has been pillaged it doesn't mean it was those three particular people who did it. All I can do, therefore, is humbly apologise and live with the fact. There are many good people at the club like Dave Dodd, Frank Woolf and the people at the Football in the Community Scheme.'

The run in the FA Cup and Auto Windshields Shield were the only highlights of a nerve-wracking season.

Orient held a minute's silence before the match with Brighton in March 1995, for former the O's star Barry Dyson, who had died at the age of 52.

Also in March, Hearn, before leaving for Las Vegas, US, to watch his boxer Herbie Hyde fight for a World title, paid off the £25,000 loan from the PFA, which enabled the club to take on loan both 21-year-old Paul Read and Scott McGleish.

In February the O's had a 4–1 win over Peterborough United, with Mark Warren scoring a hat-trick, and in March one further win occurred over Shrewsbury Town 2–1. Yet these types of display were very rare, and they lost 1–0 at Chester City during April in what was described as the battle of the bottom clubs. There was no way out for Orient, they finished bottom of Division Two, recording their worst ever total, and ended with a run of nine consecutive defeats, scoring just three goals with 17 goals against. For the first time ever in their history of League football, dating back to 1905, Orient had failed to win an away match in a season, although in one match at Cardiff City on 4 April they had led 1–0 until injury time, when the Welsh club netted twice for a 2–1 win.

It was after a 2–0 home defeat against Brentford on 17 April 1995 that both Sitton and Turner were summoned to Barry Hearn's office, and instead of him waiting until the end of the season he decided to tell them that their contracts would not be renewed, and most of the younger players were seen to be leaving the dressing room in tears.

The O's longest serving professional Danny Carter stated 'It came as a great shock when both John and Chris were told they no longer have a future at the club. It was quite emotional in the dressing room – especially for the younger players, as John had played a big part in their development as youth-team coach.'

Sitton said 'Hearn asked us to stay in charge of the team for the time being but promised the process would be accelerated. He calls it mutual consent, but I call it the sack. We've taken it bravely but it's difficult, we will not be staying.'

Sitton, in fact, thought he was on the brink of signing a new contract with the club. 'Over the last few weeks he [Hearn] intimated that I'd get a three-year contract and told me to keep it confidential from Chris. But now I've gone from a possible contract to not having any future inside the club. It's a Julius Caesar divide and conquer scenario. Totally ruthless and without integrity. I don't deserve to be treated this way. A priceless lesson has been learnt. The biggest mistake we made was not to resign during October. Since then we have never been allowed to manage properly on and off the pitch, and I've never seen such a lack of cooperation than exists at this football club. It's not sour grapes. We've never wanted a sympathy vote, just a level of understanding. But in an industry governed by fear, dishonesty, paranoia and power, you're always going to be struggling.'

According to Sitton, Hearn told him that the club's new sponsors stipulated that changes were needed and a high profile manager should be installed.

Meanwhile, Chris Turner, who joined the O's in 1991, was also told that his contract would not be renewed. Turner, who had stayed in the background during this time, said the following: 'This season's task had been mission impossible to work with a squad of 18 players, many of whom were far too young for first-team football, but because of the club's financial situation and the PFA ban on transfers, not much else could be done.

'In hindsight we maybe should never have taken it on, but one thing that possibly blinded us this year was our enthusiasm, commitment and professionalism. But now it's gone against us both.'

Turner concluded by saying 'We can walk out now with our heads held high and say that we gave it our best shot and did things for the best of Leyton Orient. But for us two and a handful of others there wouldn't be a Leyton Orient. But we will reappear.' Sitton continued 'It's hard not to be melodramatic because of the work we've put in from YTS right up to the first-team players, many of whom we've wasted our breath on. Some supporters will get what they deserve and some won't. Some of them will know what's been going on. But the club will rue the day they lost Sitton and Turner.'

Barry Hearn said in a statement 'It was a very hard decision to make, but I believe that we are at the beginning of a new era at Brisbane Road, and it is in the best interests of the club to start next season with a new managerial team. The job Chris and John have done under the most testing conditions has been greatly appreciated, and I wish them every success in the future.'

The fact that the team were relegated was hardly a surprise with the financial troubles being the root of the decline, and a large number of players appeared in the League side who would never have done so in normal circumstances, due to the PFA embargo on the purchase of new players.

Joint managers John Sitton and Chris Turner, whatever one's personal view may be, cannot be judged to have failed under such trying circumstances, although it must be added that John Sitton came in for some very strong criticism regarding the unbelievable sacking of Terry Howard in a TV documentary on the O's. In fact, a book was written by Trevor Davies and Terry Howard a year or so after his sacking that explained the goings-on between Sitton and the players.

Below are some extracts, which were printed in the local press, that gave an insight into the managerial style of John Sitton.

In his book Terry Howard revealed all about his infamous sacking from the club by Sitton and the goings-on in the dressing room on the night of Howard's sacking. Howard, who was deeply hurt over the way things were handled after eight loyal years of service, said he thought there was a conspiracy against him.

He said 'My departure from Brisbane Road had nothing to do with one night's performance. It was a conspiracy if you like.'

He goes on to accuse three people at the club, former bosses Sitton and Turner and board member Derek Weinrabe, of being the protagonists of the sensational sacking.

'It doesn't add up.' He goes on 'You just don't send a message up to the board on the spur of the moment saying you're going to sack a player who had made over 400 League and Cup appearances for the club. I'm convinced it was premeditated. It goes far deeper than that. John must have come up a couple of minutes before half-time to write up the team sheet because it takes about 20 seconds to reach the dressing room once the referee has blown his whistle. Now John couldn't have written everyone's initials and a couple of little points underneath in such a short space of time, he'd obviously come in early.

'I looked at the board and my initials were nowhere to be seen. I assumed they were going to pull me off at half-time so I started to undo my boots.

'After Chris had torn into everyone, John started on me. He said 'That performance was the straw that broke the camel's back. You've got two weeks' notice. I was without emotion. I didn't feel anything. John is such a spontaneous person. He often said things on the spur of the moment, and I thought this might be one of these occasions.'

The whole thing was caught on camera by the 'fly-on-the-wall' Channel Four Documentary *Leyton Orient yours for a fiver*, referring to Tony Wood's offer to sell the club for a fiver and takeover all the club's debts.

Howard, who was dubbed 'Oooh' by his adoring O's fans, added 'It all seemed so cold and clinical.'

Howard waited around until the end of the game when he was handed an envelope, which terminated his contract.

But the episode didn't end there. When Phil Wallace was contemplating buying the club, a circular was sent around to other clubs with nine player's names on it, and Howard's name was already listed, so other clubs knew before the Blackpool match about his availability.

Howard said 'It makes me wonder whether it was being prepared well beforehand.'

The O's cult hero also cited the sacking as the beginning of the end for the beleaguered management duo.

'He [Sitton] thought he was the Godfather who could do what he liked, but he couldn't.

'I think he forgot that football clubs have always belonged to the fans, and they will make their opinions known; the O's fans certainly did by booing Sitton at a number of home matches after Howard's sacking, which greatly upset the manager.' Howard concluded, 'I think it was the straw that broke the camel's back as far as he was concerned too.'

In his book, *The autobiography of Terry Howard*, by Howard and Trevor Davies, it was written that 'Blackpool outplayed us for 45 minutes. I'd be the first to admit I didn't have a great first half. There were not too many who could come in at half-time, put their hands on their heart, and say they had done well.

'After coming in at half-time my name had been wiped from the tactics blackboard, I assumed they were going to pull me off and so I started to undo my boots, and the rest has already been well documented. A statement from the club read "both John Sitton and Chris Turner have stressed that Howard wasn't 'sacked' but was served two weeks' notice at the half-time break.

"It should be made clear that Terry Howard was never sacked. Terry was on a week-to-week contract following our offer of a one-year contract to him in the summer. Therefore, we exercised our prerogative of serving him two weeks' notice."'

The actual letter that Howard received was a terse one that stated 'The services of Terry Howard were no longer required at Leyton Orient Football Club and that two weeks' wages would be paid.' The letter was signed by secretary David Burton

'In view of his service to the club, we felt it only right that we give him the opportunity to find a new club now, before the transfer deadline, and the possible large number of players on free transfers in the summer, and so giving him a head start in the continuance of his career.'

Many fans showed their disgust at the sacking. A number wrote to the local press, and some of the extracts read 'If Orient's management duo had sacked every player who made unacceptable performances I doubt we would be able to field a five-a-side team.'

'It was a sour and spiteful ending to an excellent career at Brisbane Road, Terry should have left the club with his head held high.'

'What Howard has been through is nothing short of a public humiliation, the way the managers handled the situation was diabolical.'

Herewith follows the scene in the dressing room, as printed in the local press. The team, 1–0 down at half-time to Blackpool on 7 February 1995, featuring Sitton and the players.

> '(Sitton pacing up and down in front of the players) Now all I'm saying to you is when the ball pops out, you've got to be crafty, you've got to drift off and when it pops out you've got to establish possession for Orient, for a red shirt.

(Calmly, Sitton continues) All I'm saying to you is get your body in the way, you were lucky you got a free-kick.

(Quickly Sitton moves through the gears to reach ballistic in 0.3 seconds) Now don't be coming back to me when I'm shouting at you above the crowd and above the next bench. Alright? (Menacing glare) 'Cause I run this f...... football club until I'm told otherwise by the f...... circus upstairs. And if you come back at me you'll be off the field and you'll be following Terry (Howard) down the road.

(Sitton turns to a somewhat surprised Terry Howard) You come and see me tomorrow! You've got a fortnight's notice 'cause that performance is the straw that broke the camel's back and that will not be tolerated in this dressing room while I'm in charge or by Chris Turner (the joint manager). That is the f...... straw that broke the camel's f...... back and that is typical f...... Leyton Orient.

(Sitton mocks players) Sitts you're too intense, 'your f...... this, your f...... that, no one can talk to you.

(Sitton speaks back to himself) Well I never f...... followed two games with a f...... game like that. The reason I was too intense was 'cause I wanted to play well again, but I'm wasting my breath on some of you.... (Sitton regains his breath) Wasting my breath on some of you. What did I say to you about good players wanting to be good players all the time? Don't you know how profound that is? Have you examined the f...... words? No, 'cause you've had two good performances and you think, I'm f...... Bertie Bollocks tonight, I'll f...... play how I like. But you wont play how you like, 'cause if you play how you like I'll f...... stick the youth team in. See, If I'm gonna take abuse from a bunch of cockroaches behind me, I'll take abuse by doing it my way – and that is f....... conformity and not f...... non-conformity.

So you (Sitton points to nippy winger), you little c... when I tell you to do something, and you (Sitton points to towering centre-half), you big c...., when I tell you to do something, do it. And if you come back at me, we'll have a f...... sort out in 'ere all right? And you can pair up if you like and you can f...... pick someone else to hold your hand, and you can bring your f...... dinner 'cause by the time I've finished with ya, you'll f...... need it. Do you f...... hear what I'm saying or not?

(Sitton points and shouts at Terry Howard) You! See me in the morning. Howard is left sitting in the dressing room all on his own, bemused. Not surprising after the negative vibes that Orient went on to lose the match 1–0 to Blackpool.'

Division Two bottom five relegation places – 1994–95

	P	W	D	L	F	A	Pts
Cambridge U	46	11	15	20	52	69	48
Plymouth Argyle	46	12	10	24	45	83	46
Cardiff C	46	9	11	26	46	74	38
Chester C	46	6	11	29	37	84	29
Leyton Orient	46	6	8	32	30	75	26

The man to take over from the duo was 44-year-old Pat Holland. He signed a three-year contract and had been reserve-team manager at Spurs that season. He also played for 13 years with West Ham and spent a few years on Orient's coaching staff between 1983–85. Former '80s O's skipper Tommy Cunningham was appointed his coaching assistant.

Colin West celebrates his hat-trick against Cardiff City on 10 February 1996.

Hearn stated 'It would have been a disaster to have a high-profile manager at Leyton Orient because they don't want to work.'

The other person in contention for the job was Billy Bonds; Hearn stated that 'Bonds would have been a good manager, but at the end of our meeting he said. "Do you think I'd give up my cushy little number with QPR for Division Three football?" He soon went out of the reckoning.'

Holland took charge for the final few League matches, with Orient already doomed to relegation.

The 1994–95 season does not make pretty reading, but with all the restrictions on the club it would have taken a genius to have saved Orient from the big drop.

Listed below are the sad facts behind what had been an O's so depressing tale of woe on the field.

Most League defeats in a season: 32.

Lowest away points tally: two.

First season in the O's history in which they have failed to win an away game.

The O's failed to score a goal in a record 26 League matches.

Leyton Orient finished with the lowest points haul of all 92 clubs this season: 26.

Club record run of consecutive defeats: nine, previous worst was eight in 1927–28.

Orient's tally of nine away goals was their lowest since World War One.

In both the 1912–13 and 1913–14 seasons, the O's travelling fans had only nine goals to celebrate. However, the team only played 19 away games in each of those seasons, and in 1913–14 they still managed to finish sixth in Division Two.

The O's tally of 11 home defeats has only been exceeded when they lost 12 at Brisbane Road in the old Division One in 1962–63, their only season in the top flight.

The players could have no excuses concerning Charlie Hasler's award-winning playing surface, it was voted the best in the land.

There was a new manager and renewed hope for the 1995–96 season, and, although most fans realised that to expect instant promotion from Division Three (the old Division Four) would be asking too much, at least a new spirit in the team could be expected under Pat Holland.

A number of changes were made to the playing staff. Manager Holland brought in players who had perhaps not been given much opportunity at other clubs, and, of course, he was still unable to spend much money in the transfer market.

The new boss Pat Holland was in a confident mood, stating 'I have set a target of First Division football within three years.'

Given that Orient were relegated the previous season, the first home match of the new season against Torquay United attracted a remarkable 8,244 spectators. There was fresh paint, new razzmatazz and noise, which included a bongo drummer in the stand, and the players reacted with a 1–0 win.

Hearn said 'I've had a lot of good days with the likes of Steve Davis and Chris Eubank, but this win will take some beating,' after watching Shaun Brooks seal the victory. 'You can't buy what I got today.' This is not altogether true: Hearn puts his financial investment at 'A few hundred thousand pounds and that's it. I've told everyone no more from where that came from. On the opposite side of my heart is my wallet. This is a business for me. I can't score the goals, I look at sets of accounts. That's how I get my buzz. I looked at our 14,000 stadium and we got 3,000 people a week. I looked at the empty seats and thought, how to fill them? Well we targeted kids. We went into the community and said "We're your club".

'Orient has for a long time run the country's most popular 'in the community scheme'. The parks are full of small boys and girls dressed in other club's kits coached by Orient's staff. Eighty thousand kids went through our scheme last year, run by 45 volunteer coaches.'

So Hearn turned it into a direct mail advertising campaign. Kids were returning with material including free match tickets for a family of four.

The results were surprising: more than 3,000 season tickets were sold, but at the end of the day business, marketing and modern accountancy practice will all make a certain amount of difference to the club, 'But only if the team stop playing like a collection of refuse. The bullshit must stop the moment the bugger blows the whistle,' admitted Hearn.

Also it was his complete overhaul of the commercial department that has put the club on a new footing and the income quadrupled in six months.

He continued, 'Leyton Orient are now making money, and debts of nearly one million pounds have been paid off, thanks partially to summer transfer deals, and in particular the cut the club got from the £2.5 million move of old boy Chris Bart-Williams (bought by former O's manager Frank Clark at Nottingham Forest from Sheffield Wednesday).

Season ticket sales rocketed, with Under-16s paying only £10 and women getting a £70 discount on the full price.

'This isn't sexism,' asserted Hearn. 'Last year we had just 12 women ticket holders, already this year we have 350.'

The team were 15/1 to get promotion in the 1995–96 season; if they achieved their goal it could have set back Hearn over £100,000. He offered the players an extra £75 for a win and £35 for a draw. If they followed that up with another victory the bonus would be doubled to £175. Another lump sum would be handed over should they gain promotion.

The early League games gave rise to considerable hope; in fact, only one defeat had been suffered from the first 10 League matches, and after a 3–1 home win over Doncaster Rovers on 30 September 1995 the O's were in third spot.

Twelve days earlier, on 12 September 1995, the O's did the unthinkable and pulled off a victory away from home after nearly two years and 42 away games (the last win being against Hull City at Boothferry Park on 30 October 1993). They finally laid their abysmal 42-League game away record without a win to rest, with a 2–1 win at Northampton Town. The magical moment came in the last minute, when Ian Hendon lobbed over a cross. Shaun Brooks volleyed back a clearance and Inglethorpe lunged forward for the winning goal. Alex Inglethorpe's winner was followed by a mass pitch invasion by the starved travelling fans, and it was a nice present for boss Holland who had celebrated his 45th birthday the previous day.

The 700-plus delirious O's fans were floating down the M1, and chairman Hearn was lining up the beers for the trip back home. A cheery Hearn had forgotten to bring the champagne, but choked 'That was marvellous. It was like our European Cup Final and great for the fans. It's about time we got the rub of the green. The atmosphere in the dressing room was electric. All the players were magnificent.'

Holland said. 'That was the best birthday present I've had. Ironically Alex Inglethorpe nearly never made the match, he was carrying a knock but we talked him into playing, now he is the great hero.'

However, the team's form went completely off the rails with only two wins from the next 11 games, and by Christmas they were down in a very disappointing 13th spot. They made a humiliating performance on 20 January 1996 at Torquay – the lowest team in the League. A draw looked a good bet, Torquay without a win in 16 matches and Orient just that one away win at Northampton from 51 away League trips.

The O's opened the scoring through an Ian Hendon half volley, but Paul Baker levelled for the home side on 52 minutes. Then on 75 minutes the O's 'keeper Ron Fearon brought down Simon Garner after a suicidal back-pass from Kevin Austin and was shown a red card. Young Darren Purse deputised in goal, and in injury time Gary Bellamy carelessly conceded a free-kick. Hathaway floated over for the unattended Alex Watson to nod past a stranded Purse. The Torquay fans were pinching themselves in disbelief, and Orient's woes continued.

A season that started in such a promising fashion and with all the off-the-field hype was at the end of the season rather a terrible let down – Orient had only three teams below them in the final League table. Some disgruntled noises came from the terraces. Far from making an instant return to Division Two, they were nearer to dropping out of the League.

In truth, bottom club Torquay United were 11 points behind second from bottom Scarborough and 18 points adrift of the O's, and as it happened Torquay remained in the League because Vauxhall Conference winners Stevenage Borough's stadium was not up to the League standard.

During the O's slump crowds dwindled, and on 19 March 1996, for the match at Brisbane Road against second from bottom Scarborough, just 2,121 turned up, the lowest crowd at the ground for nine years.

Striker Colin West topped the O's League scorer's list with 16 goals, the third time in his stay at the club that he was the top marksman.

There were some good honest pros in the side, but they just did not seem to gel as a team. However, for the record they achieved their first 'double' against Northampton Town in March 1996. A feat not achieved since 1993–94 over Hull City.

Another black day in the club's history was the banning from football of 27-year-old defender Roger Stanislaus on 1 February 1996 for 12 months, after becoming the first British-based footballer to test positive for taking a performance-enhancing drug. A 'metabolite' of cocaine showed up in his test. The Football League handed out their longest suspension in 30 years. He was caught by the FA's mobile drugs unit following Orient's 3–0 defeat at Barnet in the Endsleigh League Division Three match in November 1995.

Chairman Barry Hearn refused to show any leniency towards the player when he booted him out of the club.

Hearn rapped 'The fact that Roger's version of events that led to him testing positive was heavily contradictory left us with no alternative, Roger is a nice guy but my overall interest is with the club. Drugs have no place in football and particularly not at Leyton Orient.

Stanislaus, sounding stunned and upset, took a deep breath before sighing 'I haven't got any comment to make.'

Some people drew comparisons with the Paul Merson affair at Arsenal, but as Brendon Batson, the spokesperson for the PFA, stated, Merson admitted he had problem but Stanislaus insisted that he unwittingly took the drug.'

Most of his fellow teammates were also shocked and very upset.

Defender Ian Hendon stated 'It is unbelievable, everyone is in a state of shock. It has become a massive slur against the club. We just want it done and dusted by the FA so we can concentrate on the football. The sooner it gets out of the papers the better for the team and the club.'

The club issued an official statement, which read:

'The Board of Leyton Orient voted unanimously to terminate Roger Stanislaus's contract with immediate effect. In considering all the factors, we felt that the good name of Leyton Orient as the Littlewoods Community Club of the Year and the very high percentage of young supporters we attract were two of the overriding factors.

'In addition, the fact that Roger's version of events that led to him testing positive for cocaine was heavily contradicted by expert medical testimony has, in our opinion, left the club with no possible alternative. It is out belief that the decision of the Football Association in handing down a 12-month ban was, in our opinion, a lenient one in the circumstances.'

The statement concluded by saying 'Leyton Orient is a small Third Division club. The last thing we want is to lose the £40,000 that Roger Stanislaus cost us. However, there are much bigger issues at stake here, and we have made it clear that Leyton Orient FC will not tolerate any form of drug abuse by any of our players. I hope our message is clear.'

The Orient supporter is an eternal optimist so the forthcoming season could only get better, couldn't it?

Barry Hearn reported 'After the financial disaster that nearly took the O's to the brink, I am delighted that for the year ending 30 June 1996 the club achieved a surplus of £11,638.' That may not sound a fortune but, compared with the previous year's deficit of £502,252, I'd call it an absolute miracle. Holland warned that unless money was made available to him to buy new players, now that the PFA ban had been lifted, then our loyal fans could face another season of frustration.

Holland said 'I need to make wholesale changes, but it is going to be difficult if there is no money available. People have got to be realistic – if we are going to rely on free transfers then it is going to be a tough season.'

A number of changes were made to the playing staff prior to the commencement of the 1996–97 season.

The big story was the surprise free-transfer signings of veteran players Alvin Martin, a former England centre-half, goalkeeper Les Sealey, from West Ham United, the experienced Justin Channing, the Bristol Rovers midfielder, Dominic Naylor, who came from Gillingham, Peter Garland, an

A pre-season friendly between Leyton Orient and Tottenham Hotspur on 20 July 1996, with the captains, Howells of Spurs and Naylor.

overweight looking midfield player from Charlton Athletic, Martin Ling, a midfield forager from Swindon Town, and others. The fans had a big surprise on their return to Brisbane Road as terracing at the Coronation end of the ground had been demolished.

There was a great expectancy from the fans because the general feeling was that Division Three was not too strong a League and they appeared to have a squad to do the business, so to speak, that season. Orient played a friendly against the Wales National team at Leyton during May 1996. The Welsh included such stars as Ryan Giggs, Mark Hughes, Neville Southall, Dean Saunders, John Hartson and Barry Horne. Orient slayed the Welsh dragons 2–1. The O's fielded a makeshift side including a number of trialists such as Dutchman Erik Regtop, Udo Onwere, Greg Tello and a 15-stone player named Peter Garland. They took the lead after 15 minutes when Regtop played in a free-kick, which Welsh 'keeper Southall dropped for young defender Lee Shearer to head home. With 12 minutes remaining, the Welsh seemed to have gained a draw when John Robinson scored from close range, but in injury time Tello broke down the right, and Baker hooked the ball back for Garland to scramble home the winner before a delighted 5,055 crowd. The club made around £26,000 from the match.

The reality of the matter was that once more Orient struggled to make progress, and by the end of October 1996 the team had gone six hours without scoring a goal, with four straight defeats. Something had to be done to ignite a side that had slipped to 17th position in the League. The fans had begun calling for Holland's head, with chants of 'Holland Out' emanating from the terraces since the beginning of October. Holland urged the fans to be patient while he searched for that elusive formula, and he reminded the fans that he still had not seen the money promised for new players. However, it was obvious to the fans that Holland's formula was very defensive by nature. He strengthened the defence at the expense of a decent midfield and forward line.

It was after a 3–0 defeat at Cardiff City on 26 October that Hearn thought to himself 'enough was enough'.

Hearn revealed 'I had slept on it on Saturday, phoned Pat on Sunday and told him "This is the time."

'I'm sorry to see him go in many ways because he worked tirelessly for the club and gave it his best shot, and he's a smashing fellow. Pat clearly wanted to stay, but I think it was an amicable departure. I just thought we were going the wrong way and the club needed a kick up the backside. This has got to be a successful club and we've got to move on. I started to lose confidence in some of Pat's decisions and I told him that. I was very upset and annoyed with several issues at the Cardiff match, but it wasn't just the one game. It had been building up over the last few months. We've got one of the biggest wage bills in the Division, and I know we've had key injuries but we can't keep making excuses. I looked at myself in the mirror and said I'm not sure about this and that's a bad thing because you have to have confidence in your manager.'

A disappointed Holland was still in a state of numbness on that Monday, and he brought all the players and staff together at his Essex wine bar to say his farewells after 18 months in charge.

The players were shocked and saddened at Holland's departure. Colin West, who had played under three different managers in three years, pined 'It's very sad for any manager to be sacked. I think it was a surprise to all of us, but we're all professionals and we've got to get on with it. Holland had a lot of respect from the players and a knowledge of the game that was second to none. More time would have been nice but money would have been even better because he could only do so much with what he had.'

Teenage 'keeper Luke Weaver admitted 'We were all in a state of shock when we found out about the boss. He was a great coach and a good manager to work for.'

Head groundsman Charlie Hasler – who had worked for 10 different O's managers – said 'We are sad to see him go. Pat was too nice to be a football manager. He was Mr Nice Guy. To be honest we were expecting it to happen after the recent results.'

The affair was best summed up by Jamie Stripe, editor of the O's fanzine *Leyton Orientear*, who wrote 'the departure has come as no great shock. Unfortunately his sacking only serves to underline the club's inability to appoint anyone remotely resembling a suitable replacement for Frank Clark in 1993.'

Hearn said 'I had considered taking charge of the team myself. The thought of manager-chairman is tempting sometimes, but I've got to be led by people who understand more about football than I do.'

So, while the search for a new manager took place, it was Tommy Cunningham who took charge of the team for the two home matches against Scarborough and Torquay United, the latter being a 1–0 win. Cunningham, a close friend of Holland, did not want to be considered for the job and left at the end of the season. During the 1998–99 season he was youth-team coach at Barnet. He was appointed assistant manager in September 1999 and more recently he managed non-League side Harlow Town.

In the team for the Torquay match was loan player Carl Griffiths, who joined the club on Thursday evening from Peterborough United, met with the team and trained on Friday and soon showed what he could do on the Saturday.

The Welshman scored in the 43rd minute when Ian Hendon punted a long ball up the field for Griff to chase, it looked like 'keeper Rhys Wilmot (a former O's loan player from Arsenal in 1984–85) would gather a back pass, but instead Griff slid in to dispossess him of the ball and score into an empty net.

This was the O's first goal in over seven hours of football and their first win in seven games. Hearn interviewed a number of candidates for the 'Gaffer's' job, including Alvin Martin, Billy Bonds, and former O's defender Tommy Taylor, who was out of contract with Cambridge United having taken the U's young side to second in Division Three.

Taylor's 18-month contract with Cambridge was due to expire at Christmas, and he was originally offered a deal only until the end of the season plus a further three months. After his talks with Barry Hearn at Orient, Cambridge chairman Reg Smart suddenly came up with an extended deal that would have kept Taylor at Abbey Stadium for three and a half years.

Taylor was reported as saying 'If that had been a genuine offer a week ago I would have taken it. But the directors at Cambridge have merely been panicked into the better offer. I meant it when I said that I didn't want to leave Cambridge, but I feel I have to make the move to Orient as a matter of principle. I have been offered a two-year deal and a very good package by Barry Hearn at Orient, and I have to take it.'

Hearn eventually appointed Taylor as the new manager on 7 November 1996, due to the fact that Taylor was an Orient man through and through and had come through the junior ranks with the club while captaining the England Schoolboy and Youth teams. He, of course, went on to to help Orient to the Third Division Championship in 1970 before moving to West Ham United.

After a long career with the Hammers, he returned to Orient and played again in what was a good side, so he obviously had a 'feel and love' for the club.

Taylor said 'It's going to be a bloody big job and the potential is here, I don't think what's come out of the players so far this season is their full potential.

'That's what football is about. I like to think I can get the best out of the players.

'Barry wants to get to the top in everything he does, and I'm the same. There's no reason why Leyton Orient cannot be a Second Division, First Division or even a Premiership side in the years to come.'

Hearn admitted 'Some supporters might be surprised at his choice. I don't expect the appointment to be universally well-received, but I think most of the fans will approve. He's got a proven track record and doesn't see this as a stepping stone. He's been working on a budget about a third of ours and has done a magnificent job with Cambridge. Let's hope he can do an even better job with bigger resources.'

Taylor appointed Paul Clark as his assistant. Clark was with Taylor at Cambridge and was a former manager with Southend United, which meant the end for former assistant manager Tommy Cunningham.

Managing Leyton Orient is never the easiest of jobs in the world, as many others have found out, and Taylor certainly found difficulties in his early months in charge, similar to most of his predecessors.

There was a mixed bag of results under his charge in the first few weeks. In the FA Cup the O's had squeezed through 2–1 against Merthyr Tydfil to give Taylor his first win at the club. A difficult match for Taylor and Clark soon followed at 'old club' Cambridge, which was lost 2–0.

During December another non-League side, Stevenage Borough, put Taylor's boys out of the FA Cup at Brisbane Road, in a tie which the O's had enough chances to win, especially during the final 20 minutes, and one which saw goalie Peter Shilton receiving a rare yellow card.

Shilton said 'It's a bit disappointing. We deserved it in the second half, but it just wasn't our day, though they [Stevenage Borough] did play well.'

Midfielder Martin Ling said 'Clubs go out to non-League teams every year, but at least we went out with all guns firing.' So it was Stevenage who were rewarded with a third-round tie at home to Birmingham City, and it probably cost the O's around £60,000 because of a potential capacity 14,000 crowd, but it was not meant to be.

Orient went on a good run of results, winning seven games without defeat, which helped them finish in 16th position in the table, having spent a good deal of time in the lower reaches of the Division. They scored a total of 50 League goals during the campaign.

Alec Inglethorpe topped the goalscoring chart with eight goals from just 10 League appearances.

One fact to emerge concerning the 1996–97 campaign was that they used 40 players in the League matches – the highest number ever used in a season since the O's League entry in 1905. Taylor obviously searched far and wide for the right material. Taylor had been in charge for only two-thirds of the season so it was far too early to make any judgment on his time as the boss.

During the season the O's had three former England veterans on their books, 36-year-old Alvin Martin, 40-year-old midfielder Ray Wilkins and 47-year-old goalie Peter Shilton, and veteran Chris Whyte also played one League match.

A report was released in *Leyton Orientear* on 1 April of another big name 'veteran' signing:

'HEARN CAPTURES EX-ENGLAND STAR

Former Stoke City, Blackpool and England hero Sir Stanley Matthews has joined Leyton Orient.

Sir Stan, who has signed a three-year deal with the club, made his League debut for Stoke back in 1932. Barry Hearn swooped to sign Matthews, now 82 years old, after reading that he had always regretted retiring at the age of 50.

Hearn continued "He's got everything we look for in a player. He's one of the most skilful players of his generation, he's old and, of course, he is incredibly famous."

Orient fans are thought to be delighted at having an opportunity to see yet another living legend in action at Brisbane Road.

"Who can forget the Matthews Cup Final?" beamed Hearn. "Thousands were locked out, there was a white horse on the pitch and Geoff Hurst's shot definitely crossed the line. And then on came Matthews and – well the rest is history." The O's faithful certainly needed cheering up after watching the club sink to its lowest level in years. "The moaners will always look for an excuse to have a whinge." beamed Hearn. "I say look at the quality of players we've signed. Look at what we've already done to the ground – a terrific new car park – and look at the stability we've brought to this little 'friendly' East London family club."

And the charismatic chairman's wheeling and dealing isn't finished yet. "Watch out for a few more surprise names," he beamed.

"I'm not promising anything but Tommy wants a new defender and Bobby Moore doesn't seem to be doing anything these days."

The O's attracted a bumper crowd to see the silky skills of Matthews.

AN APRIL FOOL'S JOKE'

Seriously though, the highlights of the season seem to have centred around Brighton. There was Shilton's marvellous 1,000th League appearance match versus Brighton in December 1996, and Wilkins's second-half display to cap one of the most exciting League matches ever, also against the Seagulls in March 1997.

There was also the return of 'Super' Carl Griffiths, who joined the club in March 1997 for £100,000, after a successful loan spell the previous season. He scored six goals on his return.

Shilton celebrated his 1,000th Football League match on 22 December 1996 against the Seagulls before 7,944 fans. He only touched the ball a handful of times during the historic afternoon.

Orient gave the goalkeeper the red carpet treatment and 1,000 red balloons were released, then the band of the Coldstream Guards gave Shilton a special fanfare on the pitch, and he was presented with a special plaque by former World Cup referee Jack Taylor and a certificate from the Guinness Book of Records. Orient won the match 2–0 and both goals came from Dominic Naylor, one a penalty.

Shilton said 'The main thing was to keep a clean sheet and take the three points. It would have been nice to have a couple of fantastic saves, I didn't really have any to make, but we deserved it and it was a great feeling. The club and the fans were great, and I thank them all very much. I was a bit overwhelmed to be honest. I didn't really expect all the palaver.'

Another highlight was the match at Brighton on 8 March 1997, quite a remarkable affair, and it will go down as the match that had everything, including eight goals (see Matches to Remember).

During March 1997 it was announced that six times Embassy World snooker champion Steve Davis has joined his good friend Barry Hearn on the board of Leyton Orient.

Peter Shilton runs out to a fanfare as he competes in his 1,000th League game against Brighton on 22 December 1996. Orient won 2–0.

Davis said 'I have been watching Barry over the last two and half years and seen the excitement he has got out of this club, and I decided that maybe I should get a bit.'

Davis's role will be to promote the involvement of the club within the local community, but he will not concentrate fully on it until his snooker days are over. Davis, a Charlton supporter, added 'I will be bringing my kids to the ground and hope they will become masochistic O's fans before long.'

And so on to the 1997–98 season. Orient signed a new sponsorship deal with Marchpole PLC, a marketing company for big names like Conran and Yves Saint Laurent, and the deal was said to be the largest sponsorship deal in the two lower Divisions. The original deal was to use the name of top designer Jasper Conran (JC) on the shirts, but their management appeared unhappy to be associated with the O's after the brawl match against Brighton; however, the O's management stated this was complete nonsense. Eventually it was agreed to use the name Marchpole on the shirts.

Taylor captured three solid defenders in Simon Clark from Peterborough United, Dean Smith from Hereford United and Stuart Hicks from Scarborough, and the three were nicknamed by the fans as the 'three Amigos'. Also Roger Joseph returned to the club from a spell with West Brom, and Tony Richards signed from Taylor's old club Cambridge United.

Barry Hearn called the season 'a season of no excuses'. One sometimes wonders if supporters occasionally put chairmen and managers under extra pressure. After all, 24 teams are chasing just four promotion places so 20 must be disappointed, and, with the ever-increasing problems regarding the finances on lower Division clubs, the task for Taylor was mighty difficult.

It was difficult to assess Orient's chances, but they appeared to have a solid look about them. They started off with two defeats, but they soon settled down, maintaining a mid-table position.

Leyton Orient in 1997–98. Back row (left to right): Joseph, Howes, Channing, Warren, Morrison, Brown, Hanson. Middle row: Clark, West, Hicks, Hyde, Weaver, Shearer, Smith, Richards. Front row: Winston, McGleish, Inglethorpe, Naylor, Ling, Griffiths, Baker.

By Christmas 1997 Orient still held a mid-table position, yet they were just one point from a Play-off place. A Boxing Day single-goal defeat by Cambridge United was followed by a record-equalling 8–0 home victory over struggling Doncaster Rovers, who conceded four goals in each half, and it was only their teenage 'keeper Gary Hoggeth who prevented an even bigger rout. Carl Griffiths bagged a hat-trick, Richards two and Inglethorpe, Smith and Baker were the other scorers.

The big score should have been even bigger because when the O's notched their eighth goal there was still 26 minutes remaining in the match. One possible reason was that the O's three goal scorers, Griffiths, Richards and Inglethorpe, were all substituted during the final phase of the game.

However, a couple of events changed the fortunes of the team. On 31 January 1998 Paul Hyde suffered a very serious broken leg at Exeter City when City scored their second winning goal, which everyone thought should have been disallowed. Thirty-four-year-old Hyde cried out in pain after a terrible tackle by Exeter's substitute John Williams, which resulted in Hyde breaking his leg is three places and also sustaining considerable bruising to his chest. The first man on the scene was the O's physio Tony Flynn, who was at his side before the referee stopped play. Flynn said 'Paul knew his leg was broken and cried out to the ref in pain to stop play. He allowed play to go on, and Exeter scored into an empty net. It was ridiculous. Paul was in a tremendous amount of pain, the only painkiller strong enough was morphine, and he only got that when he arrived in hospital, there was a lot of muscle wastage so it will be a long hard road back for Hyde.' Exeter manager Peter Fox, a former 'keeper himself, praised Hyde for his bravery in challenging for the ball. He said 'it was a simple 50/50 ball and both players were brave, but sometimes players get hurt.'

It was to be Hyde's final League match after losing the fight for a full recovery, and he decided to quit League football in December 1998, although he later returned to play a few games in the

Goal celebration modern-style during the FA Cup game against Brighton in 1998. Richards, Griffiths and Walschaerts are doing their routine.

Conference with Dover Athletic. During mid-March the O's were in 10th spot with just a two-point gap to the last Play-off position. Surely a real last gasp push would have seen the team at last gain a Play-off spot. During April Orient received shock news that they were being fined £20,000 by the FA after administrative blunders by secretary David Burton.

Burton failed to keep up with the amount of bookings accrued by three players and did not tell manager Taylor when they should have been suspended. The O's boss then unwittingly allowed the trio, Mark Warren, Simon Clark and Stuart Hicks, to play when they were in fact ineligible to do so, thus breaching FA disciplinary rules.

However, the three key men need not have been suspended at all. Burton gaffed again by forgetting that they had all gone five matches without a booking, constituting good behaviour, and under the new laws that absolves one of the previous bookings, thus delaying a suspension, but the confusion arose because Burton had forgotten to fill in the relevant paperwork.

Barry Hearn, who attended the hearing, said 'I think we have been treated fairly by the FA. It was a mess up on our former secretary's part, and he has taken full responsibility. The O's have to pay up £7,500 immediately and the remaining £12,500 was suspended for 12 months, as long as the club keeps its records up to date.'

Secretary David Burton resigned over the incident. Leyton MP Harry Cohen decided to join the fight to get Orient's fine revoked, but the club decided to let the entire scenario rest. However, Cohen felt that his local team had been unjustly fined.

Shortly after, the club found that they were also to be docked three points by the Football League for the error. A shocked Barry Hearn stated 'The FA especially told us that this was not a points deductible offence, so we are asking them to overturn the Football League's decision. I am fully confident that this will be done.'

It appears that Exeter City complained to the League and that they decided to take the matter further. Exeter's complaint concerned Simon Clark, who scored the equaliser in the 2–2 draw at St James's Park. They had asked the Football League for the game to either be replayed or that they be granted the three points.

Orient spokesman Luke Riches said 'It's frustrating, we have received our punishment from the FA and accepted it, but now Exeter have thrown a spanner in the works.'

League spokesman Chris Hall said 'This decision has nothing to do with the complaints of another club. Orient could have been docked three points for each of the three players that should have been suspended, so in our view they have got off lightly with only the three points being docked off.'

The club decided to appeal against the decision, but on 24 April 1998 the FA decided to uphold their sentence.

FA spokesman Steve Double said 'Barry Hearn, the Leyton Orient chairman, made the case to the three-man appeal tribunal, but the tribunal decided that the Football League had acted within their regulations and so dismissed the appeal.' Former secretary David Burton was charged with misconduct.

Over Easter Orient won a cracking match at Barnet on a typical Easter day, with sunshine, snow and rain. The home side seemed to have victory in their grasp, but with just seven minutes remaining Orient turned up the heat and firing on all cylinders took the three points with two strikes. In the 83rd minute the O's substitute king Joe Baker levelled from close range. In the referee's optional time Carl Griffiths scored with a fine glancing header from a Channing cross.

Two days later a home defeat to Shrewsbury Town summed up Orient to a tee and so their Play-off hopes came spectacularly off the rails. They looked comfortable with a 2–0 lead through Craig Maskell and Carl Griffiths, his 21st League and Cup goal of the season. The visitors went down to 10 men through the sending-off of Berkley for a second bookable offence, and the points looked safe in the bank. Then 'Griff' missed a sitter, which should have made it 3–0. From then on the O's defence took on the appearance of a 'quivering jelly', with three goals from the visitors. The stunned crowd began a mass exit long before the Orient players, wearing haunted expressions, disappeared down the tunnel.

A day after the FA appeal, the O's went to Hull City and lost 3–2. The O's boss said 'This whole matter badly affected the players at Hull.' All in all it was not a good April for them. At the end of the season they fell four points short of a Play-off position and finished in 11th spot. So even without the three-point deduction they would have just missed out, but, on the other hand, three points at Hull would have made the world of difference to the confidence of the team, and who knows what may have happened.

The general feeling around the terraces was that Orient were at least as good as the other teams involved in the Play-offs, but somehow, like in quite a number of previous seasons over this past decade, they seemed to freeze at the inappropriate time.

Once again, they didn't make it.

It was a reasonable League campaign for the O's, but one could not say the same for their efforts in the FA Cup. In fact, their exit in the first-round replay at Brisbane Road against Isthmian Ryman League side Hendon must have been one of their poorest ever FA Cup displays.

The club gained a reported windfall of around £120,000 from a 'sell-on' of Darren Purse from Oxford United to Birmingham City, which certainly eased the club's financial position.

Hearn replied, when he was asked about his comment earlier on that it would be a season of no excuses, 'Well, we were not good enough to go up, plain and simple.'

The club's accounts for the year ending June 1998 showed an accounting loss of £57,000 down from £657,000 in the previous year. However, £446,000 of this improvement can be placed with profits arising from transfers. Transfer income for 1996 was £565,000 (1997, £253,000) and transfer expenditure was £128,000 (1997, £262,000).

Gate receipts and other related income (probably including TV money and sponsorship) increased from £1,462,000 to £1,587,000. Staff costs stayed constant at £1,188,000, and the number of playing staff remained at 40.

Barry Hearn gave an undertaking to provide financial support to enable the club to continue trading for the foreseeable future.

So on to the 1998–99 season – the final 'full season' before the new millennium. The previous season had been a campaign in which Orient had made progress; now further progress was needed to enable the club to launch a serious promotion challenge. Summer signings had been few. Wim Walschaerts, a defender/midfield player, had joined from KFC Tielen in Belgium, the former Eire Under-21 player Kwame Ampadu joined on a free transfer from Swansea City, Matthew Lockwood, an attacking wing-back renowned for his excellent crossing ability, joined from Bristol Rovers, and finally Scott Canham, a defender, came from Brentford on a free transfer.

The team made a successful start to the new season by winning the opening League match at Chester City 2–0; however, the first home match turned into something of a nightmare when visitors Rotherham United coasted to a 4–1 victory. A 1–1 draw at Swansea was followed by another below par home display, this time a 3–0 reverse at the hands of Scarborough, which did not suggest that the

O's were going to make a bold bid for promotion, with four matches played and Orient in 19th position.

Manager Taylor tried several players, like Reinelt on a non-contract basis and the lanky forward McCormick on loan from Dundee, in an attempt to strengthen the squad, but neither proved to be the answer. Soon after, Orient results started to improve considerably and a run of 10 unbeaten League games saw them zoom up the table.

Orient gained a great home win over fellow promotion candidates Brentford, winning 2–1. The O's were 1–0 down in the first half and equalised after a dubious penalty flagged by the female linesman Wendy Toms for a foul on Richards. It was quite unusual to see a player (Richards) blowing a kiss to a official, before Dean Smith put away the spot-kick. It was substitute Steve Watts who headed home the winner on his debut.

Taylor's boys were now showing real fighting character, this being the third consecutive match that they had fought back from behind.

The most notable pre-Christmas signing was that of former French international striker Amara Simba, who, just a few months from his 37th birthday, looked very skilful and fit for his age. Simba came to Orient from Mexican club Lyon after training with them while on holiday in London. Previously Simba had played for French sides Cannes, Paris St Germain and Monaco. He scored on his League debut against Exeter City with a bullet header, well captured on Orient's internet site.

Another exciting prospect was Steve Watts, who won a 'search for a striker' competition run by the *Sun* newspaper and Bravo TV. He joined Orient from Fisher Athletic. In October the long transfer saga of Billy Beall was finally settled with Cambridge United via a tribunal amounting in total to £50,000. Beall proved to be an average capture, and one cannot see why Taylor went to all that trouble to sign him.

The match against Plymouth started with the home side in control, and Matthew Joseph turned the ball into his own net in the ninth minute. Steve Watts hit the equaliser and Martin Ling gave the O's the lead in the 72nd minute with a well-struck shot from the edge of the penalty area. However, their lead was short lived as Collins beat Mackenzie with a right foot shot. The Orient team showed some tremendous character over the final 10 minutes and took the lead again on 80 minutes when Tony Richards headed home from a Lockwood corner. Five minutes later Carl Griffiths was upended in the box by Besetherick, and, taking the kick himself, his right-footed spot-kick went to the right of home 'keeper Sheffield for a wonderful 4–2 win.

At Christmas time Orient were lying in seventh position – handily placed for a promotion push in the new year.

Orient signed the experienced Cambridge United 'keeper Scott Barrett after Chris Mackenzie, who had been the number-one goalie, was going through a bad period and had lost his confidence. A run of five consecutive League victories took the O's into third position by the beginning of March. Tommy Taylor was awarded the manager of the month award for February 1999. None more pleasing for Taylor was the 2–0 win over his former club Cambridge United. This was the visitors' first defeat in nine League games. It was Carl Griffiths, back from a loan spell with Wrexham (where he scored four goals in five games), who slipped the ball past United's 'keeper Van Heusden in the 23rd minute. The inspirational Martin Ling chipped home a second, which left manager Taylor celebrating with a glass of champagne and his assistant Paul Clark saying 'We are delighted with the commitment and the two excellent goals.'

As Orient entered the vital run-in stage of the campaign, Taylor made one very controversial decision that upset many supporters: the sale of Carl Griffiths to Port Vale for £100,000. They felt that selling the top marksman at such an important stage of the season could cost the O's promotion. Although it must be stated that Griff had not enjoyed a particularly good early part to the season, there were signs that his old goalscoring touch was returning. (Older fans have long memories, which went back to the sale of Kevin Nugent back in March 1992, when he was also sold and a chance of getting into the Play-offs was lost.)

It was Watts who was brought into the side after Griff's departure.

Orient had some good results during April, including an exciting 4–3 win over Plymouth Argyle. The O's were 2–0 up after eight minutes through Watts and Morrison in one of his rare outings, a player who only had one hand, which was a birth defect. The visitors fought back to draw level by half-time. The O's longest serving player Alex Inglethorpe came on as a sub to record his 30th goal for the club since joining in 1995. The Pilgrims refused to throw in the towel and were level again in the 52nd minute through a diving header by Mauge. It was Tony Richards who headed home the winner in the 73rd minute to finally settle the seven-goal thriller.

An excellent draw at Brighton was followed by a 3–1 win at Scarborough, with Simba netting twice. Then came Orient's best win of the season, a 6–1 thrashing of Shrewsbury Town, and the O's were four goals up by half-time, with the veteran Frenchman Amara Simba looking sharp.

The rout started after just eight minutes through Simba. Then goals from defender Dean Smith, his 10th goal of the season, an own goal from Brian Gayle and another from Simba (his fourth goal in three days) made it 4–0 by half-time. Early in the second half, goals from Walschaerts and Clark put the O's 6–0 up after just 52 minutes. Chances went a begging to increase their lead, but when manager Taylor decided to take off both Watts and Simba for the 'reserve duo' of Inglethorpe and Finney Orient's attacking creativity seemed to ebb away. Simba went off to a rousing reception, replayed by Steve Finney, who must have felt like he'd arrived at the party after the drink had run out.

In fact, it was Shrewsbury who scored a late consolation goal. Quite remarkably this was only the seventh time Orient had scored six goals, in this their 1,776th home match. They have never had a final score of six goals away from home in a League match.

The O's chances of finishing in the top three did not disappear until very late into the season. So the team had to make sure of securing one of the four Play-off places at the close of the season, which they achieved with ease.

And so the O's entered into the Play-off Finals. Orient had to play Rotherham United over two legs, the first being at the Matchroom Stadium on Sunday 16 May. A crowd of 9,419 assembled for one of their most important matches over the past decade. It was a game that barely got off the ground and caution seemed the order of the day for Rotherham, which was understandable as the away team. At the end of 90 minutes neither team had managed to score – the nearest effort came from Matt Lockwood with a 25-yarder that was saved by the Rotherham 'keeper Mike Pollitt.

The fact that Orient failed to gain any sort of lead in the first leg was a worry to all, but at least they travelled to Yorkshire all square. In excess of 2,000 O's fans made the trip to cheer on their heroes, and the match was delayed for 15 minutes to enable all of the 9,529 fans to get into the ground, yet according to one local policeman well over 10,000 were in the ground. In the end the O's fans were squeezed into one section of the ground to allow hundreds of home supporters to be shoehorned in, to the intimidation of the away fans, thus breaking all the Football League's crowd segregation rules.

The match followed a similar pattern to the first leg, yet, perhaps, Orient looked a little more confident. Simba shot over the bar after just four minutes, and Watts missed a chance. The interval arrived with Orient having the better of the half. Orient did not look like conceding a goal until the dying seconds of the second half, when Roscoe looked certain to steel a last-gasp dramatic winner. From almost 30 yards he curled in a fierce free-kick, but somehow the 'keeper Scott Barrett scrambled across his goal and at full stretch finger-tipped the effort round the post to send the game into extra-time.

In extra-time Simba could have sewn it up but prodded a left-footed shot straight at Pollitt, and then Martin Ling volleyed a superb 20-yarder, but the 'keeper was well positioned to collect. And so on to a nerve wracking penalty shoot-out to decide who goes to Wembley.

The kicks were taken where the home fans were situated. Rotherham took the first kick and scored through Steve Thompson. Dean Smith levelled with a powerful shot. After a short delay, it was Roscoe who came up to see his effort saved by Barrett, diving to his right. Martin Ling strode up looking confident, and he coolly slotted the ball into the corner of the net. Orient had a 2–1 advantage.

Paul Hurst then drove low to Barrett's left, only for the veteran to leap across and push the ball away. Dave Morrison scored the vital penalty to really put Orient in the driving seat, 3–1 up. Mark Williams had to score to keep the Yorkshiremen in with a chance, and he did so with a fierce shot. Now it stood at 3–2. It was up to Lockwood to score to take Orient to the Wembley Final. The young O's defender ran up and put the ball to Pollitt's left as the 'keeper moved in the opposite direction.

Billy Beall consoles a Rotherham United player as Orient go through to the Play-off Final on penalties, 19 May 1999.

Dean Smith, Steve Watts and Roger Joseph.

THE O's HAD DONE IT.

The celebrations began, the O's players ran towards the excited fans and everyone was ecstatic. The fans could hardly believe it... WE'RE GOING TO WEMBLEY...

Every player played their part, but hats off to Scott Barrett for some remarkable saves, none much better than in the final seconds of normal time. Scunthorpe United, having beaten Swansea City in the other Play-off, were to be Orient's obstacle to gaining promotion. It was a great feeling, yet nervous times for all Orient fans awaiting a Wembley Final and a place in Division Two. Saturday 29 May was the date for the showdown.

It must have been quite an experience for all the O's fans walking down Wembley Way towards the famous old stadium. Coaches, open-top buses and private cars were all decorated with red and white on their way to the famous venue. There was quite a wonderful atmosphere around the stadium, the noise, the flags, as the teams were led out on to the hallowed turf of Wembley by their managers, and many fans had a lump in their throat to see Orient at Wembley (see Matches to Remember).

Game over for Orient and skipper Dean Smith (centre) in the Play-off Final at Wembley.

Despite the disappointment of missing out on promotion at the last hurdle by 1–0 to Scunthorpe United, the O's appeared to be heading in the right direction. Tommy Taylor said 'It starts again, we're all disappointed and the players are down at the moment, but I shall have them ready for next season.

'I told them afterwards that they need to show some real character to come back from this. A lot of sides who reach the Play-off Final often find themselves in the bottom six of the League the next season.

'I don't want that to happen to us, and I'm sure the team have got the character to make sure that it doesn't.'

Taylor informed the press that he had pledged his future to Orient and vowed to bring in some new faces.

The club appeared to be on a very sound financial footing, due to the leadership qualities of Barry Hearn and the work of his backroom team at the club. A new stand had been erected at the Coronation Gardens end of the Matchroom Stadium and extra seating installed into the main stand, which brought a capacity of 13,494 and 9,204 seats. A new 124-year lease agreement was signed with the Waltham Forest administration, which will allow further ground development at a later date. There was also a new sponsor in Bravo TV and a move back to the famous old white shirts with the red chevron, last seen some 50 years ago.

The youth policy seemed to be paying dividends with some useful players waiting in the wings. Possibly the best group of youngsters since the youth team of the early 1970s.

Taylor released six players: Maskell, Stimson, Simpson, Mackenzie, McDougald and Finney. Some new players were signed including South African-born Andy Harris from Southend United, Josh Low from Bristol Rovers and big striker Iyseden Christie, a 22-year-old from Mansfield Town, for a reported £30,000. One of the problems Orient have had over their years in the Football League has been to find a hot-shot goalscorer who could score 20 League goals in a season (only nine different players have scored 20 or more League goals in any given season since 1905–06). With strikers in the squad such as Simba, Watts, Richards and Christie, could this be the season for lots and lots of goals?

Orient had assembled a group of fine players like Matt Lockwood and Belgian player Wim Walschaerts, along with many experienced pros.

Hearn and Taylor made their intentions clear: nothing but promotion would do in the 1999–2000 season. This was shown by two serious bids for two Premier League players, having also put in bids for the goal machine Ian Wright from West Ham and Stan Collymore on loan from Aston Villa. It was reported in the press that Orient were prepared to offer Wright £20,000 a week to come to Brisbane Road. Neither deals materialised.

To secure extra income the club signed a deal with near neighbours West Ham for the Hammers to play all their midweek reserve matches at Brisbane Road in the revamped FA Premier Reserve League.

However, on the field of play, it was yet another dour struggle to avoid relegation. The first win of the season came in match five, 1–0 versus Halifax Town. By the time a visit to fellow strugglers Chester City came on Tuesday 28 December, the O's were bottom, their lowest ever position in the Football League, after five straight defeats, looking a good bet for the Conference next season.

In an effort to score some goals (only 14 goals had been scored in 22 League games), Taylor brought back home, that December, Carl Griffiths from Port Vale for £80,000, and he did the trick with a hat-trick in a 5–1 win at Chester, although injury ended the rest of his season. The team went unbeaten for the next seven games, which helped them into a safe position.

Star Man dinner in 2000 with Stan Charlton and Malcolm Graham presented with original photographs taken after a 2–0 win against Bury during April 1962, which took the O's up to the First Division. Charlton was the captain and Graham scored the two goals after being called up as a late replacement.

At the end of the season the O's were safe in 19th position, quite a few points ahead of the two relegated teams. Christie finished top scorer on seven League goals. Not the sort of position one had hoped for at the start of the new millennium.

The New Millennium

The 2000–01 season was much better, with the O's rarely out of the top six. They started the season unbeaten in seven games; their first defeat came at Kidderminster Harriers 2–1, which saw them drop from third spot to seventh.

In the end it was a 2–0 win at Macclesfield Town, with two goals from Jabo Ibehre, that secured the O's fifth spot and a place in the Play-offs against Hull City.

The first leg of the Play-off Final was played at Boothferry Park on a warm and sunny Wednesday, 13 May 2001, before 13,310 (over 1,300 O's fans made the trip). The O's boss Tommy Taylor opted for a defensive formation, which saw a rare outing for veteran Steve Castle in midfield.

In the first half both teams had chances, with Hull's big 6ft 7in striker Kevin Francis causing most of the problems and youngster Jabo Ibehre doing likewise for the O's.

The end of the half saw both defences on top. The second period started in the same fashion with Castle shooting high and wide a couple of times. Then on 69 minutes disaster struck when John Eyre,

Leyton Orient in 2000–01. Back row (left to right): Steve Castle, Brendan McElholm, Simon Downer, Matthew Lockwood, Wim Walschaerts, Neil Gough, Andrew Harris, Isyeden Christie. Middle row: David Parsons, David McGhee, Dean Smith, Scott Barrett, Steve Watts, Ashley Bayes, Tony Richards, Ray Akontoh, Richard Garcia. Front row: Nicky Shorey, Chris Dorrian, Billy Beall, Ahmet Brkovic, Carl Griffiths, Jason Brissett, Jade Murray, John Martin.

who had only been on the pitch about five minutes, appeared to control a Dean Smith clearance with his hand, but, amid all the protests, he drove the ball from fully 25-yards past Ashley Bayes into the O's goal for an important lead and what turned out to be the winner.

So to the second leg on Wednesday 16 May: there was an electric atmosphere, with 9,419 inside Brisbane Road making lots of noise. It was a match long to be remembered (see Matches to Remember).

Barry Hearn, Tommy Taylor and their players, as well as the fans, were on the way to the Millennium Stadium, Cardiff, to face Blackpool in the Play-off Final. The match started off in great fashion, but in the end they lost again in the final 4–2 (see Matches to Remember).

Another highlight of the season was the victory by the O's Under-19 youth side of the Football League Alliance Cup, which also graced the Millennium Stadium on Sunday 22 April 2001, against Bradford City. It turned out to be an outstanding team performance, with the O's dominating the match from the start. The match was played on a heavy rain-sodden pitch following the Final of the LDV Vans Trophy. The only goal of the game came on 43 minutes when, after a corner from Billy Jones, a Bradford defender Lewis Emanuel pulled Opara's shirt in the box, and referee Mr Probert awarded a penalty, and up stepped Billy Jones to slam the ball into the net.

The O's winning Under-19 side was: Morris, Dorrien, Jones, Parsons, McElholm, Stephens, Gould, Grimsdell, Ibehre (sub Morgan on 77 mins), Opara (sub Hatcher on 71 mins), Murray (sub Gough on 64 mins).

Chris Tate (third from left) celebrates Orient's first goal in the Play-off Final at the Millennium Stadium.

What would the 2001–02 season bring the long suffering O's fans, so desperate for promotion? Would it be third time lucky after two failures in the Play-off Finals in recent seasons?

The question on every fan's lips was who would boss Tommy Taylor bring in for another promotion assault in 2001–02?

The season started with a couple of draws, and the first victory came in game four with a 2–0 win over Hartlepool United and then three further wins followed. Things began to fall off the rails with four straight losses after that. The fourth, a 4–2 loss at home to Shrewsbury Town, proved to be the final straw for Barry Hearn and the end for Taylor.

After much speculation, the end of Tommy Taylor's reign as manager came in unexpected circumstances when he resigned at 10am on Monday 15 October 2001, after five years in charge. He was in charge for 271 League and Cup matches with 98 wins, 78 draws and 95 defeats. His teams scored a total of 343 goals and conceded 344. (His League record appears in the managers section of this book.)

The fans had made their minds up a few days earlier in a poll run by Mark Walters on *www.brisbaneroad.com*, with 86 percent of the voters saying Taylor should go, 10 percent wanted him to stay and four percent were undecided.

During his stay at Brisbane Road, he had named a total of 128 players, of whom he had signed 106 himself. He spent £541,000 in transfer fees and raised £583,000, making a profit on these deals of £42,000.

Leyton Orient Football Club released the following statement:

'Tommy Taylor today resigned his post as manager of the club.'

Club chairman Barry Hearn said 'The Board of Leyton Orient reluctantly agreed to accept Tommy's resignation but understand his wish to step down to allow his replacement the opportunity to improve the current playing performance and results. Tommy Taylor has been a good manager and a great friend to Leyton Orient. He has worked tirelessly under stringent budget restrictions for five years and will be sorely missed.

'The Board wish Tommy every success with his future career in football and welcome Paul Brush as the manager of Leyton Orient.'

Hearn informed the League Managers' Association:

'Obviously I'm disappointed that it had to end with Tommy putting in his resignation, but I understand his reasons, and I admired the integrity he brought to the table.

'Over the past years we've had a lot of time where I'm sure the fans would have loved to have seen him go earlier, when we had a few bad results, and, of course, the manager doesn't always get the applause when we had some good results – that goes with the job.

'We kept the ship very stable but there came a time when Tommy knew and I knew that it was time for a change and it was done very amicably between two grown up men, and that's the way business should be done.

'Quite seriously, we think he's made a major contribution to our club, to the running, we think he's changed the face of the football club.

'We think he's worked very hard, and when he resigned – you have to remember it takes two to tango – by resigning he waived any rights he had under his contract.

'He asked to be released from his contract and the board of directors considered this, accepted his resignation and felt obliged, and indeed were pleased to be obliged, to make a substantial ex-gratia payment to Tommy in respect of his past service. But it was a two-way thing, with both sides acting with integrity and honesty.'

Taylor himself stated 'I've loved my time at Orient and have had some great moments, and I would like to thank Barry and the board for their support, but now it is time to move on. I wish Paul Brush every success, and he knows I'm always available for Orient if I can help in anyway.'

Taylor later stated on the League Managers' Association website 'I'd been at the club for almost five years, and I thought to myself that's a fairly long time, (Taylor was the longest serving manager in the Third Division), and I thought to myself that's a long time for a manager at a football club.

'I thought I'd got everything right there, I mean, the youth policy, we got that right from nothing to what it is today, with many of them in the first-team squad. But it wasn't enough for the supporters, I've been to two Play-off Finals and it still wasn't enough and it came to a crunch, that, at the end of the day, if they were going to keep moaning at me it would have got to the players and it did get to them for the last three games. We were up in every game, and when we conceded a goal they started moaning and so it was time for me to walk away and give the players a chance to play the kind of football they can play.

'I went over to Barry's house on Sunday, and we just came to an arrangement where it was best I left the club so it could step forward. Initially he said "No – you're gonna be there. You've got a contract for another two and a half years, I want you to be there." 'But I said "Barry it ain't gonna work."

'Barry and myself got on so well. We never had a crossword, he treated me not like a manager but like a friend most of the time. It was a hard for me to say cheerio because it was my first club as a player, but it was just the situation, it had to be done. So we moved on and came to an arrangement.

Barry's sorted me out money wise, and I'm pleased with that because he didn't have to give me anything really because I'd just walked away from it. But he said because you've done such a good job over the five years you've got to take this money with you.'

The League Managers' Association's reaction was as follows:

> 'The Association have praised the conduct of both Leyton Orient Football Club and Tommy Taylor, having reached an amicable agreement almost immediately. The club have agreed to pay Taylor a substantial payment in recognition of his efforts over the last five years, even though they were under no contractual obligations as it was the manager's decision to leave.'

John Barnwell, the LMA director, praised both parties as an example to all football clubs on the way such negotiations should be conducted.

The O's captain Dean Smith revealed his sadness that Taylor had left the club 'I'm gutted for Tommy,' he said. 'He brought all the current players to the club, and we're sad to see him go, but he obviously felt it was the right time. I've spoken to him and thanked him for everything he's done for me – at the end of the day we're all sorry to have let him down.'

Smith looked back fondly on his four years at the O's under Taylor: 'I was so proud to lead the team out at Wembley and Cardiff in two Play-off Finals.

'His best moment was winning on penalties at Rotherham United – the reaction in the dressing room after that match was something else. We've had some good games. Spurs, Newcastle United, Hull in the Play-offs and even going to Premiership-side Bolton Wanderers and Nottingham Forest, and holding them to draws.

'It's the end of an era but also the start of a new one, and it's up to us to make it successful.'

Paul Brush was appointed as manager on 15 October 2001.

After his appointment as the O's boss, 43-year-old Paul Brush had an exclusive interview with *www.leytonorient.com* and it is reproduced with their kind permission.

'It feels very nice to be called Boss but very strange as well, it's something I'll have to get used to. I've just signed a piece of paper that says manager and thought "oh that's me now" so it hasn't really sunk in yet!

'I wasn't expecting this but obviously the run of results under Tommy we've just had would put anyone under pressure, and the same thing would happen to me if we went six games with just one point.

'You can tell there was some unrest on the terraces when the players weren't playing to the best of their ability.

'They always say a change can make a difference, and hopefully from my point of view I can install some confidence in the players. Although I'm pleased to get the opportunity to manage the O's, the circumstances that I got the job in were not the most ideal.

'I was watching my son playing football after taking the O's players for Sunday morning training, and the O's chairman Barry Hearn phoned me up. It came as a total surprise, especially as I'd been with Tommy in the morning.

'In an ideal scenario I would have liked the opportunity in a year or two with Tommy either moving upstairs or going to another club but things don't work out that way in football very often.

'I've had some chats to Tommy and he's got the confidence in me, first of all it's all about getting the team to play with some confidence and quality and getting some results. Then you look longer term at the whole squad and senior players and decide what to do.'

As a player, Brush was known for his passing ability, and he revealed that he'd like his teams to mirror that on the pitch.

He said 'I have not been handed a 'promotion or bust' by chairman Barry Hearn, but Division Two is still high on everybody's list. He's not set me targets. Whatever people think of me, the chairman knows how I can work with the players here. I know what happened in recent weeks and because of that we are now the worst team in the League.

'I want the players to give it their best shot for the club. Not for me, not themselves, but for the club. They should be proud to wear the club colours and badge of Leyton Orient. That's what we want, everyone together from the players to the supporters. I understand that people want instant success, but I'm asking the fans to be a bit patient and we'll try and make them smile again by rising up the League.' Paul Brush was ready to draw from his past personal ordeals, he has always been an honest and straightforward individual, but he has learned, the hard way, a resilience and single-minded determination the others perhaps lack.

A pivotal moment in his life came in 1985 when his first wife Mary died from leukaemia, their son Peter was six months old. He has since married again to Sue, a senior nurse who looked after his wife in the London Hospital in Whitechapel, and they now have two children.

He said 'Life has taught me not to expect things to go right all the time, but it taught me never to give in.'

With regards to Tommy Taylor, he said 'I didn't think the two Play-offs in the space of five years could be termed a failure, but the fans put the team's poor performance down to the manager rather than the players themselves.

'I'm looking forward to the challenge, I'm not a caretaker – they work in schools – and I believe I have the time to mould myself into a manager and try to give the fans the one thing they want more than anything – PROMOTION.

'It's a tough job, but I do have the confidence in my ability to make players want to do their best and to make them better players. I've had it hard before, so what have I got to be worried about.

Chairman Barry Hearn said of his new charge, 'Paul's style is completely different to that of Tommy's, so there will be changes, but there won't be a huge amount of money to spend.

'I'm delighted to have Paul, and it's my policy wherever possible to appoint from within. I hope the fans give Paul their 100 percent support as he tries to turn it around.'

Well Brush certainly got off to an excellent start in the League with a 1–0 win over Swansea City, a 1–1 draw with Hull City and a 4–2 home win over Division Three high-flyers Rochdale.

The new Brush – Ling team were rewarded after their fine start with a new contract, which would keep them at the club until at least the end of the 2003–04 season.

Brush admitted 'We are delighted to have put pen to paper. I'm pleased Barry and the board of directors have shown faith in us beyond what many classed as a temporary appointment. There is a great deal of potential at this club, and Martin and I will work long and hard to get it right.'

Hearn added 'I am confident that I have found the right men for the job in Brush and Ling. They're young managers with a lot of new ideas and bags of enthusiasm, everyone's been impressed by what they have done so far, and we're confident they can continue this improvement over the next couple of years.'

Unfortunately, the duo did not see much success in the League, with the O's battling to get out of the bottom five. At the start of the 2002–03 season they hit the fourth spot, but that success did not last, and the O's found themselves at the dangerous end of the table. However, they enjoyed some good results in Cup competition, none more so than the excellent 4–1 win – after being 1–0 down at half-time – at Portsmouth in the FA Cup in 2002 (see Matches to Remember) and a 3–2 victory over Queen's Park Rangers in the Worthington Cup, but they just could not take that kind of form over in to the League.

On the downside, after the great FA Cup win over Pompey at Fratton Park, the boys went the following week to play second from bottom in Division Three Carlisle United and were brought down to earth very quickly, being thrashed 6–1, and it was the 32-year-old veteran Ian Stevens who did the damage with a first-half hat-trick. Paul Brush apologised to the fans 'for this shambles of a display'.

After the O's poor run at the start of the 2002–03 season, chairman Barry Hearn stated in the local press 'I give the O's management team of Paul Brush and Martin Ling my vote of confidence following the club's poor start to the season. I still believe they are the right people for the job, and I look to the players to resolve the issue because once they cross that white line they are on their own.

'Man for man we have one of the best squads in this Division and certainly one of the highest paid, so there are no excuses.

'I understand the fans' concerns, and I share them, but we have got to work ourselves out of this

Loan player Jamal Campbell-Ryce celebrates a goal against Bristol Rovers, 26 October 2002.

position, and I'm confident we will do just that. We will be out of business unless we do something serious, and serious is being in control over our own finances and doing something out on the field of play.'

In an interview with Peter King of the *Waltham Forest Guardian* newspaper, Hearn stated 'After eight years in the Third Division, I'm not about to say that I'm crazily optimistic about our chances, but I'm still waiting with a mixture of trepidation and excitement for the kick-off.

'I know the fans have been frustrated in the past, I have been too, and after eight years I thought I would be in the Champions League by now, although I am one of life's biggest optimists. But I will, however, take what God gives me now, although I would be happy if he could see his way clear in letting us get automatic promotion.'

Brush himself stated in November 2003, after being knocked out of the FA Cup by Margate, dismissing calls for him to resign after he and his team were booed off the Dover pitch, that he would fight on. He said 'You don't walk away from these situations, you stand up like a man and fight on, I'm not a quitter. I can understand everyone's frustrations, from the chairman to the supporters. It's my job to get the best out of the players and you do question them after such a game, I feel empty, choked, gutted, the whole lot.'

Well he had no need to question them the following game with a gutsy 1–0 win at Boston United to gain three valuable points against their fellow strugglers, and in the end they did survive another season in Division Three but could only manage 14 wins the whole season, which left the O's languishing in 18th place.

How long will chairman Hearn's patience last? Should the O's have another poor season in 2003–04, and with a warning from Hearn to Brush – promotion or you are out of job – it would be a tough and nerve-wracking start to the new season for the O's manager and his assistant Martin Ling. And nerve-wracking it certainly was. After the first 10 League games they had managed just one win against Yeovil Town, which saw them second from bottom.

After a 3–0 defeat at Huddersfield Town on Saturday 27 September 2003, the club issued the following statement at 18.15, 'Leyton Orient officially announces that manager Paul Brush has parted company with the club with immediate effect.'

The announcement read 'Chairman Barry Hearn informed Brush of the decision after the defeat at Huddersfield, which leaves the O's in 23rd place in the Division Three table with just seven points from the first 10 games. Unfortunately results have not been good enough, and Paul has accepted that. Hearn said "Paul has been completely dedicated and professional in his approach to the job, and we're sorry things haven't worked out. I have spoken to him after the defeat at Huddersfield and we agreed to part company. It is a shame, but it is a decision that has been made with Leyton Orient's best interests at heart – our results have to improve."'

Brush was in charge for almost two years at Brisbane Road after five seasons as coach, and was devastated at leaving the club.

He said 'I feel very empty as Leyton Orient have been part of my life for seven years. It's weird to think that I won't be going in this week, and I'm sure the feeling will get worse.'

Brush was in charge of a total of 101 League and Cup games in which he named 29 players on the team sheet. His downfall was that he could manage just 29 wins. His full record read: P 101, W 29, D 26, L 46, F 118, A 151, GD 33.

The first thing Brush did was to send a message of goodwill to Martin Ling.

The O's assistant manager Martin Ling was appointed caretaker manager for the immediate future, and his first match in charge was a tough away trip to bottom of the table Carlisle United three days later, and it went much better than he could have dared for with a 1–0 win.

Ling said 'The goal was a very scrappy affair, but its the best goal I've seen in my life.'

In the meantime, a number of names were mentioned as taking the job full-time; in fact Ling was among 70 candidates to potentially succeed Brush, with a decision due by the end of October. The shortlist included Ling, Steve Parkin, Terry Dolan, Colin Todd, Joe Kinnear and the name of Bobby Gould was also bounded about in the press; however, it was Ling who had the backing of the senior squad.

In September the O's lost 2–1 at Torquay United with Gary Alexander and Matt Lockwood both getting red cards as frustrations began to take their toll.

At the end of October Ling was told to carry on until the end of the year.

By the beginning of December, under Ling, the O's had climbed to 14th in the table, collecting 18 points from 10 games as well as moving into the second round of the FA Cup. He was told by Hearn that he had to continue winning games if he was to be made full-time manager.

Touchline encouragement from Ling against Carlisle United on 30 September 2003.

On 29 November the O's romped in what proved to be their best win of the season, a 4–1 victory at Cambridge United (the first time four goals had been scored since a 4–1 win at Portsmouth in the FA Cup in January 2002), with goals from Purser (2), Thorpe and Miller.

On 20 December 2003 Ling was given the job, this after a 2–0 win over Bury on a one-year contract, and soon after Ian Culverhouse was appointed his assistant.

However, after two home wins during February 2004, against Oxford United and Southend United, things began to fall apart with 13 League games without a win (six draws and seven defeats).

The match at York City on 1 May 2004 was a vital affair to see who would be relegated into the Conference, with the O's trying to stop equalling the club record number of matches without a victory. In the end, a 2–1 victory over Exeter (and when Carlisle United failed to beat Cheltenham Town) assured another season in the League for Orient.

The match at Exeter started in terrible fashion when the home team took the lead through their central-defender Wise, who headed home from a corner, his first goal in senior football.

The nerves, both on the field and on the terracing, were evident as a defeat could end the O's membership of the Football League.

Matt Lockwood was the orchestrator of most of the O's positive play, and from one of his corners Mark Peters towered above the home defenders to head home for the equaliser.

It was after this that youngsters Brian Saah and Gabby Zakuani both grew in stature. In injury-time of the first half came another significant moment when Lockwood lofted a cross from deep on the left, and with the home goalkeeper Porter hesitating in came Gary Alexander to beat him in the air and head home into an empty net for his 16th goal of the season.

The second half proved to be a non-event as Exeter seemed to accept their fate of Conference football next season.

When the news of the Cheltenham equaliser against Carlisle came filtering through, and when the final whistle blew to record a much needed win, it was celebrated by the 418 vocal O's fans in the 3,462 crowd, as much of joy by them and the players as it was with relief.

After the final game of the season, a 1–0 home defeat by Cambridge United, the O's finished in 19th position on 53 points, eight points ahead of Carlisle United and nine points ahead of York City.

It was a disappointing season, with many feeling that the O's should have reached a top-five place, but it was not meant to be, and the O's started the new 2004–05 season in the lower tier of the Football League for their ninth consecutive season.

Manager Martin Ling secured four experienced players for the new campaign in Lee Steele, Alan White, Wayne Carlisle and Michael Simpson, and with the start of the £10 million development of Brisbane Road taking place there was a real optimism around the club.

Skipper Matt Lockwood, who had previously suffered six years of disappointments at Brisbane Road, stated 'Every year at the start of a new season I'm always optimistic that we are going to do well, but that hasn't happened in the past and you do start to wonder if it is ever going to happen. I'm hoping by May, when we face Mansfield Town, it will just be the case that everyone connected with the club will be ready for a big party for promotion.'

As in recent seasons, the O's lost the first match of the new season at home to Macclesfield Town by 3–1 before 3,227. However, results began to pick up and their away form was more impressive than in many a season, with three wins at Cheltenham Town, Kidderminster Harriers and Notts County.

Gary Alexander's goal against York City on 1 May 2004 saved the O's from relegation into the Conference.

Then came the home match against Shrewsbury Town on 16 October, with the O's lying in fourth spot of the Coca-Cola League Division Two.

The O's stormed to a one-sided 4–1 victory with two goals each from Andy Scott and Lee Steele, and the three points saw the O's leap-frog to the top of the Division for the first time since they went top of the old Second Division almost 12 years to the day (17 October 1992).

So, it had taken manager Martin Ling just over a year to take the O's from bottom to the very top of League Two, quite an achievement to the delight of all, in particular chairman Barry Hearn, who stated 'Without doubt we are playing the best football I've seen during my time with the club, so all credit to Martin Ling and the boys. All the signs are very positive, and I hope for the sake of my health that we might finally get out of this Division.'

Ling stated 'We are top so we should rejoice, but there's a long way to go.'

The top five positions of the table at 5pm on Saturday 16 October 2004 read:

	Home						Away						Goal
	P	W	D	L	F	A	W	D	L	F	A	Pts	Diff
LEYTON ORIENT	13	3	3	1	12	8	3	2	1	9	8	23	5
Swansea C	13	4	1	1	7	3	3	1	3	7	7	23	4
Scunthorpe U	13	4	1	1	12	6	2	3	2	7	7	22	7
Mansfield T	13	5	1	1	16	8	1	2	3	6	7	21	7
Yeovil T	13	4	2	1	15	6	2	1	3	8	12	21	5

On the following Tuesday came an important match at second place Swansea City, but unfortunately they lost 1–0 and also lost the top spot. The next Saturday the O's went to Lincoln City, and after trailing three times in the match they clawed back to a magnificent 4–3 victory, with Man of the Match Lee Steele scoring a hat-trick. The win took them into second spot (see Matches to Remember).

This took Lee Steele to the top spot of the goalscoring charts, the first O's player to achieve this feat since Peter Kitchen back in 1977–78. The chart read:

League and Cup

Steele	Leyton Orient	11
Agogo	Bristol R	10
Hurst	Notts County	9
Jevons	Yeovil T	9
Hayes	Scunthorpe U	9
Larkin	Mansfield T	9
Nugent	Bury	8
Parkin	Macclesfield T	8

Steele was named as the Powerade League Two player of the month for October 2004, netting seven times from six games.

By the end of November the O's had maintained a top four place, but then injuries took their toll on the side. With strikers Alexander and Steele out with long-term injuries, the team battled throughout December and January with just one win from eight League games.

With both Alexander, Steele and also Jabo Ibehre still out injured, it was time for some strikers to come in on loan, also boss Ling used youngsters like Brian Saah, Derek Duncan and Efe Echanomi, the latter proving he could score goals and celebrate in style as well.

The first loan player to come in was Lee Barnard from Tottenham Hotspur, then came David Chillingworth from Cambridge United. It was the latter who scored some goals, and in particular his late goal to secure a 2–2 draw and a point against Rushden & Diamonds was quite remarkable. In the last seconds of injury time Justin Miller swung in a cross from the right, and Chillingworth swivelled and then hit the ball high up field. The Diamonds goalkeeper Lee Worgan, expecting the ball to drop over the bar, lost track of its flight in the wind, and to his horror it was in the back of the net, with the referee pointing for a corner-kick. Those of the 3,777 fans still left in the ground could hardly believe what they had witnessed.

In early January the newspapers were full of the news that Orient were trying to sign Irish

Craig Easton celebrates after scoring in the FA Cup game against Fulham in January 2006, which the O's won 2–1.

midfielder David Savage from Bristol Rovers. Their chairman Geoff Dunford even went so far as saying that Orient had approached the player illegally after being told not to do so. In the end the player injured his hamstring, so any deal went on the backburner and all was forgotten.

By the time Grimsby Town were the visitors to Brisbane Road on 15 January, both Barnard and Chillingworth had returned to their clubs and in came another loan striker, Scott Fitzgerald from Watford. Fitzgerald had two telling moments during the match: on 75 minutes when he flicked a glancing header wide and five minutes later when he was sent off for violent conduct, so missing three games of his one-month loan spell, and that was the last the fans saw of him. So, after another home defeat by the Mariners, the O's were lying in 10th spot with just four home wins to show for their efforts at Brisbane Road.

Maybe what former manager Frank Clark wrote in the O's programme at the start of the season was proving quite a poignant statement. He wrote 'With the building going on at the ground the place looks surreal, and I believe it could be more of a hindrance than a help to the Orient team. It might be difficult for the players this season.'

And so Clark proved to be correct in his assumption. The O's battled at home. In February they were in 13th position, having dropped another two points against Lincoln City with a 1–1 draw in a match that started 30 minutes late due to a power failure on a bitterly cold evening.

At the end of February Lee Steele scored his first goal since returning from injury to win three points against Darlington, and if a good run could be put together a Play-off place was not out of the question, being just four points off the pace.

But after a poor run in March 2005, which brought four defeats and just two draws, hopes of a Play-off spot had all but faded. The season ended in May with two strikes from Gary Alexander for a 2–1 win over Mansfield Town to secure 11th place in League Two, their highest position in four seasons.

The highlights of the season were the 17 goals from Lee Steele, and for his great efforts he was voted the Player of the Year; however, on a sad note, 32-year-old midfielder Andy Scott was told to quit the game due to a serious heart problem.

For the O's 90th season in the Football League, manager Martin Ling had a backroom clear out. His assistant manager Ian Culverhouse left to take over as youth manager with Wycombe Wanderers and was replaced by former star player and later youth-team manager Dean Smith, his position going to Andy Scott. Also leaving the club physio was Jack Demetriou, who was replaced by former Army physio Dave Appanah, who had served in the armed forces for five years in both Bosnia and Germany, and fitness coach Jack Reitz.

On the player side, Ling was busy with five new signings: Joe Keith signed from Colchester United, Craig Easton from Scottish side Livingston, Welsh-born Goalie Glyn Garner came with a big reputation from Bury and Shane Tudor, an exciting winger, came from Cambridge United.

The season opened with a home match again Macclesfield Town on 6 August 2005, and it was Joe Keith who opened the scoring on his debut after just 63 seconds, but the visitors drew level early in the second half, and as the game entered added time it was young substitute Efe Echamomi who ensured victory on the day when the new £8 million West Stand was opened.

Echanomi latched on to an under-hit back pass by Danny Swailes, he rounded goalie Alan Fettis, before cheekily stopping on the goal line and tapping the ball into an empty net, causing heart palpitations to manager Ling. At the time little was thought about the significance of the goal, and the three points, but how important they proved to be nine months later. Two more victories followed at

Coca-Cola League Two match at Glansford Park, Mansfield, 15 April 2006. Leyton Orient's Wayne Corden (far left) celebrates Matt Lockwood's (second from left) winning penalty.

This really was a match to remember as captain John Mackie (left), Gary Alexander (centre) and Gabriel Zakuani (right) celebrate Leyton Orient's famous 2–1 away win at Premiership side Fulham, in the FA Cup third-round game at Craven Cottage, 8 January 2006.

Lee Steele (on floor) is congratulated by Daryl McMahon (right), Matt Lockwood (centre) and Gabriel Zakuani (left) as his injury-time goal against his former club Oxford United sees Leyton Orient promoted.

Leyton Orient's leading goalscorer for 2005–06 Gary Alexander celebrates putting his side 2–1 up against Oxford United.

Bury and Darlington to take the O's to an early top-of-the-table spot. It was during September that they showed they were promotion material, embarking on a 14-match unbeaten run, including excellent 3–2 away wins at both Carlisle United and Barnet.

The following month saw some excellent performances, and Ling was named manager of the month for October. The O's were top of the League again on 29 October, one point ahead of Wycombe Wanderers and three ahead of Grimsby Town. During November they saw a couple of home defeats but bounced back with two excellent wins at Rochdale 4–2 and at home to Rushden & Diamonds 5–1. However, at the end of the year, after losing 4–2 at Wycombe, they found themselves in third spot behind leaders Wycombe and second-placed Grimsby.

January 2006 saw the arrival of Swansea City striker Paul Connor for a £40,000 fee and Adam Tann from Notts County, and from 14 February they lost just once from the following 16 matches – surprisingly at lowly Rushden & Diamonds on 18 March.

In the final home game of the season a victory was vital to keep up the challenge for promotion and another Lockwood penalty and a strike from Wayne Corden saw the O's through 2–1 to set up an exciting last weekend of promotion and relegation football at both Oxford and Grimsby.

Well, as we all know, the Oxford match really did turn out to be a nail-biting *Match to Remember*, and features as the last report in that section of the book, and so, after 11 years of trying, O's chairman Barry Hearn has finally achieved his goal of promotion.

A Coca-Cola League Two game at the Kassam Stadium, Oxford, 6 May 2006. Adam Tann (left) and Shane Tudor (right) celebrate the victory over Oxford United that saw Leyton Orient promoted to League One.

Chairman Barry Hearn celebrates in front of the fans as Leyton Orient are promoted.

Barry Hearn – Chairman

'For the first time in my life I am lost for words. We have all endured a couple of Play-off defeats and flirtations with relegation, but after today all that is consigned to the history book. I have had 11 years of abject failure, and I've made an awful lot of mistakes. I've learned from some of them, ignored others and today feel justified.

This is the greatest day of my life and it's a wonderful warm feeling

In a sporting sense, I've never felt such a rush of euphoria as at the final whistle, and I'm so proud to be here.

We've got a good management team in place with Martin Ling and Dean Smith and the basis of a very good team, and I couldn't have asked for more from the duo. We've always said we needed something to build on.

The elevation to League One is just the first stage of my ambitions for the club, and I will be pulling out all the stops to ensure the O's can aim even higher. We have the aspirations of being bigger, and now we have the opportunity that we've been looking for for these past 11 years.

On a sad note, I have to put myself in Oxford's position and think how would I feel, we are sad for them, and I really do wish them well.'

Manager Martin Ling celebrates on the pitch with his son and daughter after Leyton Orient are promoted to League One.

Martin Ling – Manager

'To say it was nerve-shredding is an understatement. I don't think I have ever been so high and low in such a short space of time. It really was a surreal day and one I will remember for years. It's certainly one of the biggest achievements of my career.

Our topsy-turvy emotion came to its conclusion and was rewarded with a double dose of joy, all within the final 30 seconds. First news filtered through that Northampton had levelled at Grimsby and then we made absolutely sure thanks to Lee Steele's strike

The way it happened was phenomenal – the great cheer goes up that my good friend Colin Calderwood and his team had done us a favour and got that equaliser in the final few seconds of their match, so we all started going mad with joy, and then Steele put in the winning goal – you couldn't have written a better script.'

We had a phone on the bench, and we got the message that Grimsby had scored: everyone was looking dejected, at 2–2, and then when both Lee [Steele] and Jabo [Ibehre] missed those late chances I thought our chance had passed us by and we weren't going to get what we deserved after a long hard season, but then came the final twist of fate.

I have been here 10 years, and it's as much my club as anyone else's. I've been involved as a player, youth-team coach, assistant and now manager, and I've got an affinity to the club.

It's the first automatic promotion for 36 years and the first promotion since 1989 when we went up in the Play-offs, so it's nice to go into the history books as the manager who did that, it's far too long for this great club, this was our year, and we will go from strength to strength.

I've got another year on my contract, and I'm Leyton Orient through and through – I want to take us up to the Championship rather than to go into that League with another club.'

O's Early Pioneers 1881 to 1905

Today's club owes its origins to Homerton College, a theological teacher training establishment for Non-Conformists and Puritans who, in 1881, started a cricket club called Glyn CC. The name was chosen because they played on a piece of waste ground in Glyn Road, Clapton. In 1887 a new name, Eagle CC, was chosen. In March 1888 they formed themselves into a football club under the name of Orient. The man who suggested the name, a Jack Dearing, worked for the Orient Steamship Company and was with them when they launched the SS *Orient* in 1879 (a few years later that company was bought out by the P&O Group). Very little was reported in the local press at the time of the club's early days as a cricket or football club. It was only between 1893 and 1896, when playing in the Clapton & District League, and from the 1896–97 season, when Orient Football Club first entered the local London League, that the local community and press started taking notice. In match reports and articles most of the players were only mentioned by their surname.

These are the early pioneering players of London's second oldest Football League club (Fulham being founded in 1879).

1891–96

Goalkeepers: Diver, Gill, Little, Tommy Longstreeth, Ernie Stephens, Jack Turner. Full-backs: J. Archer, Evans, T. Gage, Hay, T. Hudson, Tallant, M. Williams. Half-backs: T. Carne, Chinn, Jack Dearing, Hadler, Hitch, Rodick, Edward Wiggins, H. Woods, J. Wright. Forwards: R. Barrow, W. Bradford, Sid Carr, Clarris, Harry Edgar, Field, Gage, A. Gardiner, R.P. Haines, H. Keir-Gibson, Ken Gibson, Gregory, Hadden, Hall, F. Hodder, Holmes, F. Hudson, Hughes, Lambe, Laxton, Matthews, Freddy Nesbitt, J. Rhyder, Waldron, S. Wicks, W. Wiggins, J. Wright.

1896–97

Goalkeepers: J. Coyle, Gill, Tommy Longstreeth, Ernie Stephens, L. White. Full-backs: Bentley, Colver, Hall, R. Hodder, Hudson, A. Humphries, R. Humphries, Mossford, Okenfield, T. Humphries, Stevens, F. Williams. Half-backs: Craig, Dawson, Duffill, Gubbs, F. Hodder, J. Hitch, J. Little, G. Smith, J. Shorter, W. Wiggins, R. Williams. Forwards: R. Barrow, Sid Carr, Dick, Fairhead, Field, Gage, Gardner, Gibson, Gildersen, Gregory, Hadler, R.P. Haines, F. Hodder, Lambe, Lux, Lutterlock, Molehouse, Matthews, Mulligan, Nash, Noble, Payne, Pevey, Rittman, J. Rhyder, Vine, Westleholm.
Note: The player named Matthews who was in goal and also a forward was the same man.

1897–98

Goalkeepers: J. Coyle, Gill, Matthews, Ernie Stephens, L. White. Full-backs: Archer, Bacon, Evans, J. Hall, T. Humphries, Sells, M. Williams. Half-backs: Ack, H. Dyke, Fairhead, Forsaith, Gage, A. Gardiner, J. Hitch, F. Hodder, R. Hodder, McFie, Ritchie, Weckey, Weeds, W. Wiggins, H. Woods. Forwards: R. Barrow, Bradford, Croker, Edwards, Gardner, Ken Gibson, R. Haines, Jack Hilsdon, R. McGeorge, Payne, Nash, Nicholls, J. Rhyder, Robinson, Summerville, Weston.

1898–99

Goalkeeper: Ernie Stephens. Full-backs: J. Hall, J. Marriott. Half-backs: H. Dyke, F. Hodder, J. Ratyer, W. Wiggins. Forwards: K. Gibson, R. Haines, Jack Hilsdon, G. Ratyer.

1899–1900

Goalkeeper: Tommy Longstreeth. Full-back: J. Manniger. Half-backs: A. Gardiner, F. Hodder, Hugh McLelland, W. Wiggins. Forwards: T. Aston, L. Best, Sid Carr, T. Hart, Jack Hills, Murrell, L. Nicholson.

1900–01

Goalkeeper: Tommy Longstreeth. Full-backs: T. Davies, H. Ransom. Half-backs: A. Ainger, Hugh McLelland, W. Wiggins. Forwards: Sid Carr, A. Gardiner, Ken Gibson, R.P. Haines, Jack Hills, J. Hilsdon, G. Merritt, L. Nicholson.

1901–02

Goalkeeper: Ernie Ward. Full-backs: Robert Chalkley, Gwin. Half-backs: Claude Berry, R. Haines, Hugh McLelland. Forwards: F. Berry, Carby, Clancy, Ken Gibson, Jack Hills, Jack Hilsdon, V. Routs, J. Robertson.

1902–03

Goalkeeper: Harry Liles, G. McGeorge, Ernie Ward. Half-backs: Ernie Bailey, Robert Chalkley, Price, Claude Berry, R. Haines, F. Hodder, Holland, Hugh McLelland, W. Palmer, Billy Price, J. Robertson. Forwards: Adams, J. Beedall, K. Blunden, Bush, Clancy, J. Counden T. Dwyer, Ken Gibson, W. Glenton, Jack Hills, Robert McGeorge, Ginger Merritt, J. Robertson, J. Wallace.

1903–04

Goalkeepers: Harry Liles, Ernie Ward. Full-backs: Allison, Robert Chalkley, George McGeorge, Price, Upsdale, Watson. Half-backs: Claude Berry, F. Hodder, Hugh McLelland, J. Robertson, Simpson, Upsdale. Forwards: Baker, Bodder, T. Burrage, Bush, Jack Hills, Holland, R. Janes, Jones, J. Mackie, Robert McGeorge, G. Seeley, J. Wallace, Weldon.

1904–05

Goalkeepers: Harry Liles, E. Potter, Joseph Redding. Full-backs: A. Archer, T. Hills, Lowe, Nidd, John Rance, H. Reason. Half-backs: Claude Berry, F. Hodder, William Lane, George McGeorge, Partridge, Thomas Poulton, John Rance, J. Robertson. Forwards: Baker, J. Beedall, Birkett, Cantor, Syd Cavendish, R. Elliott, George Hammond, Jack Hills, Herbert Kingaby, Robert McGeorge, William Nicol, A. Rance, J.W. Reynolds.

Orient's Grounds

Leyton Orient, like many League clubs of today, used several different grounds throughout the years. They started with cricket matches and originally played them at Victoria Park. The club moved to Whittles Athletic ground in 1900 in Glyn Road, just off Millfields Road, in Clapton. The ground was formerly known as the Whittles Firework Field because it was owned by the Bailey Firework Company.

In 1900 the club moved to the large Millfields Road ground because the council decided to build a power station on the old site.

On one side of the Millfields Road ground was a large banking referred to as the 'Spion Kop'. Accommodation was increased from 12,000 to 20,000 and a neat wooden fence was erected all around the ground. The terracing was mainly clinkers obtained from the nearby power station.

In 1914 200 new tip-up seats were installed in the grandstand, and in 1923 a new grandstand was purchased to the value of £30,000, which eventually became a large financial burden. The new grandstand could seat nearly 500 people and was situated opposite the 'Spion Kop' on the north side of the ground, where concrete terracing was laid and flowerbeds were planted all around the ground to make it more homely.

The opening of the new stand took place on 15 September 1923 for the visit of Derby County. Attending the match was the president of the Football League Mr J. McKenna, and he unveiled a bronze tablet in the boardroom commemorating the opening of the new grandstand in drizzling rain.

After a speech by the O's chairman Mr H. Gray-Robbins, McKenna stated that he was glad to know that the club had such fine quarters for the players and officials. He was also pleased to hear that good provision had been made for what one might call the 'shilling' attendance. They were the backbone of the game. 'Although I always got a seat', he said, 'one must not detract from those men and women who stand in the open.' They are the real supporters who kept the game going.

Mr McKenna was presented with a silver bowl by Mr Gray-Robbins as a souvenir of the occasion. Also among the 20,000 crowd was the Mayor of Hackney, Councillor Mr J. Genese, and the Mayor of Derby, Alderman O. Ling. They witnessed a fine match, with the O's running out 2–0 winners with goals from Waite and Green, with goalkeeper Arthur Wood having a brilliant match.

The old stand was sold to Wimbledon FC and was still used at Wimbledon's old Plough Lane ground before their move to Selhurst Park (later the club moved to Milton Keynes and changed their name to Milton Keynes Dons).

In 1927 a greyhound racing syndicate led by the former player Monty Garland-Wells purchased the ground from the local council. It was during this time that attendances began to dwindle from an average of 13,262 in 1927 down to 5,471 in 1930, and with the dog track encroaching on to the playing surface it was in 1930 that matters came to a head, and the club decided they had to move away. (The Greyhound Stadium in Millfields Road, Clapton, eventually closed in December 1973.)

The O's were actually banned in 1929–30 from using the stadium for training purposes, and the directors could not use the boardroom or its facilities on match days. The situation became intolerable, and it was no surprise that an alternative stadium in the area was being sought.

It was a sad situation. Having spent a lot of money improving facilities over the previous quarter of a century, it was a cruel blow to the club.

The stadium at Millfields enjoyed some great matches, including the famous win over the high-flying Newcastle United in 1926 before 31,400 spectators.

Orient had played at Millfields Road ground from 1900 to 3 May 1930; the final League match there was when the O's defeated Brighton & Hove Albion by 4–1 before 8,763 nostalgic spectators.

The club searched long and hard for a new home, and eventually they chose a site in Lea Bridge Road, just half a mile from the old stadium. The new ground was situated near to the Greyhound pub and the stadium had been used by a local speedway team.

The new stadium was a large but fairly barren site: it was an oval shape with wooden fencing all around and was in need of great repair. The railway line overlooked the stadium and trains would stop a little longer at Lea Bridge Station to watch the action.

The first League match at the new Lea Bridge Road stadium was against Newport County on the afternoon of Thursday 4 September 1930, the O's winning 3–1 before 5,505 spectators, the first O's goal being scored by 32-year-old Jack Fowler. In the next League match at the stadium against Coventry City two days later, Fowler notched up a hat-trick, one a penalty, in a 3–3 draw, before a larger Saturday crowd of 9,030.

It was after a match with Torquay United on 8 November 1930, when the O's won 4–0, that the visiting directors complained that the wooden fence was too near the touchline and the visiting players complained it had affected their performance.

After an inspection by the Football League, the club was ordered to close the ground for alterations. Orient's next two Division Three South fixtures were both played at the famous Wembley Stadium, a 3–0 win over Brentford before 8,319 fans and a 3–1 win over Southend United before just 1,916 fans on a very wet and windy day. One FA Cup tie against Luton Town was staged at Arsenal's stadium in Highbury, the O's losing 4–2.

The directors of the club were never really happy at Lea Bridge. The ground could have held many more, but work was never carried out. The capacity at Lea Bridge was 20,000 with room for 4,000 under cover, but with improvements and extensions it could have easily held up to 50,000. The record attendance was for the visit of Millwall on 13 March 1937; 20,288 fans witnessed the O's win 1–0. A considerable number of Millwall fans broke into the ground without paying. A crush, particularly on one side of the ground, caused spectators to almost spill on to the playing field, and fans had to line the touchline for most of the game. The police estimated at least a further 1,000 people were in the ground without having paid.

Rumours were abound of a possible move to Mitcham or even a merger with the ill-fated Thames Association Football Club, who played in the West Ham area, but chairman Frank Snewin informed the fans that after due consideration he had no intention of taking the club out of the area.

Talks were in progress with the Leyton Town Council over Leyton Amateurs' difficulty in paying their rent at their Brisbane Road ground. The two parties agreed terms and the club was to move in for the start of the 1937–38 season, and Leyton Amateurs moved to the Hare and Hounds ground. The Lea Bridge Road ground was demolished in the 1970s and today factories stand on the site, although the original Greyhound public house is still around and older fans may recall the O's players meeting there to collect their wages.

Orient played at Lea Bridge between 1930 to 1937, and the final League match there was against Southend United on 29 April 1937, ending on a winning note by 3–1 before just 2,541 fans. It was defender Ambrose 'Bud' Rossiter, playing up front, who scored twice. Unfortunately, the following week in the final match of the season at Brighton he broke his leg, which ended his playing career.

Mr Charles Sutcliffe, president of the Football League, shakes hands with Orient's skipper Frank Searle before the opening of the Brisbane Road ground in August 1937.

The ground in Osborne Road, as it was then known, was first used by Leyton FC in 1905, a professional Southern League side with the likes of Charlie Buchan among their ranks. In 1912 it became the ground for the Bryant & May Company, and then Leyton Amateurs re-rented the ground from the local council between 1929 and 1937.

The ground was in a poor state and looked very similar to how it had when Leyton first played there in 1905, being in need of great repair.

The first match took place on 28 August 1937 when the O's drew a crowd of 14,598 to witness a draw with Cardiff City 1–1. One would suppose it was fitting for Cardiff to open this new chapter in Orient's history as it was Orient, some 17 years earlier, who first played League football in Wales.

Due to the wartime period, the first major improvement to the ground took place in 1949 when a large grassy hill, which was at the side of a small main stand, was levelled and crush barriers were added to the West Stand and behind the goals. In 1951 a running track, although limited in size, was added.

In 1952 terracing behind the Coronation Gardens end was improved and extended for the visit of Arsenal for an FA Cup tie in February 1952, which allowed for a record 30,000 crowd in the stadium. Since then the terracing behind the goals was further improved in both 1959 and 1960. (The whole of the West Stand was given new smaller steps in 1962.)

When the O's gained promotion for the first time in their history in 1956 to Division Two, it was decided that the tiny seating stand, which had stood for over 50 years, was to be dismantled in the summer of 1956 and replaced with a new stand purchased from the derelict Mitcham Stadium. The new stand included new offices, a medical room and other facilities.

The old small box stand affectionately known as the 'Orange Box' held 500 people.

The new stand was to hold 2,600 spectators and it was ready in time for the start of the 1956–57 season and the visit of Nottingham Forest in August, with 25,272 in attendance.

There was a scare during the match when a small fire started in the new stand, caused by a lighted cigarette, which was thrown on the floor, but it was quickly put out. Chairman Harry Zussman joked 'For years we hoped the 'Orange Box' would catch fire so we could collect the insurance, and now the new one nearly goes up in smoke on the first day of use.'

The club installed floodlights in 1960, and the first official match under them was the League game against Brighton on 31 August 1960. The lights have been improved several times since then.

The old wooden fence, which had surrounded the ground for many years, was dismantled in 1952 and replaced with a concrete wall.

During the summer of 1962, with the O's having been promoted to the old First Division (Premiership), when the final wing to the Main Stand was added, providing an additional 900 seats, the seating total was increased to 3,500.

The highest attendance ever recorded at the ground was for the visit of West Ham United in an FA Cup tie on 25 January 1964; the crowd was 34,345.

A major concern over many years was the state of the often waterlogged and muddy pitch. It was a constant source of embarrassment to the club until 1977 when Brian Winston had the pitch dug up and re-turfed under the guidance of the curator Charlie Hasler, and it has turned out to be arguably one of the best in the Football League and a credit to Hasler and his team.

Winston had the West Stand converted into an all-seater stand in 1978, and two years earlier temporary seating to the right of the stand was introduced. Also, fencing was placed on both sides of the terracing to stop fans getting on to the pitch. These were torn down after the Hillsborough tragedy.

During the post-war boom the ground had some very large crowds. A record 24,864 assembled for the visit of Ipswich Town in March 1948. However, after a gate broke many got into the ground without paying.

The other occasion that people broke into the ground was 2 May 1971 for the match with Birmingham City, who beat Orient 1–0 to gain promotion. The win denied Millwall a chance of promotion. The official attendance was 33,383, but it was estimated by the police that around 1,000 people got in free. This figure also excludes the many people who sold prize tickets for the club, who were also allowed in free with a matchday programme through a small side door in the Main Stand. This total is a record for a League game at the ground.

Safety regulations have gradually diminished the capacity of the stadium from 26,500 (7,171 seats) in 1989 to around 18,000 a couple of years later. This was further reduced to 13,842 when 7,113 seats were removed in the mid-1990s.

The fans had a big surprise at the start of the 1996–97 season, as something drastic had taken place at the Coronation Gardens south end of the stadium.

Break contractors had demolished the terracing and had removed over 20,000 tonnes of it to make way for a planned new £4.5 million 3,500 all-seater stand. The new stand would have provided a sports and events hall capable of seating 1,000 people. The new stand was to have a top-of-the-range fitness centre and dressing rooms. Lifts would have whisked you to the first floor and a new supporters' club room. However, funds for the new stand were not forthcoming from the National Lottery, and it was put on hold for a few years. The open terracing was closed off and used as a car park.

The name of the ground was changed from Leyton Stadium to the Matchroom Stadium. Barry Hearn explained at the club's AGM in 1999 that the name came about from an idea to gain a little tax relief from the receiver of revenue. He stated that he didn't really want to use the name Matchroom, but it was unavoidable. The Matchroom Company contribute a lot to the club regarding accounting and commercial spheres.

The building of a smaller stand seating 1,336 people and a small car park began in the summer of 1999 and was partly funded by a grant from the Football Trust of a reported £900,000. Also the terrracing on the north side was to be upgraded at a cost of £50,000. The money for this was also grant funded. The enclosure under the Main Stand was upgraded to an all-seater area with 900 seats. There is also an improved facility for the disabled in the new enclosure seating area.

The ground capacity increased to 13,500 and about 10,000 seats. At this time, it was hoped that the capacity would be increased to around 20,000 in the not too distant future. The visiting section of the south wing in the Main Stand was to be increased to 2,177 seats.

So after three seasons the ground was to once again become a four-sided stadium. The upgrade of the stadium went a long way towards making it come into line with the Taylor report, which stated that grounds had to be all-seater by 2002.

The club was in discussion with the owners of the ground, the local council, for a 125-year lease on the ground for the sum of £325,000 or the club could continue to lease the ground from the council for £30,000 per annum. The lease ran out in June 2001, but the club did have a 12-year right of tenancy on the current site so there was no real rush to sign anything.

During March 2003 the club announced that plans for the redevelopment of the ground were pressing ahead and hopes were that the planning committee of the London Borough of Waltham Forest would give the green light for the project.

The cost of the redevelopment of both the West Stand and North Terrace would cost

In safe hands: pre-season preparation in 1998 with Adrian Martin (assistant groundsman), Barry Hearn and Charlie Hasler (senior groundsman).

approximately £9 million, of which around £7.5 million will come from Bellway Homes, who are purchasing four plots of land to develop flats, a further £1 million from the Football Foundation and the reminder of the money from Barry Hearn and Matchroom Sports Limited.

The end result would see a new multi-function West Stand with a capacity of 2,500 seats, and this stand would be the new headquarters of the club, incorporating a new ticket office, large shop, a relocation of the Supporters' Club, players' changing rooms, corporate hospitality areas and lettable space, which would generate extra income.

The new North Stand would be similar to the new South Stand with approximately 1,500 seats. The area underneath would be used for stewards and housing medical facilities. The stand would have an access road and provide much needed car parking for club officials and would ultimately be for away fans.

The club calculated that the current ground is only properly utilised for up to 1.7 percent of the year, and the objective is to bring in more activities to the new stadium for the remaining 98.3 percent.

Future plans are for a new East Stand with at least 4,000 seats to be built, which will be subject to separate funding, but the existing stand is likely to remain for a few years.

The old stand became decrepit and decayed and if not rebuilt would most likely face closure very soon.

The club had the full support of the local authority to remain in Leyton, and a variation to the club's current lease agreement of 999 years includes an extension on the original agreement.

Barry Hearn warned 'unless planning was granted there would be no future for the club at Brisbane Road as it is literally falling apart, we either improve or move.'

In May 2003 planning permission was granted by Waltham Forest Council. A happy Hearn said 'This safeguards the club's future in Leyton.' In August 2003 the club was informed that it was too dangerous to start demolition work during the season, and it could only commence at the end of the season on health and safety grounds. So the builders went in on 26 May 2004 to demolish both the North Terrace and the West Stand, with a plan of seven weeks for all debris to be cleared and construction work to start, which did happen on schedule.

Today, the new capacity of the all-seater Matchroom Stadium is 7,804 and the new West Stand was full (over 2,500 seats) for the visit of Oxford United in October 2005.

New plans have been submitted for the building of a new North Stand and it is hoped that it will commence in around September 2006.

Ground History:

Victoria Park	1881 to 1888
Glyn Road	1888 to 1896
Whittles Athletic	1896 to 1900
Millfields Road	1900 to 1930
Lea Bridge Road	1930 to 1937
Brisbane Road	1937 to Present

The Orient Crests

The club have had five different crests or badges on their shirts through the years.

The initial badge was first introduced to the fans on the front cover of the club programme on 28 September 1946 for the visit of Crystal Palace, when the club announced their name change from Clapton Orient to Leyton Orient.

This design was worn on the shirts for the following few seasons and was based on the arms of the Borough of Leyton, showing a Chevronel Gules with a Lion passant. On the bottom is a wreath supported by a crozier of gold with the Latin motto *Ministrando Dignitas*, meaning 'Dignity through service'. The colours on the crest were red and gold and, although not used on the shirts from 1954–55, it remained the official club crest until 1965 when the Borough of Leyton was incorporated in the new Waltham Forest Administration.

During the mid-1960s the club replaced the Latin motto by incorporating the name Leyton Orient FC on to the badge. In 1965 new manager Dave Sexton designed a small blue and white striped badge with no name on it, but when Sexton departed in December 1965 it was dropped.

From August 1966 the O's changed their official shirt colours from blue to an all-red strip and at the same time introduced two new badges. On the shirt appeared an oval badge with the colours of blue, white and yellow. This badge was the suggestion of new director Reg Briggs, a shipping company director, who knew how the club name had evolved from the Oriental Steamship Navigation Company. The colours of the badge were that of the P&O Group, the company that took over Oriental Steamship. This badge was worn in the promotion season of 1969–70. There was another badge shown on the front cover of the matchday programme, which was that of a single wyvern (an heraldic animal which resembles a dragon, except it had no hindquarters, its rear being like a serpent with a barbed tail).

The O's introduced a new left-facing motif of a single female griffin in white on the red shirt, which was first worn for the visit of Sheffield United on 15 August 1970. The mythical griffin creature was symbolic of vigilance and strength and is said to guard against all danger and keep evil spirits away.

During August 1976 the club announced a competition for the design of a new club badge to be worn on new shirts with two red stripes for the 1977–78 season.

On 27 December 1976 the final version of the crest was introduced. The winning design was based on two different suggestions submitted by Clive M. Brown and Mark Hodges. The design was completed by chairman Brian Winston. Two wyverns are the main feature of the crest, one holding a football in its claws. These were chosen by the designers to represent the eastern mystery of the Orient and the connection with the shipping company of the same name. The name of the club and the year of its formation can also be seen on the crest.

On 1 July 1997, when the club reverted back to the name of Leyton Orient Football Club, the new name was introduced on to the crest.

There have been numerous questions as to why the wyvern was chosen, and actually Brian Winston, the then chairman, wanted two griffins on the crest, but the designers, not quite sure of the difference between a griffin and a wyvern, wanted to use something of the eastern mystery of the Orient and no thought was given to the coat of arms of the City of London or to Orient's connection with the sea.

Chairmen and Directors

Directors

* Committee members before there were directors
Managing director
^^ Not the same person
+ Club chairman (not necessarily the years shown)

A. Haines *	1904–1906
R. Lovelock *	1904–1906
J. Robertson *	1904–1908
E. Wiggins * +	1904–1906
H. Woods *	1904–1906
Dr M. Jones	1905–1906
A. Unwin	1905–1925
T.S. Ludford +	1906–1928
E. Lehmann	1907–1909
S. Goodger	1912–1921
T. Wimms	1913–1924
W. Cornish	1914–1934
J. Loe	1914–1919
H. Gray-Robbins +	1914–1924
R.J. Holmes	1914–1915
P. Arber	1910–1929
D. McCarthy	1919–1925
N. Mardell	1921–1929
G.H. Harris +	1924–1949
B. Emmanuel	1926–1929
H. Bailey	1929–1934
H. Garland-Wells	1929–1934
P. Boyden +	1929–1936
N. Middleboe	1929–1930
F. Snewin +	1932–1949
G. Cowan	1932–1933
P. Showell	1932–1934
G. Foster	1932–1933
H. Botten	1933–1936 & 1940–1945
W. Baxter	1933–1936
J. Genese	1933–1934
R. Powis	1933–1934
L. Blush	1933–1934
W. Moore	1933–1946
H. Robertson	1934–1956
F. Blakemore	1935–1936
C. Hopping	1942–1943
Dr A. Byrne+	1943–1947
E. Girt	1945–1949
D. McLardy	1945–1947
R. Elliott	1945–1947
G. Kenure	1947–1949
H. Lea	1947–1967
A.E. Page +	1947–1951 & 1958–1974
R. Sharplin	1948–1953
H.S. Zussman +	1949–1981
F.F. Harris	1950–1978
D. Osborne #	1953–1955
C. Bent-Marshall	1955–1967
L. Grade	1959–1967
B. Delfont	1961–1967
N.E. Ovenden +	1966–1971 & 1982–1988
R.S. Briggs	1967–1973
M. Page	1972–1978
B.B. Winston +	1972–1985 & 1986–1987
A. Harding +	1976–1986
R. Russ	1977–1978
D.L. Weinrabe	1981–1996
A. Pincus	1981–1993
M.R. Ovenden	1982–1988
T. Wood OBE +	1985–2002
H. Linney	1987–1996
F. Clark ##	1987–1993
D. Osborne #	1988–1989
M. Pears	1989–1992
V. Marsh	1993–1996
J. Goldsmith	1993–2003
B. Hearn +	1995–
B. Goodall	1995–1998
S. Dawson	1995–
R. Cousens	1995–1996
D. Dodd	1995–
S. Davis	1997–
N. Levine	1997–
M. Porter	2006–

Note: Mr J. John Young, a man in the shoe trade and a great benefactor of Orient, was club president from 1948 to 1967, and although never a director of the club he deserves a special mention because quite often he used to foot the bill and pay for the players' trips and stays in hotels when on special training for big FA Cup ties as well as paying for other things for the club, and he was a long-time fan.

As a gift to the club, he paid the £300 transfer for Scottish international player Tommy Brown, on 4 August 1950, and he also paid the bills for various ground improvements over the years.

Mr Philip Wallace took over the running of the club and paid the bills between January and March 1995 while checking out the books. In March 1995 he pulled out of taking over the club due to the severity of their financial position.

The O's chairmen

E. Wiggins
H. Wells-Holland
T. Ludford
H. Gray-Robbins
G. Harris
P. Boyden
F. Snewin
Dr A. Byrne
H. Zussman
A.E. Page
N. Ovenden
B.B. Winston
A. Harding
T. Wood
B. Hearn

The Managers

Samuel Ormerod

April 1905–March 1906

Sam Ormerod was the man to take charge of the O's inaugural season in the Football League, having been appointed as the club's first full-time manager on 12 April 1905. He watched proudly as his team took the field at Leicester Fosse on 2 September 1905 for their first League Division Two fixture, which was lost 2–1 with a goal in the last seconds by the home team. Born in Accrington, he was an amateur player and referee in Lancashire football in the 1880s, and he rose to officiating in an international fixture.

Ormerod was secretary-manager to Manchester City for seven years between 1 June 1895 and July 1902 with a record of: P 241, W 111, D 51, L 79. In later years at Hyde Road he worked as part of a three-man committee that led City to a number of test-match positions (the old Play-offs). In 1899 he eventually led them to their first ever promotion. The local press dubbed him 'The Wizard of Longsight' on account of his prowess in guiding City to become the leading club in Lancashire.

Sam resigned in June 1902 after the City board was replaced following discontent from the shareholders, claiming that the outlay of monies on players' bonuses, wages and travelling expenses were far too high. He found it difficult working with the new committee members and found he was being pushed aside with regards to team selection, as two of the members, Joshua Parlby-Two and Lawrence Furniss, had been previous managers with the club.

Ormerod then moved to Accrington Stanley. In June 1903 he was appointed secretary-manager with Stockport County after they had failed to be re-elected back into the League and stayed for two years before resigning on 31 March 1905 when Fred Stewart was appointed in his place, and Ormerod seemed to become the forgotten man at Edgeley Park. After joining the O's, Ormerod found it increasingly difficult to mould a team to stay in the League with all the off-the-field financial problems at Millfields Road: things were not easy.

In March 1906, after a crisis meeting of the board of directors, newly-appointed chairman Captain Henry Wells-Holland stated that a number of experienced players had to be sold to keep the club afloat. Ormerod walked out of the meeting in disgust and resigned, but truth be known the pressure was getting to him as he became ill, and he returned home to Accrington to live in retirement. He died just three months later.

To judge Ormerod critically in light of the crisis at the club would be harsh indeed. He was certainly a man of vast experience, and it was doubtful if any other man could have lifted Orient off the bottom of Division Two. Ormerod made a number of astute signings during his spell in East London, one being the former Manchester City player and colleague William Holmes, and it was Holmes who was given the job as player-manager.

William Marsden Holmes

March 1906–February 1922

Billy Holmes was born in Darley Dale, Matlock, in 1875. He started his playing career with local side Darley Dale FC, before moving to Chesterfield Town of the Sheffield League, making 38 appearances. He joined Manchester City in July 1896 and stayed for nine years, making 166 senior appearances and scoring four goals.

Holmes was signed by Ormerod from his former club Manchester City on 19 August 1905 for a £10 fee. He was a steady, reliable defender with qualities of leadership, so he was the obvious choice to take over from Ormerod as player-manager in March 1906. When he joined the O's, he still had a suspension to serve, being one of 16 other

City colleagues found guilty of receiving illegal payments. He was suspended between May 1906 to the end of November 1906 and fined £50 for his part in the infamous 'Billy Meredith' illegal payment scandal of 1904–05. However, after further investigation by the FA, all charges against Holmes were eventually dropped in March 1908. He decided to retire from playing and was appointed full-time manager after making a total of 51 senior appearances.

Holmes proved to be a great leader, and his charges played with great style and ability. He brought some great players to the club, including Richard McFadden, Willie Jonas, Fred Parker, Robert Dalrymple and, after World War One, the three Tonner brothers, John Townrow, Arthur Wood and Owen Williams.

His management acumen earned his team the title of 'Holmes' Homerton Heroes', particularly between 1910 and 1912 when they finished in fourth spot in Division Two on two occasions. It came as a great shock when the club announced that Holmes had collapsed in Hackney, London, from a heart attack. He was taken to the German hospital in Dalston and died as an inpatient on 18 February 1922. His last match in charge was an emphatic 4–0 home win over Coventry City on 18 February. Three days after his passing, the O's, wearing black armbands, went to Coventry and won 2–1. 'Doc' Holmes, as he was always affectionately known, did a superb job as manager during his 16 years at Millfields Road.

Isaac Evenson

September–November 1906

Born in Manchester during November 1882, Ike Evenson was a fine centre-half who had a long and distinguished career with Glossop North End, Stockport County, Leicester Fosse and the O's, before joining West Bromwich Albion for £225 on 29 April 1907. He later played for Plymouth Argyle and Nottingham Forest. He made a career total of 210 senior appearances, scoring 42 goals. Evenson joined the O's from Leicester Fosse in August 1905. The 24-year-old was the man to take charge of the team for the first nine matches of the 1906–07 season, while Holmes was serving his suspension. His record read: P 9, W 3, D 3, L 3, F 10, A 15. He died in Manchester during 1954.

Peter Proudfoot

April 1922–April 1929, April 1930–April 1931 & January 1935–January 1939

The link between previous managers Ormerod and Holmes continued in April 1922 with the appointment of Peter Proudfoot as manager after the death of Holmes. It was Ormerod who had originally signed Proudfoot from Southern League side Millwall in August 1905 for the O's first League campaign, and Proudfoot made 26 appearances before his transfer to Chelsea in 1906 for £120. The highlight of his first spell as boss was the great 1925–26 FA Cup run. Born in Wishaw, Scotland, on 25 November 1880, he was a wing-half who started his playing career with Wishaw United in December 1900. He joined Lincoln City, and after three years he made 79 League appearances, scoring 20 goals.

In 1903 he returned to Scotland, playing for St Mirren, but made only two Scottish League appearances before moving back south of the border with Southern League side Millwall Athletic where he chalked up 16 senior appearances. He joined the O's in May 1905, and after 32 senior appearances and one goal he was sold to Chelsea for £120 in March 1906. After 12 League appearances for Chelsea, he played in the reserves for Manchester United and Stockport County (45 League appearances and one goal). Proudfoot made a career total of 186 senior appearances with 22 goals.

After a commission in the army, he was appointed the O's manager in April 1922. He stepped down as manager in 1929, after being suspended by the FA for six months due to certain irregularities, although he remained at the club as an official club representative. In 1930 he returned as manager after the departure of Arthur Grimsdell, but he found it a difficult task due to the financial problems at the club and lack of money for quality players.

After various managers came and went, it was the loyal Proudfoot who took over again in January 1935, and he stayed for a further four years, and it was no mean achievement that he kept the O's away from the bottom of the table. He was the only manager at the club to work at all three grounds: Millfields Road, Lea Bridge Road and Brisbane Road.

Proudfoot was one of the many managers who had an unenviable task during one of the club's many financial crises of the 1930s; he was the man that led the O's in the most League matches – 483 – and also had the most defeats – 218. After retirement he returned to his native Wishaw in Scotland where he died on 4 March 1941, aged 60.

Arthur Grimsdell

May 1929–March 1930

Arthur Grimsdell was one of the finest half-backs of his era, gaining six England caps while playing with Tottenham Hotspur in the 1920s. Born in Watford in March 1894, he played for Watford before joining Spurs on 17 April 1912, and he stayed at White Hart Lane for 17 years, making 417 senior appearances and scoring 38 goals. When the O's were relegated for the very first time in their history to Division Three South in 1929, 35-year-old Grimsdell was the man seen to take the O's back up to the Second Division, and he was appointed player-manager and secretary in the summer of 1929.

Grimsdell was a quiet yet determined man, with a great vision of the game and a scientific approach; however, problems soon arose when his registration was not sanctioned by the FA until the eighth match of the season, at which point the O's were bottom of the League. Their decline continued, and Grimsdell resigned in March 1930 on amicable terms after just 10 months in charge. He retired and opened a newsagent in Watford and was a director of Watford football club in 1945–51. He died in Watford on 13 March 1963, aged 68.

James Marshall Seed

April 1931–May 1933

Jimmy Seed was born in Blackhill, County Durham, on 25 March 1895. He first made his name as a brilliant inside-forward with Tottenham Hotspur. Seed started his career with Whitburn FC in the Wearside League, and it was reported that he alone scored over 80 goals in 1913–14. During April 1914 he was signed by Sunderland, but the 5ft 11in and 11st 9lb player never got his chance due to the start of the hostilities. He was severely gassed during his time in the trenches, while serving with the West Yorkshire Regiment in France. He recovered in a Sheffield Hospital but was released by Sunderland FC, as they felt he was not up to the rigours of League football.

After the war, he went to Wales to play for Mid Rhondda before joining Spurs in February 1920 for a fee of £350. He won an FA Cup-winners' medal with Spurs in 1921 and made a total of 254 senior appearances, hitting 76 goals. He was transferred to Sheffield Wednesday in June 1927, making 134 League appearances and scoring 33 goals, and skippered them to two League Championships. He won a total of five England caps.

Seed was appointed as secretary-manager on 18 April 1931 on a salary of £12 per week, the deal having been arranged by ex-Spurs man Herbert Chapman. Seed was another manager who failed to perform to his true ability due to the O's being under a constant financial cloud and struggling for survival.

During a match at Lea Bridge Road his opposing manager was his elder brother Angus Seed, manager of Aldershot, in 1932. It was only the second time in League history that brothers had been opposing managers. The first were the Chapman brothers, and also to do this in later years were the brothers Bobby and Jack Charlton.

On 17 May 1933 Seed left the O's to join the Gliksten brothers at Charlton Athletic. He had a very long and happy association with them that lasted over 23 years, lifting them from being a Third Division South club right up to the old First Division in consecutive seasons during the 1930s. He also took them to two FA Cup Finals, runners-up in 1946 and winners the following year, when he dropped the trophy and broke the top of the lid, and it required emergency repairs at a garage before the Town Hall reception.

He left the Valley after being sacked on 3 September 1956, following Charlton's 8–1 defeat at Sunderland. According to the official club minutes book, the Charlton board met two days later, and it was unanimously resolved that Seed's contract be terminated forthwith and that he be offered £6,000 in full and final settlement. The official programme on the following Saturday for the match versus Sheffield Wednesday, attended by 21,435 spectators, informed that Seed had in fact resigned and had not been sacked. It stated that 'his decision to resign was a shock to us all and was received with great regret.' To add to the confusion, the press reports stated he had retired. For someone who had been at the Valley for 23 years and taken Charlton from a Third Division club to the First Division, as runners-up, within three years and also featured in two FA Cup wartime Finals, this was a real shabby way to treat a man who had put the club on the map.

Seed was appointed as a consultant with Bristol City in January 1957 and was acting manager for 18 days in January 1958. A year later he was manager with Millwall. He was appointed as an advisor in July 1959 and a director/consultant at The Den in January 1960, before he died at the Farnborough Hospital in Kent on 16 July 1966, while still holding office, aged 71. Jimmy Seed had a stand posthumously named after him, opened at Charlton's old Valley ground on 18 August 1981.

Jimmy Seed's managerial career (League and Cup) with other clubs:

Team	*From*	*To*	*Games*	*Won*	*Drawn*	*Lost*
Charlton Ath	1 Jan 1933	1 Sep 1956	727	311	156	260
Millwall	1 Jan 1958	1 Jul 1959	70	24	17	29
			797	335	173	289

David Pratt

May 1933–December 1934

Born in Lochore, Fifeshire, Scotland, on 5 March 1896, the 5ft 11in and 11st 10lb centre-half David Pratt started off his playing career with local side Lochore Welfare FC in 1913, moving to Lochgelly United the following season. During World War One he served with Cameron Highlanders in France, winning a military medal. In 1918 he joined Fife side Hill O'Beath FC, and a year later he turned professional with Glasgow Celtic, winning a Scottish Cup medal in 1920–21.

After a loan spell with Scottish League side Bo'ness, Pratt joined Bradford City in November 1921, making 50

League appearances with five goals. In January 1923 he signed for Liverpool and played a further 77 League matches, scoring once for the Merseysiders. In November he was on the books of Bury, playing 51 senior matches, and in June 1929 he was appointed player-manager with Southern League side Yeovil & Petters United, who finished as Southern League (western section) Champions in 1932.

Yet another manager to arrive at the Orient at rather a difficult period, at the end of the 1932–33 season the club had to release almost the entire staff owing to their financial plight. Pratt was given the unenviable task of trying to rebuild the team, and he signed no less than 26 new players on free transfers, a record number for a club during the close season and for one not having been elected into the Football League. Pratt revitalised the club after his arrival in 1933. His attacking style of football gained much favour with the supporters and pundits alike.

With the likes of Ted Crawford and David Halliday now on the books, Orient were playing some sparkling football, and the fans were immensely disappointed to hear of the resignation of Pratt in December 1934. So much so, they got together a petition in the hope he would change his mind; however, it was to no avail, and it was Sid White who was appointed caretaker manager until the return of Peter Proudfoot.

Pratt, a canny Scot, was appointed manager of Notts County on 28 April 1935, but his stay at Meadow Lane was short-lived, and he resigned in June 1935 having been in charge for just seven matches, which resulted in five defeats, with only one win and a draw. On 29 June 1936 he was appointed manager-trainer of Scottish side Heart of Midlothian, his fourth club in two years, a position he held until resigning on 4 February 1937. He became manager of Birmingham League side Bangor City on 24 July 1937 but resigned just four months later.

During World War Two Pratt served as a flying officer with the RAF and was awarded a DCM. On 29 December 1944 he was appointed manager with Port Vale, but unfortunately he had to resign on 11 July 1945 because he was unable to gain his release from the services to assume his role as manager for the 1946–47 season. On leaving the forces, he became a BBC sports broadcaster.

Thomas William Halsey

January 1939–December 1939

Tom Halsey was born in Leyton, London, during 1895, and he made the unique step up from supporters' club official, as one of the early founders, to the post of club secretary during the late 1930s and finally team manager in January 1939.

He was appointed secretary to the club, but when Peter Proudfoot resigned in January 1939 due to ill health Halsey was appointed boss. His one big-name signing for the start of the 1939–40 season was that of William McFadyen, previously a record goalscorer with both Motherwell and Huddersfield Town. It was during this season that, after just three League games had been completed, war was declared and the season abandoned, with all records expunged.

Halsey served in the naval forces during World War Two in France, Egypt and Russia. He stepped down from his managerial duties in December 1939 to make way for William Peter Wright.

William Peter Wright

December 1939–September 1945

Bill Wright, as he was always known (not to be confused with Billy Wright the famous Wolves and England player and Arsenal manager or with William Bulloch Wright, later to become the O's manager for three matches between September and October 1946), was never in charge of team affairs during peacetime, but it would be a serious omission if he was not included because of his long association with the club, especially during the war years when he was in charge.

Born in Sheffield during 1903, as a player he was an amateur throughout the 1920s and turned professional in 1930, but he never quite made the grade and appeared in just one League match for the O's at wing-half against Torquay United on 10 October 1931, a 1–3 defeat. He remained on the playing staff until 1935 when he was appointed as assistant trainer, and he took over as secretary-manager in January 1939.

He guided the O's through the difficult wartime period and his dedication and hard work can not be overestimated; he even played in 18 matches, including two as a goalkeeper due to a lack of recognised 'keepers being available. He remained boss until September 1945 when Willie Hall took over, and he became coach and, during 1946, was masseur at Brisbane Road. In May 1948 he left to manage the semi-professional club Chingford Town. His namesake William Bulloch Wright joined him as coach at Chingford in July 1948.

He had a benefit match against Queen's Park Rangers awarded to him and long-serving player Fred Bartlett on 21 May 1949. Bill Wright was still playing football at the age of 65 in the Birmingham Sunday Alliance League in a team of three generations of Wrights. He died in Birmingham during October 1983, aged 80.

George William Hall

September 1945–January 1946

Willie Hall was a great player with Tottenham Hotspur and England, and he once scored five goals for his country against Northern Ireland on 16 November 1938, a 7–0 rout of the Irish.

Born in Newark, Nottinghamshire, on 12 March 1912, the 5ft 7in and 10st 7lb inside-forward started his playing career with local side Ransome & Marles FC, having previously represented Nottingham Schoolboys. He joined Notts County in November 1930, making 34 League appearances with seven goals, before moving to Spurs on 21 December 1932 for £3,000. He made 222 senior appearances at White Hart Lane, scoring 29 goals, and he also played in 136 wartime matches for Spurs, scoring a further 10 goals right up to 1943.

Hall won 10 peacetime and three wartime international caps and represented an England FA XI three times, scoring nine goals from his England peacetime appearances. He retired from playing professional football in February 1944 due to an injury.

When war ended, Hall wanted to embark on a managerial career, and he was appointed manager with the O's in September 1945, which made him the youngest manager in the Football League at that time. He was to be in charge of the team for the resumption of League football in the 1946–47 season, and he told supporters that he would do everything in his power to get them back up to Division Two.

Unfortunately, he was struck down by thrombosis in January 1946, following a life punctuated by illness, and never fulfilled his dream of managing a League side. After several operations, his right leg had to be amputated and some 13 months later he lost his left leg. Remarkably, in 1948–49 he was appointed manager of Chelmsford City, and between August and December 1949 he took over the managerial reins of Chingford Town from William P. Wright.

On leaving full-time football, he worked for a brewery, ran a sports shop with former Spurs teammate Vic Buckingham (the venture failed), and he also ran the Archers public house in Aldgate, London. Willie Hall died in his native Newark on 22 May 1967, aged 55.

Charles William Hewitt

January 1946–September 1946 & October 1946–April 1948

Captain Charles Hewitt, as he was known because of his days as a naval captain during World War Two, was born in Greatham, Cleveland, on 10 April 1884. He started playing football in his local junior Leagues before playing for a number of clubs up to World War One, including Middlesbrough, Tottenham Hotspur, Liverpool, West Bromwich Albion, Spennymoor United and Crystal Palace.

During World War One he served on a destroyer while with the Royal Navy. After the war, he had a trial with Hartlepool United but decided to turn his hand to management with Mold FC during September 1919. He was later appointed as the first manager of Wrexham on 10 November 1924 and stayed for two years without much success in the League, but they did win the Welsh Cup Final, beating Flint in 1925. Between June 1926 and 1928 he was in charge of Flint FC and then in May 1928 joined the new combined Connah's Quay and Shotton FC.

In May 1930 he was appointed at Chester, and during his first year they were runners-up in the Cheshire County League. The following season they were crowned as Champions. In May 1931 Chester were elected into the League Division Three North, they were Welsh Cup winners in 1933 and were runners-up in the Third Division North in 1936. In April 1936 he resigned and became manager with Millwall, and he took the Lions to the FA Cup semi-final, losing to Sunderland (the first ever Third Division outfit to reach that stage of the competition), and in 1938 they were Champions of Division Three South.

During November 1939 he was suspended by Millwall for allegedly making illegal payments to players, and he was eventually dismissed in April 1940. During World War Two he served as a Naval skipper in charge of a troopship with the Royal Navy and also served on a torpedo boat destroyer.

Hewitt was appointed as the O's secretary-manager on 1 January 1946, earning the highest salary the club had ever paid, yet his stay was a stormy one, and after just nine months he resigned due to the lack of money he had requested from the board of directors for new players. He actually signed a new player and was then told that the money was not available, and he walked out on the club on 20 September 1946. He also decided to change the colours from the chevron kit to blue shirts and white shorts, the same colours that his former club Millwall played in.

It was newly appointed coach William Bulloch Wright who took over the reins. However, just under three weeks later on 9 October 1946 Hewitt was reinstated with a promise of funds being made available to him for new players, and Wright was appointed his assistant manager. The O's chairman Dr Arthur Bryne resigned and his daughter also resigned as assistant secretary at the club because of the re-appointment of Hewitt. In 1947 Hewitt made a bold effort to sign Chelsea's legendary forward Tommy Lawton (the club, through Alec Stock, made another effort to sign Lawton in 1952).

It was Hewitt who was instrumental in bringing both Arthur Page and Harry Zussman to the club, both later to become chairmen of the club, whose funds helped stave off closure in 1966. Hewitt did bring many new faces, yet the much-wanted success was not forthcoming. In fact, after a 4–2 home defeat at Brisbane Road by Bristol

Rovers in October 1947, after the O's had led 2–0, Hewitt was booed by supporters, which was followed by a demonstration outside the ground after the match. It was Arthur Page who had to address the angry crowd, who eventually dispersed.

The performance of the team did not improve, and Hewitt was fired in May 1948. He returned to Millwall in August 1948 but was dismissed after much acrimony on 10 January 1956. He successfully sued Millwall FC for breach of contract and in July 1957 received £4,500 in damages.

In May 1954 he received a medal from the FA for his 20 years' service to the game. Hewitt died in Darlington on 3 December 1966, aged 82.

Charles Hewitt's managerial record (League and FA Cup) with other clubs:

Team	*From*	*To*	*Games*	*Won*	*Drawn*	*Lost*
Wrexham	1 Nov 1924	1 Dec 1929	225	81	51	93
Chester City	1 Aug 1930	30 Apr 1936	223	110	49	64
Millwall	1 Apr 1936	1 Apr 1940	146	64	39	43
Millwall	1 Aug 1948	1 Jan 1956	363	156	81	126
TOTAL			957	411	220	326

William Bulloch Wright

September–October 1946

Bill Wright, or Bert as he was also sometimes known, was born in Sheffield on 25 December 1899. He hailed from a footballing family as his father Jackie played for Sheffield Wednesday, Southend United, Plymouth and Bolton and his younger brother John was an England international while on Newcastle United's books.

Bill Wright started his professional career with Southern League side Southend United, playing either at inside-forward or half-back, before joining Bolton Wanderers in 1923, and during his 11 seasons there he made 159 senior appearances and scored 22 goals. He played alongside the legendary David Jack (brother of former 'Oriental' Rollo Jack), who was his closest schoolmate.

In 1933 he joined Reading and was ever present during his four seasons at Elm Park. They finished in the top five each season, and he made 193 senior appearances, netting five goals. In 1937 he left England to join French side Wachet Rouen as coach. The following August he returned to England, joining Crystal Palace as first-team coach.

During the war he served six years in the APTC, reaching the rank of staff sergeant. He joined the O's in June 1946 as first-team trainer but took over as manager the day after Charles Hewitt had resigned on 20 September 1946. He was in charge for three League matches, all defeats, at Reading on 21 September, at home to Crystal Palace on 28 September and away at Torquay United on 5 October, but his reign lasted just 19 days (two days less in charge than Paul Went's reign, some 35 years later).

Charles Hewitt was reinstated as secretary-manager on 9 October and took charge of the side three days later, a 3–1 win over Mansfield Town. Bert Wright was appointed as Hewitt's assistant.

In June 1948 he was appointed coach at Southern League side Chingford Town under former 'Oriental' and namesake William Peter Wright. William Bulloch Wright died in Milton, Portsmouth, on 2 May 1965, aged 55.

Neil McBain

April 1948–July 1949

Neil McBain was born in Campbelltown, Argyllshire, Scotland, on 15 November 1885. The stylish 5ft 8in and 12st 3lb full-back started off with local side Campbelltown Academicals. After a trial with Hamilton, he signed for Ayr United in 1914.

During World War One he guested for both Portsmouth and Southampton but returned to Ayr after the hostilities. In November 1921 he joined Manchester United for £4,600, a high fee in those days, making 42 League appearances and scoring two goals. He also won three Scottish international caps. He requested a transfer from United after he was continually played out of position and was snapped up by Everton in January 1923 for £4,200, where he made 97 League appearances with one goal.

McBain joined St Johnstone in July 1926 for £1,100, but after two years he returned south of the border with Liverpool in March 1928. Then after just 12 League appearances he moved to Watford that November for £900, playing 84 League matches and scoring four goals. He moved into management with Watford as player-manager in 1929 and was appointed manager in August 1937.

During the proceeding years he acted as manager with Ayr United (1937–38) and Luton Town (June 1938–July 1939). After World War Two, he became manager with New Brighton and quite remarkably appeared as an emergency goalkeeper against Hartlepools United on 15 March 1947 in a Football League Division Three North match, aged 52 years and four months, the oldest player ever to appear in a Football League match, it ended in a 0–3 defeat.

In February 1948 he was appointed as the O's assistant manager under Charles Hewitt and took over as boss with them on 22 April 1948 after Hewitt was fired. The team struggled under his leadership, finishing fourth from bottom in Division Three South.

McBain left the O's in July 1949 to take up a coaching position in Argentina with Estudianties De La Plata. In 1955 he returned to England as manager of his old

Scottish club Ayr United. The following August he took charge of Watford, a position he held until February 1959.

In January 1963 he was back in charge of Ayr for just five months. He later scouted for Watford, Mansfield Town, Everton and Chelsea.

Neil McBain had quite a remarkable career in football that spanned two World Wars and a total of 32 years. He died in Ayr, Scotland, on 13 May 1974, aged 78.

Neil McBain's managerial career (League and FA Cup) with other clubs in England:

Team	*From*	*To*	*Games*	*Won*	*Drawn*	*Lost*
Watford	1 Aug 1929	30 May 1937	364	152	77	135
Luton T	1 Jul 1939	1 Jan 1939	23	11	3	9
Watford	1 Aug 1949	28 Feb 1959	130	44	35	21
			517	207	116	165

Alexander William Alfred Stock

August 1949–February 1956, April 1956–August 1957 and March 1958–February 1959

Alec Stock was born in Peasedown St John's, near Radstock Coalfields, Bath, Somerset, on 30 March 1917 (not Surrey as incorrectly printed in the *Complete Record of Leyton Orient*, Breedon Books, October 1990).

The 5ft 10in and 10st 10lb forward first attended a rugby playing school in Somerset, but he moved after the general strike of 1926 to Dartford in Kent where his father worked down the mines. Young Alec played football for Wilmington Village FC and then Redhill FC, working as a trainee bank clerk, a job he hated.

After being spotted by Jimmy Seed, Stock played a handful of games for Tottenham Hotpsur as an amateur, and he turned professional in 1936 with Charlton Athletic where his father was the assistant groundsman. However, it was with Queen's Park Rangers that he made his League debut, making 26 appearances in 1938–39, scoring three goals. During World War Two he guested for Bristol City with four appearances, QPR with 21 appearances and 10 goals and Crystal Palace with one appearance and one goal. He also made 18 wartime appearances for the O's in 1945–46.

During the hostilities he attained the rank of Major in the Royal Armoured Corps, but he injured his back when a bazooka blew up in the tank he was commanding in the Battle of Caen. He received an injury and several pieces of shrapnel were left in his body, which lead to his ill-health in later life. After the war, he moved to Wales to convalesce, and he was put in the care of Marjorie, whom he married in 1943.

In July 1946 he was appointed player-manager with Southern League outfit Yeovil Town and was in charge during their shock 2–1 third-round FA Cup victory over First Division Sunderland at Huish Park in 1949, which catapulted him into the limelight. In the fifth round Yeovil were knocked out of the FA Cup 8–0 by Manchester United at Old Trafford, before a huge crowd of 81,565. It was within a matter of days that Gateshead had come in with an offer for him to manage them.

However, in August 1949 chairman Harry Zussman offered Stock the manager's job but that was quite a tale in itself. When Zussman threw a party at the Savoy Hotel in London to celebrate him buying the club, leading to his election as chairman, he shocked the merry-making assembly by announcing that the reigning manager Neil McBain would be leaving the club to coach in Argentina.

Within minutes a journalist whispered in Zussman's ear that he knew of a young, keen and apparently very capable player-manager by the name of Stock at Southern League giantkillers Yeovil, who had appeared for the O's in the war years. Straightaway Zussman's sharp brain started ticking, and he got in touch with Yeovil and Stock and asked to meet with him at Brisbane Road, and two days later the meeting changed the course of the club's history.

Zussman informed the author just before his death in July 1981 'I liked the look of Alec, he seemed extremely interested in the huge challenge at Orient, and I appointed him, being the youngest manager in the Football League at that time, aged 32. It was that simple and that is how I got Alec Stock to join us.'

Under Stock the team gradually improved. They reached the sixth round of the FA Cup, unluckily losing to Port Vale, one of the biggest disappointments during Stock's time in football, came in runners-up in the League in 1954–55 (only one team were promoted in those days), and won the Third Division South Championship in May 1956. It was during their great run in February 1956 that Stock declined an offer to manage Middlesbrough at £50 per week, but just a few days later, with the O's on top of the table, he decided to join Arsenal as assistant to their manager Tom Whittaker.

Stock stayed just 53 days at Highbury and returned home to Orient saying 'Hard as I tried, I could never stop thinking about Orient. My mind said Arsenal, but my heart said Orient. I realised that friendship to me is more important, much more valuable than all the progress and prestige I might have had at Highbury.'

The Gunners promised him much, and perhaps he misjudged the strength of his position. At one significant moment it was reported that he had requested one of the younger players (Danny Clapton) to go over to two of the senior players (goalie Jack Kelsey and skipper Dennis Evans) with an ashtray and tell them to stub out their cigarettes. The two players just tapped their ash into the ashtray and carried on smoking.

It was an unhappy interlude for Stock, and he was never given any backing by manager Whittaker or the board of directors, and he resigned on principle. In August 1957 Stock was on the move again, a £5,000 offer took him to AS Roma in Italy, but after eight months he was back with the O's again for a third spell during March 1958, during which time Les Gore once again took charge as manager.

In August 1959 he managed QPR, winning the League Cup while still a Third Division club, followed by two successive promotions to take Rangers to the top flight for the first time in their 51 years as a member of the Football League. Stock did not always get on well with directors at the clubs he served, and he once said 'They aren't always the sharpest tools in the box, or even pleasant individuals.'

At one of Queen's Park Rangers' games, they were 2–0 down at half-time, and in the tunnel he was abused by a director, but instead of going into the dressing room for his half-time talk he thought to himself 'I don't sodding need this' and walked out of the ground and went into a cinema. When he got back to the game it had finished, and he discovered Rangers had won 3–2, and on meeting the same director he was now singing his praises.

In December 1968 Stock was boss at Luton Town, guiding them to promotion from the Third Division as runners-up to the O's in May 1970. In April 1972 he resigned, claiming that the journey from his Epsom home was taking its toll on him.

Two months later he was the new boss at Fulham, and in May 1975, with Bobby Moore as his captain, he took Fulham to their only FA Cup Final appearance, losing 2–0 to West Ham United. He left Craven Cottage in December 1976. In April 1977 he was appointed a director at QPR and even acted as a caretaker manager in 1978.

The Rangers chairman Jim Gregory slowly demoted Stock and replaced him with Tommy Docherty, which lasted just 28 days, and they were finally relegated from the First Division on just 18 points. Stock felt that he was treated as though he had pinched the petty cash. In January 1979 he became the oldest manager in the League with his appointment at AFC Bournemouth, a position he held until October 1981 when he became general manager and later a director until his retirement in 1986.

In January 1999 he was seen by viewers on *Match of the Day* when interviewed during another of Yeovil's FA Cup giantkilling acts. In July 1999 Fulham sent their first team to play Yeovil for Stock's testimonial match.

The final word on Stock goes to Harry Zussman. 'Alec Stock (with the help of Les Gore) did it all to take Orient to promotion in May 1956, and every credit belongs to them both. Stock knew when he joined he could not afford to make mistakes. The history books written on the club by the authors have shown that he made very few.'

Alec Stock was no doubt one of the O's greatest ever managers, who took the team to their very first promotion season as Champions of Division Three South in 1955–56. Sadly, he died in a nursing home at Wimborne, Dorset, on 16 April 2001, aged 84, after battling with cancer for nearly three years. Up to his death his memory was always with him, and he recalled to former O's players who visited him his very fond years with the club.

The Stock years are bright pages in the O's history and in the history of all the clubs he has served and he was instrumental in restoring the club's and supporters' pride. Alec Stock's managerial career (League and FA Cup) with other clubs:

Team	*From*	*To*	*Games*	*Won*	*Drawn*	*Lost*
QPR	1 Aug 1959	31 May 1968	428	202	101	125
Luton T	1 Dec 1968	28 Apr 1972	156	66	52	38
Fulham	21 Jun 1972	16 Dec 1976	200	68	66	66
Bournemouth	25 Jan 1979	1 Dec 1980	92	28	29	35
			876	364	248	264

Frederick Leslie Gore

February–April 1956, August 1957–March 1958, February 1959–May 1961, September–November 1963 and December 1965–May 1966

Les Gore proved to be another of the loyal servants with the club, spending over 16 years as trainer, caretaker manager and as manager in his own right between 1951 and 1966.

He was assistant trainer in 1951–54, head trainer in 1954 to 5 March 1959, caretaker manager in October 1955, caretaker manager in February 1956 to April 1956, caretaker manager in August 1957 to March 1958, manager from 5 March 1959 to May 1961, assistant manager in May 1961 to May 1966, caretaker manager in September 1963 to November 1963, caretaker manager in December 1964 to 14 January 1965 and caretaker manager in December 1965 until being dismissed in November 1967 for economic reasons. He also appeared for the O's as a player in the war years.

Those years as manager seem to have been overlooked by the various football journals. Even the well-respected *Rothmans Football Yearbook* and the football website *www.soccerbase.com* do not record Gore's years as manager with the club in their list of O's managers since the war. (Something which has now been put right by the author after numerous letters. Gore is now listed under the O's managers section of their latest *Sky Sports Yearbook*.) The Football League managers' database on *www.soccerbase.com* still has no record of Gore as an O's manager, even after numerous letters and emails from the author.

Born on 21 January 1914, Gore started his playing career with works side Morris Metalworks before joining Fulham in June 1933, but his League debut came with

Stockport County against Port Vale in September 1936. He made seven League appearances with one goal.

The 5ft 8in and 10st 11lb winger went on to play for Carlisle United in September 1937, and made three League appearances, and Bradford City on 18 February 1938, making 33 League appearances and scoring eight goals.

Les Gore first joined the O's as a player on 8 May 1939 and scored on his debut, playing at outside-right versus Ipswich Town on 26 August 1939. He appeared in all three Football League matches of the aborted 1939–40 season, when all playing records were expunged, and in the two FA Cup legs against Newport (Isle of Wight) in November 1945, scoring in the home leg. He also appeared in 25 World War Two League games for the O's, scoring five goals. In 1946 he joined Southern League side Yeovil Town in 1946 and moved on to Gravesend & Northfleet in 1948 before rejoining the O's as assistant coach in 1951.

It was Gore who made the inspired signing of the legendary Tommy Johnston in 1956, while Alec Stock was away as assistant manager with Arsenal. Managers came and went, and it was the loyal Gore who invariably took over as caretaker. In the period between 1959 and 1961 he was manager, and with Eddie Baily as his assistant the O's played some eye-catching football. Eventually, with the club going through another financial crisis, it brought Gore's departure in November 1967. He joined Charlton Athletic as chief scout and once again became the perennial caretaker manager at times of crisis. After he retired with Charlton Athletic in November 1984, he continued to scout for them on a part-time basis and in the late 1980s was scouting for Millwall. He died on Tuesday 22 January 1991, the day after his 77th birthday, in Buckhurst Hill, Essex, and there should always be a permanent and prominent place in the history of Leyton Orient Football Club for Les Gore, the 'Gentleman and Ambassador of Football'.

John Joseph Carey

August 1961–August 1963

Johnny Carey will always be fondly remembered as the man who led the O's for the first and only time into the old First Division in 1961–62 as runners-up to Liverpool after a dramatic 2–0 win over Bury on the last day of the season in April 1962 at Brisbane Road.

Born in Westland near Dublin, Ireland, on 23 February 1919, Carey was a 5ft 11in and 12st 5lb full-back who joined Manchester United from Dublin side St James' Gate FC in November 1936, at the age of 17 years, for a fee of £250, and had the distinction of representing Eire before he established himself in United's first 11.

Carey informed the author just before his death about his early days at Old Trafford: 'My arrival at Manchester was an amazing one. After I alighted from the train at Manchester Station with my father from Dublin, I spotted a poster announcing "United's big signing" I rushed over to buy the newspaper, opened it excitedly, only to read the big signing was in fact Ernie Shepherd from Blackburn Rovers. In very small type at the end of the story was the bare announcement that United had also signed one J. Carey, a Dublin junior.'

Well, Carey went on to to become one of United's greatest players. In the 17 years he spent at Old Trafford he won every honour in the game, and after he retired from playing in 1953, while still on top, he had amassed 344 senior appearances, scoring 18 goals, appearing in every position other than number 11 (outside-left). He even appeared as an emergency goalkeeper at Sunderland in a Division One fixture during February 1953, and the match ended 2–2. Carey won 36 international caps (seven for Northern Ireland and 29 for the Republic of Ireland). He represented both Irish teams within a matter of three days during September 1946 and was captain when Eire beat England 2–0 in 1949.

He became coach at United before accepting the manager's job with Blackburn Rovers in August 1953. Carey spent five years at Ewood Park, taking them into Division One as runners-up in 1958. It was Carey that brought the O's legendary centre-forward Tommy Johnston to Blackburn for £15,000 in March 1958.

In October 1958 he took over as manager of Everton and took them, in 1961, to their highest position – fifth in Division One. However, he was surprisingly sacked in April 1961 in a taxi by their chairman John Moores in London following a Football League meeting.

He was appointed as the O's manager in August 1961, and it was a shrewd and bold appointment by chairman Harry Zussman to take on such a high-profile manager from the top flight.

It was Carey, along with his coaching staff of Les Gore and Eddie Baily, who steered the side into the old Division One for the first and only time in their history. Despite the O's lack of success, Carey was highly regarded, and although it was no surprise when he left it was a surprise that he accepted the position as manager with Second Division Nottingham Forest on 26 July 1963. He also acted as team manager of the Republic of Ireland national side in 1963–64.

The O's director Leslie Grade approached Carey after yet another defeat in the top flight, with the O's now bottom of the First Division, and said 'John, how much would it take to keep the O's in the First Division', Carey replied 'Mr Grade, may I be honest with you, please don't waste your money'. He was gone six months later, with the O's back in Division Two.

Carey informed the author 'Forest made me an offer I could not refuse, but my days at Orient were among my happiest in football, working with such wonderful men as Harry Zussman, Les Gore and Eddie Bailey.'

He took Forest to Division One as runners-up in 1967 but was dismissed in December 1968. He returned to Blackburn Rovers as administration manager in January 1969 and was appointed team boss in October 1970. He retired from football management following his dismissal on 8 June 1971. He scouted for Manchester United until his retirement from football during 1985. He worked for a tile company and later at the Trafford Treasury Department in Sale, Cheshire. He died in Manchester on 23 August 1995, aged 75.

Few O's managers have experienced such contrasting fortunes as Carey. Promotion one season, relegation the next, but the quiet, pipe-smoking Carey took it all in his stride.

Johnny Carey's managerial record (League and Cup) with other clubs:

Team	*From*	*To*	*Games*	*Won*	*Drawn*	*Lost*
Blackburn R	1 Jun 1953	30 Aug 1958	235	119	49	67
Everton	1 Oct 1958	1 Apr 1961	121	50	21	50
Nott'm Forest	1 Jul 1963	31 Dec 1968	241	91	63	87
Blackburn R	21 Oct 1970	–8 Jun 1971	29	5	9	15
			226	265	142	219

Benjamin Robert Vincent Fenton

November 1963–December 1964

Benny Fenton was given barely a year to prove his worth as manager before getting the sack. Born in West Ham, London, on Monday 28 October 1918, the 11st 6lb and 5ft 11in wing-half turned out for East London and West Ham schoolboys before signing a junior contract with Colchester United in 1934. A year later he followed his brother Ted to West Ham United, both playing in the first team four times together before World War Two.

He joined Millwall on a free transfer in March 1939, making 58 senior appearances with 12 goals. He toured South Africa with an FA XI, playing three matches. During the war years he guested for Cardiff City, Charlton Athletic, Manchester City, West Ham United and York City. In January 1947 he joined Charlton for £6,000 and made 286 senior appearances, netting 26 goals. In February 1955 he moved to Colchester United as player-manager, and he made 103 League appearances and scored 15 goals before deciding to hang up his boots in June 1958, but he remained manager until he was appointed as boss with the O's in November 1963. His two most notable signings were veterans Ted Phillips and Andy Nelson from Ipswich Town.

Fenton was often criticised for playing with two wingers in deep-lying roles, and at the time not everyone realised this was the way the game was going. There were a few high spots while he was in charge, like the magnificent FA Cup victory at Leicester City in January 1964. He was dismissed in December 1964 with the O's at the foot of Division Two.

After some years of scouting work, he was appointed manager at Millwall in May 1966. At the time they achieved promotion to Division Two.

Under him, the Lions were virtually unbeaten at The Den; however, they missed out on promotion to the old Division One after Birmingham City beat the O's at Brisbane Road 1–0 in 1972 to gain the second spot before a record League crowd of 33,363. In October 1974 he resigned and three years later returned to Charlton as secretary. He became assistant manager in March 1980 and was their general manager between June 1981 and June 1982.

In hindsight it is reasonable to say that Fenton was not given enough time to see what he could achieve for the O's. Benny Fenton died in Dorset on 29 July 2000, aged 81.

Benny Fenton's managerial record (League and Cup) with other clubs:

Team	*From*	*To*	*Games*	*Won*	*Drawn*	*Lost*
Colch'r Utd	1 Feb 1955	31 Oct 1963	422	163	107	152
Millwall	1 May 1966	3Oct 1974	350	137	101	112
			772	300	208	264

David James Sexton

January 1965–December 1965

David Sexton is yet another former O's player who became manager. Born in Islington, London, on 6 April 1930, after a long-playing career that lasted over nine years, he moved into coaching with Chelsea in February 1962 under flamboyant manager Tommy Docherty. He resigned, and on 14 January 1965 he took on the challenge as manager with the O's.

Sexton was a forward of some repute. His career started in 1949 with Newmarket Town, he then played for Chelmsford City, Luton Town and West Ham United. He joined the O's in June 1956 from the Hammers for £2,000 and scored on his debut with a header against Nottingham Forest in their return to the Second Division.

He moved to Brighton & Hove Albion in October 1957 for a £3,000 fee. He then played for Crystal Palace, before 31-year-old Sexton was forced to retire through injury in January 1962. He made a total of 181 League appearances, scoring 67 goals, between 1951 and 1962.

He made a controversial and unpopular start with the O's supporters in the 1965–66 season by releasing many of the former stalwarts, bringing in a number of youngsters and players from lower Divisions to cut the wage bill.

After a disastrous start to the new season and a lack of funds for new players, he resigned in December 1965. The directors tried to persuade him to change his mind but failed. (Maybe after a successful period as head coach at Stamford Bridge, he was not quite ready for the responsibilities of management.) Les Gore had the unenviable task of trying to keep the O's in Division Two, but it was all to no avail as they were relegated, bottom of the table, on 23 points and just five wins all season.

However, in later years Sexton had a long and distinguished career holding posts with some big clubs. He guided Chelsea to victory in the 1970 FA Cup Final and was the man in charge when the O's defeated his Chelsea star-studded team 3–2 in the FA Cup during February 1972. He took Queen's Park Rangers to within a whisker of the League Championship in 1975–76. At Manchester United, he was their fourth manager within a period of eight years and took United into another Cup Final, losing to Arsenal in 1979, and the following season they were runners-up to Liverpool.

He was sacked in April 1981, another victim of United's search for major honours during the era, even though his side won their last seven League games. He was appointed boss at Coventry City in May 1981, and his first match in charge was a satisfactory 2–1 win over Manchester United. He held the job for two years. He was the FA National School of Excellence technical director in Lilleshall between August 1984 and July 1989. After a spell as National coach to the Saudi Arabian squad, he moved back to his love of coaching with Aston Villa in July 1992. Two years later he was assistant manager with Queen's Park Rangers.

During his sojourn on the League circuit he also held various positions with the England National team, including manager of the England Under-21 side from August 1977–January 1978 and again between November 1982 and August 1989, England B team manager from 1980–1990 and Under-21 manager again from February 1994–2001. He also took over as England's caretaker manager after Terry Venables left the job and was senior advisor under Glenn Hoddle. In February 2001, a few months before his 71st birthday, he was appointed chief scout to the new England boss Sven-Goran Eriksson.

It was quite a career for the man from Islington whose first few months of his managerial career were at muddy old Brisbane Road. Former O's and Chelsea player Colin Shaw, who was with Sexton at Stamford Bridge and at Brisbane Road and is now living and working in Johannesburg, South Africa, as an MD of a Sports company, explained 'Dave Sexton was a brilliant coach at Stamford Bridge, where the pitch was true and played perfectly, but when we both moved to Brisbane Road the pitch was more like a bog, which made it impossible to play any type of good football, which frustrated the players and in particular Sexton. No wonder he decided to call it a day and move to Fulham as coach.'

Dave Sexton's managerial record (League and Cup) with other clubs:

Team	*From*	*To*	*Games*	*Won*	*Drawn*	*Lost*
Chelsea	1 Oct 1967	3 Oct 1974	323	135	97	91
QPR	16 Oct 1974	9 Jul 1977	130	57	32	41
Manch'er Utd	14 Jul 1977	1 Apr 1981	191	75	64	52
Coventry C	31 May 1981	31 May 1983	88	8	21	39
			732	295	214	223

Richard Douglas Graham

August 1966–February 1968

Dick Graham was born in Corby, Northamptonshire, on 6 May 1922, (the younger brother of former O's player Jimmy Graham). Dick, who as a 14-year-old played for Corby Town's first team, was a tall and commanding figure. He was later a goalkeeper with Northampton Town in 1937 and then with Leicester City before joining Crystal Palace in December 1945. During the war years he guested for Bristol City, Crewe Alexandra, Norwich City and Notts County.

He was in goal when Palace lost 10–2 at Reading in September 1946 but remained their first-team choice until his retirement due to a serious back injury in May 1951, after making 155 League appearances for the Eagles. He left football for a while and ran a Croydon public house and worked as a part-time sports reporter.

He was appointed coach to the Surrey Football Association, and in November 1956 he was trainer at West Bromwich Albion before being appointed assistant manager to Arthur Rowe (later a scout and consultant with the O's in the early 1970s) at Palace before becoming manager in March 1963. He stayed for three years before dressing room and supporter unrest over his selection policy led to his dismissal in January 1966, but he did take Palace to promotion to Division Three in 1964 as runners-up on goal average to Coventry City.

In January 1966 he became a consultant with Charlton Athletic and was appointed the O's manager in June 1966 after the club had been relegated down to the Third Division. The day he accepted Orient's offer, he received a better offer from a Second Division club. But he wasn't prepared to go back on his word after settling in, and he soon realised the enormity of his task. Also, at the start of the season, an old back injury kept him in hospital for the first few months of his reign, yet he still picked the team. It was Graham that swapped Harry Gregory for veterans Cliff Holton and John Snedden from Charlton in 1966.

Graham was manager at the time of the O's financial crisis of 1966 and played his part in saving the club from financial ruin. He got frustrated with the club and eventually resigned because of the lack of funds for new players in February 1968. In an interview with the *London Evening Standard* in September 1970, the story went, 'Now manager with Colchester United, Graham said that it took him nearly two years to get Orient back on track, during which time his health deteriorated. But now he confesses his regret at his decision to quit in 1968.

"I sweated my guts out, and it would have been nice to stay and get my just rewards. I'm the kind of bloke who takes things to heart, and I paid for it at Orient. After our FA Cup game at Birmingham City in 1968, I was down to nine fit professionals, and I set up a transfer deal which would have enabled us to buy two more players for a down payment of only £1,500. I was surprised when the board refused me the money because the club had made £2,000 from the Birmingham match. Consequently, I was forced to play two inexperienced youngsters in the next game against Watford, and both of them were injured. It played on my conscience, and on the Monday I handed in my resignation and advised the O's board to appoint a player-manager.

"I now wish I had stuck it out, I had to tread on a lot of peoples' toes to get the club out of its crisis, perhaps they now realise I'm not as bad as I seemed."

'When you look at the O's team that won promotion in 1970, many of that squad were signed by Graham.

"I signed Ray Goddard from Fulham, and I was criticised by some members of the Orient staff for that, I moved Dennis Rofe to full-back, he was playing at inside-forward, not that I thought he would make it, but he was a great helper to me with my general duties, and I was determined to make something of him.

"I got Fairbrother and Taylor straight from school, I remember I spent four hours with Taylor's parents, trying to convince them that Orient were a better club for the lad than West Ham United.

"I signed Terry Mancini after he returned from playing in South Africa for just £500, and I got Dave Harper for just £2,500. And finally I brought in Vic Halom from Charlton Athletic for £3,000, and they sold him for £30,000, quite a profit. Well the O's board of directors were so used to me pulling off miracles that they assumed I could do it without new players."

'This time he'd had enough and resigned.'

He joined Walsall as manager between March and May 1968 but left and took over as manager of Colchester United on 11 July 1968. He stayed for four years to became one of their most popular managers at Layer Road and was vital in their historic FA Cup run and victory over high-flying Leeds United in February 1971, and under his leadership they won the Watney Cup, also in 1971 (it was his son-in-law, Phil Bloss, who converted the penalty in a shoot-out to win the Trophy over West Bromwich Albion at the Hawthorns).

Graham resigned in September 1972 after firing a broadside at grumbling shareholders. The following month he was chief scout with Cambridge United and was appointed manager with non-League Wimbledon in July 1973 but resigned in March 1974, claiming interference in player selection from directors. He managed the Willis Faber Sports Centre in Ipswich between 1974 and 1987 and later managed the Maidstone Bowling Club.

Dick Graham was often dubbed as a 'sergeant-major' type of manager due to his tough but revolutionary training methods, which he always refuted. He did not fare badly considering the club's financial plight. Credit should go to him for sowing the seeds that bore fruit under the reign of Jimmy Bloomfield.

Dick Graham's managerial record (League and Cup) with other clubs:

Team	*From*	*To*	*Games*	*Won*	*Drawn*	*Lost*
Crystal Palace	1 Mar 1963	1 Jan 1966	131	59	38	34
Walsall	1 Mar 1968	1 May 1968	13	5	4	4
Colch'er Utd	1 Jul 1968	8 Aug 1972	189	78	48	63
			333	142	90	101

James Henry Bloomfield

March 1968–May 1971 and September 1977–August 1981

It was Dick Graham who suggested to the O's board that they appoint a player-manager in order to save some money, and that is exactly what they did with the appointment of Jimmy Bloomfield, signed from Plymouth Argyle on 8 March 1968.

He was born in North Kensington, London, on Thursday 15 February 1934, and the 5ft 9in midfield player started his career with Hayes before joining Brentford in October 1952, making 42 League appearances and scoring five goals.

He moved to Arsenal in July 1954 for £8,000 and stayed at Highbury for six years, maturing into a brilliant midfield player. He made 210 League appearances with 54 goals. He moved to Birmingham City in November 1960 for £30,000, and he later had spells with Brentford and Plymouth Argyle before being appointed as the O's player-manager on 8 March 1968. He made a total of 47(2) senior appearances with four goals before retiring to concentrate on his managerial duties in May 1969.

His playing career spanned some 17 years, and he made a career total of 494 League appearances, scoring 93 goals. Within two years of being in charge at Orient, he remarkably took the club to a Third Division Championship. It was no surprise that he would eventually end up in the old First Division. He had some

Manager Jimmy Bloomfield celebrates the club's centenary in 1981.

nice offers over the years, but the best would have been an offer from the Ethnikos club in Greece, who offered 36-year-old Bloomfield a £20,000-a-year deal to get the best young manager in the country; he decided to stay in England.

On the O's Third Division Championship-winning season of 1969–70, he once remarked 'The rewarding thing about the way we won the title was the standard of football we achieved. There was no brute force, just skilful football.' He joined Leicester City on 23 June 1971, but not before they had to pay £5,000 in compensation. The O's chairman Arthur Page was away on holiday when City approached them and the deal was handled by director Neville Ovenden, who accepted City's compensation offer. When Page returned he was so upset with the compensation package that Ovenden resigned from the O's board, although he returned in later years to run the club.

At Filbert Street, Bloomfield was reported to be the highest paid manager in the League and led Leicester to some successful seasons before he resigned on 23 May 1977. He became a marketing consultant for Admiral, the Leicester-based sportswear firm. Bloomfield was not in the soccer wilderness for long, there was talk of him taking over the England manager's job, but it was the O's chairman Brian Winston who brought him back to Brisbane Road on 12 September 1977. Winston phoned Bloomfield to ask if he wanted his old job back. He discussed the offer with his family and they were in total agreement that he should take it. He told the press 'I enjoy working with Brian Winston because he genuinely loves the club, he stood on the terracing as a boy and is consumed with ambition for Orient.'

His biggest achievement was to take the O's to the semi-final of the FA Cup, although for long periods he was in and out of hospital, and it was Peter Angell who took charge of the team. When the team were celebrating in the dressing room after the 2–1 win at Chelsea, Brian Winston slipped away to phone Bloomfield with the news, who was in a London hospital having tests, and what a tonic it was for him.

It was Bloomfield who paid out the club's largest-ever transfer fee at that time of £150,000 for former England international winger Peter Taylor from Spurs, as well as the £90,000 paid to Nottingham Forest for Stanley Bowles. After the transfer of John Chiedozie to Notts County for a record £600,000, Bloomfield had a conflict of opinion over the deal with chairman Winston and resigned as manager in May 1981. He was appointed a part-time scout with Luton Town in October 1981.

After a long battle against cancer, Jimmy Bloomfield died at his North Chingford home on 3 April 1983, aged 49.

Jimmy Bloomfield's managerial record (League and Cup) with Leicester City:

Team	*From*	*To*	*Games*	*Won*	*Drawn*	*Lost*
Leicester C	23 Jun 1971	23 May 1977	263	74	99	90

George William Petchey

July 1971–August 1977

George Petchey spent his entire playing and most of his managerial career with London teams. Born in Whitechapel, London, on Wednesday 24 June 1931, he joined West Ham United in August 1948, making just two appearances before moving to QPR during July 1953. It was with Rangers that Petchey made his name as a tough tackling wing-half, making 255 senior appearances in his six years with them, scoring 22 goals. In May 1960 he joined Crystal Palace and was ever present in the side that won promotion to Division Three.

A serious eye injury forced him to retire after making 153 senior appearances, scoring 12 goals. He was appointed youth-team manager and then assistant manager. He took over as the O's boss on 12 July 1977, and during his first season at Brisbane Road the club reached the sixth round of the FA Cup. In February 1972 he won the Bells whisky manager of the month award.

Petchey adopted the 'one-touch' style of football, made famous by Arthur Rowe, at the time an O's consultant, and the O's looked to be heading to the old First Division in 1973–74, but they eventually stumbled in the second half of the season, missing out by a single point, needing victory and two points versus Aston Villa in April. The match ended 1–1 so Carlisle United were promoted instead.

Petchey guided the O's to the Final of the Anglo-Scottish Cup before losing to Nottingham Forest in the two-leg Final by 4–1, but they gained some excellent victories along the way against Norwich City, Fulham, Chelsea, Aberdeen and Partick Thistle.

Petchey's style of football was best suited to ground passing, and he was unlucky that during most of his time as manager the Brisbane Road pitch was in a very poor condition and was hardly conducive to good football. Under his reign, many fine young players came through the ranks including Laurie Cunningham, Glenn Roeder, Tony Grealish and Bobby Fisher. One of his last duties as boss was the signing of Peter Kitchen from Doncaster Rovers; however, he did not stay long enough to enjoy his great goalscoring for the O's. Chairman Brian Winston sacked him after a 4–1 home defeat by Blackpool in August 1977.

Like most O's managers, his biggest problem was to find a forward who could hit the net on a regular basis, in fact out of a total of 254 matches under his charge 89 were drawn, quite a number goalless. Just before his sacking the author remembers receiving a phone call from Petchey. He was most upset with a letter published in the *Waltham Forest Guardian* newspaper about his boring goalless draw record, so upset that he threatened to have the author banned from home matches unless a paragraph was added stating his wonderful record of blooding young players into the team.

After his departure from Brisbane Road, he did not stay away from the game too long, being appointed manager of Millwall in January 1978, a club in desperate trouble with just three Second Division wins behind them. He worked a miracle, the Lions winning their last six games to avoid the drop by a single point. That March his Lions team defeated the O's at their Den ground by 2–0 and strode off the pitch in triumph, looking, as he left the pitch, at the O's fans with a rye smile. He remained boss at Millwall until November 1980. However, with Millwall once again fighting relegation, he was appointed their general manager.

In November 1982 Petchey became involved with Brighton & Hove Albion, looking after their youth and reserve development. A year later he was promoted to chief coach, and when their boss Chris Cattlin was fired in April 1986 he took charge for the final League match of the 1985–86 season, a 2–0 defeat at Hull City on 2 May.

He was asked to take over as manager but decided to leave them soon afterwards. He scouted for both Sunderland and Watford before retiring from the game. He was tempted to return to the Goldstone at the age of 63 in January 1994, as youth development officer under manager Liam Brady. Following Brady's departure in November 1995, he was appointed assistant to new boss Jimmy Case and took temporary charge following Case's dismissal in December 1996, although no first-team matches were played.

When Steve Gritt was appointed on 12 December 1996, Petchey left, but on reaching retirement age he continued to assist Brighton by helping with the under-14 lads for free. Today Petchey lives in retirement in Brighton, following the fortunes of the clubs he served so well over the 50 years he was in the game.

George Petchey's managerial record (League and Cup) with other clubs:

Team	*From*	*To*	*Games*	*Won*	*Drawn*	*Lost*
Millwall	5 Jan 1978	30 Nov 1980	129	42	32	55
Brighton & HA	May 1986		1	0	0	1
			130	42	32	56

Paul Francis Went

September 1981–October 1981

Paul Went was born on 12 October 1949 in Bromley-by-Bow, London. He was an England Schoolboy and Youth international while with the O's. He made his League debut versus Preston North End on 4 September 1965 at the age of 15 years and 327 days – the youngest-ever player to wear an O's shirt in a League match – just seven days younger than Tommy Taylor, who made his League debut aged 15 years and 334 days.

Went turned professional in October 1966, having a long and distinguished playing career that spanned some 14 years with the O's, Charlton Athletic, Fulham, Portsmouth and back to the O's on 7 September 1978. He retired through leg and shoulder injuries, and his last game for the club was the 7–3 home defeat by Chelsea in November 1979. He made 101(2) senior appearances for the O's, scoring eight goals, and a career total of 474(6) League appearances, scoring 42 goals. He helped as coach of the O's reserve side and was appointed first-team coach on 27 July 1981 after Jimmy Bloomfield's departure. He was caretaker manager for the start of the 1981–82 season (29 August 1981 to 19 September 1981) and after a couple of good wins was appointed manager on 22 September. But after five straight defeats, the O's had sunk to the bottom of Division Two without scoring a goal. He was sacked by the O's chairman Brian Winston on Monday 12 October after a morning training session.

Went's reign as the O's manager lasted just 21 days (some records show 19 or even 20 days, but, after intensive research and after talking to the former O's chairman Brian Winston, the man to sack Went, these have proved to be incorrect). His was not the shortest managerial reign on record, that belongs to Bill Lambton who lasted just three days in 1959 at Scunthorpe United, followed by the seven days of Tim Ward with Exeter City in 1953 and Kevin Cullis with Swansea City during 1996. (Dave Bassett's reign of four days with Crystal Palace has not been included in official Football League records as he had not signed a contract.) Went's reign with the O's was two days longer than William Bulloch Wright's some 35 years earlier.

Went could hardly be judged a failure with such little time in charge. Upon leaving football, he was a publican in Essex and later ran a guesthouse in Portsmouth. Two months after his sacking Went and Winston met at his public house, the Whalebone Inn in West Riding, Essex, to talk over old times. More recently, Went was working as a field sales manager for Courage Brewery in Essex.

Paul Went's managerial record with the O's:

As caretaker manager (29 August to 19 September 1981)

Football League

29 Aug	(a)	Derby County	W	2–1
5 Aug	(h)	Grimsby Town	W	1–0
12 Aug	(a)	Blackburn Rovers	L	0–2
19 Aug	(h)	Wrexham	D	0–0

Football League Cup

1 Sep	(h)	Millwall	D	1–1
16 Sep	(a)	Millwall	L	2–3

As manager (22 September to 12 October 1981)

Football League

22 Sep	(h)	Crystal Palace	L	0–1
26 Sep	(a)	Newcastle United	L	0–1
28 Sep	(h)	Chelsea	L	0–2
3 Oct	(h)	Luton Town	L	0–3
10 Oct	(a)	Watford	L	0–3

Kenneth Knighton

October 1981–May 1983

Ken Knighton was the man appointed on 13 October 1981 to try and get the O's off the bottom of Division Two. He started with a home point over Queen's Park Rangers. Frank Clark was appointed his assistant a month later, but in the end the O's were relegated back into the old Third Division during May 1982.

Knighton was born in Mappleworth, close to Barnsley, on 20 February 1944. He attended Mexborough Secondary School and was a former apprentice colliery worker down the local mine. After representing Barnsley schoolboys, the 5ft 9in and 11st 5lb full-back started his playing career with Mexborough Rovers in the Barnsley Amateur League, and he then joined Wath Wanderers. He became an apprentice with Wolverhampton Wanderers in July 1960, turning professional a year later.

He enjoyed a long playing career with Wolverhampton Wanderers, Hull City, Oldham Athletic, Blackburn Rovers, Preston North End and Sheffield Wednesday (he was, in fact, sent off when playing for the Owls in a Division Two match versus the O's at Brisbane Road on 28 September 1974; the O's won 1–0).

He retired from playing in January 1976 after a career that spanned 16 years and 340(9) League appearances with 30 goals. In January 1976 he was appointed coach of the youth team at Hillsborough before being appointed as manager with Sunderland – Frank Clark was his assistant. The pair took Sunderland into the old Division One in 1979–80 when the Wearsiders finished runners-up to Leicester City. Yet, both men left in April 1981.

After a brief time as scout with Manchester United between April 1981 and October 1981, he was appointed as the O's boss on 13 October 1981 with them struggling at the bottom of Division Two. The following month he appointed Frank Clark as his assistant. Knighton was a strict disciplinarian and would not tolerate a lax attitude from the players, several of whom were fined. He once had a bust-up with Tommy Taylor at half-time during an FA Cup tie against Crystal Palace. Taylor left for Belgium at the end of that season, and the O's were relegated.

Several times players found themselves the target of his criticism. After one performance at Reading, Knighton declared 'If there was a way I could stop their wages, I would.' During May 1983 he was sacked and replaced by Frank Clark. He was appointed manager of Dagenham Town in May 1984, and in October 1985 he was manager with Beazer League, Midlands Division side Trowbridge Town until he left them in January 1988.

Ken Knighton's managerial record (League and Cup) with Sunderland:

Team	*From*	*To*	*Games*	*Won*	*Drawn*	*Lost*
Sunderland	7 Jun 1979	1 Apr 1981	82	33	22	27

Frank Albert Clark

May 1983–July 1991

Frank Clark was born in Rowland's Gill, Highfield, near Gateshead in Co. Durham on Thursday 9 September 1943. He started his long, distinguished footballing career with Crook Town, winning an FA Amateur Cup-winners' medal in 1961. He was playing for Crook Town while serving his apprenticeship as a laboratory technician.

The left full-back joined Newcastle United in November 1962, making his League debut at Scunthorpe United on 18 April 1964, a 2–0 defeat, and in nearly 13 years with them he went on to make 388 League and 69 Cup appearances for the Magpies. He won a Second Division Championship medal in 1965 and a UEFA Cup-

Ken Knighton shares his Manager of the Month award with the crowd.

winners' medal in 1969. In July 1975, at the age of 32, he joined Brian Clough at Second Division Nottingham Forest on a free transfer, where he made a total of 116 League and 50 Cup appearances. He won a League Championship medal and a League Cup-winners' medal in 1978, and European Cup and League Cup-winners' medals in 1979. He appeared against the O's in the two-leg Final of the Anglo-Scottish Cup, Forest winning on aggregate by 4–1.

He joined Sunderland as assistant manager to Ken Knighton and helped them to promotion to the old First Division in 1980. In April 1981 he rejoined Forest as coach before resuming his partnership with Knighton as assistant manager with the O's during November 1981. During May 1983 Clark became the O's 15th manager since World War Two. After relegation to Division Four in 1985, the O's came close to the promotion Play-offs for the following two seasons. It was during 1988–89 that the club managed a Play-off place, with excellent performances against both Scarborough and Wrexham in the Final that saw Clark become only the fourth manager in Orient's history to lead the team to promotion (Stock, Carey and Bloomfield being the other three men). In November 1986 Clark was appointed managing director of the club with a seat on the board after Brian Winston resigned. During July 1991 Clark decided to concentrate on the administrative side of the club, handing over the managerial reins to Peter Eustace, having been appointed assistant to Clark a year earlier.

After 11 years with the O's, Clark left to take over from Brian Clough as manager of Nottingham Forest. Tributes came pouring in, and chairman Tony Wood stated 'I'm sad to see Frank leave because we had such a fine working relationship. Frank was superb at his job.'

Eustace admitted that, although Clark was always fully committed to Orient, he always had a soft spot for

Forest. 'Frank had a wonderful relationship with all at the club, not having him around will be noticed for quite a while.' Eustace added 'I hope everyone realises all the hard work Frank put into the club and what a wonderful manager and administrator he was.'

There was more than a tear shed as the departing Clark packed his bags. He officially took over at Forest on 12 May 1993, winning promotion to the Premier League in 1994 at the first attempt and reaching the quarter-finals of the UEFA Cup in 1995–96. He resigned as manager of cash-strapped Forest on 19 December 1996. On 30 December 1996 he accepted the managerial job at Manchester City. His stay lasted just over a year until he was fired on 18 February 1998. He only heard of his sacking while listening to the radio on his way to the training ground.

In recent times Clark has become a commentator with Radio Five Live and a studio guest summariser for Sky Sports. In fact, he was in the studio with Barry Fry for the O's Play-off Final match against Scunthorpe United at Wembley Stadium in May 1999. Clark also works for the League Managers' Association and completed a book a couple of years ago entitled *Kicking with both feet*, which mentions his stay with the O's. He also runs a football consultancy and does some other media work.

In a recent interview Clark looked back on his career and listed the Orient promotion season of 1969 as one of his top accomplishments. 'I always look back at my time with Orient as being rather special, it was just a wonderful moment in time. Winning promotion is something I will never forget, we had a good set of players, and they deserved their success.'

Of that squad, Alan Comfort – as club chaplain – is the only one still connected with Orient. He was a key player for O's, and it was a real tragedy that he was forced out of the game due to injury.

'To be honest I built the team around him and tried to give him a bit more freedom, and that's why Kevin Hales was such a big influence.

'Kevin was a model professional, he got a small basic salary, but he was of my best-ever signings. One of the heroes that season was the young Kevin Campbell, who I got on loan from Arsenal. It was a good side, but I can't take all the credit. Brian Eastick also deserves some credit too. It was a great season, and the players were a really good bunch of lads – I still remember all that.'

Frank Clark's managerial record (League and Cup) with other clubs:

Team	*From*	*To*	*Games*	*Won*	*Drawn*	*Lost*
Nott'm Forest	12 May 1993	19 Dec 1991	178	73	58	73
Manch'er C	29 Dec 1996	17 Feb 1998	60	20	18	22
			238	93	76	95

Peter Eustace

July 1991–April 1994

Peter Eustace was born in Stocksbridge, Sheffield, Yorkshire, on Monday 31 July 1944. He was a stylish and robust 5ft 10in and 11st wing-half during his playing days. He started his playing career as a junior with Stocksbridge Park Steelworks FC before joining Sheffield Wednesday as a 15-year-old in 1959, turning professional in June 1962 and making his League debut two months later. His two spells with the Owls spanned 12 years and 213 days. He played 268(12) senior matches, scoring 26 goals.

Ron Greenwood, at West Ham United, signed him in 1969 for £90,000 – a record fee for the Hammers in those days. He played 49 senior matches for the Hammers between January 1969 and February 1972, scoring six goals. After a long loan spell with Rotherham United in March 1972, he rejoined the Hillsborough club in August 1972 for £30,000. In July 1975 he played for Peterborough United before retiring in April 1976 and made a total of 327(13) League appearances with 36 goals in a playing career that spanned some 17 years.

In 1983 Eustace was appointed coach with Sunderland under their manager Ken Knighton and his assistant Frank Clark (both later to become managers with the O's). During 1984 he rejoined his beloved Sheffield Wednesday as assistant to Howard Wilkinson in July 1983. Eustace was given the chance to manage the club after Wilkinson left to become manager with Leeds United in October 1988. It was a surprising appointment as rumours persisted of the differences between him and a number of first-team players. His record with the Hillsborough club proved to be a disaster, Wednesday winning just two League games from 19 matches. They were also dumped out of both the Football League Cup and FA Cup by lower Division teams.

Eustace was fired as manager on 14 February 1989, ending one of the shortest managerial reins at Hillsborough. After a short spell as reserve-team coach with Charlton Athletic between October 1989 and June 1990, he was appointed as assistant to Frank Clark with Orient, taking over from Brian Eastick in July 1990. During July 1991 he took full control of the team, with Clark taking over the administrative side of the club as managing director.

His first season in charge during 1991–92 saw some success, with the O's knocking out First Division Oldham Athletic in the FA Cup. They stayed as promotion contenders until slipping up towards the end of the season. The following season saw the O's storm to the top of Division Two on 17 October 1972 after a Ricky Otto goal sealed a 1–0 win over Bournemouth; however, with poor away form they dropped down the table.

It was the club's failure to gain promotion that

resulted in Eustace being sacked in April 1994, after yet another away defeat, this time at Port Vale. In 1996 Eustace and his wife Wendy were owners of a 16th-century inn called The Cheshire Cheese in Bamford, just outside the Peak District village of Hope.

With Football still in his blood, he maintained contact with Sheffield Wednesday as a part-time scout. In 2000 he joined West Ham United as a scout and was watching about five matches each week and travelled around the world looking for good young players for the Hammers, including Belgium, France, Ireland and even South Africa.

Peter Eustace's managerial record (League and Cup) with Sheffield Wednesday:

Team	*From*	*To*	*Games*	*Won*	*Drawn*	*Lost*
Sheffield W	28 Oct 1988	14 Feb 1989	17	2	7	8

John Edmund Sitton and Christopher Robert Turner

April 1994–April 1995

John Sitton, as youth-team coach, and Chris Turner, as assistant manager to Peter Eustace, were asked to take over the managerial affairs of the club in what was described by the club as joint managers after the departure of Peter Eustace.

John Sitton was born in Hackney, London, on 21 October 1959, and the 5ft 11in and 12st 4lb defender started his career as an apprentice with Chelsea in October 1977. He went on to play for Millwall, Gillingham, and joined the O's in July 1985. He was a member of the O's team that won promotion via a two-leg Play-off against Wrexham in June 1989, and he made a total of 202(6) senior appearances, scoring six goals. He was released in May 1991, and after a short spell with Slough Town he rejoined the O's to work as a coach in the School of Excellence. Sitton made a career total of 358(15) League appearances with 13 goals.

Turner was born in Sheffield on 15 September 1958. The goalkeeper had a long and distinguished career that spanned some 15 years, making 490 League appearances. The 'keeper started his playing career with Sheffield Wednesday and made his League debut at the age of 17 during the 1976–77 season. He later played for Lincoln City (loan), Sunderland, Manchester United and Sheffield Wednesday. He joined the O's in September 1991, first on loan, then as part of the deal that took Chris Bart-Williams to Hillsborough. His final match for the O's was at the age of 36 against Hull City on 11 March 1995.

In 1992 he was appointed assistant manager to Peter Eustace, and in April 1994 he was appointed, with Sitton, as joint manager, after Eustace was sacked. What a disaster their appointments turned out to be. Although with the many financial restrictions placed upon them, is it not surprising that their managerial record looks so disastrous.

They first took control as caretaker managers of the team for the match at Huddersfield Town on 9 April 1994. The O's managed to finish in 19th position. The 1994–95 season saw the duo officially being appointed as joint managers, but it proved to be one of the worst seasons in the club's history, finishing bottom of Division Two with just six wins throughout the whole season. However, it should be stated that the club was close to liquidation, unable to pay players' wages and banned from signing any new players by the Players Football Association (PFA), so it was not surprising that the O's were in the position they were in, and one wonders if anyone could have saved the O's from the drop in such terrible circumstances.

One of the most bizarre decisions made by Sitton was the sacking of crowd favourite Terry Howard during a half-time break in a match against Blackpool on 7 February 1995, after he had made 376(6) senior appearances for the O's (chronicled in depth in the chapter on the club's history in this book).

Soon after his sacking the club was taken over by Barry Hearn. After yet another defeat on 17 April 1995, at the hands of Brentford, both Sitton and Turner were summoned by Barry Hearn to his office and fired, to the relief of all the O's fans. Glenn Cockerill and Tom Loizou took over the team for the visit to Bristol Rovers on 22 April 1995. Cockerill declined the job on a permanent basis, wanting to continue with his playing career, and soon afterwards Pat Holland was appointed as the new O's manager.

John Sitton worked as a part-time PE teacher, FA coach and did some radio work. He was later manager with non-League outfit Hillingdon Borough. He was appointed assistant manager on 14 December 2000 to his brother-in-law and former O's director at the School of Excellence Tom Loizou at Enfield. When Loizou left Enfield to join Leyton FC in July 2002, Sitton was also on his way to Lea Bridge Road but left with Loizou when he resigned in 2002. It was reported he was working as a London taxi driver in 2003 and is also often seen at Brisbane Road reporting on the O's matches. He was appointed as head coach at Ryman League Premier Division Leyton FC in June 2006.

Chris Turner was youth coach with Leicester City. He later had three successful seasons as youth coach with Wolverhampton Wanderers. On 24 February 1999 40-year-old Turner was appointed manager of Third Division Hartlepool United, signing a long-term contract, and stayed three years (he went on to bigger things with Sheffield Wednesday in November 2002 and Stockport County in December 2004).

His side managed to escape the big drop into the Nationwide Conference, and Hartlepool came strong two years later. Turner informed a press conference of the following, 'I have learnt from my experience at Orient, where things were very difficult as the club had big financial problems and went into receivership (until rescued by Barry Hearn). It was a hard time for John Sitton and myself as joint caretaker managers, but it will stand me in good stead with Hartlepool.' They got to fourth position in Division Three during the 2000–01 season, their highest in many years, but were beaten in the Play-off semi-final by Blackpool, missing out on a chance to face the O's in the Final. Instead, Turner (with Ray Wilkins) was a guest studio commentator for the Third Division Play-off Final.

After a hat-trick of near misses in the Play-offs, with some of the most successful seasons seen at Victoria Park during the past three and half years, Turner left Hartlepool to become manager of struggling First Division side Sheffield Wednesday, a few weeks later taking another former 'Oriental' Colin West as his assistant from Hartlepool.

Turner's record with Hartlepool United shows he can turn around a side staring relegation in the face and remould them into promotion contenders, and that is exactly what the Wednesday faithful were banking on. He signed the O's club captain Dean Smith to steady the defence, but Wednesday were eventually relegated to the Second Division, but went out with a bang, scoring seven goals at Burnley. They were promoted in 2004–05.

Under Turner the Owls struggled to mount any promotion challenge, and, after a home defeat by Bournemouth on 18 September 2004, 46-year-old Turner and his assistant Colin West were both fired after 22 months in charge. Turner said 'Two weeks ago the fans were ringing in to say they hadn't seen such good football from the team for a long time – and two weeks later I'm fired. That's football.'

It wasn't long before Turner was back in the hot seat, this time being appointed manager of struggling Stockport County on 19 December 2004.

Chris Turner's managerial record (League and Cups) with other clubs:

Team	*From*	*To*	*Games*	*Won*	*Drawn*	*Lost*
Hartlep'l Utd	24 Feb 1999	7 Nov 2002	194	82	48	64
Sheffield W	8 Nov 2003	19 Sep 2004	96	29	31	36
Stockport Co	19 Dec 2004	26 Dec 2005	50	7	15	28

Patrick George Holland

April 1995–October 1996

Pat Holland was born in Poplar, London, on Wednesday 13 September 1950. The 5ft 10in and 11st 7lb midfielder started his football career with West Ham United in April 1969, making his League debut versus Arsenal on 21 April 1961. 'Patsy' Holland, one of the unsung heroes at Upton Park, made 271(25) senior appearances for the Hammers, scoring 32 goals (he also played 10 League games while on loan with AFC Bournemouth in March 1971).

He was a member of the Hammers' successful 1975 FA Cup-winning team that defeated Fulham 2–0. The following season he featured in their European Cup Winning side that was beaten by Anderlecht in Brussels. He also helped them to the Second Division Championship in 1981.

His last game for the Hammers was at Notts County on 17 January 1981. He collided with County 'keeper Raddy Avronovic in the course of scoring a Hammers goal and as a result suffered a serious knee injury that ended his playing career. He remained at Upton Park, assisting in coaching their youth teams, and obtained an FA coaching badge.

In 1993 he joined the O's as a player, but due to his on-going knee troubles he never played and retired, although he was a non-playing substitute in a FA Cup tie at Wimbledon on 1 November 1983. Between December 1985 and December 1988 he was with the O's in a coaching capacity until his appointment as youth-team coach with Tottenham Hotspur. In 1992 he became their youth-team manager and in 1994, reserve-team manager. On 27 April 1995 he was unveiled by Barry Hearn as the new manager. Hearn stated that 'This kid's got the hunger and this club could become a real "Busby Babe" scenario.' Holland signed a three-year contract and straight away installed his friend and former 'Oriental' Tommy Cunningham as his assistant.

Holland took charge after the club had already been relegated. In his first full season in charge he took the team to third in the table during September 1995, and they gained their first away win in nearly two years. However, it was all downhill from there on, and the O's finished in lowly 21st spot, their lowest ever League position.

During the following October the O's were at another low ebb in their history with just one win from nine matches, and after a 3–0 defeat at Cardiff Holland received a call from chairman Hearn on Sunday 27 October 1996. This was followed by a meeting the next day where he was told to clear out his desk. It was not a great shock to the fans as his position had become more and more vulnerable with chants from the fans of 'Holland OUT'. Tommy Cunningham took charge of the team for the next two home matches versus Scarborough (29 October) and Torquay (2 November), the latter a 1–0 win with a goal from on-loan Carl Griffiths, but was reluctant to apply for the managerial position.

After a short coaching spell with Queen's Park Rangers, Holland was appointed assistant manager to Billy Bonds at Millwall for the start of the 1997–98 season. Holland left the Lions in November 1997 and rejoined the coaching staff at White Hart Lane in December 1997. He was their FA Premier Academy Under-19 coach but in May 2006 he left them. He also owned a wine bar named Holland's opposite Shenfield Station in Essex.

Thomas Frederick Taylor

November 1996–October 2001

The story of Tommy Taylor makes very interesting reading. Having joined the O's as a 10-year-old, he became the second youngest player to wear the club's colours in a first-team match, making his League debut in August 1967 at the age of 15 years and 334 days, just seven days older than Paul Went (a former O's manager, be it for just a month). At the age of 46 Taylor was to become the O's 26th manager since Football League entry back in 1905 when appointed on 7 November 1996.

Taylor has taken the O's close to promotion twice via the Play-offs, in 1999 and 2001, and he has proved to a be a loyal servant to the club through thick and thin, and he has been one manager (unlike many others over the years) who can certainly say that he has been well supported by the chairman of the club. Taylor informed the press after the Play-off Final match with Blackpool in Wales that 'I believe I can get the club into the First Division before my contract expires in three-years' time. It killed me when we first lost in the Play-off Final [1–0 to Scunthorpe in May 1999], but at least I knew what to expect after this game [a 4–2 defeat at the hands of Blackpool, after leading 2–1 at one stage]. I had to make sure all the players were right because it is very hard to take.'

Born in Hornchurch, Essex, on Wednesday 26 September 1951, he signed apprentice forms with the O's after playing for Hornchurch District Schools and captaining England Schools on six occasions. He made his O's debut versus Torquay United on 26 August 1967 – playing in the same side as John Still and Barry Fry, both later to become League managers. Taylor went on to have a wonderful career in East London for both the O's and West Ham United. He played an important part in their Third Division side of 1969–70, playing alongside Terry 'Henry' Mancini.

He was transferred to West Ham in October 1970 for £78,000, plus Peter 'Les' Bennett. He stayed at Upton Park for nine years, making over 400 senior appearances before returning to Brisbane Road in May 1982. He made a total of 254(2) senior appearances for the O's during his two-spells and scored 10 goals. After leaving the O's for the second time in May 1982, he had a spell in Belgian football with Antwerp and later was youth coach with Charlton Athletic. Taylor spent three seasons in New Zealand soccer management, returning to England in 1989 to become assistant manager to Keith Peacock at newly promoted Maidstone United, replacing John Still. They finished in fifth spot but lost in the Play-off semi-final 3–1 on aggregate to Cambridge United; both were sacked in January 1991.

After a spell with Margate, he was appointed in 1993 as youth manager with Cambridge United. The following season Cambridge, under manager Gary Johnson, were struggling, with relegation staring them in the face. With six games remaining, Johnson was sacked. Taylor took charge, and four wins were needed to avoid the drop – he got three and a draw, so United went down 'fifth from bottom'.

The 1996–97 season started off well for Cambridge, who were lying in second spot, but behind the scenes things were not well. Taylor had previously only signed a contract which took him up to December 1996. He wanted more security. Their board offered him a rolling three-month contract, but he decided not to accept their offer and instead he accepted an offer from the O's. A few days later his Cambridge assistant Paul Clark decided to join up with Taylor at Brisbane Road, to the dismay of the Cambridge board and fans. Taylor's managerial record (League and Cup) with Cambridge United between 3 April 1995 and November 1996 read: P74, W28, D17, L29.

In his first season in charge, the O's finished in 16th spot and 11th the following season, when they recorded 19 wins that yielded 66 League goals, their best total for many a season. During February 1999, with the O's swiftly moving up to the top of the table, Taylor was awarded the manager of the month, and the O's achieved a top-six place to enter the Play-offs.

After a brilliant performance against Rotherham United in the two-leg semi-final, going through 4–2 on penalties after two goalless draws, they lost 1–0 to Scunthorpe United in the Wembley Final during May 1999. After a disappointing season in 1999–2000, the O's bounced back in 2000–01, losing just 11 times all season, although it was a lack of goals that was a cause of concern after long-term injuries to both Christie and Garcia, which upset the goal prowess of the team.

The O's finished in fifth spot and went through to the finals after a wonderful display defeating Hull City 2–0, to get through 2–1 on aggregate. The rest is history. Chairman Barry Hearn stated 'We tried our best in the Final in Wales, but the first stage of any recovery is to admit your shortfalls. The most important thing is that we keep the basis of what we've got, and what Tommy needs he'll get. He's not under any pressure, but I don't want to get into a rut or hangover for next season.'

After a good start to the 2001–02 season, it all started to fall apart in September after bad home losses to both Luton Town and Torquay United, not the ideal way for Taylor to celebrate his 50th birthday, and on Monday 15 October 2001 he resigned. Memories started to flood back from two years previous when the fans were quick to call for his head. Taylor stated at that time 'I've never been flavour of the month with the supporters, but I have no intention of quitting, I'm used to all the abuse from them.'

It was not be long before Taylor found a new position, being appointed manager of Third Division Darlington with effect from Monday 29 October 2001. Taylor was away from football for just a couple of weeks. The chairman of Darlington George Reynolds stated 'There were 31 people in for the job. I went through each application thoroughly and was impressed with what Tommy had done. He's got an excellent record at Leyton Orient, where he took them to two Play-off Finals. Tommy is the right man for the job.'

Taylor was sacked by Darlington chairman George Reynolds a day short of a year in charge, winning 15, drawing 13 and losing 25 out of a total of 53 games, and the team were 20th in the Third Division. Reynolds informed a local Teeside newspaper 'We've got to move forward. He's gone thank God, but we won't rush into a new appointment.

'I find with managers you've got to get them where their heart and soul is in it. Southern managers don't seem to gel up in the North for some reason.'

Taylor stated 'I'm sad to be leaving, but that's football for you. There are a lot of things I'd like to say, but it is probably better I stay quiet, but I did find George a hard man to work with. I will return to London, where I have already been contacted about a couple of jobs.' Taylor was scouting for West Ham United in January 2003 and was hoping for a permanent job.

During February 2003 Taylor was one of a number of applicants for the manager's job at Colchester United, and following that it was rumoured he was in line for the Southend United job after the departure of Rob Newman. It was announced at the end of March 2003 that Taylor had been appointed as assistant manager to Ian McDonald at Nationwide Conference side Farnborough Town until the end of the season, this after Farnborough had appointed Vic Searle as their new chief executive. Taylor was a good friend of Searle's.

Taylor said 'We need to get a few wins to get us out of trouble, and hopefully I can help do that. They have a few players who are ex-pros, but the only players I know are Ken Charlery, who I tried to sign when at Orient, and Christian Lee, who I had on loan at the O's. It is nice to put a tracksuit back on and get down the training ground again.'

However, the 50-year-old Taylor who still lives on

Canvey Island expressed an interest in the vacant Southend United job. He stated 'I've applied for the Southend job, and I hope to get the chance to work at Roots Hall and sell myself to the board of directors. I'm helping out at Farnborough but my first priority is to be a manager of a Football League club and I would love to get the chance with Southend.'

It never materialised, so he took the Farnborough job without a contract.

Fifty-two-year-old Taylor did not get beyond the second phase of interviews and he was appointed first-team manager of Conference side Farnborough Town at the end of April 2003.Taylor commented 'I am very happy to be back in football and relishing the challenge of doing well next season.'

During October 2003 Taylor resigned from his post with Farnborough following a 3–1 defeat at Accrington Stanley, lying bottom of the Conference and without a win in 14 matches.

Then Taylor made a surprise move to Jamaica. An agent phoned wanting him to go and manage out there, and within 24 hours Taylor was flying off to manage Seba United from Montego Bay, he stayed for five months before returning to England.

In October 2004 he was appointed as manager of Southern League Premier Division side King's Lynn, taking over from former O's striker Robert Taylor, who left the club soon after. A couple of months later the directors of King's Lynn issued a statement concerning Taylor rejoining Cambridge United as boss. It stated 'King's Lynn Football Club would like to confirm that they are aware of the rumours regarding manager Tommy Taylor and the vacant managerial position at Cambridge United. We confirm that no official contact has been made and as far as we are concerned these rumours are just that.'

In a recent interview Taylor stated 'I always think of Orient as my club, and I loved the five years I had as manager. It was just a shame I couldn't get them up. They were great times, but I will always remember the two Play-off Finals for all the wrong reasons. To lose twice in three years was a terrible feeling; I just wish I could have won them promotion. It was something the club deserved, the last time they went up was back in 1989, and that's far too long.'

Taylor was back at Brisbane Road in May 2006 for O's day of celebrations after gaining promotion under Martin Ling.

Paul Brush

15 October 2001–27 September 2003

Paul Brush was the man to take over from Tommy Taylor on 15 October 2001 to become the O's 27th League manager since 1905. He was first-team coach and youth director. Paul Brush first joined the O's in the 1995–96 season, asked by then boss Pat Holland to help out coaching the youth players on a part-time basis during the school holidays and at weekends.

In July 1996 he was appointed youth-team coach, and he has been instrumental over recent seasons in seeing many of his young stars make it into the first-team squad. In November 1999 he was appointed first-team coach. Born in Plaistow, London, on Saturday 22 February 1958, Brush supported West Ham United as a boy, in fact the first match he saw was as a six-year-old watching the Hammers defeat the O's 3–0 in an FA Cup replay back in January 1974 while standing on a fold-up stool.

He started off as an apprentice with West Ham United, having represented Newham, London and Essex Boys. The 5ft 11in and 12st 2lb defender turned professional in February 1976, and he made his senior debut aged 19 at right-back against Norwich City in a 3–1 home defeat on 20 August 1977.

He won an FA Cup-winners' medal as an unused substitute in their 1–0 win over Arsenal on 10 May 1980. It was a great disappointment to him that he never played, but his Wembley chance came the following

August, playing against Liverpool in the Charity Shield and gaining a runners'-up medal.

Brush made a total of 174(8) senior appearances while at Upton Park, scoring one goal after four minutes versus QPR on 1 January 1985. He also appeared in Europe with the Hammers, playing in 1(3) European Cup-Winners' Cup matches, including a quarter-final match against Dynamo Tiblisi. Brush was a fine servant for the Hammers and a highly valued member of their senior squad for nine seasons.

He moved on to Crystal Palace in September 1985 for a £30,000 fee, making 53 senior appearances with one goal. He then went to Southend United in January 1988 and appeared in 77(7) senior matches, scoring once during his two-year stay at Roots Hall.

Quite remarkably, Brush was signed by the Shrimpers' player-manager Paul Clark (later the O's assistant manager under Taylor), and in the same side was midfielder Martin Ling, later assistant to Brush with the O's (who eventually took over when Brush left the club), and they played in eight matches together in that 1987–88 season, winning four, drawing one and losing two.

In July 1990 he was signed by former 'Oriental' Peter Taylor for Diadora Premier League side Enfield, where he later became their assistant manager. A couple of years later he was with Chelmsford City and Essex side Heybridge Swifts. He retired from playing football in 1995.

Paul Brush was in charge for almost two years at Brisbane Road after five years as a youth and first-team coach, but in September 2003 he was sacked by Barry Hearn after a poor run of results. He was sacked just two hours after a 3–0 defeat at Huddersfield Town, which left the O's second from bottom in the table, with only Carlisle United below them, having collected just seven points from the first 10 games. Hearn stated 'Unfortunately results have not been good enough, and Paul has accepted that. Paul has been completely dedicated and professional in his approach, and we're sorry things have not worked out. I spoke to him after the Huddersfield game and we have agreed to part company.'

Brush said 'I feel very empty as Leyton Orient have been part of my life for seven years. It's weird to think I won't be going in this week.'

Well, just a month later, Brush was helping out Southend caretaker manager Steve Tilson, receiving just nominal pay, or sometimes just travelling expenses. The pair took the Shrimpers out of the relegation zone up to 17th spot, and on 23 March 2004 they took them to their very first Final in their 98-year history, which they lost 2–0 to Blackpool in the LDV Vans Trophy Final at the Millennium Stadium.

A week before the Final both Tilson and Brush were awarded a two-year contract, with Brush as head coach. After a poor start to the 2004–05 season, by January 2005 Southend were among the front runners for a Play-off spot.

The two have had great success taking the Shrimpers to two successive promotions, right up to the Championship, and were rewarded with extended contracts.

It was Martin Ling who took the reins at Orient from Brush as caretaker manager.

Martin Ling

September 2003–Present

Martin Ling was a splendid midfield player, and in a career that spanned some 16 years he made a total of 637(55) senior career appearances, scoring 75 goals. (His full profile appears in the chapter on the top players in this book). After a three-month spell at the end of the 1999–2000 season with Brighton & Hove Albion, he returned to Brisbane Road as the youth-team coach in July 2000. His Under-19 O's side, having won the FA Alliance Cup Final, with a 1–0 win over Bradford City on 22 April 2001, played at the Millennium Stadium.

It was no surprise that Ling was appointed the O's joint manager with Paul Clark (Clark resigned a few weeks later) on 15 October 2001. His appointment came after his wonderful achievements with the O's Under-19 side, and he had nurtured a lot of promising youngsters into the first-team squad.

O's boss Brush stated 'Martin's got a lot of enthusiasm, and although he's only had a year as coach he can feel the pulse of the players because until a year ago he's been close around them as a player.

'He brings a different dimension. Over the past year he's had ideas about the training himself and he's very conscientious, and as a pairing we can compliment each other and put a smile back on the faces of the players, and long term we both want to get this right and give it our best shot because we both want to do our jobs for a long time.'

The new management team of Brush and Ling were handed a two-and-a-half year contract after their impressive start in the hot seat, producing seven points from their three games in charge.

Ling himself said 'We're both pleased to have been given the chance for a long-term period and we're looking forward to the challenge.'

After the departure of Brush, Ling was made caretaker manager on 28 September 2003. His first match in charge was a 1–0 win at bottom place side Carlisle United.

Although there were some big names in contention for the O's manager's job – men like, Bobby Gould, Steve Parkin, Joe Kinnear, Colin Todd and Terry Dolan – Ling had impressed chairman Barry Hearn with three wins and two draws from his first seven games in charge.

Hearn stated 'I was impressed with the other applications that we had for the job, but not impressed

Martin Ling (right) with Stuart Hicks.

enough to not have given Martin Ling his chance for a couple more months as caretaker manager.'

However, with an embarrassing 4–1 defeat at Dagenham & Redbridge in the LDV Vans Trophy, his chances of getting the job on a full-time basis looked slim. Soon after Ling was informed that he could continue as the caretaker until Christmas 2003, when a decision on a full-time appointment would be made.

The O's had climbed to 14th in the table, having collected 18 points from 10 games, including a magnificent 4–1 win at Cambridge United. Ling received an early Christmas present when on 20 December 2003 both he and his assistant Ian Culverhouse were given a full-time contract until June 2005. Ling was the O's 28th manager.

With the O's having such a great start to the 2004–05 season, having a top spot in the table during October 2004, in November they both had their contracts extended to June 2007.

Ling stated 'Both myself and Ian are delighted to have committed our futures to Leyton Orient, personally I look upon it as my club because of the length of time I have been here, and it's an honour and a privilege to be asked to work as manager for another two-and-a-half-years. We are dedicated to our aim and target of achieving promotion this season, and the hard work that's been put in looks like it is paying off.

'I'm grateful to the chairman for the faith he has shown in me and the supporters too for the backing they've given us this season – I can assure you that we are determined to repay everyone for their support.'

In 2005–06 he and his new assistant Dean Smith certainly did, leading the O's in gaining promotion for only the fifth time in the club's 90 seasons in the Football League.

Not only was promotion gained by Ling's boys, but it was achieved in style, playing bright attacking football, and the future looks even brighter for the 2006–07 season in League One.

Both Martin Ling and Dean Smith were rewarded for leading the O's into League One with new two-year contracts, which they signed on 28 June 2006. The O's boss will also be honoured for his 10 years' service to the club with a testimonial.

Ling became one of the most qualified managers in the country after completing his UEFA Pro License course at Warwickshire University, which is the highest level of coaching qualification that can be gained in England and is required for any manager hopeful of working in the Premiership.

The O's Managers' Football League Records

	P	W	D	L	F	A	Pts
Samuel Ormerod	32	5	7	20	30	65	17
Ike Evenson	9	3	3	3	10	15	9
William Holmes	452	169	100	183	515	583	438
Peter Proudfoot	483	148	117	218	566	742	413
Arthur Grimsdell	42	14	13	15	53	62	41
Jimmy Seed	88	21	25	42	142	193	67
David Pratt	58	21	13	24	96	94	55
Tom Halsey	20	6	6	8	28	22	18
Charles Hewitt	81	23	18	40	100	146	64
William Bulloch Wright	3	0	0	3	2	6	0
Neil McBain	47	13	14	20	65	87	40
Alec Stock	389	148	81	160	588	622	377
Les Gore	187	79	40	68	301	289	198
Johnny Carey	84	28	19	37	106	121	75
Benny Fenton	48	14	12	22	66	91	40
Dave Sexton	37	7	10	20	33	66	24
Dick Graham	73	20	27	26	88	106	67
Jimmy Bloomfield	316	102	106	108	350	369	310
George Petchey	254	74	89	91	257	294	237
Paul Went	9	1	1	7	3	15	4
Ken Knighton	79	24	17	38	97	134	89
Frank Clark*	372	145	88	139	547	511	516
Peter Eustace	133	52	33	48	185	169	189
John Sitton/Chris Turner	48	7	9	32	33	79	30
Pat Holland	63	16	16	31	54	78	64
Tommy Taylor† + §	232	86	67	79	296	280	317
Paul Brush#	89	24	25	40	98	128	97
Martin Ling^	128	50	40	38	171	166	190
Caretaker managers	30	7	9	14	60	50	24

Note. The above stats include Play-off matches and are, therefore, different from the lists within the statistical chapter within this book.

Note: The above managerial records are for Football League matches only between 1905–06, up to and including the 2005–06 season only. The managerial records of various Cup matches appear under the chapters on the FA Cup and Football League Cup.

* Frank Clark's record includes four promotion Play-off matches in season 1988–89, the results being: 2–0, 0–1, 0–0, 2–1.

† Tommy Taylor's record takes into account a deduction of three points for booking statistic irregularities in season 1997–98.

+ Tommy Taylor's record includes a total of six promotion Play-off matches, three matches in season 1998–99 and three matches in season 2000–01. The results being: 0–0, 0–0, 0–1 and 0–1, 2–0, 2–4.

§ Tommy Taylor's record is up to and including his final match in charge versus Shrewsbury Town on 13 October 2001.

Paul Brush's Football League record commenced on 20 October 2001.

^ Martin Ling's Football League record commenced on 28 September 2003 and he is the present manager as at June 2006.

O's Cup Records

FA Cup: 1904–05 to 2005–06

Manager	*P*	*W*	*D*	*L*	*F*	*A*
Alf Wallis*	6	3	2	1	15	7
Sam Ormerod	7	4	2	1	14	7
William Holmes	18	5	2	11	24	40
Peter Proudfoot	30	10	8	12	38	56
Arthur Grimsdell	6	3	2	1	10	6
Jimmy Seed	4	1	1	2	4	7
David Pratt	6	3	1	2	11	7
Willie Hall **	2	1	0	1	2	3
Charles Hewitt	2	0	0	2	2	3
Neil McBain	2	1	0	1	3	3
Alec Stock	27	13	6	8	52	36
Les Gore	8	3	0	5	11	15
Johnny Carey	8	3	3	2	10	6
Benny Fenton	3	1	1	1	4	6
Dave Sexton	1	0	0	1	1	3
Dick Graham	8	4	2	2	9	8
Jimmy Bloomfield	22	7	8	7	24	28
George Petchey	16	5	5	6	20	21
Ken Knighton	7	3	2	2	8	4
Frank Clark	28	13	7	8	43	36
Peter Eustace	10	5	3	2	19	18
John Sitton & Chris Turner	2	1	0	1	3	2
Pat Holland	1	0	0	1	0	1
Tommy Taylor	15	6	4	5	23	22
Paul Brush	6	3	1	2	9	8
Martin Ling	9	5	1	3	12	13

* *Alf Wallis was the trainer in 1904–05 season, there was no manager.*

** Willie Hall was manager during November 1945, the war years, when two FA Cup ties took place.

Football League Cup: 1960–61 to 2005–06

Manager	*P*	*W*	*D*	*L*	*F*	*A*
Les Gore	4	1	1	2	4	5
Johnny Carey	8	4	2	2	20	15
Benny Fenton	2	1	0	1	4	2
Dave Sexton	1	0	0	1	0	3
Dick Graham	2	0	0	2	1	4
Jimmy Bloomfield	12	2	4	6	13	17
George Petchey	17	5	5	7	16	23
Peter Angell *	1	0	0	1	1	3
Paul Went	2	0	1	1	3	4
Ken Knighton	2	1	0	1	2	3
Frank Clark	29	9	10	10	41	42
Peter Eustace	8	1	2	5	8	14
John Sitton & Chris Turner	2	0	1	1	1	5
Pat Holland	4	2	0	2	3	5
Tommy Taylor	17	5	7	5	23	29
Paul Brush	3	1	0	2	6	9
Martin Ling	2	0	0	2	2	6
Total	**115**	**32**	**33**	**50**	**147**	**186**

The Football League Cup competition commenced in October 1960.

* Peter Angell was acting manager on 31 August 1977 for League Cup tie at Derby County.

The Caretaker Managers

		Matches
Freddie Powell	February 1922 to April 1922	6
Sidney White	December 1934 to January 1935	3
Peter Angell	March 1968	1
Peter Angell	August–September 1977	3
Paul Went	March–May 1981	5
Paul Went	August–September 1981	4
John Sitton & Chris Turner	April 1994	5
Glenn Cockerill & Tom Loizou	April 1995	1
Tommy Cunningham	October–November 1996	2
Total		30

Orient's star players

There has always been much discussion among football fans over the years as to who were the best players to have played for their club, and so is the case with all the O's fans. Each have their own favourite players, and so the same can be said about the two authors of this book.

We originally selected a list of just over 250 O's players (out of a total of 950 who have worn first-team O's colours since entering the FA Cup in 1904 and the Football League in 1905) who could have been profiled for this chapter as star players; however, we were restricted to 150 players to profile. Therefore, it was a very difficult choice in having to leave many of our favourite players out, but in the end we looked at each player's record with the O's, unusual achievements and also included a few of our favourite players over the years.

ALDOUS, Stanley Elvey Reginald (1950–57)

A true leader and inspiring captain, Stan Aldous was born in Northfleet on 10 February 1923 and was one of five footballing brothers. He captained the O's in some of their greatest triumphs, including the Third Division Championship in May 1956. Aldous was a tough centre-half who stood at 6ft and weighed 12st 1lb. He started his career with Erith & Belvedere, but it was while with Bromley that he gained his reputation. He joined them almost by default, when Gravesend FC, for some reason, forgot to register him for the 1950–51 season, so he became a free agent. Fulham were interested in his signature, but it was the O's head coach Les Gore, who previously played alongside Aldous in the Gravesend side, and manager Alec Stock who persuaded him to join. So at the age of 25 he became an Oriental.

Aldous, being such a strong and powerful central-defender, dominated in the air and proved to be one of the best defenders in the lower Divisions. He was one of a handful of players to have made over 300 Football League appearances during his eight-year stay. He moved on to Headington United (nowadays Oxford United) and later was coach with QPR and manager with his old club Gravesend. During the late 1970s he owned the Royal Bingo and Social Club in Littleport, Cambridgeshire. Aldous made a great contribution to the history of the club, and it was on his suggestion that the legendary Tommy Johnston was signed after being asked who was the best centre-forward he had ever faced. He informed the author just before his death 'The most disappointing moment of my career was the 1–0 defeat by Port Vale in the sixth round of the FA Cup before 31,000 fans in March 1954. We dominated the whole match but just could not find the net.

'I suppose the greatest and most exciting moment was when we won promotion into the Second Division back in 1956. There was always a great friendship about the club from the top, chairman Harry Zussman, to the lads who cleaned the boots.

'I was proud to be associated with the O's during the 1950s when I feel, at last, we shook off the tag of being a music hall joke and took our rightful place in the Second Division.'

Stan Aldous died in Ely on 17 October 1995.

SEASON	*LEAGUE*		*FA CUP*		*TOTAL*	
	Apps	*Gls*	*Apps*	*Gls*	*Apps*	*Gls*
1950–51	30	0	0	0	30	0
1951–52	46	0	9	0	55	0
1952–53	45	2	2	0	47	2
1953–54	43	1	7	0	50	1
1954–55	45	0	2	0	47	0
1955–56	42	0	4	0	46	0
1956–57	40	0	1	0	41	0
1957–58	11	0	0	0	11	0
	302	3	25	0	327	3

ALLEN, Peter Charles (1965–78)

A great club man and true professional, aggressive, with skill and vision, Peter Allen tops the O's all-time appearances list. He broke the 45-year-old League appearance record of goalkeeper Arthur Wood against Sunderland on 13 March 1976, and he became the first player to break the 400 League appearance barrier on 26 April 1977 against Southampton (he is still the only player to have achieved this). Allen left the club in March 1978, recording a total of 424(8) League appearances, a record unlikely ever to be broken with the advent of the Bosman transfer ruling.

Born in Hove, Sussex, on 1 November 1946, Allen excelled academically, gaining seven 'O' levels and three 'A' levels at Grammar School in Brighton. He joined Tottenham Hotspur as an associated schoolboy and was still at Grammar School when the O's manager Dave Sexton spotted him playing. After a brief spell on amateur forms, he decided to turn professional in July 1965, in preference to entering Birmingham University or the London School of Economics. He made his debut as a 19-year-old in the League Cup-tie against Coventry City on 22 September 1965, and his Second Division debut came three days later at Portsmouth. Unfortunately his first season was not a happy one: it saw manager Dave Sexton resigning over Christmas and the O's relegated to Division Three, and then during the following season they were nearly close to liquidation, not the ideal time for the young man to be starting his professional career.

Allen regularly impressed as a constructive midfield player with a good, firm tackle. He played a vital role in the O's avoiding relegation over the following few seasons. The 1969–70 season saw a great improvement in the Orient fortunes, and it was no coincidence that Allen had a wonderful season playing in all 46 matches when winning the Third Division Championship. Second Division football seemed to bring out the very best in Allen's all-round play, and it was no surprise when First Division Everton came in with a big offer for his services, but he decided to stay in London and over the next few seasons was a model of consistency. During the period he had a run of 116 Football League appearances that ended in August 1971.

Allen led the team superbly during 1973–74 with the O's pushing for promotion into the old First Division, but they missed it by a single point. He was very disappointed and became unsettled at the club and rumours became rife that he would leave. Manager George Petchey persuaded him to stay and his old enthusiasm was back, but his last three seasons at the club were often troubled by injury problems. He was awarded a testimonial year in 1975–76, culminating with a match against West Ham United.

It came as a real surprise that boss Jimmy Bloomfield allowed Allen to leave and join former O's boss George Petchey at Millwall (the last club one would expect Allen to play for) during March 1978, and it was also at a time when the O's were awaiting an FA Cup quarter-final match at Middlesbrough, having a number of players out with injury problems.

In football there are usually two types of midfield players. There is the hard-tackling aggressive mould of player with a high work rate or there is the calmer, ball playing type who distributes the ball to colleagues accurately. What made Peter Allen so special? Well it was that he had a bit of both in him. He never shirked an opportunity to make a telling tackle when it was required, and when in possession of the ball he always attempted to use it methodically. He never appeared in the top Division, but it would have been very interesting to see how he would have faired. One thing is for certain – there have been a lot less talented players who have played in the top flight.

Allen was hard but always a fair and sporting player. He did get sent off once in a League match at Walsall, but that decision was so ridiculous that quite rightly no action was taken against him. He captained the team for over three seasons and always led by example both on and off the field. For younger supporters, one only has to view his performances on the *Orient the 70s* video to understand his great skill and ability.

When he joined the O's he was thought of as a more attacking player, and he did go on to score a number of goals, none more pleasing than the very early goal at Millwall in May 1971 to secure the two points. But his defensive qualities came to the fore under George Petchey. One also recalls him having a wonderful match at Tottenham Hotspur when he filled in as a central-defender, and he also filled in admirably at full-back on a number of occasions. So, versatility, leadership and sportsmanship can all be ascribed to Peter Allen.

After a short period at The Den, where he made 16(2) appearances, he suffered two serious injuries which forced him to retire from the game at the age of 32. He declined an offer of a coaching post with the Lions to undertake a three-year course to complete his articles. He qualified as a solicitor in 1984, worked for a large firm of attorneys to gain experience, and then set up his own partnership in 1988 with John Diebel, named Diebel & Allen, which is based in Portslade, East Sussex. In 2001 he completed a course on the legal aspects of Sports Management, and in 2006 he was still in the practice and still plays the odd game of 5-a-side football.

Allen informed the author in 2005:

'It was an easier decision to turn professional than to take up an academic career. I was delighted to be playing at this level of football as it obscured the fact that the O's were struggling to survive in the Second Division.

'Two matches stick in my mind from those early baptismal days. The first was at Derby County in April 1966. I was marking Frank Upton, an experienced campaigner renowned for his tough tackling. It was a remarkable match in the fact that we won 3–1, yet we had both Colin Worrell and Dennis Sorrell sent off. The second match was the last of the 1965–66 season at home to Southampton. My goal kept us in front for a long period before Terry Paine headed in an equaliser to secure their promotion to the old First Division. It was our biggest home crowd for many a year: 19,839.'

He happily remembers the 1969–70 season under Jimmy Bloomfield and Peter Angell:

'Two games I recall prove just how great a part so-called "lady luck" plays in the game of football and especially for a successful side. Over the Easter period at Doncaster Rovers we desperately needed the two points [only two in those days] as we had lost at our promotion rivals Bristol Rovers the previous day before just over 22,000 fans at Eastville.

'We won by the strangest goal I have ever seen. An up and under from our own half was dropping straight into their 'keeper's hands when their centre-half Stuart Robertson ran across to head the ball into his own net with no Orient player within 20 yards of him.

'The second match was at Bradford City when a Mickey Bullock goal clinched promotion. We had a memorable night in Leeds that night.'

Moving on to the 1973–74 season, and the club's near miss in the promotion race into Division One, he recalled, 'We played marvellously well up until the Christmas period, but then luck deserted us, an FA Cup marathon seemed to take it out of us, and we missed out by a single point.

'I was injured at Bristol City on New Year's Day and my ankle troubled me up until the end of the season and my form was not as it should have been when it was operated on. This was not an excuse but a fact.

'The biggest anti-climax was the final 1–1 draw with Aston Villa. The thought that I suffered all this pain with no end result, there were heart-breaking scenes in the dressing room. I remember the picture in one of your books [*Images of Leyton Orient FC*] of both Ricky [Heppolette] and Barrie [Fairbrother] crying their eyes out, we all shed tears. I'm sure there were many a tear on the terraces too.'

He continued 'The other side of so-called "lady luck" I think cost us promotion. We had what we thought a perfectly good goal disallowed for offside when little Terry Brisley was pushed into the back of the net by a Millwall defender after Fairbrother had scored; at worst it should have be been adjudged a penalty for pushing, but that cost us the point we needed for promotion and then the tension of the Villa match would not have been a problem. Then there was a 40-yard drive by Notts County's Don Masson that cost us another home point when it took a wicked deflection off Brisley's shoulder (clearly captured on television), then Gerry Queen's header at West Brom, which somehow never entered the net and we lost 1–0. That's how the second half of the season went for us and that's why we lost out.'

Allen happily recalls the O's various FA Cup exploits while with the club:

'The first was our 2–0 win at Leicester City managed by former boss Bloomfield. Ian Bowyer scored a beauty, and I added one, don't ask me how it went it, but it did, to earn a well deserved 2–0 win at Filbert Street. The most exciting was our 3–2 win over Chelsea, perhaps the high spot in my career. It was exciting for the crowd, but believe me just as exciting for the O's players.

'During the first 30 minutes we were 2–0 down and chasing shadows, we clawed our way back with a brilliant shot from Phil Hoadley just before half-time, which gave us great heart; we could not wait to get back on to the field. It was a great fight back in the second half, the third from Barrie Fairbrother [his name seems to crop up a lot] was just a beautiful moment. In the next round we lost 1–0 to the "lucky" Gunners, but we did hit the woodwork three times. Old Bob Wilson in their goal did not know what hit him, maybe if the crowd would have blown a little harder one might have gone in. After I left the club, I followed the O's fortunes in their great FA Cup run in 1978. It gave me great satisfaction because I had left so many friends.'

Finally he remembered with particular fondness the 1975–76 season, the year of his testimonial, and the season he broke the club's League appearance record.

'That season showed me just how many friends I had who would help when I was going through a second period of serious injury. There was my testimonial committee and also club chairman Brian Winston, who was an enormous help, and the many friends and supporters who helped me, they will always have my gratitude.

Indeed I will always have a soft spot for Orient, having spent all but a short period of my playing career with them.'

He still follows the O's progress with the greatest of interest.

SEASON	*LEAGUE*		*FA CUP*		*FL CUP*		*TOTAL*	
	Apps	*Gls*	*Apps*	*Gls*	*Apps*	*Gls*	*Apps*	*Gls*
1965–66	21 (2)	3	0	0	1	0	22 (2)	3
1966–67	34	2	2	0	0	0	36	2
1967–68	34 (2)	4	5	0	1	0	40 (2)	4
1968–69	43	3	2	0	3	0	48	3
1969–70	46	3	2	0	2	0	50	3
1970–71	42	2	3	0	1	0	46	2
1971–72	40	5	4	1	2	0	46	6
1972–73	42	3	1	0	2	0	45	3
1973–74	37	1	0	0	4	0	41	1
1974–75	31 (1)	0	2	0	1	0	34 (1)	0
1975–76	7	0	0	0	0	0	7	0
1976–77	29	1	3	0	4	0	36	1
1977–78	18 (3)	0	1	0	3	1	22 (3)	1
	424 (8)	27	25	1	24	1	473 (8)	29

 # Peter Allen also appeared in 9 matches in the Anglo-Scottish Cup.

BACON, Cyril William (1946–50)

Fair-haired Cyril Bacon, an all-action wing-half, was born in Hammersmith, London, on 9 November 1919. During the war he served as an RAF Warrant Officer Air gunner. He joined the O's in June 1946, having been spotted playing for the RAF, and guested for both Chelsea and Hayes. He made his debut versus Southend United on 4 September 1946.

A most energetic and enthusiastic performer, it was these qualities that helped the O's from having to apply for re-election at the League's AGM in 1947, scoring twice in the penultimate match at Mansfield Town. The manager Neil McBain stated in the press that he had thought of moving Bacon into a more attacking role earlier in the season. He made his 100th League appearance for the O's in the 2–1 away defeat at Notts County during April 1949. Bacon was released in May 1950 and joined Brentford on trial.

SEASON	*LEAGUE*		*FA CUP*		*TOTAL*	
	Apps	*Gls*	*Apps*	*Gls*	*Apps*	*Gls*
1946–47	40	3	1	0	41	3
1947–48	27	0	0	0	27	0
1948–49	41	0	2	0	43	0
1949–50	10	0	0	0	10	0
	118	3	3	0	121	3

BAKER, Stephen (1988–91)

A bargain buy, Steve Baker joined the O's from Southampton in March 1988 for £50,000 after 85(13) senior appearances at The Dell. He scored on his debut against Swansea City on 26 March 1988. Born in Newcastle on 16 June 1962, he started with Wallsend Boys Club, joining Southampton as an apprentice in July 1978, signing pro forms the following December. During his stay at The Dell he went on loan to Burnley in February 1983.

Baker played mostly at right full-back for the O's. This attacking player, who stood just 5ft 5in, was ever present in the promotion season of 1988–89 and featured in all four Play-off matches. In 1990–91 he was playing on a week-by-week contract basis, and the following season he did not report back for training. He joined AFC Bournemouth on a permanent basis in September 1991, making 5(1) Football League appearances. After a spell with Aldershot Town, he joined Farnborough Town in the GM Vauxhall Conference, making 16 appearances. He was still playing for Farnborough in 1998–99, having made over 150 appearances for the Hampshire club. Baker rejoined Aldershot in May 1999 and was still with them in 2002. However, in June 2002 the 40-year-old decided to call it a day after 24 years in the game, and he was appointed as a coach with Southampton's Academy along with another former Saints player, David Puckett. He was still working for the club in 2006.

SEASON	LEAGUE		FA CUP		FL CUP		TOTAL	
	Apps	*Gls*	*Apps*	*Gls*	*Apps*	*Gls*	*Apps*	*Gls*
1987–88	9	3	0	0	0	0	9	3
1988–89*	50	3	1	0	5	0	56	3
1989–90	27(5)	0	0(1)	0	3(1)	0	30(7)	0
1990–91	23(2)	0	3(1)	0	5	0	31(2)	0
	109(7)	6	4(2)	0	13(1)	0	126(10)	6

** Season 1988–89 includes four promotion Play-off matches.*

 # Baker also appeared in seven Auto Windscreens Shield matches.

BANNER, Arthur (1947–53)

Another of the O's great inspiring captains and a loyal servant with the club, Arthur Banner was a player who was voted by the supporters as one of the all-time great O's players in a millennium poll published in December 1999. Banner was an excellent captain during the late 1940s and will be remembered by older fans for the way he would roll up his sleeves, encouraging and marshalling his teammates when they were losing. Born in Sheffield on 28 June 1918, he started his career with local junior side Lopham FC before joining Doncaster Rovers as an 18-year-old in March 1937. He could never break into their senior side so he came south, joining West Ham United in May 1938. After making 27 League appearances for the Hammers, he became an Oriental during February 1948 on a free transfer, and he formed a wonderful defensive partnership with Ledger Ritson.

Banner only scored two senior goals, yet he also netted two from the penalty spot in two friendlies in 1951, one against Racing Club of Haarlem from Holland, a 3–1 win, in a Festival of Britain match, and the other against Scottish side Airdrieonians, a 2–5 home defeat. Banner proved a loyal servant and was awarded with a benefit match in 1953. He joined Kent side Sittingbourne as player-manager in May 1953 and later coached Ilford FC. Banner retired to Thorpe Bay, where he died at his home on 30 April 1980.

SEASON	LEAGUE		FA CUP		TOTAL	
	Apps	*Gls*	*Apps*	*Gls*	*Apps*	*Gls*
1947–48	12	0	0	0	12	0
1948–49	30	0	2	0	32	0
1949–50	36	1	1	0	37	1
1950–51	22	0	0	0	22	0
1951–52	40	0	9	1	49	1
1952–53	24	0	2	0	26	0
	164	1	14	1	178	2

BARRETT, Scott (1998–2003)

Scott Barrett, the 6ft and 14st 4lb goalkeeper, was born in Ilkeston on 2 April 1963. What supporter would have thought that Barrett's heroic saves would take the O's to their first Wembley Play-off appearance? Well that is exactly what did happen. His brilliant save in the dying minutes in the second leg of the Division Three Play-off at Rotherham took the match into extra-time and then into a penalty shoot-out. He saved Rotherham's second and third penalties to take the O's to a Wembley Play-off Final against Scunthorpe United in May 1999, which unfortunately was lost 1–0. This was Barrett's second appearance at Wembley, having helped Colchester United beat Witton Albion to lift the FA Trophy in 1992.

He started his long 17-year career with Ilkeston Town, but his League career started in 1984 with Wolverhampton Wanderers, playing in over 30 senior matches for them. In a League career that saw him play for Wolves, Stoke City, Colchester United, Stockport County, Gillingham and Cambridge United, this excellent shot stopper made 275 senior appearances before joining the O's on a free transfer from Cambridge United on 25 January 1999, this after a month's loan with Kingstonian. He is also on record as having scored a goal for Colchester United in a GM Vauxhall clash against Wycombe Wanderers in 1991. Barrett made his O's debut versus Darlington on 30 January 1999, but was originally expected to join in the summer of 1997. Manager Taylor wanted him but refused to pay a fee, so he signed a two-year contract with Cambridge. Their manager Roy McFarland rated 'Scottie' as one of the top 'keepers in Division Three during 1997–98.

Barrett performed consistently well after replacing the out-of-form Mackenzie in goal during the club's push for promotion in 1999. He shared the jersey in 1999–2000 with Ashley Bayes and signed a new one-year contract, but during the 2000–01 season he sat on the bench as understudy to Bayes. He came back into the side in March 2001 after Bayes looked a little weary and was rested. Barrett was back on the bench during the O's run to the Play-off Final in May 2001.

Barrett signed a one-year contract in June 2001 and also acted as the club's goalkeeping coach. He started the 2002–03 season as a reserve goalie but made his first appearance on 16 November 2002 against Margate, when coming on as a substitute goalkeeper in an FA Cup-tie for the injured Glenn Morris, to become the first substitute goalkeeper to appear for the O's in an FA Cup-tie and also being the first replacement goalie ever to come off the bench and play for the O's in a senior match.

In January 2003, at 39 years of age, he was the oldest goalkeeper playing regular League football when he appeared against Cambridge United (Dave Beasant was 44 years old but only playing reserve football); however, with the signing of Lee Harrison from Barnet in March 2003 it was the end of the road for Barrett.

On 1 April 2003, at the age of 40, he decided to call it a day and accept a settlement from the club. He was close to signing for Grays Athletic on transfer deadline, but the deal fell through and he remained at Brisbane Road as goalkeeping coach.

However, in June 2003 he was appointed assistant manager to Mark Stimson (a former O's player) with Grays. Also on the books with Grays were a number of former O's players signed by Stimson and Barrett, namely Ashley Bayes, John Martin and Aaron McLean. Barrett also ran the football academy at Palmers College a couple of evenings a week. Both Stimson and Barrett resigned in May 2006. He then joined Mark Stimson as assistant manager at Conference side Stevenage Borough.

SEASON	*LEAGUE*		*FA CUP*		*FL CUP*		*TOTAL*	
	Apps	*Gls*	*Apps*	*Gls*	*Apps*	*Gls*	*Apps*	*Gls*
1998–99*	23	0	0	0	0	0	23	0
1999–2000	29	0	1	0	2	0	32	0
2000–01	7	0	0	0	0	0	7	0
2001–02	32	0	4	0	0	0	36	0
2002–03	11	0	1 (1)	0	0	0	12 (1)	0
	102	0	6 (1)	0	2	0	110 (1)	0

** Barrett's League total includes three promotion Play-off matches in 1998–99.*

BARTLETT, Frederick Leslie (1937–48)

An elegant centre-half who holds the record for the number of wartime League appearances for the O's – 207 games between 1939–46 – Fred Bartlett was born in Reading on 5 March 1913. This tall, elegant centre-half joined the O's in May 1937, as a replacement for Dave Affleck, from Queen's Park Rangers after playing 50 senior matches for them between October 1932 and May 1937. His debut came in the first League match held at Brisbane Road (Osborne Road as it was then known) against Cardiff City on 28 August 1937. During World War Two he played in a club record 207 regional fixtures between 1939–46 and was one of a small number of players to be retained for the resumption of League football in the 1946–47 season, but played only once the following season, at Port Vale in January 1948. He enjoyed a benefit match with William P. Wright during 1948 and soon after joined Southern League outfit Gloucester City. Bartlett died in Henley-on-Thames during 1968.

SEASON	*LEAGUE*		*FA CUP*		*TOTAL*	
	Apps	*Gls*	*Apps*	*Gls*	*Apps*	*Gls*
1937–38	20	0	1	0	21	0
1938–39	39	0	2	0	41	0
1945–46*	0	0	2	0	2	0
1946–47	36	0	1	0	37	0
1947–48	1	0	0	0	1	0
	96	0	6	0	102	0

** No League competition that season.*

 # Bartlett also appeared in two Third Division Cup matches between 1937–39.

BELL, Mark Dickson (1907–10)

Bell was one of the more talented of the Scottish-born players to have played for the O's in the Edwardian era. Born in Edinburgh, Scotland, on 8 February 1881, Mark Bell started his career as a nippy winger with Roseberry FC, and then he was with Edinburgh Hibernians. His professional career commenced as a 17-year-old with the Edinburgh side St Barnards FC in 1898, making 24 Scottish League appearances. In October 1900 he joined Heart of Midlothian and made 29 senior appearances, scoring nine goals and gaining a Scottish Cup-winners' medal and a Scottish international cap in March 1901 versus Wales. During May 1902 he moved south of the border to play for Southern League Southampton and bagged two goals in their 11–0 victory over Watford in December 1902.

After just nine Southern League appearances and six goals, he returned to Hearts in April 1903, making 17 Scottish Division One appearances with three goals. In May 1904 Bell joined Fulham of the Southern League and stayed for three years, making 58 Scottish League appearances with six goals. He joined the O's in August 1907 and operated at right-half, and two years later he took over the captaincy from Jumbo Reason.

He remained with the O's for three seasons before joining the Southern League side Leyton FC, and he was later with New Brompton. Mark Bell was a good, constructive player whose best years were probably just behind him when he was at Millfields Road, but nevertheless he was a great capture. During World War One he guested for Fulham. He then emigrated to Australia in 1919 but returned to Edinburgh soon after the war. He died aged 81 on 26 October 1961.

SEASON	*LEAGUE*		*FA CUP*		*TOTAL*	
	Apps	*Gls*	*Apps*	*Gls*	*Apps*	*Gls*
1907–08	36	3	5	2	41	5
1908–09	28	1	1	0	29	1
1909–10	24	0	1	0	25	0
	88	4	7	2	95	6

BELLAMY, Gary (1992–96)

A player that brought quality and assurance to the team during his four-year stay, Gary Bellamy was a player who had been watched by the O's for some time and was eventually signed by manager Peter Eustace on a month's loan and then stayed for four seasons. This 6ft 2in defender was born in Worksop on 4 July 1962, and he started as an apprentice with Chesterfield in 1980 and went on to make 184 League appearances with seven goals. He moved to Wolverhampton Wanderers, accumulating 136 appearances with nine goals, and played in their 2–0 victory at Wembley over Burnley in the Sherpa Van Trophy before 82,000 fans.

Bellamy signed for the O's on 17 November 1992 for £30,000, after a month's loan spell, but became the first player to be released by new manager Pat Holland when he surprisingly revealed 'He's on a free transfer, and I will not be using him anymore'. (This after 140 senior appearances.) He became player-manager with Chelmsford City in 1996, and he held that position until May 2001. He was appointed new boss of Dover Athletic on 5 June 2001 but was fired from the role that November, having been in charge for just 19 matches, of which 13 were lost. He was out of work for nearly 12 months before being appointed manager of Braintree Town on 17 October 2002, but he was fired 13 months later.

SEASON	*LEAGUE*		*FA CUP*		*FL CUP*		*TOTAL*	
	Apps	*Gls*	*Apps*	*Gls*	*Apps*	*Gls*	*Apps*	*Gls*
1992–93	38 (1)	4	2	0	0	0	40 (1)	4
1993–94	27 (2)	1	2	0	1	0	30 (2)	1
1994–95	32	0	2	0	0	0	34	0
1995–96	32	1	1	0	1	0	34	1
	129 (3)	6	7	0	2	0	138 (3)	6

 # Bellamy also appeared in 14 Auto Windscreens Shield matches

BENNETT, Peter Leslie (1970–79)

A true professional who never let the team down, no matter what position he played, Peter Bennett was born in Hillingdon on 24 June 1946. This former England schoolboy came to the O's as part of the deal that took Tommy Taylor to West Ham United in October 1970 for £78,000. Les Bennett joined the Hammers as an apprentice in July 1963, making 39 League appearances and scoring three goals. He made his debut a few days after his arrival at Brisbane Road against Sheffield Wednesday and soon after was appointed club captain. He played a major part in the O's run to the semi-final of the FA Cup in 1978.

Bennett proved a very versatile player, playing at centre-half, midfield and centre-forward, scoring some important goals. Alas, he was hit by a number of serious injuries including a pelvic injury, which eventually forced him to retire from the game in 1980. He later held a coaching position with the club and was awarded a well-deserved testimonial in 1982. Bennett now lives in West London and works in the carpentry trade.

SEASON	LEAGUE		FA CUP		FL CUP		TOTAL	
	Apps	*Gls*	*Apps*	*Gls*	*Apps*	*Gls*	*Apps*	*Gls*
1970–71	30	0	3	0	0	0	33	0
1971–72	35	0	4	0	0	0	39	0
1972–73	25	1	0	0	2	0	27	1
1973–74	2	0	0	0	0	0	2	0
1974–75	15 (1)	0	2	0	1	0	18 (1)	0
1975–76	33 (1)	5	0	0	1	0	34 (1)	5
1976–77	25 (2)	5	4	0	2	0	31 (2)	5
1977–78	24	2	5	0	1	1	30	3
1978–79	6	0	0	0	1	0	7	0
	195 (4)	13	18	0	8	1	221 (4)	14

 # Bennett also played in 1(1) Texaco Cup match in 1974–75 and 6(1) Anglo-Scottish Cup matches.

BEVAN, Frederick Walter (1909–13)

Burly centre-forward Fred Bevan was born in Poplar, London, on 27 February 1879. Bevan had a long, distinguished career starting with amateurs Millwall St Johns FC before joining 'big brother' Millwall Athletic on 12 August 1899, making 17 Southern League appearances and scoring seven goals. He moved to Manchester City in May 1901, but after just eight League games he moved back into the Southern League with Reading and scored 20 goals from just 36 appearances. In June 1904 he was with Queen's Park Rangers and netted a further 30 goals from 58 appearances.

In July 1906 Bevan went off to Bury, who paid £340 for his services, ending as their leading goalscorer in 1906–07 with 18 goals from 34 senior appearances. He was with Fulham when they played their first League fixture in September 1907, but after only five games he moved to Derby County during October 1907. He stayed two seasons with the Rams, making 50 League appearances and netting 17 goals. Bevan, although a heavy man, was not a battering-ram type of player but showed neat and deft touches. He became an Oriental in November 1909, and although he was near the veteran stage of his career he led the O's line well, with the likes of McFadden and Dalrymple alongside him.

He was picked to represent the Football League against the Southern League in 1910, and he skippered the club between 1910 and 1913, before Fred Parker took over. Although not as prolific as during his younger days, he still bagged 36 goals during his four seasons at Millfields Road. Bevan left the O's in 1914 to join Chatham FC but returned to the club as reserve-team coach between 1920 and 1923. Fred Bevan died in Poplar on 10 December 1935, aged 56.

SEASON	LEAGUE		FA CUP		TOTAL	
	Apps	*Gls*	*Apps*	*Gls*	*Apps*	*Gls*
1909–10	20	7	1	0	21	7
1910–11	37	12	1	0	38	12
1911–12	34	11	1	1	35	12
1912–13	27	5	1	0	28	5
	118	35	4	1	122	36

BISHOP, Sidney Harold Richard (1953–65)

Sid Bishop was a wonderful centre-half, and would probably, along with John Townrow, be ranked as one of the best ever with the O's. He was a major factor in the club attaining promotion to the First Division. Indeed not one centre-forward scored against him for half a season in 1961–62, and he formed part of the formidable half-back line of Lucas–Bishop–Lea. Born in Tooting on 8 April 1934, his parents were supporters of Tooting & Mitcham FC, and young Sid was often their team mascot. He joined the O's groundstaff in 1953 from the club's nursery side Chase of Chertsey FC and turned pro six months later.

During the promotion season of 1955–56 he made a number of appearances including in the 2–1 victory over Millwall that clinched the Championship. During the promotion campaign of 1961–62 he was ever present. Bishop was no failure in the First Division, playing in 39 matches. Although not noted for his scoring ability, he probably netted one of the longest goals ever seen at Brisbane Road when striking a 40-year drive past the startled Bristol Rovers 'keeper Howard Radford in a 3–2 win on 4 February 1961. He also scored another memorable goal from a long shot against Liverpool in a 2–1 victory on 2 May 1963.

After 13 years with the club, he was released by new boss Dave Sexton in May 1965, joining Southern League Hastings United as player-manager. Later he held a similar position with Guildford City. Sid Bishop was beautifully balanced and majestic in the air, and he was unlucky not to be capped for England. He is still seen regularly at home games and has been seen at various player reunions.

Bishop was presented with an engraved cut-crystal decanter in celebration of his 70th birthday in April 2004 by the Leyton Orient Supporters' Club.

SEASON	LEAGUE		FA CUP		FL CUP		TOTAL	
	Apps	*Gls*	*Apps*	*Gls*	*Apps*	*Gls*	*Apps*	*Gls*
1953–54	8	0	0	0	-	-	8	0
1954–55	0	0	0	0	-	-	0	0
1955–56	15	0	1	0	-	-	16	0
1956–57	4	0	0	0	-	-	4	0
1957–58	31	0	2	0	-	-	33	0
1958–59	29	0	0	0	-	-	29	0
1959–60	42	0	1	0	-	-	43	0
1960–61*	40	3	3	0	2	0	45	3
1961–62	42	0	4	0	3	0	49	0
1962–63	39	1	4	0	3	0	46	1
1963–64	42	0	3	0	1	0	46	0
1964–65	4	0	0	0	0	0	4	0
	296	4	18	0	9	0	323	4

**Football League Cup only started in season 1960–61.*

BLAIR, James Alfred (1949–53)

James Blair excelled during his four years at Brisbane Road and had great skill and vision. Blair, whose grandfather, father and brother were professional footballers, was born in Whiteince, Glasgow, Scotland, on 6 January 1918. As a boy, he lived in South Wales and even represented Wales at Schoolboy level. He signed for Blackpool as an amateur from Cardiff City in June 1935, having played some games for Birmingham City in the Central League. He made his League debut versus Stoke City in September 1937, a few months before his 19th birthday. The *Blackpool News Chronicle* reported 'Young Jimmy Blair filled the stage and captured the limelight, a tall, well-built athlete who is surely destined for international honours.'

Well all those expectations never really materialised, and he had an 'up and down' career with Blackpool between 1935 and 1947, making 51 League appearances and scoring eight goals, but he did win one Scottish international cap versus Wales in October 1946. He was transferred to Bournemouth for £4,150 in October 1947, and after 80 League matches that yielded eight goals he became an Oriental over Christmas 1949.

Blair settled in at Brisbane Road, showing some wonderful skill to delight the O's fans over four seasons, topping the goalscoring charts with 16 goals in 1950–51. He was one of the scorers when the O's beat Dutch side Racing Club of Haarlem 3–1 in a 1951 Festival of Britain match. The O's transfer-listed him in October 1951 and a national newspaper wrote 'It doesn't make sense, he could have been one of the greatest of his time, but his football refuses to conform to the orthodox'. Well he stayed with the O's for two further years, only moving to Kent League side Ramsgate Athletic as player-manager in May 1953. Jimmy Blair died in Llanelli on 12 July 1983.

SEASON	LEAGUE		FA CUP		TOTAL	
	Apps	*Gls*	*Apps*	*Gls*	*Apps*	*Gls*
1949–50	23	3	0	0	23	3
1950–51	45	16	1	0	46	16
1951–52	21	5	1	0	22	5
1952–53	15	2	2	0	17	2
	104	26	4	0	108	26

BLIZZARD, Leslie William Benjamin (1950–56)

An excellent right-half who spent seven years at Brisbane Road, six-footer Les Blizzard became an Oriental during May 1950 from Yeovil Town and proved to be a wonderful servant, and he also kept his colleagues entertained on away trips as he was a fine pianist and vocalist. Born in Acton on 13 March 1923, he started his pro career in 1946–47 with Queen's Park Rangers, appearing four times. In May 1947 he joined Bournemouth & Boscombe, playing just once before breaking his leg, and he then moved into the Southern League with Yeovil and starred in their great FA Cup run of 1949 alongside Alec Stock, when they defeated both Bury and First Division Sunderland.

Blizzard, an excellent right-half who got up well for the ball and

had his own way of 'selling a dummy', appeared in both the O's great FA Cup runs of 1951–52 and 1953–54. He played against Nottingham Forest in August 1956, when the O's returned to Division Two, which turned out to be his final appearance in their colours before moving to Headington United (later Oxford United) in December 1956. He retired at the end of that season, aged 34. Blizzard died in Northampton during 1996.

SEASON	*LEAGUE*		*FA CUP*		*TOTAL*	
	Apps	*Gls*	*Apps*	*Gls*	*Apps*	*Gls*
1950–51	26	1	1	0	27	1
1951–52	40	2	9	0	49	2
1952–53	31	3	2	0	33	3
1953–54	37	2	7	0	44	2
1954–55	46	4	2	0	48	4
1955–56	41	0	4	0	45	0
1956–57	1	0	0	0	1	0
	222	12	25	0	247	12

BOWER, William (1905–1915)

Billy Bower, a 6ft 1in goalkeeper, who weighed over 15st, had the distinction of being the only O's player to appear in at least one League match during all the first 10 seasons of the club's League campaign. Born in Dalston, London, during September 1887 (not 1888 as previously thought), Bower was a member of the Hackney District side and also gained two England Schoolboy caps. He supported the O's in their non-League days, and a local newspaper reported that as a boy he always dreamt of playing for them. He did sign on in May 1905 from the Peel Institute club, with whom he later played cricket during the summer months between 1907 and 1909.

Bower made his League debut on 10 March 1906 after regular 'keeper Joe Redding had conceded 17 goals in four League matches. Being so upset at having let the team down, he walked out of the club. However, Bower did not fare much better, with seven goals going past him in his first two matches. His final League appearance came eight years later, on 17 October 1914, a 1–0 home defeat by Derby County. He turned out to be a very capable custodian and a grand servant to the club. He left in May 1915 to join non-League outfit New Brompton (later Gillingham). In 1919 he played in three Southern League matches and two FA Cup ties. In 1922 he became their trainer-manager, holding that position until 1947, and was then appointed their groundsman. Billy Bower died in Hackney, London, during February 1954, aged 66.

SEASON	*LEAGUE*		*FA CUP*		*TOTAL*	
	Apps	*Gls*	*Apps*	*Gls*	*Apps*	*Gls*
1905–06	11	0	0	0	11	0
1906–07	35	0	0	0	35	0
1907–08	6	0	1	0	7	0
1908–09	9	0	0	0	9	0
1909–10	8	0	0	0	8	0
1910–11	37	0	1	0	38	0
1911–12	20	0	1	0	21	0
1912–13	28	0	0	0	28	0
1913–14	16	0	2	0	18	0
1914–15	1	0	0	0	1	0
	171	0	5	0	176	0

BOWLES, Stanley (1980–81)

Stan Bowles was one of the most skilful players of his era and a delight to watch. He arrived at the club in July 1980 as Jimmy Bloomfield's biggest-name signing for £90,000. Although never quite the same outstanding player he was in his earlier days, the 5ft 10in midfielder still showed plenty of skill and quality touches in his play.

Born in Manchester on 24 December 1948, Bowles started his career as an apprentice with Manchester City in January 1967. He spent nearly four years at Maine Road, playing in just 15(2) League games, scoring twice, but he netted 34 goals from 117 appearances for their reserve side. After playing five times on loan with Bury during early 1970, he signed on a free with Crewe Alexandra on 24 September 1970, netting 18 goals from 51 League appearances.

After a spell with Carlisle United, joining for £12,000 and playing in 33 League games, scoring 12 goals, it was with Queen's Park Rangers that Bowles made his name after joining them on 16 September 1972 for £112,000, scoring 96 goals from 315 senior appearances. While with Rangers, he also gained five full England caps. Brian Clough brought him to Nottingham Forest in December 1979 for over £200,000, but after only 19 League outings and two goals he was snapped up by Bloomfield to become an Oriental. He netted one particularly memorable goal versus Preston North End in October 1980 when he nonchalantly ghosted past three defenders and hit a great left-foot shot on the turn into the roof of the net.

Stan Bowles had gained himself a reputation as being a somewhat wayward character with a weakness for gambling, and it was really no surprise that after Ken Knighton took over as manager, with his strong disciplinary code, that Bowles would be one of the first players to be on their way out of Brisbane Road. He joined Brentford in September 1981 and did wonderfully well with the Bees, being voted their Player of the Year. He netted 16 goals from 80(1) League outings before calling it a day at the end of the 1986–87 season. Although there was always doubt about his temperament, Bowles was indeed a wonderful player and left many magical moments for all supporters to savour over the years. He made a total of 507 career League appearances, netting 127 goals. Nowadays he acts on match days as 'mine host' at Queen's Park Rangers' hospitality suites, and he is ever-popular at that club.

SEASON	LEAGUE		FA CUP		FL CUP		TOTAL	
	Apps	Gls	Apps	Gls	Apps	Gls	Apps	Gls
1980–81	39	6	1	0	2	0	42	6
1981–82	7	1	0	0	1	0	8	1
	46	7	1	0	3	0	50	7

 # Bowles also appeared in three Anglo-Scottish Cup matches and three Football League Groups Cup matches.

BRISLEY, Terence William (1966–75)

An industrious midfielder who spent nine years at Brisbane Road, working his way through the ranks, Terry Brisley joined the club as a 13-year-old schoolboy along with another future O's star, Denis Rofe, in 1966. Born in Stepney, London, on 4 July 1950, he was on the small side at only 5ft 6ins, yet he was new O's boss Jimmy Bloomfield's first signing during March 1968. Brisley made steady progress through the youth and reserve ranks before making his League debut when he came on as a substitute versus Carlisle United in September 1970.

Brisley was a midfield player who was very effective in the build-up of attacks, proving most effective between 1972 and 1974. Brisley was in the side that won the national five-a-side competition when defeating QPR 6–1 in the Final during the mid-70s. He had a loan spell with Southend United in March 1975, making eight League appearances before a permanent move took him to Millwall in July 1975, as part of a deal that brought Doug Allder to Leyton. He made 106(1) League appearances, scoring 14 goals, before joining Charlton Athletic in January 1978 for £20,000, playing 44(4) League matches and notching up five goals.

He was subsequently signed by Portsmouth for £25,000, playing a major part in Pompey gaining promotion from Division Four in 1980, making 55 League appearances with 13 goals, before joining Maidstone United in the Alliance League. Brisley, who now lives in Brentwood, Essex, works in London as a Foreign Exchange broker and is still seen at Orient player reunions.

SEASON	LEAGUE		FA CUP		FL CUP		TOTAL	
	Apps	Gls	Apps	Gls	Apps	Gls	Apps	Gls
1970–71	18(4)	1	3	0	0	0	21(4)	1
1971–72	25(3)	2	0(1)	0	2	0	27(4)	2
1972–73	38(1)	5	1	0	2	0	41(1)	5
1973–74	38(1)	0	3	0	3	0	44(1)	0
1974–75	14	1	0	0	2	0	16	1
	133(9)	9	7(1)	0	9	0	149(10)	9

 # Brisley also appeared in one Texaco Cup match in 1974–75.

BROADBENT, William Henry (1925–32)

William Broadbent performed well during his stay at Millfields Road. Born in Chaddleston, Oldham, on 20 November 1901, he started his career with Wellington Athletic before making 12 League appearances for Oldham Athletic between January 1920 and April 1923. He joined Brentford in June 1924, making a further 17 League appearances. The right-half joined the O's during June 1925, and although not a regular in his first season he did feature in the great 2–0 FA Cup victory over Newcastle United in February 1926 when he came into the match as a last-minute replacement for the injured Bert Rosier. A good reliable player, he performed well during his seven-year stay at Millfields Road. He left to join Preston North End in March 1932, only playing two League matches. Broadbent died in Lancaster on 14 February 1979.

SEASON	*LEAGUE*		*FA CUP*		*TOTAL*	
	Apps	*Gls*	*Apps*	*Gls*	*Apps*	*Gls*
1925–26	9	2	2	0	11	2
1926–27	29	3	2	0	31	3
1927–28	40	1	1	0	41	1
1928–29	24	0	0	0	24	0
1929–30	27	2	3	0	30	2
1930–31	32	0	0	0	32	0
1931–32	37	0	3	0	40	0
	198	8	11	0	209	8

BROOKS, Shaun (1983–87 & 1994–96)

A cultured midfielder who had two good spells with the O's, Shaun Brooks joined an elite band of players who played more than 200 senior games for the club. Born in the south of London on 9 October 1962, this midfielder often showed a skilful first touch. He joined the O's in November 1983 from Crystal Palace where he made 54 League appearances, scoring four goals. He enjoyed some good seasons at Brisbane Road before declining a new contract in 1987, transferring to AFC Bournemouth for £20,000.

He amassed 114(14) League appearances for the Cherries, scoring four goals, during which time he also went on loan to Stockport County in December 1992 after a bust-up with their boss Tony Pulis, which left Brooks with facial cuts. Pulis was reprimanded over the incident. Brooks went on trial with Everton but was not offered a contract, then he went to Crewe Alexandra but decided not to accept their offer. In the end he joined Dorchester Town. During October 1994 he went back to AFC Bournemouth on trial, but after just one League appearance he rejoined the O's in November 1994 to bring some experience to a struggling team at the foot of the table. In May 1996 he was given a free transfer, and he joined Poole Town. During a professional career that spanned some 17 seasons, he played 394(40) matches with 52 goals.

During 1999–2000 37-year-old Brooks played for Wimborne Town in the Wessex League. In 2003 he was manager of Sydenhams Wessex League club Bournemouth Poppies, and in December 2004 he was voted Manager of Month. He resigned in May 2005 and today is

involved in coaching youth players with both AFC Bournemouth and Southampton.

SEASON	*LEAGUE*		*FA CUP*		*FL CUP*		*TOTAL*	
	Apps	*Gls*	*Apps*	*Gls*	*Apps*	*Gls*	*Apps*	*Gls*
1983–84	33 (3)	9	1	0	0	0	34 (3)	9
1984–85	27 (2)	5	1	0	4	0	32 (2)	5
1985–86	35 (3)	7	6	3	4	1	45 (3)	11
1986–87	45	5	4	1	2	0	51	6
1994–95	8 (1)	0	0 (1)	0	0	0	8 (2)	0
1995–96	34 (7)	2	1	0	2	0	37 (7)	2
	182 (16)	28	13 (1)	4	12	1	207 (17)	33

 # Brooks also appeared in 11(3) Auto Windscreens Shield matches, scoring two goals.

BROWN, Edwin (1959–1961)

A great footballer and wonderful character who gave much pleasure during his three years with the O's and throughout his football career, Eddy Brown was (along with Mark Lazarus) one of the most colourful characters ever to wear an Orient shirt. He would brighten up the dullest of matches with his eccentric, clowning antics, like having chats with the fans on the terraces, or a celebration jig around a corner flag every time he scored a goal, and I even heard him quoting Shakespeare to his opposition marker in many a match, that is if they could catch him because of his remarkable speed. Off the field, Brown even had time to work as a male model. Brown was one of the great clowns of the modern game. Goals were what Brown was all about, hitting 200 League goals from 399 career outings.

Brown was born in Preston on 28 February 1926, and his early life makes remarkable reading. He spent eight years as a religious brother at the De La Salle College in Guernsey, and he was known as 'Brother John'. It was reported that his football career started in September 1948 when he walked into the offices of Preston North End and asked for a trial. He impressed them so much that he signed professional forms with the Deepdale club, making 36 appearances with six goals. He became known as the 'Brown bomber' because of his great speed, and he went on to to play for Southampton, between 1950–52, making 57 appearances and scoring 32 goals, Coventry City, between 1951–55, with 85 League appearances netting 60 goals, and Birmingham City, between 1955–59, with 158 appearances and 74 goals. He moved to the O's in January 1959 for £6,000 after an impressive reserve match for City against them at Brisbane Road a week earlier.

He made his debut in a friendly at Brisbane Road against Queen's Park Rangers in a remarkable 9–1 victory. He built up a wonderful relationship with veteran players Eddie Baily and Tommy Johnston – between the three of them their ages totalled 99 years, yet they still managed to steer the O's clear of relegation.

Brown recorded his 200th senior career goal with the O's against Middlesbrough on 30 April 1960. He previously also put four goals past Sunderland in March 1959 and scored a hat-trick against Boro in October 1959. Brown recently informed the author from his home in Fulwood, Preston, about his stay at Orient: 'I was with the O's during the days of Lou and Leslie Grade and their brother Lord Bernard Delfont. Brisbane Road was the 'in' place to be on a Saturday afternoon, stars of stage, screen, radio, TV and 'electric shavers' came along to support the Orient boys in blue.

'I remember the American singer Pat Boone meeting us and later sending the players straw hats. I also remember such stars as the gorgeous Shirley Bassey, Cliff Richard and 'Little' Arthur Askey often at Brisbane Road. I also remember the party to end all parties taking place on a Wednesday night after we had won 1–0 at Bristol City during April 1959 to avoid relegation. The return to Paddington Station was awash with drinks. We were ushered into the Great Western Hotel. I vaguely remembered arriving home on the Friday afternoon. No wonder we lost 4–1 at Grimsby Town the next day, who cared we were still in Division Two. We had some grand players in our ranks, you may have heard of a Scotsman named Johnston, he never stopped finding the net.

'I'm told he now lives down under in Aussie, how does the Walthamstow Dog Track survive without him?'

After three seasons with the O's, Brown joined Scarborough for a four-year spell as player-manager, followed by a similar position with Stourbridge in the Lancashire League. When approaching 40 years of age, he was with Wigan Athletic, also in the Lancashire League. He retired three years later to become a part-time French tutor at All Hallows School. He was still managing Broughton Amateurs in 2001, as well as working in the family carpet business in Fulwood and as a successful compère on the after-dinner circuit.

Brown concluded 'Look at me I'm still getting a kick out of football at my age, I have one foot in the grave and the other on a banana skin.'

SEASON	*LEAGUE*		*FA CUP*		*FL CUP*		*TOTAL*	
	Apps	*Gls*	*Apps*	*Gls*	*Apps*	*Gls*	*Apps*	*Gls*
1958–59	16	10	0	0	-	-	16	10
1959–60	35	12	1	0	-	-	36	12
1960–61	12	6	0	0	2	1	14	7
	63	28	1	0	2	1	66	29

BROWN, Thomas Law (1950–53)

A brilliant schemer who caused havoc among defenders and delighted the O's fans for three years, Tommy Brown was born in Glenbuck, Ayrshire, Scotland, on 17 April 1921 and started his career with Cambuslang Rangers. The 5ft 10in player joined Heart of Midlothian in 1938, making 27 Scottish League appearances, and he also played for a Scottish representative side at the age of 17 in a wartime international against England on 2 December 1939 at Newcastle. He won three caps in total. Hailed as a 'brilliant prospect' like so many of his contemporaries, his professional career was curtailed by World War Two. After the war, he joined Millwall in January 1945, making 68 League appearances and scoring seven goals. He moved to Charlton Athletic in October 1948 for a large fee for those days of £8,500, making 36 senior appearances and scoring once.

Thomas Brown joined the O's on 4 August 1950 for a fee of just £300. One of his best displays was at Birmingham City in the fourth round of the FA Cup during February 1952, when his brilliant scheming caused havoc for the City defence. Brown was a master tactician and excellent ball distributor and captained the team in the 1951–52 season. Sadly he sustained a serious leg injury versus Bristol Rovers on 7 March 1953, which eventually forced him to retire. He became coach with Dartford in July 1953. A benefit match was staged for him in April 1954 when many top players of the day, including Stanley Matthews, appeared. Tommy Brown died in Edinburgh on 10 May 1966 at the young age of just 45.

SEASON	*LEAGUE*		*FA CUP*		*TOTAL*	
	Apps	*Gls*	*Apps*	*Gls*	*Apps*	*Gls*
1950–51	30	0	1	0	31	0
1951–52	39	3	9	2	48	5
1952–53	30	2	0	0	30	2
	99	5	10	2	109	7

BUCHANAN, David (1906–08)

Born in Bellshire, Scotland, in 1873, Dave, or 'Buck' Buchanan as he was known, was reported as being the only known outfield player to have worn a black skull cap while on the field of play. He was one of the real characters in the O's early League days, and he stood at just 5ft 7in and weighed 11st 7lb. Buchanan started his career with Third Lanark, moving to Southern League Brentford in 1903, then on to

Middlesbrough in 1904 for whom he only played reserve football. He joined Plymouth Argyle in 1905, making 17 Southern League and 12 Western League appearances, scoring twice.

The 33-year-old was a clever, grafting player who was a very consistent right-half or inside-forward. He joined the O's from Argyle in July 1906, and after two successful seasons he moved in June 1908 to Southern League outfit Leyton FC as player-manager. It was Buchanan who first signed a young Charles Buchan, later to become a very famous player with Sunderland, Arsenal and England. Having spent three years with Charlton Athletic as assistant manager and coach, he was appointed manager of the newly-formed Thames Association in 1928 and was their manager when they were elected into the Third Division South two years later.

SEASON	*LEAGUE*		*FA CUP*		*TOTAL*	
	Apps	*Gls*	*Apps*	*Gls*	*Apps*	*Gls*
1906–07*	31	2	-	-	31	2
1907–08	34	0	5	3	39	3
	65	2	5	3	70	5

** Clapton Orient did not enter into the FA Cup in 1906–07.*

BULLOCK, Michael Edwin (1968–76)

A grand club servant who, along with Tommy Johnston, ranks as one of the finest headers of a ball to play for the club, Mickey Bullock was born in Stoke on 2 October 1946. The 5ft 11in striker joined the O's as a 22-year-old from Oxford United for £8,000 during October 1968. The former England Schoolboy was apprenticed in October 1963, making his League debut as a 16-year-old with Birmingham City, scoring the winner against Manchester United in January 1964. After 27 appearances and 10 goals for the Blues, he was transferred to Oxford in June 1967 for £10,000. He was their top scorer with 13 goals from 45 appearances, helping them to win the Third Division Championship.

Bullock had some wonderful seasons with the O's, scoring 19 goals in the Third Division Championship-winning side of 1969–70. He also hit 16 goals when the O's missed promotion to Division One in 1973–74 by a single point. He scored in the vital match against Aston Villa but his last-minute effort that could have given the O's a First Division place was tipped over the bar. Mickey Bullock was never the dashing type of centre-forward, more the subtle player who seemed to 'hang' in the air when jumping for a header, and he was able to lay off the ball very well.

It was with sadness that he left the club to join Halifax Town in February 1976, staying there for nine years, firstly as a player, making 119(9) senior appearances and scoring 21 goals, then in 1979 as coach and then manager from July 1981. Bullock was sacked as manager on 22 October 1984. His managerial record with Halifax (from 13 July 1981 to October 1984) read: P148, W39, D46, L63, F169, A245, Pts163. He later managed Goole Town and Ossett Town and was a scout for Hereford United, Portsmouth and Crystal Palace. Recently he worked as an insurance consultant.

Bullock talked to the author a few years ago about his stay at the O's:

'We were always looked after at the club, and I enjoyed the close-knit family atmosphere.' About the triumphant 1969–70 season, he maintained 'We gained promotion by not trying to kick our way out of the Third Division. A lot of the credit must go to boss Jimmy Bloomfield and his assistant Peter Angell. They always stressed that if you keep playing good football promotion would come. I was saddened that both died at a young age.

'I will always remember the great FA Cup run under George Petchey in 1971–72, especially when we came back from the dead against Chelsea. We were so "unlucky" to lose against Arsenal, hitting the woodwork three times, but it was not to be our day.

'Obviously the 1973–74 season was great, yet very sad when we missed promotion in 1974 by a single point with the draw against Aston Villa. I will never forget the faces of the lads in the dressing room. I think everyone was in tears, your books depict it so very well with the pictures of both Barrie [Fairbrother] and Ricky [Heppolette] crying.'

He concluded 'I must say I still have a soft spot for the O's and always look for their results.'

Mickey Bullock scored 109 career League goals from 450(19) appearances. In 2005 it was reported that 58-year-old Bullock had been suffering from ill health for a while.

SEASON	*LEAGUE*		*FA CUP*		*FL CUP*		*TOTAL*	
	Apps	*Gls*	*Apps*	*Gls*	*Apps*	*Gls*	*Apps*	*Gls*
1968–69	33	6	2	0	0	0	35	6
1969–70	42	19	2	0	2	0	46	19
1970–71	41 (1)	5	3	0	1	0	45 (1)	5
1971–72	42	11	4	1	2	1	48	13
1972–73	25 (6)	4	0	0	2	0	27 (6)	4
1973–74	40 (1)	16	4	0	4	2	48 (1)	18
1974–75	28	3	0	0	2	0	30	3
1975–76	16 (2)	1	1	0	1	0	18 (2)	1
	267 (10)	65	16	1	14	3	297 (10)	69

 # Mickey Bullock also appeared in one Texaco Cup match in 1974–75.

CARTER, Daniel Stephen (1988–95)

A regular with the O's for six seasons, who has carved out for himself a wonderful career in Wales, wingman Danny Carter was born in Hackney, London, on 29 June 1969. He started his career with Brighton & Hove Albion as a 16-year-old. A couple of years later he left England to play in Sweden with the IS Nornan club, and the club finished runners-up in the Swedish Third Division. On his return to the UK, he joined Diadora League side Billericay before becoming an Oriental in July 1988. He made his League debut as a substitute against Scunthorpe United and also played as a substitute in the O's first promotion Play-off match at Scarborough in May 1989.

Carter played consistently for six seasons, although he suffered a nasty injury at Hull City in March 1992, which kept him on the sidelines for nearly six months. His most successful season was in 1993–94, but like the rest of his teammates he suffered a loss of form in the relegation battle of 1994–95, although he did play well in the Cup run to the Southern Area semi-final of the Auto Windscreens Shield. Carter was in the process of signing for Peterborough United in June 1995 for £35,000 when new O's boss Pat Holland was appointed. He wanted him to stay, but Carter had already put pen to paper. He made 45 League appearances for Posh that yielded one goal and was given a free transfer and joined former Oriental Gary Barnett, manager with Barry Town in Wales, on 1 September 1997, playing 31(3) matches there and scoring five goals. He was voted their Player of the Year for 1997–98.

Carter joined Merthyr Tydfil in January 1998, and in December 2004 the 34-year-old midfielder made his 200th appearance for the Southern League Premier Division side. Carter is known as one of the finest players to play for that club, winning a Dr Martens Western

League medal in 2003. He left them in May 2005 and joined Cardiff Grange Quins in the Masterfit Welsh Premier League, but after playing 10(1) games without finding the net he moved to Clevedon Town in January 2006 and made 4(2) appearances before hanging up his boots after making over 700 career appearances.

SEASON	*LEAGUE*		*FA CUP*		*FL CUP*		*TOTAL*	
	Apps	*Gls*	*Apps*	*Gls*	*Apps*	*Gls*	*Apps*	*Gls*
1988–89*	0(2)	0	0	0	0	0	0(2)	0
1989–90	29(2)	5	1	0	4	2	34(2)	7
1990–91	38(4)	5	5	1	4(1)	0	47(5)	6
1991–92	15(5)	2	0	0	3(1)	0	18(6)	2
1992–93	26(3)	3	0	0	0	0	26(3)	3
1993–94	35(1)	7	2	1	2	0	39(1)	8
1994–95	25(4)	0	2	1	0(1)	0	27(5)	1
	168(21)	22	10	3	13(3)	2	191(24)	27

** Included in the 1988–89 season is one Play-off appearance as a playing substitute.*

 # Danny Carter also appeared in 17(1) Auto Windscreens Shield matches, scoring one goal.

CASTLE, Stephen Charles (1984–92, 1996–97 (loan) & 2000–02)

A great player, who scored a remarkable 67 goals for the O's from his midfield position, Steve Castle, a 5ft 11in, tenacious and tireless midfielder, always gave 100 percent and was not afraid to go in where the boots were flying. One of just a handful to have had three spells with the club, after returning home when he re-signed on 2 July 2000 from Peterborough United, Castle had a tremendous goalscoring record for a midfielder, and it was hoped he would be able to improve on his seventh overall ranking in the O's all-time goalscoring list. He was also ranked 18th overall on the all-time appearances list, but ongoing injuries curtailed his progress on his return and he was not able to add to his total.

Born in Barkingside, Essex, on 17 May 1966, Castle joined the O's as a schoolboy, becoming an apprentice on 18 May 1984. His League debut came at full-back against Bradford City in September 1984. He had a memorable match at Rochdale in May 1985, scoring four goals, and he played a vital role in the promotion season of 1988–89. In 1990 it appeared he would be on his way with a move to Wimbledon, but the deal fell through and he signed a new two-year contract. He was the O's top goalscorer in 1990–91.

After becoming a free agent in 1992, he refused a new deal and joined Peter Shilton at Plymouth Argyle on 2 June 1992. The O's evaluation was £250,000, but Shilton's offer fell well short. In the end a tribunal fixed his fee at £195,000. He finished joint top scorer at Home Park with another former Oriental, Kevin Nugent, both on 11 goals. He netted 35 goals from 98(3) League appearances, before joining Birmingham City on 21 July 1995 for £225,000. After just 16(7) League appearances with one goal, he went on loan to Gillingham and then with the O's on 3 February 1997 after a five-year gap, scoring in his third match versus Rochdale, the O's first win from seven starts, with a rare headed goal. His loan spell was cut short after he needed cartilage surgery.

The O's boss Taylor wanted to sign Castle, but in the end he joined his former Birmingham boss Barry Fry at Peterborough United as player-coach on 14 May 1997 on a free transfer. He continued his scoring ways with Posh, reaching a wonderful career milestone of 100 League goals in 1999 and ended his career with them in a promotion Play-off Final victory at Wembley in May 2000. He declined a new contract after playing 102 matches and netting 17 goals, and re-signed for the O's, taking him back to where he started his career.

Unfortunately Castle had to undergo knee surgery but the problem was slow to clear and he had further minor surgery in October 2000. It was hoped he would return to the fray in 2001 after 'The Barkingsider' came through a reserve match on 14 February 2001 unscathed, playing in the first half against AFC Bournemouth, and came on as a substitute for the final five minutes in the 3–2 win at Lincoln City 10 days later, but he struggled with fitness, making just a handful of appearances that season. He was hoping to make it third time lucky in the Play-offs, having previously been promoted with the O's and Peterborough United, but it was not meant to be, and the O's lost in the Play-off Final at the Millennium Stadium in Wales to Blackpool 4–2.

Castle was awarded a testimonial, a match against Tottenham Hotspur in July 2001, which attracted a crowd of 6,636, with Spurs winning 2–0. In September he went on loan to Conference side Stevenage Borough and stayed for two months. After returning to Brisbane Road, he decided to retire from playing League football with a record of 458(37) League appearances and a remarkable 110 goals from his midfield position.

In June 2002 he moved to St Albans City as player-coach and appeared for them in their 4–1 first-round FA Cup defeat at Stockport County in November 2002. In January 2003 he was appointed as assistant manager under Barry Fry at Second Division Peterborough United. However, in June 2003 he was back with St Albans City as assistant manager. In June 2004 he was their manager, having signed a two-year contract. On 13 November 2004 Castle was seen playing for Hornchurch in their 5–2 FA Cup defeat at Boston United. In fact, he scored the opening goal on four minutes before 2,437 fans, having signed on the eve of the game. He resigned as player-manager of St Albans on 27 October 2005, having made 45(15) appearances with three goals. In July 2006 Castle was appointed manager of Essex Olympian League Division One side Tateley FC.

SEASON	*LEAGUE*		*FA CUP*		*FL CUP*		*TOTAL*	
	Apps	*Gls*	*Apps*	*Gls*	*Apps*	*Gls*	*Apps*	*Gls*
1984–85	20 (1)	1	3	0	0	0	23 (1)	1
1985–86	19 (4)	4	1 (1)	1	1	0	21 (5)	5
1986–87	22 (2)	5	4	1	0 (1)	0	26 (3)	6
1987–88	42	10	4	0	2	0	48	10
1988–89*	26 (2)	6	0	0	0	0	26 (2)	6
1989–90	27	7	1	0	4	2	32	9
1990–91	45	12	5	3	6	3	56	18
1991–92	35 (2)	10	5	1	2	0	42 (2)	11
1996–97**	4	1	0	0	0	0	4	1
2000–01+	4 (8)	0	0 (1)	0	0	0	4 (9)	0
2001–02	0 (1)	0	0	0	0 (1)	0	0 (2)	0
	244 (20)	56	23 (2)	6	15 (2)	5	282 (24)	67

* *Includes four promotion Play-off matches in 1988–89.*

** *On loan.*

+ *Includes 2(1) promotion Play-off matches in 2000–01.*

Castle also appeared in 14(2) Auto Windscreens Shield matches.

CHARLTON Stanley (1952–56 & 1958–65)

Stan Charlton was one of the most popular players to wear an O's shirt and a great captain. He was a wonderful left-back with a unique sliding tackle, the only O's captain to lead his men into the old First Division. Born in Exeter on 28 June 1929, he first established himself with Isthmian League side Bromley, with whom he won three England amateur caps, and he was a member of the Great Britain squad for the Helsinki Olympic Games in 1952. Charlton, who stood at 5ft 10in and weighed 12st, joined the O's as an amateur in July 1952 and was ever present in his first season. During October 1955 he and Vic Groves moved to Arsenal for a joint-fee of £30,000. He stayed three seasons at Highbury, playing 99 First Division games before returning to Brisbane Road during December 1958.

The highlight of Charlton's career was being chaired off the pitch after the match versus Bury that clinched the O's promotion to Division One in April 1962. He left in 1965 to take over as player-manager of Weymouth with 17(1) appearances, but he stopped playing after a cartilage operation. He stayed at the club until May 1972. A benefit match was staged for his service to the O's in April 1970.

Some years ago the author caught up with Stan Charlton at his home in Wimborne. He recalled his stay with Orient.

'The football played and the atmosphere at the club was most enjoyable, and I used to think how lucky I was that instead of paying 3s 6d to watch the O's, here I was being paid to play for this great little club.'

Charlton scored just two League goals for the O's, but one gave him great satisfaction, coming at his home-town club Exeter City, the O's winning 7–1. A third, a penalty, came in a friendly against Scottish side Falkirk, a 2–2 draw in 1959–60.

'I remember being very disappointed in October 1955 when the papers were full of my impending move to Tottenham Hotspur, but the deal fell through when the Spurs board wanted the money owed for the transfer of Billy Rees some years before. The O's boss Alec Stock said to me, "Don't worry Stan I'll find you another great club."

'That was on the Tuesday; on the Friday I had moved with Groves to Arsenal. I shall never forget Christmas 1958 when there was a knock on my door. There was Alec Stock; within half an hour I had rejoined the O's. Things happened quickly in those days.

'I remember most vividly the scenes when the O's were promoted to Division One in April 1962 with our 2–0 win over Bury. Promotion had to be the highlight of my career. Being chaired-off the pitch was an unforgettable moment.'

'I also remember my 100th match in Division One against the Arsenal, our first match in the Division, yet it was no fairytale, we lost 2–1 in a close-fought match. I also remember our great 1–0 win over Manchester United and Terry McDonald's last minute corker; he never stopped talking about that goal.

'Since retiring I've continued my association with football through the Dorset FA, and I was greatly surprised with my benefit staged in 1970.'

Charlton has returned to the club for a number of player reunions, and he stated they 'are the happiest moments of my life, after being in the company of the old players it was like turning the clock back to a League match all those years ago.' Charlton was recently honoured with a celebration in May 2000 for his 70th birthday. Also in attendance was Malcolm Graham, the man whose goals took the O's to promotion to Division One.

SEASON	*LEAGUE*		*FA CUP*		*FL CUP*		*TOTAL*	
	Apps	*Gls*	*Apps*	*Gls*	*Apps*	*Gls*	*Apps*	*Gls*
1952–53	46	0	2	0	-	-	48	0
1953–54	43	0	7	0	-	-	50	0
1954–55	46	1	2	0	-	-	48	1
1955–56	16	0	0	0	-	-	16	0
1958–59	17	0	1	0	-	-	18	0
1959–60	29	0	1	0	-	-	30	0
1960–61*	31	0	3	0	3	0	37	0
1961–62	41	0	4	0	3	0	48	0
1962–63	42	0	4	0	5	0	51	0
1963–64	42	1	3	0	1	0	46	1
1964–65	14	0	1	0	1	0	16	0
	367	2	28	0	13	0	408	2

* *First year of the League Cup competition.*

CHIEDOZIE, John Okechukwu 'Okay' (1976–81)

The winger John Chiedozie went on to win seven Nigerian caps while with Orient. He was awarded the Officer of the Order of Nigeria by Nigerian President Olusegun Obasanjo in late 2002 for his contribution to Nigerian football.

Born in Owerri, Nigeria, on 18 April 1960, his family relocated to England to avoid the Nigerian civil war when he was just 13 years old. He was one of many youngsters developed by the O's boss George Petchey, who was never afraid to plunge the 'boys' into first-team action. 'Chidders', as he was affectionately known, was given his chance in a Second Division match against Millwall on 8 March 1977, just before his 17th birthday, after another youngster Laurie Cunningham was sold to West Bromwich Albion.

'Chidders' had made a rapid rise through schoolboy football and was offered a trial with West Ham United, but he left and signed for the O's on apprentice forms in July 1976. He showed plenty of pace and soon established himself as a first-team regular in the 1977–78 season. At the start of the O's great FA Cup run, he laid on the pass for Peter Kitchen to score at Norwich City, but the next day he broke his leg when coming on as a substitute at Ipswich Town in a Southern floodlit Youth Cup match. That put paid to his season and allowed another young winger, Kevin Godfrey, to be given his chance of stardom.

After his return from injury, he continued to excel on the wing, and it was no surprise that newly elected First Division outfit Notts County came in with a £600,000 record bid that was too good to refuse for the O's chairman Brian Winston, although it was reported that boss Jimmy Bloomfield was against the deal. 'Chidders' won seven Nigerian caps – alongside another Oriental Tunji Banjo – during his stay at Brisbane Road, the first cap being on 12 July 1981 against Tunisia, and he scored his first goal for his country the following December against Tanzania in a World Cup Qualifier. His second goal came in the 1–1 away draw at Guinea the following April.

'Chidders' performed well in the top grade, making 110(1) appearances with 16 goals. During August 1984 he joined Tottenham Hotspur for £350,000 but suffered with injuries at White Hart Lane, making 45(8) League appearances, bagging 12 goals and winning three further Nigerian international caps against Liberia in October 1984 and twice against Tunisia during July 1995, these being his last caps. He was given a free transfer by Spurs and played out his career with Derby County, Notts County and Chesterfield before having to retire through another injury in 1990. During a career that spanned some 13 years, he made a total of 293(18) League appearances with 48 goals.

Nowadays 'Chidders' is living near Burton-on-Sea. He was one of the guests of honour at a Supporters' Club Star Man Dinner in May 2003.

SEASON	*LEAGUE*		*FA CUP*		*FL CUP*		*TOTAL*	
	Apps	*Gls*	*Apps*	*Gls*	*Apps*	*Gls*	*Apps*	*Gls*
1976–77	6(9)	0	0	0	0	0	6(9)	0
1977–78	21	2	2	0	3	0	26	2
1978–79	33(3)	6	3	1	1	0	37(3)	7
1979–80	35(2)	3	1	1	2	1	38(2)	5
1980–81	36	9	1	0	2	0	39	9
	131(14)	20	7	2	8	1	146(14)	23

 # Chiedozie also appeared in seven Anglo-Scottish Cup matches, scoring one goal, and two Football League Groups Cup matches, scoring one goal.

COATES, Ralph (1978–81)

Ralph Coates was a credit to the game, not only for his total commitment but also for his impeccable fair play. Born in Hetton-le-Hole on 26 April 1946, he started his career as an apprentice with Burnley in October 1961 after working as a colliery fitter and playing for Eppleton Colliery Welfare. He was one of a number of young talented players to come through the Turf Moor youth ranks. The stocky little winger stood at 5ft 7½in and weighed 11st 10lb and had seven wonderful years with the Clarets, making 214 League appearances, scoring 26 goals. He also won two full England caps. Coates moved to Tottenham Hotspur for £190,000 in May 1971, and he netted the goal that won the League Cup Final. He also appeared in the 1972 and 1974 UEFA Cup Finals, gaining a winners' medal in 1974.

After making 173(15) senior appearances and scoring 14 goals at White Hart Lane, Coates was signed on a free transfer by the O's boss Jimmy Bloomfield during October 1978, along with Ian Moores, after Coates had come back from a loan spell with the St George's club in Australia. He had two splendid seasons at Brisbane Road, and although aged 32 he was a key figure over the period, always giving 100 percent in his new midfield role even when playing in the reserves as player-coach.

Coates excelled when running with the ball and scored some grand goals, including two against his former club Burnley in August

1979. He retired from professional football in 1982 and moved into the non-League circuit with Hertford Heath, Ware FC and finally with Nazeing FC. Upon retirement he managed two Leisure Centres, the Marconi Sports Club in Chelmsford and then Elliott Sports & Social Club in Boreham Wood, and is trained as a sports psychology counsellor. Today he also works as a host for League games at White Hart Lane.

SEASON	*LEAGUE*		*FA CUP*		*FL CUP*		*TOTAL*	
	Apps	*Gls*	*Apps*	*Gls*	*Apps*	*Gls*	*Apps*	*Gls*
1978–79	30	3	2	0	0	0	32	3
1979–80	42	9	3	0	2	0	47	9
1980–81	4	0	0	0	1	0	5	0
	76	12	5	0	3	0	84	12

 # Coates also appeared in three Anglo-Scottish Cup matches.

COCKERILL, Glenn (1993–96)

A wonderful servant to the game of football, Glenn Cockerill joined the O's from Southampton after a very long and distinguished career and stayed for three years. This popular and very talented midfielder was born in Grimsby on 25 August 1959 and started his career with non-League Louth United. He joined the O's from Southampton in 1993 (the Saints had paid £225,000 for him from Sheffield United) and stayed at Brisbane Road for three seasons. He even became joint caretaker manager (after the Sitton/Turner duo were sacked) for the fixture at Bristol Rovers on 22 April 1995 with youth coach Tom Loizou.

Cockerill ruled himself out of the 'Gaffer's' job on a full-time basis. He said 'I enjoyed the manager's role at Bristol, but I enjoy playing more. Even though I'm 36 years old I can carry on playing for a few more years.' Cockerill would have certainly been a popular choice of manager with the fans. He enjoyed one more season at the club, but in May 1996 he was among a group of eight players to be released by new O's boss Pat Holland. The departure of Cockerill came as a big disappointment to the fans. Holland stated 'The decision to release Cockerill was taken by the board, even after he had offered to take a drop in salary to stay with the club.'

The boss added 'He has carried our midfield for the past two seasons. He's got so much experience, and he could have given us another year.' A shocked Cockerill said 'I would have loved to stay at Orient another year because things could have come right at the club.'

Cockerill joined Fulham on 5 July 1996, and despite his age he did extremely well at Craven Cottage when Fulham clinched the runners-up spot in Division Three in 1996–97. He was awarded a testimonial for his achievements in football and then followed Mickey Adams to Brentford as assistant player-manager on 6 November 1997. He became assistant manager with Bashley FC in July 1998, and in 2000 he was on the coaching staff at Crystal Palace alongside Ray Houghton, and was the assistant manager under Palace boss Alan Smith but was sacked on 18 March 2001.

In January 2002 he joined Woking and was appointed head coach two months later. During November 2002 he was appointed manager,

and seven months later he was offered a long-term contract. A wonderful servant to the game, he made a career total of 771(49) League appearances with 95 goals in a career than spanned some 21 years.

SEASON	*LEAGUE*		*FA CUP*		*FL CUP*		*TOTAL*	
	Apps	*Gls*	*Apps*	*Gls*	*Apps*	*Gls*	*Apps*	*Gls*
1993–94	19	2	0	0	0	0	19	2
1994–95	32(1)	4	2	0	2	1	36(1)	5
1995–96	38	1	1	0	2	0	41	1
	89(1)	7	3	0	4	1	96(1)	8

 # Cockerill also appeared in 10 Auto Windscreens Shield matches.

COMFORT, Alan (1986–89)

Alan Comfort was one of the great O's wingmen, voted in 1999 by the fans as the second greatest player of all time, with 11 percent of all votes cast. Today he is the club's chaplain. Alan Comfort joined the O's in March 1986 for a small fee from Cambridge United after making 61(3) appearances and netting five goals; it was good to see a decent, old-fashioned winger back at the club. Comfort was born in Aldershot on 8 December 1964, and he started his career as an apprentice with Queen's Park Rangers in October 1982. His opportunities were limited so he joined Cambridge in October 1984, scoring on his League debut against the O's. Comfort missed very few matches and can be compared with another former great O's wingman Owen Williams. Both players, with their exciting wing play, would bring a buzz around the ground with exhilarating left-wing dribbles.

After the O's great victory over Wrexham in the promotion Play-off Final at Brisbane Road in June 1989, he was rushed off to Ireland to be married. He scored 18 goals that season, a wonderful return for a winger. Like Owen Williams, back in March 1924 Comfort joined Middlesbrough in July 1989 for £175,000; however, he was close to signing for AFC Bournemouth, but the O's boss Frank Clark knew he could get a bigger club and deal for his charge.

On 4 November 1989 tragedy occurred in a League match at Newcastle United: in trying to retrieve a ball he fell badly and twisted his knee, snapping the cruciate ligament. After three knee operations his professional career was over after just 18 senior appearances and two goals for Boro. He received a cash pay-off instead of the testimonial that he hoped for.

Comfort decided to enter the clergy, and in December 1990 it was announced that he had become a vicar after studying theology in Durham. He said at the time 'I would love one day to return to East London. I feel there is a job to be done there. It is where I played most of my football with Orient. When I was badly injured it was Frank Clark who was always good to me; I don't really think there is a nicer person and club in football. When I got injured a lot of people disappeared, but Frank always kept in touch.'

Comfort became curate at St Chad's, Chadwell Heath, and more recently was vicar of St Stephen's Church in Albert Road, Buckhurst Hill, Essex. Well it is quite remarkable that the Revd Alan Comfort is today chaplain with Leyton Orient Football Club. In a recent interview about football being a beautiful game, not a religion, Comfort felt it was 'sad the way football fans become obsessed with a club or idolise players, it's sad that football has become a false God, it promises you nothing and delivers nothing. I love football and loved playing it, but there are more important things in the world. I recognise people's need to worship something, but I believe it should be God.'

SEASON	*LEAGUE*		*FA CUP*		*FL CUP*		*TOTAL*	
	Apps	*Gls*	*Apps*	*Gls*	*Apps*	*Gls*	*Apps*	*Gls*
1985–86	15	5	0	0	0	0	15	5
1986–87	40 (5)	11	2 (1)	0	2	0	44 (6)	11
1987–88	46	12	4	1	2	0	52	13
1988–89*	48	18	3	0	5	1	56	19
	149 (5)	46	9 (1)	1	9	1	167 (6)	48

 # Comfort also appeared in seven Auto Windscreens Shield matches, scoring two goals.

COOPER, Mark David (1989–94)

A master of his art Mark Cooper will go down in the annuals of the O's history as the player who scored the goal against Wrexham in that Play-off Final at Leyton in June 1989 when shooting home from 12 yards with just eight minutes remaining. The striker proved to be a quite brilliant signing by boss Frank Clark. Cooper went on to score over 50 senior goals for the club.

Born in Watford, Herts, on 5 April 1967, Cooper joined the O's in February 1989 as a 21-year-old who had already crammed an enormous amount of action into a career following spells with Cambridge United, Tottenham Hotspur, Shrewsbury Town and Gillingham.

This big bustling striker stood at 6ft 1in and weighed over 13st, and he made his League debut for Cambridge at just 17 years of age and went on to score 17 goals from 62(9) appearances. He was snapped up by Spurs in April 1987 for £50,000, but it was an unhappy period in his career and there were times when he couldn't even make the reserve team. He moved to Shrewsbury Town on loan when playing against Gillingham. Cooper impressed them so much that they paid Spurs their club-record fee of £102,500. He made 38(11) senior appearances for the Gills, scoring 11 goals.

He joined the O's in February 1989 for £21,500 and went on to become their 14th all-time senior club scorer with 54 goals over six seasons at Brisbane Road. None were more valuable than the two goals against Scarborough in the Play-offs and one, as already mentioned, against Wrexham in the Play-off Final. His goalscoring achievements were quite remarkable considering he had a number of long-term injuries. He fittingly scored the club's 4,000th League goal against Wigan Athletic on 14 April 1990 when turning and slamming the ball from fully 20 yards into the net. It is a pity it was not photographed.

He left the O's to join Barnet on 13 July 1994 on a free transfer and hit two against the O's in their 4–0 win in the Coca-Cola League Cup on 16 August 1994 (also in the Barnet side that night were two former 'Orientals' Carl Hoddle and Mickey Tomlinson). Cooper scored 23 goals for the Bees from 64(12) senior appearances. This was not the end of 'Coops', he was transferred to Northampton Town in August 1996 on a free transfer and spent a successful season with The Cobblers, which saw them reach the Play-off Finals. He played 37(4) League matches, scoring 10 goals. He played in just one Play-off match at Cardiff City on 10 May 1997, but he sustained a serious injury, missing their victory in the final at Wembley Stadium. His League career ended on a total of 107 League goals from 348 appearances, but his goalscoring achievements did not stop there.

Cooper still knocked in the goals for Welling United, scoring 19 goals from 40(1) appearances in 1997–98 and four goals from 22(4) appearances in 1998–99. In January 1999 he went on a month's loan to Bishop Stortford. The 32-year-old then joined Gravesend & Northfleet on a free transfer, scoring on his debut versus Bishop Stortford on 30 March 1999.

'Coops' special Orient memory, as recently stated, was 'Well it must be the goal against Wrexham in the Play-off Final, it will always stick in my mind'. He ranks along with Colin West and Carl Griffiths as being the most prolific striker for the O's over the past two decades. He scored 107 career League goals from 322(66) appearances.

SEASON	*LEAGUE*		*FA CUP*		*FL CUP*		*TOTAL*	
	Apps	*Gls*	*Apps*	*Gls*	*Apps*	*Gls*	*Apps*	*Gls*
1988–89*	14 (4)	7	0	0	0	0	14 (4)	7
1989–90	38 (1)	11	1	0	4	1	43 (1)	12
1990–91	18 (4)	9	0	0	0	0	18 (4)	9
1991–92	11 (7)	6	2 (2)	1	0	0	13 (9)	7
1992–93	20 (8)	7	2	2	2	1	24 (8)	10
1993–94	20 (9)	8	3	1	0	0	23 (9)	9
	121 (33)	48	8 (2)	4	6	2	135 (35)	54

** Cooper's record includes four appearances and three goals in Play-off Finals in 1988–89.*

 # Cooper also appeared in 6(2) Auto Windscreens Shield matches, scoring one goal.

CORNWELL, John Anthony (1981–87)

Blond-haired John Cornwell is in the record books as the scorer of the O's fastest ever League goal versus Torquay United on 18 March 1986, witnessed by only 1,828 spectators, scoring in just 14 seconds.

Born in Bethnal Green, London, on 13 October 1964, he was yet another youngster from West Ham's youth ranks to move across to Leyton. He was signed by Jimmy Bloomfield in July 1981 after representing both Essex and London schoolboys and was a player who had a good biting tackle and was good at running off the ball and is one of only 40 or so players to have made more than 200 senior appearances for the club.

He signed a professional contract on his 18th birthday and made his League debut at Norwich City in May 1982. The

midfielder, although often troubled by injuries, was a regular for the following five seasons before being signed by Newcastle United on 9 July 1987 for £50,000. The Magpies saw him as a utility player. He never settled at St James' Park, making 28(5) League appearances and scoring once, before a £50,000 transfer took him to Second Division Swindon Town during December 1988. He also never settled at the County Ground, making just 7(18) League appearances. In August he joined Southend United for £45,000, and during his four-year spell on the coast he played in 92(9) matches, scoring five goals. He later had loan spells with Cardiff City, in August 1993, making five appearances with two goals, Brentford, during September 1993 with four appearances, and finally with Northampton Town, in February 1994, making 13 League appearances with one goal, but he could never capture the form he had at Brisbane Road. More recently, he was running the Reindeer Public House in Black Notley, Essex, and coaching a local Sunday football side in the village.

SEASON	*LEAGUE*		*FA CUP*		*FL CUP*		*TOTAL*	
	Apps	*Gls*	*Apps*	*Gls*	*Apps*	*Gls*	*Apps*	*Gls*
1981–82	3	0	0	0	0	0	3	0
1982–83	30 (2)	3	1	0	0	0	31 (2)	3
1983–84	42	7	1	0	2	1	45	8
1984–85	33 (3)	10	2	1	2 (1)	1	37 (4)	12
1985–86	41 (3)	8	6	1	3	0	50 (3)	9
1986–87	45 (1)	7	4	0	2	0	51 (1)	7
	194 (9)	35	14	2	9 (1)	2	217 (10)	39

 # Cornwell also appeared in seven Auto Windscreens Shield matches, scoring two goals.

CRAWFORD, Edmund Charles (1933–35)

Edmund Crawford ranks as one of the O's greatest-ever strikers. A big, tough centre-forward, he stood at 5ft 11in and weighed 12st 7lb. He joined from Liverpool in July 1933 after making just seven appearances with four goals at Anfield. He previously hit the headlines with Halifax Town, where he netted 22 goals from 35 senior matches in his one season at that club, 1932–33. Born in Filey, Yorkshire, on 31 October 1906, he began his playing career with Scarborough Town in the Northern League. He then moved to the unusually named Scarborough Penguins from the Yorkshire League, then on to Filey Town in the East Riding League. It was reported that he scored over 150 goals for that club.

Twenty-eight-year-old Crawford broke the O's scoring record with 25 senior goals in 1935–36 with some fierce left-foot shooting. He notched three hat-tricks in his time at the club and a chance of a goal was always on when Crawford got into the penalty area. He is in third spot on the O's all-time goalscoring list and is one of only 10 different players to have recorded more than 20 League goals in a season. He also scored the only goal of the game in a friendly against Motherwell in 1935–36.

Besides his League efforts, he also played in 51 wartime regional matches, netting nine goals. He retired from football in May 1945 to take an appointment as coach with Swedish side Dagerfors. In 1949 he left to become coach of Italian club Bologna, leaving in 1952. Crawford died in Hendon during 1977.

SEASON	*LEAGUE*		*FA CUP*		*TOTAL*	
	Apps	*Gls*	*Apps*	*Gls*	*Apps*	*Gls*
1933–34	32	10	1	0	33	10
1934–35	29	9	0	0	29	9
1935–36	41	23	5	2	46	25
1936–37	33	11	2	2	35	13
1937–38	36	6	2	0	38	6
1938–39	29	8	2	2	31	10
	200	67	12	6	212	73

 # Crawford also appeared in six Third Division Cup matches between 1933 and 1939 without scoring.

CUNNINGHAM, Laurence Paul (1974–77)

The grace, the skill and the sheer magic was highly appreciated by all the O's fans and fans throughout Europe. Laurie Cunningham, the black pearl as he was known, was one of the most exciting talents to grace the field of Brisbane Road, and he was voted by the fans in a 1999 millennium poll joint-third with Peter Allen, behind Alan Comfort in second and Tommy Johnston on top, as the best players to play for the club. Born in Archway, London, on 8 March 1956, he was on Arsenal's books as a junior along with another former Oriental, Glenn Roeder. Both failed to make it at Highbury and were snapped up by the O's scout Len Cheesewright. Within 18 months both became first-team regulars.

Cunningham first came to the attention of the footballing public on 3 August 1974 in a Texaco Cup match at West Ham United before 16,338 spectators. His brilliant touch, natural ball control and pace were all there to be seen. His League debut came in a 3–1 win at Oldham Athletic during the following October.

Former O's boss George Petchey informed the author about Cunningham's early days at the club:

'There was a time when Peter Angell and I wondered if we could win Laurie over. He often turned up late for training, the eyes flashed when we fined him, but for all that I loved the spark that made him tick.

'We had to put his wages away for him in the bank, and we encouraged him to caress the ball instead of just always laying it off like most English players.'

Cunningham himself told the author, just before his death in Spain, 'At first I must admit I was not the sweetest person to be with, nothing stirred me, I was just a dreamer. It was George Petchey and Peter Angell who showed me that the only person who could make my dreams come true was, in fact, myself.'

The O's management team nursed him along slowly, but when the time was right Barrie Fairbrother was sold to Millwall and Cunningham was brought into the side. During the final match of the 1974–75 season against Southampton, he walked into the dressing room late for the match and was told by Petchey that unless he scored a goal, his first in the League, he would be heavily fined and

suspended. It seemed to do the trick as he scored a beauty for the winning goal.

He went on to play many magical games for the O's, but on the eve of the March 1977 transfer deadline he moved to West Bromwich Albion for £110,000, with both Joe Mayo and Allan Glover joining the O's as part of the deal. He became the first black player to represent his country when selected by Ron Greenwood for the England Under-21 side, scoring with a downward header against Scotland at Bramall Lane in April 1977, a match shown on TV. He became the second black player to win a full England cap soon after defender Viv Anderson.

Cunningham made 81(5) appearances for Albion that yielded 15 goals before joining Real Madrid for £995,000 in 1979, scoring on his debut before 100,000 fans in the Bernabeau stadium. He scored 15 goals to help them gain the Spanish League and Cup double.

After gaining six full England caps between 1979 and 1982, he seemed to lose interest in football and spent more time as a male model, fashion designer and boutique owner in Europe. He drifted from club to club, playing for Manchester United, Marseilles, Leicester City, Sporting Gijon and Charleroi in Belgium. At the age of 32 he returned to London in February 1988 to play for Wimbledon and came on as a sub in the Dons' famous FA Cup Final victory over Liverpool in May 1988.

He returned to Spain to play for Second Division side Rayo Vallecano of Madrid. Sadly, in the early hours of 15 July 1989, he was killed in a car crash in Madrid. Laurie Cunningham may not have fulfilled his early promise, yet the O's fans who were privileged to witness his wonderful talent will never forget this exciting, graceful player.

The last word goes to Cunningham himself who told the author, 'I don't think I have ever fulfilled my true potential. All the coaches I've had, with the exceptions of Petchey and Angell at Orient, have never appreciated what I can do.'

Well the O's fans and those millions who saw him play certainly did appreciate Laurie Cunningham and what he could do on the field.

SEASON	*LEAGUE*		*FA CUP*		*FL CUP*		*TOTAL*	
	Apps	*Gls*	*Apps*	*Gls*	*Apps*	*Gls*	*Apps*	*Gls*
1974–75	15(2)	1	0(1)	0	0	0	15(3)	1
1975–76	33(1)	8	1	0	1	0	33(1)	8
1976–77	24	6	4	0	4	1	32	7
	72(3)	15	5(1)	0	5	1	82(4)	16

 # Cunningham also appeared in 1(1) matches in the Texaco Cup during 1974–75 and eight matches in the Anglo-Scottish Cup scoring two goals.

CUNNINGHAM, Thomas Edward (1981–87)

Tommy Cunningham spent six seasons with the club between 1981–87, having been signed by Paul Went. He later returned as coach in 1995 when Pat Holland was fired. He was acting manager for two home League matches against Scarborough and Torquay United in October 1996. The latter, a 1–0 win, was the first victory in seven matches, and the goal was scored by loanee Carl Griffiths in his first match for the O's. Born in Bethnal Green, London, on 7 December 1955, the big, strong 6ft 1in defender started with Chelsea

as an apprentice during October 1973 but joined Queen's Park Rangers on a free transfer during May 1975. He made 27(3) League appearances for Rangers before becoming a £50,000 record signing by Wimbledon in March 1979, making 99 League appearances and scoring 12 goals.

He joined the O's for £46,000 in September 1981 and remained captain for over three seasons. He was a player who always gave 100 percent and probably his most memorable day was at Exeter City in February 1984 where he scored a hat-trick from the centre-half position in a 4–3 win. Cunningham joined Fisher Athletic in June 1987. In 1998–99 he was youth coach with Barnet and was appointed assistant manager to John Still in September 1999. Barnet were relegated to the Football Conference in May 2001. In November 2002 he left the Jewish club Wingate & Finchley, where he was manager, and was appointed director of football with Ryman League Division One side Harlow Town.

SEASON	*LEAGUE*		*FA CUP*		*FL CUP*		*TOTAL*	
	Apps	*Gls*	*Apps*	*Gls*	*Apps*	*Gls*	*Apps*	*Gls*
1981–82	18	1	0	0	1	0	19	1
1982–83	28	3	2	0	0(1)	1	30(1)	4
1983–84	36	6	1	0	2	0	39	6
1984–85	36	1	4	0	1	1	41	2
1985–86	13	2	3	0	1	0	17	2
1986–87	31	4	2	0	2	0	35	4
	162	17	12	0	7(1)	2	181(1)	19

 # Cunningham also appeared in 0(1) Football League Groups Cup match and five Auto Windscreens Shield matches, scoring one goal.

DALRYMPLE, Robert Rodie (1911–1920)

One of the great players of the Edwardian area, Bob Dalrymple, or 'Dally' as he was known, was a very classy inside-forward who was born in Glasgow, Scotland, on 2 January 1880. He started his career with youth side Westmarch & Abercom FC in May 1890, at 22 years old he turned professional with Hearts and won a Scottish Cup runners'-up medal in 1903, when they lost to Rangers. He made 13 appearances and scored three goals before he came south of the border to join Southern League outfit Plymouth Argyle in 1904, making 92 senior appearances and netting 29 goals.

After a brief spell with Glasgow Rangers with 15 appearances and eight goals, Dalrymple joined Portsmouth in 1906, notching eight goals from 40 senior appearances. It was while he was with Fulham, whom he joined in 1907, that he came to prominence, netting 44 goals from 108 senior appearances before his record transfer to the O's for £300 on 28 January 1911, a large fee for a 31-year-old player. He joined the likes of McFadden, Dix, Bevan, Parker and Jonas in the forward line, and the O's were in line for promotion to Division One for two seasons, finishing in fourth position both times. He returned to the O's in 1919 after World War One and his last League match was at Bury on 22 November 1919, approaching his 39th birthday, when he sustained an injury.

Dalyrymple was probably one of the most stylish players to appear for the O's up to World War One and gave grand service to all the clubs he played for. After six seasons at Millfields Road, he retired due to an injury and joined Welsh side Ton Pentre as coach in January 1920. He died aged 90 in Worthing, Sussex, during July 1970.

SEASON	*LEAGUE*		*FA CUP*		*TOTAL*	
	Apps	*Gls*	*Apps*	*Gls*	*Apps*	*Gls*
1910–11	17	6	0	0	17	6
1911–12	31	13	1	0	32	13
1912–13	18	3	0	0	18	3
1913–14	36	9	2	0	38	9
1914–15	30	7	1	0	31	7
1919–20	7	0	0	0	7	0
	139	38	4	0	143	38

DAY, Keith David (1987–93)

The precarious career of a professional footballer is perfectly encapsulated in Keith Day. The long-serving, 6ft 1in, speedy central-defender was sweeping all before him in the 1991–92 season, winning the O's Player of the Year award, only to be released on a free transfer 12 months later.

Born in Grays, Essex, on 29 November 1962, Day started with Aveley in the Diadora League, joining Colchester United in August 1964, making 113 League appearances with 12 goals. He joined the O's in July 1987 and played a key role in their promotion side of 1988–89. He didn't score many goals with the O's but his most memorable was a stunning volley in a home victory over Huddersfield Town in 1991–92. After being left out of the side in

1992–93, the 30-year-old defender handed in a transfer request that upset boss Peter Eustace, who released him in May 1993.

Day admitted 'I would have loved to stay with the club after six wonderful seasons; I was very angry at being released; I had high hopes for the new season, but I feel I was not given a chance by Eustace.'

He joined Beazer League side Sittingbourne in June 1993. During March 1999 he was appointed joint-caretaker manager with Dean Coney at Farnborough Town but stayed for just five months. After playing a couple of games for Aveley, he left due to a knee injury and became player-manager with the Barkabians club of the Essex Business Houses Intermediate League. In August 2002 he returned to his roots when joining the management team at Aveley.

In May 2003 the 40-year-old joined his former Aveley boss Steve Mosely as assistant manager with the Dr Martens Premier Division side Chelmsford City. Day left the Essex side in October 2004 by an amicable agreement.

SEASON	*LEAGUE*		*FA CUP*		*FL CUP*		*TOTAL*	
	Apps	*Gls*	*Apps*	*Gls*	*Apps*	*Gls*	*Apps*	*Gls*
1987–88	41	2	4	0	2	0	47	2
1988–89*	49	2	3	0	4	0	56	2
1989–90	39	1	1	0	4	1	44	2
1990–91	21 (3)	1	0	0	2	0	23 (3)	1
1991–92	31 (2)	2	5	1	3	0	39 (2)	3
1992–93	7 (3)	1	1 (1)	0	2	0	10 (4)	1
	188 (8)	9	14 (1)	1	17	1	219 (9)	11

** Includes four promotion Play-off matches in 1988–89.*

 # Day also appeared in 13(2) Auto Windscreens Shield matches, scoring two goals.

DAY, Mervyn Richard (1979–83)

The O's record signing for a goalkeeper, Mervyn Day spent six seasons at Brisbane Road. He became their most expensive 'keeper when he joined from West Ham United in July 1979 for £100,000, which saw the departure of John Jackson (after his remarkable run of 222 consecutive League appearances over five seasons). Born in Chelmsford, Essex, on 26 June 1955, Day excelled as an all-round sportsman at King Edward VI Grammar School in Chelmsford. The 6ft 2in 'keeper signed as an apprentice with the Hammers in July 1971, turning professional during March 1973. He totalled 233 senior appearances at Upton Park before losing his place to Phil Parkes. He won five England Under-23 caps, an FA Cup-winners' medal in 1975 and a European Cup runners'-up medal in 1976.

He started off well at Brisbane Road but lost form as the club drifted down to Division Three. He was skipper in 1982 and was chosen as a substitute 'keeper to Nigel Spinks for an England 'B' match versus New Zealand, played at Brisbane Road in October 1979. Day was transferred to Aston Villa for £25,000 in May 1983, making 33 appearances.

After a number of loan spells with Coventry City, Leicester City, Luton Town and Sheffield United, Day signed for Leeds United in February 1985 for £30,000 and had a successful 'second' career, winning a Second Division Championship medal in 1989–90 and making 260 senior appearances at Elland Road. He joined Carlisle United on a free transfer in July 1993, and after 16 League appearances he was appointed manager in January 1996. He couldn't prevent them from being relegated to Division Three but proved his managerial acumen by leading them straight back up again. Day was dismissed in controversial circumstances in 1997 by their chairman Michael Knighton, who wanted a more hands-on role for himself. Day's managerial record at Brunton Park read: (1 August 1996 to 11 September 1997) P62, W32, D14, L16, F97, A86, Pts110.

He was appointed goalkeeping coach with Everton but joined Alan Curbishley as first-team coach with Charlton Athletic, and he has been with them through their ups and downs to the Premiership but left the Valley in May 2006 after manager Alan Curbishley resigned. Mervyn Day made a total of 642 League appearances in a career than spanned some 23 years.

SEASON	*LEAGUE*		*FA CUP*		*FL CUP*		*TOTAL*	
	Apps	*Gls*	*Apps*	*Gls*	*Apps*	*Gls*	*Apps*	*Gls*
1979–80	42	0	2	0	2	0	46	0
1980–81	40	0	1	0	2	0	43	0
1981–82	42	0	5	0	2	0	49	0
1982–83	46	0	2	0	2	0	50	0
	170	0	10	0	8	0	188	0

 # Day also appeared in three Anglo-Scottish Cup matches and six Football League Group Cup matches.

DEVERALL, Harold Reginald (1948–53)

A prominent player in the early 1950s with his never-say-die attitude, Jackie Deverall, as he was always known, was born in Petersfield, Reading, on 5 May 1916. He was one of a few players to be allowed to remain as a part-timer throughout his playing career, being a chartered accountant by profession. As a schoolboy, he won two England caps and later played for Maidenhead United in an FA Amateur Cup semi-final match before signing part-time professional forms with Reading during November 1939, going on to make 74 senior appearances and scoring nine goals. He also made 36 wartime appearances, scoring 18 goals, 14 of which came in the 1939–40 season.

The wing-half joined the O's in May 1948 and figured prominently in the 1951–52 FA Cup run. He had a splendid never-say-die attitude and was a great example to the younger players. He had a benefit match staged for him after retiring from playing in 1953, and he joined Sittingbourne as coach. After retiring from football, he ran a newsagent's business in Tilehurst. He died in Reading on 11 June 1999.

SEASON	*LEAGUE*		*FA CUP*		*TOTAL*	
	Apps	*Gls*	*Apps*	*Gls*	*Apps*	*Gls*
1948–49	29	1	2	1	31	2
1949–50	7	0	0	0	7	0
1950–51	30	1	1	0	31	1
1951–52	22	0	8	0	30	0
1952–53	27	0	2	0	29	0
	115	2	13	1	128	3

DICKENSON, Kevin James (1985–92)

Although Kevin Dickenson signed for the O's during the summer of 1985, his association with them goes back much further, having been born in Hackney. As a youngster, his father took him down to Brisbane Road to watch them, even though Kevin supported Spurs at the time and was on their books as a junior between 1977–79. Born in Hackney, London, on 24 November 1962, Dickenson was small in stature, standing just 5ft 6in tall, but he proved a reliable and splendid servant to the club, and he was voted Player of the Year by the fans in 1985–86. He spent seven seasons with the club.

Dickenson turned professional with Charlton Athletic on 21 May 1980 and made 72(3) League appearances, scoring once. He was snapped up by the O's boss Frank Clark on 1 July 1985 on a free transfer, and he starred in their promotion season of 1988–89, playing in all four of the Play-off matches. His last couple of seasons with the O's proved to be a real nightmare, suffering some serious injuries, which eventually forced the tenacious left-back to retire.

SEASON	*LEAGUE*		*FA CUP*		*FL CUP*		*TOTAL*	
	Apps	*Gls*	*Apps*	*Gls*	*Apps*	*Gls*	*Apps*	*Gls*
1985–86	46	1	6	0	4	0	56	1
1986–87	39	0	4	0	2	0	45	0
1987–88	22	1	4	0	0	0	26	1
1988–89*	42 (1)	1	2	0	5	0	49 (1)	1
1989–90	31	0	1	0	4	0	36	0
1990–91	6 (1)	0	1	0	0	0	7 (1)	0
1991–92	8	0	0	0	2	0	10	0
	194 (2)	3	18	0	17	0	229 (2	3

* *Dickenson's record includes four promotion Play-off matches in 1988–89.*

 # Dickenson also appeared in 11 Auto Windscreens Shield matches.

DIX, Joseph Charles (1910–15)

Joseph Dix joined the O's after he walked out of Portsmouth and was a regular on the left-wing for five seasons. Born in Geddington, Kettering, in 1886, Joe Dix started his professional career with Kettering before he joined Portsmouth on 13 April 1906 and played 82 Southern League matches and eight FA Cup ties for Pompey, scoring 24 goals. He joined the O's in June 1910 on a controversial note. Dix had not informed the Hampshire club of his intention to sign, and they complained to the Football League. Orient were ordered to pay a fine as well as a transfer fee of £100. The outside-left played a major part of one of the club's best periods of their history, and he performed credibly over five seasons and will go down as one of the best left-wingers, creating many of the goals scored by the prolific goal poacher Richard McFadden. One of the negatives of his game was that he did not score enough goals; however, he played his part in the O's rise up Division Two. After World War One, he retired from the game.

SEASON	*LEAGUE*		*FA CUP*		*TOTAL*	
	Apps	*Gls*	*Apps*	*Gls*	*Apps*	*Gls*
1910–11	22	3	1	0	23	3
1911–12	38	5	1	0	39	5
1912–13	35	0	1	0	36	0
1913–14	32	1	3	0	35	1
1914–15	21	2	1	0	22	2
	148	11	7	0	155	11

DIXON, Thomas Henry (1919–27)

Tommy Dixon, born in Seaham Harbour on 17 September 1899, was a former coal miner who joined the O's in June 1919 from Murton Colliery Welfare FC after failing a trial with Sunderland and had eight wonderful seasons at Millfields Road. Dixon was a very hard working player, and the right-half figured prominently in the great FA Cup run of 1925–26. He had a brilliant game when the O's shocked the football world by knocking out Newcastle United 2–0 in a fifth-round tie during February 1926. He was a player who would have faired very well in the modern game with his dynamic midfield play. Dixon moved to Southend United in June 1927 and played 249 League and 16 FA Cup matches, scoring seven goals. He retired from football in 1933 and went to live in Australia. In 1955 it was reported that he ran the Bay Horse public house in Chelmsford.

SEASON	*LEAGUE*		*FA CUP*		*TOTAL*	
	Apps	*Gls*	*Apps*	*Gls*	*Apps*	*Gls*
1919–20	9	2	0	0	9	2
1920–21	17	3	0	0	17	3
1921–22	34	0	1	0	35	0
1922–23	32	1	1	0	33	1
1923–24	38	1	3	0	41	1
1924–25	42	2	1	0	43	2
1925–26	4	0	4	4	44	4
1926–27	22	2	0	0	22	2
	234	15	10	0	244	15

DOWNING, Derrick Graham (1972–75)

A joy to watch, a hard, crisp tackler with excellent shooting power, who never stopped chasing and running throughout 90 minutes, Derek Downing started as a winger but was converted to an attacking left wing-back by the O's boss George Petchey and had the aggression of a terrier. Born in Doncaster on 3 November 1945, he started his career as a reserve player with Doncaster Rovers but moved after only nine weeks to Frickley Colliery. Middlesbrough saw his potential and offered £1,000 for his services in February 1965 when he was only 19, and he spent seven years at Ayresome Park, making 171(11) League appearances and scoring 39 goals.

Downing became an Oriental in May 1972 for £25,000 and actually signed before a home League match. He played many splendid matches, and it was a sad day when he left the club to join York City in July 1975 on a free transfer. He stayed at Bootham Crescent for one season, making 44(3) League appearances with two goals. In July 1977 he signed for Hartlepool United, making a further 40 League appearances with four goals. In 1977 he dropped out of the Football League to play for both Scarborough and Mexborough, and later he was player-manager with Hatfield Main and in 1990 was manager with Sutton Coldfield Town of the Doncaster Premier League.

SEASON	*LEAGUE*		*FA CUP*		*FL CUP*		*TOTAL*	
	Apps	*Gls*	*Apps*	*Gls*	*Apps*	*Gls*	*Apps*	*Gls*
1972–73	38	6	1	0	2	2	41	8
1973–74	35(2)	3	1(2)	0	4	0	40(4)	3
1974–75	27(2)	3	2	0	2	0	31(2)	3
	100(4)	12	4(2)	0	8	2	112(6)	14

DUNMORE, David Gerald Ivor (1961–65)

Big centre-forward Dave Dunmore was born in Whitehaven, Cumberland, on 8 February 1934. He started off with York Boys and Cliftonville Minors. During May 1952 he joined York City and scored 25 goals from 48 senior starts before signing for First Division Tottenham Hotspur in February 1954 for £10,500. During six seasons at White Hart Lane he made 97 senior appearances, scoring 34 goals. He then moved to West Ham United during March 1960 in a deal valued at £10,000, which also saw Johnny Smith going to Spurs. During his two-year stay at Upton Park he acquitted himself very well, scoring 18 goals from 39 starts.

Dunmore became an Oriental in March 1960 after another exchange deal with young Alan Sealey, and it was Dunmore who eventually replaced the legendary Tommy Johnston. He made a dramatic impact at Brisbane Road; it was his 22 League goals that helped the O's win promotion to Division One in 1961–62, none better than his 40-yard screamer against Liverpool at Anfield in a 3–3 draw. Dunmore was playing so well that he was even mentioned by the press as a possible England candidate; however, playing for the unfashionable Orient, he was not chosen. In June 1965 31-year-old Dunmore was given a free transfer by the new O's manager Dave Sexton, and he returned to York City where he scored 13 goals from 61(2) League appearances. He moved into non-League football with Worcester City in May 1967 and ended his playing career with a team called Bridlington Trinity. Today he still resides in the York area. At his best, Dave Dunmore was a top-class forward who ranks alongside the former great forwards like Richard McFadden, Tommy Johnston and Peter Kitchen and is one of only nine different players to bag 20 or more League goals in a season for the O's. During his career, which spanned some 13 years, he made 369 League appearances, notching 132 goals.

SEASON	*LEAGUE*		*FA CUP*		*FL CUP*		*TOTAL*	
	Apps	*Gls*	*Apps*	*Gls*	*Apps*	*Gls*	*Apps*	*Gls*
1960–61	11	3	0	0	0	0	11	3
1961–62	39	22	4	0	2	0	45	22
1962–63	37	11	4	1	5	2	46	14
1963–64	28	9	3	0	0	0	31	9
1964–65	32	9	1	1	2	0	35	10
	147	54	12	2	9	2	168	58

** Dunmore also scored a number of goals in friendly matches, three goals versus Wormatia Worms FC of Germany in 1960–61, the O's won 5–1, two goals versus ADO of Hague, Holland, a 2–1 win in 1962–63, and one goal versus Scottish side Morton in a 4–0 win in 1962–63.*

DYSON, John Barry (1968–73)

A prolific goalscorer in his younger days, converted by the O's to become a great midfielder, Barry Dyson, a quick thrustful forward who forced his way to the top with some sensational scoring feats, was with Tranmere Rovers between 1962 and 1966. Few clubs could have discovered a more valuable nugget of gold in the free-transfer market. The goals flowed with abundance while he was with the Rovers, twice hitting 30 senior goals in a season with some real power shooting from the 5ft 9in and 11st player.

The blond bombshell, as he was known, was born in Oldham, Lancashire, on 6 September 1942. He started his career as a junior with Bury, but it was while with Tranmere that he notched 106 goals from 183 senior appearances. He was sold to Crystal Palace for £15,000 in September 1966, scoring a hat-trick in only his second game, and he made 33(1) League appearances with nine goals. He moved to Watford for £9,000 in January 1968, scoring twice on his debut, netting 19 goals from 38 League appearances.

He joined the O's for £8,000 in December 1968 and was converted to midfield by boss Jimmy Bloomfield and enjoyed a wonderful run of 112 consecutive League matches. He also captained the side when Terry Mancini was sidelined through injury during the Division Three Championship campaign of 1969–70. He netted from a penalty in a celebration friendly against Italian side Roma, a 3–1 defeat in May 1970.

Dyson was released in July 1973 and joined Colchester United, where he made 41(1) League appearances, scoring six goals. During 1975 he joined Chelmsford City, and in 1984 he was manager of Boreham Wood FC. Upon retirement he ran a haulage business in Colchester until he died on 26 February 1995, aged 53, a month after suffering a heart attack.

SEASON	LEAGUE		FA CUP		FL CUP		TOTAL	
	Apps	Gls	Apps	Gls	Apps	Gls	Apps	Gls
1968–69	25	10	0	0	0	0	25	10
1969–70	46	6	2	0	2	0	50	6
1970–71	41	3	3	2	1	0	45	5
1971–72	34 (3)	9	4	1	2	0	40 (3)	10
1972–73	8 (3)	0	0	0	1	0	9 (3)	0
	154 (6)	28	9	3	6	0	169 (6)	31

ELWOOD, Joseph Patrick (1958–66)

Born in Belfast, Ireland, on 26 October 1939, Joe Elwood was first spotted by the O's boss Alec Stock when captaining Ireland versus England in a Youth international played at Brisbane Road in May 1957. He scored twice that day, but he was overshadowed by a lad named Jimmy Greaves who notched four goals in England's 6–2 victory. Elwood joined the O's on 24 April 1958 from Irish League side Glenavon. He bagged all four goals against high-flying Bristol City during November 1958 and soon after was chosen to represent an Irish FA XI against the Army at Windsor Park, Belfast.

His continued good form and scoring a hat-trick against Charlton Athletic in April 1959 earned Elwood a Northern Ireland Under-23 cap. He netted a few goals against foreign and Scottish opposition in friendly matches, with two goals against Maltese side Sliema Wanderers in a 5–0 victory in 1963–64, one goal in the 4–3 win at Montrose in 1959–60 and the opener in a 4–0 win over Greenock Morton in 1962–63. Elwood became the forgotten man at Leyton, making just a few League appearances, but two appearances spring to mind: scoring within a few minutes of his First Division debut against Manchester City in February 1963 and during February 1965 scoring two excellent goals to defeat Division Two leaders Newcastle United, a performance captured on BBC's *Match of The Day*. He was the O's first-ever League playing substitute (Jimmy Scott was the first player ever to sit on the bench during the previous month against Huddersfield Town but never came on), coming on against Preston on 4 September 1965, replacing Jimmy McGeorge. He was released in May 1966, and he moved back to Ireland to join Ards. Between 1979 and 1984 Elwood was the PE master at the Upton House School in Homerton and then moved to the Homerton House Secondary School, where he stayed for over five years.

SEASON	LEAGUE		FA CUP		FL CUP		TOTAL	
	Apps	Gls	Apps	Gls	Apps	Gls	Apps	Gls
1958–59*	28	10	1	0	-	-	29	10
1959–60	18	4	0	0	-	-	18	4
1960–61	11	2	3	2	0	0	14	4
1961–62	10	2	2	1	0	0	12	3
1962–63	11	1	2	1	0	0	13	2
1963–64	7	1	0	0	0	0	7	1
1964–65	11	5	0	0	0	0	11	5
1965–66	5 (2)	0	0	0	0	0	5 (2)	0
	101 (2)	25	8	4	0	0	109 (2)	29

* *The League Cup commenced in season 1960–61.*

EVANS, John Alwyn (1950–54)

Stocky John 'Taffy' Evans, at 5ft 7in and 11st 7lb, was one of the smallest full-backs in the League during his era, yet what he lacked in inches he made up for in speed and great anticipation. Born in Aberystwyth, Wales, on 22 October 1922, after a spell with his local side he joined Millwall in September 1946 and did well for the Lions, playing 73 times and scoring two goals. He joined the O's in June 1950 and appeared on the right wing on three occasions when they had injury problems. He featured in the great FA Cup run of 1951–52 and enjoyed four wonderful seasons at Brisbane Road, until illness struck him down in the summer of 1954, forcing him to retire from the game. The O's boss Alec Stock signed Jimmy Lee from Chelsea as his replacement. Evans was always a sporting player who rarely gave away a foul. He died on 24 February 1956 after a long illness aged just 34.

SEASON	LEAGUE		FA CUP		TOTAL	
	Apps	Gls	Apps	Gls	Apps	Gls
1950–51	44	0	1	0	45	0
1951–52	42	0	9	0	51	0
1952–53	27	0	2	0	29	0
1953–54	36	0	7	0	43	0
	149	0	19	0	168	0

EVANS, Thomas John (1924–28 & 1930–31)

Born in Maerdy, Wales, on 7 April 1903, Tom Evans was a tall, athletic and skilful left-back who joined the O's from Maerdy FC in May 1924. He was injured during his first appearance at Southampton in September 1924, and after recovering from a knee injury he went on loan to Aberdare Athletic, making five League appearances. He returned to the O's in December 1925 and went on to become the O's third full international player, and first to win a cap for Wales appearing against Scotland at Ibrox on 30 October 1926. After two further Welsh caps against England and Scotland, he was transferred to Newcastle United in December 1927 for £3,650.

A player who suffered with knee injuries throughout his career, he was restricted to just 13 First Division appearances and scored once for the Magpies, but he also become their first player ever to be capped for Wales. The classy player returned to the O's again in May 1930 on a free transfer. He stayed for two further seasons before joining South Wales side Merthyr Town in July 1932, who were in the Southern League Western Section, but retired soon after. Evans died in his home town of Maerdy on 31 August 1983, aged 80.

SEASON	LEAGUE		FA CUP		TOTAL	
	Apps	Gls	Apps	Gls	Apps	Gls
1924–25	1	0	0	0	1	0
1925–26	20	1	4	0	24	1
1926–27	21	0	2	0	23	0
1927–28	11	0	0	0	11	0
1930–31	23	0	2	0	25	0
1931–32	3	0	0	0	3	0
	79	1	8	0	87	1

FACEY, Kenneth William (1952–62)

Ken Facey and Steve Castle are the only two players to appear in the top 10 of both the O's leading goalscoring and appearance charts. Another of his records: he was the O's penalty king with 23 converted spot-kicks and only four misses. Born in Millfields Road, Clapton, a stone's throw from the O's second ground, on 12 October 1927, as a 16-year-old he played for Leyton Amateurs and also had spells with Walthamstow Avenue, St Albans and Tottenham Hotspur. He spent some time on the O's books but returned to Leyton FC to feature in their 1952 FA Amateur Cup Final appearance versus Walthamstow Avenue. Facey then rejoined the O's, signing on 12 May 1952.

Facey scored on his League debut in a 1–1 draw against Reading during December 1952. His most productive season was in 1954–55, when he netted 22 League goals, one of only nine different O's players to achieve this feat in one season. He featured in the Championship-winning side of 1955–56 and skippered the team for almost three seasons.

Ken Facey retired in 1963 and coached the O's reserve side and is one of only 10 O's players to have notched 20 or more League goals in a season (a full list appears in the statistical section of this book).

Some years ago Facey informed the author about some of his special memories while with the O's.

'It's nice to know I am still remembered by the older O's fans and now the new ones. Naturally all the successful years gave me great satisfaction. A couple of matches against Leicester City stand out for me, and I shall never forget them.

'This was when they won the Second Division Championship in April 1957. We played them at home on the Saturday, and I had a stinker, putting through my own goal twice in the space of a minute, and we lost 1–5 in front of over 23,000 fans. It did not make me popular with the lads in the dressing room.

'We travelled to Leicester for the Easter Monday return fixture and we won 4–1, to the amazement of the 34,000 Filbert Street crowd; that result put me back on speaking terms.'

Facey concluded: 'After leaving football, I worked with the Post Office at Mount Pleasant but retired in 1992. However, I have always retained my interest in the Orient.

'I consider that I played for a great club, both for the way the players were always treated and for the loyalty shown by its supporters through both the good times and the bad times.'

SEASON	*LEAGUE*		*FA CUP*		*FL CUP*		*TOTAL*	
	Apps	*Gls*	*Apps*	*Gls*	*Apps*	*Gls*	*Apps*	*Gls*
1952–53	22	8	1	0	-	-	23	8
1953–54	43	12	7	2	-	-	50	14
1954–55	44	22	2	1	-	-	46	23
1955–56	26	12	3	2	-	-	29	14
1956–57	40	2	1	0	-	-	41	2
1957–58	30	2	1	0	-	-	31	2
1958–59	37	4	1	0	-	-	38	4
1959–60	38	9	1	0	-	-	39	9
1960–61*	21	3	2	0	3	0	26	3
	301	74	19	5	3	0	323	79

* *The League Cup commenced in season 1960–61.*

FAIRBROTHER, Barrie Edward (1968–75)

Barrie Fairbrother proved to be one of the most popular players in his era, a real bundle of energy, very speedy and a dangerous player in and around the penalty area. Born in Hackney, London, on 30 December 1950, after a short spell as a youth player with Tottenham Hotspur he joined the O's in 1967 and scored over 150 youth and reserve-team goals. He scored on his League debut on 48 minutes against Mansfield Town during August 1969 with a lovely half volley, and he went on to play a major part in the O's Championship-winning side of 1969–70. No older O's fan will ever forget his last-gasp winner against Chelsea in the FA Cup fifth-round match in February 1972. He was voted the first O's Player of the Year in 1974, but that meant little to him after they had failed by a single point to gain a place in the First Division, and only his tears in the dressing room after the dramatic match against Aston Villa will be remembered.

He lost heart after that disappointment, and with the introduction of young Laurie Cunningham he was sold to Millwall in June 1975. His stay at The Den was hampered by a hip injury that required two operations. He made just 12(3) League appearances, scoring one League goal. He did score one goal against the O's in a dramatic League Cup replay at Highbury in October 1975, which the Lions won 3–0. During his time in the League he was only booked once for 'a complete accident' when Johnson of West Brom was weaving in and out of tackles and seemed to trip over his own feet. Fairbrother moved to Australia in 1976 and played there for four years, including a few matches for Queensland State, but gave it up after his body said 'enough is enough'. He still wears his Third

Division Championship medal around his neck as a reminder of the wonderful season he had as an O's player.

The author caught up with Barrie in September 2004 at his Brisbane home.

'All I wanted to be was a professional footballer, and the O's gave me the chance at the age of 15. Len Cheesewright was the youth-team manager at the time; he gave me my first game, and a year later I was offered an apprenticeship, and I worked my way through the various teams until I got my chance of a first-team debut when Mickey Bullock was injured in training on the Friday, and I was picked at the age of 18 to play against Mansfield Town on 30 August 1969, and I went on to score the winner early in the second half... a schoolboy's dream. We went on to win the Third Division Championship, and I went on to score 13 League goals and win a Champions-winners' medal.

'George Petchey took over as manager the following season, and I felt I was never allowed to play to my strengths as I was picked to play out wide on the wing when I much preferred to play down the middle next to Mickey Bullock, as I had a good partnership with him. A lot of the fun went out of the game under Petchey, and of course we had a few disagreements along the way.

'What I remember the most was the help given to me by a special group of people like the coach Peter Angell, who became like a father figure to me, always helping and advising on difficult situations. There was director Harry Zussman who showed us what true supporters were like. He went everywhere with the team, and when we lost we felt we had let him down.

'The main reason I stayed so long with the club was the supporters, who always gave me the encouragement to stick it out. I remember I was on the subs' bench a lot under Petchey, yet they always chanted my name for the manager to bring me on, these were a very special group of people.

'The backroom staff, like a Mrs Lewis who washed the kit to the groundsman and the youngsters who swept the stands after a game, they all became like a big family, the backbone of the club, which made it so special for me.

'The FA Cup victory over Chelsea was something very special, a David versus Goliath tussle. After going two goals down in about 20 minutes we started to get back into the game, and Phil Hoadley's goal just before half-time gave us the lift we needed. Mickey Bullock scored after about 10 minutes to equalise, and the game turned into an end to end typical Cup tie in the mud.

'With only minutes remaining, Ian Bowyer and I chased a long ball from defence, and Ian collided with Peter Bonetti, their advancing goalkeeper. The ball fell nicely in front of me, and I was able to sneak the ball past the desperate lunge of David Webb. I can still remember the noise that erupted from the stands as I ran off to celebrate... I don't think anyone could catch me until I reached the halfway line!

'After transferring to Millwall in 1975, I had two hip operations which finished my career in England, but I was still able to play and decided to have a few years of playing in Australia.

'During September 2004 I changed jobs, and I'm now running a real estate agency not far from my home after spending many successful years with the Lend Lease Company, where I was their top salesman of the year. I had a carpal tunnel operation on both my hands during last year, but have now got over that.

'I enjoy our lifestyle here in Brisbane, Queensland, and live in the Bay Side suburbs, a bit different from the cold winter days at Brisbane Road!'

SEASON	*LEAGUE*		*FA CUP*		*FL CUP*		*TOTAL*	
	Apps	*Gls*	*Apps*	*Gls*	*Apps*	*Gls*	*Apps*	*Gls*
1969–70	35 (4)	13	2	0	0	0	37 (4)	13
1970–71	31 (4)	2	3	1	0 (1)	0	34 (5)	3
1971–72	17 (3)	0	4	2	0	0	21 (3)	2
1972–73	24 (3)	11	0	0	1	0	25 (3)	11
1973–74	41	14	4	3	4	2	49	19
1974–75	23 (3)	1	2	1	2	0	27 (3)	2
	171 (17)	41	15	7	7 (1)	2	193 (18)	50

 # Fairbrother also appeared in three Texaco Cup matches in 1974–75, scoring one goal.

FISHER, Robert Paul (1971–83)

A polished player who stayed 10 years with the club and one of only 10 players to have made more than 300 League appearances for the O's, Bobby Fisher, the Brent schools captain, was brought to Orient by his Uncle Mark Lazarus in August 1971, signing as an associate schoolboy after he had spells in the youth sides of both Queen's Park Rangers and Watford. Born in Wembley on 3 August 1956, Fisher was groomed by manager George Petchey for a midfield birth, but after David Payne broke his leg in April 1974 he was switched to the vacant full-back position, and at the age of 16 he had already sat on the substitutes' bench. He came on for his League debut as a substitute versus Sunderland in August 1973 and his first full appearance came against Bolton Wanderers the following month. He showed composure beyond his years, establishing himself in the side for eight seasons. He appeared in all eight FA Cup ties in the 1977–78 side that reached the semi-final against Arsenal.

Fisher left the club in November 1982, joining Cambridge United,

where he made 42 League appearances. He moved on to Brentford in February 1984, making his Bees debut against the O's in an Associate Members Cup tie. After a further 45 appearances, he moved into non-League football with Maidstone United during December 1985. Fisher's style of play was not always to the fans' liking. He was the type of defender who held off from making rash tackles, but there is no denying that he was a neat player who proved to be a grand servant with the club. After retiring he became an author, journalist and actor.

In July 2001 he was appointed as director of football with the new Jewish club Maccabi Lions from the Herts Senior County League. He was reserve coach with another former Oriental, Tunji Banjo. He stayed for a couple of years before joining up with another former O's player, Barry Silkman, as a players' agent. In 2004 he was with One2Eleven, an organisation helping youngsters find football clubs, and he also works as a sports psychologist and has helped a large number of footballers and top celebrities.

SEASON	*LEAGUE*		*FA CUP*		*FL CUP*		*TOTAL*	
	Apps	*Gls*	*Apps*	*Gls*	*Apps*	*Gls*	*Apps*	*Gls*
1973–74	4(4)	0	0	0	2	0	6(4)	0
1974–75	42	0	2	0	2	0	46	0
1975–76	36(1)	0	1	0	1	0	38(1)	0
1976–77	31(1)	0	4	0	3(1)	0	38(2)	0
1977–78	42	1	8	0	3	0	53	1
1978–79	37	0	3	0	1	1	41	1
1979–80	42	3	3	0	2	0	47	3
1980–81	41	0	0	0	2	0	43	0
1981–82	31	0	5	0	2	0	38	0
1982–83	2	0	0	0	1	0	3	0
	308(6)	4	26	0	19(1)	1	353(7)	5

 # Fisher also appeared in three Texaco Cup matches in 1974–75, 14(1) Anglo-Scottish Cup matches and six Football League Groups Cup matches.

FLETCHER, Charles Alfred (1930–33)

Charlie Fletcher was a great winger and one of only 10 different O's players to have scored 20 or more League goals in a season. Born in Homerton, London, on 28 October 1905, he was famed for his powerful shooting, particularly from dead ball situations, and there was always a buzz when he strode up to take a free-kick. He actually started his career with the O's in 1927–28 but didn't get a first-team chance so moved on to Crystal Palace in June 1928, making his League debut that September, and he played a total of seven League games with them. During June 1929 he moved to Division Three South outfit Merthyr Town and scored one goal from 24 League games.

Fletcher became an Oriental for the second time in June 1930. He really blossomed in 1931–32, bagging 22 senior goals, appearing mostly on the left-wing. At the start of the following season manager Jimmy Seed bought veteran Jimmy Dimmock, and Fletcher, not to his liking, played in a more defensive role, he was sold to Brentford in June 1933 and was a member of their Division Two Championship-winning side of 1934–35, making a total of 104 League appearances for the Bees, scoring 25 goals.

He later played with Burnley, scoring 21 goals from 62 League appearances, and with Plymouth Argyle, making 23 League appearances with six goals between 1937 and 1939. In July 1939 he joined Ipswich Town, scoring nine goals from 32 League games. He guested for the O's during wartime football, making 68 appearances and scoring 13 goals. Throughout his League career, which spanned 11 years, he made a total of 372 League appearances and scored 94 goals and played in a further 24 FA Cup ties, netting five goals. Charlie Fletcher died in Hither Green, Lewisham, London, on 22 August 1980.

SEASON	*LEAGUE*		*FA CUP*		*TOTAL*	
	Apps	*Gls*	*Apps*	*Gls*	*Apps*	*Gls*
1927–28	0	0	0	0	0	0
1930–31	38	3	2	0	40	3
1931–32	41	20	3	2	44	22
1932–33	41	9	1	0	42	9
	120	32	6	2	126	34

FOSTER, Colin John (1981–87)

Colin Foster was born in Chislehurst, Kent, on 16 July 1964. The 6ft 4in and 13st 10lb central-defender jumped quickly into the O's first

team at the tender age of 17 due to his physique and outstanding ability. As a schoolboy, he tended to be picked for teams far in advance of his years. Fozzie, as he was affectionately known, made his debut in an FA Cup tie against Charlton Athletic in January 1982, and his League debut came against Grimsby Town a week later. He played regularly for six seasons, and it was no surprise that he would move into the First Division. It was Brian Clough at Nottingham Forest in March 1987 who paid £50,000 for him, with Mark Smalley moving to Brisbane Road as part of the deal worth £80,000.

Foster remained at the City Ground for three seasons, making 81(4) senior appearances and scoring six goals. He returned to East London to join Second Division West Ham United for £750,000 in September 1989. He made 88(5) League appearances, scoring five goals for the Hammers. A planned £400,000 return move to Forest in 1992 fell through, so he went on loan with Notts County during January 1994 and made nine League appearances. He eventually left Upton Park for First Division Watford in March 1994 for a giveaway £100,000, and he enjoyed three good seasons at Vicarage Road, making 66 League appearances and netting eight goals. After a loan spell with Cambridge United in 1997, he joined them on a non-contract basis in August that year, but after 33 League appearances and one goal he was forced to retire from the game through injury in July 1998.

SEASON	*LEAGUE*		*FA CUP*		*FL CUP*		*TOTAL*	
	Apps	*Gls*	*Apps*	*Gls*	*Apps*	*Gls*	*Apps*	*Gls*
1981–82	23	2	5	1	0	0	28	3
1982–83	43	2	2	1	2	0	47	3
1983–84	10 (1)	1	0	0	2	0	12 (1)	1
1984–85	42	1	4	1	4	0	50	2
1985–86	36	2	4	1	2	0	42	3
1986–87	19	2	4	1	2	0	25	3
	173 (1)	10	19	5	12	0	20 (1)	15

 # Foster also appeared in three Football League Groups Cup matches and five Auto Windscreens Shield matches, scoring one goal.

GALBRAITH, John McDonald (1921–31)

John Galbraith (also known as Jack) was born in Renton, Scotland, on 4 April 1902, and the 5ft 11in defender started his career with the Vale of Leven junior club, then he moved to Shawfield FC, from whom he joined the O's in July 1921. He soon impressed as a skilful, hard-working player and remained with the O's for 10 seasons. He will be remembered by older fans for scoring a beauty against Newcastle United in the 2–0 fifth-round FA Cup victory in February 1926. He also scored in the O's final League match at the Millfields Road ground on 3 May 1930, a 4–1 win over Brighton & Hove Albion.

With the club seeking urgent funds due to a financial crisis, Galbraith was sold to Cardiff City in February 1931 for £2,000. He played in 143 League games at Ninian Park, scoring twice, before being appointed as manager of Milford United in July 1935. He returned to Orient as coach in 1938. He is ranked 13th on the clubs all-time top League appearances chart.

SEASON	*LEAGUE*		*FA CUP*		*TOTAL*	
	Apps	*Gls*	*Apps*	*Gls*	*Apps*	*Gls*
1921–22	37	3	1	0	38	3
1922–23	24	1	1	0	25	1
1923–24	4	0	0	0	4	0
1924–25	25	0	1	0	26	0
1925–26	32	1	4	1	36	2
1926–27	41	1	2	0	43	1
1927–28	33	0	1	0	34	0
1928–29	22	0	2	0	24	0
1929–30	38	1	5	0	43	1
1930–31	21	2	2	0	23	2
	277	9	19	1	296	10

GODDARD, Raymond (1967–74)

A great goalkeeper who had eight wonderful years with the O's, Ray Goddard was born in Fulham, London, on 13 February 1949. He joined Orient from Fulham in March 1967, where he began as an apprentice but never featured in their League side. He was given his O's League debut against Workington on 27 May 1976, replacing Ron Willis. The 18-year-old was soon to make the position his own, and he become one of the O's best-ever goalkeepers.

Goddard was a regular in the O's Third Division Championship-winning side of 1969–70 but was upset when the O's boss George Petchey signed John Jackson from Crystal Palace in October 1973; however, he did appear in the vital promotion-clinching match versus Aston Villa in April 1974, but unfortunately the match was drawn and it was Carlisle United who were promoted to Division One. After a short loan spell with Scottish League side Greenock Morton, he joined Millwall in November 1974 and made 80 League appearances for the Lions. He was transferred to Wimbledon for £45,000 in February 1978, where he made a further 119 League appearances, including winning a Championship medal. He scored a vital penalty against Bury in May 1981 to help secure the Dons as champions.

Older O's fans will also remember Goddard for scoring the winning penalty kick past the O's goalie Mervyn Day in a League Cup shoot-out at their old Plough Lane ground, just moments after saving Joe Mayo's kick. He ended his career with Wealdstone, whom he joined in July 1981.

Goddard informed the author a few years ago:

'My most memorable memory of my days with the O's was promotion to Division Two in 1970 and receiving a gold winners' medal.'

He remembered two matches in particular:

'One of them is a match all older O's fans will want to forget, losing promotion to a stupid penalty against Villa. Everyone was sick that night.

'To compensate, who could forget our famous FA Cup victory over Chelsea by 3–2 and then being so unlucky to lose against Arsenal in the next round during February 1972; we hit the woodwork three times that day.

'Finally, give my regards to all the O's fans and to those who remember an old codger like me, I hope they have forgiven me for hitting that winning penalty against the O's in the League Cup all those years ago.'

SEASON	LEAGUE		FA CUP		FL CUP		TOTAL	
	Apps	Gls	Apps	Gls	Apps	Gls	Apps	Gls
1966–67	1	0	0	0	0	0	1	0
1967–68	41	0	5	0	0	0	46	0
1968–69	44	0	2	0	4	0	50	0
1969–70	44	0	2	0	2	0	48	0
1970–71	42	0	3	0	1	0	46	0
1971–72	39	0	4	0	2	0	45	0
1972–73	42	0	1	0	2	0	45	0
1973–74	25	0	3	0	2	0	30	0
	278	0	20	0	13	0	311	0

 # Goddard also appeared in 0(1) Texaco Cup match in 1974–75.

GODFREY, Kevin (1976–88)

Kevin Godfrey came in as a raw 16-year-old but stayed for 11 seasons and ended as the O's fourth top goalscorer of all-time with 72 senior goals. Born in Kennington, London, on 24 February 1960, he represented South London schools before becoming an apprentice with the O's in June 1976. He was just 16½ when he made his O's first-team debut in a Anglo-Scottish Cup tie against Chelsea at Brisbane Road in August 1976. He turned professional in March 1977.

Two of Godfrey's most memorable matches were against Bolton Wanderers in April 1985 when he scored a hat-trick in the 4–3 win and two goals against Tottenham Hotspur in the first leg of the League Milk Cup in September 1985 in the 2–0 victory. His biggest disappointment was being left out of the FA Cup semi-final against Arsenal in April 1978 when the more experienced Derek Clarke was chosen ahead of him. During his last two seasons with the club he suffered from a back injury which affected his performance.

Wingman Godfrey was quick with good ball control, but in his early days he often let himself down with weak crosses, but he was a loyal clubman who achieved much with the O's.

He went on loan to Plymouth Argyle in February 1986, where he made seven League appearances, scoring once. After a short spell with Maidenhead United, he joined Brentford on a free transfer in October 1988, playing in 101(39) League games and scoring 17 goals. In May 1993 he joined non-League Yeading FC, and nowadays he is a black cab driver in London.

SEASON	LEAGUE		FA CUP		FL CUP		TOTAL	
	Apps	Gls	Apps	Gls	Apps	Gls	Apps	Gls
1977–78	11	0	5	0	0	0	16	0
1978–79	3 (3)	0	0	0	0 (1)	0	3 (4)	0
1979–80	2 (3)	1	2	0	0	0	4 (3)	1
1980–81	5 (4)	2	0	0	0	0	5 (4)	2
1981–82	42	8	5	0	2	0	49	8
1982–83	42 (3)	11	2	2	2	0	46 (3)	13
1983–84	39 (2)	10	1	0	2	1	42 (2)	11
1984–85	36 (4)	10	4	1	3	0	43 (4)	11
1985–86	13 (3)	4	4	1	3	3	20 (3)	8
1986–87	34 (2)	10	2	0	1 (1)	0	37 (3)	10
1987–88	28 (6)	7	3 (1)	1	2	0	33 (7)	8
	255 (30)	63	28 (1)	5	15 (2)	4	298 (33)	72

 # Godfrey also appeared in one Anglo-Scottish Cup match, three Football League Groups Cup matches and 6(2) Auto Windscreens Shield matches.

GRAHAM, Malcolm (1960–63)

Malcolm Graham, a short and bustling forward (he stood at just 5ft 8½in), possessed a terrific shot with both feet and is a player who will always be fondly remembered for his two goals against Bury on that emotional day back on 28 April 1962, which took the O's up to top-flight status for the only time in their history as runners-up, along with champions Liverpool. Born in Crigglestone in Wakefield on 26 January 1934, he joined Barnsley in April 1953 as a part-time professional from Hall Green FC, where he combined his football with that of working as a miner at Haigh Colliery. During his time with Barnsley he attracted the attention of several First Division clubs and a deal with Newcastle United was set-up, but in the end they refused to pay the £20,000 asking fee. He made 103 senior appearances with 35 goals at

Oakwell, including four goals against Charlton Athletic in September 1958.

Graham was one of several players to leave the South Yorkshire club following their relegation at the end of 1958–59 season, joining Bristol City along with left-winger Johnny McCann in May 1959 for a joint fee of £7,000. He scored twice on his City League debut, yet played just 14 times for the Robins, scoring eight goals, before joining the O's on 20 June 1960 for a fee of £8,000. His first goal for Orient came at Leeds United in a 3–1 win during September 1960; however, injury restricted his progress that season. Graham came into his own during the 1961–62 promotion season, striking up a wonderful partnership with big striker Dave Dunmore and scoring between them 35 League goals. He started off the season with a bang with a great hat-trick at Walsall in a 5–1 victory.

The season's climax came with the Bury match in April 1962. Graham had arrived at the ground thinking he would be watching from the stands, but when Ronnie Foster failed a very late fitness test in came Graham, and what a fairytale story it turned out to be. Graham's first goal on 14 minutes was a header, while the second came with just five minutes remaining. He picked up a loose ball, beat a defender on the right, raced into the penalty area, dribbled around Bury 'keeper Chris Harker and joyfully drove into an empty net to the roars of the 21,617 crowd. The final whistle had sounded, and the result at Swansea, where Sunderland could only manage a 1–1 draw, assured promotion for the boys in blue, and tears of joy ran down the Yorkshireman's face, still in shock when he got to the dressing room. He was told by the O's director Leslie Grade 'Malcolm, you have made me a happy man this day, name whatever you want and I will give it to you'. Still in a state of shock, Graham replied 'A glass of champagne'.

Graham informed the author 'Old Leslie was dead serious, he loved the O's, and if I would have said my bond for the house, you know, he would have paid it, he was that happy.'

During the First Division campaign he hit a notable goal against West Ham United to ensure a 2–0 victory. He also grabbed a hat-trick in the demolition of Bury in the League Cup 9–1. It was, however, to be his final season at Brisbane Road, and during July 1963 he, along with Derek Gibbs, joined Queen's Park Rangers for a joint fee of £10,000. He scored on his Rangers debut versus Oldham Athletic and made 23 senior appearances with eight goals before returning to Barnsley in July 1964, playing 22 senior matches and netting a further six goals. Graham joined Buxton FC in June 1965 and ended his playing career with Alfreton Town. He made a total of 233 League appearances that yielded 82 goals.

Mal Graham was recovering from a heart attack at his home in Barnsley in 1999, but happily in May 2000 he attended the O's Star Man Dinner awards that also celebrated the 70th birthday of Stan Charlton, the O's skipper of that promotion campaign.

SEASON	*LEAGUE*		*FA CUP*		*FL CUP*		*TOTAL*	
	Apps	*Gls*	*Apps*	*Gls*	*Apps*	*Gls*	*Apps*	*Gls*
1960–61	19	7	0	0	1	0	20	7
1961–62	29	13	2	0	2	0	33	13
1962–63	27	9	2	0	2	5	31	14
	75	29	4	0	5	5	84	34

GRAY, Nigel Robert (1974–83)

Nigel Gray performed excellently in the O's great FA Cup run of 1977–78. He was never rated as one of the club's greatest of centre-halves, yet in an organised, defensive set-up he played his part very efficiently. The 6ft player stayed with the club for over nine seasons.

Born in Fulham, London, on 2 November 1956, he signed as an associate schoolboy, having been nurtured by the local Beaumont club under the leadership of Maurice Newman, a man who brought many fine youngsters to the club. He signed with the O's on apprentice forms in July 1973.

He became a full-time professional in April 1974, making his League debut a year later against Bolton Wanderers. Gray didn't score many goals but did get on the scoresheet in a 4–1 win over a Kuwait XI in a friendly during 1982–83. Gray had loan spells with both Blackburn Rovers and Charlton Athletic before joining Swindon Town in July 1983. He made 36 senior appearances with one goal for the Robins. He went on loan to Brentford in March 1984, making 16 League appearances and scoring once, and then with Aldershot in September 1984, making a further four League appearances. He went into non-League football with Enfield and then Dagenham and later represented an England non-League representative side. He ended his non-League career with Wycombe Wanderers in 1987 and Tooting & Mitcham the following season at the age of 32. In 2002 Gray was still playing, turning out for a side called Van Dyke FC in the Kingston-upon-Thames area, aged 46. He is still seen at Orient games and functions.

SEASON	*LEAGUE*		*FA CUP*		*FL CUP*		*TOTAL*	
	Apps	*Gls*	*Apps*	*Gls*	*Apps*	*Gls*	*Apps*	*Gls*
1974–75	2	0	0	0	0	0	2	0
1975–76	1	0	0	0	0	0	1	0
1976–77	22	2	0(1)	0	0	0	22 (1)	2
1977–78	22	0	8	0	2	0	32	0
1978–79	42	0	3	0	1	0	46	0
1979–80	37	0	3	0	0	0	40	0
1980–81	39	0	1	0	2	0	42	0
1981–82	38	0	5	0	1	0	44	0
1982–83	30	2	0	0	2	0	32	2
	233	4	20(1)	0	8	0	261 (1)	4

 # Gray also appeared in seven Anglo-Scottish Cup matches, scoring one goal and six Football League Group Cup matches.

GREALISH, Anthony Patrick (1974–79)

Tony 'Paddy' Grealish was born in Paddington, London, on 21 September 1956, a product of West London football who was another from a group of players brought to the club by Maurice Newman of the Beaumont club, signing as an apprentice in June 1972 and turning professional two years later. Grealish made his League debut against Nottingham Forest in November 1974, scoring with a great goal, and he was soon to become a great crowd favourite with his all-action midfield style of play. In 1973 he featured in an England Youth XI, however, due to his Irish parentage, Eire invited

him to represent them in a UEFA youth tournament in Switzerland. He gained further Eire Youth caps in the summer of 1975, and at the age of 19 he won his first full cap in 1976 against Norway. Grealish won a total of seven full caps while at Brisbane Road, and he totalled 45 caps throughout his career, scoring eight goals, and also, under the leadership of Jack Charlton, he appeared in the 1986 World Cup Finals for Eire.

Grealish starred in the O's great FA Cup run to the semi-finals in 1977–78, but with the advent of Freedom of Contract it saw him move to Luton Town for £150,000 in July 1979, making 79 appearances for the Hatters with two goals. He then moved to Brighton & Hove Albion in July 1981 for £100,000, making 95(5) League appearances with six goals, and starred in some of their great FA Cup exploits during the period. During March 1984 he moved to West Bromwich Albion for £75,000, appearing in 55(10) League matches with five goals. In October 1976 he joined Manchester City for £20,000 but stayed only a few months, making just 11 League appearances, before he joined Rotherham United in August 1987 and featured in their promotion to Division Three two years later. During August 1990 he was appointed player-coach with Walsall, making 32(4) League appearances and scoring once.

In May 1992 Grealish moved into the Conference with newly elected Bromsgrove Rovers. In later years, while working in the insurance business, he had spells with Moor Green, Halesowen Harriers, Sutton Coldfield Town and as player-coach with Evesham United before returning as coach to Bromsgrove for the start of the 1994–95 season. In September 1994 he took over as their caretaker manager when Bobby Hope resigned, and he took over the position on a permanent basis two months later before being dismissed in March 1995. In May 2000 he was assistant manager to former Manchester City player Steve Mackenzie at Atherstone United, while also working at the youth academy of West Bromwich Albion. He now works in the scrap metal business, and he was a special guest at the O's Star Man Dinner held in May 2000. Grealish had a wonderful career that spanned some 18 years, making a total of 545(25) League appearances and scoring 31 goals.

SEASON	*LEAGUE*		*FA CUP*		*FL CUP*		*TOTAL*	
	Apps	*Gls*	*Apps*	*Gls*	*Apps*	*Gls*	*Apps*	*Gls*
1974–75	24(1)	2	2	0	0	0	26(1)	2
1975–76	38	1	1	0	1	0	40	1
1976–77	33	2	4	0	2	0	39	2
1977–78	35(1)	0	8	0	2(1)	0	45(2)	0
1978–79	39	5	2	0	1	0	42	5
	169(2)	10	17	0	6(1)	0	192(3)	10

 # Grealish also played 13 Anglo-Scottish Cup matches.

GREGORY, Gordon Harold (1961–66)

Harry Gregory was born in Hackney, London, on 24 October 1943. The former Hackney schoolboy representative became the O's first ever apprentice professional soon after winning an England Youth cap versus Switzerland, a match played at Brisbane Road in 1960. Gregory was chosen to make his League debut on 9 October 1961 at Bury, but the match was postponed and his aspirations in the League had to wait a further year when he finally made his League debut at inside-forward and scored a beauty past Roy Bailey in a First Division match versus Ipswich Town during November 1962, shortly after his 19th birthday.

He only became a regular first-team player during the 1963–64 season, forming a dangerous trio with Dave Dunmore and Ted Phillips. Gregory moved to Charlton Athletic in May 1966, a deal that brought veteran striker Cliff Holton and defender John Snedden to Brisbane Road. He made 146(3) League appearances, scoring 24 goals, at The Valley. He joined Aston Villa in October 1970 for £7,770, helping them to promotion in 1971–72, and played in 18(6) matches with two goals. In August 1972 he signed for Hereford United, making 71(2) League appearances with six goals. He moved into non-League football in 1974.

SEASON	*LEAGUE*		*FA CUP*		*FL CUP*		*TOTAL*	
	Apps	*Gls*	*Apps*	*Gls*	*Apps*	*Gls*	*Apps*	*Gls*
1961–62	0	0	0	0	0	0	0	0
1962–63	6	1	0	0	2	1	8	2
1963–64	17	3	3	0	0	0	20	3
1964–65	36	6	0	0	2	2	38	8
1965–66	20	2	0	0	1	0	21	2
	79	12	3	0	5	3	87	15

GRIFFITHS, Carl Brian (1996–97 loan, 1997–99 & 1999–2001)

A top-class striker, ranked 10th on the O's all-time leading scorers list, Carl Griffiths was born in Oswestry, Shropshire, on 16 July 1971. He was brought up in Forden near Welshpool in mid Wales. He started as a trainee with Shrewsbury Town on 26 September 1988, and he made his League debut in 1988 as a 17-year-old, scoring against both Leeds United and Manchester City. He became a firm favourite with the Shrewsbury fans, finding the net 62 times from 130(40) senior appearances and winning Welsh Youth, B and Under-21 caps. He was transferred to Premiership side Manchester City for £500,000 on 29 October 1993, but with the arrival of strikers Walsh and Rossler he soon found himself out of favour and in the reserves. On 17 August 1995 he was transferred to Portsmouth for £200,000 but never quite made it there and was soon off to Peterborough United on 28 March 1996 for £225,000.

Griffiths was virtually unused by their manager Barry Fry, and he never played a complete 90 minutes of football in over two years with Posh. He joined the O's on loan on 31 October 1996, scoring three goals from five starts. The O's boss Tommy Taylor was impressed and offered £100,000 for the player, but Fry declined the offer as he wanted £200,000, which was out of reach for the O's. In March 1997 Taylor tried again with an offer of £100,000 and was happily surprised when it was accepted by Fry.

Welshman Griffiths (known by the fans as Super Carl) became a real favourite with the Orient fans after a very successful season in 1997–98, scoring 23 senior goals. He was good with both feet and at holding up the ball. Unfortunately he could not find the net so regularly the following season, and rumours were abound of a transfer to a number of clubs including Notts County, Shrewsbury and Charlton Athletic, and this after he was fined by the club for his over exuberant celebrations after scoring at Southport in the FA Cup, which upset manager Taylor.

On 13 January 1999 he went on a month's loan to Wrexham. It seemed very clear to most supporters that Griffiths would not stay with the club, and it was just a matter of time before he moved on. After his loan spell with Wrexham, where he netted four goals from four League and one Auto Windscreens Shield appearances, goals seemed to come more frequently to Griff on his return to Brisbane Road, but as expected he was eventually sold to First Division Port Vale for a reported £115,000 just before the transfer deadline on 24 March 1999, to the disappointment of all the O's fans.

It was the Port Vale manager Brian Horton who had taken Griffiths to Manchester City from Shrewsbury some years earlier. It was rumoured that boss Taylor had offered Griffiths a new, improved contract, but it was only to be finalised in the new season. Vale offered the Welshman a much better deal, which the O's could not match. He played just three League matches for Vale, scoring once. Griffiths was in the crowd at Rotherham, cheering on the O's in their famous semi-final penalty shoot-out victory, and at the Play-off Final at Wembley to see them do battle with Scunthorpe United. Rumours were abound that he was about to rejoin the O's, and on 12 December 1999 he did, for a reported £80,000, a fee paid personally by Barry Hearn. At that time the O's were at the foot of the table, the lowest position in the club's history. He scored a hat-trick against fellow strugglers Chester City in a crushing 5–1 win, but injury derailed his season. He came back with a bang in 2000–01. The following season he was on the goal charge, and manager Taylor denied rumours in March 2001 that his ace marksman was on his way to Rotherham United as 'absolute rubbish'.

Griffiths had found the net at irregular intervals, but he climbed up the O's all-time goalscoring chart with over 50 League goals to his name. However, after his sending-off at Mansfield Town on 21 April 2001 he was unavailable for the Play-offs due to his suspension. He once again fell out with boss Tommy Taylor, who stated in the club programme 'it does not help when people are not professional enough to stay on the field', and the player promptly requested to be placed on the transfer list. The O's boss Taylor stated 'We want him at the club and scoring goals – if nobody comes in for him, I'm not worried about that. He's a great goalscorer but wants to play at a higher level, yet deep down I don't believe he really wants to leave us.'

However, Griffiths told a local paper 'I find myself unwanted at the club, and was told that I could not travel with the team for the Play-off Final in Cardiff.' In July 2001 he moved to Luton Town for £65,000 and kicked-off the season by scoring seven goals from just nine starts, but a shin injury in a League match at Orient in September kept him out of action for over a year. Tragedy struck again when he was jogging up and down the touchline waiting to come on as a substitute in a match against Notts County in September 2002 when he tweaked a calf muscle and was out of action again.

He was close to rejoining his former O's boss at Darlington, but Griffiths stated he did not want to go to the North East. In October 2002 he was put on the transfer list, and he told the Annova website that he would be willing to drop a division and that a return to Leyton Orient would be a perfect move. He said 'I have had many calls from the O's fans to return, but at the end of the day it's up to Paul Brush and Barry Hearn.'

Brush stated 'Carl Griffiths is not even fit, I have too many forwards and can't take another, he's highly thought of by the crowd, but there's nothing I can do about that.'

In January 2003 he returned to the Luton first team with a goal in a 5–0 win over Colchester United. During the close season he went on trial with Southend United but did not obtain a contract, and in the end he was signed by Tommy Cunningham at non-League Harlow Town on 15 August 2003. In March 2004 he joined Ryman Premier League side Heybridge Swifts. He was then approached to join old boss Tommy Taylor at King's Lynn, and in the 2004–05 season he ended as the Swifts top marksman with 36 goals. But in May 2005, he was appointed player-assistant manager with Ryman League side Braintree Town and has one year of his contract to run. During a Football League career that spanned some 15 years he scored 150 League and Cup goals from 303(80) appearances.

SEASON	*LEAGUE*		*FA CUP*		*FL CUP*		*TOTAL*	
	Apps	*Gls*	*Apps*	*Gls*	*Apps*	*Gls*	*Apps*	*Gls*
1996–97	13	6	0	0	0	0	13	6
1997–98	31 (2)	18	2	1	4	3	37 (2)	22
1998–99	21 (3)	8	3	1	3 (1)	0	27 (4)	9
1999–2000	11	4	0	0	0	0	11	4
2000–01	35 (2)	15	3	4	2 (1)	0	40 (3)	19
	111 (7)	51	8	6	9 (2)	3	128 (9)	60

 # Griffiths also appeared in two Auto Windscreens Shield matches, without scoring.

GROOMBRIDGE, David Henry (1951–60)

A great shot stopper, who was with the O's for nine years, David Groombridge was born in Norbury, Croydon, on 13 April 1930. At 5ft 10in, the fair-haired goalkeeper first played with the Chase of Chertsey side (Arsenal's nursery club) and was spoken of as the next England amateur international goalie while with Athenian League side Hayes FC. However, his international chance never came, so he joined the O's as a professional in 1951.

He proved to be one of the O's best-ever 'keepers, but due to the form of Pat Welton he spent a fair amount of time in the reserves. He appeared in the O's great FA Cup run of 1953–54 and during his final season he was playing better than ever. Alas, he was badly injured in a minor game and forced to retire at the age of 30 in 1960. Groombridge was not a spectacular 'keeper, but he did pull off some astonishing saves and one of those was at Sheffield Wednesday when the home players applauded him after his great display. He later managed Edgware Town between 1965 and 1967 and also coached Leyton FC for a while.

SEASON	*LEAGUE*		*FA CUP*		*TOTAL*	
	Apps	*Gls*	*Apps*	*Gls*	*Apps*	*Gls*
1951–52	5	0	0	0	5	0
1952–53	23	0	2	0	25	0
1953–54	30	0	6	0	36	0
1954–55	3	0	0	0	3	0
1955–56	0	0	0	0	0	0
1956–57	24	0	0	0	24	0
1957–58	4	0	0	0	4	0
1958–59	8	0	0	0	8	0
1959–60	36	0	1	0	37	0
	133	0	9	0	142	0

GROVES, Victor George (1954–55)

Very few have made such an impact at Orient in their first few seasons as Groves did. Vic Groves was born in Stepney, London, on 5 November 1932. He started off with Leytonstone before joining Tottenham Hotspur as an amateur in June 1952, making four League appearances and scoring three goals. He moved to Walthamstow Avenue before becoming an Oriental in May 1954, turning professional five months later. He was a key man in the O's promotion push in 1954–55 before an injury put paid to his and the O's chances, and Orient finished as runners-up to Bristol City.

The following season a move to centre-forward brought him further success as his chase-everything attitude and skill made him a firm crowd favourite. The newspapers were full of him moving to a larger club. The supporters' club started a cash fund in the hope that Orient would keep Groves. Their efforts failed, and in November 1955 both he and Stan Charlton joined Arsenal for a joint fee of £30,000. Groves had a long association with the Gunners and was converted successfully to wing-half and captained them for a while. He made 203 senior appearances with 37 goals (he also appeared in 140 other matches for the Gunners, netting a further 43 goals). In May 1964 he joined Canterbury City but retired from playing football in 1965.

While with the O's he won four England amateur caps, toured the West Indies with an FA party in 1955 and played for England B against Yugoslavia. He netted three hat-tricks away at Torquay United and Exeter City in 1954–55 and at home to Colchester United during the following season. Two of his two brothers, Bunny and Reg, were top-class amateur players.

SEASON	LEAGUE		FA CUP		TOTAL	
	Apps	Gls	Apps	Gls	Apps	Gls
1954–55	30	15	2	1	32	16
1955–56	12	9	0	0	12	9
	42	24	2	1	44	25

HALES, Kevin Peter (1983–93)

A great midfielder who spent 10 seasons with the O's, Kevin Hales was a grand, loyal servant to Leyton Orient Football Club. He was rewarded with a deserved testimonial after the club had released him at the end of the 1992–93 season with a match against West Ham United on 6 August 1993. Hales finished in 11th spot in the O's all-time appearance list, with over 330 senior appearances.

Born in Dartford, Kent, on 1 January 1961, Hales played cricket and soccer for Kent Schools before signing professional forms with Chelsea in January 1979, making 22(2) senior appearances with two goals and over 200 reserve appearances for the Blues. His League debut was against the O's on 10 November 1979 as a substitute, when the O's were crushed at home 7–3. He joined in August 1983, being Frank Clark's first signing, and was an important member of the promotion-winning side of 1988–89. His first-team opportunities were rather limited in the latter part of his stay, and the 32-year-old was given a free transfer in May 1993, just a couple of days after the departure of Frank Clark as manager at Nottingham Forest.

Hales said 'I was optimistic of staying at the club, so I was very sad on leaving after 10 years' service. It's really hard to take, but that's life.'

He reflected 'I will miss the day-to-day involvement and the dressing room banter. I have a lot of friends at Orient, and it will be very difficult to say goodbye and going out into the big wide world.'

Hales joined Welling United in 1993 and was with the Wings for seven years as player then as player-manager, signing a large number of the O's players during his stay. On 2 March 1999 Hales offered to resign as manager due to their poor run of form, but the directors requested that he stay with the club. Unfortunately Welling were relegated in 1999–2000. During May 2000 he did resign and was appointed assistant manager with Stevenage Borough. He left two years later and did some scouting for West Ham United.

In March 2003 he was appointed assistant manager to Chris Kinnear (a former O's junior player) at Nationwide Conference side Margate. A year later he took charge of Southern League Division One East side Erith & Belvedere, but after just eight games in charge he resigned to become, in June 2004, the assistant manager to Garry Hill at Hornchurch. In 2005–06 he was the head coach of Weymouth, the champions of the Nationwide Conference.

SEASON	LEAGUE		FA CUP		FL CUP		TOTAL	
	Apps	Gls	Apps	Gls	Apps	Gls	Apps	Gls
1983–84	43	2	1	0	2	0	46	2
1984–85	32 (1)	0	4	0	4	0	40 (1)	0
1985–86	31	2	6	0	4	0	41	2
1986–87	28 (5)	1	3	0	0	0	31 (5)	1
1987–88	42	6	4	0	2	1	48	7
1988–89*	39	9	3	0	5	1	47	10
1989–90	36 (3)	2	1	0	3	0	40 (3)	2
1990–91	3 (2)	0	0	0	1	0	4 (2)	0
1991–92	6 (4)	0	1 (1)	0	0	0	7 (5)	0
1992–93	29	1	2	0	2	0	33	1
	289 (15)	23	25 (1)	0	23	2	337 (16)	25

** Includes four Play-off matches during 1988–89.*

 # Hales also appeared in 16 Auto Windscreens Shield matches, scoring one goal.

HALLIDAY, David (1933–35)

Born in Dumfries, Scotland, on 11 December 1897, Dave Halliday was one of the truly great forwards to appear for the O's. The 5ft 11in and 12st player with a short shuffling stride was a legend in his day for his ability and prolific goalscoring achievements. He was a delight to watch, and it was not often that the O's fans were able to witness such a top-quality forward. He became an Oriental on 29 December 1933 for a record £1,500 fee from Manchester City and netted 19 League goals from just 21 starts. Surely he would have shattered the O's goalscoring record had he joined from the start of that season.

He started his remarkable career in December 1919 with Queen of the South and then went on to play for St Mirren, Dundee, Sunderland, Arsenal and Manchester City. Halliday was a goalscoring machine, and he held Dundee's Scottish League goalscoring record with 38 goals in a season for over 40 years, until Alan Gilzean broke it in 1963–64. He netted 92 goals in his four seasons at Dens Park. He joined Sunderland for £4,000 in April 1925 and is still the record seasonal goalscorer for them when he netted 43 Division One goals from 42 starts in 1928–29 and netted a grand total of 162 senior goals from 175 appearances. He joined Arsenal in November 1929 for a sizeable fee of £6,500, and although not a regular at Highbury he netted 53 goals from 48 League, Cup and reserve starts before joining Manchester City in November 1930 for £5,700, where he found the net 47 times from 76 appearances.

It was quite a Christmas present in December 1933 when supporters read in their newspaper 'O's surprise – Sign the great 36-year-old Dave Halliday for £1,500?' Many had thought that Halliday had passed his best, but the O's fans were not let down by the player with unusual style and splendid left foot, and he caused panic among all the Third Division defences. He netted three hat-tricks in his first season and was the top scorer. During one spell he netted in nine consecutive League matches, a feat only equalled by the O's legendary goalscorer Tommy Johnston in 1957–58. Halliday again top scored in 1934–35. However, at the age of 37 he decided to retire from League football to take up a position as player-manager with Southern League side Yeovil & Petters United in June 1935. During 1938 he took up the managerial position with Aberdeen, a position he held for 17 years, winning the Scottish Cup and in his final season the Scottish League Championship for the first time in their history.

In July 1955 he was appointed manager with Leicester City, who had been relegated the previous season. Within two years he had them back up to the old First Division and clinched promotion with a 5–1 win at Brisbane Road in April 1957. He left Filbert Street in November 1958 and in March 1959 returned to Aberdeen to run a hotel and become a shareholder of the club there.

Halliday's managerial record with Leicester City between July 1955 and October 1958 reads: P145, W64, D27, L 54. Halliday's record with Aberdeen between 1938 and 1955 (not including his time in charge during the war years) reads: P98, W54, D15, L29.

Dave Halliday died on 5 January 1970. His record shows that in 15 years in both Scottish and English League football he scored a total of 339 goals from 448 appearances and averaged 0.751 goals per game – a higher goals-to-match ratio than some of the all-time greats of British football like Hughie Gallacher (0.712) and Jimmy Greaves (0.691).

One quite remarkable fact to end with was that David Halliday could never obtain a full Scottish cap. This could be attributed to the fact that Hughie Gallacher of Airdrie, Newcastle United and Chelsea fame had won 20 caps and was holding down the place at the time, and Jimmy McGrory was also chasing international honours, but it is still a remarkable record for Halliday, who is recognised as one of the six greatest strikers Britain has ever known.

SEASON	*LEAGUE*		*FA CUP*		*TOTAL*	
	Apps	*Gls*	*Apps*	*Gls*	*Apps*	*Gls*
1933–34	21	19	1	0	22	19
1934–35	32	14	2	3	34	17
	53	33	3	3	56	36

 # Halliday also appeared in three Third Division Cup matches between 1933–35, scoring one goal at Northampton Town on 24 September 1934.

Halliday also scored a number of goals in friendly matches: three goals versus Scottish side Motherwell, a 4–6 defeat in 1933–34, three goals versus Irish side Belfast Celtic FC, a 5–1 win in 1933–34, one goal versus Austrian side Sportclub Rapid of Vienna, a 2–3 defeat in 1934–35, and one goal versus Motherwell also in 1934–35.

HARRIS, Andrew David Douglas (1999–2003)

Twenty-two-year-old Andy Harris signed for the O's from Southend United on 5 June 1999 on a non-contract basis after being released by their new manager Alan Little in June 1999. Born in Springs near Johannesburg in South Africa on 26 February 1977, he left South Africa in 1979 aged two when his parents moved back to the UK but was still eligible to play for his home country. He grew up in Liverpool and was a product of the same Liverpool youth team as Michael Owen. He turned professional on 23 March 1984 and returned home when he toured South Africa with Liverpool in the 1994–95 season and played against their top club side Kaiser Chiefs.

The 5ft 10in and 11st 11lb player was signed by Ronnie Whelan, the former Liverpool player, for Second Division Southend United on 10 July 1996 on a free transfer. In 1997–98 he took over as captain and was the kingpin at the heart of the defence. After some outstanding performances, England Under-21 manager Peter Taylor came to Roots Hall to watch him. A serious injury in February 1998 curtailed his progress, and he never won his place back, playing just once in his last season there in February 1999 against Brighton, making a total of 78(2) senior appearances for the Shrimpers.

Harris has proved to be an accomplished defender who appears more at home on the right side of the defence. He is quick in the tackle but had a tendency to over commit himself, obtaining 15 yellow and one red card during his stay on the coast. Harris made his Orient debut at Carlisle United in August 1999. He is the only known League player who is a member of Mensa, with an IQ of 153. He had excellent academic grades but chose to play football rather than continue his studies. Harris recovered from an injury in his first season and was converted to a central-midfield role in 2000–01 to excellent effect. He played in the Play-off Final, a 4–2 defeat at the hands of Blackpool at the Millennium Stadium in May 2001.

He scored his first ever League goal in the 3–1 away defeat at Hartlepool United in December 2001 with a 12-yard strike. In February 2003 he was made team captain after the departure of Dean Smith to Sheffield Wednesday. Surprisingly, he was one of three midfielders released by manager Paul Brush in 2003, and he played his final match in a 1–0 defeat at home to Wrexham on 29 April 2003. Manager Brush paid tribute to Harris, 'Andy Harris has been a virtual ever present for the past three seasons, and I have never seen a more hard working, dedicated footballer than Andy. He took over as captain and has been responsible and authoritative in that role. He's a real battler and works tirelessly and unselfishly, and it was an extremely difficult decision to release him.'

Harris himself said after his final match 'It was an emotional night, after the match I received a standing ovation from the 3,766 fans; it was then that I realised that I was going to miss the place. I did not expect to be released, it was a big shock, I thought I would be here for another couple of seasons.'

He was not without a club too long, and he was snapped up by Nationwide Conference side Chester City boss Mark Wright, who stated 'He is a leader, a talker and a no-nonsense midfielder, Orient's loss is our gain.' Harris played his part in Chester City gaining their League status back in the following season.

After a loan spell at Forrest Green (12 appearances and one goal), he was recalled by Chester City where he made a further 19(13) appearances with one goal. He signed for Weymouth in July 2005 and made 41 appearances with six goals in their Championship-winning Nationwide Conference south side. He stated the biggest influence on his career was Tommy Taylor.

SEASON	*LEAGUE*		*FA CUP*		*FL CUP*		*TOTAL*	
	Apps	*Gls*	*Apps*	*Gls*	*Apps*	*Gls*	*Apps*	*Gls*
1999–2000	11(4)	0	0	0	4	0	15(4)	0
2000–01*	45(1)	0	4	0	4	0	53(1)	0
2001–02	45	1	4	0	1	0	50	1
2002–03	43(2)	1	1	0	2	0	46(2)	1
	144(7)	2	9	0	11	0	164(7)	2

* *Harris's League record includes 1(1) Play-off matches in 2000–01.*

HARTBURN, Johnny (1954–58)

John Hartburn scored the quickest hat-trick by an O's player in three and a half minutes against Shrewsbury Town in January 1955. He was a quick-raiding left-winger who was a firm favourite with the O's fans and is also one of a handful of the O's players to have recorded four goals in a League match, achieved versus Queen's Park Rangers on 3 May 1956, and he also netted once in a 7–0 win over Scottish side East Fife, a friendly during 1957–58.

Born in Houghton-le-Spring, County Durham, on 20 December 1920, Hartburn started his career with Bishop Auckland, he then played for Yeovil before moving to Queen's Park Rangers in March 1944, winning a Third Division Championship medal in 1947–48, and he netted 13 goals from 64 senior appearances at Loftus Road. He moved to Watford in September 1949 for £1,000, making 71 senior appearances with 21 goals (including four penalties). In March 1951 he joined Millwall for £2,500 and made 110 senior appearances that yielded 29 goals. The small, speedy winger became an Oriental in June 1954 on a free transfer at the age of 33, yet some of his most outstanding achievements were to come with the O's. He scored on his debut versus Torquay United in August 1954, and he excelled in the O's Third Division Championship season of 1955–56, recording 20 League goals (one of only 10 different O's players to score more than 20 League goals in a season).

It was his goal direct from a corner-kick that sent the O's on their way to the Third Division South Championship in May 1956. Age began to catch up on him, and he was not a regular in the following two seasons, although when called upon he still performed

admirably. He left the club at the age of 38 in July 1958 to join Yiewsley, and a few months later he joined Guildford. He returned to the O's in 1963 as the first pools promoter and programme editor. He left the club in the summer of 1966, joining Fulham in a similar capacity. He was the commercial manager with Watford between July 1976 and 1981 and was then Barnet's commercial manager and honorary secretary between June 1982 and 1987. Johnny Hartburn died on Sunday 22 January 2001 in Bournemouth, aged 81.

SEASON	*LEAGUE*		*FA CUP*		*TOTAL*	
	Apps	*Gls*	*Apps*	*Gls*	*Apps*	*Gls*
1954–55	39	10	2	0	41	10
1955–56	40	20	4	3	44	23
1957–57	14	1	0	0	14	1
1957–58	19	5	1	0	20	5
	112	36	7	3	119	39

HARVEY, Lee Derek (1983–93)

Lee Harvey will go down in the annuals of the club's history for scoring a superb opening goal in the O's 2–1 victory in the promotion Play-off Final second leg against Wrexham at Brisbane Road on 3 June 1989. A 5ft 11in fair-haired midfield and wing player, he was born in Harlow, Essex, on 21 December 1966. He played for Harlow and Essex Schools and scored in an England Youth game, a 5–3 win over Iceland at Maine Road. He signed as a professional with the O's on 5 December 1984 and made his League debut as a substitute in a 6–3 defeat at Sheffield United during March 1984. After the promotion Play-off match, his career took a nosedive due to various niggling injuries, and he failed to complete a full 90 minutes during the 1991–92 season. He did, however, score a magnificent goal in a third-round FA Cup replay against First Division Oldham Athletic in an extra-time 4–2 victory in January 1992.

Harvey was on a weekly contract for two seasons; the O's boss Peter Eustace stated 'I continually tried to get Lee to sign a contract, but he wanted more than we could offer. I made it clear I did not want people playing for me who are not on a full contract'. Harvey decided after nine seasons at the club that it was time to move on and start a new career. It was former O's boss Frank Clark who took Harvey to Nottingham Forest on trial between August and November 1993; he made just two appearances as a substitute but returned to London to join Brentford on 18 November 1993. He spent four seasons at Griffin Park, making 87(18) League appearances with six goals.

He moved to Vauxhall Conference side Stevenage Borough, playing a more defensive midfield role. He made 64 appearances with no goals before being released in May 2000. He joined Ryman League side St Albans City early in August 2000 but was troubled by injury. In August 2001 he moved to Ryman League side Bedford Town and was a regular until a cruciate ligament injury ended his 19-year playing career during the 2002–03 season.

SEASON	LEAGUE		FA CUP		FL CUP		TOTAL	
	Apps	Gls	Apps	Gls	Apps	Gls	Apps	Gls
1983–84	0(4)	0	0	0	0	0	0(4)	0
1984–85	2(2)	0	0(1)	0	0	0	2(3)	0
1985–86	11(1)	2	0(1)	0	0	0	11(2)	2
1986–87	10(5)	1	1(2)	1	2	1	13(7)	2
1987–88	6(17)	1	1	0	0	0	7(17)	3
1988–89*	29(4)	7	3	0	2(2)	0	34(6)	7
1989–90	36(1)	6	0	0	4	1	40(1)	7
1990–91	21(5)	3	3	0	5	1	29(5)	4
1991–92	5(8)	0	2	1	0(1)	0	7(9)	1
1992–93	19(2)	4	0	0	0	0	19(2)	4
	139(49)	24	10(4)	2	13(3)	3	162(56)	29

** Including four promotion Play-off matches and one goal in 1988–89.*
 # Harvey also appeared in 15(4) Auto Windscreens Shield matches, scoring two goals.

HEALD, Paul Andrew (1988–95)

Paul Heald, a 6ft 2in and 12st 5lb goalkeeper, was known for his quick reaction saves and safe handling and spent seven seasons with the O's after his £2,500 transfer from Sheffield United on 2 December 1988. Born in Wath-on-Dearne, Yorkshire, on 20 August 1968, he learnt his trade with the Blades, signing as a professional on 30 June 1987. Heald was excellent in the O's promotion season of 1988–89, playing in the final 32 matches (including the four promotion Play-off matches), after making his Orient debut on 17 December 1988 against Grimsby Town, replacing veteran Peter Wells in goal.

In season 1990–91 Heald was voted Player of the Year. A couple of seasons later he ended a personal 15-month injury nightmare when he ran on to the Brisbane Road turf against Mansfield Town on 28 November 1992, and the O's celebrated with a 5–1 victory. It was Heald's first game back since he underwent major back surgery that had threatened his career. He was sent on loan to a number of different clubs in order for him to regain his confidence. These included Coventry City, Crystal Palace, Leeds United, Malmo FC in Sweden and Swindon Town. He was transferred to Premiership club Wimbledon for £250,000 on 25 July 1995 as cover for Scottish international 'keeper Neil Sullivan, but the Dons signed Kelvin Davis from Luton Town for £600,000.

In January 2002 he went on loan to Sheffield Wednesday and played in their Worthington Cup semi-final clash against Blackburn Rovers, but they failed to get through to the Millennium Stadium Final, losing 6–2 on aggregate. During his stay he conceded 12 goals and achieved two clean sheets. He sustained a serious knee injury while at Hillsborough, which needed surgery. In July 2004 he decided to retire from playing and was appointed the reserve and goalkeeping coach with Milton Keynes Dons (formerly Wimbledon). Heald had made just 36(2) League and seven League Cup appearances for the Dons during his nine years with the club, and a career total of 220(3) League appearances spanning the 17 years he was in the game.

SEASON	LEAGUE		FA CUP		FL CUP		TOTAL	
	Apps	Gls	Apps	Gls	Apps	Gls	Apps	Gls
1988–89*	32	0	0	0	0	0	32	0
1989–90	37	0	1	0	4	0	42	0
1990–91	38	0	5	0	6	0	49	0
1991–92	2	0	0	0	1	0	3	0
1992–93	26	0	1	0	0	0	27	0
1993–94	0	0	0	0	0	0	0	0
1994–95	45	0	2	0	2	0	49	0
	180	0	9	0	13	0	202	0

* *Includes four promotion Play-off matches in 1988–89.*

 # Heald also appeared in 17 Auto Windscreens Shield matches.

HECKMAN, Ronald Ernest (1955–58)

The only O's player to have scored five goals in a first-team match, Ronnie Heckman bagged five against Lovells Athletic in a first-round FA Cup tie at Brisbane Road on 19 November 1955, which the O's won 7–1. He is also one of only nine players to have notched more than 20 Football League goals in a season, scoring 23 League goals in 1955–56 (he also hit six FA Cup goals that season) to end the season on 29 goals. Born in Peckham, London, on 23 November 1929, Heckman was a latecomer to the professional game, having shown his tremendous talent with amateur clubs Ilford and Southall.

He joined the O's in July 1955 from Bromley (he gained seven England amateur international caps between 1953 and 1955) and showed excellent ball playing ability with some devastating finishing from the inside-left position. Some of his goals in the Championship-winning 1955–56 side were out of the top drawer. He played most of the season with a broken wrist, but a broken jaw he suffered at Brighton in April 1956 kept him out of the O's vital run-in to eventually winning the Third Division South Championship. He was chosen to tour South Africa with an FA touring party, but due to his injury he missed out. Heckman never quite recaptured his early form and joined Millwall in November 1957, netting 21 League goals from 90 appearances.

During July 1960 he was with Crystal Palace and was a member of their Division Three promotion team of 1960–61, scoring 25 League goals from 84 appearances. He was later player-manager with Bedford Town. Heckman died in Bracknell on 26 November 1990, three days after his 61st birthday.

SEASON	LEAGUE		FA CUP		TOTAL	
	Apps	Gls	Apps	Gls	Apps	Gls
1955–56	36	23	4	6	40	29
1956–57	37	11	1	0	38	11
1957–58	14	4	0	0	14	4
	87	38	5	6	92	44

HENDON, Ian Michael (1991–92 loan & 1993–97)

An excellent attacking wing-back who had two spells with the O's before joining Notts County for £100,000, this former England Under-21 skipper made just 0(4) League and one League Cup appearances with Tottenham Hotspur, having joined them as a 10-year-old and then signing apprentice forms with them on 20 December 1989. He represented Havering Schools and captained their youth side that won the FA Youth Cup and also skippered the England Youth side that appeared in the Youth World Cup competition in Portugal. Hendon also tasted European Cup action for Spurs when he came on as a substitute against Sparkasse Stockerau in Austria and against Hadjuk Split at White Hart Lane. Born on 5 December 1971 in Ilford, Essex, he moved to Romford at an early age and had a number of loan spells in his early days at White Hart Lane, with Portsmouth (four apps), the O's and then with Barnsley (six apps) before signing for the O's on 5 August 1993 for £50,000.

During his loan spell with the O's the 6ft and 12st 11lb Hendon played in midfield, but it was as an attacking wing-back that he made his mark, and manager Taylor said that he was one of the best wing-backs in the Third Division. After four seasons in East London, Hendon's contract was coming up for renewal, and he was soon to become a free agent. Orient were concerned they would not receive a fee for him so he went on loan to Birmingham City on 23 March 1995 with a view to a permanent move. He made four League appearances at St Andrew's but was not signed, and so he returned to Brisbane Road. He was eventually transferred to Notts County on 24 February 1997 for £100,000.

Hendon sensationally revealed that he didn't want to leave Leyton Orient. He stated 'I'm choked and disappointed to be going. I would have stayed at Brisbane Road had I been offered a new contract. I wouldn't say I've been pushed out, but I certainly haven't left because I wanted to.'

Hendon continued 'I'm surprised at the fee, which was £50,000 now and £50,000 after a set number of appearances.' Orient also has a sell on clause. He continued 'A few months ago Orient wanted half a million pounds for me, and now I've really only gone for £100,000. I don't understand it.'

Hendon played under four managers at the club and chalked up 150 senior appearances. He was voted Player of the Year by the fans in 1995–96. The O's chairman Barry Hearn stated 'Tommy Taylor felt it was the right time to sell: we've got a bit of money, Ian can get on with his career and County have got a super deal.' Taylor commented 'As far as I'm concerned, having £100,000 is better than having nothing at the end of the season.'

Hendon was appointed as Notts County's club captain in 1997–98 and had the distinction of leading them to the Third Division Championship. He proved to be an inspirational leader and was selected for the PFA squad for two successive years, and he made 95 senior appearances, and scored six goals. He also gained seven England Under-21 caps. He was transferred to Northampton Town on 25 March 1999 for £25,000, making 60 League appearances and scoring three goals. With Hendon's contract running out at the end of the 2000–01 season, the Cobblers decided to cash in by selling him to First Division strugglers Sheffield Wednesday for £55,000 on 12 October 2000, and he made over 30 senior appearances in that season.

At the end of the 2001–02 season he made his 450th career League appearance. However, things began to go sour for him at Hillsborough, and he was arrested over a night club incident and was suspended by Sheffield Wednesday. He went on a month's loan to Conference side Barnet in 2002 but returned to Hillsborough and promptly had his contract cancelled by mutual consent. He joined Peterborough United in January 2003 but damaged his knee and was out for a few months. He eventually made seven League appearances for Posh, scoring once, but was then released. He returned to Barnet in May 2003 and made a significant contribution to helping the Bees to keep their League status, and at the end of the 2005–06 season he had made a total of 124 appearances and scored 17 goals for them. During his League career, which has spanned some 17 years so far, he has played a total of 577 League and Cup appearances, scoring 38 goals.

SEASON	*LEAGUE*		*FA CUP*		*FL CUP*		*TOTAL*	
	Apps	*Gls*	*Apps*	*Gls*	*Apps*	*Gls*	*Apps*	*Gls*
1991–92*	5 (1)	0	0	0	0	0	5 (1)	0
1993–94	35 (1)	2	3	0	2	0	40 (1)	2
1994–95	29	0	1	0	2	0	32	0
1995–96	38	2	1	0	2	0	41	2
1996–97	28	1	2	0	2	0	32	1
	135 (2)	5	7	0	8	0	150 (2)	5

** Hendon was on loan.*

 # Hendon also appeared in 12 Auto Windscreens Shield matches, scoring one goal.

HEPPOLETTE, Richard, Alfred William (1972–77)

A classy midfielder, Ricky Heppolette certainly lived up to his nickname of 'Tricky Ricky', being a clever and constructive player. Even though he sometimes looked a shade slow, there was a touch of class about him and everything he did on a football field. Born in Bhusawal, Bombay, India, on 8 April 1949, he came to England as a three-year-old and was brought up in Bolton. He arrived at Preston North End straight from school and signed apprentice forms at Deepdale in September 1964. He made his League debut in April 1968, making 149(5) senior appearances and scoring 12 goals. His headed goal against leaders Fulham on May Day 1971 gave Preston promotion to Division Two; however, with Preston heavily in debt he was sold to the O's for a bargain fee of £43,000 in December 1972.

He played very well on the left side of midfield and eventually linked up excellently with Laurie Cunningham. He was a member of the side that narrowly missed out on promotion to Division One in 1974 and will be remembered for the picture of him and Barrie Fairbrother both crying in the dressing room after the match. He lost his place in the 1976–77 season to a fit-again Peter Bennett and was transferred to Crystal Palace in October 1976 for £15,000. After just a few months and only 13(2) League appearances, he moved to Chesterfield in February 1977 for another £15,000 fee. He stayed for two years, making 46(1) League appearances, scoring three goals. In August 1979 he joined Peterborough United, but after just five appearances he went to play in Hong Kong for the Eastern Athletic club before moving back to the Peterborough area to set up a business

in 1982, and more recently he worked as a toy salesman in the Northampton area.

SEASON	LEAGUE		FA CUP		FL CUP		TOTAL	
	Apps	Gls	Apps	Gls	Apps	Gls	Apps	Gls
1972–73	15	0	1	0	0	0	16	0
1973–74	34	6	4	0	1	0	39	0
1974–75	22	2	0	0	0	0	22	2
1975–76	34	2	1	0	0	0	35	2
1976–77	8	0	0	0	2	0	10	0
	113	10	6	0	3	0	122	10

 # Heppolette also appeared in three Texaco Cup matches in 1974–75 and three Anglo-Scottish Cup matches.

HILLAM, Charles Emmanuel (1934–38)

One of the O's best goalkeepers during the 1930s, being fearless and strong in the air, Charlie Hillam was born in Burnley on 6 October 1908 and played for Burnley Schools. In 1922 he was working in the local collieries and played football as an amateur with Nelson, then in Division Three North, and with Clitheroe in the Lancashire Combination. He joined Burnley in May 1932 and made his League debut in a 4–4 draw against West Ham United during October 1932. He made 21 senior appearances at Turf Moor before joining Manchester United during May 1933, along with Tommy Manns, making just eight appearances for United.

In May 1934 both Hillam and Manns joined the O's for a joint fee of £100. He eventually ousted out regular 'keeper Alf Robertson in 1935–36 and played in the famous third-round FA Cup-tie victory over high-flying Charlton Athletic by 3–0 at Lea Bridge Road in January 1936. He was also in goal when the O's played their first League match at Brisbane Road against Cardiff City in August 1937 and played 116 consecutive League games for them. He was transferred to Southend United in June 1938 and was appointed trainer with Chingford Town during 1948–49. Charlie Hillam died in Southend on 16 June 1958.

SEASON	LEAGUE		FA CUP		TOTAL	
	Apps	Gls	Apps	Gls	Apps	Gls
1934–35	15	0	0	0	15	0
1935–36	42	0	5	0	47	0
1936–37	42	0	2	0	44	0
1937–38	26	0	2	0	28	0
	125	0	9	0	134	0

 # Hillam also appeared in four Third Division Cup matches between 1935 and 1937.

HIND, William (1908–20)

Billy Hind was born in Percy Main, Newcastle-upon-Tyne, during April 1885, and he was a gangly wing-half who stood at 5ft 9in and weighed 11st 9lb. Occasionally he also played at full-back, serving the O's splendidly over eight seasons. He started his career with Wellington Athletic before joining Fulham in May 1907, making his League debut against Clapton Orient on 26 October 1907. He made two further League appearances at Craven Cottage before signing for the O's in June 1908. He was a regular member of the team that finished in fourth spot in Division Two in both 1910–11 and 1911–12. He was also in the side that won the London Challenge Cup in 1911–12, a 3–0 win over Millwall.

After World War One he was back at Millfields for the 1919–20 season but had lost much of his pace and so decided to retire from the game. He was appointed trainer with Welsh side Ton Pentre in 1920, and he rejoined the O's as assistant trainer in 1921, a position he held for four years.

SEASON	LEAGUE		FA CUP		TOTAL	
	Apps	Gls	Apps	Gls	Apps	Gls
1908–09	37	1	1	0	38	1
1909–10	19	0	0	0	19	0
1910–11	24	0	1	0	25	0
1911–12	38	3	1	0	39	3
1912–13	26	1	1	0	27	1
1913–14	31	2	2	0	33	2
1914–15	15	0	0	0	15	0
1919–20	8	0	0	0	8	0
	198	7	6	0	204	7

HOADLEY, Philip Frederick William (1971–78)

A strong, solid and very consistent central-defender who had a fierce free-kick and shot and who skippered the O's for several seasons, Phil Hoadley was born in Battersea, London, on 6 January 1952, and he represented Surrey, Southampton and South of England as a schoolboy. He signed as a professional with Crystal Palace in January 1969, although he made his League debut at Bolton in April 1968 when only 16 years of age, and at that time he was the youngest ever player to appear for the Eagles in the Football League. He made 63(11) senior appearances for them, scoring one goal, before being released by their manager Malcolm Allison in September 1971. He joined the O's for a bargain £30,000, signed by boss George Petchey from his old club Crystal Palace, and he proved to be a fine player and captain.

He made his O's debut at full-back in a 3–2 win over Charlton Athletic on 2 October 1971, but he was soon converted to the centre of the defence, forming a highly effective partnership with Tom Walley. It was his unforgettable goal against Chelsea in the FA Cup in February 1972 that started the memorable comeback which led to a famous 3–2 victory. Hoadley was the first player in the Football League to a make a freedom-of-contract-move, this being to Norwich City in 1979, the £110,000 fee being fixed by a tribunal. He made 89 senior appearances for the Canaries before going on loan in 1982 to Hong Kong side Eastern Athletic, but he sustained a serious knee injury, which ended his professional playing career.

Hoadley moved into non-League football with Loudon United, Norwich United and Holt United as manager. He was assistant manager with Jewson Eastern League side Fakenham Town. He started a building business and also ran a public house for three years. In August 1987 he returned to Carrow Road as Norwich's football in the community officer and was still involved with the club in 2005.

Hoadley informed the author 'I loved my time with Orient, more than anywhere else I played; I learnt my trade at Palace and was happy there, yet at the O's I had a terrific time there with a great bunch of lads. When I moved to Norwich it was a very sad day for me.'

He remembered his outstanding moment at the O's: not the great Chelsea FA Cup win but the FA Cup semi-final against Arsenal when 'Lucky Arsenal got two rebounded goals to kill us off. I was a proud man when leading the players on to the Stamford Bridge turf with the Cockney Pearly King and Queen'. His biggest disappointment 'of course the match against Aston Villa in May 1974, to miss out on promotion, sad, yes it was very sad'.

He was also saddened that the team were not kept together; the players wanted a bit more money, the club could not meet the wage bill and some of the players were sold.

SEASON	*LEAGUE*		*FA CUP*		*FL CUP*		*TOTAL*	
	Apps	*Gls*	*Apps*	*Gls*	*Apps*	*Gls*	*Apps*	*Gls*
1971–72	32	0	4	1	0	0	36	1
1972–73	42	3	1	0	2	0	45	3
1973–74	42	1	4	0	4	0	50	1
1974–75	38	1	2	0	2	1	42	2
1975–76	40	1	1	0	1	0	42	1
1976–77	22	3	4	1	4	0	30	4
1977–78	39	0	8	0	3	0	50	0
	255	9	24	2	16	1	295	12

 # Hoadley also appeared in three Texaco Cup matches in 1974–75 and 12 Anglo-Scottish Cup matches with one goal.

HOLTON, Clifford Charles (1966–67)

Born in Oxford on 29 April 1929, Clifford Holton started as a full-back with junior side Marston Minors. He joined Arsenal in November 1947 from Isthmian League side Oxford City, where his potential as a dangerous striker came to the fore, making his Gunners debut on Boxing Day in 1950. He made 198 League appearances for Arsenal, scoring 82 goals, winning a League Championship medal and an FA Cup runners'-up medal. He moved to Watford in October 1958 for £10,000 and broke their goalscoring record with 42 League goals in 1959–60. He joined Northampton Town for £7,000 in September 1961, where he also broke their club record with 36 goals from 41 League appearances. (Both of these records were still, at the time of writing, unbroken.)

In December 1962 he moved to Crystal Palace for £4,000, netting a further 40 goals from 101 League appearances. He returned to Watford in May 1965 for £5,000 and then on to Charlton Athletic in February 1966. Holton joined the O's in June 1966, along with defender John Snedden, in exchange for the young O's favourite Harry Gregory. The O's were having financial difficulties, and it was the veteran Holton who inspired the players to beat off the threat of relegation with his skilful play and power shooting: such power had not been seen at the club since the days of Frank Neary in the 1940s, and, in fact, Holton is reported to have had the hardest shot of any player in the Football League.

A leg injury and a vein problem ended his playing career, falling just six goals short of a remarkable 300 League career goals. His 294 goals came from 570 League appearances in a career that spanned some 20 years and seven clubs. Cliff Holton died from a heart attack while in Almeria, Spain, on 4 June 1996, aged 67.

SEASON	*LEAGUE*		*FA CUP*		*FL CUP*		*TOTAL*	
	Apps	*Gls*	*Apps*	*Gls*	*Apps*	*Gls*	*Apps*	*Gls*
1966–67	44	17	3	0	1	0	48	17
1967–68	3	0	0	0	1	1	4	1
	47	17	3	0	1	1	52	18

HOWARD, Terence (1987–95)

Quite remarkably, the O's cult hero and stalwart Terry Howard, dubbed by fans as 'Oooh', was sensationally sacked by joint manager John Sitton during the half-time break in the home match against Blackpool on Tuesday 7 February 1995, after nine seasons of loyal service with Orient. (Further detail on this appears in the chapter on the history of the club.) He is one of only a handful of players to have made over 300 League appearances for the club. After his sacking, Howard was left sitting in the dressing room all on his own, bemused. Not surprisingly, the O's went on to lose the match 1–0 and were eventually relegated in bottom place on just 26 points, three adrift of Chester City and 12 points behind Cardiff City.

Born in Stepney, London, on 26 February 1966, Howard started as an apprentice with Chelsea in February 1984, making six League appearances. After a loan spell with Crystal Palace and Chester City, he joined the O's in March 1987 for £10,000.

Howard, a big man, who stood at 6ft 1in, showed good touches and was accurate with his passing. He played 50 matches in the O's promotion season of 1988–89, including four Play-off matches. His run of 114 consecutive League matches ended on the final day of the 1991–92 season because of blisters on his feet. (His run of 100 consecutive League appearances started against Shrewsbury on 13 January 1990, and on 29 February 1992 at Shrewsbury he scored the only goal of the match, a stunning 25-yarder, in celebration.)

He scored his first ever hat-trick playing in a midfield role against Mansfield Town on 28 November 1992, his third coming from the penalty spot. Howard was a player who had stayed very fit and free from any serious injuries and was on course to possibly break Peter Allen's long-standing League appearance record until that remarkable sacking – a sad time in the club's history.

Wycombe Wanderers manager Martin O'Neill signed him on 11 February 1995, and he made 20 appearances for the Chairboys in the 1994–95 season (making him one of just a handful of players to have made more than the 46 full League appearances in one season, excluding Play-off matches, playing 47 times, another former O's player Mickey Bullock also played 47 League matches for both Oxford and the O's in 1968–69). Howard made an emotional return to Brisbane Road with Wycombe for the final League match of the 1994–95 season. He said 'Despite what happened I still have a great affection for Orient, I still see a lot of people connected with the club, and I got a lot of letters from fans when I left.'

His last Wycombe match was on 6 August 1996 at Hull City, and he was substituted for the first time during his 63-match run, scoring three goals. Howard joined Woking in the Football Conference and made 43(2) appearances, scoring once during the 1996–97 and 1997–98 seasons. He won an FA Trophy-winners' medal for Woking at Wembley in 1997. After a short spell with Yeovil, he joined Aldershot Town, making his debut on 21 March 1998, and was appointed club captain. Howard made 60 appearances with four goals for the Shots, but he requested a transfer and left them at the end of the 1998–99 season. He joined Boreham Wood for the start of the 1999–2000 season, and then he was with Braintree Town FC for the 2000–01 season.

The 36-year-old was released by Braintree in May 2002 and teamed up with former Orient player Alan Hull at Ryman Division One side Great Wakering Rovers; however, when Hull was fired in January 2004 Howard, who was player-coach, resigned from his position. The author caught up with Terry Howard when still with Great Wakering Rovers back in December 2003, just before he left, and he talked about his early days, the fateful days when he was sensationally sacked and his hopes for the future as his playing days were coming to an end.

'Firstly, I will fill you in on my early days as a young lad playing football. I started with my school team Emerson Park Comprehensive in Hornchurch, and I represented Havering District and Essex Schools teams. I played with two junior teams, County Park in Hornchurch and Valence United in Dagenham.'

With regards to the sacking during the Blackpool match in 1995, 'Firstly, I would like to say it was a disgraceful way to treat a player who had given eight years of, I think, very good service to the club. I believe John Sitton wasn't the only person that wanted me out. Looking back, I think the chairman's attitude towards me changed, mainly because I truly believe people told him a few tales about me that were not at all true.

'Secondly, I don't think football had much to do with my sacking. When new managers take over invariably they want to bring their own players, and to that end Sitton and Chris Turner were no different, but if I was to be totally honest I think John was always a bit jealous of my popularity at Leyton Orient, even though as teammates, I must say, we got on reasonably well. In the end I suppose it was poetic justice that the sacking was the beginning of the end for them both as joint managers, as the fans, who until then had tolerated them because of the dire financial predicament the club was in, finally turned on them for their handling of me.

'After leaving Wycombe, I played at Wembley with Woking, which was a most enjoyable experience, in the 1997 FA Trophy Final; we defeated Dagenham & Redbridge 1–0, then I had various spells, which you know about, on the non-League circuit.

'As for my plans after football, I have to say I don't really know; my playing days, at the age of 38, are almost over, and I suppose it would be nice to stay in the game in a coaching capacity, having had some experience with Great Wakering Rovers. However, as for football management, in view of how some managers have treated me, I know I would treat players with a lot more respect.

'Finally, regards to the O's fans who remember me, and thank you for your support over the many years I was with the club, and I hope the club and its players can attain the success I did with the O's, especially in June 1989 when we were promoted under Frank Clark.'

SEASON	*LEAGUE*		*FA CUP*		*FL CUP*		*TOTAL*	
	Apps	*Gls*	*Apps*	*Gls*	*Apps*	*Gls*	*Apps*	*Gls*
1986–87	12	2	0	0	0	0	12	2
1987–88	41	2	4	0	2	0	47	2
1988–89*	50	5	3	0	5	0	58	5
1989–90	45	7	1	0	4	1	50	8
1990–91	46	3	5	1	6	0	57	4
1991–92	45	4	5	1	4	0	54	5
1992–93	41	5	2	1	2	0	45	6
1993–94	20 (5)	2	1 (1)	0	2	0	23 (6)	2
1994–95	27	1	2	0	1	0	30	1
	327 (5)	31	23 (1)	3	26	1	376 (6)	35

** Includes four promotion Play-off matches in 1988–89.*

 # Howard also appeared in 25 Auto Windscreens Shield matches (an O's record), scoring one goal.

HUGALL, James Cockburn (1910–21)

One of the O's finest goalkeepers who returned after World War One, having obtained multiple injuries, Jimmy Hugall was unquestionably one of the greats, who would rank alongside the likes of both Arthur Wood and John Jackson. He was born in Whitburn, Sunderland, on 26 April 1889 and started his career with Sunderland Co-Operative FC. He joined the O's from Whitburn FC of the Wearside League in July 1910, and during his early days at Millfields Road he was deputy to Billy Bower. He made his League debut against Stockport County in December 1910, a 1–0 victory, but shared the green jersey with Bower for a number of seasons until finally displacing him in 1914–15.

During World War One he joined the Durham Light Infantry, receiving serious wounds to his leg, eye and shoulder, which many thought would end his playing career, yet in the 1919–20 season he remarkably missed only seven matches. Hugall received a benefit in 1920 in a match versus Tottenham Hotspur that attracted over 10,000 spectators to honour the big custodian. During 1921–22 he lost his place to Arthur Wood, and in 1922 he moved to Scottish side Hamilton Academicals. In July 1923 he joined Durham City for only their third season in the Football League, making 35 League appearances in Division Three North. The team finished in 15th place, and due to their dire financial position only nine players were retained, so he left. Hugall died in Sunderland during 1927, aged just 38.

SEASON	*LEAGUE*		*FA CUP*		*TOTAL*	
	Apps	*Gls*	*Apps*	*Gls*	*Apps*	*Gls*
1910–11	1	0	0	0	1	0
1911–12	18	0	0	0	18	0
1912–13	4	0	0	0	4	0
1913–14	14	0	0	0	14	0
1914–15	31	0	1	0	32	0
1919–20	35	0	1	0	36	0
1920–21	35	0	1	0	36	0
1921–22	2	0	0	0	2	0
	140	0	3	0	143	0

JACKSON, Brian Harvill (1950–52)

Brian Jackson was a great young O's player who went on to stardom with Liverpool. Born in Walton-on-Thames, Surrey, on 1 April 1933, young Brian Jackson was just 17 years old when given his League debut and was hailed as a great prospect and was better than any other young O's star up to that time, even better than Tommy Mills or Billy Gray. Some newspapers even dare to suggest that he was better than Stanley Matthews at the same age. He joined the O's from Chase of Chertsey, Arsenal's famous junior club, in October 1950 and made his League debut at Brisbane Road versus Southend United in December 1950, and he performed so well at outside-right that he soon became a target of scouts from First Division clubs. He would take on and beat opposing defenders with ease, and he certainly benefitted from playing alongside ex-internationals like Billy Rees, Jimmy Blair and Tommy Brown.

In November 1951 he was eventually sold to Liverpool for £7,500 with winger Don Woan coming to Brisbane Road. Jackson scored on his Liverpool debut against Bolton Wanderers. He stayed seven seasons at Anfield, making 124 League appearances with 12 goals. In July 1958 he joined Port Vale for £1,700 and won a Division Four Championship-winners' medal with them in 1959. He went on to make 178 senior appearances with 34 goals, including nine penalties.

In July 1962 he signed for Peterborough United for £2,000, making a further 51 senior appearances and scoring four goals. Jackson had a short spell with Lincoln City between May and December 1964 with just 10 League appearances with one goal. He acted as assistant manager at Sincil Bank and later held managerial positions with both Burton Albion and Boston United in 1965–66, aged 32. Playing in a more defensive role, he played in every game that season in the United Counties League, scoring six goals, but retired at that end of the season.

SEASON	*LEAGUE*		*FA CUP*		*TOTAL*	
	Apps	*Gls*	*Apps*	*Gls*	*Apps*	*Gls*
1950–51	21	2	0	0	21	2
1951–52	17	0	0	0	17	0
	38	2	0	0	38	2

JACKSON, John Keith (1973–79)

Goalkeeper John Jackson joined the O's in October 1973, but his move was not greeted at first with loud cheers by the O's fans because he displaced popular 'keeper Ray Goddard, yet over time the 6ft and 14st Jackson went on to become one of the O's finest 'keepers, along with the likes of legendary Arthur Wood of the 1920s. Born in Hammersmith, London, on 5 September 1942, he joined Crystal Palace after leaving Westminster School and excelled at Selhurst Park, making 346 League appearances, including 222 consecutive appearances between August 1967 and October 1972, missing just 12 matches over eight seasons with the Glaziers.

His first season at Brisbane Road was not one of his best, being troubled with a leg injury, but from 1974–75 he did not miss a League match for five seasons, 210 consecutive League appearances. He was quite superb during the O's great FA Cup run in 1977–78 including one magnificent save at home to Chelsea in the dying minutes to ensure a replay. When Jimmy Bloomfield signed Mervyn Day from West Ham United for £100,000 in July 1979, 36-year-old Jackson became unsettled, and he joined his former O's boss George Petchey at Millwall the following August for £7,500. He made his 600th League career appearance while at The Den against Oxford United, and after 79 appearances for the Lions he joined Ipswich Town in August 1981, making his League debut and only appearance at the age of 39 in a win over Manchester United in July 1982. He moved to Hereford United in August 1982, making a further four League appearances in his 40th year before retiring.

Altogether he totalled 656 League appearances, spanning 18 seasons. Only the form of Gordon Banks and Ray Clemence denied him a full England cap, and he had to be content with England Youth caps and one appearance for a Football League XI versus the Scottish League XI at Hampden Park. He was the youth development officer with Brighton & Hove Albion between June 1996 and May 1998, while his old friend George Petchey was the Seagulls' assistant manager. In January 2005 he was not involved in football coaching anymore, but was working at Lewes District Council as their development officer.

SEASON	*LEAGUE*		*FA CUP*		*FL CUP*		*TOTAL*	
	Apps	*Gls*	*Apps*	*Gls*	*Apps*	*Gls*	*Apps*	*Gls*
1973–74	16	0	1	0	2	0	19	0
1974–75	42	0	2	0	2	0	46	0
1975–76	42	0	1	0	1	0	44	0
1976–77	42	0	4	0	4	0	50	0
1977–78	42	0	8	0	1	0	51	0
1978–79	42	0	3	0	1	0	46	0
	226	0	19	0	11	0	256	0

 # Jackson also appeared in three Texaco Cup matches in 1974–75 and nine Anglo-Scottish Cup matches.

JOHNSTON, John Thompson (1908–15)

J.T. Johnston was one of the O's finest full-backs, who had to give up the game due to wounds received in World War One. Born in Sunderland in 1886, he was a small but strong full-back who was renowned for his excellent passing skills and was regarded as one of the O's finest up to World War One. He started with Sunderland Royal Rovers and joined the O's from Middlesbrough's ground staff, having played only reserve football. He made his League debut against Hull City during September 1908, and he missed just 10 League matches in four seasons. Many of the sports writers of his day suggested that he should be picked for England, but he had to be content representing a Football League XI versus the Southern League at White Hart Lane on 14 November 1910, a 3–2 win for the Southern Leaguers.

Johnston joined both Fred Parker and George Scott as the only O's players to have made over 200 League appearances before World

War One. He was awarded a benefit in 1914 for his grand service to the club. His one senior goal came against Oldham Athletic in December 1909.

SEASON	LEAGUE		FA CUP		TOTAL	
	Apps	Gls	Apps	Gls	Apps	Gls
1908–09	38	0	1	0	39	0
1909–10	36	1	1	0	37	1
1910–11	36	0	1	0	37	0
1911–12	36	0	1	0	37	0
1912–13	34	0	0	0	34	0
1913–14	11	0	1	0	12	0
1914–15	27	0	1	0	28	0
	218	1	6	0	224	1

JOHNSTON, Thomas Bourhill (1956–58 & 1959–61)

This brief biography and statistical record of the O's seasonal and aggregate goalscoring record holder can hardly do justice to a player who was voted in a 1999 millennium poll by supporters as the greatest all-time O's player, gaining over 20 percent of all the votes cast. He will go down in the record books as one of the country's most remarkable players. He played in every class of professional football with three Scottish League clubs, one Welsh and seven English clubs. That equates to First, Second, Third (North & South) and Fourth Divisions as well as in the Southern League. Tommy Johnston is still ranked joint 53rd on the all-time leading goalscorers list for the English Football League and is also joint 114th of the leading all-time League goalscorers of world football, with the great Pele sitting on the top. The Tommy Johnston biography *The Happy Wanderer* by the authors was published in 2004 by Breedon Books Publishing.

Thomas Bourhill Johnston (Bourhill was his Mother's maiden name) was born in Loanhead, a small mining village five miles from Edinburgh, Scotland, on 18 August 1927. As a boy, Tommy, along with his father and brother, worked down the local coal mine. He wanted to follow in the footsteps of his two brothers who had played for Falkirk and Hibernian. At the age of 11 he played for his school team in a Cup Final, winning 4–2, and then against Roslin School he bagged 19 goals in their 26–0 victory. At 13 he captained the school Under-12 team on a Saturday morning and in the same afternoon played for the Under-17 side.

At the age of 17 a serious mining accident nearly ended his plans to be a professional footballer. Tommy suffered a badly crushed arm, and he was out of action for two years. It was touch and go whether his left arm would have to be amputated, but the doctors managed to save it after a series of skin grafts. He subsequently wore a bandage on his wrist for every match to protect it in case he should fall on it. Tommy sailed away to fame when he joined juvenile team Gilmerton Drumbirds and then moved on to Scottish junior side Loanhead Mayflower, where he was paid 6s 6d (35 pence) a match. He progressed to Peebles Rovers in 1947–48, who played in the East of Scotland League, and trials with Falkirk and Third Lanark soon followed. Bolton Wanderers offered him a month's trial, but he turned down the chance of playing in the English League as he wanted to stay in Scotland.

In 1949, at the age of 20, he joined Scottish First Division side Kilmarnock. He stayed two seasons at Rugby Park but then asked for a transfer, feeling the time was now right to try his hand south of the border. He had short spells with Third Division North side Darlington in 1950–51, but he could not settle and returned to Scotland. The following week he received telegrams from Oldham Athletic, Arbroath and Dundee United. He decided on Oldham, joining in March 1952 on a free transfer. He scored two goals in the final match of the season, a 5–3 win over Mansfield Town. In the crowd was Tom Bradshaw, a scout for Norwich City. It was Norwich City who offered £2,500, and he scored on his League debut for the Canaries on 23 August 1952. He started off very well, netting 10 goals from 10 matches, but a serious muscle injury to his leg kept him out of the side.

The years were drifting by for Tommy, and it did not seem possible that he would ever be more than a moderately successful Third Division player, but one match seemed to turn it all around. It was the end of January 1954 and Norwich were facing a fourth-round FA Cup tie against Arsenal at Highbury. Due to a number of injuries, he was drafted into the side to lead the attack and soon shot to fame by rocketing home two wonderful headers for a 2–1 victory.

He scored 33 goals in two seasons at Carrow Road, yet it wasn't until he joined Billy Lucas at Newport County for £2,100 in October 1954 that he became a nationally-recognised player. The Welsh air seemed to agree with him, and he bagged 26 goals in the 1954–55 season and a further 21 goals followed up to February 1956, including a hat-trick against the O's.

At the end of January 1956, when the O's were returning home from an away fixture, the players and management were discussing with chairman Harry Zussman the need for a quality striker to cement their push for the Third Division Championship title. Zussman asked captain Stan Aldous if he had any suggestions. He said 'Yes. I reckon we ought to go for that fellow Johnston at Newport, he always plays a blinder against me, in fact he is an absolute menace to play against and in the air he is unplayable.' Well no one was more surprised than Aldous when he was told by caretaker manager Les Gore that Zussman had paid the money from his own pocket to get Johnston on board. On 24 February 1956 Zussman had heard that Newport were desperate for cash to make ends meet, and they accepted an offer of £4,500 plus the O's Canadian-born forward Mike Burgess as part of the deal.

So started the extraordinary goalscoring feats of Tommy Johnston. He scored on his debut at Swindon Town on 25 February 1956 with a wonderful trademark header, and he also scored the goal that clinched the title against Millwall the following April with a stunning shot, thus winning a Championship medal for the first time in his career. In one spell of 82 matches he found the net 67 times. In a spate of 10 consecutive games from November 1957 he notched 19 goals, the sequence reading: 2, 1, 2, 1, 3, 4, 1, 1, 1, 3. The four goals were on Christmas Day 1957 in a 6–2 victory over Rotherham United.

He took Second Division football in his stride and finished the 1956–57 season on 27 League goals, surpassing Frank Neary's record of 25 League goals for the O's in 1948–49. During the following season Johnston looked the complete centre-forward, rattling in goal after goal, and some of his headed goals were truly magnificent. There was much talk of him surpassing Dixie Dean's record of 60 goals in a season from just 39 matches, achieved some 30 years earlier. He was the talk of the country, having scored a remarkable 36 goals from just 27 matches. He was itching to represent his country, and he felt he could only achieve this by playing First Division football, and he became unsettled at Brisbane Road.

Three clubs, Newcastle United, Sunderland and Blackburn Rovers, were showing interest, and it was Rovers who came in with a £15,000 offer and their manager Johnny Carey got his man. Blackburn Rovers were pushing for promotion to Division One, and in the final match of that campaign they had to win at Charlton's Valley ground to go up. If not then it would be the Londoners who would be promoted in second spot. Quite a match, and it was the Lancashire side who got through in an exciting tussle by 4–3 before 56,000 fans. So, Tommy had achieved his goal of First Division football, he netted eight goals from 11 starts, ending the 1957–58 season as the Football League's top scorer on 43 League goals. He also scored one FA Cup goal for the O's that season, so it was 44 goals for the season.

His baptism in the First Division proved a successful one: he scored twice on the opening day of the season in a 5–1 win over Newcastle United and netted five times from the opening three fixtures, proving, at the age of 31, he was well up for the big time. However, as the season progressed one thing was noticeable, he was slowing a little in the higher grade, but he continued to play well and of course score goals. Rovers started to give more youngsters a run in their side, and they began to struggle, and Tommy was not happy at losing his first-team place.

The O's were in the middle of a relegation battle, and Johnston phoned boss Les Gore and asked about rejoining. Gore met with Harry Zussman, he put in a bid of £7,500 and Tommy was on his way back 'home' to Brisbane Road, re-signing on 14 February 1959, but his dream of a Scottish cap now becoming a thing of the past. He was certainly no failure with Rovers, scoring 23 goals from 36 senior appearances. He joined up with fellow veterans Eddie Baily and Eddie Brown, who combined to steer the O's out of the relegation zone. Tommy had a fine season in 1959–60, notching 25 League goals, but he was clearly slowing and with the arrival of Johnny Carey as new manager in the summer of 1961 it was to be the end of Johnston's wonderful O's career, with his number-nine jersey going to new signing Dave Dunmore.

Carey called Johnston into his office and informed him that he may call him up into the first team from time-to-time, but he mainly wanted him to play in the reserves and help the younger players. Johnston agreed as long as he received first-team wages; Carey said no and Johnston was on his way out of Brisbane Road. At the end of September 1961 he joined Gillingham for £3,000, scoring on his League debut for the Gills, but he did not enjoy his stay at Priestfield Stadium, and in July 1962 he was appointed player-coach with Folkestone Town. Within one season they had won the Southern League Championship. He spent two happy seasons with them, scoring 40 goals from 68 Kent League and FA Cup appearances. He never played in any Southern League matches.

In 1964 he retired and moved to Poulton le Flyde just outside Blackpool to open a betting shop, but in October 1965 he was approached by Lytham St Annes FC to play for them, so, at the age of 38, he made 10 appearances. On 3 January 1972 he and his family emigrated to Australia, and he coached the Lysaghts Works football team. He and his son Neil played a few games and netted 15 goals between them.

Tommy's fondest memory at the O's: 'I'll never forget Christmas 1957, for that is when I broke the club's goalscoring record. Soon after I joined Blackburn Rovers, and the O's supporters' club presented me with a musical tankard playing *Auld Lang Syne*. More recently, when I returned to England for a holiday, I was guest of honour at the O's for their match versus Blackpool in October 1989. I think I signed more autographs that day than I did in my whole career.

'In August 1997 the O's supporters' club again kindly sent over to me in Australia a tankard in celebration of my 70th birthday; they both hold pride of place in my lounge.'

Johnston was one of only a handful of great headers of a football to play for Orient, and many of the others were only good at heading a ball with the front of the forehead (the powerful nodded type), but with Johnston he was brilliant at it from all angles. It didn't matter whether the crosses came from the left, right or from behind. And, of course, as previously mentioned, it was his great understanding with splendid right-winger Phil White which meant that the majority of his headed goals came from right-wing crosses.

For a man who was so badly injured and who failed to reach the top with his first four senior clubs, Tommy Johnston has every reason to feel proud of his achievements in football. In 1991 he was diagnosed with cancer, and in September 2004 Tommy underwent open heart surgery and recovered well at home.

Tommy Johnston's record speaks for itself: he scored a total of 290 League and Cup goals from 464 appearances.

SEASON	*LEAGUE*		*FA CUP*		*FL CUP*		*TOTAL*	
	Apps	*Gls*	*Apps*	*Gls*	*Apps*	*Gls*	*Apps*	*Gls*
1955–56	15	8	0	0	-	-	15	8
1956–57	42	27	1	0	-	-	43	27
1957–58	30	*35	2	1	-	-	32	36
1958–59	14	10	0	0	-	-	14	10
1959–60	39	25	1	0	-	-	40	25
1960–61†	40	16	3	1	3	0	46	17
	180	121	7	2	3	0	190	123

** Club record.*

† First season of the Football League Cup.

JONAS, William (1912–15)

A fine player, 22-year-old Willie Jonas joined the O's in 1912 after a personal recommendation from his friend and brilliant forward Richard McFadden; they had both grown up together in Blyth. Jonas proved to be a great capture and played his part as the O's rose to be one of the top teams in Division Two over the following few seasons leading up to World War One. Born in Blyth, Northumberland, in 1892, he started his career with Jarrow Croft FC, scoring two goals for them in the Gateshead Charity Cup Final. He turned down an offer of a trial with Barnsley, and instead he joined Havanna Rovers in 1910 and netted 68 goals in two seasons. He became an Oriental in June 1912 and his fearless and dashing play made him a firm favourite with the fans. He showed great skill and his distribution of the ball was excellent, and he was often the target of crude tackles by defenders. He also donned the goalkeeper's jersey when Hugall was injured during a number of League matches.

He came to the fore in 1913–14, scoring 10 League and 17 reserve goals. Jonas became a great heart-throb of the lady supporters, and it was reported that he received over 50 letters a week from his adoring fans.

Things got so bad that he requested the club to place a special notice within the programme to the effect that he was happily married to his sweetheart, a charming young lady called Mary Jane. Jonas was once sent off in an FA Cup tie at Millwall in January 1915 for fighting with home 'keeper Joseph Orme. The incident resulted in a riot on the terraces, and the local newspaper reported that police on horseback had to be brought in to stop the fighting and escort the O's fans out of the old Den Stadium. Jonas and friend McFadden were among 41 Orient players and officials to enlist in the Footballers' Battalion of the Middlesex Regiment. Both men were killed in action along with a third player, George Scott. Although Jonas never reached the heights of his friend McFadden, he was still a very impressive player and his contribution to the O's cause will not be forgotten.

Private William Jonas, F162 of the 17th Battalion of the Middlesex Regiment, was killed in action on 27 July 1916 in Flanders, France.

SEASON	*LEAGUE*		*FA CUP*		*TOTAL*	
	Apps	*Gls*	*Apps*	*Gls*	*Apps*	*Gls*
1912–13	13	0	0	0	13	0
1913–14	26	10	3	1	29	11
1914–15	31	11	1	1	32	12
	70	21	4	2	74	23

JONES, Michael Keith (1966–71)

An attacking full-back who performed well for seven years, the 5ft 8in and 12st right full-back Mike Jones arrived at Orient at the end of February 1966 as a replacement for David Webb and did a first-rate job for the seven seasons that he was at Brisbane Road. Born in Birkhampstead on 8 January 1945, he started his career with Slough-based junior side Pathfinders FC, representing Berkshire, Buckinghamshire and Oxon County Schoolboys. He joined Fulham as an apprentice in 1961 and turned professional in January 1963. He only played one League Cup tie against Reading in October 1964 before joining Chelsea two months later for £3,000, yet he only played reserve football at Stamford Bridge.

He became an Oriental in February 1966 for a £3,000 fee and soon became a crowd favourite with his never-give-up attitude and wonderful overlapping runs down the right wing. With the club short of strikers, he was moved up front and scored a great hat-trick against Doncaster Rovers in April 1967. Jones was ever present in the 1969–70 Championship-winning season, and he netted a remarkable goal versus Stockport County in March 1971 with a shot-come-cross from the right-hand touchline, captured so well on the promotion celebration programme covers for the matches versus both Gillingham and Roma of Italy. He moved to Charlton Athletic for £7,000 on 28 December 1971, making 66(2) senior appearances without scoring, before joining Burnham FC in June 1974. Later he was appointed their player-manager.

SEASON	*LEAGUE*		*FA CUP*		*FL CUP*		*TOTAL*	
	Apps	*Gls*	*Apps*	*Gls*	*Apps*	*Gls*	*Apps*	*Gls*
1965–66	13	0	0	0	0	0	13	0
1966–67	43	7	3	0	1	0	47	0
1967–68	39 (1)	2	5	0	0	0	44 (1)	2
1968–69	31 (3)	3	2	0	4	0	37 (3)	3
1969–70	46	3	2	0	2	0	50	3
1970–71	41	1	3	0	1	0	45	1
1971–72	10 (1)	0	0	0	2	0	12 (1)	0
	223 (5)	16	15	0	10	0	248 (5)	16

JOSEPH, Matthew Nathan Adolphus (1988–2004)

A great clubman with the O's for seven seasons, Matthew Joseph won two caps for Barbados during his stay. Despite a lack of height, standing at 5ft 8in and weighing 10st 7lb, the former England Youth international has proved to be an excellent right wing-back and a tenacious tackler, being difficult to beat in the air with good ball control. He was rewarded after many fine displays when he was voted the O's Player of the Year on more than one occasion. He also won two full international caps for Barbados during 2000. Born in Bethnal Green, London, on 30 September 1972, he joined the O's on 22 January 1988 for £20,000 from Cambridge United (another of Tommy Taylor's signings from his former club).

Matthew Joseph began as a first year YTS trainee with Arsenal on 11 November 1990. He moved on a free transfer to Gillingham on 12 December 1992, yet seemed to be lost to League football when he joined Finnish side Ilves FC in May 1993 without playing any matches in the Football League. It was Cambridge manager Gary Johnson that gave Joseph his chance in November 1993, and he went on to make 175(3) senior appearances for the U's, scoring six goals, before being snapped up by the O's boss Taylor. He was the mainstay in the team during the O's push for promotion in the 1998–99 season and in subsequent years proved to be one of the best defenders in the Third Division. He signed a new three-year contract in February 2000 and captained the side in the absence of Dean Smith for the Worthington Cup tie versus Reading in August 2000. Joseph was rewarded after some wonderful displays for his club with his first full international cap, a highlight of his career, for Barbados against Guatemala in the semi-final of the Football Confederation qualifying round (World Cup) on 9 October 2000 to become the O's 13th full international player. He won a second cap on 15 November against USA at the Waterford National Stadium in Bridgetown, losing 0–4.

After being voted Player of the Year he was presented with the bronze trophy before the match against Cheltenham on 28 April. He appeared in all three Play-off matches, including the 4–2 defeat by Blackpool at the Millennium Stadium in Cardiff on 26 May 2001. Joseph, after a series of niggling injures, was released in May 2004. After a trial with Cambridge United, he eventually signed for Nationwide Conference side Canvey Island in July 2004 and played 11(3) Conference games up to mid-December 2004. During January 2005 the non-League paper reported that Joseph had held talks with both Southern League side Histon, and Tommy Taylor's new club King's Lynn; however, he chose to go on loan with Histon, as it was just down the road from his home.

SEASON	*LEAGUE*		*FA CUP*		*FL CUP*		*TOTAL*	
	Apps	*Gls*	*Apps*	*Gls*	*Apps*	*Gls*	*Apps*	*Gls*
1997–98	14	1	0	0	0	0	14	1
1998–99	*35	0	3(1)	0	2	0	40(1)	0
1999–2000	38(3)	0	2	0	3	0	45(3)	0
2000–01	+47	0	4	0	3	0	54	0
2001–02	29(1)	1	3	0	1	0	33(1)	1
2002–03	37	0	1	0	1	0	39	0
2003–04	23(1)	0	2	0	0	0	25(1)	0
	223(5)	2	15(1)	0	9(1)	0	247(7)	2

** Joseph's League record in 1998–99 includes one promotion Play-off appearance.*

+ Joseph's League record in 2000–01 includes three promotion Play-off appearances.

Joseph also played in 0(1) Auto Windscreens Shield match in 1999–2000 and one LDV Vans Trophy match in 2000–01.

JULIANS, Leonard Bruce (1955–59)

A great striker who played second fiddle at the O's to Tommy Johnston, Len Julians was born in Tottenham, London, on 19 June 1933, and he followed Spurs as a youngster. He represented Rowland High School and Tottenham Boys. On leaving school he joined Harris Lebus youth club and then played for Spurs juniors. He moved from White Hart Lane after leaving the Army and joined Leytonstone. Shortly after he moved to Walthamstow Avenue and was their leading scorer with over 40 goals. He joined the O's in June 1955 and made an excellent start when he scored two goals against Brentford in January 1956. He scored 11 League goals from just nine starts in the O's League Championship success in 1955–56 and netted one of the goals in a 7–0 trouncing of East Fife in a friendly during 1957–58.

However, despite scoring 69 reserve goals in two seasons, 22 goals in 1955–56 and 47 in 1956–57, he could never get a regular first-team place due to the brilliant form of Tommy Johnston, yet he still managed 36 senior goals for the club. He was transferred to Arsenal for £12,000 in December 1958 but made just 18 League appearances, scoring seven goals, before signing for Nottingham Forest for £10,000 in June 1960. He stayed at the City Ground for three seasons, making 59 League appearances with 24 goals. In January 1964 he moved on to Millwall and made 125 League appearances, notching 58 goals for the Lions. He left the League in May 1967 to become player-coach for the Detroit Cougars in the US.

He also had a successful period between 1983 and 1986 in Kenya as coach with the Gor Mahia club, winning a number of League titles. Julians could include Middlesbrough as one of his favourite opponents; he scored four goals against them in 1957–58 and a hat-trick in 1958–59. He was a deceptive player who scored 124 League goals from 269 appearances, in a career that spanned some 11 years. Len Julians died at Southend-on-Sea on 17 December 1993, aged 60.

SEASON	*LEAGUE*		*FA CUP*		*TOTAL*	
	Apps	*Gls*	*Apps*	*Gls*	*Apps*	*Gls*
1955–56	9	11	0	0	9	11
1956–57	1	0	0	0	1	0
1957–58	34	16	2	1	36	17
1958–59	22	8	0	0	22	8
	66	35	2	1	68	36

JURYEFF, Ian Martin (1984–89)

Remembered for a wonderful spell he had between Christmas 1987 and May 1988, scoring 16 League goals from just 21 starts, Ian Juryeff spent five seasons at Brisbane Road without being called a regular, yet he still netted 55 senior goals. One of his goals, witnessed by millions around the world, was an FA Cup strike, officially credited to him by the FA, against Nottingham Forest on 30 January 1988. Born in Gosport, Hampshire, on 24 November 1962, he graduated through Southampton's youth and reserve sides. He went on loan to Mansfield Town in March 1984, scoring five goals from 12 starts, and on loan to Reading in November 1984, making seven appearances with two goals.

He joined the O's in February 1985 for £10,000, and when picked he gave some classy displays early during his stay, but he never quite recaptured that form later in his career, and Second Division side Ipswich Town took him on trial in February 1989. He was named substitute seven times and played twice, and he also scored three goals in six reserve appearances at Portman Road but returned to Brisbane Road in April 1989. Juryeff holds one record: he is the O's leading goalscorer in the Auto Windscreens Shield/LDV competition with six goals.

He declined a move to Gillingham but eventually signed for Halifax Town in August 1989 for £40,000. He made 15(2) League appearances and scored seven goals. In December 1989 he was transferred to Hereford United for £50,000 and netted a further 13 goals from 72 League starts. In June 1991 he was back with Halifax Town and netted four goals from 37 starts during the 1991–92 season. In August 1992 Juryeff joined Darlington on a free transfer, netting six goals from 26(8) senior matches. A further transfer took him to Scunthorpe United for £5,000, where he made 41(3) League appearances and scored 13 goals between 1993 and 1995. In the 1995–96 season he played for non-League Havant Town and in 1997 was a coach with Charlton Athletics' football in the community scheme.

In July 2003 40-year-old Juryeff, who holds a UEFA 'A' grade coaching badge, was appointed on to the coaching staff of Dr Martens Premier Division side Bath City; however, after a few months he quit to continue his job as football in the community officer and assistant reserve-team manager with Southampton. He also turned out for the Saints' Masters side in national competitions. In February 2005 he took up a temporary position as a coach with the Global Scouting Network in Long Island, New York, and also coaching there was the former the O's youth player and England international Warren Barton. In June 2006 he was still involved with the Saints' community scheme.

SEASON	*LEAGUE*		*FA CUP*		*FL CUP*		*TOTAL*	
	Apps	*Gls*	*Apps*	*Gls*	*Apps*	*Gls*	*Apps*	*Gls*
1984–85	19	7	0	0	0	0	19	7
1985–86	25(2)	10	5	3	1	0	31(2)	13
1986–87	11(2)	2	0	0	2	1	13(2)	3
1987–88	23	16	2	2	1	0	26	18
1988–89	28(1)	10	3	2	5	2	36(1)	14
	106(5)	45	10	7	9	3	125(5)	55

 # Juryeff also appeared in 9(1) Auto Windscreens Shield matches, scoring six goals.

KINGABY, Herbert Charles Lawrence James (1904–06)

He went into the record books as the scorer of the O's first ever goal in the Football League at Leicester Fosse on 2 September 1905, when heading home from a Richard Bourne cross in the 62nd minute of the match; however, he is best remembered by football historians as the man who took Aston Villa to court and lost a case that lasted six years. Bert Kingaby was born in Hackney, London, in January 1880. He joined the O's from the West Hampstead club in 1904 and played extremely well in the only season played in the Second Division of the Southern League. He was also on the team sheet in their first venture in the FA Cup, a tie against Enfield on 17 September 1904. He netted twice in an FA Cup replay against Cheshunt in a 4–1 win the following month. He remained a part-timer, earning £2 per week (the normal wage for professional players was £4) and also worked for a woollen merchant which meant he could hardly play any weekday matches and was classed as an amateur player.

Kingaby, who was known as 'rabbit', was a very fast right-winger with excellent ball control and tricky dribbling skills. His form was such that he attracted scouts from the First Division clubs, and both Arsenal and Aston Villa were following his every move. On news of his possible departure, one supporter wrote to a local newspaper with the following ditty.

Please Mr Kingaby stay with us, do
Your wing work is A1, tricky and true
If you, fleetest of runners
Did go to the Gunners
You would leave the poor O's in a stew.

However, with the O's in a serious financial crisis, Kingaby was sold to Aston Villa for £300 on 7 March 1906, and he received a £10 signing-on fee. He did not fare too well at Villa Park, making just four League appearances. In fact Villa offered him back to the O's for £150, but they just could not afford it.

Kingaby is remembered by football historians for the landmark legal case against Villa, claiming that he was denied freedom to move to another League club. Under the retain-and-transfer system, it allowed Villa to keep him on their retained players' list, even though they had no intention of giving him a new contract after his one-year deal had expired, and he was not receiving a salary. He went to the High Court in 1906, but the protracted legal case only reached the King's bench on 26 March 1912. Throughout this long period Kingaby was only allowed to play for teams outside of the League. He eventually lost the case against Villa, and it was the Players' Union who paid the legal costs of £725, which caused their near bankruptcy.

On reflection, a solicitor friend, who, looking at the case and arguments today, informed me 'Herbert Kingaby's case was a strong one; however, his Counsel made a gross and inexplicable error of judgement, by not having made any reference to the law of restrictive practices and restraint of trade, if this had been done, it appears to me that certainly Kingaby and the Players' Union would have won the case.'

During September 1906 Kingaby joined Southern League Fulham and was a member of their side that won the Southern League

Championship. He made 37 senior appearances for Fulham, scoring three goals, but had to leave Craven Cottage in 1907 when they were elected to the Football League Division Two. The Villa board refused Fulham's plea to allow him to play for them in the League.

He joined Southern League side Leyton FC in 1907, staying with them for three seasons, but he was forced to leave them due to an agreement reached in 1910 between the Southern League and the Football League, which prevented players moving from one League to another without a club's permission. Kingaby, by now a bitter man, whose registration was still held by Aston Villa, joined Southern League Division Two side Peterborough City in 1910, playing in their reserve side in the Western League, earning just 30 shillings a week, and later joined another Southern League side, Croydon Common, during 1913, also playing for their reserve side. He stayed for two years before the start of World War One, but, at 35, he was now too old to go into the forces and had to retire from playing, so he went back to work full-time at the woollen merchants in Hackney, London. Unfortunately Kingaby is remembered only for the legal wrangle with Aston Villa, yet during his time at Millfields Road he looked a wonderfully balanced player who could have gone a long way in the higher echelons of the professional game. Kingaby died in Hackney, London, during 1957, aged 77.

SEASON	*LEAGUE*		*FA CUP*		*TOTAL*	
	Apps	*Gls*	*Apps*	*Gls*	*Apps*	*Gls*
1904–05 *	-	-	5	3	5	3
1905–06	26	4	5	0	31	4
	26	4	10	3	36	7

* *Clapton Orient first entered the Football League in 1905–06.*

KITCHEN, Michael Peter (1977–79 & 1982–84)

Peter Kitchen joined the O's in July 1977 from Doncaster Rovers for £45,000 – Rovers were hoping to receive £75,000 from Ipswich Town, but after a four-day trial he returned to Yorkshire. The offer of cash up front from George Petchey was too great for Rovers to turn down. Upon his arrival the 5ft 8in and 11st player promised the fans goals after already notching 89 from 221(7) League appearances, also having notched 13 Cup goals from 28 matches, so his record at Belle Vue spoke for itself. He is recorded on Rovers' website as one of their top legendary players and is the club's fourth-highest League goalscorer.

Most certainly he lived up to his promise and was arguably the O's greatest forward of the past few decades. Many of his goals were sheer magic, and older fans will never forget his two marvellous strikes at Stamford Bridge that knocked Chelsea out of the FA Cup, nor his goal against Middlesbrough that helped to take the O's to a semi-final match against Arsenal at Stamford Bridge in April 1978, a goal he himself ranks as his greatest scored for the club.

Born in Mexborough, South Yorkshire, on 16 February 1952, he attended Mexborough Grammar School and played for Don & Dearne Boys at national schools level before joining Rovers under manager Lawrie McMenemy, and he made his debut on 27 November 1974 at Shrewsbury Town and scored. He built up a wonderful partnership with striker Brendan O'Callaghan, and in the 1976–77 season he hit 27 goals.

He was signed by manager George Petchey just before Petchey was fired. After his wonderful first spell with the O's, he moved to Fulham for £150,000 in February 1979, and also included in the deal was Fulham youngster Mark Gray. His stay at Craven Cottage was not a happy one and he netted just six goals from 21(3) appearances, so he moved on to Cardiff City for £150,000 in August 1980. He topped City's goalscoring chart in his first season and netted a total of 21 League goals from 64(3) outings. He was given a free transfer in May 1982 and went to team up with former O's colleague Joe Mayo at the Happy Valley club in Hong Kong; however, a few days after signing he was approached by top Dutch side Sparta Rotterdam for a trial, but it was too late, he was on his way to Hong Kong.

During December 1982 it was manager Ken Knighton who brought 'Kitch' back to Brisbane Road. After one match in the reserves against Southend United, he returned to first-team action against Preston North End, scoring the winner. If not the Kitchen of old, he certainly had not lost his knack of scoring goals, as was evident in a match against Millwall in April 1984 when he bagged four goals in a thrilling 5–3 win. He left the club in May 1984 and went to play indoor soccer in the US for a couple of months. In July 1984 he joined Dagenham & Redbridge, and in March 1985 he briefly returned to the League with Chester City, scoring one goal from 3(2) League appearances.

At the age of 49 'Kitch' was still doing his thing, when playing the Corinthian Casuals Vets on a charity tour of Brazil and China and some friendly games throughout England. During the 2001–02 season he netted four goals against the Paulistano Vets in a 6–1 victory in Brazil. Also in the side was another former Oriental, Mickey Tomlinson, and during the season 'Kitch' bagged a goal in China during June 2002 in a 5–3 defeat by Shanghai. He scored 14 goals for the CC-Vets from just nine appearances, including a hat-trick against Highgate on 31 October 2001.

During May 2003 he was one of the guests of honour at the supporters' club Star Man Dinner, and he was also the guest of honour for the O's opening fixture in August 2003 against Doncaster Rovers, bringing back some great memories for both sets of supporters.

Kitchen coached at the Wimbledon Football Academy and also managed the under-13s to 15s for about eight years on a part-time basis. Nowadays, Kitchen, who lives in Farningham, Kent, is the operations director for a leisure company called Sencio Community Leisure, who manage four leisure centres and a golf course on behalf of the District Council of Sevenoaks.

Kitchen informed the author some years ago about his stay with the O's: 'The whole of the 1977–78 season is a wonderful memory for me. From the first day to the very last when I scored the winner at Cardiff City to secure our Division Two status.

'I particularly remember my two hat-tricks against Mansfield Town and Sheffield United, they gave me a tremendous kick.' 'Kitch', will never forget that FA Cup.

'All the goals I scored gave me great satisfaction, the goal versus Middlesbrough I thought was the best, although many supporters rated the goals against Chelsea as top-notch.'

Kitch continued 'Every game seemed like a Cup Final. We had great support from the fans and the spirit among the players was just terrific.

'We were always the underdogs, yet every player played above himself. Everyone chased and ran for each other, which is something

I never experienced before. I think Joe Mayo was just great, and the save that John Jackson pulled out of a hat in the final seconds against Chelsea gave us heart for the replay at Stamford Bridge.

'I left the O's for the first time under, it must be said, unhappy circumstances. But I still had great affection for the club and its supporters. The Orient are a very friendly club.

'I made remarks in the press at the time of my departure, which was not a criticism of the club, players or supporters. Now all that's in the past, and I still have a great deal of satisfaction about my stay with the O's. They were successful for me and me for them.'

Peter Kitchen scored a League career total of 166 League goals from 419(19) appearances during a career that spanned some 11 years.

SEASON	*LEAGUE*		*FA CUP*		*FL CUP*		*TOTAL*	
	Apps	*Gls*	*Apps*	*Gls*	*Apps*	*Gls*	*Apps*	*Gls*
1977–78	42	21	8	7	3	1	53	29
1978–79	22(1)	7	3	2	1	0	29(1)	9
1982–83	20	9	0	0	0	0	20	9
1983–84	26(3)	12	1	0	1(1)	1	28(4)	13
	110(4)	49	12	9	5(1)	2	127(5)	60

 # Kitchen also appeared in six Anglo-Scottish Cup matches, without scoring, and one Auto Windscreens Shield match, scoring two goals.

LAZARUS, Mark (1957–60 & 1969–72)

One of the great Jewish players to play in the Football League and the only League footballer to win four promotions in successive seasons, Mark Lazarus, along with players like George Cohen (Fulham and England) and former O's stars Barry Silkman, David Metchick and Dave Morris, is listed on the Jewish sports personality website as one of the greatest Jewish-born footballers to have graced the Football League. One of the great characters of the game, he gave much pleasure in a long career, yet as a Jew he had to endure taunts and insults from opposing fans and players alike, one of the worst being against Millwall at The Den on 6 March 1971, yet he came through it all with honour. He collected a Division Three Championship-winners' medal with Queen's Park Rangers in 1967, Division Two runners'-up medals with QPR and Crystal Palace in seasons 1968 and 1969 respectively and then figured in the O's Third Division Championship triumph in 1970. Into the bargain he also gained a League Cup-winners' medal with QPR in 1967 when he scored the winning goal against West Bromwich Albion at Wembley.

Born in Stepney, London, on 5 December 1958, Lazarus is a member of a great Jewish sporting family of 13 brothers, of whom two were famous boxers, Harry and Lew Lazar. His nephew Bobby Fisher also played for the O's and his second nephew Paul Lazarus was associated with both Charlton Athletic and Wimbledon in the early 1980s before playing in Finland.

Mark Lazarus joined the O's from Barking as an amateur while serving in the armed forces and made his debut in a London Challenge Cup match against Charlton Athletic, scoring two brilliant goals. He signed professional forms on 26 November 1957 and played his first professional match for the reserves against Southend United, scoring in the 35th minute. His first-team debut came in an FA Cup tie against Reading in January 1958. His League debut came in the following season at Swansea City on Thursday 11 September 1958, the match ending 3–3. Two days later, during his home debut versus Scunthorpe United, he set up the first for Len Julians and then scored himself from one of his 'specials', the O's winning 2–1.

However, Lazarus could not establish himself in the side and jumped at the chance of joining former O's boss Alec Stock at Queen's Park Rangers for £3,000 in September 1960. The following September he moved to Wolves for £27,500, and from there Lazarus did the rounds in London with QPR, Brentford, Crystal Palace and again with the O's, giving great pleasure to many. In 1971–72 he retired from League football and played for a while with Folkestone Town in the Southern League and then was with the Jewish club Wingate from the Athenian League.

Mark Lazarus will always be fondly remembered as a colourful character; he always enjoyed his a 'lap of honour' in celebration every time he scored a goal. No older O's fans will forget his two glorious goals against Sheffield United during the O's return to Division Two on 15 August 1970, to see Mark run right round the ground during his lap of honour; it was a great sight and worth the entrance fee alone.

Recently Lazarus gave a very interesting account of his career on one of the QPR websites in the Rangers' legends series, and, in particular, he mentioned the following on his career and about some of the managers he served under:

'The deciding factor on joining QPR in 1960 from Orient was going back with Alec Stock. A year or so later Wolves manager Stan Cullis came in for me; he told me if I turned down the move to Molineux then he was going to sign Mike Summerbee instead, I couldn't believe he would pick me over him and so the deal, valued at £27,000, went through. At the time it was a lot of money.

'Unfortunately, I made the wrong decision, and Wolves became the only club I ever asked to leave. Cullis was a sergeant major type, he talked to people like s**t, but I used to answer him back and stick up for the other players when he started on them. We were never going to get along, so QPR bought me back.

'It was a perfect move for me as I was training with the Rangers players during the week and travelled to Wolverhampton on the Friday and then back to London the following evening. I wish I'd never moved to Wolves.

'I later found out that both Tottenham and West Ham had enquired about me, but Alec Stock didn't let on, as the money they had offered was below that of Wolves.

'I hold Alec Stock in high esteem, I really do. While he didn't have a good football brain, he was a tremendous influence on me and was a tremendous motivator. Mind you, we had some terrible rows – sometimes he would literally slap me around at half-time! The next day he would have his arm around me and ask how I was. You would never walk into his dressing room and wonder who was the boss – you knew. He had that sort of great presence about him.

'I had a good time at QPR, then Brentford came in for me in January 1964. They were a good side in those days, and they swapped me for George McLeod and £8,000, and I enjoyed my football down at Griffin Park and had a good relationship with the crowd. Then Stock came in for me for the third time in November 1965; he was trying to build up the side again and wanted me in.

'The great moment for me with Rangers was the winning of a League Cup-Final medal, we were 2–0 down at half-time in the Wembley Final against West Bromwich Albion, then came back to win 3–2, and I scored the winning goal.

'A couple of years later Crystal Palace wanted me, so in November 1967 I was at Selhurst Park, and I had a great time with Palace, we got promoted and the crowd were brilliant towards me, and I had some great success, so Rangers had made around £50,000 on me over all the years. They did well out of me.

'We got to the First Division, but I started to have problems with coach George Petchey, I couldn't stand the man and he didn't like me – actually he didn't like anyone – I used to offer to go outside with him at least three times a day.

'Then Jimmy Bloomfield, an old mate of mine when at Brentford, had taken over as manager at Orient. He begged me to go back there where it all started for me, and that's what I did. In doing so we got promoted, which was the fourth time for me, my fourth season in a row, which I believe is still a record to this day.'

Mark Lazarus's League career tally was 134 goals from 439(3) appearances, not bad for a player whose transfer fees totalled only £154,000 from seven moves. Thanks for the wonderful memories Mark.

SEASON	*LEAGUE*		*FA CUP*		*FL CUP*		*TOTAL*	
	Apps	*Gls*	*Apps*	*Gls*	*Apps*	*Gls*	*Apps*	*Gls*
1957–58	0	0	1	0	-	-	1	0
1958–59	15	4	0	0	-	-	15	4
1959–60	0	0	0	0	-	-	0	0
1960–61*	5	0	0	0	0	0	5	0
1969–70	29	7	2	0	0	0	31	7
1970–71	32	6	3	1	1	0	36	7
1971–72	20(1)	1	0	0	2	1	22(1)	2
	101(1)	18	6	1	3	1	110(1)	20

* *The League Cup commenced in 1960–61.*

LEA, Cyril (1957–64)

A great left-half who starred in the O's promotion season of 1961–62, it was a mystery why he was never capped by Wales when with the O's. Born in Moss near Wrexham, in Wales, on 5 August 1934, Cyril Lea, who stood at just 5ft 9in and weighed 11st 2lb, was strong in the tackle and was noted for his excellent ball distribution. As an amateur, he played in the Wrexham Area League with Bradley Rangers. A Welsh Amateur international who played as a full-back, he later blossomed as a left-half at Brisbane Road. On 11 May 1957, when Caernarfon Town reached the Final of the North Wales Coast FA Cup, their usual full-back was called away to play cricket for his side in the Lancashire League, so they approached Bradley Rangers to ask if Lea could play for them in the Final. He was signed for the one match and won himself a winners' medal. A few days later he signed for the O's.

He formed an important part of the famous Lucas, Bishop and Lea half-back line, who were considered to be as good as any middle line fielded previously in the club's history. Their most successful season came in 1961–62 when all three were ever present in the promotion season that took the O's into the old First Division. It was something of a mystery why he never gained a full Welsh cap while with the O's, although his partner Mal Lucas did. He was transferred to Ipswich Town on 17 November 1964 for £20,000 and did eventually gain two deserved full Welsh caps. He had a long stay at Portman Road, making 103(4) League appearances and scoring two goals.

During May 1969, after he retired from playing, he joined the Ipswich coaching staff and went on to coach the Welsh national squad. Lea left Portman Road on 13 August 1979 to become assistant manager to Alan Durban at Stoke City, and he then managed Hull City in 1983 and Colchester United between 1983 and 1986 when they just missed out on promotion in each of the three seasons he was in charge. But he was sacked along with assistant Stewart Houston. His record at Layer Road read: P158, W63, D44, L51.

Later he became youth development officer with Leicester City, between May 1987 and May 1989, then youth coach with West Bromwich Albion in July 1989, and more recently he held the chief scout position with Rushden & Diamonds FC until the 70-year-old moved to rejoin his former boss Brian Talbot as chief scout with Oldham Athletic during August 2004. He returned to the Diamonds in 2005 but left in January 2006. Cyril Lea will be fondly remembered by older O's fans for his rugged defensive play as well as being a highly skilful player.

SEASON	*LEAGUE*		*FA CUP*		*FL CUP*		*TOTAL*	
	Apps	*Gls*	*Apps*	*Gls*	*Apps*	*Gls*	*Apps*	*Gls*
1957–58	13	0	0	0	-	-	13	0
1958–59	14	0	0	0	-	-	14	0
1959–60	14	0	0	0	-	-	14	0
1960–61*	33	0	3	0	-	-	36	0
1961–62	42	0	4	0	3	0	49	0
1962–63	40	0	4	0	4	0	48	0
1963–64	42	0	3	0	1	0	46	0
1964–65	7	0	0	0	1	0	8	0
	205	0	14	0	9	0	228	0

* *The League Cup commenced in 1960–61.*

LEIGH, Walter Herbert (1905–06 & 1907–08)

Walter Leigh was born in Yardley near Smethwick on 18 November 1874. He was a dashing 5ft 11in and 12st forward who was the leading goalscorer during the O's first season in Division Two in 1905–06. 'Swappy', as he was known, started his career with amateur side Cadishead Athletic and was on Aston Villa's books in the 1898–89 season, making just a single First Division appearance versus Everton. The following season he turned out for the Broadheath club. He joined Altrincham in May 1899 to become their first full-time professional player, and he moved to Grimsby Town in June 1900, where his stay was more productive with 12 goals from 48 senior appearances, gaining a Division Two Championship-winners' medal. In May 1902 he signed for Bristol City, making 30 League and three FA Cup appearances, scoring six goals in total.

He moved to Southern League side New Brompton (later Gillingham) in June 1903, with whom he made 38 appearances, netting 14 goals. He came to Millfields Road in May 1905 and was a team member in the O's first League match at Leicester Fosse in September 1905 and scored four goals in the League match against Bradford City during April 1906. It was rather a surprise that he was allowed to move to Hastings & St Leonards United in May 1906, but he returned to Millfields in June 1907 and found the net twice in the FA Cup ties against both Romford and Old Newportonians. At the end of the 1907–08 season he moved on again, assisting Kettering Town. Leigh died in his native Yardley during 1938, aged 64.

SEASON	*LEAGUE*		*FA CUP*		*TOTAL*	
	Apps	*Gls*	*Apps*	*Gls*	*Apps*	*Gls*
1905–06	23	8	2	0	25	8
1907–08	17	3	5	4	22	7
	40	11	7	4	47	15

LEWIS, Edward (1958–64)

Eddie Lewis was one of the 'Busby babes' of the 1950s. He was the full-back in the O's great side that won promotion to the old First Division in April 1962, and over the past 30 years he has become one of the great coaches in South African football, until his retirement in 2001. Lewis was born in Manchester on 3 January 1935 and joined Manchester United as an amateur after playing just four matches for local side Goslings FC in 1950. He made his name as a centre-forward and scored on his League debut at the age of 17 at West Bromwich Albion in November 1952 and went on to score nine goals from 20 appearances, netting a further two FA Cup goals. He was transferred to Preston North End in December 1955 for £9,000, making 12 League appearances and scoring twice. He came south to join West Ham United during November 1956, a deal resulting in Frank O'Farrell going to Deepdale, and he helped the Hammers win promotion from Division Two, having a credible record with 15 goals from 36 senior appearances. He also netted 23 goals from 29 reserve outings that season.

Lewis joined the O's together with George Wright and was converted to full-back by manager Alec Stock. In 1958–59 he was given an extended run in the team at left-back and held that position for several seasons. He was at his peak during that promotion season of 1961–62, missing only one match through injury, and his display at Stoke City against Stanley Matthews brought rave reviews. He was in the side for the start of the First Division campaign until being ousted by Billy Taylor, but he soon regained his position. Lewis moved to Folkestone Town in May 1964 and later managed Ford Sports FC in the Greater London League, and in 1965 he coached Clapton FC.

Lewis emigrated to South Africa during April 1970 to begin a long and successful coaching career, and he first coached Border Schools. In 1971 he coached Jewish Guild FC and a year later was manager of Highlands North. In 1973 he was coaching Lusitano FC and in 1974 was coaching the famous Soweto side Kaiser Chiefs. A year later he was appointed director of soccer of the famous Wits University. It was Lewis who sent over youngsters Gary Bailey and Richard Gough to play in England; they both went on to have great careers in the British game. Lewis also coached the SA Continental XI in the first ever multi-racial tournament held in South Africa.

In 1988 he took Giant Blackpool FC to promotion to the SA Premier League, and in 1989 he took over the reins of Moroko Swallows and acted as director of soccer at Ellis Park for the former Rugby supremo Louis Luyt. During recent years he has coached a number of clubs including D'Alberton Callies, Moroko Swallows, Manning Rangers, Wits FC and Free State Stars. He was part of the South African Football Association's technical team for the 1998 World Cup Finals in France and for the African Cup of Nations Finals during early 2000, held in both Ghana and Nigeria.

On 5 April 2000 he celebrated 30 years of service to South African football. After his retirement in 2001, he took up coaching at a number of local schools each week and helps run a family garden service company in Johannesburg. Lewis still follows the fortunes of his two favourite teams: Manchester United and the O's. In 2005 Lewis was working for the South African private TV station M-net on their soccer channel as a studio analyser along with Gary Bailey and Terry Paine.

SEASON	*LEAGUE*		*FA CUP*		*FL CUP*		*TOTAL*	
	Apps	*Gls*	*Apps*	*Gls*	*Apps*	*Gls*	*Apps*	*Gls*
1958–59	14	2	1	2	-	-	15	4
1959–60	13	0	0	0	-	-	13	0
1960–61*	17	2	3	2	0	0	20	4
1961–62	41	1	4	0	3	0	48	1
1962–63	28	0	4	0	2	0	34	0
1963–64	30	0	3	0	1	0	34	0
	143	5	15	4	6	0	164	9

** The League Cup commenced in 1960–61.*

LIDDELL, Edward (1907–13)

A great centre-half who spent over 60 years in the game, as a player, manager, coach and scout, Ned Liddell (his surname has also been referred to as Liddle, but this is incorrect) was born in Sunderland on 27 May 1878. He was a strong and powerful centre-half who weighed 12st 6lb and stood at over 6ft tall. He graduated through the local Wearside Leagues with East End Blackwatch FC in 1901 and was then with Whitburn FC in 1903 and Seaham White Stars during the same year, while working at the same time for Wearside Shipyards, before signing for Sunderland in 1904. He never played any first-team games at Roker Park. Liddell was about to sign for Lincoln City when he heard that Southern League side Southampton wanted to give him a trial. He signed on for 30s a week in August 1905 but played just one Southern League match at The Dell in January 1906, a 9–1 win over Northampton Town. In August 1906 he spent a year with

Gainsborough Trinity, making 10 League appearances. He then became an Oriental in July 1907, playing at left-half, but he soon settled in at centre-half to form the wonderful defensive trio of Hind-Liddell-Willis, who were a prominent force for several seasons. During the 1909–10 season he was chosen to keep goal in a League match at Glossop North End on 13 November 1909, when both the O's goalkeepers, Bower and Whittaker, were injured. The O's lost 3–1. After six seasons at Millfields Road, he joined Southend United in October 1913, appearing 26 times in the Southern League, then he was transferred to Arsenal on 1 September 1914. He made two League appearances and also played in 46 reserve matches, scoring twice for the Gunners. He also featured in 68 matches for the Gunners during wartime football.

In July 1919, after the end of World War One, he was appointed manager of Southend United, yet he also made one Southern League appearance for them. Between 1920 and 1922 he was manager of Queen's Park Rangers. He was Fulham's scout in 1922, manager at Craven Cottage in 1929 and West Ham United's assistant manager and scout from 1931 until his appointment as manager with Luton Town. He later scouted for Chelsea, Portsmouth and Brentford.

Liddell's managerial career:

Team	*From*	*To*	*Games*	*Won*	*Drawn*	*Lost*
Southend Utd*	Aug 1919	May 1920	42	13	17	13
QPR	April 1920	May 1924	177	71	42	71
Fulham	May 1829	April 1931	87	39	19	29
Luton Town	Aug 1936	Feb 1938	74	39	12	23

** Southend United were a Southern League side in 1919–20, joining the Football League only in the following season.*

He eventually retired in January 1966, after serving Tottenham Hotspur as a scout for the previous 13 years, but continued to work for Spurs on a part-time basis until his death. Ned Liddell died in Redbridge, Essex, on 22 November 1968, aged 90, having been involved in the game for a remarkable 67 years.

SEASON	*LEAGUE*		*FA CUP*		*TOTAL*	
	Apps	*Gls*	*Apps*	*Gls*	*Apps*	*Gls*
1907–08	30	0	3	0	33	0
1908–09	35	0	1	0	36	0
1909–10	27	1	1	0	28	1
1910–11	37	2	1	0	38	2
1911–12	35	0	1	0	36	0
1912–13	29	0	1	0	30	0
1913–14	0	0	0	0	0	0
	193	3	8	0	201	3

LING, Martin (1996–2000)

A talented midfielder, like a number of former O's players before him, he went on to manage the club. Martin Ling, a 5ft 7in and 10st 2lb midfielder who showed great balance, captured the imagination of all the O's fans with a wonderful display of sparkling performances in 1997–98 with excellent passing, recapturing the form that made him a top-class Premiership player a few years before. This form earned him a place in the PFA award-winning Third Division team of 1998, and he was also the O's Player of the Year. Born in West Ham, London, on 15 July 1966, he started as a junior with the Hammers but gained his apprenticeship with Exeter City in January 1984 where he made 109(8) League appearances and scored 14 goals.

He joined Swindon Town – for his first spell – for £25,000 in July 1986, but after just 3(1) senior appearances he moved on to Southend United for £15,000 on 16 October 1986. Ling had a wonderful spell with the Shrimpers, scoring 31 goals from 126(12) games. After a loan spell with Mansfield Town in January 1991 of just three matches, he returned to Swindon Town for £15,000 on 28 March 1991 and had six wonderful seasons in Wiltshire, yielding 10 goals from 132(18) League appearances. He won the Man of the Match award in Swindon's First Division Play-off Final at Wembley Stadium in 1995.

Ling joined the O's on a free transfer on 22 July 1996. In his first season he did not play too well under the tactics of the manager Pat Holland, but under new boss Tommy Taylor he seemed to blossom and was ever present in 1997–98, playing in all 52 senior matches. At the age of 33 Ling found his form again in the 1998–99 season, and he was one of the stars when the O's climbed up the League table in their push for promotion and performed credibly in the O's second-half fight back in the Play-off Final against Scunthorpe at Wembley in May 1999, and he will be remembered for one remarkable clearance off the line, but it was to no avail as the O's lost 1–0.

He continued in the line-up for the 1999–2000 season, even though it was reported that he would mostly be sitting on the bench. Ling was sent off in a last-minute incident during the O's second-leg Worthington Cup tie over Swindon Town in August 1999, and he scored the winner at Rotherham on 13 November 1999, so ending another terrible run of matches without a win. Due to a large number of youth players being given their chance in the side, he held talks in January 2000 to return to old club Swindon Town, but he refused their terms and instead joined Brighton & Hove Albion on a short-term contract on 23 March 2000, making 3(6) senior appearances with one goal. At the end of his playing days, Ling made a total of 605(53) League and Cup appearances, scoring 70 goals, in a playing career that spanned some 17 years.

The O's fans were happy to read that Ling had rejoined them on 6 June 2000 as youth-team coach as well as being on non-contract terms should the need arise for first-team duty. To stay match fit he went on loan in February 2001 to Purfleet; the situation of a League team coach playing elsewhere was not unique as another former Oriental, Paul Raynor, combined a coaching job at Sheffield United with playing for non-League Boston United.

Ling's Under-19 youth side won the FA Alliance Cup Final 1–0 over Bradford City at the Millennium Stadium, Cardiff, on Sunday 22 April 2001. Ling signed a new three-year contract during May 2001, but there came a twist in his career during September 2003 when after a poor run of results manager Paul Brush was fired, and the man to take the helm was Ling. (*Refer to the chapter on Managers earlier in this book*).

SEASON	LEAGUE		FA CUP		FL CUP		TOTAL	
	Apps	Gls	Apps	Gls	Apps	Gls	Apps	Gls
1996–97	39 (5)	1	2	0	2	0	43 (5)	1
1997–98	46	2	2	0	4	0	52	2
1998–99*	47	4	5	0	4	0	56	4
1999–2000	14	1	0 (1)	0	3	0	17 (1)	1
2000–01	0	0	0	0	0	0	0	0
	146 (5)	8	9 (1)	0	13	0	168 (6)	8

** Ling's League record includes three promotion Play-off matches in 1998–99.*

 # Ling also appeared in two Auto Windscreens Shield matches, scoring one goal.

LOCKWOOD, Matthew Dominic (1998-present)

Matt Lockwood is a talented and highly-rated 5ft 9in and 10st 12lb left wing-back and midfield player who joined the O's from Bristol Rovers on a free transfer on 7 August 1998, having turned down an approach from First Division Bury. Lockwood has proved to be a versatile and talented player. A creator of goals, his accurate crosses provided many opportunities for the strikers, and more recently he became a deadly penalty taker who is now in his ninth year with the club. Born in Rochford near Southend-on-Sea on 17 October 1976, he spent six years with West Ham as a schoolboy but served his apprenticeship with Southend United. He was offered a contract by Queen's Park Rangers on 2 May 1995, although he did not figure in the first team at Loftus Road. He was one of three Rangers players recruited by Bristol Rovers' new manager Ian Holloway, a former player with Rangers himself, on 24 July 1996.

Lockwood made a total of 66(6) senior appearances with Rovers, scoring once against Wycombe, while turning in some outstanding performances both at left-back and on the left of midfield. Quite remarkably, his first season with the O's saw him face his old club Bristol Rovers twice, in the League Cup and FA Cup. Lockwood said 'I never dreamed when I left Rovers that I'd face them in both Cup competitions within six months. Rovers offered me a new two-year contract, but we couldn't agree personal terms. From being a first-team player I was looking for a new club just 10 days before the new season. Bury were not the right club for me; I have never regretted joining Orient.'

Rovers' loss has undoubtedly been the O's gain: Lockwood has given the O's good balance by offering astute defensive qualities and an attacking option down the left flank and has proved to be one of the star players of the 1998–99 season. He also played well in the 1–0 defeat by Scunthorpe at Wembley in the Play-off Final in May 1999 and was rewarded with a new three-year contract with the club in February 2000. The player was valued in the £1 million bracket and could become one of the O's highest transfers since the £600,000 deal with Notts County for John Chiedozie back in August 1981. It was reported but unconfirmed that during February 2001 the club turned down a £750,000 offer from Reading, and he had been watched by Charlton Athletic, Ipswich Town, Tottenham Hotspur and West Ham United. There have been many stories about

Lockwood moving on, but nothing concrete has ever materialised, and in 2006 he was still a firm fixture at Brisbane Road.

Lockwood obtained a nasty facial injury in a League match against York City in March 2001 which required plastic surgery, and he was not able to play until the wound had completely healed. He was rewarded for his consistent play by being voted for two consecutive seasons into the PFA Third Division team. It was his stunning goal against Hull City that took the O's to the Play-off Final against Blackpool at the Millennium Stadium in Cardiff, but unfortunately the final was lost 4–2.

Lockwood informed the press before the Final, 'There have been lots of rumours about a possible move to a higher level. It's always nice to have your name linked with big clubs, but much nicer if they'd actually come in and make a bid for me.

'That goal against Hull City helped me, and getting in the PFA Divisional team for the last two years helps too. In an ideal world, I would like to move up Divisions with Orient, but should that fail to happen, well it is every player's dream to play at the highest level. I know I'm good enough, I just need someone to give me the chance.'

Lockwood was a regular during the 2003–04 season, which saw him become one of around just 30 players to have achieved 200 or more League appearances for the club. During the 2005–06 season he broke a number of O's records – the most number of penalties scored with 27, breaking the previous record of Ken Facey; the most goals scored by a defender, breaking the previous record held by Dean Smith; being voted for a third time into the PFA's Divisional team of the year, and to top it all he was voted the club's Player of the Year. The 29-year-old was delighted and he informed www.leytonorient.premiumtv.co.uk 'This is the first time I have picked up this award and I'm delighted to have been recognised in this way. Everyone had a fantastic season and there were probably five or six players who could have won the award, so I'm honoured to have won it.' He was voted for the third time into the League Two Team of the Year 2005–06, having previously won the honour in 1999–2000 and 2000–01. It has also been a season to remember for him on becoming the club's highest-ever scoring defender and penalty taker.

SEASON	*LEAGUE*		*FA CUP*		*FL CUP*		*TOTAL*	
	Apps	*Gls*	*Apps*	*Gls*	*Apps*	*Gls*	*Apps*	*Gls*
1998–99*	39 (1)	3	4	0	2	0	45 (1)	3
1999–2000	41	6	2	0	4	2	47	8
2000–01+	34 (1)	7	4	0	4	0	42 (1)	7
2001–02	20 (4)	2	1	0	1	0	22 (4)	2
2002–03	42 (1)	5	2	0	1	0	45 (1)	5
2003–04	24 (1)	2	2	1	1	0	27 (1)	3
2004–05	45	2	2	0	1	0	48	2
2005–06	42	8	5	0	1	0	48	8
	286 (9)	40	22	2	14	2	321 (9)	44

** Lockwood's League record includes three promotion Play-off appearances in 1998–99.*

+ Lockwood's League record includes three promotion Play-off appearances in 2000–01.

Lockwood also appeared in eight LDV Van Trophy matches between 2002 and 2005, scoring two goals (one a penalty).

LUCAS, Peter Malcolm (1958–64)

A great half-back who gained four Welsh caps while at Brisbane Road, Welshman Mal Lucas was born in Bradley near Wrexham on 7 October 1938. He started off as a youth player with Wrexham, but after a short trial with Bolton Wanderers he returned to Wales to play for Bradley Rangers in the Wrexham & District League, gaining a number of Welsh Youth caps. The 5ft 7in and 11st 5lb half-back joined Liverpool on trial and played a few reserve games, but, on the recommendation of his friend Cyril Lea, he came to the O's for a trial in August 1958. Having impressed, he signed professional forms on 5 September 1958.

Lucas progressed rapidly and excelled as a quick-tackling and hard-working player. He didn't score many goals but did grab one in a friendly against German side Wormatia Worms, a 5–1 victory in 1960–61. Lucas formed part of arguably the O's best half-back line of Lucas, Bishop and Lea, and they played such an important role in the O's promotion to the old Division One in 1962. He gained his first of four full Welsh caps in 1962 against Northern Ireland. The other caps came against Mexico in 1962 and Scotland and England at Wembley in 1963.

He was transferred to Norwich City in September 1964 for £15,000, with full-back Colin Worrell coming to Brisbane Road. Lucas made 201 senior appearances at Carrow Road, scoring 10 goals. He moved to Torquay United in March 1970 and stayed for four seasons, making 118(4) League appearances with three goals. He retired in 1964, having made a career total of 454(7) League appearances, netting 17 goals. A few years ago he assisted Dale Gordon, the manager at Gorleston. More recently he was living in the Norwich area and worked for Brent Leisure and was a regular visitor to Carrow Road to watch the Canaries.

Lucas informed the author some years ago about his career with the O's: 'Leyton Orient were a terrific club to be with. I had such a good time with the O's and it was absolutely marvellous when we won promotion to the top flight.

'My best memory was winning the match against Bury in April 1962 to clinch promotion, and going up with Liverpool.'

He stressed 'The First Division-bound side was a complete team rather than one that contained outstanding individuals,' yet he did suggest that it was David Dunmore's goalscoring prowess that transformed the team into a successful one.

He felt 'The club should have brought in some big name stars and consolidated in the higher Division One, but all that's history now, yet it was a big disappointment to us all that we got relegated after just one season.'

SEASON	*LEAGUE*		*FA CUP*		*FL CUP*		*TOTAL*	
	Apps	*Gls*	*Apps*	*Gls*	*Apps*	*Gls*	*Apps*	*Gls*
1958–59	17	0	1	0	-	-	18	0
1959–60	3	0	0	0	-	-	3	0
1960–61*	13	0	1	0	1	0	15	0
1961–62	42	3	4	0	3	0	49	3
1962–63	37	0	2	0	3	0	42	0
1963–64	40	3	3	0	1	0	44	3
1964–65	5	0	0	0	0	0	5	0
	157	6	11	0	8	0	176	6

** The League Cup commenced in 1960–61.*

McDonald, Terence James (1959–65)

Little outside-left Terry McDonald, who stood at only 5ft 6in, turned professional with West Ham United in April 1956 and was a member of the team that reached the 1957 Youth Cup Final against Manchester United and was also an England Youth international. He played just one match for Manchester's first team, a friendly against Sparta Prague of Czechoslovakia. Born in Stepney, London, on 12 November 1938, McDonald joined the O's in July 1959 while completing his National Service. He made a promising League debut by scoring direct from a corner-kick against Hull City in October 1959, but it was his sparkling performance in the 5–0 defeat of Middlesbrough a few weeks later that saw him emerge as a top-class wingman.

He played a major part in the O's promotion campaign of 1961–62, and the highlight of his career was his scorching last-minute winner against Manchester United on 8 September 1962. He was not quite as effective in his last season with the O's, and so in May 1965 he moved to Reading, making 13 League appearances and scoring two goals during his one season at Elm Park. He moved to non-League Wimbledon and later joined Southern League Folkestone Town. He ran a string of betting shops in the Hornchurch area. Having now retired at the age of 66, he still works part-time in central London. Terry McDonald, with his son Tony (a keen West Ham fan), is often seen at Brisbane Road and at player reunions, living just a short bus ride from the ground, and still to this day he never stops talking about his winning goal against Manchester United some 45 years ago.

SEASON	LEAGUE		FA CUP		FL CUP		TOTAL	
	Apps	Gls	Apps	Gls	Apps	Gls	Apps	Gls
1959–60	28	9	1	0	-	-	29	9
1960–61	26	3	1	1	3	1	30	5
1961–62	36	6	4	0	3	2	43	8
1962–63	20	2	0	0	4	0	24	2
1963–64	16	0	0	0	0	0	16	0
1964–65	26	3	1	0	2	0	29	3
	152	23	7	1	12	3	171	27

McFADDEN, Richard (1911–15)

Skilful striker Dicky McFadden, who stood only 5ft 7in tall and weighed 10st 10lb, was a brilliant player and one of only a handful of truly prolific goalscorers to have played for the O's since entry into the Football League in 1905. Born in Cambuslang, Lanarkshire, Scotland, during 1889, he moved to Blyth as a boy and became best friends with William Jonas, and they later teamed up together at Millfields Road. McFadden started with Blyth in the Northern League and made his debut against Newburn in the Northern Alliance at Croft Park on 26 November 1910 and then was with Wallsend Park Villa, joining them for a fee of £2. He joined the O's during May 1911 and made his League debut and scored against Derby County on 2 September.

McFadden broke Bill Martin's O's goalscoring record of 17 goals when bagging 19 goals in the 1911–12 season, a record he himself surpassed in 1914–15 with 21 goals. He represented a Southern XI versus England at Craven Cottage in November 1914, obtaining rave reviews from the national press, and scored the only goal of the game.

The football editor of the *Daily Express* newspaper wrote 'A magnificent goal was scored by Dick McFadden of Clapton Orient. He took the ball as it came over to him and swung it into the net. He was the outstanding player on the field. I have heard about this inside-right but never seen him before. He is rather short for a forward, yet sturdily built, and he certainly knows how to make the best of his weight, a very tricky player who always troubled the England defence. I hope we see a lot more of him, especially in an England shirt.'

It was during the same week that Middlesbrough offered the O's over £2,000 for his services; however, after Orient chairman Captain Henry Wells-Holland consulted the player they informed the Boro board that the offer had been declined, to the delight of all the O's fans. McFadden told the O's chairman that he did not want to leave Orient. He was very popular with the fans and even more so when it was reported that he saved the life of a small boy he saw floundering in the River Lea. Jumping in the water, he pulled the boy out, for which he received a medal of bravery from the Mayor of Hackney.

McFadden, along with friend Willie Jonas and Jimmy Hugall and Fred Parker, was one of the first footballers to enlist in the Footballers Battalion of the 17th Middlesex Regiment to fight in World War One, four of over 40 O's players and officials to enlist.

Company Sergeant Major F/162 Richard McFadden, wounded on Sunday 22 October 1916, died in hospital from injuries received in battle, aged 27, on Monday 23 October in Flanders, France, one of three O's players to be killed in action in the Battle of the Somme (his friend Jonas and also George Scott being the other two killed) during hostilities in World War One. He was buried on 25 October 1916 at the Couin British Cemetery, Pas De Calais, 15 kilometres east of Doullens, France. As one enters the cemetery it states 'remembered with honour'.

McFadden was top scorer for the four seasons that he played with the O's, yet his only hat-trick came during their first overseas tour to Denmark when they beat a Copenhagen XI 4–0 in May 1912. Had he survived World War One, he surely would have topped 100 League goals for the club. McFadden was a rare O's player of quality who will be long remembered and never forgotten for his efforts both on and off the field of play.

SEASON	LEAGUE		FA CUP		TOTAL	
	Apps	Gls	Apps	Gls	Apps	Gls
1911–12	37	19	1	0	38	19
1912–13	30	10	1	0	31	10
1913–14	33	16	3	2	36	18
1914–15	37	21	0	0	37	21
	137	66	5	2	142	68

McKNIGHT, Philip (1954–57)

A model of consistency over five seasons at Brisbane Road, Phil McKnight was one of the most underrated members of the O's 1955–56 promotion team and was well known for having a long throw-in. He seldom hit the headlines, yet his steady consistent play with fellow half-backs Blizzard and Aldous were a major factor in many great League performances, and the trio must rank just behind the Lucas-Bishop-Lea half-back combination of the early 1960s as the finest in the club's history. Born in Camlachie, Glasgow, Scotland, on 15 June 1924, he played for Alloa Athletic before moving south of the border to join Chelsea in January 1947. A hard-working defender, he stayed at Stamford Bridge for eight seasons but managed just 33 League appearances, but he did win five Combination-winning medals.

McKnight joined the O's in July 1954, proving to be a wonderful defensive player, and played well in the Second Division. While at Brisbane Road, he represented London versus Lausanne in the Inter Cities Fairs Cup. In 1960 he was appointed coach to the O's 'A' side and later managed Hendon FC. In 1965–66 he was manager with Hayes FC.

McKnight informed the author some years ago about his days at Brisbane Road. 'My years at Orient under manager Alec Stock and coach Les Gore were the best years I had in football. I have many fond memories, the most memorable being the 2–1 victory over Millwall in April 1956 to clinch the Third Division South Championship. Remember, in those days, only one club went up to Division Two from the southern section and one from the northern.'

He continued, 'I especially remember when we played Liverpool at Anfield on Christmas day 1956. Our goalkeeper Dave Groombridge was badly injured and had to be carried off on a stretcher with the score at 0–0.

'It was decided by the boss and skipper Aldous that I should keep goal; I must have been mad to agree. I played all through the second half in front of the famous Kop. The noise was terrific.

'I kept everything out until a few minutes from the end when a shot from Billy Liddell hit a lump of frozen ice and shot away from me. I looked back, and it ended up in the back of the net.

'Still it was a great feeling to be cheered off the pitch by the 22,001 Liverpool crowd, I think the one extra on the attendance figure was the O's chairman Harry Zussman. Both sets of players had to get back to London for the next day's return fixture. We missed the train back due to the icy weather, and Zussman personally arranged for the Scottish Express train to stop over to pick us all up.

'We wish he never, we got thumped 0–4 by Liverpool, with veteran goalie Pat Welton having a nightmare. Zussman laughingly joked in the dressing room, after the match, that I should have played in goal and Welton in the half-back line, typical Zussman, always had a joke for every situation, win, lose or draw.'

SEASON	*LEAGUE*		*FA CUP*		*TOTAL*	
	Apps	*Gls*	*Apps*	*Gls*	*Apps*	*Gls*
1954–55	42	0	2	0	44	0
1955–56	39	0	3	0	42	0
1956–57	33	1	1	0	34	1
1957–58	29	0	2	0	31	0
1958–59	18	1	0	0	18	1
	161	2	8	0	169	2

MANCINI, Terence John (1967–71)

A great captain who led the O's to the Third Division Championship in April 1970, Terry Mancini walked into the office of the O's boss Dick Graham during October 1967 with a letter from old friend Cliff Holton asking for a trial. Three years later he captained the side that won promotion as champions of the Third Division, and later in his career he gained five Eire international caps while with Queen's Park Rangers and Arsenal. Born in Camden Town, London, on 4 October 1942, he is related to former British boxing greats Alf and Tony Mancini, and his younger brother Michael also had a couple of League outings with the O's in March 1984. After a short time on the groundstaff of Fulham, he joined Watford as a junior in September 1959 and turned professional in July 1961. The tall centre-half made 75(1) senior appearances for the Hertfordshire club.

In 1965 he was one of a number of British players who received attractive offers to play in South Africa, and he skippered Port Elizabeth FC to the local Championship. He contacted the O's because three former colleagues who played with him in South Africa were on their books, namely Tom Anderson, Roger Hugo (on trial) and Eddie Werge. Mancini impressed Dick Graham, and within two weeks he had signed a contract and so began his long association with the O's. He was skipper for nearly four seasons leading up to the Championship year in 1970. Mancini broke a leg on 31 January 1970 against Tranmere Rovers, but remarkably he returned just two months later to lead the side on to the Championship. The broken leg ended a run of 105 consecutive League games.

On 16 October 1971 he signed for Queen's Park Rangers for £25,000 and made 94 League appearances, scoring three goals. It was while at Loftus Road that he won the first of five Eire international caps. During October 1974 came the surprise announcement that he had signed for Arsenal for £22,500, and he played 52 League matches for the Gunners, scoring once. Between April and August 1977 he played in the US for the Los Angeles Aztecs. Mancini later held coaching positions with Fulham in September 1978 and was assistant manager with Luton Town in 1989. He also acted as a scout for Blackburn Rovers in the 1981–82 season.

Terry Mancini informed the author, 'My greatest recollection of Orient was the happy atmosphere and friendly attitude of players and supporters. It was a pleasure to get up in the morning and go to work.

'I've always said that Queen's Park Rangers were the best team I have played for, Arsenal were the greatest club and Orient the friendliest I've been associated with. The four years with the O's were the happiest of my career.

'The great success we had, well, it was to win the Third Division Championship under boss Jimmy Bloomfield and trainer Peter Angell, other than that we always struggled, yet it is nice to be a winner at any time in one's career, and that Championship was worth waiting for. Lifting that Cup was just a great feeling, not only for me but the rest of the lads, for the club and its loyal supporters.

'I had a special relationship with the O's fans, they were marvellous towards me and got me started with my nickname 'Henry', after the famous music composer.

'I have many memories of my years with Orient, and I cannot think of one from that time that would make me want to erase them from my mind. They were truly wonderful.

'After leaving the game of football, I ran a number of different businesses, including a sandwich bar, public house, clothes shop, betting shop, ladies' hairdressers and a chauffeur company; over the years all these have been sold and now for over 10 years I have been a director of Barwell Leisure, the leading sports tour operator to La Manga in Spain.'

SEASON	LEAGUE		FA CUP		FL CUP		TOTAL	
	Apps	Gls	Apps	Gls	Apps	Gls	Apps	Gls
1967–68	31	3	5	1	0	0	36	4
1968–69	46	7	2	0	4	0	52	7
1969–70	38	4	2	0	2	0	42	4
1970–71	42	1	3	0	1	0	46	1
1971–72	10	1	0	0	2	0	12	1
	167	16	12	1	9	0	188	17

MAYO, Joseph (1977–81)

Joseph Mayo formed a splendid partnership with Peter Kitchen that took the O's to the semi-final of the FA Cup in 1978. He came to the O's on 10 March 1977 from West Bromwich Albion, along with Allan Glover, as part of the deal that took Laurie Cunningham to The Hawthorns worth £135,000 (the two cost the O's £25,000). The 6ft 3in striker made a significant contribution, proving to be a great 'target man' in the O's great FA Cup run to the semi-finals during 1977–78, scoring one of the goals against Middlesbrough in the quarters.

Born in Tipton, Staffs, on 25 May 1952, Mayo started off with Dudley Town in the Midlands League, having represented both Dudley and Kingswinford Boys while at school and working as a trainee accountant. After a trial with Oxford United, he moved to Walsall on a free transfer in August 1972, making just 2(5) League appearances and scoring his one goal on his debut as a substitute at Notts County in September 1972. He moved on to West Bromwich Albion in February 1973 for £10,000, staying for four years and netting 17 goals from 67(5) League games, and he was a member of Johnny Giles's promotion-winning side with eight goals, which saw them return to the old First Division (Premiership).

Both Mayo and Glover scored on their O's League debuts at Blackburn Rovers, but soon after Mayo sustained a bad knee injury that ruled him out for the remainder of the season. The following season he came to the fore and was voted Player of the Year. He proved to be as very versatile clubman and also played at centre-half on numerous occasions due to injuries in the squad. His wife Pam was secretary to the O's chairman Brian Winston.

Mayo moved to Cambridge United during September 1981 for £100,000, making 39(1) senior appearances and scoring 14 goals. After a brief loan spell with Blackpool in October 1982, scoring once from five starts, he went to team up once again with Peter Kitchen at the Happy Valley club in Hong Kong during June 1983.

He ran the award-winning Plas Isa Guest House in Criccieth, North Wales, for 13 years before selling it. Mayo now lives in Nantwich, Cheshire, and is working as a sales representative for Imperial Tobacco.

SEASON	LEAGUE		FA CUP		FL CUP		TOTAL	
	Apps	Gls	Apps	Gls	Apps	Gls	Apps	Gls
1976–77	4	1	0	0	0	0	4	1
1977–78	35 (1)	9	8	2	3	0	46 (1)	11
1978–79	40	11	3	0	1	0	44	11
1979–80	39	11	2	1	2	1	43	13
1980–81	32 (3)	4	0	0	2	0	34 (3)	4
1981–82	0 (1)	0	0	0	0 (1)	0	0 (2)	0
	150 (5)	36	13	3	8 (1)	1	171 (6)	40

 # Mayo also appeared in nine Anglo-Scottish Cup matches, scoring one goal, and 2(1) Football League Groups Cup matches.

MILLS, Thomas James Edward (1929–34)

A brilliant and creative inside forward, who was picked for Wales in 1933, Tommy Mills was born in Ton Pentre, Wales, on 28 December 1911. Having worked as a miner in Wales, he moved to London and worked in the Trocadero Hotel. He was first spotted by an O's scout playing for Welsh Schoolboys against both England and Scotland, and, when the same scout saw him playing a match for the hotel staff team, the O's boss Arthur Grimsdell signed him up straight away. He made his League debut at Brighton & Hove Albion on 25 September 1929, just before his 18th birthday, and he blossomed into a brilliant and creative inside-forward with splendid ball control. He played a major part in the O's 9–2 trouncing of Aldershot in February 1934.

Mills gained his first full Welsh cap and scored the winning goal against England at Newcastle in November 1933, and he won one further cap against Northern Ireland (he won two further caps later in his career while with Leicester City). Mills was transferred to Leicester in May 1934 for over £1,500 but struggled to gain a regular first-team spot in their relegation-bound team. He could not find the form he enjoyed at Millfields and played just 18 senior matches and scored five goals. He moved in 1936 to Bristol Rovers for £575, which saw a revival of his career, and while at Eastville he made 99 League appearances and netted 17 goals. In 1939 he moved to Chester, and in 1946 he was on the coaching staff with Notts County. Sadly Tommy Mills died in Bristol on 15 May 1979 after being knocked down by a lorry.

SEASON	LEAGUE		FA CUP		TOTAL	
	Apps	Gls	Apps	Gls	Apps	Gls
1929–30	19	2	6	3	25	5
1930–31	7	0	0	0	7	0
1931–32	37	6	3	0	40	6
1932–33	27	7	1	0	28	7
1933–34	29	5	3	0	32	5
	119	20	13	3	132	23

MOORES, Ian Richard (1978–82)

Ian Moores joined the O's for £55,000 along with Ralph Coates, who came on a free transfer from Tottenham Hotspur at the end of September 1978 and scored two goals on his debut, a day after celebrating his 24th birthday in a Division Two fixture at Charlton

Athletic on 6 October 1978. He was born in Newcastle-under-Lyme on 5 October 1954 and attended the local Edward Orme Secondary School and was first spotted by Stoke City while playing for Staffordshire Schools. The 6ft 2in and 13st 8lb forward joined the Potters as an apprentice and signed professional forms in June 1972, having supported the club from the terraces. He made his League debut in a 1–1 draw at Leicester City on 16 April 1974 and scored 14 goals from 50 League games.

Moores netted twice for England Under-23 against Wales during January 1975 at Wrexham, and on that form he joined Tottenham Hotspur on 28 August 1976 for £75,000, making 32 senior appearances with eight goals. One of the highlights of his spell in north London was his hat-trick in Spurs' 9–0 win over Bristol Rovers. During the summer of 1977 he went on loan with Coates to the Western Suburbs Club in Sydney, Australia, before joining Orient.

Moores finished his first season at Brisbane Road as leading goalscorer on 13 goals. He spent much of his second season either in midfield or as an emergency centre-half. With the O's relegated to Division Three during 1992, he was one of several players to be released, and he moved to Bolton Wanderers, scoring five goals from 30 starts. He also had a three-month loan stint with Barnsley. After Bolton were relegated to the Third Division, he started a wonderful five-year stint with APOEL in Nicosia, Cyprus, during 1983, gaining a Cypriot Cup-winners' medal and helping them to a League title in 1986, and he played in games in Europe. Moores teamed up with the former Liverpool player Terry McDermott to form the most prolific strike force that APOEL have ever had. The team were managed by the former Newcastle player Tommy Cassidy.

On returning to the UK in 1988, he had a loan spell with Port Vale and at non-League Newcastle Town before signing for Southern League Tamworth. He played in the 1989 FA Vase Final at Wembley Stadium, and the match ended as a draw. In the replay he opened the scoring in their 3–0 victory over Sudbury Town at Peterborough four days later. Ian Moores made 254 senior career appearances with his five clubs, scoring 59 goals.

SEASON	*LEAGUE*		*FA CUP*		*FL CUP*		*TOTAL*	
	Apps	*Gls*	*Apps*	*Gls*	*Apps*	*Gls*	*Apps*	*Gls*
1978–79	30	13	3	0	0	0	33	13
1979–80	21 (5)	0	3	0	0	0	24 (5)	0
1980–81	36 (1)	9	1	0	0 (1)	0	37 (2)	9
1991–82	23 (1)	4	5	3	2	2	30 (1)	9
	110 (7)	26	12	3	2 (1)	2	124 (8)	31

 # Moores also appeared in 1(1) Anglo-Scottish Cup matches and three Football League Groups Cup matches, scoring one goal.

MORGAN, Alfred Stanley (1953–56)

Stan Morgan was born in Abergwynfi, Wales, on 10 October 1920. He was signed by Arsenal as an outstanding prospect from Welsh junior side Gwynfi Welfare in 1938, turning professional during December 1941. During war service with the Commandos, he made guest appearances during World War Two regional football for both Brighton & Hove Albion and Swindon Town. He appeared in the Gunners League side twice at outside-left in 1946–47 before moving to Walsall in June 1948, making 10 League appearances with one goal. He joined Millwall in December 1948, and while at Cold Blow Lane he came to the public's attention, having five great seasons, making 156 senior appearances and scoring 40 goals.

O's boss Alec Stock brought him to Brisbane Road in May 1953, and his subtle, clever play impressed the fans. He figured in the great FA Cup run of 1953–54, and his coolly taken goal in the fifth round against Doncaster Rovers was typical of the man. He missed only five matches when they finished runners-up in 1954–55, and he netted four goals against Exeter City in March 1955. Although 35 years old, he made 12 appearances in the O's Championship-winning side of 1955–56. He moved to Falmouth Town in May 1956 and soon after moved on to Tunbridge Wells. After retiring from the game Morgan worked for the Kenwood company as a sales rep.

SEASON	*LEAGUE*		*FA CUP*		*TOTAL*	
	Apps	*Gls*	*Apps*	*Gls*	*Apps*	*Gls*
1953–54	43	9	7	2	50	11
1954–55	41	12	2	0	43	12
1955–56	12	3	0	0	12	3
	96	24	9	2	105	26

MORLEY, Ernest James (1928–31)

A quality right-back who appeared three times for Wales while at Millfields Road, Ernie Morley was born in Sketty, Swansea, Wales, on 11 September 1901. The 5ft 9in and 11st 6lb player started with his local side Sketty FC and made his League debut with Swansea Town on 3 September 1921 versus Watford. He won his first full Welsh cap at right-back against England on 28 February 1925 and also won a Division Three South Championship-winners' medal in 1924–25 with Swansea. After playing in 123 League games for the Swans, he joined the O's for £500 in June 1928 and was capped a further three times while at Millfields Road against England, Scotland and Ireland in 1929. He also appeared in the O's two League matches played at Wembley Stadium against Brentford on 2 November 1930 and Southend United on 6 December 1930.

Morley, who marked his opposition very tightly, was rarely beaten for pace, was a good tackler and used the ball well and was quick and accurate in distribution. He broke his leg in a Division Three South match at Watford on 7 February 1931, and he decided to retire from the game due to the after-effects of the injury. He returned to live in his native Swansea, and the Swans management offered him a chance of a return to League action in June 1931, but he decided against it. Ernie Morley died in Swansea on 26 January 1975, aged 73.

SEASON	*LEAGUE*		*FA CUP*		*TOTAL*	
	Apps	*Gls*	*Apps*	*Gls*	*Apps*	*Gls*
1928–29	27	0	4	0	31	0
1929–30	25	0	4	0	29	0
1930–31	19	0	2	0	21	0
	71	0	10	0	81	0

MUSGROVE, Malcolm (1962–66)

Malcolm Musgrove is another player who made the journey from Upton Park to Brisbane Road. He was born in Lynemouth, Newcastle-upon-Tyne, on 8 July 1933. The left-winger started with his local side Lynemouth Colliery before joining West Ham United in December 1952 after his demob. He became second only to the legendary Jimmy Ruffell (164 goals) to score the highest number of goals as a winger for the Hammers, with 89 goals from 301 senior appearances during his 10-year stay at Upton Park. He also won a Second Division Championship medal.

Musgrove joined the O's on 20 December 1962 for £11,000 and scored with his first kick against Birmingham City, just two days later, in a First Division game. He didn't enjoy the O's crowd and came in for some unnecessary barracking, and he appeared to perform much better away from home. He had a wonderful match at Leicester City in the shock 3–2 victory at Filbert Street in the FA Cup when netting two goals. Another golden moment was when he scored against Cardiff City at Brisbane Road in April 1964, probably one of his best performances in a home fixture. The following season he was appointed player-coach, and during his four-year stay he served under five different O's managers.

While with the O's, Musgrove succeeded Tommy Cummings as chairman of the Professional Footballers Association (PFA). He left the O's in May 1966 and retired from playing but has remained in football, holding various managerial, coaching and physio positions with Charlton Athletic, Aston Villa, Leicester City, Manchester United, Torquay United, Exeter City and Plymouth Argyle. He went to America and worked in the NASL with Connecticut Bi-Continentals in 1977 and with the Chicago Stings in 1978. He stayed for two years in the States and spent three years as physiotherapist with Exeter City. After a spell as coach to the Qatar National side in 1994, he was appointed reserve coach with Plymouth Argyle and then was physiotherapist with Shrewsbury Town.

SEASON	*LEAGUE*		*FA CUP*		*FL CUP*		*TOTAL*	
	Apps	*Gls*	*Apps*	*Gls*	*Apps*	*Gls*	*Apps*	*Gls*
1962–63	18	3	3	2	0	0	21	5
1963–64	42	11	3	2	1	0	46	13
1964–65	16	0	1	0	0	0	17	0
1965–66	7	0	0	0	0	0	7	0
	83	14	7	4	1	0	91	18

NEARY, Harold Frank (1947–49)

A great striker with a very powerful shot, as many a goalkeeper found to their misfortune, big centre-forward Frank Neary, nicknamed the 'Brown Bomber', proved to be one of the most popular players to wear the O's colours in the 1940s, mainly due to his very powerful shooting from all angles and distances, his excellent goalscoring ability (he had one of the hardest shots in the game) and his never-say-die attitude. He came at a time when the O's were in the doldrums, and he not only helped them to rise up the table, but he also brought back the crowds to Brisbane Road, averaging 13,500 during his stay. Born in Aldershot, Hants, on 6 March 1921, he was one of six children, born to an Irish father and a South African mother. Neary could have excelled at a number of sports, having been good at boxing, football, cricket and swimming. He chose football and initially joined West Ham United as an amateur but left and played for Finchley early in the war years.

He then joined Fulham on amateur forms but joined the Army, and while stationed in Ireland he played for Glentoran. On leaving the armed forces, he joined Queen's Park Rangers in July 1945 and netted 23 goals from 30 regional wartime matches, helping them to win the Division Three South regional war northern section. In the 1946–47 season, the first season after the war, he scored four goals from nine League appearances when they finished runners-up to Cardiff City. He moved to West Ham United for £4,000 in January 1947. They needed a goalscorer in their fight against relegation, and his 15 League goals from just 14 games helped the Hammers in that fight. Neary was a real hard man, and it was reported that after being heavily fouled by an opponent in a League match for the Hammers, out of sight of the referee, he turned around and poleaxed the defender. The Hammers chairman took exception to Neary's actions and was only to happy to let him go at a loss.

Neary became an Oriental in November 1947, signing for £2,000, and he soon showed his ability by becoming the club's leading goalscorer for two seasons, breaking Ted Crawford's record of 23 League goals back in 1935–36, with 25 goals in the 1948–49 season. Neary's shooting was so powerful that he once knocked out Torquay United's goalkeeper Archie McFeat when he got in the way of a drive, and Bristol Rovers 'keeper Jack Weare, in trying to stop a Neary penalty-kick, not only found the ball in the back of the net but himself as well.

It was a sad day when he was allowed to leave in October 1949. It appeared he was on his way to Newcastle United, but Neary refused to talk to them, not wanting to leave London, and instead he returned for a second spell to Queen's Park Rangers for £7,000, yet he only made 19 senior appearances, scoring five goals, including a goal scored from the halfway line. He then moved to Millwall in August 1950 for £6,000, signed by the former O's boss Charles Hewitt, and he netted 50 goals from 123 League appearances. He ended his career in non-League football with Gravesend in May 1954.

Frank Neary, who died in London during 2003, aged 82, scored a total of 118 career goals from 245 League appearances.

SEASON	*LEAGUE*		*FA CUP*		*TOTAL*	
	Apps	*Gls*	*Apps*	*Gls*	*Apps*	*Gls*
1947–48	26	15	1	0	27	15
1948–49	39	25	2	0	41	25
1949–50	13	4	0	0	13	4
	78	44	3	0	81	44

NICHOLLS, Joseph Edward (1919–1925)

An aggressive left-back who had four good seasons at Millfields Road, born in Bilston near Wolverhampton during 1895, Joe Nicholls started off with Bilston United and then played as a reserve during World War One in the Midland Victory League with Wolverhampton Wanderers. The 24-year-old joined the O's in June 1919 and made his League debut at Huddersfield Town on 30 August 1919, the first League match on resumption after the hostilities. He performed credibly, usually at left-back, for four seasons until being replaced by Bert Rosier, and he will be remembered for his consistency and aggressive play rather than any flamboyant displays. He was a reserve for his final two seasons at Millfields Road and moved back to his local side Bilston United in August 1925.

SEASON	*LEAGUE*		*FA CUP*		*TOTAL*	
	Apps	*Gls*	*Apps*	*Gls*	*Apps*	*Gls*
1919–20	42	1	1	0	43	1
1920–21	24	1	1	0	25	1
1921–22	17	0	0	0	17	0
1922–23	31	0	1	0	32	0
1923–24	1	0	0	0	1	0
1924–25	2	0	0	0	2	0
	117	2	3	0	120	2

NICHOLSON, Joseph Robinson (1919–24)

Joe Nicholson was born in Ryhope near Sunderland on 4 June 1898 and started off with his home-town club Ryhope Colliery, joining the O's in July 1919 as a wing-half. A player who loved to venture forward and have a shot at goal, he proved over his four years at Millfields Road to be a great trier, but he moved to Cardiff City in May 1924, where he made 48 League appearances and also appeared for the Welshmen in the 1925 FA Cup Final, losing 1–0 to Sheffield United. He later moved to Aston Villa in an exchange deal with George Blackburn, yet only played once, in the League match for Villa, before moving to Bangor City. He ended his career with Spennymoor United. Joe Nicholson died in Durham during 1974, aged 76.

SEASON	LEAGUE		FA CUP		TOTAL	
	Apps	Gls	Apps	Gls	Apps	Gls
1919–20	30	1	0	0	30	1
1920–21	39	1	0	0	39	1
1921–22	32	0	1	0	33	0
1922–23	35	2	1	0	36	2
1923–24	9	0	0	0	9	0
	145	4	2	0	147	4

OTTO, Ricky (1990–93)

The emergence of Ricky Otto tearing opposition defences apart from his left-wing position was one of the major highlights in the O's history during the early 1990s. He was born in Hackney, London, on 9 November 1967. During his early days in Hackney he played for local sides Clapton Rangers FC and Puma FC. After trials with both Tottenham Hotspur and West Ham, he served three years in prison for robbery. He played football for the prison team and became a gym orderly, which meant he could work out everyday. After leaving prison, he played for Haringey Borough and Dartford and was watched by a number of the O's personnel, and eventually he signed for the club on 6 November 1990.

Otto stated 'I'll never forget my first taste of Football League action, when I came on as a substitute at Fulham, running all around the ground hearing the vibe of the crowd before entering the fray.'

He continued 'I got a great buzz when I made my full League debut at Brentford in the first match of the 1991–92 season [he set up the first goal for Burnett], but turning professional with Orient is something that really made me happy. I owe a great deal to both Frank Clark and Peter Eustace, they were tremendous with me.'

Otto, with his unusual hairstyle (having it tied up in a bun), his great pace, his ability to get behind defences and the mystique of his past, soon became a cult figure at the club. He surprisingly turned down a move to Coventry City in the summer of 1992 to stay with the O's, his most memorable match was at Brighton & Hove Albion on 6 February 1993, scoring a brilliant hat-trick. He also scored the goal against AFC Bournemouth on 17 October 1992 that took the O's to the top of Division Two, the first time the O's had reached such heights in over 21 years.

It was no real surprise that he would move on, the surprise was that it was to Southend United for £100,000 on 9 July 1993. He continued with his brilliance at Roots Hall, scoring 17 goals from 63(1) appearances. In December 1994 he moved on to Birmingham City for £800,000. Otto struggled to find a regular first-team spot at St Andrew's, playing 25(21) League matches and scoring six goals. He was loaned out to Charlton Athletic in June 1996, playing 5(2) League games, and to Peterborough United in February 1997, making 16 appearances with four goals. On 3 September 1997 he went to Notts

County on trial with a view to a permanent move, but he suffered a serious knee ligament injury after just six matches that put him out of action for the remainder of the 1997–98 season. He returned to Birmingham but was released from his contract by mutual consent in December 1997.

This great wingman was a real crowd pleaser everywhere he played, and many soccer fans around the country were both saddened and shocked by his enforced long-term absence from the game for personal reasons. It was reported that 32-year-old Otto was training with Peterborough United in July 1999 with a view to getting fit and returning to League action; however, he soon left and his whereabouts remained a mystery. He was located running a dry cleaning business with former Birmingham City player Peter Shearer in the Birmingham area.

During January 2001 Otto turned up again with Tamworth, and the following March he was on the move again to Halesowen Town, making 29(8) appearances with two goals. He then joined Midlands Combination side Romulas before signing for Dr Martens League side Bloxham United. In 2002 35-year-old Otto went to play in Wales for Rhyl, but he left after just two appearances, saying that the long rail trip he had to make was just too troublesome, having been stranded once for eight hours. Otto decided to call it a day and hung up his boots.

SEASON	*LEAGUE*		*FA CUP*		*FL CUP*		*TOTAL*	
	Apps	*Gls*	*Apps*	*Gls*	*Apps*	*Gls*	*Apps*	*Gls*
1990–91	0(1)	0	0	0	0	0	0(1)	0
1991–92	23(9)	4	2	0	3	0	28(9)	4
1992–93	18(5)	8	0(1)	0	0	0	18(6)	8
	41(15)	12	2(1)	0	3	0	46(16)	12

 # Otto also featured in 5(1) Auto Windscreens Shield matches, scoring two goals.

PACEY, Dennis Frank (1951–54)

Dennis Pacey bagged a hat-trick on his Orient debut and never looked back and is still the leading goalscorer in the FA Cup competition for the O's on 12 goals. The signing of the 22-year-old from Walton & Hersham in November 1951 almost went unnoticed. Three weeks after he had joined he remarkably burst on to the scene with his hat-trick in an FA Cup second-round replay against Gorleston at Highbury in December 1951, the O's winning 5–4.

Born in Feltham on 22 September 1928, Pacey was yet another product from the Chase of Chertsey club. Once he finished his two-year National Service he played as an amateur with Woking. After unsuccessful trials with both Tottenham Hotspur and Arsenal, he was invited to Brisbane Road by the O's boss Alec Stock. Although not doing particularly well, Stock saw something in the lad, and he was offered a contract.

The 6ft 2in and 12st 7lb striker was no flash in the pan, and although he looked ungainly he was very fast for a big man with a powerful shot, and as the seasons went by he scored some tremendous goals, including four in a match against Colchester United in a 5–3 win on 30 April 1953. He played a major part in the O's great FA Cup runs of 1951–52 and 1953–54, when he achieved the O's FA Cup goalscoring record. He moved to Millwall in October 1954, scoring on his debut, and he scored 13 goals from just 13 matches. He netted 36 goals for the Lions from his 132 League appearances before a transfer took him to Aldershot in September 1958, where he scored a further 13 goals from 32 appearances. He later played for Dartford and Yeovil. More recently Pacey was living in Chertsey and worked at Heathrow Airport within the baggage-handling department before his retirement.

A few years ago Pacey recalled his days with the O's: 'My three years with the O's were the most enjoyable I had in football. My wife enjoyed the socialising and everyone was very friendly. Alec Stock was a tremendous motivator and the chairman Harry Zussman was always cheerful. He was only in the game for the enjoyment, even when we lost he always had a smile, he was never any different win, lose or draw.'

Pacey has attended various O's reunion functions in recent years.

SEASON	*LEAGUE*		*FA CUP*		*TOTAL*	
	Apps	*Gls*	*Apps*	*Gls*	*Apps*	*Gls*
1951–52	25	11	7	6	32	17
1952–53	37	19	1	1	38	20
1953–54	45	16	7	5	52	21
1954–55	13	0	0	0	13	0
	120	46	15	12	135	58

PARKER, Frederick George (1907–22)

One of the O's all-time greats, he was at Millfields Road for 11 seasons, and Fred 'Spider' Parker was one of the most popular pre-World War One players, a real character whose antics often had the O's fans in fits of laughter. Yet, for all that, he was a wonderful inside-forward. Parker reached a number of milestones while with the O's. He was the first O's player to reach 100 League appearances on 30 April 1910 at Fulham. His 200th appearance was on 11 October 1913 at Leicester Fosse and his 300th League appearance came on 2 October 1920 at Millfields Road versus Nottingham Forest, when aged 35, and fittingly the O's won 2–1.

Parker was born in Weymouth on 18 June 1885, and he started his career off with local side Portland Grove FC before moving to Weymouth, where he remained for two years before joining Salisbury. He joined the O's on trial on his 22nd birthday in June 1907. Manager Billy Holmes was so impressed that he was chosen for the side to play Hull City in September 1907, and he set up the winning goal for Bill Martin. He picked up the nickname 'Spider' when after that match Holmes told the press that his new charge was just magnificent, the visitors were knocking him down so much that while he was on the floor he crawled around just like a spider. The account was published in the club programme and local newspapers and the nickname was taken up by all. There had been only one player to enjoy greater popularity than Parker up to World War Two and that man was Arthur Wood.

Parker was at the club for 11 seasons, and he was awarded a well-

deserved benefit in 1921. It was a sad day when he decided to retire at the age of 36, when age appeared to catch up on him, although for most of the 1921–22 season he was a member of the coaching staff, and his final appearance came versus Leicester Fosse on 21 January 1922; it was his 350th senior appearance. He won a number of honours while with the O's, including winners' medals in the London Challenge Cup, London Professional Cup and West Ham Charity Cup. He also captained the side to victory over Millwall in May 1911 to lift the Dubonnet Cup in Paris, France, and he captained a London XI versus Birmingham.

It was rumoured that he would stay with the club as a coach, but in the end he was appointed manager of Folkestone Town in June 1922. In later years it was reported that he worked as a porter at Kings Cross Station. Fred Parker died in the New Forest area during 1949, aged 64.

SEASON	*LEAGUE*		*FA CUP*		*TOTAL*	
	Apps	*Gls*	*Apps*	*Gls*	*Apps*	*Gls*
1907–08	31	6	3	0	34	6
1908–09	36	6	1	0	37	6
1909–10	33	5	1	0	34	5
1910–11	22	1	0	0	22	1
1911–12	34	4	1	0	35	4
1912–13	38	4	1	0	39	4
1913–14	37	3	3	0	40	3
1914–15	37	2	1	0	38	2
1919–20	28	2	1	0	29	2
1920–21	33	1	2	0	35	1
1921–22	7	0	0	0	7	0
	336	34	14	0	350	34

PINNER, Michael John (1962–65)

A solicitor by profession, Michael Pinner was one of the outstanding amateur goalkeepers of his era, having gained over 50 England amateur international caps and also representing Great Britain at the 1956 Melbourne Olympics and in the Rome Olympics of 1960. Mike Pinner was born in Boston, Lincolnshire, on 16 February 1934. He attended Boston Grammar School and started playing football with local side Wyberton Rangers. He then played for Boston United in 1953 and was with them again during the 1957–58 season. He represented Cambridge University four times in the annual varsity matches versus Oxford.

Besides playing for amateur sides Pegasus, Corinthian Casuals and Hendon, Pinner also helped out a number of Football League clubs, including Notts County Reserves in the Midlands League (1949), this before his 16th birthday, Aston Villa (1954), Sheffield Wednesday (1957), Queen's Park Rangers (1959), Manchester United (1961), Chelsea (1961) and Swansea Town (1962), making a total of 36 League appearances with those clubs. He joined the O's on amateur forms in October 1962, making his debut in the 5–1 home defeat by Tottenham Hotspur before 30,987 fans, and while with the club he also represented Great Britain versus Iceland in an Olympic Games qualifying match.

Pinner signed as a part-time professional in October 1963, but when Dave Sexton joined as the O's boss he was not keen on having part-timers on the books, so in July 1965 Pinner was allowed to leave, joining Belfast Distillery of the Irish League, where he stayed for two years. Had he stayed with Orient he would surely have given them many more years of good service. Today, Pinner is an experienced property development and investment lawyer and works for the firm of Marshall Hatchick Solicitors in London.

SEASON	*LEAGUE*		*FA CUP*		*FL CUP*		*TOTAL*	
	Apps	*Gls*	*Apps*	*Gls*	*Apps*	*Gls*	*Apps*	*Gls*
1962–63	19	0	0	0	1	0	20	0
1963–64	31	0	3	0	0	0	34	0
1964–65	27	0	1	0	1	0	29	0
	77	0	4	0	2	0	83	0

PULLEN, Walter Ernest (1946–50)

Wally Pullen was born in Ripley, Surrey, on 2 August 1919, and was an inside-forward who joined the O's in January 1946 from the Army, having previously been registered with Fulham as an amateur, but he never appeared for them during the war years. He played for the O's in the 1945–46 Regional Wartime League, making 20 appearances and scoring four goals. He established himself in the first team during the first peacetime season of 1946–47. He always had an eye for goal and supported big Frank Neary admirably during the O's 11-match unbeaten run that saved them from relegation in 1947–48. He will be remembered most for the goal he scored with the last kick of the match at Southend United, which saved the embarrassment of having to apply for re-election in 1949–50.

The club awarded him a benefit match against West Ham United in May 1950. He joined his former colleague Doug Hunt, who was boss at Gloucester City in the Southern League. Wally Pullen died in Luton during 1977, aged 58.

SEASON	LEAGUE		FA CUP		TOTAL	
	Apps	Gls	Apps	Gls	Apps	Gls
1946–47	30	13	1	0	31	13
1947–48	37	10	1	0	38	10
1948–49	17	5	0	0	17	5
1949–50	31	9	1	0	32	9
1950–51	2	0	0	0	2	0
	117	37	3	0	120	37

QUEEN, Gerald (1972–77)

Striker Gerry Queen was born in Paisley, West Glasgow, Scotland, on 15 January 1945. He was spotted by St Mirren while playing in youth-club football and made his Scottish League debut in 1962–63. After 63 games, in which he scored 10 goals, he moved the short distance to Kilmarnock in 1966 and made 94 appearances, scoring 29 goals. His excellent performances were rewarded with Scottish Under-23 honours. He moved south of the border in July 1969 to join Crystal Palace for £80,000, scoring on his First Division debut versus Manchester United before a near-50,000 crowd. He was at Selhurst Park for three years and made 149(7) senior appearances, scoring 34 goals.

Queen joined the O's for a then club-record fee of £70,000 in September 1972, making his debut versus Queen's Park Rangers. He was hailed as quite a capture, although sometimes an enigma, and yet there were times that he lived up to the high expectations with some wonderful performances. He had his best spell with the O's during the early stages of the 1973–74 season and played well in the front line along with Bullock and Fairbrother. A back injury at Notts County checked his progress, and he was never quite the same player after his return. His career gradually went into decline and fans can remember him missing a 'sitter' at West Bromwich Albion that denied the O's a vital point in their push for promotion, and also his jumping in that split second too early when going up for a header: one was never quite sure if this was being done on purpose to put the defender off or just poor timing on behalf of Queen himself.

During the 1976–77 season Queen recaptured his earlier form and scored some vital goals in the O's run to the Anglo-Scottish Cup Final. He hit the winner versus Aberdeen in the second leg of the quarter-final to secure a place in the semi-final and another two goals (one a penalty) against Partick Thistle for a place in the two-leg Final against Nottingham Forest. Queen played in eight Anglo-Scottish matches that season and enjoyed the experience of once again playing against top Scottish sides.

In 1977 Queen went to try his luck in South Africa and played for Arcadia Shepherds in Pretoria, but he returned to the UK a year later. He moved to America in the 1980s and managed such clubs as Orlando Nighthawks and Boca Raton Sabres. In March 2005 he was living and successfully coaching soccer at the Coco Expo Sports Center in Florida, US.

SEASON	LEAGUE		FA CUP		FL CUP		TOTAL	
	Apps	Gls	Apps	Gls	Apps	Gls	Apps	Gls
1972–73	33	10	1	0	0	0	34	10
1973–74	34(2)	12	3	0	3	1	40(2)	13
1974–75	32(2)	4	2	1	0	0	34(2)	5
1975–76	32	6	1	0	0	0	33	6
1976–77	18(3)	2	2(1)	0	4	0	24(4)	2
	149(7)	34	9(1)	1	7	1	165(8)	36

 # Queen also appeared in three Texaco Cup matches in 1974–75 and eight Anglo-Scottish Cup matches, scoring three goals.

REES, William Derek (1950–55)

A big name signing in 1950, adding thousands on to the attendance figures, inside-forward Billy Rees, the 5ft 11in and 12st 6lb Welsh international, caused a sensation when joining the O's for a then club-record fee of £14,500 from Tottenham Hotspur in July 1950, having outbid both Fulham and West Ham United. The O's paid the fee off in instalments and over 21,000 fans witnessed his debut at Brisbane Road. Born in Blaengarw, near Bridgend, Wales, on 10 March 1924, he spent seven years on the coal face while turning out for Carn Rovers FC and Blaengarw FC before joining Cardiff City in February 1944, making 101 League appearances and scoring 33 goals during his five-year stay at Ninian Park. He was a member of their

Division Three South Championship side of 1947 and won a wartime Welsh international cap within six months of turning professional.

Rees was involved in one unusual match for Cardiff City against Bristol City in a Wartime Cup tie. Matches during that period had to be played until a goal was scored, and that particular match lasted just over 200 minutes before Rees popped in a header to the relief of all concerned, so much so that Rees was chaired off the field by the Cardiff supporters. He won three full Welsh caps in 1949 against Northern Ireland, Belgium and Switzerland. Rees moved to Tottenham Hotspur in June 1949 for £14,000 but made just 11 appearances with three goals during his one year at White Hart Lane, also winning one further Welsh cap against Northern Ireland in 1950.

Rees made a big impact at Brisbane Road, proving his quality with some fine forceful play and scoring many excellent goals. He suffered from many injuries during his time with Orient, but always gave 100 percent. He left in December 1955, joining Headington United, and in 1959 he moved to Kettering Town. Rees informed the author just before his death about some of his memories while with the club: 'I had a rough time in the first few years at Leyton, because of my reputation the opposition seemed to kick me more than the football.

'I always found Orient to be a very happy club, and I never regretted joining them back in 1950, even though it was expected that I would join a First Division club.' Billy Rees worked for a pharmaceutical company until his death in Bridgend on 25 July 1996, aged 72.

SEASON	*LEAGUE*		*FA CUP*		*TOTAL*	
	Apps	*Gls*	*Apps*	*Gls*	*Apps*	*Gls*
1950–51	39	10	1	1	40	11
1951–52	39	13	6	3	45	16
1952–53	30	3	0	0	30	3
1953–54	36	15	5	4	41	19
1954–55	35	17	2	0	37	17
1955–56	5	0	0	0	5	0
	184	58	14	8	198	66

RENNOX, Clatworthy (1921–25)

Clatworthy 'Charlie' Rennox was born in Shotts, Lanarkshire, Scotland, on 25 February 1897. He started off with Dykehead FC and then played for Wishaw FC before joining the O's in July 1921. He went on to top the O's goalscoring charts during his first season on 11 goals. He was a forceful type of forward who had broad shoulders and was difficult to knock off the ball, and also he was a brilliant header of a ball. Both he and Albert Pape formed a formidable partnership upfront and came under the watchful eye of Manchester United during 1925, and both did move to Old Trafford within a month of each other to help United clinch promotion as runners-up in Division Two.

He moved to Manchester for £1,250 and had a wonderful first full season in the First Division during 1926–27, netting 17 goals from 34 League appearances and helping the Reds to finish ninth in the table. He scored 25 goals for them from 68 senior appearances before moving to Grimsby Town in July 1927 for £400, but rather surprisingly he did not feature in the Mariners first team; he was injured during pre-season training. He moved on to Bangor City during the following season and was with Accrington Stanley in 1928 before retiring from the game.

SEASON	*LEAGUE*		*FA CUP*		*TOTAL*	
	Apps	*Gls*	*Apps*	*Gls*	*Apps*	*Gls*
1921–22	34	11	1	0	35	11
1922–23	13	2	0	0	13	2
1923–24	24	6	3	1	27	7
1925–26	30	5	0	0	30	5
	101	24	4	1	105	25

ROEDER, Glenn Victor (1974–78 & 1992)

An elegant player with a touch of arrogance and a delightful double shuffle, Glenn Roeder, the 6ft 2in and 12st 8lb defender, had a long and distinguished career. No O's fan would forget the elegant upright player who had style and plenty of class, especially when going forward, which was tinged with a touch of arrogance. Born in Woodford, Essex, on 13 December 1955, Roeder joined Arsenal as a schoolboy in December 1969. He came to the O's along with Laurie Cunningham after both were released by Arsenal as schoolboys in August 1972, and they were spotted by the O's scout Len Cheesewright. Roeder first played for Gidea Park Rangers and represented both Essex and London schools. He started his Orient career in midfield, but was later switched to central-defender and sometimes played as sweeper. He was a vital member of the club's exciting Division Two squad and helped steer the O's to their only FA Cup semi-final appearance at Stamford Bridge against Arsenal in 1978.

Roeder was transferred to Queen's Park Rangers for £250,000 in August 1978 after he toured New Zealand with an England party. He captained Rangers to promotion and to an FA Cup Final and made 181 senior appearances for them and was on the fringe of a full England cap. After a loan spell with Notts County in November 1983, making four appearances, he joined Newcastle United in December 1983 for a bargain £125,000 and captained them for nearly six years, making 219 senior appearances with 10 goals. He won six England 'B' caps between 1978 and 1982, a League Division Two Championship medal in 1983 and also won promotion from Division Two in 1984. He moved to Watford on a free transfer in July 1989 and was at Vicarage Road for two years, playing 74(4) matches with two goals. He later acted as reserve-team coach until August 1991.

When Roeder retired from football he went to Italy to act as Paul Gasgoine's 'minder', but he soon changed his mind and returned home. After a couple of reserve outings for Millwall, he joined the O's. It was quite remarkable that Glenn Roeder, the former O's favourite, should return to Brisbane Road in January 1992, and he played for five months, some 13 years and eight months after his last League match for them at Cardiff City on 8 May 1978. After a handful of appearances during his second spell, the 32-year-old Roeder joined Purfleet FC in October 1992 and later moved to Gillingham in

November 1992 as player-manager, where he made six appearances, including one against the O's. In July 1993 he was appointed manager with Watford and stayed for three years before being sacked in February 1996, and he then joined the England scouting team.

Roeder joined Burnley as assistant manager to Chris Waddle in July 1997. In 1998 he was part of England's coaching staff under boss Glenn Hoddle. In February 1999 he joined the coaching staff of West Ham United, a week before Hoddle's departure as the England boss. After the shock departure of Harry Redknapp as the Hammers boss, it was Roeder who took charge as caretaker manager of the team for the final match of the season at Middlesbrough, a 2–1 defeat in May 2001. The 45-year-old was appointed as manager on 14 June 2001 to become only their ninth manager. However, Roeder was under enormous pressure during his spell in charge to keep the Hammers away from relegation, and eventually it took its toll and he collapsed with chest pains moments after a press conference just after they had defeated Middlesbrough 1–0 at Upton Park on 21 April 2003.

He returned to office in July 2003, but with the Hammers having been relegated into the First Division his job was under threat. Sadly, after just a few weeks into the new season, he was sacked as manager, but he is now back in management as boss of Premiership side Newcastle United and looks forward to the 2006–07 season with great confidence.

Roeder's managerial career:

Team	*From*	*To*	*Games*	*Won*	*Drawn*	*Lost*
Gillingham	Aug 1992	to July 1993	51	13	16	22
Watford	Aug 1993	to Feb 199	139	44	40	55
West Ham Utd	May 2001	to Aug 2003	86	27	23	36
Newcastle Utd	Feb 2006	to present	17	11	2	4

Roeder recalled his early days with the O's and his footballing career: 'I had a little bit of luck when I first joined Orient. There were 15 apprentices at the club, and I was the last one to be chosen. It was a choice between me and a player named John Cook, who I'm told ended up as a postman.

'I knew my second spell at Orient would be the last few League games of my career, and I did my best to enjoy them. I felt very lucky to be able to play football for a living at the age of 38.

'I think it was quite an achievement to have played over 650 League and Cup matches. I never ever had a knee or ankle injury.'

Glenn's career had turned full circle in January 1991, and he was delighted to be back at Orient: 'It's no secret I'm a Cockney.'

Glenn Roeder made 547(14) Football League appearances, scoring 31 goals in a career that spanned some 20 years.

SEASON	*LEAGUE*		*FA CUP*		*FL CUP*		*TOTAL*	
	Apps	*Gls*	*Apps*	*Gls*	*Apps*	*Gls*	*Apps*	*Gls*
1974–75	3 (3)	0	0	0	0	0	3 (3)	0
1975–76	20 (5)	2	1	0	1	0	22 (5)	2
1976–77	42	2	4	0	4	0	50	2
1977–78	42	0	8	0	3	0	53	0
1991–92	6 (2)	0	1	0	0	0	7 (2)	0
	113 (10)	4	14	0	8	0	135 (10)	4

 # Roeder also appeared in 12 Anglo-Scottish Cup matches and one Auto Windscreens Shield match.

ROFE, Dennis (1967–72)

A fast, tough tackling left-back who was one of the most admired Second Division defenders of his era, the 5ft 7in and 10st 11lb full-back Rofe was born in Epping, Essex, on 1 June 1950 and was a classmate of another O's youth player, Terry Brisley, and also appeared in the same East London schools side as another former Oriental, Paul Went. Rofe started as an inside-forward in the O's youth side but was converted to a full-back by manager Dick Graham. He was given his League debut by boss Jimmy Bloomfield on a cold winter's night in April 1968 at Bristol Rovers – a club he was to later manage – when he came on as a substitute for winger John Key and scored when playing a quick one-two with Dave Harper, picking up the return to slide the ball past the advancing 'keeper. Rofe was a key member of the O's Championship-winning side of 1969–70.

Dennis Rofe left Orient to join his former O's boss Jimmy Bloomfield at Leicester City on 23 August 1972 for a then record fee for a full-back of £112,000. After eight years with Leicester, making 323 senior appearances with six goals, he joined Chelsea in February 1980 for £80,000 and was appointed club captain. He made 58(1) League appearances before joining Southampton on a free transfer in July 1982, where he made a further 18(2) League appearances. Rofe won just one England Under-23 international cap during his career.

After retiring from playing, he was appointed on to the coaching staff at Southampton. In January 1992 he was appointed manager of Bristol Rovers, but 10 months later Malcolm Allison was drafted in as a coaching consultant, and soon after Rofe was asked to relinquish control of the first team, which he refused and resigned. He was then appointed as coach with Stoke City, but at the end of the 2000–01 season he was back at Southampton in a managerial and coaching capacity after the departure of both Glenn Hoddle and John Gorman to Spurs. In 2002 he turned down a chance of joining Wolverhampton Wanderers in a coaching capacity, and in the 2004–05 season he was assistant manager at then Premiership side Southampton.

SEASON	LEAGUE		FA CUP		FL CUP		TOTAL	
	Apps	Gls	Apps	Gls	Apps	Gls	Apps	Gls
1967–68	3(1)	1	0	0	0	0	3(1)	1
1968–69	38	2	2	0	1	0	41	2
1969–70	45	3	2	0	2	0	49	3
1970–71	42	0	3	0	1	0	46	0
1971–72	40	0	4	0	2	0	46	0
1972–73	2	0	0	0	1	0	3	0
	170(1)	6	11	0	7	0	188(1)	6

ROFFEY, William Robert (1973–84)

William Roffey was an attacking full-back with a very powerful kick, who joined the O's from Crystal Palace in October 1973 and stayed for 11 seasons. During his first few seasons at the club he was often overlooked by boss George Petchey, which caused him to miss out on becoming only one of a handful of players to have reached 400 senior appearances for the club. Only Peter Allen and Stan Charlton have achieved this wonderful feat. Roffey goes in the record books, though, as the scorer of the O's 3,500th Football League goal when he scored his second against Brentford in a 3–3 draw on 18 September 1982.

Born in Stepney, London, on 6 February 1954, Bill Roffey signed as an apprentice with Crystal Palace in May 1971 and made 24 League appearances before joining the O's for a modest £5,000. He performed very well and was in the side that reached the semi-final of the FA Cup versus Arsenal in April 1978; in fact, the second of the Gunners goals was deflected off Roffey and past John Jackson into the net after a shot from Malcolm MacDonald. In March 1984 he went on loan to Brentford, making 13 League appearances with one goal. He went on a free transfer to Millwall in August 1984 and stayed at The Den for two years, making 36(1) appearances and scoring once. In June 1986 he went to play in the US, and upon his return he managed both Tonbridge Angels and Margate. He now spends a lot of time in America at various coaching clinics.

SEASON	LEAGUE		FA CUP		FL CUP		TOTAL	
	Apps	Gls	Apps	Gls	Apps	Gls	Apps	Gls
1973–74	20(1)	1	0	0	1	0	21(1)	1
1974–75	6	0	0	0	0	0	6	0
1975–76	13(1)	0	0	0	1	0	14(1)	0
1976–77	34(1)	2	0(1)	1	3	0	37(2)	3
1977–78	42	1	8	0	1(1)	0	51(1)	1
1978–79	39	0	3	0	1	0	43	0
1979–80	40	1	3	0	2	0	45	1
1980–81	42	0	1	0	2	0	45	0
1981–82	18	0	0	0	2	0	20	0
1982–83	42	3	2	0	2	0	46	0
1983–84	28(1)	0	1	0	1	0	30(1)	0
	324(4)	8	18(1)	1	16(1)	0	358(6)	9

 # Roffey also appeared in three Texaco Cup matches in 1974–75, 13(1) Anglo-Scottish Cup matches, three Football League Groups Cup matches and one Auto Windscreens Shield match.

ROSIER, Bertram Leonard (1923–27)

One of the O's better full-backs during the 1920s, Bertie Rosier was born in Hanwell on 21 March 1893. He was a small but tenacious left-back who attended St Anne's School in Hanwell and played for Hanwell North End, Uxbridge Town and Southall before signing for Brentford as a professional in July 1914. Rosier spent 17 months in a prisoner of war camp before being released, and he helped the Bees take the London Combination title in 1918–19. He made 127 senior appearances for Brentford before the O's boss Peter Proudfoot signed him in March 1923. He made his debut in a 3–1 defeat at Notts County on 17 March 1923.

He was noted for his no-nonsense approach and was one of the better full-backs for the O's during the 1920s. He was transferred to Southend United in June 1927, making 41 League appearances, and then moved to Fulham in July 1928, making 57 senior appearances. He moved into non-League football with Folkestone Town in September 1930. His only career League goal, out of a total of 367 senior appearances, came for the O's against Wolves in April 1925 from the penalty spot to secure a 2–1 win. Bert Rosier died in Ealing, London, on 18 February 1939, aged 55 years.

SEASON	LEAGUE		FA CUP		TOTAL	
	Apps	Gls	Apps	Gls	Apps	Gls
1922–23	10	0	0	0	10	0
1923–24	34	0	0	0	34	0
1924–25	33	1	1	0	34	1
1925–26	26	0	2	0	28	0
1926–27	33	0	2	0	35	0
	136	1	5	0	141	1

SCOTT, George (1908–1915)

One of the great pre-World War One players and one of three O's players to be killed in action, George Scott was born in West Stanley near Sunderland on 29 September 1885. He started his career with local sides Braeside FC and Sunderland West End FC, both of the Sunderland District Amateur League. The bandy-legged Scott, who stood at 5ft 8in and weighed 10st 9lb, joined the O's in July 1908. He made his League debut at centre-half in a 2–0 win over Oldham Athletic on 12 December 1908, yet he also appeared in various forward positions later that season.

Scott was a model of consistency and his fine play was rewarded when he was picked to represent a London FA XI versus a Paris XI in France during 1911. Scott was a splendid servant over the years, and he scored many wonderful goals, but none better than the winning goal he scored against Tottenham Hotspur at White Hart Lane on Boxing Day 1909. He also hit a hat-trick versus Leicester Fosse on 30 September 1911. He was a vital member of a great O's squad that finished in the top 10 during four seasons before World War One.

Private George Scott was sadly killed in action on 16 August 1916 during the Battle of the Somme and is buried in St Souplet British Cemetery about six kilometres south of Le Cateau in France.

SEASON	*LEAGUE*		*FA CUP*		*TOTAL*	
	Apps	*Gls*	*Apps*	*Gls*	*Apps*	*Gls*
1908–09	21	6	1	0	22	6
1909–10	30	6	1	0	31	6
1910–11	32	9	1	0	33	9
1911–12	21	5	0	0	21	5
1912–13	37	4	1	0	38	4
1913–14	27	1	3	1	30	2
1914–15	37	2	1	0	38	2
	205	33	8	1	213	34

SEARLE, Frank Burnett (1934–38)

O's captain during the 1930s, Frank Searle was born in Hednesford, Staffs, on 30 January 1906. The 5ft 9in and 11st 7lb defender started off as an amateur with Stoke City in 1924 before joining Willenhall FC in 1925.

It was with Bristol City that Searle made his League debut in a 5–0 defeat at Fulham in March 1926, his only senior appearance before he joined Charlton Athletic in May 1928 for £200, where he made 70 senior appearances and scored twice. After a four-match loan spell with Chester in February 1933, he moved to Watford in July 1933 on a free transfer and made one appearance at left-half. He was pushed up to centre-forward later in the season for three matches in an effort to beef up their attack, but he was soon relieved of his duties as he failed to score.

Searle joined the O's in September 1934 and was in the side that defeated his former club Charlton Athletic 3–0, an epic third-round FA Cup tie during January 1936, when they were beating all before them in their rise to Division One. He also captained the side that drew 1–1 with Cardiff City in the first-ever League fixture at Brisbane Road on 28 August 1937. Searle retired in 1938 and died in Wanstead, London, on 16 June 1977, aged 71.

SEASON	*LEAGUE*		*FA CUP*		*TOTAL*	
	Apps	*Gls*	*Apps*	*Gls*	*Apps*	*Gls*
1934–35	33	0	0	0	33	0
1935–36	38	1	5	0	43	1
1936–37	26	0	0	0	26	0
1937–38	25	0	3	0	28	0
	122	1	8	0	130	1

 # Searle also appeared in three Third Division Cup matches between 1935 and 1937.

SILKMAN, Barry (1981–85)

One of a handful of successful Jewish players to play for the O's through the years, Barry Silkman was born in Stepney, London, on 29 June 1952. He was a man of many clubs, and his four-year stint at Brisbane Road was one of the longest in his League career, which spanned some 12 years and 340 League appearances with 32 goals. He commenced his playing career as an amateur, with Wimbledon between 1971 and 1973 and Barnet in 1973–74. Silkman played for Hereford United (1974–75), Crystal Palace (1978), Plymouth Argyle (1978), Luton Town (loan in 1978), Manchester City (1978–79), Maccabi Tel Aviv in Israel (loan in January 1980, but he quickly left before he played a single game after he learned that his status made

him eligible to be called up into the Israeli army), Brentford (1980) and Queen's Park Rangers (1980).

Silkman was signed for Orient by manager Paul Went, and the flamboyant and natty dresser proved to be a skilful and stylish midfield player who was unfortunate to have been with the O's during some of their most unsuccessful seasons going from Division Two down to Division Four. During the latter part of his spell he undertook coaching duties but moved to Southend United in July 1985, making 38(2) League appearances, before joining Crewe Alexandra in September 1986, but after just 1(1) appearances he moved into the non-League circuit, playing six times with Isthmian League Wycombe Wanderers in 1987. One of his best games was against Tooting & Mitcham where he set up four goals and then was substituted in the second half because he had to attend a greyhound meeting. He then moved on to Jewish club Wingate & Finchley FC at the age 45 in the Icis Third Division.

Silkman turned his hand to greyhound racing with much success, and in recent years he was training at the Canterbury Stadium in Kent. He also acts as a leading player's agent, and it was Silkman who tried to get pop singer Rod Stewart to buy the O's in January 1995 and was also instrumental in bringing Aussie winger Steve Riches to Brisbane Road in September 1996. The Association of Football Statisticians (AFS) report No.111 of Spring 2001 stated that Silkman became the oldest player at that time, since Sir Stanley Matthews in the 1960s, to appear in the FA Cup competition when he came on as a substitute for Harrow Borough versus Wycombe Wanderers on 18 November 2000, aged 48 years and 142 days.

SEASON	LEAGUE		FA CUP		FL CUP		TOTAL	
	Apps	Gls	Apps	Gls	Apps	Gls	Apps	Gls
1981–82	33(2)	5	4(1)	0	0	0	37(3)	5
1982–83	17(5)	2	0	0	1	0	18(5)	2
1983–84	41	4	1	0	2	0	44	4
1984–85	42	3	4	1	4	1	50	5
	133(7)	14	9(1)	1	7	1	149(8)	16

 # Silkman also appeared in two Football League Groups Cup matches and six Auto Windscreens Shield matches.

SITTON, John Edmund (1985–91)

Born in Hackney, London, on 21 October 1959, the 5ft 11in and 12st 4lb defender John Sitton started his career with Chelsea as an apprentice in October 1977, making 11(2) League appearances. In February 1980 he joined Millwall for £10,000, making 43(2) League appearances with one goal. During September 1981 he moved on to Gillingham for another £10,000 fee, and during his four-year stay he made 102(5) League appearances with five goals.

Sitton joined the O's on a free transfer from Gillingham in July 1985 and was captain for some of the games of the O's promotion-winning team of 1988–89, playing in all four promotion Play-off matches. He was released on a free transfer in May 1991. He applied for a number of coaching jobs, having a full FA coaching badge, including player-coach at Exeter City and the manager's job with Maidstone United, but neither came to fruition. He worked in a part-

time capacity with the O's School of Excellence Academy while playing for Slough Town, making four appearances in 1991–92. He was appointed joint manager with Chris Turner in the 1994–95 season. Today, he is often seen in the press box covering O's matches, and is also often heard on the radio.

SEASON	LEAGUE		FA CUP		FL CUP		TOTAL	
	Apps	Gls	Apps	Gls	Apps	Gls	Apps	Gls
1985–86	39	0	2	0	4	0	45	0
1986–87	13	0	2	0	2	0	17	0
1987–88	19(1)	1	0(1)	0	1(1)	0	20(3)	1
1988–89*	41	4	3	0	2	0	46	4
1989–90	36(1)	2	1	0	4	0	41(1)	2
1990–91	22(2)	0	5	0	6	0	33(2)	0
	170(4)	7	13(1)	0	19(1)	0	202(6)	7

** Sitton's record includes four matches in promotion Play-offs in 1988–89.*

He also appeared in 10 Auto Windscreens matches, scoring one goal.

SMITH, Dean (1997–2003 & 2005–present)

A great professional and former captain who sadly led the O's to two Play-off Final defeats, 'Deano', as he is affectionately known by the O's fans, joined on 2 June 1997, proving to be a strong defender and equally good in the air. He shouldered the responsibility of taking the penalties with his style of 'busting the net', although he missed a vital spot-kick versus Southend in April 1999 and thereafter was reluctant to take them, eventually giving up the task to Matthew Lockwood. A confident leader and good professional, he was appointed club captain in 1998–99.

Smith was born in West Bromwich on 19 March 1971, and he started as a trainee with Walsall in July 1989, getting a professional contract as an 18-year-old and playing regularly for the Saddlers for over five years, making 137(5) League appearances with two goals and also playing in 24 Cup matches.

The 6ft 1in and 12st 10lb defender became Hereford United's record signing on 17 June 1974 at £75,000. He found the net 19 times from 116(1) League appearances and in 28(1) Cup matches scored a further seven goals. When the Worcestershire side dropped out of the Football League on the last day of the 1996–97 season, the O's manager Taylor quickly moved in for his signature. Hereford wanted £200,000 for Smith and the matter went to a tribunal. Hereford's manager Graham Turner was angry at the tribunal's decision to take the Bosman ruling into account for the first-time ever when cutting the price from the required £200,000 to only £42,500 on 16 June 1997.

Graham Turner said 'I'm staggered and gob-smacked at the low valuation of our record signing, this is going to send shockwaves throughout football.'

Smith proved to be an excellent capture and skipper, and he converted one of the penalties in the shoot-out at Rotherham to take the O's into the Play-off Final. He had the honour of leading out the team at Wembley in the Third Division Play-off Final against Scunthorpe United in May 1999, but the tears visibly flowed when the O's went down 1–0.

Smith was one of the longest serving players at the club and has an enviable record of scoring one goal in nearly every six games, not bad for a central-defender. His 50th career League goal came at Rochdale on 28 January 2001, and his 200th senior appearance for the O's came in a 2–0 victory over Hull City, a match that took the O's to the Play-off Finals. Sadly, Smith captained them to his second Play-off Final defeat in three years, this time losing 4–2 to Blackpool at the Millennium Stadium in Cardiff during May 2001. In the 2001–02 season he was voted by the Leyton Orient supporters club as their Star Man Player of the Year.

Smith opened his scoring account for the 2002–03 season with a goal against Mansfield Town on 13 August 2002, his 34th League goal for the O's. After six years at the club, the 31-year-old defender was allowed to sign for First Division side Sheffield Wednesday on a free transfer on 21 February 2003; however, the Owls were relegated.

O's boss Paul Brush stated at the time of Smith's transfer 'It will be a blow to lose the captain and leader, but he's given us brilliant service and it would have been wrong to stop him. He got offered a massive deal by Wednesday, which we were unable to match, and his contract is up in the summer. I wish him well.'

Smith himself stated 'I didn't know a lot about the move. I was on the way back to Birmingham with my kid to see my parents when I got a phone call – would I like to go to Sheffield Wednesday?

'I thought about it a few seconds and headed off to the M1 straight away. The deal happened very quickly and to be fair to both the O's chairman Barry Hearn and manager Paul Brush they allowed me to leave on a free transfer because of my service to the club. I had talks on the Friday morning and headed back to London to play for Wednesday against Crystal Palace the next day.

'We have already bought a house in Sheffield, but with an eight-week-old baby it was a big upheaval, but at least I have a 12-month contract. He was made their team captain for the start of the 2003–04 season. The 33-year-old made 55 League appearances with one goal while at Hillsborough, and at the end of his contract he moved on a free transfer to Port Vale on 6 July 2004. He was a regular during the season with 12(1) League appearances and no goals, but in December he was offered the chance to return to the Matchroom Stadium as Orient's youth-team manager, which he grabbed with both hands.

Vale manager Martin Foyle stated 'Dean has decided to retire from the game and go into coaching, and the sort of offer he was given does not come along too often. He has been a pleasure to coach and a good professional, it's a good opportunity for him at Orient, and we wish him all the best for the future.'

Smith was given a two-and-half year contract and has also been registered as a player should he be needed next season in an emergency. However, he was appointed as Martin Ling's assistant manager after the departure of Ian Culverhouse in June 2006 and helped to take the O's to promotion to League One in his first season in the position.

SEASON	*LEAGUE*		*FA CUP*		*FL CUP*		*TOTAL*	
	Apps	*Gls*	*Apps*	*Gls*	*Apps*	*Gls*	*Apps*	*Gls*
1997–98	43	9	2	1	4	0	49	10
1998–99*	40	9	5	1	4	0	49	10
1999–2000	44	4	2	1	4	0	50	5
2000–01+	46	5	4	0	3	0	53	5
2001–02	45	2	4	1	1	0	50	3
2002–03	27	3	2	0	2	0	31	3
	245	32	19	4	18	0	282	36

** Smith's League record includes three Play-off matches in 1998–99.*

+ Smith's League record includes three Play-off matches in 2000–01.

 # He also appeared in two Auto Windscreens Shield matches.

He also appeared in four LDV Vans Trophy matches between 2000 and 2003, with one goal.

SMITH, Harold McPherson (1934–39)

A lively inside-forward for five seasons with Orient during the 1930s, Harry Smith was born in Dundee, Scotland, on 14 October 1911 (not 5 May 1911 as previously recorded). He started off with Dundee in 1928 and after a spell with Dunfermline signed for near neighbours Dundee United in December 1933, playing 12 senior matches for The Terrors, scoring twice. After a short spell with Raith Rovers, the inside-forward, who stood at 5ft 10in and weighed 12st, came south of the border to join the O's in August 1934, signed by boss David Pratt, a Scotsman himself.

Smith made a slow start but did score in a friendly against Austrian side Sportclub Rapid, a 2–3 defeat in 1934–35, and was in the side that defeated high-flying Charlton Athletic in an FA Cup third-round tie in January 1936 before a ground record attendance at Lea Bridge Road of 18,658. He also appeared in the first fixture at Brisbane Road against Cardiff City on 28 August 1937 and was in the side on 2 September 1939 at Watford, the last match before the outbreak of World War Two, which ended 1–1. This result, like the previous two matches, was expunged from the record books. Smith played in 12 regional wartime matches, scoring six goals, before deciding to retire from playing after the war.

SEASON	*LEAGUE*		*FA CUP*		*TOTAL*	
	Apps	*Gls*	*Apps*	*Gls*	*Apps*	*Gls*
1934–35	11	1	2	0	13	1
1935–36	28	5	5	0	33	5
1936–37	38	10	2	1	40	11
1937–38	40	11	3	1	43	12
1939–39	31	7	2	1	33	8
	148	34	14	3	162	37

 # Smith also appeared in six Third Division Cup matches between 1934 and 1939, scoring once.

SMITH, Henry Harold (1919–1925)

Harry, as he was known, was born in Walthamstow, London, on 14 October 1901, and he appeared as a guest for the O's on 21 April 1919, in the final London Combination wartime match of that season, the inside-forward scoring in a 4–2 win over Brentford, only the third win from 36 wartime matches played. Seventeen-year-old Smith signed professional forms for the O's in June 1919 for the start of the first League campaign after the hostilities. Manager Holmes converted Smith to a right-winger, and he became a regular for six seasons. Smith was a grand player, a little underrated, fast and strong, and he cut out the frills and made direct runs down the wing, creating quite a number of goals for others.

He had a cartilage operation during the summer of 1925, which proved slow to mend, and even though he played a couple of League games in April it put an end to his professional career and he was released in May 1925. In 1932–33 he turned out for amateur side Royal London United Sports FC.

SEASON	*LEAGUE*		*FA CUP*		*TOTAL*	
	Apps	*Gls*	*Apps*	*Gls*	*Apps*	*Gls*
1919–20	18	1	0	0	18	1
1920–21	31	4	2	1	33	5
1921–22	32	3	1	0	33	3
1922–23	22	0	0	0	22	0
1923–24	40	1	1	0	41	1
1924–25	24	0	1	0	25	0
	167	9	5	1	172	10

SUSSEX, Andrew Robert (1981–88)

Andy Sussex, who was born in Islington, London, on 23 September 1964, hit the headlines when making his O's League debut at the age of 16 years and 10 months when starring in a 3–0 win over Sheffield Wednesday on 7 November 1981, scoring one of the goals with a superb chip from 16 yards. He signed professional forms one year later. The tall, lanky, constructive left-sided midfielder often had a casual look about him, and he played for seven seasons, yet was never really considered a regular; in fact, he was in and out of the team for long periods, his place being given to a more all-action type of player. During his stay he was often played out of position.

His best season at Brisbane Road was in the Fourth Division during 1985–86, but he was transferred to Crewe Alexandra in June 1988 for £16,000, who were managed by former O's youth-team manager Dario Gradi, and Sussex helped them to gain promotion in 1988–89. He stayed for three seasons at Gresty Road, making 125

appearances and scoring 36 goals. He was transferred to Southend United in July 1991 for £100,000 and made 63(13) appearances with 14 goals. In December 1995 he had a loan spell with Brentford where he made just three League appearances. After six years with the Shrimpers, he signed for Canvey Island in January 1997 and then joined Barking in May 2000.

Thirty-seven-year-old Sussex joined Ryman League side Grays Athletic during August 2001, while also working as a tiler. He won both Ryman League First and Second Division Championship medals. In May 2002 it was reported that he had left Grays and decided to retire from the game at the age of 38.

SEASON	*LEAGUE*		*FA CUP*		*FL CUP*		*TOTAL*	
	Apps	*Gls*	*Apps*	*Gls*	*Apps*	*Gls*	*Apps*	*Gls*
1981–82	8	1	0	0	0	0	8	1
1982–83	24	2	2	1	0	0	26	3
1983–84	24(5)	6	0	0	0(1)	0	24(6)	6
1984–85	15(4)	2	1	0	3	1	19(4)	3
1985–86	35(1)	4	5	0	4	1	44(1)	5
1986–87	15(5)	1	0	0	0	0	15(5)	1
1987–88	5(3)	1	0	0	0	0	5(3)	1
	126(18)	17	8	1	7(1)	2	141(19)	20

 # Sussex also appeared in three Football League Groups Cup matches and 5(3) Auto Windscreens Shield matches.

TAYLOR, Harold William (1933–39)

Harold Taylor, the 5ft 10in and 10st 10lb player, was affectionately referred to as 'Lal' during his playing career and was one of the most impressive wing-halves on the club's books during the 1930s. His consistency was a feature of the O's play during those years, and he proved to be a wonderful servant for seven seasons. Born in Boston, Lincs, on 20 December 1910, he moved with his family from Lincolnshire to Southport in 1921 and started his amateur career with a local Southport side called Vulcans FC and was then with High Park FC. He joined Southport in November 1929 and made his senior debut with two goals against New Brighton in the Lancashire Senior Cup on 13 October 1931. His League debut, his only first-team appearance, came four days later against Gateshead, yet he notched two reserve hat-tricks during his stay at Haig Avenue.

Taylor joined the O's in a double transfer on 16 July 1933, along with Jackie Mayson. His first opportunity came in attack, but he soon established himself in the half-back line during 1936–37. He played in the first League match at Brisbane Road against Cardiff City in August 1937, and two years later he was in the side that faced Ipswich Town and Southend United in a season that lasted just three matches due to World War Two, these two appearances being expunged from the record books. He appeared in 29 wartime matches in 1939–40 before returning to play for Southport as a guest player, then he retired after the war. He died in Southport Infirmary on 15 November 1970, aged 59.

SEASON	*LEAGUE*		*FA CUP*		*TOTAL*	
	Apps	*Gls*	*Apps*	*Gls*	*Apps*	*Gls*
1933–34	15	4	4	2	19	6
1934–35	19	3	1	0	20	3
1935–36	27	3	4	1	31	4
1936–37	40	2	2	0	42	2
1937–38	40	1	3	0	43	1
1938–39	33	0	2	0	35	0
	174	13	16	3	190	16

 # Taylor also appeared in four Third Division Cup matches between 1934–39.

TAYLOR, Thomas Frederick (1967–70 & 1979–82)

Thomas Taylor was the second youngest-ever player to appear in the Football League for the O's at the age of 15 years and 334 days (after Paul Went who was just seven days younger than Taylor). His debut was alongside another debutante John Still (nowadays manager and director with Barnet, and funnily enough also in the side was current Peterborough manager Barry Fry) against Torquay United on 26 August 1967, which led to a wonderful career in East London with both Orient and West Ham United and to him being appointed the O's manager on 7 November 1996 staying in charge for nearly five years.

Taylor was born in Hornchurch, Essex, on 26 September 1951, and he joined the O's as a 10-year-old, having played for Hornchurch District Schools and captained England Schools on six occasions. He showed a maturity way beyond his years and teamed up well with Terry Mancini in the centre of defence, especially during the O's Championship-winning side of 1969–70. He was transferred to West Ham United in October 1970 for £78,000, and the deal included Peter Bennett. Taylor had a wonderful career at Upton Park, winning an FA Cup-winners' medal in 1975 and totalling 340 League and 58 Cup appearances. During his stay at Upton Park he also won 16 England Under-23 caps (some of those appearances were made as part of the over-age rule) and was often on the verge of a full cap.

He rejoined the O's in May 1979 after losing his place at Upton Park to Alvin Martin, and he was appointed team captain, staying for three years. It was during an infamous row with manager Ken Knighton at half-time in an FA Cup tie versus Crystal Palace on 16 February 1982 that he lost his place for a while. In May 1982 he was released on a free transfer, and he joined Belgian side Antwerp and also played for Beerschot.

** Tommy Taylor's managerial record appears in the managers section in this book.*

SEASON	LEAGUE		FA CUP		FL CUP		TOTAL	
	Apps	Gls	Apps	Gls	Apps	Gls	Apps	Gls
1967–68	16 (1)	0	0	0	0	0	16 (1)	0
1968–69	39 (1)	2	2	0	4	0	45 (1)	2
1969–70	46	2	2	0	2	0	50	2
1970–71	11	0	0	0	1	0	12	0
1979–80	42	5	3	1	2	0	47	6
1980–81	41	0	1	0	2	0	44	0
1981–82	33	0	5	0	2	0	40	0
	228 (2)	9	13	1	13	0	254 (2)	10

 # Taylor also appeared in two Anglo-Scottish Cup matches and three Football League Groups Cup matches.

TONER, Ciaran 2002–04

Capped twice by Northern Ireland in June 2003 to become the O's 14th internationally-capped player (joined in 2005–06 by both Gabrial Zakuani and Glyn Garner), Irishman Ciaran Toner became the O's second signing for the new 2002–03 season, the 20-year-old joining from Bristol Rovers on 4 May 2002. One of the reasons he joined the O's was that he lives in Buckhurst Hill, so it suited him down to the ground.

Born in Craigavon, Northern Ireland, on 30 June 1981, Toner signed as a trainee with Tottenham Hotspur during July 1997, turning professional two years later. The 6ft 1in and 12st 2lb midfielder joined Peterborough United on loan in December 2001, making six League appearances, and on 28 March 2002 he signed a short-term contract with Bristol Rovers after being released by Spurs, saying he had no future with the White Hart Lane club after making 13 reserve appearances with one goal in the 2001–02 season. He made six League appearances for the Pirates, helping them to stay in Division Three.

Toner has been a regular Northern Ireland Under-21 international and has captained the side on a number of occasions. He has also represented his country at both Under-16 and Under-17 level, with seven caps. He has been a Northern Ireland senior-team member and has been an unused substitute twice. It was quite a week for the young Toner when once again he captained the Under-21 side in their 1–1 draw versus Scotland, a match played at St Mirren's Loveday Street ground, and he also netted his first ever League goal in the O's 1–1 draw at Hull City on 31 August 2002. He was chosen again for the Northern Ireland Under-21 squad for their European Championship qualifiers against Spain and Ukraine.

Toner become the O's first ever full Northern Ireland international player when he gained two caps against France and Spain in the summer of 2003. When he was picked to gain his 15th cap for the Northern Ireland Under-21 side to take on Finland, he wasn't even picked for the O's first team; he was placed on the list of players available on loan.

Paul Brush stated 'Ciaran has worked very hard on his fitness and defensive duties and has been excellent in training, a loan spell could benefit him. I have a lot of faith in him as a player and there's no doubt that he's got a future at this club, I see him in my long-term plans.'

However, Toner returned to first-team action with some excellent displays: none better than in the 2–0 win at Oxford United on 4 March 2003. Toner was in the Northern Ireland first-team squad for their two European Championship matches during April 2003 in Armenia and at home to Greece, but he did not come on to the field of play in either match. However, after being on the bench five times, he eventually made his full international debut in a 2–0 defeat in Campobasso, Italy, on 3 June 2003, coming on as substitute in the 69th minute and replacing Damien Johnson, and he also appeared as a substitute a few days later in their excellent 0–0 draw with Spain.

He was released in the summer of 2004, and he joined Football League Two side Lincoln City on 3 August. After playing 10(5) League games he went on loan to struggling Cambridge United on 19 March 2005 to help in their fight against relegation down into the Conference. During the 2005–06 season he was in the Grimsby Town side that missed out on promotion from League Two after a Play-off Final defeat.

SEASON	LEAGUE		FA CUP		FL CUP		TOTAL	
	Apps	Gls	Apps	Gls	Apps	Gls	Apps	Gls
2002–03	22 (3)	1	1	0	1	0	24 (3)	1
2003–04	19 (8)	1	0	0	1	0	20 (8)	1
	41 (11)	2	1	0	2	0	48 (11)	2

Toner also appeared in two LDV Vans Trophy matches in 2002–03.

The Tonner Brothers

The Scottish-born Tonner brothers hold quite a unique O's record when the three – James, John and Samuel – played together in 12 Football League matches and one FA Cup tie at Manchester City on 10 January 1920 before 25,878 fans during the 1919–20 season. The only other known sets of three brothers to appear together for the same side during the same season for a football League club are recorded as:

Ernest, Harold and Richard Greenhalgh of Notts County, 1877–78 and 1878–79.

Arthur, Charles and Harry Carsham of Notts County, FA Cup 1878–79 (the Football League started in 1888).

Alec, Danny and Bobby Steel, 1909–10, one League match for Tottenham Hotspur.

Andrew, George and Tom Browell of Hull City, 1910–11, two League matches.

George, John and Willie Carr of Middlesbrough, 1919–20, 24 League matches.

Harold, Joseph and John Keetley of Doncaster Rovers, 1925–26, three League matches.

Frank, Harold and Thomas Keetley of Doncaster Rovers, 1926–27, 14 League matches.

Danny, Ray and Rodney Wallace of Southampton, 1988 to 1989, 25 League matches.

Two of the Tonner brothers, John and Samuel, also equalled another League record by firstly appearing with the Duffus brothers, John and Robert in a League match for the O's versus Bury on 9 December 1922 and then with the Williams brothers, Owen and Thomas, in a League match for the O's at Stockport County on 25 December 1922.

TONNER, James Edward (1919–20)

The least known of the three Tonner brothers, James was born in Bridgetown, Glasgow, Scotland, on 31 March 1896, and unlike the other two he was not a regular in the O's first XI due to the form of veteran Fred Parker. Jimmy Tonner started his career playing in Fife junior football with Bungalow City in Forsyth and with Linlithgow Port FC. He then joined Dunfermline Athletic in 1912. He joined the O's in 1919 and made his League debut alongside his two brothers in a 1–0 win over Nottingham Forest on 13 December 1919. He left in July 1920 to join Lochgelly United during their first season in the 'rebel' Central League, but they ended the season at the foot of the table. The following season, when all Central League sides were admitted to the Scottish Football League, he joined one of those sides, Bo'ness FC. In 1923–24 he appeared for them against his former club Lochgelly in a home Scottish League fixture on 8 March 1924 in a match that was later found out to have been fixed. Two Lochgelly players – Browning and Kyle – had approached and offered the Bo'ness skipper Peter Brown £30 to 'throw' the match. Lochgelly managed to win 2–0 and when they came to give Brown the money they were arrested and received 60 days' hard labour.

Many Bo'ness players were unhappy at the situation, and Tonner was transferred to English Division One side Burnley in October 1924 and was more or less a regular in the 1924–25 season, playing 27 League matches and scoring twice. He played just 10 League matches the following season without scoring. He did not feature at all in the following season and was eventually transferred to Hamilton Academicals in October 1926, making his debut on 9 October at Douglas Park against Dundee United, when it was reported that he shaped up well and could not be criticised following his first appearance for the men in hoops. He made 44 Scottish League appearances, scoring six goals, scored one goal from two Scottish Cup matches and also made one appearance in the Lanarkshire Cup.

Tonner was another of the Scots, during the period, who sought fame and fortune in America but returned in 1932 and then turned out for Portsmouth reserves. When Dunfermline played Aberdeen on 7 August 1985 to celebrate their centenary, Jimmy Tonner, aged 89, was guest of honour, believed to be the oldest living Dunfermline player at that time, having first played in 1912. He died shortly after in 1985, at the ripe old age of 99.

SEASON	*LEAGUE*		*FA CUP*		*TOTAL*	
	Apps	*Gls*	*Apps*	*Gls*	*Apps*	*Gls*
1919–20	12	0	1	0	13	0
	12	0	1	0	13	0

TONNER, John (1919–26)

Born in Holytown, Lanarkshire, Scotland, on 20 February 1898, the youngest of the three brothers, Jack, as he was always affectionately known, also progressed through local junior football in Fife before signing for Dunfermline, and he joined the O's in September 1919. He proved to be a full-blooded footballer who seldom shirked a hard tackle and loved to hassle the opposition. The 5ft 8in and 11st 7lb inside-right scored on his League debut at Hull City on 13 October 1919, and he topped the goalscoring charts during his first season. The following season, playing in more than half of the first-team matches, he still managed to notch 23 goals for the reserves. In December 1922 he bagged a League hat-trick against Rotherham County in a 5–1 win but suffered from injuries between 1923 and 1925, which affected his progress.

After seven seasons at Millfields Road he joined Fulham in June 1926, also scoring on his debut at Craven Cottage against Manchester City on 28 August 1926, where he made 30 senior appearances with 15 goals. In May 1927 he moved on to Crystal Palace and netted eight goals from 24 appearances. The 30-year-old Tonner left the Football League scene when he joined the newly formed Southern League Eastern Section side Thames Association in June 1928. He appeared in their very first home match on 30 August 1928 in a 2–0 defeat against Brighton Reserves before 3,000 fans. Tonner had left them by the time Thames joined the Football League in 1930. He was later the O's groundsman at Brisbane Road between 1951 and 1966. During a career that lasted nine seasons, Jack Tonner recorded a career total of 208 League appearances, scoring 62 goals. He died at Southend-on-Sea, Essex, in 1978, aged 80.

SEASON	*LEAGUE*		*FA CUP*		*TOTAL*	
	Apps	*Gls*	*Apps*	*Gls*	*Apps*	*Gls*
1919–20	30	12	1	1	31	13
1920–21	24	5	2	0	26	5
1921–22	13	2	0	0	13	2
1922–23	22	7	1	0	23	7
1923–24	7	2	3	0	10	2
1924–25	16	3	0	0	16	3
1925–36	31	4	4	3	35	7
	143	35	11	4	154	39

TONNER, Samuel (1919–25)

Sam Tonner was born in Dunfermline on 10 August 1894 and was the eldest of the three brothers. He started with junior side Inverkeithing FC before joining Dunfermline Athletic as a junior. He turned professional in 1914 and then moved to East Fife in 1918, joining the O's in May 1919. The 5ft 7in and 11st 7lb Tonner made his League debut for the O's at Huddersfield Town on 30 August, and he soon became known for his powerful long-range shooting and scored a great goal from fully 35 yards at Wolves on 20 September to help them secure their first win of the 1919–20 campaign.

He was a full-back who could play on either flank, possessing remarkable speed, and during World War One he was the quarter mile champion for the British Army for four years. Tonner was in a number of record books, and in an O's magazine of 1956 he was credited with scoring a rare hat-trick by a full-back versus Stockport County on 18 September 1920, but after checking a number of local newspapers for the period it was found that one report clearly stated that his 'third' was his cross-shot, which was touched into the net by Forrest, and another report stated Sam Tonner might be said to have scored a third, but it was Forrest who could clearly be seen helping Sam's cross-shot into the corner of the net. But it was no surprise that the club might have reported that Tonner scored three as it was a very rare feat indeed in that era for a full-back to hit three goals in a match.

One thing that could not be taken away from Tonner was that he was a member of the O's side that won the London Challenge Cup Final. (Even in 1955, at the age of 55, he won a medal while playing in the Manchester Hotels League.) Tonner's rather robust defensive play subjected him to barracking at most away grounds and even this spilled over to the away fans at Millfields Road in a number of matches, which upset him so much that he asked for a transfer, but instead the O's directors awarded him a benefit match during August 1924 against Spurs reserves, which attracted many thousands of fans.

In July 1925, after six seasons at Millfields, he was eventually transferred to Bristol City, and he made his debut during the following month against Norwich City. His only goal for City came from a penalty in October against Brentford, and he made just six League appearances before joining Crystal Palace in August 1926. His debut came in a 5–3 win over Southend United on 13 November 1926, but he could only manage two further senior appearances before joining non-League side Armadale FC in 1927.

As mentioned, the mid-1950s still saw Tonner playing football at the age of 65 in the Manchester Hotels League, while he was running a family-owned wholesale ice cream business with a cousin. In 1956 he told the club his one great ambition was to see the O's in Division Two. They did achieve that the following May. Well Sam what can we say, it is now over 4,000 O's fans' ambition as well. Sam Tonner died in Fleetwood during 1976, aged 82.

SEASON	*LEAGUE*		*FA CUP*		*TOTAL*	
	Apps	*Gls*	*Apps*	*Gls*	*Apps*	*Gls*
1919–20	36	6	1	0	37	6
1920–21	31	5	2	0	33	5
1921–22	17	1	0	0	17	1
1922–23	40	1	1	0	41	1
1923–24	37	0	3	0	40	0
1924–25	25	0	1	0	26	0
	186	13	8	0	194	13

TOWNROW, John Ernest (1919–27)

John Townrow was one of the finest defenders in the history of the club, and it was a surprise that he never won more than two full England international caps during his career. He was born in Stratford, London, on 28 March 1901, and he started as a schoolboy with Pelly Memorial School. He was first spotted by the O's boss William Holmes as a 15-year-old, playing for England Schoolboys against both Scotland and Wales in 1915, and was one of the first players to be signed by the O's as a youth player while still playing for Fairburn House as an amateur, turning professional after World War One in July 1919. The 5ft 11in and 13st 6lb centre-half made his League debut at just 18 years old in a 2–1 defeat at Fulham on 15 September 1919, taking over from another youngster Alf Worboys. Townrow made the position his own over the next seven seasons.

His class was obvious, and he was a player of resource and power and noted for his coolness, great heading and passing ability and was often referred to by the local press as the great all-round player. He became the second O's player to gain full England international honours after Owen Williams, gaining caps against Scotland in 1925 where he subdued the legendary Hughie Gallacher at Hampden Park on 4 April 1925 before a crowd of 92,000, the Scots winning 2–0. His second cap came against Wales on 1 March 1926 at Selhurst Park before 23,000 fans, the Welsh winning 3–1. He also represented the Football League.

Townrow was a tower of strength in the O's famous 2–0 FA Cup fifth-round victory over Newcastle United on 20 February 1926, once again outplaying Gallacher. In February 1927 Chelsea came in with a record £4,000 offer for him, which the O's directors just could not refuse, and he went on to make 140 senior appearances while at Stamford Bridge, scoring three goals, before the 31-year-old Townrow moved to Bristol Rovers in May 1932, playing just 10 senior games. In later years he became coach and groundsman at Fairbairn House School, and later he worked at Becton Gas Works and was also a publican in Harrogate. He died in Knarsborough on 11 April 1969, aged 68.

SEASON	*LEAGUE*		*FA CUP*		*TOTAL*	
	Apps	*Gls*	*Apps*	*Gls*	*Apps*	*Gls*
1919–20	29	1	0	0	29	1
1920–21	37	1	2	0	39	1
1921–22	20	0	0	0	20	0
1922–23	23	1	0	0	23	1
1923–24	39	1	3	0	42	1
1924–25	39	0	1	0	40	0
1925–26	40	1	4	0	44	1
1926–27	26	0	2	0	28	0
	253	5	12	0	265	5

TRICKER, Reginald William (1929–33)

Reg Tricker was born in Karachi, India, on 5 October 1904 (Karachi became part of the newly-formed Pakistan in 1947), and his parents returned to England in 1908 when he was a four-year-old and settled in Suffolk. He was a fine athlete and held the Norfolk and Suffolk 120-yard hurdles championship for two years. His football career started with Beccles Town in the Suffolk amateur League. He moved south to study at the Borough Road Training College in Islewoth, Middlesex, and was appointed schoolteacher at Crouch Hill School. He played for Alexandra Park before joining Luton Town on amateur forms in 1924, making his League debut at centre-forward against Watford on 25 December 1924, making a total of four senior appearances.

Tricker moved to Charlton Athletic in June 1925, still combining his football with that of teaching, a vocation he pursued throughout his playing career. He scored his first League goal after 50 minutes versus Exeter City on 12 September 1925, and he netted 18 goals from 41 senior appearances. Just before signing for Arsenal on 12 March 1927 for £2,250, he turned professional and made his debut against Everton, but he could never gain a regular first-team spot during his three-year stay at Highbury, making just 12 League appearances and scoring five goals, but made 40 appearances for the Gunners in the London Combination, netting 10 goals and winning a London Combination Championship medal in 1927–28. He joined the O's on 8 February 1929 for £1,000, a substantial fee for them, which was payable in instalments and linked to the number of senior appearances he made.

It took Tricker a while to settle down in the Third Division, but the 5ft 11in and 11st 7lb forward came to the fore in the 1930–31 season, showing some skilful touches with an eye for goal. He top scored with 18 goals from just 29 appearances, and the following two seasons he remained the club's top marksman, and also netted in both the O's League matches played at Wembley Stadium in 1930. He moved to Margate FC in October 1933 and later played for Ramsgate. In September 1954 he was appointed coach of Old Owens FC. Reg Tricker died in Hendon on 9 June 1990, aged 85.

SEASON	*LEAGUE*		*FA CUP*		*TOTAL*	
	Apps	*Gls*	*Apps*	*Gls*	*Apps*	*Gls*
1928–29	11	0	0	0	11	0
1929–30	23	9	1	0	24	9
1930–31	29	18	2	2	31	20
1931–32	39	19	3	1	42	20
1932–33	29	14	0	0	29	14
	131	60	6	3	137	63

WALLEY, John Thomas (1971–76)

A model professional, who stayed at Brisbane Road for five seasons, Tom Walley was born in Caernarvon, North Wales, on 27 February 1945, and as a boy he was encouraged to play football by his older brother Ernie, then a professional with Tottenham Hotspur and later coach at Crystal Palace. He was an amateur with Caernarvon Town before joining Wrexham in November 1963. He was not keen to move out of Wales but was lured by an offer to join Arsenal and signed for the Gunners for £3,000 in December 1964. He made 10(4) First Division appearances with one goal and also gained Welsh Under-23 honours.

After 18 months at Highbury, where he was never given the

opportunity to establish himself, Walley moved to Watford in March 1967 and soon made a big impact, playing a major role in their team that won the Third Division Championship in 1969 and in the following year reached the semi-final of the FA Cup before going out to Chelsea. The following season in an FA Cup tie against Manchester United he gained rave reviews for marking George Best out of the match. He gained his one full international cap during October 1971 against Czechoslovakia, a 1–0 defeat in Prague.

Walley stepped out at Watford to play against the O's on 4 December 1971, not dreaming that 48 hours later he would be an Oriental, but that is just what happened. The two clubs had agreed a £25,000 fee, but the player wasn't told until after the match, and he happily signed on 6 December. Walley was a determined and hard working professional, and after a spell in midfield, where he scored a cracking 25-yard goal against Sunderland, he formed a very effective partnership in defence with Phil Hoadley, and he missed just one match during his last three seasons at the club and was always on the verge of another full Welsh cap.

He was appointed captain of the side in 1975–76, and it was a surprise when, at the age of 31, he joined Watford for £3,000 in May 1976, the first signing under their new chairman, singer Elton John. After playing 12(1) League matches a serious injury ended his career, and he was appointed youth-team coach in August 1977. The following year he was appointed first-team coach, a position he held until March 1990. During the period his older brother was reserve coach. In August 1990 he was appointed youth coach with Millwall until he left in February 1996 when he took up a position as the Welsh Under-21 manager and as youth manager with Arsenal. He left Highbury in May 1997 and returned to Watford as reserve-team manager in July 1997, and in July 2001 he was appointed first-team coach. To characterise his wonderful work, he took both his Watford and Millwall charges to the Finals of the FA Youth Cup. Tom Walley retired from football in June 2002.

SEASON	*LEAGUE*		*FA CUP*		*FL CUP*		*TOTAL*	
	Apps	*Gls*	*Apps*	*Gls*	*Apps*	*Gls*	*Apps*	*Gls*
1971–72	22	2	4	0	0	0	26	2
1972–73	8(2)	0	0	0	0	0	8(2)	0
1973–74	42	1	4	0	4	0	50	1
1974–75	41	2	2	0	2	0	45	2
1975–76	42	1	1	0	1	0	44	1
	155(2)	6	11	0	7	0	173(2)	6

 # Walley also appeared in three Texaco Cup matches in 1974–75.

WALSCHAERTS, Wim (1998–2001)

Wim Walschaerts, a midfielder who could also play at right wing-back, was signed by the O's boss Tommy Taylor from Belgian Second Division side KFC Tielen of Antwerp, who had withdrawn from the professional League during 1998 due to financial problems. He joined the O's on a free transfer on 1 July 1998 under the Bosman ruling, having declined a move to another Belgian Premier side, Oostende, and he made an immediate impression with his tremendous stamina, energy and hard work, and he also weighed in with some important goals over his three years at Brisbane Road.

Born in Antwerp, Belgium, on 5 November 1972, Walschaerts started his career in 1994 with FC Beerschot, appearing in their youth team on the right wing. He made his first first-team appearance in 1995–96 and was voted their most valuable player in that season, and he joined KFC Tielen in June 1996. He proved to be a more than useful player for the O's, turning in many excellent performances on a regular basis. He opened his goal account against old foes Brighton & Hove Albion in an FA Cup tie and also scored a vital goal against Kingstonian in an FA Cup replay to secure a 2–1 win.

Walschaerts stated 'I was brought here to play in midfield, that is my true position, I do not mind playing wing-back, wherever I am asked to play I will give 100 percent for the team.' He originally signed a two-year contract with the club in February 1999, which was later extended.

He sadly missed all three promotion Play-off matches in May 1999 due to suspension after receiving a rather harsh red card at Peterborough United. Walschaerts was voted by members of the 'Fantastic O's' email group and the *Cheery O's* fanzine as their player of the year for 1998–99. He missed the early part of the 1999–2000 season after breaking his arm in a training mishap with Simon Clark during September 1999 and was one of 12 first-team players out for the start of the 1999–2000 season. Although linked to Luton Town, he has remained committed to the O's.

He continued to be a regular during the 2000–01 season and was in the side that lost 4–2 in the Play-off Final against Blackpool at the Millennium Stadium in May 2001. He was released under the Bosman ruling in June 2001, and it was reported that he was only informed of his release by letter while on holiday in his native Belgium. The O's boss Tommy Taylor reported 'His agent said he is talking to Second Division side KFC Strombeek in Belgium, which is fair enough.' He signed for them in June 2001. In July 2002 he moved to Koninklijk Bercham-Sport (KFC), on 1 July 2003 he was on the books of another Belgian League side KV Red Star Waasland, and in 2006 he was with RC Lebbeke.

SEASON	*LEAGUE*		*FA CUP*		*FL CUP*		*TOTAL*	
	Apps	*Gls*	*Apps*	*Gls*	*Apps*	*Gls*	*Apps*	*Gls*
1998–99	44	3	5	2	4	0	53	5
1999–2000	32 (4)	3	1	0	2 (1)	0	35 (5)	3
2000–01*	47 (1)	3	4	0	3	0	54 (1)	3
	123 (5)	9	10	2	9 (1)	0	142 (6)	11

** Walschaerts League record includes three Play-off appearances in 2000–01. He also played in one Auto Windscreens Shield match in 1999–2000 and one LDV Vans Trophy match in 2000–01.*

WARREN, Mark Wayne (1991–99)

It's quite ironic that Mark Warren should have played in Nottingham for Notts County, with whom he signed in January 1999 for £35,000, because some six years earlier a proposed £170,000 transfer to Nottingham Forest (to be Frank Clark's first signing as boss) was scuppered because a scan revealed an injury on the left side of his back, which was a bitter blow at the time for the youngster.

Warren was, until his transfer in 1999, the longest-serving player on the O's books, having signed professional forms with the club on 8 July 1991. He made his O's League debut at Chester City on 2 May 1992, aged just 17. He made just over 150 League appearances during his eight seasons with the club, and was a player with good pace who always gave 100 percent, and sometimes got into trouble with referees for his robust play. Born in Hackney, London, on 12 November 1974, the 5ft 9in and 10st 5lb defender was first spotted by the O's scout Jimmy Hallybone while playing for the Cornet FC Under-12 team and then he trained with the O's before signing on as a YTS player. He played district football for Barking and Dagenham and represented Essex Schools at both Under-15 and Under-16 levels.

Warren had an impressive run in the 1992–93 season before injuring his back at Bolton Wanderers in March 1993, and in February 1995 he scored a hat-trick playing up front in the O's 4–1 win over Peterborough United. He was voted Player of the Year in 1996–97 and carried on where he left off the previous season, having his most productive season at the club, playing 41 matches. In September 1997 he scored the O's fourth goal in a thrilling 4–4 draw against Bolton Wanderers at their new Reebok Stadium, and in August 1998 he hit the O's extra-time winner in a 2–1 League Cup win at Bristol Rovers.

During 1998–99 he refused to sign a new contract and had loan spells with West Ham United, Northampton Town and with Oxford United in December 1998, playing four League games. Twenty-four-year-old Warren was snapped up by the Notts County manager Sam Allardyce on 28 January 1999. Allardyce stated that he long admired the player and that he had bought him for a 'steal'. Warren was a regular, making 76(8) League appearances with one goal, before being released in April 2002.

After a trial with Colchester United in July 2002, playing 62 minutes in a friendly against Tottenham Hotspur, Warren eventually signed a one-year contract with them. He made 21 League appearances from January 2003, but was left out of the team and was given a free transfer in May 2003. He signed for the Shrimpers on 1 June, making 27(5) League appearances and scoring twice before being released in May 2004. He joined Southern League Division One East side Fisher Athletic in July 2004 to team up with former Orient players Wayne Burnett, the manager, and his assistant Warren Hackett. During his 12 years in League football, Warren made a total of 270(13) League appearances, scoring eight goals.

SEASON	*LEAGUE*		*FA CUP*		*FL CUP*		*TOTAL*	
	Apps	*Gls*	*Apps*	*Gls*	*Apps*	*Gls*	*Apps*	*Gls*
1991–92	0 (1)	0	0	0	0	0	0 (1)	0
1992–93	14	0	1	0	0	0	15	0
1993–94	5 (1)	0	0	0	0	0	5 (1)	0
1994–95	24 (7)	3	0	0	1	0	25 (7)	3
1995–96	15 (7)	1	0	0	2	0	17 (7)	1
1996–97	25 (2)	1	2	0	0	0	27 (2)	1
1997–98	41	0	2	0	4	1	47	1
1998–99	10	0	0 (1)	0	1 (1)	1	11 (2)	1
	134 (18)	5	5 (1)	0	8 (1)	2	147 (20)	7

 # Warren also appeared in 10(4) Auto Windscreens Shield matches, scoring one goal.

WEBB, David James (1964–66)

He joined the O's from West Ham juniors in May 1963 to become one of their great full-backs of the post-war era. David Webb, known for his famous crew-cut hairstyle, was an all-action player, a hard runner and strong tackler. He was to become the darling of the O's fans and he had a great sense of humour and would do anything for a laugh. Born in Stratford, London, on Tuesday 9 April 1946, he made his League debut in a 5–2 victory over Portsmouth on 22 August 1964; also making his first-team debut on the same day was another youngster, Terry Price. Webb played at centre-half that day but soon settled down in the full-back position. He played his part in the O's battle to avoid relegation in 1965–66, and it was no surprise that with the O's close to the drop into the Third Division he was transferred to Southampton in March 1966 for £23,000, with striker George O'Brien making the trip to London as part of the deal.

Webb stayed at The Dell for two seasons, making 75 League appearances with two goals. He joined Chelsea in February 1968 for £40,000, with defender Joe Kirkup going to The Dell. He scored the Blues winner when he rose to head home after extra-time in the 104th minute in an FA Cup Final replay against Leeds United at Old Trafford in May 1970, the first ever replayed Final. He was in the winning side that beat Real Madrid in the 1971 European Cup-winners' Cup Final after a replay, and he was also in their side that were dumped out of the FA Cup by the O's at Brisbane Road by 3–2. It was Barrie Fairbrother who slipped the ball past a diving and despairing Webb to secure a famous victory in the final minute in February 1972. As a midfielder he played in their League Cup Final defeat against Stoke City in 1972.

He remained at Stamford Bridge for six seasons, making 299 senior appearances with 33 goals. In July 1974 he moved on to Queen's Park Rangers for £100,000 and made a further 116 League appearances, scoring seven goals. He moved to Leicester City in September 1977 for £50,000, making 32(1) League appearances. Webb later played for Derby County in December 1978, AFC Bournemouth in May 1980 as player-coach and Torquay United. Webb made a career total of 550(2) League appearances and scored 34 goals.

In 1993 he had a brief spell at Chelsea as caretaker boss for three months before Glenn Hoddle was appointed at Stamford Bridge. He started his League management career with AFC Bournemouth from December 1980 and stayed for 14 months. His record read: P48, W21, D11, L16. He then took the reins of Torquay United for 18 months, with 70 games in charge, which resulted in 19 wins, 18 draws and 33 losses. A year after leaving Torquay he began a long association with Southend United, and for part of the 1986–87 season he took them to 20 wins from 37 games with 10 losses. After a short time away he rejoined the Shrimpers in November 1988 and stayed until May 1992 for 181 games.

After the short time at Stamford Bridge, he went to Brentford and stayed for over four years, until August 1997, with a further 216 games under his belt, winning 85 and losing 66. He was given a place on their board but left Griffin Park under a cloud when Ron Noades took over. After a successful six months with Football Conference side Yeovil Town, he went back to the Shrimpers in October 2000, saying he wanted to bring back the fun, laughter and joy of his previous time on the coast. He stayed in charge for a year. In November 2003 he returned to Roots Hall for a brief spell of four games as caretaker manager. Webb also runs a wholesale/retail business and a successful property company in Dorset.

Webb's managerial career in the Football League and senior Cup matches between December 1980 and November 2003 reads: P628, W252, D168, L208 (not including his managerial career with then Conference side Yeovil Town).

SEASON	*LEAGUE*		*FA CUP*		*FL CUP*		*TOTAL*	
	Apps	*Gls*	*Apps*	*Gls*	*Apps*	*Gls*	*Apps*	*Gls*
1964–65	33	0	0	0	2	0	35	0
1965–66	29	3	1	0	1	0	66	3
	63	3	1	0	3	0	66	3

WELLS, Peter Alan (1985–89)

Born in Nottingham on Monday 13 August 1956, Peter Wells, a 6ft 1in and 13st goalkeeper, started off as an apprentice with Nottingham Forest in October 1974, making his debut in May 1975 in a 3–3 draw against Blackpool, and chalked up 27 League appearances. He joined Southampton in December 1976 for £8,000 and stayed for seven years, making 141 League appearances before losing his place to Peter Shilton. He joined Millwall in February 1983 and let in five goals on his debut at Huddersfield Town. After playing 33 League matches for the Lions, he joined the O's in July 1985 and proved to be a very reliable goalie for four seasons until he broke a bone in his ankle during training and was replaced by David Cass. His days were numbered with the arrival of young Paul Heald from Sheffield United in December 1988, and he was released in May 1989, joining Fisher Athletic.

SEASON	*LEAGUE*		*FA CUP*		*FL CUP*		*TOTAL*	
	Apps	*Gls*	*Apps*	*Gls*	*Apps*	*Gls*	*Apps*	*Gls*
1985–86	45	0	6	0	4	0	55	0
1986–87	39	0	4	0	2	0	45	0
1987–88	46	0	4	0	2	0	52	0
1988–89	18	0	3	0	5	0	26	0
	148	0	17	0	13	0	178	0

 # Wells also appeared in eight Auto Windscreens Shield matches.

WELTON, Roy Patrick (1949–58)

One of the O's finest goalkeepers of the post-war era, playing for nine seasons, Pat Welton was born in Eltham on 3 May 1928. He started off with Chiselhurst FC before joining the O's in May 1949 as an amateur. He was a PE teacher at a public school and at a school in Highbury before turning professional as a footballer later that season. The solidly-built 6ft goalkeeper had a traumatic baptism to the League when Notts County hit seven goals past him on 1 October

1949, and the following week they lost 2–0 at Aldershot. He was replaced by Polish 'keeper Stan Gerula, but the O's boss Alec Stock restored Welton to the team in December. However, after two further defeats he was yet again replaced, this time by Sid Hobbins.

Welton came back in March 1950 and was the regular 'keeper for the following six seasons, before sharing the green jersey with Dave Groombridge and Frank George between 1956 and 1958. He was a member of the team that won the Third Division South Championship in May 1956. Thirty-year-old Welton was transferred to Queen's Park Rangers in March 1958, playing just three League matches and letting in seven goals. He was appointed manager with St Albans FC and later managed Walthamstow Avenue. He held a coaching position with the England Youth side and was a coach with Tottenham Hotspur before taking his skills overseas.

SEASON	*LEAGUE*		*FA CUP*		*TOTAL*	
	Apps	*Gls*	*Apps*	*Gls*	*Apps*	*Gls*
1949–50	16	0	0	0	16	0
1950–51	46	0	1	0	47	0
1951–52	41	0	9	0	50	0
1952–53	23	0	0	0	23	0
1953–54	16	0	1	0	17	0
1954–55	43	0	2	0	45	0
1955–56	46	0	4	0	50	0
1956–57	17	0	1	0	18	0
1957–58	15	0	0	0	15	0
	263	0	18	0	281	0

WENT, Paul Frank (1965–67 & 1978–81)

Went holds some unique records in the folklore of the club, being the youngest ever player to appear for the O's in the Football League aged 15 years and 327 days (the youngest known players ever to appear in League football were Ken Roberts at 15 years and 157 days for Wrexham on 1 September 1951 against Bradford Park Avenue and Albert Geldard at 15 years and 158 days for Bradford Park Avenue versus Millwall on 16 September 1929) to being the manager between September and October 1981, just 21 days in charge, one of the shortest reigns ever in League history. Went also spent his whole career playing for a series of hard-up clubs and often found himself being sold to keep clubs like the O's, Fulham and Portsmouth afloat.

Paul Went was born in Bromley-by-Bow, London, on 12 October 1949. The son of an Italian mother, he attended a number of local schools in the area including schools in Whitechapel, St Agnes School, St Bernard's Secondary School and Morpeth School in Bethnal Green, and he represented East London Schools. The England Schoolboy won six caps and also 10 youth international caps and started with the O's as an apprentice in August 1965. Big and strong for his age, standing at 6ft and weighing 12st 10lb, he made his League debut on 4 September 1965 versus Preston North End in a 2–2 draw, the O's first point of that season.

Went signed professional forms in October 1966 and he shone regularly during the following season. He was sold to Charlton Athletic on 8 June 1967 for a then record fee of £24,250 to help the O's out of one of their worst financial crises, and it was this money which saved the club from closure. He was a kingpin at the Valley for five seasons, making 160(3) League appearances and scoring 15 goals. He was signed by Fulham on 7 July 1982 for £80,000 by boss Alec Stock on the same day as Alan Mullery in an attempt to strengthen an ailing side, but 18 months later, after appearing in 58 League matches with three goals, he moved to Portsmouth in December 1973 for £155,000, a then club record fee, in an effort to repay some of the monies due on their new Riverside Stand. Both he and Steve Earle were sacrificed to keep Fulham afloat.

Went stayed with Pompey for nearly three years, making 92 League appearances with five goals, and yet again Went was sold for a give-away fee of £30,000 to Cardiff City on 8 October 1976 to help them stave off the threat of bankruptcy. He was with the Bluebirds for two years and played in 71(1) League matches with 11 goals before returning 'home' to become an Oriental for the second time on 7 September 1978 for £20,000, a month before his 29th birthday. Went was troubled during his second spell with leg and shoulder injuries and his last League appearance came in a 7–3 home defeat by Chelsea in November 1979. He retired from playing and was appointed reserve-team coach and club scout. He took charge of the side as caretaker manager during the latter part of the 1980–81 season, when boss Jimmy Bloomfield was hospitalised, and eventually he took over as manager when Bloomfield left over the transfer of John Chiedozie to Notts County. Went made a career total of 474(6) League appearances and scored 42 goals between 1965 and 1979. Nowadays he is a manager for Courage Breweries in Essex.

* The remainder of Paul Went's story appears under the managers section of this book.

SEASON	*LEAGUE*		*FA CUP*		*FL CUP*		*TOTAL*	
	Apps	*Gls*	*Apps*	*Gls*	*Apps*	*Gls*	*Apps*	*Gls*
1965–66	9(2)	0	0	0	1	0	10(2)	0
1966–67	39	5	3	0	1	0	43	5
1978–79	37	2	3	0	0	0	40	2
1979–80	8	1	0	0	0	0	8	1
	93(2)	8	6	0	2	0	101(2)	8

WEST, Colin (1993–98)

A proven striker over the years who has not always been a crowd pleaser but has let his goalscoring ability do his talking for him, with 50 goals for the club, Colin West was a quality striker, who stood at 6ft 1in and weighed 14st. The 30-year-old linked up again with both Peter Eustace and Chris Turner, following his days with them at Sunderland and Sheffield Wednesday. He joined from Swansea City on 9 July 1993 after a long and distinguished career, scoring 86 League goals with seven clubs. His goalscoring didn't stop there, and he went on to become a member of the 100 Football League goals club.

Born in Wallsend on 13 November 1962, West started his career with Sunderland as an apprentice and made 81(14) League appearances, scoring 21 goals. He joined Watford in March 1985 for £115,000, and after 14 months he scored 20 goals from 45 League appearances.

Perhaps the highlight of his career came in the 1986–87 season

when he joined Glasgow Rangers from Watford for £180,000 and won both a Scottish League title and a Scottish Cup-winners' medal with them. He moved to Sheffield Wednesday in September 1987 for £150,000, scoring just eight goals from 40(50) League appearances. He fared better after moving to Sunderland in July 1990 with 21 goals from 81(14) League appearances. In 1992 he was with Swansea City and during his one season in Wales he notched 12 goals from 29(4) League appearances.

It was reported that 'Westie', as he was known, came on a free transfer. In fact, the friendly Geordie had another year to run on his contract at Vetch Field and, according to the O's boss Eustace, the club had to pay a 'reasonably high fee for him'.

Eustace said 'I wanted to bring Colin to this club when he was at West Bromwich Albion last year, but we didn't have the financial resources at the time. He is vastly experienced, has power and a brilliant goalscoring record, an ability that is just what this club needs.'

West scored on his O's debut versus Burnley, and he certainly didn't let them down, scoring 50 senior goals while at the club. He seemed to come in for some rough treatment from the fans and was barracked on numerous occasions. In one match versus Hartlepool United he gave them the proverbial two fingers after scoring twice and setting up two more goals in a 4–1 win on 16 September 1995. Westie's goals rank him in the top 20 in the O's all-time goalscoring list since 1905, and as he once said 'They can boo me as much as they want, but at the end of the day goals speak louder than them'. After a loan spell with Rushden & Diamonds in the Football Conference during January 1998, the move was made permanent a month later for the same fee that the O's paid for him to Swansea back in 1993. At the age of 36 he was still among the goals, hitting two for the Diamonds in a 4–2 FA Cup victory that gave them a place in the third round against Leeds United in January 1999. He netted five League and Cup goals in 1998–99 from 19 starts. He was appointed their reserve-team manager and his charges were reserve League champions, also winning the Capital League Cup.

He moved to Northwich Victoria before being appointed as assistant manager and coach under former Oriental Chris Turner at Hartlepool United on 2 November 1999. They retained his player registration, and he made two substitute appearances in the 1999–2000 season. He retired from playing in August 2001 with a wonderful record of 494(68) Football League, Conference and Cup appearances, scoring 168 goals.

Turner stated 'I am delighted to have Colin on the staff here at Hartlepool. He will be a major help to myself, but most importantly to the players. His experience within the game is there for all to see, and the list of clubs and managers he has played with speaks for itself, he scored over 150 senior goals.' They took Hartlepool to a top-four spot within two years but were knocked out by Blackpool in the Play-off semi-final, losing 5–1 on aggregate.

After the departure of Chris Turner from Hartlepool United to become manager of Sheffield Wednesday in November 2002, West was appointed their caretaker manager, and after just two matches in charge he was offered a chance to team up with Turner again at Hillsborough as his assistant, this after being offered the job at Hartlepool.

West stated 'It was a tough decision to leave Hartlepool, but Sheffield Wednesday is a massive club and a chance to further my career and team up again with Chris.'

However, the Turner and West partnership failed to prevent them from dropping out of the Second Division, although they went out with a bang, winning 7–2 at Burnley in April 2003. The Owls failed to mount any promotion challenge, and after a home defeat against AFC Bournemouth on 18 September 2004 both Turner and West were fired after being in charge for 22 months. On 19 December 2004 Chris Turner was appointed manager of struggling Stockport County, and for the third time in their management careers the two teamed up when West was appointed as Turner's number two at Stockport on 27 January 2005, until both were dismissed in December 2005.

SEASON	*LEAGUE*		*FA CUP*		*FL CUP*		*TOTAL*	
	Apps	*Gls*	*Apps*	*Gls*	*Apps*	*Gls*	*Apps*	*Gls*
1993–94	42(1)	14	2	0	0	0	44(1)	14
1994–95	27(3)	9	2	1	2	0	31(3)	10
1995–96	39	16	1	0	1	1	41	17
1996–97	22(1)	3	2	1	2	1	26(1)	5
1997–98	2(5)	0	0	0	1	0	3(5)	0
	132(10)	42	7	2	6	2	145(10)	46

 # West also appeared in nine Auto Windscreens Shield matches, scoring four goals.

WHITBREAD, Adrian Richard (1989–93)

Adrian Whitbread was handed the team captaincy in 1992 when just 20 years old to become the youngest skipper at that time throughout the League. Adrian Whitbread was a dominant centre-back, and at 6ft 2in and 12st he proved difficult to beat and was always cool under pressure. He was born in Epping, Essex, on 22 October 1971, and came through the club's School of Excellence Academy from the age of 12 to serve his apprenticeship and finally signed as a professional on 13 November 1989. He made his League debut at Brentford on 3 December 1989, and he was made team captain in 1992 (the role was to be awarded to Terry Howard, but at the time he was out of contract).

After four seasons at the club, he was transferred on 30 July 1993 to newly-promoted Premiership side Swindon Town for £500,000. The O's boss Peter Eustace stated 'Adrian has done everything I've asked of him since I joined the club, now he's going to a Premier League side, he deserves his chance, Whitbread had two years left on his contract.'

Whitbread made 35(1) League appearances for the Wiltshire side, scoring one goal, before being transferred to West Ham United for £650,000 on 17 August 1994. A foot injury sidelined him for six months at Upton Park, and he failed to break into the first team, playing just 5(7) senior matches. He went on a three-month loan spell to Portsmouth from November 1995, making 13 League appearances, before the move was made permanent in October 1996 for £250,000. He was Pompey's team captain and made 133(1) League appearances with two goals. A knee injury ruled him out of the start of the 2000–01 season, and he fell out of favour with player-manager Steve Claridge and was told he could leave. He went on a two-month loan to Second Division Luton Town in November 2000, making 13 senior appearances.

Twenty-nine-year-old Whitbread went on loan with Second Division side Reading, making his debut in their 2–1 win at Brentford on 10 February 2001. He made over 20 League appearances up to the end of the season. In November 2001 he sustained a serious knee injury which kept him out of the game for nearly a year. He returned in a pre-season match in July 2002 but sustained another injury, which saw him out until he went on loan in January 2003 to Third Division side Exeter City, making seven League appearances for them. He returned to Reading in March 2003 but had to finally quit after picking up another injury in training. So, after nearly 14 years in the Football League, he made a total of 404(10) senior appearances and scored seven goals. His final League appearance came for Exeter in their 2–0 defeat against AFC Bournemouth on 22 February 2003.

In June 2003 he was appointed first-team player-coach with Conference outfit Barnet while he was in rehabilitation after yet another knee operation. In the summer of 2003 he was appointed assistant manager of Barnet under Martin Allen, and in February 2004 he helped out his brother Neil, who was the manager of the Epping reserve side and played a few games for fun with the Essex Intermediate Senior side. In March 2004 Whitbread was put in charge of the Bees affairs with physiotherapist Damien Coyle after Martin Allen was appointed manager of Brentford, and soon after both Whitbread and Coyle had joined Brentford, with Whitbread appointed as the first-team coach.

SEASON	*LEAGUE*		*FA CUP*		*FL CUP*		*TOTAL*	
	Apps	*Gls*	*Apps*	*Gls*	*Apps*	*Gls*	*Apps*	*Gls*
1989–90	8	0	0	0	0	0	8	0
1990–91	38	0	5	0	5(1)	0	48 (1)	0
1991–92	43	1	5	0	3	0	51	1
1992–93	36	1	1	1	2	0	39	2
	125	2	11	1	10(1)	0	146 (1)	3

 # Whitbread also appeared in eight Auto Windscreens matches.

WHITE, Philip George John (1953–64)

Phil White was an exceptionally gifted right-winger who would have received international honours had he been with a more glamorous club. When his chance did come with a planned move to Liverpool for £15,000 plus former O's player Brian Jackson, White himself turned down the chance, deciding to remain with the O's throughout his professional career. He was a frail-looking player who relied on skill as well as speed. White was born near Craven Cottage in Fulham on 29 December 1930. He was signed by Alec Stock from Wealdstone FC, and when Vic Groves moved to Arsenal he became an automatic choice for the first team. He came to the fore during the Championship-winning season of 1955–56, turning in some scintillating displays, and was a major player during the late 1950s.

There can be no doubt that the Johnston–White partnership was a high-class combination. There was always a high level of expectancy when White had the ball on the right wing and Johnston was waiting in the middle. When the two were in the O's team, you knew there was a good chance of a win. White was an excellent dribbler of the ball and the word 'bamboozled' was used in many match reports in describing White's mastery over full-backs and defenders.

He played a major part in the O's promotion side to the First Division in 1961–62, but he sustained a very bad leg injury which denied him a run in the First Division, and after a handful of matches between October and November 1963 he was eventually forced to retire in 1964. The club staged a well-earned benefit for him on 21 April 1964 against an ex-Leyton Orient XI, and many of his former colleagues turned out for him including Tommy Johnston. The match ended 3–3.

Outside of Brisbane Road, Phil White was hardly known, which was a travesty of justice for such a brilliant player. The last word on Phil White goes to the legendary Tommy Johnston from his biography *The Happy Wanderer*:

'Whitey was a superb player, brilliant at crossing a ball, and I headed many goals from his passes. We had an understanding that's hard to explain, the ball seemed to come at just the right angle and speed. Whitey was a top man and a top player.'

Phil White sadly died in June 2000, a few months before his 70th birthday.

SEASON	*LEAGUE*		*FA CUP*		*FL CUP*		*TOTAL*	
	Apps	*Gls*	*Apps*	*Gls*	*Apps*	*Gls*	*Apps*	*Gls*
1953–54	5	2	0	0	-	-	5	2
1954–55	3	0	0	0	-	-	3	0
1955–56	28	3	2	0	-	-	30	3
1956–57	36	6	1	0	-	-	37	6
1957–58	29	5	1	0	-	-	30	5
1958–59	35	5	0	0	-	-	35	5
1959–60	23	0	1	0	-	-	24	0
1960–61	23	1	1	0	3	0	27	1
1961–62	30	6	4	0	3	0	37	6
1962–63	0	0	0	0	0	0	0	0
1963–64	5	0	0	0	0	0	5	0
	217	28	10	0	6	0	233	28

+ *The League Cup commenced in 1960–61.*

WILLIAMS, Owen (1919–24)

One of the finest left-wingers in the club's history, and the O's first full international player, Owen Williams, a small stocky player, was arguably the finest outside-left in the club's history. He was fast, tricky and direct, causing havoc to opposing defenders.

Born in Ryhope, County Durham, on 23 September 1895, Owen Williams was an England Schoolboy before joining his local side Ryhope Colliery. After unsuccessful trials with both Sunderland and Manchester United, he joined Easington Colliery. He was spotted by an O's scout and came for a trial at Millfields Road in July 1919 and signed professional forms in August. He made his debut on the right wing against Wolverhampton Wanderers on 17 September 1919 but soon found himself as reserve to Ben Ives. Once Ives was injured at the end of November, Williams came in and played for the remainder of the season.

He proved to be one of the speediest wingers of his day, with excellent ball-control, and often went on long dribbling runs, drifting past full-backs with ease, and his perfect crosses proved crucial for the likes of Rennox, Whipp and Green over the years. There was reluctance by the England selectors to pick a player from the lower Divisions, but in the end they just couldn't leave him out, and really he should have won more than the two caps. He moved to Middlesbrough in March 1924 for a record fee of £2,525 but experienced relegation in his first season, but they bounced back and won two Division Two Championships in 1927 and 1929.

He experienced the humiliation of defeat with Boro against the O's in a fourth-round FA Cup tie at Millfields Road when defeated 4–2 on 30 January 1926, but still received a rousing reception from the 24,247 O's fans, who he acknowledged with a wave to each corner of the ground from the middle of the pitch. He stayed at Ayresome Park for seven seasons, making 194 senior appearances with 43 goals, but he was now approaching 35 years of age and was placed on the transfer list at £400. He joined Southend United for a cut price £200 in July 1930, making 16 League appearances with four goals before retiring in May 1931. On 1 September 1931 he joined Shildon FC.

He lived in Easington, Co. Durham, until he died on 9 December 1960, aged 65. His younger brother Tom played with the O's between 1921 and 1923, and he died just days after his brother on the 14 December 1960, aged 61.

SEASON	*LEAGUE*		*FA CUP*		*TOTAL*	
	Apps	*Gls*	*Apps*	*Gls*	*Apps*	*Gls*
1919–20	28	6	1	0	29	6
1920–21	40	9	2	0	42	9
1921–22	33	6	1	0	34	6
1922–23	37	7	1	0	38	7
1923–24	24	5	3	2	27	7
	162	33	8	2	170	35

WOOD, Arthur (1921–31)

Legendary goalkeeper Arthur Wood was born in Walsall on 14 January 1894, the son of the great Southampton stalwart Harry Wood (a great forward who also played for Wolverhampton Wanderers and won two caps for England, making 180 Southern League and FA Cup appearances for the Saints with 65 goals). Arthur Wood first watched his father at Southampton as a boy, and he then represented Portsmouth Schoolboys before joining Portsmouth as a 16-year-old amateur in 1910, where his father was trainer. He first played as a full-back, but due to his heavy weight he was converted to a goalkeeper. When his father retired from football to run the Milton Arms Public House near Fratton Park, Wood went to The Dell for a trial in 1913.

He was duly taken on and made his senior debut in a 3–2 defeat at Luton Town in a Southern League fixture on 9 September 1914, with his proud father in attendance. Wood had his career interrupted, like so many young players, by World War One and served in the Royal Engineers but still played for the Saints in wartime matches. He served in France, Palestine and Salonika and received two medals for bravery. He rejoined the Southampton groundstaff after his demobilisation and made his League debut, a 1–1 draw at Brentford, on 30 October 1920. He seemed to have a long career ahead of him at The Dell, but with the arrival of goalie Tommy Allen from Sunderland he lost his place. Not being content with reserve football, the opportunity arose to come to London, and he signed for the O's in May 1921 after making 41 Southern League, two League and four FA Cup appearances for the Saints.

His first outing was in a public trial match at Millfields Road in July 1921, and the 5ft 10in and 14st Wood, to the amazement of the 12,000 crowd, wore a large poachers pocket sewn on to his tent-like shorts, and the newspaper reported that Wood kept fruit in it and it was nothing to see him whip out an apple when the home players were up the field. During the match he was challenged by centre-forward Clatworthy Rennox, and Wood lost his temper but was restrained from hitting him, quite a debut the paper reported. The reporter concluded by asking the question, did manager Holmes have a few too many when he signed this Arthur Wood on?

Well, Wood made his League debut in a 0–0 draw at Bury on 3 September 1921, after first-choice goalie Hugall was injured, and Wood kept the jersey for the following nine seasons, during which time his weight increased to over 18 stone.

He was a massive obstacle to opposing forwards, and in those days, when outfield players were allowed to barge a goalkeeper, not many tried it with Wood; he was truly a magnificent custodian. The *Southern Press* campaigned for his England call-up, but he could never replace Taylor of Huddersfield Town, Sewell of Blackburn Rovers and later Ted Hufton at West Ham United, so Wood was often referred to in match reports as the best uncapped goalkeeper in England, and after many splendid performances around the country he was often applauded off the pitch by home fans.

Wood still holds the O's record for consecutive League appearances for the club, appearing in 225 matches. The run started in that first match at Bury until the game against Grimsby Town on 4 December 1926. During this five-year spell, he also played in 10 FA Cup ties, until a thigh strain sidelined him for the match at Blackpool. In came amateur goalie John Leather for his only senior appearance, a 6–0 defeat.

Wood had an excellent match as captain versus Newcastle United in the fifth round of the FA Cup at Millfields Road, a brilliant 2–0 victory, and he was chaired off the pitch by ecstatic fans. He also played in the two League matches played at Wembley Stadium in 1930. His final League match was at Newport County, a 1–1 draw on 2 May 1931, and he held the O's League record of 373 appearances, which stood for 45 years until being surpassed by Peter Allen in March 1976.

Wood left the O's at the age of 37 and joined Ryde Sports on the Isle of Wight in June 1931 and later coached Newport Isle of Wight. He returned to London to watch the O's play Crystal Palace on 26 February 1936, and the club programme of 7 March stated that it was splendid to see Arthur Wood at the ground again, also saying that he was now over 20 stones in weight.

This was a possible reason for him dying at the young age of 47 in Portsmouth on 8 April 1941. His father, Harry, died later on 5 July 1951, aged 83. The last word on Arthur Wood goes to a former colleague and Welsh international Eddie Lawrence, who spoke to the author from his home in Nottingham just before he died in July 1989.

'Firstly a lot has been written about Arthur Wood that you are not always sure what is truth and what is fiction, one thing, though, I was told by the O's directors that they, like the local press, wondered what they had bought from Southampton because in his first public trial match he did indeed eat fruit brought out from the largest pair of shorts ever seen down Millfields Road, but Wood wasn't worried, after all he had already signed a one-year contract, and manager Holmes had known of his worth down at The Dell, having spoken to his father and others at the club.

'Woody, as he was known by his colleagues, soon became respected by all, he had a great ability between the sticks, which got him selected season after season at Orient. It was surprising he was never picked for his country. Why was he so loved by the fans? Well it certainly wasn't for his bulk or the fact that he was one of the few players who ran a motor car, the secret is in one word... Charisma.

'He had it, and the O's fans just loved him, and I remember in so many away fixtures how he was clapped off the field. He was a very special player and a special man. I'll never forget Arthur Wood, he was probably one of the first, what they would call today a cult figure.

'To bring this into perspective, I clearly remember I was in the stands for the thrashing we received at the hands of Aston Villa in an FA Cup replay by 0–8, but do you know Woody was actually cheered off the field by the fans. I thought to myself, as I was leaving for the dressing room, "quite remarkable", although he himself was not a happy man that evening, he felt he let the fans, his colleagues and the club he loved so much down, but truth be told they were just too good for us on the day, remember only a few days earlier we held them at Villa Park 0–0 before a massive 50,000 crowd, and Woody and the team had a blinder.

'I played with Woody in his final home League match versus Luton Town in 1931 (18 April), it was also the first match under new boss Jimmy Seed, we won 3–2 and the ovation Woody received lasted for over five minutes, I stood next to him and saw tears streaming down his cheek, it was a sight to behold.

'I can remember when I returned to the club for a second spell in 1937, some seven years after Woody left, the fans still talked of him with great affection, and it was a sad day for everyone when hearing of his death in April 1941.'

SEASON	LEAGUE		FA CUP		TOTAL	
	Apps	Gls	Apps	Gls	Apps	Gls
1921–22	40	0	1	0	41	0
1922–23	42	0	1	0	43	0
1923–24	42	0	3	0	45	0
1924–25	42	0	1	0	43	0
1925–26	42	0	4	0	46	0
1926–27	40	0	0	0	40	0
1927–28	37	0	1	0	38	0
1928–29	36	0	4	0	40	0
1929–30	22	0	6	0	28	0
1930–31	30	0	1	0	31	0
	373	0	22	0	395	0

WOOSNAM, Philip Abraham (1954–58)

As one newspaper put it, 'he was like watching poetry in motion'. Philip Woosnam was one of a small band to have been capped for Wales at Schoolboy, Youth, Amateur and Professional levels. He was born in the small scenic mid-Wales village of Caersws, Montgomeryshire, on 22 December 1932, a farmer's son who showed considerable academic ability. He won a scholarship to Newton Grammar School and went to the University of Wales in Bangor during 1950, and after four years he gained degrees in Physics, Mathematics and Education. During this time he played in the university team and for a number of Welsh representative sides.

Woosnam gained an Under-18 cap against Northern Ireland in 1950–51 and 15 Amateur caps. The first Amateur cap came against England, a 4–3 defeat at Bangor in 1951. In 1953–54 he scored against South Africa to secure a 1–0 victory, he scored against Scotland in 1955–56 and his last Amateur cap came in 1956–57, with a goal against Northern Ireland. He also captained the Varsity side to the Welsh Universities' Championship. He played his early football with Wrexham, Peritas FC and Middlesex Wanderers before joining Manchester City on amateur forms while still at university in 1952, making one League appearance against Cardiff City in February 1953, a 6–0 defeat. He represented an Army XI with such famous names as Maurice Setters (WBA), Eddie Colman and Duncan Edwards of Manchester United.

Woosnam joined the O's as an amateur from Sutton United in January 1955 and took up a science teaching post at Leyton County High School. Not the quickest of footballers, he never failed to create space for himself, and he radiated class whenever on the ball and was one of the best midfielders in the country. He made his O's debut in a 2–0 defeat at Brentford on 8 April 1954 but came to the fore in the following season when the O's won the Third Division South Championship. In his later seasons he became a cult figure with his distinctive crew-cut hairstyle. Woosnam turned professional in January 1957 and was a member of an O's side that demolished Scottish side East Fife by 7–0 in 1957–58, Woosnam bagging a pair. He was rewarded when winning his first full Welsh cap against Scotland in October 1958. Twenty-six-year-old Woosnam moved to West Ham United for a then record fee of £30,000 in November 1958, making his debut against Arsenal, and was capped a further 15 times during his two-year stay at the Boleyn, and he was picked on 1 November 1960 for a Football League XI against an Italian XI played in Milan before 40,000 fans, playing alongside the greats of European football, an honour he considers to be one of his greatest achievements as a player.

The arrival of Johnny Byrne to Upton Park hastened Woosnam's departure to Aston Villa for £27,000 in November 1962 after making 153 senior appearances with 29 goals. He gained another two Welsh caps while in the Midlands and scored 24 goals from 111 League appearances.

'I read a story by Clive Toye in the *Daily Express* that a new League was starting up in the States. After speaking to Clive, I met a representative from the new League in London. The following day I told Villa that I wanted to go over to the States to evaluate the possibility of spending two years there in management.'

In January 1966, at the age of 33, he emigrated to the US to take the post of player-coach with Atlanta Chiefs, but he nearly didn't make it when, a week after accepting the post, Tommy Docherty at Chelsea offered him (and Tony Hateley) a chance to remain in the First Division. As Woosnam explained 'I hadn't signed for Atlanta, but I had given them my word and I stuck to it.' If Chelsea had put in their offer a week or so earlier I would have accepted it. I had very fond memories of playing for Villa, in particular with Vic Crowe.

In 1968 Atlanta won the League, and he was voted coach of the year and was appointed Commissioner to the North American Soccer League and vice-president of the United States Soccer Federation between 1969 and 1983. He probably did more to further the game of football in America than anyone else. He put together the plan to get Pele to play with New York Cosmos and led the campaign with Henry Kissinger, which eventually saw the 1994 World Cup Finals held successfully in America. He worked as a marketing consultant in Atlanta and held a management position with the Atlanta Committee for the Olympic Games. During 1999, aged 67 and now retired, he oversaw the Women's World Cup Finals held in America.

Today, with more than 30 years of soccer leadership experience in the US, he has been one of the driving forces behind the growth of soccer there at all levels. He was inducted into the US National Soccer Hall of Fame in Oneonta, New York, on 14 June 1997, and he was also inducted in the Georgia Soccer Hall of Fame on 10 January 1997.

SEASON	LEAGUE		FA CUP		TOTAL	
	Apps	Gls	Apps	Gls	Apps	Gls
1954–55	5	0	0	0	5	0
1955–56	29	9	2	0	31	9
1956–57	23	4	0	0	23	4
1957–58	37	3	2	0	39	3
1958–59	14	3	0	0	14	3
	108	19	4	0	112	19

Matches to Remember

2 September 1905
Leicester Fosse 2 Clapton Orient 1

Orient opened their League account with a match at Leicester Fosse. The players, officials and around 100 supporters travelled to Leicester by train for the 3.30pm kick-off at Filbert Street.

There were around 6,000 spectators in the ground by the time the two teams walked on to the field, Leicester in blue and Orient wearing white shirts with red and green stripes and white shorts. It was the home team who started off strongly with the visitors looking a bit disjointed in their play. It appeared the O's would hold their own and go in at half-time at 0–0, but on 31 minutes the ball found left-winger Durrant, who centred for the former Luton Town player Herbert Moody to head past Butler. With Leicester on the attack again, the referee blew for half-time.

The second half saw Orient on the attack in an effort to score an equaliser, with shots from Boden and Bourne going close, and on 62 minutes their efforts were rewarded when the O's recorded their first goal in the Football League. Winger Richard Bourne beat Ashby, who had slipped over when in possession, and Bourne swung the ball over into the goalmouth, and there was Bert Kingaby who rose majestically to head powerfully past goalkeeper Walter Smith.

With the crowd filing out of the ground with literally just seconds remaining, a draw seemed certain. However, the ball found its way to Bill Cox, who smashed a long shot at Butler in the O's goal. He saved it and the ball went out to right-half Billy Morgan, who was standing to the right of the goal, and from 25 yards he let fly, and the ball sailed into the top right-hand corner of the rigging for the winner, out of the reach of Butler, to the delight of the home players.

The ball was quickly taken to the centre circle for the restart, but the whistle blew, to the annoyance of the O's players. Manager Ormerod informed the press 'On the run of the play a draw would have been a fair result, especially with our second-half display and, though beaten, we were not disgraced.'

Leicester Fosse: Smith, Ashby, Oakes, Morgan, Bannister, Trueman, Durrant, Blessington, Cox, Moody, Hodgkinson.

Clapton Orient: Butler, J. Lamberton, Boyle, Boden, Codling, Holmes, Kingaby, Wootton, Leigh, G. Lamberton, Bourne.

Referee: A.E. Farrant

Attendance: 6,000

---

9 April 1909
Tottenham Hotspur 0 Clapton Orient 1

For the first-ever League clash between the two teams, a big Good Friday crowd were at White Hart Lane, and the gates were closed half an hour before kick-off, with thousands outside wanting to get in.

The game was played at an incredible pace considering it was a very warm and sunny day, and the O's were playing far more aggressively than their neighbours, and some even remarked that their play was rather rough.

Spurs' England international centre-forward Vivian Woodward was completely marked out of the game by centre-half Mark Bell, and John Johnston and Ned Liddell also excelled in defence. Up front George Scott and amateur international Lionel Louch gave the Spurs defence plenty to worry about.

The game seemed to be drifting towards a draw when on 76 minutes a move down the left inspired by the inimitable Fred Parker ended with George Scott sweeping the ball past Spurs goalkeeper Fred Boreham and into the net for a well-deserved victory.

Spurs were lying second in the Second Division at the time and were eventually promoted, and Orient were at the lower end of the table, finishing in 15th position that season.

Tottenham Hotspur: Boreham, Coquet, Burton, Bull, D. Steel, Darnell, Walton, Minter, Woodward, R. Steel, Middlemass.

Clapton Orient: Whittaker, Johnston, Reason, Hind, Bell, Liddell, Parker, McLean, Louch, Scott, Ward.

Referee: A.E. Farrant

Attendance: 32,821

---

18 April 1914
Woolwich Arsenal 2 Clapton Orient 2

Arsenal's move from Plumstead to Highbury at the start of the season was not greeted with much enthusiasm by either of their new neighbours, Orient or Tottenham Hotspur.

The Gunners needed to win this match to stay in the promotion race and keep ahead of arch rivals Bradford Park Avenue. The early exchanges were even, although left-winger Charlie Lewis was giving the O's defence some difficult moments. However, it was Fred Parker who came closest to scoring when his shot struck a post.

It was on 20 minutes that Jock Rutherford – who in later years played for Orient – floated over a cross for Pat Flanagan to drive the ball home for the Gunners' opener. Eight minutes before the interval the O's goalkeeper William Bower had to leave the field after receiving an injury, and forward Willie Jonas went in goal, although Bower did return after the interval.

Arsenal's promotion hopes were boosted when Flanagan scored a second soon after the restart. It was still 2–0 with just five minutes remaining when Parker slammed the ball home after a goalmouth scramble.

With seconds remaining, and the Gunners holding on, Orient were awarded a free-kick, and all the O's players went up field, including the Belgian international centre-half Ike Van den Eynden. Forrest took the kick, the ball rebounded to Parker, and he slipped it to Richard McFadden, who hooked the ball past Joe Leivesley for the equaliser.

Both the Arsenal players and fans alike were absolutely stunned by Orient's great comeback, and it was the Gunners' failure to win this match that lost them promotion to Division One at the hands of Bradford Park Avenue.

Woolwich Arsenal: Leivesley, Shaw, Benson, Grant, Sands, Graham, Rutherford, Flanagan, Stonely, Slade, Lewis.

Clapton Orient: Bower, Hind, Evans, Forrest, Van Den Eynden, Gibson, Parker, Dalrymple, Jonas, McFadden, Dix.

Referee: H. Swift

Attendance: 35,500

---

20 February 1915
Derby County 0 Clapton Orient 3

Orient went to top-of-the-table Derby County with little hope, having lost their previous away encounter 5–1 at Lincoln City and having gained only one away victory in their previous nine encounters.

Although there was one ray of hope, the O's had defeated promotion-chasing Arsenal at Homerton the previous week by 1–0. The opening minutes saw the home side going forward for all their worth for an opening goal. However, on 10 minutes the O's took the early lead when half-back Eddie King burst down the middle of the pitch. He slipped the ball to Fred Parker, who scored with a powerful shot past George Lawrence in the Derby goal.

The O's held on to their slender lead at half-time, mainly due to the wonderful display of goalie Jimmy Hugall. The Second Division leaders enjoyed the territorial advantage during the early stages of the second half, but, as the O's defence stood firm, there were signs of frustrations in the Derby players and among the crowd after an incredible save by Hugall from a shot by inside-forward Jim Moore.

The Derby defence was caught napping on 86 minutes, and Parker got away down the left. His cross found Willie Jonas alone, who had an easy job of beating Lawrence in goal for the O's second.

There was a sting in the tail from the O's; in the closing minutes a weak back pass from full-back Tom Barbour to the goalkeeper, which fell short, was seized upon by Dickie McFadden to knock in the third.

The whole of the Orient team were magnificent, but undoubtedly the star man was goalkeeper Hugall. Derby were eventually promoted to Division One, and Orient finished in ninth spot.

Derby County: Lawrence, Atkin, Barbour, Walker, Eadie, Bagshaw, Grimes, Benfield, Leonard, Moore, Baker.

Clapton Orient: Hugall, Johnston, Evans, Forrest, Steel, Scott, Parker, King, Jonas, McFadden, Ridley.

Referee: W.J. Heath

Attendance: 6,000

---

20 February 1926
Clapton Orient 2 Newcastle United 0

This FA Cup tie turned out to be one of the most memorable victories in the club's history. The star-studded First Division Newcastle United side came to London with one thing on their mind: victory over the Second Division minnows. The fans gave the O's skipper and legendary goalkeeper Arthur Wood a loud ovation as he led the team on to the Millfields Road pitch, this being his 202nd consecutive League and FA Cup appearance. He even wore a new, bright-green jersey for the occasion.

The visitors were on form in the early stages with their Scottish international centre-forward Hughie Gallacher going close with a header just wide of the post.

Orient were battling well and on orders from manager Doc Holmes to get in some early, robust tackles to upset the rhythm of the Newcastle players, and his instructions certainly worked.

On 23 minutes the ball was picked by John Galbraith and from fully 25 yards he smashed the ball all along the ground and past a crowd of players and goalkeeper Willie Wilson into the net – this was Galbraith's only goal in the FA Cup from 19 appearances.

This spurred on the O's as they fought for every ball, rattling the famous Geordies, and then three minutes before half-time they increased their lead when Peter Gavigan sped down the right-wing, crossing for Donald Cock to steer the ball into the net, and the O's faithful erupted.

As expected, the visitors came at Orient with everything they had and got right on top, but they could not get past the inspired Arthur Wood in the O's goal, who saved shots in the closing minutes from Tommy Urwin, Billy Cowan and Willie Gibson. The frustration was showing when Gallacher was severely spoken to by the referee for some stiff tackles on John Townrow.

In the end victory was secured, and the team were magnificent. However, there were a few outstanding performances, like Townrow's total eclipse of Hughie Gallacher, the defending of Billy Broadbent and Tom Evans, Gavigan's and Bob McLaughlan's play down the wings and the wing-half play of both Tommy Dixon and Broadbent and, of course, the splendid Arthur Wood.

As the final whistle sounded, the O's fans invaded the pitch to chair-off their heroes, and it took quite a number of them to carry Arthur Wood all the way to the tunnel because of his weight.

Clapton Orient: Wood, Broadbent, Evans, Dixon, Townrow, Galbraith, Gavigan, Henderson, Cock, Tonner, McLaughlan.
Newcastle United: Wilson, Chandler, Hudspeth, Harris, Spencer, Gibson, Urwin, Cowan, Gallacher, McDonald, Seymour.
Referee: A. Haworth
Attendance: 31,420

---

30 January 1929
Clapton Orient 0 Aston Villa 8

After a wonderful display in drawing 0–0 at Villa Park on an icy pitch before a massive 58,086 crowd, the FA Cup fourth-round replay was held on the following Wednesday afternoon, and the O's were demolished by 8–0, their heaviest ever first-class defeat.

The replay opened in bright fashion for the home side with plenty of attacking play, with Whipp and Dennison coming close to scoring, but gradually their First Division opponents got on top and by the interval were 2–0 up through Waring and Swailes.

Beresford scored straight after the interval with a scorching shot, and that was followed by a goal from Dorrell, York and then Waring (2), which completed his hat-trick, followed with a tap-in goal from Cook for Villa's eighth. All that can be said was that the Orient never gave up trying, but in the end there was a vast gap between the two teams. One thing's for sure, the O's goalkeeper Arthur Wood was not a happy man as he left the Millfields Road pitch, and he had a few choice words for his teammates in the dressing room.

Villa finished their season third in the First Division just two points behind the champions Sheffield Wednesday, and the O's came 12th in Division Three South.
Clapton Orient: Wood, Morley, Gay, Galbraith, Eastman, Duffy, Collins, Whipp, Turnbull, Dennison, Corkindale.
Aston Villa: Olney, Smart, Bowen, Kingdon, Talbot, Swales, York, Beresford, Waring, Cook, Dorrell.
Referee: Unknown
Attendance: 27,532

---

10 February 1934
Clapton Orient 9 Aldershot 2

The 1933–34 season was an entertaining one for the fans at Lea Bridge Road. After hitting Southend United for five in January 1934, the fans were in for a treat for the visit of Aldershot on a grey Saturday afternoon.

Early exchanges in the match did not suggest that a goal avalanche would follow, although Orient looked by far the better side from the start.

The match saw the return to the side of schemer Tommy Mills, after a two-month absence through injury, and his play was as good as the outstanding display of Eddie Ware at left-half, and the deadly shooting of veteran David Halliday was to spell disaster for the Shots.

In goal for the Shots was the former Birmingham City and Glasgow Rangers player and Scottish international Willie Robb. In fact, he made some fine saves during the game, which prevented the score being even higher.

Seldom have Orient looked so dangerous and goal-hungry, and it was Halliday who grabbed a hat-trick. The goals came as follows in the O's record total in a Football League match: Halliday (10 minutes), Mayson (16), Mills (42), Ware (54), Rigby (62), Crawford (71), Ware (80), Halliday (83) and Halliday (86). Aldershot: Smithson (36) and Lee (49).

Clapton Orient: Robertson, Keen, Crompton, Fogg, Fellowes, Ware, Mayson, Mills, Halliday, Crawford, Rigby.
Aldershot: Robb, Bann, McDougall, White, Middleton, Lawson, Izzard, Simmons, Smithson, Sharpe, Lee.
Referee: J.M. Wiltshire
Attendance: 9,832

---

7 February 1948
Notts County 1 Leyton Orient 4

The legendary Tommy Lawton held talks with the O's boss Charles Hewitt in November 1947 with a view to a record transfer from Chelsea, but instead he chose to sign for Notts County for £17,500 plus the Irish international wing-half Bill Dickson. Lawton added 10,000 on to County's attendances.

Three months later Orient, who had been going through a terrible run in the League, showing a number of heavy away defeats, visited County and came up against Tommy Lawton. Few gave the O's any chance.

The first half saw the County team throw everything at the boys from London, and it took a series of wonderful saves from Stan Tolliday in the O's goal to keep out the impressive County forwards. Three of his saves from Lawton, Sewell and Gannon could be described as amazing, and his brilliance acted as a tonic to the boys in royal blue.

Then in the O's first real attack, Frank Neary broke through, on to Wally Pullen, who put the O's one up with a fine cross-come-shot two minutes before the half-time break.

In the second half County mounted more attacks, and from one, on 58 minutes, Lawton scored with a cracking drive. However, instead of capitulating, the O's players appeared to grow in confidence and went back into the lead on 65 minutes, the County goalkeeper Harry Brown appeared to misjudge the flight of Johnny Baynham's corner-kick, and Vernon Chapman ran in to hit a low shot into the corner of the net.

They really grew in confidence and looked the better attacking side, and it was no surprise when Wally Pullen, on 75 minutes, and Frank Neary, on 77 minutes, extended the O's lead to 4–1. Indeed, near the end Orient should have made it five.

A shrewd pre-match plan for the O's boss Hewitt to cut out the service to Lawton worked, and Orient gained a splendid win, with Tolliday and Ronnie Sales made Man of the Match for marking out Lawton.
Notts County: Brown, Southwell, Howe, Gannon, Bagnall, Baxter, Freeman, Sewell, Lawton, Marsh, Lyman.
Leyton Orient: Tolliday, Brown, Ritson, Bacon, Sales, Stroud, Chapman, Hunt, Neary, Pullen, Baynham.
Referee: H. Pearce
Attendance: 28,875

---

6 May 1950
Leyton Orient 2 Southend United 2

Orient were in a situation where they needed a point to avoid having to apply for re-election, and the visitors, Southend United, required a victory to finish as runners-up of Division Three South. Although only one side went up as champions, the runners-up would receive extra money.

The weather was not very kind, with torrential rain during the morning, and the Brisbane Road pitch looked very muddy indeed. The O's leading goalscorer George Sutherland failed a late fitness test, so in came Wally Pullen.

The first half was a stalemate, with both defences dominating; however, the deadlock was broken on 61 minutes when a Pullen free-kick was headed in by Billy McEwan. For a short spell it looked as though the O's would increase their lead as they got the upper hand, despite the very heavy conditions, with Jimmy Blair playing well.

It was, therefore, a big blow when the visitors broke away on 75 minutes to score from Reg Davies and an even bigger shock just five minutes later when their big, dangerous centre-forward Albert Wakefield tucked the ball away for the lead.

All seemed lost for the O's, but skipper Arthur Banner urged his men on for one last effort, and with seconds remaining Banner pumped the ball into the Southend penalty area for Pullen to latch on to it and knock it home past Frank Nash. There was only time for Southend to restart before the final whistle went.

So, Orient had escaped, and their fans cheered them off the pitch, although a number had given up on the match and left before the final whistle had sounded.

Leyton Orient: Welton, Walton, Banner, Taylor, Rooney, Trailor, McEwan, Blair, Pullen, Deverall, Pattison.
Southend United: Nash, Lindsay, Horsfall, Wallbanks, Sheard, French, Butler, McAlinden, Wakefield, Lawler, Davies.
Referee: F.S. Fiander
Attendance: 13,197

---

2 February 1952
Birmingham City 0 Leyton Orient 1

Orient had established themselves as giantkillers in the 1951–52 FA Cup competition after a 3–1 third-round replay victory at Second Division Everton. In the fourth round they had to visit Sunderland, who were second in Division Two.

The win at Goodison Park in the previous round saw some great rearguard action with splendid counter attacking football that brought the goals. This match was a different story (and manager), and the O's took the initiative straight from the kick-off.

The match will be remembered for the brilliant display of inside-left and skipper Tommy Brown, who played magnificently throughout the 90 minutes. He was ably assisted by the O's fast-raiding wingers in Don Woan and Paddy Blatchford. Also in the action were the reserve forward Tommy Harris and young Dennis Pacey, who formed a dangerous striking duo.

Orient's early pressure inevitably led to a goal, and it came in the 26th minute. Receiving a ball from Blatchford, Brown made a clever run through the defence, and as the Birmingham goalkeeper Gil Merrick advanced from his line Brown pushed the ball to Harris who scored with a firm shot.

Orient were now full of confidence, and Pacey forced Merrick into a great save, and with the forwards now buzzing it was the Londoners who looked most likely to score. It was only late into the second half that the home side looked at all dangerous, but skipper Stan Aldous marshalled his defence superbly, and the big goalscoring centre-forward Tommy Briggs was kept quiet.

In the end the O's held out for another excellent FA Cup victory for a fifth-round home tie versus Arsenal (which in the end was lost 3–0 three weeks later).

At the end of the Birmingham match there were some remarkable scenes when the O's fans ran out on to the St Andrew's pitch and hoisted the gallant O's players to the tunnel.

Birmingham City: Merrick, Green, Martin, Badham, Atkins, Warhurst, Stewart, Smith, Briggs, Murphy, Wardle.
Leyton Orient: Welton, Evans, Banner, Blizzard, Aldous, Deverall, Woan, Pacey, Harris, Brown, Blatchford.
Referee: B.J. Flanagan
Attendance: 49,500

---

20 February 1954
Leyton Orient 3 Doncaster Rovers 1

For sheer excitement this fifth-round FA Cup tie takes a lot of beating. Orient were having a fine Cup run, having already disposed of Kettering Town, Weymouth, Tranmere Rovers and Fulham.

Second Division Doncaster Rovers seemed a tough hurdle, and Alec Stock's men were playing below par for much of the first half, and indeed Rovers took a 1–0 lead after 16 minutes through their Irish international forward Ted McMorran from a Herbert Tindill corner-kick

After 32 minutes the O's had a good chance when 38-year-old Joe Mallett hit a wonderful drive that smacked against the crossbar. The ball bounced down to the feet of Canadian-born centre-forward Mike Burgess – only playing because of an injury to Billy Rees – and with the goal at his mercy he hit a weak shot straight at goalkeeper Ken Hardwick.

After the interval the O's came storming forward and scored within five minutes of the restart when veteran Stan Morgan took an Aldous pass in his stride and cleverly screwed the ball into the corner of the net.

The loud roar of the crowd spurred on the O's, and in the 59th minute they went ahead when Burgess and Ken Facey, who was playing a blinder, set up Dennis Pacey to score.

Orient were now swarming all over Rovers, and a third goal followed in the 65th minute. Facey made a great run before cutting inside to hit a cracking low drive, which Hardwick could parry. Burgess followed up to prod the ball home.

The continuous ear-splitting roar of the home fans during the second half seemed to upset the visitors from Doncaster. Pacey hit the crossbar, but no further goals were scored, and so it was Orient who advanced to the sixth round of the FA Cup for the first time since 1926, but they went out in a most disappointing fashion: 1–0 to Port Vale before a packed Brisbane Road crowd.

Leyton Orient: Groombridge, Evans, Charlton, Blizzard, Aldous, Mallett, Facey, Morgan, Pacey, Burgess, Poulton.

Doncaster Rovers: Hardwick, Makepeace, Graham, Brown, Paterson, Teasdale, Tindill, McMorran, Harrison, Lawlor, Walker.

Referee: F. Cowen

Attendance: 29,191

---

6 November 1954
Exeter City 1 Leyton Orient 7

Orient gave their promotion chances a massive boost when they went down to St Jame's Park and came back to East London having achieved their highest ever away victory in a Football League match.

Alex Stock's men got into their stride from the very first minute when Ken Facey ran down the wing and laid on a goal for Stan Morgan, and from that moment they turned in a skilful display of attacking football. The O's went further ahead with goals from Vic Groves, a free-kick, and a rare strike from Exeter-born full-back Stan Charlton, who strode up field, received a back pass from Facey and scored with a blistering 30-yard shot. Exeter inside-forward Charlie McClellan pulled one back from a twice-taken penalty for the Devonians, but by half-time the O's had a 3–1 lead.

The second half was one-way traffic, and a brace each from Billy Rees and Vic Groves made it a record away victory and sent the travelling O's fans away almost in disbelief. It had been a superb team display but special mention should go to Vic Groves for a brilliant hat-trick and Ken Facey, who, although he did not get on to the score sheet, had a great game that had class written all over it. It was no fluke; the following month they went to Torquay United and won 7–2.

Exeter's former Irish international goalkeeper Hugh Kelly had no chance on the day, and unsung O's hero George Poulton had a good game down the left-wing.

Quotes on the match: O's boss Alec Stock said 'Our boys did waste opportunities, but in the end it really was promotion football.' O's forward hat-trick hero Vic Groves said 'Exeter were lucky that I wasn't trying.'

Exeter City: Kelly, B. Doyle, L. Doyle, Setters, Davey, Dodgin, McClelland, Dunne, Donaldson, Murphy, Kalle.

Leyton Orient: Welton, Lee, Charlton, Blizzard, Aldous, McKnight, Groves, Facey, Rees, Morgan, Poulton.

Referee: Unknown

Attendance: 8,748

1 January 1955
Leyton Orient 4 Bristol City 1

This was the O's biggest match of the 1954–55 League season so far against the leaders of Division Three South. A win would take them to the top of the table, and Orient turned on a scintillating display with an abundance of good football cheered on by the large Brisbane Road crowd.

From the kick-off, the O's took hold of the game but could not score, and against the run of play City took the lead on 30 minutes when a low drive from left-winger Jack Boxley struck the O's captain Stan Aldous on the foot, and the ball flew past Pat Welton and into the net.

Orient hit back within two minutes with a great goal: Johnny Hartburn received the ball from Les Blizzard, he broke down the left wing and his inch-perfect cross was crashed home by Vic Groves. Just six minutes later the O's were ahead, Hartburn slamming the ball in from a shrewd pass by Billy Rees.

Orient were full of fire in the second half, and on 53 minutes Hartburn netted after fine play from Blizzard. Then, minutes later, Blizzard himself scored the O's fourth from their 13th corner of the match. The O's kept up the pressure and went close to adding a fifth goal.

This near-perfect display seemed to set Orient on the road to promotion, but later on in the season they were hit by injuries to key players and eventually finished as runners–up to Bristol City, with only one team promoted in those days.

Leyton Orient: Welton, Lee, Charlton, Blizzard, Aldous, McKnight, Groves, Facey, Rees, Morgan, Hartburn.

Bristol City: Anderson, Guy, Thresher, Burden, Peacock, White, Rogers, Ateyo, Rodgers, Eisentrager, Boxley.

Referee: E.T. Jennings

Attendance: 20,347

---

12 February 1955
Leyton Orient 2 Gillingham 2

This match was a great advert for Division Three South football. Quite simply, it had everything: superb goals, a great referee in Mervyn Griffiths, Paddy Sowden, the Gills' great attack leader, two sporting teams and a raging snow blizzard during the game, which lent a certain atmosphere to the occasion.

Orient commenced in fine style, but the Gills defence stood firm, and after some real exciting end-to-end play the Gills took the lead when Ernie Morgan converted Jimmy Scarth's pass. Despite many goalmouth tussles at both ends, that remained the only goal of the first half.

The teams kept up the tremendous pace after the break, and Les Blizzard almost levelled for the O's, but Gillingham broke away and Morgan again scored for a two-goal lead.

The O's Stan Morgan – no relation to the Gills man – broke but was fouled; he carried on to score, but referee Griffiths had already blown for a penalty, so up stepped Ken Facey to convert the kick. It was now all Orient's play, and Stan Morgan headed home Vic Groves's cross on 86 minutes to equalise. Almost on time, Morgan had looked to win the match for the O's when he scored from close range, but the referee disallowed the goal, indicating handball. Nobody complained as referee Griffiths had given a great performance. But it was the two teams who must take the main plaudits. The crowds, even in a snow blizzard, would flood back with matches of this calibre – whatever Division it was played in.

Leyton Orient: Welton, Lee, Charlton, Blizzard, Aldous, McKnight, Groves, Facey, Rees, S. Morgan, Hartburn.

Gillingham: Rigg, Marks, West, Boswell, Niblett, Riggs, Scarth, Evans, Sowden, E. Morgan, Miller.

Referee: M. Griffiths

Attendance: 19,775

26 April 1956
Leyton Orient 2 Millwall 1

Supporters queued for well over an hour in the rain before the start of this vital match in which the prize for the O's was a victory to ensure promotion to Division Two and the clubs first major honour since entering the League in 1905. They would be back for the first time since relegation in 1929. Their opponents, Millwall, were still in danger of having to apply for re-election to stay in the League.

On the run of play, Orient should have won by several goals, but by half-time it was still goalless, and it was becoming a frustrating time for the O's players and their supporters when both Tommy Johnston and Phil White hit the post.

Five minutes after the break Orient forced a corner-kick. The Lions goalie Tony Brewer misjudged Johnny Hartburn's kick, and the ball dipped just inside the near post for the opener. Orient's joy was short lived, in fact for just six minutes, when a mix up in the O's defence meant Jack Gregory missed a long ball from Alec Jardine. It was picked up by Joe Tyrell, and from his cross Johnny Summers took his chance splendidly.

Then on 60 minutes, after shots from Woosnam, Facey and White had been blocked, the high-spinning ball was headed forward by Aldous, Tommy Johnston fastened on to it and smashed the ball into the net for the all-important winner.

When the final whistle was sounded by Newport referee Mervyn Griffiths at 7.50pm, there followed scenes never witnessed at Brisbane Road before when thousands of the O's fans swarmed on to the pitch. The players were mobbed, and the longest 90 minutes for the O's players and fans were over. The crowd gathered in front of the ramshackle wooden stand shouting non-stop, 'We want Alec... We want the players.'

Out came the smiling manager Alec Stock, the chairman Harry Zussman and the players in their tracksuits.

Alec Stock said 'There is only one thing I can do, and I know it is what you want me to do – pay our most gracious thanks to 11 wonderful footballers.'

Chairman Zussman told the press 'That was the toughest game of the season, I'm glad it's over, now, at long last, I can sleep.' The players and officials went back to the dressing room to celebrate, and the champagne flowed down Leyton way that night.

The victory crowned a wonderful season for Orient, who scored 106 League goals, the only time they have scored more than 100 goals in a League season

Leyton Orient: Welton, Bishop, Gregory, Blizzard, Aldous, McKnight, White, Facey, Johnston, P. Woosnam, Hartburn.

Millwall: Brewer, Jardine, J. Smith, Veitch, Brand, Rawson, Hazlett, F. Smith, Summers, Tyrrell, Prior.

Referee: M. Griffiths

Attendance: 22,377

---

30 March 1959
Leyton Orient 6 Sunderland 0

Orient put on an Easter Monday treat for the fans in this Second Division fixture by actually hitting the net nine times, with three goals being disallowed. Had they scored 10 goals, it would not have flattered the boys in royal blue. Tommy Johnston started the rout in the 18th minute with a low drive after a Brown left-wing cross, which was touched back into the middle by Phil White. Two more goals followed within a minute of each other from Eddy Brown before the interval, the first when a Joe Elwood shot was blocked and the ball span back in the middle and Brown was on-hand to head in, then Baily put a perfect through-pass for Brown who scored with a fierce shot. The O's standard of play actually improved after the restart and Sunderland were being totally outclassed.

Leyton Orient in 1959 wearing the hats sent to them by Pat Boone. From left to right: Joe Elwood, Tommy Johnston, Dave Groombridge, Eddie Brown, Stan Charlton, Ronnie Foster, Les Gore, Ken Facey, Terry McDonald, Sid Bishop, Nick Collins, Alan Eagles, Dennis Sorrell.

Within three minutes of the restart, Joe Elwood laid on the O's fourth for Phil White just after the break; however, the best of the bunch was the fifth goal. Ken Facey started the move, he passed on to Cyril Lea, and the Welshman found veteran Eddie Baily with an astute pass. Baily sent a peach of a ball through to Brown, who flashed round a defender as if he wasn't there and crashed a sizzling 15-yarder past Peter Wakeham, which flashed into the net. One could hear the thud as it smacked against the netting.

Brown completed the scoring to grab his fourth goal on 85 minutes and record his 200th career League goal as he scored from point-blank range from another White centre. Both Johnston, twice, and Brown had goals ruled out. Every Orient player performed very well on this day, but it was, however, Baily who almost made the ball talk with his delightful play, while Brown's devastating lethal finishing and his scintillating speed made him look the complete striker, and Johnston was his usual explosive self.

Leyton Orient: George, Wright, Charlton, Facey, Bishop, Lea, White, Brown, Johnston, Baily, Elwood.
Sunderland: Wakeham, Nelson, Ashurst, Anderson, Hurley, Pearce, Bircham, Goodchild, Kichenbrand, Taylor, Godbold.
Referee: E. Crawford
Attendance: 15,613

---

31 October 1959
Leyton Orient 5 Middlesbrough 0

Although there was nothing really counting on the result of this match, with Boro in fourth position with some star-studded players in their ranks like Brian Clough, Mick McNeil, Alan Peacock and Edwin Holliday, and Orient lying in seventh spot in Division Two, it rates as a match to remember because of the way Orient served up some brilliant attacking football.

Orient were blossoming all the time under the leadership of manager Les Gore and the coaching of Eddie Baily. He was a member of the great Tottenham Hotspur 'push and run' team of the early 1950s, and he must have been proud of the O's display, of which the Spurs side of his time would have also been proud.

Orient played splendidly during the first half and were 3–0 up by half-time, with goals from Eddy Brown (2) and a Ken Facey penalty, after Johnston's header had been fisted off the line by defender Harris.

The second half opened with a brief flurry by the visitors, but the O's soon got back into their stride and turned on a performance that had the disbelieving Orient faithful open-mouthed in admiration. It was scintillating stuff.

Although only two more goals were scored, Brown completed his hat-trick and Johnston netted with another of his glorious headers from another perfect Phil White centre. The positive attacking football served up was right out of the top drawer, with the ball moving quickly from man to man.

Orient had never received such wonderful praise from the press or from a visiting manager as they did on the following morning, and they deserved every bit of it, for displays such as this one are rare anywhere – and at Orient particularly so.

Leyton Orient: Groombridge, Wright, Charlton, Facey, Bishop, Sorrell, White, Brown, Johnston, Foster, McDonald.
Middlesbrough: Taylor, Bilcliff, McNeil, Harris, Phillips, Yeoman, Day, Fernie, Clough, Peacock, Holliday.
Referee: F. Collinge
Attendance: 15,700

---

28 October 1961
Liverpool 3 Leyton Orient 3

Division Two leaders Liverpool were a little fortunate to salvage a point from a fast-improving Leyton Orient team. The home side had slightly the better of the early exchanges, but the O's started to cause the Liverpool defence problems. In the 26th minute the O's big centre-forward Dave Dunmore electrified the crowd when he nonchalantly strolled in the centre circle, slipped the ball between Ron Yeats's legs, skipped round him from all of 40 yards and crashed a glorious shot past Bill Slater and into the net.

It was thrill-a-minute stuff, and Roger Hunt equalised for Liverpool from 18-yards on 34 minutes. Orient strode back up field, won a corner, and from Terry McDonald's kick Ronnie Foster poked the ball into the net for a 2–1 lead.

After the interval, Roger Hunt again levelled the scores when the O's 'keeper Frank George let a downward header by Hunt slip through his hands and into the net. Orient came roaring back and on 75 minutes McDonald put over a pinpoint kick, and Dunmore rose, majestically beating Yates, to head the ball, which roared into the net. Unfortunately, Tommy Leishman made it 3–3 with a header with just four minutes remaining. Both sides were given a standing ovation by the crowd at the finish, and all 22 players deserved credit for their part in a truly wonderful game of football. Few did better than Dave Dunmore, but in the end the Man of the Match award went to the O's right-half Malcolm Lucas, who played a blinder in the middle of the park.

Liverpool: Slater, White, Byrne, Milne, Yeats, Leishman, Lewis, Hunt, St John, Melia, A'Court.
Leyton Orient: George, Charlton, Lewis, Lucas, Bishop, Lea, White, Foster, Dunmore, Graham, McDonald.
Referee: V. James
Attendance: 36,612

---

6 February 1962
Leyton Orient 0 Burnley 1

Orient enjoyed two epic FA Cup ties against First Division leaders Burnley in the 1961–62 season, a 1–1 draw at Turf Moor before 37,932 fans, with Ron Foster scoring. Orient wore, for the first time, an all-white strip similar to that of Real Madrid.

The replay was at a packed Brisbane Road, and although they lost the tie Orient have seldom received such accolades as they did after this encounter.

At the time Burnley were a great team and on top of the First Division with some truly magnificent players in their ranks like Ray Pointer, Jimmy Adamson, and Jimmy McIlroy, but the way Orient outplayed them on this occasion without any reward was really a travesty of justice.

Orient attacked them from the start, and the visitors defended well, but they also enjoyed slices of luck. Adam Blacklaw made some great saves, one from a cracking drive from Malcolm Graham, and somehow the first half ended with no goals being scored.

After the interval the O's got more and more on top, and it took a lot of good fortune and more stout defending to keep them out. On the hour it was, however, Burnley who took the lead when a corner from Connelly was headed goalwards by Brian Miller. In an effort to stop the ball the O's goalie Frank George had accidentally punched his defender Eddie Lewis in the face, and Lewis stood on the goal line, with his hands clutching his face, in a daze. In the meantime the ball had hit the underside of the bar, bounced past Lewis and rolled agonisingly over the line for a rather 'lucky' goal.

Orient responded with wave after wave of attacks and several times only last-ditch clearances saved Burnley. Then in the 85th minute came Orient's cruellest piece of misfortune: Terry McDonald centred from the left and Dave Dunmore rose majestically – Tommy Johnston style – to meet the ball and send a glorious header soaring towards goal. But the ball crashed against the underside of the bar, bounced down and was cleared.

The game ended with Burnley desperately hanging on, and the Orient players were cheered all the way off the pitch. Orient boss Johnny Carey summed it up very well when he told the boys in the dressing room 'You weren't meant to win tonight.'

Leyton Orient: George, Charlton, Lewis, Lucas, Bishop, Lea, White, Foster, Dunmore, Graham, McDonald.
Burnley: Blacklaw, Angus, Elder, Adamson, Cummings, Miller, Connelly, McIlroy, Pointer, Robson, Harris.
Referee: C.W. Kingston
Attendance: 31,000

---

28 April 1962
Leyton Orient 2 Bury 0

No O's fan at this match will ever forget the victory that secured a First Division place. Orient had to rely on Sunderland not winning at relegation threatened Swansea Town as well as getting a win themselves. The atmosphere at Brisbane Road was tense as the match progressed.

The first goal came after 14 minutes. Malcolm Graham, playing as a late replacement for the injured Ron Foster, headed into the roof of the net after good work by Dave Dunmore and Derek Gibbs.

Orient's all-out attack brought no further goals, and a great save by Bill Robertson just before the break prevented Bury's equaliser.

Orient stepped up the pressure on the visitors, but goalie Chris Harker made several fine saves, and the news that Sunderland were now leading at Swansea made the agony of the players and fans unbearable until word came that the Welsh side had equalised.

Dunmore, Deeley and Gibbs had all come close to a second before that man Graham did it again with just five minutes remaining. Picking up the ball on the right, he cut inside and rounded a defender before slamming a low drive past a diving Harker and into the net.

The scenes that greeted the goal and the after-match scenes are another wonderful memory for older O's fans. The skipper Stan Charlton was chaired off the pitch in an emotional climax and there were tears and cheers alike, but none more so than from goal hero Mal Graham. The quietly spoken O's manager Johnny Carey and his players appeared before the fans and they saluted their heroes.

Orient had made it into the First Division for the very first time in their history

Leyton Orient: Robertson, Charlton, Lewis, Lucas, Bishop, Lea, Deeley, Gibbs, Dunmore, Graham, McDonald.
Bury: Harker, Gallagher, Eastham, Turner, Stokoe, Atherton, Leech, Beaumont, Calder, Jackson, Bartley.
Referee: C.W. Kingston
Attendance: 21,617

---

12 September 1962
Leyton Orient 3 Everton 0

Having come from a terrific 1–0 victory over Manchester United – a cracking last-minute goal by O's winger Terry McDonald – four days later they recorded their best victory in the First Division and what turned out to be Everton's, the eventual League champions, worst defeat of the season.

There was a great atmosphere at Brisbane Road, and the O's players were keen to win for manager Johnny Carey, who learnt of his sacking as Everton boss in a taxi-cab prior to joining Orient.

The first half gave no indication of what was to come when neither side took control in the first 45 minutes; however, what a difference in the second-half. The first O's goal came after 53 minutes when little Norman Deeley nipped to crash the ball home after good work from McDonald and Eddie Lewis. Four minutes later McDonald broke down the left and Gordon Bolland converted his accurate centre. Orient went on the rampage, roared on by the excited crowd, and began to run the League leaders ragged. The third came on 80 minutes when McDonald floated over a free-kick, and Dave Dunmore glanced the ball into the net past goalie Gordon West.

The Orient team left the pitch with the sound of cheering and applause ringing in their ears, and how well deserved it was, for theirs had been a truly inspiring week, having beaten the likes of Manchester United and Everton in a matter of four days.
Leyton Orient: Robertson, Charlton, Lewis, Lucas, Bishop, Lea, Deeley, Bolland, Dunmore, Graham, McDonald.
Everton: West, Meagan, Thomson, Sharples, Labone, Harris, Bingham, Stevens, Young, Vernon, Morrissey.
Referee: T.W. Dawes
Attendance: 21,756

---

17 October 1962
Leyton Orient 9 Chester 2

The Fourth Division visitors came to Brisbane Road on a foggy Wednesday evening to play a third-round football League Cup tie without their hot-shot centre-forward Ron Davies, who had been sold to Luton Town for £10,000 just a few days before.

Orient took time off from their First Division campaign to give a severe beating to their opponents. Twenty-one-year-old George Waites opened the scoring with a close-range effort after seven minutes.

For nearly half an hour there was little between the two teams, and, in fact, Chester could have taken the lead but Bill Myerscough blasted the ball over the bar. Then the O's took control; on 37 minutes Dave Dunmore unleashed a 20-yarder into the net.

Dunmore laid on a third for Norman Deeley, who had no trouble side-footing the ball past the advancing Chester 'keeper John Hardie.

After the break, Orient turned on the heat and the flood gates opened, and it was only the brave goalkeeping of 6ft 2in Scottish-born Hardie that prevented the score reaching cricketing proportions. The O's scored their fourth within a few seconds of the restart when Malcolm Graham went clean through the defence to score.

Dunmore added a fifth with the pick of the goals, a scorching, low 30-yarder. Nine minutes later Graham pounced for the sixth. On 73 minutes Waites thumped in number seven, and eight minutes later he completed his hat-trick, his first goal since his transfer back from Norwich City.

Chester had the audacity to pull one back when John Gregson scored with a neat effort on 83 minutes, but there was still time for Graham to complete his hat-trick. With two minutes remaining Myerscough scored a second goal for the visitors, a soft goal which the O's goalie Bill Robertson should have stopped.

Orient gave a first-team debut to 17-year-old left-winger Roger Wedge, who was the only O's forward on the night not to have scored. Wedge was never seen again in the first team.

Leyton Orient: Robertson, Charlton, Taylor, Gibbs, Bishop, Lea, Deeley, Waites, Dunmore, Graham, Wedge.
Chester: Hardie, Molyneux, Fleming, Wilson, Butler, Corbishley, Gregson, Myerscough, Fitzgerald, Clarke, Jones.
Referee: J.E. Cooke
Attendance: 7,428

---

15 September 1969
Orient 2 Bradford City 1

This was a magnificent game and both teams are to be complimented on the high standard of football and a good sporting contest. It took City just seven minutes to open the scoring when the O's failed to clear their lines, and Barry Swallow volleyed home. Orient missed a great opportunity to equalise after 18 minutes when Ron Bayliss handled Peter Brabrook's cross, but goalie Pat Linney smothered Terry Mancini's spot-kick. After strong pressure, Mickey Bullock levelled the score, turning in Mick Jones's cross on 28 minutes. Orient had the edge, both at the end of the first half and at the start of the second half, with both teams playing splendid attacking football. Then on 76 minutes Jimmy Bloomfield's lads snatched a winner. Linney mishandled Dennis Rofe's cross, and 18-year-old Barrie Fairbrother pounced to score, and the young striker almost added another soon after.

Orient just about deserved the two points, but few would have begrudged City a point for their grand display. The referee John Osborne and his linesman joined in the applause for the players, as did the policemen on duty and even the hot-dog salesmen and the like. It was that kind of match.

Orient: Goddard, Jones, Rofe, Taylor, Mancini, Harper, Bullock, Fairbrother, Allen, Dyson, Brabrook.
Bradford City: Linney, Bayliss, Cooper, Stowell, Hallett, Swallow, Hall, Ham, Corner, McConnell, Bannister.
Referee: J. Osborne
Attendance: 7,365

---

26 February 1972
Orient 3 Chelsea 2

Having overcome Jimmy Bloomfield's First Division outfit Leicester City at Filbert Street in the fourth round of the FA Cup by 2–0, Orient had to take on another side from the top flight at home, the star-studded Chelsea side, managed by former O's player and manager Dave Sexton, in the fifth round.

In the early stages the O's seemed to be chasing shadows as the boys from south London made all the running on a muddy pitch, which did not prevent some grand football being played.

It was no surprise when Chelsea took the lead through former O's favourite David Webb, who beat Ray Goddard with a looping header on 27 minutes from a Peter Houseman centre.

Chelsea were in full control and scored a second goal in the 36th minute when Peter Osgood headed home a Charlie Cook well-flighted corner.

Then came the start of the turn around in fortunes. On the stroke of half-time, the ground erupted as

Phil Hoadley, latching on to a loose ball, hammered a glorious 30-yard drive into the net, and even though Peter Bonetti touched the ball he could not stop it fizzing into the net. The goal came at the perfect time to give George Petchey's boys a lift during the break.

Orient were level within three minutes of the restart, when Peter Allen's long pass into the Chelsea penalty area saw both Webb and Bonetti momentarily hesitate, and the ball spun off Webb's foot, straight into the path of Mickey Bullock, who gleefully side footed the ball home from four yards

It was Orient, having gained in confidence, who were now looking the more dangerous with their long passes to the front men, and the O's midfield trio of Peter Allen, Barry Dyson and Tom Walley were now dictating the game.

With just 60 seconds remaining, Bullock cleverly controlled a clearance and touched the ball to Walley, who sent a great ball through the middle. Bonetti came out as Bowyer ran on and the ball broke loose to Fairbrother, who clipped it into the net with defender Webb sprawling in the mud. A number of fans ran on to the pitch to mob their hero Fairbrother.

The cameras were clicking from all angles in order to capture one of Orient's greatest goals for posterity.

In the last seconds, well, it was sheer pandemonium: the O's fans were cheering and celebrating victory and the Chelsea supporters invaded the pitch in an effort to get the game stopped, holding up play for a few minutes. The game was restarted and the O's players seemed to lose concentration, and Chelsea nearly equalised with almost the last kick of the match when Webb scooped the ball over the bar.

At the final whistle, Orient supporters celebrated a famous victory, and the Chelsea boss Dave Sexton congratulated the Orient players and manager George Petchey on a fine win.

That evening the whole country could experience the excitement when BBC *Match of the Day* showed the highlights of the match.

Orient: Goddard, Hoadley, Bennett, P. Harris, Rofe, Allen, Dyson, Walley, Fairbrother, Bullock, Bowyer (Brisley 90 mins).

Chelsea: Bonetti, Mulligan, Dempsey, Webb, R. Harris, Hudson, Hollins, Kember, Cooke, Osgood, Houseman.

Referee: R. Tinkler

Attendance: 30,329

---

24 February 1973
Orient 4 Aston Villa 0

Orient were at the start of an excellent run of home form in the Second Division, and this victory was as decisive as the score suggests as the O's treated their fans to a sparkling performance. Gerry Queen opened the scoring on eight minutes after a clever move.

Villa posed little threat, and the O's should have added more goals in the first half. The second goal only came in the first minute of the second half from a Paul Harris header after a Terry Brisley corner-kick.

The rest of the match was a joy for the O's fans as they watched their team turn on the magic and totally outplay the boys from the Midlands. Transfer-listed Barrie Fairbrother netted two further goals to complete the tally, and Ian Bowyer almost added a fifth just before the end. It would be unfair to pick out players in this grand team display, but Fairbrother and Bowyer were both superb.

Orient: Goddard, Hoadley, Wall, Bennett, Harris, Brisley, Allen, Heppolette, Fairbrother, Bowyer, Queen. Sub: Bullock (unused).

Aston Villa: Cumbes, Robson, Aitken, Rioch, Nicholl, Ross (Lochhead), Graydon, Brown, Evans, Vowden, Little.

Referee: C. Nicholls

Attendance: 9,085

14 March 1978
Orient 2 Middlesbrough 1

This was another of Orient's most memorable and emotional occasions in their FA Cup history. They continued their fine run in the FA Cup that season, with a superb performance at First Division Middlesbrough, to gain a 0–0 draw and replay in this sixth-round encounter.

Boro manager John Neal vowed that his team would make amends for failing to win the first tie, and few O's fans really expected them to reach the semi-final.

Barely five minutes had elapsed when Orient took the lead with a stunning goal. Phil Hoadley pushed the ball to Peter Kitchen, who was well marked, and, with his back to goal, he flicked it into the air and then he hooked an amazing shot over his shoulder from more than 20 yards – a goal that Kitchen himself described as the best career goal he had ever scored – he turned to see the ball spinning into the roof of the net and away he went, hand raised in celebration.

The goal gave the O's great confidence as they powered forward, and their reward came in the 12th minute when David Payne sent a pass through to Joe Mayo, who took the ball ahead before hitting what looked a speculative zippy shot from fully 25 yards. The ball bounced just before it reached the Boro goalie Jim Platt, and it spun over his arm and high into the net for the second goal.

The crowd continually roared as the O's went in search of a third and decisive goal, but at the break the score remained 2–0. In the second half the third nearly came when a Kevin Godfrey shot was deflected off a Boro defender's boot, going just inches over the bar.

The Boro players, now under pressure, were making some crude tackles, but with just five minutes remaining Dave Armstrong scored for the visitors after a goalmouth scramble. Despite this set-back, the O's players saw out the final minutes without any trouble.

It was an occasion to savour for all Orient fans, for their club had made it to the semi-final of the FA Cup to play the mighty Arsenal at Stamford Bridge for the first time in their history, and although the match was lost 3–0, letting the occasion get to them, it had been a really tremendous FA Cup journey.

Orient: Jackson, Fisher, Gray, Hoadley, Roeder, Roffey, Grealish, Payne, Godfrey, Mayo, Kitchen.

Middlesbrough: Platt, Craggs, Ramage, Boam, Bailey, Mahoney, Armstrong, McAndrew, Cummins (Johnston), Ashcroft, Mills.

Referee: J. Hunting

Attendance: 18,051

---

20 October 1987
Leyton Orient 8 Rochdale 0

Orient moved into second place in Division Four with this emphatic win against lowly Rochdale. They had slightly the better exchanges up until the 19th minute when Mark Smalley shot home following an Alan Comfort corner. From here on there was no holding the O's. Paul Shinners soon added a second from a poor back pass and then Kevin Hales added two further goals, the first from a penalty after 36 minutes, and then his second with a 20-yard drive, for a comfortable 4–0 half-time lead.

The scoring spree continued after the break with a goal from full-back Kevin Dickenson and two from Alan Comfort. There were still 15 minutes remaining when Shinners headed in number eight.

Orient looked in devastating form that night and seemed a good bet for promotion, but somehow they managed to only end up in eighth position.

Goal chart: Smalley (19 minutes), Shinners (33 and 75), Hales (36 pen, 44), Dickenson (60), Comfort (62, 72).

Leyton Orient: Wells, Howard, Dickenson, Smalley, Day, Hales, Castle (Sussex 87 mins), Godfrey (Harvey 74 mins), Shinners, Hull, Comfort.

Rochdale: Welsh, Lomax, Hampton, Mycock, Bramhall, Smart, Parker, Simmonds, Parlane, Coyle, Gavin. Subs not used: Holden, Hughes.
Referee: W.K. Burge
Attendance: 2,995

---

3 June 1989
Leyton Orient 2 Wrexham 1

A well earned 0–0 draw in North Wales on Thursday 30 May, in the first leg of the Division Four Play-off Final, made for a very tense atmosphere for all concerned in the second leg at Brisbane Road.

At the start both teams were showing a lot of tension and there were few clear-cut chances at either end. The match was nearing the interval when good play on the left-wing by Alan Comfort led to Orient taking the lead. The ball was helped on to Lee Harvey, and without hesitation the fair-haired winger slammed a magnificent 20-yard shot into the far corner of the net past Salmon.

The second half had been running just two minutes when Jon Bowden darted in to head home from close range to put Wrexham on level terms. This was a real blow to Orient's hopes, and the match seemed destined for extra-time and the possibility of the Welsh side going through on the away-goals rule, when on 82 minutes Steve Baker fed Harvey through on the right-wing, who crossed the ball and Mark Cooper hooked the ball into the net for the winner.

After the final whistle the scenes were reminiscent of the previous promotion years of 1956, 1962 and 1970. Despite gaining promotion via the Play-offs, the team were really good enough for this honour and deserved their success.

Leyton Orient: Heald, Baker, Dickenson (Ward 17 mins), Sitton, Day, Hales, Harvey, Howard, Castle, Cooper, Comfort. Sub not used: Hull.
Wrexham: Salmon, Salathiel, Wright, Hunter, Beaumont, Jones, Thackeray, Flynn, Kearns, Russell, Bowden Subs: Buxton, G. Cooper.
Referee: J.E. Martin
Attendance: 13,355

---

28 December 1991
Leyton Orient 4 Brentford 2

Brentford came to Brisbane Road as Division Three leaders, but Orient looked the better team in what turned out to be, in the latter stages, a highly explosive match. The match saw the return to Brisbane Road of old favourite Kevin Godfrey.

The O's winger Greg Berry opened the scoring after six minutes, but it took Brentford, through Les Luscombe, just five minutes to equalise. The same two players scored again, Berry on 18 minutes and Luscombe levelling on 30 minutes.

When Adrian Whitbread had to leave the field shortly before half-time, the O's moved Berry to left-back. Many felt this was a strange move, with Berry looking so dangerous in attack; however, it made no difference, and two minutes after the interval Steve Castle restored Orient's lead.

Despite a few attacks by the Bees, O's substitute Andy Jones sealed the game with a goal on 70 minutes to make it 4–2. About five minutes before the final whistle there was a big flare-up when a player fouled Kenny Achampong, who retaliated, and suddenly there was a big brawl involving 16 players. When calm had been restored, Achampong was sent off by referee David Elleray, which seemed very unfair as in truth any one of at least 10 players could have been shown the red card; however, it was a good victory for the O's and manager Peter Eustace could be satisfied with the effort and skill of his team.

It is not very often that you hear a home crowd booing the referee off the field after their team had gained such an emphatic win, such was the anger of the O's fans. The match attracted the O's highest League crowd since their return to Division Three.

The O's boss Eustace stated after the match 'I have no idea why Kenny was the only player to be sent off. I think five or six others could have gone as well.'

Leyton Orient: Turner, Howard, Hackett, Whitbread (Burnett 37 mins), Day, Castle, Achampong, Berry, Cooper, Nugent (Jones 75 mins), Otto.

Brentford: Benstead, Bates, Rostron, Millen, Evans, Ratcliffe, Sealy, Godfrey, Luscombe, Smillie, Buckle. Subs: Manuel, Holdsworth.

Referee: D. Elleray

Attendance: 7,347

---

15 January 1992
Leyton Orient 4 Oldham Athletic 2

Occasionally Brisbane Road has been set alight by one of those electric evenings where the on-the-pitch happenings set the pulse racing: this was one such occasion.

Oldham Athletic, a top team at the time in Division One, managed by Joe Royle, were in for a rude shock in this FA Cup third-round replay. The O's had already drawn 1–1 at Boundary Park, and, being two divisions above the Londoners, Oldham were expected to cruise past the O's. The Lancashire outfit were in fact one goal ahead when the half-time whistle sounded through Adams.

Orient surged forward after the resumption, and a Lee Harvey cross-come-shot levelled the scores after centre-half Marshall missed the ball and it trickled past goalie Hallworth and into the net. Orient then began to call all the shots when Kevin Nugent slotted home after good play on the left by Greg Berry. Excitement was mounting when the O's fans began to sense a famous victory. However, Roger Palmer had other ideas, not that he knew much about the goal, and he equalised on 80 minutes. Marshall's shot was cleared by Keith Day, but his clearance hit Palmer and bounced into the net.

Orient were not to be denied, and during extra-time Steve Castle put the O's back in front with a twice-taken penalty after 95 minutes. Jobson had body-checked Jones in the box, and from the first spot-kick Hallworth saved it, but an Oldham player had moved into the box and Castle converted the re-take. Even though Oldham threw five men forward in attack, victory was sealed by Kevin Nugent when he picked up a poor back pass from Jobson, and waltzed through 13 minutes from time to score for a 4–2 victory. Joyous scenes followed the final whistle, and the O's supporters celebrated another famous FA Cup victory.

The O's boss Peter Eustace said 'There were a lot of 19 and 20-year-old legs out there, it was the biggest night of their footballing lives, and they came through it very very well.'

Leyton Orient: Turner, Howard, Hackett, Burnett, Day, Whitbread, Harvey (Taylor 73 mins), Castle, Jones, Nugent, Berry. Subs not used: Otto.

Oldham Athletic: Hallworth, Fleming, Bernard, Henry, Barrett, Jobson, Adams, Marshall, Sharp, Palmer, Holden.

Referee: S.J. Lodge

Attendance: 10,056

---

8 March 1997
Brighton & Hove Albion 4 Leyton Orient 4

The match at Brighton was quite a remarkable affair. It will go down as the match that had everything and was possibly the most entertaining match of the past few decades.

It had eight goals, umpteen chances, bookings, a controversial sending-off, pitch invasion and three O's players attacked by a number of idiotic, so-called Brighton fans.

Brighton were bottom of the table, and Orient were also fighting for safety in the relegation zone. The memoirs of the match are listed:

3.00pm – Crowd congestion delays kick-off.
3.05pm – Over 9,000 are eventually packed in, their biggest crowd of the season.
3.10pm – Craig Maskell lifts the ball over the O's goalie Luke Weaver to open the scoring for the Seagulls.
3.11pm – Alec Inglethorpe misses a good chance to equalise.
3.12pm – Maskell's glancing header makes it 2–0.
3.19pm – Inglethorpe goes wide with a header.
3.21pm – Weaver saves from Stuart Storer.
3.31pm – Lee Hodges fires from over 25-yards for the O's.
3.35pm – Carl Griffiths has a penalty appeal turned down after being dragged down in the box.
3.40pm – Scott McGleish and Ian Baird go close at either end.
3.48pm – Mark Warren, the O's defender, is restrained after being held by Baird.
3.51pm – Weaver pulls down Brighton's Paul McDonald in the box, but the penalty appeal is declined. The half-time whistle goes and it is 2–0 to Brighton.
3.55pm – The home crowd sings 'it's just like watching Brazil', and the O's fans think this could be a thrashing.
4.07pm – Ray Wilkins takes control of the midfield; Griffiths side-foots home a Hodges cross, 2–1.
4.10pm – Inglethorpe glances home a Channing cross for the O's, 2–2.
4.13pm – Warren is booked for a bad tackle.
4.15pm – Griffiths has a goal ruled out for a trip.
4.17pm – Griffiths makes it 3–2, scoring from a Baker cross.
4.19pm – Baird has a goal ruled out for climbing on to an O's defender.
4.22pm – Inglethorpe plants a header just over the bar.
4.27pm – The O's boss is booed for not passing the ball back to a Brighton player.
4.35pm – Baird climbs to head home for Brighton, 3–3.
4.36pm – The O's play one-touch football, McGleish to Wilkins to Baker to Griffiths, and McGleish makes it 4–3, prompting a pitch invasion by the Brighton hooligans, who start kicking McGleish and Wilkins, police cart off the offenders, and play resumes after five minutes.
4.46pm – Danny Chapman slides into Maskell in the box, first the referee awards a corner, but he dramatically changes his mind and awards a penalty.
4.47pm – Referee spots Warren pushing Baird before the penalty is taken. Warren is shown a red card.
4.48pm – McDonald shoots past Weaver from the penalty spot, 4–4.
4.50pm – Maskell shoots into the side netting for the home side.
4.52pm – Brighton force two quick corners.
4.55pm – O's defender Chapman clears off the line with Weaver beaten.
4.56pm – Final whistle goes and the match ends 4–4.

The O's boss Taylor gave his verdict on the match: 'It was unbelievable, during the second half I told the lads to go out there and play with a bit of spirit and get into them, and to their credit they tore Brighton apart. During that second-half I turned round to ask what the score was. I didn't know if we were winning, losing or what was going on.'

Taylor said 'O's were rocked back in the closing minutes after the pitch attack, and the referee buckled under the pressure to firstly giving a dubious penalty and then the Warren sending-off. It was reported that Orient players could be hauled before the FA following accusations that they incited the pitch invasion at Brighton.'

However, as far as Orient were concerned two fans attacked three of their players, McGleish, Wilkins and Hodges, after their fourth goal went in. The O's boss Taylor fiercely defended his players and said he would kick Brighton out of the League. They already had two points deducted for a pitch invasion against Lincoln in October 1996. Taylor fumed, 'Three of my players got struck by people who invaded the pitch. It's ludicrous to blame Orient. I was worried about my players and myself. Aren't you allowed to celebrate a goal now?'

The coolest head during Saturday's mayhem was the O's former England International Ray Wilkins who even prevented one fan from getting to the referee with a deft trip.

Wilkins said 'It's taken the gloss off what was a super game. It's very sad.'

The O's chairman Barry Hearn is ranking the match alongside some of his all-time boxing classics. He raved 'It was the most amazing 90 minutes of football I've ever seen in my life.'

The FA did hold an inquiry and both clubs were severely warned as to their future conduct, but no further action was taken, but many thought that Brighton should have lost their League status or had points deducted over the incident.

Brighton & Hove Albion: Rust, Humphrey (Johnson), Tuck, Reinelt, Allan, Hobson, Storer, Peake, Baird, Maskell, McDonald.

Leyton Orient: Weaver, Channing (McCarthy 83 mins), Naylor, Chapman, Warren, Wilkins (Ling 89 mins), Hodges, Griffiths (Hanson 88 mins), Inglethorpe, McGleish, Baker.

Referee: F. Stretton

Attendance: 9,298

---

29 May 1999
Leyton Orient 0 Scunthorpe United 1

The Division Three Play-off Final at Wembley Stadium started off in sunshine before nearly 37,000 fans. Orient took it to Scunthorpe United, and the first chance came when a Steve Watts header flashed just wide. Then both Amara Simba and Matt Lockwood had shots blocked. But in Scunthorpe's very first attack they took the lead. Good play by Gareth Sheldon on the left-wing put the O's under pressure and from his cross Alex Calvo-Garcia headed the ball just inside Scott Barrett's inside post, with no chance of him getting to the ball.

After the goal the O's seemed to resort to long, high balls into the penalty area, with little threat to Scunthorpe's goal, and neither side looked likely to find the net.

The O's manager Tommy Taylor decided to change things around in the second-half with both Tony Richards and Stuart Hicks being replaced by veteran Craig Maskell and Alex Inglethorpe, and the O's players stepped it up in an effort for a quick equaliser, and they dominated the second half. The two substitutes made a big, immediate impression and there were several near chances around the Scunthorpe goal, all of which were scrambled away and would just not go into the net.

Time appeared to be running out for the O's, and, with just a few minutes remaining, Inglethorpe ran on to a Simba prodded pass, but he was at an angle and his powerful strike was parried away by goalkeeper Evans.

With the O's committed to attack, Scunthorpe almost scored a second goal, but Barrett and then Martin Ling somehow managed to keep the ball out of the net with superb stops.

The final whistle blew, and Orient were beaten 1–0 and were left to reflect on what might have been; the players were devastated. Orient's second-half performance certainly deserved a goal, but it was not meant to be. Scunthorpe defended stoutly and had a long spell when 'lady luck' appeared on their side, but that's football, and Orient hoped for better things in the new millennium.

Leyton Orient: Barrett, R. Joseph, Lockwood, Smith, Hicks (Inglethorpe 46 mins), Clark, Ling, Richards (Maskell 46 mins), Watts, Simba, Beall.

Scunthorpe United: Evans, Wilcox, Dawson, Logan, Harlsey, Hope, Walker, Forrester (Bull), Gayle (Stamp), Sheldon, Calvo-Garcia (Housham).

Referee: C. Wilkes

Attendance: 36,985

---

6 May 2001
Leyton Orient 2 Hull City 0

For the first leg of the Play-off semi-final, played on a warm day at Boothferry Park on 13 May, O's boss Tommy Taylor played a defensive pattern, but on 69 minutes John Eyre, who had only been on the pitch for five minutes, seemed to control a Dean Smith clearance with his hand, but, amid Orient's protests, he drove home the all-important winner from 25 yards past Ashley Bayes before 13,310 fans.

So to the second leg at Brisbane Road three days later, and the pattern of play was much as expected with the visitors out to defend their lead.

It was Scott Houghton down the left wing who caused the Hull defence most trouble, and from one of his crosses Paul Musselwhite tipped over a Steve Watts header. As time went by, the anxiety began to show on the Orient players with both McGhee and Castle getting booked.

However, with just seconds remaining of the first half, a poor Hull clearance after a mix-up between Eyre and giant striker Kevin Francis was picked up by Houghton midway inside the visitors half, and, as three O's forwards ran back from offside positions, Watts made a forward run to meet Houghton's precise cross to head past Musselwhite and level the scores on aggregate at one each.

The O's manager Tommy Taylor made his first change of the night on 66 minutes when Andy Harris replaced veteran Steve Castle, and the goal that settled the match came just four minutes later when Matt Lockwood picked up the ball in the centre of the pitch and ran straight down the middle to unleash from fully 30 yards with his left foot, and it flew past Musselwhite into the top right-hand corner. The stadium erupted as the final at the Millennium Stadium in Cardiff seemed very close.

A jubilant Steve Watts has just scored to make it all square in the second leg against Hull City.

Barry Hearn was obviously confident that Orient were going to the Millennium Stadium.

The O's defence held firm, and with just seconds remaining of the four minutes of added time a cross came over into the Orient box with Bayes and his defenders looking at each other until Matthew Joseph took control to hoof the ball over for a corner. Hull had one last chance to level the aggregate scores, and all of the 22 players were in the O's penalty box, the ball was cleared and the referee Pugh blew his whistle before any player could take advantage of Hull's empty net. The scenes were one of jubilation, with the ground being rocked by the post match anthem of *Rocking all over the World* followed by a reprise of the club anthem of *Tijuana Taxi* by Herb Alpert and his Tijuana Brass all fired up by DJ Buono.

Hull fought hard, but this was Orient's night, and a great one for the players, officials and fans who combined to make it something special that no one who was present will ever forget.

And so it was off to the Play-off Final in Cardiff to face Blackpool, but with two of their strikers, Griffiths and Watts, suspended it was not going to be easy.

Leyton Orient: Bayes, Joseph, Lockwood, Smith, McGhee, Downer, Ibehre (Tate 86 mins), Castle (Harris 67 mins), Walschaerts, Watts, Houghton (Brkovic 87 mins).

Hull City: Musselwhite, Edwards, Whitney, Whittle, Greaves, Matthews (Brown 69 mins), Atkins, Brabin, Holt (Philpott 38 mins), Francis (Rowe), Eyre.

Referee: D. Pugh

Attendance: 9,419

---

26 May 2001
Leyton Orient 2 Blackpool 4

The crowd of nearly 24,000, rather disappointing for this Division Three Play-off Final, who were hardly settled in their seats after being delayed by a traffic jam on the M25 motorway, witnessed the O's dream

In front of a crowd of 23,600 fans, Tommy Taylor leads the players out for the Division Three Play-off Final.

start, when after only 27 seconds a hopeful punt downfield by Jabo Ibehre was knocked back by a Blackpool defender to goalie Phil Barnes, but he slipped on the lush surface as he teed up the ball to make a clearance upfield. It was Chris Tate who was running in to pressure the expected kick that was able to take the ball around Barnes and slip it into an empty net, recording the fastest goal scored at the Millennium Stadium.

Orient's defence seemed untroubled, but then on 34 minutes the scores were level when from a corner-kick Hughes was unmarked and easily headed in past Bayes. The defending was abysmal.

To their credit, the O's came storming back and went ahead three minutes later when, from a Matt Lockwood corner, the ball came to him, and he hit the ball across field to Scott Houghton, who fired home past Barnes for a 2–1 lead. He ran straight over to the O's crowd to celebrate in style.

With just seconds of the interval remaining, Blackpool were level again from a poorly-defended corner. The ball was turned in at the far post by Reid.

The second half started with the O's on the attack from an Andy Harris pass. Houghton gathered the ball in midfield, beat a Blackpool player and slipped the ball to Ibehre on the left wing. The youngster ran on and cut into the box, wrong-footed two defenders and, with a deft touch, slipped the ball past goalie Barnes, only to see the ball hit the upright and bounce clear.

This was the last moment of the match for the O's; from then on the Blackpool midfield took a strong grip on the game, and the O's seldom looked like scoring. In one rare attack, Houghton stumbled over the ball, the ball went to Blackpool midfielder Wellens, he raced clear, and, with the O's defence stretched, the ball was passed to Simpson, who slotted home past Bayes for a 3–2 lead.

Scott Houghton celebrates after putting the O's 2–1 ahead.

With the O's now committed to attack, Hills set up big striker Brett Ormerod, and he netted easily on 88 minutes for a 4–2 victory, so in the end it was the O's defence who could not cope with the corner-kicks of Blackpool and their strike power and so left Orient still trying to find a way out of the lower reaches of the Football League.

The O's boss Tommy Taylor stated after the match 'It was like Wembley all over again – the second half was like a mirror image of the first-half at Wembley two years ago. We got caught out at set pieces, something that hasn't happened at all this season. I can't fault the players for their effort today.'

Leyton Orient: Bayes, Joseph, Lockwood, Smith, Downer, Harris, Walschaerts (Castle 67 mins), McGhee, Houghton (Martin 82 mins), Ibehre, Tate (Brkovic 66 mins).

Blackpool: Barnes, Hills, Parkinson, Hughes, Reid, Coid, Wellens (M. Milligan 90 mins), Clarkson, Simpson (J. Milligan 90 mins), Ormerod (Thompson 90 mins), J. Murphy.

Referee: D. Pugh

Attendance: 23,600

5 January 2002
Portsmouth 1 Leyton Orient 4

A visit to Fratton Park for this third-round FA Cup tie looked a difficult one, even though Pompey were struggling in the First Division.

The home team held the upper hand in the first half and led after 12 minutes when O's skipper Dean Smith turned Courtney Pitt's cross into his own goal, as their big 6ft 7in centre-forward Peter Crouch caused confusion in the penalty area, and from then on in it was all one-way traffic to Scott Barrett's goal.

However, in the second half it was a totally different story when the O's turned on a scintillating display to dump Portsmouth unceremoniously out of the Cup.

It took Orient less than two minutes to equalise. Wayne Gray was shoved over by Scott Hiley, and, while the Japanese international goalkeeper Yoshikatsu Kawaguchi was organising his defence, Dean Smith stepped up to curl the ball home from 25 yards and send the O's travelling contingent of 1,468 fans wild.

Three minutes later the home fans thought they had regained the lead when Crouch had touched home a cross from the former Croatian World Cup star Robert Prosinecki, but the linesman had his flag up for offside.

O's midfield trio of Minton, Martin and an inspirational Andy Harris were running the show, and in the 66th minute they went ahead. Harris played a long ball down the middle, and Steve Watts ran past two defenders to chip past Kawaguchi from 15 yards.

Ten minutes later Gray almost sealed the Cup tie. He picked a long Barrett goal-kick, holding off his marker before placing the ball into the bottom right-hand corner of the goal from 18 yards, which saw a mass exodus of home fans, who missed the O's fourth goal in the final minute.

Mikele Leigertwood ran down the left touchline and on the halfway line he passed to Minton, who advanced towards the box and slid a cross to Iyseden Christie, who gleefully smashed the ball into the net.

They say the FA Cup is full of fairytales, and it certainly was for the O's, and in particular Christie, sidelined for 15 months with a leg injury, who came on as a sub in the 88th minute and with his first kick scored a great goal.

The O's fans were happy travelling home that night, as was the O's chairman Barry Hearn, who told Sky Sports live from the club coach 'Well, as we all know, football is a funny game'. The following week the O's went to struggling Division Three side Carlisle United and got thrashed 6–1.

Portsmouth: Kawaguchi, O'Neill (Derry 78 mins), Tiler, Primus, Hiley (Crowe 80 mins), Harper, Prosinecki, Quashie, Pitt, Lovell, Crouch.

Leyton Orient: Barrett, McGhee, Smith, Leigertwood, Dorrian (Barnard 45 mins), Harris, Minton, Martin, Jones, Watts (Christie 88 mins), Gray (Ibehre 90 mins).

Referee: P. Prosser

Attendance: 12,936

---

23 October 2004
Lincoln City 3 Leyton Orient 4

It's not very often that you would see an O's team trailing three times away from home and still come out on top. Well, that is what did happen in this remarkable Coca-Cola League Two fixture at Sincil Bank, with the irrepressible Lee Steele bagging a hat-trick to keep the O's, at the time, in second position in the table. Yet the game did not start too well, with the home team going ahead after just a minute through Gareth McAuley, who headed home unchallenged.

Orient were level within 10 minutes when Steele scored from a tap in after a fine O's move, when Stuart Wardley headed against the bar from a Wayne Carlisle cross.

However, after sloppy defending by the O's, Simon Yeo nipped for Lincoln's second. Seven minutes before the break the O's were level again when Jabo Ibehre volleyed home from a Michael Simpson cross.

Just a minute after the break, the home side were ahead again when McAuley headed home from a free-kick. Orient got more into the game and 13 minutes from time Steele got his second when he headed home from a Lockwood free-kick.

There were less than 30 seconds remaining on the clock when Lockwood strongly carried the ball forward from defence. He put a vintage ball through, splitting the Lincoln defence, Steele timing his run perfectly and arriving to the ball before goalie Alan Marriott, and he planted it into the net for a remarkable 4–3 win.

This was a truly unique match witnessed by 543 elated O's fans, and the after-match scenes were something to behold, especially when Steele ran towards and greeted the O's fans, holding the match ball aloft for one of the more memorable O's moments in recent seasons, and it will remain planted in the memory for those who were fortunate enough to witness it.

On the bench for Lincoln was the former O's and Northern Ireland international player Ciaran Toner.

Lincoln City: Marriott, Sandwith, Morgan, Butcher, Yeo (Peat 74 mins), Carruthers (McNamara 74 mins), Gain, Bloomer, McAuley, McCombe, Green.

Leyton Orient: Harrison, Lockwood, Simpson, White, Zakuani, Carlisle (Newey 69 mins), Steele, Scott, Miller, Wardley (Hunt 69 mins), Ibehre.

Referee: T. Leake

Attendance: 4,246

Travelling in style: Leyton Orient's leading goalscorer for 2005–06 Gary Alexander on his way to a match on the London Underground against Fulham in the FA Cup.

9 January 2006
Fulham 1 Leyton Orient 2

The O's were drawn out of the hat with a plumb tie at Premiership side Fulham, and with more than 6,000 fans sitting in the Putney end of Craven Cottage – almost half of the 13,339 attendance – and with the team

A sensational win for the Orient team.

on top form, the Cottagers seemed ripe for the taking and even their manager Chris Coleman appeared a worried man during the week when speaking to the press. Maybe many of their fans felt the same and stayed away?

Orient took the lead on 16 minutes when the Premiership side's new signing, the New Zealand international player Simon Elliott, failed to clear a Joe Keith cross from the left. Craig Easton, who was having a brilliant game, shot powerfully and the ball found the top right-hand corner of the net, which deflected past goalkeeper Tony Warner off Elliott's boot.

With the O's full of confidence and spurred on by their vocal fans, it was no surprise that they would take a two-goal advantage a minute before half-time, with Elliott once again at fault when losing the ball to Justin Miller about 40 yards out, who quickly passed to Gary Alexander, who then gave it to Joe Keith whose shot was slightly deflected by Liam Rosenior's boot on its way past Warner.

Whatever Fulham manager Chris Coleman said to his boys at half-time, it certainly worked; four minutes after the break they pulled a goal back when Rosenior found himself in space. He passed to Collins John, who beat Gabriel Zakuani and easily beat goalie Garner.

Then on 67 minutes the O's defence was caught sleeping, and when Luis Boa Morte got into the box he was shoved over by Zakuani and referee Peter Walton awarded a penalty. Up stepped Collins John to take the spot-kick, but his effort was saved by Garner to the delight of the O's players and fans.

The O's held out for another memorable and most famous FA Cup victory of their 102 years of playing in the competition.

Barry Hearn celebrates the FA Cup win over Fulham.

Fulham: Warner, Jensen, Knight, Pearce (Goma), Rosenior, Elliott, Elrich (Timlin), Legwinski, Boa Morte, John, Radzinski
Leyton Orient: Garner, Lockwood, Mackie, Miller, Zakuani, Easton, Keith (Carlisle), Simpson, Tudor (McMahon), Alexander (Barnard), Ibehre.
Referee: P. Walton
Attendance: 13,339

---

6 May 2006
Oxford United 2 Leyton Orient 3

There have been a number of classical, nail-biting games in the history of this grand old club – the games versus Millwall that secured promotion in May 1956, versus Bury in April 1962, versus Aston Villa in May 1974, the Play-off Final against Wrexham in June 1989 and the two recent Play-off Final defeats all spring to mind.

The scene was set as the teams strode onto the pitch. The boys from East London were quick out of the starting blocks, and within two minutes the former O's goalkeeper Billy Turley saved a left-foot volley from Joe Keith and then three minutes later he brilliantly pushed a Lee Steele shot on to a post, and with just 10 minutes on the clock he pulled off another wonder-save from the highly-impressive Wayne Corden.

Surely it was only a matter of time before the O's would score the opening goal. Well football is an unpredictable game, and on 14 minutes the home team won a free-kick in a dangerous area, Andy Burgess delivered a curling kick into the box, and after some sloppy defending there was Eric Sabin, who bundled the ball home past Glyn Garner. Within just three minutes Corden crossed from the right for Scotsman Craig Easton to rise above the Oxford defence and head powerfully towards the goal. It appeared Turley had it covered, but somehow in his attempt to stop the ball he let it squirm from his grasp and clearly go over the line for the equaliser and his first mistake of the match.

The O's were now playing some of their best, free-flowing football with Wayne Corden proving to be a real menace down the right wing with his dribbling skill and powerful shooting, but the O's could not find another way past Turley and the first half ended all-square.

On 64 minutes Alexander latched on to a fine pass from Steele to produce a delightful finish, lobbing Turley as he advanced out of his goal for a 2–1 lead, his first goal in three months.

However, they were soon brought down to earth with a massive bump, when, just two minutes later, Oxford had equalised from another set-piece from Burgess, met by Chris Hargreaves, which was brilliantly stopped by Garner, but in came Chris Willmott to powerfully head into the net.

Then, with 15 minutes of normal time remaining, news was filtering through that Grimsby had a penalty, so the O's needed another goal to ensure they got the third promotion spot, but it looked like the

Inspirational captain and Player of the Season (and Players' Player of the Season) John Mackie celebrates promotion.

O's had missed the boat when on 74 minutes Oxford striker Steve Basham rose high to a cross and his powerful header seemed to be sneaking into the corner of the right-hand post, but Garner sprang across his goal to push away for a corner.

Then on 85 minutes, after a skirmish in the O's penalty area between Chris Willmott and O's skipper John Mackie, the Oxford man was sent off and Mackie received just a yellow card.

Then came the announcement of five minutes of added time and both teams just went for it in their do-or-die effort; both teams had five up front with no midfield to be seen. Then substitute Jabo Ibehre burst on goal, and with just Turley to beat and two unmarked O's forwards to his right he shot straight at Turley, and a header from Lee Steele went just over.

A gloom descended over the Kassam Stadium and tears were seen from men, women and children, but after three minutes of added time came an amazing twist in the tale: news was coming through of a Northampton goal at Grimsby and a deafening noise erupted from the O's fans when their hopes had been confirmed.

As everything was happening and with just 16 seconds remaining of the match, the ball came out to Gary Alexander down the left, and with three O's players left unmarked in the Oxford penalty area he passed the ball into the path of Lee Steele to gleefully fire past Turley for the third and winning goal, and soon after the final whistle blew. The fans started their chant of 'We Are Going Up' as the O's players and management danced with joy before them.

Oxford United: Turley, Mansell (Brooks 76), Willmott, Dempster, Robinson, Quinn, Hargreaves, Smith (Beechers 89), N'Toya, Sabin (Basham 69), Burgess.

Leyton Orient: Garner, Tann, Mackie, Zakuani, Lockwood, Corden (Ibehre 82), Simpson (McMahon 87), Easton, Keith (Tudor 79), Steele, Alexander.

Referee: Mr. K Woolmer (Northamptonshire)

Attendance: 12,243

Leyton Orient Chairman Barry Hearn celebrates promotion with John Mackie.

Football League Record

1905–06 up to and including 2005–06

	Played	Won	Drawn	Lost	For	Against	Points
Home*	1,938	941	516	481	3,105	2,056	2,674
Away	1,938	363	486	1,827	1,827	3,519	1,336
Totals	3,876	1,304	1,002	1,570	4,932	5,575	4,010

* Includes two League matches played at Wembley Stadium.

Note:
The above totals exclude four promotion Play-off matches in season 1988–89, two at home and two away, and three promotion Play-off matches in season 1998–99, one at home and one away, one Play-off Final match played at Wembley Stadium and three promotion Play-off matches in season 2000–01, one away and one at home, and one Play-off Final at the Millennium Stadium. It also excludes three abandoned matches in 1939–40 when war intervened.

The points total reflects three points deducted due to booking irregularities in season 1997–98.

Number of seasons: 90
Goal difference: -643

Home League Record Ground by Ground

		Played	Won	Drawn	Lost	For	Against	Points
Millfields Road	1905–30	421	219	108	94	633	362	546
Lea Bridge Road	1930–37	145	74	36	35	291	180	184
Wembley Stadium	Nov–Dec 1930	2	2	0	0	6	1	4
Brisbane Road	28 August 1937 to 2005–06	1,370	646	372	352	2,175	1,513	1,940
Totals		1,938	941	516	481	3,105	2,056	2,674

Highest League Wins and Defeats

Highest League wins at home

Score	*Opponents*	*Season*
9–2	Aldershot	1933–34
8–0	Rochdale	1987–88
8–0	Crystal Palace	1955–56
8–0	Colchester United	1988–89
8–0	Doncaster Rovers	1997–98
8–3	Aldershot	1955–56
7–0	Colchester United	1951–52
7–1	Swindon Town	1932–33
7–1	Queen's Park Rangers	1955–56
6–0	Brighton & Hove Albion	1934–35
6–0	Colchester United	1955–56
6–0	Sunderland	1958–59
6–1	Luton Town	1929–30
6–1	Charlton Athletic	1958–59
6–1	Shrewsbury Town	1998–99
6–2	Rotherham United	1957–58

Highest League wins away

Score	*Opponents*	*Season*
7–1	Exeter City	1954–55
7–2	Torquay United	1954–55
5–0	Torquay United	1929–30
5–1	Luton Town	1931–32
5–1	Walsall	1961–62
5–1	Chester City	1999–2000
5–2	Swansea City	1963–64

Highest League defeats at home

Score	*Opponents*	*Season*
2–7	Aldershot	1949–50
3–7	Chelsea	1979–80
2–6	Wimbledon	1983–84
3–6	Portsmouth	1963–64

Highest League defeats away

Score	*Opponents*	*Season*
1–7	Torquay United	1948–49
1–7	Notts County	1949–50
1–7	Stoke City	1956–57
2–7	Grimsby Town	1957–58
0–6	Stockport County	1920–21
0–6	Darlington	1925–26
0–6	Blackpool	1926–27
0–6	Middlesbrough	1926–27
0–6	Watford	1933–34
0–6	Bristol City	1947–48
0–6	Manchester City	1964–65
0–6	Huddesfield Town	1982–83

Other League records 1905–06 to 2003–2004 only

Most Wins in a Season	*Most Draws in a Season*	*Most Defeats in a Season*
1955–56 – 29	1974–75 – 20	1994–95 – 32
1954–55 – 26	1966–67 – 18	1962–63 – 27
1969–70 – 25	1973–74 – 18	1905–06 – 24
2005–06 – 22	1977–78 – 18	1965–66 – 24
1961–62 – 22	1967–68 – 17	1926–27 – 23
1911–12 – 21	1979–80 – 17	1950–51 – 23
1988–89 – 21		1981–82 – 23
1992–93 – 21		1995–96 – 23
1985–86 – 20		1928–29 – 22
1986–87 – 20		1946–47 – 22
		1982–83 – 22
		1984–85 – 22

Highest number of League goals scored in a season

1955–56 – 106
1954–55 – 89
1988–89 – 86
1987–88 – 85
1953–54 – 79
1985–86 – 79
1931–32 – 77
1957–58 – 77
1959–60 – 76
1933–34 – 75
1983–84 – 71

Against other clubs

Opponents		Home					Away					Total		Percentage of		
	P	W	D	L	F	A	W	D	L	F	A	F	A	wins	draws	losses
Aldershot	38	7	2	10	40	40	4	9	6	13	21	53	61	28.95	28.95	42.11
Arsenal	6	2	0	1	3	2	0	1	2	3	6	6	8	33.33	16.67	50.00
Aston Villa	10	2	2	1	6	3	0	1	4	3	8	9	11	20.00	30.00	50.00
Barnet	16	3	4	1	14	9	3	2	3	12	15	26	24	37.50	37.50	25.00
Barnsley	52	18	5	3	53	20	3	4	19	25	55	78	75	40.38	17.31	42.31
Barrow	6	2	0	1	7	4	0	1	2	2	5	9	9	33.33	16.67	50.00
Birmingham City	36	7	7	4	26	22	2	6	10	13	29	39	51	25.00	36.11	38.89
Blackburn Rovers	20	2	7	1	12	7	0	5	5	8	19	20	26	10.00	60.00	30.00
Blackpool	66	17	7	9	40	28	4	10	19	24	66	64	94	31.82	25.76	42.42
Bolton Wanderers	40	9	7	4	28	18	2	4	14	8	27	36	45	27.50	27.50	45.00
Boston United	8	1	1	1	6	5	2	1	1	5	6	11	11	50.00	25.00	25.00
AFC Bournemouth	66	19	10	4	56	20	6	6	21	28	63	84	83	37.88	24.24	37.88
Bradford City	34	9	6	2	25	16	5	4	8	17	29	42	45	41.18	29.41	29.41
Bradord Park Av	16	8	0	0	10	0	1	0	7	5	17	15	17	56.25	0.00	43.75
Brentford	30	5	4	6	22	23	2	2	11	14	34	36	57	23.33	20.00	56.67
Brighton & Hove A	78	22	5	12	69	51	6	13	20	33	58	102	109	35.90	23.08	41.03
Bristol City	82	21	9	11	71	39	3	10	28	26	86	97	125	29.27	23.17	47.56
Bristol Rovers	90	20	11	14	71	65	9	13	23	49	77	120	142	32.22	26.66	41.12
Burnley	46	13	2	8	38	22	5	4	14	18	48	56	70	39.13	13.04	47.83
Burton United	4	1	0	1	1	1	0	0	2	1	3	2	4	25.00	0.00	75.00
Bury	46	13	4	6	36	23	7	6	10	17	30	53	53	43.48	21.73	34.79
Cambridge United	36	8	6	4	27	17	3	3	12	15	29	42	46	30.56	25.00	44.44
Cardiff City	76	18	13	7	74	38	5	11	22	26	65	100	103	30.26	31.58	38.16
Carlisle United	34	10	5	2	22	11	4	1	12	12	30	34	41	41.17	17.66	41.17
Charlton Athletic	36	7	6	5	28	23	5	3	10	18	32	46	55	33.33	30.56	41.67
Chelsea	28	4	2	8	14	23	3	4	7	15	23	29	46	25.00	21.43	53.57
Cheltenham Town	12	2	1	3	5	9	1	3	2	5	7	10	16	25.00	33.33	41.67
Chester City	26	6	3	4	14	13	5	3	5	16	13	30	26	42.30	23.08	34.62
Chesterfield	12	3	2	1	14	7	1	2	3	6	11	20	18	33.33	33.33	33.33
Colchester United	30	7	5	3	39	15	1	7	7	10	20	49	35	26.67	40.00	33.33
Coventry City	38	8	6	5	32	20	1	6	12	14	47	46	67	23.68	31.58	44.74
Crewe Alexandra	16	3	3	2	10	10	2	2	4	13	17	23	27	31.25	31.25	37.50
Crystal Palace	60	15	8	7	48	25	3	9	18	26	48	74	73	30.00	28.33	41.67
Darlington	34	11	3	3	23	17	3	6	8	15	30	38	47	41.17	26.48	32.35
Derby County	44	12	4	6	31	20	5	3	14	18	38	49	58	38.64	15.91	45.45
Doncaster Rovers	22	9	1	1	30	8	3	2	6	14	24	44	32	54.55	13.64	31.82
Everton	2	1	0	0	3	0	0	0	1	0	3	3	3	50.00	0.00	50.00
Exeter City	76	21	10	7	86	46	9	11	18	51	70	137	116	39.47	27.63	32.89
Fulham	82	19	11	11	51	38	9	14	18	41	66	92	104	34.15	30.49	35.37
Gainsborough Trinity	14	6	1	0	14	3	2	1	4	6	10	20	13	57.14	14.29	28.57
Gateshead	18	4	3	2	12	5	0	3	6	5	17	17	22	22.22	33.33	44.44
Gillingham	46	11	5	7	38	27	7	7	9	22	31	60	58	39.13	26.09	34.78
Glossop North End	20	7	2	1	22	6	2	1	7	12	27	34	33	45.00	15.00	40.00
Grimsby Town	50	11	6	8	36	25	5	8	12	25	49	61	74	32.00	28.00	40.00
Halifax Town	18	8	0	1	17	5	2	4	3	10	13	27	18	55.56	22.22	22.22
Hartlepool United	32	9	3	4	29	16	4	4	8	20	28	49	44	40.63	21.88	37.50
Hereford United	14	3	2	2	12	8	2	2	3	12	12	24	20	35.71	28.57	35.71
Huddersfield Town	48	15	3	6	39	25	0	10	14	9	35	48	60	31.25	27.08	41.67
Hull City	86	15	19	9	50	38	6	11	26	36	81	86	119	24.42	34.88	40.70
Ipswich Town	34	7	5	5	29	20	1	6	10	23	42	52	62	23.53	32.35	44.12
Kidderminster Harriers	10	1	3	1	4	5	2	0	3	7	8	11	13	30.00	30.00	40.00
Leeds City	20	5	4	1	11	5	2	2	6	10	20	21	25	35.00	30.00	35.00
Leeds United	16	4	1	3	10	7	1	2	5	5	12	15	19	31.25	18.75	50.00
Leicester City	42	11	2	8	27	17	4	3	14	23	43	50	60	35.71	11.90	52.38
Lincoln City	58	16	7	6	51	25	5	11	13	22	41	73	66	36.20	31.03	32.77

Opponents		*Home*					*Away*					*Total*		*Percentage of*		
	P	*W*	*D*	*L*	*F*	*A*	*W*	*D*	*L*	*F*	*A*	*F*	*A*	*wins*	*draws*	*losses*
Liverpool	14	3	1	3	9	13	0	1	6	6	24	15	37	21.43	14.29	64.29
Luton Town	48	9	10	5	30	21	5	2	17	24	47	54	68	29.17	25.00	45.83
Macclesfield Town	16	5	2	1	13	8	1	1	6	5	11	18	19	37.50	25.00	37.50
Manchester City	14	2	2	3	12	16	0	0	7	5	28	17	44	14.29	14.29	71.43
Manchester United	12	2	1	3	3	5	0	3	3	5	13	8	18	16.67	33.33	50.00
Mansfield Town	46	16	4	3	47	22	6	9	8	26	31	73	53	47.83	28.26	23.91
Merthyr Town	2	1	0	0	1	0	1	0	0	1	0	2	0	100.00	0.00	0.00
Middlesbrough	36	9	6	3	35	15	4	2	12	19	41	54	56	36.11	22.22	41.67
Millwall	48	11	10	3	35	28	5	4	15	16	37	51	65	33.33	29.17	37.50
Milton Keynes Dons	2	0	0	1	2	6	0	1	0	2	2	4	8	0.00	50.00	50.00
Nelson	2	1	0	0	5	1	0	1	0	1	1	6	2	50.00	50.00	0.00
Newcastle United	14	5	1	1	10	6	0	2	5	1	14	11	20	35.71	21.43	42.86
Newport County	44	12	4	6	49	32	4	9	9	24	34	73	66	36.36	29.55	34.01
Northampton Town	66	17	10	6	55	32	6	8	19	32	70	87	102	34.84	27.28	37.88
Norwich City	48	10	7	7	36	31	1	5	18	15	54	51	85	22.92	25.00	52.08
Nottingham Forest	42	5	7	9	23	32	3	7	11	17	33	40	65	19.05	33.33	47.62
Notts County	60	13	9	8	39	34	7	6	17	26	51	65	85	33.33	25.00	41.67
Oldham Athletic	40	10	3	7	37	25	1	7	12	15	41	52	66	27.50	25.00	47.50
Oxford United	32	6	7	3	18	16	4	6	6	22	26	40	42	31.25	37.50	31.25
Peterborough United	24	6	3	3	20	12	5	3	4	14	14	34	26	45.83	25.00	29.17
Plymouth Argyle	48	11	4	9	35	28	3	5	16	20	48	55	76	29.17	18.75	52.08
Port Vale	48	12	5	7	35	24	1	2	21	16	60	51	84	27.08	14.58	58.33
Portsmouth	30	5	5	5	25	25	2	6	7	19	27	44	52	23.33	36.67	40.00
Preston North End	52	11	10	5	40	29	7	8	11	32	43	72	72	34.62	34.62	30.77
QPR	46	9	10	4	47	26	3	4	16	21	51	68	77	26.09	30.43	43.48
Reading	64	15	10	7	60	44	5	8	19	29	73	89	117	31.25	28.13	40.63
Rochdale	32	11	3	2	40	13	7	1	8	25	21	65	34	56.25	12.50	31.25
Rotherham United	54	10	8	9	45	38	3	8	16	23	47	68	85	24.07	29.63	46.31
Rushden & Diamonds	8	2	2	0	9	4	0	0	4	0	6	9	10	25.00	25.00	50.00
Scarborough	12	3	0	3	9	9	1	1	4	6	10	15	19	33.33	8.33	58.33
Scunthorpe United	42	11	8	2	31	15	3	8	10	23	34	54	49	33.34	38.09	28.57
Sheffield United	24	4	4	4	19	17	5	1	6	18	26	37	43	37.50	20.83	41.67
Sheffield Wednesday	30	6	5	4	17	16	2	4	9	10	26	27	42	26.67	30.00	43.33
Shrewsbury Town	48	15	3	6	52	24	5	6	13	27	47	79	71	41.67	18.75	39.58
Southampton	38	10	6	3	28	18	4	3	12	17	39	45	57	36.84	23.68	39.47
Southend United	62	18	8	5	61	30	8	9	14	32	45	93	75	41.94	27.42	30.65
Southport	6	2	0	1	6	4	0	2	1	2	3	8	7	33.33	33.33	33.33
Stockport County	56	15	9	4	55	24	7	8	13	31	53	86	77	39.28	30.36	30.36
Stoke City	40	12	1	7	30	20	7	2	11	19	37	49	57	47.50	7.50	45.00
Sunderland	28	6	5	3	27	16	1	3	10	11	29	38	45	25.00	28.57	46.43
Swansea City	66	17	8	8	58	35	10	8	15	32	49	90	84	40.91	24.24	35.85
Swindon Town	60	16	8	6	45	26	5	10	15	28	59	73	85	35.00	30.00	35.00
Thames Assoc	4	1	1	0	3	2	0	1	1	3	6	6	8	25.00	50.00	25.00
Torquay United	78	24	5	10	72	42	7	14	18	51	75	123	117	39.74	24.36	35.90
Tottenham Hotspur	10	0	2	3	4	13	1	1	3	4	7	8	20	10.00	30.00	60.00
Tranmere Rovers	18	5	2	2	16	6	2	1	6	8	19	24	25	38.89	16.67	44.44
Walsall	48	11	8	5	38	26	9	2	13	39	50	77	76	41.67	20.83	37.50
Watford	56	8	13	7	32	27	7	5	16	27	47	59	74	26.79	32.14	41.07
West Bromwich A	28	3	6	5	12	16	1	2	11	8	31	20	47	14.29	28.57	57.14
West Ham United	20	2	1	7	5	17	3	0	7	9	14	14	31	25.00	5.00	70.00
Wigan Athletic	18	2	5	2	10	9	4	1	4	11	15	21	24	33.33	33.33	33.33
Wolverhampton W	46	11	6	6	32	26	6	2	15	25	49	57	75	36.96	17.39	45.65
Workington	2	1	0	0	2	1	0	0	1	1	3	3	4	50.00	0.00	50.00
Wrexham	26	3	5	5	15	16	4	3	6	16	22	31	38	26.92	30.78	42.30
Wycombe Wanderers	6	1	0	2	2	3	0	0	3	5	9	7	12	16.67	16.67	66.66
Yeovil Town	2	1	0	0	2	0	1	0	0	2	1	4	1	100.00	0.00	0.00
York City	22	4	3	4	13	10	3	2	6	13	19	26	29	31.82	22.73	45.45
	3,876	**941**	**516**	**481**	**3,105**	**2,056**	**363**	**486**	**1,089**	**1,827**	**3,519**	**4,932**	**5,575**	**33.64**	**25.86**	**40.50**

Not including three expunged games from the 1939–40 season or any Play-off games.

In the Football League

		Home					Away							Average home League
	P	W	D	L	F	A	W	D	L	F	A	Pts	Position	Attendance
Division Two														
1905–06	38	6	4	9	19	22	1	3	15	16	56	21	20th	3,916
1906–07	38	9	7	3	25	13	2	1	16	20	54	30	17th	6,784
1907–08	38	10	5	4	28	13	1	5	13	12	52	32	14th	7,413
1908–09	38	7	7	5	25	19	5	2	12	12	30	33	15th	10,373
1909–10	38	10	4	5	26	15	2	2	15	11	45	30	16th	8,766
1910–11	38	14	4	1	28	7	5	3	11	16	28	45	4th	10,968
1911–12	38	16	0	3	44	14	5	3	11	17	30	45	4th	12,016
1912–13	38	8	6	5	25	20	2	8	9	9	27	34	14th	11,142
1913–14	38	14	5	0	38	11	2	6	11	9	24	43	6th	13,424
1914–15	38	12	5	2	36	17	4	4	11	14	31	41	9th	7,975
1919–20	42	14	3	4	34	17	2	3	16	17	42	38	15th	14,385
1920–21	42	13	6	2	31	9	3	7	11	12	33	45	7th	18,166
1921–22	42	12	4	5	33	18	3	5	13	10	32	39	15th	16,093
1922–23	42	9	6	6	26	17	3	6	12	14	33	36	19th	14,789
1923–24	42	11	7	3	27	10	3	8	10	13	26	43	10th	17,404
1924–25	42	8	7	6	22	13	6	5	10	20	29	40	11th	16,914
1925–26	42	8	6	7	30	21	4	3	14	20	44	33	20th	12,757
1926–27	42	9	3	9	37	35	3	4	14	23	61	31	20th	12,929
1927–28	42	9	7	5	32	25	2	5	14	23	60	34	20th	13,262
1928–29	42	10	4	7	29	25	2	4	15	16	47	32	22nd Relegated	12,172
Division Three South														
1929–30	42	10	8	3	38	21	4	5	12	17	41	41	12th	9,967
1930–31	42	12	3	6	47	33	2	4	15	16	58	35	19th	5,471
1931–32	42	7	0	C	41	35	5	3	13	36	55	35	16th	7,593
1932–33	42	7	8	6	39	35	1	5	15	20	58	29	20th	6,064
1933–34	42	14	4	3	60	25	2	6	13	15	44	42	11th	9,119
1934–35	42	13	3	5	47	21	2	7	12	18	44	40	14th	8,652
1935–36	42	13	2	6	34	15	3	4	14	21	46	38	14th	7,586
1936–37	42	10	8	3	29	17	4	7	10	23	35	43	12th	8,027
1937–38	42	10	7	4	27	19	3	0	18	15	42	33	19th	7,835
1938–39	42	10	9	2	40	16	1	4	16	13	39	35	20th	7,943
1946–47	42	10	5	6	40	28	2	3	16	14	47	32	19th	10,048
1947–48	42	8	5	8	31	32	5	5	11	20	41	36	17th	13,345
1948–49	42	9	6	6	36	29	2	6	13	22	51	34	19th	12,444
1949–50	42	10	6	5	33	30	2	5	14	20	55	35	18th	12,587
1950–51	46	13	2	8	36	28	2	6	15	17	47	38	19th	11,914
1951–52	46	12	5	6	39	26	4	4	15	16	42	41	18th	11,487
1952–53	46	1	7	4	52	28	4	3	16	16	45	42	14th	10,562
1953–54	46	14	5	4	48	26	4	6	13	31	47	47	11th	11,218
1954–55	46	16	2	5	48	20	10	7	6	41	27	61	2nd	15,216
1955–56	46	18	3	2	76	20	11	5	7	30	29	66	1st Promoted Champions	16,061

Division Two															
1956–57	42	7	8	6	34	38	8	2	11	32	46	40	15th		17,524
1957–58	42	14	2	5	53	27	4	3	14	24	52	41	12th		14,839
1958–59	42	9	4	8	43	30	5	4	12	28	48	36	17th		13,323
1959–60	42	12	4	5	47	25	3	10	8	29	36	44	10th		13,250
1960–61	42	10	5	6	31	29	4	3	14	24	49	36	19th		10,539
1961–62	42	11	5	5	34	17	11	5	5	35	23	54	2nd	Promoted	14,751
Division One															
1962–63	42	4	5	12	22	37	2	4	15	15	44	21	22nd	Relegated	16,406
Division Two															
1963–64	42	8	6	7	32	32	5	4	12	22	40	36	16th		10,359
1964–65	42	10	4	7	36	34	2	7	12	14	38	35	19th		8,920
1965–66	42	3	9	9	19	36	2	4	15	19	44	23	22nd		7,378
Division Three															
1966–67	46	10	9	4	36	27	3	9	11	22	41	44	14th		5,981
1967–68	46	10	6	7	27	24	2	11	10	19	38	41	19th		4,715
1968–69	46	10	8	5	31	19	4	6	13	20	39	42	18th		5,695
1969–70	46	16	5	2	43	15	9	7	7	24	21	62	1st	Promoted Champions	11,369
Division Two															
1970–71	42	5	11	5	16	15	4	5	12	13	36	34	17th		9,119
1971–72	42	12	4	5	32	19	2	5	14	18	42	37	17th		9,530
1972–73	42	11	6	4	33	18	1	6	14	16	35	36	15th		6,449
1973–74	42	9	8	4	28	17	6	10	5	27	25	48	4th		11,793
1974–75	42	8	9	4	1	16	3	11	7	11	23	42	12th		7,605
1975–76	42	10	6	5	21	12	3	8	10	16	27	40	13th		6,386
1976–77	42	4	8	9	18	23	5	8	8	19	32	34	19th		6,222
1977–78	42	8	11	2	30	20	2	7	12	13	29	38	14th		8,400
1978–79	42	11	5	5	32	18	4	5	12	19	33	40	11th		7,323
1979–80	42	7	9	5	29	31	5	8	8	19	23	41	14th		7,245
1980–81	42	9	8	4	34	20	4	4	13	18	36	38	17th		6,076
1981–82	42	6	8	7	23	24	4	1	16	13	37	39	22nd	Relegated	4,419
Division Three															
1982–83	46	10	6	7	44	38	5	3	15	20	50	54	20th		2,718
1983–84	46	13	5	5	40	27	5	4	14	31	54	63	11th		3,222
1984–85	46	7	7	9	30	36	4	6	13	21	40	46	22nd	Relegated	2,640
Division Four															
1985–86	46	11	6	6	39	21	9	6	8	40	43	72	5th		2,629
1986–87	46	15	2	6	40	25	5	7	11	24	36	69	7th		2,857
1987–88	46	13	4	6	55	27	6	8	9	30	36	69	8th		3,933
1988–89	46	16	2	5	61	19	5	10	8	25	31	75	6th	Promoted Play-offs	3,794
Division Three															
1989–90	46	9	6	8	28	24	7	4	12	24	32	58	14th		4,365
1990–91	46	15	2	6	35	19	3	8	12	20	39	64	13th		4,194
1991–92	46	12	7	4	36	18	6	4	13	26	34	65	10th		4,460

Division Two (Note: this Division was called Division Three until 1992–93)															
1992–93	46	16	4	3	49	20	5	5	13	20	33	72	7th		5,377
1993–94	46	11	9	3	38	26	3	5	15	19	45	56	18th		4,237
1994–95	46	6	6	11	21	29	0	2	21	9	46	26	24th	Relegated	3,436
Division Three (Note: this Division was called Division Four until 1992–93)															
1995–96	46	11	4	8	29	22	1	7	15	15	41	47	21st		4,478
1996–97	46	11	6	6	28	20	4	6	13	22	38	57	16th		4,336
1997–98 *	46	14	5	4	40	20	5	7	11	22	27	66	11th		4,374
1998–99	46	12	6	5	40	30	7	9	7	28	29	72	6th	Play-offs Lost in Final	4,689
1999–00	46	7	7	9	22	22	6	6	11	25	30	52	19th		4,355
2000–01	46	13	7	3	31	18	7	8	8	28	33	75	5th	Play-offs Lost in Final	4,633
2001–02	46	10	7	6	37	25	3	6	13	18	46	52	18th		4,540
2002–03	46	9	6	8	28	24	5	5	13	23	37	53	18th		4,257
2003–04	46	8	9	6	28	27	5	5	13	20	38	53	19th		4,157
Football League Two (Note: this Division was called Division Three until 2004–05)															
2004–05	46	10	8	5	40	30	6	7	10	25	37	63	11th		3,642
2005–06	46	11	6	6	29	21	11	9	3	38	30	81	3rd	Promoted	4,714

* Leyton Orient had three points deducted.

1904-05

Southern League Division Two

Match No.	Date		Opponents	Result	Scorers	Attenda
1	Oct	8	BRIGHTON & HOVE ALBION	0-0		2,9
2		22	Southampton	3-3	Cavendish 3	4,0
3	Nov	12	Brighton & Hove Albion	2-1	Nicol, Cavendish	2,2
4		19	WEST HAM UNITED	2-0	Kingaby, Cavendish	3,5
5		26	FULHAM	2-2	Cavendish, Kingaby	2,0
6	Dec	3	Swindon Town	1-4	Cavendish	1,5
7		17	Reading	0-0		1,2
8	Jan	7	Fulham	2-4	McGeorge, Cavendish	2,5
9		14	WATFORD	5-7	Reynolds, Hammond 2, McGeorge 2,	1,1
10		21	Wycombe Wanderers	4-6	Reynolds, Kingaby, J. Hills, Hammond	2
11	Feb	18	West Ham United	2-2	J. Hills 2	5,0
12		25	SOUTHALL	3-0	Hammond, Berry, Nicol (pen)	1,5
13	Mar	4	WYCOMBE WANDERERS	1-1	Poulton	1,7
14		8	Watford	3-3	Cavendish, Nicol 2	1,1
15		11	PORTSMOUTH	1-2	J. Hills	2,0
16		22	Southall	3-0	Hammond, Robertson, Bedell	6
17		25	READING	3-0	Reynolds, Cavendish, J. Hills	1,2
18		29	Portsmouth	0-13		4,5
19	Apr	1	SWINDON TOWN	3-0	Hammond, Cavendish 2	2,5
20		10	GRAYS ATHLETIC	7-1	Cavendish 2, Hammond 2, Reynolds 2, Berry	2
21		22	SOUTHAMPTON	0-5		3,0
22		24	Grays Athletic	0-2		1,0

Appearanc

Go

FA Cup

Q1	Sep	17	ENFIELD	4-1	Reynolds, Hammond, McGeorge, Lane	1,0
Q2	Oct	1	Cheshunt	0-0		5
R		6	CHESHUNT	4-1	Kingaby 2, Reynolds, Nicol	1,1
Q3		15	LEYTONSTONE	1-1	Kingaby	3,0
R		20	Leytonstone	5-2	White, Hammond, Reynolds, McGeorge, Nicol (pen)	2,0
Q4		29	Hitchen Town	1-2	Nicol	7

Appearanc

Gc

Note:

One local newspaper credited Herbert Kingaby with a hat-trick against Cheshunt on 6 October 1904, however, most agreed o goal was scored by Bill Reynolds.

Rance, J	Archer	Berry	McGeorge	Lane	Kingaby	Nicol	Cavendish	Reynolds	Hills, JC	Robertson	Hammond	Hodder	Hills, TC	Reason	Poulton	Nidd	Beedell	Cantor	Rance, A	White, T	
2	3	4	5	6	7	8	9	10	11												1
2	3		5	6	7		9	10	11	4	8										2
2	3	4	5	6	7	10	9		11		8										3
2	3	4	5	6	7	8	9		11		10										4
2	3	4	5	6	7	8	9		11		10										5
2	3	4	5	6	7	8	9		11		10										6
2	3	4	5	6	7	8	9		11		10										7
2	3		5	6	7		9	10	11		8	4									8
2	3		5	6	7		9	10	11		8	4									9
2			5	6	7	10		9	11	4	8		3								10
2		6	5		7	8	9	10	11					3	4						11
2		6			7	10	9		11	5	8			3	4						12
2		6	5		7	8	9		11		10			3	4						13
2		11		6	7	8	9			5	10			3	4						14
2		6			7	8	9		11	5	10			3	4						15
		4		6	7	8	9			5	10			3		2	11				16
		4		6			9	10	11	3	10				5	2	7				17
	5		6	7	8	9	10		3	11				4							18
3		6				7	9	10	11	5	8				4	2					19
		4		6		7	9	10	11	5	8			3		2					20
		4		6		7	9	10	11					3	5	2		8			21
				6	7		9	10		5	8			3	4	2			11		22
16	9	16	13	17	18	17	21	11	19	11	18	2	1	10	9	6	2	1	1		
		2	3		3	4	14	5	5	1	8				1		1				

Rance, J	Archer	Berry	McGeorge	Lane	Kingaby	Nicol	Cavendish	Reynolds	Hills, JC	Robertson	Hammond	Hodder	Hills, TC	Reason	Poulton	Nidd	Beedell	Cantor	Rance, A	White, T	
2	3	4	5	6	7	8		10	11		9										Q1
2	3	4	5	6	7	8	9	10	11												Q2
2	3	4	5	6	7	8	9	10	11												R
2	3	4	5	6	7	8	9	10	11												Q3
2	3	4	5	6		9		10		11	8									7	R
2	3	4	5	6	7	9		10	11		8										Q4
6	6	6	6	6	5	6	3	6	5	1	3									1	
			2	1	3	3		3			2									1	

1905-06

Manager: Sep 1905–Mar 1906 Samuel Ormerod; Mar–Apr 1906 William Holmes

	P	W	D	L	F	A	Pts
Bristol City	38	30	6	2	83	28	66
Manchester United	38	28	6	4	90	28	62
Chelsea	38	22	9	7	90	37	53
West Bromwich Albion	38	22	8	8	79	36	52
Hull City	38	19	6	13	67	54	44
Leeds City	38	17	9	12	59	47	43
Leicester Fosse	38	15	12	11	53	48	42
Grimsby Town	38	15	10	13	46	46	40
Burnley	38	15	8	15	42	53	38
Stockport County	38	13	9	16	44	56	35
Bradford City	38	13	8	17	46	60	34
Barnsley	38	12	9	17	60	62	33
Lincoln City	38	12	6	20	69	72	30
Blackpool	38	10	9	19	37	62	29
Gainsborough Trinity	38	12	4	22	44	57	28
Glossop North End	38	10	8	20	49	71	28
Burslem Port Vale	38	12	4	22	49	82	28
Chesterfield Town	38	10	8	20	40	72	28
Burton United	38	10	6	22	34	67	26
Clapton Orient	38	7	7	24	35	78	21

Football League Division Two

Match No.	Date		Opponents	Result	Scorers	Attend
1	Sep	2	Leicester Fosse	1-2	Kingaby	6
2		9	HULL CITY	0-1		3
3		11	GLOSSOP NORTH END	2-0	Leigh 2	2,
4		16	Lincoln City	3-2	Evenson, Leigh, Kingaby	5
5		23	CHESTERFIELD TOWN	3-3	Evenson 3	5,
6		30	Burslem Port Vale	1-2	Boden (pen)	2,
7	Oct	7	BARNSLEY	0-0		6,
8		14	GRIMSBY TOWN	1-2	Codling	6,
9		21	Burnley	0-3		4,
10	Nov	4	Burton United	0-1		2,
11		11	CHELSEA	0-3		8,
12		25	BRISTOL CITY	0-2		7,
13	Dec	2	Manchester United	0-4		12,
14		4	Gainsborough Trinity	1-2	Dougal	4,
15		16	Stockport County	3-3	G. Lamberton 2, Wootten	5,
16		23	BLACKPOOL	0-0		2,
17		25	West Bromwich Albion	1-1	Wootten	18,
18		26	Bradford City	0-3		13,
19		30	LEICESTER FOSSE	0-2		2,
20	Jan	6	Hull City	1-3	Bourne	5,
21		20	LINCOLN CITY	3-0	Halse, Boden, Gibson	3,
22		27	Chesterfield Town	1-1	Boden	5,
23	Feb	3	BURSLEM PORT VALE	1-3	Boden	4,
24		10	Barnsley	1-4	G. Lamberton	4,
25		17	Grimsby Town	1-4	Evenson	3,
26		24	BURNLEY	3-0	Leigh, Kingaby 2	5,
27	Mar	3	Leeds City	1-6	Boden	8,
28		10	BURTON UNITED	0-1		3,
29		17	Chelsea	1-6	Haigh-Brown	15,
30		24	GAINSBOROUGH TRINITY	1-0	Orton	2,
31		29	LEEDS CITY	0-0		4,
32		31	Bristol City	0-1		8,
33	Apr	7	MANCHESTER UNITED	0-1		9,
34		13	BRADFORD CITY	4-2	Leigh 4	6,
35		14	Glossop North End	0-5		3,
36		16	WEST BROMWICH ALBION	0-2		3,
37		21	STOCKPORT COUNTY	1-0	Simons	3,
38		28	Blackpool	0-3		4,

Appearan

Go

FA Cup

Q1	Oct	7	Felstead	1-1	Dougal	
R		12	FELSTEAD	5-1	G. Lamberton 2, Boden, Evenson, Dougal	1,
Q2		28	BARKING	3-1	G. Lamberton, Proudfoot, Dougal	3,
Q3	Nov	18	Leyton	3-1	Bourne, Boden, G. Lamberton	5,
Q4	Dec	9	Clapton	2-0	Evenson, Boden (pen)	4,
R 1	Jan	13	CHESTERFIELD TOWN	0-0		6,
R		17	Chesterfield Town	0-3		3,

Appearan

Go

Lamberton, J	Boyle	Holmes	Boden	Codling	Kingaby	Wootten	Leigh	Lamberton, G	Bourne	Evenson	McGeorge	Proudfoot	Dougal	Redding	Reason	Halse	Gibson	Hills	Hammond	Haigh-Brown	Gilson	Bower	Orton	Simons	Hunt	Wightman	Poulton	Roach	Elliott	Westcott	Cavendish	
2	3	4	5	6	7	8	9	10	11																							1
2	3	4	5	6	7		10	8	11	9																						2
2	3	4	5	6	7	8	10		11	9																						3
2	3	4	5	6	7		10	8	11	9																						4
2	3	4	5	6	7		10	8	11	9																						5
2	3	4	5	6	7		10	8	11	9																						6
2	3		5	6	7	8		9	11	10	4																					7
2	3		9	6	7			8	11	10	5	4																				8
2		3	5	6	7				11	10	4	8	9																			9
2	3		5	6	7			8	11	10		4	9	1																		10
2	3		5	6	7		9	8	11	10		4		1																		11
2			5	6	7		9	8	11	10		4			3																	12
2			5	6	7			8	11	10		4			3	9																13
2			5	6		11	9	8		10		4	7		3																	14
2	3		5	6	7	9		8	11	10		4																				15
2		3	5	6	7	9		8	11	10		4																				16
2		3	5	6	7	9		8	11	10		4																				17
2		3	5	6	7	9		8	11	10		4																				18
2		3	5	6	7	9		8	11	10		4																				19
2		3	5	6	7		10	9	11			4	8																			20
2		3	5	6	8				10			4				9	7	11														21
2		3	9	6	8				11		5	4					7		10													22
		3	9	6	8				11		5	4		1	2		7	10														23
		3	5	6	7			9	11	10		4		1	2				8													24
			5	6	7			9	11	10	3	4		1	2				8													25
		3	5	6	8		9		11			4	10	1	2					7												26
3			5	6	8		9		11			4	10	1			7				2											27
2				6			9	8	11		5	4	10		3					7		1										28
		5					8		11	6		4	10		3					7	2	1	9									29
2		3					9		11	6	5	4	7									1	10	8								30
2		3				8	9		11	6	5	4	7									1	10									31
2		3					10		11	6	5	4	7									1	8		9							32
2		3					10		11	6	5	4	8							7		1	9									33
2		3					10	4	11	6	5		7									1	9	8								34
2		3					10	4	11	6	5		7									1	9	8								35
2		3					10	4	11	6	5		7									1	9	8								36
2		3					10	4	11	5			9		6		7					1		8								37
2		3					10	4	11	5			7		6				9			1		8								38
33	11	27	27	28	26	10	23	26	37	30	14	26	17	7	11	2	5	2	4	4	2	11	8	6	1							
			5	1	4	2	8	3	1	5			1			1	1			1			1	1								
		4					11						8	1	2											3	5	6	7	9	10	Q1
2	3		5	6				8	11	10	4	7	9																			R
2			5	6	7			8	11	10		4	9	1	3																	Q2
2	3		5	6	7		9	8	11	10		4		1																		Q3
2			5	6	7	9		8	11	10		4			3																	Q4
2		3	5	6	7			9	10			4	8					11														R1
2		3	5	6	7			9	11			4	8					10														R
6	2	3	6	6	5	1	2	6	6	4	1	6	5	3	3			2								1	1	1	1	1	1	
			3					4	1	2		1	3																			

1906-07

Manager: Sep–Nov 1906 Isaac Evenson; Nov 1906–Apr 1907 William Holmes

	P	W	D	L	F	A	Pts
Nottingham Forest	38	28	4	6	74	36	60
Chelsea	38	26	5	7	80	34	57
Leicester Fosse	38	20	8	10	62	39	48
West Bromwich Albion	38	21	5	12	83	45	47
Bradford City	38	21	5	12	70	53	47
Wolverhampton W	38	17	7	14	66	53	41
Burnley	38	17	6	15	62	47	40
Barnsley	38	15	8	15	73	55	38
Hull City	38	15	7	16	65	57	37
Leeds City	38	13	10	15	55	63	36
Grimsby Town	38	16	3	19	57	62	35
Stockport County	38	12	11	15	42	52	35
Blackpool	38	11	11	16	33	51	33
Gainsborough Trinity	38	14	5	19	45	72	33
Glossop North End	38	13	6	19	53	79	32
Burslem Port Vale	38	12	7	19	60	83	310
Clapton Orient	38	11	8	19	45	67	30
Chesterfield Town	38	11	7	20	50	66	29
Lincoln City	38	12	4	22	46	73	28
Burton United	38	8	7	23	34	68	23

Division Two

Match No.	Date		Opponents	Result	Scorers	Attenc
1	Sep	1	STOCKPORT COUNTY	1-1	Thomas	5
2		8	Hull City	0-2		5
3		15	GLOSSOP NORTH END	3-0	Leonard, Evenson, Oliver	6
4		22	Blackpool	3-1	Oliver, Bourne, Leonard	4
5		29	BRADFORD CITY	1-1	Leonard	9
6	Oct	6	West Bromwich Albion	0-5		10
7		13	LEICESTER FOSSE	1-0	Thacker	4
8		20	Nottingham Forest	0-4		8
9		27	LINCOLN CITY	1-1	Oliver	5
10	Nov	3	Burton United	1-2	Oliver	7
11		10	GRIMSBY TOWN	1-0	Oliver	5
12		17	Burslem Port Vale	2-3	Martin 2	5
13		24	BURNLEY	2-1	Martin 2	6
14	Dec	1	Leeds City	2-3	Martin 2	10
15		15	Chelsea	1-2	Martin	15
16		22	WOLVERHAMPTON W	4-0	Martin 3, Leonard	6
17		25	Gainsborough Trinity	1-3	Martin	4
18		26	CHESTERFIELD TOWN	1-2	Evenson	6
19		27	Wolverhampton W	1-6	Evenson	5
20		29	Stockport County	1-1	Dougal	3
21	Jan	1	Barnsley	2-3	Martin, Leonard (pen)	4
22		5	HULL CITY	2-1	Lappin, Martin	7
23		19	Glossop North End	0-3		
24		26	BLACKPOOL	0-0		5
25	Feb	9	WEST BROMWICH ALBION	1-1	Buchanan	3
26		16	Leicester Fosse	1-2	Oliver	8
27		23	NOTTINGHAM FOREST	0-1		6
28	Mar	2	Lincoln City	0-3		2
29		9	BURTON UNITED	1-0	Dougal	5
30		12	Bradford City	2-5	Martin, Buchanan	5
31		16	Grimsby Town	2-1	Oliver, Martin	3
32		23	BURSLEM PORT VALE	1-1	Leonard (pen)	7
33		29	Chesterfield Town	1-2	Oliver	8
34		30	Burnley	0-3		6
35	Apr	1	GAINSBOROUGH TRINITY	3-1	Leonard, Martin, Birkbeck (og)	6
36		6	LEEDS CITY	1-1	Martin	6
37		13	BARNSLEY	1-0	Oliver	7
38		20	CHELSEA	0-1		18

Appearar

G

Final League Position: 17th in Division Two

Clapton Orient did not enter the FA Cup competition in 1906-07.

Henderson	Stewart	Gates	Evenson	Martin	Dougal	Thomas	Oliver	Simons	Lappin	Leonard	Reason	Pemberton	Bourne	Thacker	Buchanan	Thompson	Holmes	Watts	
2	3	4	5	6	7	8	9	10	11										1
2	3	4	5	6	7	10	9		11	8									2
	2	4	5		7		9		11	8	3	6	10						3
2	3	4	5		7		9		11	8			10	6					4
2	3	4	5		7		9		11	8			10	6					5
		2	5	4	7		9		11	8		6	10	3					6
2	3	4	5		9				11	8			7	6	10				7
2	3	4	5		7		9		11	8				6	10				8
2	3	4	5		7		9		11	8				6	10	1			9
2	3	4	5		7		9		11	8				6	10				10
2	3	4	5		7		9		11	8			10	6					11
	2	4	5	9	7				11	8	3		10		6				12
	3	4	5	9	7				11	8			10		6		2		13
	3	4	5	9	7				11	8			10		6		2		14
	3	4	5	9	7				11	8			10		6		2		15
	3	4	5	9		10			7	8			11		6		2		16
	3	4	5	9		10			7	8			11		6		2		17
	3	4	5	9		10			7	8			11		6		2		18
	3	4	5	9		10			7	8			11		6		2		19
2	3		5	9	10				7	8			11	6	4			1	20
2	3		5	9	10				7	8			11	6	4			1	21
2	3		5	9	10				7	8			11	6	4				22
2	3		5	9	10				7	8			11	6	4				23
2		10	5	9	7				11	8	3			6	4				24
2	3		5	9			10		7	8			11	6	4				25
2	3		5	9	7		10		11	8				6	4				26
	3		5	9	7		10		11	8	2			6	4				27
	3		5	9	7		10		11	8	2			6	4				28
2			5	9	7		10		11	8				6	4		3		29
2			5	9	7		10		11	8				6	4		3		30
2	5	4		9	7		10		11	8					6		3		31
2	5	4		9	7		10		11	8					6		3		32
2		5		9	7		10		11	8				6	4		3		33
2		5		9	7		10		11	8				6	4		3		34
2	5	4		9	7				11	8				6	10		3		35
2		4	5	9	7				11	8				6	10		3		36
	3		5	9	7		10		11	8				6	4		2		37
	3		5	9	7		10		11	8				6	4		2		38
24	31	26	33	30	33	6	22	1	38	37	5	2	19	25	31	1	17	2	
			3	17	2	1	9		1	7			1	1	2				

One own-goal

1907-08

Manager: William Holmes

	P	W	D	L	F	A	Pts
Bradford City	38	24	6	8	90	42	54
Leicester Fosse	38	21	10	7	72	47	52
Oldham Athletic	38	22	6	10	76	42	50
Fulham	38	22	5	11	82	49	49
West Bromwich Albion	38	19	9	10	61	39	47
Derby County	38	21	4	13	77	45	46
Burnley	38	20	6	12	67	50	46
Hull City	38	21	4	13	73	62	46
Wolverhampton W	38	15	7	16	50	45	37
Stoke	38	16	5	17	57	52	37
Gainsborough Trinity	38	14	7	17	47	71	35
Leeds City	38	12	8	18	53	65	32
Stockport County	38	12	8	18	48	67	32
Clapton Orient	38	11	10	17	40	65	32
Blackpool	38	11	9	18	51	58	31
Barnsley	38	12	6	20	54	68	30
Glossop North End	38	11	8	19	54	74	30
Grimsby Town	38	11	8	19	43	71	30
Chesterfield Town	38	6	11	21	46	92	23
Lincoln City	38	9	3	26	46	83	21

Division Two

Match No.	Date		Opponents	Result	Scorers	Atten
1	Sep	2	HULL CITY	1-0	Martin	5
2		5	Barnsley	2-2	Leigh, J. Whittaker	3
3		7	Blackpool	0-5		4
4		9	Leeds United	2-5	Bell 2	6
5		14	STOKE	3-0	Parker, Leigh, Martin	9
6		21	West Bromwich Albion	0-3		12
7		28	BRADFORD CITY	0-3		10
8	Oct	10	Hull City	0-5		4
9		12	DERBY COUNTY	1-0	Parker	7
10		26	FULHAM	0-1		15
11	Nov	9	CHESTERFIELD TOWN	5-1	Greechan 2, Martin, Goffin, Parker	5
12		11	Stoke	0-3		5
13		16	Burnley	0-3		8
14		23	OLDHAM ATHLETIC	2-0	Leigh, Parker	5
15		30	GRIMSBY TOWN	2-1	Martin, Goffin	6
16	Dec	14	WOLVERHAMPTON W	1-1	Martin	7
17		21	Gainsborough Trinity	0-0		4
18		25	Glossop North End	1-2	Greechan	4
19		26	Leicester Fosse	2-0	Goffin, Parker	12
20		28	STOCKPORT COUNTY	4-1	Martin 3, Bell	8
21	Jan	4	BLACKPOOL	1-1	Goffin	5
22		18	WEST BROMWICH ALBION	2-2	Goffin 2	15
23		25	Bradford City	0-1		10
24	Feb	8	Derby County	0-4		12
25		15	Lincoln City	2-2	Martin 2	1
26		29	BARNSLEY	2-0	Greechan, Goffin	7
27	Mar	7	Chesterfield Town	1-1	Greechan	5
28		14	BURNLEY	0-1		9
29		18	Fulham	0-4		8
30		21	Oldham Athletic	1-4	Greechan	6
31		26	LINCOLN CITY	2-0	Greechan, Parker	3
32		28	Grimsby Town	0-0		5
33	Apr	4	LEEDS CITY	0-0		8
34		9	GLOSSOP NORTH END	0-0		6
35		11	Wolverhampton W	0-2		15
36		18	GAINSBOROUGH TRINITY	2-0	Greechan, Martin	4
37		20	LEICESTER FOSSE	0-1		8
38		25	Stockport County	1-6	Goffin	5

Appearar

G

FA Cup

Q1	Sep	21	CUSTOM HOUSE	3-0	Martin, Whittaker, Buchanan	3
Q2	Oct	5	ROMFORD	6-3	Leigh 2, Greechan 2, Buchanan, Bell	2
Q3		19	OLD NEWPORTONIANS	5-2	Leigh 2, Bell, Buchanan, Greechan (pen)	2
Q4	Nov	2	SOUTHEND UNITED	1-1	Whittaker	7,
R		6	Southend United	3-1	Martin	4,

Appearar

G

Final League Position: 14th in Division Two

Note: Some reports credit Goffin as the scorer in Match 30.

Henderson	Stewart	Buchanan	Shelley	Thacker	Bell	Leigh	Martin	Oliver	Whittaker, J	Gates	Parker	Bower	Reason	Liddell	Pemberton	Roach	Goffin	Greechan	Caldwell, J	Holmes	Williams	Caldwell, T	Howshell	Edley	
2	3	4	5	6	7	8	9	10	11																1
2	3	4	5	6	7	8	9	10	11																2
2	3	4	5	6	7	8	9		11	10															3
2	3	4	5	6	10	8	9		11		7														4
2	3	5		6	10	8	9		11	4	7														5
2			5								7	1	3	4	6	8	9	10	11						6
2	3	5		6	7	10	9		11	4								8							7
2		4	5	6	7	10	9		11									8		3					8
2		4		6	10	9			11		7	1		5				8		3					9
2	3	4		6	10	9			11		7	1		5				8							10
	3	4			5		9		11		7	1	2		6		8	10							11
	3	4			5		9		11		7	1	2	6			8	10							12
2		4			5	8	9				7	1	3	6				10	11						13
2		4			5	8	9				7		3	6				10	11						14
2		4			5		9				7		3	6			8	10	11						15
2		4			5		9				7		3	6			8	10	11						16
		4			5		9				7		3	6			8	10	11		2				17
		4			5		9				7		3	6			8	10	11		2				18
		4			5		9				7		3	6			8	10	11		2				19
		4			5		9				7		3	6			8	10	11		2				20
					6		9			4	7		3	5			8	10	11		2				21
2		4			5		9				7		3	6			8	10	11						22
2		4			5		9				7		3	6			8	10	11						23
2					5		9		11	4	7		3	6			8	10							24
2	3				5		9	10	11	4	7			6			8								25
2		4			5		9		11		7		3	6			8	10							26
2		4			5		9		11		7		3	6			8	10							27
2		4			5		9		11		7		3	6			8	10							28
2		4			5		9				7		3	6			8	10				11			29
	3	4			5	7	9						2	6			8	10				11			30
	3	4			5			9			7		2	6			8	10				11			31
	3	4	5			7		9		2				6			8	10				11			32
	3	4			5	8	9			2	7			6				10				11			33
	3	4			5	9					7		2	6			8	10					11		34
	3	4			5	9			11		7		2	6			8	10							35
	3	4			5		9				7		2	6			8	10				11			36
	3	4			5	10	9				7		2	6			8					11			37
2	3	4			5		9	10			7			6			8						11		38
23	19	34	7	9	36	17	31	6	17	8	31	6	25	30	2	1	26	30	12	2	5	7	2		
					3	3	11		1		6						8	8							

Henderson	Stewart	Buchanan	Shelley	Thacker	Bell	Leigh	Martin	Oliver	Whittaker, J	Gates	Parker	Bower	Reason	Liddell	Pemberton	Roach	Goffin	Greechan	Caldwell, J	Holmes	Williams	Caldwell, T	Howshell	Edley	
	3	5		6	10	8	9		11	4										2			7		Q1
2		5		6	7	10	9		11	4								8		3					Q2
2	3	4		6	10	9			11		7			5				8							Q3
2	3	4			10	9			11		7	1		5				8						6	Q4
2	3	6			8	10	9		11	4	7			5											R
4	4	5		3	5	5	3		5	3	3	1		3				3		2			1	1	
		3			2	4	2		2									3							

1908-09

Manager: William Holmes

	P	W	D	L	F	A	Pts
Bolton Wanderers	38	24	4	10	59	28	52
Tottenham Hotspur	38	20	11	7	67	32	51
West Bromwich Albion	38	19	13	6	56	27	51
Hull City	38	19	6	13	63	39	44
Derby County	38	16	11	11	55	41	43
Oldham Athletic	38	17	6	15	55	43	40
Wolverhampton W	38	14	11	13	56	48	39
Glossop North End	38	15	8	15	57	53	38
Gainsborough Trinity	38	15	8	15	49	70	38
Fulham	38	13	11	14	58	48	37
Birmingham	38	14	9	15	58	61	37
Leeds City	38	14	7	17	43	53	35
Grimsby Town	38	14	7	17	41	54	35
Burnley	38	13	7	18	51	58	33
Clapton Orient	38	12	9	17	37	49	33
Bradford Park Avenue	38	13	6	19	51	59	32
Barnsley	38	11	10	17	48	57	32
Stockport County	38	14	3	21	39	71	31
Chesterfield Town	38	11	8	19	37	67	30
Blackpool	38	9	11	18	46	68	29

Division Two

Match No.	Date		Opponents	Result	Scorers	Atten
1	Sep	5	Hull City	2-3	Ward, Parker	9
2		7	Leeds City	0-0		8
3		12	Derby County	0-1		6
4		19	BLACKPOOL	1-1	Reason (pen)	16
5		26	Chesterfield Town	0-2		5
6	Oct	3	GLOSSOP NORTH END	0-2		8
7		10	Stcokport County	1-1	Gates	4
8		17	WEST BROMWICH ALBION	1-0	Reason (pen)	10
9		24	Birmingham	0-1		14
10		31	GAINSBOROUGH TRINITY	2-2	Gates, Shaw	7
11	Nov	7	Grimsby Town	0-1		5
12		14	FULHAM	1-1	Parker	15
13		21	Burnley	1-0	Parker	6
14		28	BRADFORD PARK AVENUE	2-0	Parker, Gates	6
15	Dec	5	Wolverhampton W	1-5	Gates	8
16		12	OLDHAM ATHLETIC	2-0	Shaw, Gates	4
17		19	Bolton Wanderers	0-2		7
18		25	BARNSLEY	1-1	Louch	20
19		26	Barnsley	0-3		5
20	Jan	2	HULL CITY	1-2	Louch	10
21		9	DERBY COUNTY	2-0	Oliver, Reason (pen)	8
22		23	Blackpool	3-1	Gates, Beale, McLean	2
23		30	CHESTERFIELD TOWN	1-1	Gates	9
24	Feb	13	STOCKPORT COUNTY	5-0	McLean , Scott 2, Louch 2	7
25		20	West Bromwich Albion	0-1		14
26		27	BIRMINGHAM	3-2	Scott, Parker 2	8
27	Mar	13	GRIMSBY TOWN	2-1	Bell, Reason (pen)	7
28		20	Fulham	2-1	Hind (pen), Scott	25
29		27	BURNLEY	0-1		12
30	Apr	3	Bradford Park Avenue	1-0	Louch	10
31		9	Tottenham Hotspur	1-0	Scott	32
32		10	WOLVERHAMPTON W	1-3	Scott	16
33		12	TOTTENHAM HOTSPUR	0-0		26
34		13	LEEDS CITY	0-0		12
35		17	Oldham Athletic	0-2		7
36		20	Glossop North End	0-4		1
37		24	BOLTON WANDERERS	0-2		13
38		28	Gainsborough Trinity	0-2		2

Appeara

G

FA Cup

1	Jan	16	Newcastle United	0-5		23

Appeara

G

Final League Position: 15th in Division Two

Note: Some reports credit Parker with both goals in Match 14.

Johnston	Reason	Hind	Bell	Liddell	Ward	Parker	Goffin	Oliver	Thompson	Bower	O'Gara	Shaw	Candy	Willis	McLean	Gates	Scott	Louch	Beale	Johnson	Shelley	
2	3	4	5	6	7	8	9	10	11													1
2	3	4	5	6	7	8	9	10	11	1												2
2	3	4	5	6	7	8	9	10	11	1												3
2	3	4	5	6	7	8	9	10	11	1												4
2	3	4	5	6	11	7	8	9		1	10											5
2	3	4	5	6	7	8			10	1		9	11									6
2	3	4		5	11	7						9		6	8	10						7
2	3	4	5	6	11	7						9			8	10						8
2	3	4	5	6	11	7						9			8	10						9
2	3	4	5	6	11	7						9			8	10						10
2	3	4	5	6	11	7						9			8	10						11
2	3	4	5	6	11	7						9			8	10						12
2	3	4	5	6	11	7						9			8	10						13
2	3	4	5	6	11	7						9			8	10						14
2	3	4	5	6	11	7						9			8	10						15
2	3	4		6	11	7						9			8	10	5					16
2	3	4		6	11	7						9			8	10	5					17
2	3	4	5	6	11	7									8	10		9				18
2	3	4	5	6	11	7	8					9				10						19
2	3	4		6		7		10		1					8		5	9	11			20
2	3	4	5	6		7		10									8	9	11			21
2		4				7				1				6	8	10	9		11	3	5	22
2		4				7				1				6	8	10	9		11	3	5	23
2	3	4	5	6	11	7									8		10	9				24
2	3	4	5	6		7							11		8		10	9				25
2	3	4	5	6	11	7									8		10	9				26
2	3	4	5	6	11	7									8		10	9				27
2	3	4	5	6	11	7						10			8		9					28
2	3	4	5	6	11	7									8		10	9				29
2	3	4	5	6	11	7									8		10	9				30
2	3	4	5	6	11	7									8		10	9				31
2	3	4	5	6	11	7									8		10	9				32
2	3	4	5	6	11	7						8					10	9				33
2	3	4			7				11	1		9	6			5	10	8				34
2		4		6	7			8				9				5	10		11	3		35
2		4		6	11	7		8				9				5	10			3		36
2	3	4	5	6	11	7									8		10	9				37
2	3			6	11	7	5	8				9				4	10					38
38	34	37	28	35	33	36	7	10	6	9	1	19	3	3	25	19	21	14	5	4	2	
	4	1	1		1	6		1				2			2	7	6	5	1			

Johnston	Reason	Hind	Bell	Liddell	Ward	Parker	Goffin	Oliver	Thompson	Bower	O'Gara	Shaw	Candy	Willis	McLean	Gates	Scott	Louch	Beale	Johnson	Shelley	
2	3	4	5	6		7		10									8	9	11			1
1	1	1	1	1		1		1									1	1	1			

1909-10

Manager: William Holmes

	P	W	D	L	F	A	Pts
Manchester City	38	23	8	7	81	40	54
Oldham Athletic	38	23	7	8	79	39	53
Hull City	38	23	7	8	80	46	53
Derby County	38	22	9	7	72	47	53
Leicester Fosse	38	20	4	14	79	58	44
Glossop North End	38	18	7	13	64	57	43
Fulham	38	14	13	11	51	43	41
Wolverhampton W	38	17	6	15	64	63	40
Barnsley	38	16	7	15	62	59	39
Bradford Park Avenue	38	17	4	17	64	59	38
West Bromwich Albion	38	16	5	17	58	56	37
Blackpool	38	14	8	16	50	52	36
Stockport County	38	13	8	17	50	47	34
Burnley	38	14	6	18	62	61	34
Lincoln City	38	10	11	17	42	69	31
Clapton Orient	38	12	6	20	37	60	30
Leeds City	38	10	7	21	46	80	27
Gainsborough Trinity	38	10	6	22	33	75	26
Grimsby Town	38	9	6	23	50	77	24
Birmingham	38	8	7	23	42	78	23

Division Two

Match No.	Date		Opponents	Result	Scorers	Atten
1	Sept	4	GAINSBOROUGH TRINITY	2-0	Parker 2	14
2		11	Grimsby Town	0-2		5
3		13	Wolverhampton W	1-3	Williams	6
4		18	MANCHESTER CITY	3-2	Parker 2, Underwood	21
5		25	Leicester Fosse	0-4		10
6	Oct	2	LINCOLN CITY	1-2	Liddell	9
7		9	Bradford Park Avenue	1-3	Scott	10
8		16	Blackpool	2-2	Henderson 2	4
9		23	HULL CITY	0-0		8
10		25	WOLVERHAMPTON W	1-0	Scott	9
11		30	Derby County	0-1		6
12	Nov	6	STOCKPORT COUNTY	2-0	Scott, Henderson	7
13		13	Glossop North End	1-3	Louch	5
14		20	BIRMINGHAM	3-0	Scott, Meynell, Louch	7
15		27	West Bromwich Albion	0-3		12
16	Dec	4	OLDHAM ATHLETIC	1-2	Johnston	7
17		11	Barnsley	1-2	Bevan	6
18		18	FULHAM	0-0		11
19		25	Leeds City	1-2	Bevan	6
20		27	BURNLEY	2-1	Scott, Louch	13
21	Jan	1	Burnley	0-2		6
22		8	Gainsborough Trinity	1-0	Scott	5
23		22	GRIMSBY TOWN	0-0		7
24	Feb	12	Lincoln City	0-4		5
25		19	BRADFORD PARK AVENUE	1-0	Williams	8
26		26	BLACKPOOL	2-1	Henderson, Williams	5
27	Mar	5	Hull City	0-3		8
28		12	DERBY COUNTY	0-2		5
29		19	Stockport County	0-3		4
30		26	GLOSSOP NORTH END	0-0		5
31		28	LEEDS CITY	0-2		7
32	Apr	2	Birmingham	2-1	Goffin, Bevan	8
33		7	BARNSLEY	4-0	Bevan 2, Louch, Parker	5
34		9	WEST BROMWICH ALBION	1-3	Goffin	15
35		13	Manchester City	1-2	Meynell	12
36		16	Oldham Athletic	0-5		5
37		25	LEICESTER FOSSE	3-0	Louch, Bevan 2	4
38		30	Fulham	0-0		12

Appearar

G

FA Cup

1	Jan	15	West Bromwich Albion	0-2	7

Appearar

G

Final League Position: 16th in Division Two

Johnston	Reason	Hind	Bell	Liddell	Parker	McLean	Williams	Scott	Underwood	Louch	Henderson	Tully	Johnson	Goffin	Meynell	Bower	Bevan	Prior	Willis	Reed	Lee	
2	3	4	5	6	7	8	9	10	11													1
2	3	4	5	6	7	8		10	11	9												2
2	3	4	5		7	8	9		11		6	10										3
2	3	4	5		7	8	9	10	11		6											4
2		4		5	7	8		10	11		6		3	9								5
2	3		5	6	7	10	9		11	8	4											6
2	3		5	6	7		9	10	11	8	4											7
2		4	8	6	7			10	11		9		3		5							8
2		4	5	6	7			10	11	8	9		3									9
2		4	7	6				10	11	8	9		3		5	1						10
2		4	7	6		8		10	11		9		3		5							11
2		4				8		10	11	7	6		3		5		9					12
2		4		1				10	11	8	6		3		5		9	7				13
2				4	7			10	11	8	6		3		5		9					14
2				4	7	8		10	11		6		3		5		9					15
2				4	7			10	11	8	6		3		5		9					16
2	3		5	4	7			10	11	8	6					1	9					17
2	3		5	4	7	8		10	11	9	6					1						18
2	3	4	5	6	7	8		10	11							1	9					19
2	3		5	4	7			10	11	9	6						8					20
2	3		5	4	7		9	10	11		6						8					21
2			5	4	7			10	11	9	6		3				8					22
2			5	4		8	9	10	11		6		3				7					23
2				4	7	8			11		6	10	3		5		9					24
2	3		5	4	7		8	10	11		9								6			25
2	3		5	4	7		8	10	11		9								6			26
2			5	4	7		8	10	11		9		3						6			27
2	3		5	4	7			10	11	9							8		6			28
2			5	4	7	8		10	11	9	6		3									29
2			5	4	7		8	10	11	9			3						6			30
2			5		7		8	10	11	9	4		3						6			31
	2	4			7				11	9			3	8	5		10		6			32
	2	4			7				11	9				8	5		10		6	3		33
2		4			7				11	9				8	5		10		6	3		34
2		4			7			9	11				3	8	5	1	10		6			35
2		4			7			9	11				3	8	5	1	10		6			36
2		4			7					9			3	8	5	1	10		6		11	37
2		4			7				11	9			3	8	5	1	10		6			38
36	16	19	24	27	33	14	12	30	37	22	26	2	22	8	16	8	20	1	13	2	1	
1				1	5		3	6	1	5	4			2	2		7					

Johnston	Reason	Hind	Bell	Liddell	Parker	McLean	Williams	Scott	Underwood	Louch	Henderson	Tully	Johnson	Goffin	Meynell	Bower	Bevan	Prior	Willis	Reed	Lee	
2			5	6	7			10	11	9	4		3				8					1
1			1	1	1			1	1	1	1		1				1					

1910-11

Manager: William Holmes

	P	W	D	L	F	A	Pts
West Bromwich Albion	38	22	9	7	67	41	53
Bolton Wanderers	38	21	9	8	69	40	51
Chelsea	38	20	9	9	71	35	49
Clapton Orient	38	19	7	12	44	35	45
Hull City	38	14	16	8	55	39	44
Derby County	38	17	8	13	73	52	42
Blackpool	38	16	10	12	49	38	42
Burnley	38	13	15	10	45	45	41
Wolverhampton W	38	15	8	15	51	52	38
Fulham	38	15	7	16	52	48	37
Leeds City	38	15	7	16	58	56	37
Bradford Park Avenue	38	14	9	15	53	55	37
Huddersfield Town	38	13	8	17	57	58	34
Glossop North End	38	13	8	17	48	62	34
Leicester Fosse	38	14	5	19	52	62	33
Birmingham	38	12	8	18	42	64	32
Stockport County	38	11	8	19	47	79	30
Gainsborough Trinity	38	9	11	18	37	55	29
Barnsley	38	7	14	17	52	62	28
Lincoln City	38	7	10	21	28	72	24

Division Two

Match No.	Date		Opponents	Result	Scorers	Atten
1	Sep	3	Stockport County	3-0	Scott, Bevan, Goffin	[illegible]
2		10	DERBY COUNTY	1-0	Bevan	1
3		17	Barnsley	2-1	Scott, Parker	[illegible]
4		24	LEICESTER FOSSE	3-1	Scott 2, Goffin	15
5	Oct	1	Wolverhampton W	0-1		[illegible]
6		8	CHELSEA	0-0		25
7		15	BOLTON WANDERERS	0-0		15
8		22	Blackpool	1-1	Liddell	6
9		29	GLOSSOP NORTH END	4-0	Scott 2, Dix 2	15
10	Nov	5	Lincoln City	0-0		5
11		12	HUDDERSFIELD TOWN	2-0	Bevan, Prior	16
12		19	Birmingham	1-0	Scott	14
13		26	WEST BROMWICH ALBION	0-0		1
14	Dec	3	Hull City	2-1	Dix, Prior	1
15		10	FULHAM	1-0	Prior	16
16		17	Bradford Park Avenue	0-3		9
17		24	BURNLEY	0-2		12
18		26	GAINSBOROUGH TRINITY	1-0	Liddell	12
19		27	Leeds City	0-1		13
20		31	STOCKPORT COUNTY	1-0	Bevan	9
21	Jan	7	Derby County	1-3	Bevan	9
22		21	BARNSLEY	3-0	Bevan 2, Dalrymple	10
23		28	Leicester Fosse	1-2	Dalrymple	10
24	Feb	11	Chelsea	0-1		47
25		18	Bolton Wanderers	0-2		11
26		25	BLACKPOOL	2-1	Bevan 2	9
27	Mar	4	Glossop North End	3-1	Bevan, Dalrymple, Scott	3
28		11	LINCOLN CITY	2-0	Lee, Johnson (pen)	8
29		18	Huddersfield Town	0-2		3
30		20	WOLVERHAMPTON W	3-1	Dalrymple 2, Scott	7
31		25	BIRMINGHAM	2-1	Johnson 2 (2 pens)	8
32	Apr	1	West Bromwich Albion	0-3		12
33		8	HULL CITY	1-1	Dalrymple	9
34		14	Gainsborough Trinity	1-3	Bevan	6
35		15	Fulham	1-1	Johnson (pen)	16
36		17	LEEDS CITY	1-0	Tully	6
37		22	BRADFORD PARK AVENUE	1-0	Bevan	9
38		29	Burnley	0-2		3

Appearar

G

FA Cup

1	Jan	16	WOOLWICH ARSENAL *	1-2	Goffin	9

Appearar

G

Final League Position: 4th in Division Two

Note: For Match 38 a number of local newspapers had player number 7 as FISKE, research shows that player was DIX.

* After an abandoned game after 55 minutes due to fog on Saturday 14 January before an attendance of 13,416, the Gunners were leading 1-0.

Johnston	Johnson	Hind	Liddell	Willis	Parker	Goffin	Scott	Bevan	Lee	Dix	Prior	Tully	Hugull	Willingham	Dalrymple	Henderson	Holmes	Hales	
2	3	4	5	6	7	8	9	10	11										1
2	3	4	5	6	7	8	9	10		11									2
2	3	4	5	6	7	8	9	10		11									3
2	3	4	5	6	7	8	9	10		11									4
2	3	4	5	6	7	8	9	10		11									5
2	3	4	5	6	7	8	9	10		11									6
2	3	4	5	6		8	9	10		11	7								7
2	3	4	5	6		8	9	10		11	7								8
2	3	4	5	6		8	9	10		11	7								9
2	3	4	5	6		8	9	10		11	7								10
2	3	4	5	6		8	9	10		11	7								11
2	3	4	5	6		8	9	10		11	7								12
2	3	4	5	6		8	9	10		11	7								13
2	3	4	5	6		8	9	10		11	7								14
2	3	4	5	6		8	9	10		11	7								15
2	3	4	5	6		8	9	10		11	7								16
2	3	4	5	6		8	9	10		11	7								17
2	3	4	5	6		8	9			11	7	10							18
2	3	4	5	6			9	8	11		7	10							19
2	3	4	5	6		8		10	11		7		1	9					20
2	3	4	5	6			9	10	11		7				8				21
2	3	4	5	6	7	8		9		11					10				22
2	3	4	5	6	7	8		9		11					10				23
2	3		5	6	7	8		9		11					10	4			24
2	3		5	6	7	8		9	11						10	4			25
2	3		5	6	7	8	9	10	11							4			26
	3		5	6	7		9	10	11						8	4	2		27
	3		5	6	7		9	10	11						8	4	2		28
2	3		5	6	7		9	10	11						8	4			29
2	3		5	6	7		9	10	11						8	4			30
2	3		5	6	7		9	10	11						8	4			31
2	3		5	6	7		9	10	11						8	4			32
2	3		5	6	7		9	10	11						8	4			33
2	3		5	6	7		9	10	11						8	4			34
2	3	4			7		9	10		11					8	6		5	35
2	3		5	6	7			9	11			10			8	4			36
2	3		5	6	7		9	10	11						8	4			37
2	3		5	6			9	10	11	7					8	4			38
36	38	24	37	37	22	24	32	37	17	22	15	3	1	1	17	15	2	1	
	4		2		1	2	9	12	1	3	3	1			6				

Johnston	Johnson	Hind	Liddell	Willis	Parker	Goffin	Scott	Bevan	Lee	Dix	Prior	
2	3	4	5	6		8	9	10		11	7	1
1	1	1	1	1		1	1	1		1	1	
						1						

1911-12

Manager: William Holmes

	P	W	D	L	F	A	Pts
Derby County	38	23	8	7	74	28	54
Chelsea	38	24	6	8	64	34	54
Burnley	38	22	8	8	77	41	52
Clapton Orient	38	21	3	14	61	44	45
Wolverhampton W	38	16	10	12	57	33	42
Barnsley	38	15	12	11	45	42	42
Hull City	38	17	8	13	54	51	42
Fulham	38	16	7	15	66	58	39
Grimsby Town	38	15	9	14	48	55	39
Leicester Fosse	38	15	7	16	49	66	37
Bradford Park Avenue	38	13	9	16	44	45	35
Birmingham	38	14	6	18	55	59	34
Bristol City	38	14	6	18	41	60	34
Blackpool	38	13	8	17	32	52	34
Nottingham Forest	38	13	7	18	46	48	33
Stockport County	38	11	11	16	47	54	33
Huddersfield Town	38	13	6	19	50	64	32
Glossop North End	38	8	12	18	42	56	28
Leeds City	38	10	8	20	50	78	28
Gainsborough Trinity	38	5	13	20	30	64	23

Division Two

Match No.	Date		Opponents	Result	Scorers	Atter
1	Sep	2	DERBY COUNTY	3-0	Dix, McFadden, Scott	1
2		9	Stockport County	1-1	McFadden	
3		16	LEEDS CITY	2-1	Dalrymple, McFadden	1
4		23	Wolverhampton W	1-0	McFadden	1
5		30	LEICESTER FOSSE	4-1	Scott 3, Willis	1
6	Oct	7	Gainsborough Trinity	2-0	McFadden, Dix	
7		14	GRIMSBY TOWN	1-0	Bevan	1
8		21	Nottingham Forest	0-3		
9		28	CHELSEA	1-4	McFadden	2
10	Nov	4	Burnley	0-1		1
11		11	Bristol City	0-1		
12		18	BIRMINGHAM	2-0	Parker, Bevan	
13		25	Huddersfield Town	0-0		
14	Dec	2	BLACKPOOL	2-0	Bevan, McFadden	1
15		9	Glossop North End	3-3	Parker, McFadden 2	
16		16	HULL CITY	4-0	McFadden 2, Dalrymple 2	1
17		23	Barnsley	1-2	McFadden	
18		25	Bradford Park Avenue	1-2	McFadden	3
19		26	BRADFORD PARK AVENUE	2-0	Dalrymple 2	1
20		30	Derby County	1-5	Dalrymple	1
21	Jan	6	STOCKPORT COUNTY	4-2	Hind, Parker, Scott, McFadden	
22		20	Leeds City	2-0	Bevan, McFadden	
23		27	WOLVERHAMPTON W	1-0	Bevan	
24	Feb	10	GAINSBOROUGH TRINITY	3-0	Dalrymple, Bevan, Hind (pen)	
25		17	Grimsby Town	1-2	Bevan	
26		24	NOTTINGHAM FOREST	0-2		1
27	Mar	2	Chelsea	0-3		4
28		9	BURNLEY	1-2	Dix	2
29		16	BRISTOL CITY	4-0	Bevan, Hind, McFadden (pen), Dalrymple	
30		23	Birmingham	0-4		1
31		30	HUDDERSFIELD TOWN	2-1	Dix, McFadden	
32	Apr	5	Fulham	2-0	Dalrymple, Dix	2
33		6	Blackpool	0-1		1
34		8	FULHAM	4-0	Bevan 2, Dalrymple 2	1
35		9	Leicester Fosse	0-2		1
36		13	GLOSSOP NORTH END	2-1	Dalrymple 2	
37		20	Hull City	2-0	McFadden 2 (1 pen)	
38		27	BARNSLEY	2-0	Bevan, Parker	9

Appeara

G

FA Cup

1	Jan	13	EVERTON	1-2	Bevan	1

Appeara

G

Final League position: 4th in Division Two

Bower	Dalrymple	Dix	Henderson	Hind	Holmes	Hugull	Johnson	Johnston	Liddell	McFadden	Parker	Prior	Riddell	Scott	Silvester	Stonehouse	Willis	
1	8	11		4				2	5	10	7		3	9			6	1
1	8	11		4				2	5	10	7		3	9			6	2
1	8	11		4				2	5	10	7		3	9			6	3
1		11		4				2	5	10	7		3	9			6	4
1		11		4				2	5	10	7		3	9			6	5
1		11		4			3	2	5	10	7			9			6	6
1		11		4			3	2	5	10	7			9			6	7
1		11		4			3	2	5	10	7			9			6	8
1	7	11		4			3	2	5	10				9			6	9
1		11		4			3	2	5	10	7			9			6	10
1	8	11		4			3	2	5	10	7			6				11
1	8	11		4			3	2	5	10	7						6	12
1	8	11		4			3	2	5	10	7						6	13
1	8	11		4			3	2	5	10	7						6	14
1	8	11		4				2	5	10	7		3				6	15
1	8	11		4				2	5	10	7		3				6	16
1	8	11		4				2	5	10	7		3				6	17
1	8	11		4			3	2	5	10	7						6	18
1	8	11		4				2	5	10	7		3				6	19
1	8	11		4			3	2	5	10	7						6	20
	8	11		4		1		2	5	10	7		3	9			6	21
	8	11		4		1	3	2	5	10	7						6	22
	8	11		4		1	3	2	5	10	7						6	23
	8	11		4		1	3	2	5		7			9			6	24
	8	11		4		1	3	2	5	10	7						6	25
	8	11		4		1	3	2	5	10	7						6	26
		11		4		1	3	2	5	10	7			8			6	27
	8	11		4		1	3	2	5	10		7					6	28
	8	11		4	2	1		3		10		7				5	6	29
	8	11		3	2	1				10		7			4	5	6	30
	8	11		2		1			5	10	7		3	4			6	31
	8	11		2		1		3	5	10	7			4			6	32
	8	11		2		1		3	5	10	7			4			6	33
	8	11		2		1		3	5	10	7			4			6	34
	8	11	4	2		1		3		10	7					5	6	35
	8	11		2		1		3	5	10	7			4			6	36
	8	11		2		1		3	5	10	7			4			6	37
	8	11		2		1		3	5	10	7			4			6	38
20	31	38	1	38	2	18	18	36	35	37	34	3	11	21	1	3	37	
	13	5		3						19	4			5			1	

Bower	Dalrymple	Dix	Henderson	Hind	Holmes	Hugull	Johnson	Johnston	Liddell	McFadden	Parker	Prior	Riddell	Scott	Silvester	Stonehouse	Willis	
1	8	11		4				2	5	10	7		3				6	1
1	1	1		1				1	1	1	1		1				1	

1912-13

Manager: William Holmes

	P	W	D	L	F	A	Pts
Preston North End	38	19	15	4	56	33	53
Burnley	38	21	8	9	88	53	50
Birmingham	38	18	10	10	59	44	46
Barnsley	38	19	7	12	57	47	45
Huddersfield Town	38	17	9	12	66	40	43
Leeds City	38	15	10	13	70	64	40
Grimsby Town	38	15	10	13	51	50	40
Lincoln City	38	15	10	13	50	52	40
Fulham	38	17	5	16	65	55	39
Wolverhampton W	38	14	10	14	56	54	38
Bury	38	15	8	15	53	57	38
Hull City	38	15	6	17	60	56	36
Bradford Park Avenue	38	14	8	16	60	60	36
Clapton Orient	38	10	14	14	34	47	34
Leicester Fosse	38	13	7	18	50	65	33
Bristol City	38	9	15	14	46	72	33
Nottingham Forest	38	12	8	18	58	59	32
Glossop North End	38	12	8	18	49	68	32
Stockport County	38	8	10	20	56	78	26
Blackpool	38	9	8	21	39	69	26

Division Two

Match No.	Date		Opponents	Result	Scorers	Atten
1	Sep	7	Preston North End	1-0	Scott	[illegible]
2		14	BURNLEY	2-0	Scott, Dalrymple	2
3		16	STOCKPORT COUNTY	4-1	McFadden 2, Dalrymple, Bevan	[illegible]
4		21	Hull City	1-2	Hendry (og)	1[illegible]
5		28	GLOSSOP NORTH END	1-0	McFadden	1[illegible]
6	Oct	5	BLACKPOOL	1-0	Bevan	1[illegible]
7		12	Lincoln City	1-1	McFadden	[illegible]
8		19	NOTTINGHAM FOREST	2-2	Bevan 2	2[illegible]
9		26	Bristol City	0-1		1[illegible]
10	Nov	2	BIRMINGHAM	0-2		1[illegible]
11		9	Huddersfield Town	0-0		[illegible]
12		16	LEEDS CITY	2-0	McFadden 2	1[illegible]
13		23	Grimsby Town	2-1	Scott, Parker	[illegible]
14		30	BURY	1-2	Bevan	[illegible]
15	Dec	7	Fulham	1-1	Dryden	20[illegible]
16		14	BURNLEY	2-2	Dryden 2	1[illegible]
17		21	Bradford Park Avenue	0-3		1[illegible]
18		25	LEICESTER FOSSE	1-1	Dryden	1[illegible]
19		26	Wolverhampton W	1-1	Dalrymple	[illegible]
20		28	PRESTON NORTH END	1-2	Dryden	1[illegible]
21	Jan	1	Stockport County	0-2		[illegible]
22		4	Burnley	0-5		1[illegible]
23		18	HULL CITY	2-1	Scott, Hind	[illegible]
24		25	Glossop North End	0-3		[illegible]
25	Feb	8	Blackpool	0-2		[illegible]
26		15	LINCOLN CITY	1-2	McFadden (pen)	[illegible]
27		22	Nottingham Forest	0-0		[illegible]
28	Mar	1	BRISTOL CITY	0-0		1[illegible]
29		8	Birmingham	1-1	Parker	1[illegible]
30		15	HUDDERSFIELD TOWN	1-1	McFadden	[illegible]
31		21	WOLVERHAMPTON W	0-0		[illegible]
32		22	Leeds City	1-3	McFadden	[illegible]
33		24	Leicester Fosse	0-1		[illegible]
34		29	GRIMSBY TOWN	1-3	McFadden	[illegible]
35	Apr	5	Bury	0-0		[illegible]
36		12	FULHAM	2-1	Dryden, Parker	14[illegible]
37		19	Barnsley	0-0		4[illegible]
38		26	BRADFORD PARK AVENUE	1-0	Parker	[illegible]

Appeara[illegible]

G[illegible]

FA Cup

1	Jan	11	Sunderland	0-6		12[illegible]

Appeara[illegible]

G[illegible]

Final League Position: 14th in Division Two

Johnston	Evans	Hind	Liddell	Willis	Parker	Scott	Bevan	McFadden	Dix	Dalrymple	Grapes	Bower	Dryden	Benson	Lee	Davis	Jonas	Johnson	Oliver	Griffiths	Tilley	
2	3	4	5	6	7	8	9	10	11													1
2	3		5	6	7	4	9	10	11	8												2
2	3		5	6	7	4	9	10	11	8												3
2	3		5	6	7	4	9	10	11	8												4
2	3		5	6	7	4	9	10	11	8	1											5
2	3		5	6	7	4	9	10	11	8	1											6
2	3		5	6	7	4	9	10	11	8		1										7
2	3		5	6	7	4	9	10	11	8		1										8
2	3		5	6	7	4	9	10	11	8		1										9
2	3		5	6	7	4	9	10	11	8		1										10
2	3	4	5	6	7	10	8	9	11			1										11
2	3	4	5	6	7	9	8	10	11			1										12
2	3	4	5	6	7	9	8	10	11			1										13
2	3	4	5	6	7	9	8	10	11			1										14
2	3	4	5	6	7	8		10	11			1	9									15
2	3	4	5	6	7	8	10		11			1	9									16
2	3		5	6	7	4	8	10	11			1	9									17
2	3		5	6	7	4	8	10	11			1	9									18
2	3	4		6	7	5		10	11	8		1	9									19
2	3	4		6	7	5		10		8		1	9	11								20
2	3	4		6	7	5	10			8		1	9		11							21
2	3	4		6	7	5	8	10		9		1			11							22
3		2	5	6	7	9	8		11							1	4	10				23
	3	2	5	6	7	9	8		11							1	4	10				24
	3	2	5		7	6	8		11							1	4	10	9			25
2	3		5	6	7	9	8	10	11							1	4					26
2	3	4	5		7	6	8		11			1	9				10					27
2	3	4	5		7	6	8		11			1	9				10					28
2	3	4	5		7	9		8	11			1					10			6		29
2	3	4	5		7	9		8	11			1					10			6		30
2	3	4	5		7	9		8	11			1					10			6		31
2	3	4	5		7	9		8	11			1					10			6		32
2	3	4		6	7	5	9		11	8		1					10					33
2	3	4	5	6	8		9	10	11			1									7	34
	3	2			7	5		10	11	8		1	9				4			6		35
	3	2			7	5		10	11	8		1	9				4			6		36
2	3	4			7	5		10	11	8		1	9							6		37
2	3	4			7	5		10	11	8		1	9							6		38
34	37	26	29	27	38	37	27	30	35	18	2	28	13	1	2	4	13	3	1	8	1	
		1			4	4	5	10		3			6									

One own-goal

Johnston	Evans	Hind	Liddell	Willis	Parker	Scott	Bevan	McFadden	Dix	Dalrymple	Grapes	Bower	Dryden	Benson	Lee	Davis	Jonas	Johnson	Oliver	Griffiths	Tilley	
	3	2	5	4	7	6	8	10	11				9			1						1
	1	1	1	1	1	1	1	1	1				1			1						

1913-14

Manager: William Holmes

	P	W	D	L	F	A	Pts
Notts County	38	23	7	8	77	36	53
Bradford Park Avenue	38	23	3	12	71	47	49
Woolwich Arsenal	38	20	9	9	54	38	49
Leeds City	38	20	7	11	76	46	47
Barnsley	38	19	7	12	51	45	45
Clapton Orient	38	16	11	11	47	35	43
Hull City	38	16	9	13	53	37	41
Bristol City	38	16	9	13	52	50	41
Wolverhampton W	38	18	5	15	51	52	41
Bury	38	15	10	13	39	40	40
Fulham	38	16	6	16	46	43	38
Stockport County	38	13	10	15	55	57	36
Huddersfield Town	38	13	8	17	47	53	34
Birmingham	38	12	10	16	48	60	34
Grimsby Town	38	13	8	17	42	58	34
Blackpool	38	9	14	15	33	44	32
Glossop North End	38	11	6	21	51	67	28
Leicester Fosse	38	11	4	23	45	61	26
Lincoln City	38	10	6	22	36	66	26
Nottingham Forest	38	7	9	22	37	76	23

Division Two

Match No.	Date		Opponents	Result	Scorers	Attend
1	Sep	6	FULHAM	1-0	McFadden (pen)	18
2		13	Glossop North End	3-0	Hunter, Dalrymple, Parker	8
3		20	STOCKPORT COUNTY	1-1	McFadden (pen)	11
4		27	Bradford Park Avenue	0-1		15
5	Oct	4	NOTTS COUNTY	1-0	Dalrymple	16
6		11	Leicester Fosse	0-1		10
7		18	WOLVERHAMPTON W	2-2	McFadden 2	14
8		25	Hull City	0-2		8
9	Nov	1	BARNSLEY	1-0	Dalrymple	11
10		8	Bury	0-0		5
11		15	HUDDERSFIELD TOWN	0-0		11
12		22	Lincoln City	0-0		6
13		29	BLACKPOOL	2-0	Jonas 2	10
14	Dec	6	Nottingham Forest	1-1	McFadden	6
15		13	WOOLWICH ARSENAL	1-0	McFadden	26
16		20	Grimsby Town	0-2		6
17		25	BRISTOL CITY	5-2	Dalrymple 3, Forrest, Jonas	20
18		26	Bristol City	0-3		14
19		27	Fulham	0-2		21
20	Jan	3	GLOSSOP NORTH END	5-1	McFadden 2, Dalrymple, Forrest, Scott	6
21		17	Stockport County	1-0	Parker	5
22		24	BRADFORD PARK AVENUE	1-0	Jonas	12
23	Feb	7	Notts County	0-3		9
24		14	LEICESTER FOSSE	1-0	Jonas	11
25		21	Wolverhampton W	1-2	Jonas	6
26		28	HULL CITY	3-0	McFadden 2 (1 pen), Jonas	18
27	Mar	2	LEEDS CITY	3-1	Hind 2, Evans	13
28		7	Barnsley	1-2	Dix	7
29		14	BURY	1-0	Dalrymple	10
30		21	Huddersfield Town	0-1		2
31		28	LINCOLN CITY	5-1	Dalrymple, McFadden 2, Jonas 2	9
32	Apr	4	Blackpool	0-0		3
33		10	Birmingham	0-2		30
34		11	NOTTINGHAM FOREST	3-1	Jonas, Forrest, McFadden	12
35		13	BIRMINGHAM	2-2	McFadden 2	11
36		14	Leeds City	0-0		12
37		18	Woolwich Arsenal	2-2	Parker, McFadden	35
38		25	GRIMSBY TOWN	0-0		10

Appeara

G

FA Cup

1	Jan	10	NOTTINGHAM FOREST	2-2	McFadden, Jonas	15
R		14	Nottingham Forest	1-0	McFadden	9
2		31	Brighton & Hove Albion	1-3	Scott	15

Appeara

G

Final League Position: 6th in Division Two

Johnston	Evans	Forrest	Scott	Willis	Parker	Dalrymple	Hunter	McFadden	Dix	Hind	Pattison	Lomas	Griffiths	Jonas	Clegg	Bower	McMahon	Gibson	Spencer	Van den Eynden	
2	3	4	5	6	7	8	9	10	11												1
	3	4	5	6	7	8	9	10	11	2											2
	3	4	5	6	7	8	9	10	11	2											3
2	3	4	5	6	7	8	9	10			11										4
2	3		5	6	7	8		10		4	11	9									5
2	3		5	6	7	8		10		4	11	9									6
2	3	4	5	6	7	8		10	11			9									7
2	3		5	6	7	8		10	11	4		9									8
	3	4	5	6	7	8		10	11	2		9									9
	3	4	5		7	8	9	10	11	2			6								10
	3	4	5		7	8	9	10	11	2			6								11
	3	4	5			8	9		11	2	7		6	10							12
	3	4	5	6	7	8		10		2	11			9							13
	3	4	5	6	7	8		10		2	11			9							14
	3	4	5	6	7	8		10		2	11			9	1						15
	3	4	5	6	7	9		10	11	2				8	1						16
	3	4	5	6	7	9		10	11	2				8	1						17
2	3	4	5	6	7	9		10	11					8	1						18
2	3	4	5	6	7	8			11					9	1		10				19
2	3	4	5	6	7	8		10	11					9	1						20
	3	4	5		7		9	10	11	2			6	8		1					21
	3	4	5	6	7	8		10	11	2				9		1					22
	3	4	5	6	7	8	9		11	2						1	10				23
	3	4	5		7			10	11	2				9		1		6	8		24
	3	4	5		7	9		10	11	2				8		1		6			25
	3	4			7	8		10	11	2				9		1		6		5	26
	3	4			7	8			11	2				9		1	10	6		5	27
	3	4			7	8		10	11	2				9	1			6		5	28
3		4			7	8		10	11	2				9		1		6		5	29
	3	4			7	8		10	11	2				9		1		6		5	30
	3	4			7	8		10	11	2				9		1		6		5	31
	3	4			7	8		10	11	2				9		1		6		5	32
	3	4			7	8		10	11	2				9		1		6		5	33
2	3	4			7	8		10	11					9		1		6		5	34
	3	4			7	8		10	11	2				9		1		6		5	35
	3	4	10		7	8			11	2				9		1		6		5	36
	3	4			7	8		10	11	2				9		1		6		5	37
	3	4	5		7	8		10	11	2				9	1			6			38
11	37	35	27	19	37	36	9	33	32	31	7	5	4	26	8	16	3	15	1	12	
	1	3	1		3	9	1	16	1	2				10							

Johnston	Evans	Forrest	Scott	Willis	Parker	Dalrymple	Hunter	McFadden	Dix	Hind	Pattison	Lomas	Griffiths	Jonas	Clegg	Bower	McMahon	Gibson	Spencer	Van den Eynden	
2	3	4	5	6	7	8		10	11					9	1						1
	3	4	5		7		9	10	11	2			6	8		1					R
	3	4	5	6	7	8		10	11	2				9		1					2
1	3	3	3	2	3	2	1	3	3	2			1	3	1	2					
			1					2						1							

1914-15

Manager: William Holmes

	P	W	D	L	F	A	Pts
Derby County	38	23	7	8	71	33	53
Preston North End	38	20	10	8	61	42	50
Barnsley	38	22	3	13	51	51	47
Wolverhampton W	38	19	7	12	77	52	45
Arsenal	38	19	5	14	69	41	43
Birmingham	38	17	9	12	62	39	43
Hull City	38	19	5	14	65	54	43
Huddersfield Town	38	17	8	13	61	42	42
Clapton Orient	38	16	9	13	50	48	41
Blackpool	38	17	5	16	58	57	39
Bury	38	15	8	15	61	56	38
Fulham	38	15	7	16	53	47	37
Bristol City	38	15	7	16	62	56	37
Stockport County	38	15	7	16	54	60	37
Leeds City	38	14	4	20	65	64	32
Lincoln City	38	11	9	18	46	65	31
Grimsby Town	38	11	9	18	48	76	31
Nottingham Forest	38	10	9	19	43	77	29
Leicester Fosse	38	10	4	24	47	88	24
Glossop North End	38	6	6	26	31	87	18

Division Two

Match No.	Date		Opponents	Result	Scorers	Atten
1	Sep	1	WOLVERHAMPTON W	1-1	McFadden	10
2		5	Fulham	0-4		12
3		7	Wolverhampton W	0-0		13
4		12	STOCKPORT COUNTY	3-0	Dix, McFadden, Jonas	6
5		19	Hull City	1-0	McFadden	6
6		26	LEEDS CITY	2-0	McFadden, Jonas	9
7	Oct	3	BLACKPOOL	2-0	Jonas (pen), Dalrymple	10
8		10	Arsenal	1-2	Forrest	30
9		17	DERBY COUNTY	0-1		9
10		24	Lincoln City	0-1		6
11		31	BIRMINGHAM	1-1	Jonas	8
12	Nov	7	Grimsby Town	1-2	Jonas	7
13		14	HUDDERSFIELD TOWN	3-1	Jonas, Dix, McFadden	8
14		21	Bristol City	0-3		7
15		28	BURY	2-2	McFadden 2 (1 pen)	1
16	Dec	5	Preston North End	2-2	McFadden, Dalrymple	5
17		12	NOTTINGHAM FOREST	0-0		4
18		25	BARNSLEY	4-2	McFadden 2, Dalrymple 2	8
19		26	Barnsley	0-1		6
20	Jan	2	FULHAM	2-1	McFadden 2	11
21		16	Stockport County	0-2		7
22		23	HULL CITY	0-3		9
23		30	Leicester Fosse	1-1	Scott	8
24	Feb	3	Leeds City	1-0	McFadden	4
25		6	Blackpool	1-5	Jonas	5
26		13	ARSENAL	1-0	McFadden	13
27		20	Derby County	3-0	Parker, Jonas, McFadden	6
28		27	LINCOLN CITY	3-1	McFadden 2 (1 pen), Dalrymple	11
29	Mar	6	Birmingham	0-1		15
30		13	GRIMSBY TOWN	2-1	Ridley, Parker	6
31		20	Huddersfield Town	1-1	McFadden (pen)	4
32		27	BRISTOL CITY	2-0	McFadden, Jonas	8
33	Apr	2	Glossop North End	1-3	McFadden	2
34		3	Bury	0-3		1
35		5	GLOSSOP NORTH END	5-2	Scott, Forrest, Dalrymple, McFadden, Jonas	6
36		10	PRESTON NORTH END	1-1	Dalrymple	8
37		17	Nottingham Forest	1-0	Jonas	4
38		24	LEICESTER FOSSE	2-0	Barron (og), Layton	21

Appearar

G

FA Cup

1	Jan	9	Millwall	1-2	Jonas (pen)	16

Appearar

G

Final League Position: 9th in Division Two

Hind	Evans	Forrest	Scott	Gibson	Parker	Dalrymple	Jonas	McFadden	Dix	King	Bower	Johnston	Steel	Ridley	Layton	Jeyes	Stevens	Morris	Smith	
2	3	4	5	6	7	8	9	10	11											1
2	3	4	5	6	7	8	9	10	11											2
2	3		5	6	7	8	9	10	11	4										3
2	3		5	6	7	8	9	10	11	4										4
2	3		5	6	7	8	9	10	11	4										5
2	3		5	6	7	8	9	10	11	4										6
2	3		5	6	7	8	9	10	11	4										7
2	3	8	5	6	7		9	10	11	4										8
2	3		5	6	7	8	9	10	11	4	1									9
2	3		5	6	7	8	9	10	11	4										10
2	3	8	5	6	7		9	10	11	4										11
2	3	8	5	6	7		9	10	11			4								12
	3	8	5	6	7		9	10	11	4		2								13
	3	8	5	6	7		9	10	11	4		2								14
	3	4	6		7	8	9	10	11			2	5							15
	3	4	6		7	8	9	10	11			2	5							16
	3	4	6		7	8	9	10	11			2	5							17
	3	4	6		7	8	9	10	11			2	5							18
	3	4	6		7	8	9	10	11			2	5							19
	3	4	6		7	8	9	10				2	5	11						20
	3	4	6		7	8	9	10				2	5	11						21
4	3	9	6		7	8		10				2	5	11						22
	3	4	6		7	8		10	11			2	5		9					23
	3	4	5		7	8	9	10	11			2				6				24
7	3	4	6			8	9					2	5	11			10			25
	3	4	6		7	8	9	10				2	5	11						26
	3	4	6		7		9	10		8		2	5	11						27
	3	4	6		7	8		10		9		2	5	11						28
	3	4	6		7	8		10		9		2	5	11						29
	3	4	6		7	8		10		9		2	5	11				1		30
	3	4	6		7	8	9	10				2	5	11				1		31
	3	4	6		7	8	9	10				2	5	11				1		32
	3	4	6		7		9	10		8		2	5	11					1	33
	3	4	6		7		9	10		8		2	5	11					1	34
2		4	6		7	8	9	10				3	5	11				1		35
	3	4	6		7	8		10				2	5	11	9					36
	3	4	6		7	8	9	10				2	5	11						37
	3	4		6	7	8		10				2	5	11	9					38
15	37	31	37	15	37	30	31	37	21	17	1	27	23	17	3	1	1	4	2	
		2	2		2	7	11	21	2					1	1					

One own-goal

Hind	Evans	Forrest	Scott	Gibson	Parker	Dalrymple	Jonas	McFadden	Dix	King	Bower	Johnston	Steel	Ridley	Layton	Jeyes	Stevens	Morris	Smith	
	3	4	6		7	8	10		11			2	5		9					1
	1	1	1		1	1	1		1			1	1		1					
							1													

1915-16

Manager: William Holmes

London Combination

Match No.	Date		Opponents	Result	Scorers
1	Sep	4	Chelsea	1-3	Barber
2		11	WATFORD	2-0	Jones, Dalrymple
3		18	Millwall	1-0	Layton
4		25	CROYDON COMMON	0-0	
5	Oct	2	Arsenal	0-2	
6		9	BRENTFORD	1-3	Turner
7		16	West Ham United	2-5	Lamb, Layton
8		23	TOTTENHAM HOTSPUR	0-0	
9		30	Crystal Palace	2-1	Williams, Whalley
10	Nov	6	QUEEN'S PARK RANGERS	0-2	
11		13	CHELSEA	1-6	Layton
12		20	Watford	1-3	Taylor
13		27	MILLWALL	2-0	Dun, Layton
14	Dec	4	Croydon Common	3-3	Turnbull 3
15		11	ARSENAL	0-2	
16		18	Brentford	1-1	Beech
17		25	Fulham	0-4	
18		27	FULHAM	1-3	Lamb
19	Jan	1	WEST HAM UNITED	1-2	Beech
20		8	Tottenham Hotspur	1-1	Caldwell
21		15	CRYSTAL PALACE	2-3	Upex, Beech
22		22	Queen's Park Rangers	0-0	

Supplementary Tournament

Match No.	Date		Opponents	Result	Scorers
23	Feb	5	Croydon Common	0-3	
24		12	FULHAM	0-3	
25		19	Luton Town	2-1	Layton 2
26		26	ARSENAL	1-1	Craddock
27	Mar	4	Queen's Park Rangers	1-1	Bailey
28		11	CRYSTAL PALACE	1-5	Ashurst
29		18	Fulham	0-4	
30		25	LUTON TOWN	4-0	Beech 2, Layton 2
31	Apr	1	Arsenal	1-2	Beech
32		8	QUEEN'S PARK RANGERS	1-1	Layton
33		15	Crystal Palace	1-2	Bailey
34		21	WEST HAM UNITED	3-1	Layton 2, Beech
35		22	West Ham United	1-2	Odger
36		29	CROYDON COMMON	1-1	Layton

1916-17

Manager: William Holmes

London Combination

Match No.	Date		Opponents	Result	Scorers
1	Sep	2	MILLWALL	3-0	Walden, Bailey, Layton
2		9	Watford	2-2	Layton, H. Simon
3		16	Southampton	1-1	Bailey
4		23	FULHAM	0-3	
5		28	Millwall	0-3	
6		30	Queen's Park Rangers	0-0	
7	Oct	7	WEST HAM UNITED	0-4	
8		14	Tottenham Hotspur	2-4	Chapman, Layton
9		21	CRYSTAL PALACE	2-2	Layton, Bailey
10		28	Brentford	0-3	
11	Nov	4	CHELSEA	0-2	
12		11	Arsenal	0-4	
13		18	LUTON TOWN	1-7	Bailey
14		25	Millwall	0-2	
15	Dec	2	WATFORD	1-1	Upex
16		9	SOUTHAMPTON	1-2	Stevens
17		23	QUEEN'S PARK RANGERS	2-1	Walden, Little
18		25	PORTSMOUTH	1-1	Goodman
19		26	Portsmouth	0-2	
20		30	West Ham United	1-6	Goodman
21	Jan	6	TOTTENHAM HOTSPUR	1-2	Goodman
22		13	Crystal Palace	0-3	
23		20	BRENTFORD	5-2	Layton 4, Goodman
24		27	Chelsea	0-1	
25	Feb	3	ARSENAL	2-2	Layton, Bailey
26		10	Luton Town	3-2	Blake, Stevens, Bailey
27		17	Crystal Palace	0-3	
28		24	WEST HAM UNITED	3-4	Cheriton, Layton 2
29	Mar	3	Arsenal	1-3	Goodman
30		10	PORTSMOUTH	6-1	Blake 3, Cheriton 2, Bailey
31		17	Tottenham Hotspur	2-5	Bailey 2
32		24	MILLWALL	1-2	Cheriton
33		31	CRYSTAL PALACE	1-4	Barlow
34	Apr	6	SOUTHAMPTON	4-0	Layton 2, Blake, Cheriton
35		7	West Ham United	0-2	
36		9	Southampton	1-2	Stevens
37		10	Fulham	1-2	Layton
38		14	ARSENAL	1-3	Chamberlain
39		21	Portsmouth	0-3	
40		28	TOTTENHAM HOTSPUR	0-8	

1917-18

Manager: William Holmes

London Combination

Match No.	Date		Opponents	Result	Scorers
1	Sep	1	Brentford	0-1	
2		8	ARSENAL	0-5	
3		15	West Ham United	2-1	Layton, Powell
4		22	FULHAM	1-5	Layton
5		29	Queen's Park Rangers	0-2	
6	Oct	6	CRYSTAL PALACE	2-3	Nisbitt, Layton
7		13	MILLWALL	2-3	Powell, Tyler
8		20	Tottenham Hotspur	1-2	Powell
9		27	BRENTFORD	1-3	Hodgson
10	Nov	3	Arsenal	1-3	Layton
11		10	WEST HAM UNITED	1-4	Stevens
12		17	Fulham	0-3	
13		24	QUEEN'S PARK RANGERS	1-2	Goodwin
14	Dec	1	Crystal Palace	1-3	Fifield
15		8	Millwall	1-2	Fifield
16		15	TOTTENHAM HOTSPUR	2-4	Nisbitt, Goodwin
17		22	Brentford	0-5	
18		25	CHELSEA	1-4	Fifield
19		26	Chelsea	2-0	Scorers unknown
20		29	ARSENAL	1-2	Parkes
21	Jan	5	West Ham United	0-3	
22		12	FULHAM	1-1	Gray
23		19	Queen's Park Rangers	1-6	Fifield
24		26	CRYSTAL PALACE	0-0	
25	Feb	2	MILLWALL	0-1	
26		9	Chelsea	0-3	
27		16	BRENTFORD	1-1	Fifield
28		23	Arsenal	1-7	Fifield
29	Mar	2	WEST HAM UNITED	1-3	Fifield
30		9	Fulham	2-3	Smith, Nisbitt
31		16	QUEEN'S PARK RANGERS	0-1	
32		23	Crystal Palace	1-3	White
33		29	TOTTENHAM HOTSPUR	2-3	Stevens, Burke
34		30	Millwall	1-1	Gibson
35	Apr	1	Tottenham Hotspur	2-5	Goodman, Nisbitt
36		6	CHELSEA	1-6	Blake

1918-19

Manager: William Holmes

London Combination

Match No.	Date		Opponents	Result	Scorers
1	Sep	7	CRYSTAL PALACE	1-2	Roe
2		14	West Ham United	1-3	Blake
3		21	QUEEN'S PARK RANGERS	1-5	Nesbit
4		28	Tottenham Hotspur	0-2	
5	Oct	5	MILLWALL	0-1	
6		12	Chelsea	0-6	
7		19	FULHAM	1-4	Brightwell
8		26	BRENTFORD	1-2	Nesbit
9	Nov	2	Crystal Palace	1-6	Nash
10		9	WEST HAM UNITED	1-5	White
11		16	Queen's Park Rangers	1-3	White
12		23	TOTTENHAM HOTSPUR	0-3	
13		30	Millwall	1-1	Wiseman
14	Dec	7	CHELSEA	0-5	
15		14	Fulham	1-5	Chesney
16		21	Brentford	0-7	
17		25	ARSENAL	3-2	Dimmock 2, Eves
18		26	Arsenal	2-9	Dimmock, own-goal
19		28	CRYSTAL PALACE	0-4	
20	Jan	4	West Ham United	0-7	
21		11	QUEEN'S PARK RANGERS	1-5	Dimmock
22		18	Tottenham Hotspur	4-2	Moore 2, Dimmock, Jones
23		25	MILLWALL	1-3	Bowyer
24	Feb	1	Chelsea	3-3	Bowyer, Nash, Lee
25		8	FULHAM	0-4	
26		15	Arsenal	0-4	
27		22	Crystal Palace	1-4	Moore
28	Mar	1	WEST HAM UNITED	0-0	
29		8	Queen's Park Rangers	2-5	Dalrymple, Moore
30		15	TOTTENHAM HOTSPUR	1-2	Dalrymple
31		22	Millwall	1-1	own-goal
32		29	CHELSEA	0-0	
33	Apr	5	Fulham	0-2	
34		12	ARSENAL	2-2	Bowyer, Dalrymple
35		18	Brentford	0-2	
36		21	BRENTFORD	4-2	Dimmock, Dalrymple, Bowyer, Smith

London Victory Cup

Match No.	Date		Opponents	Result	Scorers
1	Dec	30	Brentford	2-3	Dimmock, Bowyer

1919-20

Manager: William Holmes

	P	W	D	L	F	A	Pts
Tottenham Hotspur	42	32	6	4	102	32	70
Huddersfield Town	42	28	8	6	97	38	64
Birmingham	42	24	8	10	85	34	56
Blackpool	42	21	10	11	65	47	52
Bury	42	20	8	14	60	44	48
Fulham	42	19	9	14	61	50	47
West Ham United	42	19	9	14	47	40	47
Bristol City	42	13	17	12	46	43	43
South Shields	42	15	12	15	58	48	42
Stoke	42	18	6	18	60	54	42
Hull City	42	18	6	18	78	72	42
Barnsley	42	15	10	17	61	55	40
Port Vale*	42	16	8	18	59	62	40
Leicester City	42	15	10	17	41	61	40
Clapton Orient	42	16	6	20	51	59	38
Stockport County	42	14	9	19	52	61	37
Rotherham County	42	13	8	21	51	83	34
Nottingham Forest	42	11	9	22	43	73	31
Wolverhampton W	42	10	10	22	55	80	30
Coventry City	42	9	11	22	35	73	29
Lincoln City	42	9	9	24	44	101	27
Grimsby Town	42	10	5	27	34	75	25

*Port Vale replaced Leeds City

Division Two

Match No.	Date		Opponents	Result	Scorers	Attenda
1	Aug	30	Huddersfield Town	1-2	Bowyer	5,
2	Sep	4	FULHAM	0-1		19,
3		6	HUDDERSFIELD TOWN	0-1		12,
4		13	WOLVERHAMPTON W	0-0		11,
5		15	Fulham	1-2	Bowyer	10,
6		20	Wolverhampton W	2-1	S. Tonner, Ives	11,
7		27	SOUTH SHIELDS	4-0	Ives 3, Layton	15,
8	Oct	4	South Shields	0-2		18,
9		11	Tottenham Hotspur	1-2	Layton	44,
10		13	Hull City	1-3	J. Tonner	7,
11		18	TOTTENHAM HOTSPUR	0-4		*32,
12		25	Lincoln City	1-2	Nicholls (pen)	7,
13	Nov	1	LINCOLN CITY	1-0	Forrest	20,
14		15	PORT VALE	2-1	Chapman, Townrow	8,
15		22	Bury	0-3		5,
16		24	Port Vale	2-4	Forrest, Bowyer	7,
17		29	BURY	2-1	S. Tonner, J. Tonner	8,
18	Dec	6	Nottingham Forest	1-2	J. Tonner	6,
19		13	NOTTINGHAM FOREST	1-0	Forrest	10,
20		20	Coventry City	0-0		18,
21		25	STOCKPORT COUNTY	2-1	Bowyer (pen), J. Tonner	14,
22		26	Stockport County	1-3	Bowyer	10,
23		27	COVENTRY CITY	2-2	J. Tonner, Roberts (og)	13,
24	Jan	3	Barnsley	1-2	Williams	4,
25		17	BARNSLEY	2-0	Parker, Williams	13,
26		24	Blackpool	0-3		5,
27	Feb	7	Bristol City	1-1	J. Tonner	12,
28		14	BRISTOL CITY	1-0	Parker	14,
29		28	WEST HAM UNITED	1-0	Williams	28,
30	Mar	4	West Ham United	1-0	J. Tonner	15,
31		6	ROTHERHAM COUNTY	1-2	S. Tonner	12,
32		13	Rotherham County	1-3	S. Tonner	7,
33		18	BLACKPOOL	3-0	Williams, Bowyer, J. Tonner	8,
34		20	STOKE	2-1	Nicholson, Williams	16,
35		27	Stoke	0-2		7,
36	Apr	2	HULL CITY	2-2	S. Tonner (pen), Williams	12,
37		3	GRIMSBY TOWN	3-0	J. Tonner 2, Chapman	10,
38		10	Grimsby Town	0-2		5,
39		17	BIRMINGHAM	2-1	Smith, Layton	18,
40		24	Birmingham	1-2	J. Tonner	20,
41		26	LEICESTER CITY	3-0	S. Tonner, J. Tonner, Dixon	8,
42	May	1	Leicester City	1-1	Dixon	12,
						Appearan
						Go

FA Cup

1	Jan	10	Manchester City	1-4	J. Tonner	25,
						Appearan
						Go

Final League Position: 15th in Division Two

* Ground Record at Millfields Road

Nicholls	Tonner, S	Forrest	Worboys	Hind	Parker	Dalrymple	Smith	Bowyer	Ives	Carrington	Layton	Gray	Francis	Calderhead	Williams	Townrow	Nicholson	Tonner, J	Spottiswood	Chapman	Osmond	Ing	Tonner, JE	Dixon	
2	3	4	5	6	7	8	9	10	11																1
3	2	6	5	4	7		9	10	11	1	8														2
3	2	6		4	7	8	9	10	11			1	5												3
3	2	4	5			8	9	10	11			1		6	7										4
3	2	4					10	8	11		9	1			7	5	6								5
3	2	4			7		10	8	11		9					5	6								6
3	2	4			7		10	8	11		9					5	6								7
3	2	4			7		9	8	11		10					5	6								8
3	2	4	6		7		10	8	11		9					5									9
3		4	5	2	7		10		11		9						6	8							10
3	2		6		7		9	8	11							5		10	4						11
3		4	6	2	7	8			11		9					5		10							12
3		4	10	2	7	8			11		9					5	6								13
3		4		2	7	8			11		10					5	6			9					14
3		4		2	7	8	10		11							5	6			9					15
3		4			7			8	11							5	6	10		9	2				16
3	2	4	5		7						8				11		6	10		9					17
3	2	4	5		7						8				11			10		9		6			18
3	2	4	5								8				11			10		9		6	7		19
3	2	4	5								8				11			10		9		6	7		20
3	2	4	5					8			9				11			10				6	7		21
3	2							8			9				11	5	6	10				4	7		22
3	2							8			9				11	5	6	10				4	7		23
3	2		5					8			9				11		6	10				4	7		24
3	2	9	5		8										11		6	10				4	7		25
3	2	9	5		8										11		6	10				4	7		26
3	2	9			8										11	5	6	10				4	7		27
3	2	9			8							1			11	5	6	10				4	7		28
3	2	9			8										11	5	6	10				4	7		29
3	2	9			7		8								11	5	6	10				4			30
3	2	9					7				8				11	5	6	10				4			31
3	2							8	11						7	5	6	10				4		9	32
3	2	4			8			7							11	5	6	10						9	33
3	2	4			8			7							11	5	6	10						9	34
3	2	4			8			7							11	5	6	10						9	35
3	2				8			7							11	5	6	10				4		9	36
3	2	4			8			7							11	5		10		9		6			37
3	2	4			8										11	5	6	10		9			7		38
3	2	4					7				8	1			11	5	6	10						9	39
3	2	4					7				8	1			11	5	6	10						9	40
3	2	4					7				8				11	5	6	10						9	41
3	2	4					7				8				11	5	6	10						9	42
42	36	36	16	8	28	7	18	21	17	1	23	6	1	1	28	29	30	30	1	9	1	17	12	9	
1	6	3			2		1	6	4		3				6	1	1	12		2				2	

One own-goal

Nicholls	Tonner, S	Forrest	Worboys	Hind	Parker	Dalrymple	Smith	Bowyer	Ives	Carrington	Layton	Gray	Francis	Calderhead	Williams	Townrow	Nicholson	Tonner, J	Spottiswood	Chapman	Osmond	Ing	Tonner, JE	Dixon	
3	2	4	5		8						9				11			10				6	7		1
1	1	1	1		1						1				1			1				1	1		
																		1							

1920-21

Manager: William Holmes

	P	W	D	L	F	A	Pts
Birmingham	42	24	10	8	79	38	58
Cardiff City	42	24	10	8	59	32	58
Bristol City	42	19	13	10	49	29	51
Blackpool	42	20	10	12	54	42	50
West Ham United	42	19	10	13	51	30	48
Notts County	42	18	11	13	55	40	47
Clapton Orient	42	16	13	13	43	42	45
South Shields	42	17	10	15	61	46	44
Fulham	42	16	10	16	43	47	42
The Wednesday	42	15	11	16	48	48	41
Bury	42	15	10	17	45	49	40
Leicester City	42	12	16	14	39	46	40
Hull City	42	10	20	12	43	53	40
Leeds United	42	14	10	18	40	45	38
Wolverhampton W	42	16	6	20	49	66	38
Barnsley	42	10	16	16	48	50	36
Port Vale	42	11	14	17	43	49	36
Nottingham Forest	42	12	12	18	48	55	36
Rotherham County	42	12	12	18	37	53	36
Stoke	42	12	11	19	46	56	35
Coventry City	42	12	11	19	39	70	35
Stockport County	42	9	12	21	42	75	30

Division Two

Match No.	Date		Opponents	Result	Scorers	Attenda
1	Aug	28	LEICESTER CITY	2-0	Williams, Smith	18,0
2		30	Cardiff City	0-0		25,0
3	Sep	4	Leicester City	1-2	Smith	17,6
4		6	CARDIFF CITY	2-0	J. Tonner, Gillatt	12,0
5		11	Stockport County	0-6		7,0
6		13	Blackpool	2-2	Juniper, Nicholson	8,0
7		18	STOCKPORT COUNTY	5-0	Parker, S. Tonner 2, J. Tonner, Forrest	10,0
8		25	Nottingham Forest	1-1	Nicholls	12,0
9	Oct	2	NOTTINGHAM FOREST	2-1	S. Tonner (pen), Cockle	17,5
10		9	Bury	1-0	J. Tonner	13,2
11		16	BURY	1-0	J. Tonner	14,1
12		23	BRISTOL CITY	0-0		25,0
13		30	Bristol City	0-2		26,0
14	Nov	13	Barnsley	0-1		10,4
15		20	ROTHERHAM COUNTY	2-0	Worboys, Cockle	17,0
16		25	BARNSLEY	3-2	S. Tonner (pen), Cockle, Williams	19,0
17		27	Rotherham County	0-0		12,0
18	Dec	4	FULHAM	3-0	J. Tonner, Williams, Cockle	22,0
19		11	Fulham	0-1		25,0
20		25	HULL CITY	1-1	S. Tonner	30,0
21		27	Hull City	0-3		14,0
22	Jan	1	Port Vale	0-4		12,0
23		15	WEST HAM UNITED	0-1		24,0
24		22	West Ham United	0-1		27,8
25	Feb	2	South Shields	0-3		5,0
26		5	SOUTH SHIELDS	1-0	Williams	20,0
27		12	BIRMINGHAM	1-1	Williams	18,0
28		16	Birmingham	0-0		20,0
29		26	LEEDS UNITED	1-0	Bradley	17,0
30	Mar	5	Leeds United	1-2	Williams	18,0
31		12	COVENTRY CITY	0-0		15,0
32		19	Coventry City	1-1	Bradbury (pen)	16,0
33		25	WOLVERHAMPTON W	0-1		27,0
34		26	Stoke	1-0	Dixon	14,0
35		28	Wolverhampton W	2-0	Bradbury (pen), Townrow	30,0
36	Apr	2	STOKE	3-2	Dixon, Smith, Williams	16,0
37		9	The Wednesday	1-1	Smith	15,0
38		16	THE WEDNESDAY	1-0	Williams	16,0
39		23	Notts County	1-3	Williams	9,0
40		25	PORT VALE	0-0		15,0
41		30	NOTTS COUNTY	3-0	Dixon, Forrest, Gillatt	19,0
42	May	7	BLACKPOOL	0-0		12,0
						Appearanc
						Go

FA Cup

Q6	Dec	18	PORT VALE	1-0	Smith	15,7
1	Jan	4	Bradford Park Avenue	0-1		13,0
						Appearnc
						Go

Final League Position: 7th in Division Two

	Tonner, S	Nicholls	Forrest	Townrow	Nicholson	Smith	Gillatt	Juniper	Tonner, J	Williams	Bradbury	Worboys	Parker	Leggett	Denton	Cockle	Dale	Gray	Osmond	Bradley	Dixon	Shearer	Bratby	Nunn
1	2	3	4	5	6	7	8	9	10	11														
2	2	3	4	5	6	7	8	9	10	11														
3	2	3	4	5	6	7	8	9	10	11														
4	2	3	4	5	6	7	8	9	10	11														
5	2	3	4	5	6	7	8	9	10	11														
6		3	4		6			9		11	2	5	7	8	10									
7	2	3	4	5	6	7		9	10	11			8											
8	2	3	4	5	6	7		9	10	11			8											
9	2	3	4	5	6		7		10	11			8			9								
10	2	3	4	5	6		7		10	11			8			9	1							
11	2	3	4	5	6		7		10	11			8			9								
12	2	3	4	5	6		7		10	11			8			9								
13	2	3	4	5	6		7		10	11			8			9								
14	2	3	4	5	6		7		10	11			8			9								
15	2	3		5	6		7		10	11		4	8			9								
16	2	3		5	6		7		10	11		4	8			9								
17	2	3		5	6		7		10	11		4	8			9								
18	2	3	4	5	6	7			10	11			8			9								
19	2	3	4	5	6	7			10	11			8			9								
20	2	3	4	5		7			10	11		6	8			9								
21	2	3	6			7		4	10	11		5	8			9								
22		3	4			7	8		10	11		5	6			9		1	2					
23	2	3	4	5	6	7	8		10	11						9		1						
24	2	3	4	5	6	9	7		10	11			8					1						
25	2		4	5	6	7			9	11			10					1	3	8				
26	2			5	6	9				11			10					1	3	8	4	7		
27	2			5	6	9				11			10					1	3	8	4	7		
28	2			5	6	9				11			10						3	8	4	7		
29	2			5	6	7				11			10			9			3	8	4			
30	2			5	6	7	8			11					10	9			3		4			
31				5	6	7	8			11	2				10	9			3		4			
32				5	6	7	8			11	2		10			9			3		4			
33				5	6	7	8			11	2		10			9			3		4			
34				5	6	7	8			11	2	4	10						3		9			
35				5	6	7	8			11	2	4	10						3		9			
36				5	6	7	8			11	2	4	10						3		9			
37				5	6	7	8			11	2	4	10						3		9			
38				5	6		8			11	2	4	10						3		9	7		
39				5	6	7	8			11	2		10						3		4		9	
40	2				6	7	8					5	10						3		4		9	11
41	2		4		6	7	8					5	10						3		9			11
42	2		4	5	6	7	8			11									3		9		10	
	31	24	24	37	39	31	30	9	24	40	10	14	33	1	3	20	1	6	19	5	17	4	3	2
	5	1	2	1	1	4	2	1	5	9	2	1	1			4				1	3			

	Tonner, S	Nicholls	Forrest	Townrow	Nicholson	Smith	Gillatt	Juniper	Tonner, J	Williams	Bradbury	Worboys	Parker	Leggett	Denton	Cockle	Dale	Gray	Osmond	Bradley	Dixon	Shearer	Bratby	Nunn
Q6	2	3	4	5		7			10	11		6	8			9								
1	2		4	5		7			10	11		6	8			9		1	3					
	2	1	2	2		2			2	2		2	2			2		1	1					
						1																		

1921-22

Manager: Aug 1921–Feb 1922 William Holmes; Feb 1922 Freddie Powell (acting); Apr 1922–May 1922 Peter Proudfoot.

	P	W	D	L	F	A	Pts
Nottingham Forest	42	22	12	8	51	30	56
Stoke	42	18	16	8	60	44	52
Barnsley	42	22	8	12	67	52	52
West Ham United	42	20	8	14	52	39	48
Hull City	42	19	10	13	51	41	48
South Shields	42	17	12	13	43	38	46
Fulham	42	18	9	15	57	38	45
Leeds United	42	16	13	13	48	38	45
Leicester City	42	14	17	11	39	34	45
The Wednesday	42	15	14	13	47	50	44
Bury	42	15	10	17	54	55	40
Derby County	42	15	9	18	60	64	39
Notts County	42	12	15	15	47	51	39
Crystal Palace	42	13	13	16	45	51	39
Clapton Orient	42	15	9	18	43	50	39
Rotherham County	42	14	11	17	32	43	39
Wolverhampton W	42	13	11	18	44	49	37
Port Vale	42	14	8	20	43	57	36
Blackpool	42	15	5	22	44	57	35
Coventry City	42	12	10	20	51	60	34
Bradford Park Avenue	42	12	9	21	46	62	33
Bristol City	42	12	9	21	37	58	33

Division Two

Match No.	Date		Opponents	Result	Scorers	Attenda
1	Aug	27	BURY	3-1	Bratby, Smith, S. Tonner	20,7
2		29	Port Vale	0-3		17,0
3	Sep	3	Bury	0-0		12,4
4		10	Stoke	0-0		16,0
5		12	PORT VALE	2-0	Rennox 2	17,1
6		17	STOKE	1-0	Rennox	17,5
7		24	Leeds United	0-2		20,0
8	Oct	1	LEEDS UNITED	4-2	Rennox 2, O. Williams, Gillatt	10,5
9		8	Hull City	1-2	O. Williams	12,0
10		15	HULL CITY	0-2		21,0
11		22	Notts County	0-0		10,0
12		29	NOTTS COUNTY	2-1	O. Williiams, Rennox	15,0
13	Nov	5	Crystal Palace	0-1		18,0
14		12	CRYSTAL PALACE	0-0		19,0
15		19	ROTHERHAM COUNTY	1-2	Galbraith	12,0
16		26	Rotherham County	0-2		9,0
17	Dec	3	The Wednesday	0-0		18,0
18		10	THE WEDNESDAY	1-1	Smith	12,0
19		17	Fulham	0-2		26,0
20		24	FULHAM	4-2	Whipp, Rennox, Gillatt 2	21,0
21		26	Bradford Park Avenue	1-3	O. Williams	20,0
22		27	BRADFORD PARK AVENUE	1-0	Galbraith	8,0
23		31	BLACKPOOL	3-0	Whipp 2, Gillatt	15,0
24	Jan	14	Blackpool	0-2		6,0
25		21	LEICESTER CITY	0-0		8,0
26	Feb	4	DERBY COUNTY	3-2	T. Williams 2, Whipp	9,6
27		9	Leicester City	0-1		11,3
28		11	Derby County	0-3		10,0
29		18	COVENTRY CITY	4-0	Whipp 2, Rennox, O. Williams	16,5
30		25	Coventry City	2-1	Whipp, Rennox	15,0
31	Mar	4	BARNSLEY	2-1	Tindall (og), O. Williams	14,0
32		11	Barnsley	0-4		10,0
33		18	Wolverhampton W	2-0	Rennox, J. Tonner	11,4
34		25	WOLVERHAMPTON W	1-0	Rennox	16,0
35	Apr	1	Nottingham Forest	0-2		8,0
36		8	NOTTINGHAM FOREST	1-2	J. Tonner	14,0
37		14	West Ham United	2-1	Smith, T. Williams	30,0
38		15	Bristol City	1-2	Galbraith	14,0
39		17	WEST HAM UNITED	0-0		27,0
40		22	BRISTOL CITY	0-1		12,0
41		29	South Shields	1-1	Whipp	10,0
42	May	6	SOUTH SHIELDS	0-1		13,0

Appearanc

Go

FA Cup

1	Jan	7	Leicester City	0-2		20,7

Appearanc

Go

Final League Position: 15th in Division Two

Tonner, S	Osmond	Dixon	Worboys	Nicholson	Smith	Bratby	Rennox	Kean	Williams, O	Wood	Bradbury	Galbraith	Townrow	Nunn	Gillatt	Whipp	Parker	Tonner, J	Nicholls	Williams, T	
2	3	4	5	6	7	8	9	10	11												1
2	3	4	5	6	7	8	9	10	11												2
2				6	7	8	9	10	11	1	3	4	5								3
2				6	7	8	9	10		1	3	4	5	11							4
2				6	7	8	9	10		1	3	4	5	11							5
2				6	7	8	9	10		1	3	4	5	11							6
2				6		8	9	10	11	1	3	4	5		7						7
2				6		8	9	10	11	1	3	4	5		7						8
2				6		7	9	10	11	1	3	4	5		8						9
2				6	7		9	10	11	1	3	4	5		8						10
2		4		6		7	9		11	1	3		5			8	10				11
2		4		6		7	9		11	1	3		5			8	10				12
2		4		6		7	9		11	1	3		5			8	10				13
2		6					9		11	1	3	4	5			8	7	10			14
2		6			8		9		11	1	3	4	5				7	10			15
2		9		4	10				11	1	3	6	5			8	7				16
	3	4		6	10				11	1	2	5	9		7	8					17
	3	4		6	10				11	1	2	5	9		7	8					18
	3	9		6	10					1	2	4	5	11	7	8					19
	3	4		6	10		9		11	1	2	5			7	8					20
	3	4		6	10		9		11	1	2	5			7	8					21
	3	4		6	10		9		11	1	2	5			7	8					22
	3	4		6	10		9		11	1	2	5			7	8					23
2	3	4		6	8		9	10	11	1		5			7						24
	2	4		6		10			11	1		5			7		8		3	9	25
	2	4				10			11	1		6	5		7	8			3	9	26
	2	4				10			11	1		6	5		7	8			3	9	27
	2	4			10				11	1	3	6	5		7			8		9	28
	2	4		6	7		10		11	1		5				8			3	9	29
	2	4		6	7		10		11	1		5				8			3	9	30
	2	4		6	7		10		11	1		5				8			3	9	31
	2	4	6		7		10		11	1		5				8			3	9	32
	2	4	6		7		10		11	1		5						8	3	9	33
	2	4	6		7		10		11	1		5						8	3	9	34
	2	4	6		7		10			1		5		11				8	3	9	35
	2	4	6		7		10		11	1		5						8	3	9	36
	2	4		6	7	11	10			1		5						8	3	9	37
	2	4		6	7	11	10			1		5						8	3	9	38
	2	4		6	7	11	10			1		5						8	3	9	39
	2	4		6	7	11	10			1		5						8	3	9	40
	2	4		6	7		10		11	1		5				8		8	3		41
	2	4		6	7		10		11	1		5				8		8	3		42
17	28	34	7	32	32	19	34	11	33	40	22	37	20	5	16	20	7	13	17	16	
1					3	1	11		6			3			4	8		2		3	

One own-goal

Tonner, S	Osmond	Dixon	Worboys	Nicholson	Smith	Bratby	Rennox	Kean	Williams, O	Wood	Bradbury	Galbraith	Townrow	Nunn	Gillatt	Whipp	Parker	Tonner, J	Nicholls	Williams, T	
	3	4		6	10		9		11	1	2	5			7	8					1
	1	1		1	1		1		1	1	1	1			1	1					

1922-23

Manager: Peter Proudfoot

	P	W	D	L	F	A	Pts
Notts County	42	23	7	12	46	34	53
West Ham United	42	20	11	11	63	38	51
Leicester City	42	21	9	12	65	44	51
Manchester United	42	17	14	11	51	36	48
Blackpool	42	18	11	13	60	43	47
Bury	42	18	11	13	55	46	47
Leeds United	42	18	11	13	43	36	47
The Wednesday	42	17	12	13	54	47	46
Barnsley	42	17	11	14	62	51	45
Fulham	42	16	12	14	43	32	44
Southampton	42	14	14	14	40	40	42
Hull City	42	14	14	14	43	45	42
South Shields	42	15	10	17	35	44	40
Derby County	42	14	11	17	46	50	39
Bradford City	42	12	13	17	41	45	37
Crystal Palace	42	13	11	18	54	62	37
Port Vale	42	14	9	19	39	51	37
Coventry City	42	15	7	20	46	63	37
Clapton Orient	42	12	12	18	40	50	36
Stockport County	42	14	8	20	43	58	36
Rotherham County	42	13	9	20	44	63	35
Wolverhampton W	42	9	9	24	42	77	27

Division Two

Match No.	Date		Opponents	Result	Scorers	Attendar
1	Aug	26	BARNSLEY	0-1		16,0
2		28	Blackpool	0-0		8,0
3	Sep	2	Barnsley	1-2	J. Tonner	12,0
4		4	BLACKPOOL	0-1		9,0
5		9	LEICESTER CITY	2-0	J. Tonner, Galbraith	14,0
6		16	Leicester City	0-2		17,0
7		23	PORT VALE	0-0		11,0
8		30	Port Vale	1-3	Nicholson	10,2
9	Oct	7	LEEDS UNITED	3-0	Jacques, Rennox, O. Williams	14,5
10		14	Leeds United	0-0		15,0
11		21	THE WEDNESDAY	2-2	J. Tonner, Jacques	16,0
12		28	The Wednesday	1-4	Rennox	15,6
13	Nov	4	Manchester United	0-0		20,0
14		11	MANCHESTER UNITED	1-1	S. Tonner	16,0
15		18	West Ham United	0-1		24,0
16		25	WEST HAM UNITED	0-2		21,0
17	Dec	2	Bury	1-5	Bailey	10,0
18		9	BURY	0-2		5,0
19		16	SOUTH SHIELDS	0-0		9,0
20		23	South Shields	0-3		10,0
21		25	Stockport County	2-0	J. Tonner, O. Williams	9,5
22		26	STOCKPORT COUNTY	0-2		15,0
23		30	ROTHERHAM COUNTY	5-1	J. Tonner 3, Bailey, O. Williams	17,0
24	Jan	6	Rotherham County	0-0		10,3
25		20	Wolverhampton W	3-1	O. Williams, T. Williams, Bliss	13,7
26		27	WOLVERHAMPTON W	4-1	Bailey, O. Williams (pen), Bliss, Dixon	8,5
27	Feb	3	HULL CITY	2-0	Townrow, T. Williams	12,5
28		10	Hull City	1-2	Bailey	8,0
29		17	CRYSTAL PALACE	3-1	Bliss, Nicholson, T. Williams	25,0
30		24	Crystal Palace	0-2		22,0
31	Mar	3	FULHAM	0-2		16,0
32		10	Fulham	0-0		22,0
33		17	Notts County	1-3	O. Williams	14,0
34		24	NOTTS COUNTY	2-1	Waite, Higginbotham	17,0
35		31	Derby County	0-0		8,0
36	Apr	2	COVENTRY CITY	0-0		20,0
37		3	Coventry City	1-2	Waite	18,0
38		7	DERBY COUNTY	0-0		15,0
39		14	Southampton	0-2		9,0
40		21	SOUTHAMPTON	1-0	O. Williams	14,6
41		23	Bradford City	2-1	Bliss 2	11,0
42	May	5	BRADFORD CITY	1-0	Bliss	18,0

Appearanc

Go

FA Cup

1	Jan	12	MILLWALL	0-2		36,8

Appearanc

Go

Final League Position: 19th in Division Two

Osmond	Nicholls	Dixon	Galbraith	Nicholson	Smith	Gillatt	Rennox	Bratby	Williams, O	Worboys	Bailey	Williams, T	Tonner, S	Tonner, J	Rose	Barr	Townrow	Duffus, J	Jacques	Nunn	Duffus,R	Bliss	Higginbotham	Rosier	Waite	
2	3	4	5	6	7	8	9	10	11																	1
2	3	4	5		7		10		11	6	8	9														2
	3	4	5		7		10		11	6	8		2	9												3
	3	4	5		7		10		11	6	8		2	9												4
	3	4	5		8			10	11				2	9	6	7										5
	3	4	5		8			10	11				2	9	6	7										6
	3		5	6				10	11		8		2	9	4	7										7
	3		4	6			10		11				2	8		7	5	9								8
	3		4	6			10		11				2	8		7	5		9							9
	3		4	6			10		11				2	8		7	5		9							10
	3		4	6			10						2	8		7	5		9	11						11
	3		4	6		7	10		11				2	8			5		9							12
	3		4	5		7	9		11		10		2	8							6					13
	3		4	5		7	9		11		10		2	8							6					14
	3	4		6			10		11	5			2	8				9		7						15
	3	4		6					11	5			2	10			8	9		7						16
	3	4	5	9				11			8		2			10				7	6					17
	3	4	5			7					8		2	10				9		11	6					18
	3	4	5	6	7	8							2	10				9		11						19
	3	4	5	6	7	10			11		8		2	9												20
	3	4	5	6		7			11		8	9	2	10												21
	3	4	5	6		7			11		8	9	2	10												22
	3	4	5	6	7				11		8		2	9								10				23
	3	4	5	6		7			11		8		2	9								10				24
	3		4	6	7				11		8	9	2				5					10				25
	3	4		6	7				11		8	9	2				5					10				26
	3	4			7				11		8	9	2				5				6	10				27
	3		4	6	7				11		8	9	2					5				10				28
	3	4		6	7				11			9	2				5					10	8			29
	3	4		6	7				11			9	2				5					10	8			30
	3	4		6	7				11				2	9			5					10	8			31
		4		6	7					3		9	2				5			11		10	8			32
		4		6	7				11				2				5					10	8	3	9	33
		4		6		7			11				2				5					10	8	3	9	34
		4		6		7			11				2				5					10	8	3	9	35
		4		6		7			11				2				5					10	8	3	9	36
		4		6		7			11				2				5					10	8	3	9	37
		4		6		7			11		8		2				5						10	3	9	38
		4		6	7		10		11				2				5						8	3	9	39
		4		6	7				11				2				5					10	8	3	9	40
		4		6	7				11				2				5					10	8	3	9	41
		4		6	7				11				2				5					10	8	3	9	42
2	31	32	24	35	22	15	13	5	37	6	18	10	40	22	3	8	23	6	4	7	5	18	14	10	10	
		1	1	2			2		7		4	3	1	7			1		2			6	1		2	

Osmond	Nicholls	Dixon	Galbraith	Nicholson	Smith	Gillatt	Rennox	Bratby	Williams, O	Worboys	Bailey	Williams, T	Tonner, S	Tonner, J	Rose	Barr	Townrow	Duffus, J	Jacques	Nunn	Duffus,R	Bliss	Higginbotham	Rosier	Waite	
	3	4	5	6		7			11		8		2	9								10				1
	1	1	1	1		1			1		1		1	1								1				

1923-24

Manager: Peter Proudfoot

	P	W	D	L	F	A	Pts
Leeds United	42	21	12	9	61	35	54
Bury	42	21	9	12	63	35	51
Derby County	42	21	9	12	75	42	51
Blackpool	42	18	13	11	72	47	49
Southampton	42	17	14	11	52	31	48
Stoke	42	14	18	10	44	42	46
Oldham Athletic	42	14	17	11	45	52	45
The Wednesday	42	16	12	14	54	51	44
South Shields	42	17	10	15	49	50	44
Clapton Orient	42	14	15	13	40	36	43
Barnsley	42	16	11	15	57	61	43
Leicester City	42	17	8	17	64	54	42
Stockport County	42	13	16	13	44	52	42
Manchester United	42	13	14	15	52	44	40
Crystal Palace	42	13	13	16	53	65	39
Port Vale	42	13	12	17	50	66	38
Hull City	42	10	17	15	46	51	37
Bradford City	42	11	15	16	35	48	37
Coventry City	42	11	13	18	52	68	35
Fulham	42	10	14	18	45	56	34
Nelson	42	10	13	19	40	74	33
Bristol City	42	7	15	20	32	65	29

Division Two

Match No.	Date		Opponents	Result	Scorers	Atten
1	Aug	25	Nelson	1-1	Bliss	12
2		27	HULL CITY	0-0		18
3	Sep	1	NELSON	5-1	Green 3, Smith, Williams	22
4		3	Hull City	2-2	Dixon, Williams	10
5		8	Derby County	0-1		12
6		15	DERBY COUNTY	2-0	Waite, Green	21
7		22	Bury	0-0		12
8		29	BURY	1-0	Williams	25
9	Oct	6	LEEDS UNITED	0-1		22
10		13	Leeds United	0-1		15
11		20	SOUTH SHIELDS	3-0	Williams, Rennox, Waite	25
12		27	South Shields	1-1	Green	10
13	Nov	3	PORT VALE	1-1	Williams	20
14		10	Port Vale	0-1		7
15		17	OLDHAM ATHLETIC	1-2	Green	16
16	Dec	3	Oldham Athletic	0-1		4
17		8	BRADFORD CITY	1-1	Green	16,
18		22	STOCKPORT COUNTY	1-1	Green	8,
19		25	LEICESTER CITY	1-0	Townrow	15,
20		26	Leicester City	2-1	Bliss 2	23,
21		29	Barnsley	0-1		12,
22	Jan	5	BARNSLEY	2-1	Green 2	8,
23		19	Stoke	1-0	Rennox	10,
24		26	STOKE	0-2		17,
25	Feb	9	CRYSTAL PALACE	1-0	Bliss	11,
26		16	The Wednesday	0-1		14,
27		23	THE WEDNESDAY	0-0		20,
28	Mar	1	Coventry City	1-1	Bliss	13,
29		8	COVENTRY CITY	4-0	Waite, Hannaford, Rennox 2	16,
30		12	Bradford City	0-0		12,
31		15	BRISTOL CITY	2-0	Bliss 2	16,
32		22	Bristol City	2-0	Bliss, Rennox	10,
33		29	SOUTHAMPTON	0-0		18,
34		31	Stockport County	0-2		4,
35	Apr	5	Southampton	0-5		9,
36		12	Fulham	0-0		10,
37		18	MANCHESTER UNITED	1-0	Bliss	22,
38		19	FULHAM	0-0		19,
39		21	Manchester United	2-2	Rennox, Waite	16,
40		22	Crystal Palace	1-2	J. Tonner	6,
41		26	BLACKPOOL	1-0	J. Tonner	10,
42	May	3	Blackpool	0-3		8,

Appearan

G

FA Cup

1	Jan	12	Swansea Town	1-1	Williams	15,
R		17	SWANSEA TOWN*	1-1	Rennox	17,
2R		21	Swansea Town**	1-2	Williams (pen)	12,

Appearan

G

Final League Position: 10th in Division Two

* After extra-time

** Played at White Hart Lane, Tottenham

Tonner, S	Rosier	Dixon	Townrow	Archibald	Smith	Higginbotham	Green	Bliss	Williams	Waite	McKechnie	Rennox	Nicholls	Galbraith	Tonner, J	Nicholson	Nunn	Hannaford	Roseboom	
2	3	4	5	6	7	8	9	10	11											1
2	3	4	5	6	7	8	9	10	11											2
2	3	4	5	6	7	8	9	10	11											3
2	3	4	5	6	7	8		10	11	9										4
2	3	4	5	6	7	8	9	10	11											5
2	3	4	5	6	7		9	10	11	8										6
2	3	4	5	6	7		9	10	11	8										7
2	3	4	5	6	7		9	10	11	8										8
2	3	4	5	6	7		9	10	11	8										9
	3	4	5	6	7		9		11	8	2	10								10
	3	4	5	6	7		9		11	8	2	10								11
	3	4	5	6	7		9		11	8	2	10								12
	3	4	5	6			9	10	11	7	2	8								13
	3	4	5	6	7		9		11	8	2	10								14
2	3	4	5	6	7		9	10	11	8										15
2		4		6	7		9	8	11			10	3	5						16
2		4	5	6	7		9	8	11		3	10								17
2		4	5	6	7		9	10	11	8	3									18
2		4	5	6	7		9	10	11	8	3									19
2		4		6	7			10	11	8	3			5	9					20
2		4		6	7			10	11	8	3			5	9					21
2		4	5	6			9	10	11	7	3	8								22
2			5	6	7		9		11		3	10			8	4				23
2	3	4	5	6	7		9		11			10			8					24
2	3	4	5	6	7		9	10		8							11			25
2	3		5	6	7		9	10		4		8					11			26
2	3	4	5	6	7		9	10		8							11			27
2	3	4	5	6	7			10		8		9					11			28
2	3	4	5	6	7			10		8		9						11		29
2	3	4	5		7			10		8		9				6		11		30
2	3	4	5		7			10		8		9		6				11		31
2	3	4	5		7			10		8		9				6		11		32
2	3	4	5		7			10				9				6		11	8	33
2	3	4	5		7			10				9				6		11	8	34
2	3	4	5		7			10				9				6		11	8	35
2	3	4	5	6	7			10		8		9						11		36
2	3	4	5	6	7			10		8		9						11		37
2	3	4	5	6	7			10		8		9					11			38
2	3	4	5	6	7			10		8		9						11		39
2	3	4	5	6	7							10			9	8		11		40
2	3		5	4	7			10		8					9	6		11		41
2	3		5	4	7			10		8					9	6		11		42
37	34	38	39	36	40	5	24	35	24	30	12	24	1	4	7	9	5	13	3	
		1	1		1		10	9	5	4		6			2			1		

Tonner, S	Rosier	Dixon	Townrow	Archibald	Smith	Higginbotham	Green	Bliss	Williams	Waite	McKechnie	Rennox	Nicholls	Galbraith	Tonner, J	Nicholson	Nunn	Hannaford	Roseboom	
2		4	5	6			9		11	7	3	10			8					1
2		4	5	6	7		9		11		3	10			8					R
2		4	5	6			9		11	7	3	10			8					2R
3		3	3	3	1		3		3	2	3	3			3					
									2			1								

1924-25

Manager: Peter Proudfoot

	P	W	D	L	F	A	Pts
Leicester City	42	24	11	7	90	32	59
Manchester United	42	23	11	8	57	23	57
Derby County	42	22	11	9	71	36	55
Portsmouth	42	15	18	9	58	50	48
Chelsea	42	16	15	11	51	37	47
Wolverhampton W	42	20	6	16	55	51	46
Southampton	42	13	18	11	40	36	44
Port Vale	42	17	8	17	48	56	42
South Shields	42	12	17	13	42	38	41
Hull City	42	15	11	16	50	49	41
Clapton Orient	42	14	12	16	42	42	40
Fulham	42	15	10	17	41	56	40
Middlesbrough	42	10	19	13	36	44	39
The Wednesday	42	15	8	19	50	56	38
Barnsley	42	13	12	17	46	59	38
Bradford City	42	13	12	17	37	50	38
Blackpool	42	14	9	19	65	61	37
Oldham Athletic	42	13	11	18	35	51	37
Stockport County	42	13	11	18	37	57	37
Stoke	42	12	11	19	34	46	35
Crystal Palace	42	12	10	20	38	54	34
Coventry City	42	11	9	22	45	84	31

Division Two

Match No.	Date		Opponents	Result	Scorers	Atten
1	Aug	30	Blackpool	0-1		15
2	Sep	1	OLDHAM ATHLETIC	5-1	Pape 4, Bliss	12
3		6	CRYSTAL PALACE	3-0	Rennox, Pape, Bliss	30
4		8	Oldham Athletic	1-2	Bliss	5
5		13	Southampton	0-2		9
6		20	CHELSEA	0-0		33
7		27	Stockport County	1-0	Rennox	12
8	Oct	2	THE WEDNESDAY	1-0	Rennox	11
9		4	MANCHESTER UNITED	0-1		22
10		11	Leicester City	2-4	Rennox, Bliss	15
11		18	STOKE	0-2		13
12		25	Derby County	0-3		15
13	Nov	1	SOUTH SHIELDS	0-0		15
14		8	Bradford City	0-0		11
15		15	PORT VALE	3-1	Finlayson, McKay 2	10
16		22	Middlesbrough	1-1	Pape	10
17		29	BARNSLEY	0-0		14
18	Dec	6	Wolverhampton W	2-1	Pape, Hannaford	18
19		13	FULHAM	3-0	Finlayson, Waite, Hannaford	19
20		20	Portsmouth	2-0	Pape 2	10
21		25	HULL CITY	0-0		26
22		26	Hull City	1-2	Waite	14,
23		27	BLACKPOOL	1-0	Hannaford	15,
24	Jan	3	Crystal Palace	1-0	Pape	16,
25		17	SOUTHAMPTON	1-0	Pape (pen)	12,
26		24	Chelsea	1-1	Hannaford	36
27	Feb	7	Manchester United	2-4	Rennox, Bliss	18
28		14	LEICESTER CITY	0-1		20,
29		16	STOCKPORT COUNTY	1-1	J. Tonner	18,
30		21	Stoke	1-0	J. Tonner	10,
31		28	DERBY COUNTY	0-1		25,
32	Mar	7	South Shields	0-2		10,
33		14	BRADFORD CITY	0-0		18,
34		21	Port Vale	2-4	J. Tonner, Hannaford	10,
35		28	MIDDLESBROUGH	0-1		8,
36	Apr	4	Barnsley	1-1	Dixon	8,
37		10	COVENTRY CITY	1-2	Shea	14,
38		11	WOLVERHAMPTON W	2-1	Dixon, Rosier (pen)	9,
39		14	Coventry City	0-1		13,
40		18	Fulham	2-0	Waite, Shea	16,
41		25	PORTSMOUTH	1-1	Shea	12,
42	May	2	The Wednesday	0-0		14,

Appearan

G

FA Cup

1	Jan	10	Nottingham Forest	0-1		16,

Appearan

G

Final League Position: 11th in Division Two

McKechnie	Rosier	Dixon	Townrow	Archibald	Hannaford	Rennox	Pape	Bliss	Thompson	Tonner, S	Smith	Evans	Roulson	Tonner, J	Waite	McKay	Finlayson	Galbraith	Nicholls	Wingham	Shea	Bell	Clark	Dunn	Yardley	
2	3	4	5	6	7	8	9	10	11																	1
	3	4	5	6	11	8	9	10		2	7															2
	3	4	5	6	11	8	9	10		2	7															3
	3	4	5	6	11	8	9	10		2	7															4
		4	5	6	11	8	9	10		2	7	3														5
	3	4	5		11	8	9	10		2	7		6													6
	3	4	5		11	8	9	10		2	7		6													7
	3	4	5		11	8	9	10		2	7		6													8
	3	4	5		11	8	9	10		2	7		6													9
		4	5		11	8	9	10		2	7		3	6												10
	3	4	5		11	8	9	10		2			6		7											11
2	3	4	5		11	8	9				7		6	10												12
2	3	4	5		11	8	9	10			7		6													13
2	3	4	5		11	8					7		6			9	10									14
2	3	4	5		11	8					7		6			9	10									15
2	3	4	5		11	8	9				7		6				10									16
2	3	4	5		11	8	9						6		7		10									17
2	3	4	5		11	8	9								7		10	6								18
2	3	4	5		11	8	9								7		10	6								19
3	2	4	5		11	8	9								7		10	6								20
3	2	4	5		11	8	9								7		10	6								21
2	3	4	5		11	8	9								7		10	6								22
		4	5		11		9			2	7				8		10	6	3							23
	3	4	5		11		9			2	7				8		10	6								24
	3	4	5		11	8	9			2	7						10	6								25
	3	4	5		11	8	9			2	7						10	6								26
	3	4	5		11	8		10		2	7						9	6								27
	3	4	5		11	8		10		2	7					9		6								28
		4	5		11	8		10		2				7		9		6		3						29
		4	5			8		10						11	7		9	6	3	2						30
	3	4		6	11	8				2				9	7		10	5								31
	3	4	5		11	10				2	7			9	8			6								32
	3	4	5		11			10		2	7			9				6			8					33
3		4	5		11					2				9			10	6			8	7				34
		4	5		7					2				11		9	10	6		3	8					35
		4								2			6	9	7		10	5		3	8		11			36
		4								2			6	9	7		10	5		3	8		11			37
	3	4	5							2	7		6	10				9			8		11			38
2	3	4	5								7		6	10				9			8		11			39
2	3	4	5											11	9			6			10			7	8	40
2	3	4	5											11	9			6			10			7	8	41
2	3	4	5											11			9	6			10			7	8	42
17	33	42	39	6	34	30	24	17	1	25	24	1	16	16	16	5	21	25	2	5	10	1	4	3	3	
	1	2			5	5	11	5						3	3	2	2				3					

McKechnie	Rosier	Dixon	Townrow	Archibald	Hannaford	Rennox	Pape	Bliss	Thompson	Tonner, S	Smith	Evans	Roulson	Tonner, J	Waite	McKay	Finlayson	Galbraith	Nicholls	Wingham	Shea	Bell	Clark	Dunn	Yardley	
	3	4	5		11		9			2	7				8		10	6								1
	1	1	1		1		1			1	1				1		1	1								

1925-26

Manager: Peter Proudfoot

	P	W	D	L	F	A	Pts
The Wednesday	42	27	6	9	88	48	60
Derby County	42	25	7	10	77	42	57
Chelsea	42	19	14	9	76	49	52
Wolverhampton W	42	21	7	14	84	60	49
Swansea Town	42	19	11	12	77	57	49
Blackpool	42	17	11	14	76	69	45
Oldham Athletic	42	18	8	16	74	62	44
Port Vale	42	19	6	17	79	69	44
South Shields	42	18	8	16	74	65	44
Middlesbrough	42	21	2	19	77	68	44
Portsmouth	42	17	10	15	79	74	44
Preston North End	42	18	7	17	71	84	43
Hull City	42	16	9	17	63	61	41
Southampton	42	15	8	19	63	63	38
Darlington	42	14	10	18	72	77	38
Bradford City	42	13	10	19	47	66	36
Nottingham Forest	42	14	8	20	51	73	36
Barnsley	42	12	12	18	58	84	36
Fulham	42	11	12	19	46	77	34
Clapton Orient	42	12	9	21	50	65	33
Stoke City	42	12	8	22	54	77	32
Stockport County	42	8	9	25	51	97	25

Division Two

Match No.	Date		Opponents	Result	Scorers	Atten
1	Aug	29	PORT VALE	1-2	J. Tonner	16
2		31	Derby County	1-3	Henderson	13
3	Sep	5	Barnsley	1-3	Henderson	5
4		12	STOCKPORT COUNTY	2-1	Shea, Henderson	12
5		19	CHELSEA	1-2	Shea	15
6		24	DERBY COUNTY	0-1		7
7		26	Hull City	0-2		9
8	Oct	3	DARLINGTON	1-2	Shea	17
9		7	Bradford City	3-0	Hannaford, Gavigan, Cock	6
10		10	Blackpool	0-3		9
11		17	Fulham	2-0	Hannaford, Cock	26
12		24	SOUTH SHIELDS	1-2	Broadbent	13
13		31	Stoke City	0-0		9
14	Nov	7	OLDHAM ATHLETIC	1-2	Hannaford	9
15		14	Portsmouth	2-3	Shea, Dixon	12
16		21	WOLVERHAMPTON W	2-1	Shea, Hannaford	11
17	Dec	5	THE WEDNESDAY	0-0		11
18		12	Preston North End	1-4	Cock	14
19		19	MIDDLESBROUGH	1-0	Cock	10
20		25	SOUTHAMPTON	2-1	Henderson, Cock	13
21		26	Southampton	0-2		15
22	Jan	2	Port Vale	2-4	Henderson 2	8
23		16	BARNSLEY	4-0	J. Tonner 2, McLaughlan, Galbraith	8
24		23	Stockport County	2-3	Cock, McLaughlan	7
25	Feb	6	HULL CITY	0-0		14
26		10	Chelsea	3-1	Cock, McKay, McLaughlan	14
27		13	Darlington	0-6		8
28		27	FULHAM	1-1	Dixon	20
29	Mar	8	BLACKPOOL	2-2	Yardley, Dixon	4
30		13	STOKE CITY	4-0	Cock 3, Yardley	12
31		20	Oldham Athletic	1-1	Evans	11
32		24	South Shields	0-1		2
33		27	PORTSMOUTH	1-1	Townrow	13
34	Apr	2	NOTTINGHAM FOREST	0-1		15
35		3	Wolverhampton W	0-3		14
36		5	Nottingham Forest	0-1		13
37		10	SWANSEA TOWN	2-0	Henderson, Cock	14
38		12	Swansea Town	0-0		8
39		17	The Wednesday	0-3		21,
40		19	BRADFORD CITY	3-1	Archibald, Cock, J. Tonner	8,
41		24	PRESTON NORTH END	1-1	Dixon	13
42	May	1	Middlesbrough	2-1	Cock, Broadbent	7,

Appearar

G

FA Cup

3	Jan	9	Chesterfield	1-0	J. Tonner	17,
4		30	MIDDLESBROUGH	4-2	J. Tonner 2, Henderson, Cock	24,
5	Feb	20	NEWCASTLE UNITED	2-0	Galbraith, Cock	31,
6	Mar	6	MANCHESTER CITY	1-6	Cock	24,

Appearar

G

Final League Position: 20th in Division Two

Mckechnie	Rosier	Dixon	Townrow	Gailbraith	Dunn	Yardley	Henderson	Shea	Tonner, J	Lillie	Gavigan	Hannaford	Bell	Gough	Cock	Broadbent	McLaughlan	Evans	Waite	Archibald	McKay	Goodman	Streets	
2	3	4	5	6	7	8	9	10	11															1
	3	4	5	6		8	9	10	11	2	7													2
	3	4	5	6			9	8	10	2	7	11												3
2	3	4		5			9	8	10		7	11	6											4
2	3	4	5	6			9	8	10		7	11												5
2	3		5	6			9	8	10		7	11		4										6
2			5	6			9	8	10	3	7	11		4										7
2	3	4	5	6			10	8			7	11			9									8
2	3	4	5	6			10	8			7	11			9									9
2	3	4	5	6			10	8			7	11			9									10
2	3	4	5	6				8			7	11			9	10								11
2	3	4	5	6				8				11			9	10	7							12
2	3	4	5	6		8	10					11			9		7							13
2	3	4	5	6		8	10					11			9		7							14
2	3	4	5	6				8	10		7	11			9									15
2	3	4	5	6				8	10		7	11			9									16
2		4	5	6				8	10	3	7	9			11									17
	2	4	5	6				8	10	3	7	11			9									18
	2	4	5	6				8	10		7				9		11	3						19
	2	4	5	6			9	8	10		7				11			3						20
		4	5	6		8	9		10						11	2		3	7					21
	3	4	5	6			9	8	10						11	2			7					22
	3	4	5	6				8	10		7				9	2	11							23
	3	4	5					8	10		7				9	2	11			6				24
	2	4	5				8	10			7			6	9		11	3						25
2		4	5				8				7			6	9		11	3			10			26
2		4	5				8				7			6	9		11	3			10			27
		4	5	6			8		10		7					2	11	3			9			28
		4	5	6		8	9		10		7						11	3				2		29
		4	5	6		10	8				7				9		11	3				2		30
		4	5	6		10			11		7				9			3				2	8	31
		4	5	6		10			11		7				9			3				2	8	32
		4	5	6					10		7				9		11	3				2	8	33
		4	5	6			9	8	10		7				11			3				2		34
		4		5			9		10		8			6		2	11	3	7					35
2		4	5				8		10								11	3	7	6		9		36
	2	4	5				8		10		7				9		11	3		6				37
		4	5				8		10		7				9		11	3		6		2		38
	2	4	5				8		10		7				9		11	3		6				39
	2	4	5				8		10						9		11		7	6		3		40
	2	4	5				8		10		11				9			3	7	6				41
		4	5	6		8			10		7				11	9		3				2		42
18	26	40	40	32	1	10	29	23	31	5	34	16	1	6	31	9	19	20	6	7	3	10	3	
		4	1	1		2	7	5	4		1	4			13	2	3	1		1	1			

Mckechnie	Rosier	Dixon	Townrow	Gailbraith	Dunn	Yardley	Henderson	Shea	Tonner, J	Lillie	Gavigan	Hannaford	Bell	Gough	Cock	Broadbent	McLaughlan	Evans	Waite	Archibald	McKay	Goodman	Streets	
	3	4	5	6			8		10		7				9		11	2						1
	2	4	5	6			8		10		7				9		11	3						R
		4	5	6			8		10		7				9	2	11	3						2R
		4	5	6			8		10		7				9	2	11	3						
	2	4	4	4			4		4		4				4	2	4	4						
				1			1		3						3									

1926-27

Manager: Peter Proudfoot

	P	W	D	L	F	A	Pts
Middlesbrough	42	27	8	7	122	60	62
Portsmouth	42	23	8	11	87	49	54
Manchester City	42	22	10	10	108	61	54
Chelsea	42	20	12	10	62	52	52
Nottingham Forest	42	18	14	10	80	55	50
Preston North End	42	20	9	13	74	72	49
Hull City	42	20	7	15	63	52	47
Port Vale	42	16	13	13	88	78	45
Blackpool	42	18	8	16	95	80	44
Oldham Athletic	42	19	6	17	74	84	44
Barnsley	42	17	9	16	88	87	43
Swansea Town	42	16	11	15	68	72	43
Southampton	42	15	12	15	60	62	42
Reading	42	16	8	18	64	72	40
Wolverhampton W	42	14	7	21	73	75	35
Notts County	42	15	5	22	70	96	35
Grimsby Town	42	11	12	19	74	91	34
Fulham	42	13	8	21	58	92	34
South Shields	42	11	11	20	71	96	33
Clapton Orient	42	12	7	23	60	96	31
Darlington	42	12	6	24	79	98	30
Bradford City	42	7	9	26	50	88	23

Division Two

Match No.	Date		Opponents	Result	Scorers	Atten
1	Aug	28	Preston North End	2-2	Cock 2	19
2	Sep	2	BRADFORD CITY	1-1	Dixon	7
3		4	SOUTH SHIELDS	1-0	Dennison	19
4		8	Bradford City	3-1	Corkindale, Dennison, Cock	8
5		11	Hull City	0-4		8
6		18	WOLVERHAMPTON W	2-0	Cock 2 (I pen)	15
7		25	Notts County	1-3	Dennison	8
8	Oct	2	BARNSLEY	0-1		13
9		9	MIDDLESBROUGH	2-3	Cock, Dennison	12
10		16	Swansea Town	2-3	Dennison, Broadbent	14
11		23	NOTTINGHAM FOREST	2-2	Dennison, Waterall	12
12		30	Manchester City	1-6	Cock	28
13	Nov	6	DARLINGTON	0-4		11
14		20	OLDHAM ATHLETIC	3-1	Yardley, Cock	7
15		24	Portsmouth	1-1	Cock	9
16		27	Fulham	0-2		18
17	Dec	4	GRIMSBY TOWN	2-4	Cock, Dennison	11
18		11	Blackpool	0-6		7
19		18	READING	5-1	Dennison 2, Gavigan 2, Inglis (og)	9
20		25	PORT VALE	1-2	Broadbent	14
21		27	Port Vale	0-3		16
22	Jan	1	Chelsea	1-2	Broadbent	28
23		15	PRESTON NORTH END	1-1	Cock	14
24		22	South Shields	1-2	Reid	5
25	Feb	5	Wolverhampton W	0-5		18
26		12	NOTTS COUNTY	2-1	Corkindale, Dixon	10
27		19	Barnsley	2-4	Cock, Dennison	6
28		23	HULL CITY	1-2	Cock	4
29		26	Middlesbrough	0-6		21
30	Mar	12	Nottingham Forest	1-1	Thomson	11
31		19	MANCHESTER CITY	2-4	Corkindale, Gardner	15
32		21	SWANSEA TOWN	1-0	Gardner	5
33		26	Darlington	1-2	Gardner	5
34	Apr	2	PORTSMOUTH	4-5	Gardner 2, Corkindale, Thomson	14
35		9	Oldham Athletic	2-5	Gavigan, Galbraith	4
36		15	SOUTHAMPTON	1-0	Gardner	13
37		16	FULHAM	2-3	Corkindale, Gardner	16
38		18	Southampton	2-1	Dennison, Gardner	7
39		23	Grimsby Town	2-2	Dennison, Corkindale	10
40		28	CHELSEA	3-0	Dennison, Corkindale, Cock	25
41		30	BLACKPOOL	1-0	Reid	16
42	May	7	Reading	1-0	Gardner (pen)	8
						Appearar
						G

FA Cup

3	Jan	8	PORT VALE	1-1	Dennison	17
R		12	Port Vale	1-5	Dennison	11
						Appearar
						G

Final League Position: 20th in Division Two

Rosier	Evans	Dixon	Townrow	Galbraith	Rutherford	Yardley	Cock	Dennison	Corkindale	Gardner	Gavigan	Carey	Lyons	Broadbent	Waterall	Goodman	Findlay	Leather	Ashton	Spence	Livingstone	Slater	Thomson	Streets	Ames	Reid	Hayward	Armstrong	Duffy	Campbell	Mooney	
2	3	4	5	6	7	8	9	10	11																							1
2	3	4	5	6	7	8	9	10	11																							2
2	3	4	5	6	7	8	9	10	11																							3
2	3	4	5	6		8	9	10	11	7																						4
2	3	4	5	6		8	9	10	11	7																						5
2	3	4	5	6		8	9	10	11		7																					6
2	3		5	6		8	9	10	11		7	4																				7
	3		5	6		8	9	10	11		7	4	2																			8
2	3	4	5	6			9	10	11		7			8																		9
2	3	4	5	6			9	10	11		7			8																		10
2	3		5	6			9	8	11		7			10	4																	11
2				6			9	8	11		7	4		10	5	3																12
2	3		5	6			9	8	11		7			10			4															13
2	3	4	5	6		8	9		11		7			10																		14
2	3	4	5	6		8	9		11		7			10																		15
2	3	4	5	6		8	9		11		7			10																		16
2	3	4	5	6		8	9	10	11		7																					17
	3		5	6		8	9	10			7							1	2	4	11											18
2	3	4	5	6		8		10	11		7			9																		19
2	3	4	5	6		8		10	11		7			9																		20
2		4	5	6	7			10	11		8			9					3			1										21
2	3	4	5	6		8	11	10			7			9																		22
2			5	6			9				7			4					3				8	10	11							23
2			5	6			10			7									3				8	4	11	9						24
		7	5	3			10		11				2	4									8	6		9						25
		4	5	6				10	11	7				2					3				8			9						26
3		4	5				11	10			7			2									8			9	6					27
2	3			6			9	10	11		7			4		5	8															28
2		4		6			9		11		7		3	5									8			10						29
2				5	7					9			3	4									10	8	11			6				30
2				5	7				11	9			3	4									10	8					6			31
2				5	7				11	9			3	4									10	8					6			32
2				5	7					9			3	4										8	11	10			6			33
2				5	7				11	9			3	10									8					6	4			34
2		4		5			8	10	11	9	7		3																6			35
3				5			8	10	11	9	7		2	4															6			36
2				5			8	10	11	9	7		3	4															6			37
		4		5			8	10	11	9	7		2																6	3		38
				5			8	10	11	9	7		3	4															6	2		39
				5			8	10	11	9	7		3	4															6	2		40
				5			8	10	11				3	4											7	9			6	2		41
				5			8	10	11	9	7		3	4															6	2		42
33	21	22	26	41	9	16	33	30	35	16	28	3	16	29	2	2	2	1	5	1	1	1	10	7	5	7	1	2	12	5		
		2		1		1	15	13	7	9	3			3	1								2			2						

One own-goal

Rosier	Evans	Dixon	Townrow	Galbraith	Rutherford	Yardley	Cock	Dennison	Corkindale	Gardner	Gavigan	Carey	Lyons	Broadbent	Waterall	Goodman	Findlay	Leather	Ashton	Spence	Livingstone	Slater	Thomson	Streets	Ames	Reid	Hayward	Armstrong	Duffy	Campbell	Mooney	
2	3		5	6			9	10	11		7			4								1									8	3
2	3		5	6			9	10	11		7			4								1		8								R
2	2		2	2			2	2	2		2			2								2		1							1	
								2																								

1927-28

Manager: Peter Proudfoot

	P	W	D	L	F	A	Pts
Manchester City	42	25	9	8	100	59	59
Leeds United	42	25	7	10	98	49	57
Chelsea	42	23	8	11	75	45	54
Preston North End	42	22	9	11	100	66	53
Stoke City	42	22	8	12	78	59	52
Swansea Town	42	18	12	12	75	63	48
Oldham Athletic	42	19	8	15	75	51	46
West Bromwich Albion	42	17	12	13	90	70	46
Port Vale	42	18	8	16	68	57	44
Nottingham Forest	42	15	10	17	83	84	40
Grimsby Town	42	14	12	16	69	83	40
Bristol City	42	15	9	18	76	79	39
Barnsley	42	14	11	17	65	85	39
Hull City	42	12	15	15	41	54	39
Notts County	42	13	12	17	68	74	38
Wolverhampton W	42	13	10	19	63	91	36
Southampton	42	14	7	21	68	77	35
Reading	42	11	13	18	53	75	35
Blackpool	42	13	8	21	83	101	34
Clapton Orient	42	11	12	19	55	85	34
Fulham	42	13	7	22	68	89	33
South Shields	42	7	9	26	56	111	23

Division Two

Match No.	Date		Opponents	Result	Scorers	Attenc
1	Aug	27	Grimsby Town	2-2	Kerr, Dennison	15
2		29	SOUTHAMPTON	2-0	Dennison, Corkindale	13
3	Sep	3	READING	3-0	Duffy, Whipp, Kerr	18
4		5	Southampton	3-1	Dennison 2, Whipp	7
5		10	Blackpool	1-0	Kerr	12
6		17	CHELSEA	2-1	Whipp, Kerr	34
7		24	Barnsley	2-4	Gardner 2	11
8	Oct	1	West Bromwich Albion	1-4	Corkindale	19
9		8	BRISTOL CITY	4-2	Dennison 3, Whipp	21
10		15	Stoke City	0-2		15
11		22	PRESTON NORTH END	1-1	Dennison	10
12		29	Swansea Town	0-5		12
13	Nov	5	FULHAM	3-2	Gardner 2, Dennison	15
14		12	Hull City	2-2	Gardner, Smith	6
15		19	MANCHESTER CITY	0-2		14,
16		26	South Shields	2-2	Whipp 2	5,
17	Dec	3	LEEDS UNITED	2-1	Kerr 2	12,
18		10	Nottingham Forest	3-4	Collins, Whipp 2	7
19		17	PORT VALE	0-1		9
20		24	Wolverhampton W	3-5	Whipp, Holland, McDougall (og)	6
21		27	Oldham Athletic	0-5		23
22		31	GRIMSBY TOWN	1-2	Holland	8,
23		7	Reading	0-4		10,
24	Jan	21	BLACKPOOL	2-5	Gardner 2 (1 pen)	11,
25		28	Chelsea	0-1		17
26		4	BARNSLEY	2-0	Broadbent, Whipp	8,
27	Feb	11	WEST BROMWICH ALBION	0-0		11,
28		18	Bristol City	1-5	Streets	15,
29		25	STOKE CITY	3-2	Turnbull, Whipp, Williams	20,
30		3	Preston North End	0-0		18,
31	Mar	10	SWANSEA TOWN	1-1	Turnbull	11,
32		17	Fulham	0-2		21,
33		24	HULL CITY	0-0		8,
34		31	Manchester City	3-5	Turnbull 2, Batten	38,
35		6	Notts County	0-3		13,
36	Apr	7	SOUTH SHIELDS	2-2	Dennison, Turnbull	11,
37		9	NOTTS COUNTY	0-1		10,
38		14	Leeds United	0-4		22,
39		16	OLDHAM ATHLETIC	2-0	Corkindale, Kerr	2,
40		21	NOTTINGHAM FOREST	2-2	Whipp, Kerr	9,
41		28	Port Vale	0-0		5,
42	May	5	WOLVERHAMPTON W	0-0		12,
						Appearan
						G

FA Cup

3	Jan	14	Swindon Town	1-2	Whipp	19,
						Appearan
						G

Final League Position: 20th in Division Two

Campbell	Evans	Broadbent	Galbraith	Duffy	Collins	Whipp	Kerr	Dennison	Corkindale	Hope	Spence	Sage	Gardner	Lyons	Streets	MacDonald	Woodward	Smith	Jewhurst	Holland	Ames	Surtees	Williams	Turnbull	Batten	Slater	
2	3	4	5	6	7	8	9	10	11																		1
2		4		6	7	8	9	10	11	3	5																2
2	3	4		6	7	8	9	10	11			5															3
2	3	4		6	7	8	9	10	11		5																4
2	3	4		6	7	8	9	10	11		5																5
	3	4		6	7	8	9	10	11	2	5																6
	3	4		6	7	8		10	11	2	5		9														7
	3	4		6	7	8		10	11	2	5		9														8
	3	4	5		7	8	9	10	11	2		6															9
	3	4	5		7	8	9	10	11	2		6															10
	3	4	5	6	7	8	9	10	11	2																	11
		4	5	6	7		9	10	11	2				3	8												12
		4	5	6	7	8		10	11	2			9			3											13
		4	5	6	7	8		10		2			9			3	1	11									14
			6		7	8		10	11	2	5		9			3			4								15
		4	5	6	7	8		10		2			9			3		11									16
	3	4	5		7	8	9				6					2		11		10							17
		4	5		7	8	9	10			6			3		2		11									18
		4	5		7	8	9	10		3	6					2		11									19
		4	5		7	8	9		11	3	6					2				10							20
		4	5		7	8	10		11	3	6		9			2											21
2		4	5	6		8		9	11							3				10	7						22
2		4	5	6	7	8	9							3						10	11						23
		4	6			8			7		5		9	2		3						10	11				24
2		10	5	6	7	8	9					4				3							11				25
2		10	5	6	7	8	9					4				3							11				26
2		10	5	6	7	8						4	9			3							11				27
2		10	5	6	7	8						4			9	3							11				28
2			5	6	7	8						4				3							11	9	10		29
2		6	5		7	8						4				3							11	9	10		30
2		6	5		7	8						4				3							11	9	10		31
2		6	5		7	8						4				3							11	9	10		32
2		4	5		7	8										3				6			11	9	10		33
2		4	5		7	8										3				6			11	9	10		34
2		4	5	6	7	8										3							11	9	10		35
		4		6	7	8		10		2						3							11	9	5		36
		4	5	6	7			8		2						3							11	9	10	1	37
		4		6		8	9	10		2		5		3				11			7					1	38
		4	5	6		8	9	10	11					3		2					7					1	39
		4	5	6		8	9	10	11					3		2					7						40
		4	5	6		8	9	10	11					3		2					7						41
		4	5	6			9	10	11					3		2							7		8	1	42
18	11	40	33	28	35	39	23	26	22	18	13	12	9	9	2	28	1	6	1	6	6	1	15	9	10	4	
		1		1	1	12	8	10	3				7		1			1		2			1	5	1		

One own-goal

Campbell	Evans	Broadbent	Galbraith	Duffy	Collins	Whipp	Kerr	Dennison	Corkindale	Hope	Spence	Sage	Gardner	Lyons	Streets	MacDonald	Woodward	Smith	Jewhurst	Holland	Ames	Surtees	Williams	Turnbull	Batten	Slater	
		4	6		7	8				3	5		9			2		11				10					3
		1	1		1	1				1	1		1			1		1				1					
						1																					

1928-29

Manager: Peter Proudfoot

	P	W	D	L	F	A	Pts
Middlesbrough	42	22	11	9	92	57	55
Grimsby Town	42	24	5	13	82	61	53
Bradford Park Avenue	42	22	4	16	88	70	48
Southampton	42	17	14	11	74	60	48
Notts County	42	19	9	14	78	65	47
Stoke City	42	17	12	13	74	51	46
West Bromwich Albion	42	19	8	15	80	79	46
Blackpool	42	19	7	16	92	76	45
Chelsea	42	17	10	15	64	65	44
Tottenham Hotspur	42	17	9	16	75	81	43
Nottingham Forest	42	15	12	15	71	70	42
Hull City	42	13	14	15	58	63	40
Preston North End	42	15	9	18	78	79	39
Millwall	42	16	7	19	71	86	39
Reading	42	15	9	18	63	86	39
Barnsley	42	16	6	20	69	66	38
Wolverhampton W	42	15	7	20	77	81	37
Oldham Athletic	42	16	5	21	54	75	37
Swansea Town	42	13	10	19	62	75	36
Bristol City	42	13	10	19	58	72	36
Port Vale	42	15	4	23	71	86	34
Clapton Orient	42	12	8	22	45	72	32

Division Two

Match No.	Date		Opponents	Result	Scorers	Atter
1	Aug	25	West Bromwich Albion	1-3	Batten	1
2		27	NOTTINGHAM FOREST	1-4	Turnbull	
3	Sep	1	MILLWALL	1-1	Spence (pen)	3
4		5	Nottingham Forest	0-0		
5		8	STOKE CITY	1-0	Holland	1
6		15	Grimsby Town	1-6	Whipp	1
7		22	BRADFORD PARK AVENUE	1-0	Turnbull	1
8		29	Swansea Town	1-0	Spence (pen)	1
9	Oct	6	BLACKPOOL	2-4	Turnbull 2	1
10		13	Chelsea	2-2	Turnbull, Spence (pen)	3
11		20	Port Vale	0-3		1
12		27	HULL CITY	0-2		
13	Nov	3	Tottenham Hotspur	1-2	Turnbull	3
14		10	NOTTS COUNTY	2-2	J. Williams 2	
15		17	Preston North End	2-5	Dennison, E. Williams	1
16		24	MIDDLESBROUGH	3-0	Turnbull 3	
17	Dec	1	Oldham Athletic	1-1	Corkindale	
18		8	SOUTHAMPTON	1-1	Corkindale (pen)	
19		15	Wolverhampton W	2-3	Corkindale, Dennison	
20		22	READING	1-1	Dennison	
21		25	BARNSLEY	3-1	Batten, Turnbull, Dennison	
22		26	Barnsley	0-2		
23		29	WEST BROMWICH ALBION	0-2		10
24	Jan	5	Millwall	0-2		16
25		19	Stoke City	1-3	Corkindale	10
26	Feb	2	Bradford Park Avenue	1-2	Dennison	12
27		9	SWANSEA TOWN	1-2	Corkindale (pen)	10
28		16	Blackpool	1-0	Turnbull	6
29		23	CHELSEA	1-0	Whipp	18
30	Mar	2	PORT VALE	1-0	Turnbull	15
31		4	GRIMSBY TOWN	3-1	Whipp, Corkindale, Turnbull	5
32		9	Hull City	0-0		7
33		16	TOTTENHAM HOTSPUR	2-3	McMillan, Corkindale	37
34		23	Notts County	0-2		10
35		29	BRISTOL CITY	0-1		12
36		30	PRESTON NORTH END	1-0	Gardner (pen)	9
37	Apr	1	Bristol City	0-1		15
38		6	Middlesbrough	0-4		16
39		13	OLDHAM ATHLETIC	2-0	Whipp, Batten	6
40		20	Southampton	0-2		8
41		27	WOLVERHAMPTON W	2-0	Batten, Holland	5
42	May	4	Reading	2-4	Batten, Whipp	7

Appearar

G

FA Cup

3	Jan	12	Southampton	0-0		21
R		17	SOUTHAMPTON	2-1	Dennison, Corkindale	17
4		26	Aston Villa	0-0		*53
R		30	ASTON VILLA	0-8**		27

Appearar

G

Final League Position: 22nd in Division Two

* Record attendance to watch an Orient match.

** Orient's heaviest ever defeat.

Morley	MacDonald	Broadbent	Galbraith	Duffy	McMillan	Batten	Turnbull	Dennison	Corkindale	Lyons	Spence	Whipp	Kerr	Slater	Williams, J	Holland	Collins	Gay	Williams, E	Lawrence	Eastman	Gough	Gardner	Hannaford	Tricker	
2	3	4	5	6	7	8	9	10	11																	1
2	3	4	5	6	7	8	9	10	11																	2
2			4	6	7			10	11	3	5	8	9													3
2		4		6	7			10		3	5	8	9	1	11											4
2	3	4		6	7						5	8	9	1	11	10										5
2	3	4		6							5	8	9		11	10	7									6
2		4		6			9		11		5	8			7	10		3								7
2		4		6			9		11		5	8			7	10		3								8
2		4		6			9		11		5	8			7	10		3								9
2		4		6			9		11		5	8		1	7	10		3								10
2		4		6					11		5	8	9	1	7	10		3								11
	2	4		6	7		9		11		5	8		1		10		3								12
2		4	6			10	9		11		5	8			7			3								13
2		4	6			10	9		11		5	8			7			3								14
		4	5	6		9		10	11	2					7			3	8							15
2				6		8	9	10	11		5				7			3		4						16
2				6		8	9	10	11		5				7			3		4						17
2				6		10	9		11			8			7			3		4	5					18
2				6		8	9	10	11						7			3		4	5					19
2				6		8	9	10	11						7			3		4	5					20
	2			6		8	9	10	11								7	3		4	5					21
	2			6		8	9		11								7	3	10	4	5					22
	2					8	9	10	11									3		4	5	6	7			23
2				6				10	11			8	9					3		4	5		7			24
2			5	6	7		9		11	3		8							10	4						25
			5	6		9	2	10	11	3		8		1						4				7		26
2			5	6		9	3	10	11											4				7	8	27
2		6			7		9		11			8						3		4	5				10	28
2		6	5		7		9		11			8						3		4					10	29
2		6			7		9		11			8						3		4	5				10	30
2		6	5		7		9		11			8						3		4					10	31
2		6	5		7		9		11			8						3		4					10	32
2		6	5		7		9		11			8						3		4					10	33
		6	5		7		2		11			8						3	10	4					9	34
	2	6	5				9		11			8					7	3		4					10	35
		6	5			10			11	2			7			8		3		4			9			36
			5	6					11	2		8	7			10		3		4			9			37
			5	6		8			11	2								3		4			9	7	10	38
			5	6		9			11	2		8						3		4				7	10	39
			5	6		10			11	2		8					7	3		4			9			40
			5	6	7	9			11	2		8				10		3		4						41
		4	5	6	7	9			11	2		8				10		3								42
27	9	24	22	30	16	21	28	14	39	12	14	29	8	6	16	12	5	33	4	26	9	1	6	4	11	
					1	5	13	5	7		3	5			2	2			1				1			

Morley	MacDonald	Broadbent	Galbraith	Duffy	McMillan	Batten	Turnbull	Dennison	Corkindale	Lyons	Spence	Whipp	Kerr	Slater	Williams, J	Holland	Collins	Gay	Williams, E	Lawrence	Eastman	Gough	Gardner	Hannaford	Tricker	
2				6			9	10	11			8			7			3		4	5					3
2				6	7		9	10	11			8						3		4	5					R
2			4	6			9	10	11			8					7	3			5					4
2			4	6			9	10	11			8					7	3			5					R
4			2	4	1		4	4	4			4			1		2	4		2	4					
								1	1																	

1929-30

Manager: Aug 1929–Mar 1930 Arthur Grimsdell; Apr 1930 Peter Proudfoot

	P	W	D	L	F	A	Pts
Plymouth Argyle	42	30	8	4	98	38	68
Brentford	42	28	5	9	94	44	61
Queen's Park Rangers	42	21	9	12	80	68	51
Northampton Town	42	21	8	13	82	58	50
Brighton & Hove Albion	42	21	8	13	87	63	50
Coventry City	42	19	9	14	88	73	47
Fulham	42	18	11	13	87	83	47
Norwich City	42	18	10	14	88	77	46
Crystal Palace	42	17	12	13	81	74	46
Bournemouth & B A	42	15	13	14	72	61	43
Southend United	42	15	13	14	69	59	43
Clapton Orient	42	14	13	15	55	62	41
Luton Town	42	14	12	16	64	78	40
Swindon Town	42	13	12	17	73	83	38
Watford	42	15	8	19	60	73	38
Exeter City	42	12	11	19	67	73	35
Walsall	42	13	8	21	71	78	34
Newport County	42	12	10	20	74	85	34
Torquay United	42	10	11	21	64	94	31
Bristol Rovers	42	11	8	23	67	93	30
Gillingham	42	11	8	23	51	80	30
Merthyr Town	42	6	9	27	60	135	21

Division Three South

Match No.	Date		Opponents	Result	Scorers	Atten
1	Aug	31	PLYMOUTH ARGYLE	0-2		1
2	Sep	4	Brentford	1-3	Jack	
3		7	Merthyr Town	1-0	Edmonds	
4		14	TORQUAY UNITED	1-1	Edmonds	1
5		16	BRENTFORD	1-1	Hoar	
6		21	Newport County	0-0		
7		25	Brighton & Hove Albion	0-1		
8		28	WATFORD	1-1	Tricker	1
9	Oct	5	Coventry City	2-5	Jack, Tricker	1
10		12	WALSALL	1-1	Broadbent (pen)	1
11		19	Queen's Park Rangers	1-1	Edmonds	1
12		26	FULHAM	2-4	Edmonds, Tricker	1
13	Nov	2	Norwich City	0-1		
14		9	CRYSTAL PALACE	2-1	Campbell 2	1
15		16	Gillingham	0-2		
16		23	NORTHAMPTON TOWN	0-0		
17	Dec	7	SOUTHEND UNITED	1-1	Edmonds	
18		21	BOURNEMOUTH & B A	0-0		
19		25	SWINDON TOWN	2-1	Hughes, Campbell	1
20		26	Swindon Town	0-0		1
21		28	Plymouth Argyle	0-3		
22	Jan	4	MERTHYR TOWN	1-0	Campbell	
23		18	Torquay United	5-0	Dominy, Hoar, Campbell 3	
24	Feb	1	Watford	0-3		
25		5	Exeter City	0-4		
26		8	COVENTRY CITY	3-1	Broadbent (pen), Sanders 2	
27		15	Walsall	1-0	Tricker	
28		22	QUEEN'S PARK RANGERS	2-4	Lawrence, Sanders	12
29	Mar	1	Fulham	2-2	Campbell, Hoar	17
30		8	NORWICH CITY	0-0		
31		10	Luton Town	2-1	Smith (og), Edmonds	2
32		15	Crystal Palace	0-3		14
33		22	GILLINGHAM	2-0	Lawrence, Edmonds (pen)	9
34		29	Northampton Town	0-3		6
35		31	NEWPORT COUNTY	3-1	Campbell, Mills, Edmonds	2
36	Apr	5	EXETER CITY	3-0	Tricker, Townley, Edmonds	7
37		12	Southend United	1-4	Edmonds	6
38		18	Bristol Rovers	0-0		10
39		19	LUTON TOWN	6-1	Jack 2, Tricker 2, Edmonds 2	6
40		21	BRISTOL ROVERS	3-0	Tricker 2, Edmonds	10
41		26	Bournemouth & B A	1-5	Jack	3
42	May	3	BRIGHTON & HOVE ALBION	4-1	Edmonds, Mills, Galbraith, Vanner	8

Appearar

G

FA Cup

Round	Date		Opponents	Result	Scorers	Atten
1	Nov	30	FOLKESTONE TOWN	0-0		10
R	Dec	4	Folkestone Town	2-2	Mills, Campbell	4
2R		9	Folkestone Town*	4-1	Eastman, Vanner, Campbell, Grimsdell	3
2		14	NORTHFLEET	2-0	Grimsdell, Mills	12
3	Jan	11	BRISTOL ROVERS	1-0	Lyons (pen)	13
4		25	Newcastle United	1-3	Mills	48

Appearar

G

Final League Position: 12th in Division Three South

* Played at Highbury Stadium, Highbury, London.

	Gay	Lawrence	Eastman	Galbraith	McMillian	Dominy	Turnbull	Tricker	Edwards	Little	Jack	Slater	Lyons	Edmonds	Hoar	Spence	Broadbent	Campbell	Mills	Grimsdell	Sanders	Ames	Vanner	Hughes	Townley	Garland-Wells	Menlove	
	3	4	5	6	7	8	9	10	11																			1
	3	4		5	7		9	10	11	6	8																	2
		4		5	7			10	11	6	8	1	3	9														3
		4		5	7			10		6	8	1	3	9	11													4
		4		5	7			10		6	8	1	3	9	11													5
		4		5				10	11	6	8	1	3	9	7													6
		4								6	8	1	3		11	5	7	9	10									7
		4						10		6	8	1	3		11	5	7	9										8
		4		5				10		6	8		3		11		7	9										9
		4		5				10			8	1	3		11		7	9		6								10
		4		5				10			7	1	3	8	11					6	9							11
		4		5				10			7	1	3	8	11					6	9							12
				4				10		6	7		3	8	11			9		5								13
				5							7		3	8	11		4	9	10	6								14
				5	8					6	7		3		11		4	9	10									15
				5	8						7		3				4	9	10	6		11						16
		4	5					10			7		3	8	11			9		6								17
	3	4		5											11		6	8	10	9			7					18
		4		5							9		3				6	8	10				7	11				19
		4		5		8							3				6	9	10				7	11				20
		4		5							8		3				6	9	10				7	11				21
	3	4		5							8		2				6	9	10				7	11				22
		4		5		7							3	8	11		2	9	10	6								23
	3			5		7							2	8	11			9	10	6				4				24
	3	4	5	6							9		2	8	7									10	11			25
		4		5				10					3	8	11		2			6	9		7			1		26
		4		5				10		6			3	8	11		2				9		7			1		27
	3	4		5				10		6	8		2		11						9		7			1		28
		4		5						6			3	8	11		2	9	10				7			1		29
		4		5		8		10		6			3	9			2						7		11	1		30
		4		5				9		6			3	8			2		10				7		11	1		31
		4		5						6			3	8			2	9	10				7		11			32
		8		5						6			3	4	11		2	9	10				7			1		33
		8		5						6			3	4	11		2	9	10				7			1		34
		4		5						6			3	8	7		2	9	10						11	1		35
		4		5				10		6			3	8	7		2	9							11	1		36
		4		5				10		6			3	8	7		2	9							11	1		37
		4		5				10		6			3	8			2	9					7		11			38
2		4		5				10			8		3	9			6						7		11			39
2		4	5					10		6	8		3	9									7		11			40
2		4		5							8		3	9			6		10				7		11			41
2		4		5						6			3	8				9	10				7		11			42
25	7	37	4	38	7	5	2	23	4	24	24	9	39	28	26	2	27	25	19	11	5	1	19	6	12	11		
		2		1		1		9			5			14	3		2	9	2		3		1	1	1			

One own-goal

	Gay	Lawrence	Eastman	Galbraith	McMillian	Dominy	Turnbull	Tricker	Edwards	Little	Jack	Slater	Lyons	Edmonds	Hoar	Spence	Broadbent	Campbell	Mills	Grimsdell	Sanders	Ames	Vanner	Hughes	Townley	Garland-Wells	Menlove	
2				5				8					3		11		4	7	10	6							9	1
2		4		5						11	7		3	8				9	10	6								R
2		4	5										3	8	11			9	10	6			7					2R
2		4		5									3	6	11			8	10	9			7					2
		4		5		7					9		3		11		2	8	10	6								3
		4		5		7							3	8	11		2	9	10	6								4
4		5	1	5		2		1		1	2		6	4	5		3	6	6	6			2				1	
			1										1					2	3	2			1					

1930-31

Manager: Aug 1930–Apr 1931 Peter Proudfoot; Apr 1931–May 1931 Jimmy Seed

	P	W	D	L	F	A	Pts
Notts County	42	24	11	7	97	46	59
Crystal Palace	42	22	7	13	107	71	51
Brentford	42	22	6	14	90	64	50
Brighton & Hove Albion	42	17	15	10	68	53	49
Southend United	42	22	5	15	76	60	49
Northampton Town	42	18	12	12	77	59	48
Luton Town	42	19	8	15	76	51	46
Queen's Park Rangers	42	20	3	19	82	75	43
Fulham	42	18	7	17	77	75	43
Bournemouth & B A	42	15	13	14	72	73	43
Torquay United	42	17	9	16	80	84	43
Swindon Town	42	18	6	18	89	94	42
Exeter City	42	17	8	17	84	90	42
Coventry City	42	16	9	17	75	65	41
Bristol Rovers	42	16	8	18	75	92	40
Gillingham	42	14	10	18	61	76	38
Walsall	42	14	9	19	78	95	37
Watford	42	14	7	21	72	75	35
Clapton Orient	42	14	7	21	63	91	35
Thames	42	13	8	21	54	93	34
Newport County	42	11	6	25	69	111	28
Norwich City	42	10	8	24	47	76	28

Division Three South

Match No.	Date		Opponents	Result	Scorers
1	Aug	30	Walsall	2-4	Fowler, Tricker
2	Sep	4	NEWPORT COUNTY	3-1	Fowler, Fletcher, Galbraith
3		6	COVENTRY CITY	3-3	Fowler 3 (1 pen)
4		11	Thames	0-3	
5		13	Fulham	0-2	
6		18	THAMES	2-1	Vanner, Edmonds
7		20	SWINDON TOWN	2-3	Vanner, Fowler
8		27	Bournemouth & B A	1-1	Fowler
9	Oct	4	WATFORD	4-0	Sanders, Tricker 2, Fowler
10		11	Notts County	0-5	
11		18	Gillingham	0-0	
12		25	EXETER CITY	2-3	Cropper, Sanders
13	Nov	1	Brighton & Hove Albion	1-3	Cropper
14		8	TORQUAY UNITED	4-0	Jack, Cropper, Bolton, Tricker
15		15	Northampton Town	0-0	
16		22	BRENTFORD*	3-0	Cropper 2, Tricker
17	Dec	6	SOUTHEND UNITED*	3-1	Fowler 2, Tricker
18		20	BRISTOL ROVERS	3-1	Tricker 3
19		25	Norwich City	0-2	
20		26	NORWICH CITY	2-0	Vanner, Tricker
21		27	WALSALL	2-5	Fletcher, Tricker
22	Jan	3	Coventry City	0-4	
23		17	FULHAM	2-0	Galbraith, Cropper
24		24	Swindon Town	1-5	Cropper
25		31	BOURNEMOUTH & B A	0-0	
26	Feb	7	Watford	2-1	Garbutt, Jack (pen)
27		14	NOTTS COUNTY	1-4	Townley
28		21	GILLINGHAM	0-2	
29	Mar	7	BRIGHTON & HOVE ALBION	1-0	Cropper
30		14	Torquay United	2-5	Fletcher, Cropper
31		21	NORTHAMPTON TOWN	2-2	Tricker 2
32		23	Luton Town	1-0	Dudley
33		28	Brentford	0-3	
34	Apr	3	Queen's Park Rangers	2-4	Fowler, Cropper
35		4	CRYSTAL PALACE	3-2	Tricker, Jack 2
36		6	QUEEN'S PARK RANGERS	2-3	Jack, Harris (og)
37		11	Southend United	0-2	
38		15	Exeter City	1-6	Edmonds
39		18	LUTON TOWN	3-2	Tricker 2, Fowler
40		20	Crystal Palace	1-3	Tricker
41		25	Bristol Rovers	1-4	Tricker
42	May	2	Newport County	1-1	Jack

Appearan
G

FA Cup

1	Nov	29	Luton Town	2-2	Tricker, McGinnigle (og)
R	Dec	4	Luton Town**	2-4	Tricker, Cropper

Appearar
G

Final League Position: 19th in Division Three South

* Matches 16 and 17 both played at Wembley Stadium.

** Played at Highbury Stadium, Highbury , London.

Morley	Broadbent	Lawrence	Galbraith	Bolton	Sanders	Tricker	Fowler	Mills	Fletcher	Edmonds	Vanner	Garbutt	McGrae	Hull	Jack	Wood	Jennings	Townley	Evans	Cropper	Ames	Dudley	
2	3	4	5	6	7	8	9	10	11														1
3	2	4	5			8	10		11	6	7	9											2
3	2	4	5			8	10		11	6	7	9											3
	2	4					10		11	6	7	9	3	5	8								4
2		4	5			10	9		11	6	7		3		8	1							5
	2	4	5			10	9		11	6	7				8	1	3						6
	2	4	5		9		10			6	7				8	1	3	11					7
3	2	4	5		8		9		10	6	7					1		11					8
3	2	4		6	8	9	10		11	5	7					1							9
3	2	4		6	8	9	10		11	5	7					1							10
2	4			6	9				10	5	7					1		11	3	8			11
2	4			6	9		10			5						1		11	3	8	7		12
2	4		5	6			10		11	8						1			3	9	7		13
2		4	5	6		9	10		11						7	1			3	8			14
2		4	5	6		9	10		11						7	1			3	8			15
2		4	5	6		9	10		11						7	1			3	8			16
2	3	4	5	6		9	10		11						7					8			17
2		4	5	6		9	10		11						7				3	8			18
	2	4	5	6		9	10		11						7				3	8			19
	3	4	5	6		9	10		11		7						2			8			20
	3	4	5	6		9	10		11		7						2			8			21
	2	4	5	6		9	10		11		7								3	8			22
2		4	5	6		9	10		11						7	1			3	8			23
2		4	5	6		9	10		11						7	1			3	8			24
2	3	4	5	6		9	10		11						7	1				8			25
2	3		5	6			10		11	4		8			7	1				9			26
	2	4		6			10		11	5	7	8				1		9	3				27
	3	4		6			10		11	5	7	8				1	2			9			28
	2	5		6			8	10	11	4					7	1			3	9			29
	2	5		6	4		8	10	11						7	1			3	9			30
	2	4		6		9	10		11	5	7					1			3	8			31
	3	4		6		9	10		11	5						1	2			8		7	32
	2	4		6		9	10		11	5						1			3	8		7	33
	3	4		6		9	10		11	5					7	1	2			8			34
	2	4		6		9	10		11	5					7	1			3	8			35
	3	4		6		9	10			8			5		7	1	2	11					36
		4				9	10			5		8			7	1	2	11	3			6	37
		4					10		11	9		8	5		7	1	2		3			6	38
	2	4				9	8	10	11	5					7	1			3			6	39
	2	4				9		10	11	5		8			7				3			6	40
	2	4				9	8	10	11	5					7				3			6	41
					4		8	10	11	5					7	1	2		3	9		6	42
9	32	37	21	29	9	29	40	7	38	28	16	9	4	1	25	30	11	7	23	25	2	8	
			2	1	2	18	12		3	2	3	1			6			1		10		1	

One own-goal

Morley	Broadbent	Lawrence	Galbraith	Bolton	Sanders	Tricker	Fowler	Mills	Fletcher	Edmonds	Vanner	Garbutt	McGrae	Hull	Jack	Wood	Jennings	Townley	Evans	Cropper	Ames	Dudley	
2		4	5	6		9	10		11						7	1			3	8			3
2		4	5	6		9	10		11						7				3	8			R
2		2	2	2		2	2		2						2	1			2	2			
						2														1			

One own-goal

1931-32

Manager: Jimmy Seed

	P	W	D	L	F	A	Pts
Fulham	42	24	9	9	111	62	57
Reading	42	23	9	10	97	67	55
Southend United	42	21	11	10	77	53	53
Crystal Palace	42	20	11	11	74	63	51
Brentford	42	19	10	13	68	52	48
Luton Town	42	20	7	15	95	70	47
Exeter City	42	20	7	15	77	62	47
Brighton & Hove Albion	42	17	12	13	73	58	46
Cardiff City	42	19	8	15	87	73	46
Norwich City	42	17	12	13	76	67	46
Watford	42	19	8	15	81	79	46
Coventry City	42	18	8	16	108	97	44
Queen's Park Rangers	42	15	12	15	79	73	42
Northampton Town	42	16	7	19	69	69	39
Bournemouth & B A	42	13	12	17	70	78	38
Clapton Orient	42	12	11	19	77	90	35
Swindon Town	42	14	6	22	70	84	34
Bristol Rovers	42	13	8	21	65	92	34
Torquay United	42	12	9	21	72	106	33
Mansfield Town	42	11	10	21	75	108	32
Gillingham	42	10	8	24	40	82	28
Thames	42	7	9	26	53	109	23

Division Three South

Match No.	Date		Opponents	Result	Scorers	Atten
1	Aug	29	Watford	1-2	Fowler	10
2		31	CRYSTAL PALACE	1-3	Tricker	7
3	Sep	5	MANSFIELD TOWN	4-0	Tricker 2, Mills, Fletcher	8
4		7	BRISTOL ROVERS	1-0	Jack	5
5		12	Brighton & Hove Albion	1-1	Jack	5
6		16	Bristol Rovers	1-2	Fletcher	6
7		19	NORWICH CITY	1-3	Tricker	10
8		26	Swindon Town	3-2	Jack 2, Mills	4
9	Oct	3	SOUTHEND UNITED	2-4	Jack, Fowler	17
10		10	TORQUAY UNITED	1-3	Fowler	8
11		17	Fulham	1-5	Best	16
12		24	THAMES	1-1	Tricker	7
13		31	Brentford	0-3		11
14	Nov	7	EXETER CITY	2-2	Fletcher, Tricker	7
15		14	Coventry City	2-4	Fletcher 2	13
16		21	GILLINGHAM	3-1	Fletcher 2, Tricker	5
17	Dec	5	CARDIFF CITY	1-1	Jack	6
18		19	READING	2-2	Fletcher, Hodgkiss (og)	1
19		25	BOURNEMOUTH & B A	1-2	Best	7
20		26	Bournemouth & B A	1-0	Tricker	10
21	Jan	2	WATFORD	2-2	Best, Fletcher	4
22		11	Luton Town	5-1	Mills 2, Best 2, Jack	1
23		16	Mansfield Town	3-4	Mills, Fletcher, Tricker	6
24		23	BRIGHTON & HOVE ALBION	2-2	Tricker 2	5
25		30	Norwich City	2-3	Fletcher 2	8
26	Feb	6	SWINDON TOWN	4-2	Fletcher (pen), Hales 2, Tricker	6
27		13	Southend United	3-1	Best, Tricker, Fletcher	4
28		20	Torquay United	0-3		2
29		27	FULHAM	0-1		11
30	Mar	5	Thames	3-3	Fletcher 2, Edmonds	3
31		12	BRENTFORD	2-2	Best, Mills	10
32		19	Exeter City	3-4	Best, Edmonds, Jack	5
33		25	QUEEN'S PARK RANGERS	3-0	Jack, Tricker, Fletcher	9
34		26	COVENTRY CITY	5-2	Fletcher 2 (1 pen), Tricker 2, Jack	7
35		28	Queen's Park Rangers	2-3	Best 2	11
36	Apr	2	Gillingham	2-0	Tricker 2,	4
37		9	LUTON TOWN	0-0		5
38		16	Cardiff City	0-5		5
39		21	Northampton Town	3-4	Imrie 3	2
40		23	NORTHAMPTON TOWN	3-2	Fletcher, Tricker, Jack	4
41		30	Reading	0-5		7
42	May	7	Crystal Palace	0-0		10
						Appeara
						G

FA Cup

1	Nov	28	Coventry City	2-2	Fletcher, Sanders	19
R	Dec	3	COVENTRY CITY	2-0	Tricker, Fletcher	20
2		12	Cardiff City	0-4		10
						Appeara
						G

Final League Positon: 16th in Division Three South

Broadbent	Evans	Peacock	Edmonds	Dudley	Reynolds	Jack	Tricker	Fowler	Fletcher	Allison	Cropper	Jennings	Hayward	Imrie	Mills	Bolton	Wright	Jones	Best	Blackwell	Sanders	Roberts	Watson	Hales	Witheridge	
2	3	4	5	6	7	8	9	10	11																	1
2		4	5	6	7		9	10	11	3	8															2
2		4	5			7	8		11			3	6	9	10											3
2		4	5			7	8		11			3	6	9	10											4
2		4	5			7	8		11			3	6	9	10											5
2		4	5			7		8	11			3	6	9	10											6
2		4	5			7	8		11			3	6	9	10											7
2		4	5			7	9	8	11			3			10	6										8
2		4	5			7	9	8	11			3			10	6										9
2	3	6	4			7	9	8	11						10		5									10
3		4	5			7	8	9					6		10			2	11							11
3		4	5			7	8		9				6		10			2	11							12
3		4	5			7	8		9				6		10			2	11							13
3		4				7	8	5	9						10	6		2	11	1						14
3		4				7	8	5	9						10	6		2	11							15
2						7	8	5	9						10	6		2			4	11				16
	3			6		10	8	5	9									2	7		4	11				17
3		6				7	8	5	9						10			2	11		4					18
3		6					9	5	10		8							2	11		4		7			19
		6					8	5	9	3					10			2	11		4		7			20
		6				7	8	5	9	3					10			2	11		4					21
2		6	4			7	8	5	9	3					10				11							22
2		6	4			7	8	5	9	3					10				11							23
2		6	4				8	5	9	3					10				11					7		24
2		6	4				8	5	11	3					10				9					7		25
2		6	4				8	5	11	3					10				9					7		26
2		6	4				8	5	11	3					10				9					7		27
2		6	4				8	5	11	3					10				9					7		28
2		6	4				8	5	11	3					10				9	1				7		29
2		6	4				8	5	11	3					10				9	1				7		30
2		6	4				8	5	11						10			3	9					7		31
2		6	4			8		5	11						10			3	9					7		32
2			4			8	9	5	11						10	6		3	7							33
2						8	9	5	11						10	6		3	7		4					34
2			4			8	9	5	11						10	6		3	7							35
2		6	4			8	9	5	11						10			3	7							36
2		6	4			8	9	5	11						10			3	7							37
2		6	4			8	9	5	11	3					10				7							38
		6	4	10					11	2			5	9				3	7						8	39
2		6	4			8	9	5	11						10			3	7							40
		6	4			8	9	5	11			2			10			3	7							41
2		6	4			8	9	5	11						10			3	7							42
37	3	37	33	4	2	30	39	35	41	14	2	8	9	6	37	8	1	22	31	3	7	2	2	9	1	
			2			11	19	3	20					3	6				10					2		

One own-goal

Broadbent	Evans	Peacock	Edmonds	Dudley	Reynolds	Jack	Tricker	Fowler	Fletcher	Allison	Cropper	Jennings	Hayward	Imrie	Mills	Bolton	Wright	Jones	Best	Blackwell	Sanders	Roberts	Watson	Hales	Witheridge	
3							8	5	9						10	6		2	7		4	11				1
3							8	5	9						10	6		2	7		4	11				R
3							8	5	9						10	6		2	7		4	11				2R
3							3	3	3						3	3		3	3		3	3				
							1		2												1					

1932-33

Manager: Jimmy Seed

	P	W	D	L	F	A	Pts
Brentford	42	26	10	6	90	49	62
Exeter City	42	24	10	8	88	48	58
Norwich City	42	22	13	7	88	55	57
Reading	42	19	13	10	103	71	51
Crystal Palace	42	19	8	15	78	64	46
Coventry City	42	19	6	17	106	77	44
Gillingham	42	18	8	16	72	61	44
Northampton Town	42	18	8	16	76	66	44
Bristol Rovers	42	15	14	13	61	56	44
Torquay United	42	16	12	14	72	67	44
Watford	42	16	12	14	66	63	44
Brighton & Hove Albion	42	17	8	17	66	65	42
Southend United	42	15	11	16	65	82	41
Luton Town	42	13	13	16	78	78	39
Bristol City	42	12	13	17	83	90	37
Queen's Park Rangers	42	13	11	18	72	87	37
Aldershot	42	13	10	19	61	72	36
Bournemouth & B A	42	12	12	18	60	81	36
Cardiff City	42	12	7	23	69	99	31
Clapton Orient	42	8	13	21	59	93	29
Newport County	42	11	7	24	61	105	29
Swindon Town	42	9	11	22	60	105	29

Division Three South

Match No.	Date		Opponents	Result	Scorers	Atten
1	Aug	27	Newport County	2-0	Tricker, Best	7
2		29	LUTON TOWN	0-0		7
3	Sep	3	BOURNEMOUTH & B A	1-1	Tricker	7
4		5	Luton Town	1-4	Best	4
5		10	Swindon Town	3-3	Tricker 2, Earle	5
6		17	NORWICH CITY	0-0		9
7		24	NORTHAMPTON TOWN	2-2	Tricker 2	8
8	Oct	1	Bristol City	0-3		7
9		8	COVENTRY CITY	2-1	Imrie, Best	7
10		15	Brentford	2-4	Imrie, Dimmock	14
11		22	Brighton & Hove Albion	0-0		4
12		29	BRISTOL ROVERS	0-3		7
13	Nov	5	Aldershot	0-4		5
14		12	QUEEN'S PARK RANGERS	2-2	Best 2	6
15		19	Southend United	3-3	Dimmock, Best, G. Phillips	4
16	Dec	3	Gillingham	1-3	Mills	5
17		10	WATFORD	2-0	Mills, Tricker	4
18		17	Cardiff City	1-6	Dimmock	4
19		24	READING	2-5	Tricker 2	6
20		26	TORQUAY UNITED	1-4	Robinson (og)	5
21		27	Torquay United	1-1	Hales	4
22		31	NEWPORT COUNTY	3-1	Best, Mills, Fletcher	4
23	Jan	7	Bournemouth & B A	2-4	Fletcher, Thompson	4
24		14	CRYSTAL PALACE	4-1	Thompson 2, Fletcher, W. Phillips	3
25		21	SWINDON TOWN	7-1	Keen 2, Mills 2, Fletcher 2, Thompson	5
26		28	Norwich City	0-2		6
27	Feb	4	Northampton Town	0-3		5
28		11	BRISTOL CITY	2-2	Tricker 2	5
29		18	Coventry City	0-5		10
30		25	BRENTFORD	1-5	Mills	7
31	Mar	4	BRIGHTON & HOVE ALBION	2-0	Thompson, Mills	6
32		11	Bristol Rovers	0-2		9
33		18	ALDERSHOT	2-3	W. Phillips, Tricker	6
34		25	Queen's Park Rangers	1-2	Tricker	5
35	Apr	1	SOUTHEND UNITED	0-0		4
36		8	Crystal Palace	1-2	Tricker	8
37		14	EXETER CITY	2-2	W. Phillips, Fletcher	4
38		15	GILLINGHAM	1-2	Fletcher	5
39		17	Exeter City	0-3		10
40		22	Watford	1-1	Fletcher	5
41		29	CARDIFF CITY	3-0	Imrie 2, Fletcher	3
42	May	6	Reading	1-3	W. Phillips	3

Appeara

(

FA Cup

No.	Date		Opponents	Result	Scorers	Atten
1	Nov	26	ALDERSHOT	0-1		11

Appeara

(

Final League Position: 20th in Division Three South

Hebdon	Jones	Sanders	Keen	Ellis	Best	Earle	Tricker	Phillip,s W	Fletcher	Peacock	Cooper	Chisem	Mills	Dawson	Vango	Smith	Imrie	Dimmock	Thompson	Bruce	Phillips, G	Le May	Pickering	Hales	
2	3	4	5	6	7	8	9	10	11																1
2	3	4	5	6	7	8	9	10	11																2
2	3	4	5	6	7	8	9	10	11																3
2	3		5	6	7	8		10	11	4	9														4
	3	4	5	6	7	8	9		11			2	10												5
	2	4	5	6	7	8	9		11				10	3											6
	2	4	5		7	8	9	10	11	6				3											7
	2	4	5		7	8	9		11	6			10	3											8
	2				7	8			10	6				3	4	5	9	11							9
	2				7				10	6			8	3	4	5	9	11							10
	2	4	5		7		9		10	6				3				11	8						11
	2	4	5		7		9		10	6				3				11	8						12
	2	4	5		11		9		10	6				3				7	8	1					13
	2		5		9				6	4			10	3				11	7	1	8				14
			5	2	9				6	4			10	3				11	7	1	8				15
	2		5		9				6	4			10	3				11	7	1	8				16
		4	5	2		8	9		6				10	3				11		1		7			17
		4	5	2		8	9		6				10	3				11		1		7			18
		4	5	2			9	8	6				10	3				11				7			19
	2	4	5	3			9	8	10									11				7	6		20
	2	4	5	3			9	8	10									11					6	7	21
	2	4		3	9			8	6				10		5			11						7	22
	2	4		3	11			8	6				10		5				9					7	23
	2	4		3				8	11	6			10		5				9	1		7			24
	2		4	3				8	11	6			10		5				9	1		7			25
	2		4	3				8	11	6			10		5				9	1		7			26
	2		4	3				8	11	6			10		5				9	1		7			27
	2	6	4	3			9	8	11				10		5					1		7			28
	2	6	4	3			9	8	11				10		5					1				7	29
	2		4	3				8	11	6			10		5			7	9	1					30
	2	4		3	7		9		11	6			10		5				8	1					31
	2	4		3	7		9		11				10		5				8	1			6		32
	2	4		3			9	8	11		7		10		5					1			6		33
	2	4		3			8	10	11		7				5				9				6		34
	2	4		3			9		11		7		10		5				8	1			6		35
	2	4		3		9	7		11				10		5				8	1			6		36
		4	2			9	7	8	11				10	3	5					1			6		37
		4	2			9	10	8	11					3	5							7	6		38
	3	4	2			8	6						10		5		9	11	7						39
		4	2				7	8	10					3	5		9	11					6		40
		4	2				7	8	10					3	5		9	11					6		41
		4	2				7	8	11				10	3	5		9						6		42
4	33	32	31	27	20	15	29	24	41	17	4	1	27	19	23	2	6	18	18	19	3	10	12	4	
			2		7	1	14	4	9				7				4	3	5		1			1	

One own-goal

Hebdon	Jones	Sanders	Keen	Ellis	Best	Earle	Tricker	Phillip,s W	Fletcher	Peacock	Cooper	Chisem	Mills	Dawson	Vango	Smith	Imrie	Dimmock	Thompson	Bruce	Phillips, G	Le May	Pickering	Hales	
	2		5		9	8			6	4			10	3				11	7	1					3
	1		1		1	1			1	1			1	1				1	1	1					

1933-34

Manager: David Pratt

	P	W	D	L	F	A	Pts
Norwich City	42	25	11	6	88	49	61
Coventry City	42	21	12	9	100	54	54
Reading	42	21	12	9	82	50	54
Queen's Park Rangers	42	24	6	12	70	51	54
Charlton Athletic	42	22	8	12	83	56	52
Luton Town	42	21	10	11	83	61	52
Bristol Rovers	42	20	11	11	77	47	51
Swindon Town	42	17	11	14	64	68	45
Exeter City	42	16	11	15	68	57	43
Brighton & Hove Albion	42	15	13	14	68	60	43
Clapton Orient	42	16	10	16	75	69	42
Crystal Palace	42	16	9	17	71	67	41
Northampton Town	42	14	12	16	71	78	40
Aldershot	42	13	12	17	52	71	38
Watford	42	15	7	20	71	63	37
Southend United	42	12	10	20	51	74	34
Gillingham	42	11	11	20	75	96	33
Newport County	42	8	17	17	49	70	33
Bristol City	42	10	13	19	58	85	33
Torquay United	42	13	7	22	53	93	33
Bournemouth & B A	42	9	9	24	60	102	27
Cardiff City	42	9	6	27	57	105	24

Division Three South

Match No.	Date		Opponents	Result	Scorers	Attend
1	Aug	26	Norwich City	0-3		14
2		28	NEWPORT COUNTY	3-0	Morris, Crawford, Mayson	6
3	Sep	2	BRISTOL CITY	4-0	Morris 2, Davin, Rigby	10
4		4	Newport County	1-1	Mayson	5
5		9	Southend United	1-2	Morris	8
6		16	Swindon Town	0-3		12
7		23	BRIGHTON & HOVE ALBION	2-1	Davin, French	6
8		30	Aldershot	0-0		7
9	Oct	7	LUTON TOWN	1-1	Mills	10
10		14	Northampton Town	0-3		5
11		21	BRISTOL ROVERS	0-0		8
12		28	Crystal Palace	2-3	Rigby 2	11
13	Nov	4	GILLINGHAM	2-1	Taylor, Crawford	7
14		11	Exeter City	3-0	Taylor, Morris, Mayson	6
15		18	CARDIFF CITY	4-2	Morris 3, Taylor	8
16	Dec	2	CHARLTON ATHLETIC	1-3	Mills	10
17		16	READING	2-3	Mills 2	7
18		20	Watford	0-6		1
19		23	Coventry City	1-3	Taylor	14
20		25	Queen's Park Rangers	0-2		19
21		26	QUEEN'S PARK RANGERS	2-2	Rigby, Mayson	6
22		30	NORWICH CITY	3-2	Crawford 2, Mayson	10
23	Jan	6	Bristol City	0-3		7
24		17	Bournemouth & B A	0-2		2
25		20	SOUTHEND UNITED	5-2	Halliday 3, Rigby 2	8
26		27	SWINDON TOWN	1-0	Halliday	8
27	Feb	3	Brighton & Hove Albion	0-0		5
28		10	ALDERSHOT	9-2	Halliday 3, Ware 2, Mayson, Mills, Rigby, Crawford	9
29		17	Luton Town	0-2		7
30		24	NORTHAMPTON TOWN	5-1	Crawford 2, Mayson 2, Halliday	8
31	Mar	3	Bristol Rovers	2-2	Halliday, Fellowes	10
32		10	CRYSTAL PALACE	2-0	Halliday, Rigby	11
33		17	Gillingham	1-1	Halliday	5
34		24	EXETER CITY	4-0	Halliday 3, Rigby	8
35		30	TORQUAY UNITED	4-1	Mayson 2, Halliday, Crawford	12
36		31	Cardiff City	2-1	Rigby, Halliday	5
37	Apr	2	Torquay United	1-2	Halliday	3
38		7	BOURNEMOUTH & B A	4-1	Crawford 2, Halliday, Mayson	11
39		14	Charlton Athletic	1-1	Rigby	12
40		21	WATFORD	2-3	Halliday, Fogg	10
41		28	Reading	0-4		5
42	May	5	COVENTRY CITY	0-0		8

Appeara
G

FA Cup

1	Nov	25	EPSOM TOWN	4-2	Rigby (pen), Morris 2, Taylor	9
2	Dec	9	Walsall	0-0		11
R		14	WALSALL	2-0	Morris, Taylor	8
3	Jan	3	Grimsby Town	0-1		13

Appeara
G

Final League Position: 11th in Division Three South

Lucas	Crompton	Henderson	Fellowes	Ware	Mayson	Davin	Crawford	Mills	Rigby	Yews	Morris	Fogg	French	Taylor	Robertson	Keen	Rogers	Finlayson	Halliday	Allen	Robinson	
2	3	4	5	6	7	8	9	10	11													1
2	3	4	5	6	11	8	10			7	9											2
2	3	4	5	6	7	8	10		11		9											3
2	3		5	6	7	8	10		11		9	4										4
2	3		5	6	7	8	10		11		9	4										5
2	3	4	5	6	7	8	10		11		9											6
2	3	4	5	6		8		10	11	7			9									7
2	3	4	5	6	7	8	9	10	11													8
2	3		5	6	7	8	9	10	11			4										9
2	3	4	5	6	7	8		10	11		9											10
2	3		5	6	7		9	10	11			4		8								11
2	3		5	6		8		10	11	7		4		9								12
2	3		5	6	7	8	10		11			4		9								13
2	3		5	6	7			10	11		9	4		8								14
2	3		5	6	7			10	11		9	4		8								15
2	3		5	6	7			10	11			4	9	8								16
2	3	4	5	6	7			10	11		9			8								17
2	3	4	5	6	7	8		10	11					9								18
	3	4	5	6	7		10		11		9			8	1	2						19
	3		5	6	7			10	11		9			8	1	2	4					20
	3		5	6	7			10	11		9				1	2	4	8				21
	3		5	6	7		10		11					8	1	2	4		9			22
	3	4	5	6	7		11				9			8	1	2			10			23
2	3	6		5	7	8	10		11			4			1				9			24
	3		5	6	7		10		11			4		8	1	2			9			25
	3		5	6	7		10		11			4		8	1	2			9			26
	3		5	6	7		10		11			4	8		1	2			9			27
	3		5	6	7		8	10	11			4			1	2			9			28
	3		5	6	7		10	8				4	11		1	2			9			29
	3		5	6	7		10	8				4			1	2			9	11		30
2	3		5	6	7		10	8	11			4			1				9			31
2	3		5	6	7		10	8	11			4			1				9			32
	3		5	6	7		10	8	11			4			1	2			9			33
	3		5	6	7		10	8	11			4			1	2			9			34
	3		5	6	7		10	8	11			4				2			9			35
	3		5	6	7		10	8	11			4			1	2			9			36
	3		5	6	7		10	8	11			4			1	2			9			37
	3		5	6	7		10	8	11			4			1	2			9			38
	3		5	6	7		10	8	11			4			1	2			9			39
	3		5	6	7		10	8	11			4			1				9		2	40
	3	4	5	6		8	11	10						7	1				9		2	41
	3	8	5	6	7		11	10				4			1	2			9			42
21	42	14	41	42	39	15	32	29	36	3	13	27	4	15	23	19	3	1	21	1	2	
			1	2	11	2	10	5	11		8	1	1	4					19			

Lucas	Crompton	Henderson	Fellowes	Ware	Mayson	Davin	Crawford	Mills	Rigby	Yews	Morris	Fogg	French	Taylor	Robertson	Keen	Rogers	Finlayson	Halliday	Allen	Robinson	
2	3	6	5		7			10	11		9	4		8								1
2	3	4	5	6	7			10	11			9		8								2
2	3	4	5	6	7			10	11		9			8								R
2	3		5	6	7		10		11			4		8	1				9			3
4	4	3	4	3	4		1	3	4		2	3		4	1				1			
									1		3			2								

1934-35

Manager: Aug 1934–Dec 1934 David Pratt; Dec 1934–Jan 1935 Sidney White (acting); Jan 1935–May 1935 Peter Proudfoot

	P	W	D	L	F	A	Pts
Charlton Athletic	42	27	7	8	103	52	61
Reading	42	21	11	10	89	65	53
Coventry City	42	21	9	12	86	50	51
Luton Town	42	19	12	11	92	60	50
Crystal Palace	42	19	10	13	86	64	48
Watford	42	19	9	14	76	49	47
Northampton Town	42	19	8	15	65	67	46
Bristol Rovers	42	17	10	15	73	77	44
Brighton & Hove Albion	42	17	9	16	69	62	43
Torquay United	42	18	6	18	81	75	42
Exeter City	42	16	9	17	70	75	41
Millwall	42	17	7	18	57	62	41
Queen's Park Rangers	42	16	9	17	63	72	41
Clapton Orient	42	15	10	17	65	65	40
Bristol City	42	15	9	18	52	68	39
Swindon Town	42	13	12	17	67	78	38
Bournemouth & B A	42	15	7	20	54	71	37
Aldershot	42	13	10	19	50	75	36
Cardiff City	42	13	9	20	62	82	35
Gillingham	42	11	13	18	55	75	35
Southend United	42	11	9	22	65	78	31
Newport County	42	10	5	27	54	112	25

Division Three South

Match No.	Date		Opponents	Result	Scorers	Attend
1	Aug	25	READING	2-1	Halliday, Mayson	14,
2		30	COVENTRY CITY	0-1		8,
3	Sep	1	Northampton Town	1-3	Mayson (pen)	9,
4		3	Coventry City	0-4		20,
5		8	BOURNEMOUTH & B A	0-1		10,
6		15	Watford	0-5		7,
7		22	NEWPORT COUNTY	4-0	Taylor, Halliday, Crawford, Mayson	4,
8		29	Exeter City	1-1	Halliday	4,
9	Oct	6	BRISTOL CITY	4-0	Halliday 2, Mayson, Rigby	8,
10		13	Millwall	1-1	Rigby	17,
11		20	CRYSTAL PALACE	2-0	Crawford, Foster	12,
12		27	Charlton Athletic	1-2	Mayson	17,
13	Nov	3	SWINDON TOWN	2-0	Foster 2	10,
14		10	Torquay United	2-4	Mayson, Foster	3,
15		17	LUTON TOWN	1-1	Foster	8,
16	Dec	1	CARDIFF CITY	0-1		8,
17		15	BRISTOL ROVERS	5-2	Farrell, Halliday 3, Smith	3,
18		22	Southend United	2-0	Taylor, Mayson	5,
19		25	Queen's Park Rangers	3-6	Mayson, Halliday 2	9,
20		26	QUEEN'S PARK RANGERS	3-1	Farell, Halliday, Taylor	11,
21		29	Reading	0-0		9,
22	Jan	5	NORTHAMPTON TOWN	3-2	Farrell 2, Mayson	8,
23		16	Brighton & Hove Albion	0-3		4,
24		19	Bournemouth & B A	0-1		4,
25		26	WATFORD	1-1	Farrell	8,
26	Feb	2	Newport County	3-3	Rigby 2, Halliday	2,
27		9	EXETER CITY	0-3		7,
28		23	MILLWALL	2-1	Farrell, Halliday	10,
29	Mar	2	Crystal Palace	0-1		13,
30		9	CHARLTON ATHLETIC	1-2	Ware (pen)	13,
31		13	Bristol City	0-0		3,
32		16	Swindon Town	1-1	Farrell	5,
33		23	TORQUAY UNITED	3-1	Crawford 2, Farrell	5,
34		30	Luton Town	0-3		7,
35	Apr	6	BRIGHTON & HOVE ALBION	6-0	Foster 3, Crawford 2, King (og)	6,
36		13	Cardiff City	0-3		7,
37		19	GILLINGHAM	2-2	Foster, Rigby	8,
38		20	ALDERSHOT	3-1	Rigby 2, Halliday	6,
39		22	Gillingham	0-1		7,
40		27	Bristol Rovers	2-1	Crawford, Mayson	5,
41	May	1	Aldershot	1-1	Manns	2,
42		4	SOUTHEND UNITED	3-0	Crawford 2, Foster	6,

Appearar

G

FA Cup

1	Nov	24	Ashford Town	4-1	Halliday 2, Mayson, Ware	5,
2	Dec	8	CHESTER	1-3	Halliday	12,

Appearar

G

Final League Position: 14th in Division Three South

Finlayson	Crompton	Fogg	Fellowes	Ware	Mayson	Smith	Halliday	Crawford	Rigby	Henderson	Taylor	Farrell	Millington	Keen	Searle	Foster	Manns	Coull	Hillam	Miles	Bow	
2	3	4	5	6	7	8	9	10	11													1
2	3		5	6	7	8	9	10	11	4												2
2	3	4	5	6	7	8		10	11		9											3
2	3		5	6	7	8				4	9	10	11									4
2	3		5	6	7	8	9		11	4		10										5
	2	4	5	6	7	8	9					10	11	3								6
	3	4	5	6	7		9	10	11		8			2								7
	3	4	5	6	7		9	10	11		8			2								8
	3	4	5	6	7		9	10	11		8				2							9
	3	4	5	6	7		9	10	11		8				2							10
	3	4	5	6	7			10	11		8				2	9						11
	3	4	5		7		9	10	11	6	8				2							12
	3	4	5	6	7		8	10	11						2	9						13
	3	4	5	6	7		8	10	11						2	9						14
	3	4	5	6	7		8	10	11						2	9						15
	3	4	5	6	7	10	9	11			8						2					16
	3	4	5	6	7	11	9				8	10			2							17
	3	4	5	6	7		9		11		8	10			2							18
	3	4	5	6	7	11	9				8	10			2							19
	3	4	5	6	7	11	9				8	10			2							20
	3	4	5	6	7	11	9				8	10			2							21
	3	4	5	6	7		9		11		8	10			2							22
	3	4	5	6	7		9		11		8	10			2							23
		4		6	7		9	8	11			10			2		3	5				24
	3	4		6	7		9		11		8	10			2			5				25
	3	4		6	7		9		11		8	10			2			5				26
	3	4		6	7		9		11		8	10			2			5				27
	3	4	5	6	7		9	10	11			8			2				1			28
	3	4	5	6	7		9	10	11			8			2				1			29
	3	4	5	6			9	10	11			8			2				1	7		30
	3	4	5	6	11		9	10				8			2				1	7		31
	3	4	5	6				10	11			8			2	9			1	7		32
	3	4	5	6				10	11			8			2	9			1	7		33
	3	4	5	6				10	11			8			2	9			1	7		34
	3	4	5	6				10	11			8			2	9			1	7		35
	3	4	5	6	11			10				8			2	9			1	7		36
	3	4	5	6				10	11			8			2	9			1	7		37
2		4	5	6			9	10	11			8			3				1	7		38
2		4	5	6			9	10	11			8			3				1	7		39
2		4	5	6	7		9	10	11			8			3				1			40
2		4	5	6			9	10	11			8			3		7		1			41
5	3	4		6	7	8		10	11						2	9			1			42
10	37	39	37	41	33	12	32	29	33	4	19	28	2	3	33	11	3	4	15	10		
				1	10	1	14	9	7		3	8				10	1					

One own-goal

Finlayson	Crompton	Fogg	Fellowes	Ware	Mayson	Smith	Halliday	Crawford	Rigby	Henderson	Taylor	Farrell	Millington	Keen	Searle	Foster	Manns	Coull	Hillam	Miles	Bow	
	3	4	5	6	7	11	9				8					10	2					1
	3	4	5	6	7	11	8									9	2				10	2
	2	2	2	2	2	2	2				1					2	2				1	
				1	1		3															

1935-36

Manager: Peter Proudfoot

	P	W	D	L	F	A	Pts
Coventry City	42	24	9	9	102	45	57
Luton Town	42	22	12	8	81	45	56
Reading	42	26	2	14	87	62	54
Queen's Park Rangers	42	22	9	11	84	53	53
Watford	42	20	9	13	80	54	49
Crystal Palace	42	22	5	15	96	74	49
Brighton & Hove Albion	42	18	8	16	70	63	44
Bournemouth & B A	42	16	11	15	60	56	43
Notts County	42	15	12	15	60	57	42
Torquay United	42	16	9	17	62	62	41
Aldershot	42	14	12	16	53	61	40
Millwall	42	14	12	16	58	71	40
Bristol City	42	15	10	17	48	59	40
Clapton Orient	42	16	6	20	55	61	38
Northampton Town	42	15	8	19	62	90	38
Gillingham	42	14	9	19	66	77	37
Bristol Rovers	42	14	9	19	69	95	37
Southend United	42	13	10	19	61	62	36
Swindon Town	42	14	8	20	64	73	36
Cardiff City	42	13	10	19	60	73	36
Newport County	42	11	9	22	60	111	31
Exeter City	42	8	11	23	59	93	27

Division Three South

Match No.	Date		Opponents	Result	Scorers	Attend
1	Aug	31	LUTON TOWN	3-0	Crawford 3	12,
2	Sep	5	READING	1-0	Crawford	8,
3		7	Notts County	0-2		11,
4		11	Reading	1-4	H. Taylor	10,
5		14	BRISTOL ROVERS	2-0	Searle (pen), Farrell	9,
6		16	Cardiff City	1-4	Crawford	7,
7		21	Millwall	0-1		13,
8		28	Southend United	1-2	Fogg	10,
9	Oct	5	NOTHAMPTON TOWN	4-0	Crawford 3, Pateman	8,
10		12	Crystal Palace	2-2	Crawford, Smith	16,
11		19	BRISTOL CITY	2-0	Miles, Farrell	8,
12		26	Watford	1-1	Crawford	8,
13	Nov	2	QUEEN'S PARK RANGERS	1-0	Smith	12,
14		9	Torquay United	0-1		3,
15		16	EXETER CITY	1-2	Miller (og)	7,
16		23	Newport County	3-2	McAleer, Crawford, Farrell	4,
17	Dec	7	Swindon Town	2-2	Foster, Smith	5,
18		21	Brighton & Hove Albion	3-1	Crawford 2, Smith	5,
19		25	GILLINGHAM	3-1	Crawford, Campbell, Farrell	9,
20		26	Gillingham	0-3		10,
21		28	Luton Town	3-5	Crawford 2, Smith	13,
22	Jan	4	NOTTS COUNTY	0-2		9,
23		16	COVENTRY CITY	0-1		2,
24		18	Bristol Rovers	1-1	Crawford	5,
25	Feb	1	SOUTHEND UNITED	3-0	Crawford 3	9,
26		8	Northampton Town	0-2		6,
27		22	Bristol City	0-2		4,8
28		26	CRYSTAL PALACE	1-0	Crawford	5,
29		29	TORQUAY UNITED	1-1	Crawford	7,5
30	Mar	7	Aldershot	0-1		3,
31		14	WATFORD	0-2		8,
32		21	Exeter City	3-2	H. Taylor, McAleer, Robinson (og)	3,6
33		28	NEWPORT COUNTY	4-0	Farrell 2, Miles 2	7,4
34	Apr	2	MILLWALL	1-0	Crawford	4,3
35		4	Coventry City	0-2		12,4
36		10	BOURNEMOUTH & B A	1-1	H. Taylor	8,3
37		11	SWINDON TOWN	1-2	Mayson	6,1
38		13	Bournemouth & B A	0-2		7,9
39		18	Queen's Park Rangers	0-4		10,8
40		23	ALDERSHOT	0-1		2,8
41		25	BRIGHTON & HOVE ALBION	3-1	Farrell 3	3,4
42	May	2	CARDIFF CITY	2-1	McAleer 2	5,4

Appearan

Go

FA Cup

1	Nov	20	ALDERSHOT	0-0		12,0
R	Dec	4	Aldershot	1-0	Crawford	5,0
2		14	Folkestone Town	2-1	McAleer, Crawford	7,0
3	Jan	11	CHARLTON ATHLETIC	3-0	H. Taylor, Foster 2	*18,6
4		25	Middlesbrough	0-3		34,4

Appearan

Go

Final League Position: 14th in Division Three South

* Ground attendance record at Lea Bridge Road

Searle	Herod	Heinemann	Affleck	Ware	Miles	Pateman	Crawford	Farrell	Edwards	Campbell	Taylor, H	Mayson	Taylor, J	Smith	Fogg	McAleer	Foster	Davis	Hurst	Reed	
2	3	4	5	6	7	8	9	10	11												1
2	3	4	5	6	7	8	9	10		11											2
2	3	4	5	6	7	8	9	10		11											3
2	3	4	5		7	8	9	10		11	6										4
2	3	4	5		7	10	9	8			6	11									5
2	3	4	5		7	10	9	8			6	11									6
2		4	5		7		9	8			6	11	3	10							7
2		6	5			10	9					7	3	8	4	11					8
2		6	5		7	10	9					11	3	8	4						9
2		6	5		7	10	9						3	8	4	11					10
2	3	6	5		7		9	8						10	4	11					11
2	3	6	5		7		9	8						10	4	11					12
2	3	6	5		7		9	8						10	4	11					13
2	3	6	5		7		9	8						10	4	11					14
2	3	6	5		7		9	8						10	4	11					15
2	3	6	5				11	10			4			8		7	9				16
2	3	6	5		7		11	10			4			8			9				17
2	3	6	5		7		9	10			4			8		11					18
2	3	6	5		7		9	10		11	8				4						19
2	3	6	5		7		9	10		11	8				4						20
2		6	5		7		9				8	11	3	10	4						21
2		6	5		7		9	10		11			3	8	4						22
2	3	4		6	7		11				8		5	10			9				23
2	3	4		6	7		11				8		5	10			9				24
2	3	4		6	7		9				8		5	10		11					25
2	3	4		6	7		9				8		5	10		11					26
2	3	4		6	7		9				8		5	10		11					27
2	3	4		6	7		9				8		5	10				11			28
2	3	4		6	7		9			11	8		5	10							29
2	3	4		6	7		9	8		11			5	10							30
2	3	4		6			11	8					5	10	7		9				31
2	3	4		6	7		9	10			8		5			11					32
2	3	4		6	7			10			8		5			11	9				33
2	3	4		6	7		9	10			8		5					11			34
2	3	4		6	7		9	10			8		5			11					35
2	3	4		6	7		9	10			8		5			11					36
2	3	4		6	7		9				8	11	5	10							37
2	3	4		6	7		9				8		5	10		11					38
	3	4		6			10	8			5		2	11	7		9				39
	3	4	5	6			10	8					2	11	7		9				40
	3		5	6	7		9	10			8			11					2	4	41
	2	4	5	6	7		9	10			8		3			11					42
38	36	41	25	23	37	9	41	29	1	8	27	7	25	28	15	18	8	2	1	1	
1					3	1	23	9		1	3	1		5	1	4	1				

Two own-goals

Searle	Herod	Heinemann	Affleck	Ware	Miles	Pateman	Crawford	Farrell	Edwards	Campbell	Taylor, H	Mayson	Taylor, J	Smith	Fogg	McAleer	Foster	Davis	Hurst	Reed	
2	3	6	5				11	10			4			8		7	9				1
2	3	6	5		7		9	10			4			8		11					R
2	3	6	5	4	7		9	8						10		11					2
2	3	4		6	7		11				8		5	10			9				3
2	3	4		6	7		11				8		5	10			9				4
5	5	5	3	3	4		5	3			4		2	5		3	3				
							2				1					1	2				

1936-37

Manager: Peter Proudfoot

	P	W	D	L	F	A	Pts
Luton Town	42	27	4	11	103	53	58
Notts County	42	23	10	9	74	52	56
Brighton & Hove Albion	42	24	5	13	74	43	53
Watford	42	19	11	12	85	60	49
Reading	42	19	11	12	76	60	49
Bournemouth & B A	42	20	9	13	65	59	49
Northampton Town	42	20	6	16	85	68	46
Millwall	42	18	10	14	64	54	46
Queen's Park Rangers	42	18	9	15	73	52	45
Southend United	42	17	11	14	78	67	45
Gillingham	42	18	8	16	52	66	44
Clapton Orient	42	14	15	13	52	52	43
Swindon Town	42	14	11	17	75	73	39
Crystal Palace	42	13	12	17	62	61	38
Bristol Rovers	42	16	4	22	71	80	36
Bristol City	42	15	6	21	58	70	36
Walsall	42	13	10	19	63	85	36
Cardiff City	42	14	7	21	54	87	35
Newport County	42	12	10	20	67	98	34
Torquay United	42	11	10	21	57	80	32
Exeter City	42	10	12	20	59	88	32
Aldershot	42	7	9	26	50	89	23

Division Three South

Match No.	Date		Opponents	Result	Scorers	Attendar
1	Aug	29	CRYSTAL PALACE	1-1	McCombe	12,6
2		31	Cardiff City	1-2	McCombe	16,6
3	Sep	5	Exeter City	2-0	McCombe, Fletcher	7,6
4		10	CARDIFF CITY	0-1		5,4
5		12	READING	3-2	Crawford, Farrell, Heinemann	7,9
6		17	BRIGHTON & HOVE ALBION	2-0	Crawford, Farrell	6,1
7		19	Queen's Park Rangers	1-2	Crawford	15,4
8		26	BRISTOL CITY	0-0		8,7
9	Oct	3	Torquay United	1-4	H. Smith	4,5
10		10	NOTTS COUNTY	1-1	Wells	10,4
11		17	BOURNEMOUTH & B A	2-1	Miles, Farrell	7,8
12		24	Northampton Town	1-1	McCombe	8,0
13		31	BRISTOL ROVERS	2-1	H. Taylor, H. Smith	5,5
14	Nov	7	Millwall	1-2	Crawford	19,0
15		14	SWINDON TOWN	1-1	H. Smith	7,4
16		21	Aldershot	1-1	Crawford	3,6
17	Dec	5	Newport County	1-1	Low (og)	8,6
18		19	Watford	1-2	McCombe	6,3
19		25	Walsall	2-3	McCombe 2	8,4
20		26	Crystal Palace	3-2	McCombe, H. Smith 2	15,1
21		28	WALSALL	2-2	Crawford 2	3,8
22	Jan	2	EXETER CITY	1-0	H. Smith	5,5
23		9	Reading	1-1	H. Smith	7,0
24		16	GILLINGHAM	2-0	Codling, Crawford	8,3
25		23	QUEEN'S PARK RANGERS	0-0		7,6
26		30	Bristol City	0-4		4,5
27	Feb	6	TORQUAY UNITED	2-0	Crawford, H. Taylor	7,4
28		13	Notts County	0-0		14,3
29		20	Bournemouth & B A	1-2	Fletcher	5,5
30		27	NORTHAMPTON TOWN	3-1	H. Smith, Crawford, Miles	5,0
31	Mar	6	Bristol Rovers	0-4		6,5
32		13	MILLWALL	1-0	Crawford	*20,2
33		20	Swindon Town	3-1	Farrell, H. Smith 2	5,8
34		26	LUTON TOWN	0-2		17,4
35		27	ALDERSHOT	1-1	Fletcher	6,3
36		29	Luton Town	0-2		18,2
37	Apr	3	Gillingham	2-0	Codling, Miles	6,2
38		10	NEWPORT COUNTY	1-2	Fletcher	6,0
39		17	Southend United	0-0		5,1
40		24	WATFORD	1-1	Fletcher	5,7
41		29	SOUTHEND UNITED	3-0	Rossiter 2, Fletcher	2,5
42	May	1	Brighton & Hove Albion	1-1	Hearty	5,6

Appearanc

Goa

FA Cup

1	Nov	28	TORQUAY UNITED	2-1	H. Smith, Crawford	8,72
2	Dec	12	Carlisle United	1-4	Crawford	13,31

Appearanc

Goa

Final League Position: 12th in Division Three South

* Ground attendance record at Lea Bridge Road.

Taylor, J	Herod	Taylor, H	Affleck	Heinemann	McCombe	Fletcher	Crawford	Smith, H	Wells	Codling	Farrell	Rossiter	Brown	Hearty	Miles	Smith, J	Searle	Boyd	Fisher	
2	3	4	5	6	7	8	9	10	11											1
2	3	4	5	6	7	8	9	10	11											2
2	3	4	5	6	7	8	9	10		11										3
2	3	4	5	6	7	8	9	10		11										4
2	3	4	5	6	7	8	9			11	10									5
	3	4	5	6	7	8	9			11	10	2								6
	3		5	6	7	8	9			11	10	2	4							7
	3	4	5	6	7	8	9	10		11				2						8
	3	4	5	6	7	8	9	10		11				2						9
	3	5		6	7	8	9	10	11		4			2						10
	3	4	5	6	7	9		10			8			2	11					11
	3	4	5	6	7	8	9	10						2	11					12
	3	4	5	6	7	9		10						2	11	8				13
	3	4	5	6	7		9	10						2	11	8				14
	3	4	5	6	7		9	10						2	11	8				15
	3	4	5	6	7	9	11	10						2		8				16
	3	4	5			10	9	11						2	7	8	6			17
		4	5		7		9	10			8			3	11		2	6		18
		4	5		11		9	10			8			3	7		2	6		19
		4	5		7	10	9	8			6			3	11		2			20
		4	5		11	8	9	10			6			3	7		2			21
		4	5		7	10	9	8			6			3	11		2			22
		4	5			8	9	10		11	6			3	7		2			23
		4	5			8	9	10		11	6			3	7		2			24
		4	5			8	9	10		11	6			3	7		2			25
		4	5			8		10		11	6			3	7		2		9	26
		4	5	6		8	9	10		11				3	7		2			27
		4	5	6		8	9	10			11			3	7		2			28
		4	5			8	9	10		11	6			3	7		2			29
		4	5			8	9	10		11	6			3	7		2			30
			5	6		8	9			11	4			3	7		2		10	31
		4	5	6		8	9	10	11					3	7		2			32
		4	5	6	7	8	9	10			11			3			2			33
		4	5	6	7	8	9	10			11			3			2			34
		4	5	6		8	9	10			11			3	7		2			35
		4	5	6		9		10		11	8			3	7		2			36
		4	5	6		8		10		11		9		3	7		2			37
		4	5	6		8		10		11		9		3	7		2			38
		4	5	6	7	8		10		11		9		3			2			39
		4	5	6	7	8	9	10						3	11		2			40
		4	5	6	7	8		10		11		9		3			2			41
		4	5	6	7	8		10		11		9		3			2			42
5	17	40	41	30	27	38	33	38	4	21	22	7	1	35	26	5	26	2	2	
		2		1	8	6	11	10	1	2	4	2		1	3					

One own-goal

Taylor, J	Herod	Taylor, H	Affleck	Heinemann	McCombe	Fletcher	Crawford	Smith, H	Wells	Codling	Farrell	Rossiter	Brown	Hearty	Miles	Smith, J	Searle	Boyd	Fisher	
	3	4	5	6	7		9	10						2	11	8				1
	3	4	5	6	7		9	10						2	11	8				2
	2	2	2	2	2		2	2						2	2	2				
							2	1												

1937-38

Manager: Peter Proudfoot

	P	W	D	L	F	A	Pts
Millwall	42	23	10	9	83	37	56
Bristol City	42	21	13	8	68	40	55
Queen's Park Rangers	42	22	9	11	80	47	53
Watford	42	21	11	10	73	43	53
Brighton & Hove Albion	42	21	9	12	64	44	51
Reading	42	20	11	11	71	63	51
Crystal Palace	42	18	12	12	67	47	48
Swindon Town	42	17	10	15	49	49	44
Northampton Town	42	17	9	16	51	57	43
Cardiff City	42	15	12	15	67	54	42
Notts County	42	16	9	17	50	50	41
Southend United	42	15	10	17	70	68	40
Bournemouth & B A	42	14	12	16	56	57	40
Mansfield Town	42	15	9	18	62	67	39
Bristol Rovers	42	13	13	16	46	61	39
Newport County	42	11	16	15	43	52	38
Exeter City	42	13	12	17	57	70	38
Aldershot	42	15	5	22	39	59	35
Clapton Orient	42	13	7	22	42	61	33
Torquay United	42	9	12	21	38	73	30
Walsall	42	11	7	24	52	88	29
Gillingham	42	10	6	26	36	77	26

Division Three South

Match No.	Date		Opponents	Result	Scorers	Attenda
1	Aug	28	CARDIFF CITY	1-1	Tully	14,5
2	Sept	1	Bournemouth & B A	1-2	H. Smith	6,8
3		4	Walsall	0-2		8,0
4		9	BOURNEMOUTH & B A	3-0	Fletcher 3	2,8
5		11	NORTHAMPTON TOWN	1-0	Fletcher	8,9
6		15	Southend United	2-1	Crawford 2	5,5
7		18	Bristol Rovers	2-3	Fletcher, H. Smith	8,2
8		25	MANSFIELD TOWN	1-2	Hearty	8,5
9	Oct	2	Torquay United	1-3	Codling	3,8
10		9	SWINDON TOWN	1-0	Crawford	8,8
11		16	Aldershot	2-1	Crawford, Tully	5,9
12		23	MILLWALL	2-1	Lane, Tully	19,8
13		30	Reading	0-2		7,1
14	Nov	6	CRYSTAL PALACE	0-2		11,1
15		13	Notts County	0-1		11,0
16		20	NEWPORT COUNTY	0-2		6,7
17	Dec	4	WATFORD	1-1	Tully	6,4
18		18	EXETER CITY	2-1	Tully 2	4,3
19		27	Brighton & Hove Albion	1-2	Crawford	18,3
20		28	BRIGHTON & HOVE ALBION	0-3		4,6
21	Jan	1	Cardiff City	0-2		19,5
22		8	Bristol City	0-2		7,7
23		15	WALSALL	2-2	H. Smith, Taylor	4,6
24		22	Northampton Town	0-2		6,7
25		29	BRISTOL ROVERS	1-0	Graham	4,4
26	Feb	5	Mansfield Town	1-3	Tully	5,3
27		12	TORQUAY UNITED	2-0	Tully, H. Smith	4,8
28		19	Swindon Town	0-1		6,6
29		23	Gillingham	2-1	Tully 2	1,7
30		26	ALDERSHOT	2-1	Crawford, H. Smith	5,7
31	Mar	5	Millwall	0-3		25,7
32		12	READING	1-1	Tully	7,3
33		19	Crystal Palace	0-1		15,3
34		26	NOTTS COUNTY	2-0	Dodds, Dodgin	7,4
35	Apr	2	Newport County	1-3	Tully	7,0
36		9	BRISTOL CITY	0-0		8,7
37		15	QUEEN'S PARK RANGERS	1-1	H. Smith	12,8
38		16	Watford	0-2		11,9
39		18	Queen's Park Rangers	2-3	H. Smith 2	15,8
40		23	GILLINGHAM	3-0	H. Smith 2, Tully	5,9
41		30	Exeter City	0-2		2,7
42	May	7	SOUTHEND UNITED	1-1	H. Smith	5,5

Appearanc

Go

FA Cup

1	Nov	27	Torquay United	2-1	Tully, Graham	7,0
2	Dec	11	YORK CITY	2-2	Lane, H. Smith	7,7
R		15	York City	0-1		7,5

Appearanc

Go

Final League Position: 19th in Division Three South

	Searle	Hearty	Taylor	Bartlett	Lawrence	Tully	Fletcher	Lane	Smith, H	Codling	Heinemann	McCombe	Crawford	Shankly	Dodds	Dodgin	Graham	Allen	Landells	Brooks	Iceton	Rumbold	Smith, M	Tidman
1	2	3	4	5	6	7	8	9	10	11														
2	2	3	5		4		8	9	10	11	6	7												
3	2	3	5		4		8		10	11	6	7	9											
4	2	3	5		4		8		10	11	6	7	9											
5	2	3	5		4		8		10	11	6	7	9											
6	2	3	5		4		8			11	6	7	9	10										
7	2	3	5		4		8		10	11	6	7	9											
8	2	3	5		4		8		10	11	6	7	9											
9	2	3	5		4	7	8		10	11	6		9											
10	2	3	5		4	7	8		10		6		9		11									
11	2	3	5		4	7	8						9	10	11	6								
12	2	3	5		4	11		8	10		6	7	9											
13	2	3	5		4	11		8	10		6	7					9							
14	2	3	5		4	11		8	10		6	7	9											
15	2	3		5	6	11		8	10				9					4	7					
16	2	3	6	5		7	8		10	11			9					4						
17	3		5		6	7	8		10				11				9	4		2				
18	2	3	5		4	7		8	10		6		9		11						1			
19	2	3	5		4	7		8	10		6		9		11						1			
20	2	3	5		4				10		6	7	9	8	11						1			
21			5						10	11				8	7	6	9	4		2	1	3		
22			4					8	10					7	11	6	9			2	1	3	5	
23			4					8	10				11		7	6	9			2	1	3	5	
24	2	3	4			7	8		10				11			6	9						5	
25	2	3	4	5		7	8		10				11			6	9							
26	2	3	4	5		7	8		10				11			6	9							
27	2	3	4	5		7	8		10						11	6	9							
28		3	4	5		7		8	10				9		11	6						2		
29		3	4	5		7		8	10				9		11	6						2		
30		3	4	5		7			10				9		11	6			8			2		
31		3	4	5		7			10				9		11	6		8				2		
32	2	3	4	5		8			10			7	9		11	6					1			
33		3	4	5		8			10			7	9		11	6					1	2		
34		3	4	5		8			10			7	9		11	6					1	2		
35			4	5	2	8			10			7	9		11	6					1	3		
36		3	4	5		8			10			7	9		11	6					1	2		
37		3	4	5		8			10			7	9		11	6					1	2		
38		3		5					10			7	9	8	11	6					1	2		4
39		3	5		4	7			10				9	8	11	6						2		
40		3	4	5		7			10				9	8	11	6					1	2		
41		3	4	5		7			10				9	8	11	6					1	2		
42		3	4	5		7			10				9	8	11	6					1	2		
	25	37	40	20	21	30	17	12	40	11	15	18	36	10	24	23	9	5	2	4	16	17	3	1
		1	1			13	5	1	11	1			6		1	1	1							

	Searle	Hearty	Taylor	Bartlett	Lawrence	Tully	Fletcher	Lane	Smith, H	Codling	Heinemann	McCombe	Crawford	Shankly	Dodds	Dodgin	Graham	Allen	Landells	Brooks	Iceton	Rumbold	Smith, M	Tidman
1	3		8	5	6	7			10				11				9	4		2				
2	2	3	5		6	7		8	10				9		11			4						
R	2	3	5		6	7	8	9	10						11			4			1			
	3	2	3	1	3	3	1	2	3				2		2		1	3		1	1			
						1		1	1								1							

1938-39

Manager: Aug 1938–Jan 1939 Peter Proudfoot; Jan 1939–May 1939 Tom Halsey

	P	W	D	L	F	A	Pts
Newport County	42	22	11	9	58	45	55
Crystal Palace	42	20	12	10	71	52	52
Brighton & Hove Albion	42	19	11	12	68	49	49
Watford	42	17	12	13	62	51	46
Reading	42	16	14	12	69	59	46
Queen's Park Rangers	42	15	14	13	68	49	44
Ipswich Town	42	16	12	14	62	52	44
Bristol City	42	16	12	14	61	63	44
Swindon Town	42	18	8	16	72	77	44
Aldershot	42	16	12	14	53	66	44
Notts County	42	17	9	16	59	54	43
Southend United	42	16	9	17	61	64	41
Cardiff City	42	15	11	16	61	65	41
Exeter City	42	13	14	15	65	82	40
Bournemouth & B A	42	13	13	16	52	58	39
Mansfield Town	42	12	15	15	44	62	39
Northampton Town	42	15	8	19	51	58	38
Port Vale	42	14	9	19	52	58	37
Torquay United	42	14	9	19	54	70	37
Clapton Orient	42	11	13	18	53	55	35
Walsall	42	11	11	20	68	69	33
Bristol Rovers	42	10	13	19	55	61	33

Division Three South

Match No.	Date		Opponents	Result	Scorers	Attenda
1	Aug	27	NEWPORT COUNTY	1-3	Tully (pen)	10,5
2		31	Swindon Town	0-2		10,3
3	Sep	3	Northampton Town	0-3		13,2
4		8	PORT VALE	1-0	Walters	4,3
5		10	NOTTS COUNTY	1-1	H. Smith	8,5
6		17	Aldershot	0-1		7,6
7		24	BRISTOL CITY	1-1	H. Smith	8,9
8	Oct	1	Crystal Palace	2-4	Crawford, Williams	19,1
9		8	WATFORD	0-0		8,9
10		15	Cardiff City	2-1	H. Smith, Dodds (pen)	16,3
11		22	SOUTHEND UNITED	5-0	Williams 3, Dodds, H. Smith	9,7
12		29	Reading	2-2	Crawford, Grant	11,4
13	Nov	5	BRISTOL ROVERS	2-1	Crawford 2	11,6
14		12	Brighton & Hove Albion	0-2		7,6
15		19	BOURNEMOUTH & B A	1-1	Williams	9,8
16	Dec	3	MANSFIELD TOWN	0-0		8,2
17		17	IPSWICH TOWN	1-1	Williams	6,4
18		24	Newport County	1-2	Crawford	9,3
19		27	Torquay United	1-2	Dodds	4,1
20		31	NORTHAMPTON TOWN	3-0	Tully 2, H. Smith	6,9
21	Jan	12	Walsall	1-5	Williams	3,6
22		14	Notts County	0-1		10,8
23		21	ALDERSHOT	2-0	Williams, Crawford	6,7
24		28	Bristol City	1-3	H. Smith	7,7
25	Feb	4	CRYSTAL PALACE	4-0	Williams, Crawford, Walters, Tully	8,8
26		11	Watford	0-1		8,8
27		18	CARDIFF CITY	1-1	Walters	9,0
28		25	Southend United	0-1		4,4
29	Mar	4	READING	1-2	Tully	6,6
30		11	Bristol Rovers	0-1		3,7
31		18	BRIGHTON & HOVE ALBION	2-0	Walters 2	7,3
32		25	Bournemouth & B A	0-0		4,6
33	Apr	1	WALSALL	1-1	Crawford	7,2
34		7	EXETER CITY	3-3	Williams 2 (1 pen), Walters	8,9
35		8	Mansfield Town	0-1		4,1
36		10	Exeter City	1-2	Williams	7,3
37		15	QUEEN'S PARK RANGERS	2-1	Grant, Williams	8,0
38		17	TORQUAY UNITED	3-0	Williams 2 (1 pen), Walters	3,8
39		22	Ipswich Town	0-3		10,4
40		24	Queen's Park Rangers	1-1	Grant	2,8
41		29	SWINDON TOWN	5-0	Walters 2, H. Smith, Williams, Grant	5,7
42	May	6	Port Vale	1-1	Rowe (og)	3,4

Appearanc

Go

FA Cup

1	Nov	26	HAYES	3-1	H. Smith, Williams, Crawford	11,4
2	Dec	10	Walsall	2-4	Crawford, Williams	13,5

Appearanc

Go

Final League Position: 20th in Division Three South

Rumbold	Hearty	Taylor	Bartlett	Dodgin	Tully	Smith, H	Walters	Galloway	Dodds	Crawford	Rennie	Smith, M	Grant	Pateman	Shankly	Black	Williams	Hall	Farrell	Richmond	Percy	Whyte	Pritchard	No.
2	3	4	5	6	7	8	9	10	11															1
2	3	4	5	6	7	8	10		11	9														2
2	3	4	5	6	7	8		10	11	9														3
	3	4		6	11		9			10	2	5	7	8										4
	3	4		6	11	10	9				2	5	7		8									5
2	3	4	5	6	11	8	9			10			7											6
2	3		5	6	11	8	10			9			7			4								7
2	3	4	5	6	11	8				10			7				9							8
2	3	4	5	6	11	8				10			7				9							9
2	3	4	5	6		8			11	10			7				9							10
2	3	4	5	6		8			11	10			7				9							11
2	3	4	5	6		8			11	10			7				9							12
2	3	4	5	6					11	10			7		8		9							13
2	3	4	5	6					11	10			7	8			9							14
2	3	4	5	6		8			11				7	10			9							15
2	3	4	5	6		8			11	10			7				9							16
2	3	8	5	4	7				11	10						6	9							17
2	3	4	5	6	7	8			11	10							9							18
2	3	4	5	6	7	8			11	10							9							19
2	3		5	4	7	8			11	10						6	9							20
2	3	4	5	6	7	8			11	10							9							21
2	3	5		4	7	8			11	10						6	9							22
2	3		5	4	7	8			11	10						6	9							23
2	3	4	5	6	7	8			11	10							9							24
3		2	5	4	7		9		11	10						6	8	1						25
3		2	5	4	7		9		11	10						6	8	1						26
3		2	5	4	7		9		11						10	6	8	1						27
3		2	5	4	7		9		11							6	8	1	10					28
3		2	5		7		9		11							6	8	1	10	4				29
3		2	5	4	7	10	8									6	9	1			11			30
3		2	5	4	7	10	8									6	9	1			11			31
3		2	5	4	7	10	8									6	9	1			11			32
	3	2	5	4	7	10	8			11						6	9	1						33
	3	2	5	4	7		8			10						6	9	1			11			34
		2	5	4			9		11	10	3			7		6	8	1						35
			5	4		10	8			11	2			7		6	9	1				3		36
3			5	4		8			11	10	2		7			6	9	1						37
			5	4		10	8		11		2		7			6	9	1				3		38
2			5	4		10	8			11			7			6	9	1				3		39
2			5			10	8		11				7			6	9	1				3	4	40
2			5	4		10	8		11				7			6	9	1				3		41
2		4	5			10	8		11				7			6	9	1				3		42
35	26	33	39	39	27	31	23	2	29	29	6	2	19	5	3	23	35	18	2	1	4	6	1	
					5	7	9		3	8			4				16							

One own-goal

Rumbold	Hearty	Taylor	Bartlett	Dodgin	Tully	Smith, H	Walters	Galloway	Dodds	Crawford	Rennie	Smith, M	Grant	Pateman	Shankly	Black	Williams	Hall	Farrell	Richmond	Percy	Whyte	Pritchard	No.
2	3	4	5	6		8			11	10			7				9							1
2	3	4	5	6	7	8			11	10							9							2
2	2	2	2	2	1	2			2	2			1				2							
						1				2							2							

Orient in World War Two

When Britain declared war on Germany on 3 September 1939, the Football League programme, then only three games old, was abandoned, and Clapton Orient, like every other professional sporting organisation in the country, found themselves in a state of limbo.

The Government ordered an immediate ban on all outdoor sporting activity until the dangers posed by air-raids could be assessed. When there was no immediate threat of attack from the air, during the period known as the 'Phoney War', soccer clubs were allowed to play friendly matches, although with a limit of 5,000 on the number of spectators who could attend.

Eventually, some form of competitive football got underway again, and Orient joined the South 'A' Division for the remainder of the 1939–40 season. It was not only the Third Division, of course, that was now regionalised. Even First Division clubs played in geographical regions to cut down on travelling in such difficult times.

Thus, Orient found themselves with such attractive opposition as Arsenal, Tottenham Hotspur and West Ham United. They also had the benefit of some well-known names in the game such as Welsh international Dai Astley, the former Charlton Athletic, Derby County and Aston Villa star who guested for them. Rules of qualification had to be adjusted to allow players who were either stationed in the Armed Forces or on essential war work to play for a club near to their base.

By 1945–46 the war was over, but League football still needed time to adjust and another season of 'wartime' football was arranged, only this time the First and Second Division clubs of the pre-war era were placed in two sections, Football League North and Football League South. So, Orient lost their attractive opposition and went to play in the Third Division South (North). There was also a Third Division South (South).

In 1945–46 the FA Cup returned although it was run on a two-leg basis up to and including the sixth round. Charlton Athletic became the first, and so far only, team to make it to Wembley after losing a game. Orient were on the end of the first post-war FA Cup giantkilling shocks, losing 3–2 on aggregate to non-League Newport FC from the Isle of Wight.

The following seven pages chart Orient's results, scorers and attendances from 1939 to 1946. Unfortunately it has not been possible to provide team line-ups, such was the vague nature of reporting these things in wartime. Orient's teams were often made up entirely of guest players and sometimes even spectators were called in to make up the numbers.

From 1946–47, when normal League football resumed, full-line-ups are again provided.

1939-40

Managers: Aug 1939–Dec 1939 Tom Halsey; Dec 1939–May 1940 William Peter Wright

South 'A' Division

Match No.	Date		Opponents	Result	Scorers	Attendance
1	Oct	21	Watford	2-1	Shankly, Fletcher	3,000
2		28	ARSENAL	1-6	Shankly	8,000
3	Nov	4	Charlton Athletic	1-8	Shankly	2,000
4		11	SOUTHEND UNITED	5-1	Shankly 3, Fletcher, Smith	2,500
5		18	CRYSTAL PALACE	5-3	Shankly 2, Fletcher 2, Willshaw	5,000
6		25	Norwich City	0-4		5,000
7	Dec	2	TOTTENHAM HOTSPUR	2-1	Shankly 2	8,000
8		9	Millwall	1-1	Shankly	7,830
9		16	WEST HAM UNITED	1-6	Shankly	8,000
10		25	Arsenal	0-3		4,000
11		26	CHARLTON ATHLETIC	2-7	Shankly 2	3,000
12		30	Southend United	0-7		2,000
13	Jan	6	Crystal Palace	1-1	Astley	3,600
14		13	NORWICH CITY	1-1	Astley	3,000
15		20	Tottenham Hotspur	3-2	Devine, Astley, Tully	2,881
16		27	MILLWALL	1-2	Astley	2,000
17	Feb	15	WATFORD	1-2	Willshaw	1,800
18		22	West Ham United	1-4	Thomas	2,300

South 'D' Division

Match No.	Date		Opponents	Result	Scorers	Attendance
1	Feb	10	Norwich City	2-2	Fletcher, Smith	2,000
2		17	WATFORD	1-1	Willshaw	990
3		24	Aldershot	1-4	Shankly	3,000
4	Mar	2	BRIGHTON & HOVE ALBION	5-1	Shankly 3, Astley, Opponents own-goal	2,000
5		9	SOUTHEND UNITED	5-1	Shankly 2, Smith 2, Tully	2,500
6		16	Bournemouth & B A	0-4		4,000
7		22	CRYSTAL PALACE	0-1		5,000
8		23	Reading	2-0	Fletcher, Willshaw	3,500
9		25	Crystal Palace	1-7	Smith	7,892
10		30	QUEEN'S PARK RANGERS	4-3	Smith 3, Willshaw	3,000
11	Apr	4	READING	0-3		3,100
12		6	NORWICH CITY	4-3	Thomas 2, Tully, Shankly	3,000
13		11	BOURNEMOUTH & B A	2-0	Willshaw, Thomas	3,800
14	May	4	ALDERSHOT	4-3	Perry 2, Willshaw 2	4,500
15		11	Watford	2-2	Shankly	2,800
16		18	Queen's Park Rangers	0-4		2,100
17		25	Southend United	0-3		2,200
18	Jun	8	Brighton & Hove Albion	0-3		3,500

League Cup

Match No.	Date		Opponents	Result	Scorers	Attendance
	Apr	13	Brighton & Hove Albion	2-1	Willshaw 2	3,000
		20	Leicester City (1st leg)	2-5	Smith 2	5,500
		27	LEICESTER CITY (2nd leg)	2-0	Smith, Shankly	4,800

1940-41

Manager: William Peter Wright

South Regional League

Match No.	Date		Opponents	Result	Scorers	Attend
1	Aug	31	Brentford	2-2	Muttitt, Smith	1
2	Sep	7	Queen's Park Rangers	3-3	Astley, Shankly 2	1
3		14	SOUTHEND UNITED	1-2	Astley	
4		28	WEST HAM UNITED	3-3	Tully, Willshaw, Smith	
5	Oct	5	BRENTFORD	1-0	Smith	1
6		12	Fulham	1-3	Shankly	
7		19	Crystal Palace	2-6	Gregory, C. Fletcher	1
8	Nov	2	QUEEN'S PARK RANGERS	0-3		
9		9	Reading	0-6		1
10		16	CRYSTAL PALACE	2-4	Gillespie, Fletcher	1
11	Dec	7	Luton Town	0-4		
12		14	West Ham United	1-5	Willshaw	1
13		21	Tottenham Hotspur *	0-9		1
14		25	Southend United **	3-9	Houston 2, Rawlings	
15		28	Tottenham Hotspur	0-7		1

London Cup 'B' Division

The table is listed within the history section under 1940–41.

Match No.	Date		Opponents	Result	Scorers	Attend
1	Jan	4	Tottenham Hotspur	0-3		1
2		11	TOTTENHAM HOTSPUR	1-9	C. Fletcher	
3		25	READING	0-4		
4	Feb	1	ARSENAL	3-3	McNeil 3	1,
5		8	Arsenal	2-15	Rawlings, McNeil	2,
6	Mar	1	MILLWALL	0-1		
7		29	Reading	0-9		3,
8	Apr	4	Millwall	0-4		1,
9		12	West Ham United	1-8	Rawlings	2,
10		19	WEST HAM UNITED	2-3	Fisher, C. Fletcher	1,

League War Cup

The table is shown under the history section under 1940–41.

Match No.	Date		Opponents	Result	Scorers	Attend
	Feb	15	ALDERSHOT (1st Leg)	3-2	C. Fletcher, Astley, Fisher	
		22	Aldershot (2nd leg)	0-4		2,

* Orient fielded only 10 men in the first half. In the second half Spurs player Jimmy Sperrin played for the O's, having scored twice for Spurs in the first half.

** The match was played at Chelmsford's ground, which counted as an away game; Orient had 10 men, and Houston, a Chelmsford player at the ground, turned out for the O's

The Southern Group comprised of 34 clubs, but because of the war and the logistics it was not possible for all the clubs to p each other, so there was no League table. The League, therefore, was decided on goal averages. The O's finished bottom of table with an average of 0.287

1941-42

Manager: William Peter Wright

London League

Match No.	Date		Opponents	Result	Scorers	Attendance
1	Aug	30	READING	3-8	Armstrong 2, Fletcher	2,000
2	Sep	6	Charlton Athletic	0-4		4,000
3		13	BRIGHTON & HOVE ALBION	3-3	Crawford, Willshaw 2	2,000
4		20	West Ham United	1-3	Willshaw	4,500
5		27	BRENTFORD	1-3	Fletcher	3,500
6	Oct	4	Watford	2-2	Bestwick, Willshaw	2,000
7		11	Brentford	0-2		4,000
8		18	Aldershot	1-1	Crawford	2,500
9		25	FULHAM	2-1	Willshaw 2	2,000
10	Nov	1	Millwall	2-2	Shankly 2	2,200
11		8	Tottenham Hotspur	0-2		5,685
12		15	Arsenal	2-5	Armstrong 2	7,036
13		22	PORTSMOUTH	0-4		3,000
14		29	QUEEN'S PARK RANGERS	0-0		2,500
15	Dec	6	Chelsea	3-1	Willshaw, O'Dell, Armstrong	2,718
16		13	Reading	0-2		3,500
17		20	CHARLTON ATHLETIC	1-1	Tully	2,000
18		25	Brighton & Hove Albion	1-4	Willshaw	3,500
19		27	WEST HAM UNITED	3-1	Tully 2, Armstrong	3,800
20	Jan	3	Brentford	2-5	Armstong, Opponents own-goal	3,420
21		10	WATFORD	2-0	Dryden, Crawford	1,200
22		17	CRYSTAL PALACE	4-0	Dryden, Tully, O'Dell, Fletcher	2,200
23		24	ALDERSHOT	0-5		2,500
24		31	Fulham	1-5	Armstrong	1,921
25	Feb	14	TOTTENHAM HOTSPUR	2-3	Barnes, Crawford	2,500
26		21	ARSENAL	1-3	O'Dell	6,000
27		28	Portsmouth	1-16	Barnes	5,000
28	Mar	7	Queen's Park Rangers	1-2	Fletcher	2,000
29		14	CHELSEA	0-3		2,800
30	May	2	MILLWALL	3-3	O'Dell, Armstrong, Dryden	1,200

London Cup

Match No.	Date		Opponents	Result	Scorers	Attendance
1	Marc	21	Arsenal	1-4	Fletcher	6,790
2		28	BRIGHTON & HOVE ALBION	3-2	Crawford, Armstrong, Fletcher	1,500
3	Apr	4	ARSENAL	1-2	Crawford	6,000
4		6	Brighton & Hove Albion	2-5	Armstrong, O'Dell	6,500
5		11	West Ham United	3-5	Armstrong 2, Dryden	7,000
6		18	WEST HAM UNITED	0-1		8,600

1942-43

Manager: William Peter Wright

League South

Match No.	Date		Opponents	Result	Scorers	Atten
1	Aug	29	Brentford	2-2	Armstrong, Willshaw	3
2	Sep	5	Crystal Palace	3-5	Tully, Fletcher, Dryden	4
3		12	QUEEN'S PARK RANGERS	0-4		1
4		19	Charlton Athletic	2-1	Hewitt, Willshaw	3
5		26	WEST HAM UNITED	0-5		5
6	Oct	3	Southampton	2-5	Armstrong, Crawford	5
7		10	ARSENAL	1-4	Dryden	4
8		17	Watford	3-2	Armstrong 3	1
9		24	Luton Town	2-2	Dodgin, Armstrong	3
10		31	READING	2-3	Dryden, Armstrong	1
11	Nov	7	Chelsea	2-0	Hewitt, Armstrong	4
12		14	PORTSMOUTH	3-2	Dryden, Black, Hewitt	2
13		21	FULHAM	4-2	Hewitt 4	2
14		28	BRENTFORD	2-0	Hewitt 2	3
15	Dec	5	CRYSTAL PALACE	1-2	Hewitt	2
16		12	Queen's Park Rangers	1-3	Armstrong	4
17		19	CHARLTON ATHLETIC	4-2	Willshaw 2, Summersett, Lucas	2
18		25	BRIGHTON & HOVE ALBION	3-1	Willshaw 2, Summersett	6
19		26	Brighton & Hove Albion	0-1		6
20	Jan	2	West Ham United	3-10	Willshaw, Armstrong, Hewitt	7
21		9	SOUTHAMPTON	2-2	Armstrong, Willshaw	2
22		16	Arsenal	0-6		8
23		23	WATFORD	4-3	Hewitt, Barnes, Dodgin, Opponents own-goal	1
24		30	LUTON TOWN	4-2	Armstrong 2, O'Dell, Summersett	1
25	Feb	6	Reading	0-0		3
26		13	CHELSEA	3-1	Crawford, Saul, O'Dell	5
27		20	Portsmouth	0-1		6
28		27	Fulham	1-1	Armstrong	4

League Cup South, Group 2

Match No.	Date		Opponents	Result	Scorers	Atten
1	Mar	6	Southampton	0-1		10
2		13	BRENTFORD	1-1	Hewitt	3
3		20	QUEEN'S PARK RANGERS	1-1	O'Dell	3
4		27	SOUTHAMPTON	1-0	Summersett	4
5	Apr	3	Brentford	2-3	McLuckie, Hewitt	4
6		10	Queen's Park Rangers	1-8	Summersett	5

1943-44

Manager: William Peter Wright

League South

Match No.	Date		Opponents	Result	Scorers	Attendance
1	Aug	28	Brentford	2-4	C. Smith, O'Dell	4,820
2	Sep	4	Crystal Palace	2-5	C. Smith, Gillespie	4,653
3		11	QUEEN'S PARK RANGERS	2-3	O'Dell, Robson	3,000
4		18	Brighton & Hove Albion	0-2		3,400
5		25	WEST HAM UNITED	0-4		6,000
6	Oct	2	PORTSMOUTH	1-1	Blackman	2,000
7		9	ARSENAL	1-1	Ayres	7,500
8		16	Watford	1-6	Bryant	2,886
9		23	MILLWALL	0-1		3,000
10		30	Reading	2-8	Bryant, Clarke	4,000
11	Nov	6	Luton Town	1-2	Parry	3,000
12		13	TOTTENHAM HOTSPUR	0-4		5,500
13		20	FULHAM	1-3	Crawford	2,000
14		27	BRENTFORD	1-4	Bryant	950
15	Dec	4	CRYSTAL PALACE	1-6	Saunders	1,200
16		11	Queen's Park Rangers	2-6	Lowes, Bryant	4,000
17		18	ALDERSHOT	1-3	Bryant	800
18		25	CHARLTON ATHLETIC	1-7	Bryant	2,000
19		26	Charlton Athletic	0-1		5,000
20	Jan	1	BRIGHTON & HOVE ALBION	3-0	Bryant, Sual, O'Dell	1,500
21		8	LUTON TOWN	2-1	C. Smith, Bryant	3,000
22		22	Portsmouth	1-2	Lucas	3,200
23		29	Arsenal	0-1		8,971
24	Feb	5	WATFORD	0-0		2,000
25		12	Millwall	1-5	Liddell	2,100
26	Apr	10	West Ham United	1-3	Summersett	3,000
27		22	Aldershot	3-0	Ford 2, Opponents own-goal	5,000
28		29	Tottenham Hotspur	0-1		7,952
29	May	6	Fulham	1-3	Saunders	2,000
30		13	READING	1-0	C. Smith	2,500

League Cup South, Group D

Match No.	Date		Opponents	Result	Scorers	Attendance
1	Feb	19	QUEEN'S PARK RANGERS	2-5	C. Smith, Sharpe	2,000
2		26	Reading	0-3		4,000
3	Mar	4	FULHAM	0-4		2,000
4		11	Queen's Park Rangers	0-6		7,000
5		18	READING	0-5		3,000
6		25	Fulham	5-4	Kelly, Ford 3, Opponents own-goal	5,000

1944-45

Manager: William Peter Wright

League South

Match No.	Date		Opponents	Result	Scorers	Atten
1	Aug	26	Portsmouth	1-5	Browne	10
2	Sep	2	Brighton & Hove Albion	1-3	G. Kelly	2
3		9	LUTON TOWN	3-3	Ford 2, O'Dell	[illegible]
4		16	Aldershot	0-1		4
5		23	READING	2-1	O'Dell, G. Kelly	3
6		30	Chelsea	0-5		12
7	Oct	7	WATFORD	4-4	Daniels, Colloff 2, O'Dell	2
8		14	QUEEN'S PARK RANGERS	0-3		3
9		21	Southampton	2-6	Pond, Daniels	6
10		28	Fulham	2-5	Ford 2	6
11	Nov	4	WEST HAM UNITED	0-3		10
12		11	Crystal Palace	1-6	Pond	4
13		18	TOTTENHAM HOTSPUR	0-2		7
14		25	MILLWALL	3-2	Parry, Cross, Daniels	3
15	Dec	2	PORTSMOUTH	2-1	Foreman, Dugnolle	2
16		9	BRIGHTON & HOVE ALBION	2-2	O'Dell, Ford	2
17		16	Luton Town	2-4	Daniels, Parry	3
18		23	CHARLTON ATHLETIC	1-3	O'Dell	3
19		25	Charlton Athletic	0-4		6
20		30	ALDERSHOT	1-1	Daniels	2
21	Jan	6	Reading	1-3	Walters	3
22		13	CHELSEA	2-6	Daniels, Opponents own-goal	3
23		20	Watford	3-0	Younger, Liddell, Blackman	1
24		27	Queen's Park Rangers	3-3	Younger 3	2
25	Mar	17	SOUTHAMPTON	1-0	Ford	1
26		24	FULHAM	0-0		2
27		31	West Ham United	0-1		8
28	Apr	14	CRYSTAL PALACE	1-1	Liddell	2
		21	Tottenham Hotspur	0-4		10
		28	Millwall	1-4	Morrad	3

League Cup South

Match No.	Date		Opponents	Result	Scorers	Atten
1	Feb	3	PORTSMOUTH	0-1		2
2		10	Arsenal	0-5		10
3		17	Reading	2-2	Ford, Daniels	3
4		24	Portsmouth	1-4	Blackman	12
5	Mar	3	ARSENAL	1-3	Ford	7
6		10	READING	1-1	Ford	2

1945-46

Managers: Aug 1945–Sep 1945 William Peter Wright; Sep 1945–Jan 1946 Willie Hall; Jan 1946–May 1946 Charles Hewitt

Division Three South (North Region)

Match No.	Date		Opponents	Result	Scorers	Attendance
1	Aug	25	Mansfield Town	2-2	Dinnen, Morrad	4,000
2	Sep	1	MANSFIELD TOWN	0-0		5,000
3		5	QUEEN'S PARK RANGERS	0-2		4,000
4		8	SOUTHEND UNITED	2-2	Stock 2	4,000
5		13	Norwich City	0-4		7,000
6		15	Southend United	1-1	Dinnen	8,000
7		19	Queen's Park Rangers	0-3		6,485
8		22	Walsall	3-5	Robson 3	5,000
9		29	WALSALL	2-0	Stock, Dinnen	4,089
10	Oct	6	PORT VALE	1-1	Stock	4,817
11		13	Port Vale	0-4		7,000
12		20	Ipswich Town	1-3	Gore	13,000
13		27	IPSWICH TOWN	2-1	Stock, Parr	5,000
14	Nov	3	NORTHAMPTON TOWN	1-0	Gore	5,600
15		10	Northampton Town	1-6	Parr	5,100
16	Dec	1	Notts County	0-1		8,000
17		20	NOTTS COUNTY	3-3	Parr, Campbell 2	5,400
18		22	Watford	2-5	Pullen, Gore	2,883
19		29	NORWICH CITY	3-0	Gore, Pullen, Fletcher	5,000
20	Jan	10	WATFORD	4-0	Pullen 2, Parr, Somerfield	6,000

Division Three South (North Region) Cup

Match No.	Date		Opponents	Result	Scorers	Attendance
1	Jan	5	Walsall	3-4	Campbell 2, Howshall	4,000
2		12	NORWICH CITY	2-1	Gore, Somerfield	8,000
3		19	Norwich City	4-3	Medley 2, Pullen, Parr	6,000
4	Feb	2	WATFORD	4-3	Parr 2, Robson 2	5,922
5		9	MANSFIELD TOWN	0-2		9,000
6		16	Mansfield Town	2-1	Smith 2	4,000
7		23	WALSALL	0-1		10,000
8	Mar	9	PORT VALE	0-0		8,000
9		16	Port Vale	2-2	Froom, Taylor	9,000
10		23	Southend United	1-2	Parr	8,000
11		30	SOUTHEND UNITED	0-3		10,000
12	Apr	6	Northampton Town	2-0	Baynham, Pullen	5,000
13		13	NORTHAMPTON TOWN	2-1	Merritt, Hunt	10,900
14		19	Watford	0-2		3,435
15		20	QUEEN'S PARK RANGERS	0-0		14,000
16		22	Queen's Park Rangers	0-6		17,000

FA Cup

Date		Opponents	Result		Scorers	Attendance
Nov	17	NEWPORT ISLE OF WIGHT	2-1	1st leg	Gore, Parr (pen)	6,000
	24	Newport Isle of Wight	0-2	2nd leg		4,300

1946-47

Managers: Aug 1946–Sep 1946 Charles Hewitt; Sep 1946–Oct 1946 William Bulloch Wright; Oct 1946–Jun 1947 Charles Hewitt

	P	W	D	L	F	A	Pts
Cardiff City	42	30	6	6	93	30	66
Queen's Park Rangers	42	23	11	8	74	40	57
Bristol City	42	20	11	11	94	56	51
Swindon Town	42	19	11	12	84	73	49
Walsall	42	17	12	13	74	59	46
Ipswich Town	42	16	14	12	61	53	46
Bournemouth & B A	42	18	8	16	72	54	44
Southend United	42	17	10	15	71	60	44
Reading	42	16	11	15	83	74	43
Port Vale	42	17	9	16	68	63	43
Torquay United	42	15	12	15	52	61	42
Notts County	42	15	10	17	63	63	40
Northampton Town	42	15	10	17	72	75	40
Bristol Rovers	42	16	8	18	59	69	40
Exeter City	42	15	9	18	60	69	39
Watford	42	17	5	20	61	76	39
Brighton & Hove Albion	42	13	12	17	54	72	38
Crystal Palace	42	13	11	18	49	62	37
Leyton Orient	42	12	8	22	54	75	32
Aldershot	42	10	12	20	48	78	32
Norwich City	42	10	8	24	64	100	28
Mansfield Town	42	9	10	23	48	96	28

Division Three South

Match No.	Date		Opponents	Result	Scorers	Atten
1	Aug	31	IPSWICH TOWN	2-2	Willshaw, W.C. Brown	12
2	Sep	4	SOUTHEND UNITED	1-1	Baynham	6
3		7	Watford	1-3	Ballard	9
4		11	Queen's Park Rangers	0-2		15
5		14	WALSALL	1-0	Willshaw	8
6		19	Southend United	0-0		7
7		21	Reading	0-2		12
8		28	CRYSTAL PALACE	0-1		11
9	Oct	5	Torquay United	2-3	Hunt 2	5
10		12	MANSFIELD TOWN	3-1	Baynham, Fullbrook, Hunt	9
11		19	Norwich City	0-5		15
12		26	NOTTS COUNTY	1-3	Pullen	7
13	Nov	2	Northampton Town	1-4	Hunt	10
14		9	ALDERSHOT	1-3	Bacon	7
15		16	Brighton & Hove Albion	1-2	Hunt	9
16	Dec	7	BRISTOL CITY	4-1	Pullen 3, Morrad	7,
17		25	CARDIFF CITY	0-1		12,
18		28	Ipswich Town	0-0		13,
19	Jan	4	WATFORD	3-1	Pullen 2, Morrad	9,
20		11	EXETER CITY	3-1	Baynham, Hunt, Morrad	8,
21		16	Port Vale	1-2	Pullen	6,
22		18	Walsall	1-3	Hunt (pen)	12,
23		25	READING	3-3	Morrad 2, Pullen	9,
24	Feb	1	Crystal Palace	0-2		8,
25		22	NORWICH CITY	3-0	Pullen, Hunt, Smith	7,
26	Mar	8	NORTHAMPTON TOWN	2-1	Pullen, Roberts	8,
27		15	Aldershot	0-0		3,
28		22	BRIGHTON & HOVE ALBION	2-1	Morrad 2	10,
29		29	Exeter City	1-3	Pullen	7,
30	Apr	4	BRISTOL ROVERS	3-0	Hunt, Morrad, Davidson	13,
31		5	PORT VALE	5-3	Pullen 2, Hunt, Roberts, Morrad	12,
32		7	Bristol Rovers	1-6	Morrad	14,
33		12	Bristol City	0-3		16,
34		19	SWINDON TOWN	0-0		9,
35		26	Bournemouth & B A	0-2		7,
36	May	3	QUEEN'S PARK RANGERS	1-1	Morrad	13,
37		10	TORQUAY UNITED	0-1		11,
38		17	Swindon Town	0-2		12,
39		24	BOURNEMOUTH & B A	2-3	Smith, Hunt	9,
40		26	Notts County	2-1	Baynham, Hunt	10,
41		31	Mansfield Town	3-1	Bacon 2, Hunt	4,
42	June	7	Cardiff City	0-1		24,

Appearan

Gc

FA Cup

1	Nov	30	NOTTS COUNTY	1-2	Hunt	10,

Appearan

Gc

Final League Position: 19th in Division Three South

Clark	Ritson	Fullbrook	Fenton	Ballard	Smith	Hunt	Brown,WC	Pullen	Willshaw	Seigel	Bacon	Baynham	Bartlett	Farley	Hall	McKeeman	Merritt	King	Morrad	Roberts	Tolliday	Davidson	Canvin	Brown, WI	
2	3	4	5	6	7	8	9	10	11																1
2	3		5		7	4	9	10		6	8	11													2
2	3		5	6	7	4		10	9		8	11													3
2	3	4				9		10	11	6	8	7	5												4
	2	4				8		11	9	6	10	7	5	3											5
2	6	4			7				9	10	8	11	5	3	1										6
2	6		4		7				9	10	8	11	5	3	1										7
2	6	4			7				9		10	11	5	3	1	8									8
2		4		6	7	9			10		8	11	5	3	1										9
2		4		6		8			11	9	10	7	5	3	1										10
2		4		6	7	8		10		9		11	5	3	1										11
2		4	5			9		11		6	10	7		3	1		8								12
2		4	5	6		9		11			8	7		3				1	10						13
2		4	5	6		9		10	11		8	7		3	1										14
2		9		6		8		10			4	11	5	3						7	1				15
	3	2		6		8		10	11		4		5						9	7	1				16
	3	2		6		8		10	11		4		5						9	7	1				17
	3	2		6		8		10			4	11	5						9	7	1				18
	3	2		6		8		10			4	11	5						9	7	1				19
	3	2		6		8		10			4	11	5						9	7	1				20
	3	2		6		8		10			4	11	5						9	7	1				21
2	3			6		8		10			4	11	5						9	7	1				22
	3	2				8		10			4	11	5						9	7	1	6			23
	3	2				8		10			4	11	5						9	7	1	6			24
	3	2			7	8		10			4	11	5						9		1	6			25
	3	2				8		10			4	11	5						9	7	1	6			26
	2			3		8		10			4	11	5						9	7	1	6			27
	3	2				8		10			4	11	5						9	7	1	6			28
	3	2		4		8		10			6		5						9	7	1	11			29
2	3			6		8		11			4		5						9	7	1	10			30
2	3			6		8		11			4		5						9	7	1	10			31
	3			2		8		11		9	4	7	5						10		1	6			32
	3	2				8		10			4	11	5						9	7	1	6			33
	3	2				8		10			4	11	5						9	7	1	6			34
	3	2		4	7	8					10	11	5						9		1	6			35
	3	2		4	7	8					10	11	5						9		1	6			36
	3	2		6	7	8		10			4	11	5						9		1				37
	3	2		4	7	8					10	11	5						9		1	6			38
2	3	4			7	8					10	11	5						9		1	6			39
	3	2		4	7	9					8	11	5								1	6	10		40
	3	2		4	7	9					8	11	5								1	6	10		41
	3	4			7	9					8	11	5								1	6	10	2	42
18	35	34	7	26	17	39	2	30	12	9	40	36	36	11	8	1	1	1	25	18	28	19	3	1	
		1		1	2	13	1	13	2		3	4							11	2		1			

Clark	Ritson	Fullbrook	Fenton	Ballard	Smith	Hunt	Brown,WC	Pullen	Willshaw	Seigel	Bacon	Baynham	Bartlett	Farley	Hall	McKeeman	Merritt	King	Morrad	Roberts	Tolliday	Davidson	Canvin	Brown, WI	
2		9		6		8		10			4	11	5	3						7	1				1
1		1		1		1		1			1	1	1	1						1	1				
						1																			

1947-48

Managers: Aug 1947–Apr 1948 Charles Hewitt; Apr 1948–May 1948 Neil McBain

	P	W	D	L	F	A	Pts
Queen's Park Rangers	42	26	9	7	74	37	61
Bournemouth & B A	42	24	9	9	76	35	57
Walsall	42	21	9	12	70	40	51
Ipswich Town	42	23	3	16	67	61	49
Swansea Town	42	18	12	12	70	52	48
Notts County	42	19	8	15	68	59	46
Bristol City	42	18	7	17	77	65	43
Port Vale	42	16	11	15	63	54	43
Southend United	42	15	13	14	51	58	43
Reading	42	15	11	16	56	58	41
Exeter City	42	15	11	16	55	63	41
Newport County	42	14	13	15	61	73	41
Crystal Palace	42	13	13	16	49	49	39
Northampton Town	42	14	11	17	58	72	39
Watford	42	14	10	18	57	79	38
Swindon Town	42	10	16	16	41	46	36
Leyton Orient	42	13	10	19	51	73	36
Torquay United	42	11	13	18	63	62	35
Aldershot	42	10	15	17	45	67	35
Bristol Rovers	42	13	8	21	71	75	34
Norwich City	42	13	8	21	61	76	34
Brighton & Hove Albion	42	11	12	19	43	73	34

Division Three South

Match No.	Date		Opponents	Result	Scorers	Atte
1	Aug	23	CRYSTAL PALACE	1-1	Sales (pen)	1
2		28	Walsall	1-3	Baynham	1
3		30	Exeter City	1-1	Thompson (og)	
4	Sep	4	WALSALL	0-1		1
5		6	NEWPORT COUNTY	2-2	Naylor, Gray	1
6		11	BRISTOL CITY	0-2		1
7		13	Southend United	1-2	Hunt	1
8		17	Bristol City	0-6		1
9		20	NOTTS COUNTY	2-1	Naylor, Sales (pen)	1
10		27	Swansea Town	0-5		1
11	Oct	4	BOURNEMOUTH & B A	2-0	Johnson, Hunt	1
12		11	ALDERSHOT	0-3		1
13		18	Northampton Town	1-1	Smith	9
14		25	BRISTOL ROVERS	2-4	Sales (pen), Pullen	1
15	Nov	1	Norwich City	0-3		1
16		8	BRIGHTON & HOVE ALBION	2-1	Pullen 2	1
17		15	Watford	1-2	Neary	8
18		22	QUEEN'S PARK RANGERS	1-3	Baynham	1
19	Dec	6	SWINDON TOWN	0-3		6
20		20	Crystal Palace	0-2		9
21		26	Reading	2-6	Pullen, Chapman	13
22		27	READING	2-2	Neary, Baynham	5
23	Jan	3	EXETER CITY	2-4	Chapman, Neary (pen)	9
24		10	Port Vale	0-3		12
25		17	Newport County	2-3	Pullen 2	10
26		24	Torquay United	1-0	Chapman	6
27		31	SOUTHEND UNITED	2-0	Neary, Pullen	13
28	Feb	7	Notts County	4-1	Pullen 2, Neary, Chapman	28
29		14	SWANSEA TOWN	1-0	Neary	16
30		21	Bournemouth & B A	1-1	Hunt	13
31		28	Aldershot	0-0		7
32	Mar	6	NORTHAMPTON TOWN	5-0	Naylor 2, Neary, Pullen, Smalley (og)	14
33		13	Bristol Rovers	2-0	Chapman, Neary	12
34		20	NORWICH CITY	2-1	Naylor, Chapman	18
35		26	IPSWICH TOWN	1-1	Neary	*24
36		27	Brighton & Hove Albion	0-0		19
37		29	Ipswich Town	0-1		16,
38	Apr	3	WATFORD	0-2		13,
39		10	Queen's Park Rangers	2-1	Neary 2	27,
40		17	PORT VALE	0-0		12,
41		24	Swindon Town	1-0	Neary	10,
42	May	1	TORQUAY UNITED	4-1	Neary 3 (1 pen), Naylor	12,

Appearar

G

FA Cup

1	Nov	29	Gillingham	0-1		15,

Appearar

G

Final League Position: 17th in Division Three South

* Ground record at the time

Brown	Ritson	Waller	Sales	Stroud	Chapman	Skelton	Hunt	Naylor	Pullen	Baynham	Bacon	Gray	Fullbrook	Johnson	Morrison	Farley	Davidson	Smith	Neary	Bartlett	Richardson	Banner	
2	3	4	5	6	7	8	9	10	11														1
2	3	4	5	6		8	9	10	11	7													2
2	3	4	5	6	7		9	10	11		8												3
2	3	4	5	6			9	10	11		8	7											4
	3	4	5	6				10	11		8	7	2	9									5
2	3	4	5	6	9		8	10		11		7											6
	2		5	4			8	10	11	7				9	1	3	6						7
5	2			6		8	9		10	11	4	7				3							8
2	3	4	5	6			9	8	10	11		7											9
2	3	4	5	6			8	10	11			7					9						10
2	3	4		6			8	10				11		9	1		5	7					11
2	3	4		6			8	10				11		9	1		5	7					12
2	3	4	5	6				10	8			11			1		9	7					13
2	3	4	5	6	11			10	8			7			1		9						14
	3	4		6	7			10	8	11			2		1		5		9				15
2	3	4		6			8		10	11					1		5	7	9				16
2	3			6				10	8	11	4				1		5	7	9				17
2	3		5	4	7		8		10	11							6		9				18
2	3	4		6				10	11	7	8						5		9				19
2	3			6			8		10	11	4	7					5		9				20
2	3			6	7		8		10	11	4						5		9				21
2	3			6	7		8		10	11	4				1		5		9				22
2	3			6	7		8		10	11	4						5		9				23
	3			6	7				10	11	4			9	1	2				5	8		24
	3		5	6	7				10	11	4					2			9		8		25
2	3		5	6	7				10	11	4								9		8		26
2	3		5	6	7				10	11	4								9		8		27
2	3		5	6	7		8		10	11	4								9				28
2	3		5	6	7		8		10	11	4								9				29
	3		5	6	7		9		10	11	4										8	2	30
	3		5	6	7				10	11	4								9		8	2	31
	3		5	6	7			10	11		4								9		8	2	32
	3		5	6	7			10	11		4								9		8	2	33
	3		5	6	7			10	11		4								9		8	2	34
	3		5	6	7			10	11		4								9		8	2	35
	3	4	5	6	7		8	10	11										9			2	36
	3	4	5	6	7			10	11										9		8	2	37
	3		5	6	7		8	10	11		4								9			2	38
2	3			6	7			10		11	4						5		9		8		39
	3			6	7			10		11	4						5		9		8	2	40
	3			6	7			10	11		4						5		9		8	2	41
	3			6	7			10	11		4						5		9		8	2	42
25	42	17	26	42	28	3	22	27	37	24	27	11	2	5	10	4	19	5	26	1	15	12	
			3		6		3	6	10	3		1		1				1	15				

Two own-goals

Brown	Ritson	Waller	Sales	Stroud	Chapman	Skelton	Hunt	Naylor	Pullen	Baynham	Bacon	Gray	Fullbrook	Johnson	Morrison	Farley	Davidson	Smith	Neary	Bartlett	Richardson	Banner	
2	3	4		6			8		10	11		7					5		9				1
1	1	1		1			1		1	1		1					1		1				

1948-49

Manager: Neil McBain

	P	W	D	L	F	A	Pts
Swansea Town	42	27	8	7	87	34	62
Reading	42	25	5	12	77	50	55
Bournemouth & B A	42	22	8	12	69	48	52
Swindon Town	42	18	15	9	64	56	51
Bristol Rovers	42	19	10	13	61	51	48
Brighton & Hove Albion	42	15	18	9	55	55	48
Ipswich Town	42	18	9	15	78	77	45
Millwall	42	17	11	14	63	64	45
Torquay United	42	17	11	14	65	70	45
Norwich City	42	16	12	14	67	49	44
Notts County	42	19	5	18	102	68	43
Exeter City	42	15	10	17	63	76	40
Port Vale	42	14	11	17	51	54	39
Walsall	42	15	8	19	56	64	38
Newport County	42	14	9	19	68	92	37
Bristol City	42	11	14	17	44	62	36
Watford	42	10	15	17	41	54	35
Southend United	42	9	16	17	41	46	34
Leyton Orient	42	11	12	19	58	80	34
Northampton Town	42	12	9	21	51	62	33
Aldershot	42	11	11	20	48	59	33
Crystal Palace	42	8	11	23	38	76	27

Division Three South

Match No.	Date		Opponents	Result	Scorers	Atter
1	Aug	21	Aldershot	1-1	Neary	9
2		26	MILLWALL	2-2	Taylor, Chapman	22
3		28	BRIGHTON & HOVE ALBION	0-3		16
4		30	Millwall	0-0		22
5	Sep	4	Southend United	2-2	Neary, Dryden	13
6		9	Swansea Town	1-3	Johnson	24
7		11	NORTHAMPTON TOWN	0-3		12
8		16	SWANSEA TOWN	3-1	Connelly, Deverall, Neary	9
9		18	Norwich City	0-0		24
10		25	EXETER CITY	5-2	Neary 2, Dryden 2, Naylor	12
11	Oct	2	Bristol City	0-3		13
12		9	NEWPORT COUNTY	5-2	Neary 2, Dryden 2, Naylor	14
13		16	Bristol Rovers	3-2	Connelly, Naylor 2	14
14		23	BOURNEMOUTH & B A	1-2	Neary (pen)	18
15		30	Watford	1-2	Dryden	13
16	Nov	6	NOTTS COUNTY	3-1	Neary 3	16
17		13	Ipswich Town	2-2	Neary, Dryden	12
18		20	TORQUAY UNITED	3-1	McGeachy, Dryden, Neary	14
19	Dec	4	CRYSTAL PALACE	1-1	Neary	12
20		18	ALDERSHOT	1-2	Neary	9
21		25	Port Vale	0-3		9
22		27	PORT VALE	2-0	Neary 2	8
23	Jan	1	Brighton & Hove Albion	1-3	Naylor	11
24		15	SOUTHEND UNITED	2-0	Naylor, McGeachy	9
25		22	Northampton Town	1-4	Neary	8
26	Feb	5	NORWICH CITY	0-3		12
27		12	Reading	0-3		13
28		19	Exeter City	1-3	Connelly	9
29		26	BRISTOL CITY	3-1	Connelly, Neary, Naylor	8
30	Mar	5	Newport County	2-3	Pullen 2	6
31		12	BRISTOL ROVERS	1-1	Neary (pen)	10
32		19	Bournemouth & B A	0-3		13
33		26	WATFORD	1-0	Connelly	8
34	Apr	2	Notts County	1-2	Pullen	29
35		9	IPSWICH TOWN	1-1	Pullen	9
36		15	SWINDON TOWN	1-1	Neary	12
37		16	Torquay United	1-7	Neary	7
38		18	Swindon Town	1-1	Brinton	14
39		23	WALSALL	1-1	Naylor	9
40		28	Walsall	3-2	Pullen, Neary 2	5
41		30	Crystal Palace	1-2	Neary (pen)	7
42	May	7	READING	0-1		11,

Appearar

G

FA Cup

1	Nov	27	Dartford	3-2	Connelly, Deverall, McGeachy	11,
2	Dec	11	Darlington	0-1		12,

Appearar

G

Final League Position: 19th in Division Three South

	Ritson	Bacon	Davidson	Stroud	Chapman	Taylor	Neary	Connelly	McGeachy	Naylor	Deverall	Dryden	Pullen	Newton	Johnson	Sales	Haslam	Rooney	Gray	Gerula	Brinton	Walton	Lucas	
	3	4	5	6	7	8	9	10	11															1
	3	4	5	6	7	8	9	10	11															2
	3	4	5	6	7	8	9		11	10														3
	3	4	5			8	9		11		6	7	10											4
	3	4	5			8	9	10	11		6	7		1										5
	3	4	5					10	11		6	7	8	1	9									6
	3	4	5			8		10	11		6	7		1	9									7
		4	3				9	8	11	10	6	7		1		5								8
		4	3				9	8	11	10	6	7		1		5								9
		4	3				9	8	11	10	6	7		1		5								10
		4	3				9	8	11	10	6	7		1		5								11
		4	3				9	8	11	10	6	7		1		5								12
		4	3				9	8	11	10	6	7		1		5								13
		4	3				9	8	11	10	6	7		1		5								14
		4	3				9	8	11	10	6	7		1		5								15
		4	3				9	8	11	10	6	7		1		5								16
		4	3				9	8	11	10	6	7		1		5								17
		4	3				9	8	11	10	6	7		1		5	2							18
		4	3				9	8	11	10	6	7		1		5								19
		4	3			8	9		11		6	7	10	1		5								20
		4	3				9	8	11	10	6	7		1		5	2							21
		4	3				9	8	11		6	7		1			2	5	10					22
			3				9	8	11	10	6	7		1		5	2	4						23
		4	3				9	8	11	10	6	7		1			2	5						24
		4	3				9	8	11	10	6	7		1			2	5						25
		4	3			8	9		11	10	6	7		1			2	5						26
2		4	3			8	9		11		6		10	1				5	7					27
2		4	3				9	8			6		10					5	7	1	11			28
2		4	3				9	8		10	6					5			7	1	11			29
2		4	3					8	11	10	6		9			5			7	1				30
2		4					9			10	6		8			5			7	1	11	3		31
2		4	5				9		11	10	6		8						7	1		3		32
		4	3	6			9	8		10			11			5			7	1		2		33
		4	3	6			9	8	11	10			7			5				1		2		34
2		4	3	6			9	8	11			7	10					5		1				35
2		4	3	6			7	8	11	10			9					5		1				36
2		4		6			9		11	10		7	8					5		1		3		37
		4	3	6			9	8	11			7						5		1	10	2		38
2		4		6			9		11	8		7	10					5		1		3		39
		4	3	6			9		11	8		7	10					5		1		2		40
2		4		6			9		11	8		7	10					5		1		3		41
		4		6			9	8	11			7	10					5		1		3	2	42
0	7	41	37	13	3	9	39	31	38	29	29	30	17	23	2	20	7	15	8	15	4	10	1	
					1	1	25	5	2	8	1	8	5		1						1			

	Ritson	Bacon	Davidson	Stroud	Chapman	Taylor	Neary	Connelly	McGeachy	Naylor	Deverall	Dryden	Pullen	Newton	Johnson	Sales	
2		4	3				9	8	11	10	6	7		1		5	1
2		4	3				9	8	11	10	6	7		1		5	2
2		2	2				2	2	2	2	2	2		2		2	
								1	1		1						

1949-50

Manager: Alec Stock

	P	W	D	L	F	A	Pts
Notts County	42	25	8	9	95	50	58
Northampton Town	42	20	11	11	72	50	51
Southend United	42	19	13	10	66	48	51
Nottingham Forest	42	20	9	13	67	39	49
Torquay United	42	19	10	13	66	63	48
Watford	42	16	13	13	45	35	45
Crystal Palace	42	15	14	13	55	54	44
Brighton & Hove Albion	42	16	12	14	57	69	44
Bristol Rovers	42	19	5	18	51	51	43
Reading	42	17	8	17	70	64	42
Norwich City	42	16	10	16	65	63	42
Bournemouth & B A	42	16	10	16	57	56	42
Port Vale	42	15	11	16	47	42	41
Swindon Town	42	15	11	16	59	62	41
Bristol City	42	15	10	17	60	61	40
Exeter City	42	14	11	17	63	75	39
Ipswich Town	42	12	11	19	57	86	35
Leyton Orient	42	12	11	19	53	85	35
Walsall	42	9	16	17	61	62	34
Aldershot	42	13	8	21	48	60	34
Newport County	42	13	8	21	67	98	34
Millwall	42	14	4	24	55	63	32

Division Three South

Match No.	Date		Opponents	Result	Scorers	Atten
1	Aug	20	WATFORD	0-0		16
2		24	Crystal Palace	1-1	Neary	17
3		27	Reading	1-5	Neary	16
4	Sep	1	CRYSTAL PALACE	2-2	Neary (pen), Pullen	14
5		3	TORQUAY UNITED	2-1	Pullen 2	14
6		6	Southend United	0-2		12
7		10	EXETER CITY	4-1	Pullen 2, Smith, Sutherland	13
8		17	Ipswich Town	4-4	Sutherland 3, Rooney	13
9		24	PORT VALE	1-0	Rooney	15
10	Oct	1	Notts County	1-7	Sutherland	36
11		8	Aldershot	0-2		7
12		15	NOTTINGHAM FOREST	1-1	Neary	15
13		22	Northampton Town	0-3		11
14		29	NORWICH CITY	1-2	Sherratt	13
15	Nov	5	Newport County	2-3	Sherratt 2	11
16		12	BRISTOL CITY	1-0	Wood	9
17		19	Brighton & Hove Albion	2-2	Dryden 2	13
18	Dec	3	Millwall	1-3	McGeachy	16
19		17	Watford	1-2	Sutherland	9
20		24	READING	2-1	Sutherland 2	9
21		26	BRISTOL ROVERS	1-0	Banner (pen)	11
22		27	Bristol Rovers	0-3		19
23		31	Torquay United	1-4	Sutherland	7
24	Jan	14	Exeter City	1-1	Clark (og)	8
25		21	IPSWICH TOWN	4-0	Sutherland 3, Blair	9
26		28	WALSALL	2-2	Sutherland, Pullen	7
27	Feb	4	Port Vale	0-2		14
28		11	SWINDON TOWN	1-3	Stroud	9
29		18	NOTTS COUNTY	1-4	Sutherland	21
30		25	ALDERSHOT	2-7	Pullen, McEwan	8
31	Mar	4	Nottingham Forest	1-2	McEwan	19
32		11	NORTHAMPTON TOWN	1-0	Sutherland	9
33		18	Norwich City	0-4		20
34		25	NEWPORT COUNTY	2-1	Campbell, Pattison	8
35	Apr	1	Bristol City	0-0		16
36		7	BOURNEMOUTH & B A	2-1	Pattison 2	13
37		8	BRIGHTON & HOVE ALBION	0-1		10
38		10	Bournemouth & B A	1-4	Pattison	9
39		15	Walsall	2-1	Pullen, Blair	7
40		22	MILLWALL	1-1	Sutherland	16,
41		29	Swindon Town	1-0	Blair	5
42	May	6	SOUTHEND UNITED	2-2	McEwan, Pullen	13,

Appearar

G

FA Cup

1	Nov	26	SOUTHEND UNITED	0-2		17,

Appearar

G

Final League Position: 18th in Division Three South

[illegible]	Walton	Taylor	Rooney	Trailor	Neary	Pullen	Sutherland	Naylor	McGeachy	Stroud	Smith	Welton	Connelly	Lucas	Wood	Bacon	Sherratt	Dryden	Davidson	Campbell	Hobbins	Blair	Skivington	McEwan	Pattison	Higgins	Adams	Deverall	
2	3	4	5	6	7	8	9	10	11																				1
2	3	4	5	6	7	8	9	10	11																				2
2	3	4	5		7	8	9	10	11	6																			3
2	3	4	5	6	7	8	9	10	11																				4
2	3	4	5	6	7	8	9	10	11																				5
2	3	4	5	6	7	8	9	10	11																				6
2	3	4	5	6	7	8	9	10			11																		7
2	3	4	5	6	7	8	9	10			11																		8
2	3	4	5	6	7	8	9		10		11																		9
2	3	4	5	6	7	10	9				11	1	8																10
	3	4	5	6	7	8	9				11	1		2	10														11
2	3	8	5	6	7	10									11	4	9												12
2	3	4	5	6	7	10									11	8	9												13
3	2	4	5	6					11						10	8	9	7											14
3	2	4	5	6					11						10	8	9	7											15
3	2	4	5	6					11						10	8	9	7											16
2		4	5	6					11						10	8	9	7	3										17
2		4	5	8					11	6		1			10		9	7	3										18
2		4	5	6		10	9		11			1						7	3	8									19
2		4	5	6		10	9		11									7	3		1	8							20
2		4	5	6		10	9		11									7	3		1	8							21
2			5			10	9		11	6						4		7	3		1	8							22
2		4	5	6		10	9		11						7				3		1	8							23
2		4	3	6		10	9		11								7				1	8	5						24
2		4	3			10	9		11	6							7				1	8	5						25
2		4	3	6		10	9				11						7				1	8	5						26
2	9	4	3			10			11	6							7				1	8	5						27
2		4	3	10			9			6											1	8	5	7	11				28
	2	4	3	6		10	9												5		1	8		7	11				29
	2	4	3			10				6							9		5		1	8		7	11				30
3	2		5	6								1				4		7				10		8	11	9			31
	2		5	3		10	9			6		1				4						8		7	11				32
	2		5	3		10	9			6		1				4						8		7	11				33
3	2		5				9					1								8		10		7	11		4	6	34
3	2		5				9					1								8		10		7	11		4	6	35
3	2		5				9					1								8		10		7	11		4	6	36
3	2		5				9					1								8		10		7	11		4	6	37
	3	4	5	6		7				8		1					2					10			11	9			38
3	2	4	5	6		7	9					1										8			11			10	39
3	2	4	5	0		10	0					1										8		7	11				40
3	2	4	5	6		9						1										8		7	11			10	41
3	2	4	5	6		9						1										8		7	11			10	42
36	31	34	42	33	13	31	29	8	20	10	6	16	1	1	9	10	13	10	9	5	11	23	5	13	15	2	4	7	
1			2		4	9	16		1	1	1				1		3	2		1		3		3	4				

One own-goal

[illegible]	Walton	Taylor	Rooney	Trailor	Neary	Pullen	Sutherland	Naylor	McGeachy	Stroud	Smith	Welton	Connelly	Lucas	Wood	Bacon	Sherratt	Dryden	Davidson	Campbell	Hobbins	Blair	Skivington	McEwan	Pattison	Higgins	Adams	Deverall	
2		4	5	6		8			11						10		9	7	3										1
1		1	1	1		1			1						1		1	1	1										

1950-51

Manager: Alec Stock

	P	W	D	L	F	A	Pts
Nottingham Forest	46	30	10	6	110	40	70
Norwich City	46	25	14	7	82	45	64
Reading	46	21	15	10	88	53	57
Plymouth Argyle	46	24	9	13	85	55	57
Millwall	46	23	10	13	80	57	56
Bristol Rovers	46	20	15	11	64	42	55
Southend United	46	21	10	15	92	69	52
Ipswich Town	46	23	6	17	69	58	52
Bournemouth & B A	46	22	7	17	65	57	51
Bristol City	46	20	11	15	64	59	51
Newport County	46	19	9	18	77	70	47
Port Vale	46	16	13	17	60	65	45
Brighton & Hove Albion	46	13	17	16	71	79	43
Exeter City	46	18	6	22	62	85	42
Walsall	46	15	10	21	52	62	40
Colchester United	46	14	12	20	63	76	40
Swindon Town	46	18	4	24	55	67	40
Aldershot	46	15	10	21	56	88	40
Leyton Orient	46	15	8	23	53	75	38
Torquay United	46	14	9	23	64	81	37
Northampton Town	46	10	16	20	55	67	36
Gillingham	46	13	9	24	69	101	35
Watford	46	9	11	26	54	88	29
Crystal Palace	46	8	11	27	33	84	27

Division Three South

Match No.	Date		Opponents	Result	Scorers	Atter
1	Aug	19	Plymouth Argyle	1-2	Blair	2
2		23	Ipswich Town	2-2	Blair, Pattison	1
3		26	READING	2-0	Pattison, Simmonds	2
4		31	IPSWICH TOWN	2-0	Blair 2	1
5	Sep	2	Southend United	1-0	Pattison	1
6		7	NORTHAMPTON TOWN	1-0	Blair	1
7		9	EXETER CITY	1-3	Pattison	1
8		14	Northampton Town	3-3	Sutherland 2, Pattison	1
9		16	Bournemouth & B A	0-5		1
10		18	Millwall	1-3	Sutherland	2
11		23	GILLINGHAM	4-0	Rees 2, Davies, Blair	1
12		30	Bristol City	1-4	Blair	1
13	Oct	7	Port Vale	1-3	Rees	1
14		14	NOTTINGHAM FOREST	0-4		1
15		21	Torquay United	1-2	Sherratt	
16		28	ALDERSHOT	1-0	Blair	1
17	Nov	4	Swindon Town	0-2		
18		18	Bristol Rovers	1-2	Blair	14
19	Dec	2	Brighton & Hove Albion	0-3		
20		9	COLCHESTER UNITED	1-1	Sutherland	8
21		23	Reading	0-4		10
22		25	Watford	0-2		7
23		26	WATFORD	1-2	Sherratt (pen)	9
24		30	SOUTHEND UNITED	1-1	McGeachy	7
25	Jan	11	NORWICH CITY	3-1	Blair 2, Sutherland	4
26		13	Exeter City	0-0		9
27		20	BOURNEMOUTH & B A	2-0	Sutherland, Jackson	9
28	Feb	1	Norwich City	1-3	Rees	12
29		3	Gillingham	0-1		8
30		10	CRYSTAL PALACE	2-0	Jackson, Walton	11
31		24	PORT VALE	2-3	Sherratt, Blizzard	6
32	Mar	3	Nottingham Forest	1-0	Sherratt	22
33		10	TORQUAY UNITED	5-1	Blair 3, Rees 2	6
34		17	Aldershot	1-3	Rees	7
35		23	WALSALL	2-1	Deverall, Blair	9
36		24	SWINDON TOWN	2-1	Blair, Pattison	10
37		26	Walsall	1-1	Walton	8
38		31	Colchester United	0-1		9
39	Apr	7	BRISTOL ROVERS	1-0	Walton	6
40		12	NEWPORT COUNTY	0-3		8
41		14	Crystal Palace	1-1	Rees	10
42		19	MILLWALL	0-2		16
43		21	BRIGHTON & HOVE ALBION	2-1	Rees, Walton	9
44		26	PLYMOUTH ARGYLE	1-2	Rees	8
45		28	Newport County	0-0		7
46	May	3	BRISTOL CITY	0-2		6

Appearar
G

FA Cup

1	Nov	25	IPSWICH TOWN	1-2	Rees	10

Appearan
G

Final League Position: 19th in Division Three South

Evans	Banner	Deverall	Rooney	Brown	Davies	Rees	Simmonds	Blair	Pattison	Taylor	McEwan	Sutherland	Robb	Aldous	Blizzard	Trailor	Sherratt	Pullen	McGeachy	Cairney	Walton	Lewis	Jackson	Francis	Glidden	
2	3	4	5	6	7	8	9	10	11																	1
2	3	4	5	6	7	8	9	10	11																	2
2	3	4	5	6	7	8	9	10	11																	3
2	3	4	5	6	7	8	9	10	11																	4
2	3	4	5	6	7	9	8	10	11																	5
2	3		5	6	7	8	9	10	11	4																6
2	3	4	5	6	7	8	9	10	11																	7
2	3		5	6			8	10	11	4	7	9														8
2	3		5	6			8	10	11	4	7	9														9
2	3			6		10		8	11		7	9	4	5												10
2	3			6	7	8		10	11			9	4	5												11
2	3			6	7	8		10	11			9	4		5											12
2	3			6	7	8	9	10	11						5	4										13
2	3			6		9	8	10	11		7				5	4										14
2	3	6						8	11		7			5		4	9	10								15
2		10		6	7			8	11			9		5		4	3									16
3				6				8	11		7	9		5		4	2		10							17
3		4		6	7		9	10	11						5		2			8						18
3		4		6	7	8	9	10	11						5		2									19
3		4		6		8		10				9			5		2		11	7						20
3		4		6		8	9	10						5			2		11	7						21
3		4				9		8						5		6	2	10	11	7						22
3		4				8			11		10			5	6		9				2	7				23
3		4				8	9	10						5	6		2		11				7			24
3		4				8		10				9		5	6		2		11				7			25
3		4				8		10				9		5	6				11		2		7			26
3		4		6				10			8	9		5					11		2		7			27
3	2	4		6		8		10						5					11		9		7			28
3		4		10		9		8						5	6				11		2		7			29
3		4				8		10				9		5	6				11		2		7			30
3		4				8		10						5	6		9		11		2		7			31
	3	4				8		10	11					5	6		9				2		7			32
	3	4				8		10	11					5	6		9				2		7			33
3		4				8		10	11					5	6		9				2		7			34
3		11		6		8		10						5	4						2	9	7			35
3				6		8		10	11					5	4		9				2		7			36
3		4			7	8		10						5	6		9		11		2					37
3		4				8		10	11					5	6		9				2		7			38
3				6		8		10						5	4		2		11		9		7			39
3				6		8		10	11					5	4		2					9	7			40
3				6		8		10	11					5	4		2				9		7			41
3				6		8		10	11					5	4		2				9	7				42
2	3	11				8		10						5	6						9		7	4		43
2	3	11				8		10				9	6	5									7	4		44
2	5					8		10					6						11		9		7	4	3	45
2	3			6		8		10						5	4				11		9		7			46
44	22	30	9	30	14	39	15	45	28	3	8	13	5	30	26	6	22	2	16	4	20	4	21	3	1	
		1			1	10	1	16	6			6			1		4		1		4		2			

Evans	Banner	Deverall	Rooney	Brown	Davies	Rees	Simmonds	Blair	Pattison	Taylor	McEwan	Sutherland	Robb	Aldous	Blizzard	Trailor	Sherratt	Pullen	McGeachy	Cairney	Walton	Lewis	Jackson	Francis	Glidden	
3		4		6	7	8	9	10	11						5		2									1
1		1		1	1	1	1	1	1						1		1									
						1																				

1951-52

Manager: Alec Stock

	P	W	D	L	F	A	Pts
Plymouth Argyle	46	29	8	9	107	53	66
Reading	46	29	3	14	112	60	61
Norwich City	46	26	9	11	89	50	61
Millwall	46	23	12	11	74	53	58
Brighton & Hove Albion	46	24	10	12	87	63	58
Newport County	46	21	12	13	77	76	54
Bristol Rovers	46	20	12	14	89	53	52
Northampton Town	46	22	5	19	93	74	49
Southend United	46	19	10	17	75	66	48
Colchester United	46	17	12	17	56	77	46
Torquay United	46	17	10	19	86	98	44
Aldershot	46	18	8	20	78	89	44
Port Vale	46	14	15	17	50	66	43
Bournemouth & B A	46	16	10	20	69	75	42
Bristol City	46	15	12	19	58	69	42
Swindon Town	46	14	14	18	51	68	42
Ipswich Town	46	16	9	21	63	74	41
Leyton Orient	46	16	9	21	55	68	41
Crystal Palace	46	15	9	22	61	80	39
Shrewsbury Town	46	13	10	23	62	86	36
Watford	46	13	10	23	57	81	36
Gillingham	46	11	13	22	71	81	35
Exeter City	46	13	9	24	65	86	35
Walsall	46	13	5	28	55	94	31

Division Three South

Match No.	Date		Opponents	Result	Scorers	Attend
1	Aug	18	PLYMOUTH ARGYLE	1-0	Rees	15,
2		23	Watford	1-0	Blatchford	12,
3		25	Norwich City	0-1		28,
4		29	WATFORD	0-0		11,
5	Sep	1	EXETER CITY	3-0	Rees 3 (1 pen)	14,
6		5	Aldershot	1-0	Blair	6,
7		8	Colchester United	1-0	Rees (pen)	10,
8		12	ALDERSHOT	0-1		12,
9		15	CRYSTAL PALACE	0-4		12,
10		19	WALSALL	3-0	Brown, Blair, Walters (og)	7,
11		22	Swindon Town	0-2		10,
12		24	Shrewsbury Town	0-3		9,
13		29	Southend United	0-1		11,
14	Oct	6	MILLWALL	0-0		21,
15		13	Brighton & Hove Albion	1-3	Blizzard	17,
16		20	GILLINGHAM	1-0	Blair	13,
17		27	Torquay United	1-1	Blatchford	6,
18	Nov	3	IPSWICH TOWN	2-0	Rees, Blair	10,
19		10	Bristol City	1-1	Rees	17,
20		17	PORT VALE	2-0	Woan 2	7,
21	Dec	1	READING	0-4		11,
22		22	NORWICH CITY	3-3	Pacey, Rees, Blair	10,
23		25	Bournemouth & B A	2-3	Sherratt (pen), Woan	10,
24		26	BOURNEMOUTH & B A	1-0	Pacey	13,
25		29	Exeter City	1-6	Bryant	7,
26	Jan	5	COLCHESTER UNITED	7-0	Pacey 2, Harris 2, Brown, Rees, Blatchford	11,
27		19	Crystal Palace	1-2	Blatchford	14,
28		24	Walsall	4-2	Pacey, Davies, Harris 2	2,
29		26	SWINDON TOWN	1-0	Harris	11,
30	Feb	7	BRISTOL ROVERS	3-3	Blizzard, Pacey, Harris	10,
31		9	SOUTHEND UNITED	1-4	Harris	16,
32		16	Millwall	0-2		24,
33		27	Bristol Rovers	0-1		7,
34	Mar	1	BRIGHTON & HOVE ALBION	2-3	Rees, Woan	13,
35		8	Gillingham	1-1	Pacey	13,
36		15	TORQUAY UNITED	0-1		9,
37		19	Plymouth Argyle	0-3		15,
38		22	Ipswich Town	0-1		11,
39	Apr	3	Newport County	0-1		7,
40		5	Port Vale	0-3		7,
41		12	NORTHAMPTON TOWN	2-1	Rees, Brown	8,
42		14	SHREWSBURY TOWN	4-1	Rees 2, Pacey 2	6,
43		19	Reading	1-1	Harris	12,
44		24	Northampton Town	0-4		6,
45		26	NEWPORT COUNTY	1-1	Blatchford	6,
46	May	1	BRISTOL CITY	2-0	Pacey	5,

Appearan

Go

FA Cup

1	Nov	24	GORLESTON	2-2	Banner (pen), Blatchford	11,7
R		29	Gorleston	0-0		4,4
2R	Dec	3	Gorleston*	5-4	Pacey 3, Brown 2	12,0
2		15	Wrexham	1-1	Pacey	14,7
R		19	WREXHAM	3-2	Rees 3	10,7
3	Jan	12	EVERTON	0-0		21,2
R		16	Everton	3-1	Harris, Pacey 2	39,7
4	Feb	2	Birmingham City	1-0	Harris	49,5
5		23	ARSENAL	0-3		30,0

Appearan

Go

Final League Position: 18th in Division Three South

* Played at Arsenal Stadium, Highbury, London

Evans	Banner	Blizzard	Aldous	Brown	Jackson	Rees	Bryant	Blair	Blatchford	Davies	Cater	Pole	Harris	Walton	Hawkins	Deverall	Woan	Sherratt	Pacey	Groombridge	McMahon	Bruce	
2	3	4	5	6	7	8	9	10	11														1
2	3	4	5	6	7	8	9	10	11														2
2	3	4	5	6	7	8	9	10	11														3
2	3	4	5	6	7	8	9	10	11														4
2	3	4	5	6	7	8	9	10	11														5
2	3	4	5	6	7	8	9	10	11														6
2	3	4	5	6	7	8	9	10	11														7
2	3	4	5	6		8	9	10	11	7													8
2		4	5	6	7	8			11		3	9	10										9
	3	4	5	6	7	8		10	11		2	9											10
	3	4	5	6	7			8	11		2	9	10										11
	3		5	6	7	8		10	11		4	9		2									12
	3		5	6	7	8		10	11		4			2	9								13
2	3	4	5	6	7	8		10	11						9								14
2	3	4	5	6	7	8		10	11						9								15
2	3	4	5	6	7	9		10		11	8												16
2	3	4	5	6	7	9		10	11		8												17
2	3	4	5	6	7	9		10	11		8												18
2	3	4	5			9		10	11		8					6	7						19
2	3	4	5			9		10	11		8					6	7						20
2	3	4	5	6		9		10	11		8						7						21
3		4	5	6		9		10	11								7	2	8				22
3		4	5	6		10	9		11								7	2	8	1			23
3			5	6		10	9		11							4	7	2	8	1			24
2	3	4	5	6		10	9		11				7						8	1			25
2	3	4	5	10		9			11				7			6			8				26
2	3	4	5	10					11				9				7		8		6		27
2	3	4	5	10						11			9			6	7		8				28
2		4	5	10					11		6	3	9				7		8				29
2	3	4	5	10					11				9			6	7		8				30
2	3	10	5						11		4		9			6	7		8				31
2	3	4	5			10			11				9			6	7		8				32
2	3	4	5	10		9							7			6			8			11	33
2	3		5	6		10			11				9			4	7		8				34
2	3	4	5	10		9			11				7			6			8	1			35
2	3		5	10		9			11			4	7			6			8				36
2	3		5	10					11			4	9			6	7		8				37
2	3	4	5	10		9			11			3				6			8	1			38
2	3	4	5	10		9						11				6	7		8				39
2	3	4	5	10		9			11			7				6			8				40
2	3	4	5	10		9			11				7			6			8				41
2		4	5	10		9			11				7			6		3	8				42
2	3	4	5			10			11				9			6	7		8				43
2	3	4	5			10			11				9			6	7		8				44
2	3	4	5	10		9			11				7			6			8				45
2	3	4	5			10	9		11							6	7		8				46
42	40	40	46	39	17	39	12	21	42	3	13	10	20	2	3	22	18	4	25	5	1	1	
		2		3		13	1	5	5	1			8				4	1	11				

One own-goal

Evans	Banner	Blizzard	Aldous	Brown	Jackson	Rees	Bryant	Blair	Blatchford	Davies	Cater	Pole	Harris	Walton	Hawkins	Deverall	Woan	Sherratt	Pacey	Groombridge	McMahon	Bruce	
2	3	4	5	6		9		10	11		8						7						1
2	3	4	5	10		8			11						9	6	7						R
2	3	4	5	10		9			11							6	7		8				2R
2	3	4	5	10		9			11							6	7		8				2
2	3	4	5	10		9			11							6	7		8				R
2	3	4	5	10		9			11							6	7		8				3
2	3	4	5	10					11				9			6	7		8				R
2	3	4	5	10					11				9			6	7		8				4
2	3	4	5	10					11				9			6	7		8				5
9	9	9	9	9		6		1	9		1		3		1	8	9		7				
	1			2		3			1				2						6				

1952-53

Manager: Alec Stock

	P	W	D	L	F	A	Pts
Bristol Rovers	46	26	12	8	92	46	64
Millwall	46	24	14	8	82	44	62
Northampton Town	46	26	10	10	109	70	62
Norwich City	46	25	10	11	99	55	60
Bristol City	46	22	15	9	95	61	59
Coventry City	46	19	12	15	77	62	50
Brighton & Hove Albion	46	19	12	15	81	75	50
Southend United	46	18	13	15	69	74	49
Bournemouth & B A	46	19	9	18	74	69	47
Watford	46	15	17	14	62	63	47
Reading	46	19	8	19	69	64	46
Torquay United	46	18	9	19	87	88	45
Crystal Palace	46	15	13	18	66	82	43
Leyton Orient	46	16	10	20	68	73	42
Newport County	46	16	10	20	70	82	42
Ipswich Town	46	13	15	18	60	69	41
Exeter City	46	13	14	19	61	71	40
Swindon Town	46	14	12	20	64	79	40
Aldershot	46	12	15	19	61	77	39
Queen's Park Rangers	46	12	15	19	61	82	39
Gillingham	46	12	15	19	55	74	39
Colchester United	46	12	14	20	59	76	38
Shrewsbury Town	46	12	12	22	68	91	36
Walsall	46	7	10	29	56	118	24

Division Three South

Match No.	Date		Opponents	Result	Scorers	Attend.
1	Aug	23	Reading	0-2		17,
2		28	COVENTRY CITY	1-2	Blair	11,
3		30	BOURNEMOUTH & B A	2-2	Aldous, Pacey	10,
4	Sep	1	Coventry City	0-3		17,
5		6	Southend United	0-1		14,
6		8	TORQUAY UNITED	4-1	Pacey 2, Poulton 2	7,
7		13	WATFORD	2-0	Rees, Poulton	16,
8		17	Torquay United	0-5		6,
9		20	Brighton & Hove Albion	1-3	Poulton	20,
10		25	QUEEN'S PARK RANGERS	5-0	Pacey 2, Poulton, Woan, Blair	8,
11		27	NEWPORT COUNTY	2-1	Poulton, Brown	11,
12	Oct	2	BRISTOL CITY	1-3	Blizzard	7,
13		4	Crystal Palace	2-2	Blizzard, Poulton	16,
14		11	EXETER CITY	2-0	Pacey, Rowe (og)	12,
15		18	Bristol Rovers	1-2	Pacey	23,
16		25	MILLWALL	1-4	Blizzard	19,
17	Nov	1	Gillingham	2-3	Poulton, Niblett (og)	11,
18		8	WALSALL	4-1	Poulton 2 (1 pen), Harris, Lusted	9,
19		15	Shrewsbury Town	0-2		6,
20	Dec	13	Colchester United	1-3	Blatchford	6,
21		20	READING	1-1	Facey	4,
22		26	IPSWICH TOWN	3-1	Blatchford 2, Harris	6,
23	Jan	3	Bournemouth & B A	1-4	Harris	8,
24		10	NORTHAMPTON TOWN	0-1		8,
25		17	SOUTHEND UNITED	3-0	Pacey, Poulton (pen), Brown	13,
26		24	Watford	0-1		10,
27		31	Northampton Town	1-3	Pacey	9,
28	Feb	7	BRIGHTON & HOVE ALBION	3-0	Facey 2, Lusted	8,
29		14	Newport County	1-0	Lusted	5,1
30		21	CRYSTAL PALACE	0-0		12,
31		28	Exeter City	1-0	Facey	8,
32	Mar	7	BRISTOL ROVERS	3-3	Facey, Pacey 2	16,
33		14	Millwall	0-0		23,7
34		18	Swindon Town	1-1	Whiteley	3,
35		21	GILLINGHAM	1-1	Facey	11,4
36		25	Ipswich Town	1-0	Lusted	3,1
37		28	Walsall	0-1		3,
38	Apr	3	NORWICH CITY	3-1	Aldous, Lusted, Pacey	18,5
39		4	SHREWSBURY TOWN	0-0		10,6
40		6	Norwich City	1-5	Whiteley	23,3
41		11	Queen's Park Rangers	1-0	Rees	10,8
42		16	ALDERSHOT	4-1	Facey 2, Pacey 2	6,0
43		18	SWINDON TOWN	2-2	Lusted, Pacey	11,1
44		21	Bristol City	1-2	Rees	9,3
45		25	Aldershot	0-2		6,2
46		30	COLCHESTER UNITED	5-3	Pacey 4, Whiteley	2,5

Appearanc

Go

FA Cup

1	Nov	22	BRISTOL ROVERS	1-1	Pacey	10,7
R		24	Bristol Rovers	0-1		15,0

Appearanc

Go

Final League Position: 14th in Division Three South

Charlton	Banner	Blizzard	Aldous	Brown	Woan	Pacey	Rees	Harris	Blatchford	Evans	Blair	Groombridge	Deverall	Jones	Hawkins	Mansley	Poulton	Lusted	Facey	McMahon	Whiteley	Pole	
2	3	4	5	6	7	8	9	10	11														1
2		4	5	6	7	8	9		11	3	10												2
2		4	5	6	7	8	9		11	3	10												3
2		4	5	10		8		9	11	3		1	6	7									4
2	3		5	6	7	8	10		11			1	4		9								5
2			5	10		9	8			3		1	4	7		6	11						6
2			5	10		9	8			3		1	6	7		4	11						7
2			5	10		9				3	8	1	6	7		4	11						8
2			5	10		8		7		3		1	6		9	4	11						9
2		4	5	10	7	9				3	8	1				6	11						10
2		4	5	10	7	9				3	8	1				6	11						11
2		4	5	10	7	9				3	8	1				6	11						12
2		4	5	6		9	8			3	10	1		7			11						13
2		4	5	6		9	8			3	10	1		7			11						14
2		4	5	6		9	8		7	3	10	1					11						15
2		6	5	10		9			7	3	8	1				4	11						16
2		10	5	6		9			7	3	8	1				4	11						17
2		4	5			9		7		3	8	1	6				11	10					18
2	3	4	5			8		9		7	10	1	6				11						19
2	3	4	5	10				9	7		8	1	6				11						20
8	3	4	5	10		9			11	2		1	6						7				21
8	3	4	5	10				9	11	2		1	6						7				22
8	3	5		6				9	11	2	10	1	4						7				23
8	3	4	5	10				9	11	2		1	6						7				24
3		4	5	10		9	8		11	2		1	6				7						25
3			5	10		9	8			2		1	6				7			4	11		26
3		8	5	10		9			11	2			6			4	7						27
3	2		5	6		9	10											8	7	4	11		28
3	2		5	6		9	10											8	7	4	11		29
3	2		5	6		9	10											8	7	4	11		30
3	2		5	6		9	10											8	7	4	11		31
3	2		5	6		9	10											8	7	4	11		32
3	2	4	5			9	10						6					8	7		11		33
3	2	4	5			9	10						6					8	7		11		34
3	2	4	5				10	9					6					8	7		11		35
3	2	4	5				10						6					8	7		11	9	36
3	2	4	5				10											8	7	6	11	9	37
3			5			9	10			2			6				11	8	7	4			38
3			5			9	10			2			6				11	8	7	4			39
3		4	5				8	9	7	2								10		6	11		40
3	2	4	5				9		8				6					10	7		11		41
3	2	4	5			9	10						6					8	7		11		42
3	2	4	5			9	8											10	7	6	11		43
3	2	4	5			9	10						6					8	7		11		44
3	2		5			9	10		8				6						7	4	11		45
3	2	6	5			9	8											10	7	4	11		46
46	24	32	45	30	7	37	30	11	18	27	15	23	26	6	2	10	20	19	22	13	18	2	
		3	2	2	1	19	3	3	3		2						11	6	8		3		

Two own-goals

Charlton	Banner	Blizzard	Aldous	Brown	Woan	Pacey	Rees	Harris	Blatchford	Evans	Blair	Groombridge	Deverall	Jones	Hawkins	Mansley	Poulton	Lusted	Facey	McMahon	Whiteley	Pole	
2	3	4	5			9		10		7	8	1	6				11						1
2	3	4	5					9		7	10	1	6				11		8				R
2	2	2	2			1		2		2	2	2	2				2		1				
						1																	

1953-54

Manager: Alec Stock

	P	W	D	L	F	A	Pts
Ipswich Town	46	27	10	9	82	51	64
Brighton & Hove Albion	46	26	9	11	86	61	61
Bristol City	46	25	6	15	88	66	56
Watford	46	21	10	15	85	69	52
Northampton Town	46	20	11	15	82	55	51
Southampton	46	22	7	17	76	63	51
Norwich City	46	20	11	15	73	66	51
Reading	46	20	9	17	86	73	49
Exeter City	46	20	8	18	68	58	48
Gillingham	46	19	10	17	61	66	48
Leyton Orient	46	18	11	17	79	73	47
Millwall	46	19	9	18	74	77	47
Torquay United	46	17	12	17	81	88	46
Coventry City	46	18	9	19	61	56	45
Newport County	46	19	6	21	61	81	44
Southend United	46	18	7	21	69	71	43
Aldershot	46	17	9	20	74	86	43
Queen's Park Rangers	46	16	10	20	60	68	42
Bournemouth & B A	46	16	8	22	67	70	40
Swindon Town	46	15	10	21	67	70	40
Shrewsbury Town	46	14	12	20	65	76	40
Crystal Palace	46	14	12	20	60	86	40
Colchester United	46	10	10	26	50	78	30
Walsall	46	9	8	29	40	87	26

Division Three South

Match No.	Date		Opponents	Result	Scorers	Attenda
1	Aug	19	Exeter City	1-2	Rees	10,4
2		22	Coventry City	0-4		11,6
3		26	Brighton & Hove Albion	1-2	Facey	18,3
4		29	BOURNEMOUTH & B A	5-0	Pacey 3, Morgan, Rees	10,8
5	Sep	3	BRIGHTON & HOVE ALBION	0-2		13,8
6		5	Ipswich Town	1-3	Facey	13,8
7		10	TORQUAY UNITED	3-2	Poulton, Blizzard, Rees	8,9
8		12	MILLWALL	2-2	Morgan 2	16,3
9		16	Torquay United	3-2	Pacey, Morgan, Rees	6,2
10		19	BRISTOL CITY	4-1	Poulton, Rees 2, Facey	13,1
11		24	GILLINGHAM	3-1	Mallett, Poulton, Pacey	8,2
12		26	Reading	1-1	Poulton	14,2
13		30	Gillingham	2-1	Poulton, Rees	6,3
14	Oct	3	SOUTHEND UNITED	1-1	Pacey	16,9
15		10	Swindon Town	1-2	Johnstone (og)	12,6
16		17	WALSALL	2-1	Blizzard, Rees	7,6
17		24	Shrewsbury Town	3-3	Morgan, Pacey, Edwards	9,8
18		31	EXETER CITY	3-1	Morgan, Pacey 2	11,3
19	Nov	7	Newport County	1-1	Pacey	7,7
20		14	NORWICH CITY	3-1	Poulton 2, Rees	15,6
21		28	SOUTHAMPTON	1-4	Rees	15,7
22	Dec	5	Colchester United	0-1		6,8
23		19	COVENTRY CITY	1-0	Facey	8,0
24		25	Northampton Town	2-2	Rees 2	13,8
25		26	NORTHAMPTON TOWN	2-0	Rees, Pacey	14,5
26	Jan	2	Bournemouth & B A	2-1	Facey 2 (1 pen)	9,0
27		16	IPSWICH TOWN	1-2	Poulton	17,3
28		23	Millwall	3-0	Rees 2, Bowler (og)	15,1
29	Feb	6	Bristol City	0-1		15,6
30		13	READING	2-1	Facey, Morgan	13,3
31		24	Southend United	1-2	Facey	4,5
32		27	SWINDON TOWN	1-1	White	12,4
33	Mar	6	Walsall	2-4	Facey (pen), Burgess	9,7
34		18	QUEEN'S PARK RANGERS	2-2	Burgess, Facey	4,1
35		20	Southampton	1-4	Aldous	14,5
36		27	NEWPORT COUNTY	3-0	Facey, Burgess, White	9,6
37	Apr	3	Norwich City	1-3	Burgess	14,7
38		8	CRYSTAL PALACE	2-0	Pacey, Poulton	5,2
39		10	COLCHESTER UNITED	3-1	Harrison (og), Pacey 2	9,3
40		16	Aldershot	1-1	Pacey	7,9
41		17	Crystal Palace	2-2	Facey (pen), Burgess	12,4
42		19	ALDERSHOT	1-2	Morgan	9,3
43		22	WATFORD	1-1	Pacey	7,0
44		24	SHREWSBURY TOWN	2-0	Poulton 2	9,0
45		26	Queen's Park Rangers	1-2	Poulton	9,3
46		30	Watford	1-3	Morgan	5,5

Appearanc

Go

FA Cup

1	Nov	21	KETTERING TOWN	3-0	Poulton 2, Facey	15,0
2	Dec	12	WEYMOUTH	4-0	Rees 2, Morgan, Pacey	14,3
3	Jan	9	Tranmere Rovers	2-2	Rees, Facey (pen)	12,3
R		14	TRANMERE ROVERS	4-1	Pacey 3, Rees	14,2
4		30	FULHAM	2-1	Poulton, Davies	25,8
5	Feb	20	DONCASTER ROVERS	3-1	Morgan, Pacey, Burgess	29,1
6	Mar	13	PORT VALE	0-1		31,0

Appearanc

Go

Final League Position: 11th in Division Three South

Evans	Earl	McMahon	Aldous	Mallett	Facey	Rees	Pacey	Morgan	Lusted	Charlton	Davies	Whiteley	Jackett	Welton	Blizzard	Poulton	White	Edwards	Burgess	Bishop	
2	3	4	5	6	7	8	9	10	11												1
2	3	4	5	6	7	8	9	10	11												2
	3	4	5	6	7	10	8		11	2	9										3
	3	4	5	6	7	10	9	8		2		11									4
	3	4	5	6	7	8	9	10		2		11									5
	3		5	6	7		8	10		2	9	11	4								6
2		6	5		7	8	9	10		3				1	4	11					7
2		6	5		7	8	9	10		3				1	4	11					8
2			5	6	7	8	9	10		3				1	4	11					9
2		4	5		7	8	9	10		3				1	6	11					10
2			5	6	7	8	9	10		3				1	4	11					11
2		6	5		7	8	9	10		3				1	4	11					12
2			5	6	7	8	9	10		3				1	4	11					13
2			5	6	7	8	9	10		3				1	4	11					14
2		6	5		8		9	10		3				1	4	11	7				15
2		6	5		7	8	9	10		3				1	4	11					16
2		6	5		7		9	10		3				1	4	11		8			17
2		6	5		7	9	8	10		3				1	4	11					18
2		6	5		7	9	8	10		3				1	4	11					19
2		6	5		7	9	8	10		3				1	4	11					20
2		6	5		7	9	8	10		3				1	4	11					21
2		6	5		7		8	10		3				1	4	11		9			22
2		6	5		7	9	8	10		3					4	11					23
2		6	5		7	9	8	10		3					4	11					24
2		6	5		7	9	8	10		3					4	11					25
2		6	5		7	9	8	10		3					4	11					26
2		6	5		7	9	8	10		3					4	11					27
2			5	6	7	9	8	10		3					4	11					28
2			5	6	7		8	10		3	9				4	11					29
2			5	4	7		8	10		3	9					11			6		30
2			5	6	7		9	8		3					4	11			10		31
2	3			4			9	8	10							11	7		6	5	32
2			5	4	7		9	8		3			6			11			10		33
2			5	6	7	9	8			3		11			4				10		34
2			5	6	7	8	9			3					4	11			10		35
2			5	6	8	9		11		3					4		7		10		36
2			5	6	7	8	9	11		3					4				10		37
			5	6		8	9	7		3					4	11			10	2	38
			5	6		8	9	7		3					4	11			10	2	39
		4		6	7		9	8		3		11			5				10	2	40
			5		7	8	9	11		3			6		4				10	2	41
			5		7	8	9	10		3			6		4	11				2	42
		6	5		7	9	8	11		3					4				10	2	43
2					8	4	9	10		3					6	11	7			5	44
2			5		8	4	9	10		3					6	11	7				45
2		6	5		7	8	9	10		3					4	11					46
36	7	25	43	23	43	36	45	43	4	43	4	5	4	16	37	34	5	2	13	8	
			1	1	12	15	16	9							2	12	2	1	5		

Three own-goals

Evans	Earl	McMahon	Aldous	Mallett	Facey	Rees	Pacey	Morgan	Lusted	Charlton	Davies	Whiteley	Jackett	Welton	Blizzard	Poulton	White	Edwards	Burgess	Bishop	
2		6	5		7	9	8	10		3				1	4	11					1
2		6	5		7	9	8	10		3					4	11					2
2		6	5		7	9	8	10		3					4	11					3
2		6	5		7	9	8	10		3					4	11					R
2			5	6	7		8	10		3	9				4	11					4
2			5	6	7		9	8		3					4	11			10		5
2			5	6	7	9	8	10		3					4	11					6
7		4	7	3	7	5	7	7		7	1			1	7	7			1		
					2	4	5	2			1					3			1		

1954-55

Manager: Alec Stock

	P	W	D	L	F	A	Pts
Bristol City	46	30	10	6	101	47	70
Leyton Orient	46	26	9	11	89	47	61
Southampton	46	24	11	11	75	51	59
Gillingham	46	20	15	11	77	66	55
Millwall	46	20	11	15	72	68	51
Brighton & Hove Albion	46	20	10	16	76	63	50
Watford	46	18	14	14	71	62	50
Torquay United	46	18	12	16	82	82	48
Coventry City	46	18	11	17	67	59	47
Southend United	46	17	12	17	83	80	46
Brentford	46	16	14	16	82	82	46
Norwich City	46	18	10	18	60	60	46
Northampton Town	46	19	8	19	73	81	46
Aldershot	46	16	13	17	75	71	45
Queen's Park Rangers	46	15	14	17	69	75	44
Shrewsbury Town	46	16	10	20	70	78	42
Bournemouth & B A	46	12	18	16	57	65	42
Reading	46	13	15	18	65	73	41
Newport County	46	11	16	19	60	73	38
Crystal Palace	46	11	16	19	52	80	38
Swindon Town	46	11	15	20	46	64	37
Exeter City	46	11	15	20	47	73	37
Walsall	46	10	14	22	75	86	34
Colchester United	46	9	13	24	53	91	31

Division Three South

Match No.	Date		Opponents	Result	Scorers	Attenda
1	Aug	21	TORQUAY UNITED	2-1	Hartburn, Towers (og)	18,7
2		26	MILLWALL	1-0	Burgess	18,9
3		28	Bristol City	0-5		19,4
4		30	Millwall	0-1		16,0
5	Sep	4	WALSALL	1-0	Facey	12,1
6		9	SOUTHAMPTON	4-1	Groves 2, Facey 2	11,1
7		11	Shrewsbury Town	2-0	Facey 2 (1pen)	9,2
8		15	Southampton	0-1		11,9
9		18	READING	2-0	Facey 2	14,1
10		20	Coventry City	2-2	Kirk 2 (2 ogs)	14,8
11		25	Gillingham	0-0		11,6
12		30	COVENTRY CITY	1-0	Poulton	8,8
13	Oct	2	CRYSTAL PALACE	2-1	Facey, Morgan	16,4
14		9	Watford	3-1	Facey 2 (1 pen), Rees	17,5
15		16	BOURNEMOUTH & B A	3-1	Blizzard, Groves, Facey (pen)	15,8
16		23	Queen's Park Rangers	0-2		22,1
17		30	SWINDON TOWN	1-0	Blizzard	15,0
18	Nov	6	Exeter City	7-1	Morgan, Groves 3, Rees 2, Charlton	8,7
19		13	COLCHESTER UNITED	2-0	Facey, Rees	16,0
20		27	SOUTHEND UNITED	5-1	Facey (pen), Morgan, Rees 2, Blizzard	16,1
21	Dec	4	Aldershot	1-0	Morgan	7,5
22		18	Torquay United	7-2	Rees, Facey 2, Hartburn, Groves 3	6,3
23		27	BRIGHTON & HOVE ALBION	0-0		25,0
24	Jan	1	BRISTOL CITY	4-1	Groves, Hartburn 2, Blizzard	20,3
25		8	Northampton Town	2-2	Rees, Groves	8,8
26		22	SHREWSBURY TOWN	5-0	Facey, Morgan, Hartburn 3	11,7
27		29	NORTHAMPTON TOWN	2-1	Groves, Facey	17,9
28	Feb	5	Reading	2-0	Facey, Rees	12,0
29		12	GILLINGHAM	2-2	Facey (pen), Morgan	19,7
30		19	Crystal Palace	1-1	Hartburn	12,7
31		26	WATFORD	0-1		17,4
32	Mar	5	Bournemouth & B A	3-0	Groves, Morgan, Brown (og)	12,7
33		12	QUEEN'S PARK RANGERS	3-0	Facey (pen), Hartburn, Morgan	17,5
34		17	NEWPORT COUNTY	1-2	Facey	10,3
35		19	Swindon Town	0-0		8,4
36		26	EXETER CITY	5-0	Morgan 4, Facey	11,9
37	Apr	2	Colchester United	2-2	Rees 2	9,4
38		8	Brentford	0-2		18,0
39		9	NORWICH CITY	1-2	Rees	15,2
40		11	BRENTFORD	0-1		9,5
41		16	Southend United	2-1	Rees, Fisher	9,0
42		20	Brighton & Hove Albion	0-1		11,3
43		23	ALDERSHOT	1-5	Lee	8,2
44		27	Norwich City	1-1	Hartburn	9,1
45		30	Newport County	2-1	Rees, Groves	5,8
46	May	5	Walsall	4-1	Rees 3, Groves	17,5
						Appearan
						Go

FA Cup

1	Nov	20	Frome Town	3-0	Facey, Groves, Fitz (og)	8,0
2	Dec	11	WORKINGTON	0-1		15,4
						Appearan
						Go

Final League position: 2nd in Division Three South
(only top team promoted)

Lee	Charlton	Blizzard	Aldous	McKnight	Facey	Groves	Rees	Pacey	Hartburn	Burgess	Poulton	Mallett	Morgan	White	McMahon	Woosnam	Groombridge	Fisher	Earl	
2	3	4	5	6	7	8	9	10	11											1
2	3	4	5	6	7		8	9	11	10										2
2	3	4	5	6	7		8	9	11	10										3
2	3	4	5	6	8		9	10	7		11									4
2	3	5		6	8	7		9	11			4	10							5
2	3	4	5	6	8	7		9	11				10							6
2	3	4	5	6	8	7		9	11				10							7
2	3	4	5	6	7			9	11			8	10							8
2	3	4	5		8			9	11			6	10	7						9
2	3	4	5		8	7		9	11			6	10							10
2	3	4	5	6	8	7		9	11				10							11
2	3	4	5	6	8	7		9			11		10							12
2	3	4	5	6	8			9			11		10	7						13
2	3	4	5	6	8	7	9		11				10							14
2	3	4	5	6	8	7	9		11				10							15
2	3	4	5	6	8	7	9		11				10							16
2	3	4	5	6	8	7	9				11		10							17
2	3	4	5	6	8	7	9				11		10							18
2	3	4	5	6	8	7	9				11		10							19
2	3	4	5	6	8	7	9		11				10							20
2	3	4	5	6	8	7	9		11				10							21
2	3	4	5	6	8	7	9		11				10							22
2	3	4	5	6	8	7	9		11				10							23
2	3	4	5	6	8	7	9		11				10							24
2	3	4	5	6	8	7	9		11				10							25
2	3	4	5	6	8	7	9		11				10							26
2	3	4	5		8	7	9		11				10		6					27
2	3	4	5		8	7	9		11				10		6					28
2	3	4	5	6	8	7	9		11				10							29
2	3	4	5	6	8	7	9		11				10							30
2	3	4	5	6	8	7			11	9			10							31
2	3	4	5	6	8	7	9		11				10							32
2	3	4	5	6	8	7	9		11				10							33
2	3	4	5	6	8		9		11				10	7						34
2	3	4	5	6	8	7			11	9			10							35
2	3	4	5	6	7		8		11	9			10							36
2	3	4	5	6	7		8		11	9			10							37
2	3	4	5	6	7		9		11				10			8				38
2	3	4	5	6	7		9				11		10			8				39
2	3	4	5	6	7		8		11	9			10							40
2	3	9	5	6			8		11				10		4		1	7		41
2	3	9	5	6			8		11				10		4		1	7		42
2	3	9	5	6	7		8		11				10		4		1			43
	2	4	5	6	7		9		11				10			8			3	44
	2	4	5	6	8	7	9						11			10			3	45
	2	4	5	6	8	7	9		11							10			3	46
43	46	46	45	42	44	30	35	13	39	7	7	4	41	3	5	5	3	2	3	
1	1	4			22	15	17		10	1	1		12					1		

Four own-goals

Lee	Charlton	Blizzard	Aldous	McKnight	Facey	Groves	Rees	Pacey	Hartburn	Burgess	Poulton	Mallett	Morgan	
2	3	4	5	6	8	7	9		11				10	1
2	3	4	5	6	8	7	9		11				10	2
2	2	2	2	2	2	2	2		2				2	
					1	1								

One own-goal

1955-56

Managers: Aug 1955–Feb 1956 Alec Stock; Feb–Apr 1956 Les Gore; Apr–May 1956 Alec Stock

	P	W	D	L	F	A	Pts
Leyton Orient	46	29	8	9	106	49	66
Brighton & Hove Albion	46	29	7	10	112	50	65
Ipswich Town	46	25	14	7	106	60	64
Southend United	46	21	11	14	88	80	53
Torquay United	46	20	12	14	86	63	52
Brentford	46	19	14	13	69	66	52
Norwich City	46	19	13	14	86	82	51
Coventry City	46	20	9	17	73	60	49
Bournemouth & B A	46	19	10	17	63	51	48
Gillingham	46	19	10	17	69	71	48
Northampton Town	46	20	7	19	67	71	47
Colchester United	46	18	11	17	76	81	47
Shrewsbury Town	46	17	12	17	69	66	46
Southampton	46	18	8	20	91	81	44
Aldershot	46	12	16	18	70	90	40
Exeter City	46	15	10	21	58	77	40
Reading	46	15	9	22	70	79	39
Queen's Park Rangers	46	14	11	21	64	86	39
Newport County	46	15	9	22	58	79	39
Walsall	46	15	8	23	68	84	38
Watford	46	13	11	22	52	85	37
Millwall	46	15	6	25	83	100	36
Crystal Palace	46	12	10	24	54	83	34
Swindon Town	46	8	14	24	34	78	30

Division Three South

Match No.	Date		Opponents	Result	Scorers	Attend
1	Aug	20	Walsall	2-0	Woosnam, Morgan	18,
2		24	Gillingham	1-0	Groves	14,
3		27	EXETER CITY	1-1	Hartburn	15,
4	Sep	1	GILLINGHAM	2-0	Facey, Woosnam	13,
5		3	Southend United	0-0		21,
6		8	COLCHESTER UNITED	6-0	Groves 3, Hartburn (pen), Woosnam, Fenton (og)	13,
7		10	COVENTRY CITY	3-1	Kirk (og), Groves, Hartburn	18,
8		15	Colchester United	1-2	Heckman	7,
9		17	Brentford	0-1		17,
10		22	BOURNEMOUTH & B A	3-0	Morgan, Groves 2	9,
11		24	WATFORD	3-1	Heckman, Groves 2	16,
12	Oct	1	Reading	1-0	Morgan	14,
13		8	Newport County	0-3		8,
14		15	SWINDON TOWN	4-0	Heckman, Facey 3	14,
15		22	Queen's Park Rangers	1-0	Woosnam	11,
16		29	NORTHAMPTON TOWN	1-1	Hartburn	23,
17	Nov	5	Aldershot	1-1	Burgess	7,
18		12	CRYSTAL PALACE	8-0	Facey 3, Hartburn 2, Burgess 2, White	13,
19		26	SOUTHAMPTON	4-0	Heckman 2, Facey 2	14,
20	Dec	3	Shrewsbury Town	4-1	Burgess, Heckman 3	10
21		17	WALSALL	4-0	Heckman, Facey, Hartburn (pen), Burgess	11,
22		24	Exeter City	1-1	Heckman	11,
23		26	NORWICH CITY	2-2	Hartburn 2	16
24		27	Norwich City	2-2	Facey, Heckman	30
25		31	SOUTHEND UNITED	3-0	Heckman 2, Burgess	19
26	Jan	14	Coventry City	0-3		23
27		21	BRENTFORD	2-1	Julians 2	14
28	Feb	4	Watford	4-0	Julians 2, Woosnam, Hartburn (pen)	6
29		11	READING	1-0	Hartburn	9
30		18	NEWPORT COUNTY	3-1	Julians 2, White	11
31		25	Swindon Town	2-1	Woosnam, Johnston	9
32	Mar	3	QUEEN'S PARK RANGERS	7-1	Hartburn 4, Heckman 3	12
33		10	Northampton Town	1-0	Facey	13
34		17	ALDERSHOT	8-3	Johnston 3, Heckman 2, Woosnam 2, Hartburn	18
35		24	Crystal Palace	2-1	White, Johnston	19
36		30	TORQUAY UNITED	3-2	Heckman 2, Hartburn	26
37		31	BRIGHTON & HOVE ALBION	0-1		25
38	Apr	2	Torquay United	3-1	Julians 2, Heckman	9
39		7	Southampton	2-1	Julians 2	18
40		14	SHREWSBURY TOWN	5-2	Heckman 2, Johnston 2, Hartburn	13
41		18	Brighton & Hove Albion	1-1	Hartburn	30
42		21	Ipswich Town	0-2		22
43		26	MILLWALL	2-1	Hartburn, Johnston	22
44		28	Bournemouth & B A	1-3	Julians	10
45		30	Millwall	0-5		16
46	May	3	Ipswich Town	1-2	Woosnam	15
						Appeara
						G

FA Cup

1	Nov	19	LOVELLS ATHLETIC	7-1	Heckman 5, Facey, Hartburn	12
2	Dec	10	BRENTFORD	4-1	Heckman, Facey, Hartburn, Burgess	17
3	Jan	7	PLYMOUTH ARGYLE	1-0	Hartburn	15
4		28	BIRMINGHAM CITY	0-4		24
						Appeara
						G

Final League position: 1st in Division Three South (promoted as champions)

Lee	Charlton	Blizzard	Aldous	McKnight	Groves	Woosnam	Rees	Morgan	Hartburn	Facey	Brahan	Heckman	Bishop	White	Gregory	McMahon	Earl	Burgess	Smith	Julians	Johnston	
2	3	4	5	6	7	8	9	10	11													1
2	3	4	5	6	7	8	9	10	11													2
2	3	4	5	6	7	8	9	10	11													3
2	3	4	5	6		8	9	10	11	7												4
2	3	4		6		8		10	7	9	5	11										5
2	3	4		6	9	8			11			10	5	7								6
2	3	4		6	9	8			11			10	5	7								7
2	3	4		6	9	8			11	7		10	5									8
	2	4	5	6		8		11		9		10		7	3							9
2	3	4	5	6	9			10		8		11		7								10
2	3	4	5	6	9	10				8		11		7								11
2	3	4	5	6		10		9		8		11		7								12
2	3	4	5	6	7		9	10		8		11										13
2	3		5	6	9	8			11	7		10				4						14
2	3		5	6	9	8			11	7		10				4						15
2	3		5	6	9	8			11	7		10				4						16
2		4	5	6		8			11	7		10					3	9				17
2		4	5	6					11	8		10		7			3	9				18
		4	5	6					11	8		10	2	7			3	9				19
		4	5						11	8		10	2	7		6	3	9				20
		4	5						11	8		10	2	7		6	3	9				21
		4	5	6		8			11			10	2	7			3	9				22
		4	5	6					11	8		10	2				3	9	7			23
		4	5	6		8				7		10			2		3	9	11			24
		4	5	6		8			11	7		10			2		3	9				25
		4	5	6				8	11			10			2		3	9	7			26
		4	5	6					11			10			2		3	9	7	8		27
2		4	5	6		8		10	11					7			3			9		28
2		4	5	6					11	8		10		7			3			9		29
2		4	5	6				8	11			10		7			3			9		30
2		4	5	6		8			11			10		7			3				9	31
2		4	5	6		8			11			10		7			3				9	32
2		4	5	6					11	8		10		7			3				9	33
2		4	5	6		8			11			10		7			3				9	34
		4	5	6		8			11			10		7	2		3				9	35
		4	5	6		8			11			10		7	2		3				9	36
			5	6		8			11	7		10			2	4	3				9	37
		6	5						11			10	2		3	4			7	8	9	38
		6	5						11			10		7	2	4	3			8	9	39
		6	5						11			10		7	2	4	3			8	9	40
		6	5			8			11			10	2	7	3	4					9	41
		4	5						11	8			2	7	3	6				10	9	42
		4	5	6		10			11	8			2	7	3						9	43
			5	6					11	8			2	7	3	4			10	9		44
		4	5	6		8			11				2	7	3				10		9	45
		4	5	6		10			11	8			2	7	3						9	46
24	16	41	42	39	12	29	5	12	40	26	1	36	15	28	17	12	23	11	7	9	15	
					9	9		3	20	12		23		3				6		11	8	

Two own-goals

Lee	Charlton	Blizzard	Aldous	McKnight	Groves	Woosnam	Rees	Morgan	Hartburn	Facey	Brahan	Heckman	Bishop	White	Gregory	McMahon	Earl	Burgess	Smith	Julians	Johnston	
		4	5	6					11	8		10	2	7			3	9				1
2		4	5						11	8		10		7		6	3	9				2
		4	5	6		8			11	7		10			2		3	9				3
2		4	5	6		8			11			10					3	9	7			4
2		4	4	3		2			4	3		4	1	2	1	1	4	4	1			
									3	2		6						1				

1956-57

Manager: Alec Stock

	P	W	D	L	F	A	Pts
Leicester City	42	25	11	6	109	67	61
Nottingham Forest	42	22	10	10	94	55	54
Liverpool	42	21	11	10	82	54	53
Blackburn Rovers	42	21	10	11	83	75	52
Stoke City	42	20	8	14	83	58	48
Middlesbrough	42	19	10	13	84	60	48
Sheffield United	42	19	8	15	87	76	46
West Ham United	42	19	8	15	59	63	46
Bristol Rovers	42	18	9	15	81	67	45
Swansea Town	42	19	7	16	90	90	45
Fulham	42	19	4	19	84	76	42
Huddersfield Town	42	18	6	18	68	74	42
Bristol City	42	16	9	17	74	79	41
Doncaster Rovers	42	15	10	17	77	77	40
Leyton Orient	42	15	10	17	66	84	40
Grimsby Town	42	17	5	20	61	62	39
Rotherham United	42	13	11	18	74	75	37
Lincoln City	42	14	6	22	54	80	34
Barnsley	42	12	10	20	59	89	34
Notts County	42	9	12	21	58	86	30
Bury	42	8	9	25	60	96	25
Port Vale	42	8	6	28	57	101	22

Division Two

Match No.	Date		Opponents	Result	Scorers	Attenda
1	Aug	18	NOTTINGHAM FOREST	1-4	Sexton	25,2
2		23	BRISTOL ROVERS	1-1	White	20,1
3		25	Huddersfield Town	0-3		15,1
4		27	Bristol Rovers	2-3	White, Heckman	24,7
5	Sep	1	BURY	4-3	White, Hartburn, Willemse, Johnston	17,5
6		8	Grimsby Town	0-0		18,2
7		13	Notts County	3-1	Johnston, Heckman, Groome (og)	10,5
8		15	DONCASTER ROVERS	1-1	Woosnam	19,9
9		22	Stoke City	1-7	Johnston	19,9
10		29	MIDDLESBROUGH	1-1	Facey	17,0
11	Oct	6	WEST HAM UNITED	1-2	Heckman	24,6
12		13	Blackburn Rovers	3-3	Heckman 2, Johnston	20,2
13		20	SWANSEA TOWN	3-0	Johnston, Smith, Heckman	16,7
14		27	Sheffield United	3-2	Johnston, Heckman 2	22,4
15	Nov	3	BARNSLEY	2-0	Johnston 2	17,3
16		10	Port Vale	2-1	Johnston, White	8,4
17		17	ROTHERHAM UNITED	2-1	Sexton, Johnston	16,4
18		24	Lincoln City	2-0	Smith 2	10,3
19	Dec	1	BRISTOL CITY	2-2	White, Johnston	17,5
20		8	Fulham	1-3	Johnston	26,8
21		15	Nottingham Forest	2-1	Johnston 2	13,8
22		22	HUDDERSFIELD TOWN	3-1	Sexton 2, Johnston	15,2
23		25	Liverpool	0-1		22,0
24		26	LIVERPOOL	0-4		10,3
25		29	Bury	3-1	Andrews, Johnston 2	12,0
26	Jan	12	GRIMSBY TOWN	1-1	Johnston	16,4
27		19	Doncaster Rovers	1-6	Johnston	10,0
28	Feb	2	STOKE CITY	2-2	Johnston 2	18,7
29		9	Middlesbrough	2-1	Woosnam, Johnston	30,0
30		16	West Ham United	1-2	Johnston	36,5
31		23	BLACKBURN ROVERS	1-1	Facey	9,5
32	Mar	2	Swansea Town	0-1		18,0
33		9	SHEFFIELD UNITED	1-2	Heckman	17,7
34		16	Barnsley	0-3		12,9
35		23	PORT VALE	3-2	Heckman 2, Johnston	14,2
36		30	Rotherham United	0-2		8,0
37	Apr	6	LINCOLN CITY	2-1	Woosnam, Jackson (og)	13,0
38		13	Bristol City	2-4	Andrews, Woosnam	19,1
39		19	LEICESTER CITY	1-5	Johnston	23,6
40		20	FULHAM	0-2		16,4
41		22	Leicester City	4-1	White, McKnight, Andrews, Johnston	27,5
42		27	NOTTS COUNTY	2-2	Johnston, Andrews	12,3

Appearanc

Go

FA Cup

3	Jan	5	CHELSEA	0-2		27,5

Appearanc

Go

Final League Position: 15th in Division Two

Gregory	Willemse	Blizzard	Aldous	Forbes	White	Sexton	Johnston	Heckman	Hartburn	Facey	Woosnam	McKnight	Carey	Groombridge	Rossiter	McMahon	Smith	Andrews	Bishop	Julians	Cook	George	
2	3	4	5	6	7	8	9	10	11														1
2	3		5	6	7		9	10	11	4	8												2
2	3		5	6	7		9	10	11	4	8												3
2	3		5		7		9	10	11	4	8	6											4
2	3		5		7		9	10	11	4	8	6											5
2	3				7		9	10	11	4	8	6	5										6
2	3		5		7		9	10	11	4	8	6											7
2	3		5		7		9	10	11	4	8	6		1									8
2	3		5		7		9		11	4	10	6		1	8								9
2	3		5				9	10		8		6		1		4	7	11					10
2	3		5	6	7		9	10		8		4		1			11						11
2	3		5	6	7	8	9	10		4				1			11						12
2	3		5		7	8	9	10		4		6		1			11						13
2	3		5		7	8	9	10		4		6		1			11						14
2	3		5		7	8	9	10		4		6		1			11						15
2	3		5		7	8	9	10		4		6		1				11					16
2	3		5			8	9	10	7	4		6		1			11						17
2	3		5		7	8	9	10		4		6		1			11						18
2	3		5		7	8	9	10		4		6		1			11						19
2	3		5		7	8	9			4	10	6		1			11						20
2	3		5		7	8	9	10		4		6		1			11						21
2	3		5		7	8	9	10		4		6		1			11						22
2	3		5		7	8	9	10		4		6		1			11						23
2	3		5		7	8	9	10		4		6					11						24
3			5		7	8	9			4		6					11	10	2				25
	3		5		7	8	9	10		4		6					11		2				26
	3		5		7	8	9	11		4		6						10	2				27
2	3		5		7		9	11		4	8	6						10					28
2	3		5		7		9	11		4	8	6						10					29
2	3		5		7		9	11		4	8	6						10					30
2	3		5				9	11		4	8	6					7	10					31
2	3		5				9	10		4	8	6					7	11					32
2	3		5	6			9	10	11	4	8						7						33
2	3		5	6			9	10	11	4	8			1						7			34
2	3		5		7		9	10	11	4	8	6		1									35
2	3		5		7		9	10		4	8	6		1			11						36
2	3				7	10	9			4	8		5	1				11			6		37
2	3		5		7	10	9			4	8			1				11			6		38
2	3		5	6	7		9	10	11	4	8			1									39
2	3		5		7		9	10			8	4				6		11				1	40
2	3		5		7	8	9	10		4		6		1				11					41
3			5		7		9	10		4	8	6		1				11	2				42
40	40	1	40	8	36	20	42	37	14	40	23	33	2	24	1	2	20	14	4	1	2	1	
	1				6	4	27	11	1	2	4	1					3	4					

Two own-goals

Gregory	Willemse	Blizzard	Aldous	Forbes	White	Sexton	Johnston	Heckman	Hartburn	Facey	Woosnam	McKnight	Carey	Groombridge	Rossiter	McMahon	Smith	Andrews	Bishop	Julians	Cook	George	
2	3		5		7	8	9	10		4		6					11						3
1	1		1		1	1	1	1		1		1					1						

1957-58

Managers: Aug 1957–Mar 1958 Les Gore; Mar–May 1958 Alec Stock

	P	W	D	L	F	A	Pts
West Ham United	42	23	11	8	101	54	57
Blackburn Rovers	42	22	12	8	93	57	56
Charlton Athletic	42	24	7	11	107	69	55
Liverpool	42	22	10	10	79	54	54
Fulham	42	20	12	10	97	59	52
Sheffield United	42	21	10	11	75	50	52
Middlesbrough	42	19	7	16	83	74	45
Ipswich Town	42	16	12	14	68	69	44
Huddersfield Town	42	14	16	12	63	66	44
Bristol Rovers	42	17	8	17	85	80	42
Stoke City	42	18	6	18	75	73	42
Leyton Orient	42	18	5	19	77	79	41
Grimsby Town	42	17	6	19	86	83	40
Barnsley	42	14	12	16	70	74	40
Cardiff City	42	14	9	19	63	77	37
Derby County	42	14	8	20	60	81	36
Bristol City	42	13	9	20	63	88	35
Rotherham United	42	14	5	23	65	101	33
Swansea Town	42	11	9	22	72	99	31
Lincoln City	42	11	9	22	55	82	31
Notts County	42	12	6	24	44	80	30
Doncaster Rovers	42	8	11	23	56	88	27

Division Two

Match No.	Date		Opponents	Result	Scorers	Attend
1	Aug	24	Grimsby Town	2-7	Johnston 2	14,
2		28	Doncaster Rovers	0-2		12,
3		31	STOKE CITY	0-2		17,
4	Sep	5	DONCASTER ROVERS	2-0	Johnston 2	16,
5		7	Bristol City	2-2	Heckman, Johnston	23,
6		12	Charlton Athletic	2-3	Johnston 2	17,
7		14	CARDIFF CITY	4-2	Johnston 2 (1 pen), Julians, Milne (og)	16,
8		19	CHARLTON ATHLETIC	3-2	Johnston 2, Heckman	18,
9		21	Liverpool	0-3		36,
10		28	MIDDLESBROUGH	4-0	Julians 4	18,
11	Oct	5	West Ham United	2-3	Johnston, Heckman	26,
12		12	BARNSLEY	2-1	Johnston 2 (1 pen)	15,
13		19	Fulham	1-3	Julians	26,
14		26	SWANSEA TOWN	5-1	Johnston 3, Heckman, White	16,
15	Nov	2	Derby County	0-2		20,
16		9	BRISTOL ROVERS	1-3	Carey	14,
17		16	Lincoln City	0-2		6,
18		23	NOTTS COUNTY	2-2	Johnston 2	12,
19		30	Ipswich Town	3-5	Hartburn, Julians, Johnston	17,
20	Dec	7	BLACKBURN ROVERS	5-1	Johnston 2, Julians 2, White	11,
21		14	Sheffield United	2-0	Julians, Johnston	14
22		21	GRIMSBY TOWN	5-1	Johnston 3, Julians, Hartburn	13,
23		25	ROTHERHAM UNITED	6-2	Woosnam, Johnston 4, Hartburn	13,
24		26	Rotherham United	2-2	White, Johnston	10,
25		28	Stoke City	3-1	Johnston, Julians, Woosnam	27,
26	Jan	11	BRISTOL CITY	4-0	Johnston 3, Woosnam	15
27		18	Cardiff City	1-1	Julians	13
28	Feb	1	LIVERPOOL	1-0	Hartburn (pen)	18,
29		20	WEST HAM UNITED	1-4	Julians	25,
30		22	Notts County	1-0	Pritchard (og)	11,
31	Mar	8	Swansea Town	2-1	White, Hartburn	15,
32		13	FULHAM	1-3	Facey	12,
33		15	DERBY COUNTY	1-1	Julians	13
34		19	Middlesbrough	0-2		22,
35		22	Bristol Rovers	0-4		15,
36		29	LINCOLN CITY	1-0	McMahon	9,
37	Apr	4	HUDDERSFIELD TOWN	3-1	Willemse, White, Andrews	16,
38		5	Barnsley	0-3		8,
39		8	Huddersfield Town	0-2		14,
40		12	IPSWICH TOWN	2-0	Julians, Facey	10,
41		19	Blackburn Rovers	1-4	Carey	24,
42		26	SHEFFIELD UNITED	0-1		8

Appearar

G

FA Cup

3	Jan	4	READING	1-0	Johnston	20,
4		25	Cardiff City	1-4	Julians	35

Appearar

G

Final League Position: 12th in Division Two

		Gregory	Willemse	Facey	Aldous	McKnight	White	Sexton	Johnston	Woosnam	Smith	Heckman	Nicholson	Welton	Bishop	Julians	Eagles	Carey	Andrews	Hartburn	George	Lea	McMahon	Lazarus
1		2	3	4	5	6	7	8	9	10	11													
2		2	3	4	5	6	7		9	8	11	10												
3		2	3	4	5	6		8	9	10	11		7											
4		2	3	4		6			10	8		11	7	1	5	9								
5		2	3	4		6			10	8		11	7	1	5	9								
6		2	3	4		6			10	8		11	7	1	5	9								
7		2	3	4		6			10	8	7	11		1	5	9								
8		2	3	4		6		9	10	8	7	11		1	5									
9		2	3	4		6		9	10	8	7	11		1	5									
10		2	3	4		6			10	8	7	11		1	5	9								
11		2	3	4		6			10	8	7	11		1	5	9								
12			3	4		6			10	8	7	11		1	5	9	2							
13		3		4		6			10	8	7	11		1	5	9	2							
14		3	11	4	5		7		9			8		1			2	6	10					
15		3			5	4	7		9	10		8		1			2	6	11					
16		3		4	5		7		10			8		1		9	2	6	11					
17			3	8	5	4	7		9					1		10	2	6	11					
18			3		5	4	7		10					1		9	2	6	8	11				
19			3		5	4	7		10							9	2	6	8	11	1			
20		3			5	4	7		9	8						10	2	6		11	1			
21		3			5	4	7		9	8						10	2	6		11	1			
22		3				4	7		9	8					5	10	2	6		11	1			
23		3				4	7		9	8					5	10	2	6		11	1			
24		3				4	7		9	8					5	10	2	6		11	1			
25		3		4			7		9	8					5	10	2	6		11	1			
26		3				4	7		9	8					5		2	6	10	11	1			
27		3				4	7		9	8					5	10	2	6		11	1			
28		3				4	7		9	8					5	10	2	6		11	1			
29		3				4	7		9	8					5	10	2	6		11	1			
30				4			7		9	8					5	10	2	6		11	1	3		
31				8		4	7			10					5	9	2	6		11	1	3		
32				8		4	7			10					5	9	2	6		11	1	3		
33				10		4	7			8					5	9	2	6		11	1	3		
34				4						8			7		5	9	2	6	10	11	1	3		
35				10						8					5	9	2	6	11	7	1	3	4	
36				4			7			8			9		5	10	2		11		1	3	6	
37			9	4			7			8					5	10	2		11		1	3	6	
38			9	4			7			8					5	10	2		11		1	3	6	
39				4			7			8					5	9	2		10	11		3	6	
40		2	9	4			7			8					5	10			11		1	3	6	
41		2		4			7			8					5	10		9	11		1	3	6	
42				4			7			8					5	10	2	9	11		1	3	6	
	4	27	19	30	11	29	29	4	30	37	10	14	6	15	31	34	29	24	16	19	23	13	8	
			1	2			5		35	3		4				16		2	1	5			1	

Two own-goals

	Gregory	Willemse	Facey	Aldous	McKnight	White	Sexton	Johnston	Woosnam	Smith	Heckman	Nicholson	Welton	Bishop	Julians	Eagles	Carey	Andrews	Hartburn	George	Lea	McMahon	Lazarus
1	3		7		4			9	8					5	10	2	6			1			11
2	3				4	7		9	8					5	10	2	6		11	1			
	2		1		2	1		2	2					2	2	2	2		1	2			1
								1							1								

1958-59

Managers: Aug 1958–Feb 1959 Alec Stock; Feb–May 1959 Les Gore

	P	W	D	L	F	A	Pts
Sheffield Wednesday	42	28	6	8	106	48	62
Fulham	42	27	6	9	96	61	60
Sheffield United	42	23	7	12	82	48	53
Liverpool	42	24	5	13	87	62	53
Stoke City	42	21	7	14	72	58	49
Bristol Rovers	42	18	12	12	80	64	48
Derby County	42	20	8	14	74	71	48
Charlton Athletic	42	18	7	17	92	90	43
Cardiff City	42	18	7	17	65	65	43
Bristol City	42	17	7	18	74	70	41
Swansea Town	42	16	9	17	79	81	41
Brighton & Hove Albion	42	15	11	16	74	90	41
Middlesbrough	42	15	10	17	87	71	40
Huddersfield Town	42	16	8	18	62	55	40
Sunderland	42	16	8	18	64	75	40
Ipswich Town	42	17	6	19	62	77	40
Leyton Orient	42	14	8	20	71	78	36
Scunthorpe United	42	12	9	21	55	84	33
Lincoln City	42	11	7	24	63	93	29
Rotherham United	42	10	9	23	42	82	29
Grimsby Town	42	9	10	23	62	90	28
Barnsley	42	10	7	25	55	91	27

Division Two

Match No.	Date		Opponents	Result	Scorers	Attenda
1	Aug	23	BRISTOL ROVERS	1-3	Julians	17,3
2		27	Ipswich Town	1-2	Elwood	16,7
3		30	Derby County	2-1	McClellan, Julians	22,6
4	Sep	4	IPSWICH TOWN	2-0	McClellan, White	11,7
5		6	BARNSLEY	5-1	Woosnam 3, Julians 2	13,2
6		11	Swansea Town	3-3	Hasty 2, McKnight	20,0
7		13	SCUNTHORPE UNITED	2-1	Julians, Lazarus	15,9
8		18	SWANSEA TOWN	0-0		12,3
9		20	Sheffield Wednesday	0-2		28,4
10		27	FULHAM	0-2		24,6
11	Oct	4	Lincoln City	0-2		9,7
12		11	Rotherham United	1-1	Andrews	6,7
13		18	SHEFFIELD UNITED	1-1	Andrews	13,5
14		25	Brighton & Hove Albion	2-2	McClellan 2	26,2
15	Nov	1	HUDDERSFIELD TOWN	2-5	Facey 2	13,9
16		8	Liverpool	0-3		34,9
17		15	MIDDLESBROUGH	5-2	Julians 3, White, Lazarus	10,2
18		22	Charlton Athletic	1-4	Lararus	15,8
19		29	BRISTOL CITY	4-2	Elwood 4	9,5
20	Dec	6	Cardiff City	1-2	Lewis	15,1
21		13	GRIMSBY TOWN	0-1		7,6
22		20	Bristol Rovers	3-1	White, Lewis, Lazarus	10,0
23		26	STOKE CITY	0-1		12,1
24		27	Stoke City	2-3	Burridge, White	30,0
25	Jan	1	Sunderland	0-4		33,0
26		3	DERBY COUNTY	1-3	Elwood	11,7
27		31	Scunthorpe United	0-2		10,2
28	Feb	7	SHEFFIELD WEDNESDAY	0-2		11,8
29		14	Fulham	2-5	Baily, Andrews	20,47
30		21	LINCOLN CITY	0-0		10,10
31		28	LIVERPOOL	1-3	Facey (pen)	14,06
32	Mar	7	Sheffield United	3-2	Brown, Johnston 2	14,76
33		14	BRIGHTON & HOVE ALBION	2-2	Brown, Johnston	15,81
34		21	Huddersfield Town	0-0		10,06
35		28	ROTHERHAM UNITED	2-0	Baily, Brown	11,86
36		30	SUNDERLAND	6-0	Johnston, Brown 4, White	15,61
37	Apr	4	Middlesbrough	2-4	Wright (pen), Elwood	20,43
38		11	CHARLTON ATHLETIC	6-1	Elwood 3, Facey (pen), Brown, Baily	15,28
39		18	Bristol City	1-0	Johnston	14,44
40		21	Grimsby Town	1-4	Johnston	8,00
41		25	CARDIFF CITY	3-0	Brown, Johnston 2	11,46
42		29	Barnsley	3-1	Johnston 2, Brown	7,78
						Appearance
						Goal

FA Cup

Match No.	Date		Opponents	Result	Scorers	Attendance
3	Jan	10	Blackburn Rovers	2-4	Lewis 2	27,72
						Appearance
						Goal

Final League Position: 17th in Division Two

Wright	Lea	McKnight	Owen	Facey	White	Woosnam	Lewis	Julians	Elwood	Groombridge	Eagles	McClellan	Flint	Lazarus	Hasty	Gregory	Carey	Andrews	Bishop	Lucas	Charlton	Baily	Burridge	Biggs	Waites	Brown	Johnston	Sorrell	
2	3	4	5	6	7	8	9	10	11																				1
2	3	4	5	6	7	8	9	10	11	1																			2
3		6	5	4	7	8		10	11	1	2	9																	3
3		6	5	4	7	8		10		1	2	9	11																4
3		6	5	4	7	8		10		1	2	9	11																5
3		6	5	4		8		10		1	2		11	7	9														6
3		6	5	4	7	8	9	10		1	2			11															7
3		6	5	4	7	8		10		1	2			11	9														8
3		6	5	4		8		10		1	2	9	11	7															9
2	3	6	5	4	7	8		10				9		11															10
3		6	5	4	7	8		10	11		2	9																	11
2			5	4		8	9	10				7				3	6	11											12
3		4		8	7			9			2	10					6	11	5										13
3		4			7	8		9			2	10					6	11	5										14
3		4		10	7	8		9			2	11					6		5										15
2		4		8	7		3	9	11			10					6		5										16
2	3			4	7		10	9	11					8					5	6									17
2	3			4	7		10	9	11					8					5	6									18
2				4	7		10	9	11					8		3			5	6									19
2				4	7		10	9	11					8		3			5	6									20
2				4	7		10	9	11					8		3			5	6									21
2				4	7		10	9	11					8		3			5	6									22
2				4	7		9		11					8					5	6	3	10							23
2				4	7				11					8					5	6	3	10	9						24
2				4	7				11					8					5	6	3	10		9					25
2			5	4					11					8				10		6	3			9	7				26
3				4	7						2	10							5	6		8	11			9			27
		6		4	7		10				2							11	5		3	8				9			28
		6			7						2					3		11	5	4		8				10	9		29
2				4	7		10		11							3			5	6						8	9		30
2				4					11										5	6	3	10			7	8	9		31
2				4	7				11										5	6	3	8				10	9		32
2				4	7				11										5	6	3	10				8	9		33
2	6			4	7				11										5		3	10				8	9		34
2	6			4	7				11										5		3	10				8	9		35
2	6			4	7				11										5		3	10				8	9		36
2	6	4			7				11										5		3	10				8	9		37
2	6			4	7				11										5		3	10				8	9		38
2	6			4	7				11										5		3	10				8	9		39
2	6			4					11										5		3	10			7	8	9		40
2	6				7				11										5	4	3	10				8	9		41
2	6								11										5		3	10			7	8	9	4	42
40	14	18	13	37	35	14	14	22	28	8	14	12	4	15	2	7	5	6	29	17	17	18	2	2	4	16	14	1	
1		1		4	5	3	2	8	10			4		4	2			3				3	1			10	10		

Wright	Lea	McKnight	Owen	Facey	White	Woosnam	Lewis	Julians	Elwood	Groombridge	Eagles	McClellan	Flint	Lazarus	Hasty	Gregory	Carey	Andrews	Bishop	Lucas	Charlton	Baily	Burridge	Biggs	Waites	Brown	Johnston	Sorrell	
2			5	4			10		11			7								6	3	8	9						3
1			1	1			1		1			1								1	1	1	1						
							2																						

1959-60

Manager: Les Gore

	P	W	D	L	F	A	Pts
Aston Villa	42	25	9	8	89	43	59
Cardiff City	42	23	12	7	90	62	58
Liverpool	42	20	10	12	90	66	50
Sheffield United	42	19	12	11	68	51	50
Middlesbrough	42	19	10	13	90	64	48
Huddersfield Town	42	19	9	14	73	52	47
Charlton Athletic	42	17	13	12	90	87	47
Rotherham United	42	17	13	12	61	60	47
Bristol Rovers	42	18	11	13	72	78	47
Leyton Orient	42	15	14	13	76	61	44
Ipswich Town	42	19	6	17	78	68	44
Swansea Town	42	15	10	17	82	84	40
Lincoln City	42	16	7	19	75	78	39
Brighton & Hove Albion	42	13	12	17	67	76	38
Scunthorpe United	42	13	10	19	57	71	36
Sunderland	42	12	12	18	52	65	36
Stoke City	42	14	7	21	66	83	35
Derby County	42	14	7	21	61	77	35
Plymouth Argyle	42	13	9	20	61	89	35
Portsmouth	42	10	12	20	59	77	32
Hull City	42	10	10	22	48	76	30
Bristol City	42	11	5	26	60	97	27

Division Two

Match No.	Date		Opponents	Result	Scorers	Atten
1	Aug	22	Bristol Rovers	2-2	Brown, Johnston	20
2		27	STOKE CITY	2-1	Johnston, Elwood	13
3		29	IPSWICH TOWN	4-1	Waites 2, Johnston 2	14
4	Sep	2	Stoke City	1-2	Johnston	19
5		5	Huddersfield Town	1-1	Facey (pen)	15
6		10	BRIGHTON & HOVE ALBION	3-2	Facey (pen), Johnston, Waites	13
7		12	ROTHERHAM UNITED	2-3	Johnston 2	14
8		16	Brighton & Hove Albion	1-1	Johnston	21
9		19	LINCOLN CITY	4-0	Waites 2, Facey, Brown	11
10		26	Aston Villa	0-1		39
11	Oct	3	SUNDERLAND	1-1	Elwood	16
12		10	Cardiff City	1-5	Johnston	18
13		17	HULL CITY	3-1	McDonald, Johnston 2	13
14		24	Sheffield United	2-0	Foster, Johnston	11
15		31	MIDDLESBROUGH	5-0	Brown 3, Facey (pen), Johnston	15
16	Nov	7	Derby County	1-1	Facey (pen)	13
17		14	PLYMOUTH ARGYLE	2-3	Foster, Facey (pen)	11
18		21	Liverpool	3-4	Johnston 2, Sorrell	34
19		28	CHARLTON ATHLETIC	2-0	Sewell (og), Brown	17,
20	Dec	5	Bristol City	1-1	Johnston	13,
21		12	SCUNTHORPE UNITED	1-1	Brown	9,
22		19	BRISTOL ROVERS	1-2	Brown	6,
23		26	PORTSMOUTH	1-2	Brown	14,
24		28	Portsmouth	1-1	Elwood	21,
25	Jan	2	Ipswich Town	3-6	Foster 2, Elwood	11,
26		16	HUDDERSFIELD TOWN	2-1	Facey (pen), Johnston	11,
27		23	Rotherham United	1-1	Biggs	16,
28	Feb	6	Lincoln City	2-2	Foster, Johnston	9,
29		13	ASTON VILLA	0-0		16,
30		20	Sunderland	4-1	McDonald, Waites, Facey (pen), Johnston	16,
31		27	CARDIFF CITY	3-4	Johnston 2, McDonald	22,
32	Mar	5	Hull City	2-1	Johnston, McDonald	10,
33		17	SHEFFIELD UNITED	1-1	Facey (pen)	7,
34		19	Charlton Athletic	0-0		17,
35		26	DERBY COUNTY	3-0	Burridge, McDonald 2	10,
36	Apr	2	Plymouth Argyle	0-1		11,
37		9	LIVERPOOL	2-0	McDonald, Johnston	13,
38		15	SWANSEA TOWN	2-1	Waites, McDonald	15,
39		16	Scunthorpe United	1-2	Foster	8,
40		18	Swansea Town	0-1		10,
41		23	BRISTOL CITY	3-1	Brown 2, McDonald	9,
42		30	Middlesbrough	2-2	Brown, Johnston	13,

Appearan

Go

FA Cup

3	Jan	9	Liverpool	1-2	Foster	40,3

Appearan

Go

Final League Position: 10th in Division Two

Wright	Charlton	Facey	Bishop	Lea	White	Brown	Johnston	Baily	Elwood	Waites	Lewis	George	Burridge	Lucas	Foster	McDonald	Sorrell	Eagles	Biggs	Carey	Nicholson	
2	3	4	5	6	7	8	9	10	11													1
2	3	4	5	6		8	9	10	11	7												2
2	3	4	5	6		8	9	10	11	7												3
2	3	4	5	6		8	9	10	11	7												4
2	3	4	5	6		8	9	10	11	7												5
2	3	4	5	6		8	9	10	11	7												6
2		4	5	6		8	9	10	11	7	3											7
2		4	5	6		8	9	10	11	7	3	1										8
2		4	5	6		8	9	10	11	7	3	1										9
2		4	5	6		8	9	10	7		3		11									10
2	3	4	5			8	9	10	11	7				6								11
2	3	4	5			8	9		11	7				6	10							12
2	3	4	5	6		8	9			7					10	11						13
2	3	4	5	6		8	9			7					10	11						14
2	3	4	5		7	8	9								10	11	6					15
2	3	4	5		7	8	9								10	11	6					16
2	3	4	5		7	8	9								10	11	6					17
2	3	4	5		7	8	9								10	11	6					18
2	3	4	5		7	8	9								10	11	6					19
2	3	4	5		7	8	9								10	11	6					20
2	3	4	5		7	8	9								10	11	6					21
2	3	4	5		7	8	9								10	11	6					22
2	3	4	5		7	8	9								10	11	6					23
2	3	4	5	6		8	9		11	7			10									24
2	3	4	5	6		8	9		11	7					10							25
	3	4	5			8	9		7						10	11	6	2				26
	3	4	5			8			7						10	11	6	2	9			27
	3	4	5			8	9		7						10	11	6	2				28
	3	4	5			8	9		7						10	11	6	2				29
		4	5		7		9			8	3				10	11	6	2				30
	3	4	5		7		9			8					10	11	6	2				31
	3	4	5		7		9			8					10	11	6	2				32
	3	4	5		7		9			8					10	11	6	2				33
	3	4	5		7					8					10	11	6	2	9			34
		4	5		7					8	3		9		10	11	6	2				35
		4	5		7		10			8	3		9			11	6	2				36
		4	5		7	10	9			8	3					11	6	2				37
			5		7	10	9			8	3					11	6	2		4		38
			5		7	10	9				3			4	8	11	6	2			1	39
			5		7	10	9			8	3					11	6	2		4	1	40
			5		7	10	9			8	3					11	6	2		4	1	41
		4	5		7	10	9			8	3					11	6	2			1	42
25	29	38	42	14	23	35	39	11	18	26	13	2	4	3	24	28	26	17	2	3	4	
		9				12	25		4	7			1		6	9	1		1			

One own-goal

Wright	Charlton	Facey	Bishop	Lea	White	Brown	Johnston	Baily	Elwood	Waites	Lewis	George	Burridge	Lucas	Foster	McDonald	Sorrell	Eagles	Biggs	Carey	Nicholson	
	3	4	5		7	8	9								10	11	6	2				3
	1	1	1		1	1	1								1	1	1	1				
															1							

1960-61

Manager: Les Gore

	P	W	D	L	F	A	Pts
Ipswich Town	42	26	7	9	100	55	59
Sheffield United	42	26	6	10	81	51	58
Liverpool	42	21	10	11	87	58	52
Norwich City	42	20	9	13	70	53	49
Middlesbrough	42	18	12	12	83	74	48
Sunderland	42	17	13	12	75	60	47
Swansea Town	42	18	11	13	77	73	47
Southampton	42	18	8	16	84	81	44
Scunthorpe United	42	14	15	13	69	64	43
Charlton Athletic	42	16	11	15	97	91	43
Plymouth Argyle	42	17	8	17	81	82	42
Derby County	42	15	10	17	80	80	40
Luton Town	42	15	9	18	71	79	39
Leeds United	42	14	10	18	75	83	38
Rotherham United	42	12	13	17	65	64	37
Brighton & Hove Albion	42	14	9	19	61	75	37
Bristol Rovers	42	15	7	20	73	92	37
Stoke City	42	12	12	18	51	59	36
Leyton Orient	42	14	8	20	55	78	36
Huddersfield Town	42	13	9	20	62	71	35
Portsmouth	42	11	11	20	64	91	33
Lincoln City	42	8	8	26	48	95	24

Division Two

Match No.	Date		Opponents	Result	Scorers	Attend
1	Aug	20	IPSWICH TOWN	1-3	Johnston	14
2		24	Brighton & Hove Albion	1-1	Johnston	17,
3		27	Scunthorpe United	2-2	Johnston 2	10,
4		31	BRIGHTON & HOVE ALBION	2-1	Bishop, Facey (pen)	12,
5	Sep	3	SHEFFIELD UNITED	1-4	Brown	10,
6		7	Leeds United	3-1	Waites, Johnston, Graham	17,
7		10	DERBY COUNTY	2-1	Johnston 2	10,
8		14	LEEDS UNITED	0-1		8,
9		17	Bristol Rovers	2-4	Elwood, Graham	15,
10		24	LIVERPOOL	1-3	Graham	10,
11	Oct	1	Rotherham United	1-2	Facey	7,
12		8	Stoke City	2-1	Brown, Johnston	8,
13		15	SWANSEA TOWN	2-2	Johnston, Brown	9,
14		22	Luton Town	1-0	Brown	10,
15		29	LINCOLN CITY	1-2	Brown	5,
16	Nov	5	Portsmouth	2-1	White, Johnston	11,
17		19	Sunderland	1-4	Brown	16,
18	Dec	3	Norwich City	2-3	Johnston, Waites	19,
19		10	CHARLTON ATHLETIC	1-1	Gibbs	9,
20		17	Ipswich Town	2-6	Johnston, McDonald	9,
21		26	Middlesbrough	0-2		15,
22		31	SCUNTHORPE UNITED	2-1	Foster, Johnston	8,
23	Jan	14	Sheffield United	1-4	Elwood,	17,
24		21	Derby County	1-3	Crossan	11,
25	Feb	4	BRISTOL ROVERS	3-2	Bishop, Newman, Lewis (pen)	12,
26		11	Liverpool	0-5		22,
27		20	ROTHERHAM UNITED	2-1	Lambert (og), Lewis (pen)	9,6
28	Mar	4	Swansea Town	0-1		14,0
29		7	PLYMOUTH ARGYLE	1-1	Crossan	9,6
30		11	LUTON TOWN	2-1	Bishop, Sealey	11,9
31		14	MIDDLESBROUGH	1-1	McDonald	11,6
32		18	Charlton Athletic	0-2		12,3
33		21	HUDDERSFIELD TOWN	2-0	Graham, Dunmore	10,0
34		25	PORTSMOUTH	2-1	Graham, Johnston	10,1
35		29	SOUTHAMPTON	1-1	McDonald	11,2
36	Apr	1	Plymouth Argyle	2-3	Dunmore, Facey (pen)	14,8
37		3	Southampton	1-1	Dunmore	12,1
38		8	SUNDERLAND	0-1		12,7
39		10	STOKE CITY	3-1	Graham 2, Johnston	8,3
40		15	Huddersfield Town	0-1		12,2
41		22	NORWICH CITY	1-0	Johnston	12,1
42		29	Lincoln City	0-2		3,9

Appearanc

Goa

FA Cup

3	Jan	7	Gillingham	6-2	Elwood 2, Lewis 2 (2 pens), Johnston, McDonald	13,16
4		28	Southampton	1-0	Gibbs	21,3
5	Feb	18	SHEFFIELD WEDNESDAY	0-2		31,0

Appearance

Goa

League Cup

1	Oct	12	Chester	2-2	Foster, Brown	9,07
R		17	CHESTER	1-0	McDonald	5,00
2	Nov	14	CHESTERFIELD	0-1		5,24

Appearance

Goa

Final League Position: 19th in Division Two

Eagles	Lewis	Facey	Bishop	Sorrell	White	Foster	Johnston	Graham	McDonald	Brown	Lea	Lazarus	Waites	Gibson	Wright	Elwood	Robertson	Charlton	Gibbs	Owen	Lucas	Crossan	Newman	Sealey	Dunmore	Cochran	Taylor	
2	3	4	5	6	7	8	9	10	11																			1
2	3	4	5	6	7	10	9		11	8																		2
2	3	4	5	6	7	10	9		11	8																		3
2	3	4	5				9		11	10	6	7	8															4
2	3	4	5				9		11	10	6	7	8															5
	3		5				9	10	11		6	7	8	4	2													6
	3		5				9	10	11		6	7	8	4	2													7
	3		5				9	10	11		6	7	8	4	2													8
	3		5		7		9	10			6		8	4	2	11												9
	3	4	5		7		9	10			6		8		2	11	1											10
2	3	8	5	4			9	10		7	6		11															11
2		4	5	6	7	10	9		11	8								3										12
2		4	5	6	7	10	9		11	8								3										13
2		4	5	6	7	10	9		11	8								3										14
2		4	5	6	7	10	9		11	8								3										15
2		4	5	6	7	10	9		11	8								3										16
2		4	5	6	7		9		11	8								3	10									17
2			5				8	10	11		6		7	4				3	9									18
2							8	10	11		6		7	4				3	9	5								19
2							9		10		6		7	4		11		3	8	5								20
	3		5				9		11	10	6		7	4				2	8									21
	3		5			10	9		11		6		7			8		2			4							22
	3		5			10	9				6					8		2			4	7	11					23
	3		5			10	9				6					8		2			4	7	11					24
	3	4	5				9				6					8		2	10			7	11					25
		4	5				9				6				3	8		2	10			7	11					26
	3		5				9				6					8		2	10		4	7	11					27
		4	5								6				2	8	1	3	10			7	11	9				28
		4	5								6				2	8	1	3	10			7	11	9				29
		4	5				9				6				2		1	3	10			7	11	8				30
		4	5		7		9	10	11		6				2		1	3						8				31
		4	5		7		9	10	11		6				2		1	3							8			32
			5		7		9	10	11		6				2		1	3			4				8			33
			5		7		9	10	11		6				2		1	3			4				8			34
			5		7		9	10	11		6				2		1	3			4				8			35
		4	5		7		9	10	11		6				2		1	3							8			36
			5		7		9				6				2		1	3	10		4		11		8			37
			5		7		9		11		6				2		1	3	10		4				8			38
			5		7		9	10			6				2		1	3			4		11		8			39
			5		7		9	10			6				2		1	3			4		11		8			40
			5		7		9	10			6				2		1	3			4		11		8			41
			5		7		9	11			6				2			3			4				10	1	8	42
15	17	21	40	10	23	11	40	19	26	12	33	5	13	8	21	11	15	31	13	2	13	8	12	4	11	1	1	
	2	3	3		1	1	16	7	3	6			2			2			1			2	1	1	3			

One own-goal

Eagles	Lewis	Facey	Bishop	Sorrell	White	Foster	Johnston	Graham	McDonald	Brown	Lea	Lazarus	Waites	Gibson	Wright	Elwood	Robertson	Charlton	Gibbs	Owen	Lucas	Crossan	Newman	Sealey	Dunmore	Cochran	Taylor	
	3		5		7	10	9		11		6					8		2			4							3
	3	4	5				9				6					8		2	10			7	11					4
	3	4	5				9				6					8		2	10			7	11					5
	3	2	3		1	1	3		1		3					3		3	2		1	2	2					
	2						1		1							2			1									

Eagles	Lewis	Facey	Bishop	Sorrell	White	Foster	Johnston	Graham	McDonald	Brown	Lea	Lazarus	Waites	Gibson	Wright	Elwood	Robertson	Charlton	Gibbs	Owen	Lucas	Crossan	Newman	Sealey	Dunmore	Cochran	Taylor	
2		4		6	7	10	9		11	8								3		5								1
2		4	5	6	7	10	9	8	11									3										R
		4	5	6	7	10	9		11	8								3			2							2
2		3	2	3	3	3	3	1	3	2								3		1	1							
						1			1	1																		

1961-62

Manager: Johnny Carey

	P	W	D	L	F	A	Pts
Liverpool	42	27	8	7	99	43	62
Leyton Orient	42	22	10	10	69	40	54
Sunderland	42	22	9	11	85	50	53
Scunthorpe United	42	21	7	14	86	71	49
Plymouth Argyle	42	19	8	15	75	75	46
Southampton	42	18	9	15	77	62	45
Huddersfield Town	42	16	12	14	67	59	44
Stoke City	42	17	8	17	55	57	42
Rotherham United	42	16	9	17	70	76	41
Preston North End	42	15	10	17	55	57	40
Newcastle United	42	15	9	18	64	58	39
Middlesbrough	42	16	7	19	76	72	39
Luton Town	42	17	5	20	69	71	39
Walsall	42	14	11	17	70	75	39
Charlton Athletic	42	15	9	18	69	75	39
Derby County	42	14	11	17	68	75	39
Norwich City	42	14	11	17	61	70	39
Bury	42	17	5	20	52	76	39
Leeds United	42	12	12	18	50	61	36
Swansea Town	42	12	12	18	61	83	36
Bristol Rovers	42	13	7	22	53	81	33
Brighton & Hove Albion	42	10	11	21	42	86	31

Division Two

Match No.	Date		Opponents	Result	Scorers	Atten
1	Aug	19	Newcastle United	0-0		2
2		21	SOUTHAMPTON	1-3	Foster	1
3		26	MIDDLESBROUGH	2-0	White, Lucas	9
4		30	Southampton	2-1	Foster McDonald	14
5	Sep	2	Walsall	5-1	Foster, Dunmore, Graham 3	15
6		9	DERBY COUNTY	2-0	Swallow (og), Dunmore (pen)	12
7		16	Bristol Rovers	1-2	Dunmore (pen)	11
8		20	HUDDERSFIELD TOWN	3-0	McDonald, Foster, Graham	9
9		23	Preston North End	2-3	McDonald, Foster	9
10		27	Huddersfield Town	1-1	White	16
11		29	PLYMOUTH ARGYLE	1-2	Dunmore	13
12	Oct	7	STOKE CITY	3-0	Foster, Graham, Dunmore	10
13		14	Sunderland	1-2	Dunmore	36
14		21	ROTHERHAM UNITED	1-1	Graham	10
15		28	Liverpool	3-3	Dunmore 2, Foster	36
16	Nov	4	CHARLTON ATHLETIC	2-1	Dunmore 2 (1 pen)	13
17		11	Leeds United	0-0		7
18		18	BRIGHTON & HOVE ALBION	4-1	Dunmore, Elwood, White, Sitford (og)	10
19		24	Scunthorpe United	2-0	McDonald, White	11
20	Dec	2	NORWICH CITY	2-0	Dunmore 2	12
21		16	NEWCASTLE UNITED	2-0	White, Elwood	13
22		23	Middlesbrough	3-2	Dunmore, Foster 2	9
23		26	SWANSEA TOWN	1-0	Dunmore	14
24		30	Swansea Town	3-1	Dunmore 3	9
25	Jan	13	WALSALL	3-0	Dunmore (pen), Graham, White	15,
26		20	Derby County	2-1	Dunmore (pen), Graham	22,
27	Feb	3	BRISTOL ROVERS	2-3	McDonald, Graham	14,
28		9	PRESTON NORTH END	0-2		18,
29		17	Plymouth Argyle	1-2	Dunmore	20
30		24	Stoke City	1-0	Dunmore	21,
31	Mar	3	SUNDERLAND	1-1	Deeley	19,
32		9	Rotherham United	1-2	Lucas	10,
33		13	Bury	1-0	McDonald	9,
34		17	LIVERPOOL	2-2	Graham, Lewis	25,
35		24	Charlton Athletic	2-1	Deeley, Graham	29,
36		31	LEEDS UNITED	0-0		13,
37	Apr	7	Brighton & Hove Albion	1-0	Foster	12,
38		14	SCUNTHORPE UNITED	0-1		16,
39		20	LUTON TOWN	0-0		21,
40		21	Norwich City	0-0		20,
41		23	Luton Town	3-1	Gibbs 2, Lucas	13,
42		28	BURY	2-0	Graham 2	21,

Appearan

Go

FA Cup

3	Jan	6	Brentford	1-1	Foster	19,
R		8	BRENTFORD	2-1	Foster, Elwood	22,
4		30	Burnley	1-1	Foster	37,
R	Feb	6	BURNLEY	0-1		31,

Appearan

Go

League Cup

1	Sep	11	Stockport County	1-0	McDonald	7,
2	Oct	4	BLACKPOOL	1-1	Gibbs	9,
R		30	Blackpool	1-5	McDonald	6,

Appearan

Go

Final League Position: 2nd in Division Two

[illegible]	Lewis	Lucas	Bishop	Lea	White	Foster	Dunmore	Graham	McDonald	Gibbs	Elwood	Robertson	Newman	Deeley	Wright	Taylor	Bolland	Clark	
	3	4	5	6	7	8	9	10	11										1
	3	4	5	6	7	8	9	10	11										2
	3	4	5	6	7	8	9	10	11										3
	3	4	5	6	7	8	9	10	11										4
	3	4	5	6	7	8	9	10	11										5
	3	4	5	6	7	8	9	10	11										6
	3	4	5	6	7	8	9	10	11										7
	3	4	5	6	7	8	9	10	11										8
	3	4	5	6	7	8	9	10	11										9
	3	4	5	6	7	8	9	10	11										10
	3	4	5	6	7	8	9	10	11										11
	3	4	5	6	7	8	9	10	11										12
	3	4	5	6	7	8	9		11	10									13
	3	4	5	6	7	8	9	10	11										14
	3	4	5	6	7	8	9	10	11										15
	3	4	5	6	7	8	9	10	11										16
	3	4	5	6	7		9	10	11		8								17
	3	4	5	6	7	8	9		11		10								18
2	3	4	5	6	7	8	9		11		10								19
2	3	4	5	6	7	8	9		11		10								20
2	3	4	5	6	7	8	9		11		10	1							21
2	3	4	5	6	7	8	9		11		10								22
2	3	4	5	6	7	8	9		11		10								23
2	3	4	5	6	7	8	9		11		10								24
2	3	4	5	6	7	8	9	10					11						25
2	3	4	5	6	7	8	9	10					11						26
2	3	4	5	6	7	8	9	10	11										27
2	3	4	5	6	7	8	9	10	11			1							28
2	3	4	5	6	7	8	9	10				1		11					29
	3	4	5	6		10	9				11	1		7	2	8			30
2	3	4	5	6		8	9				11	1		7			10		31
2	3	4	5	6	7		9					1		11		8	10		32
2	3	4	5	6			9	10	11			1		7			8		33
2	3	4	5	6				10	11			1		7		8	9		34
2	3	4	5	6			9	10	11			1		7			8		35
2	3	4	5	6				10	11			1		7		8	9		36
2		4	5	6		8		10	11			1		7			9	3	37
2	3	4	5	6		8	9	10	11			1		7					38
2	3	4	5	6			9	10	11			1		7		8			39
2	3	4	5	6			9		11			1		7		8	10		40
2	3	4	5	6		10	9		11	8		1		7					41
2	3	4	5	6			9	10	11	8		1		7					42
1	41	42	42	42	30	33	39	29	36	3	10	16	2	14	1	6	8	1	
	1	3			6	10	22	13	6	2	2			2					

Two own-goals

[illegible]	Lewis	Lucas	Bishop	Lea	White	Foster	Dunmore	Graham	McDonald	Gibbs	Elwood	
2	3	4	5	6	7	8	9		11		10	3
2	3	4	5	6	7	8	9		11		10	R
2	3	4	5	6	7	8	9	10	11			4
2	3	4	5	6	7	8	9	10	11			R
4	4	4	4	4	4	4	4	2	4		2	
						3					1	

[illegible]	Lewis	Lucas	Bishop	Lea	White	Foster	Dunmore	Graham	McDonald	Gibbs	Elwood	Robertson	Newman	
2	3	4	5	6	7	8	9	10	11					1
2	3	4	5	6	7	8		10	11	9				2
2	3	4	5	6	7	8	9		11				10	R
3	3	3	3	3	3	3	2	2	3	1			1	
									2	1				

1962-63

Manager: Johnny Carey

	P	W	D	L	F	A	Pts
Everton	42	25	11	6	84	42	61
Tottenham Hotspur	42	23	9	10	111	62	55
Burnley	42	22	10	10	78	57	54
Leicester City	42	20	12	10	79	53	52
Wolverhampton W	42	20	10	12	93	65	50
Sheffield Wednesday	42	19	10	13	77	63	48
Arsenal	42	18	10	14	86	77	46
Liverpool	42	17	10	15	71	59	44
Nottingham Forest	42	17	10	15	67	69	44
Sheffield United	42	16	12	14	58	60	44
Blackburn Rovers	42	15	12	15	79	71	42
West Ham United	42	14	12	16	73	69	40
Blackpool	42	13	14	15	58	64	40
West Bromwich Albion	42	16	7	19	71	79	39
Aston Villa	42	15	8	19	62	68	38
Fulham	42	14	10	18	50	71	38
Ipswich Town	42	12	11	19	59	78	35
Bolton Wanderers	42	15	5	22	55	75	35
Manchester United	42	12	10	20	67	81	34
Birmingham City	42	10	13	19	63	90	33
Manchester City	42	10	11	21	58	102	31
Leyton Orient	42	6	9	27	37	81	21

Division One

Match No.	Date		Opponents	Result	Scorers	Atte
1	Aug	18	ARSENAL	1-2	Gibbs	2
2		22	West Bromwich Albion	1-2	Dunmore	2
3		25	Birmingham City	2-2	Graham, Dunmore (pen)	2
4		29	WEST BROMWICH ALBION	2-3	Deeley, Dunmore	1
5	Sep	1	WEST HAM UNITED	2-0	Dunmore, Graham	2
6		5	Everton	0-3		5
7		8	MANCHESTER UNITED	1-0	McDonald	2
8		12	EVERTON	3-0	Deeley, Bolland, Dunmore	2
9		15	Burnley	0-2		2
10		22	SHEFFIELD WEDNESDAY	2-4	Bolland, Deeley	2
11		29	Fulham	2-0	Graham, McDonald	2
12	Oct	6	Manchester City	0-2		1
13		13	BLACKPOOL	0-2		1
14		20	Aston Villa	0-1		2
15		27	TOTTENHAM HOTSPUR	1-5	Deeley	3
16	Nov	3	Nottingham Forest	1-1	Dunmore	1
17		10	IPSWICH TOWN	1-2	Gregory	1
18		17	Liverpool	0-5		3
19		24	WOLVERHAMPTON W	0-4		1
20	Dec	1	Blackburn Rovers	1-1	Graham	1
21		8	SHEFFIELD UNITED	2-2	Graham, Dunmore	
22		15	Arsenal	0-2		2
23		22	BIRMINGHAM CITY	2-2	Musgrove, Bolland	1
24		26	Leicester City	1-5	Musgrove	1
25	Feb	16	FULHAM	1-1	Graham	1
26		23	MANCHESTER CITY	1-1	Elwood	1
27	Mar	2	Blackpool	2-3	Dunmore, Deeley (pen)	1
28		9	ASTON VILLA	0-2		1
29		23	NOTTINGHAM FOREST	0-1		1
30		27	Tottenham Hotspur	0-2		4
31		30	Wolverhampton W	1-2	Graham	1
32	Apr	3	LEICESTER CITY	0-2		1
33		12	BOLTON WANDERERS	0-1		1
34		13	Ipswich Town	1-1	Musgrove	1
35		15	Bolton Wanderers	1-0	Dunmore	1
36		20	BLACKBURN ROVERS	1-1	Dunmore	8
37		26	Sheffield United	0-2		2
38	May	2	LIVERPOOL	2-1	Graham, Bishop	8
39		4	Sheffield Wednesday	1-3	Graham	2
40		7	BURNLEY	0-1		1
41		11	West Ham United	0-2		1
42		18	Manchester United	1-3	Dunmore	3

Appeara

FA Cup

3	Feb	11	HULL CITY	1-1	Musgrove	9
R		19	Hull City	2-0*	Musgrove, Gibbs	14
4	Mar	4	DERBY COUNTY	3-0	Dunmore, Elwood, Deeley	12
5		16	LEICESTER CITY	0-1		25

Appeara

League Cup

2	Sep	26	Newcastle United	1-1	Bolland	22
R	Oct	1	NEWCASTLE UNITED	4-2*	Graham 2, Deeley, Bolland	8
3		17	CHESTER	9-2	Graham 3, Waites 3, Dunmore 2, Deeley	7
4	Nov	12	CHARLTON ATHLETIC	3-2	Foster 2, Gregory	9
5	Dec	3	BURY	0-2		6

Appeara

Final League Position: 22nd in Division One

* After extra-time

Charlton	Lewis	Lucas	Bishop	Lea	Deeley	Gibbs	Dunmore	Graham	McDonald	Bolland	Clark	Waites	Taylor	Pinner	Foster	Gregory	George	Musgrove	Elwood	Mason	Wedge	
2	3	4	5	6	7	8	9	10	11													1
2	3	4	5	6	7	8	9	10	11													2
2	3	4	5	6	7	8	9	10	11													3
2	3	4	5	6	7	8	9	10	11													4
2	3	4	5	6	7		9	10	11	8												5
2	3	4	5	6	7		9	10	11	8												6
2	3	4	5	6	7		9	10	11	8												7
2	3	4	5	6	7		9	10	11	8												8
2	3	4	5	6	7		9	10	11	8												9
2	3	4	5	6	7		9	10	11	8												10
2	3	4		6	7		9	10	11	8	5											11
2	3	4		6	7		9	10	11	8	5											12
2	3	4		6	7		9	10	11		5	8										13
2			5	6	11	4	9	10		8		7	3									14
2		4	5	6	7		9		11	8			3	1	10							15
2		4	5	6	7		9		11	8			3	1	10							16
2		4	5	6	7		9		11				3	1	10	8						17
2		4	5	6	7		9		11				3		10	8	1					18
2	3	10	5	6	11	4	7						8			9	1					19
2	3	4	5	6	7		9	10	11					1		8						20
2	3		5	6	7	4	9	10	11				8	1								21
2	3		5	6	7	4		10	11	9				1		8						22
2	3	4	5	6	7	8		10		9				1				11				23
2	3		5	6	7	4	9	10		8				1				11				24
2	3		5	6	7	4	9	10		8							1	11				25
2	3	4	5	6	7		9			8							1	11	10			26
2	3	4	5	6	7	8	9			10							1		11			27
2	3	4	5	6	7		9			10								11		8		28
2	3	4	5	6	7		9			10								11		8		29
2	3	4	5	6	7		9	10						1				11		8		30
2	3	4	5		7	6	9	10						1				11		8		31
2	3	4	5		7	6	9	10						1				11		8		32
2	3	4	5	6			9	10						1		7			11	8		33
2		4	5	6			8			10			3	1				9	11	7		34
2		4	5	6			8	10					3	1				9	11	7		35
2		4	5	6	10		8						3	1				9	11	7		36
2		4	5	6	10		8						3	1				9	11	7		37
2		4	5	6	8			10					3	1				9	11	7		38
2		4	5	6	8			10		7			3	1				9	11			39
2		4	5	6		8	9			10			3				1	11	7			40
2		4	5	6		8				10			3	1				9	11	7		41
2		4	5	6		8	9			10			3				1	11		7		42
2	28	37	39	40	36	17	37	27	20	24	3	2	16	19	4	6	7	18	11	13		
			1		5	1	11	9	2	3						1		3	1			

Charlton	Lewis	Lucas	Bishop	Lea	Deeley	Gibbs	Dunmore	Graham	McDonald	Bolland	Clark	Waites	Taylor	Pinner	Foster	Gregory	George	Musgrove	Elwood	Mason	Wedge	
2	3		5	6	7	4	9	10		8							1	11				3
2	3		5	6	7	4	9	10		8							1	11				R
2	3	4	5	6	7	8	9			10									11			4
2	3	4	5	6	7		9			8								11	10			5
4	4	2	4	4	4	3	4	2		4							2	3	2			
					1	1	1											2	1			

Charlton	Lewis	Lucas	Bishop	Lea	Deeley	Gibbs	Dunmore	Graham	McDonald	Bolland	Clark	Waites	Taylor	Pinner	Foster	Gregory	George	Musgrove	Elwood	Mason	Wedge	
2		4		6	7		9		11	8	5	10	3				1					2
2	3	4		6	7		9	10	11	8	5											R
2			5	6	7	4	9	10				8	3								11	3
2		4	5		7	6	9		11				3		10	8	1					4
2	3		5	6	7	4	9		11				10	1		8						5
5	2	3	3	4	5	3	5	2	4	2	2	2	4	1	1	2	2				1	
					2		2	5		2		3			2	1						

1963-64

Managers: Aug 1963 Johnny Carey; Sep–Nov 1963 Les Gore; Nov 1963–Apr 1964 Benny Fenton

	P	W	D	L	F	A	Pts
Leeds United	42	24	15	3	71	34	63
Sunderland	42	25	11	6	81	37	61
Preston North End	42	23	10	9	79	54	56
Charlton Athletic	42	19	10	13	76	70	48
Southampton	42	19	9	14	100	73	47
Manchester City	42	18	10	14	84	66	46
Rotherham United	42	19	7	16	90	78	45
Newcastle United	42	20	5	17	74	69	45
Portsmouth	42	16	11	15	79	70	43
Middlesbrough	42	15	11	16	67	52	41
Northampton Town	42	16	9	17	58	60	41
Huddersfield Town	42	15	10	17	57	64	40
Derby County	42	14	11	17	56	67	39
Swindon Town	42	14	10	18	57	69	38
Cardiff City	42	14	10	18	56	81	38
Leyton Orient	42	13	10	19	54	72	36
Norwich City	42	11	13	18	64	80	35
Bury	42	13	9	20	57	73	35
Swansea Town	42	12	9	21	63	74	33
Plymouth Argyle	42	8	16	18	45	67	32
Grimsby Town	42	9	14	19	47	75	32
Scunthorpe United	42	10	10	22	52	82	30

Division Two

Match No.	Date		Opponents	Result	Scorers	Atten
1	Aug	24	PRESTON NORTH END	2-2	Bolland, Lucas	12
2		28	Plymouth Argyle	2-2	Bolland, Musgrove	15
3		31	Norwich City	2-1	Bolland, Dunmore	18
4	Sep	3	PLYMOUTH ARGYLE	1-0	Lucas	14
5		7	Swansea Town	0-1		9
6		11	Derby County	0-1		17
7		14	SOUTHAMPTON	1-0	Williams (og)	12
8		18	DERBY COUNTY	3-0	Bolland 2, Ward	11
9		21	Middlesbrough	0-2		23
10		28	NEWCASTLE UNITED	1-0	Deeley	12
11	Oct	1	Scunthorpe United	0-0		6
12		5	Huddersfield Town	1-2	Bolland	10
13		19	Swindon Town	0-5		18
14		26	PORTSMOUTH	3-6	Charlton, Bolland 2	12
15	Nov	2	Bury	2-1	Bolland 2	6
16		9	NORTHAMPTON TOWN	0-0		11
17		16	Sunderland	1-4	Elwood	35
18		23	LEEDS UNITED	0-2		12
19		30	Rotherham United	4-2	Dunmore, Musgrove 2, Ward	6
20	Dec	7	MANCHESTER CITY	0-2		9
21		14	Preston North End	0-0		13
22		21	NORWICH CITY	1-1	Bolland	6
23		26	Grimsby Town	1-1	Deeley	8
24		28	GRIMSBY TOWN	0-0		9
25	Jan	11	SWANSEA TOWN	4-0	Dunmore, Bolland 2, Lucas	12
26		18	Southampton	0-3		14
27	Feb	1	MIDDLESBROUGH	3-2	Bolland, Musgrove 2	8
28		8	Newcastle United	0-3		20
29		22	Cardiff City	1-2	Musgrove	8
30		24	HUDDERSFIELD TOWN	2-3	Balderstone (og), Gregory	7
31	Mar	7	Portsmouth	3-4	Musgrove, Dunmore, Bolland	10
32		14	SCUNTHORPE UNITED	2-2	Bolland, Dunmore	4
33		21	Northampton Town	2-1	Musgrove 2	9
34		26	CHARLTON ATHLETIC	0-3		12
35		28	SWINDON TOWN	2-1	Dunmore (pen), Gregory	7
36		30	Charlton Athletic	2-1	Musgrove, Dunmore	15
37	Apr	4	Leeds United	1-2	Gregory	30
38		6	SUNDERLAND	2-5	Phillips 2	16
39		11	ROTHERHAM UNITED	0-2		7
40		13	CARDIFF CITY	4-0	Musgrove, Dunmore, Phillips 2	7
41		18	Manchester City	0-2		15
42		25	BURY	1-1	Dunmore	6

Appeara

G

FA Cup

No.	Date		Opponents	Result	Scorers	Atten
3	Jan	4	Leicester City	3-2	Musgrove 2, King (og)	21
4		25	WEST HAM UNITED	1-1	Deeley	34
R		29	West Ham United	0-3		35

Appeara

G

League Cup

No.	Date		Opponents	Result	Scorers	Atten
2	Sep	25	West Ham United	1-2	Bolland	11

Appeara

G

Final League Position: 16th in Division Two

Lewis	Lucas	Bishop	Lea	Deeley	Bolland	Dunmore	Ward	Musgrove	Davies	Mason	Gregory	McDonald	Elwood	White	Scott	Hollow	Phillips	
3	4	5	6	7	8	9	10	11										1
3	4	5	6	7	8	9	10	11										2
3	4	5	6	7	8	9	10	11										3
3	4	5	6	7	8	9		11	1	10								4
3	4	5	6	7	8	9	10	11	1									5
3	4	5	6		8		10	9	1		7	11						6
3	4	5	6	7	9		10	11	1	8								7
3	4	5	6	7	9		10	11	1	8								8
3	4	5	6	7	9		10	11	1	8								9
3	4	5	6	7	9		10	11	1				8					10
3	4	5	6	7	9		10	11	1				8					11
3	4	5	6	7	9		10	11	1				8					12
3	4	5	6	7	9		10	8	1	11								13
3	4	5	6		9		10	8	1	11				7				14
3		5	6	8	9		4	11					10	7				15
3		5	6	8	9		4	11					10	7				16
3	8	5	6		9			11					10	7	4			17
3	4	5	6		9		8	11					10	7				18
3	4	5	6	7	10	9	8	11										19
3	4	5	6	7	10	9	8	11										20
3	4	5	6	7	10		8	11			9							21
3	4	5	6	7	10	9		11		8								22
3	4	5	6	7		10		11		8	9							23
3	4	5	6	7	10	9		11		8								24
3	4	5	6	7	10	8		11			9							25
3	4	5	6	7	10	8		11			9							26
3	4	5	6	7	8	10		11			9							27
3	4	5	6		8	9		11		10		7						28
3	4	5	6		8	9		11			10	7						29
3	4	5	6		10	9		11			8	7						30
	4	5	6		10	9		11			8	7				3		31
	4	5	6		10	9		11			8	7				3		32
	4	5	6			9		11			8	7				3	10	33
	4	5	6			9		11			8	7				3	10	34
	4	5	6			8		11			9	7				3	10	35
	4	5	6			8		11			9	7				3	10	36
	4	5	6			8		11			9	7				3	10	37
	4	5	6			8		11			9	7				3	10	38
	4	5	6			8		11			9	7				3	10	39
	4	5	6			9	8	11				7				3	10	40
	4	5	6			9	8	11				7				3	10	41
	4	5	6			9	8	11				7				3	10	42
30	40	42	42	23	31	28	22	42	11	10	17	16	7	5	1	12	10	
	3			2	16	9	2	11			3		1				4	

Two own-goals

Lewis	Lucas	Bishop	Lea	Deeley	Bolland	Dunmore	Ward	Musgrove	Davies	Mason	Gregory	McDonald	Elwood	White	Scott	Hollow	Phillips	
3	4	5	6	7	10	8		11			9							3
3	4	5	6	7	10	8		11			9							4
3	4	5	6	7	10	8		11			9							R
3	3	3	3	3	3	3		3			3							
				1				2										

One own-goal

Lewis	Lucas	Bishop	Lea	Deeley	Bolland	Dunmore	Ward	Musgrove	Davies	Mason	Gregory	McDonald	Elwood	White	Scott	Hollow	Phillips	
3	4	5	6	7	9		10	11	1	8								2
1	1	1	1	1	1		1	1	1	1								
					1													

1964-65

Managers: Aug–Dec 1964 Benny Fenton; Dec 1964 Les Gore; Jan 1965–Apr 1965 Dave Sexton

	P	W	D	L	F	A	Pts
Newcastle United	42	24	9	9	81	45	57
Northampton Town	42	20	16	6	66	50	56
Bolton Wanderers	42	20	10	12	80	58	50
Southampton	42	17	14	11	83	63	48
Ipswich Town	42	15	17	10	74	67	47
Norwich City	42	20	7	15	61	57	47
Crystal Palace	42	16	13	13	55	51	45
Huddersfield Town	42	17	10	15	53	51	44
Derby County	42	16	11	15	84	79	43
Coventry City	42	17	9	16	72	70	43
Manchester City	42	16	9	17	63	62	41
Preston North End	42	14	13	15	76	81	41
Cardiff City	42	13	14	15	64	57	40
Rotherham United	42	14	12	16	70	69	40
Plymouth Argyle	42	16	8	18	63	79	40
Bury	42	14	10	18	60	66	38
Middlesbrough	42	13	9	20	70	76	35
Charlton Athletic	42	13	9	20	64	75	35
Leyton Orient	42	12	11	19	50	72	35
Portsmouth	42	12	10	20	56	77	34
Swindon Town	42	14	5	23	63	81	33
Swansea Town	42	11	10	21	62	84	32

Division Two

Match No.	Date		Opponents	Result	Scorers	Atte
1	Aug	22	PORTSMOUTH	5-2	Phillips 3, Dunmore, Price	1
2		26	Manchester City	0-6		2
3		29	Swindon Town	0-1		1
4		31	MANCHESTER CITY	4-3	Phillips 2, Dunmore 2	1
5	Sep	5	DERBY COUNTY	1-4	Price	
6		8	Bury	1-2	Dunmore (pen)	
7		12	Swansea Town	5-2	McDonald 2, Price , Phillips 2	
8		14	BURY	1-0	Price	1
9		19	ROTHERHAM UNITED	2-1	Phillips 2	
10		26	Norwich City	0-2		2
11		28	BOLTON WANDERERS	3-1	Phillips, Dunmore 2	1
12	Oct	3	CRYSTAL PALACE	0-1		1
13		10	Newcastle United	0-5		2
14		17	NORTHAMPTON TOWN	2-2	Price 2	
15		24	Southampton	2-2	Price 2	1
16		31	HUDDERSFIELD TOWN	1-0	Phillips	
17	Nov	7	Coventry City	1-1	Dunmore	2
18		14	CARDIFF CITY	1-3	McDonald	
19		21	Preston North End	0-3		1
20		28	IPSWICH TOWN	0-0		
21	Dec	5	Plymouth Argyle	1-1	Newman (og)	1
22		12	Portsmouth	1-1	Scott	
23		19	SWINDON TOWN	0-3		
24		26	CHARLTON ATHLETIC	4-2	Phillips 2, Dunmore, Metchick	
25		28	Charlton Athletic	0-2		
26	Jan	2	Derby County	0-1		1
27		16	SWANSEA TOWN	2-3	Gregory 2	
28	Feb	6	NORWICH CITY	2-3	Gregory, Dunmore	
29		13	Crystal Palace	0-1		1
30		20	NEWCASTLE UNITED	2-1	Elwood 2	
31		27	Northampton Town	0-2		1
32	Mar	13	Huddersfield Town	0-0		1
33		27	Cardiff City	2-0	Gregory (pen), Elwood	
34		31	PLYMOUTH ARGYLE	2-0	Elwood 2	
35	Apr	3	PRESTON NORTH END	2-1	Sorrell, Gregory	
36		6	Rotherham United	0-3		
37		10	Ipswich Town	1-1	Gregory	1
38		16	MIDDLESBROUGH	1-1	Metchick	1
39		17	SOUTHAMPTON	0-0		
40		19	Middlesbrough	0-2		1
41		24	Bolton Wanderers	0-0		8
42		28	COVENTRY CITY	1-3	Scott	6

Appeara

G

FA Cup

3	Jan	9	Southampton	1-3	Dunmore	20

Appeara

G

League Cup

2	Sep	23	BARNSLEY	3-0	Phillips 2, Gregory	5
3	Oct	14	Charlton Athletic	1-2	Gregory	5

Appeara

G

Final League Position: 19th in Division Two

Charlton	Hollow	Lucas	Webb	Lea	Price	Gregory	Dunmore	Phillips	McDonald	Bishop	Ward	Sorrell	Elwood	Nelson	Ramage	Dunne	Musgrove	Worrell	Scott	Metchick	Harris	Davies	McGeorge	
2	3	4	5	6	7	8	9	10	11															1
2	3	4	5	6	7	8	9	10	11															2
	3	4	2	6	7	8	9	10	11	5														3
	3	4	2	6	7	8	9	10	11	5														4
	3	4	2	6	7	8	9	10	11	5														5
2	3				7		9	10	11	5	4	6	8											6
2	3				7	8	9	10	11		4	6		5										7
2	3				7	8	9	10	11		4	6		5										8
2			3		7	8	9	10	11		4	6		5										9
2			3		7	8	9	10	11		4	6		5										10
2			3		7	8	9	10	11		4	6		5										11
2			3		7	8	9	10	11		4	6		5										12
2			3		7	8	9	10	11		4	6		5										13
	2		3		7	10	9	8	11		4	6		5	1									14
	2		3		7	8	10	9	11		4	6		5										15
	2		3		7	8	10	9	11		4	6		5										16
	2		3	6	7	8	10	9	11		4			5										17
	2		3	6	7	8		9	11		4			5		10								18
	2		3			8	9	10	7		4	6		5			11							19
	2				7	8	9	10	11		4	6		5				3						20
	2		3		7		9	10	11		4	6		5					8					21
	2		3		7		9	10	11		4	6		5					8					22
	2		3		7		9	10	11		4	6		5					8					23
2			3		7		9	10	11		4	6		5						8				24
2			3		7		9	10			4	6		5			11			8				25
2			3			7	9		11		4	6		5			10			8				26
	2				7	8	9		11		4	6		5				3		10				27
	2				7	8	9					4		5			11	3		10	6			28
	2					7	9	8				4		5	1		11	3		10	6			29
	2					8	9					4	7	5	1		11	3		10	6			30
2						8	9					4	7	5	1		11	3		10	6			31
			2			9						4	7	5				3	10	8	6	1	11	32
			2			9						4	8	5			11	3	10		6	1	7	33
			2			9						4	8	5			11	3	10		6	1	7	34
			2			9						4	8	5			11	3	10		6	1	7	35
			2			9						4	8	5			11	3	10		6	1	7	36
			2			8	9					4		5			11	3	6	10		1	7	37
			2			9						4	8	5			11	3		10	6	1	7	38
			2			8	9					4	7	5			11	3		10	6	1		39
			2			9						4		5			11	3	8	10	6	1	7	40
			2			9						4		5			11	3	8	10	6	1	7	41
			2			9						4	11	5				3	10	8	6	1	7	42
4	22	5	33	7	26	36	32	26	26	4	22	35	11	36	4	1	16	17	12	15	14	11	10	
					8	6	9	13	3			1	5						2	2				

One own-goal

Charlton	Hollow	Lucas	Webb	Lea	Price	Gregory	Dunmore	Phillips	McDonald	Bishop	Ward	Sorrell	Elwood	Nelson	Ramage	Dunne	Musgrove	Worrell	Scott	Metchick	Harris	Davies	McGeorge	
2					7		9		11		4	6		5			10	3		8				3
1					1		1		1		1	1		1			1	1		1				
							1																	

Charlton	Hollow	Lucas	Webb	Lea	Price	Gregory	Dunmore	Phillips	McDonald	Bishop	Ward	Sorrell	Elwood	Nelson	Ramage	Dunne	Musgrove	Worrell	Scott	Metchick	Harris	Davies	McGeorge	
2			3		7	8	9	10	11		4	6		5										2
	2		3	6	7	8	9	10	11		4			5	1									3
1	1		2	1	2	2	2	2	2		2	1		2	1									
						2		2																

1965-66

Manager: Aug–Dec 1965 Dave Sexton; Dec 1965–May 1966 Les Gore

	P	W	D	L	F	A	Pts
Manchester City	42	22	15	5	76	44	59
Southampton	42	22	10	10	85	56	54
Coventry City	42	20	13	9	73	53	53
Huddersfield Town	42	19	13	10	62	36	51
Bristol City	42	17	17	8	63	48	51
Wolverhampton W	42	20	10	12	87	61	50
Rotherham United	42	16	14	12	75	74	46
Derby County	42	16	11	15	71	68	43
Bolton Wanderers	42	16	9	17	62	59	41
Birmingham City	42	16	9	17	70	75	41
Crystal Palace	42	14	13	15	47	52	41
Portsmouth	42	16	8	18	74	78	40
Norwich City	42	12	15	15	52	52	39
Carlisle United	42	17	5	20	60	63	39
Ipswich Town	42	15	9	18	58	66	39
Charlton Athletic	42	12	14	16	61	70	38
Preston North End	42	11	15	16	62	70	37
Plymouth Argyle	42	12	13	17	54	63	37
Bury	42	14	7	21	62	76	35
Cardiff City	42	12	10	20	71	91	34
Middlesbrough	42	10	13	19	58	86	33
Leyton Orient	42	5	13	24	38	80	23

Note: 12 replaced * as the first substitute, 13 replaced + as the second substitute and 14 replaced # as the third substitute.

Division Two

Match No.	Date		Opponents	Result	Scorers	Atten
1	Aug	21	HUDDERSFIELD TOWN	0-2		7
2		24	Rotherham United	1-2	Flatt	[illegible]
3		28	Crystal Palace	1-2	Scott	16
4		30	ROTHERHAM UNITED	1-4	Scott	[illegible]
5	Sep	4	PRESTON NORTH END	2-2	Flatt 2	6
6		8	Birmingham City	2-2	Scott 2	[illegible]
7		11	Charlton Athletic	0-3		11
8		13	BIRMINGHAM CITY	2-1	Flatt 2	7
9		18	PLYMOUTH ARGYLE	0-1		6
10		25	Portsmouth	1-4	Flatt	10
11	Oct	2	BOLTON WANDERERS	1-0	Smith	[illegible]
12		9	WOLVERHAMPTON W	0-3		11
13		16	Norwich City	1-2	Sorrell	13
14		23	BURY	2-2	Webb, Price	6
15		30	Southampton	0-1		15
16	Nov	6	DERBY COUNTY	0-0		5
17		13	Cardiff City	1-3	Allen	9
18		20	CARLISLE UNITED	2-1	Flatt 2	3
19		27	Coventry City	1-1	Gregory	20
20	Dec	4	BRISTOL CITY	0-4		5
21		11	Manchester City	0-5		16
22		27	Middlesbrough	1-2	Allen	21
23	Jan	1	Wolverhampton W	1-2	Metchick	20
24		8	CARDIFF CITY	1-1	Nicholas	5
25		15	Bury	0-3		4
26		29	Huddersfield Town	1-1	Webb	16
27	Feb	5	CRYSTAL PALACE	0-2		7
28		19	Preston North End	2-1	Webb, Metchick	10
29		26	CHARLTON ATHLETIC	1-2	Nicholas	13
30	Mar	12	Plymouth Argyle	1-1	Gregory (pen)	11
31		19	PORTSMOUTH	0-0		6
32		26	Bolton Wanderers	0-2		8
33		28	NORWICH CITY	0-0		4
34	Apr	2	Derby County	3-1	Metchick 2, Le Flem	6
35		8	IPSWICH TOWN	1-4	Le Flem	7
36		11	Ipswich Town	2-3	Metchick 2	13
37		15	Carlisle United	0-1		9
38		18	MIDDLESBROUGH	2-3	Price 2	2
39		23	COVENTRY CITY	1-1	Metchick	5
40		30	Bristol City	0-2		11
41	May	7	MANCHESTER CITY	2-2	Metchick, Smith	6
42		9	SOUTHAMPTON	1-1	Allen	19

Appeara
Sub appeara
G

FA Cup

3	Jan	22	NORWICH CITY	1-3	Price	9

Appeara
G

League Cup

2	Sep	22	COVENTRY CITY	0-3		5

Appeara
G

Final League Position: 22nd in Division Two

	Worrell	Ferry	Nelson	Webb	Metchick	Nicholas	Flatt	Elwood	Thorne	Gregory	Scott	Rouse	Went	McGeorge	Shaw	Price	Sorrell	Allen	Smith	Musgrove	Carter	Jones	O'Brien	Le Flem	Jenkins	
	3	4	5	6	7	8	9	10	11																	1
	3	4	5	6	7		9	11		8	10															2
	3	4	5	6	7		9	11		8	10															3
	3	4	5	6	7		9	11		8	10															4
	3	5		6			9	12	11		7	1	4	8*	10											5
	3	5		6	7		9				11	1	4		10	8										6
	3	5		6	7		9				11	1	4		10	8										7
	3*	5		6	7		9	12			11	1	4		10	8										8
	3	5		6	7		9				11	1	4		10	8										9
	3	5		2	8		9			10		1	4	11			6	7								10
	3	4	5	2	8		9			10		1		11			6		7							11
	3	4	5	2	8		9*			10	12	1				11	6		7							12
	3	4	5	2	8	11				9		1				10	6		7							13
	3	5		2	8					9		1			11	10	4	7	6							14
	3	5		2	8					9		1				10	4	7	6	11						15
	3	5		2	8					9		1				10	4	7	6	11						16
	3	5		2	10					9		1	4				6	7	8	11						17
	3	5		2	8		9			10		1					4	7	6	11						18
	3	5		2			9			10		1	4				6	7	8	11						19
	3	5		2			9	11				1			10		4	6	7	8						20
	3	5		2	8		9				10	1	4				6	7		11						21
2		5		3	10	11	9					1				7	6	8	4							22
2		5		3	10	11	9					1				7	6	8	4							23
2		5		3		11	9					1				7	6	8	4		10					24
2		5		3		11	9			8		1				7	6		4		10					25
2		5		3	10	11	9					1				7	6		8		4					26
2		5		3	10	11	9									7	6		8		4					27
	3	5		2	8		9					1		11		7	6		10		4					28
	3	5		2	8	12	9*					1		11		7	6		10		4					29
	3	5			8		7			9		1					6		4			2	10	11		30
	3	5			10		7			9		1					4		6			2	8	11		31
	3	5			10		9			8		1				7		6	4		12	2		11*		32
	3	5			10		9					1		11		7	4	6	8			2				33
	3	5			10		9					1				7	4	6	8			2		11		34
	3	5			10		9					1				7		6	4			2	8	11		35
	3	5			10							1				7	6	12	9		4	2	8	11*		36
	3	5			11		12					1				7	6	10	9		4*	2	8			37
	3	5			10		9					1				7	6	12	4			2	8	11		38
	3	5			11		9			10		1	12			7	6	4				2	8*			39
	3	5			10*							1	12			7	6	4	9		8	2			11	40
3		5			10					7		1					6	4	9		8	2		11		41
3		5			10					7		1					6	4	9		8	2		11		42
7	34	42	7	29	37	8	32	5	2	20	9	37	9	6	7	26	31	21	30	7	11	13	7	9	1	
						1	1	2			1		2					2			1					
				3	8	2	8			2	4					3	1	3	2					2		

	Worrell	Ferry	Nelson	Webb	Metchick	Nicholas	Flatt	Elwood	Thorne	Gregory	Scott	Rouse	Went	McGeorge	Shaw	Price	Sorrell	Allen	Smith	Musgrove	Carter	Jones	O'Brien	Le Flem	Jenkins	
2		5		3	10	11	9					1				7	6		4		8					3
1		1		1	1	1	1					1				1	1		1		1					
																1										

	Worrell	Ferry	Nelson	Webb	Metchick	Nicholas	Flatt	Elwood	Thorne	Gregory	Scott	Rouse	Went	McGeorge	Shaw	Price	Sorrell	Allen	Smith	Musgrove	Carter	Jones	O'Brien	Le Flem	Jenkins	
	3	5		2	8		9			10		1	4	11			6	7								2
	1	1		1	1		1			1		1	1	1			1	1								

1966-67

Manager: Dick Graham

	P	W	D	L	F	A	Pts
Queen's Park Rangers	46	26	15	5	103	38	67
Middlesbrough	46	23	9	14	87	64	55
Watford	46	20	14	12	61	46	54
Reading	46	22	9	15	76	57	53
Bristol Rovers	46	20	13	13	76	67	53
Shrewsbury Town	46	20	12	14	77	62	52
Torquay United	46	21	9	16	73	54	51
Swindon Town	46	20	10	16	81	59	50
Mansfield Town	46	20	9	17	84	79	49
Oldham Athletic	46	19	10	17	80	63	48
Gillingham	46	15	16	15	58	62	46
Walsall	46	18	10	18	65	72	46
Colchester United	46	17	10	19	76	73	44
Orient	46	13	18	15	58	68	44
Peterborough United	46	14	15	17	66	71	43
Oxford United	46	15	13	18	61	66	43
Grimsby Town	46	17	9	20	61	68	43
Scunthorpe United	46	17	8	21	58	73	42
Brighton & Hove Albion	46	13	15	18	61	71	41
Bournemouth & B A	46	12	17	17	39	57	41
Swansea Town	46	12	15	19	85	89	39
Darlington	46	13	11	22	47	81	37
Doncaster Rovers	46	12	8	26	58	117	32
Workington	46	12	7	27	55	89	31

Division Three

Match No.	Date		Opponents	Result	Scorers	Atten
1	Aug	20	Oldham Athletic	1-3	Metchick	
2		27	SCUNTHORPE UNITED	3-1	Price, Metchick, Whitehouse	5
3	Sep	2	Workington	1-3	Metchick	
4		5	TORQUAY UNITED	0-0		
5		9	GILLINGHAM	0-1		
6		17	PETERBOROUGH UNITED	1-1	Price	5
7		24	Bournemouth & B A	0-1		6
8		28	Torquay United	1-1	J. Smith	6
9	Oct	1	SWANSEA TOWN	1-0	Holton	3
10		8	Brighton & Hove Albion	0-1		13
11		15	DARLINGTON	1-2	Carter	4
12		17	Colchester United	2-2	Carter, Sorrell	8
13		22	Queen's Park Rangers	1-4	Holton	16
14		29	WATFORD	1-1	Price	5
15	Nov	5	Swindon Town	1-5	Jones	8
16		11	READING	3-2	Price, Holton 2	4
17		14	COLCHESTER UNITED	3-3	O'Brien 2, Price	5
18		18	Doncaster Rovers	2-2	Jones, O'Brien	6
19	Dec	3	Grimsby Town	2-1	Holton, Price	3
20		17	OLDHAM ATHLETIC	2-2	Holton (pen), Carter	4
21		26	BRISTOL ROVERS	0-2		6
22		27	Bristol Rovers	0-1		15
23		30	Scunthorpe United	2-2	Holton, Metchick	5
24	Jan	14	Gillingham	0-0		6
25		21	Peterborough United	2-0	Slater, Wood	7
26	Feb	4	BOURNEMOUTH & B A	1-0	Went	5
27		11	Swansea Town	0-2		6
28		18	SHREWSBURY TOWN	2-2	Holton, Jones	5
29		25	BRIGHTON & HOVE ALBION	3-2	Went 2, Holton	5
30	Mar	4	Darlington	0-0		5
31		11	Shrewsbury Town	1-6	Metchick	3
32		18	QUEEN'S PARK RANGERS	0-0		14
33		24	Oxford United	0-0		8
34		25	Watford	3-1	Went, Snedden 2	10
35		27	OXFORD UNITED	2-1	Whitehouse, Holton	7
36	Apr	1	SWINDON TOWN	0-0		7
37		8	Reading	0-1		6
38		10	MIDDLESBROUGH	2-0	Holton 2 (1 pen)	5
39		15	DONCASTER ROVERS	4-1	Holton, Jones 3	6
40		22	Mansfield Town	1-1	Allen	8
41		24	Middlesbrough	1-3	Holton	15
42		29	GRIMSBY TOWN	1-1	Whitehouse	6
43	May	6	Walsall	1-1	Jones	5
44		12	MANSFIELD TOWN	4-2	Holton 3 (1 pen), Price	4
45		19	WALSALL	0-2		3
46		27	WORKINGTON	2-1	Allen, Went	6

Appearar
Sub appearar
G

FA Cup

1	Nov	26	LOWESTOFT TOWN	2-1	Whitehouse, Metchick	6
2	Jan	7	BRENTFORD	0-0		8,
R		10	Brentford	1-3	Metchick	10

Appearar
Sub appearar
G

League Cup

1	Aug	24	Brighton & Hove Albion	0-1		7

Appearar
Sub appearar
G

Final League Position: 14th in Division Three

Jones	Forsyth	Whitehouse	Snedden	Bradbury	Carter	Smith, J	Metchick	Holton	O'Brien	Price	Sorrell	Rouse	LeFlem	Went	Goodgame	Woodward	Allen	Ackerman	Werge	Fry	Street	Wood	Howe	Slater	Parkinson	Smith, K	Goddard	
2	3	4	5	6	7	8	9	10	11																			1
2	3	10	5	4	7	6	8	9		11																		2
2	3	10	5*	4	12	6	8	9		11	7																	3
2	3	5		4		6	7	9	10	8		1	11															4
2	3	10		4	7	6	8	9		11		1		5														5
2		10		4	12		7	9	8	11	6			5	3*													6
2		8		4	7	12		5	9	10*				6	3	11												7
3	5	2				7	8	9	10	11	6			4														8
	3	2		4		7	8*	9	10	11	6			5	12													9
	3	4		5		7	8	9		10	6		11		2													10
2	3	10		4	7			9	8	11				5			6											11
2		4		6	7		11	9			8			5	3		10											12
3		2		4	7		11	9			10			5	6		8											13
11		2			7			9		10	8			4	3		6	5										14
11	3	2			7			9		10		1		4	8		6	5										15
2	3			4			8	9	10	11				5			6		7									16
2		4		6			8	9	10	11				5			3		7									17
2		4		6			8	9	10	11				5			3		7									18
2	3	4		6	7		8	9		10				5					11									19
2	3	4		6	7		8	9		10				5					11									20
2		4		6	7		8	9						5			3		11	10								21
2	3*	10		4	7			9						5			8		11	12	6							22
2		10		6	7		8	9		11				5			3					4						23
2		10					8	9						5			6		7			4	3	11				24
2		10					8	9						5			6		7			4	3	11				25
2		10		7				9						5			6		8			4	3	11				26
2		10		7				9						5			6		8			4	3	11				27
10	2							9						5			6		7	11		4	3	8				28
11				3			8	9						5			6		7			4	2	10				29
		2	4				10	9						5			8		7			6	3	11				30
11		2					10	9						5			6		8			4	3	7				31
2		9	5							11				6			10	7				4	3	8				32
10		7						9		11				5			6		2			4	3	8				33
2			10	12				9		11				5			6		7*			4	3	8				34
2		10			7			9		11				5			6					4	3	8				35
2		10	4	7				9		11				5			6						3	8				36
2		8	10	7				9						5			6					4	3	11				37
10		2						9		11				5			6		7			4	3	8				38
10		2	7*	12				9		11				5			6					4	3	8				39
10			3					9		11				5			6		7			4	2	8	1			40
2		8						9		11				5			6		7			4	3	10				41
8		2	5					9		11				10			6					4	3	7				42
8		10	5					9		11*							6		2			4	3	7				43
8		2	5					9		11							6					4	3	7		10		44
10		2	5											9			6		7			4	3	8		11		45
2		7	5					8		11				9			6					4	3			10	1	46
43	15	41	15	25	15	8	23	44	10	31	8	3	2	39	7	1	34	3	22	2	1	23	23	22	1	3	1	
				2	2	1									1					1								
7		3	2		3	1	5	17	3	7	1			5			2					1		1				

Jones	Forsyth	Whitehouse	Snedden	Bradbury	Carter	Smith, J	Metchick	Holton	O'Brien	Price	Sorrell	Rouse	LeFlem	Went	Goodgame	Woodward	Allen	Ackerman	Werge	Fry	Street	Wood	Howe	Slater	Parkinson	Smith, K	Goddard	
2	3	6		4	12		8	9	10*	11				5					7									1
2	3	10		4	7		8	9		11				5			6											2
2	3	10		4	7		8	9		11				5			6											R
3	3	3		3	2		3	3	1	3				3			2		1									
					1																							
		1					2																					

Jones	Forsyth	Whitehouse	Snedden	Bradbury	Carter	Smith, J	Metchick	Holton	O'Brien	Price	Sorrell	Rouse	LeFlem	Went	Goodgame	Woodward	Allen	Ackerman	Werge	Fry	Street	Wood	Howe	Slater	Parkinson	Smith, K	Goddard	
10	3	2	5	4	7		8	9		11				6														1
1	1	1	1	1	1		1	1		1				1														

1967-68

Managers: Aug 1967–Feb 1968 Dick Graham; Feb–Mar 1968 Peter Angell (acting); Mar–May 1968 Jimmy Bloomfield

	P	W	D	L	F	A	Pts
Oxford United	46	22	13	11	69	47	57
Bury	46	24	8	14	91	66	56
Shrewsbury Town	46	20	15	11	61	49	55
Torquay United	46	21	11	14	60	56	53
Reading	46	21	9	16	70	60	51
Watford	46	21	8	17	74	50	50
Walsall	46	19	12	15	74	61	50
Barrow	46	21	8	17	65	54	50
Peterborough United*	46	20	10	16	79	67	50
Swindon Town	46	16	17	13	74	51	49
Brighton & Hove Albion	46	16	16	14	57	55	48
Gillingham	46	18	12	16	59	63	48
Bournemouth & B A	46	16	15	15	56	51	47
Stockport County	46	19	9	18	70	75	47
Southport	46	17	12	17	65	65	46
Bristol Rovers	46	17	9	20	72	78	43
Oldham Athletic	46	18	7	21	60	65	43
Northampton Town	46	14	13	19	58	72	41
Orient	46	12	17	17	46	62	41
Tranmere Rovers	46	14	12	20	62	74	40
Mansfield Town	46	12	13	21	51	67	37
Grimsby Town	46	14	9	23	52	69	37
Colchester United	46	9	15	22	50	87	33
Scunthorpe United	46	10	12	24	56	87	32

* Peterborough United were deducted 19 points for irregular bonuses and automatically demoted to Division Four.

Division Three

Match No.	Date		Opponents	Result	Scorers	Atten
1	Aug	19	Grimsby Town	0-0		6,
2		26	TORQUAY UNITED	0-2		4,
3	Sep	2	Reading	2-4	Allen 2	9
4		5	Walsall	0-5		7,
5		9	SWINDON TOWN	0-0		4,
6		16	Shrewsbury Town	2-2	Snedden, Jones	4,
7		23	BRIGHTON & HOVE ALBION	1-2	Massey	4,
8		25	WALSALL	2-0	Jones, Whitehouse	3,
9		29	Stockport County	0-2		8,
10	Oct	3	Northampton Town	1-2	Thomas	8,
11		7	Watford	1-1	Whitehouse (pen)	9
12		14	SOUTHPORT	3-0	Massey, Whitehouse, Thomas	3
13		21	Scunthorpe United	1-1	Halom	3,
14		24	NORTHAMPTON TOWN	1-3	Allen	4,
15		28	OLDHAM ATHLETIC	0-2		3,
16	Nov	11	BARROW	4-2	Massey 2, Wood, Mancini	3,
17		13	READING	1-0	D. Allen (og)	4,
18		18	Oxford United	0-2		7
19		25	BURY	1-0	Wood	3,
20	Dec	2	Bournemouth & B A	0-0		5,
21		16	GRIMSBY TOWN	1-0	Simpson	3,
22		26	Peterborough United	2-3	Massey, Mancini	8,
23		30	PETERBOROUGH UNITED	3-0	Simpson, Massey, Mancini	4,
24	Jan	20	SHREWSBURY TOWN	1-1	Massey	5,
25	Feb	3	Brighton & Hove Albion	1-1	Halom	8,
26		10	STOCKPORT COUNTY	2-2	Massey, Slater	6,
27		24	WATFORD	0-1		5,
28	Mar	1	Southport	0-0		4,
29		9	Gillingham	3-2	Arnott 2 (2 og's), Massey	5,
30		12	Swindon Town	0-4		14,
31		16	SCUNTHORPE UNITED	2-1	Halom 2	5,
32		23	Oldham Athletic	2-2	Massey, Simpson	3,
33		25	Tranmere Rovers	0-3		5,
34		30	BRISTOL ROVERS	2-2`	Halom, Massey	4,
35	Apr	1	Torquay United	1-1	Slater	9,
36		6	Barrow	0-1		4,
37		13	OXFORD UNITED	1-0	Halom	6,
38		15	MANSFIELD TOWN	0-0		6,
39		16	Mansfield Town	0-0		6,
40		19	Bury	0-1		10,
41		22	COLCHESTER UNITED	1-1	Halom	6,
42		27	BOURNEMOUTH & B A	1-0	Massey	5,
43		30	Bristol Rovers	2-0	Simpson, Rofe	5,
44	May	4	Colchester United	1-1	Allen	3,
45		7	GILLINGHAM	0-4		4,
46		11	TRANMERE ROVERS	0-1		3,

Appearan
Sub appearan
G

FA Cup

1	Dec	9	Weymouth	2-0	Halom 2	4,
2	Jan	6	Boston United	1-1	Simpson	7,
R		15	BOSTON UNITED	2-1	Mancini, Halom	11,
3		27	BURY	1-0	Massey	11,
4	Feb	4	Birmingham City	0-3		29,

Appearan
Sub appearan
G

League Cup

1	Aug	22	GILLINGHAM	1-3	Holton (pen)	4,

Appearan
Sub appearan
G

Final League Position: 19th in Division Three

Jones	Howe	Wood	Snedden	Allen	Werge	Slater	Holton	Anderson	Price	Fry	Taylor	Still	Goddard	Simpson	Whitehouse	Halom	Massey	Thomas	Eadie	Ackerman	Harper	Mancini	Archell	Bloomfield	Key	Rofe	Bowtell	
*	3	4	5	6	7	8	9	10	11	12																		1
	3	4	5	7	10	8*		12	11	9	2	6																2
	2	5		8	7				12				1	3	4	6	9	10	11*									3
	2	5	12	6			9	8						3	4	7	10		11*									4
	3		5	10	12		9	2	11				1	6	4	8				7*								5
3	3	4*	7	6				2		12			1	11	10	5	9											6
3	4		7	6	12			2					1	11	3	5	9	10*										7
3	2	4			6			9		11			1	3	7	5	10											8
3	2	5			6			9		11			1	3	7	4	10											9
3	2	5	4	6	11					10				3	7		12	9*										10
3	3	4		7						12			1	11	2*	5	9	10			6							11
	2	5		6		8				12			1	3	11	4	9	10			7*							12
	2	5		6	7	8				11			1	3		4	9	10										13
2	2	4	5	6*		11							1	3		7	9	10			8							14
1	2			6	7			8		12			1	3	4	5	9	10*										15
2	3	4	6	10		8							1	7			9					5	11					16
0	3	4	2	6		8							1	7			9					5	11					17
0	3	4	2	7	12	8							1	11		6	9*					5						18
2	3	4		6		8							1	11			9	10			7	5						19
2	3	4		6		8							1	11			9	10			7	5						20
2	3	4		6									1	11		10	9	8			7	5						21
2	3	4		6		8							1	11		10	9				7	5						22
2	3	4		6		8							1	11		10	9				7	5						23
2		4	3	6		8							1	11		10	9				7	5						24
2	3	4		6		8							1	11		10	9				7	5						25
2	3	4		6		8							1	11		10	9				7	5						26
2	3	4		6		8					12		1	11		10	9					5	7*					27
2	3	6		7		8					4		1	11		10	9					5						28
2	3	6		7		8					4		1	11		10	9					5						29
2	3	6		7		8					4		1	11*		10	9					5		12				30
2	3	6				8					4		1	11		10	9					5		7				31
2	3	6				8					4		1	11		10	9					5		7				32
2	3	6*		12		8					4		1	11		10	9					5		7				33
2	3	4				11							1			10	9				6	5		7	8			34
2	3					11					4		1			10	9				6	5		7	8			35
2	3			6		11					4		1			9					8	5		7	10			36
2	3					11					4		1			10	9				6	5		7	8			37
2	3					11					4		1			10	9				6	5		7	8			38
2	3	4		6		11							1			10	9				8	5		7				39
2	3	4		6		11							1			10	9				8	5		7				40
2	3	4		12		11							1			10	9				7*	5		6	8			41
2				6		11					4		1	3		10	9					5		7	8			42
2				6		11					4		1	3		10	9				7	5			8*	12		43
2				6		8					4		1	11		10	9				7	5				3		44
2						8					4			11		10	9				6	5		7		3	1	45
2		6				8					4		1	11		10	9					5		7		3		46
39	40	35	11	34	8	35	3	8	3	5	16	1	41	36	11	39	41	11	2	1	22	31	3	14	8	3	1	
1			1	2	3			1	1	5	1						1							1		1		
2		2	1	4		2								4	3	7	12	2				3				1		

Three own-goals

Jones	Howe	Wood	Snedden	Allen	Werge	Slater	Holton	Anderson	Price	Fry	Taylor	Still	Goddard	Simpson	Whitehouse	Halom	Massey	Thomas	Eadie	Ackerman	Harper	Mancini	Archell	Bloomfield	Key	Rofe	Bowtell	
2	3	4		6		8							1	11		10	9				7	5						1
2	3	4		6		8							1	11		10	9				7	5						2
2	3	4		6		8							1	11		10	9				7	5						R
2	3	4		6		8							1	11		10	9				7	5						3
2	3	4		6	12	8							1	11		10	9				7*	5						4
5	5	5		5		5							5	5		5	5				5	5						
					1																							
														1		3	1					1						

Jones	Howe	Wood	Snedden	Allen	Werge	Slater	Holton	Anderson	Price	Fry	Taylor	Still	Goddard	Simpson	Whitehouse	Halom	Massey	Thomas	Eadie	Ackerman	Harper	Mancini	Archell	Bloomfield	Key	Rofe	Bowtell	
	3	4	5	6	2	8	9	10	11	7																		1
	1	1	1	1	1	1	1	1	1	1																		
							1																					

1968-69

Manager: Jimmy Bloomfield

	P	W	D	L	F	A	Pts
Watford	46	27	10	9	74	34	64
Swindon Town	46	27	10	9	71	35	64
Luton Town	46	25	11	10	74	38	61
Bournemouth & B A	46	21	9	16	60	45	51
Plymouth Argyle	46	17	15	14	53	49	49
Torquay United	46	18	12	16	54	46	48
Tranmere Rovers	46	19	10	17	70	68	48
Southport	46	17	13	16	71	64	47
Stockport County	46	16	14	16	67	68	46
Barnsley	46	16	14	16	58	63	46
Rotherham United	46	16	13	17	56	50	45
Brighton & Hove Albion	46	16	13	17	72	65	45
Walsall	46	14	16	16	50	49	44
Reading	46	15	13	18	67	66	43
Mansfield Town	46	16	11	19	58	62	43
Bristol Rovers	46	16	11	19	63	71	43
Shrewsbury Town	46	16	11	19	51	67	43
Orient	46	14	14	18	51	58	42
Barrow	46	17	8	21	56	75	42
Gillingham	46	13	15	18	54	63	41
Northampton Town	46	14	12	20	54	61	40
Hartlepool United	46	10	19	17	40	70	39
Crewe Alexandra	46	13	9	24	52	76	35
Oldham Athletic	46	13	9	24	50	83	35

Division Three

Match No.	Date		Opponents	Result	Scorers	Atten
1	Aug	10	ROTHERHAM UNITED	3-3	Halom, Jones, Brabrook	7
2		17	Gillingham	2-2	Brabrook, Bloomfield	5
3		24	MANSFIELD TOWN	1-0	Halom	7
4		30	Southport	2-2	Halom, Taylor	4
5	Sep	7	LUTON TOWN	0-0		13
6		9	TRANMERE ROVERS	0-0		8
7		14	Barnsley	2-2	Allen, Halom	9
8		21	OLDHAM ATHLETIC	3-0	Halom, Slater, Allen	6
9		28	Barrow	1-3	Taylor	5
10	Oct	5	Swindon Town	0-1		12
11		7	Tranmere Rovers	0-3		6
12		18	Stockport County	2-5	Jones, Mancini	7
13		21	BRIGHTON & HOVE ALBION	3-2	Bloomfield, Mancini 2 (1 pen)	5
14		26	HARTLEPOOL UNITED	0-1		6
15	Nov	2	Shrewsbury Town	0-1		3
16		6	Reading	1-0	Massey	5
17		9	WATFORD	1-1	Cross	6
18		23	BRISTOL ROVERS	2-1	Mancini, Bloomfield	3
19		30	Plymouth Argyle	1-2	Bullock	7
20	Dec	9	NORTHAMPTON TOWN	0-0		3
21		14	Northampton Town	1-4	Cross	5
22		26	SWINDON TOWN	1-0	Allen	7
23	Jan	4	Crewe Alexandra	0-2		4
24		18	Watford	0-0		13
25		25	READING	4-2	Dyson 2, Bullock, Jones	4
26	Feb	1	WALSALL	0-0		5
27		15	PLYMOUTH ARGYLE	1-2	Dyson	4
28		24	Bristol Rovers	1-0	Dyson	10
29	Mar	1	Rotherham United	1-3	Rofe	6
30		3	CREWE ALEXANDRA	2-0	Bullock, Dyson	3,
31		8	GILLINGHAM	1-1	Parmenter	4
32		11	Walsall	1-2	Dyson	5,
33		15	Mansfield Town	2-0	Mancini (pen), Dyson	5,
34		17	BOURNEMOUTH & B A	1-0	Mancini	4,
35		22	SOUTHPORT	0-2		4,
36		26	STOCKPORT COUNTY	2-0	Bullock 2	3,
37		29	Luton Town	1-2	Rofe	13,
38	Apr	4	Brighton & Hove Albion	0-2		16,
39		5	BARROW	1-2	Harper	5,
40		9	TORQUAY UNITED	0-1		4,
41		12	Oldham Athletic	1-3	Harper	3,
42		16	Torquay United	0-0		5,
43		19	BARNSLEY	1-1	Dyson	3,
44		21	Hartlepool United	0-0		4,
45		25	Bournemouth & B A	1-0	Dyson	4,
46		28	SHREWSWBURY TOWN	4-0	Bullock, Dyson, Mancini, Harper	6,

Appearan
Sub appearan
G

FA Cup

1	Nov	16	GILLINGHAM	1-1	Bloomfield	4,
R		20	Gillingham	1-2	Slater	9,

Appearan
Sub appearan
G

League Cup

1	Aug	14	Gillingham	2-2	Halom 2	5,
R		20	GILLINGHAM	3-0	Halom 2, Bailey (og)	7,
2	Sep	3	FULHAM	1-0	Massey	12,
3		24	CRYSTAL PALACE	0-1		13,

Appearan
Sub appearan
G

Final League Position: 18th in Division Three

Jones	Howe	Harper	Mancini	Taylor	Slater	Massey	Bloomfield	Halom	Brabrook	Goddard	Allen	Key	Rofe	Archell	Bullock	Cross	Dyson	Parmenter	
2	3	4	5	6	7	8	9	10	11										1
2	3	4	5	6	7	8	9	10	11	1									2
2	3	4	5	6	7	8		10	11	1	9								3
2	3	4	5	6	7	8		10	11*	1	9	12							4
2	3	4	5	6	7	8*	12	10	11	1	9								5
2	3	4	5	6	7		8	10		1	9	11							6
2	3	4	5	6	7		8	10	11	1	9								7
2	3	12	5	6	7	8	9	10	11*	1	4								8
2	3		5	6	7	8	9	10		1	4		11						9
2	3		5	6	7	8	9	10		1	4		11						10
2	3*	8	5	6	7		9	10		1	4		11	12					11
2	3		5	6	7	8	9	10		1	4		11*	12					12
2			5	6	7	8	9	10		1	4		3	11					13
2			5	6	7		8	10			4		3		9	11			14
2		8	5	6	7	10*	11			1	4		3		9	12			15
2		8	5	6	7	10	11			1	4		3		9				16
2		8	5	6	7	10*	11			1	4		3		9	12			17
2		8	5	6	7		11			1	4		3		9	10			18
2		8	5	6	7		11			1	4		3		9	10			19
12	2	8	5	6	7	10	11			1	4*		3		9				20
2	3	4	5	6	7	12				1			3*	11	9	10			21
2		8	5	6	7		11			1	4		3		9		10		22
2		8	5	6	7		11			1	4		3		9		10		23
2		8	5	6	7		11			1	4		3		9		10		24
2		8*	5	6	7	12	11			1	4		3		9		10		25
2		8	5	6	7		11			1	4		3		9		10		26
2		8	5	6	7					1	4		3		9		10	11	27
	2	8	5	6	7					1	4		3		9		10	11	28
	2	8	5	6	7	12				1	4		3		9*		10	11	29
	2	8	5	6	7					1	4		3		9		10	11	30
	2	8	5	6	7					1	4		3		9		10	11	31
	2	8	5	6	7					1	4		3		9		10	11	32
	2	8	5	6	7					1	4		3		9		10	11	33
	2	8	5	6	7					1	4		3		9		10	11	34
12	2*	8	5	6	7					1	4		3		9		10	11	35
	2	8	5		7	11	6			1	4		3		9		10		36
	2	8	5	6	7*	12				1	4		3		9		10	11	37
	2	8	5	6	7					1	4		3		9		10	11	38
12	2*	8	5			7	6			1	4		3		9		10	11	39
	2	8	5	6	7					1	4		3		9		10	11	40
	2	8	5	6	7	11				1	4		3		9		10		41
2		8	5		7		6			1	4		3		9		10	11	42
2		8	5	12	7		6			1	4		3		9		10	11*	43
2		8	5		7		6			1	4		3		9		10	11	44
2		8	5		7		6			1	4		3		9		10	11	45
2		8	5		7		6			1	4		3		9		10	11	46
31	28	40	46	39	45	17	29	14	7	44	43	1	38	2	33	4	25	18	
3		1		1		4	1					1		2		2			
3		3	7	2	1	1	3	5	2		3		2		6	2	10	1	

Jones	Howe	Harper	Mancini	Taylor	Slater	Massey	Bloomfield	Halom	Brabrook	Goddard	Allen	Key	Rofe	Archell	Bullock	Cross	Dyson	Parmenter	
2		8	5	6	7		10			1	4		3	11	9				1
2			5	6	7	8	10			1	4		3	11	9				R
2		1	2	2	2	1	2			2	2		2	2	2				
					1		1												

Jones	Howe	Harper	Mancini	Taylor	Slater	Massey	Bloomfield	Halom	Brabrook	Goddard	Allen	Key	Rofe	Archell	Bullock	Cross	Dyson	Parmenter	
2	3	4	5	6	7	9	8	10	11	1									1
2	3	8	5	6	7	9*		10	11	1	4	12							R
2	3	8	5	6	7	9		10	11*	1	4	12							2
2	3		5	6	7	9	8	10		1	4		11						3
4	4	3	4	4	4	4	2	4	3	4	3		1						
												2							
						1		4											

One own-goal

1969-70

Manager: Jimmy Bloomfield

	P	W	D	L	F	A	Pts
Orient	46	25	12	9	67	36	62
Luton Town	46	23	14	9	77	43	60
Bristol Rovers	46	20	16	10	80	59	56
Fulham	46	20	15	11	81	55	55
Brighton & Hove Albion	46	23	9	14	57	43	55
Mansfield Town	46	21	11	14	70	49	53
Barnsley	46	19	15	12	68	59	53
Reading	46	21	11	14	87	77	53
Rochdale	46	18	10	18	69	60	46
Bradford City	46	17	12	17	57	50	46
Doncaster Rovers	46	17	12	17	52	54	46
Walsall	46	17	12	17	54	67	46
Torquay United	46	14	17	15	62	59	45
Rotherham United	46	15	14	17	62	54	44
Shrewsbury Town	46	13	18	15	62	63	44
Tranmere Rovers	46	14	16	16	56	72	44
Plymouth Argyle	46	16	11	19	56	64	43
Halifax Town	46	14	15	17	47	63	43
Bury	46	15	11	20	75	80	41
Gillingham	46	13	13	20	52	64	39
Bournemouth & B A	46	12	15	19	48	71	39
Southport	46	14	10	22	48	66	38
Barrow	46	8	14	24	46	81	30
Stockport County	46	6	11	29	27	71	23

Division Three

Match No.	Date		Opponents	Result	Scorers	Attend
1	Aug	9	Rochdale	3-0	Rofe, Dyson, Bullock	7,
2		16	HALIFAX TOWN	1-0	Bullock	6,
3		23	Luton Town	2-3	Jones, Bullock	14,
4		25	Barrow	1-1	Mancini	4,
5		30	MANSFIELD TOWN	1-0	Fairbrother	6,
6	Sep	6	Rotherham United	0-0		6,
7		13	BRIGHTON & HOVE ALBION	1-1	Mancini	8,
8		15	BRADFORD CITY	2-1	Bullock, Fairbrother	7,
9		20	Barnsley	2-1	Fairbrother, Plume	11,
10		27	TORQUAY UNITED	1-1	Allen	9,
11		29	FULHAM	3-1	Mancini, Allen, Fairbrother	18,
12	Oct	4	Tranmere Rovers	1-1	Bullock	4,
13		7	Halifax Town	1-1	Bullock	4,
14		11	READING	0-1		9,
15		18	DONCASTER ROVERS	2-0	Mancini, Bullock	9,
16		25	Gillingham	1-0	Fairbrother	5,
17	Nov	1	BOURNEMOUTH & B A	3-0	Dyson, Bullock 2	9,
18		8	Plymouth Argyle	0-1		7,
19		22	Shrewsbury Town	1-1	Bullock	4,
20		24	WALSALL	2-0	Dyson, Bullock	6,
21	Dec	13	Brighton & Hove Albion	0-0		9,
22		20	ROTHERHAM UNITED	1-1	Brabrook	4,
23		26	LUTON TOWN	1-0	Allen	17,
24		27	Mansfield Town	1-4	Lazarus	7,
25	Jan	2	Fulham	1-1	Lazarus	12,
26		17	Torquay United	1-0	Jones	5,
27		26	BURY	3-0	Fairbrother 2, Bullock	10,
28		31	TRANMERE ROVERS	2-0	Bullock, Rofe	11,
29	Feb	7	Reading	2-3	Bullock 2	17,
30		16	BARNSLEY	4-2	Bullock, Rofe, Lazarus, Dyson	10,
31		28	Bournemouth & B A	2-0	Fairbrother, Parmenter	5,
32	Mar	2	Stockport County	2-0	Fairbrother 2	2,
33		9	BRISTOL ROVERS	0-0		14,
34		14	Bury	1-0	Fairbrother	4,
35		17	Southport	0-1		3,
36		21	STOCKPORT COUNTY	3-0	Coddington (og), Jones, Taylor	10,
37		27	PLYMOUTH ARGYLE	4-1	Dyson, Brabrook, Fairbrother 2	19,8
38		28	Bristol Rovers	0-1		22,
39		30	Doncaster Rovers	1-0	Robertson (og)	5,
40	Apr	4	BARROW	2-0	Lazarus, Taylor	11,
41		7	Walsall	0-2		5,
42		11	ROCHDALE	2-2	Brabrook, Lazarus	13,
43		15	Bradford City	1-0	Bullock	5,
44		20	SOUTHPORT	3-2	Lazarus, Bullock 2	14,
45		25	SHREWSBURY TOWN	1-0	Lazarus	13,
46		27	GILLINGHAM	1-2	Dyson	16,

Appearan
Sub appearan
Go

FA Cup

1	Nov	15	Walsall	0-0		5,
R		17	WALSALL	0-2		10,

Appearan
Sub appearan
Go

League Cup

1	Aug	13	FULHAM	0-0		8,
R		18	Fulham	1-3	Harper	11,4

Appearan
Sub appearan
Go

Final League Position: 1st in Division Three

Jones	Rofe	Taylor	Mancini	Harper	Slater	Bullock	Allen	Dyson	Brabrook	Fairbrother	Plume	Parmenter	Bowtell	Lazarus	
2	3	4	5	6	7	8	9	10	11						1
2	3	4	5	6	7	8	9	10	11						2
2	3	4	5	6	7	8	9	10	11						3
2	3	4	5	6	7	8	9	10	11						4
2	3	4	5	6	7		9	10	11*	8	12				5
2	3	4	5	6	7		9	10	11	8					6
2	3	4	5	6	7		9	10	11	8					7
2	3	4	5	6		7	9	10	11	8					8
2	3	4	5	6		7	9	10		8	12	11*			9
2	3	4	5	6	7		9	10	11	8					10
2	3	4	5	6		7	9	10	11	8					11
2	3	4	5	6*		7	9	10	11	8	12		1		12
2	3*	4	5			8	6	10	7	9	12	11	1		13
2		4	5		7	8	6	10		9	3	11			14
2	3	4	5			8	6	10		9		11		7	15
2	3	4	5			8	6	10		9		11		7	16
2	3	4	5			8	6	10		9		11		7	17
2	3	4	5			8	6	10		9		11		7	18
2	3	4	5			8	6	10	11	9				7	19
2	3	4	5	9		8	6	10	11					7	20
2	3	4	5	6		8	9	10				11		7	21
2	3	4	5	6		8*	9	10	11	12				7	22
2	3	4	5	6*		8	9	10	11	12				7	23
2	3	4	5			8	9	10	11		6			7	24
2	3	4	5			8	6	10	11	9				7	25
2	3	4	5			8	6	10	11	9				7	26
2	3	4	5			8	6	10	11	9				7	27
2	3	4	5*			8	6	10	11	9	12			7	28
2	3	5				8	4	10	11	9	6			7	29
2*	3	5				8	4	10	11	9	6	12		7	30
2	3	5				8	4	10	7	9	6	11			31
2	3	5				8	4	10	7	9	6	11			32
2	3	5				8	4	10	11	9	6			7	33
2	3	5				8	4	10	11	9	6			7	34
2	3	5				8	4	10	11	9	6	12		7*	35
2	3	5		7		8	4	10	11	9	6				36
2	3	4	5			8	6	10	11	9				7	37
2	3	4	5			8	6	10	11	9				7	38
2	3	4	5			8	6	10	11	9				7	39
2	3	4	5			8	6	10		9		11		7	40
2	3	4	5	12		8	6	10		9		11*		7	41
2	3	4*	5	12		8	6	10	11	9				7	42
2	3	4	5	9*		8	6	10	11	12				7	43
2	3	4	5			8	6	10	11	9				7	44
2	3	4	5			8	6	10	11	9				7	45
2	3	4	5	9*		8	6	10	11	12				7	46
46	45	46	38	19	9	42	46	46	37	35	10	12	2	29	
				2						4	5	2			
3	3	2	4			19	3	6	3	13	1	1		7	

Two own-goals

Jones	Rofe	Taylor	Mancini	Harper	Slater	Bullock	Allen	Dyson	Brabrook	Fairbrother	Plume	Parmenter	Bowtell	Lazarus	
2	3	4	5			8	6	10	11	9				7	1
2	3	4	5			8	6	10	11	9				7	R
2	2	2	2			2	2	2	2	2				2	

Jones	Rofe	Taylor	Mancini	Harper	Slater	Bullock	Allen	Dyson	Brabrook	Fairbrother	Plume	Parmenter	Bowtell	Lazarus	
2	3	4	5	6	7	8	9	10	11						1
2	3	4	5	6	7	8	9	10	11						R
2	2	2	2	2	2	2	2	2	2						
				1											

1970-71

Manager: Jimmy Bloomfield

	P	W	D	L	F	A	Pts
Leicester City	42	23	13	6	57	30	59
Sheffield United	42	21	14	7	73	39	56
Cardiff City	42	20	13	9	64	41	53
Carlisle United	42	20	13	9	65	43	53
Hull City	42	19	13	10	54	41	51
Luton Town	42	18	13	11	62	43	49
Middlesbrough	42	17	14	11	60	43	48
Millwall	42	19	9	14	59	42	47
Birmingham City	42	17	12	13	58	48	46
Norwich City	42	15	14	13	54	52	44
Queen's Park Rangers	42	16	11	15	58	53	43
Swindon Town	42	15	12	15	61	51	42
Sunderland	42	15	12	15	52	54	42
Oxford United	42	14	14	14	41	48	42
Sheffield Wednesday	42	12	12	18	51	69	36
Portsmouth	42	10	14	18	46	61	34
Orient	42	9	16	17	29	51	34
Watford	42	10	13	19	38	60	33
Bristol City	42	10	11	21	46	64	31
Charlton Athletic	42	8	14	20	41	65	30
Blackburn Rovers	42	6	15	21	37	69	27
Bolton Wanderers	42	7	10	25	35	74	24

Division Two

Match No.	Date		Opponents	Result	Scorers	Attend
1	Aug	15	SHEFFIELD UNITED	3-1	Harper, Lazarus 2	10,
2		22	Blackburn Rovers	0-0		9,
3		29	CHARLTON ATHLETIC	0-0		14,
4	Sep	2	Portsmouth	1-1	Bullock	15,
5		5	Carlisle United	0-2		8,
6		12	SUNDERLAND	1-0	Parmenter	8,
7		19	Luton Town	0-4		16,
8		26	CARDIFF CITY	0-0		11
9		30	Bolton Wanderers	1-0	Fairbrother	6,
10	Oct	3	Queen's Park Rangers	1-5	Fairbrother	14,
11		10	HULL CITY	0-1		9,
12		17	Sheffield United	1-3	Bullock	20,
13		19	SHEFFIELD WEDNESDAY	1-1	Dyson	10
14		24	MILLWALL	0-0		14,
15		31	Norwich City	2-4	Allen, Payne (og)	11
16	Nov	7	MIDDLESBROUGH	0-0		6,
17		14	Birmingham City	0-1		14,
18		21	WATFORD	1-1	Moss	8,
19		28	Leicester City	0-4		23,
20	Dec	5	BRISTOL CITY	1-1	Riddick	6,
21		12	Swindon Town	1-1	Mancini	13,
22		19	BLACKBURN ROVERS	1-1	Brisley	5
23	Jan	9	BOLTON WANDERERS	3-1	Jones, Bullock, Lazarus	6,
24		16	Sheffield Wednesday	1-2	Lazarus	11,
25	Feb	6	Bristol City	0-0		11,
26		13	SWINDON TOWN	1-0	Riddick	7,
27		20	Watford	0-0		14,
28		26	NORWICH CITY	1-0	Dyson (pen)	8,
29	Mar	6	Millwall	1-0	Allen	7,
30		10	Oxford United	1-0	Dyson	7
31		13	BIRMINGHAM CITY	0-2		11,
32		20	Middlesbrough	1-0	Riddick	17,
33		27	CARLISLE UNITED	1-1	Bullock	7,
34		29	LEICESTER CITY	0-1		12,
35	Apr	3	Charlton Athletic	0-2		8,
36		9	Sunderland	0-1		15,
37		10	OXFORD UNITED	0-0		6
38		12	QUEEN'S PARK RANGERS	0-1		11,
39		17	Hull City	2-5	Bullock, Lazarus	19,
40		24	LUTON TOWN	1-2	Brabrook	6,
41		26	PORTSMOUTH	1-1	Lazarus	3,
42	May	1	Cardiff City	0-1		15,
						Appearan
						Sub appearan
						G

FA Cup

3	Jan	11	Sunderland	3-0	Fairbrother, Dyson, Lazarus	18,
4		23	Nottingham Forest	1-1	Dyson	25,
R	Feb	1	NOTTINGHAM FOREST	0-1		18,
						Appearan
						Sub appearan
						G

League Cup

1	Aug	19	Fulham	0-1		10,
						Appearan
						Sub appearan
						G

Final League Position: 17th in Division Two

Note: FA Cup replay against Nottingham Forest was first played on 25 January when the game was abandoned at half-time (waterlogged pitch) with the score at 0–0 before another 18,000 strong crowd.

Jones	Rofe	Taylor	Mancini	Allen	Harper	Dyson	Bullock	Lazarus	Brabrook	Fairbrother	Parmenter	Brisley	Plume	Riddick	Bennett	Moss	Harris	
2	3	4	5	6	7	8	9	10	11									1
2	3	4	5	6		7	9		8	10	11							2
2	3	4	5	6		7	10	8	11	9								3
2	3	4	5	6		7	9	8	11	10								4
2	3	4	5	6*		7	9	8	11	10		12						5
2	3	4	5	6		7	9	8	11*	10	12							6
2	3	4	5	6		7	9	8		10	11*		12					7
2	3	4	5	6		7	9	10		11			8					8
2	3	4	5	6		7	9	8	11	10								9
2	3	4	5	6		7	10	8	9	11								10
2	3	4	5	6		7	10		9*	11		12	8					11
2	3		5	4		7	9	8	11	10				6				12
2	3		5	6		8	9	10	11					7	4			13
2	3		5	6		8	9	10	11					7	4			14
2	3		5	6		8	9	10		11				7	4			15
2	3		5	6		8	9*	10	11	12				7	4			16
2	3		5	6		8	9	10	11*	12				7	4			17
2	3		5	6		7	9		11	10					4	8		18
2	3		5	6		7	9		11	10					4	8		19
2	3		5	6		7	12	8	11*	9				10	4			20
2	3		5	6		7	9	8	11	10*		12			4			21
2	3		5	6		7*	9	8	11			12		10	4			22
2	3		5	7		8	9	10		11		6			4			23
2	3		5	7		8	9	10		11		6			4			24
2	3		5	7		8	9	10*		11		6		12	4			25
2	3		5	7		8	9			11		6		10	4*	12		26
2*	3		5	7		8	9		11	10		6		12	4			27
2	3		5	7		8	9		10	11*		6		12	4			28
2	3		5	7		8	9	10		11		6			4			29
2	3		5	7		8	9	10		11		6			4			30
2	3		5	7		8	9	10	12	11		6*			4			31
2	3		5	7		8	9	10*		11		6		12	4			32
2	3		5	7		8	9		10	11		6			4			33
2	3		5	7		8	9		10*	11		6		12	4			34
2	3		5	7		8	9	10		11		6			4			35
2	11		5	7		8	9			12	3	6		10*	4			36
2	3		5	7		8	9*	10	11	12		6			4			37
2	3		5	7		8*	9	10		11		6			4			38
2	3		5*	6		7	9	8	11					10	4	12		39
2	3		5	7		8	9	10	11			6*		12	4	12		40
2	3		5	6		8	9	10	12	11				7*	4			41
	3		5	9			10	11			2	8		7	4		6	42
41	42	11	42	42	1	41	41	32	26	31	4	18	2	13	30	2	1	
							1		2	4	1	4	1	6		3		
1			1	2	1	3	5	6	1	2	1	1		3		1		

One own-goal

Jones	Rofe	Taylor	Mancini	Allen	Harper	Dyson	Bullock	Lazarus	Brabrook	Fairbrother	Parmenter	Brisley	Plume	Riddick	Bennett	Moss	Harris	
2	3		5	7		8	9	10		11		6			4			3
2	3		5	7		8	9	10		11		6			4			4
2	3		5	7*		8	9	10	12	11		6			4			R
3	3		3	3		3	3	3		3		3			3			
									1									
						2		1		1								

Jones	Rofe	Taylor	Mancini	Allen	Harper	Dyson	Bullock	Lazarus	Brabrook	Fairbrother	Parmenter	Brisley	Plume	Riddick	Bennett	Moss	Harris	
2	3	4	5	6	7*	8	9	10	11	12								1
1	1	1	1	1	1	1	1	1	1									
										1								

1971-72

Manager: George Petchey

	P	W	D	L	F	A	Pts
Norwich City	42	21	15	6	60	36	57
Birmingham City	42	19	18	5	60	31	56
Millwall	42	19	17	6	64	46	55
Queen's Park Rangers	42	20	14	8	57	28	54
Sunderland	42	17	16	9	67	57	50
Blackpool	42	20	7	15	70	50	47
Burnley	42	20	6	16	70	55	46
Bristol City	42	18	10	14	61	49	46
Middlesbrough	42	19	8	15	50	48	46
Carlisle United	42	17	9	16	61	57	43
Swindon Town	42	15	12	15	47	47	42
Hull City	42	14	10	18	49	53	38
Luton Town	42	10	18	14	43	48	38
Sheffield Wednesday	42	13	12	17	51	58	38
Oxford United	42	12	14	16	43	55	38
Portsmouth	42	12	13	17	59	68	37
Orient	42	14	9	19	50	61	37
Preston North End	42	12	12	18	52	58	36
Cardiff City	42	10	14	18	56	69	34
Fulham	42	12	10	20	45	68	34
Charlton Athletic	42	12	9	21	55	77	33
Watford	42	5	9	28	24	75	19

Division Two

Match No.	Date		Opponents	Result	Scorers	Attend
1	Aug	14	Oxford United	1-1	Bullock	7
2		21	CARDIFF CITY	4-1	Bowyer 3, Mancini	7
3		28	Sunderland	0-2		14
4	Sep	1	Norwich City	0-0		13
5		4	LUTON TOWN	0-0		8
6		11	Portsmouth	2-3	Brisley, Bowyer	10
7		18	CARLISLE UNITED	2-1	Allen, Dyson	7
8		25	Fulham	1-2	Dyson (pen)	9
9		28	Burnley	1-6	Bowyer	12
10	Oct	2	CHARLTON ATHLETIC	3-2	Harris, Allen, Bullock	9
11		9	Blackpool	1-4	Bowyer	14
12		16	OXFORD UNITED	1-1	Dyson (pen)	5
13		18	PRESTON NORTH END	3-2	Bullock 2, Bowyer	7
14		23	Bristol City	3-5	Brisley, Bowyer 2	17
15		30	MILLWALL	2-2	Dyson, Lazarus	13
16	Nov	6	Birmingham City	0-2		27
17		13	HULL CITY	1-0	Bowyer	6
18		20	Middlesbrough	0-1		13
19		27	SHEFFIELD WEDNESDAY	0-3		6
20	Dec	4	Watford	1-0	Harris	9
21		11	SWINDON TOWN	0-1		6
22		18	Luton Town	0-2		9
23		27	QUEEN'S PARK RANGERS	2-0	Dyson, Bullock	19
24	Jan	1	Carlisle United	0-2		11
25		8	SUNDERLAND	5-0	Bullock 2, Walley, Bowyer 2	6
26		22	BURNLEY	1-0	Bullock	9
27		29	Preston North End	1-1	Bullock	19
28	Feb	12	BRISTOL CITY	2-0	Bullock 2	13
29		19	Millwall	1-2	Dyson	18
30	Mar	4	Hull City	1-1	Allen	12
31		11	BLACKPOOL	0-1		11
32		24	PORTSMOUTH	2-1	Hand (og), Allen	9
33		31	Charlton Athletic	2-1	Dyson (pen), Shipperley (og)	12
34	Apr	1	Queen's Park Rangers	0-1		12
35		3	FULHAM	1-0	Bowyer	16
36		8	MIDDLESBROUGH	1-1	Dyson (pen)	7
37		12	Cardiff City	0-1		16
38		17	Sheffield Wednesday	1-3	Dyson	15
39		22	WATFORD	1-0	Bowyer	7
40		24	NORWICH CITY	1-2	Bowyer	15
41		29	Swindon Town	2-2	Walley, Allen	8
42	May	2	BIRMINGHAM CITY	0-1		33
						Appearar
						Sub appearar
						G

FA Cup

3	Jan	15	WREXHAM	3-0	Dyson (pen), Fairbrother, Bowyer	8
4	Feb	5	Leicester City	2-0	Bowyer, Allen	31
5		25	CHELSEA	3-2	Hoadley, Bullock, Fairbrother	30
6	Mar	18	ARSENAL	0-1		31
						Appearar
						Sub appearar
						G

League Cup

1	Aug	17	NOTTS COUNTY	1-1	Lazarus	8
R		25	Notts County	1-3	Bullock	13
						Appearar
						Sub appearar
						G

Final League Position: 17th in Division Two

Jones	Rofe	Allen	Mancini	Harris	Lazarus	Brisley	Bullock	Dyson	Bowyer	Sewell	Fairbrother	Bennett	Hoadley	Riddick	Walley	Bowtell	Arber	Johnson	
2	3	4	5	6	7	8	9	10	11										1
2	3	4*	5	6	7	8	9	10	11	12									2
12	3	4*	5	6	7	8	9	10	11	2									3
2	3		5	6	7	8	9	10	11	4									4
2	3		5	6	7	8	9	10*	11	4	12								5
2	3	4	5	6	7	8	9*	10	11	12									6
	3	4*	5	6	7	8	9	12	11	2		10							7
	3	4	5	6	7	8	9	12	11	2		10*							8
2	3	4	5	6		8	9	7	11			10							9
2	3	4	5	6		8	9	7	11*		12	10							10
2	3	4		6		8	9	7	11			10	5						11
	3	2		6	7	8	9	10	11			4	5						12
	3	2		6	7	8	9	4	11			10	5						13
	3	4		2	7	8	9	10	11			5	6						14
	3	2		6	7*	8	9	10	11		12	4	5						15
	3	2		10	7	8	9	4	11			5	6						16
	3	2*		5	7	8	9	4	11			6	10	12					17
	3	2		5	7	10	9	8	11			4	6						18
	3	2		6	7	8	9	4	11			10	5						19
2	3	10		5	7	8	9		11			6	4						20
	3	2		5	7	8	9		11			6	4		10				21
2	3	8		5			9		11		7	4	6		10				22
	3	2		6			9	8	11		7	4	5		10				23
	3	2		5		12	9	8	11		7*	6	4		10				24
	3	6		5			9	8	11		7	4	2		10				25
	3	6		5			9	8	11		7	4	2		10				26
	3	6		5			9	8	11		7	4	2		10				27
	3	6		5			9	8	11		7	4	2		10	1			28
	3	6		5			9	6	11		7	4	2		10	1			29
	3	6		5			9	8	11		7	4	2		10				30
	3	6		5		12	9	8	11		7*	4	2		10				31
	3	6		5			9	8	11		7	4	2		10				32
	3	6		5			9	8	11		7	4	2		10				33
	3	6		5			9	8	11		7	4	2		10				34
	3	6		5			9	8	11		7	4	2		10				35
	3	6		5			9	8	11		7	4	2		10				36
	3	6		5			9	8	11		7	4	2		10				37
	3*	6		5		12	9	8	11		7	4	2		10				38
		6		5		7	9	8	11			4	3		10		2		39
		6		5	7	8	9		11			4	3		10		2		40
	3	6		5	12	8	9		11			4*	2		10	1		7	41
	3	6*		5	7	8	9	12	11				4		10		2		42
10	40	40	10	42	20	25	42	34	42	5	17	35	32		22	3	3	1	
1					1	3		3		2	3			1					
		5	1	2	1	2	11	9	15						2				

Two own-goals

Jones	Rofe	Allen	Mancini	Harris	Lazarus	Brisley	Bullock	Dyson	Bowyer	Sewell	Fairbrother	Bennett	Hoadley	Riddick	Walley	Bowtell	Arber	Johnson	
	3	6		5			9	8	11		7	4	2		10				3
	3	6		5			9	8	11		7	4	2		10				4
	3	6		5		12	9	8	11*		7	4	2		10				5
	3	6		5			9	8	11		7	4	2		10				6
	4	4		4			4	4	4		4	4	4		4				
						1													
		1					1	1	2		2		1						

Jones	Rofe	Allen	Mancini	Harris	Lazarus	Brisley	Bullock	Dyson	Bowyer	Sewell	Fairbrother	Bennett	Hoadley	Riddick	Walley	Bowtell	Arber	Johnson	
2	3	4	5	6	7	8	9	10	11										1
2	3	4*	5	6	7	8	9	10	11	12									R
2	2	2	2	2	2	2	2	2	2										
										1									
					1		1												

1972-73

Manager: George Petchey

	P	W	D	L	F	A	Pts
Burnley	42	24	14	4	72	35	62
Queen's Park Rangers	42	24	13	5	81	37	61
Aston Villa	42	18	14	10	51	47	50
Middlesbrough	42	17	13	12	46	43	47
Bristol City	42	17	12	13	63	51	46
Sunderland	42	17	12	13	59	49	46
Blackpool	42	18	10	14	56	51	46
Oxford United	42	19	7	16	52	43	45
Fulham	42	16	12	14	58	49	44
Sheffield Wednesday	42	17	10	15	59	55	44
Millwall	42	16	10	16	55	47	42
Luton Town	42	15	11	16	44	53	41
Hull City	42	14	12	16	64	59	40
Nottingham Forest	42	14	12	16	47	52	40
Orient	42	12	12	18	49	53	36
Swindon Town	42	10	16	16	46	60	36
Portsmouth	42	12	11	19	42	59	35
Carlisle United	42	11	12	19	50	52	34
Preston North End	42	11	12	19	37	64	34
Cardiff City	42	11	11	20	43	58	33
Huddersfield Town	42	8	17	17	36	56	33
Brighton & Hove Albion	42	8	13	21	46	83	29

Division Two

Match No.	Date		Opponents	Result	Scorers	Attendar
1	Aug	12	OXFORD UNITED	1-1	Bowyer	7,2
2		19	Sunderland	0-1		12,5
3		26	LUTON TOWN	0-1		6,4
4		28	MIDDLESBROUGH	2-0	Bullock, Allen	5,1
5	Sep	2	Hull City	0-2		7,9
6		9	BRISTOL CITY	0-2		4,4
7		16	Blackpool	1-1	Bullock	10,4
8		18	BURNLEY	1-1	Fairbrother	4,9
9		23	QUEEN'S PARK RANGERS	2-2	Fairbrother, Downing	9,4
10		25	Preston North End	0-0		10,7
11		30	Fulham	1-1	Queen	10,9
12	Oct	7	CARDIFF CITY	0-0		6,2
13		14	Millwall	0-2		10,0
14		21	CARLISLE UNITED	2-1	Queen, Bennett	4,6
15		28	Huddersfield Town	1-1	Downing	6,2
16	Nov	3	PRESTON NORTH END	1-2	Fairbrother	5,6
17		11	Burnley	2-1	Harris, Queen	12,0
18		18	Swindon Town	1-3	Brisley	7,9
19		25	SHEFFIELD WEDNESDAY	3-2	Bowyer, Hoadley, Queen	5,2
20	Dec	2	Nottingham Forest	1-2	Downing	7,9
21		9	BRIGHTON & HOVE ALBION	1-0	Downing	5,3
22		16	Aston Villa	0-1		20,5
23		23	PORTSMOUTH	0-1		4,4
24		26	Queen's Park Rangers	1-3	Brisley	15,0
25	Jan	6	Luton Town	1-1	Brisley	8,3
26		20	HULL CITY	0-0		3,8
27		27	Bristol City	2-2	Allen, Queen	11,7
28	Feb	10	BLACKPOOL	2-0	Brisley, Queen	4,9
29		16	Oxford United	1-2	Fairbrother	7,0
30		24	ASTON VILLA	4-0	Queen, Harris, Fairbrother 2	9,0
31	Mar	3	Cardiff City	1-3	Bullock	8,4
32		10	MILLWALL	3-1	Downing, Brisley, Bowyer	10,5
33		17	Carlisle United	0-1		5,6
34		24	HUDDERSFIELD TOWN	3-1	Fairbrother, Allen, Hoadley	5,4
35		31	Sheffield Wednesday	0-2		10,0
36	Apr	7	NOTTINGHAM FOREST	3-0	Hoadley, Queen, Bullock	6,3
37		14	Brighton & Hove Albion	1-2	Queen	14,7
38		20	Portsmouth	0-1		8,9
39		21	SWINDON TOWN	1-0	Queen	6,3
40		23	FULHAM	3-2	Fairbrother 2, Bowyer	9,9
41		28	Middlesbrough	2-3	Fairbrother 2	7,9
42		30	SUNDERLAND	1-1	Downing	9,1
						Appearanc
						Sub appearanc
						Goa

FA Cup

3	Jan	13	COVENTRY CITY	1-4	Arber (pen)	12,2
						Appearanc
						Sub appearanc
						Goa

League Cup

1	Aug	16	WATFORD	2-0	Downing, Bowyer	5,1
2	Sep	5	Wolverhampton W	1-2	Downing	15,9
						Appearanc
						Sub appearanc
						Goa

Final League Position: 15th in Division Two

Hoadley	Rofe	Bennett	Harris	Brisley	Allen	Dyson	Bullock	Bowyer	Downing	Fairbrother	Arber	Riddick	Walley	Queen	Fulton	Lewis	Wall	Linton	Heppolette	Johnson	
2	3	4	5	6	7	8	9	10	11												1
2	3	4	5		6	7	9	11	8	10											2
3		4	5	6	7	8	9	11	10		2										3
3		4	5	6	7	8	9	11*	10	12	2										4
3		4*	5	6	7	8	9	11	10	12	2										5
3		4	5	6*	7		9	11	10	8	2	12									6
2		4*	5	6	7		9	11	10	8	3		12								7
2			5	6	7	8	9		11	10	3		4								8
2			5	6	7	12	9		11	8*	3		4	10							9
3			5	6	7	8	9		11		2		4	10							10
3			5	12	6		9	11	7	8	2		4*	10							11
2			5		6	12	9	11	7	8	3*		4	10							12
3		4	5	6	7		9*	11	8	12	2			10							13
2		4	5	6	7		9	11	8		3			10							14
2		6	5	7	8				11	9	3		4	10							15
2		6	5	7	8			12	11	9	3		4*	10							16
2		4	5	6	7		9	12	8	11*	3			10							17
5		4		6	7		9	12	11	8*	2			10	3						18
2		4	5	6	7		9	11	8		3*			10		12					19
2		4	5	6	7		9	11	8		3			10							20
2		4*	5	6	7		9	11	8		3			10		12					21
5				6	7		9	11	8		2		4	10			3				22
5				6	7		9	11	8		2			10			3	4			23
4			5	6	7	12		9	11		2			10			3		8*		24
4			5	6	7			9	11		2			10			3		8		25
2			5	6	7	8		9	11					10			3	4			26
2		4	5	6	7			9	11					10			3		8		27
2		4		6	7			9		10				11			3	5	8		28
2		4		6	7			10		9				11			3	5	8		29
2		4	5	6	7			10		9				11			3		8		30
2		4	5	6	7		12	10		9				11			3*		8		31
2		4	5	6	7			8	11	9	3			10							32
2		4	5	6	7*		12	8	11	9				10							33
2		4	5		6		8	7	11	9	3			10					3		34
2		4*	5	6	7		12		11	9	3			10					8		35
2			5	6	7		9		10		3*			11				4	8	12	36
2			5	6	7		9	11*	3					10				4	8	12	37
2			5	6	7		12	11	3	9				10				4	8		38
2			5	6*	7		12	11	3	9				10				4	8*		39
2			5	6	7		12	11	3	9				10				4*	8		40
2			5	6	7		9	11	3	10								4	8		41
2			5	6	7			8	11	9*	3		12	10				4			42
42	2	25	37	38	42	8	25	33	38	24	28		8	33	1		10	11	15		
				1		3	6	3		3		1	2			2				2	
3		1	2	5	3		4	4	6	11				10							

Hoadley	Rofe	Bennett	Harris	Brisley	Allen	Dyson	Bullock	Bowyer	Downing	Fairbrother	Arber	Riddick	Walley	Queen	Fulton	Lewis	Wall	Linton	Heppolette	Johnson	
2			5	6	7			9	11		3			10				4	8		3
1			1	1	1			1	1		1			1				1	1		
											1										

Hoadley	Rofe	Bennett	Harris	Brisley	Allen	Dyson	Bullock	Bowyer	Downing	Fairbrother	Arber	Riddick	Walley	Queen	Fulton	Lewis	Wall	Linton	Heppolette	Johnson	
2	3	4	5	6	7	8	9	11	10												1
2		4	5	6	7		9	11	10	8	3										2
2	1	2	2	2	2	1	2	2	2	1	1										
								1	2												

1973-74

Manager: George Petchey

	P	W	D	L	F	A	Pts
Middlesbrough	42	27	11	4	77	30	65
Luton Town	42	19	12	11	64	51	50
Carlisle United	42	20	9	13	61	48	49
Orient	42	15	18	9	55	42	48
Blackpool	42	17	13	12	57	40	47
Sunderland	42	19	9	14	58	44	47
Nottingham Forest	42	15	15	12	57	43	45
West Bromwich Albion	42	14	16	12	48	45	44
Hull City	42	13	17	12	46	47	43
Notts County	42	15	13	14	55	60	43
Bolton Wanderers	42	15	12	15	44	40	42
Millwall	42	14	14	14	51	51	42
Fulham	42	16	10	16	39	43	42
Aston Villa	42	13	15	14	48	45	41
Portsmouth	42	14	12	16	45	62	40
Bristol City	42	14	10	18	47	54	38
Cardiff City	42	10	16	16	49	62	36
Oxford United	42	10	16	16	35	46	36
Sheffield Wednesday	42	12	11	19	51	63	35
Crystal Palace	42	11	12	19	43	56	34
Preston North End*	42	9	14	19	40	62	31
Swindon Town	42	7	11	24	36	72	25

*Preston North End had one point deducted for fielding an ineligible player

Division Two

Match No.	Date		Opponents	Result	Scorers	Attenda
1	Aug	25	Sunderland	1-1	Queen	28,
2	Sep	1	BRISTOL CITY	0-1		7,
3		8	Fulham	3-0	Bullock 2, Queen	10,
4		11	Bolton Wanderers	1-1	Queen (pen)	16,
5		15	BLACKPOOL	3-2	Bullock, Allen, Queen (pen)	7,
6		17	MIDDLESBROUGH	0-0		9,
7		22	Aston Villa	2-2	Bullock, Heppolette	26,
8		29	SWINDON TOWN	0-0		7,
9	Oct	2	Middlesbrough	2-3	Bullock, Heppolette	22,
10		6	Hull City	1-1	Bullock	7,
11		13	NOTTINGHAM FOREST	2-1	Fairbrother, Heppolette	8,
12		20	LUTON TOWN	2-0	Queen, Fairbrother	11,
13		22	BOLTON WANDERERS	3-0	Queen 2 (1 pen), Fairbrother	11,
14		27	Oxford United	1-1	Bullock	8,
15	Nov	3	PRESTON NORTH END	2-2	Fairbrother, Bullock	12,
16		10	Sheffield Wednesday	2-1	Bullock, Fairbrother	9,
17		17	WEST BROMWICH ALBION	2-0	Fairbrother, Heppolette	11,
18		24	Millwall	1-0	Bullock	13,
19	Dec	1	CARDIFF CITY	1-2	Fairbrother	9,
20		8	Notts County	4-2	Bullock, Queen 2, Fairbrother	11,
21		15	CARLISLE UNITED	0-1		7,
22		22	Swindon Town	2-2	Bullock, Fairbrother	5,
23		26	CRYSTAL PALACE	3-0	Bullock, Fairbrother 2	20,
24		29	FULHAM	1-0	Roffey	14,
25	Jan	1	Bristol City	2-0	Walley, Downing	19,
26		12	Blackpool	1-1	Bullock (pen)	8,
27		19	SUNDERLAND	2-1	Queen, Fairbrother	14,
28	Feb	2	Carlisle United	0-3		9,
29		23	HULL CITY	1-1	Heppolette	9,
30		26	Nottingham Forest	1-2	Heppolette	16,
31	Mar	3	Crystal Palace	0-0		29,
32		10	OXFORD UNITED	1-1	Downing	10,
33		16	Luton Town	1-3	Hoadley	17,
34		23	SHEFFIELD WEDNESDAY	0-1		9,
35		30	Preston North End	1-0	Downing	7,
36	Apr	6	MILLWALL	1-1	Fairbrother	10,
37		12	Portsmouth	0-0		10,
38		13	West Bromwich Albion	0-1		11,
39		15	PORTSMOUTH	2-1	Queen 2	11,
40		20	NOTTS COUNTY	1-1	Fairbrother	11,
41		27	Cardiff City	1-1	Bullock	11,
42	May	3	ASTON VILLA	1-1	Bullock	29,

Appearan
Sub appearan
Go

FA Cup

3	Jan	5	BOURNEMOUTH	2-1	Fairbrother 2	9,
4		27	Portsmouth	0-0		32,
R		29	PORTSMOUTH	1-1*	Fairbrother	14,
2R	Feb	5	Portsmouth **	0-2		19,

Appearan
Sub appearan
Go

League Cup

1	Aug	28	Brentford	2-1	Bowyer, Fairbrother	6,
2	Oct	9	BLACKBURN ROVERS	2-0	Fairbrother, Bullock	7,
3		31	YORK CITY	1-1	Queen	12,
R	Nov	6	York City	1-2*	Bullock	11,

Appearan
Sub appearan
Go

Final League Position: 4th in Division Two

* After extra-time.

** Played at Selhurst Park, London.

	Hoadley	Downing	Walley	Linton	Brisley	Allen	Payne	Bullock	Fairbrother	Queen	Fisher	Heppolette	O'Shaugnessy	Jackson	Roffey	Harris	Boyle	Bennett	Arber	Bowyer	
	2	3	4	5	6	7	8	9	10	11*	12										1
	2*	3	4	5	6	7	8	9	10	11	12										2
	5	3	4		6	7	2	9	10	11		8									3
	5	3	4		6	8	2	9	10	11	7										4
	5	3	4		6	8	2	9	10	11	7										5
	5	3	4		6	7	2	9	10	11		8									6
	5	3	4		6	7	2	9	10	11		8									7
	5	3	4		6	7	2	9	10	11		8									8
	5	3	4	12	6*	7	2	9	10	11		8									9
	5		4	12	6*	7	2	9	10	11	3	8	1								10
	5	3	4			7	2	9	10	11	6	8									11
	5	3	4		6	7	2	9	10	11		8		1							12
	5*	3	4	12	6	7	2	9	10	11		8		1							13
	5	3	4		6	7	2	9	10	11		8		1							14
	5		4	12	6	7	2	9	10	11		8*		1	3						15
	5		4		6*	7	2	9	10	11	12	8		1	3						16
	5	3	4			6	7	9	10	11		8		1	2						17
	5	3	4		6	7		9	10	11		8		1	2						18
	5	12	4		6*	7	2	9	10	11		8		1	3						19
	5	2	4	12	6	7		9	10	11*		8		1	3						20
	2	11	4		6	7		9	10			8			3	5					21
	5	11	4		6	7		9	10			8		1	3		2				22
	5	11	4		6	7		9	10			8			3		2				23
	5	11	4		6	7		9	10			8			3		2				24
	5	11	4		6	7*	12	9	10			8			3		2				25
	5	11	6		7		3	9	10			8				4	2				26
	5	3	4		7		2	9	10	11		8					6				27
	5	12	4		6	7*	2	9	10	11		8		1			3				28
	5		4		7		2	9	10	11		8		1	3		6				29
	5		4		7		2	9	10	11		8		1	3		6				30
	5	11	4			7	2	9	10	12		8*		1	3			6			31
	5	8	4		12	7	2	9*	10	11				1	3			6			32
	5	11	4		7	8	2		9	10				1	3		6				33
	5	11	4		7	8	2	9	10*	12					3		6				34
	5	11	4		7	8	2	9*		10	12				3		6				35
	5	11	4		6	7	2	12	9	10		8			3*						36
	5	3	4		6	7	2	9	10	11		8									37
	5	3	4		7		2	9	10	11		8					6				38
	5	3	4		6	7	2	9	10	11		8									39
	5	3	4		6	7	2	9	10	11		8									40
	5	3	4		6	7	2*	9	10	11		8			12						41
	5	2	4		6	7		9	10	11		8			3						42
5	42	35	42	2	38	37	34	40	41	34	4	34	1	16	20	2	13	2			
		2		5	1		1	1		2	4				1						
	1	3	1			1		16	14	12		6			1						

	Hoadley	Downing	Walley	Linton	Brisley	Allen	Payne	Bullock	Fairbrother	Queen	Fisher	Heppolette	O'Shaugnessy	Jackson	Roffey	Harris	Boyle	Bennett	Arber	Bowyer	
	5	11	6				2	9	10			8				4	7		3		3
	2		4	5	7		3	9	10	11		8					6				4
	2	12	4	5	7*		3	9	10	11		8					6				R
	2	12	4		7		3	9*	10	11		8		1		5	6				2R
3	4	1	4	2	3		4	4	4	3		4		1		2	4		1		
		2																			
									3												

	Hoadley	Downing	Walley	Linton	Brisley	Allen	Payne	Bullock	Fairbrother	Queen	Fisher	Heppolette	O'Shaugnessy	Jackson	Roffey	Harris	Boyle	Bennett	Arber	Bowyer	
	2	3	4		6	8	7	9	10							5				11	1
	5	3*	4			7	2	9	10	11	6	8				12					2
	5	3*	4		6	8	2	9	10	11	7			1		12					3
	5	2*	4	12	6	8	7	9	10	11				1	3						R
2	4	4	4		3	4	4	4	4	3	2	1		2	1	1				1	
				1												2					
								2	2	1										1	

1974-75

Manager: George Petchey

	P	W	D	L	F	A	Pts
Manchester United	42	26	9	7	66	30	61
Aston Villa	42	25	8	9	79	32	58
Norwich City	42	20	13	9	58	37	53
Sunderland	42	19	13	10	65	35	51
Bristol City	42	21	8	13	47	33	50
West Bromwich Albion	42	18	9	15	54	42	45
Blackpool	42	14	17	11	38	33	45
Hull City	42	15	14	13	40	53	44
Fulham	42	13	16	13	44	39	42
Bolton Wanderers	42	15	12	15	45	41	42
Oxford United	42	15	12	15	41	51	42
Orient	42	11	20	11	28	39	42
Southampton	42	15	11	16	53	54	41
Notts County	42	12	16	14	49	59	40
York City	42	14	10	18	51	55	38
Nottingham Forest	42	12	14	16	43	55	38
Portsmouth	42	12	13	17	44	54	37
Oldham Athletic	42	10	15	17	40	48	35
Bristol Rovers	42	12	11	19	42	64	35
Millwall	42	10	12	20	44	56	32
Cardiff City	42	9	14	19	36	62	32
Sheffield Wednesday	42	5	11	26	29	64	21

Division Two

Match No.	Date		Opponents	Result	Scorers	Attend
1	Aug	17	MANCHESTER UNITED	0-2		17,
2		20	Blackpool	0-0		9,
3		24	Bristol City	0-0		10,
4		27	BLACKPOOL	0-0		7,
5		31	PORTSMOUTH	1-1	Bullock	6,
6	Sep	7	Aston Villa	1-3	Downing	16,
7		14	FULHAM	0-0		8,
8		21	Oxford United	2-1	Downing, Walley	6,
9		24	Notts County	1-1	Possee	7,
10		28	SHEFFIELD WEDNESDAY	1-0	Bullock (pen)	7,
11	Oct	5	Bolton Wanderers	0-2		9,
12		12	OLDHAM ATHLETIC	3-1	Possee, Bullock, Walley	6,
13		19	Southampton	2-4	Brisley, Possee	14,
14		26	NORWICH CITY	0-3		8,
15	Nov	1	York City	1-0	Possee	7,
16		9	CARDIFF CITY	1-1	Queen	6,
17		16	Bristol Rovers	0-0		10,
18		23	WEST BROMWICH ALBION	0-2		6,
19		30	NOTTINGHAM FOREST	1-1	Grealish	5,
20	Dec	7	Millwall	1-1	Fairbrother	8,
21		14	Manchester United	0-0		41,
22		21	HULL CITY	0-0		4,
23		26	Fulham	0-0		9,
24		28	SUNDERLAND	1-1	Downing	10,
25	Jan	11	MILLWALL	2-1	Possee, Grealish	9,
26		18	Nottingham Forest	2-2	Possee, Chapman (og)	17,
27	Feb	1	Cardiff City	0-0		8,
28		8	YORK CITY	1-0	Heppolette	6,
29		15	West Bromwich Albion	0-1		9,3
30		22	BRISTOL ROVERS	1-0	Hoadley	6,5
31		28	Portsmouth	0-3		11,6
32	Mar	8	NOTTS COUNTY	0-1		4,3
33		15	Sheffield Wednesday	1-0	Queen	8,4
34		22	ASTON VILLA	1-0	Heppolette	9,4
35		28	Sunderland	0-3		30,9
36		29	Hull City	0-0		5,2
37		31	OXFORD UNITED	1-1	Queen	6,5
38	Apr	5	Norwich City	0-2		18,1
39		12	BOLTON WANDERERS	0-0		5,4
40		15	BRISTOL CITY	1-0	Possee	6,4
41		19	Oldham Athletic	0-0		9,6
42		26	SOUTHAMPTON	2-1	Queen, Cunningham	7,5

Appearanc
Sub appearanc
Goa

FA Cup

3	Jan	4	DERBY COUNTY	2-2	Possee, Queen	12,4
R		8	Derby County	1-2	Fairbrother	26,5

Appearanc
Sub appearanc
Goa

League Cup

2	Sep	10	Queen's Park Rangers	1-1	Hoadley	14,3
R		17	QUEEN'S PARK RANGERS	0-3		11,7

Appearanc
Sub appearanc
Goa

Final League Position: 12th in Division Two

Fisher	Roffey	Hoadley	Harris	Walley	Fairbrother	Heppolette	Bullock	Queen	Possee	Downing	Brisley	Bennett	Allen	Grealish	Cunningham	Boyle	Linton	Payne	Mooney	Roeder	Gray	
2	3	4	5	6	7	8	9	10	11													1
2	3	5	4	6	7	8	9	10	11													2
2	3	4	5	6*	7	8	9	10	11	12												3
2	3	4	5	6	7	8	9	10*	11	12												4
2	3	4	5	6	7		9	10	11		8											5
2	3	4	5	6	7		9	10*		11	8	12										6
2		4	5	6	7*		9		11	3	8	10	12									7
2		4	5	6	7		9		11	3	8		10									8
2		4	5	6	7		9		11	3	8		10									9
2		4	5	6	7*		9		11	3	8		10	12								10
2		4	5	6	7		9	12	11*	3	8		10									11
2		4	5	6			9		11	3	8		10		7							12
2		4	5	6			9		11	3	8		10		7							13
2		5		10			9		11	3	8		4		7	6						14
2		5		6			9	7	11	3	5		4			10						15
2			5	6	12		9	11*	7	3	10		4			8						16
2		5		6	12		9	11	7*	3	8		4			10						17
2		5		6	12		9	11	7	3	8		4			10*						18
2		5		6	7			9	11	3		10	4	8								19
2		5		6	7			9		3		8	4	10	11							20
2		5		6	7			9	11	3		8	4	10								21
2		5		6	7			9	11	3		10	4	8								22
2		5		6	7			9	11	3		8	4	10								23
2		5			7			9	11	3		8	4	10			6					24
2		5		6	7	8*		9	11	3			4	10	12							25
2		5		6	7*	8		9	11	3			4	10	12							26
2		5		6	7	8		9	11	3			4	10								27
2		5		6	7	10		9	11	3			4	8								28
2		5		6	7	10		9	11*	3			4	8				12				29
2		5		6	7*	10		9	11				4	8				3	12			30
2		5		6		10		9	11*				4	8	7			3	12			31
2		5		6		10		9	7				4	3					11	8		32
3		5		6		11	9	10				8*	4	2	7					12		33
2		5		6		11	9	10				8	4	3	7							34
3		5		6		11	9	10*	12			8	4	2	7							35
3		5		6		11	9	10				8	4	2	7							36
3		5		6		11	9	10				8	4	2	7							37
3		5		6		11	9		10	2			4*	8	7					12		38
2				6		10	9	12	11	3				4	7					8*	5	39
2				6		11	9	10	8			4		3	7					12	5*	40
3				6		11	9	10	8			4		2	7					5		41
2		5		6		10	9	8		11		4		3	7							42
42	6	38	14	41	23	22	28	32	34	27	14	15	31	24	15	5	1	2	1	3	2	
					3			2	1	2		1	1	1	2			1	2	3		
		1		2	1	2	3	4	7	3	1			2	1							

One own-goal

Fisher	Roffey	Hoadley	Harris	Walley	Fairbrother	Heppolette	Bullock	Queen	Possee	Downing	Brisley	Bennett	Allen	Grealish	Cunningham	
2		5		6	7			9	11	3		8	4	10		3
2		5		6	7			9	11	3		8*	4	10	12	R
2		2		2	2			2	2	2		2	2	2		
															1	
					1			1	1							

Fisher	Roffey	Hoadley	Harris	Walley	Fairbrother	Heppolette	Bullock	Queen	Possee	Downing	Brisley	Bennett	Allen	
2		4	5	6	7		9		11	3	8	10		2
2		4	5	6	7		9		11	3	8		10	R
2		2	2	2	2		2		2	2	2	1	1	
		1												

1975-76

Manager: George Petchey

	P	W	D	L	F	A	Pts
Sunderland	42	24	8	10	67	36	56
Bristol City	42	19	15	8	59	35	53
West Bromwich Albion	42	20	13	9	50	33	53
Bolton Wanderers	42	20	12	10	64	38	52
Notts County	42	19	11	12	60	41	49
Southampton	42	21	7	14	66	50	49
Luton Town	42	19	10	13	61	51	48
Nottingham Forest	42	17	12	13	55	40	46
Charlton Athletic	42	15	12	15	61	72	42
Blackpool	42	14	14	14	40	49	42
Chelsea	42	12	16	14	53	54	40
Fulham	42	13	14	15	45	47	40
Orient	42	13	14	15	37	39	40
Hull City	42	14	11	17	45	49	39
Blackburn Rovers	42	12	14	16	45	50	38
Plymouth Argyle	42	13	12	17	48	54	38
Oldham Athletic	42	13	12	17	57	68	38
Bristol Rovers	42	11	16	15	38	50	38
Carlisle United	42	12	13	17	45	59	37
Oxford United	42	11	11	20	39	59	33
York City	42	10	8	24	39	71	28
Portsmouth	42	9	7	26	32	61	25

Division Two

Match No.	Date		Opponents	Result	Scorers	Atten
1	Aug	16	BLACKBURN ROVERS	1-1	Waddington (og)	
2		19	NOTTS COUNTY	1-1	Bullock	
3		23	Blackpool	0-1		6
4		29	PORTSMOUTH	0-1		5
5	Sep	6	Hull City	0-1		5
6		13	PLYMOUTH ARGYLE	1-0	Grealish	5
7		20	Bolton Wanderers	1-1	Roeder	10
8		23	YORK CITY	1-0	Bennett	4
9		26	BRISTOL ROVERS	0-0		4
10	Oct	4	Oxford United	1-2	Bennett	4
11		11	Sunderland	1-3	Queen	28
12		18	CARLISLE UNITED	1-0	Heppolette	4
13		25	Fulham	1-1	Cunningham	10
14	Nov	1	OLDHAM ATHLETIC	2-0	Roeder, Holt (og)	4
15		7	Bristol City	0-0		14
16		15	SOUTHAMPTON	2-1	Queen, Rodrigues (og)	6
17		22	Carlisle United	2-1	Mooney, Cunningham	6
18		29	Luton Town	0-1		7
19	Dec	6	NOTTINGHAM FOREST	1-1	Cunningham	5
20		12	BLACKPOOL	0-1		4
21		20	Blackburn Rovers	1-1	Hoadley	7
22		26	CHELSEA	3-1	Possee, Bennett, Cunningham	15
23		27	West Bromwich Albion	1-1	Possee	20
24	Jan	10	Plymouth Argyle	0-3		11
25		17	HULL CITY	1-0	Cunningham	3
26	Feb	14	BRISTOL CITY	0-1		5
27		21	Southampton	0-3		17
28		24	York City	2-0	Scott (og), Queen	2
29		28	FULHAM	2-0	Cunningham, Queen	7
30	Mar	2	CHARLTON ATHLETIC	0-1		9
31		6	Oldham Athletic	1-1	Walley	6
32		13	SUNDERLAND	0-2		7
33		20	LUTON TOWN	3-0	Bennett 2, Heppolette	5
34		23	Charlton Athletic	1-1	Queen	10
35		27	Nottingham Forest	0-1		11
36	Apr	3	Bristol Rovers	1-1	Mooney	5
37		10	BOLTON WANDERERS	0-0		6
38		13	Portsmouth	1-2	Queen	5
39		17	Chelsea	2-0	Possee, Cunningham	17
40		20	WEST BROMWICH ALBION	0-0		10
41		24	OXFORD UNITED	2-1	Cunningham, Mooney	5
42		27	Notts County	0-2		8,

Appearar
Sub appearan
G

FA Cup

3	Jan	3	CARDIFF CITY	0-1		8,

Appearan
Sub appearan
G

League Cup

2	Sep	9	Birmingham City	0-4		18,

Appearan
Sub appearan
G

Final League Position: 13th in Division Two

Fisher	Grealish	Allen	Hoadley	Walley	Cunningham	Bennett	Bullock	Heppolette	Allder	Roffey	Roeder	Queen	Mooney	Cotton	Possee	Beason	Gray	Payne	Everett	Hibbs	
2	3	4	5	6	7	8	9	10	11												1
2	4		5	6	7	8	9	10	11	3											2
2	4		5	6	7	8*	9	10	11	3	12										3
2	3		5	6	7	8	9	10	11			4									4
2	8		5	6	7	4	9	10	11*	3	12										5
2	8		5	6		4			11	3	7	9*	10	12							6
2	8		5	6		4	12		11*	3	7	9	10								7
2	8		5	6	11	4	12			3*	7	10	9								8
2	8*		5	6		4	9		11	3	7	10			12						9
2	8		5	6	12	4	9		11*	3	7	10									10
2	3		5	6	11	4	9	8			7	10									11
2	3		5	6	11	4	9*	8			7	10	12								12
2	3		5	6	11	4		10			7	9	8								13
2	3		5	6	11	4*		10			7	9	8			12					14
2	3		5	6	7	4		11			8	10	9								15
2	3		5	6	11	4		10			7	9	8								16
2	3		5	6	11	4		10			7	9	8								17
2	3		5	6	7	4		11	12		8	9	10*								18
2	3		5	6	7	4		11			8	10*	12		9						19
2	3		5	6	7	4*	9	11	12		8				10						20
2	3		5	6	7	4	9			12	8	10			11*						21
2	3		5	6	7	4	9				8	11			10						22
2	3		5	6	7	4	9	11			8				10						23
2				6	7	4	9	11			8	10					5	3			24
			5	6	7	4	9	10		3		8			11			2			25
2*	4		5	6	7		9	10	12			8			11			3			26
2	8		5	6	7	9		10				4*	12		11			3			27
2	8		5	6	7	4		10				9			11			3			28
	8*		5	6	7			11	4	2		9			10			3	12		29
12		4	5	6	7*			11	8	2		9			10			3			30
	8	4	5	6				11	7	3		9			10			2			31
	8*	4	5	6				10	11	3		9	7	12				2			32
	5	7	4	3	9*	10		6	8			11		12				2			33
2		4	5	6		8		11	10*		12	9			7			3			34
2	8*	3		6	11	9		10			5		12		7			4			35
2	8		5	6	11	4		10					9		7			3			36
3	8		5	6		4		11				10	9		7			2			37
2	8		5	6		4		10	12			11	9*		7			3			38
2	8		5	6	7	12		10	4*			9			11			3			39
2	8		5	6	7			10	4			9			11			3			40
3	8		5	6	7			10*	4		12		9		11			2			41
3	8		5	6	7				4		12		9*		11			2		10	42
36	38	7	40	42	33	33	16	34	19	13	20	32	15		21		1	19		1	
1					1	1	2		4	1	5		4	3	1	1			1		
	1		1	1	8	5	1	2			2	6	3		3						

Four own-goals

Fisher	Grealish	Allen	Hoadley	Walley	Cunningham	Bennett	Bullock	Heppolette	Allder	Roffey	Roeder	Queen	Mooney	Cotton	Possee	Beason	Gray	Payne	Everett	Hibbs	
2	3		5	6	7		9	11	4		8	10									3
1	1		1	1	1		1	1	1		1	1									

Fisher	Grealish	Allen	Hoadley	Walley	Cunningham	Bennett	Bullock	Heppolette	Allder	Roffey	Roeder	Queen	Mooney	Cotton	Possee	Beason	Gray	Payne	Everett	Hibbs	
2	8		5	6	11*	4	9		12	3	7			10							2
1	1		1	1	1	1	1			1	1			1							
									1												

1976-77

Manager: George Petchey

	P	W	D	L	F	A	Pts
Wolverhampton W	42	22	13	7	84	45	57
Chelsea	42	21	13	8	73	53	55
Nottingham Forest	42	21	10	11	77	43	52
Bolton Wanderers	42	20	11	11	75	54	51
Blackpool	42	17	17	8	58	42	51
Luton Town	42	21	6	15	67	48	48
Charlton Athletic	42	16	16	10	71	58	48
Notts County	42	19	10	13	65	60	48
Southampton	42	17	10	15	72	67	44
Millwall	42	15	13	14	57	53	43
Sheffield United	42	14	12	16	54	63	40
Blackburn Rovers	42	15	9	18	42	54	39
Oldham Athletic	42	14	10	18	52	64	38
Hull City	42	10	17	15	45	53	37
Bristol Rovers	42	12	13	17	53	68	37
Burnley	42	11	14	17	46	64	36
Fulham	42	11	13	18	54	61	35
Cardiff City	42	12	10	20	56	67	34
Orient	42	9	16	17	37	55	34
Carlisle United	42	11	12	19	49	75	34
Plymouth Argyle	42	8	16	18	46	65	32
Hereford United	42	8	15	19	57	78	31

Division Two

Match No.	Date		Opponents	Result	Scorers	Attend.
1	Aug	21	CHELSEA	0-1		11,
2		24	Bolton Wanderers	0-2		11,
3		28	Blackpool	0-3		7,
4	Sep	4	PLYMOUTH ARGYLE	2-2	Hoadley 2	4,
5		11	Bristol Rovers	0-1		5,
6		18	CARDIFF CITY	3-0	Cunningham 2, Whittle	5,
7		25	Oldham Athletic	0-0		7,
8	Oct	2	BLACKBURN ROVERS	0-1		5,
9		9	Burnley	3-3	Hoadley, Clarke 2	9,
10		16	Notts County	1-0	Roffey	8,
11	Nov	6	Southampton	2-2	Cunningham, Queen	16,
12		13	NOTTINGHAM FOREST	0-1		5,
13		20	Sheffield United	1-1	Allen	14,
14		27	WOLVERHAMPTON W	2-4	Queen (pen), Cunningham	6,
15	Dec	4	Carlisle United	0-1		5,
16		11	FULHAM	0-0		11,
17		18	Hereford United	3-2	Whittle 2, Bennett	5,
18		27	LUTON TOWN	1-0	Bennett	8,
19	Jan	22	Chelsea	1-1	Whittle	25,
20	Feb	12	Plymouth Argyle	2-1	Possee, Cunningham	9,
21		15	Charlton Athletic	0-2		10,
22		19	BRISTOL ROVERS	2-0	Gray, Whittle (pen)	4,
23	Mar	2	Cardiff City	1-0	Cunningham	9,3
24		5	OLDHAM ATHLETIC	0-2		5,2
25		8	MILLWALL	1-1	Bennett	7,4
26		12	Blackburn Rovers	2-2	Mayo, Glover	7,7
27		15	BOLTON WANDERERS	2-2	Grealish, Roeder	5,4
28		19	BURNLEY	0-1		5,6
29		26	NOTTS COUNTY	1-0	Stubbs (og)	4,6
30		29	Nottingham Forest	0-3		16,2
31	Apr	2	Millwall	1-0	Bennett	6,7
32		9	CHARLTON ATHLETIC	0-0		6,6
33		11	Luton Town	0-0		11,0
34		16	SHEFFIELD UNITED	0-2		4,7
35		19	Hull City	1-1	Roeder	4,4
36		23	Wolverhampton W	0-1		19,8
37		26	SOUTHAMPTON	2-3	Gray, Bennett	5,2
38		30	CARLISLE UNITED	0-0		4,1
39	May	7	Fulham	1-6	Grealish	11,8
40		10	BLACKPOOL	0-1		4,7
41		14	HEREFORD UNITED	1-1	Roffey	4,9
42		17	HULL CITY	1-1	Glover	8,4

Appearanc
Sub appearanc
Goa

FA Cup

3	Jan	8	Darlington	2-2	Possee, Hoadley	8,1
R		11	DARLINGTON	0-0†		5,62
2R		17	Darlington *	3-0	Whittle 2, Roffey	4,34
4		29	Blackburn Rovers	0-3		12,36

Appearance
Sub appearance
Goa

League Cup

2	Aug	31	HULL CITY	1-0	Cunningham	3,57
3	Sep	21	Millwall	0-0		11,63
R	Oct	12	MILLWALL	0-0†		9,20
2R		19	Millwall ‡	0-3		8,84

Appearance
Sub appearance
Goal

Final League Position: 19th in Division Two

* Played at White Hart Lane, London

† After extra-time

‡ Played ar Highbury Stadium, London

	Payne	Fisher	Allen	Hoadley	Roeder	Cunningham	Heppolette	Queen	Possee	Allder	Clarke	Grealish	Roffey	Gray	Whittle	Bennett	Glynn	Chiedozie	Glover	Mayo	Hurley
1	2	3	4	5	6	7	8	9	10	11											
2	2	3	4	5	6	7	8	9	10*	11	12										
3	2	3*	4	5	6	7	8	9		12	11	10									
4		3	4	5	6	7	8		10		9	11	2								
5		2	4	5	8*	7	11	12	10		9	6		3							
6		2	4	5	6	7	8	11			10	3			9						
7		2	4	5	6	7	8	10			9		3		11						
8	2		4*	5	6	7	8	10		12	9		3		11						
9	2		4	5	6	7		8		11	9		3			10					
10	2	8	11	5	6	7		10			9		3			4					
11		12	4	5	6	7		10		11*	9	2	3			8					
12		2	4*	5	6	7		10			9	11	3		12	8					
13	2		4	5	6	7		10			9	8	3		11						
14	2		4	5	6	7		10			9	8	3*		11	12					
15	2			5	6	7*		10		11	9	8	3		12	4					
16	4			5	6	7		10		11	9*	2	3			8	12				
17	2	3	11	5	6	7		12	10			8*			9	4					
18	2	3	4	5	6	7		11	9						10	8					
19		2	9	5	6	7*		10		3		8	12		11	4					
20		2	8	5	6	7		10	9			4	3		11						
21		2*	8	5	6	7		10	9	12		4	3		11						
22		2	9	5	6	7		12	11*			8	3	4	10						
23		2	8		6	7			9	10		4	3	5	11						
24		2	4		6	7			9*	10		8	3	5	11	12					
25		2			6					10		4	3	5	11	8	9	7			
26		3			6					10		4	2	5	11	8			7	9	
27		2			6				12	11		8	3	5	7	4			10	9*	
28		2			6				9	11*		8	3	5	7	4		12	10		
29	2	4			6				7*			8	3	5	11	9		12	10		
30	3	2*			6				10			8	4	5	7	9		12	11		
31	7	2			6				10			4	3	5	8*	9		12	11		
32	8*	2			6				7			4	3	5	11	9		12	10		
33	4	2			6				7			10*	3	5	11	9		12	8		
34	2	3			4				7	10			6	5	11*	9		12	8		
35	2	4			6				7	8			3	5	11			12	10		9*
36	2	4	8		6				7			9	3	5	11				10		
37	2	8	4		6				11*			9	3	5	7	10		12			
38	2		4		6							10	3	5	11	9		7	8		
39		2	4		6							10	3	5	11*	9		7	8		12
40			4		6				10			2	3	5	11	9		7	8		
41			4		6							10	3	5	11	2		7	8	9	
42			10		6							2	3	5	11	4		7	8	9	
Apps	22	31	29	22	42	24	8	18	22	15	14	33	34	22	31	25	1	6	16	4	1
Sub apps		1						3	1	3	1		1		2	2	1	9			1
Goals			1	3	2	6		2	1		2	2	2	2	5	5			2	1	

One own-goal

	Payne	Fisher	Allen	Hoadley	Roeder	Cunningham	Heppolette	Queen	Possee	Allder	Clarke	Grealish	Roffey	Gray	Whittle	Bennett	Glynn	Chiedozie	Glover	Mayo	Hurley
3	2	3	9	5	6	7			10			8		12	11*	4					
R	2*	3	9	5	6	7		11	10	12		8				4					
2R		3		5	6	7		11	10*	8		2	12		9	4					
4		3	9	5	6	7		12	10	8*		2			11	4					
Apps	2	4	3	4	4	4		2	4	2		4			3	4					
Sub apps								1		1			1	1							
Goals				1					1				1		2						

	Payne	Fisher	Allen	Hoadley	Roeder	Cunningham	Heppolette	Queen	Possee	Allder	Clarke	Grealish	Roffey	Gray	Whittle	Bennett	Glynn	Chiedozie	Glover	Mayo	Hurley
2		3	4	5	6	7	8	9	10			11	2								
3		3	4	5	6	7	8	9	10	12		2*			11						
R	2	12	4	5	6	7		9		11*			3		10	8					
2R	2	11	4	5	6	7		9	10*				3		12	8					
Apps	2	3	4	4	4	4	2	4	3	1		2	3		2	2					
Sub apps		1								1					1						
Goals						1															

1977-78

Managers: Aug 1977 George Petchey; Aug–Sep 1977 Peter Angell (acting); Sep 1977–May 1978 Jimmy Bloomfield

	P	W	D	L	F	A	Pts
Bolton Wanderers	42	24	10	8	63	33	58
Southampton	42	22	13	7	70	39	57
Tottenham Hotspur	42	20	16	6	83	49	56
Brighton & Hove Albion	42	22	12	8	63	38	56
Blackburn Rovers	42	16	13	13	56	60	45
Sunderland	42	14	16	12	67	59	44
Stoke City	42	16	10	16	53	49	42
Oldham Athletic	42	13	16	13	54	58	42
Crystal Palace	42	13	15	14	50	47	41
Fulham	42	14	13	15	49	49	41
Burnley	42	15	10	17	56	64	40
Sheffield United	42	16	8	18	62	73	40
Luton Town	42	14	10	18	54	52	38
Orient	42	10	18	14	43	49	38
Notts County	42	11	16	15	54	62	38
Millwall	42	12	14	16	49	57	38
Charlton Athletic	42	13	12	17	55	68	38
Bristol Rovers	42	13	12	17	61	77	38
Cardiff City	42	13	12	17	51	71	38
Blackpool	42	12	13	17	59	60	37
Mansfield Town	42	10	11	21	49	69	31
Hull City	42	8	12	22	34	52	28

Division Two

Match No.	Date		Opponents	Result	Scorers	Atten
1	Aug	20	Luton Town	0-1		8
2		23	BLACKPOOL	1-4	Glover	5
3		27	Sunderland	1-1	Kitchen	28
4	Sep	3	OLDHAM ATHLETIC	5-3	Kitchen 2, Glover, Clarke, Bennett	4
5		10	Charlton Athletic	1-2	Glover	8
6		17	BRISTOL ROVERS	2-1	Fisher, Kitchen (pen)	5
7		24	Blackburn Rovers	0-1		6
8	Oct	1	TOTTENHAM HOTSPUR	1-1	Mayo	24
9		4	Southampton	0-1		15
10		8	Notts County	1-1	Kitchen	7
11		15	CARDIFF CITY	2-1	Kitchen 2	5
12		22	Fulham	2-1	Kitchen, Mayo	9
13		29	MILLWALL	0-0		8
14	Nov	5	BOLTON WANDERERS	1-1	Roffey	7,
15		12	Brighton & Hove Albion	0-1		20
16		19	CRYSTAL PALACE	0-0		10
17		26	Burnley	0-0		8,
18	Dec	3	MANSFIELD TOWN	4-2	Chiedozie, Kitchen 3	4,
19		10	Hull City	2-2	Mayo, Kitchen	4,
20		17	BRIGHTON & HOVE ALBION	0-1		9,
21		26	Sheffield United	0-2		18,
22		27	STOKE CITY	2-0	Kitchen 2	6,
23		31	Blackpool	0-0		6,
24	Jan	2	LUTON TOWN	0-0		9,
25		14	SUNDERLAND	2-2	Kitchen, Chiedozie	6
26		21	Oldham Athletic	1-2	Mayo	8,
27	Feb	11	Bristol Rovers	1-2	Mayo	9,
28		25	Tottenham Hotspur	1-1	Mayo	32,
29	Mar	4	NOTTS COUNTY	0-0		5,
30		17	FULHAM	1-1	Kitchen	7,
31		21	Millwall	0-2		6,
32		25	Stoke City	1-5	Mayo	14,
33		27	SHEFFIELD UNITED	3-1	Kitchen 3 (1 pen)	6,
34	Apr	1	Bolton Wanderers	0-2		17,
35		4	BLACKBURN ROVERS	0-0		7,
36		15	Crystal Palace	0-1		15,
37		18	BURNLEY	3-0	Bennett, Clarke 2	5,
38		22	HULL CITY	2-1	Kitchen, Clarke	5,
39		25	SOUTHAMPTON	1-1	Mayo	19,2
40		29	Mansfield Town	1-1	Mayo	6,3
41	May	3	CHARLTON ATHLETIC	0-0		10,2
42		9	Cardiff City	1-0	Kitchen	8,2
						Appearanc
						Sub appearanc
						Go

FA Cup

3	Jan	6	NORWICH CITY	1-1	Kitchen	14,5
R		16	Norwich City	1-0	Kitchen	20,4
4		28	BLACKBURN ROVERS	3-1	Kitchen 2, Mayo	9,5
5	Feb	18	CHELSEA	0-0		25,1
R		27	Chelsea	2-1	Kitchen 2	36,3
6	Mar	11	Middlesbrough	0-0		33,4
R		14	MIDDLESBROUGH	2-1	Kitchen, Mayo	18,0
SF	Apr	8	Arsenal *	0-3		49,6
						Appearanc
						Sub appearanc
						Goa

League Cup

1	Aug	13	FULHAM †	2-0	Kitchen, Lacy (og)	4,7
2		16	Fulham	1-2	Allen	4,3
3		31	Derby County	1-3	Bennett	16,9
						Appearanc
						Sub appearanc
						Goa

Final League Position: 14th in Division Two

* Semi-final played at Stamford Bridge, London

† Home tie played at Craven Cottage, Fulham

Fisher	Roffey	Allen	Hoadley	Roeder	Chiedozie	Glover	Mayo	Kitchen	Payne	Grealish	Bennett	Clarke	Gray	Godfrey	Banjo	Smeulders	
2	3	4	5	6	7	8	9	10	11*	12							1
2	3	4	5	6	7	8	9	10			11						2
2	3	4	5	6	7	8	9	10			11						3
2	3	4	5	6		8		10		7	11	9					4
2	3	4	5	6		7		10		8	11	9					5
2	3	4	5	6		7	9	10		8	11						6
2	3	4	5	6		7	9	10		8	11						7
2	3		5	6	7	8	9	10		4	11						8
2	3		5	6	7	8	9	10		4	11						9
2	3	12	5	6	7	8*	9	10		11	4						10
2	3	12	5	6	7	8	9	10		11	4*						11
2	3	4*	5	6	7	8	9	10	12	11							12
2	3	4	5	6	7	8	9	10		11							13
2	3	12	5	6	7	8	9	10		11	4*						14
2	3	4	5	6	7		9	10		8	11						15
2	3	8	5	6	7	11		10		4		9					16
2	3	11	5	6	7	8		10	4			9					17
2	3	8	5	6	7	11	9	10		4							18
2	3	4	5	6	7	8	9	10		11							19
2	3	8	5	6	7	11	9	10		4							20
2	3	8*		6	7	11	9	10	12	4			5				21
2	3			6	7	11*	9	10		4	8	12	5				22
2	3		5	6	7		9	10		4	11		8				23
2	3		5	6	7		9	10		4	11		8				24
2	3		5	6	7			10	12	11	4	9*	8				25
2	3		5	6			9	10	11	4			8	7			26
2	3		5	6			9	10	11	4			8	7			27
2	3	4		6			9	10	5	11			8	7			28
2	3	11	5	6			9	10		4			8	7			29
2	3		5	6			9	10	11	4		12	8	7*			30
2	3		5	6			9	10	4	11			8	7			31
2	3		5	6			9	10	4*	11		12	8	7			32
2	3		5	6			9	10		4		11	8	7			33
2	3		5	6			9	10	4*			11	8	7	12		34
2	3		5	6			9	10		4	11		8	7			35
2	3		5	6			9	10		4	11		8	7*	12		36
2	3		5	6				10		4	9	7	8		11		37
2	3		5	6			12	10		4	11	9	8		7*		38
2	3		5	6			11	10	4		9	7	8				39
2	3		5	6			9	10	4		11	7*	8		12		40
2	3		5	6			11	10		4	9		8		7		41
2	3		5	6			11	10		4	9	7	8				42
42	42	18	39	42	21	21	35	42	11	35	24	12	22	11	3		
		3					1		3	1		3			3		
1					2	3	9	21			2	4					

Fisher	Roffey	Allen	Hoadley	Roeder	Chiedozie	Glover	Mayo	Kitchen	Payne	Grealish	Bennett	Clarke	Gray	Godfrey	Banjo	Smeulders	
2	3		5	6	7		9	10		4	11		8				3
2	3		5	6	7		9	10		4	11		8				R
2	3		5	6			9	10	12	4	11*		8	7			4
2	3		5	6			9	10		4	11		8	7			5
2	3	11	5	6			9	10		4			8	7			R
2	3		5	6			9	10	11	4			8	7			6
2	3		5	6			9	10	11	4			8	7			R
2	3		5	6			9	10		4	11	7	8*		12		SF
8	8	1	8	8	2		8	8	2	8	5	1	8	5			
									1						1		
							2	7									

Fisher	Roffey	Allen	Hoadley	Roeder	Chiedozie	Glover	Mayo	Kitchen	Payne	Grealish	Bennett	Clarke	Gray	Godfrey	Banjo	Smeulders	
2	12	4	5	6	7		9	10	11*	8			3			1	1
2		4	5	6	7		9	10	11	8			3			1	2
2	3	4	5	6	7	8*	9	10		12	11						3
3	1	3	3	3	3	1	3	3	2	2	1		2			2	
	1									1							
		1						1			1						

One own-goal

1978-79

Manager: Jimmy Bloomfield

	P	W	D	L	F	A	Pts
Crystal Palace	42	19	19	4	51	24	57
Brighton & Hove Albion	42	23	10	9	72	39	56
Stoke City	42	20	16	6	58	31	56
Sunderland	42	22	11	9	70	44	55
West Ham United	42	18	14	10	70	39	50
Notts County	42	14	16	12	48	60	44
Preston North End	42	12	18	12	59	57	42
Newcastle United	42	17	8	17	51	55	42
Cardiff City	42	16	10	16	56	70	42
Fulham	42	13	15	14	50	47	41
Orient	42	15	10	17	51	51	40
Cambridge United	42	12	16	14	44	52	40
Burnley	42	14	12	16	51	62	40
Oldham Athletic	42	13	13	16	52	61	39
Wrexham	42	12	14	16	45	42	38
Bristol Rovers	42	14	10	18	48	60	38
Leicester City	42	10	17	15	43	52	37
Luton Town	42	13	10	19	60	57	36
Charlton Athletic	42	11	13	18	60	69	35
Sheffield United	42	11	12	19	52	69	34
Millwall	42	11	10	21	42	61	32
Blackburn Rovers	42	10	10	22	41	72	30

Division Two

Match No.	Date		Opponents	Result	Scorers	Atten
1	Aug	19	Sheffield United	2-1	Mayo, Kitchen	19
2		22	SUNDERLAND	3-0	Hughton, Mayo, Grealish	7
3		26	WREXHAM	0-1		6
4	Sep	2	Blackburn Rovers	0-3		6
5		9	STOKE CITY	0-1		6
6		16	Notts County	0-1		8
7		23	Newcastle United	0-0		26
8		30	LEICESTER CITY	0-1		5
9	Oct	6	Charlton Athletic	2-0	Moores 2	11
10		14	CARDIFF CITY	2-2	Mayo, Grealish	6
11		21	Bristol Rovers	1-2	Moores	7
12		28	LUTON TOWN	3-2	Coates, Kitchen 2	7
13	Nov	4	Cambridge United	1-3	Grealish	6
14		11	SHEFFIELD UNITED	1-1	Kitchen (pen)	5
15		18	Wrexham	1-3	Moores	9
16		21	BLACKBURN ROVERS	2-0	Mayo, Moores	4
17		25	PRESTON NORTH END	2-0	Hughton, Moores	4
18	Dec	2	Brighton & Hove Albion	0-2		16
19		9	BURNLEY	2-1	Grealish, Kitchen	4
20		16	Oldham Athletic	0-0		5
21		23	MILLWALL	2-1	Went, Chiedozie	6
22		26	West Ham United	2-0	Mayo, Chiedozie	29
23		30	Crystal Palace	1-1	Mayo	20
24	Jan	20	NOTTS COUNTY	3-0	Moores 2, Chiedozie	4
25	Feb	3	NEWCASTLE UNITED	2-0	Mayo, Kitchen (pen)	7
26		10	Leicester City	3-5	Chiedozie 2, Kitchen	12
27		24	Cardiff City	0-1		8
28	Mar	3	BRISTOL ROVERS	1-1	Moores (pen)	5
29		10	Luton Town	1-2	Moores	6
30		14	Stoke City	1-3	Mayo	16,
31		17	CAMBRIDGE UNITED	3-0	Grealish, Mayo, Coates	4,
32		20	CHARLTON ATHLETIC	2-1	Chiedozie, Whittle	6
33		24	Sunderland	0-1		21,
34		27	FULHAM	1-0	Went (pen)	6
35		31	Preston North End	1-1	Moores	9,
36	Apr	7	BRIGHTON & HOVE ALBION	3-3	Mayo, Coates, Moores	11,
37		10	Millwall	0-2		6,
38		14	WEST HAM UNITED	0-2		17,
39		16	Fulham	2-2	Moores, Banjo	6,
40		21	OLDHAM ATHLETIC	0-0		4,
41		28	Burnley	1-0	Mayo	7,
42	May	5	CRYSTAL PALACE	0-1		19,

Appearan
Sub appearan
Go

FA Cup

3	Jan	9	BURY	3-2	Kitchen 2, Chiedozie	6,
4		27	Ipswich Town	0-0		23,
R		30	IPSWICH TOWN	0-2		18,

Appearan
Sub appearan
Go

League Cup

2	Aug	30	CHESTERFIELD	1-2	Fisher	4,

Appearan
Sub appearan
Go

Final League Position: 11th in Division Two

Fisher	Roffey	Grealish	Gray, N	Hughton	Chiedozie	Banjo	Mayo	Kitchen	Bennett	Godfrey	Smith	Kane	Went	Moores	Coates	Whittle	Clarke	Gray, M	
2	3	4	5	6	7	8	9	10	11										1
2	3	4	5	6	7*	8	9	10	11	12									2
2		4	5	6	7	8	9	10	11	12	3*								3
2	3	4	5	6		8	9	10	11*	7		12							4
2	3	4	5	8	7		9	10	11				6						5
2	3	4	5	8*	7	12	9	10	11				6						6
2	3	4	5		7	8	9	10		11			6						7
2	3	4	5		7	8	9	10		11			6						8
2	3	4	5	7			9	10					6	8	11				9
2	3	4	5	7	12		9	10*					6	8	11				10
2	3	4	5	7	11	10	9						6	8					11
2	3	4	5	7			9	10					6	8	11				12
2	3*	4	5	7	12		9	10					6	8	11				13
2	3	4	5	8			9	10					6	11	7				14
2	3	4	5	7			9	10					6	8	11				15
2	3	4	5	7	12		9	10*					6	8	11				16
2	3	4	5	10	7		9						6	8	11				17
2	3	4	5	7	10		9						6	8	11				18
2*	3	4	5	7	10		9	12					6	8	11				19
2	3	4	5	7*	10	12	9	6						8	11				20
2	3	4	5		10	7	9	8					6		11				21
2	3	4	5		10	12	9	7					6	8	11*				22
2	3	4	5	7	10		9	11					6	8					23
2	3	4	5		7		9	10					6	8	11				24
2	3		5	4	7		9	10					6	8	11				25
2	3		5	4	7		9	10					6	8	11				26
2	3		5	4	7		9*						6	10	11	8	12		27
2	3	4	5		7		9						6	10	11	8			28
2	3	4	5	8	7		9						6	10	11				29
2	3	4	5	10			9						6	8	11	7			30
2	3	4	5		7		9						6	10	11	8			31
2	3	4	5		7	11	9						6	8		10			32
2	3	4	5		7	11	9			12			6			10*	8		33
2	3	4	5	8	7*		9						6		11		10	12	34
3		4	5	8	7	4							6	9	11		10		35
	3	4	5	2	7		9						6	8	11	10			36
	3	4	5	2	7		9						6	8	11	10			37
	3	4	5	2	7		9*						6	8	11	10	12		38
	3	4	5	2	7	9							6	8	11		10		39
	3	4	5	2	7	9	10						6	8	11				40
3	8	4	5	2	7	12	9						6		11			10*	41
3		4	5	2	7		9						6	8	11	10			42
37	39	39	42	33	33	13	40	22	6	3	1		37	30	30	10	4	1	
					3	4		1		3		1					2	1	
		5		2	6	1	11	7					2	13	3	1			

Fisher	Roffey	Grealish	Gray, N	Hughton	Chiedozie	Banjo	Mayo	Kitchen	Bennett	Godfrey	Smith	Kane	Went	Moores	Coates	Whittle	Clarke	Gray, M	
2	3	4	5	7	11		9	10					6	8					3
2	3	4	5		7		9	10					6	8	11				4
2	3*		5	4	7	12	9	10					6	8	11				R
3	3	2	3	2	3		3	3					3	3	2				
						1													
					1			2											

Fisher	Roffey	Grealish	Gray, N	Hughton	Chiedozie	Banjo	Mayo	Kitchen	Bennett	Godfrey	Smith	Kane	Went	Moores	Coates	Whittle	Clarke	Gray, M	
2	3	4	5	11	7*	8	9	10	6	12									2
1	1	1	1	1	1	1	1	1	1										
										1									
1																			

1979-80

Manager: Jimmy Bloomfield

	P	W	D	L	F	A	Pts
Leicester City	42	21	13	8	58	38	55
Sunderland	42	21	12	9	69	42	54
Birmingham City	42	21	11	10	58	38	53
Chelsea	42	23	7	12	66	52	53
Queen's Park Rangers	42	18	13	11	75	53	49
Luton Town	42	16	17	9	66	45	49
West Ham United	42	20	7	15	54	43	47
Cambridge United	42	14	16	12	61	53	44
Newcastle United	42	15	14	13	53	49	44
Preston North End	42	12	19	11	56	52	43
Oldham Athletic	42	16	11	15	49	53	43
Swansea City	42	17	9	16	48	53	43
Shrewsbury Town	42	18	5	19	60	53	41
Orient	42	12	17	13	48	54	41
Cardiff City	42	16	8	18	41	48	40
Wrexham	42	16	6	20	40	49	38
Notts County	42	11	15	16	51	52	37
Watford	42	12	13	17	39	46	37
Bristol Rovers	42	11	13	18	50	64	35
Fulham	42	11	7	24	42	74	29
Burnley	42	6	15	21	39	73	27
Charlton Athletic	42	6	10	26	39	78	22

Division Two

Match No.	Date		Opponents	Result	Scorers	Atten
1	Aug	18	BURNLEY	2-2	Coates 2	6
2		22	Fulham	0-0		9
3		25	Luton Town	1-2	Margerrison	6
4	Sep	1	CHARLTON ATHLETIC	1-1	Jennings	6
5		8	NEWCASTLE UNITED	1-4	Jennings	5
6		15	Wrexham	1-2	Mayo	8
7		22	BIRMINGHAM CITY	2-2	Mayo 2	5
8		29	Shrewsbury Town	0-1		6
9	Oct	6	Oldham Athletic	0-1		6
10		9	FULHAM	1-0	Coates	5
11		13	WATFORD	1-0	Mayo	7
12		20	Cambridge United	1-1	Chiedozie	5
13		27	BRISTOL ROVERS	2-1	Coates, Went (pen)	4
14	Nov	3	Burnley	2-1	Mayo, Coates	6
15		10	CHELSEA	3-7	Jennings 2, Fisher	13
16		17	Cardiff City	0-0		8
17		24	Preston North End	2-2	Penfold, Taylor	7
18	Dec	1	SUNDERLAND	2-1	Jennings, Taylor	6
19		8	Leicester City	2-2	Mayo, Margerrison	16
20		15	NOTTS COUNTY	1-0	Jennings	4
21		21	Swansea City	1-0	Taylor	10
22		29	LUTON TOWN	2-2	Jennings, Godfrey	9
23	Jan	1	WEST HAM UNITED	0-4		23
24		12	Charlton Athletic	1-0	Coates	6
25		19	Newcastle United	0-2		20
26	Feb	2	WREXHAM	4-0	Jennings 2, Mayo, Taylor (pen)	4
27		9	Birmingham City	1-3	Mayo	17
28		12	Queen's Park Rangers	0-0		11
29		16	SHREWSBURY TOWN	0-1		4
30		23	Watford	3-0	Jennings, Chiedozie, Coates	15
31	Mar	1	CAMBRIDGE UNITED	2-0	Coates, Mayo	5,
32		8	Bristol Rovers	2-1	Mayo, Jennings	5,
33		14	OLDHAM ATHLETIC	1-1	Mayo	4,
34		22	Chelsea	0-1		19,
35		29	CARDIFF CITY	1-1	Roffey	4,
36	Apr	5	West Ham United	0-2		22,
37		8	QUEEN'S PARK RANGERS	1-1	Fisher	9,
38		12	Sunderland	1-1	Coates	33,
39		19	PRESTON NORTH END	2-2	Fisher, Taylor (pen)	4,
40		26	Notts County	1-1	Chiedozie	5,
41		30	SWANSEA CITY	0-0		3,
42	May	3	LEICESTER CITY	0-1		13,

Appearan
Sub appearar
G

FA Cup

3	Jan	5	Altrincham	1-1	Jennings	7,
R		9	ALTRINCHAM	2-1	Mayo, Jennings	8,
4		26	WEST HAM UNITED	2-3	Taylor (pen), Chiedozie	21,

Appearan
Sub appearan
Gc

League Cup

2	Aug	29	WIMBLEDON	2-2	Chiedozie, Hughton	4,
R	Sep	4	Wimbledon	2-2*	Mayo, Margerrison	3,

Appearan
Sub appearan
Gc

Final League Position: 14th in Division Two

* Wimbledon won 5–4 on penalties after extra-time

Fisher	Roffey	Hughton	Gray	Taylor	Whittle	Margerrison	Mayo	Jennings	Coates	Chiedozie	Banjo	Penfold	Went	Moores	Godfrey	Smith	Parsons	Rafter	Hamberger	
2	3	4	5	6	7	8	9	10	11											1
2	3	10	5*	6	7	4	9	8	11	12										2
2	3	10		6	8	4	5	9	11	7										3
2	3	10		6	5	4	9	8	11	7										4
2	3	10		5		4	9	8	11	7	6									5
8	3			5	7	4	9	10	11			2	6							6
2	3	10	5	6	12	4	9	8*	11					7						7
2	3	8	5	6	7	4*	9		11	12				10						8
2	3	8	5	6			9		11	7			4	10						9
2	3	8	5	6			9		11	7			4	10						10
2	3	8	5	6			9		11	7			4	10						11
2	3	8	5	6			9	12	11	7			4	10*						12
2	3	8	5	6			9	10	11	7			4							13
2	3	8	5	6			9	10	11	7			4							14
2	3	8*	5	6			9	10	11	7			4	12						15
2	3	8	5	6		4		10	11	7				9						16
2	3	8		6			4	10	11	7		5		9						17
2	3	8	5	4			9	10	11	7				6						18
2	3	8	5	4		12	9	10*	11	7				6						19
2	3	8	5	4		12	9	10	11	7*				6						20
2	3	8	5	4		10	9		11					6	7					21
2		8	5	4			9	10	11	7*				6	12	3				22
2		8	5	4			9	10	11	7				6	12	3*				23
2	3	8	5	4			9	10	11					6	7					24
2	3	8	5	4		10*		9	11	7				6	12					25
2	3	6	5	4		10	9	8	11	7										26
2	3	6	5	4		8*	10	9	11	7				12						27
2	3	6	5	4		10	9	8	11	7										28
2	3	6	5	4		8	10	9*	11	7				12						29
2	3	6	5	4		10	9	8	11	7										30
2	3	6	5	4		10	9	8	11	7										31
2	3	6	5	4		10	9	8	11	7										32
2	3		5	4		10	9	8	11	7		6								33
2	3	6	5	4		10	9	8	11	7										34
2	3	6	5	4		10	9	8*	11	7				12						35
2	3	6	5	4		10		8	11	7				9						36
2	3	6	5	4			9		11	7				8			10			37
2	3	6	5	4			9		11	7				8			10			38
2	3	6	5	4			9		11	7				8			10			39
2	3	6	5	4			9	8	11	7							10			40
2	3	6	5	4			9*	12	11	7				8			10			41
2	3	6	5*	4			9	8	11	7				12			10			42
42	40	40	37	42	6	22	39	32	42	35	1	3	8	21	2	2	6			
					1	2		2		2				5	3					
3	1			5		2	11	11	9	3		1	1		1					

Fisher	Roffey	Hughton	Gray	Taylor	Whittle	Margerrison	Mayo	Jennings	Coates	Chiedozie	Banjo	Penfold	Went	Moores	Godfrey	Smith	Parsons	Rafter	Hamberger	
2	3	8	5	4			9	10	11					6	7					3
2	3	8	5	4			9	10	11					6	7					R
2	3	8	5	4		10		9	11	7				6				1		4
3	3	3	3	3		1	2	3	3	1				3	2			1		
				1			1	2		1										

Fisher	Roffey	Hughton	Gray	Taylor	Whittle	Margerrison	Mayo	Jennings	Coates	Chiedozie	Banjo	Penfold	Went	Moores	Godfrey	Smith	Parsons	Rafter	Hamberger	
2	3	10		6	12	4	9	8	11	7									5*	2
2	3	10		5	12	4	9	8	11	7*	6									
2	2	2		2		2	2	2	2	2	1								1	
					2															
		1				1	1			1										

1980-81

Manager: Jimmy Bloomfield

	P	W	D	L	F	A	Pts
West Ham United	42	28	10	4	79	29	66
Notts County	42	18	17	7	49	38	53
Swansea City	42	18	14	10	64	44	50
Blackburn Rovers	42	16	18	8	42	29	50
Luton Town	42	18	12	12	61	46	48
Derby County	42	15	15	12	57	52	45
Grimsby Town	42	15	15	12	44	42	45
Queen's Park Rangers	42	15	13	14	56	46	43
Watford	42	16	11	15	50	45	43
Sheffield Wednesday	42	17	8	17	53	51	42
Newcastle United	42	14	14	14	30	45	42
Chelsea	42	14	12	16	46	41	40
Cambridge United	42	17	6	19	53	65	40
Shrewsbury Town	42	11	17	14	46	47	39
Oldham Athletic	42	12	15	15	39	48	39
Wrexham	42	12	14	16	43	45	38
Orient	42	13	12	17	52	56	38
Bolton Wanderers	42	14	10	18	61	66	38
Cardiff City	42	12	12	18	44	60	36
Preston North End	42	11	14	17	41	62	36
Bristol City	42	7	16	19	29	51	30
Bristol Rovers	42	5	13	24	34	65	23

Division Two

Match No.	Date		Opponents	Result	Scorers	Atter
1	Aug	16	Bristol Rovers	1-1	Chiedozie	
2		19	CAMBRIDGE UNITED	3-0	Jennings, Parsons, Chiedozie	
3		23	BLACKBURN ROVERS	1-1	Bowles	
4		30	Cardiff City	2-4	Parsons, Jennings	
5	Sep	6	GRIMSBY TOWN	2-0	Moores, Bowles (pen)	
6		13	Wrexham	1-3	Bowles	
7		20	Luton Town	1-2	Moores	
8		27	DERBY COUNTY	1-0	Moores	
9	Oct	4	PRESTON NORTH END	4-0	Moores, Parsons, Chiedozie, Bowles	
10		7	Queen's Park Rangers	0-0		
11		11	Shrewsbury Town	2-1	Chiedozie, Moores	
12		18	NOTTS COUNTY	0-2		
13		21	CHELSEA	0-1		1
14		25	Sheffield Wednesday	2-2	Moores, Chiedozie	1
15	Nov	1	BRISTOL CITY	3-1	Chiedozie, Parsons, Moores	4
16		8	Swansea City	2-0	Moores, Chiedozie	1
17		11	Cambridge United	0-1		5
18		15	BRISTOL ROVERS	2-2	Moores, P. Taylor	5
19		22	Oldham Athletic	1-0	Parsons	5
20		29	NEWCASTLE UNITED	1-1	P. Taylor	5
21	Dec	6	Bolton Wanderers	1-3	P. Taylor	8
22		13	SHREWSBURY TOWN	1-0	P. Taylor	4
23		20	Chelsea	1-0	Mayo	15
24		26	WATFORD	1-1	P. Taylor	10
25		27	West Ham United	1-2	Chiedozie	34
26	Jan	10	OLDHAM ATHLETIC	2-3	Jennings, Bowles (pen)	4
27		17	CARDIFF CITY	2-2	Mayo, P. Taylor	3
28		31	Blackburn Rovers	0-2		9
29	Feb	7	WREXHAM	2-1	Bowles (pen), Parsons	4
30		14	Grimsby Town	0-2		10
31		21	Derby County	1-1	Margerrison	15
32	Mar	1	LUTON TOWN	0-0		8
33		7	Preston North End	0-3		5
34		21	Notts County	0-1		6
35		28	SHEFFIELD WEDNESDAY	2-0	Jennings, P. Taylor	6
36		31	QUEEN'S PARK RANGERS	4-0	Chiedozie, Jennings 2, P. Taylor	6
37	Apr	4	Bristol City	1-3	Jennings	5
38		11	SWANSEA CITY	1-1	Godfrey	4
39		17	Watford	0-2		12
40		18	WEST HAM UNITED	0-2		14
41		26	BOLTON WANDERERS	2-2	Mayo, Godfrey	3
42	May	2	Newcastle United	1-3	Mayo	11

Appearar
Sub appearar
G

FA Cup

3	Jan	3	LUTON TOWN	1-3	Jennings	9,

Appearan
Sub appearan
G

League Cup

2/1	Aug	27	TOTTENHAM HOTSPUR	0-1		20,
2/2	Sep	3	Tottenham Hotspur	1-3	Jennings	25,

Appearan
Sub appearan
G

Final League Position: 17th in Division Two

Fisher	Roffey	Taylor, T	Gray	Parsons	Chiedozie	Jennings	Mayo	Bowles	Coates	Moores	Margerrison	Hughton	Godfrey	Taylor, P	Rafter	
2	3	4	5	6	7*	8	9	10	11	12						1
2	3	4	5	6	7	8	9	10	11							2
2	3	4	5	6	7	8	9	10	11							3
2	3	4	5	6	7	8	9	10	11*		12					4
2	3	4	5	6	7		9	10		8	11					5
2	3		5	6*	7		9	10		8	11	4	12			6
2	3	4	5	6	7		9	10		8	11					7
2	3	4	5	6	7		9	10		8	11					8
2	3	4	5	6	7		9	10		8	11					9
2	3	4	5	6	7		9	10		8	11					10
2	3	4	5	6	7		9	10		8	11					11
2	3	4	5	6	7		9	10		8	11					12
2	3	4	5	6*	7	12	9	10		8	11					13
2	3	4*	5	6	7		9	10		8	11	12				14
2	3	4	5	6	7		9	10		8	11					15
2	3	4	5	6	7		9			8	11	10				16
2	3	4	5	6	7		9	10		8	11					17
2	3	4	5	6	7		9	10		8				11		18
2	3	4	5	6	7		9	10		8				11		19
2	3	4	5	6	7		9	10		8*		12		11		20
2	3	4	5	6		9		10		8		7		11		21
2	3	4	5	6	7		9	10		8				11		22
2	3	4	5	6			9	10		8			7	11		23
2	3	4	5	6	7		9	10		8				11		24
2	3	4	5	6	7		9	10		8				11		25
	3	4	5	6	7	9	8	10				2		11		26
2	3	4	5	6	7	9	8	10						11		27
2	3	4		6	7	9		10		5	8			11		28
2	3	4		6	7	9*		10		5	8	12		11		29
2	3	4		6*	7	9		10		5	8		12	11		30
2	3	4	5		7	9		10		6	8			11		31
2	3	4	5		7	9		10		6	8			11		32
2	3	4	5		7	9	12	10		6	8*			11		33
2	3	4	5		7	9	10			6	8*		12	11		34
2	3	4	5		7	9	10	8		6				11		35
2	3	4	5		7*	9		8		6		10	12	11		36
2	3	4	5		7*	9	12	8		6		10		11		37
2	3	4	5			8	9	10		6			7	11		38
2	3	4	5			8	9	10		6			7	11		39
2	3	4*	5		7	9	12	10		6		8		11		40
2	3	4	5			8	9	10		6			7	11	1	41
2	3	4	5			8	9			6	10	7	11		1	42
41	42	41	39	30	36	22	32	39	4	36	21	8	5	24	2	
						1	3			1	1	3	4			
				6	9	7	4	6		9	1		2	8		

Fisher	Roffey	Taylor, T	Gray	Parsons	Chiedozie	Jennings	Mayo	Bowles	Coates	Moores	Margerrison	Hughton	Godfrey	Taylor, P	Rafter	
	3	4	5	6	7	9		10		8		2		11		3
	1	1	1	1	1	1		1		1		1		1		
						1										

Fisher	Roffey	Taylor, T	Gray	Parsons	Chiedozie	Jennings	Mayo	Bowles	Coates	Moores	Margerrison	Hughton	Godfrey	Taylor, P	Rafter	
2	3	4	5	6	7	8	9	10	11							2/1
2	3	4	5	6	7	8*	9	10		12	11					2/2
2	2	2	2	2	2	2	2	2	1		1					
										1						
						1										

1981-82

Managers: Aug–Oct 1981 Paul Went; Oct 1981–May 1982 Ken Knighton

	P	W	D	L	F	A	Pts
Luton Town	42	25	13	4	86	46	88
Watford	42	23	11	8	76	42	80
Norwich City	42	22	5	15	64	50	71
Sheffield Wednesday	42	20	10	12	55	51	70
Queen's Park Rangers	42	21	6	15	65	43	69
Barnsley	42	19	10	13	59	41	67
Rotherham United	42	20	7	15	66	54	67
Leicester City	42	18	12	12	56	48	66
Newcastle United	42	18	8	16	52	50	62
Blackburn Rovers	42	16	11	15	47	43	59
Oldham Athletic	42	15	14	13	50	51	59
Chelsea	42	15	12	15	60	60	57
Charlton Athletic	42	13	12	17	50	65	51
Cambridge United	42	13	9	20	48	53	48
Crystal Palace	42	13	9	20	34	45	48
Derby County	42	12	12	18	53	68	48
Grimsby Town	42	11	13	18	53	65	46
Shrewsbury Town	42	11	13	18	37	57	46
Bolton Wanderers	42	13	7	22	39	61	46
Cardiff City	42	12	8	22	45	61	44
Wrexham	42	11	11	20	40	56	44
Orient	42	10	9	23	36	61	39

Division Two

Match No.	Date		Opponents	Result	Scorers	Atten
1	Aug	29	Derby County	2-1	P. Taylor, Jennings	1
2	Sep	5	GRIMSBY TOWN	1-2	P. Taylor	
3		12	Blackburn Rovers	0-2		
4		19	WREXHAM	0-0		
5		22	Crystal Palace	0-1		1
6		26	Newcastle United	0-1		1
7		28	CHELSEA	0-2		
8	Oct	3	LUTON TOWN	0-3		
9		10	Watford	0-3		1
10		18	QUEEN'S PARK RANGERS	1-1	Cunningham	
11		25	CHARLTON ATHLETIC	1-1	Bowles (pen)	
12		31	Barnsley	0-1		1
13	Nov	7	SHEFFIELD WEDNESDAY	3-0	Margerrison, Sussex, Silkman	
14		14	Leicester City	1-0	McNeil	1
15		21	Bolton Wanderers	0-1		
16		24	NEWCASTLE UNITED	1-0	Margerrison	
17		28	SHREWSBURY TOWN	2-0	Godfrey 2	
18	Dec	5	Rotherham United	0-1		
19		19	Oldham Athletic	2-3	Giles 2	
20	Jan	9	Grimsby Town	2-1	Godfrey, Moores	
21		16	DERBY COUNTY	3-2	Moores 2, Godfrey	4
22		23	BARNSLEY	1-3	Moores	
23		30	Wrexham	1-0	Godfrey	4
24	Feb	6	BLACKBURN ROVERS	0-0		3
25		21	CRYSTAL PALACE	0-0		5
26		27	WATFORD	1-3	Silkman (pen)	6
27	Mar	12	Charlton Athletic	2-5	Jennings, Silkman	5
28		16	NORWICH CITY	1-1	Jennings	2
29		27	Sheffield Wednesday	0-2		16
30		30	Luton Town	0-2		9
31	Apr	6	Queen's Park Rangers	0-3		10
32		10	Cardiff City	1-2	Foster	5
33		12	CAMBRIDGE UNITED	0-0		3
34		17	BOLTON WANDERERS	3-0	Godfrey, McNeil, Silkman (pen)	2
35		20	Cambridge United	0-2		3
36		24	Shrewsbury Town	0-2		2
37		28	CARDIFF CITY	1-1	Foster	2
38	May	1	ROTHERHAM UNITED	1-2	Godfrey	3
39		5	Chelsea	2-2	Houchen, Margerrison	6
40		8	Norwich City	0-2		19
41		15	OLDHAM ATHLETIC	0-3		2
42		18	LEICESTER CITY	3-0	Godfrey, Silkman, McNeil	2

Appearar
Sub appearar
G

FA Cup

3	Jan	2	CHARLTON ATHLETIC	1-0	Moores	6,
4		26	Huddersfield Town	1-1	Moores	13,
R	Feb	1	HUDDERSFIELD TOWN	2-0	Foster, Moores	6,
5		13	Crystal Palace	0-0		14,
R		16	CRYSTAL PALACE	0-1		10,

Appearan
Sub appearan
G

League Cup

1/1	Sep	1	MILLWALL	1-1	Moores	4,
1/2		16	Millwall	2-3	Moores, Jennings	4,

Appearan
Sub appearan
G

Final League Position: 22nd in Division Two

Fisher	Roffey	Taylor, T	Gray	Margerrison	Godfrey	Moores	Jennings	Bowles	Taylor, P	Mayo	Hughton	Cunningham	Hallybone	Silkman	McNeill	Sussex	Giles	Foster	Osgood	Blackhall	Houchen	Peach	Banjo	Cornwell	Vincent	
2	3	4	5	6*	7	8	9	10	11	12																1
2	3	4	5	6	7	8	9	10	11																	2
2	3	4	5	6	7	9	8	10*	11		12															3
2	3	4		6*	7	9	8	10	11		12	5														4
2	3	4	5		8	9	7				10	6	11													5
	3	4	5	10	7	9	8				2	6		11												6
	3	4	5	10	7*	9	8		12		2	6		11												7
	3	4	5	10	7	9*	8		11		2	6		12												8
	3	4	5	10	7			9	11		2	6		8												9
	3	4	5	10*	7			9			2	6	12	8	11											10
	3	4	5*	10	7			9	12		2	6		8	11											11
	3	4	5	10	7				9		2	6		8	11											12
3		4	5	10	7				9		2			8	11	6										13
3		4	5	10	7				9		2			8	11	6										14
3		4	5	10	7				9		2			8	11	6										15
6	3*	4	5	10	7	9					2		12	8	11											16
6		4	5	10	7						2	3		8	11		9									17
6		4	5	10	7						2	3		8	11		9									18
6		4	5	10	7						2	3		8	11		9									19
11		4	5	8	7	9					3			10				2	6							20
1*		4	5	8	7	9					3			10				2	6	12						21
		4	5*	8	7	9					3		11	10				2	6	12						22
3		4	5	8	7	9							11	10*	12			2	6							23
3		4	5	8	7	9							11	12	10*			2	6							24
4	3		5	8	7	9					11		6*	10	12			2								25
4	3		5		7	9					11			10	8			2	6							26
4	3		5	6	7	9	8				11			10				2								27
4	3		5	7*	9	10	11				2		12	8				6								28
4	3		5		7	9								10		11		2			8		6			29
4			5		7	9*					12			10		11		2			8	3	6			30
4		8	5		7									10	12	11*		2			9	3	6			31
4		8	5	6	7									10	11			2			9	3				32
4		8	5	6*	7	12								10	11			2			9	3				33
4		8	5	6	7									10	11			2			9	3				34
4		8	5	6	7						12			10*	11			2			9	3				35
4		8	5		7*				12		10	6			11			2			9	3				36
4		5		11	7	10						6		8				2			9	3				37
4		5		11	7	10						6		8				2			9	3				38
4		5		11	7	10*						6		8	12			2			9	3				39
			5	11	7							6			10	8		2			9	3		4		40
			5		7							6		11	10	8*		2		12	9	3		4		41
			5		7									11	10			2		6	9	3		4	8	42
31	18	33	38	34	42	23	10	7	10		23	18	5	33	20	8	3	23	6	1	14	13	3	3	1	
						1			3	1	4		3	2	4					3						
				3	8	4	3	1	2			1		5	3	1	2	2			1					

Fisher	Roffey	Taylor, T	Gray	Margerrison	Godfrey	Moores	Jennings	Bowles	Taylor, P	Mayo	Hughton	Cunningham	Hallybone	Silkman	McNeill	Sussex	Giles	Foster	Osgood	Blackhall	Houchen	Peach	Banjo	Cornwell	Vincent	
6		4	5	8	7	9	11*				3			10				2		12						3
3		4	5	8	7	9							11	10				2	6							4
3		4	5	8	7	9							11	12	10*			2	6							R
3		4	5	8	7	9					11			10				2	6							5
3		4	5	8	7	9					11		6	10*	12			2								R
5		5	5	5	5	5	1				3		3	4	1			5	3							
														1	1					1						
						3												1								

Fisher	Roffey	Taylor, T	Gray	Margerrison	Godfrey	Moores	Jennings	Bowles	Taylor, P	Mayo	Hughton	Cunningham	Hallybone	Silkman	McNeill	Sussex	Giles	Foster	Osgood	Blackhall	Houchen	Peach	Banjo	Cornwell	Vincent	
2	3	4	5	6	7*	8	9	10	11	12																1/1
2	3	4		6	7	8	9		11		10	5														1/2
2	2	2	1	2	2	2	2	1	2		1	1														
										1																
						2	1																			

1982-83

Manager: Ken Knighton

	P	W	D	L	F	A	Pts
Portsmouth	46	27	10	9	74	41	91
Cardiff City	46	25	11	10	76	50	86
Huddersfield Town	46	23	13	10	84	49	82
Newport County	46	23	9	14	76	54	78
Oxford United	46	22	12	12	71	53	78
Lincoln City	46	23	7	16	77	51	76
Bristol Rovers	46	22	9	15	84	58	75
Plymouth Argyle	46	19	8	19	61	66	65
Brentford	46	18	10	18	88	77	64
Walsall	46	17	13	16	64	63	64
Sheffield United	46	19	7	20	62	64	64
Bradford City	46	16	13	17	68	69	61
Gillingham	46	16	13	17	58	59	61
Bournemouth	46	16	13	17	59	68	61
Southend United	46	15	14	17	66	65	59
Preston North End	46	15	13	18	60	69	58
Millwall	46	14	13	19	64	77	55
Wigan Athletic	46	15	9	22	60	72	54
Exeter City	46	14	12	20	81	104	54
Orient	46	15	9	22	64	88	54
Reading	46	12	17	17	64	79	53
Wrexham	46	12	15	19	56	76	51
Doncaster Rovers	46	9	11	26	57	97	38
Chesterfield	46	8	13	25	43	68	37

Division Three

Match No.	Date		Opponents	Result	Scorers	Atten
1	Aug	28	Chesterfield	2-1	Taylor, Godfrey	2
2	Sep	4	BRADFORD CITY	0-1		2
3		8	CARDIFF CITY	4-0	Foster, Godfrey 2, Silkman	2
4		11	Plymouth Argyle	0-2		3
5		18	BRENTFORD	3-3	Donn, Roffey 2	3
6		25	Lincoln City	0-2		3
7		28	Huddersfield Town	0-6		6
8	Oct	2	DONCASTER ROVERS	1-0	Donn	1
9		9	Reading	0-3		2
10		16	NEWPORT COUNTY	1-5	McNeil	2
11		19	Gillingham	0-4		3
12		23	BRISTOL ROVERS	1-5	Peach	2
13		29	Southend United	1-1	Cunningham	5
14	Nov	2	WALSALL	2-1	Hawley, Sussex	1
15		6	WIGAN ATHLETIC	1-1	Godfrey	2
16		13	Wrexham	0-1		2
17		27	Exeter City	0-2		2
18	Dec	4	OXFORD UNITED	1-5	Houchen	2
19		17	PRESTON NORTH END	2-1	Peach (pen), Kitchen	1
20		26	Millwall	1-0	Houchen	4
21		28	BOURNEMOUTH	5-0	Kitchen, Godfrey 2, Cornwell, Houchen	3
22	Jan	1	Sheffield United	0-3		10
23		12	Bradford City	3-2	Kitchen, Gray, Peach (pen)	3
24		15	CHESTERFIELD	2-0	Peach (pen), Kitchen	2
25		18	PORTSMOUTH	2-1	Peach (pen), Sussex	3
26		22	Brentford	2-5	Blackhall, Godfrey	5
27		29	PLYMOUTH ARGYLE	0-2		2
28	Feb	5	LINCOLN CITY	1-1	Peach	2
29		15	Walsall	0-2		2
30		20	READING	3-3	Godfrey, Cunningham 2	2,
31		26	Newport County	1-4	Silkman	3,
32	Mar	1	GILLINGHAM	2-0	Gray, Houchen (pen)	2
33		5	Bristol Rovers	1-2	Godfrey	6,
34		13	SOUTHEND UNITED	1-1	Houchen	3,
35		19	Wigan Athletic	1-0	Godfrey	2,
36		25	WREXHAM	0-0		1,
37	Apr	2	Bournemouth	0-2		7,
38		4	MILLWALL	2-3	Cornwell, Houchen	4,
39		9	Oxford United	2-2	Houchen, Kitchen	4,
40		12	Doncaster Rovers	3-0	Kitchen 2, Cornwell	2,
41		16	HUDDERSFIELD TOWN	1-3	McNeil	3,
42		23	Preston North End	1-2	Foster,	5,
43		30	EXETER CITY	5-1	Houchen 2, McNeil 2, Viney (og)	2,
44	May	2	Portsmouth	2-2	McNeil, Kitchen	16,
45		7	Cardiff City	0-2		11,
46		14	SHEFFIELD UNITED	4-1	Houchen, Kitchen, Godfrey, Roffey	4,

Appearan
Sub appearan
G

FA Cup

1	Nov	20	BRISTOL CITY	4-1	Foster, Godfrey 2, Sussex	2,
2	Dec	11	Newport County	0-1		4,

Appearan
Sub appearan
G

League Cup

1/1	Aug	31	Gillingham	0-3		2,
1/2	Sep	14	GILLINGHAM	2-0	Osgood, Cunningham	2,

Appearan
Sub appearan
G

Final League Position: 20th in Division Three

	Fisher	Peach	Foster	Gray	Roffey	Godfrey	Donn	Houchen	Silkman	Taylor	Blackhall	Osgood	Vincent	Smith	Cornwell	Cunningham	McNeil	Sussex	Lee	Hawley	Kitchen	Mankelow	Price	Match
	2	3	4	5	6	7	8	9*	10	11	12													1
	2	3	4	5	6	7	8	9	10	11														2
		3	4	5		7	8		10	11	9	2	6											3
		3*	4	5		7	8			11	9	2	6	10	12									4
			4	5	3	7	8		10	11	9	2				6								5
			4	5	3	7	8		10	11*	9	2				6	12							6
			4		3	7	8		10		9*	2	12	5		6	11							7
			4		3	7	8		10	12	9	2		5		6	11*							8
			4	6	3	7	8		10	12	9	2	11*	5										9
			4	5	3	7			10	11	12	2		6*	8		9							10
			4		3	7				11		2		5	8	6	9	10						11
		5	4		3	7			12	11		2*				6		10	8	9				12
		3	4		2		6			11			7			5		10	8	9				13
		3	4		2	12	6			11			7			5		10	8	9*				14
		3	4		2	9	6			11			7			5		10	8					15
		3	4		2	12	6			11*			7			5		10	8	9				16
		3	4		2	8	6*	9		11		7			12	5		10						17
		3	4		2	8	6	9		11*	12	7				5		10						18
		3	4		2	8		9				7			6	5		10			11			19
		3	4		2	8		9				7		12	6	5		11*			10			20
		3	4		2	8		9				7*		12	6	5		11			10			21
		3	4		2	8		9				7			6	5		11			10			22
		3	4	6	2	8		9							7	5		11			10			23
		3	4	7	2	8		9							6	5		11			10			24
		3	4	7	2	8		9						12	6	5		11			10*			25
		3	4	7	2	8		9			10				6	5		11						26
		3	4		2	8		9			10*	7		12	6	5		11						27
		3	4		2	8		9			10	7*			6	5		11				12		28
		3		7	2	8	4	9	12		10*				6	5		11						29
		3		7	2	8	4	9	12						6	5		11				10*		30
		3*	4	7	2	8	12	9	10						6	5		11						31
			4	7	2	8	3	9	10	12					6	5		11*						32
			4	7	2	8	3	9	10*	12				11	6	5								33
		3	4	5		11	7	9							2		12	6			10		8*	34
		5	3	4		11	7	9							2		12	6*			10		8	35
			4	5	3	11	7	9							2		6				10		8	36
		7	4	5	3	11		9							2		6				10		8	37
		7	4	5	3	11		9	12						2		6				10*		8	38
		7	4	5	3	11		9							2		6				10		8	39
		3	4	5	2	6		9							8		11				10		7	40
		3	4	5	2	7		9	12						8		11				10		6*	41
			5	4	2	8*		9	7					12	6		11				10		3	42
			5	4	2	8		9	7						6		11				10		3	43
		3	4	5	2	7*		9	6					12	8		11				10			44
		3	4	5	2	12		9	6					7*	8		11				10			45
		3		5	2	7		9	6						8	4	11				10			46
	2	34	43	30	42	42	22	32	17	15	11	18	7	8	30	28	15	24	5	4	20	1	10	
						3	1		5	4	3		1	6	2		3					1		
		6	2	2	3	11	2	10	2	1	1				3	3	5	2		1	9			

One own-goal

	Fisher	Peach	Foster	Gray	Roffey	Godfrey	Donn	Houchen	Silkman	Taylor	Blackhall	Osgood	Vincent	Smith	Cornwell	Cunningham	McNeil	Sussex	Lee	Hawley	Kitchen	Mankelow	Price	Match
		3	4		2	8	6	9		11		7				5		10						1
		3	4		2	8		9			11	7			6	5		10						2
		2	2		2	2	1	2		1	1	2			1	2		2						
			1			2												1						

	Fisher	Peach	Foster	Gray	Roffey	Godfrey	Donn	Houchen	Silkman	Taylor	Blackhall	Osgood	Vincent	Smith	Cornwell	Cunningham	McNeil	Sussex	Lee	Hawley	Kitchen	Mankelow	Price	Match
	2	3	4	5	6	10	8	9		11*	12		7											1/1
			4	5	6	10	8		10	11*	9	2	7			12								1/2
	1	1	2	2	2	2	2	1	1	2	1	1	2											
											1					1								
												1				1								

1983-84

Manager: Frank Clark

	P	W	D	L	F	A	Pts
Oxford United	46	28	11	7	91	50	95
Wimbledon	46	26	9	11	97	76	87
Hull City	46	23	14	9	71	38	83
Sheffield United	46	24	11	11	86	53	83
Bristol Rovers	46	22	13	11	68	54	79
Walsall	46	22	9	15	68	61	75
Bradford City	46	20	11	15	73	65	71
Gillingham	46	20	10	16	74	69	70
Millwall	46	18	13	15	71	65	67
Bolton Wanderers	46	18	10	18	56	60	64
Orient	46	18	9	19	71	81	63
Burnley	46	16	14	16	76	61	62
Newport County	46	16	14	16	58	75	62
Lincoln City	46	17	10	19	59	62	61
Wigan Athletic	46	16	13	17	46	56	61
Preston North End	46	15	11	20	66	66	56
Bournemouth	46	16	7	23	63	73	55
Rotherham United	46	15	9	22	57	64	54
Plymouth Argyle	46	13	12	21	56	62	51
Brentford	46	11	16	19	69	79	49
Scunthorpe United	46	9	19	18	54	73	46
Southend United	46	10	14	22	55	76	44
Port Vale	46	11	10	25	51	83	43
Exeter City	46	6	15	25	50	84	33

Division Three

Match No.	Date		Opponents	Result	Scorers	Attenda
1	Aug	27	BRADFORD CITY	2-0	Foster, Cunningham	2,6
2	Sep	3	Walsall	1-0	Godfrey	3,0
3		7	Lincoln City	0-2		2,8
4		9	SCUNTHORPE UNITED	1-0	Houchen	2,7
5		17	Rotherham United	1-0	Godfrey	5,5
6		23	BRISTOL ROVERS	0-1		4,2
7	Oct	1	Wimbledon	2-2	McNeil, Houchen	3,3
8		8	Newport County	0-0		3,2
9		14	PORT VALE	3-0	Hales, McNeil, Houchen (pen)	3,0
10		18	SHEFFIELD UNITED	2-0	Godfrey, Houchen	4,0
11		21	Southend United	0-3		4,1
12		24	GILLINGHAM	1-1	Silkman	4,0
13		29	EXETER CITY	2-2	Houchen (pen), Silkman	3,1
14	Nov	1	Wigan Athletic	1-0	Cunningham	3,3
15		5	Bolton Wanderers	2-3	Godfrey, Houchen (pen)	5,8
16		12	BRENTFORD	2-0	Godfrey, Brooks	3,6
17		26	Hull City	1-2	Kitchen	6,8
18	Dec	3	PRESTON NORTH END	2-1	Kitchen, McNeil	2,6
19		17	PLYMOUTH ARGYLE	3-2	McNeil, Cornwell 2	2,6
20		26	Millwall	3-4	Sussex, Kitchen, Godfrey	5,1
21		27	BOURNEMOUTH	2-0	Cornwell, Sussex	4,0
22		31	Oxford United	2-5	Houchen (pen), Cornwell	11,1
23	Jan	2	BURNLEY	1-2	Houchen	4,4
24		7	WALSALL	0-1		3,1
25		14	Bradford City	1-4	Cunningham	3,9
26		22	ROTHERHAM UNITED	2-1	Brooks, Houchen (pen)	2,2
27		27	WIGAN ATHLETIC	0-0		2,1
28	Feb	4	WIMBLEDON	2-6	Kitchen, Corbett	3,3
29		11	Bristol Rovers	0-0		4,7
30		18	Exeter City	4-3	Cunningham 3, Godfrey	2,3
31		26	SOUTHEND UNITED	1-0	Brooks	3,0
32	Mar	3	Sheffield United	3-6	Silkman, Cornwell, Kitchen	10,0
33		6	BOLTON WANDERERS	2-1	Godfrey, Kitchen	2,4
34		10	Brentford	1-1	Kitchen	4,3
35		17	NEWPORT COUNTY	2-2	Godfrey, Silkman	2,3
36		31	Gillingham	1-3	Godfrey	3,0
37	Apr	7	LINCOLN CITY	1-1	Brooks	2,1
38		9	Port Vale	0-2		3,1
39		14	Preston North End	1-3	Cornwell	3,1
40		21	MILLWALL	5-3	Cornwell, Kitchen 4	3,8
41		24	Bournemouth	2-3	Kitchen (pen), Brooks	3,7
42		28	HULL CITY	3-1	Sussex 2, Brooks	3,0
43	May	1	Scunthorpe United	1-3	Brooks	2,2
44		5	Burnley	3-2	Sussex, Hales, Brooks (pen)	3,2
45		7	OXFORD UNITED	1-2	Brooks (pen)	5,6
46		12	Plymouth Argyle	1-3	Sussex	7,6

Appearan
Sub appearan
Gc

FA Cup

1	Nov	19	Wimbledon	1-2	Smith (og)	4,3

Appearan
Sub appearan
Gc

League Cup

1/1	Aug	30	Aldershot	1-3	Houchen	1,9
1/2	Sep	13	ALDERSHOT	3-3	Godfrey, Cornwell, Kitchen	2,2

Appearan
Sub appearan
Gc

Final League Position: 11th in Division Three

Cornwell	Corbett	Foster	Cunningham	Hales	Godfrey	Silkman	Houchen	Kitchen	McNeil	Roffey	Sussex	Brooks	Osgood	Harvey	Banfield	Wilkins	Mancini	Shoemake	
2	3	4	5	6	7	8	9	10	11										1
2	3	4	5	6	7	8	9		11	10									2
7	5	4		6*	10	8	9	12	11	2	3								3
2	3	4	5	6	7	8	9		11	10									4
2	3	4	5	6	7	8	9		11	10									5
2	3	4*	5		7	8	9	10	11	6	12								6
2	3		5	4	7	8	9		11	6	10								7
2	3	8	5	6	7		9		11	10	4								8
2	3	8	5	6	7	4	9		11	10									9
2	3	8	5	6	7	4	9		11	10									10
2	3	8*	5	6	7	4	9		11	10		12							11
2	3		5	6*	7	4	9		11	10	8	12							12
2	3		5	6	7	4	9		11	10*	8	12							13
2	3	12	5	6	7*	4	9		11		8	10							14
2	3		5	6	7	4	9		11		8	10							15
2*	3		5	6	7	4	9		11	12	8	10							16
2	3		5	6	7	4	9	10		11		8							17
2	3		5	6	7	4	9	12	11	10		8*							18
2	3			6	7		9	10	11	4	5	8							19
2	3			6	7		9	10	11	4	5	8							20
2	3		5	6	7		9	10	11*	4	12	8							21
2	3		5	6	7		9		11	4	10	8							22
2	3		5	6	7	4	9	10		11		8							23
2	3		5	6*	7	4	9	10		11	12	8							24
2	3		5	6	7	10	9		11	4		8							25
2	3		5	6		7	9	10	11	4		8							26
2	3		5	6	12	7	9*	10	11	4		8							27
2	3		5	6	12	7	9	10	11	4		8*							28
2			5	6	9	7		10	11	4		8	3						29
2			5	6	9	7		10*	11	4	12	8	3						30
2				6	9	7	12	10	11*	4	5	8	3						31
2	4			6	9	7		10	11*		5	8	3	12					32
2	4			6	9	7	12	10	11*			8	3		5				33
2	4		5	6	9	7		10*	12	11		8	3						34
2	4		5	6	9	7		10			11	8	3						35
6	4		5		9	7		10			11	8	3		2				36
6	4		5	2	9	7		10	12		11*	8				3			37
6	4		5	2	9	7		12			11	8*				3	10		38
6	4		5		9*	7		10			12	8			2	3	11		39
6	4			2		7		10	11		9	8	5			3			40
6	4			2		7		10	11		9	8	5			3		1	41
6*	4			2		7		10	11		9	8	5	12		3		1	42
	4			2		7		10	11		9	8	5	12	6*	3		1	43
	4		5	2	9	7			11		10	8			6	3			44
	4		5	2	6	7		10	11		9	8				3			45
	4		5	2	10	7*			11		9	8		12	6	3		1	46
42	43	10	36	43	39	41	28	26	37	28	24	33	12		6	10	2	4	
		1			2		2	3	2	1	5	3		4					
7	1	1	6	2	10	4	9	12	4		6	9							

Cornwell	Corbett	Foster	Cunningham	Hales	Godfrey	Silkman	Houchen	Kitchen	McNeil	Roffey	Sussex	Brooks	Osgood	Harvey	Banfield	Wilkins	Mancini	Shoemake	
2	3		5	6	7	4	9	10		11		8							1
1	1		1	1	1	1	1	1		1		1							

One own-goal

Cornwell	Corbett	Foster	Cunningham	Hales	Godfrey	Silkman	Houchen	Kitchen	McNeil	Roffey	Sussex	Brooks	Osgood	Harvey	Banfield	Wilkins	Mancini	Shoemake	
2	3	4	5	6	7	8	9	10*	11		12								1/1
2	3	4	5	6	7	8	9	12	11	10*									1/2
2	2	2	2	2	2	2	2	1	2	1									
								1			1								
1					1		1	1											

1984-85

Manager: Frank Clark

	P	W	D	L	F	A	Pts
Bradford City*	46	28	10	8	77	45	94
Millwall	46	26	12	8	73	42	90
Hull City	46	25	12	9	78	49	87
Gillingham	46	25	8	13	80	62	83
Bristol City	46	24	9	13	74	47	81
Bristol Rovers	46	21	12	13	66	48	75
Derby County	46	19	13	14	65	54	70
York City	46	20	9	17	70	57	69
Reading	46	19	12	15	68	62	69
Bournemouth	46	19	11	16	57	46	68
Walsall	46	18	13	15	58	52	67
Rotherham United	46	18	11	17	55	55	65
Brentford	46	16	14	16	62	64	62
Doncaster Rovers	46	17	8	21	72	74	59
Plymouth Argyle	46	15	14	17	62	65	59
Wigan Athletic	46	15	14	17	60	64	59
Bolton Wanderers	46	16	6	24	69	75	54
Newport County	46	13	13	20	55	67	52
Lincoln City	46	11	18	17	50	51	51
Swansea City	46	12	11	23	53	80	47
Burnley	46	11	13	22	60	73	46
Orient	46	11	13	22	51	76	46
Preston North End	46	13	7	26	51	100	46
Cambridge United	46	4	9	33	37	95	21

*Includes one match abandoned at 0–0 after 40 minutes. Result stands.

Division Three

Match No.	Date		Opponents	Result	Scorers	Attend
1	Aug	25	Brentford	1-0	Foster	4
2	Sep	1	GILLINGHAM	2-4	Godfrey, Cornwell	2
3		9	Millwall	0-1		5
4		15	YORK CITY	1-3	Cadette	2
5		18	BURNLEY	0-2		2
6		22	Bristol City	2-3	Silkman, Cornwell	6,
7		29	BRADFORD CITY	1-0	Brooks	2,
8	Oct	2	Preston North End	1-0	Castle	3
9		6	Swansea City	1-3	Brooks (pen)	4,
10		13	CAMBRIDGE UNITED	2-2	Cornwell 2	2
11		20	Newport County	0-2		2
12		23	PLYMOUTH ARGYLE	3-0	Godfrey 2, Brooks	2
13		27	Wigan Athletic	2-4	Cornwell 2	3,
14	Nov	3	WALSALL	0-3		2,
15		7	Reading	1-1	Jones	2
16		10	HULL CITY	4-5	Godfrey, Jones, Cornwell, Silkman	2
17		24	Rotherham United	1-2	Cunningham	3,
18		30	BRISTOL ROVERS	1-4	Cornwell	2,
19	Dec	15	Derby County	0-1		10,
20		21	Bournemouth	0-1		3,
21		26	LINCOLN CITY	1-0	Cadette	2,
22		29	DONCASTER ROVERS	2-1	Cadette 2	2,
23	Jan	1	Bolton Wanderers	0-0		4,
24		12	Gillingham	0-2		4,
25		29	MILLWALL	1-0	Cusack (og)	4,
26	Feb	2	Bradford City	1-4	Jones	5,
27		9	BRISTOL CITY	0-1		2,
28		16	Burnley	1-1	Juryeff	3,
29		23	Walsall	2-4	Corbett, Silkman (pen)	4,
30	Mar	2	WIGAN ATHLETIC	1-1	Godfrey	2,
31		5	Plymouth Argyle	1-1	Sussex	4,
32		9	NEWPORT COUNTY	1-1	Godfrey	2,
33		16	Cambridge United	3-2	Juryeff 2, Mountford	2,
34		23	SWANSEA CITY	4-2	Juryeff 2, Godfrey, Jones	2,
35		30	READING	0-0		2,
36	Apr	2	York City	1-2	Cornwell	3,
37		6	Lincoln City	0-0		2,
38		9	BOLTON WANDERERS	4-3	Brooks, Godfrey 3	2,
39		13	Hull City	1-5	Brooks (pen)	7,
40		16	BRENTFORD	0-1		3,
41		20	ROTHERHAM UNITED	0-1		2,
42		27	Bristol Rovers	1-0	Juryeff	2,5
43		30	PRESTON NORTH END	0-0		3,1
44	May	4	DERBY COUNTY	2-2	Juryeff, Cornwell	3,0
45		6	Doncaster Rovers	1-1	Sussex	2,
46		11	BOURNEMOUTH	0-0		3,5

Appearan
Sub appearan
Go

FA Cup

1	Nov	19	Buckingham Town	2-1	Cornwell (pen), McNeil	3,0
2	Dec	8	TORQUAY UNITED	3-0	Godfrey, Jones, Foster	2,7
3	Jan	5	WEST BROMWICH ALBION	2-1	Silkman, Cadette	7,0
4		26	SOUTHAMPTON	0-2		17,6

Appearan
Sub appearan
Go

League Cup

1/1	Aug	28	SOUTHEND UNITED	2-1	Cunningham, Sussex	2,6
1/2	Sep	5	Southend United	0-0		2,3
2/1		25	LUTON TOWN	1-4	Cornwell	3,0
2/2	Oct	9	Luton Town	1-3	Silkman	3,3

Appearanc
Sub appearanc
Go

Final League Position: 22nd in Division Three – Relegated

Hales	Stride	Cunningham	Foster	Corbett	Silkman	Brooks	Sussex	Godfrey	Cadette	McNeil	Cornwell	Banfield	Castle	Jones	Harvey	Donnellan	Juryeff	Mountford	
2	3	4	5	6	7	8	9	10*	11	12									1
2	3	4*	5	6	7	8	9	10	11		12								2
2	3		5		7	8	9	10		11	4	6							3
2	3		5		7	8	9	12	10	11	4	6*							4
2*	3		5	10	7	8	9		11	12	4	6							5
2	3		5	4	7	8	9	11	10*		12	6							6
2			5	4	7	8			11	12	10	6*	3	9					7
2			5	4	7	8			11		10	6	3	9					8
2			5	4	7	8			11	12	10	6*	3	9					9
2	3			4	6	8		12	11		10	5		9	7*				10
2	3	5	6	4	7	8		11			10			9					11
2	3	5	6	4	7	8		11			10			9					12
2	3	5	6	4	7	8		9	11*		10	12							13
2	3	6	5	4*	7			11			10	8		9	12				14
2	3	6	5*	4	7	12		11		8	10			9					15
2	3	6		4	7			11		8	10	5		9					16
2	3	5	4	6		8		7	11		10			9					17
2		4	5	3	6	8		7	11		10			9					18
2	3*	4	5		6	8		7			10	11	12	9					19
2		4		5	6	8		7			10	11	3	9					20
2		4	5		6			7	8		10	11	3	9					21
2		4	5		6			7	8			11	3	9		10			22
2		4	5		6			7	8			11	3	9		10			23
2		4	5		6			7	8			11	3	9		10			24
2		4	5		6		8	7				11	3	9		10			25
2		4	5		6		8	7				11	3	9	12	10*			26
2*		4	5	11	6		12	7					3	9	8	10			27
2		4	5		6			7			10	11	3	9			8		28
2			5	4	6		12	7			10*	11	3	9			8		29
			5	4	6		2	7			10	11*	3	9			8	12	30
		2	5	4	6		11	7			10*		3	9			8	12	31
	3	2	5	4	6		11	7						9			8	10	32
	3	2	5	4	6		11	7						9			8	10	33
		2	5	4	6		11*	7			12		3	9			8	10	34
	3	2	5		6	12	11*	7			4			9			8	10	35
	11*	2	5					7	12		4	6	3	9			8	10	36
12	3	2	5		6	11		7			4			9*			8	10	37
	3	2			6	11		7			4	5		9			8	10	38
	3	2	5		6	11					4	7		9			8	10	39
	3	2	5		6	11		7			4			9			8	10	40
	3	2	5		6	11		7	12		4			9*			8	10	41
	3	2	5		6	11					4		7	9			8	10	42
	3*	2	5		6	11		12			4		7	9			8	10	43
6	3	2	5			11	12	7	9		4*						8	10	44
4	3	2	5			11	6	12	9				7*				8	10	45
4	3	2	5		7	11	12	10*	9		6						8		46
32	29	36	42	24	42	27	15	36	19	4	33	24	20	36	2	6	19	14	
1						2	4	4	2	4	3	1	1		2			2	
		1	1	1	3	5	2	10	4		10		1	4			7	1	

One own-goal

Hales	Stride	Cunningham	Foster	Corbett	Silkman	Brooks	Sussex	Godfrey	Cadette	McNeil	Cornwell	Banfield	Castle	Jones	Harvey	Donnellan	Juryeff	Mountford	
2		4	5	3	6			7		8	10	11		9					1
2	11	4	5		6	8		7			10		3	9					2
2		4	5		6			7	8			11	3	9		10			3
2		4	5		6		8*	7				11	3	9	12	10			4
4	1	4	4	1	4	1	1	4	1	1	2	3	3	4		2			
															1				
			1		1			1	1	1	1			1					

Hales	Stride	Cunningham	Foster	Corbett	Silkman	Brooks	Sussex	Godfrey	Cadette	McNeil	Cornwell	Banfield	Castle	Jones	Harvey	Donnellan	Juryeff	Mountford	
2	3	4	5	6	7	8	9	10	11*	12									1/1
2	3		5	6	7	8	9	10	11		4								1/2
2	3*		5	4	7	8	9	10	11		12	6							2/1
2	3		5*	4	7	8			11	12	10	6		9					2/2
4	4	1	4	4	4	4	3	3	4		2	2		1					
										2	1								
		1			1		1				1								

1985-86

Manager: Frank Clark

	P	W	D	L	F	A	Pts
Swindon Town	46	32	6	8	82	43	102
Chester City	46	23	15	8	83	50	84
Mansfield Town	46	23	12	11	74	47	81
Port Vale	46	21	16	9	67	37	79
Orient	46	20	12	14	79	64	72
Colchester United	46	19	13	14	88	63	70
Hartlepool United	46	20	10	16	68	67	70
Northampton Town	46	18	10	18	79	58	64
Southend United	46	18	10	18	69	67	64
Hereford United	46	18	10	18	74	73	64
Stockport County	46	17	13	16	63	71	64
Crewe Alexandra	46	18	9	19	54	61	63
Wrexham	46	17	9	20	68	80	60
Burnley	46	16	11	19	60	65	59
Scunthorpe United	46	15	14	17	50	55	59
Aldershot	46	17	7	22	66	74	58
Peterborough United	46	13	17	16	52	64	56
Rochdale	46	14	13	19	57	77	55
Tranmere Rovers	46	15	9	22	74	73	54
Halifax Town	46	14	12	20	60	71	54
Exeter City	46	13	15	18	47	59	54
Cambridge United	46	15	9	22	65	80	54
Preston North End	46	11	10	25	54	89	43
Torquay United	46	9	10	27	43	88	37

Final League Position: 5th in Division Four

Division Four

Match No.	Date		Opponents	Result	Scorers	Attenda
1	Aug	17	TRANMERE ROVERS	3-1	Godfrey, Brooks, Cornwell	2,
2		23	Southend United	1-5	Jones	3,6
3		27	PETERBOROUGH UNITED	2-2	Mountford, Hales	2,5
4		31	Hartlepool United	2-1	Cornwell 2	2,
5	Sep	7	PORT VALE	1-0	Cornwell	2,4
6		13	Halifax Town	1-2	Shinners	1,2
7		18	Mansfield Town	1-1	Shinners	4,1
8		21	COLCHESTER UNITED	1-2	Shinners	2,5
9		28	Wrexham	3-1	Shinners 2, Godfrey	1,8
10	Oct	1	ROCHDALE	5-0	Juryeff, Shinners, Jones 2, Brooks (pen)	2,6
11		5	SCUNTHORPE UNITED	3-0	Shinners 2, Brooks (pen)	2,8
12		12	Exeter City	1-1	Godfrey	2,0
13		19	Cambridge United	2-1	Jones, Dowman (og)	2,7
14		22	ALDERSHOT	1-1	Shinners	2,8
15		26	STOCKPORT COUNTY	0-1		3,0
16	Nov	2	Torquay United	2-2	Brooks, Sussex	1,2
17		5	Crewe Alexandra	3-1	Juryeff, Sussex, Brooks	1,2
18		9	PRESTON NORTH END	2-0	Cornwell, Juryeff	2,8
19		23	Chester City	0-3		2,6
20		30	SWINDON TOWN	1-0	Cornwell	3,1
21	Dec	14	Burnley	0-1		3,0
22		21	SOUTHEND UNITED	3-0	Brooks (pen), Shinners, Juryeff	3,5
23		26	HEREFORD UNITED	2-2	Juryeff, Hales	2,7
24		28	Peterborough United	2-2	Cunningham, Sussex	3,2
25	Jan	11	HARTLEPOOL UNITED	1-1	Brooks	3,6
26		17	Tranmere Rovers	3-0	Shinners, Juryeff, Cornwell	1,6
27	Feb	1	Port Vale	0-2		3,0
28		4	Aldershot	1-1	Shinners	1,2
29		8	CAMBRIDGE UNITED	3-1	Juryeff, Shinners, Jones	2,7
30		15	MANSFIELD TOWN	0-1		3,7
31	Mar	1	WREXHAM	1-3	Juryeff	2,1
32		8	Scunthorpe United	2-2	Shinners, Jones	1,4
33		15	EXETER CITY	2-2	Cunningham, Sussex	2,2
34		18	TORQUAY UNITED	4-2	Cornwell, Jones, Wright (og), Shinners	1,8
35		21	Stockport County	3-2	Shinners, Jones, Comfort	3,1
36		29	NORTHAMPTON TOWN	0-1		2,9
37		31	Hereford United	2-3	Dickenson, Foster	2,8
38	Apr	5	CREWE ALEXANDRA	0-1		1,9
39		8	Colchester United	0-4		1,7
40		12	Preston North End	3-1	Juryeff 2, Comfort	4,7
41		15	Northampton Town	3-2	Jones, Comfort, Foster	1,7
42		19	CHESTER CITY	0-0		2,6
43		22	HALIFAX TOWN	1-0	Godfrey	1,4
44		27	Swindon Town	1-4	Comfort	8,0
45	May	3	BURNLEY	3-0	Harvey 2, Comfort	1,9
46		5	Rochdale	4-1	Castle 4	1,2

Appearanc
Sub appearanc
Go

FA Cup

1	Nov	16	VS Rugby	2-2	Brooks 2 (1 pen)	2,5
R		19	VS RUGBY	4-1	Jones, Castle, Juryeff, Brooks	2,3
2	Dec	7	SLOUGH TOWN	2-2	Cornwell, Juryeff	3,4
R		10	Slough Town	3-2	Juryeff, Godfrey, Shinners	3,0
3	Jan	6	Oldham Athletic	2-1	Shinners, Foster	3,6
4		25	Sheffield Wednesday	0-5		19,0

Appearanc
Sub appearanc
Go

League Cup

1/1	Aug	20	Aldershot	3-1	Godfrey, Jones, Sussex	1,4
1/2	Sep	3	ALDERSHOT	2-2	Shinners, Brooks	1,7
2/1		23	TOTTENHAM HOTSPUR	2-0	Godfrey 2	13,8
2/2		30	Tottenham Hotspur	0-4		21,0

Appearanc
Sub appearanc
Go

Hales	Dickenson	Sussex	Sitton	Cornwell	Godfrey	Brooks	Jones	Castle	Mountford	Shinners	Corbett	Cunningham	Foster	Juryeff	John	Greygoose	Harvey	Comfort	
2	3	4	5	6	7	8	9*	10	11	12									1
2	3	4	5	6	7	8	9	10*	11	12									2
2	3	4	5	6		8	9		11	7	10								3
2	3	4	5	6		8		10		9	11	7							4
2	3	4*	5	6		8	12		11	9	10	7							5
2	3	4	5	6		8	11			9	10	7							6
2	3	4	5	6		8*	11	10		9			7	12					7
2	3	4	5	6*	10	8		11		9			7	12					8
2	3	4	5	12	10	8	11			9	6		7						9
2	3	4	5			8	11			9	6		7	10					10
2	3*	4	5	12		8	11			9	6		7	10					11
2	3	4	5*	8	10		11	12		9	6		7						12
2	3	4		6	10	8	11			9		5	7						13
2	3	4	5	6	10*	8	11	12		9			7						14
2	3	4	5	6		8	11	12		9*			7	10					15
2	3	4	5	6		8	11	9					7	10					16
2	3	4	5	6		8	9	10					7	11					17
2	3	4	5	6		8	9	10	12				7*	11					18
2	3	4	7	6	10	8	9					5		11					19
2	3	4	5	6	10*	8	9		12					11	7				20
2	3	4	7	6	10	8	9*		12				5	11					21
2	3	4	7	6		8	10			9			5	11					22
2	3	4	7	6	12	8*	10			9			5	11					23
2	3	4		6		8	10			9		7	5	11					24
2	3	4		6		8	10		12	9		7*	5	11					25
2	3	4		6		8	10			9		7	5	11					26
	3		4	6		8	10	7	2	9			5	11					27
	3		2	6		8	10	7	4	9			5	11		1			28
	3		2			8	10	7	4	9	6		5	11					29
	3		2	12		8	10*	7	4	9	6		5	11					303
2	3	10	6	7		8*			4	9		5		11			12		1
2	3	10		7			4			9		6	5				8	11	32
2*	3	10		7		12	4			9		6	5				8	11	33
	3*	10	2	7		12	4			9		6	5				8	11	34
	3	10	2	7			4			9		6	5				8	11	35
6	3	10	2	7			4			9			5				8	11	36
	3	10	6	7			4		2	9			5				8	11	37
	3	10	6	7			4		2	9			5				8	11	38
2	3	10	6	7				12		9			5	4			8*	11	39
	3	12	6	7			4	10					5	9	2		8	11*	40
	3		6	7		8	4	10					5	9	2			11	41
	3		6	7	12	8	4	10*					5	9	2			11	42
	3			6	7	8	4	10					5	9	2			11	43
	3		6	7	12	8	4*	10					5	9	2			11	44
	3		6	7	4	12		10		9*			5		2		8	11	45
	3		6	7	5	8	4	10							2		9	11	46
31	46	35	39	41	13	35	40	19	11	32	10	13	36	25	8	1	11	15	
		1		3	3	3	1	4	4	2				2			1		
2	1	4		8	4	7	9	4	1	16		2	2	10			2	5	

Two own-goals

Hales	Dickenson	Sussex	Sitton	Cornwell	Godfrey	Brooks	Jones	Castle	Mountford	Shinners	Corbett	Cunningham	Foster	Juryeff	John	Greygoose	Harvey	Comfort	
2	3	4*		6		8	10	12	7	9		5		11					1
2	3			6	7*	8	9	10	4					11	5		12		R
2	3	10	5	6	7	8				9			4	11					2
2	3	10	5	6	7	8			12	9			4	11*					R
2	3	4		6		8	10			9		7	5	11					3
2*	3	4		6	11	8	10		12	9		7	5						4
6	6	5	2	6	4	6	4	1	2	5		3	4	5	1				
								1	2								1		
				1	1	3	1	1		2			1	3					

Hales	Dickenson	Sussex	Sitton	Cornwell	Godfrey	Brooks	Jones	Castle	Mountford	Shinners	Corbett	Cunningham	Foster	Juryeff	John	Greygoose	Harvey	Comfort	
2	3	4	5	6	7	8	9*		11	12	10								1/1
2	3	4	5	6		8		10		9	11	7							1/2
2	3	4	5		10	8	11			9	6		7						2/1
2	3	4	5	6	11*	8	9		12				7	10					2/2
4	4	4	4	3	3	4	3	1	1	2	3	1	2	1					
									1	1									
		1			3	1	1			1									

1986-87

Manager: Frank Clark

	P	W	D	L	F	A	Pts
Northampton Town	46	30	9	7	103	53	99
Preston North End	46	26	12	8	72	47	90
Southend United	46	25	5	16	68	55	80
Wolverhampton W	46	24	7	15	69	50	79
Colchester United	46	21	7	18	64	56	70
Aldershot	46	20	10	16	64	57	70
Orient	46	20	9	17	64	61	69
Scunthorpe United	46	18	12	16	73	57	66
Wrexham	46	15	20	11	70	51	65
Peterborough United	46	17	14	15	57	50	65
Cambridge United	46	17	11	18	60	62	62
Swansea City	46	17	11	18	56	61	62
Cardiff City	46	15	16	15	48	50	61
Exeter City	46	11	23	12	53	49	56
Halifax Town	46	15	10	21	59	74	55
Hereford United	46	14	11	21	60	61	53
Crewe Alexandra	46	13	14	19	70	72	53
Hartlepool United	46	11	18	17	44	65	51
Stockport County	46	13	12	21	40	69	51
Tranmere Rovers	46	11	17	18	54	72	50
Rochdale	46	11	17	18	54	73	50
Burnley	46	12	13	21	53	74	49
Torquay United	46	10	18	18	56	72	48
Lincoln City	46	12	12	22	45	65	48

Division Four

Match No.	Date		Opponents	Result	Scorers	Attenda
1	Aug	23	Exeter City	0-1		2,1
2		30	PETERBOROUGH UNITED	1-0	Foster	2,4
3	Sep	6	Swansea City	1-4	Cunningham	4,
4		13	SCUNTHORPE UNITED	3-1	Jones, Godfrey, Comfort	1,8
5		16	ROCHDALE	3-0	Cornwell (pen), Castle, Jones	2,1
6		20	Hereford United	1-1	Cunningham	2,4
7		27	HARTLEPOOL UNITED	2-0	Juryeff, Comfort	2,6
8		30	Lincoln City	0-2		1,4
9	Oct	4	SOUTHEND UNITED	1-0	Cornwell	3,0
10		10	Crewe Alexandra	2-3	Cornwell, Brooks	2,2
11		18	WREXHAM	2-4	Castle 2	2,6
12		25	Wolverhampton W	1-3	Castle	4,
13		31	STOCKPORT COUNTY	1-0	Harvey	2,7
14	Nov	4	NORTHAMPTON TOWN	0-1		3,4
15		7	Colchester United	0-0		3,
16		21	Halifax Town	0-4		1,4
17		29	TRANMERE ROVERS	2-2	Hales, Brooks	2,
18	Dec	13	BURNLEY	2-0	Jones 2	2,4
19		20	Preston North End	0-1		5,9
20		26	ALDERSHOT	1-3	Cornwell	2,
21		27	Torquay United	2-2	Godfrey, Foster	1,3
22	Jan	3	HALIFAX TOWN	1-3	Castle	2,2
23		17	Peterborough United	1-0	Godfrey	3,5
24		24	SWANSEA CITY	1-4	Godfrey	2,6
25	Feb	7	Rochdale	0-0		1,4
26		10	Scunthorpe United	2-0	Shinners, Comfort	2,0
27		14	HEREFORD UNITED	2-0	Brooks, Dalziel (og)	2,
28		21	Hartlepool United	3-1	Godfrey 2, Shinners	1,4
29		28	LINCOLN CITY	2-1	Godfrey, Comfort	2,9
30	Mar	2	Stockport County	2-2	Smalley, Shinners	1,8
31		7	WOLVERHAMPTON W	3-1	Godfrey, Brooks, Shinners (pen)	4,6
32		10	Cambridge United	0-2		2,8
33		14	Wrexham	1-1	Comfort	1,7
34		17	CARDIFF CITY	2-0	Comfort 2	2,4
35		21	CREWE ALEXANDRA	1-1	Shinners	2,9
36		24	Cardiff City	1-1	Sussex	1,5
37		27	Southend United	1-2	Cunningham	4,1
38	Apr	3	COLCHESTER UNITED	1-0	Jones	3,1
39		7	EXETER CITY	2-0	Jones, Godfrey	2,4
40		12	Northampton Town	0-2		6,
41		18	CAMBRIDGE UNITED	3-0	Godfrey, Cornwell, Comfort	2,9
42		20	Aldershot	2-1	Cornwell, Juryeff	3,1
43		25	PRESTON NORTH END	1-2	Cornwell (pen)	5,2
44	May	1	Tranmere Rovers	3-1	Comfort 2, Brooks	1,
45		4	TORQUAY UNITED	3-2	Howard 2, Cunningham	4,
46		9	Burnley	1-2	Comfort	15,

Appearan
Sub appearan
Gc

FA Cup

1	Nov	15	Woodford Town	1-0	Foster	2,4
2	Dec	6	Bournemouth	1-0	Harvey	4,3
3	Jan	10	WEST HAM UNITED	1-1	Castle (pen)	19,2
R		31	West Ham United	1-4	Brooks	19,4

Appearan
Sub appearan
Gc

League Cup

1/1	Aug	26	CAMBRIDGE UNITED	2-2	Juryeff, Harvey	1,5
1/2	Sep	2	Cambridge United	0-1		2,6

Appearan
Sub appearan
Gc

Final League Position: 7th in Division Four

Sitton	Dickenson	Cunningham	Foster	Cornwell	Harvey	Brooks	Juryeff	Jones	Comfort	Castle	Godfrey	John	Hales	Sussex	Fishenden	Mountford	Hughton	Smalley	Shinners	Howard	Cass	
2	3	4*	5	6	7	8	9	10	11	12												1
2	3	4	5	6	7	8	9		11		10											2
2	3	4		6	7*	8	9		11	12	10	5										3
	3	4		6	12	8		9*	11	7	10	5	2									4
	3	4		6		8		9	11	7	10	5	2									5
	3	4		6	12	8		9	11	7	10	5	2*									6
	3		4	6		8	2	9	11	7	10*	5		12								7
	3		4	6		8	2	9*	11	7	10	5		12								8
2	3		4	6			8	9	11	7	10*	5		12								9
2	3		4	6		8	10	9*	11	7	12	5										10
2*	3		4	6	12	8	10	9	11	7		5										11
2	3		4	6	12	8	10	9	11	7		5*										12
2	3		4	6	5	8		9	11	7					10							13
2			4	6	5	8		9	11*	7				12	10	3						14
2	3		4	6	12	8		9	11	7					10*	5						15
2	3		4	6		8	9		11	7			5*	12	10							16
2	3		4	6	10	8	9*		11	7	12		5									17
2	3		4	6	10	8		9	11	7			5									18
	3	2	4	6	10	8		9	11	7			5									19
	3	2	4	6	9	7		8	12	10*			5				11					20
	3	2	4	6	10	8*			12	7	9		5				11					21
	3	6	4	12		8		10*	9	7	11		5				2					22
	3	6		4		8		9		7	10	11	5				2					23
	3	6*	2	4		8		9	12	7	10	11	5									24
	3	6		2		8		11	12	7	10*		5					4	9			25
	3	6		2		8		11*	12		10		5	7				4	9			26
	3	6		2		8			11		10		5	7				4	9			27
	3	2		6		8			11		10		5	7				4	9			28
	3	2		6		8			11		10		5	7				4	9			29
	3	2		6		8			11		10		5	7				4	9			30
	3			6		8			11		10	2	5	7				4	9			31
	3			6		8			11		10	2	5	7				4	9			32
	3	2		6		8			11		10		5	7				4	9			33
	3	2		6		8			11		10		5	7				4	9			34
	3	2		6		8			11		10			7				4	9	5		35
	3	2		6		8			11*		10		12	7				4	9	5		36
	3	2		6		8			11		10		12	7				4	9*	5		37
	3	2*		6		8		9	11		10		12	7				4		5		38
	3*			6		8		9	11		10	2	12	7				4		5		39
	3	2		6		8*		9	11		10		12	7				4		5	1	40
		2		6		8		9	11		10		3				7	4		5	1	41
		2		6		8	12	9*	11		10		3				7	4		5	1	42
		2		6		8	12	9	11		10		3*				7	4		5	1	43
		2		6		8		9	11		10		3				7	4		5	1	44
		2		6		8		9	11		10		3				7	4		5	1	45
		2		6		8		9	11		10		3				7	4		5	1	46
13	39	31	19	45	10	45	11	30	40	22	34	15	28	15	4	2	10	22	13	12	7	
				1	5		2		5	2	2		5	5								
		4	2	7	1	5	2	6	11	5	10		1	1				1	5	2		

One own-goal

Sitton	Dickenson	Cunningham	Foster	Cornwell	Harvey	Brooks	Juryeff	Jones	Comfort	Castle	Godfrey	John	Hales	Sussex	Fishenden	Mountford	Hughton	Smalley	Shinners	Howard	Cass	
2	3		4	6	12	8		9	11	7					10	5*						1
2	3		4	6	10*	8			11	7			5			12			9			2
	3	6	4	2	12	8		9	13	7	10+	11	5*									3
	3	6*	4	2		8		9		7	10	11	5						12			R
2	4	2	4	4	1	4		3	2	4	2	2	3		1	1			1			
					2				1							1			1			
			1		1	1				1												

Sitton	Dickenson	Cunningham	Foster	Cornwell	Harvey	Brooks	Juryeff	Jones	Comfort	Castle	Godfrey	
2	3	4	5	6	7	8	9	10*	11		12	1/1
2	3	4	5	6	7*	8	9		11	12	10	1/2
2	2	2	2	2	2	2	2	1	2		1	
										1	1	
					1		1					

1987-88

Manager: Frank Clark

	P	W	D	L	F	A	Pts
Wolverhampton W	46	27	9	10	82	43	90
Cardiff City	46	24	13	9	66	41	85
Bolton Wanderers	46	22	12	12	66	42	78
Torquay United	46	21	14	11	66	41	77
Scunthorpe United	46	20	17	9	76	51	77
Swansea City	46	20	10	16	62	56	70
Peterborough United	46	20	10	16	52	53	70
Leyton Orient	46	19	12	15	85	63	69
Colchester United	46	19	10	17	47	51	67
Burnley	46	20	7	19	57	62	67
Wrexham	46	20	6	20	69	58	66
Scarborough	46	17	14	15	56	48	65
Darlington	46	18	11	17	71	69	65
Tranmere Rovers*	46	19	9	18	61	53	64
Cambridge United	46	16	13	17	50	52	61
Hartlepool United	46	15	14	17	50	57	59
Crewe Alexandra	46	13	19	14	57	53	58
Halifax Town**	46	14	14	18	54	59	55
Hereford United	46	14	12	20	41	59	54
Stockport County	46	12	15	19	44	58	51
Rochdale	46	11	15	20	47	76	48
Exeter City	46	11	13	22	53	68	46
Carlisle United	46	12	8	26	57	86	44
Newport County	46	6	7	33	35	105	25

*Two points deducted for failing to meet a fixture.
**One point deducted for fielding an unregistered player

Division Four

Match No.	Date		Opponents	Result	Scorers	Attend
1	Aug	15	Cardiff City	1-1	Smalley	3,
2		22	SCARBOROUGH	3-1	Day, Comfort, Nugent	3,
3		29	Torquay United	1-1	Castle	2,
4	Sep	1	BURNLEY	4-1	Comfort, Hull 2, Godfrey	3,
5		5	Hartlepool United	2-2	Godfrey, Shinners	1,
6		12	EXETER CITY	2-3	Godfrey, Day	3,
7		15	Stockport County	2-1	Hull 2	2
8		18	Crewe Alexandra	3-3	Godfrey 2, Comfort	2,
9		26	PETERBOROUGH UNITED	2-0	Smalley, Comfort	3
10		29	NEWPORT COUNTY	4-1	Howard, Shinners, Hull, Harvey	3,
11	Oct	3	Wrexham	2-2	Nugent, Comfort	2,
12		9	Colchester United	0-0		1,
13		17	CAMBRIDGE UNITED	0-2		4,
14		20	ROCHDALE	8-0	Smalley, Hales 2 (1 pen), Shinners 2, Comfort 2, Dickenson	2
15		24	Swansea City	0-3		3
16		31	HALIFAX TOWN	4-1	Shinners 2, Hales (pen), Hull	3
17	Nov	3	Carlisle United	2-1	Shinners	2,
18		7	Bolton Wanderers	0-1		5,
19		20	DARLINGTON	4-3	Hales (pen), Comfort, Sussex, Shinners	3
20		28	Hereford United	3-0	Shinners, Godfrey, Castle	1,
21	Dec	12	TRANMERE ROVERS	3-1	Castle 2, Shinners	3,
22		19	Wolverhampton W	0-2		12,
23		26	Peterborough United	2-1	Castle, Hales (pen)	3
24		28	SCUNTHORPE UNITED	1-1	Juryeff	5,
25	Jan	1	TORQUAY UNITED	0-2		4
26		2	Exeter City	3-2	Juryeff 2, Comfort	2,
27		16	CREWE ALEXANDRA	1-1	Nugent	4,
28		23	STOCKPORT COUNTY	1-1	Juryeff	4,
29	Feb	6	HARTLEPOOL UNITED	0-2		4,
30		13	Scunthorpe United	2-3	Castle (pen), Juryeff	2
31		20	CARDIFF CITY	4-1	Hales (pen), Castle, Howard, Juryeff	3,
32		24	Scarborough	1-3	Castle	2,
33		27	WREXHAM	2-1	Comfort, Sitton	3
34	Mar	1	Newport County	0-0		1,
35		5	Cambridge United	0-2		2
36		12	COLCHESTER UNITED	0-0		3
37		22	Burnley	0-2		5
38		26	SWANSEA CITY	3-0	Comfort, Juryeff, Baker	3
39	Apr	2	BOLTON WANDERERS	1-2	Comfort	4,
40		4	Darlington	2-2	Juryeff 2	2,
41		9	CARLISLE UNITED	4-1	Juryeff 2, Castle, Baker	2
42		14	Halifax Town	0-1		1
43		23	Rochdale	3-1	Juryeff 2, Castle	1,
44		30	HEREFORD UNITED	4-0	Godfrey, Baker, Juryeff 2	3,
45	May	2	Tranmere Rovers	1-2	Juryeff	3,
46		7	WOLVERHAMPTON W	0-2		7,

Appearar
Sub appearar
G

FA Cup

1	Nov	14	EXETER CITY	2-0	Godfrey, Hull	3,
2	Dec	5	SWANSEA CITY	2-0	Shinners, Comfort	4
3	Jan	9	Stockport County	2-1	Juryeff, Shinners	4,
4		30	NOTTINGHAM FOREST	1-2	Juryeff	19,

Appearar
Sub appearar
G

League Cup

1/1	Aug	18	MILLWALL	1-1	Hales (pen)	4
1/2		25	Millwall	0-1		4,

Appearar
Sub appeara
G

Final League Position: 8th in Division Four

Howard	Hughton	Smalley	Day	Hales	Ketteridge	Castle	Godfrey	Juryeff	Comfort	Hull	Nugent	Shinners	Sitton	Sussex	Harvey	Dickenson	Conroy	Marks	Stimson	Baker	
2	3	4	5	6	7	8	9*	10	11	12											1
2		4	5	3	6	7	8	10*	11	12	9										2
2		4	5	3	6	7	8		11		10*	9	12								3
2*	12	4	5	3	6	7	8		11	10		9									4
	2	4	5	3	6	7	8		11	10		9*		12							5
	2	4	5	3	6	7	8		11	10	9										6
2		4	5	3	6	7	8*		11	10		9			12						7
2		4	5	3	6	7	8		11	10*		9			12						8
2		4	5	3	6	7	8*		11	10		9			12						9
2		4	5	3	6	7	8		11	10		9*			12						10
2		4	5		6	7	8		11	10*	9				12	3					11
		4	5	2	6	7	8*		11		10	9			12	3					12
		4	5	2	6	7	8*		11	10		9			12	3					13
2		4	5	6		7+	8*		11	10		9		13	12	3					14
2		4	5	6		7	8		11	10*		9			12	3					15
2		4	5	6		7			11	10		9			8	3					16
2		4	5	6		7	12		11	10*		9		13	8+	3					17
2		4	5	6		7	8*		11	10		9			12	3					18
2		4	5	6			8		11	10		9		7		3					19
2		4	5	6		7	8		11	10		9				3					20
2		4	5	6		7	8		11	10*		9			12	3					21
2		4	5	6		7	8*		11	10		9			12	3					22
2		4	5	6		7	8*		11	10		9			12	3					23
2		4	5	6+	13	7		9*	11	10	12				8	3					24
2+		4	5	6	13	7	8*		11	10	9				12	3					25
		4	5	2	6	7		10	11	12	9*				8	3					26
2		4	5	6	13	7*	8+	10	11		9				12	3					27
2*			5	6		7		10	11	13		9	4		8+	3	12				28
2		4			6	7	8	10	11	12			5		9*	3					29
2		12	5*		6	7	8	9	11	10+			4		13	3					30
2		4		7	6	8		10	11	9			5			3					31
2	13	4		7*	6	8	12	10	11	9			5			3+					32
2	3	13	5	7	6	8		10+	11	12			4					9*			33
2	3	4		7	6*	8	12		11	9			5					10			34
2	3	4		6		8		10	11	9			5		12		7*				35
2		3	5	6		8		10	11	9			4				7				36
2			5	6		7	12	10	11			9	4	8*					3		37
2			5	6		7		10	11			9	4						3	8	38
2			5	6		7		10	11			9	4						3	8	39
2			5		6	7		10	11		9		4						3	8	40
2			5	6		7	12	10	11			9*	4						3	8	41
2			5	6		7	12	10	11		9		4						3	8*	42
2			5	6		7		10	11				4					9	3	8	43
2			5	6	13		9*	10	11	12			4	7					3	8+	44
2			5	6			9*	10	11	12			4	7					3	8	45
2*			5	6	13		9	10	11	12			4	7+					3	8	46
41	6	33	41	42	21	42	28	23	46	27	10	24	19	5	6	22	2	3	10	9	
	2	2			5		6			9	1		1	3	17		1				
2		3	2	6		10	7	16	12	6	3	11	1	1	1	1				3	

Howard	Hughton	Smalley	Day	Hales	Ketteridge	Castle	Godfrey	Juryeff	Comfort	Hull	Nugent	Shinners	Sitton	Sussex	Harvey	Dickenson	Conroy	Marks	Stimson	Baker	
2		4	5	6		7	8		11	10		9				3					1
2		4	5	6		7	8		11	10		9				3					2
2		4+	5	6	13	7	12	10	11			9			8*	3					3
2		4	5	6*		7	8	10	11	13		9+	12			3					4
4		4	4	4		4	3	2	4	2		4			1	4					
					1		1			1			1								
							1	2	1	1		2									

Howard	Hughton	Smalley	Day	Hales	Ketteridge	Castle	Godfrey	Juryeff	Comfort	Hull	Nugent	Shinners	Sitton	Sussex	Harvey	Dickenson	Conroy	Marks	Stimson	Baker	
2	3*	4	5	7+	6	8	9	10	11	13			12								1/1
2		6	5*	3	7	8	9		11	12	10		4								1/2
2	1	2	2	2	2	2	2	1	2		1		1								
										2			1								
				1																	

1988-89

Manager: Frank Clark

	P	W	D	L	F	A	Pts
Rotherham United	46	22	16	8	76	35	82
Tranmere Rovers	46	21	17	8	62	43	80
Crewe Alexandra	46	21	15	10	67	48	78
Scunthorpe United	46	21	14	11	77	57	77
Scarborough	46	21	14	11	67	52	77
Leyton Orient	46	21	12	13	86	50	75
Wrexham	46	19	14	13	77	63	71
Cambridge United	46	18	14	14	71	62	68
Grimsby Town	46	17	15	14	65	59	66
Lincoln City	46	18	10	18	64	60	64
York City	46	17	13	16	62	63	64
Carlisle United	46	15	15	16	53	52	60
Exeter City	46	18	6	22	65	68	60
Torquay United	46	17	8	21	45	60	59
Hereford United	46	14	16	16	66	72	58
Burnley	46	14	13	19	52	61	55
Peterborough United	46	14	12	20	52	74	54
Rochdale	46	13	14	19	56	82	53
Hartlepool United	46	14	10	22	50	78	52
Stockport County	46	10	21	15	54	52	51
Halifax Town	46	13	11	22	69	75	50
Colchester United	46	12	14	20	60	78	50
Doncaster Rovers	46	13	10	23	49	78	49
Darlington	46	8	18	20	53	76	42

Final League Position: 6th in Division Four
Promoted to Division Three
* After extra-time
** After extra-time, Leyton Orient won on penalties

Division Four

Match No.	Date		Opponents	Result	Scorers	Attendan
1	Aug	27	CREWE ALEXANDRA	0-0		3,93
2	Sep	3	Stockport County	0-0		2,10
3		10	HEREFORD UNITED	1-3	Hull	3,08
4		17	Hartlepool United	0-1		1,82
5		20	Rotherham United	1-4	Ketteridge	4,28
6		23	DARLINGTON	1-0	Juryeff	2,75
7	Oct	1	Torquay United	0-3		2,52
8		4	YORK CITY	4-0	Sitton, Comfort, Hales, Juryeff	2,48
9		8	Scarborough	0-0		2,37
10		15	COLCHESTER UNITED	8-0	Hull 3, Sitton, Baker, Comfort, Hales (pen), Day	3,42
11		22	Burnley	2-2	Juryeff, Comfort	8,52
12		25	EXETER CITY	4-0	Hull, Dickenson, Comfort, Juryeff	3,87
13		29	Doncaster Rovers	0-1		2,18
14	Nov	5	PETERBOROUGH UNITED	1-2	Juryeff	3,69
15		8	CARLISLE UNITED	2-0	Baker, Comfort	2,87
16		12	Scunthorpe United	2-2	Harvey, Juryeff	4,23
17		26	Cambridge United	2-2	Juryeff, Hales	2,67
18	Dec	3	LINCOLN CITY	3-1	Hales, Juryeff, Ward	3,09
19		17	Grimsby Town	2-2	Juryeff, Comfort	3,44
20		26	TRANMERE ROVERS	2-0	Howard, O'Shea	4,24
21		31	WREXHAM	0-1		4,02
22	Jan	2	Rochdale	3-0	Harvey 2, Juryeff	2,03
23		14	STOCKPORT COUNTY	1-2	Howard	3,82
24		21	Crewe Alexandra	1-2	Campbell	2,93
25	Feb	4	ROTHERHAM UNITED	3-1	Campbell 2, Comfort	3,29
26		11	Darlington	3-1	Comfort, Howard, Cooper	1,83
27		14	Halifax Town	2-2	Comfort 2	1,47
28		18	SCARBOROUGH	2-3	Campbell, Castle	3,87
29		24	Colchester United	0-1		4,26
30	Mar	1	Exeter City	1-1	Campbell	2,89
31		4	BURNLEY	3-0	Comfort 2, Campbell	3,94
32		11	Peterborough United	1-0	Howard	3,30
33		14	DONCASTER ROVERS	4-0	Campbell, Harvey, Castle, Comfort	2,82
34		18	Hereford United	1-1	Comfort	2,06
35		21	HARTLEPOOL UNITED	4-3	Howard, Day, Campbell, Sitton	3,40
36		25	ROCHDALE	3-0	Comfort, Hales, Castle	4,59
37		27	Tranmere Rovers	0-3		6,87
38	Apr	1	GRIMSBY TOWN	5-0	Harvey 2, Agnew (og), Comfort, Campbell	4,14
39		4	HALIFAX TOWN	2-0	Hales 2 (1 pen)	3,28
40		8	Wrexham	1-0	Comfort	2,43
41		15	TORQUAY UNITED	3-1	Hales, Comfort, Baker	4,64
42		22	York City	1-1	Sitton	2,74
43		29	CAMBRIDGE UNITED	1-1	Hales (pen)	5,65
44	May	1	Carlisle United	1-2	Castle	2,41
45		6	Lincoln City	1-0	Castle	3,57
46		13	SCUNTHORPE UNITED	4-1	Cooper 3, Castle	6,36

Appearanc
Sub appearanc
Goa

Play-Offs

SF1	May	21	SCARBOROUGH	2-0	Cooper 2	9,28
SF2		24	Scarborough	0-1		4,37
F		30	Wrexham	0-0		7,91
R	June	3	WREXHAM	2-1	Harvey, Cooper	13,35

Appearanc
Sub appearanc
Goa

FA Cup

1	Nov	19	Enfield	1-1	Ward	4,03
R		23	ENFIELD	2-2*	Juryeff 2	4,82
2R		28	ENFIELD	0-1		5,94

Appearanc
Sub appearanc
Goa

League Cup

1/1	Aug	30	ALDERSHOT	2-0	Hull, Juryeff	2,33
1/2	Sep	6	Aldershot	0-0		1,70
2/1		27	STOKE CITY	1-2	Juryeff	3,15
2/2	Oct	11	Stoke City	2-1**	Hales (pen), Comfort	5,75
3	Nov	1	Ipswich Town	0-2		9,75

Appearanc
Sub appearanc
Goa

	Howard	Dickenson	Hales	Corner	Day	Baker	Ward	Shinners	Juryeff	Comfort	Hull	Ketteridge	Nugent	Harvey	Sitton	O'Shea	Heald	Smalley	Jones	Castle	Campbell	Cooper	Kerrins	Carter
1	2	3	4	5	6	7	8	9*	10	11	12													
2	2	3	4	5	6	7	8	12	10*	11	9													
3	2	3	4	5		7	8		10	11	9	6*	12											
4	2	3	4		5	7		12	10*	11	9	6		8										
5	2	3	4		5	7		9	10	11		6		8										
6	2	3	4		5	7		9	10	11		6		8										
7	2	3	4		5	7	8		10	11	12		9*		6									
8	2	3	4		5	7	8	9	10	11					6									
9	2	3	4		5	7	8		10	11	9				6									
10	2	3	4		5	7	8		10	11	9				6									
11	2	3			5	7	8		10	11	9				6	4								
12	2	3	4		5	7	8		10	11	9				6									
13	2	3	4		5	7*	8		10	11	9			12	6									
14	2	3	4		5	7	8*		10	11	9			6		12								
15	2		4	6	5	7	8		10	11	9					3								
16	2		4		5	7	8		10	11	9*			12	6	3								
17	2	3	4		5	11	8		10		9			7	6									
18	2	3	4		5	9	8		10			11		7	6									
19	2	3	4		5	9	8		10	11				7	6		1							
20	2	3	4*		5	9	8		10	11				7	6	12	1							
21	2	3*			5	9	8		10	11				7		4	1	6	12					
22	2				5	9	8		10*	11				7	6	4	1	3	12					
23	2				5	9*	8		10	11			7		6	4	1	3		12				
24	2	3			5	9	8		10	11					6	4*	1			12	7			
25	2	3			5	7	8		10*	11					6		1			4	9	12		
26	2	3			5	7	8			11					6		1			4	10	9		
27	2	3			5	7	8			11					6		1			4	10	9		
28	2	3			5	7	8			11					6		1			4	10	9		
29	2	3			5	7	8			11	12				6		1			4	10	9*		
30	2	3			5	7	8			11				12	6		1			4	10	9*		
31	2		3		5	7	8*			11				12	6		1			4	10	9		
32	2	3	8		5	7				11				9*	6		1			4	10	12		
33	2	3	4		5	7				11				9	6		1			8	10			
34	2	3	4*		5	7				11				9	6		1			8	10	12		
35	2	3	4		5	7				11				9	6		1			8	10			
36	2	3	4		5	7				11				9	6		1			8	10			
37	2	3	4*		5	7				11				9	6		1			8	10	12		
38	2	3	4		5	7				11	12			9	6		1			8	10*			
39	2	3	4		5	7				11				9	6		1			8	10			
40	2	3	4		5	7				11				9	6		1			8		10		
41	2	3*	4		5	7				11				9	6		1	12		8		10		
42	2		4		5	7			10	11				9	6		1			8			3	
43	2		4		5	7			10	11				9	6		1			8			3	
44	2	12	4*		5	7			10+	11	13			9	6		1			8			3	
45	2	3	4		5	7				11				9	6		1			8		10		
46	2	3	4		5	7			12	11+				9*	6		1			8		10		13
(totals)	46	38	35	4	45	46	28	4	28	44	12	5	2	25	37	7	28	3		22	16	10	3	
		1						2	1		5		1	4		2		1	2	2		4		1
	5	1	9		2	3	1		10	18	5	1		6	4	1				6	9	4		

One own-goal

	Howard	Dickenson	Hales	Corner	Day	Baker	Ward	Shinners	Juryeff	Comfort	Hull	Ketteridge	Nugent	Harvey	Sitton	O'Shea	Heald	Smalley	Jones	Castle	Campbell	Cooper	Kerrins	Carter
SF1	2	3	4*		5	7				11				9	6		1			8		10		12
SF2	2	3	4		5	7	12			11*				9	6		1			8		10		
F	2	3	4		5	7*	12			11				9	6		1			8		10		
R	2	3*	4		5	7	12			11				9	6		1			8		10		
(totals)	4	4	4		4	4				4				4	4		4			4		4		
							3																	1
														1								3		

	Howard	Dickenson	Hales	Corner	Day	Baker	Ward	Shinners	Juryeff	Comfort	Hull	Ketteridge	Nugent	Harvey	Sitton	O'Shea	Heald	Smalley	Jones	Castle	Campbell	Cooper	Kerrins	Carter
1	2	3	4		5		8		10	11	12			7	6	9*								
R	2		4		5	3	8		10	11	12			7	6	9*								
2R	2	3	4		5		8		10	11	9			7	6									
(totals)	3	2	3		3	1	3		3	3	1			3	3	2								
											2													
							1		2															

	Howard	Dickenson	Hales	Corner	Day	Baker	Ward	Shinners	Juryeff	Comfort	Hull	Ketteridge	Nugent	Harvey	Sitton	O'Shea	Heald	Smalley	Jones	Castle	Campbell	Cooper	Kerrins	Carter
1/1	2	3	4	5		7	8		10+	11	9	12	13	6*										
1/2	2	3	4	5	6*	7	8	13	10+	11	9	12												
2/1	2	3	4		5	7	6	9	10	11		12		8*										
2/2	2	3	4		5	7*	8		10	11	9			12	6									
3	2	3	4		5	7	8		10	11	9			12	6*									
(totals)	5	5	5	2	4	5	5	1	5	5	4			2	2									
								1				3	1	2										
			1						2	1	1													

1989-90

Manager: Frank Clark

	P	W	D	L	F	A	Pts
Bristol Rovers	46	26	15	5	71	35	93
Bristol City	46	27	10	9	76	40	91
Notts County	46	25	12	9	73	53	87
Tranmere Rovers	46	23	11	12	86	49	80
Bury	46	21	11	14	70	49	74
Bolton Wanderers	46	18	15	13	59	48	69
Birmingham City	46	18	12	16	60	59	66
Huddersfield Town	46	17	14	15	61	62	65
Rotherham United	46	17	13	16	71	62	64
Reading	46	15	19	12	57	53	64
Shrewsbury Town	46	16	15	15	59	54	63
Crewe Alexandra	46	15	17	14	56	53	62
Brentford	46	18	7	21	66	66	61
Leyton Orient	46	16	10	20	52	56	58
Mansfield Town	46	16	7	23	50	65	55
Chester City	46	13	15	18	43	55	54
Swansea City	46	14	12	20	45	63	54
Wigan Athletic	46	13	14	19	48	64	53
Preston North End	46	14	10	22	65	79	52
Fulham	46	12	15	19	55	66	51
Cardiff City	46	12	14	20	51	70	50
Northampton Town	46	11	14	21	51	68	47
Blackpool	46	10	16	20	49	73	46
Walsall	46	9	14	23	40	72	41

Division Three

Match No.	Date		Opponents	Result	Scorers	Attenda
1	Aug	19	NOTTS COUNTY	0-1		5,3
2		26	Shrewsbury Town	2-4	Cooper 2	3,2
3	Sep	2	PRESTON NORTH END	3-1	Castle, Sitton, Hull	4,8
4		9	Walsall	3-1	Castle 2, Harvey	3,8
5		16	WIGAN ATHLETIC	1-0	Cooper	4,2
6		23	Bolton Wanderers	1-2	Carter	5,9
7		26	BRISTOL ROVERS	0-1		4,6
8		30	Huddersfield Town	0-2		5,2
9	Oct	6	Tranmere Rovers	0-3		8,2
10		14	BLACKPOOL	2-0	Howard 2	4,1
11		17	Rotherham United	2-5	Harvey, Cooper	5,7
12		21	READING	4-1	Castle, Hoddle, Berry, Cooper	4,2
13		28	Cardiff City	1-1	Harvey,	2,3
14		31	CHESTER CITY	0-3		3,9
15	Nov	5	FULHAM	1-1	Cooper	5,8
16		11	Birmingham City	0-0		7,4
17		25	MANSFIELD TOWN	3-1	Cooper, Howard, Harvey	3,3
18	Dec	3	Brentford	3-4	Howard, Castle 2 (1 pen)	6,4
19		16	Bristol City	1-2	Castle	7,4
20		26	NORTHAMPTON TOWN	1-1	Cooper	4,7
21		30	CREWE ALEXANDRA	2-1	Hull, Cooper	3,7
22	Jan	1	Bury	0-2		2,5
23		6	Chester City	0-1		1,7
24		13	SHREWSBURY TOWN	1-0	Hales (pen)	3,7
25		20	Notts County	0-1		5,3
26		27	WALSALL	1-1	Hull	3,5
27	Feb	10	Wigan Athletic	2-0	Hull 2	2,3
28		13	Preston North End	3-0	Cooper, Hull, Day	4,4
29		18	BRENTFORD	0-1		6,5
30		24	Mansfield Town	0-1		2,5
31	Mar	3	SWANSEA CITY	0-2		3,6
32		6	HUDDERSFIELD TOWN	1-0	Sayer	3,0
33		11	Bristol Rovers	0-0		7,0
34		17	TRANMERE ROVERS	0-1		4,0
35		20	Blackpool	0-1		2,7
36		24	ROTHERHAM UNITED	1-1	Carter	3,3
37		27	BOLTON WANDERERS	0-0		3,2
38		31	Reading	1-1	Sitton	4,1
39	Apr	3	Swansea City	1-0	Carter	2,5
40		7	CARDIFF CITY	3-1	Hales (pen), Beesley, Harvey	3,4
41		14	BURY	2-3	Howard, Cooper	3,5
42		16	Northampton Town	1-0	Carter	3,2
43		21	BRISTOL CITY	1-1	Howard	7,2
44		24	Crewe Alexandra	1-0	Hoddle	3,8
45		28	BIRMINGHAM CITY	1-2	Harvey	5,6
46	May	5	Fulham	2-1	Howard, Carter	7,1
						Appearanc
						Sub appearanc
						Go

FA Cup

1	Nov	18	BIRMINGHAM CITY	0-1		4,3
						Appearanc
						Sub appearanc
						Go

League Cup

1/1	Aug	22	Gillingham	4-1	Howard, Harvey, Cooper, Castle	3,2
1/2		29	GILLINGHAM	3-0	Day, Castle, Carter	2,8
2/1	Sep	19	EVERTON	0-2		8,2
2\2	Oct	3	Everton	2-2	Carter, Pike	10,1
						Appearanc
						Sub appearanc
						Go

Final League Position: 14th in Division Three

	Baker	Dickenson	Hales	Day	Sitton	Howard	Castle	Harvey	Cooper	Ward	Carter	Hull	Pike	Smalley	Hoddle	Berry	Beesley	Whitbread	Nugent	Hedman	Rees	Campbell	Sayer	Fashanu	Burnett	
	2	3	4	5	6	7	8	9	10	11*	12															1
	2	3	4*	5	6	7	8	9	10		11	12														2
	2	3	4	5	6	7	8	9	10		11*	12														3
	2	3	4	5	6	7	8+	9	10*		11	12	13													4
	2	3	4	5	6	7	8	9	10		11*	12														5
	2	3	4+	5*	6	7	8	9	10		11	13	12													6
	2	3	4*		6	7	8	9	10		11	12		5												7
	2	3		5	6	7	8	9	10		11	12	4*													8
		3		5	6	7	8		10	12	11	9	4		2*											9
	13	3		5	6	7	8		10		11	9*	4+		2	12										10
	12	3		5	6	7		9	10*	8	11		4		2											11
	4	3	12	5*		7	8	9	10						2	11	6									12
	4	3			6	7	8	9	10						2	11	5									13
	4	3	12	5	13	7	8+	9	10						2*	11	6									14
	4	3	8	5	2	7		9+	10					12	13	11	6*									15
		3	2	5	6	7	8		10		9			12		11*	4									16
	6	3	2	5*		7	8	11	10		9+		12			13	4									17
	6	3	2*			7	8	11	10		9	12					4	5								18
		3		5	2	7	8		10			9	11*		6		4		12							19
		3		5		7	8	9	10			6				11	4			2						20
	12	3+	6	5		7	8	11	10*			9	13				4			2						21
	6		2	5		7+	8	11*				10	9		12	13	4	3								22
	6		2	5	3		8	11			9	10*	12		7		4				1					23
			2	5	3	7	8*	11	10			9+			12		4		13	6	1					24
	9*		2	5	3	7		11	10						8		4		12	6	1					25
			2	5	3	7	8	11*	10			9					4		12	6	1					26
		3	2	5	6	7	8		10		11*	9			12		4				1					27
		3	2	5	6	7	8		10		11*	9			12		4				1					28
		3	2	5	6	7	8		10		11	9			12		4*				1					29
		3	2	5	6	7	8		10+		11	9			4*				13		1	12				30
	13	3	2	5	6	7		8	10*						4						1	11+	9	12		31
	11	3	2	5	6	7		8	10						4								9			32
	11	3	2	5	6	7			10						8		4						9*	12		33
	11	3	2*	5		7		6	10						8		4					12		9		34
	11		2	5		7		6	10		12				8		4					3*		9		35
			2	5	3	7		12			11				8		4					6	10	9*		36
	13		2	5	6	7		9	12		11				8		4					3+	10*			37
	6		2	5	3	7		9	10		11				8*		4						12			38
	6		2		3*	7		9	10		11		12				4	5					8			39
	6		2	5	3	7		9	10		11+	12	13				4						8*			40
	6		2	5	3	7		9	10		11	8*					4		12							41
	6		2+		3	7		9	10*		11		12		13		4	5	8							42
	6		2		3	7		9			11	10*					4	5	8			12				43
			2	5+	3	7		9			11				10		4	6*	8			13			12	44
		3	2	5		7		8			11						4	6	9				10*		12	45
		3	12		5	7		8			11						4	6	9*				10		2	46
7	27	31	36	39	36	45	27	36	38	2	29	15	6	1	19	6	32	8	5	5	9	4	9	3	1	
	5		3		1			1	1	1	2	9	8	2	7	3			6			4	1	2	2	
			2	1	2	7	7	6	11		5	6			2	1	1						1			

	Baker	Dickenson	Hales	Day	Sitton	Howard	Castle	Harvey	Cooper	Ward	Carter	Hull	Pike	Smalley	Hoddle	Berry	Beesley	Whitbread	Nugent	Hedman	Rees	Campbell	Sayer	Fashanu	Burnett	
1	12	3	2	5	6*	7	8		10		9					11	4									1
1		1	1	1	1	1	1		1		1					1	1									
	1																									

	Baker	Dickenson	Hales	Day	Sitton	Howard	Castle	Harvey	Cooper	Ward	Carter	Hull	Pike	Smalley	Hoddle	Berry	Beesley	Whitbread	Nugent	Hedman	Rees	Campbell	Sayer	Fashanu	Burnett	
1	2	3	4	5	6	7	8	9	10		11															1/1
1	2	3	4	5	6	7	8	9*	10		11	12														1/2
1	2	3	4	5	6	7	8	9*	10		11	12														2/1
1	12	3		5*	6	7	8	9	10		11		4		2											2/2
4	3	4	3	4	4	4	4	4	4		4		1		1											
	1											2														
				1		1	2	1	1		2		1													

1990-91

Manager: Frank Clark

	P	W	D	L	F	A	Pts
Cambridge United	46	25	11	10	75	45	86
Southend United	46	26	7	13	67	51	85
Grimsby Town	46	24	11	11	66	34	83
Bolton Wanderers	46	24	11	11	64	50	83
Tranmere Rovers	46	23	9	14	64	46	78
Brentford	46	21	13	12	59	47	76
Bury	46	20	13	13	67	56	73
Bradford City	46	20	10	16	62	54	70
Bournemouth	46	19	13	14	58	58	70
Wigan Athletic	46	20	9	17	71	54	69
Huddersfield Town	46	18	13	15	57	51	67
Birmingham City	46	16	17	13	45	49	65
Leyton Orient	46	18	10	18	55	58	64
Stoke City	46	16	12	18	55	59	60
Reading	46	17	8	21	53	66	59
Exeter City	46	16	9	21	58	52	57
Preston North End	46	15	11	20	54	67	56
Shrewsbury Town	46	14	10	22	61	68	52
Chester City	46	14	9	23	46	58	51
Swansea City	46	13	9	24	49	72	48
Fulham	46	10	16	20	41	56	46
Crewe Alexandra	46	11	11	24	62	80	44
Rotherham United	46	10	12	24	50	87	42
Mansfield Town	46	8	14	24	42	63	38

Division Three

Match No.	Date		Opponents	Result	Scorers	Attenda
1	Aug	25	SWANSEA CITY	3-0	Harvey, Castle, Sayer	4,5
2	Sep	1	Birmingham City	1-3	Sayer	5,8
3		8	MANSFIELD TOWN	2-1	Harvey, Castle	3,6
4		15	Chester City	0-2		1,7
5		17	Tranmere Rovers	0-3		5,5
6		22	ROTHERHAM UNITED	3-0	Castle 2 (1 pen), Berry	3,4
7		29	BRADFORD CITY	2-1	Castle 2	3,7
8	Oct	2	Cambridge United	0-1		4,9
9		6	Huddersfield Town	0-1		4,6
10		13	SHREWSBURY TOWN	3-2	Harvey, Nugent, Achampong	4,3
11		20	BOLTON WANDERERS	0-1		4,1
12		23	Grimsby Town	2-2	Achampong, Carter	6,6
13		27	Reading	2-1	Nugent, Carter	4,5
14	Nov	4	FULHAM	1-0	Berry	6,1
15		10	EXETER CITY	1-0	Nugent	3,7
16		24	Wigan Athletic	2-1	Nugent, Berry	2,2
17	Dec	2	Brentford	0-1		7,3
18		15	PRESTON NORTH END	1-0	Achampong	3,2
19		22	CREWE ALEXANDRA	3-2	Howard, Berry, Carter	3,8
20		29	Bournemouth	2-2	Castle, Achampong	6,1
21	Jan	1	STOKE CITY	0-2		6,36
22		12	BIRMINGHAM CITY	1-1	Castle	4,70
23		26	CHESTER CITY	1-0	Castle	3,43
24	Feb	2	TRANMERE ROVERS	4-0	Castle, Pike, Bart-Williams, Cooper	4,31
25		5	Rotherham United	0-0		4,06
26		19	Bury	0-1		2,20
27		23	Exeter City	0-2		3,21
28	Mar	3	BRENTFORD	1-2	Cooper	5,31
29		9	Preston North End	1-2	Bart-Williams	3,65
30		12	CAMBRIDGE UNITED	0-3		4,28
31		16	Bradford City	0-4		5,05
32		19	Shrewsbury Town	0-3		2,23
33		23	HUDDERSFIELD TOWN	1-0	Nugent	3,28
34		30	BURY	1-0	Cooper	3,53
35	Apr	1	Crewe Alexandra	3-3	Cooper 2, Taylor	3,04
36		6	BOURNEMOUTH	2-0	Bond (og), Carter	4,29
37		9	SOUTHEND UNITED	0-1		6,29
38		13	Stoke City	2-1	Cooper 2	8,07
39		16	Mansfield Town	3-3	Castle, Cooper 2	2,05
40		20	Bolton Wanderers	0-1		7,92
41		23	WIGAN ATHLETIC	1-1	Tomlinson	2,61
42		27	GRIMSBY TOWN	0-2		4,30
43		30	Swansea City	0-0		2,13
44	May	4	READING	4-0	Howard, Castle (pen), Berry, Carter	2,64
45		7	Southend United	1-1	Day	8,75
46		11	Fulham	1-1	Howard	6,59

Appearances
Sub appearances
Goals

FA Cup

1	Nov	17	SOUTHEND UNITED	3-2	Castle 2, Nugent	6,095
2	Dec	12	Colchester United	0-0		6,150
R		17	COLCHESTER UNITED	4-1	Howard, Castle, Carter, Pike	4,615
3	Jan	5	SWINDON TOWN	1-1	Pike	6,697
R		21	Swindon Town	0-1		7,395

Appearances
Sub appearances
Goals

League Cup

1/1	Aug	29	Maidstone United	2-2	Nugent, Berry	2,225
1/2	Sep	4	MAIDSTONE UNITED	4-1	Harvey, Castle 2, Nugent	3,429
2/1		26	Charlton Athletic	2-2	Nugent, Berry	3,238
2/2	Oct	9	CHARLTON ATHLETIC	1-0	Castle (pen)	6,811
3		30	Crystal Palace	0-0		12,958
R	Nov	7	CRYSTAL PALACE	0-1		10,158

Appearances
Sub appearances
Goals

Final League Position: 13th in Division Three

Note: FA Cup replay against Swindon Town was first played on 14 January at Swindon, the game was abandoned after 54 minutes with the score at 1–1.

Baker	Howard	Sitton	Day	Hales	Harvey	Castle	Nugent	Sayer	Berry	Achampong	Carter	Whitbread	Pike	Zoricich	Hull	Bart-Williams	Burnett	Dickenson	Cooper	Newell	Fee	Hoddle	Taylor	Cobb	Tomlinson	Hackett	Otto	
2	3	4	5	6*	7	8	9	10	11+	12	13																	1
2	3	4			7	8+	9	10	11*	12	13	5	6															2
2	3	4			7	8	9	10	11*		12	5	6															3
2	3	4			7	8	9	10*	11		12	5	6															4
2	3	4			7*	8	9		11	12	10	5	6															5
2	3	4				8	9	10	11	12	7*	5	6															6
2	3	4				8	9		11	10	7	5	6															7
	3	4	13			8	9	12	11+	7*	10	5	6	2														8
	3	4			11	8	9			10*	7	5	6	2	12													9
	3	4			11*	8	9	12		10	7	5	6	2														10
	3		4		11	8	9		12	10*	7	5	6	2														11
	3		4			8	9		11*	10	7	5	6	2		12												12
	3		4		12	8	9		11	10*	7	5	6	2														13
2	3	12	4*		10+	8	9		11	13	7	5	6															14
2	3	4			10	8	9		11*	12	7	5	6															15
2	3	4			10*	8	9		11+	13	7	5	6	12														16
2	3				10	8*	9			11+	7	5	6	4			12	13										17
2	3	4				8	9		11*	10	7	5	6	12														18
2	3	4			12	8	9		11*	10	7	5	6															19
2	3	4			11*	8	9			10	7	5	6	12														20
2	3	4			12	8	9		11*	10	7	5	6															21
2	3	4			12+	8	9		11*	10	7	5	6	13														22
2	3		5		11	8			13	10+	7		4	9				6*	12									23
13	3	2			11	8			10		7*	5	4			9+		6	12									24
2	3				11+	8			10*	13	7	5	4	9				6	12									25
2	3	9			11	8			10		7	5*	4					6	12	1								26
12	3	4				8			10	11	7	5				2		6*	9	1								27
2	3	4*			11+	8			10		7	5	6			13			9	1	12							28
	3		12		11*	8				13	7	5	6			10		2+	9	1	4							29
	3					8		12		11	7	5	6	2		10*			9	1	4							30
	3		12			8		13		11	7	5*	6	2		10+			9	1	4							31
	3		5			8		9		11	7		6	2	12	10*				1	4							32
	3		4			8	9	12	6*	11	7	5		2		10				1								33
	3		4			8	9+			11	7*	5		2		6			10			12	13					34
	3		4			8*	9			11+	7	5		2		6			10			12	13					35
	3		4			8	9			11	7	5		2		6			10*				12					36
	3		4			8			9*	11	7	5		2		6			10					12				37
2	3		4	13	12	8	9		11+		7*	5				6			10									38
2	3		4		7	8	9		11			5				6			10									39
2	3		4	12	11+	8*	9		13			5		7		6			10									40
	3	12	4	8					11+	7		5*		2		6			10					9	13			41
	3	5	4			8			11	7				2		6			10					9				42
	3		4	6		8	9		11		7			2					10							5		43
	3		4			8	9		11		7			2		6			10*					12		5		44
	3		4			8	9		11		7			2		6			10							5		45
	3		4			8	9		11		7			2		6			10*							5	12	46
23	46	22	21	3	21	45	33	6	32	25	38	38	30	24		19		6	18	8	4			2		4		
2		2	3	2	5			5	3	9	4			4	2	2	1	1	4		1	2	3	2	1		1	
	3		1		3	12	5	2	5	4	5		1			2			9				1		1			

One own-goal

Baker	Howard	Sitton	Day	Hales	Harvey	Castle	Nugent	Sayer	Berry	Achampong	Carter	Whitbread	Pike	Zoricich	Hull	Bart-Williams	Burnett	Dickenson	Cooper	Newell	Fee	Hoddle	Taylor	Cobb	Tomlinson	Hackett	Otto	
2	3	4			10	8	9		11		7	5	6															1
2	3	10				8	9		11		7	5	6	4														2
2	3	4				8+	9		11	10	7*	5	6	13	12													R
	3	4			11	8	9		12	10	7*	5	6	2														3
13	3	2			11	8	9		10+		7	5*	4	12				6										R
3	5	5			3	5	5		4	2	5	5	5	2				1										
1									1					2	1													
	1					3	1				1		2															

Baker	Howard	Sitton	Day	Hales	Harvey	Castle	Nugent	Sayer	Berry	Achampong	Carter	Whitbread	Pike	Zoricich	Hull	Bart-Williams	Burnett	Dickenson	Cooper	Newell	Fee	Hoddle	Taylor	Cobb	Tomlinson	Hackett	Otto	
2	3	4	5*	6	7	8	9	10	11+		13	12																1/1
2	3	4			7	8	9	10	11			5	6															1/2
2	3	4				8	9		11	7	10	5	6															2/1
	3	4			11	8	9			10	7	5	6	2														2/2
10	3	2	4		11	8	12		9*		7	5	6															3
2	3	4			10	8	13		11+	12	7	5	6	9*														R
5	6	6	2	1	5	6	4	2	5	2	4	5	5	2														
							2			1	1	1																
					1	3	3		2																			

1991-92

Manager: Peter Eustace

	P	W	D	L	F	A	Pts
Brentford	46	25	7	14	81	55	82
Birmingham City	46	23	12	11	69	52	81
Huddersfield Town	46	22	12	12	59	38	78
Stoke City	46	21	14	11	69	49	77
Stockport County	46	22	10	14	75	51	76
Peterborough United	46	20	14	12	65	58	74
West Bromwich Albion	46	19	14	13	64	49	71
Bournemouth	46	20	11	15	52	48	71
Fulham	46	19	13	14	57	53	70
Leyton Orient	46	18	11	17	62	52	65
Hartlepool United	46	18	11	17	57	57	65
Reading	46	16	13	17	59	62	61
Bolton Wanderers	46	14	17	15	57	56	59
Hull City	46	16	11	19	54	54	59
Wigan Athletic	46	15	14	17	58	64	59
Bradford City	46	13	19	14	62	61	58
Preston North End	46	15	12	19	61	72	57
Chester City	46	14	14	18	56	59	56
Swansea City	46	14	14	18	55	65	56
Exeter City	46	14	11	21	57	80	53
Bury	46	13	12	21	55	74	51
Shrewsbury Town	46	12	11	23	53	68	47
Torquay United	46	13	8	25	42	68	47
Darlington	46	10	7	29	56	90	37

Division Three

Match No.	Date		Opponents	Result	Scorers	Atten
1	Aug	17	Brentford	3-4	Nugent 2, Sayer	6
2		24	STOCKPORT COUNTY	3-3	Nugent 2, Sayer	3
3		31	Bolton Wanderers	0-1		5
4	Sep	3	BRADFORD CITY	1-1	Sayer	3
5		7	Hartlepool United	3-2	Otto, Carter, Castle	3
6		14	DARLINGTON	2-1	Otto 2	3
7		17	PRESTON NORTH END	0-0		3
8		21	Fulham	1-2	Nugent	4
9		28	HUDDERSFIELD TOWN	1-0	Day	3,
10	Oct	5	Peterborough United	2-0	Nugent 2	4,
11		12	CHESTER CITY	1-0	Jones	4,
12		19	BOURNEMOUTH	1-1	Castle	3
13		26	Stoke City	0-2		9,
14	Nov	2	EXETER CITY	1-0	Castle	2,
15		5	Swansea City	2-2	Howard, Otto	2,
16		9	Torquay United	0-1		2,
17		23	HULL CITY	1-0	Howard	3,
18		30	Wigan Athletic	1-1	Berry	2,
19	Dec	20	Stockport County	0-1		2,
20		26	BOLTON WANDERERS	2-1	Cooper 2	4,
21		28	BRENTFORD	4-2	Berry 2, Castle, Jones	7,
22	Jan	1	Bradford City	1-1	Castle	6,
23		11	Birmingham City	2-2	Nugent, Castle	10,
24		18	WEST BROMWICH ALBION	1-1	Jones	6,
25		28	SHREWSBURY TOWN	2-0	Castle, Achampong	3,
26	Feb	1	Bournemouth	1-0	Nugent	6,
27		8	STOKE CITY	0-1		7,
28		11	WIGAN ATHLETIC	3-1	Whitbread, Berry, Jones	3,
29		15	Bury	2-4	Carter, Taylor	2,
30		22	BIRMINGHAM CITY	0-0		6,
31		29	Shrewsbury Town	1-0	Howard	2,8
32	Mar	3	West Bromwich Albion	3-1	Howard, Berry, Nugent	11,
33		7	READING	1-1	Nugent	4,4
34		10	SWANSEA CITY	1-2	Castle	3,3
35		14	Exeter City	0-2		3,0
36		21	TORQUAY UNITED	2-0	Nugent, Otto	3,6
37		24	BURY	4-0	Berry 3, Wilder	3,0
38		28	Hull City	0-1		3,8
39		31	Darlington	1-0	Cooper	1,7
40	Apr	4	HARTLEPOOL UNITED	4-0	Castle, Achampong, Jones, Cooper	4,2
41		11	Preston North End	1-2	Castle	3,9
42		18	FULHAM	0-1		7,0
43		20	Huddersfield Town	0-1		10,0
44		25	PETERBOROUGH UNITED	1-2	Cooper	6,1
45		29	Reading	2-3	Cooper, Okai	2,6
46	May	2	Chester City	0-1		2,0

Appearanc
Sub appearanc
Goa

FA Cup

1	Nov	16	WELLING UNITED	2-1	Howard, Cooper	4,6
2	Dec	9	WEST BROMWICH ALBION	2-1	Berry 2	6,1
3	Jan	4	Oldham Athletic	1-1	Day	10,7
R		15	OLDHAM ATHLETIC	4-2e	Nugent 2, Castle (pen), Harvey	10,0
4	Jan	25	Portsmouth	0-2		16,1

Appearance
Sub appearance
Goa

League Cup

1/1	Aug	20	NORTHAMPTON TOWN	5-0	Berry, Burnett, Nugent 2, Sayer	2,9
1/2	Sep	10	Northampton Town	0-2		1,4
2/1		24	SHEFFIELD WEDNESDAY	0-0		6,2
2/2	Oct	9	Sheffield Wednesday	1-4	Nugent	14,3

Appearance
Sub appearance
Goa

Final League Position: 10th in Division Three
10th in Division Three

	Howard	Dickenson	Whitbread	Day	Bart-Williams	Berry	Burnett	Nugent	Sayer	Otto	Zoricich	Carter	Castle	Newell	Harvey	Achampong	Hackett	Jones	Turner	Hales	Cooper	Roeder	Taylor	Wilder	Hendon	Okai	Cobb	Warren	Tomlinson	
	2	3	4*	5	6	7+	8	9	10	11	12	13																		1
	2	3		5	6	7+	8*	9	10	11	4		12																	2
	2*	3	5	12	6	13	8+	9	10	11	4		7	1																3
	2	3	5		6	7	12	9	10	11	4		8*	1																4
	2	3	5*	12	6		7	9	10+	11	4	13	8	1																5
	2	3	5	4	6*	13	12	9	10	11		7+	8	1																6
	2	3	5	4	6	12		9	10*	11		7	8	1																7
	2		4	5	6	11	3	9	10*		13	7	8	1	12+															8
	2	3	4	5	6			9		11*		7	8	1	12		10													9
	2		4	5	6*			9			3	7	10	1	12	13	8	11+												10
	2		4	5			6	9		11		7*	10	1	12		3	8												11
	2		4	5	6		7*	9		11+			10	1	12	13	3	8												12
	2			5	7			9		11			10		12	4	3	8	1	6*										13
	2		4		6	13		9		11+	5		10		7*		3	8	1	12										14
	2		4		6	12		9		11	5		10		7*		3	8	1											15
	2		4	5	6	13		9		11			10		7+		3*	8	1	12										16
	2		4	5		11	6	10					8			7	3	9*	1		12									17
	2		4	5		11	6	10					8+		13	7	3	9*	1	12										18
	2		4	5		11		10		12			8		6*	7	3		1		9									19
	2		4	5		11		10		6*			8			7	3	12	1		9									20
	2		4*	5		11	12	10+		6			8			7	3	13	1		9									21
	2			5		11	4*	10		6+			8			7	3	13	1	12	9									22
	2		6	5		11	4*	10					8		13		3	12	1		9+	7								23
	2		6	5		11	4	10		12			8				3	9	1				7*							24
	2		6	5		11	4	10		7			8*			12	3	9+	1		13									25
	2		6	5		11+	4	10		13		7				8	3	9*	1		12									26
	2*		6	5		11	4	10				7+	12			8	3	9	1		13									27
	2		6	5		11	4	10+				12	8			7*	3	9	1		13									28
	2		6	5+		11	4	10				7	8				3*	9	1			12	13							29
	2		6			11	4	10			12		8		7+		3*	9	1			5	13							30
	2		6			11	4	10				12	8			7*		9+	1			5	13	3						31
	2		6			11	4	10			5	12	8					13	1	7*			9+	3						32
	2		6	5		11	4	10				7	8					12	1				9*	3						33
	2		6	5		11+	4	9		13		7	8*						1		10		12	3						34
	2		6	5		11+	4	9		13		7	8					10	1				12	3*						35
	2		6	5		11*	4	9		10	8	7				12			1					3						36
	2		6	5		11	4			12	8	7*				9		10+	1		13			3						37
	2		6	5		11	4			12	8	7*				9		10+	1					3	13					38
	2		6	5		11	4				8					9			1		10			3	7					39
	2		6			11+	4			13	8		7			9		12	1	5	10*			3						40
	2		6				4			11	8		7			9		13	1	5*		12	10+	3						41
	2		6				4			11	8		7			9		12	1	5*			10	3						42
	2		6			10				11+	8		7*			9		12	1		13	5		3	4					43
	2		6			11	5		12		8					9			1		10		7*	3	4					44
	2		6				4			12	8					9			1		10	5		3	7	11*				45
			6				5			11	8								1	7	10	2		3	4*		9	12	13	46
2	45	8	43	31	15	30	33	36	8	23	19	15	35	10	5	20	22	20	34	6	11	6	6	16	5	1	1			
				2		6	3		1	9	3	5	2		8	4		10		4	7	2	5		1			1	1	
	4		1	1		8		12	3	5		2	10			2		5			6		1	1		1				

	Howard	Dickenson	Whitbread	Day	Bart-Williams	Berry	Burnett	Nugent	Sayer	Otto	Zoricich	Carter	Castle	Newell	Harvey	Achampong	Hackett	Jones	Turner	Hales	Cooper	Roeder	Taylor	Wilder	Hendon	Okai	Cobb	Warren	Tomlinson	
	2		4	5		13	12			11+			8			7	3	9	1	6*	10									1
	2		4	5		11		10					8		6	7	3	9*	1		12									2
	2		6	5		11	4	10					8			7+	3	12	1	13	9*									3
	2		6	5		11	4	10					8		7*		3	9	1				12							R
	2		6	5			4	10		11*			8			12	3	9+	1		13	7								4
	5		5	5		3	3	4		2			5		2	3	5	4	5	1	2	1								
						1	1									1		1		1	2		1							
	1			1		2		2					1		1						1									

	Howard	Dickenson	Whitbread	Day	Bart-Williams	Berry	Burnett	Nugent	Sayer	Otto	Zoricich	Carter	Castle	Newell	Harvey	Achampong	Hackett	Jones	Turner	Hales	Cooper	Roeder	Taylor	Wilder	Hendon	Okai	Cobb	Warren	Tomlinson	
1	2	3		5	6	7*	8	9	10	11	4	12																		1/1
	2	3	5		6		12	9	10	11*	4	7	8	1																1/2
	2		4	5	6		10	9		11	12	7		1		3*	8													2/1
	2		4	5	6		3*	9				7	8	1	12	11	10													2/2
1	4	2	3	3	4	1	3	4	2	3	2	3	2	3		2	2													
							1				1	1			1															
						1	1	3	1																					

1992-93

Manager: Peter Eustace

	P	W	D	L	F	A	Pts
Stoke City	46	27	12	7	73	34	93
Bolton Wanderers	46	27	9	10	80	41	90
Port Vale	46	26	11	9	79	44	89
West Bromwich Albion	46	25	10	11	88	54	85
Swansea City	46	20	13	13	65	47	73
Stockport County	46	19	15	12	81	57	72
Leyton Orient	46	21	9	16	69	53	72
Reading	46	18	15	13	66	51	69
Brighton & Hove Albion	46	20	9	17	63	59	69
Bradford City	46	18	14	14	69	67	68
Rotherham United	46	17	14	15	60	60	65
Fulham	46	16	17	13	57	55	65
Burnley	46	15	16	15	57	59	61
Plymouth Argyle	46	16	12	18	59	64	60
Huddersfield Town	46	17	9	20	54	61	60
Hartlepool United	46	14	12	20	42	60	54
Bournemouth	46	12	17	17	45	52	53
Blackpool	46	12	15	19	63	75	51
Exeter City	46	11	17	18	54	69	50
Hull City	46	13	11	22	46	69	50
Preston North End	46	13	8	25	65	94	47
Mansfield Town	46	11	11	24	52	80	44
Wigan Athletic	46	10	11	25	43	72	41
Chester City	46	8	5	33	49	102	29

Division Two

Match No.	Date		Opponents	Result	Scorers	Attenda
1	Aug	15	BRIGHTON & HOVE ALBION	3-2	Zoricich, Jones 2	5,6
2		22	Reading	1-1	Day	4,2
3		29	BLACKPOOL	1-0	Howard	4,3
4	Sep	1	HUDDERSFIELD TOWN	4-1	Jones 2, Taylor, Ludden	3,7
5		5	Plymouth Argyle	0-2		7,3
6		12	CHESTER CITY	4-3	Hales (pen), Jones, Taylor 2	4,1
7		15	Hartlepool United	2-0	Taylor 2	3,2
8		19	Exeter City	0-1		2,7
9		26	HULL CITY	0-0		4,9
10	Oct	3	BOLTON WANDERERS	1-0	Okai	3,9
11		10	Stoke City	1-2	Otto	12,6
12		17	BOURNEMOUTH	1-0	Otto	4,5
13		24	Bradford City	0-1		7,2
14		31	SWANSEA CITY	4-2	Cooper 2, Taylor 2	5,6
15	Nov	3	Port Vale	0-2		7,3
16		7	WEST BROMWICH ALBION	2-0	Kitchen, Taylor	8,6
17		21	Wigan Athletic	1-3	Cooper	1,8
18		28	MANSFIELD TOWN	5-1	Howard 3 (1 pen), Cooper, Taylor	4,5
19	Dec	12	Burnley	0-2		8,7
20		18	PRESTON NORTH END	3-1	Flynn (og), Jones, Cooper	3,4
21		26	FULHAM	0-0		8,4
22		28	Stockport County	1-1	Taylor	6,3
23	Jan	2	Chester City	3-1	Jones, Cooper, Harvey	2,5
24		9	HARTLEPOOL UNITED	0-0		5,5
25		16	Hull City	0-0		3,8
26		23	EXETER CITY	5-0	Jones, Taylor 3, Carter	5,24
27		26	Blackpool	1-3	Gore (og)	3,1
28		30	READING	1-2	Howard	5,46
29	Feb	6	Brighton & Hove Albion	3-1	Otto 3	7,85
30		13	PLYMOUTH ARGYLE	2-0	Achampong, Otto	5,80
31		20	Huddersfield Town	1-1	Bellamy	5,11
32		27	STOKE CITY	1-0	Cooper	10,80
33	Mar	6	Bolton Wanderers	0-1		7,76
34		9	ROTHERHAM UNITED	1-1	Bellamy	4,40
35		13	West Bromwich Albion	0-2		15,02
36		20	PORT VALE	0-1		5,95
37		23	Mansfield Town	0-3		2,77
38		27	WIGAN ATHLETIC	1-2	Carter	4,10
39	Apr	3	Rotherham United	1-1	Taylor	3,23
40		6	BURNLEY	3-2	Whitbread, Bellamy, Harvey	4,23
41		10	Fulham	0-1		5,97
42		12	STOCKPORT COUNTY	3-0	Bellamy, Carter, Lakin	4,641
43		17	Preston North End	4-1	Taylor 2, Lakin, Harvey	5,89
44		24	Bournemouth	0-3		4,59
45	May	1	BRADFORD CITY	4-2	Taylor 2, Otto, Harvey	5,504
46		8	Swansea City	1-0	Otto	6,543
						Appearances
						Sub appearances
						Goals

FA Cup

1	Nov	14	Dagenham & Redbridge	5-4	Howard, Whitbread, Jones, Cooper 2	5,300
2	Dec	5	Reading	0-3		7,213
						Appearances
						Sub appearances
						Goals

League Cup

1/1	Aug	18	MILLWALL	2-2	Tomlinson, Cooper	4,939
1/2		26	Millwall	0-3		5,444
						Appearances
						Sub appearances
						Goals

Final League Position: 7th in Division Two

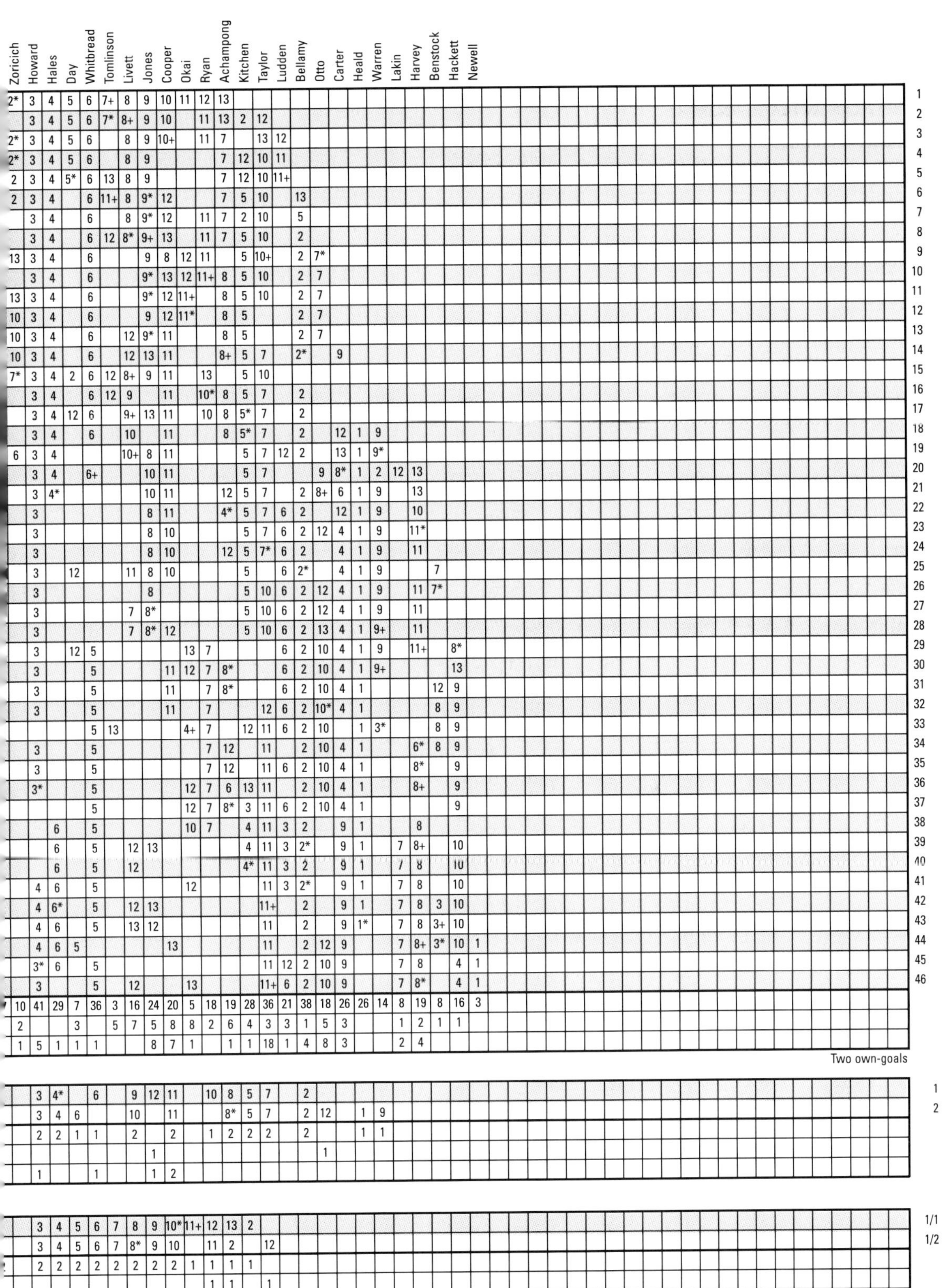

Zoricich	Howard	Hales	Day	Whitbread	Tomlinson	Livett	Jones	Cooper	Okai	Ryan	Achampong	Kitchen	Taylor	Ludden	Bellamy	Otto	Carter	Heald	Warren	Lakin	Harvey	Benstock	Hackett	Newell	
2*	3	4	5	6	7+	8	9	10	11	12	13														1
	3	4	5	6	7*	8+	9	10		11	13	2	12												2
2*	3	4	5	6		8	9	10+		11	7		13	12											3
2*	3	4	5	6		8	9				7	12	10	11											4
2	3	4	5*	6	13	8	9				7	12	10	11+											5
2	3	4		6	11+	8	9*	12			7	5	10		13										6
	3	4		6		8	9*	12		11	7	2	10		5										7
	3	4		6	12	8*	9+	13		11	7	5	10		2										8
13	3	4		6			9	8	12	11		5	10+		2	7*									9
	3	4		6			9*	13	12	11+	8	5	10		2	7									10
13	3	4		6			9*	12	11+		8	5	10		2	7									11
10	3	4		6			9	12	11*		8	5			2	7									12
10	3	4		6		12	9*	11			8	5			2	7									13
10	3	4		6		12	13	11			8+	5	7		2*		9								14
7*	3	4	2	6	12	8+	9	11		13		5	10												15
	3	4		6	12	9		11		10*	8	5	7		2										16
	3	4	12	6		9+	13	11		10	8	5*	7		2										17
	3	4		6		10		11			8	5*	7		2		12	1	9						18
6	3	4				10+	8	11				5	7	12	2		13	1	9*						19
	3	4		6+			10	11				5	7			9	8*	1	2	12	13				20
	3	4*					10	11			12	5	7		2	8+	6	1	9		13				21
	3						8	11			4*	5	7	6	2		12	1	9		10				22
	3						8	10				5	7	6	2	12	4	1	9		11*				23
	3						8	10			12	5	7*	6	2		4	1	9		11				24
	3		12			11	8	10				5		6	2*		4	1	9			7			25
	3						8					5	10	6	2	12	4	1	9		11	7*			26
	3					7	8*					5	10	6	2	12	4	1	9		11				27
	3					7	8*	12				5	10	6	2	13	4	1	9+		11				28
	3		12	5					13	7				6	2	10	4	1	9		11+		8*		29
	3			5				11	12	7	8*			6	2	10	4	1	9+				13		30
	3			5				11		7	8*			6	2	10	4	1				12	9		31
	3			5				11		7			12	6	2	10*	4	1				8	9		32
				5	13				4+	7		12	11	6	2	10		1	3*			8	9		33
	3			5						7	12		11		2	10	4	1			6*	8	9		34
	3			5						7	12		11	6	2	10	4	1			8*		9		35
	3*			5					12	7	6	13	11		2	10	4	1			8+		9		36
				5					12	7	8*	3	11	6	2	10	4	1					9		37
		6		5					10	7		4	11	3	2		9	1			8				38
		6		5		12	13					4	11	3	2*		9	1		7	8+		10		39
		6		5		12						4*	11	3	2		9	1		7	8		10		40
	4	6		5					12				11	3	2*		9	1		7	8		10		41
	4	6*		5		12	13						11+		2		9	1		7	8	3	10		42
	4	6		5		13	12						11		2		9	1*		7	8	3+	10		43
	4	6	5					13					11		2	12	9			7	8+	3*	10	1	44
	3*	6		5									11	12	2	10	9			7	8		4	1	45
	3			5		12			13				11+	6	2	10	9			7	8*		4	1	46
10	41	29	7	36	3	16	24	20	5	18	19	28	36	21	38	18	26	26	14	8	19	8	16	3	
2			3		5	7	5	8	8	2	6	4	3	3	1	5	3			1	2	1	1		
1	5	1	1	1			8	7	1		1	1	18	1	4	8	3			2	4				

Two own-goals

Zoricich	Howard	Hales	Day	Whitbread	Tomlinson	Livett	Jones	Cooper	Okai	Ryan	Achampong	Kitchen	Taylor	Ludden	Bellamy	Otto	Carter	Heald	Warren	Lakin	Harvey	Benstock	Hackett	Newell	
	3	4*		6		9	12	11		10	8	5	7		2										1
	3	4	6			10		11			8*	5	7		2	12		1	9						2
	2	2	1	1		2		2		1	2	2	2		2			1	1						
							1									1									
	1			1			1	2																	

Zoricich	Howard	Hales	Day	Whitbread	Tomlinson	Livett	Jones	Cooper	Okai	Ryan	Achampong	Kitchen	Taylor	Ludden	Bellamy	Otto	Carter	Heald	Warren	Lakin	Harvey	Benstock	Hackett	Newell	
	3	4	5	6	7	8	9	10*	11+	12	13	2													1/1
	3	4	5	6	7	8*	9	10		11	2		12												1/2
	2	2	2	2	2	2	2	2	1	1	1	1													
										1	1		1												
					1			1																	

1993-94

Managers: Aug 1993–Apr 1994 Peter Eustace; Apr–May 1994 John Sitton & Chris Turner (acting)

	P	W	D	L	F	A	Pts
Reading	46	26	11	9	81	44	89
Port Vale	46	26	10	10	79	46	88
Plymouth Argyle	46	25	10	11	88	56	85
Stockport County	46	24	13	9	74	44	85
York City	46	21	12	13	64	40	75
Burnley	46	21	10	15	79	58	73
Bradford City	46	19	13	14	61	53	70
Bristol Rovers	46	20	10	16	60	59	70
Hull City	46	18	14	14	62	54	68
Cambridge United	46	19	9	18	79	73	66
Huddersfield Town	46	17	14	15	58	61	65
Wrexham	46	17	11	18	66	77	62
Swansea City	46	16	12	18	56	58	60
Brighton & Hove Albion	46	15	14	17	60	67	59
Rotherham United	46	15	13	18	63	60	58
Brentford	46	13	19	14	57	55	58
Bournemouth	46	14	15	17	51	59	57
Leyton Orient	46	14	14	18	57	71	56
Cardiff City	46	13	15	18	66	79	54
Blackpool	46	16	5	25	63	75	53
Fulham	46	14	10	22	50	63	52
Exeter City	46	11	12	23	52	83	45
Hartlepool United	46	9	9	28	41	87	36
Barnet	46	5	13	28	41	86	28

Division Two

Match No.	Date		Opponents	Result	Scorers	Attend
1	Aug	14	Cardiff City	0-2		9,
2		21	BRISTOL ROVERS	1-0	Taylor	4,
3		28	Burnley	1-4	West	10,
4		31	HARTLEPOOL UNITED	1-2	Howard	3,
5	Sep	4	YORK CITY	2-0	West 2	3,
6		11	Plymouth Argyle	1-3	Barnett	5,
7		14	Brentford	1-0	Carter	5,
8		18	BARNET	4-2	Bellamy, Carter, Barnett, Okai	4,
9		25	BRIGHTON & HOVE ALBION	1-3	Hackett	4,
10	Oct	2	Fulham	3-2	Hendon 2, Putney	4,
11		9	ROTHERHAM UNITED	1-1	Howard	4,
12		16	Reading	1-2	West	6,
13		23	BOURNEMOUTH	0-0		3,
14		30	Hull City	1-0	West	5,
15	Nov	2	Stockport County	0-3		4,
16		6	EXETER CITY	1-1	Cooper	3,
17		20	Swansea City	1-1	Cooper	3,1
18		27	BLACKPOOL	2-0	West, Cooper	3,
19	Dec	11	Bristol Rovers	1-1	Cooper	4,5
20		18	CARDIFF CITY	2-2	Cooper, Cockerill	3,6
21		27	CAMBRIDGE UNITED	2-1	Okai, Cockerill	6,
22		29	Port Vale	1-2	Barnett	8,9
23	Jan	1	HUDDERSFIELD TOWN	1-0	Carter	4,5
24		3	Wrexham	2-4	Hackett, West	3,5
25		8	Bradford City	0-0		5,2
26		15	READING	1-1	West	6,2
27		22	Rotherham United	1-2	West	3,3
28		29	HULL CITY	3-1	Barnett, West 2	4,3
29	Feb	5	Bournemouth	1-1	Pennock (og)	4,0
30		12	BRADFORD CITY	2-1	Carter, Bogie	3,6
31		19	BURNLEY	3-1	Carter, Putney, Bogie	5,2
32		26	York City	0-3		3,4
33	Mar	5	PLYMOUTH ARGYLE	2-1	Carter, Bogie	5,3
34		8	Hartlepool United	1-1	Barnett	1,2
35		12	Barnet	1-3	West	2,7
36		15	BRENTFORD	1-1	Barnett	3,1
37		19	Brighton & Hove Albion	0-2		8,2
38		26	FULHAM	2-2	Carter, Thomas	5,0
39		29	WREXHAM	2-2	Barnett, Cooper	2,6
40	Apr	2	Cambridge United	1-3	Cooper	3,7
41		4	PORT VALE	2-3	Cooper, Thomas	3,4
42		9	Huddersfield Town	0-1		4,9
43		16	STOCKPORT COUNTY	0-0		3,9
44		23	Exeter City	0-1		1,9
45		30	SWANSEA CITY	2-1	West 2 (1 pen)	3,5
46	May	7	Blackpool	1-4	Hackett	5,4

Appearance
Sub appearance
Goa

FA Cup

1	Nov	13	GRAVESEND & NORTHFLEET	2-1	Hackett, Lakin	5,46
2	Dec	4	EXETER CITY	1-1	Cooper	4,36
R		14	Exeter City	2-2	Hackett, Carter	3,62

Second replay lost on penalties after extra-time

Appearance
Sub appearance
Goal

League Cup

1/1	Aug	17	WYCOMBE WANDERERS	0-2		4,15
1/2		24	Wycombe Wanderers	0-1		4,90

Appearances
Sub appearances
Goals

Final League Position: 18th in Division Two

* After extra-time Exeter City won 5–4 on penalties

Hendon	Howard	Hackett	Bellamy	Ryan	Carter	Lakin	Taylor	Tomlinson	Putney	Ludden	Benstock	Kitchen	Barnett	Okai	West	Newell	Austin	Cooper	Livett	Harriott	Bogie	Cockerill	Gamble	Warren	Purse	Thomas	
2	3	4	5	6*	7	8	9	10	11	12																	1
2	3	4		6	7		9	10*	11	8		5	12														2
2	3*	4			7	12	9		11	8	13	5	6+		10												3
2	3	4			7	6	9			8		5	11		10												4
2	3	4	6		7	13	9+		11	8*		5	12		10												5
2	3*	4	6		7	13	9+		11		12	5	8		10												6
2		4	6		7	5			11				9	8	10	1	3										7
2*	12	4	6		7	5			11				9	8+	10	1	3	13									8
2		4	6*		7	5			11				9	8+	10	1	3	13	12								9
2		4	6	8*	7		12		11						10	1	3	9		5							10
2	4		6	8*	7		13		11	12					10	1	3	9+		5							11
2		4		8	7*	12	13			11					10	1	3	9+		5	6						12
2	11+	4		8	7		9*			13					10	1	3	12		5	6						13
2		4		8	7	11	9*								10	1	3	12		5	6						14
2		4		8		11+	9*	7				13			10	1	3	12		5	6						15
2		4		8		11		7							10	1	3	9		5	6						16
2		4	12	8		11								6	10	1	3	9		5*	7						17
2		4	5			11	12						8	6*	10	1	3	9			7						18
2	12	4	5		7								8		10*	1	3	9			11	6					19
2		4	5		7*					3		12	8		10	1		9			11	6					20
2	12	4	5			7*				3			8	13	10	1					11	6	9+				21
2	9	4*	5							3		7	8	12	10	1					11	6					22
2	8	4	5		7								9		10	1	3				11	6					23
2	9+	4	5		7*					3		12	8	13	10	1					11	6					24
2	9	4	5		7					3			8		10	1					11	6					25
2*	9	4	5		7+		13			3		12	8		10	1					11	6					26
	9	4	5	12	7+		13			3		2*	8		10	1					11	6					27
3	4		5		8		9*			2	12		7		10	1					11	6					28
3	4		5		8*		9+		12	2			7		10	1		13			11	6					29
2	4		5		7		12			3	9		8			1		10*			11	6					30
2			5		7				8*	3	9		12		13	1	4	10+			11	6					31
2			5*		7				8	3	9+		13		10	1	4	12			11	6					32
2*	3				7		12		8+	13	9		6		5	1	4	10			11						33
	3				7		12		8*	13	9		6		5	1	4	10+			11			2			34
				6	7		9			3			8*	12	5	1	4	10			11			2			35
			6		7		12			3	9		8*		5	1	4	10			11			2			36
			2	6	7		13			3	9+		8		5	1	4*	10			11				12		37
			6		7				2*	3			8	13	5	1	4	10+			11				12	9	38
			12		7				2+	3	11		8		5	1	4	10							6	9	39
		13			7					3	6+		8	12	5	1	4	10			11				2*	9	40
		4	6	2						3			8		9	1	5	10			11					7	41
	5	4		2					12	3					9	1	6	10+			11	8			13	7*	42
13		4		2	7+				6*	3			9		10	1	5	12			11	8					43
7		4		2*					6+	3			9		10	1	5	13			11	8		12			44
7	12	4							6	3			9*		10	1	5				11	8		2			45
7	12	4			13				6	3			9+		10	1	5*				11	8		2			46
35	20	32	27	16	35	11	12	4	20	29	9	7	32	5	42	40	30	20		8	34	19	1	5	2	5	
1	5	1	2	1	1	4	11		2	5	3	4	4	6	1			9	1					1	3		
2	2	3	1		7		1		2				7	2	14			8			3	2				2	

One own-goal

Hendon	Howard	Hackett	Bellamy	Ryan	Carter	Lakin	Taylor	Tomlinson	Putney	Ludden	Benstock	Kitchen	Barnett	Okai	West	Newell	Austin	Cooper	Livett	Harriott	Bogie	Cockerill	Gamble	Warren	Purse	Thomas	
2		4		8		11		7						6	10	1	3	9		5							1
2	13	4	5		7*	11+						6	8	12	10	1	3	9									2
2	10	4	5	6	7					12		11	8			1	3*	9									R
3	1	3	2	2	2	2		1				2	2	1	2	3	3	3		1							
	1									1				1													
		2			1	1												1									

Hendon	Howard	Hackett	Bellamy	Ryan	Carter	Lakin	Taylor	Tomlinson	Putney	Ludden	Benstock	Kitchen	Barnett	Okai	West	Newell	Austin	Cooper	Livett	Harriott	Bogie	Cockerill	Gamble	Warren	Purse	Thomas	
2	3	4	5	6	7	8*	9	10	11		12																1/1
2	3	4			7	6*		10	11	8+	12	5	9	13													1/2
2	2	2	1	1	2	2	1	2	2	1		1	1														
											2			1													

1994-95

Managers: Aug 1994–Apr 1995 John Sitton & Chris Turner (joint); Apr 1995 Glenn Cockerill & Tom Loizou (caretaker); Apr–May 1995 Pat Holland

	P	W	D	L	F	A	Pts
Birmingham City	46	25	14	7	84	37	89
Brentford	46	25	10	11	81	39	85
Crewe Alexandra	46	25	8	13	80	68	83
Bristol Rovers	46	22	16	8	70	40	82
Huddersfield Town	46	22	15	9	79	49	81
Wycombe	46	21	15	10	60	46	78
Oxford United	46	21	12	13	66	52	75
Hull City	46	21	11	14	70	57	74
York City	46	21	9	16	67	51	72
Swansea City	46	19	14	13	57	45	71
Stockport County	46	19	8	19	63	60	65
Blackpool	46	18	10	18	64	70	64
Wrexham	46	16	15	15	65	64	63
Bradford City	46	16	12	18	57	64	60
Peterborough United	46	14	18	14	54	69	60
Brighton & Hove Albion	46	14	17	15	54	53	59
Rotherham United	46	14	14	18	57	61	56
Shrewsbury Town	46	13	14	19	54	62	53
Bournemouth	46	13	11	22	49	69	50
Cambridge United	46	11	15	20	52	69	48
Plymouth Argyle	46	12	10	24	45	83	46
Cardiff City	46	9	11	26	46	74	38
Chester City	46	6	11	29	37	84	29
Leyton Orient	46	6	8	32	30	75	26

Division Two

Match No.	Date		Opponents	Result	Scorers	Attend
1	Aug	13	BIRMINGHAM CITY	2-1	Purse, Bogie	7
2		20	Bradford City	0-2		7,
3		27	HULL CITY	1-1	Gray	3,
4		30	Huddersfield Town	1-2	Purse	8
5	Sep	3	Brighton & Hove Albion	0-1		8
6		10	CAMBRIDGE UNITED	1-1	West	3
7		13	BOURNEMOUTH	3-2	West 2 (2 pens), Cockerill	2,
8		17	Shrewsbury Town	0-3		3,
9		24	Oxford United	2-3	Howard, Hague	5,
10	Oct	1	PLYMOUTH ARGYLE	0-2		4,
11		8	Wycombe Wanderers	1-2	Gray	5,
12		15	CHESTER CITY	2-0	West, Cockerill	3,
13		22	Rotherham United	0-2		2,
14		29	STOCKPORT COUNTY	0-1		3,
15	Nov	1	CARDIFF CITY	2-0	Purse, West	2,
16		5	Blackpool	1-2	West	4,
17		19	YORK CITY	0-1		3,
18		26	Peterborough United	0-0		5,
19	Dec	10	BRADFORD CITY	0-0		2,
20		17	Birmingham City	0-2		20,
21		26	Brentford	0-3		6,
22		27	SWANSEA CITY	0-1		3,
23		31	Crewe Alexandra	0-3		3,
24	Jan	7	ROTHERHAM UNITED	0-0		2,
25		14	Wrexham	1-4	Bogie (pen)	6,
26		28	Stockport County	1-2	West	4,
27	Feb	4	PETERBOROUGH UNITED	4-1	Warren 3, West	3,
28		7	BLACKPOOL	0-1		3,
29		18	WREXHAM	1-1	Cockerill	3,
30		21	York City	1-4	Cockerill	2,
31		25	Plymouth Argyle	0-1		5,1
32	Mar	4	OXFORD UNITED	1-1	West	4,
33		7	BRIGHTON & HOVE ALBION	0-3		3,
34		11	Hull City	0-2		4,
35		18	HUDDERSFIELD TOWN	0-2		3,1
36		21	Cambridge United	0-0		3,
37		25	SHREWSBURY TOWN	2-1	Austin, Gray	2,7
38	Apr	1	Bournemouth	0-2		4,1
39		4	Cardiff City	1-2	McGleish	4,3
40		8	CREWE ALEXANDRA	1-4	Austin	2,7
41		11	BRISTOL ROVERS	1-2	Dempsey	2,3
42		15	Swansea City	0-2		3,2
43		17	BRENTFORD	0-2		4,4
44		22	Bristol Rovers	0-1		5,0
45		29	Chester City	0-1		1,5
46	May	6	WYCOMBE WANDERERS	0-1		4,6

Appearanc

Sub appearanc

Goa

FA Cup

1	Nov	12	Tiverton Town	3-1	West, Gray, Carter	3,0
2	Dec	3	BRISTOL ROVERS	0-2		5,0

Appearanc

Sub appearanc

Goa

League Cup

1/1	Aug	16	Barnet	0-4		2,1
1/2		23	BARNET	1-1	Cockerill	2,4

Appearanc

Sub appearanc

Goa

Final League Position: 24th in Division Two

Relegated

Warren	Austin	Purse	Hendon	Lakin	Barnett	Ryan	Bogie	West	Dempsey	Gray	Cockerill	Howard	Carter	Martin	Hague	Bellamy	Brooks	Wilkie	Read	McGleish	Turner	Barry	Perifimou	Rufus	Shearer	Putney	
2	3	4	5	6	7*	8+	9	10	11	12	13																1
	3	4	5	12	7*	6	13	10	11		8	2	9+														2
	3	4	5	12			6	10	11	9	8	2	7*														3
13	3	4	2	12		6*	7+	10	11	9	8	5															4
2	3	4		6	12	7*		10	11	9+	8	5	13														5
	3	4	2	6		7*		10	11	9+	8	5	12	13													6
	3	4	2		12	7		10	11	9+	8	5	6*	13													7
	3	4*	2	7		13		10	11		8	5	6	9+	12												8
	3	4	2	7*				10	11+	12	8	6	9	13	5												9
	3	4		7	13		12	10	11+	9	8	2	6*		5												10
13	3	12		7			6	10	11	9+	8	2			5*	4											11
	3	9*	5	7			6	10	11		8	2	12			4											12
12	3	9	5	7			6	10	11			2	8*			4											13
	3	9*	5	7	12		6	10	11			2	8			4											14
	3	9	5	7	12		6	10	11			2	8*			4											15
2*	3	9+		7	12		6	10	11	13	8	5				4											16
	3		2	12	7*		6	10	11	9	8	5				4											17
	3		2	13	7*		6	10	11	9+	8	5				4	12										18
	3	5		7*	12		6		11	13	8	2	9			4	10+										19
13		5	2	8+	7*		6		11	12		3	9			4	10										20
12			2				6		11	7	8	3	9*		5	4	10										21
10			2		12		6		11	7*	8	3	9		5	4											22
10	3	5			13		6		11	7*	8	2+	9			4		12									23
9+	3	4			7*		6		11	13	8	2	12		5		10										24
9*	3	4	8				6	12	11			2	7		5		10										25
		5	2				12	10	11	9*	8	3	7			4	6										26
10		5	2	6*			9	12	11		8	3	7			4											27
10		5	2	6			9	12	11		8	3*	7			4											28
9*	3	5	2		12		6	10	11		8		7			4											29
9	3	5	2				6	10	11		8		7			4											30
9	3	5	2				6	10	11		8		7			4											31
12	3	5	2				6	10+	11	13	8		7*			4			9								32
10	3	5	2		7*		6		11		8					4			9	12							33
12	3	5	2				6	10	11		8					4			9	7*	1						34
9	3		2	7			6	10	11		8				5	4											35
9+			2		12		6	10	11	13	8				5			4		7*		3					36
9*	3	4			13			10+	11	12	8				5			6		7		2					37
9	3	4			8				11*						5	7		6	10	12		2					38
9	3	4			8					12					5	7			10*	6		2	11+	13			39
10*	3	4							11	12	8				5	7		6	9			2					40
10	3	4			8*				11	13						5		2	9+			12	7	6			41
10	3				8				11						5	4		2	9				7	6			42
10	3				8				11				7			4		2	9					6	5		43
	3	9			8				11				7		5	4		2	10					6			44
2	3	9			7								11*		5	6	4	8	10					12			45
2	3	9			7										5	6	4	8*					12	11	10		46
24	39	37	29	17	15	6	28	27	43	13	32	27	25	1	17	32	8	10	11	4	1	5	3	5	2		
7		1		5	12	1	3	3		12	1		4	3	1		1	1		2		1	1	2			
3	2	3					2	9	1	3	4	1			1					1							

Warren	Austin	Purse	Hendon	Lakin	Barnett	Ryan	Bogie	West	Dempsey	Gray	Cockerill	Howard	Carter	Martin	Hague	Bellamy	Brooks	Wilkie	Read	McGleish	Turner	Barry	Perifimou	Rufus	Shearer	Putney	
	3		2	12	7*		6	10	13	9+	8	5	11			4											1
	3	5		12	7+		6	10	11		8	2	9			4*	13										2
	2	1	1		2		2	2	1	1	2	2	2			2											
				2					1								1										
								1		1			1														

Warren	Austin	Purse	Hendon	Lakin	Barnett	Ryan	Bogie	West	Dempsey	Gray	Cockerill	Howard	Carter	Martin	Hague	Bellamy	Brooks	Wilkie	Read	McGleish	Turner	Barry	Perifimou	Rufus	Shearer	Putney	
2	3	4	5	6	7*		9	10	11	12	8																1/1
	3	4	5	6*	7+		9	10	11	12	8	2	13														1/2
1	2	2	2	2	2		2	2	2		2	1															
										2			1														
											1																

1995-96

Manager: Pat Holland

	P	W	D	L	F	A	Pts
Preston North End	46	23	17	6	78	38	86
Gillingham	46	22	17	7	49	20	83
Bury	46	22	13	11	66	48	79
Plymouth Argyle	46	22	12	12	68	49	78
Darlington	46	20	18	8	60	42	78
Hereford	46	20	14	12	65	47	74
Colchester United	46	18	18	10	61	51	72
Chester City	46	18	16	12	72	53	70
Barnet	46	18	16	12	65	45	70
Wigan Athletic	46	20	10	16	62	56	70
Northampton Town	46	18	13	15	51	44	67
Scunthorpe United	46	15	15	16	67	61	60
Doncaster Rovers	46	16	11	19	49	60	59
Exeter City	46	13	18	15	46	53	57
Rochdale	46	14	13	19	57	61	55
Cambridge United	46	14	12	20	61	71	54
Fulham	46	12	17	17	57	63	53
Lincoln City	46	13	14	19	57	73	53
Mansfield Town	46	11	20	15	54	64	53
Hartlepool United	46	12	13	21	47	67	49
Leyton Orient	46	12	11	23	44	63	47
Cardiff City	46	11	12	23	41	64	45
Scarborough	46	8	16	22	39	69	40
Torquay United	46	5	14	27	30	84	29

Division Three

Match No.	Date		Opponents	Result	Scorers	Attend
1	Aug	12	TORQUAY UNITED	1-0	Brooks	7,
2		19	Mansfield Town	0-0		2,
3		26	DARLINGTON	1-1	Inglethorpe	4,
4		30	Scarborough	1-2	Cockerill	1,
5	Sep	2	FULHAM	1-0	Inglethorpe	7,
6		9	Plymouth Argyle	1-1	Watson	6,
7		12	Northampton Town	2-1	Hendon, Inglethorpe	5,
8		16	HARTLEPOOL UNITED	4-1	Bellamy, Inglethorpe, West 2	4,
9		23	Exeter City	2-2	Inglethorpe 2	5,
10		30	DONCASTER ROVERS	3-1	Chapman, Kelly A, West	5,
11	Oct	7	Bury	1-2	West	3,
12		14	CHESTER CITY	0-2		6,
13		21	Scunthorpe United	0-2		2,
14		28	WIGAN ATHLETIC	1-1	Brooks	4,
15		31	HEREFORD UNITED	0-1		3,
16	Nov	4	Preston North End	0-4		9,
17		18	CAMBRIDGE UNITED	3-1	Inglethorpe, West 2	4,
18		25	Barnet	0-3		2,
19	Dec	9	EXETER CITY	0-3		3,
20		16	Doncaster Rovers	1-4	Chapman	1,
21		22	ROCHDALE	2-0	West 2	5,
22		26	Colchester United	0-0		4,
23	Jan	1	GILLINGHAM	0-1		7,
24		6	Cardiff City	0-0		2,
25		13	MANSFIELD TOWN	1-0	Kelly A	3,
26		16	Lincoln City	0-1		1,
27		20	Torquay United	1-2	Hendon	2,
28	Feb	3	Darlington	0-2		1,
29		10	CARDIFF CITY	4-1	Inglethorpe, West 3 (1 pen)	3,
30		17	NORTHAMPTON TOWN	2-0	West, Arnott	4,
31		24	Hartlepool United	1-4	Kelly A	1,
32		27	PLYMOUTH ARGYLE	0-1		3,
33	Mar	2	COLCHESTER UNITED	0-1		4,
34		9	Rochdale	0-1		1,
35		16	LINCOLN CITY	2-0	Austin, Inglethorpe	3,
36		19	SCARBOROUGH	1-0	Warren	2,
37		23	Gillingham	1-1	Arnott	8,
38		26	Fulham	1-2	Shearer	3,6
39		30	BURY	0-2		3,4
40	Apr	2	Chester City	1-1	West	2,
41		6	Wigan Athletic	0-1		3,
42		8	SCUNTHORPE UNITED	0-0		2,8
43		13	Hereford United	2-3	West 2	3,4
44		20	PRESTON NORTH END	0-2		5,1
45		27	BARNET	3-3	West, Hanson, Arnott	4,0
46	May	4	Cambridge United	0-2		3,8

Appearanc
Sub appearanc
Goa

FA Cup

1	Nov	11	Torquay United	0-1		2,4

Appearanc
Sub appearanc
Goa

League Cup

1\1	Aug	15	Wycombe Wanderers	0-3		3,3
1\2		22	WYCOMBE WANDERERS	2-0	Austin, West (pen)	2,4

Appearanc
Sub appearanc
Goa

Final League Position: 21st in Division Three

Warren	Austin	Chapman	Hendon	Bellamy	Brooks	Cockerill	Inglethorpe	Gray	Stanislaus	Baker	Shearer	McCarthy	Kelly	West	Watson	Hanson	Purse	Lakin	Fearon	Williams	Currie	Arnott	Berry	Kelly	Ayorinde	
2	3*	4	5	6	7	8	9	10	11	12																1
2	3	4	5		11	8	9					6	7	10												2
	3	4	5	2	11	8	9*			12		6	7	10												3
	3	4*		5	11	8	9			12	2	6	7	10												4
		4	2	5	11	8	9		3			6	7	10												5
	12	4	2*	5	11	8	9+		3			6	7	10	13											6
		4	2	5	11	8*	9		3	12		6	7	10												7
		4	2	5	11	8	9		3			6	7	10												8
2	13	4	2	5	11+	8	9		3			6	7*	10												9
2	13	4	2	5	11+	8	9		3			6	7*	10												10
2	11*	4	8	5			9		3			6	7+	10		12	13									11
2	12	4	6	5*			9		3	13		11	7	10+				8								12
1	8	4	2	5			9*		3	12		6	7			10										13
3	12	4*	2	5+	11	8	9		3			6	7	10												14
2		4	5		11	8	9		3			6	7			10										15
3	3	4	5		11	8			12	7*		6	9			10+	2									16
	6		2	5	4*	8	9+		3			12	7	10					1	13	11					17
	6		2	5	4*	8	9		3			13		10				7+	1	12	11					18
	6		5		12	8	9	13	3					10			2	4*	1	7+	11					19
	7*	4	2	5	12	8	9		3			6		10					1		11					20
		2	4	5		8	9		3			6	7	10					1		11					21
	11+			5	4*	8	9	13	3			6	7	10		12	2		1							22
				5	4	8	9*		3			6	7	10		12	2		1		11					23
	12			5	4	8		10*	3			6	7			9	2		1		11					24
	3	2	4	5*	13	8		14				6	7	10		9+	12		1		11#					25
	3	2	7	5	4	8*		9+		12		6	11	10					1		13					26
	3	2	7	5	4		9	12		13		6	11+				8		1		10*					27
	13		4	5	11	8	9			12		3	7+	10			2*					6				28
	3		2	5	11	8*	9					6	7	10			12		1			4				29
	3	11	2	5		8	9					6	7	10					1			4				30
	3	11	2	5	12	8	9*					6	7	10					1			4				31
	3	11+	2	5	12	8	9*			13		6	7	10					1			4				32
12	3	11	2	5	9	8						6	7*	10					1			4				33
9	3	4		5	11+	8*					12	13	7	10			2					6				34
11	3	4		5	12		9			13		8	7+			10	2*					6				35
11	3	4	2	5	12		9+					6	7*	10		13						8				36
7+	3	4*	2		11	8					5	6	12	10				14				9#	13			37
7*	3	4	2		11+	8					5	6	12	10								9	13			38
	3	4	2		7*	8				12	5	6		10								9	11+	13		39
7*	3	4	2		11	8				12		6		10								9		5		40
11	3	4			7+	8				13		6		10				2*				5	12	9		41
12	3*	4	2		8					7		6		10								5	9	11		42
11	3	4			7					12	8	6		10				2*				5	9			43
	3*	4+	2		7	8				12		6		10				13				5	9	11		44
12	3	4	2		7	8+				11	14	6*		10		9#		13	1			5				45
6	12	4	2		7+	8				11	13			10					1			5		3*	9	46
15	32	38	38	32	34	38	30	3	20	4	5	40	32	39		7	9	5	18	1	9	19	4	5	1	
7	8				7			4	1	16	3	3	2		1	4	3	3		2	1		3	1		
1	1	2	2	1	2	1	9				1		3	16	1	1						3				

Warren	Austin	Chapman	Hendon	Bellamy	Brooks	Cockerill	Inglethorpe	Gray	Stanislaus	Baker	Shearer	McCarthy	Kelly	West	Watson	Hanson	Purse	Lakin	Fearon	Williams	Currie	Arnott	Berry	Kelly	Ayorinde	
	6	4	2	5	11*	8			3	12			7	10					1	9						1
	1	1	1	1	1	1			1				1	1					1	1						
										1																

Warren	Austin	Chapman	Hendon	Bellamy	Brooks	Cockerill	Inglethorpe	Gray	Stanislaus	Baker	Shearer	McCarthy	Kelly	West	Watson	Hanson	Purse	Lakin	Fearon	Williams	Currie	Arnott	Berry	Kelly	Ayorinde	
2	3	4	5	6	7	8	9		11*	12	10															1/1
2*	3	4	5		11+	8	9			13	12	6	7	10												1/2
2	2	2	2	1	2	2	2		1		1	1	1	1												
										2	1															
	1													1												

1996-97

Managers: Aug–Oct 1996 Pat Holland; Oct–Nov 1996 Tommy Cunningham (caretaker); Nov 1996–May 1997 Tommy Taylor

	P	W	D	L	F	A	Pts
Wigan Athletic	46	26	9	11	84	51	87
Fulham	46	25	12	9	72	38	87
Carlisle United	46	24	12	10	67	44	84
Northampton Town	46	20	12	14	67	44	72
Swansea City	46	21	8	17	62	58	71
Chester City	46	18	16	12	55	43	70
Cardiff City	46	20	9	17	56	54	69
Colchester United	46	17	17	12	62	51	68
Lincoln City	46	18	12	16	70	69	66
Cambridge United	46	18	11	17	53	59	65
Mansfield Town	46	16	16	14	47	45	64
Scarborough	46	16	15	15	65	68	63
Scunthorpe United	46	18	9	19	59	62	63
Rochdale	46	14	16	16	58	58	58
Barnet	46	14	16	16	46	51	58
Leyton Orient	46	15	12	19	50	58	57
Hull City	46	13	18	15	44	50	57
Darlington	46	14	10	22	64	78	52
Doncaster	46	14	10	22	52	66	52
Hartlepool United	46	14	9	23	53	66	51
Torquay United	46	13	11	22	46	62	50
Exeter City	46	12	12	22	48	73	48
Brighton & Hove Albion*	46	13	10	23	53	70	47
Hereford	46	11	14	21	50	65	47

*Brighton & Hove Albion deducted 2 points.

Division Three

Match No.	Date		Opponents	Result	Scorers	Atter
1	Aug	17	SCUNTHORPE UNITED	0-1		[illegible]
2		24	Lincoln City	1-1	Hendon	3
3		27	Carlisle United	0-1		4
4		31	HARTLEPOOL UNITED	2-0	West, Kelly	4
5	Sep	7	DARLINGTON	0-0		3
6		10	Northampton Town	1-0	Chapman	3
7		14	Mansfield Town	2-0	Hanson 2	1
8		21	COLCHESTER UNITED	1-1	Channing	5
9		28	Rochdale	0-1		1
10	Oct	1	SWANSEA CITY	1-0	Hanson	3
11		5	Doncaster Rovers	1-2	Ayorinde	1
12		12	HULL CITY	1-1	Naylor (pen)	4
13		15	CHESTER CITY	0-0		3
14		19	Hereford United	0-2		2
15		26	Cardiff City	0-3		3
16		29	SCARBOROUGH	0-1		2
17	Nov	2	TORQUAY UNITED	1-0	Griffiths	3
18		9	Exeter City	2-3	Ayorinde, Griffiths	3
19		23	Cambridge United	0-2		4
20		30	CARDIFF CITY	3-0	Arnott, Griffiths, McGleish	4
21	Dec	3	Barnet	0-0		2
22		14	Fulham	1-1	Warren	7
23		22	BRIGHTON & HOVE ALBION	2-0	Naylor 2 (1 pen)	7,
24		26	NORTHAMPTON TOWN	2-1	Channing, Inglethorpe	4
25		28	Darlington	1-1	West	2
26	Jan	4	MANSFIELD TOWN	2-1	West, McGleish	3
27		18	Swansea City	0-1		3
28		21	WIGAN ATHLETIC	1-2	McGleish	3
29		25	Scarborough	1-2	Chapman	2,
30	Feb	1	EXETER CITY	1-1	Winston	3,
31		4	Colchester United	1-2	Channing	3
32		8	Torquay United	0-0		3
33		11	ROCHDALE	2-1	Inglethorpe, Castle	2,
34		15	CAMBRIDGE UNITED	1-1	McGleish	4,
35		22	Wigan Athletic	1-5	Inglethorpe	3,
36	Mar	1	BARNET	0-1		4,
37		8	Brighton & Hove Albion	4-4	Griffiths 2, McGleish, Inglethorpe	8,
38		16	FULHAM	0-2		7,
39		22	LINCOLN CITY	2-3	Arnott, Timons	4,
40		29	Scunthorpe United	2-1	Timons, Channing	3,
41		31	CARLISLE UNITED	2-1	McGleish 2	4,
42	Apr	5	Hartlepool United	1-3	Channing	2,
43		12	DONCASTER ROVERS	2-1	Arnott, Inglethorpe	4,
44		19	Hull City	2-3	Griffiths, Inglethorpe	2,
45		26	HEREFORD UNITED	2-1	Ling, Inglethorpe	5,
46	May	3	Chester City	1-0	Inglethorpe	3,

Appearanc
Sub appearanc
Go

FA Cup

1	Nov	16	MERTHYR TYDFIL	2-1	West, Winston	4,4
2	Dec	7	STEVENAGE BOROUGH	1-2	Channing	6,9

Appearanc
Sub appearanc
Goa

League Cup

1/1	Aug	20	Portsmouth	0-2		3,1
1/2	Sep	4	PORTSMOUTH	1-0	West	3,1

Appearanc
Sub appearanc
Goa

Final League Position: 16th in Division Three

Hendon	Naylor	Garland	Martin	Arnott	Martin	Ling	Ayorinde	West	Baker	Hanson	Chapman	McCarthy	Caldwell	Kelly	Channing	Riches	Warren	Shearer	Weaver	Griffiths	Winston	Joseph	McGleish	Shilton	Inglethorpe	Howes	Heidenstrom	Ansah	Clapham	Whyte	Hyde	Castle	Wilkins	Hodges	Atkin	Timons	Morrison	Fortune-West	
2	3	4	5	6	7	8	9	10*	11+	12	13																												1
2	3	4	5	6	7	8	9*	10	11+	12			1	13																									2
2	3	4*	5	6	7	8	9+	10#		14	13			12	11																								3
2	3		5	6	7	8		10		9	12			11	4*																								4
2	3		5	6	7	8	13	10		9+	12			11	4*																								5
2	3	13	5	6	7	8*		10	12	9	4			11+																									6
2	3		5	6	7	8		10	11	9	4																												7
2	3		5	6	7*	8		10		9	4			12	11																								8
2	3		5	6		8	13	10		9+	4			7*	11	12																							9
2	3	13	5	6		8		10		9	4			7*	11+	12																							10
2	3	12	5*	6+		8	13	10	11	9	4	7																											11
2	3	7				8	10		12	9	4	6			11		5*																						12
2	3	7				8	10		13	9+	4	6*			11		12	5																					13
2	3	6*				8		10	7	9	4		1		11	12		5																					14
2	3	6		5		8	12		7	9	4		1		11	10*																							15
2	3	14		6*		8+	12		7	9	4				10	11#	13	5	1																				16
2	3	7		6		8	11				4				10			5	1	9																			17
2	3	13	5*	6		8+	12	11			4				10		7		1	9																			18
	3			6		8		11						5*	7			2	1	10	12	4	9																19
2	3	13		6		8		11+							7		5			10	12	4	9*	1															20
2	3	11		6		8		12							7		5			10*		4	9	1															21
	3		12	6*		8		11+			4				7		5					10	9	1	13	2													22
2	3		4			8		9*			13				7		5					6	10	1	12		11+												23
2	3					8		9*			4				7		5				14	6	10+	1	13	12	11#												24
2	3					8		9+			4				7		5					6	10	1	12	13	11*												25
2	3		11*			8		9			4				7		5					6	10	1				12											26
	3		2*	12		8		9+		13	4						5					6	10	1	7	11#	14												27
2	3		11*			8		9+			4				7		5				13	6	10	1	12														28
2	3					8				9*	4				7		5		1			6	10		11			12											29
		2		12		8			11		13				7		5		1*		9	6	10						3	4+									30
						8			11		4				7		5				2	10	9						3		1	6							31
	3					8			12		4				7		5				9*	2	10						11		1	6							32
2*	3			9#		8+			4		12				7		5				13		10		14				11		1	6							33
2	3					8*			9+	13					7		5				12		10		4				11		1	6							34
	3					8			11	12	4				7			5*	1			6	10		9				2										35
	3					8*			11	12	5				4				1				10		9	2							6	7					36
	3					14			11	13	4	12			2*		5		1	8+			10		9								6#	7					37
	3			14		12			11#		4				2		5	9+		8	13		10								1		6	7*					38
	3			7		8+					4*				2			12		9	13		10								1				5	6	11		39
	3			7		12					4				2		5			9			10*								1				8	6	11+	13	40
	3	12		7		14					4*				2		5			9+			10								1				8	6	11#	13	41
	3	14		7		12					4*				2		5			9			10								1				8#	6	11+	13	42
	3	6		7											2		5			9			10		4						1				8		11		43
	3	6*		7						12	8+				2		5			9			10		4						1						11	13	44
	3	6*		7		8			13	9	12				2								10		4						1					5	11+		45
	3			7		8*				13	12				2		6						10		4						1					5	11	9+	46
28	44	13	16	28	8	39	6	22	15	15	31	3	3	6	40	2	25	7	9	13	3	15	28	9	10	3	3		6	1	13	4	3	3	5	6	8	1	
		8	1	3		5	6	1	5	10	9	1		3		3	2	1			8				6	2	1	2										4	
1	3			3		1	2	3		3	2			1	5		1			6	1		7		8							1				2			

Hendon	Naylor	Garland	Martin	Arnott	Martin	Ling	Ayorinde	West	Baker	Hanson	Chapman	McCarthy	Caldwell	Kelly	Channing	Riches	Warren	Shearer	Weaver	Griffiths	Winston	Joseph	McGleish	Shilton	Inglethorpe	Howes	Heidenstrom	Ansah	Clapham	Whyte	Hyde	Castle	Wilkins	Hodges	Atkin	Timons	Morrison	Fortune-West	
2	3	5*		6		8	9+	11	12		4				10		7		1		13																		1
2	3	10#		6+		8		11			14				7		5	4*			12		9	1	13														2
2	2	2		2		2	1	2			1				2		2	1	1				1	1															
									1		1										2				1														
								1							1						1																		

Hendon	Naylor	Garland	Martin	Arnott	Martin	Ling	Ayorinde	West	Baker	Hanson	Chapman	McCarthy	Caldwell	Kelly	Channing	Riches	Warren	Shearer	Weaver	Griffiths	Winston	Joseph	McGleish	Shilton	Inglethorpe	Howes	Heidenstrom	Ansah	Clapham	Whyte	Hyde	Castle	Wilkins	Hodges	Atkin	Timons	Morrison	Fortune-West	
2	3	4	5	6	7	8*	9+	10		12	13	11																											1/1
2	3		5	6	7*	8	12	10		9				11	4																								1/2
2	2	1	2	2	2	2	1	2		1		1		1	1																								
							1			1	1																												
								1																															

1997-98

Manager: Tommy Taylor

	P	W	D	L	F	A	Pts
Notts County	46	29	12	5	82	43	99
Macclesfield	46	23	13	10	63	44	82
Lincoln City	46	20	15	11	60	51	75
Colchester United	46	21	11	14	72	60	74
Torquay United	46	21	11	14	68	59	74
Scarborough	46	19	15	12	67	58	72
Barnet	46	19	13	14	61	51	70
Scunthorpe United	46	19	12	15	56	52	69
Rotherham United	46	16	19	11	67	61	67
Peterborough United	46	18	13	15	63	51	67
Leyton Orient*	46	19	12	15	62	47	66
Mansfield Town	46	16	17	13	64	55	65
Shrewsbury Town	46	16	13	17	61	62	61
Chester City	46	17	10	19	60	61	61
Exeter City	46	15	15	16	68	63	60
Cambridge United	46	14	18	14	63	57	60
Hartlepool United	46	12	23	11	61	53	59
Rochdale	46	17	7	22	56	55	58
Darlington	46	14	12	20	56	72	54
Swansea City	46	13	11	22	49	62	50
Cardiff City	46	9	23	14	48	52	50
Hull City	46	11	8	27	56	83	41
Brighton & Hove Albion	46	6	17	23	38	66	35
Doncaster	46	4	8	34	30	113	20

* Leyton Orient deducted 3 points.

Division Three

Match No.	Date		Opponents	Result	Scorers	Atten
1	Aug	9	CARDIFF CITY	0-1		5
2		16	Scunthorpe United	0-1		3
3		23	ROCHDALE	2-0	Smith 2	3
4		30	Brighton & Hove Albion	1-0	Griffiths	2
5	Sep	2	Doncaster Rovers	4-1	Hicks, Clark 2, Griffiths	1
6		5	CAMBRIDGE UNITED	0-2		4
7		13	EXETER CITY	1-0	Griffiths	4
8		20	Peterborough United	0-2		6,
9		27	Swansea City	1-1	Clark	3
10	Oct	4	MACCESFIELD TOWN	1-1	Griffiths	4
11		11	ROTHERHAM UNITED	1-1	Griffiths	3
12		18	Hartlepool United	2-2	Griffiths, Inglethorpe	2
13		21	Torquay United	1-1	Harris	1,
14		25	COLCHESTER UNITED	0-2		4
15	Nov	1	Lincoln City	0-1		4,
16		4	SCARBOROUGH	3-1	Inglethorpe 2, Harris	2,
17		8	CHESTER CITY	1-0	Smith	3
18		18	Darlington	0-1		1,
19		22	NOTTS COUNTY	1-1	Harris	4,
20		29	Mansfield Town	0-0		2
21	Dec	2	BARNET	2-0	Smith, Hanson	2
22		13	Shrewsbury Town	2-1	Smith, Simpson	2,
23		20	HULL CITY	2-1	Smith, Harris	4,
24		26	Cambridge United	0-1		4,
25		28	DONCASTER ROVERS	8-0	Smith, Richards 2, Griffiths 3, Baker, Inglethorpe	4,
26	Jan	10	Cardiff City	0-1		4,
27		17	BRIGHTON & HOVE ALBION	3-1	Griffiths, Simpson 2	6,
28		24	Rochdale	2-0	Griffiths, Inglethorpe	1,
29		31	Exeter City	2-2	Clark, Ling	4,
30	Feb	6	PETERBOROUGH UNITED	1-0	Baker	6,
31		14	Macclesfield Town	0-1		2,
32		21	SWANSEA CITY	2-2	Griffiths, Harris	4,
33		24	HARTLEPOOL UNITED	2-1	Harris, Joseph M	3,
34		28	Rotherham United	1-2	Griffiths	3,
35	Mar	3	Chester City	1-1	Smith	1,
36		7	LINCOLN CITY	1-0	Inglethorpe	4,
37		14	Scarborough	0-2		2,
38		21	DARLINGTON	2-0	Naylor, Inglethorpe	4,
39		28	Notts County	0-1		8,
40	Apr	4	MANSFIELD TOWN	2-2	Griffiths 2	4,
41		11	Barnet	2-1	Griffiths, Baker	3,
42		13	SHREWSBURY TOWN	2-3	Griffiths, Maskell	4,
43		18	Hull City	2-3	Griffiths, Inglethorpe	3,
44		21	SCUNTHORPE UNITED	1-0	Ling	2,
45		25	Colchester United	1-1	Inglethorpe	5,
46	May	2	TORQUAY UNITED	2-1	Smith, Maskell	6,5

Appearanc
Sub appearanc
Go

FA Cup

1	Nov	15	Hendon	2-2	Smith, Harris	2,4
R		25	HENDON	0-1		3,3

Appearanc
Sub appearanc
Goa

League Cup

1/1	Aug	13	Brighton & Hove Albion	1-1	Griffiths	1,0
1/2		26	BRIGHTON & HOVE ALbion	3-1	McGleish, Griffiths, Baker	3,6
2/1	Sep	16	BOLTON WANDERERS	1-3	Inglethorpe	4,1
2/2		30	Bolton Wanderers	4-4	Warren, Griffiths, Baker, Inglethorpe	6,4

Appearanc
Sub appearanc
Goa

Final League Position: 11th in Division Three

Channing	Naylor	Smith	Hicks	Clark	Ling	Warren	McGleish	West	Morrison	Richards	Hanson	Joseph	Griffiths	Hodge	Baker	Richardson	Colkin	Inglethorpe	Harris	Williams	Linger	Regis	Mackenzie	Simpson	Pitcher	Cooper	Joseph	Bennett	Fenn	Turley	Raynor	Maskell	Martin	
2	3	4	5*	6	7	8	9	10+	11#	12	13	14																						1
2*	3	4	5		7	8	9	10#		11	12	13		6+	14																			2
	3	4	5	6	7	8*	10+	13		12		2	9		14	11#																		3
	3	4	5	6	7*	8	10			11+		2	9		12		13																	4
	3	4	5	6	7	8	10+	13		11#		2	9*		14		12																	5
	3	4	5*	6	7	8	10	12		11			9+		13		2																	6
11	3	4	5	6	7		10+	13				12	9#		14		2	8*																7
2*	3	4		6	7	8	10			5+	12	13	9					11																8
2*	3	4	5	6	7	8							9		12		13	11	10+															9
12	3	4	5*	6	7	2							9		8		13	11	10+															10
5	3*	4		6	7	2						14	9		12		8+	11	10#	13														11
5*	3	4		6	7	2						11#	9		14		13	8	10+		12													12
5	3	4		6	7	2						12	9*		13		11	8	10+															13
6*	3	4	5		7	2		13					9		10		11+	8			12													14
2*	3	4	5	6	7	8					10						12	11+	13			9												15
2*	3	4	5	6	7	8					10+	12						11	13			9												16
2	3	4	5*	6	7	8					10	12						11	13			9+												17
2	3		5	6	7	8					10		9					4*	12			11												18
2	3	4	5	6	7	8									12			9	10		11*													19
2	3	4	5	6	7	8					12		9		11				10*															20
2	3	4	5	6	7	8					12	13	9		11+				10*															21
2	3	4	5	6	7	8					13+	12			14			11	10*				1	9+										22
2	3	4	5		7	8					12	6	13					11	10*					9+										23
2	3	4	5+		7	8				14	12	6	13					11*	10					9#										24
2	3	4	5	6	7					10+		8	9*		13			11#	12					14										25
2+	3	4#	5	6	7	8				13			9					11	12						10*	14								26
2+	3	4		6	7	8				11*			9		12			5	10					13										27
2	3	4		6	7	8							9					5	12					11*			10							28
	3	4		6	7	8				13		12	9					5+	14								10	2#	11					29
	3	4		6	7	8						2*	9		12			5+	13								10		11	1				30
	3			6	7	8				4		2*			12			5	9								10	13	11+	1				31
	3		5*	6	7	8				11+		2	9		12			4	13								10			1				32
	3	4	5*	6	7	8							9+		12			11	10					13			2			1				33
12	3	4	5	6	7	8						13	9*					11	14								2+			1	10#			34
12	3	4	5	6	7	8							9					11									2			1	10*			35
12	3	4	5+	6	7*	8							9		13			11	14								2			1	10#			36
12	3	4	5+	6	7	8				9					13			11	10								2*			1				37
2	3	4	5	6	7	8				12								11	10+					9*						1	13			38
2	3	4*	5	6	7					12			9					11	10#					8+						1	13	14		39
2	3	4	5	6	7								9		12			11+	13					8						1		10*		40
2	3	4	5+	6	7								9		12			11	8											1	13	10*		41
2+	3	4	5		7	6							9		12			11	8											1	13	10*		42
8*	3	4	5+		7	6							9		12			11						13			2			1		10		43
		4	5		7	6						8*			12			11	13				1	9+			2				3#	10	14	44
		4		6	7	5						2			12			11	9				1	13			8				3+	10*		45
		4		6	7	5			12			2			13			11	9+				1	8#			3				14	10*		46
29	43	43	35	39	46	41	8	2	1	10	4	13	31	1	4	1	5	38	21		1	4	4	9	1		14	1	3	14	5	7		
5								5	1	7	8	12	2		27		6		14	1	2			5		1		1			5	1	1	
	1	9	1	4	2					2	1		18		3			9	6					3			1					2		

Channing	Naylor	Smith	Hicks	Clark	Ling	Warren	McGleish	West	Morrison	Richards	Hanson	Joseph	Griffiths	Hodge	Baker	Richardson	Colkin	Inglethorpe	Harris	Williams	Linger	Regis	Mackenzie	Simpson	Pitcher	Cooper	Joseph	Bennett	Fenn	Turley	Raynor	Maskell	Martin	
11	3	4*	5	6	7	2		13			10	12	9						8															1
11#	3	4	5	6	7	2					14		9		13			8*	10+		12													R
2	2	2	2	2	2	2					1		2					1	2															
								1			1	1			1						1													
		1																	1															

Channing	Naylor	Smith	Hicks	Clark	Ling	Warren	McGleish	West	Morrison	Richards	Hanson	Joseph	Griffiths	Hodge	Baker	Richardson	Colkin	Inglethorpe	Harris	Williams	Linger	Regis	Mackenzie	Simpson	Pitcher	Cooper	Joseph	Bennett	Fenn	Turley	Raynor	Maskell	Martin	
2	3	4	5		7	8	9	10		12		6	11*																					1
	3	4	5	6	7	8	10			11		2	9*		12																			
2	3	4	5*	6	7	8	10			12			9					11																2
12	3	4	5	6	7	2						13	9		8*		14	11#	10+															
2	4	4	4	3	4	4	3	1		1		2	4		1			2	1															
1										2		1			1		1																	
						1	1						3		2			2																

1998-99

Manager: Tommy Taylor

	P	W	D	L	F	A	Pts
Brentford	46	26	7	13	79	56	85
Cambridge United	46	23	12	11	78	48	81
Cardiff City	46	22	14	10	60	39	80
Scunthorpe United	46	22	8	16	69	58	74
Rotherham United	46	20	13	13	79	61	73
Leyton Orient	46	19	15	12	68	59	72
Swansea City	46	19	14	13	56	48	71
Mansfield Town	46	19	10	17	60	58	67
Peterborough United	46	18	12	16	72	56	66
Halifax Town	46	17	15	14	58	56	66
Darlington	46	18	11	17	69	58	65
Exeter City	46	17	12	17	47	50	63
Plymouth Argyle	46	17	10	19	58	54	61
Chester City	46	13	18	15	57	66	57
Shrewsbury Town	46	14	14	18	52	63	56
Barnet	46	14	13	19	54	71	55
Brighton & Hove Albion	46	16	7	23	49	66	55
Southend United	46	14	12	20	52	58	54
Rochdale	46	13	15	18	42	55	54
Torquay United	46	12	17	17	47	58	53
Hull City	46	14	11	21	44	62	53
Hartlepool United	46	13	12	21	52	65	51
Carlisle United	46	11	16	19	43	53	49
Scarborough	46	14	6	26	50	77	48

Final League Position: 6th in Division Three

*Second semi-final won 4–2 on penalties after extra-time

**The Final was played at Wembley Stadium

Division Three

Match No.		Date	Opponents	Result	Scorers	Atten
1	Aug	8	Chester City	2-0	Richards, Harris	2
2		15	ROTHERHAM UNITED	1-4	Smith	4
3		22	Swansea City	1-1	Morrison	4
4		29	SCARBOROUGH	0-3		3
5	Sep	1	Torquay United	1-1	Griffiths	2
6		5	CARLISLE UNITED	2-1	Griffiths (pen), Morrison	3
7		8	MANSFIELD TOWN	1-1	Clark	3
8		12	Cambridge United	0-1		3
9		19	BRIGHTON & HOVE ALBION	1-0	Smith	5
10		26	Rochdale	1-2	Smith	1
11	Oct	3	HARTLEPOOL UNITED	1-1	Clark	3
12		9	EXETER CITY	2-0	Inglethorpe, Simba	3
13		17	Southend United	2-2	Lockwood, Inglethorpe	6
14		20	Cardiff City	0-0		5
15		24	HALIFAX TOWN	1-0	Inglethorpe	3
16		31	SCUNTHORPE UNITED	1-0	Griffiths	3
17	Nov	7	Hull City	1-0	Beall	5
18		10	Shrewsbury Town	1-1	Smith	2
19		21	BRENTFORD	2-1	Smith (pen), Watts	6
20		28	Plymouth Argyle	4-2	Ling, Richards, Griffiths (pen), Watts	4
21	Dec	12	PETERBOROUGH UNITED	1-2	Smith (pen)	4
22		19	Barnet	2-3	Simba, Beall	3
23		26	SWANSEA CITY	1-1	Smith (pen)	5,
24		28	Darlington	1-1	Ling	3
25	Jan	9	CHESTER CITY	2-2	Simba 2	4,
26		16	Rotherham United	1-3	Watts	3,
27		30	DARLINGTON	3-2	Walschaerts, Smith, Richards	3,
28	Feb	6	Carlisle United	1-1	Watts	2,
29		13	Mansfield Town	2-1	Ling, Richards	2,
30		20	CAMBRIDGE UNITED	2-0	Ling, Griffiths	6
31		27	Brighton & Hove Albion	2-1	Lockwood, Griffiths (pen)	4,
32	Mar	2	TORQUAY UNITED	2-0	Lockwood, Watts	4,
33		6	ROCHDALE	3-0	Ampadu, Griffiths 2	4,
34		13	HULL CITY	1-2	Richards	5,
35		20	Scunthorpe United	0-2		4,
36		26	Halifax Town	2-1	Clark, Omoyinmi	2,
37	Apr	3	SOUTHEND UNITED	0-3		6,
38		5	Exeter City	1-1	Walschaerts	2,
39		10	CARDIFF CITY	1-1	Eckhardt (og)	5,
40		13	PLYMOUTH ARGYLE	4-3	Richards, Morrison, Inglethorpe, Watts	4,
41		17	Brentford	0-0		8,
42		21	Scarborough	3-1	Richards, Simba 2	1,
43		24	SHREWSBURY TOWN	6-1	Walschaerts, Smith, Clark, Simba 2, Gayle (og)	4,
44		27	Hartlepool United	0-1		3,
45	May	1	Peterborough United	0-3		6,
46		8	BARNET	2-2	Simba 2	6,

Appearan
Sub appearan
Gc

Play-offs

SF	May	16	ROTHERHAM UNITED	0-0		9,
SF2		19	Rotherham United	0-0*		9,
F**		29	Scunthorpe United	0-1		36,

Appearan
Sub appearan
Go

FA Cup

1	Nov	14	BRIGHTON & HOVE ALBION	4-2	Walschaerts, Richards 3	7,
2	Dec	6	Kingstonian	0-0		3,
R		15	KINGSTONIAN	2-1	Walschaerts, Simba	3,
3	Jan	2	Southport	2-0	Smith (pen), Griffiths	4,
4		23	Bristol Rovers	0-3		9,

Appearan
Sub appearan
Go

League Cup

1/1	Aug	11	BRISTOL ROVERS	1-1	Richards	2,
1/2		18	Bristol Rovers	2-1e	Warren, Inglethorpe	4,
2/1	Sep	15	NOTTINGHAM FOREST	1-5	Reinelt	4,
2/1		22	Nottingham Forest	0-0		6,

Appearan
Sub appearan
Go

Walschaerts	Lockwood	Smith	Hicks	Clark	Ling	Ampadu	Richards	Maskell	Martin	Reinelt	Harris	Warren	Griffiths	Baker	Canham	Inglethorpe	Morrison	Raynor	Joseph, M	Joseph, R	McCormick	McDougald	Simba	Watts	Beall	Curran	Barrett	Stimson	Omoyinmi	Finney	Downer	Capleton	
2	3	4	5	6	7	8	9*	10	11+	12	13																						1
2	3	4	5*	6	7	8		10		9+		11	12	13																			2
2	3		5*	6	7	8		10				4	9+		12	14	13	11#															3
2		4	5+	6	7	8		10*			12	3	9#		13	14		11															4
2			5	6	7	8		10			12	3	9*		4	11+	13																5
2	11		5	6	7	8		10*			12	3	9			13			4+														6
2	11		5+	6	7	8					10*	3	9			14			4	12	13#												7
2*	11		5#	6+	7	8					12	3	9			13			4	10	14												8
2		4	5		7	8					10#	3	9		12	11+			6*	14	13												9
2		4			7	8		10#				3	9		13		12	11+	6	14	5*												10
2	10	4		6	7*	8	9+	13				3		12				11	5														11
2	3	4		6	7		9+							12				11	5		8		10*	13									12
2*	3	4		6	7	12	9											11	5+		8		10#	13	14								13
2	3	4	5	6	7		9						12					11	8+		13		10*										14
2	3	4	5	6	7	12	9+						13					11*			8		10#		14								15
2*	3	4	5	6	7	8	12						9										10+	13		11							16
2	3	4	5	6	7	8+	10*	12					9								13					11							17
2+	3*	4	5	6	7	8	10						9								12				13	11							18
2	3	4	5	6	7		10+	12					9*						8						13	11							19
2#	3	4+	5*	6	7	12	10	13					9						8						14	11							20
2*	3	4	5+	6	7			13					9					12	8				10#		14	11							21
2+	3	4	5	6	7		9											12	8				10*			11							22
2	3	4		6	7		9+						10*					5	8				12		13	11							23
2	3+	4		6	7	9											12	5*	8				10#		13	11	14						24
	3	4		6	7	5	8												2				10*	9	12	11							25
5+	3	4		6	7											13		12	2				10*	9	8	11							26
2		4	5		7		9*									13#	3	8+			6		10	12	14	11		1					27
2		4	5*	6	7	8	9										3#	12			13		10		14	11+		1					28
2		4	5+	6	7	8	9									14		11#	3		13		12		10*			1					29
2		4	5	3	7	8	9						10*			11					6		12					1					30
2	12	4	5+	3	7	8	9						10			11*			6						13			1					31
2	11+	4	5*	3	7	8	9						10			12			6						13			1					32
2	3	4			7	8	9+						10*			13		12	6		5		11#		14			1					33
2	3				7	8*	9						10			13		4+	6		5		11#		14	12		1					34
2	3		5	6	7+								10					9	8		12				14	13		1	11*			4#	35
2	3		5	6		4	10	12								13			8#		14				9+	7		1	11*				36
	3	4	5+	6	7	8	11												2				10*		12			1	13	9			37
2	3	4		6	7	5*	10									12			8						13			1	11	9+			38
2#	3	4		6	7		11	10*						12		5+	14		8		13				9			1					39
2*	3	4		6	7		10									5		12	8				13		9+	11		1					40
2			5	6	7		10									4*	12		8		3				9	11		1					41
2	3	4	5	6	7		10*												8				12		9+	11		1		13			42
2	3	4		6	7											13		12	8		5		10#		9*	11+		1		14			43
2	3	4		6	7											12			8		5		10+		9	11*		1		13			44
2	3	4		6*	7											12		9	8		5		10+	13		11		1					45
2	3	4						12										13	8		5		10	7+	9#	11		1			14	6*	46
44	36	37	29	40	44	26	28	8	1	1	2	10	21		1	7	2	15	34	1	13		19	3	10	21		20	3	2		2	
	1					3	1	7		1	5		3	4	4	16	6	8		3	11		5	5	18	2	1		1	3	1		
3	3	9		4	4	1	7			1			8			3		4					10		6	2			1				

Two own-goals

Walschaerts	Lockwood	Smith	Hicks	Clark	Ling	Ampadu	Richards	Maskell	Martin	Reinelt	Harris	Warren	Griffiths	Baker	Canham	Inglethorpe	Morrison	Raynor	Joseph, M	Joseph, R	McCormick	McDougald	Simba	Watts	Beall	Curran	Barrett	Stimson	Omoyinmi	Finney	Downer	Capleton	
	3	4		6	7		8	13											2+		5		10		9+	11		1				12	SF
	3	4	12	6	7		8+									13		14			5		10		9#	11		1				2*	SF2
	3	4	5*	6	7		8+	12										13			2		10		9	11		1					F
	3	3	1	3	3		3												1		3		3		3	3		3				1	
			1					2								1		2														1	

Walschaerts	Lockwood	Smith	Hicks	Clark	Ling	Ampadu	Richards	Maskell	Martin	Reinelt	Harris	Warren	Griffiths	Baker	Canham	Inglethorpe	Morrison	Raynor	Joseph, M	Joseph, R	McCormick	McDougald	Simba	Watts	Beall	Curran	Barrett	Stimson	Omoyinmi	Finney	Downer	Capleton	
2	3	4	5	6	7	8*	10+						9						12		14		13			11#							1
2		4	5	6	7			13					9+			3*		12	8				10			11							2
2	3	4	5	6	7			13				12						9*	8				10+			11							R
2	3	4		6	7*	14	10#						9+					12	5				13	8		11							3
2	3*	4		6	7	8+												9	5				10	12		11	13						4
5	4	5	3	5	5	2	2						3			1		2	4				3	1		5							
						1		2				1						2	1		1		2	1			1						
2		1					3						1										1										

Walschaerts	Lockwood	Smith	Hicks	Clark	Ling	Ampadu	Richards	Maskell	Martin	Reinelt	Harris	Warren	Griffiths	Baker	Canham	Inglethorpe	Morrison	Raynor	Joseph, M	Joseph, R	McCormick	McDougald	Simba	Watts	Beall	Curran	Barrett	Stimson	Omoyinmi	Finney	Downer	Capleton	
2	3	4		6*	7	8	9+	10	11#		12		13		5	14																	1/1
2	3	4	5	6	7	8		10			14	12	9*			13#		11+															1/2
2		4	5*		7+	8					14	3	9	13		11			6	10#	12												2/1
2		4	5		7	8			11#		12		9*		13	14			6	10+	3	1											2/2
4	2	4	3	2	4	4	1	2	2			1	3		1	1		1	2	2	1	1											
											4	1	1	1	1	3					1												
						1					1	1						1															

1999-2000

Manager: Tommy Taylor

	P	W	D	L	F	A	Pts
Swansea City	46	24	13	9	51	30	85
Rotherham United	46	24	12	10	72	36	84
Northampton Town	46	25	7	14	63	45	82
Darlington	46	21	16	9	66	36	79
Peterborough United	46	22	12	12	63	54	78
Barnet	46	21	12	13	59	53	75
Hartlepool United	46	21	9	16	60	49	72
Cheltenham Town	46	20	10	16	50	42	70
Torquay United	46	19	12	15	62	52	69
Rochdale	46	18	14	14	57	54	68
Brighton & Hove Albion	46	17	16	13	64	46	67
Plymouth Argyle	46	16	18	12	55	51	66
Macclesfield Town	46	18	11	17	66	61	65
Hull City	46	15	14	17	43	43	59
Lincoln City	46	15	14	17	67	69	59
Southend United	46	15	11	20	53	61	56
Mansfield Town	46	16	8	22	50	65	-56
Halifax Town	46	15	9	22	44	58	54
Leyton Orient	46	13	13	20	47	52	52
York City	46	12	16	18	39	53	52
Exeter City	46	11	11	24	46	72	44
Shrewsbury Town	46	9	13	24	40	67	-40
Carlisle United	46	9	12	25	42	75	39
Chester City	46	10	9	27	44	79	39

Division Three

Match No.	Date		Opponents	Result	Scorers	Attend
1	Aug	7	Carlisle United	1-2	Inglethorpe	3,
2		14	BRIGHTON & HOVE ALBION	1-2	Richards	7,
3		21	Peterborough United	1-2	Lockwood	6,
4		28	HALIFAX TOWN	1-0	Simba	3,
5		30	Southend United	1-1	Walschaerts	5,
6	Sep	3	SHREWSBURY TOWN	1-2	Inglethorpe	3,
7		11	Mansfield Town	1-1	Simba	2,
8		18	TORQUAY UNITED	0-2		4,
9		25	HARTLEPOOL UNITED	2-1	Smith, Low	3,
10	Oct	2	Plymouth Argyle	0-5		3,
11		9	York City	1-2	Clark	2,
12		16	LINCOLN CITY	2-3	Lockwood (pen), Simba	4,
13		19	BARNET	0-0		3,
14		23	Hartlepool United	0-1		2,
15	Nov	2	Darlington	1-3	Brkovic	4,
16		6	NORTHAMPTON TOWN	0-0		3,
17		12	Rotherham United	1-0	Ling	4,
18		23	ROCHDALE	0-0		2,
19		27	Cheltenham Town	0-2		3,
20	Dec	4	CARLISLE UNITED	0-1		3,8
21		18	Macclesfield Town	0-1		2,
22		26	SWANSEA CITY	0-1		4,4
23		28	Chester City	5-1	Christie, Watts, Griffiths 3 (2 pens)	2,8
24	Jan	3	HULL CITY	0-0		5,
25		8	Exeter City	3-1	Smith, Christie, Watts	2,
26		15	Brighton & Hove Albion	1-0	Brkovic	5,
27		22	PETERBOROUGH UNITED	1-1	Brkovic	4,
28		29	Halifax Town	2-0	Christie, Watts	2,
29	Feb	5	SOUTHEND UNITED	2-1	Watts, Brkovic	5,
30		8	EXETER CITY	4-1	Lockwood, Richards, Walschaerts, Watts	3,8
31		12	Shrewsbury Town	0-1		2,7
32		19	CHELTENHAM TOWN	1-0	Walschaerts	4,8
33		26	Torquay United	0-0		2,
34	Mar	4	MANSFIELD TOWN	1-3	Smith	4,
35		7	Northampton Town	1-2	Christie	5,1
36		11	DARLINGTON	2-1	Lockwood, Watts	4,0
37		18	Rochdale	4-1	Lockwood, Smith, Christie 2	2,4
38		21	ROTHERHAM UNITED	0-1		3,
39		25	Swansea City	0-0		5,3
40	Apr	1	MACCESFIELD TOWN	0-0		4,3
41		8	Hull City	0-2		4,4
42		15	CHESTER CITY	1-2	Griffiths	4,1
43		22	Lincoln City	0-0		2,7
44		24	PLYMOUTH ARGYLE	3-0	Christie, Brkovic, McGhee	4,1
45		29	Barnet	2-2	Lockwood (pen), Beall	4,0
46	May	6	YORK CITY	0-0		4,5

Appearanc
Sub appearanc
Goa

FA Cup

1	Oct	30	CARDIFF CITY	1-1	Ampadu	3,1
R	Nov	9	Cardiff City	1-3	Smith	3,0

Appearanc
Sub appearanc
Goa

League Cup

1/1	Aug	10	Swindon Town	1-0	Inglethorpe	3,5
1/2		24	SWINDON TOWN	1-1	Lockwood	2,7
2/1	Sep	14	Grimsby Town	1-4	Lockwood (pen)	2,2
2/2		21	GRIMSBY TOWN	1-0	Watts	1,0

Appearanc
Sub appearanc
Goa

Final League Position: 19th in Division Three

Joseph	Lockwood	McGhee	Downer	Walschaerts	Brkovic	Ampadu	Richards	Watts	Martin	Christie	Beall	Harris	Bayes	Smith	Inglethorpe	Ling	Morrison	Low	Hicks	
	3		6			8	12			10	11	2	1	4	5	7*	9+	13		1
	3			6*		8	13	14		10	11+	2		4	9	7#	12		5	2
6+	3			13		8*	9	14		10	11	2		4		7#	12		5	3
14	3			5		8		9+			11	2		4	13	7#	12			4
12	3			5		8		9+			11	2		4	10	7*	14	13#		5
14	3			5		8		13			11*	2	1	4	9	7	12			6
7	3			5		8		12				2	1	4	9		11			7
6	3					8#						2	1	4		7*		12	5+	8
5	3		6			8	14	12			13	2	1	4	9*		11	7#		9
2			3			8	12	13			5		1	4	9+		11#	7*		10
5	3						9+	12			11	2	1	4	7					11
7	3				14					10#	11	2+		4	9				5	12
3						2				10	11			4		7			5	13
2	3				14	8*				10+	11			4	9	7#	12		5+	14
2	3				7	8		13		10	11		1	4	9*		12		5+	15
2	3			11+	9#	8				10	13			4		7	12		5*	16
2		11	3	5#		8				10+	13			4	12	7				17
	3	2		13		8+				10#	11			4	12	7			5	18
		3		2		8				12	11			4	9	7*			5+	19
		3	5	2		8	13							4#	12	7	11		14	20
2	3	11*			7	8	12			10									5	21
7	3			2+	13	8		10*			11			4					5	22
11	3		5	2	7	8		10+		12				4						23
11	3		6	2	7	8		10*		12				4					5	24
2	3	14	5	11	7	8		10#		12	13			4						25
2	3	13	5	11	7*	8		9		10	12			4						26
6	3		5	2	7	8	12	9	11	10*				4						27
2	3	4	5	6	7#	8	9*	10	11+	12	13	14								28
2	3	13	5	6	7	8	9+	10	11*	12				4						29
2	3	13	5+	6	7	8	9	10	11*	12				4						30
2	3	5+		6	7	8	9	10#	11*	12		13		4						31
2	3	13	5	6	7	8+	9	10	11*	12				4						32
2	3	11*	5	6	7+	8	9	10		12	13			4						33
2	3		5	6	7#	8	9	10+	11*	12	14			4						34
2	3	13	5	6#	7	8+		12		10	11			4						35
2	3	10	5	6	7+	8	13	9		12	11*		1	4						36
2*	3	6	5	13	7	8		9+		10		12	1	4						37
2	3	11	5	6#	7+	8*		9		10	12		1	4						38
2	3#	8	5	6	7			9		10+	12		1	4						39
2	3	10	5	6	7#	8			11*	12	13		1	4						40
2	3	7*	5	6		8#		9+		10	11		1	4						41
2	3		5	6	7	8*		10+		12				4						42
2	3	5		6	7	8				10	11		1	4						43
2	3	5		6*	7	8		12		10	11			4						44
2	3			5*	7	8+		13		10	11	12	1	4						45
2	3	5		12	13	8				10	11#		1	4						46
38	41	17	24	32	25	43	9	21	8	22	22	11	17	44	12	14	5	2	13	
3		6		4	4		8	11		14	11	4			4		8	3	1	
	6	1		3	5		2	6		7	1			4	2	1		1		

Simba	Clark	Hockton	Curran	Holligan	Canham	Carter	Gough	Webb	Rowbotham	McElholm	Griffiths	Shorey	Ibehre	Murray	Joseph	Gould	McLean	Parsons	
																			1
																			2
																			3
10*	6																		4
	6																		5
10+	6#																		6
10*	6																		7
10				9	11	14	13												8
10+																			9
10	6	14																	10
13	6	10#				14		8*											11
12	6*	13						8											12
9	6							8											13
	6	13																	14
	6																		15
14	6																		16
	6	14							9*										17
14	6								9*										18
14	6							13	10#										19
10+	6								9*										20
	6									4	9								21
	6								12		9								22
	6								13		9*								23
											9								24
										6+	9*								25
										6+									26
																			27
																			28
																			29
																			30
												14							31
																			32
																			33
												13							34
												9*	14						35
																			36
												11							37
												13		14					38
												11*	13		14				39
							14				9+								40
							12						13			14			41
							11				9			13					42
											9*						12		43
											9+						13		44
	6										9#						14		45
											9	7+				14		6*	46
8	19	1		1	1		1	3	4	3	11	4						1	
5		4				2	3	1	2			3	3	2	1	2	3		
3	1										4								

Joseph	Lockwood	McGhee	Downer	Walschaerts	Brkovic	Ampadu	Richards	Watts	Martin	Christie	Beall	Harris	Bayes	Smith	Inglethorpe	Ling	Morrison	Low	Hicks	Simba	Clark	
2	3				7*	8		13		10	11		1	4	12				5	9+	6	1
2	3		5	11#	7*	8		9		12				4	13	14				10+	6	R
2	2		1	1	2	2		1		1	1		1	2					1	2	2	
								1		1					2	1						
						1								1								

Joseph	Lockwood	McGhee	Downer	Walschaerts	Brkovic	Ampadu	Richards	Watts	Martin	Christie	Beall	Harris	Bayes	Smith	Inglethorpe	Ling	Morrison	Low	Hicks	Simba	Clark	Hockton	Curran	Holligan	Canham	Carter	Gough	
	3			6*		8	13			10#	11	2		4	9+	7	12		5	14								1
12	3			6*		8	9+	14		10#	11	2		4		7			5	13								
5	3		12	14		8		9*				2	1	4		7	11#				6	10+	13					2
5	3		6			8*		9+				2	1	4			14	7						10	12	11#	13	
2	4		1	2		4	1	2		2	2	4	2	4	1	3	1	1	2		1	1		1		1		
1			1	1			1	1									2			2			1		1		1	
	2							1							1													

2000-01

Manager: Tommy Taylor

	P	W	D	L	F	A	Pts
Brighton & Hove Albion	46	28	8	10	73	35	92
Cardiff City	46	23	13	10	95	58	82
Chesterfield*	46	25	14	7	79	42	80
Hartlepool United	46	21	14	11	71	54	77
Leyton Orient	46	20	15	11	59	51	75
Hull City	46	19	17	10	47	39	74
Blackpool	46	22	6	18	74	58	72
Rochdale	46	18	17	11	59	48	71
Cheltenham Town	46	18	14	14	59	52	68
Scunthorpe United	46	18	11	17	62	52	65
Southend United	46	15	18	13	55	53	63
Mansfield Town	46	15	13	18	64	72	58
Plymouth Argyle	46	15	13	18	54	61	58
Macclesfield Town	46	14	14	18	51	62	56
Shrewsbury Town	46	15	10	21	49	65	55
Kidderminster Harriers	46	13	14	19	47	61	53
York City	46	13	13	20	42	63	52
Lincoln City	46	12	15	19	58	66	51
Exeter City	46	12	14	20	40	58	40
Darlington	46	12	13	21	44	56	49
Torquay United	46	12	13	21	52	77	49
Carlisle United	46	11	15	20	42	65	48
Halifax Town	46	12	11	23	54	68	47
Barnet	46	12	9	25	67	81	45

* Chesterfield 9 points deducted

Final League Position: 5th in Division Three

Note: 12 Replaced † as the first sub, 13 Replaced ‡ as the second sub and 14 Replaced § as the third sub

*Leyton Orient won 2–1 on aggregate
**Final played at Millennium Stadium, Cardiff
#After extra-time

Division Three

Match No.	Date		Opponents	Result	Scorers	Attend
1	Aug	12	Plymouth Argyle	1-0	Griffiths	5,
2		19	CARLISLE UNITED	1-0	Lockwood	4,
3		26	Blackpool	2-2	Garcia 2	4,
4		28	EXETER CITY	2-1	Lockwood, McGhee	4,
5	Sep	2	Halifax Town	2-2	Smith, Griffiths	1,
6		9	HULL CITY	2-2	Griffiths, Christie	5,
7		12	SCUNTHORPE UNITED	1-1	Lockwood	3,
8		16	Kidderminster Harriers	1-2	Christie	3,
9		23	LINCOLN CITY	1-0	Griffiths	3,
10		30	Brighton & Hove Albion	0-2		6,
11	Oct	8	Torquay United	2-1	Griffiths, Garcia	1,
12		14	CARDIFF CITY	2-1	Lockwood, Smith	4,
13		17	SHREWSBURY TOWN	2-0	Walschaerts, Watts	3,
14		21	York City	1-1	Garcia	2,
15		24	BARNET	3-1	Lockwood, Walschaerts, Griffiths	4,
16		28	Hartlepool United	1-2	Watts	2,
17	Nov	4	MANSFIELD TOWN	2-1	Lockwood, Griffiths	4,
18		11	Cheltenham Town	1-1	McGhee	3,
19		25	MACCLESFIELD TOWN	2-1	Brkovic, Watts	4,
20	Dec	2	Chesterfield	1-4	Watts	4,
21		16	DARLINGTON	1-0	Houghton	4,
22		23	ROCHDALE	1-1	Walschaerts	4,
23		26	Southend United	1-0	Griffiths	9,
24	Jan	13	Exeter City	3-2	Griffiths 2, Tate	3,
25		20	SOUTHEND UNITED	0-2		6,
26		28	Rochdale	1-3	Smith	3,
27	Feb	3	HALIFAX TOWN	3-0	Brkovic, Watts, Pinamonte	3,
28		10	Hull City	0-1		8,
29		17	KIDDERMINSTER HARRIERS	0-0		4,
30		20	Scunthorpe United	1-1	Griffiths	2,
31		24	Lincoln City	3-2	Brkovic, Watts, Pinamonte	3,
32	Mar	3	BRIGHTON & HOVE ALBION	0-2		7,
33		6	Cardiff City	1-1	Opinel	9,
34		10	TORQUAY UNITED	0-2		4,
35		13	Carlisle United	0-1		2,
36		17	Shrewsbury Town	1-1	McLean	2,
37		20	BLACKPOOL	1-0	Lockwood	4,
38		24	YORK CITY	1-1	Griffiths	4,
39		31	Darlington	1-1	Smith	3,
40	Apr	7	CHESTERFIELD	2-0	McGhee, Griffiths	4,
41		10	PLYMOUTH ARGYLE	1-1	Watts	4,
42		14	Barnet	2-1	Tate 2	3,
43		16	HARTLEPOOL UNITED	3-1	Smith, Griffiths, Watts	5,
44		21	Mansfield Town	0-2		3,
45		28	CHELTENHAM TOWN	0-0		5,
46	May	5	Macclesfield Town	2-0	Ibehre 2	2,

Appearanc
Sub appearanc
Go

Play-offs

SF	May	13	Hull City	0-1		13,
SF2		16	HULL CITY	2-0*	Lockwood, Watts	9,
F**		26	Blackpool	2-4#	Houghton, Tate	23,

Appearanc
Sub Appearanc
Go

FA Cup

1	Nov	18	Barrow	2-0	Griffiths, Watts	3,6
2	Dec	9	Northwich Victoria	3-3	Griffiths 2, Tate	2,7
R		20	NORTHWICH VICTORIA	3-2e	Griffiths, Simpson (og), Houghton	4,0
3	Jan	6	TOTTENHAM HOTSPUR	0-1		12,3

Appearanc
Sub Appearanc
Goa

League Cup

1/1	Aug	22	READING	1-1	Brkovic	2,3
1/2	Sep	5	Reading	2-0	Brkovic, Christie	4,3
2/1		20	Newcastle United	0-2		37,2
2/2		26	NEWCASTLE UNITED	1-1	Watts	9,5

Appearanc
Sub appearanc
Goa

Harris	Lockwood	Smith	McGhee	Walschaerts	Brkovic	Dorrian	Griffiths	Garcia	Martin	Brissett	Downer	Watts	Joseph	McElholm	Christie	Shorey	Ibehre	Murray	Houghton	Cadiou	Beall	Tate	Castle	Opara	Mansley	Hatcher	Pinamonte	Vasseur	Jones	Opinel	Forge	McLean	Lee	Barrett	
2	3	4	5	6	7#	8*	9	10	11+	14	12	13																							1
8	3	4	5	6	7#		9	10+	11*	12		13	2	14																					2
8	3	4		6	7*		9#	10	11		5+	12	2	13	14																				3
8	3	4	5	6	7*		9	10	11+			12	2		13																				4
2		4	5	6	7*		9	10	11+			12	3		13	8																			5
8	3	4	5	6	7+		9	10	12	11#		14	2*		13																				6
8	3	4	5	6	7		9	10	11*				2		12																				7
8	3	4	5	6	7*		12	10				9	2		11+		13																		8
8	3	4	5	6	7#		9*	10	11+			12	2	14	13																				9
8	3	4	5	6	7		9	10#	12+	11*		13	2				14																		10
2	3	4*	8	6		7	9	10	13		5	12							11+																11
8	3	4	5	6	7+		9#	10*			13	12	2			11				14															12
8	3	4	5	6	7		9*	10+				12	2			11#				13	14														13
8	3	4	5	6+	7*		9	10			13	12	2			11																			14
8	3	4+	5	6	7		9	10			13	12	2			11*																			15
8	3	4	5	6	7*		9	10				12	2							13	11+														16
8	3	4	5	6*	7		9	10			12		2			11+						13													17
8	3	4	5	6	7+			10#			12		2			11*	14				13	9													18
	3	4	5	6	7#		9				12	13	2	8					11*		14	10+													19
8	3	4	5	6	7+		9				12	10#	2						11*		13	14													20
8	3	4	5	6	9						12		2						7		11+			10*	13										21
8	3	4	5	6			9					10+	2						7		11*	12		13											22
8	3		4	6	12		9#				5	13	2						11		14	7+		10*											23
8	3+	4		6	7		9#				5	12	2	13					11			10*				14									24
2		4	5	6	7*		9					10	3			8			11+			12				13									25
8	3	4	5	6	12		9				13	10+	2	7*					11#			14													26
8		4	3	6	7#		9		12		5	13	2						11*								10+	14							27
8		4	3	6	7+		9		11		5*	12	2						13								10								28
8		4	5	6	7		9		11+			12	2#						13								10*		3	14					29
2		4	5	6	7		12				13	10	3	8#					11+			9*					14								30
8		4	5	6	7		9					10*	2+						11				13				12			3					31
8	12	4	5	6	7							9+	2						11			13	14				10#			3*					32
	11	4			7						5		2	12									8*				10			3	6	9+	13		33
6*	3	4		12	7						5		2						11#			9+	8				13	14					10		34
8	3	4		6	7		9		11*		5		2						12+								14			13			10#	1	35
8	3	4		6			9				5		2	12							11+	13		10#						7*		14		1	36
8	3		4	6			9				5		2	12							11	10								7*				1	37
8	3#		4	6	12		9				5	13	2	14							11	10+								7*				1	38
8		4	9	6					7*		5	12+	2								11	10#		14			13			3				1	39
8		4	3	6			9		7		5	10*	2								11	12												1	40
8		4		6+	12		9#		7		5	10	2	13							11			14						3*				1	41
8		4	3	6	7				9*		5#	10+	2						12		11	13	14												42
8		4	3	6	12		9				5	10+	2						7*		11#	13	14												43
8		4	3	6	10+		9				5#		2						7*		11	12	14				13								44
8		4	11	6	7*				9#		5	10	2				12					13	14							3+					45
8	3	4	7	6	12						5	10+	2				9*		11#			13	14												46
44	31	43	39	44	34	2	35	18	15	2	20	14	44	3	1	8	1		17		12	9	2	3			5		1	9	1	1	2	7	
	1			1	6		2		4	2	11	22		9	6		4		4	3	5	13	7	3	1	2	6	2		2		1	1		
	7	5	3	3	3		14	4				8			2		2		1			3					2			1		1			

Harris	Lockwood	Smith	McGhee	Walschaerts	Brkovic	Dorrian	Griffiths	Garcia	Martin	Brissett	Downer	Watts	Joseph	McElholm	Christie	Shorey	Ibehre	Murray	Houghton	Cadiou	Beall	Tate	Castle	Opara	Mansley	Hatcher	Pinamonte	Vasseur	Jones	Opinel	Forge	McLean	Lee	Barrett	
	3	4	7	6					13		5	10*	2				9		11+			12	8												SF
12	3	4	7	6	14						5	10	2				9+		11#			13	8*												SF2
8	3	4	7	6*	13				14		5		2				9		11#			10+	12												F
1	3	3	3	3							3	2	3				3		3			1	2	0											
1					2				2													2	1												
	1											1							1			1													

Harris	Lockwood	Smith	McGhee	Walschaerts	Brkovic	Dorrian	Griffiths	Garcia	Martin	Brissett	Downer	Watts	Joseph	McElholm	Christie	Shorey	Ibehre	Murray	Houghton	Cadiou	Beall	Tate	Castle	Opara	Mansley	Hatcher	Pinamonte	Vasseur	Jones	Opinel	Forge	McLean	Lee	Barrett	
8	3	4	5	6*	7		9				14	13	2			11#						10+	12												1
8	3	4	7	6	13		9*				5	10	2						11+			12													2
8	3	4	7	6	14		9				5*	10#	2+						11		12				13										R
8	3	4	5	6	7*							9	2						11		12	13		10+											3
4	4	4	4	4	2		3				2	3	4			1			3			1		1											
					2						1	1									2	2	1		1										
							4					1							1			1													

One own-goal

Harris	Lockwood	Smith	McGhee	Walschaerts	Brkovic	Dorrian	Griffiths	Garcia	Martin	Brissett	Downer	Watts	Joseph	McElholm	Christie	Shorey	Ibehre	Murray	Houghton	Cadiou	Beall	Tate	Castle	Opara	Mansley	Hatcher	Pinamonte	Vasseur	Jones	Opinel	Forge	McLean	Lee	Barrett	
8	3		6		7		9*	10	11		5	12	2	4																					1/1
2	3	4	5	6	7	8*	12		11#	14		9		13	10+																				1/2
8	3	4	5	6	7		9*	10	11+				2	12	13																				2/1
8	3	4	5	6				10		11#	13	9+	2		7*		14	12																	2/2
4	4	3	4	3	3	1	2	3	3	1	1	2	3	1	2																				
							1			1	1	1		2	1		1	1																	
					2							1			1																				

2001-02

Managers: Aug–Oct 2001 Tommy Taylor; Oct 2001–May 2002 Paul Brush

	P	W	D	L	F	A	Pts
Plymouth Argyle	46	31	9	6	71	28	102
Luton Town	46	30	7	9	96	48	97
Mansfield Town	46	24	7	15	72	60	79
Cheltenham Town	46	21	15	10	66	49	78
Rochdale	46	21	15	10	65	52	78
Rushden & Diamonds	46	20	13	13	69	53	73
Hartlepool United	46	20	11	15	74	48	71
Scunthorpe United	46	19	14	13	74	56	71
Shrewsbury Town	46	20	10	16	64	53	70
Kidderminster Harriers	46	19	9	18	56	47	66
Hull City	46	16	13	17	57	51	61
Southend United	46	15	13	18	51	54	58
Macclesfield Town	46	15	13	18	41	52	58
York City	46	16	9	21	54	67	57
Darlington	46	15	11	20	60	71	56
Exeter City	46	14	13	19	48	73	55
Carlisle United	46	12	16	18	48	56	52
Leyton Orient	46	13	13	20	55	71	52
Torquay United	46	12	15	19	46	63	51
Swansea City	46	13	12	21	53	76	51
Oxford United	46	11	14	21	53	62	47
Lincoln City	46	10	16	20	44	62	46
Bristol Rovers	46	11	12	23	40	60	45
Halifax Town	46	8	12	26	39	84	36

Division Three

Match No.	Date		Opponents	Result	Scorers	Attenda
1	Aug	11	Cheltenham Town	1-1	Lockwood	4,
2		18	CARLISLE UNITED	0-0		4,6
3		25	York City	1-2	McLean	2,6
4		27	HARTLEPOOL UNITED	2-0	Ibehre, Houghton	3,
5	Sep	1	Southend United	2-1	Smith, Constantine	5,8
6		8	BRISTOL ROVERS	3-1	Minton, Gough, Constantine	5,4
7		15	RUSHDEN & DIAMONDS	2-1	Ibehre, Houghton (pen)	5,2
8		18	Darlington	0-3		3,3
9		22	Halifax Town	0-0		2,0
10		25	LUTON TOWN	1-3	Houghton (pen)	6,6
11		29	TORQUAY UNITED	1-2	Constantine	4,4
12	Oct	5	Mansfield Town	2-3	Houghton, Watts	5,
13		13	SHREWSBURY TOWN	2-4	Watts 2	4,4
14		20	Swansea City	1-0	Minton	3,6
15		23	Hull City	1-1	Whittle (og)	9,8
16		27	ROCHDALE	4-2	Joseph, Minton, Ibehre, Watts	4,6
17	Nov	3	Scunthorpe United	1-4	Minton	3,3
18		10	KIDDERMINSTER HARRIERS	1-3	Minton	4,3
19		20	OXFORD UNITED	3-0	Ibehre, Watts, Martin	3,7
20		24	Exeter City	0-0		3,3
21	Dec	1	PLYMOUTH ARGYLE	0-0		6,3
22		15	Macclesfield Town	1-2	Watts	2,6
23		22	LINCOLN CITY	5-0	Houghton, Watts 2, Canham, Gray	3,8
24		26	Bristol Rovers	3-5	Watts, Gray 2	7,4
25		29	Hartlepool United	1-3	Harris	3,8
26	Jan	12	Carlisle United	1-6	Gray	2,9
27		19	CHELTENHAM TOWN	0-2		4,8
28		22	Lincoln City	0-2		1,9
29	Feb	2	Torquay United	1-1	Canham	1,9
30		9	SWANSEA CITY	2-2	McGhee, Gray	4,5
31		16	Shrewsbury Town	0-1		3,2
32		19	YORK CITY	1-2	Hadland	3,6
33		23	Rushden & Diamonds	0-1		4,5
34		26	DARLINGTON	0-0		3,2
35	Mar	2	HALIFAX TOWN	3-1	Canham 2, Christie	4,7
36		5	Luton Town	0-3		6,6
37		9	MACCLESFIELD TOWN	2-0	Lockwood (pen), Christie	3,8
38		12	SOUTHEND UNITED	2-1	Christie, Nugent	4,8
39		16	Plymouth Argyle	0-3		9,4
40		19	MANSFIELD TOWN	2-0	Hutchings, Martin	3,3
41		23	HULL CITY	0-0		4,6
42		30	Rochdale	0-3		3,0
43	Apr	1	SCUNTHORPE UNITED	0-0		4,2
44		6	Oxford United	1-1	McGhee	5,7
45		13	EXETER CITY	1-1	Newton	5,3
46		20	Kidderminster Harriers	1-0	Smith	3,1

Appearance
Sub appearance
Goa

FA Cup

1	Nov	17	Bristol City	1-0	Watts	6,3
2	Dec	8	LINCOLN CITY	2-1	Ibehre, Watts	4,1
3	Jan	5	Portsmouth	4-1	Smith, Watts, Gray, Christie	12,9
4		26	Everton	1-4	Canham	35,8

Appearance
Sub appearance
Goa

League Cup

1	Aug	21	CRYSTAL PALACE	2-4	Minton, Houghton	4,2

Appearance
Sub appearance
Goa

Final League Position: 18th in Division Three

Joseph	Lockwood	Smith	Downer	McGhee	Minton	Harris	Tate	Ibehre	Oakes	Houghton	McLean	Castle	Watts	Fletcher	Hadland	Martin	Gough	Constantine	Beall	Barnard	Barrett	Jones	Herrera	Canham	McElholm	Dorrian	Hatcher	Leigertwood	Gray	Christie	Partridge	Brazier	Nugent	Hutchings	Newton	Morris	
2	3	4	5	6	7#	8	9*	10	11+	14	12	13																									1
2	3	4	5	6	7	8	12		10*	11			9+	13																							2
2	3*	4	5			8		10+	6	7	13		9#		12	11	14																				3
2		4	5	3	7	8	12	10+	6#	11	13							9*	14																		4
2		4	5	3	7	8		10*	6+	11							12	9		13																	5
2		4	5	3	7	8		10*	6	11							12	9																			6
2		4	5		7	8		10*	6	11							12	9		3	1																7
2		4	5		7	8#		10*	6+	11					13		12	9	14	3	1																8
2		4	5		7	8		10	6*							11		9	12			3															9
2		4	5	3	7	8		10	6+	12				14		11*	13	9#																			10
2		4	12	5	7	8				11	13			10+				9	6		1	3*															11
2		4*	5	12	7	8		10+	6#	11	13		14					9			1	3															12
2+		4		5	7	8					12		9	10+			11*	13			1	6	3	12													13
2		4		5	7	8	13	12			10*		9+			11			6		1		3#		14												14
2		4		5	7	8	14	10+		12	13		9			11*			6#		1	3															15
2#		4		5	7	8		10+		12	13		9			11			6*		1	3			14												16
2		4		5	7	8*	14	10#		12	13		9+			11			6		1	3															17
2		4		5	7	8	12			13	10*		9			11#	14		6+		1	3															18
2		4		5	7	8		10+			12		9*			11					1	3#				14	13	6									19
	12	4		5	7	2		10#		13			9			11+					1	3*				8	14	6									20
2	12	4		5		8		10		7+			9#			11					1	3*					13	6	14								21
2	12	4		5	7	8+#		10+		13			9			11*					1	3+						6	14								22
2		4		5		8		12		14	13		9+			11					1	3		7#				6	10*								23
2	12	4#		5		8		13		14			9			11					1	3*		7+				6	10								24
	3			5		2		12		13			9*			11#			4		1			7+		8	14	6	10								25
		4		5	7			10#								11+			13	2*	1	3		8			12	6	9	14							26
6	3	4		5	7	8							9			11*				2+	1						12		10	13							27
6	3	4#		5	7	8*					9				14	12+					1			11					10	13	2						28
6		4		5	7	8							12								1			11					10+	13	2	3	9*				29
6		4		5	7	8							13			12					1			11*					10		2	3	9+				30
6#		4		5	7*	8					13			12							1			11					10		2	3	9+	14			31
		4				8					13		9#		12	11					1	5*		7+					10		2	3	14	6			32
	3	4		5	13	8					14		9#		12					2*	1			7+					10			11		6			33
	3	4		5	7	8							12				13				1			6					9*	10		11+		2			34
	3	4		5	7	8							12				14				1			6#					9+	10*		11	13	2			35
	3	4		5		8					13		12			7#	14				1			6						10+		11	9*	2			36
	3	4		5		8					13		12			11					1#			6						10+			9*	2	7		37
	3	4		5		8							12			11				13				6						10			9*	2	7+		38
	3	4				8					12		9*			11				13				6+						10	5			2	7		39
	3	4		5		8		12			13		9+			11					1			6						10*				2	7		40
	3	4		5	8	2		12			13		9*			11								6						10+					7		41
	3	4		5	8	2		13			14		9#	12		11*								6						10+					7		42
	3	4		5	8	2		10			9+			13		11					1			6						12					7*		43
	3	4#		5	8	2		10+			13			9*		11					1			6						12	14				7		44
12	3	4		5		8		10#			14			13		11+				2*				6			9								7	1	45
2	3	4+		5		8					12					11				13				6			10*						9		7	1	46
29	20	45	11	39	32	45	1	21	11	10	4		22	3		29	1	9	7	6	32	16	2	23		2	2	8	13	9	6	8	7	9	10	2	
1	4		1	1	1		6	7		11	23	1	8	6	5	2	10	1	4	4				1	2	1	6		2	6	1		2	1			
1	2	2		2	5	1		4		5	1		9		1	2	1	3						4					5	3			1	1	1		

One own-goal

Joseph	Lockwood	Smith	Downer	McGhee	Minton	Harris	Tate	Ibehre	Oakes	Houghton	McLean	Castle	Watts	Fletcher	Hadland	Martin	Gough	Constantine	Beall	Barnard	Barrett	Jones	Herrera	Canham	McElholm	Dorrian	Hatcher	Leigertwood	Gray	Christie	Partridge	Brazier	Nugent	Hutchings	Newton	Morris	
2		4		5	7	8		10+			13		9*			11#					1	3	14			6	12										1
2		4		5	7	8		10			12		9*			11					1	3						6									2
		4		5	7	2		14					9+			11				12	1	3				8*		6	10#	13							3
6	3+	4		5	7	8					14		9#			12					1	13		11					10		2*						4
3	1	4		4	4	4		2					4			3					4	3		1		2		2	2		1						
								1			3					1				1		1	1				1			1							
		1						1					3											1					1	1							

Joseph	Lockwood	Smith	Downer	McGhee	Minton	Harris	Tate	Ibehre	Oakes	Houghton	McLean	Castle	Watts	Fletcher	Hadland	Martin	Gough	Constantine	Beall	Barnard	Barrett	Jones	Herrera	Canham	McElholm	Dorrian	Hatcher	Leigertwood	Gray	Christie	Partridge	Brazier	Nugent	Hutchings	Newton	Morris	
2	3	4	5		7*	8		10	6	11+		12	9		13																						1
1	1	1	1		1	1		1	1	1			1																								
												1			1																						
					1					1																											

2002-03

Manager: Paul Brush

	P	W	D	L	F	A	Pts
Rushden & Diamonds	46	24	15	7	73	47	87
Hartlepool United	46	24	13	9	71	51	85
Wrexham	46	23	15	8	84	50	84
AFC Bournemouth	46	20	14	12	60	48	74
Scunthorpe United	46	19	15	12	68	49	72
Lincoln City	46	18	16	12	46	37	70
Bury	46	18	16	12	57	56	70
Oxford United	46	19	12	15	57	47	69
Torquay United	46	16	18	12	71	71	66
York City	46	17	15	14	52	53	66
Kidderminster Harriers	46	16	15	15	62	63	63
Cambridge United	46	16	13	17	67	70	61
Hull City	46	14	17	15	58	53	59
Darlington	46	12	18	16	58	59	54
Boston United*	46	15	13	18	55	56	54
Macclesfield Town	46	14	12	20	57	63	54
Southend United	46	17	3	26	47	59	54
Leyton Orient	46	14	11	21	51	61	53
Rochdale	46	12	16	18	63	70	52
Bristol Rovers	46	12	15	19	50	57	51
Swansea City	46	12	13	21	48	65	49
Carlisle United	46	13	10	23	52	78	49
Exeter City	46	11	15	20	50	64	48
Shrewsbury Town	46	9	14	23	62	92	41

Division Three

Match No.	Date		Opponents	Result	Scorers	Attenda
1	Aug	10	Rochdale	0-1		3,
2		13	MACCESFIELD TOWN	3-2	Lockwood (pen), Smith, Thorpe	3,
3		17	SCUNTHORPE UNITED	2-0	Lockwood (pen), Martin	4,
4		24	Cambridge United	1-2	Campbell-Ryce	4,
5		26	KIDDERMINSTER HARRIERS	0-0		4,
6		31	Hull City	1-1	Toner	7,
7	Sep	7	Shrewsbury Town	1-2	Lockwood	2,
8		14	LINCOLN CITY	1-1	Thorpe	4,
9		17	OXFORD UNITED	1-2	Thorpe*	3,
10		21	Exeter City	0-1		2,
11		28	DARLINGTON	2-1	Hutchings, Nugent	3,
12	Oct	5	Rushden & Diamonds	0-2		4,
13		12	Wrexham	0-0		3,
14		19	BOURNEMOUTH	0-0		5,
15		26	Bristol Rovers	2-1	Campbell-Ryce, Nugent	6,
16		29	SOUTHEND UNITED	2-1	Iriekpen, Whelan (og)	5,
17	Nov	2	BURY	1-2	Thorpe	4,
18		9	York City	2-3	Martin, Nugent	3,
19		23	HARTLEPOOL UNITED	1-2	Canham	4,
20		30	Boston United	1-0	Tate	2,
21	Dec	14	TORQUAY UNITED	2-0	Canham, Tate	4,
22		21	Swansea City	1-0	Tate	4,
23		26	Kidderminster Harriers	2-3	Ibehre 2	3,
24		28	CARLISLE UNITED	2-1	Smith, Ibehre	4,
25	Jan	11	Scunthorpe United	1-2	Smith	3,
26		18	HULL CITY	2-0	Thorpe, Ibehre	5,
27		25	Carlisle United	0-3		4,
28		28	CAMBRIDGE UNITED	1-1	Ibehre	3,
29	Feb	8	YORK CITY	0-1		4,
30		15	Bury	1-0	Martin	2,
31		22	SHREWSBURY TOWN	0-2		3,
32		25	ROCHDALE	0-1		2,
33	Mar	1	Lincoln City	1-1	Brazier	3,
34		4	Oxford United	2-0	Harris, Tate	5,
35		8	EXETER CITY	1-1	Thorpe	3,
36		11	Macclesfield Town	1-3	Thorpe	1,
37		15	BRISTOL ROVERS	1-2	Lockwood (pen)	4,
38		18	Bournemouth	1-3	Thorpe	5,
39		22	Southend United	0-1		4,
40	Apr	5	BOSTON UNITED	3-2	Purser 3	3,
41		12	Hartlepool United	1-4	Heald	4,
42		19	SWANSEA CITY	3-1	Tate 2, Turner	4,
43		21	Torquay United	2-2	Fletcher, Alexander	3,
44		26	RUSHDEN & DIAMONDS	0-0		5,
45		29	WREXHAM	0-1		3,
46	May	3	Darlington	2-2	Lockwood, Alexander	5,

*Match No 9: A goal was first awarded to Thorpe but was later credited as an own-goal to Crosby.

Appearan
Sub Appearan
G

FA Cup

1	Nov	16	MARGATE	1-1	Martin	3,
R*		26	Margate	0-1		2,

* Match played at Dover Athletic's ground

Appearan
Sub appearan
G

League Cup

1	Sep	10	QUEEN'S PARK RANGERS	3-2	Campbell-Ryce, Fletcher, Thorpe	4
2	Oct	2	BIRMINGHAM CITY	2-3	Nugent, Ibehre	3

Appearan
Sub appearan
G

Final League Position: 18th in Division Three

Joseph	Lockwood	Smith	Campbell-Ryce	Hutchings	Martin	Harris	Fletcher	Thorpe	Brazier	McLean	Canham	Nugent	Toner	Barnard	McGhee	Watts	Morris	Jones	Ibehre	Miller	Forbes	Hatcher	Iriekpen	Stephens	Barrett	Tate	Alexander	Downer	Harrison	Zakuani	Turner	Heald	Purser	
2	3	4	5*	6	7+	8	9#	10	11	12	13	14																						1
2	3*	4	5+	6	7	8	9#	10	11			14	12	13																				2
2	3	4	5*	6	7	8	9+	10	11	13			12																					3
2	3	4	5	6	7*	8	9+	10	11			13	12																					4
	3	4	6	2	12	8		10	11*	13		9+	7		5																			5
2+	3	4	12	6		8		10	11				7	13	5	9*																		6
2	3	4	7	6	12	8		10	11*	13					5	9+																		7
2		4	5	6	7*	8	9+	10	11			12					1	3	13															8
2*		4	7	6	12	8	9#	10	11			13					1	3+	14	5														9
2		4	10+	6	7#	8					11*	9		12			1	3	13	5	14													10
	3	4	8	6		2		10	11			9	7*	12			1			5														11
	3	4	7	6		8		12	11			9		2*			1		10	5														12
	3	4	7	6		8		10+	11			9*		2			1		12	5		13												13
	3	4	7	6	12	8		10+	11*			9#		2		14	1		13	5														14
	3	4	10#		11	8					12	9+	7*	2		13	1			5		14	6											15
	3	4	10#		11	8					12	9+	7*	2		13	1			5		14	6											16
	3		10+		11	8		12			7	9*	6#	2		13	1			5		14	4											17
	3	4			11	8		10*			12	9	6+	2			1			5		13		7										18
2	3				11	8	10				12		6*							5	13	7+	4		1	9								19
2	3					8			11	12	7	13		6				14	10*	5#			4		1	9+								20
2	3	4				8		12	11		7	13		6					10+	5					1	9*								21
2	3	4			12	8		13	11		7			6				5	10*						1	9+								22
2*	3	4			13	8		12	11+		7			6				5	10						1	9								23
2	3	4			11	8		12			7	13		6				5	10+						1	9*								24
2	3	4		12	7	8		9	11*	13		14		6+				5#	10						1									25
2	3	4		12	7*	8		9	11	13				6				5	10+						1									26
2	3	4		12	7+	8		9+	11	13	14			6*				5	10						1									27
2*	3	4		12	7#	8		9+	11					6				5	10						1	13	14							28
2	3	4		7*	12	8		13	11#					6					10+	5					1	14	9							29
2	3	4		12	11	8		10+			7*			6			1	5	13							14	9#							30
2*	3			12	11	8		10#			7+			6			1	5	13							14	9	4						31
2	3				11	8		12			13		7	6#			1	5	14							9	10*	4+						32
2	3			6		8		10	11				7				1	5								9		4						33
2	3			6		8		10+	11				7*	12			1	5	13							9		4						34
2	3			6		8		10#	11				7*	12			1	5	13							9+	14	4						35
2	12			6		8		10	11				7	3+			1	5	13							9#	14	4*						36
2	3			6	12	8		10	11*				7					5	13							9#	14	4+	1					37
2	3			12	11	8		10					7	6*				5						4#		9+	13		1	14				38
2	3			6	12	8		10	11+				7*					5	13					14			9	4#	1					39
2	3					8	13		6				7*	12												9+	10		1		4	5	11	40
2	3				12	8		13	6				7*					14								9	10+		1		4#	5	11	41
2	3				12			13	8				7*				14			6						9+	10		1#		4	5	11	42
2	3				7*	12	13	10#	8								1		14	6+							9				4	5	11	43
2	3					12	13		8+				7				1			6*						9	10				4	5	11	44
2	3					8	13	12					7+				1	5		6	14					9*	10#				4		11	45
2	3					8	12						7				1	5*		6						9	10				4		11	46
37	42	27	16	21	21	43	7	27	33		9	10	22	22	3	2	22	22	11	19		1	5	2	11	19	12	8	6		7	5	7	
	1		1	7	11	2	5	11		8	7	9	3	7		4	1	2	14		3	5		1		4	5			1				
	5	3	2	1	3	1	1	8	1		2	3	1						5				1			6	2				1	1	3	

One own-goal

Joseph	Lockwood	Smith	Campbell-Ryce	Hutchings	Martin	Harris	Fletcher	Thorpe	Brazier	McLean	Canham	Nugent	Toner	Barnard	McGhee	Watts	Morris	Jones	Ibehre	Miller	Forbes	Hatcher	Iriekpen	Stephens	Barrett	
	3	4			11		10#				7	9	8	2+		14	1*			5		13	6		12	1
2	3	4*			11	8	10#		12		6	9							14	5	13	7+			1	R
1	2	2			2	1	2				2	2	1	1			1			2		1	1		1	
									1							1			1		1	1			1	
					1																					

Joseph	Lockwood	Smith	Campbell-Ryce	Hutchings	Martin	Harris	Fletcher	Thorpe	Brazier	McLean	Canham	Nugent	Toner	Barnard	McGhee	Watts	Morris	Jones	Ibehre	Miller	
2		4	7	6	12	8	9+	10	11					13	5*		1	3			1
	3	4	8#	6*	12	2		10	11			9	7+	13			1		14	5	2
1	1	2	2	2		2	1	2	2			1	1		1		2	1		1	
					2									2					1		
			1				1	1				1							1		

2003-04

Managers: Aug 2003–Oct 2003 Paul Brush; Oct 2003–May 2004 Martin Ling

	P	W	D	L	F	A	Pts
Doncaster Rovers	46	27	11	8	79	37	92
Hull City	46	25	13	8	82	44	88
Torquay United	46	23	12	11	68	44	81
Huddersfield Town	46	23	12	11	68	52	81
Mansfield Town	46	22	9	15	76	62	75
Northampton Town	46	22	9	15	58	51	75
Lincoln City	46	19	17	10	68	47	74
Yeovil Town	46	23	5	18	70	57	74
Oxford United	46	18	17	11	55	44	71
Swansea City	46	15	14	17	58	61	59
Boston United	46	16	11	19	50	54	59
Bury	46	15	11	20	54	64	56
Cambridge United	46	14	14	18	55	67	56
Cheltenham Town	46	14	14	18	57	71	56
Bristol Rovers	46	14	13	19	50	61	55
Kidderminster Harriers	46	14	13	19	45	59	55
Southend United	46	14	12	20	51	63	54
Darlington	46	14	11	21	53	61	53
Leyton Orient	46	13	14	19	48	65	53
Macclesfield Town	46	13	13	20	54	69	52
Rochdale	46	12	14	20	49	58	50
Scunthorpe United	46	11	16	19	69	72	49
Carlisle United	46	12	9	25	46	69	45
York City	46	10	14	22	35	66	44

Division Three

Match No.	Date		Opponents	Result	Scorers	Attend
1	Aug	9	DONCASTER ROVERS	1-3	Lockwood (pen)	5,
2		16	Mansfield Town	1-1	Alexander	3,
3		23	YEOVIL TOWN	2-0	Brazier, Thorpe	4,
4		25	Darlington	1-2	Thorpe	4,
5		30	CHELTENHAM TOWN	1-4	Purser	3,
6	Sep	6	Torquay United	1-2	Newey	2,
7		13	Lincoln City	0-0		3,
8		16	HULL CITY	1-1	Hunt D	3,
9		20	SCUNTHORPE UNITED	1-1	Ibehre	3,
10		27	Huddersfield Town	0-3		8,
11		30	Carlisle United	1-0	Ibehre	4,
12	Oct	4	MACCLESFIELD TOWN	2-0	Alexander, McGhee	3
13		11	SWANSEA CITY	1-2	Tate	4
14		18	Southend United	2-1	Alexander, McSweeney (og)	6
15		21	Bristol Rovers	1-1	Ibehre	5
16		25	NORTHAMPTON TOWN	1-1	Alexander	4
17	Nov	1	ROCHDALE	2-1	Lockwood (pen), Alexander	3
18		15	Boston United	0-3		2
19		22	YORK CITY	2-2	Miller, Thorpe	3
20		29	Cambridge United	4-1	Miller, Purser 2, Thorpe	3
21	Dec	13	Kidderminster Harriers	1-2	Zakuani	2
22		20	BURY	2-0	Alexander, Zakuani	3
23		26	Oxford United	1-2	Alexander	9
24		28	TORQUAY UNITED	0-0		4
25	Jan	3	DARLINGTON	1-0	Toner	3
26		10	Doncaster Rovers	0-5		6
27		17	MANSFIELD TOWN	3-1	Alexander 2, Newey	4
28		24	Yeovil Town	2-1	Alexander, Peters	6
29		31	Cheltenham Town	0-1		3
30	Feb	7	OXFORD UNITED	1-0	Alexander	5
31		21	SOUTHEND UNITED	2-1	Broughton (og), Bramble (og)	6
32		24	Swansea City	1-2	Purser	4
33		28	Northampton Town	0-1		5
34	Mar	2	BRISTOL ROVERS	1-1	Ibehre	3
35		6	Bury	1-1	Mackie	2
36		13	KIDDERMINSTER HARRIERS	1-1	Alexander	3
37		16	Hull City	0-3		15
38		20	LINCOLN CITY	0-2		3
39		27	Scunthorpe United	1-1	Purser	2
40	Apr	3	HUDDERSFIELD TOWN	1-1	Alexander	4
41		10	Macclesfield Town	0-1		2
42		12	CARLISLE UNITED	1-1	Alexander	4
43		17	Rochdale	0-3		2
44		24	BOSTON UNITED	1-3	Scott	3
45	May	1	York City	2-1	Alexander, Peters	3
46		8	CAMBRIDGE UNITED	0-1		5

Appearar

Sub Appearar

G

FA Cup

1	Nov	8	Grantham Town	2-1	Purser, Alexander	2
2	Dec	6	Cheltenham Town	1-3	Lockwood	3

Appeara

Sub appeara

G

League Cup

1	Aug	12	Cardiff City	1-4	Ibehre	4

Appeara

Sub appeara

G

Final League Position: 19th in Division Three

	Hunt	Lockwood	Jones	Miller	Brazier	Purser	Ebdon	Tate	Alexander	Newey T	Harnwell	Ibehre	Toner	Morris	Joseph	Stephens	Thorpe	Heald	McCormack	Peters	Downer	Forbes	McGhee	Saah	Zakuani	Cooper	Hammond	Akinfenwa	Barnard	Mackie	Sam	Hunt	Scott	Duncan	
	2*	3	4	5	6	7	8+	9	10	11#	12	13	14																						1
	7	3	4	5	6	9	8*	12	10	11#				1	2+	13	14																		2
	12	3	4	8	6	7+	13		9	11#	14			1	2*		10	5																	3
	13	3	4	8	6	7#	12	14	9	11*				1	2		10+	5																	4
	12	3	4+	8#	11	7			9		6			1	2		10*	5	13																5
	7	3		4*		13	8		9	11		12			2		10	5	6+																6
	7+	3	4			12	8		9	11*					2		10		6	5	13														7
	7	3	4	12			8	13	9+	11					2		10		6*	5															8
	7		4	3			8#	9	10*	11		12			2				6	5+	13	14													9
	7		4#	6		12	8	13	9	3+		10								5		14	2	11*											10
	7		4#			11+	8		9	3*		10								5	6	12	2	13	14										11
	2	3	4			7	8	12	9+	11#		10*								5		13	6	14											12
	2	3	4#			7*	8	12	9+			10					13		11	5		14	6												13
	7	3*	12			11			9								10		6	5			4			2	8								14
	7		3*			11+	12		9	13		14					10#		6	5			4			2	8								15
	7		3#			13	12		9	11+		10							6	5		14	4			2*	8								16
	7*	3		12		6+			9	11		10			2				14	5		13	4				8#								17
		3+		6		7			9	11		10	12		2					5		13	4				8*								18
		3		6		7*			9	11#			12		2		10			5		13			4		8+	14							19
	8	3		6		7+			9	11		12		1	2#		10*			5					4		13		14						20
	8	3		6		7+			9	11		12	13	1	2		10*			5					4#		14								21
	8	3		6					9	11			7		2		10			5					4										22
	8	3		6		12			9*	11		13	7		2		10+			5					4#				14						23
	8	3		4		6		12	9	11+		10*	7#	1	2					5		13							14						24
	8	3		6				12		11		10	7+	1	2		9*			5					4				13						25
	8	3*	12	6		11			9			13	7	1	2#		10+			5					4				14						26
	8		3	6		12			9	11+		10*	7	1	2					5										4	13				27
	8		3	6		12			9	11		10*	7	1	2+					5									13	4					28
	8		3	6		10*		12	9	11+			7	1						5									2	4	13				29
	8		3	6*		10		13	9	12			7	1						5									2	4	11+				30
	8		3	6		10			9	11		12		1						5									2	4	7*				31
	8		3	6#		11		13	9	12		10+	7*	1						5									2	4	14				32
	8		3+			10		13	9	11		12	7	1						5									2	4	6*				33
	8		3+	12		10		14	9	11#		13	7	1						5									2*	4	6				34
	8			12		6*			9	11+		10	7	1	2					5									3	4	13				35
	8			13		6*			9	11+		10	7	1	2					5									3	4	12				36
	8			12		13		14	9	11		10#	7	1	2					5			6*						3+	4					37
			3	6		8		13	9	11#		14	7+	1	12					5				10					2*	4					38
			3	6		12		10				13	7+	1						5						2				4	11*	8	9		39
			3	6		12		10#	7			14	13	1						5						2			11+	4		8	9*		40
			3	6+		12		10#	7			14	13	1						5						2			11	4		8*	9		41
			3			11		12	7			10*	13							5						2			6	4		8	9+		42
		12	3*			11		13	7			10#	14							5						2			6	4		8+	9		43
	7	3		12		11+		13	10			14		1						5						2*			6	4		8#	9		44
	8	3							10			12	7	1						5				6	2				11	4			9*		45
	8	3	2*			12			10			13	7	1										6+	5				11	4			9#	14	46
9	35	24	29	27	5	29	10	5	44	31	1	17	19	27	23		15	4	8	39	1		10	4	9	9	6		17	20	5	6	8		
	3	1	2	7		12	4	18		3	2	18	8		1	1	2		2		2	10		2	1		2	1	6		5			1	
	1	2		2	1	5		1	15	2		4	1				4			2			1		2					1			1		

Three own-goals

	Hunt	Lockwood	Jones	Miller	Brazier	Purser	Ebdon	Tate	Alexander	Newey T	Harnwell	Ibehre	Toner	Morris	Joseph	Stephens	Thorpe	Heald	McCormack	Peters	Downer	Forbes	McGhee	Saah	Zakuani	Cooper	Hammond	Akinfenwa	
	7	3		13		6			9	11#		10			2*					5		14	4				8+	12	1
2	8	3		6		7*			9	11+		13		1	2		10			5					4				2
	2	2		1		2			2	2		1		1	2		1			2			1		1		1		
				1								1										1						1	
		1				1			1																				

	Hunt	Lockwood	Jones	Miller	Brazier	Purser	Ebdon	Tate	Alexander	Newey T	Harnwell	Ibehre	Toner	Morris	
*	2	3	4	5	6	9	8	14	10#	11		13	7+	12	1
	1	1	1	1	1	1	1		1	1			1		
								1				1		1	
												1			

2004-05

Manager: Martin Ling

	P	W	D	L	F	A	Pts
Yeovil Town	46	25	8	13	90	65	83
Scunthorpe United	46	22	14	10	69	42	80
Swansea City	46	24	8	14	62	43	80
Southend United	46	22	12	12	65	46	78
Macclesfield Town	46	22	9	15	60	49	75
Lincoln City	46	20	12	14	64	47	72
Northampton Town	46	20	12	14	62	51	72
Darlington	46	20	12	14	57	49	72
Rochdale	46	16	18	12	54	48	66
Wycombe Wanderers	46	17	14	15	58	52	65
Leyton Orient	46	16	15	15	65	67	63
Bristol Rovers	46	13	21	12	60	57	60
Mansfield Town	46	15	15	16	56	56	60
Cheltenham Town	46	16	12	18	51	54	60
Oxford United	46	16	11	19	50	63	59
Boston United	46	14	16	16	62	58	58
Bury	46	14	16	16	54	54	58
Grimsby Town	46	13	17	16	47	51	56
Notts County	46	13	13	20	46	62	52
Chester City	46	12	16	18	43	69	52
Shrewsbury Town	46	11	16	19	48	53	49
Rushden & Diamonds	46	10	14	22	42	63	44
Cambridge United*	46	8	16	22	39	62	40
Kidderminster Harriers	46	10	9	27	38	81	39

* Cambridge United had 10 points deducted for entering administration and were relegated to the Conference League.

League Two

Match No.	Date		Opponents	Result	Scorers	Attendan
1	Aug	7	MACCLESFIELD TOWN	1-3	Purser	4,54
2		10	Cambridge United	1-1	Scott	4,11
3		14	Cheltenham Town	2-1	Steele, Ibehre	3,34
4		21	OXFORD UNITED	0-0		3,42
5		28	Northampton Town	2-2	Carlisle 2	5,57
6		30	ROCHDALE	2-1	Steele, Newey	3,24
7	Sep	4	Kidderminster Harriers	2-1	Lockwood (pen), Alexander	2,36
8		11	BRISTOL ROVERS	4-2	Steele, Simpson, Alexander 2	3,97
9		18	Grimsby Town	0-2		5,08
10		25	BOSTON UNITED	0-0		4,75
11	Oct	2	Notts County	2-1	Steele, Alexander	5,14
12		9	BURY	1-1	Steele	3,39
13		16	SHREWSBURY TOWN	4-1	Steele 2, Scott 2	3,71
14		19	Swansea City	0-1		8,48
15		23	Lincoln City	4-3	Steele 3, Ibehre	4,24
16		30	SCUNTHORPE UNITED	1-1	Scott	4,35
17	Nov	6	Chester City	1-1	Steele	3,12
18		20	WYCOMBE WANDERERS	1-2	Carlisle	4,04
19		27	Mansfield Town	1-0	Scott	3,80
20	Dec	7	SOUTHEND UNITED	2-2	Lockwood (pen), Scott	3,85
21		11	Darlington	0-3		3,70
22		18	YEOVIL TOWN	2-3	Chillingworth, Echanomi	3,86
23		26	Bristol Rovers	1-1	Lockwood (pen)	8,41
24		28	RUSHDEN & DIAMONDS	2-2	Chillingworth, Echanomi	3,77
25	Jan	1	KIDDERMINSTER HARRIERS	2-1	Scott 2	3,57
26		3	Boston United	2-2	McMahon 2	3,18
27		8	Bury	0-0		2,19
28		15	GRIMSBY TOWN	1-2	Echanomi	3,81
29		22	Rushden & Diamonds	0-2		3,28
30		29	NOTTS COUNTY	2-0	Barnard D, Youngs	3,44
31	Feb	5	Shrewsbury Town	1-4	Echanomi	3,49
32		12	SWANSEA CITY	3-1	Lockwood (pen), Scott, McMahon	4,05
33		19	Scunthorpe United	0-1		5,16
34		22	LINCOLN CITY	1-1	Mackie	2,43
35		26	DARLINGTON	1-0	Steele	3,43
36	Mar	5	Yeovil Town	0-1		6,54
37		12	CAMBRIDGE UNITED	1-1	Lockwood	3,75
38		19	Macclesfield Town	1-3	Steele	2,23
39		25	CHELTENHAM TOWN	2-3	Mackie, Alexander	3,26
40		28	Oxford United	2-2	Steele, Simpson	5,32
41	Apr	2	NORTHAMPTON TOWN	3-2	Mackie, Steele 2	3,58
42		9	Rochdale	0-2		2,25
43		15	Southend United	1-0	Mackie	9,18
44		23	CHESTER CITY	2-0	Lockwood (pen), Echanomi	3,19
45		30	Wycombe Wanderers	2-3	Alexander 2	5,33
46	May	7	MANSFIELD TOWN	2-1	Alexander 2	3,88

Appearance
Sub Appearance
Goal

FA Cup

1	Nov	13	DAGENHAM & REDBRIDGE	3-1	Lockwood, Hunt, Carlisle	4,15
2	Dec	4	Oldham Athletic	0-4		4,65

Appearance
Sub Appearance
Goal

League Cup

1	Aug	24	BOURNEMOUTH	1-3	Steele	1,70

Appearance
Sub Appearance
Goal

Final League Position: 11th in League Two

Barnard	Lockwood	Mackie	White	Hunt	Steele	Simpson	Scott	Alexander	Carlisle	Purser	Ibehre	Newey T	Miller	Zakuani	Saah	Harrison	Peters	Duncan	Wardley	Barnard	McMahon	Chillingworth	Echanomi	Fitzgerald	Youngs T	Palmer	Wallis	
2	3	4	5	6	7	8	9#	10+	11*	12	13	14																1
	3		5	6	7	8	9+		11	12	10*	13	2	4														2
	3		5	6	7	8	9+	12	11		10*	13	2	4														3
	3		5	6	7	8	9	12	11*		10		2	4														4
	3		5	6	7*	8	9+	10	11		12	13	2	4														5
12	3		5	6	7	8	9#	10+	11*		13	14	2	4														6
12	3		5	6#	7	8	9+	10	11*			13	2	4	14	1												7
12	3		5	6	7#	8	9+	10	11*		14	13	2	4		1												8
	3		5	6	7	8	9	10*	11+		12	13	2	4		1												9
2	3		5	6	7*	8	9+	10	11#		12	13	4			1	14											10
2	3			6	7	8	9	10	11				5	4*		1	12											11
2	3			6*	7	8	9#	10+	11		13	12	5	4		1			14									12
2	3		5	12	7	8	9#	10+	11		13	14	4			1			6*									13
2#	3		5	12	7	8	9+	10	11		13		4	14		1			6*									14
	3		5	12	7	8	9		11+		10	13	2	4		1			6*									15
12	3		5		7	8	9		11+		10	13	2	4		1			6*									16
	3		5	6	7	8	9		11		10		2	4		1												17
	3		5	6	7	8	9#		11*		10	12	2+	4		1			13	14								18
2	3	4	5			8	9		11		10				6	1				7								19
2	3*	4	5	6		8	11		7		10	12				1						9+	13					20
	3	4	5	6		8	11+		7*		10	12	2							13		9						21
	3	4		6+		8	10					11	2	5	7*						13	9	12					22
2	3		5			8	11+		12			13	6	4*	7	1				10#		9	14					23
	3	12	5			8	7					11	2	4*	6+	1				10#	13	9	14					24
	3	4*	5	12	13	8	7						2			1		11+		14	6	9	10#					25
2	3	4		6	12		7						5		11	1				13	8	9+	10*					26
2	3	4	5	12	7#	8	10						6			1				13	11*	9+	14					27
	3	4	5		9	8	7*					11+	2			1		12			6		13	10				28
2	3	4	5	11	9	8	13	12					6			1					7+		10*					29
12	3	4		2	9	8	7+	10					5			1		13			6				11*			30
12	3	4		2#	9	8	7	10					5			1		13			6*		14		11+			31
12	3	4			9	8	7	10					2	5		1					6				11*			32
3		4			9	8	7	10					2	5		1					6		12		11*			33
12	3	4			9	8	10						2	5		1		7+			6		13		11*			34
2#	3		4	7+	9	8	10*						6	5		1		12			11		13		14			35
12	3*	4			9	8	10		7+				2	5		1					6		13		11			36
12	3	4			9	8	11+	10	7#				2	5		1		13			6*				14			37
2+	3*	4			9	8	12	10	13				6	5	7	1					11							38
12	3*	4			9	8	11+	10	7#				2	5				13			6				14			39
2+		4			9	8		10					6	5	7			12			11*					3	13	40
2	12	4			9	8		10					6*	5	7+			13			11#					3	14	41
2#		4			9	8		10					6	5	7			13			11+		12			3*	14	42
2	3*	4			9	8		10					6	5		1		7			11					12		43
2	3	4				8		10	12				6	5		1		7*			11		9+		13			44
2	3*	4			9	8		10					6	5	12	1		7#			11+		13			14		45
2	3	4*			9#	8		10	12				6	5	13	1		7+			11		14					46
22	42	26	26	22	37	45	37	25	24		10	3	43	32	9	34		6	4	3	22	8	4	1	6	3		
11	1	1		5	2		2	3	4	2	9	17		1	3		2	9	2	5	2		14		4	2	3	
1	6	4			16	2	9	9	3	1	2	1									3	2	5		1			

Barnard	Lockwood	Mackie	White	Hunt	Steele	Simpson	Scott	Alexander	Carlisle	Purser	Ibehre	Newey T	Miller	Zakuani	Saah	Harrison	Peters	Duncan	Wardley	Barnard	McMahon	Chillingworth	Echanomi	Fitzgerald	Youngs T	Palmer	Wallis	
12	3+		5	6	7#	8	9		11		10	13	2*	4		1			14									1
2	3	4	5			8	9		11#		10+	13			6*	1		14		7	12							2
1	2	1	2	1	1	2	2		2		2		1	1	1	2				1								
1												2						1	1		1							
	1			1					1																			

Barnard	Lockwood	Mackie	White	Hunt	Steele	Simpson	Scott	Alexander	Carlisle	Purser	Ibehre	Newey T	Miller	Zakuani	Saah	Harrison	Peters	Duncan	Wardley	Barnard	McMahon	Chillingworth	Echanomi	Fitzgerald	Youngs T	Palmer	Wallis	
	3		5	6*	7	8	9+	14	11#		10	13	2	4	12													1
	1		1	1	1	1	1		1		1		1	1														
								1				1			1													
					1																							

2005-06

Manager: Martin Ling

	P	W	D	L	F	A	Pts
Carlisle United	46	25	11	10	84	42	86
Northampton Town	46	22	17	7	63	37	83
Leyton Orient	46	22	15	9	67	51	81
Grimsby Town	46	22	12	12	64	44	78
Cheltenham Town	46	19	15	12	65	53	72
Wycombe Wanderers	46	18	17	11	72	56	71
Lincoln City	46	15	21	10	65	53	66
Darlington	46	16	15	15	58	52	63
Peterborough United	46	17	11	18	57	49	62
Shrewsbury Town	46	16	13	17	55	55	61
Boston United	46	15	16	15	50	60	61
Bristol Rovers	46	17	9	20	59	67	60
Wrexham	46	15	14	17	61	54	59
Rochdale	46	14	14	18	66	69	56
Chester City	46	14	12	20	53	59	54
Mansfield Town	46	13	15	18	59	66	54
Macclesfield Town	46	12	18	16	60	71	54
Barnet	46	12	18	16	44	57	54
Bury	46	12	17	17	45	57	52
Torquay United	46	13	13	20	53	66	52
Notts County	46	12	16	18	48	63	52
Stockport County	46	11	19	16	57	78	52
Oxford United	46	11	16	19	43	57	49
Rushden & Diamonds	46	11	12	23	44	76	45

League Two

Match No.	Date		Opponents	Result	Scorers	Attendar
1	Aug	6	MACCLESFIELD TOWN	2-1	Keith, Echanomi	3,6
2		9	Bury	2-1	Zakuani, Tudor	2,0
3		13	Darlington	1-0	Lockwood (pen)	4,0
4		20	ROCHDALE	1-4	Echanomi	4,2
5		27	Cheltenham Town	1-1	Mackie	3,2
6		29	SHREWSBURY TOWN	0-1		3,7
7	Sep	3	BRISTOL ROVERS	2-3	McMahon, Alexander	3,4
8		10	Barnet	3-2	Alexander 2, Ibehre	3,7
9		17	WREXHAM	1-1	Alexander	3,7
10		24	Carlisle United	3-2	Lockwood (pen), Alexander, Ibehre	6,5
11		27	TORQUAY UNITED	2-1	Alexander, Ibehre	4,0
12	Oct	1	MANSFIELD TOWN	3-1	Alexander, Keith, Echanomi	4,1
13		8	Stockport County	1-1	Alexander	3,9
14		15	LINCOLN CITY	1-1	Alexander	4,8
15		22	Grimsby Town	1-0	Easton	4,9
16		29	OXFORD UNITED	1-0	Easton	5,2
17	Nov	12	Peterborough United	1-1	Miller	5,3
18		19	STOCKPORT COUNTY	2-2	Raynes (og), Mackie	4,9
19		26	Macclesfield Town	0-0		1,6
20	Dec	6	CHESTER CITY	0-1		3,4
21		10	BURY	0-1		4,0
22		17	Rochdale	4-2	Alexander 2, Tudor, Mackie	2,6
23		26	RUSHDEN & DIAMONDS	5-1	Steele 2, Mackie, Ibehre, Easton	4,5
24		29	Wycombe Wanderers	2-4	Steele, Tudor	6,2
25		31	NOTTS COUNTY	1-0	Ibehre	3,7
26	Jan	2	Boston United	2-1	Ibehre, Alexander	2,6
27		14	NORTHAMPTON TOWN	1-2	McMahon	5,4
28		21	Wrexham	2-1	Alexander, Lockwood (pen)	5,0
29		31	Bristol Rovers	3-3	Ibehre 2, Simpson	5,9
30	Feb	4	Torquay United	0-2		2,6
31		11	CARLISLE UNITED	0-0		5,8
32		14	Northampton Town	1-1	Mackie	5,5
33		18	Chester City	2-0	Lockwood (pen), Connor	2,2
34		25	DARLINGTON	1-0	Tudor	4,7
35		28	BARNET	0-0		4,9
36	Mar	4	Shrewsbury Town	3-3	Lockwood, Connor, Tann	3,4
37		11	CHELTENHAM TOWN	1-0	Connor	4,8
38		18	Rushden & Diamonds	0-1		3,6
39		25	WYCOMBE WANDERERS	1-0	Connor	6,7
40	Apr	1	Notts County	1-1	Corden	5,0
41		8	BOSTON UNITED	2-0	Lockwood (pen), Connor	4,3
42		15	Mansfield Town	1-0	Lockwood (pen)	4,7
43		17	GRIMSBY TOWN	0-0		6,5
44		22	Lincoln City	1-1	Mackie	5,6
45		29	PETERBOROUGH UNITED	2-1	Lockwood (pen), Corden	6,5
46	May	6	Oxford United	3-2	Easton, Alexander, Steele	12,2

Appearance
Sub appearance
Goa

FA Cup

1	Nov	5	CHESTERFIELD	0-0		3,5
R		16	Chesterfield	2-1	Mackie, Tudor	4,8
2	Dec	3	Rushden & Diamonds	1-0	Steele	3,2
3	Jan	8	Fulham	2-1	Easton, Keith	13,3
4		28	Charlton Athletic	1-2	Steele	22,0

Appearance
Sub appearance
Goa

League Cup

1	Aug	23	LUTON TOWN	1-3	McMahon	2,38

Appearance
Sub appearance
Goa

Final League Position: 3rd League Two

	Barnard	Lockwood	Zakuani	Mackie	McMahon	Tudor	Simpson	Steele	Alexander	Keith	Carlisle	Easton	Echanomi	Miller	Palmer	Dolan	Ibehre	Morris	Hanson	Duncan	Demetriou	Saah	Tann	Connor	Corden	
	2	3*	4	5	6	7+	8	9#	10	11	12	13	14													1
	2	3	4	5	6	7+	8	9*	10	11		13	12													2
	2	3	4	5	6	7*	8	9+	10	11		12	13													3
	2#	3	4	5	6*	7	8	9	10	11+		12	13	14												4
	2		4	5	6		8	9*	10			11	12	7	3											5
	13		4	5+	12	7	8	9	10#	11		6	14	2	3*											6
	2*			5	11	12	8+	9#	10	3	13	6	14	7		4										7
		3	4	5	11		8		10		7	6	12	2			9*									8
		3	4	5	11	12	8		10		7*	6	13	2			9+									9
		3	4	5		7+*	8		10	11	12	6		2			9									10
	12	3	4	5		7*	8		10	11		6	13	2			9+									11
		3	4	5		7	8		10	11		6	12	2			9*									12
	2*	3		5	14	7	8		10	11#	12	6	13	4			9+									13
	2*	3	4		14	7	8		10	11#	12	6	13	5			9+									14
		3	4	5		7+	8		10	11		6	12	2			9*		13							15
		3	4	5	12	7	8		10	11+*		6		2			9									16
		3	4	5	12	7	8		10	11*		6	13	2			9+#									17
		3	4#	5	12	7*	8		10	11*		6	13	2			9+		14							18
	12*	3	4	5		7*	8		10	11		6+		2			9									19
	2+	3	4		14	7	5*	12	10	11#	13	6					9					8				20
	2	3#	4		14	7*	8	13	10+	11#	12*	6					9					5				21
	12	3	4	5		8	7	11	10	9*		6		2												22
		3	4	5	12		7	11	10+	9#	8*	6		2			13			14						23
		3	4	5	13	8	7	11*	10	9+	14	6		2#			12									24
		3	4	5		8	7		10	9		6		2			11									25
		3	4	5	7	8			10	9		6		2			11									26
#		3	4	5	6	8	7	12	10	9*	13			2+			11	14								27
		3	4*	5	6	8	7	13	10	9				2			11+					12				28
	14	3	4	5	6	8#	7	11+	10	9				2*			13						12			29
			4	5	6	8	7	14	10*	9+		13			3		11#						2	12		30
		3	4	5	12	8*	7	14	10#	9		6		2			13							11+		31
		3	4	5			7	10*	12	9		6		2			8							11		32
	12	3	4	5	8#		7	13	10	9*		6		2							14			11+		33
	13	3	4	5	8	6	7		10*	9+				2			12							11		34
	14	3	4	5	8#	6	7	12	10+	9				2			13	1						11*		35
		3	4		6		7	12	10+	9*		8		2			13						5	11		36
	13	3	4		12		7*		14	9		8		2			10#				6+		5	11		37
	6	3	4		14		7#	13	12	9+		8		2			10*	1					5	11		38
	12	3	4	5			7		10	9		8		2				1						11	6*	39
		3	4	5		12	7		10+	9		8		2			13							11	6#	40
1	12	3	4	5		9+	7		10	13		8		2*										11	6	41
1	2	3	4*	5			7	13	10+	9#		8									14		12	11	6	42
1	2*	3		5			7	14	10#	9		8		12			13						4	11+	6	43
1	2#	3	4	5	14		7	12	10*			8					13						9	11+	6	44
1	12	3	4	5	14		7	10+	13	9		8											2*	11	6#	45
1		3	4	5	14	12	7#	10	11	9*		8					13						2		6+	46
43	14	42	43	40	17	29	45	14	42	41	3	36		34	3	1	22	3			1	2	8	15	8	
	13				16	4		13	4	1	9	5	16	2			11	1	2		2	1	2	1		
		8	1	6	2	4	1	4	14	2		4	3	1			8						1	5	2	

One own-goal

	Barnard	Lockwood	Zakuani	Mackie	McMahon	Tudor	Simpson	Steele	Alexander	Keith	Carlisle	Easton	Echanomi	Miller	Palmer	Dolan	Ibehre	Morris	Hanson	Duncan	Demetriou	Saah	Tann	Connor	Corden	
1		3	4	5	12	8	7*		10	9+	13	6	14	2			11#									1
1		3	4	5		8	7		10	9		6		2			11									R
1	5	3	4		6	8#	7	13	10	9	14			2*			11+					12				2
1	14	3	4	5	12	8*	7		10#	6+	13	9		2			11									3
1		3	4	5	6	8	7	11*	10	9				2						12						4
5	1	5	5	4	2	5	5	1	5	5		3		5			4									
	1				2			1			3		1							1		1				
				1		1		2		1		1														

	Barnard	Lockwood	Zakuani	Mackie	McMahon	Tudor	Simpson	Steele	Alexander	Keith	Carlisle	Easton	Echanomi	Miller	Palmer	Dolan	
1			4	5*	6	8#	7	13	10	14		11	9+	2	3	12	1
1			1	1	1	1	1		1			1	1	1	1		
								1		1						1	
					1												

Players on the bench

These 21 players only appeared on the bench, never making a Football League or senior Cup appearance for the club.

Name	*Born*	*Pos*	*From*	*To*	*No of times sat on the bench*
Abbey, Nathan	Islington, London 11 Jul 1978	G	Boston U (loan) 2005	Boston U Jan 2006	7 games 2005
Andrews, Barry	Skerries, Ireland 30 Aug 1980	G	QPR 1999	Bohemians (Ireland) 2000	7 games 1999–2000 (5) League (2) League Cup
Bankole, Ademola	Lagos, Nigeria 9 Sep 1969	G	Doncaster R 1995	Crewe A 1996	1 game 1996
Bird, Matthew	Barking, Essex 4 Mar 1978	M	O's youth 1994	Dagenham & Redbridge 1996	1 game 1995
Bray, Thomas John	Salisbury 9 Dec 1983	G	O's youth 2000	Gave up the game 2001	1 game 2000
Brazier, Jeffrey Charles	Ascot, Surrey 27 May 1979	M	O's youth 1994	Canvey Island 1998	1 game 1998
Brown, Daniel	Mile End, London 12 Sep 1980	M	Watford 1997	Barnet 1999 (£40,000)	1 game FA Cup 1989
Everitt, David	Chertsey 30 Dec 1976	D	Tottenham (junior) 1995	Sutton United 1997	1 game 1996
Ramis-Hayrettin, Hakan	Enfield 4 Feb 1970	M	O's youth 1986	Barnet 1989	1 game 1988
Henney, Christopher	Forest Gate, London 1959	D	O's youth 1975	Clapton 1980	2 games 1978
Holland, Patrick George	Poplar, London, 13 Sep 1950	M	O's player-coach 1983	Tottenham (youth coach) 1984	1 game FA Cup 1983
Holmes, John	Astratford, London 1959	G	O's youth 1974	Not retained 1977	1 game at Partick Thistle Anglo-Scottish Cup 1976
Honeyball, Scott	London 9 Mar 1979	D	O's youth 1983	Gravesend & Northfleet 1997	1 game 1997
Jones, Anthony	London 28 Jan 1979	M	O's youth 1993	Chelmsford City 1997	1 game 1996
Jones, Paul	Maidstone, Kent 28 Jun 1986	G	O's youth 2002	Exeter City 2005	2 games 2002–03, 8 games 2003–04 (1 in League Cup)
Morgan, Thomas	Enfield 8 Apr 1983	F	O's youth 2000	Billericay Town 2001	1 game in LDV Cup 2001
Sopp, Darryl	Barking 12 Aug 1978	G	O's youth 1993	Charlton Athletic (trial) 1996	3 games 1995
Stephenson, Alan Charles	Chesham 26 Sep 1944	D	Durban U (S. Africa) 1976	Development officer 1981	2 games 1977
Uka, Niam	Kosovo, Croatia 26 Oct 1981	F	O's youth 1992	Returned home to Croatia 2002	1 game 2000
Whittington, Eric Richard	Brighton 18 Sep 1946	F	Highlands Park (SA) 1970	Crawley Town 1970	1 game 1970
Wigg, Ronald George	Dunmow 18 May 1949	F	O's youth 1965	Ipswich Town 1967	1 game 1966

Club Sponsors

Season/Period	*Name of Sponsor*
Jan 1981–June 1981	E.O. PAPERS
1981–82	E.O. PAPERS
1982–83	TAYLOR WALKER
1983–84	NO SPONSOR
1984–85	NO SPONSOR
1985–86	OVENDEN PAPERS
1986–87	LEGGETT FREIGHTWAYS
1987–88	LEGGETT FREIGHTWAYS
1988–89	COMET ROOFING
1989–90	COMET ROOFING
1990–91	COMET ROOFING
1991–92	BAMAN
1992–93	INDEPENDENT TRANSPORT
1993–94	HEAT
1994–95	HEAT
1995–96	ACCLAIM

Season/Period	*Name of Sponsor*
1996–97	ACCLAIM
1997–98	MARCHPOLE
1998–99	MARCHPOLE
1999–2000	BRAVO TV
2000–01	MATCHROOM SPORTS
2001–02	MATCHROOM SPORTS
2002–03	MATCHROOM SPORTS
2002–07	MATCHROOM SPORTS and POKERMILLION.COM (jointly)

The club also signed a new three-year deal with Haart Estate agency in June 2006 for their name to appear on the back of the new blue third kit above the player's name.

FA Cup Records

	P	W	D	L	F	A
Aldershot	3	1	1	1	1	1
Altrincham	2	1	1	0	3	2
Arsenal	4	0	0	4	1	9
Ashford Town	1	1	0	0	4	1
Aston Villa	2	0	1	1	0	8
Barking	1	1	0	0	3	1
Barrow	1	1	0	0	2	0
Birmingham City	4	1	0	3	1	8
Blackburn Rovers	3	1	0	2	5	8
Boston United	2	1	1	0	3	2
AFC Bournemouth	2	2	0	0	3	1
Bradford Park Avenue	1	0	0	1	0	1
Brentford	5	2	2	1	8	6
Brighton & Hove Albion	2	1	0	1	5	5
Bristol City	2	2	0	0	5	1
Bristol Rovers	5	1	1	3	2	7
Buckingham Town	1	1	0	0	2	0
Burnley	2	0	1	1	1	2
Bury	2	2	0	0	4	2
Cardiff City	5	0	1	4	3	13
Carlisle United	1	0	0	1	1	4
Charlton Athletic	3	2	0	1	5	2
Chelsea	4	2	1	1	5	5
Cheltenham Town	1	0	0	1	1	3
Cheshunt	2	1	1	0	4	1
Chester City	1	0	0	1	1	3
Chesterfield	5	2	2	1	3	4
Clapton	1	1	0	0	2	0
Colchester United	2	1	1	0	4	1
Coventry City	3	1	1	1	5	6
Crystal Palace	2	0	1	1	0	1
Custom House	1	1	0	0	3	0
Dagenham & Red.	2	2	0	0	8	5
Darlington	4	1	2	1	5	3
Dartford	1	1	0	0	3	2
Derby County	3	1	1	1	0	4
Doncaster Rovers	1	1	0	0	3	1
Enfield	4	1	2	1	7	5
Epsom Town	1	1	0	0	4	2
Everton	4	1	1	2	5	7
Exeter City	3	1	2	0	5	3
Felstead	2	1	1	0	6	2
Folkestone Town	4	2	2	0	8	4
Frome Town	1	1	0	0	3	0
Fulham	2	2	0	0	4	2
Gillingham	4	1	1	2	8	6
Gorleston	3	1	2	0	7	6
Grantham Town	1	1	0	0	2	1
Grimsby Town	1	0	0	1	0	1
Gravesend & Northfleet**	2	2	0	0	4	1
Hayes	1	1	0	0	3	1
Hendon	2	0	1	1	2	3
Hitchen	1	0	0	1	1	2
Huddersfield Town	2	1	1	0	3	1
Hull City	2	1	1	0	3	1
Ipswich Town	3	0	1	2	1	4
Kettering	1	1	0	0	3	0
Kingstonian	2	1	1	0	2	1
Leicester City	4	2	0	2	5	5
Leyton Amateurs	1	1	0	0	3	1
Leytonstone	2	1	1	0	6	3

	P	W	D	L	F	A
Lincoln City	1	1	0	0	2	1
Liverpool	1	0	0	1	1	2
Lovells Athletic	1	1	0	0	7	1
Lowestoft	1	1	0	0	2	1
Luton Town	3	0	1	2	5	9
Manchester City	2	0	0	2	2	10
Margate	2	0	1	1	1	2
Merthyr Tydfil	1	1	0	0	2	1
Middlesbrough	4	2	1	1	6	6
Millwall	2	0	0	2	1	4
Newcastle United	3	1	0	2	3	8
Newport County	1	0	0	1	0	1
Newport (I O W)	2	1	0	1	2	3
Northwich Victoria	2	1	1	0	6	5
Norwich City	3	1	1	1	3	4
Nottingham Forest	6	1	2	3	5	7
Notts County	1	0	0	1	1	2
Old Newportonians	1	1	0	0	5	2
Oldham	4	2	1	1	7	8
Plymouth Argyle	1	1	0	0	1	0
Port Vale	4	1	1	2	3	7
Portsmouth	5	1	2	2	5	6
Reading	2	1	0	1	1	3
Romford	1	1	0	0	6	3
Rushden & Diamonds	1	1	0	0	1	0
Sheffield Wednesday	2	0	0	2	0	7
Slough Town	2	1	1	0	5	4
Southampton	5	2	1	2	4	6
Southend United	4	1	1	2	5	8
Southport	1	1	0	0	2	0
Stevenage Borough	1	0	0	1	1	2
Stockport County	1	1	0	0	2	1
Sunderland	2	1	0	1	3	6
Swansea City	4	1	2	1	5	4
Swindon Town	3	0	1	2	2	4
Tiveton	1	1	0	0	3	1
Torquay United	4	3	0	1	7	3
Tottenham Hotspur	1	0	0	1	0	1
Tranmere Rovers	2	1	1	0	6	3
V.S. Rugby	2	1	1	0	6	3
Walsall	5	1	2	2	4	6
Welling United	1	1	0	0	2	1
West Bromwich Albion	3	2	0	1	4	4
West Ham United	5	0	2	3	5	12
Weymouth	2	2	0	0	6	0
Wimbledon	1	0	0	1	1	2
Woodford Town	1	1	0	0	1	0
Workington Town	1	0	0	1	0	1
Wrexham	3	2	1	0	7	3
York City	2	0	1	1	2	3
Totals	254	103	61	90	371	366

** FA Cup tie in 1929, played under previous name of Gravesend FC
(Gravesend & Northfleet FC was an amalgamation of Northfleet United and Gravesend United, formed in April 1946.)

	P	W	D	L	Goals F	Goals A
HOME	127	63	28	36	214	159
AWAY	120	37	33	50	142	191
NEUTRAL	7	3	0	4	15	16
	254	100	60	89	371	366

FA Cup ties played on neutral grounds

v Swansea, played at White Hart Lane, 1–2 on 21 January 1924.

v Folkestone, played at Highbury, 4–1 on 9 December 1929.

v Luton Town, played at Highbury, 2–4 on 4 December 1930.

(*Orient's Lea Bridge Ground was closed for alterations*).

v Gorleston, played at Highbury, 5–4 on 3 December 1951.

v Portsmouth, played at Selhurst Park, 0–2 on 5 February 1994.

v Darlington, played at White Hart Lane, 3–0 on 17 January 1977.

v Arsenal, played at Stamford Bridge, semi-final 0–3 on 8 April 1978.

FA Cup Milestones

Orient first entered the FA Cup in 1904–05 when they were members of the Second Division of the Southern League. They first became members of the Football League in 1905–06. Clapton Orient did not enter the competition in season 1906–07.

1st	FA Cup tie	(H)	versus	Enfield	4–1	1904–05
50th	FA Cup tie	(A)	versus	Folkestone	2–2	1929–30
100th	FA Cup tie	(H)	versus	Tranmere R	2–2	1953–54
150th	FA Cup tie	(H)	versus	Arsenal	0–1	1971–72
200th	FA Cup tie	(H)	versus	Swansea City	2–0	1987–88
250th	FA Cup tie	(H)	versus	Chesterfield	0–0	2005–06

1st	FA Cup goal scored by William Reynolds	17 September 1904
50th	FA Cup goal scored by Richard McFadden	14 January 1914
100th	FA Cup goal scored by Ted Crawford	4 December 1935
200th	FA Cup goal scored by Dave Dunmore	9 January 1965
250th	FA Cup goal scored by Joe Mayo	9 January 1980
300th	FA Cup goal scored by Steve Castle	17 November 1990
350th	FA Cup goal scored by Scott Houghton	20 December 2000

Giant Killings

Club O's beat	*Venue*	*Score*	*Round*	*O's scorers*	*Div of Opp*	*Div of O's*	*Season*
Newcastle United	H	2–0	5	Galbraith, Cock	1	2	1925–26
Charlton Athletic	H	3–0	3	Foster 2, Taylor	2	3 South	1935–36
Everton (Replay)	A	3–1	3	Pacey 2, Harris	2	3 South	1951–52
Birmingham City	A	1–0	4	Harris	2	3 South	1951–52

Club O's beat	*Venue*	*Score*	*Round*	*O's scorers*	*Div of Opp*	*Div of O's*	*Season*
Fulham	H	2–1	4	Poulton, Davies	2	3 South	1953–54
Doncaster Rovers	H	3–1	5	Morgan, Pacey, Burgess	2	3 South	1953–54
Plymouth Argyle	H	1–0	3	Hartburn	2	3 South	1955–56
Leicester City	A	3–2	3	Musgrove 2, King (og)	1	2	1963–64
Leicester City	A	2–0	4	Bowyer, Allen	1	2	1971–72
Chelsea	H	3–2	5	Hoadley, Bullock, Fairbrother	1	2	1971–72
Norwich City (R)	A	1–0	3	Kitchen	1	2	1977–78
Chelsea (R)	A	2–1	5	Kitchen 2	1	2	1977–78
Middlesbrough(R)	H	2–1	6	Kitchen, Mayo	1	2	1977–78
W.B.A.	H	2–1	3	Silkman, Cadette	1	3	1984–85
Oldham Athletic (R)	H	4–2*	3	Nugent 2, Castle(pen Harvey	1	3	1991–92
Bristol City	A	1–0	1	Watts	2	3	2001–02
Portsmouth	A	4–1	3	Smith, Watts, Gray, Christie	1	3	2001–02
Chesterfield	A	2–1	1	Mackie, Tudor	L1	L2	2005–06
Fulham	A	2–1	3	Easton, Keith	Prem	L2	2005–06

*(after extra-time)

Leading Goalscorers

Denis Pacey	12
Peter Kitchen	9
Billy Rees	8
Barrie Fairbrother	7
Ian Juryeff	7
Steve Castle	6
Ted Crawford	6
Carl Griffiths	6
Ronnie Heckman *	6
Ken Facey	5
Colin Foster	5
Kevin Godfrey	5

* Ron Heckman is the only player to have scored five goals in a match during any major competition for Orient (the League, FA Cup or League Cup). He scored his five goals versus Lovells Athletic in a first-round FA Cup tie during November 1955.

Leading Appearances

Kevin Godfrey	28 /1
Stan Charlton	28
Bobby Fisher	26
Kevin Hales	25 /1
Stan Aldous	25
Peter Allen	25
Les Blizzard	25
Phil Hoadley	24
Steve Castle	23 /2
Terry Howard	23 /1
Matthew Lockwood	22 /2
Arthur Wood	22
Nigel Gray	20 /1
Ray Goddard	20

League Cup Records

	P	W	D	L	F	A
Aldershot	6	2	3	1	11	9
Barnet	2	0	1	1	1	5
Barnsley	1	1	0	0	3	0
Birmingham	2	0	0	2	2	7
Blackburn Rovers	1	1	0	0	2	0
Blackpool	2	0	1	1	2	6
Bolton Wanderers	2	0	1	1	5	7
Bournemouth	1	0	0	1	1	3
Brentford	1	1	0	0	2	1
Brighton	3	1	1	1	4	3
Bristol Rovers	2	1	1	0	3	2
Bury	1	0	0	1	0	2
Cambridge United	2	0	1	1	2	3
Cardiff City	1	0	0	1	1	4
Charlton Athletic	4	2	1	1	7	6
Chester City	3	2	1	0	12	4
Chesterfield	2	0	0	2	1	3
Coventry City	1	0	0	1	0	3
Crystal Palace	4	0	1	3	2	6
Derby County	1	0	0	1	1	3
Everton	2	0	1	1	2	4
Fulham	6	2	1	3	5	6
Gillingham	7	4	1	2	15	9
Grimsby Town	2	1	0	1	2	4
Hull City	1	1	0	0	1	0
Ipswich Town	1	0	0	1	0	2
Luton Town	3	0	0	3	1	10
Maidstone United	2	1	1	0	6	3
Millwall	9	0	5	4	6	14
Newcastle United	4	1	1	1	6	6
Northampton	2	1	1	0	5	2
Nottm Forest	2	0	1	1	1	5
Notts County	2	0	1	1	2	4
Portsmouth	2	1	0	1	1	2
QPR	3	1	1	1	4	6
Reading	2	1	1	0	3	1
Sheffield Wednesday	2	0	1	1	1	4
Southend United	2	1	1	0	2	1
Stockport County	1	1	0	0	1	0
Stoke City**	2	1	0	1	3	3
Swindon Town	2	1	1	0	2	1
Tottenham Hotspur	4	1	0	3	3	8
Watford	1	1	0	0	2	0
West Ham United	1	0	0	1	1	2
Wimbledon*	2	0	2	0	4	4
Wolverhampton Wanderers	1	0	0	1	1	2
Wycombe Wanderers	4	1	0	3	2	6
York City	2	0	1	1	2	3
TOTALS	**116**	**32**	**33**	**51**	**148**	**189**

* The tie at Plough Lane, Wimbledon, in 1979–80 was won by Wimbledon 5–4 on penalties. The Dons' winning penalty was scored by former Orient goalkeeper Ray Goddard.

** The tie at Stoke City's Victoria Ground, in 1988–89, Orient won 6–5 on penalties.

(Milton Keynes Dons listed under their previous name of Wimbledon)

Leading Appearances

Terry Howard	26
Peter Allen	24
Kevin Hales	23
Bobby Fisher	19/1
John Sitton	19/1
Dean Smith	18

Leading Goalcscorers

Kevin Nugent	7
Steve Castle	5
Malcolm Graham	5
Kevin Godfrey	4
Vic Halom	4

Milestones

Highest home win 9–2 v Chester City 17 October 1962
Highest away win 4–1 v Gillingham 1 August 1989
Heaviest home defeat 1–5 v Nottingham Forest 15 September 1998
Heaviest away defeat 1–5 v Blackpool 30 October 1961

Best win over a higher Division opponent: 2–0 v Tottenham Hotspur 23 September 1985 (O's lost 4–0 at White Hart Lane in second leg).

The first player to score for Orient in the competition was Ronnie Foster in a 2–2 draw at Chester City on 12 October 1960. In the replay the O's obtained their first victory in the competition 1–0 with a goal from Terry McDonald.

O's best run in the competition was in 1962–63, reaching the quarter-finals.

In Other Competitions

Southern Section Cup

From 1933 there was a Cup competition for all Division Three Southern and Northern teams called the Southern Section Cup. It ran from 1933–34 to 1938–39 and Orient played in the Southern section.
Orient had a dismal record in this competition, winning just one match – 2–0 at Southend United in October 1936 – from the nine Cup games played.

1933–34
First round: Bye
Second round: Thursday 8 February 1934 v Norwich City (a) 0–3
Robertson, Keen, Crompton, Fogg, Fellowes, Ware, Mayson, French, Halliday, Crawford, Rigby
Att: 2,561

1934–35
First round: Monday 24 September 1934 v Northampton Town (h) 1–1 (*This match was played at home by arrangement between the two clubs)*
Robertson, Keen, Crompton, Fogg, Fellowes, Ware, Mayson, Taylor, Halliday, Crawford, Rigby
Scorer: Halliday
Att: 3,600
First-round replay: Monday 1 October 1934 v Northampton Town (a) 0–4
Robertson, Finlayson, Crompton, Fogg, Fellowes, Manns, Mayson, Smith, Halliday, Crawford, Millington
Att: 3,000

1935–36
First round: Thursday 26 September 1935 v Bournemouth (h) 1–1
Hillam, Searle, Taylor, J. Fogg, Taylor, H. Heinemann, Mayson, Smith, Crawford, Edwards, Campbell
Scorer: Campbell
Att: 5,200
First round replay: Wednesday 9 October 1935 v Bournemouth (a) 2–6
Hillam, Searle, Taylor, Fogg, Affleck, Heinemann, Miles, Smith, Crawford, Pateman, Mayson
Scorers: King (own-goal), Mayson
Att: 996

1936–37
First round: Bye
Second round: Wednesday 28 October 1936 v Southend United (a) 2–0
Hillam, Hearty, Herod, Taylor, Affleck, Heinemann, McCombe, Fletcher, Fisher, Smith, Miles
Scorer: Fisher (2)
Att: 2,068
Third round: Monday 16 November 1936 v Millwall (a) 2–3
Hillam, Hearty, Herod, Searle, Affleck, Heinemann, McCombe, Farrell, Fletcher, Smith, Wells
Scorers: Smith, Wells
Att: 4,100

1937–38
First round: Thursday 11 November 1937 v Queen's Park Rangers (h) 0–2
Gilfillan, Brooks, Hearty, Allen, Bartlett, Dodgin, McCombe, Fletcher, Graham, Shankly, Codling
Att: 3,500

1938–39
First round: Bye
Second round: Saturday 7 January 1939 v Reading (a) 0–4
Iceton, Rumbold, Hearty, Taylor, Bartlett, Dodgin, Tully, Smith, Williams, Crawford, Dodds
Att: 2,335

Southern Floodlit Challenge Cup

The Cup was played between 1955–56 and 1959–60 (inclusive). All O's ties were played away due to the fact that they didn't had floodlights.

1955–56
First round: Monday 31 October 1955 v Queen's Park Rangers 1–0
Welton, Gregory, Charlton, Rees, Aldous, McKnight, Facey, Webb, Burgess, Heckman, Hartburn
Scorer: Hartburn
Att: 2,790
Second round: Monday 30 January 1956 v Aldershot 0–1
Groombridge, Lee, Earl, Cook, Bishop, McMahon, White, Woosnam, Julians, Webb, Smith
Att: 1,800

1956–57
First round: Tuesday 2 October 1956 v West Ham United 1–4
Groombridge, Earl, Willemse, Cini, Carey, McMahon, Smith, Facey, Sexton, Heckman, Andrews
Scorer: Andrews
Att: 14,500

1957–58
First round: Monday 23 September 1957 v West Ham United 0–1
George, Eagles, Willemse, Facey, Carey, McMahon.

Smith, Woosnam, Julians, Johnston, Andrews
Att: 10,000

1958–59
First round: Tuesday 14 October 1958 v Brentford 2–3
George, Wright, Lea, Facey, Bishop, Carey, McLellan, Elwood, Lewis, Julians, Andrews
Scorers: McLellan, Lewis
Att: 6,500

1959–60
First round: Monday 26 October 1959 v Queen's Park Rangers 2–1
Groombridge, Eagles, Charlton, Facey, Bishop, Sorrell, Waites, Brown, Johnston, Lucas, McDonald
Scorers: Brown, Facey (pen)
Att: 5,758
Second round: Tuesday 3 November 1959 v Watford 2–0
Groombridge, Wright, Charlton, Facey, Bishop, Sorrell, White, Brown, Johnston, Foster, McDonald
Scorers: Johnston, Brown
Att: 4,064
Third round: Monday 7 December 1959 v West Ham United 3–4
Groombridge, Wright, Charlton, Facey, Bishop, Sorrell, White, Brown, Johnston, Foster, McDonald
Scorers: Johnston, McDonald, White
Att: 8,606

London Challenge Cup

Orient's involvement in this competition goes back to 1910, but it was in the 1911–12 season that they defeated Millwall 3–1 in the Final.

Between 1946 and 1974 the O's competed in the competition, which in the latter seasons involved all the Football League clubs in the London area plus the four semi-finalists from the London Senior Cup, a competition for leading amateur clubs in London, so 16 clubs took part. In 1954 the O's recorded a great 4–1 victory over Wimbledon's first team, with Phil White being made Man of the Match. In the 1957–58 season the O's lost 2–0 in a semi-final tie at Arsenal. O's goalie Pat Welton was injured in the sixth minute, and Sid Bishop played in goal.

Orient's record in the competition was largely uneventful, but they did win the competition in 1971–72. The O's beat Dagenham 2–1 at home; Gordon Riddick hit both of the goals after a 1–1 replay on the way to the Final. Their other Final appearance in the competition in 1972–73 was against Enfield, and they won 2–1.

Winners

1911–12 Clapton Orient 3 Millwall 0
1971–72 Orient 2 Dagenham 1 (after a 1–1 draw at Dagenham)
1972–73 Enfield 1 Orient 2

Runners-up

1920–21 Crystal Palace 1 Clapton Orient 0
1924–25 West Ham United 2 Clapton Orient 1
1926–27 Chelsea 2 Clapton Orient 1

Essex Professional Cup

This competition was inaugurated in 1949 by the Essex County FA, and Orient competed from its first season in 1949–50. Orient decided to withdraw from the competition in 1965–66.

This was considered mainly as a reserve competition (for League clubs, but non-League clubs also entered). Instead of awarding the usual medals or plaques, the winners were awarded a pair of cufflinks with the County crest on. Orient appeared in 16 semi-finals and appeared in nine Finals, against Southend United four times, Chelmsford City three times and against West Ham United twice, Colchester United twice, and once each against Romford and Clacton Town.

Winners

1–0 v Southend United (h) 1955–56 (played at Upton Park)
4–2 v Colchester United (h) 1962–63
2–0 v Chelmsford City (a) 1963–64

Orient enjoyed some big wins over the years in the early rounds, including 7–1 over Clacton Town in 1948–49, with goals from Adams (2), Connelly (2), Smith (2) and Dryden.

Texaco Cup

This competition was introduced in 1974–75.

1974–75
Group Two
3 August v West Ham United (a) 0–1
Jackson, Fisher, Hoadley, Walley, Roffey, Boyle, (Bennett), Brisley, Heppolette, Cunningham, Fairbrother, Queen
Att: 16,338
6 August v Southampton (a) 1–2
Fairbrother, Jackson, Fisher, Hoadley, Harris, Walley, Roffey, Bennett (Boyle), Heppolette, Queen, Possee
Scorer: Fairbrother
Att: 9,932
10 Aug v Luton Town (h) 2–2
Jackson (Goddard), Fisher, Hoadley, Harris, Roffey, Walley, Heppolette (Cunningham), Fairbrother, Bullock, Queen, Possee
Scorers: Walley, Queen
Att: 5,443

Anglo-Scottish Cup

The competition started in 1971 when Wolves were the winners. It was introduced to encourage attacking football, and in the earlier rounds teams who scored three or more goals were awarded an extra point. The competition gave an opportunity in later rounds for teams from both England and Scotland to play each other.

Orient progressed to the Final of the competition during their first attempt in the 1976–77 season. In the group stages they finished top and knocked out two Scottish sides, both over two legs, Aberdeen and Partick Thistle. The O's lost in the Final to Nottingham Forest, 5–1 over the two legs. Orient's lone goal in the home leg was scored by Derek Possee, who eluded Forest full-back Frank Clark to score with a flashing header past 'keeper Middleton, replying to a penalty by Robertson. In the second leg Orient were outplayed, losing 4–0, their scorers being Barrett (2), Chapman and former 'Oriental' Ian Bowyer.

1976–77
Group C
7 August v Norwich City (a) 0–0
Jackson, Fisher, Roeder, Hoadley, Roffey, Allen, Grealish, Allder, Cunningham, Queen, Possee
Att: 6,285
11 August v Fulham (h) 2–1
Jackson, Fisher, Roeder, Hoadley, Roffey, Grealish, Hibbs (Bennett), Allder, Cunningham, Queen, Possee
Scorers: Possee, Hoadley
Att: 3,357
14 August v Chelsea (h) 2–1
Jackson, Payne, Hoadley, Roeder, Fisher, Allen, Heppolette, Allder (Roffey), Cunningham, Possee, Godfrey
Scorers: Possee, Cunningham
Att: 6,591
Quarter-final (first leg): 15 September v Aberdeen (a) 1-0
Jackson, Fisher, Hoadley, Roeder, Grealish, Allen, Whittle, Heppolette, Cunningham, Clarke, Queen
Scorer: Clarke
Att: 9,569
Quarter-final (second leg): 29 September v Aberdeen (h) 1–0
Jackson, Fisher (Allder), Hoadley, Roeder, Roffey, Allen, Whittle, Heppolette, Cunningham, Clarke, Queen
Scorer: Queen
Att: 5,005
Semi-final (first leg): 8 November v Partick Thistle (a) 1–0
Jackson, Fisher, Hoadley, Roeder, Roffey, Allen, Bennett (Whittle), Grealish, Cunningham, Clarke, Queen
Scorer: Cunningham
Att: 3,885
Semi-final (second leg): 24 November v Partick Thistle (h) 3–2
Jackson, Payne, Hoadley, Roeder, Roffey, Allen, Grealish, Whittle, Cunningham, Clarke, Queen
Scorer: Whittle, Queen (2) (1 pen)
Att: 3,541
Final (first leg): 13 December v Nottingham Forest (h) 1–1
Jackson, Payne, Hoadley, Roeder, Roffey, Bennett, Grealish, Allder, Cunningham (Whittle), Possee, Queen
Scorer: Possee
Att: 5,058
Final (second leg): 15 December v Nottingham Forest (a) 0–4
Jackson, Payne, Hoadley, Roeder, Bennett, Roffey, Grealish, Whittle, Allder (Fisher), Possee, Queen
Att: 12,717

1977–78
Group Two
2 August v Fulham (a) 0–1
Smeulders, Payne, Hoadley, Roeder, Gray, Allen, Grealish, Glover (Banjo), Chiedozie, Mayo, Kitchen
Att: 3,700
6 August v Norwich City (a) 1–1
Smeulders, Payne, Hoadley, Roeder, Fisher, Allen, Grealish, Glover, Chiedozie, Mayo, Kitchen
Scorer: Mayo
Att: 3,124
9 August v Chelsea (h) 0–2
Smeulders, Payne, Hoadley, Roder, Fisher, Allen, Grealish, Glover, Chiedozie, Mayo, Kitchen
Att: 5,702

1978–79
Group C
5 August v Mansfield Town (h) 0–1
Smeulders, Fisher, Gray, Kane, Roffey, Banjo, Bennett, Grealish, Chiedozie, Mayo, Kitchen
Att: 3,385
8 August v Notts County (h) 2–3
Smeulders, Fisher, Gray, Hughton, Roffey, Bennett, Banjo, Grealish, Chiedozie, Mayo, Kitchen
Scorer: Banjo, Gray
Att: 2,511
12 August v Norwich City (a) 0–0
Smeulders, Fisher, Gray, Hughton, Roffey, Bennett, (Godfrey), Banjo, Grealish, Chiedozie, Mayo, Kitchen.
Att: 2,870

Orient did not enter the competition in 1979–80

1980–81
Group B
2 August v Notts County (a) 2–2
Day, Fisher, T. Taylor, Gray, Roffey, Coates, Margerrison, Parsons, Bowles, Jennings (Moores), Mayo
Scorers: Jennings, Margerrison
Att: 2,450

5 August v Fulham (h) 1–2
Day, Fisher, T. Taylor, Gray, Roffey, Coates, Margerrison, Parsons, Bowles, Jennings, Mayo
Scorer: Margerrison
Att: 2,906
9 August v Bristol City (h) 1–0
Day, Fisher, Moores, Gray, Roffey, Coates, Parsons, Bowles, Chiedozie, Mayo, Jennings
Scorer: Chiedozie
Att: 1,999

Football League Groups Cup

This competition was launched in season 1981–82 to replace the Anglo-Scottish Cup and lasted just two seasons. In 1982–83 it was renamed the Football League Trophy.

1981–82
Group One
15 August v Southend United (h) 2–0
Day, Fisher, T. Taylor, Gray, Roffey, Moores, Bowles, Chiedozie, Jennings, Mayo, P. Taylor
Scorers: Jennings, Chiedozie
Att: 1,806
18 August v Wimbledon (h) 0–1
Day, Fisher, T. Taylor, Gray, Roffey, Moores, Bowles, Chiedozie, Jennings, Mayo, P. Taylor
Att: 1,777
22 August v Gillingham (a) 1–1
Day, Fisher, T. Taylor, Gray, Roffey, Margerrison, Bowles, Godfrey (Hallybone), Jennings (Mayo), Moores, P. Taylor
Scorer: Moores
Att: 2,234

1982–83
Group One
14 August v Watford (a) 1–4
Day, Fisher, Osgood, Foster (Silkman), Gray, Peach, Vincent, Sussex, Houchen, Blackhall, P. Taylor
Scorer: Rice (og)
Att: 4,063
16 August v Southend United (a) 1–1
Day, Fisher, Foster, Gray (Cunningham), Peach, Vincent, Silkman (Blackhall), Sussex, Godfrey, Houchen, P. Taylor
Scorer: P. Taylor
Att: 2,069
21 August v Colchester United (h) 0–2
Day, Fisher, (McNeil), Foster, Gray, Peach, Donn, Silkman, Godfrey (Blackhall), Houchen, Taylor, Sussex
Att: 1,384

LDV Vans Trophy

The current LDV Vans Trophy was launched in the 1983–84 season as the Associate Members Cup (AMC) for teams in the old Third and Fourth Divisions.

The AMC was initially organised into mini-leagues of three clubs, who played each other in knock-out stages, and it was split into two regions (North and South).

In 1996–97 the competition became a straight knock-out tournament. In 2000–01 seven clubs from the Nationwide Conference also played in the competition.

The competition has had various sponsors throughout the years. Namely:

The Associate Members' Cup	1983–84
Freight Rover Trophy	1984–87
Sherpa Van Trophy	1987–89
Leyland DAF Cup	1989–91
Autoglass Trophy	1991–94
Auto Windscreens Shield	1994–2000
LDV Vans Trophy	2000–present

Associate Members' Cup

1983–84
First round: 21 February v Brentford (a) 2–3
Key, Corbett, Sussex, Osgood, Roffey, Brooks, Hales, Silkman, Godfrey, Kitchen, McNeil (Houchen)
Scorer: Kitchen (2)
Att: 2,301

Freight Rover Trophy

1984–85
First round (first leg): 22 January v Aldershot (h) 0–0
Wilmot, Hales, Cunningham (Sussex), Foster, Banfield, Castle, Donnellan, Silkman, Godfrey, Jones, Cadette (Brooks).
Att: 804
First round (second leg): 5 February v Aldershot (a) 1–0
Wilmot, Hales, Cunningham, Foster, Corbett, Castle, Donnellan, Silkman, Harvey, Godfrey, Jones (Sussex)
Scorer: Jones
Att: 1,569
Second round: 25 March v Millwall (a) 3–2
Wilmot, Cornwell, Foster (Corbett), Banfield, Castle, Brooks, Silkman, Mountford, Harvey, Juryeff, Jones
Scorers: Juryeff, Foster, Harvey
Att: 1,170

Third round: 23 April v Millwall (h) 4–2
Greygoose, Cornwell, Corbett, Banfield, Stride, Brooks, Mountford, Castle, Silkman, Juryeff, Cadette
Scorers: Juryeff (2), Brooks, Cornwell
Att: 1,647
Southern area semi-final: 8 May v Newport County (h) (after extra-time)
Newport won 4–2 on pens.
Greygoose, Hales, Banfield, Corbett, Castle (Sussex), Brooks, Silkman, Harvey, Jones, Juryeff, Godfrey
Scorer: Corbett
Att: 1,279
Note: In the penalty shoot-out Brooks and Hales converted their spot kicks, but Silkman and Banfield both missed.

1985–86
Southern group
First round: 14 Jan v AFC Bournemouth (h) 3–1
Greygoose, Corbett, John, Foster, Dickenson, Brooks, Cornwell, Mountford, Godfrey (Harvey), Shinners, Juryeff (Castle)
Scorers: Shinners 2, Juryeff
Att: 947
6 March v Reading (a) 3–0
Wells, Corbett, John, Cunningham, Dickinson, Cornwell, Mountford, Sussex, Harvey (Brooks), Shinners, Juryeff (Jones)
Scorers: Juryeff, Cunningham, Jones
Att: 1,403
Second round: 24 March v Hereford United (h) 1–2 (after extra-time)
Wells, Sitton, Cunningham (John), Foster, Dickenson, Cornwell, Mountford, Sussex (Brooks), Harvey, Shinners, Juryeff
Scorer: Cornwell
Att: 1,133

1986–87
Preliminary group
9 December v Swindon Town (a) 0–3
Wells, Cornwell, Cunningham, Sitton, Castle, Brooks, Hales, Mountford, Harvey, Shinners, Comfort (Godfrey)
Att: 3,085
15 December v Brentford (h) 1–5
Wells, Hales, Sitton (Mountford), John, Dickenson, Brooks, Cornwell, Castle, Harvey (Godfrey), Jones, Comfort
Scorer: Mountford
Att: 749

Sherpa Van Trophy

1987–88
Preliminary group
27 October v Gillingham (a) 2–2
Wells, Howard, John, Day, Hughton, Hales, Sussex, Harvey, Shinners, Hull, (Juryeff), Comfort
Scorer: Comfort, Hull
Att: 2,558
24 November v Aldershot (h) 2–2
Wells, Howard, Smalley, Day, Dickenson, Hales, Sussex, Godfrey (Harvey), Nugent, Hull, Comfort
Scorers: Comfort, Hull
Att: 1,606
First round: 19 January v Colchester United (a) 1–1 (after extra-time)
Colchester won 6–5 on penalties
Penalty shoot-out: spot kicks converted by Hales, Comfort, Juryeff, Conroy and Hull. (*Lee Harvey crashed his kick against the crossbar, and John Sitton also missed his kick).*
Wells, Howard, Sitton, Day, Dickenson, Ketteridge, (Conroy), Hales, Harvey, Nugent (Hull), Juryeff, Comfort
Scorer: Juryeff
Att: 1,351

1988–89
Preliminary groups
6 December v Reading (h) 1–1
Wells, Howard, Day, Sitton, Smalley, Dickenson, (Hull), Hales, Ward, Baker, Jones
(Marks)
Scorer: Hales (pen)
Att: 1,174
10 January v Aldershot (a) 3–1
Heald, Howard, Day, Sitton, Smalley, O'Shea, Baker, Ward, Harvey (Jones), Juryeff, Comfort
Scorers: O'Shea, Ward, Jones
Att: 1,310
17 January v Colchester United (a) 1–3
Heald, Howard, Day, Sitton, Dickenson, O'Shea (Castle), Baker, Ward, Hull, Juryeff, Comfort
Scorer: Hull
Att: 1,736

Leyland DAF Cup

1989–90
Preliminary rounds
7 November v Brentford (a) 0–3
Heald, Hoddle, Dickenson, Baker, Day, Sitton, Howard, Pike (Nugent), Smalley, Cooper, Berry
Att; 2,544
28 November v Mansfield Town (h) 2–0
Heald, Hales, Dickenson, Beesley, Whitbread, Baker, Howard, Castle, Carter, Cooper (Berry), Harvey
Scorers: Beesley, Hunt (og)
Att; 1,133
Preliminary round play-off: 9 January v Mansfield Town (a) 1–2
Rees, Hales (Berry), Sitton, Beesley, Day, Baker, Hoddle, Castle, Carter, Nugent, Harvey
Scorer: Sitton
Att: 1,983

1990–91
Preliminary rounds
12 November v Fulham (h) 0–2
Heald, Howard, Baker (Zoricich), Sitton, Whitbread, Achampong, Castle, Carter (Hull), Nugent, Sayer, Berry
Att: 1,359
29 January v Brentford (a) 0–2
Heald, Zoricich, Dickenson (Berry), Howard, Hoddle, Pike, Bart-Williams, Castle, Achampong, Carter, Harvey
Att: 2,526

Autoglass Trophy

1991–92
Preliminary rounds
22 October v Reading (h) 1–0
Newell, Howard, Hackett, Whitbread, Day, Bart-Williams, Castle, Achampong, Jones, Nugent, Otto (Harvey)
Scorer: Otto
Att: 1,054
2 December v Northampton Town (a) 2–1
Turner, Day, Hackett, Hales, Whitbread, Howard, Burnett, Castle (Harvey), Jones, Nugent, Otto
Scorers: Jones, Berry
Att: 1,193
First round: 21 January v Brentford (h) 3–2
Turner, Howard, Hackett, Day, Roeder, Burnett, Hales, Castle (Achampong), Jones (Cooper), Nugent, Otto
Scorers: Otto, Nugent, Day
Att: 1,861
Second round: 4 February v Barnet (a) 1–0
Turner, Howard, Hackett, Whitbread, Day, Burnett, Achampong, Carter, Nugent, Jones, Berry
Scorer: Jones
Att: 2,969
Southern area semi-final: 17 March v Stoke City (h) 0–1
Turner, Wilder, Zoricich, Day, Whitbread, Howard, Burnett (Taylor), Berry, Carter (Jones), Nugent, Otto
Att: 3,792

1992–93
Preliminary rounds
1 December v Gillingham (h) 4–1
Heald, Warren, Kitchen, Bellamy, Whitbread (Day), Hales, Howard, Achampong, Livett, Jones, Cooper
Scorers: Achampong, Day, Cooper, Livett
Att: 1,677
15 December v Fulham (a) 2–2
Heald, Warren, Ludden, Bellamy, Kitchen, Hales, Lakin, Carter (Tomlinson), Jones, Cooper, Otto (Zoricich)
Scorer: Jones 2
Att: 1,267
Second round: 12 January v Wrexham (h) 4–1
Heald, Warren, Ludden, Bellamy, Kitchen, Benstock, Howard, Carter (Day), Taylor (Otto), Jones, Harvey
Scorers: Carter, Harvey, Jones, Howard
Att: 1,513
Third round: 16 February v Swansea City (a) 0–1
Heald, Howard, Ludden, Bellamy, Whitbread, Hackett, Ryan, Achampong, Carter,
Cooper, Otto
Att: 3,339

1993–94
Second round: 21 December v AFC Bournemouth (a) 1–1
Newell, Hendon, Ludden, Hackett, Bellamy, Cockerill, Bogie, Carter (Kitchen), Barnett, Cooper (Gamble), West
Scorer: Barnett
After extra-time, Orient won 5–3 on penalties. The O's penalties, all of which were converted, were taken by Ian Bogie, Glenn Cockerill, Ian Hendon, Warren Hackett and Gary Bellamy.
Att: 1,383
Third round: 11 January v Brentford (h) 1–0
Newell, Hendon, Ludden, Hackett, Bellamy, Howard, Cockerill, Bogie, Barnett, Carter, West
Scorer: Ludden
Att: 3,683
Southern area semi-final: 8 February v Swansea City (h) 0–2
Newell, Hendon, Ludden, Howard, Bellamy, Cockerill, Bogie (Putney), Carter, Barnett (Cooper), Taylor, West
Att: 7,010

Auto Windscreens Shield

1994–95
First round: 27 September v Colchester United (a) 0–1
Heald, Warren (Barnett), Austin, Purse, Howard, Hague, Putney, Cockerill, Carter, West, Martin (Lakin)
Att: 1,486
18 October v Fulham (h) 5–2
Heald, Howard (Warren), Austin, Bellamy, Hendon, Lakin, Bogie, Cockerill, Purse (Carter), West, Dempsey
Scorers: Purse, Dempsey, West 3 (1 pen)
Att: 1,282
Second round: 29 November v Fulham (h) 1–0
Heald, Hendon, Austin, Bellamy, Howard, Brooks, Cockerill, Barnett, Purse (Bogie), West (Warren), Carter
Scorer: West
Att: 1,757
Southern area quarter-final: Jan 10 v Bristol Rovers (h) 0–0
After extra-time, Orient won 4–3 on penalties. Bogie, Dempsey, Barnett and Brooks all converted and Hendon missed his kick.
Heald, Howard, Austin, Purse, Hague, Hendon, Brooks, Carter, Bogie, Warren (Barnett), Dempsey

Southern area semi-final: 31 January v Shrewsbury Town (h) 2–1
Heald, Hendon, Howard, Bellamy, Purse, Austin, Barnett, Bogie (Gray), Carter, Warren, Dempsey
Scorers: Warren, Brooks
Att: 2,913

Southern areas Final (first leg): 28 February v Birmingham City (a) 0–1
Heald, Hendon, Dempsey, Bellamy, Purse, Austin, Barnett (Warren), Bogie, Cockerill, Carter, West
Att: 24,002

Southern area Final (second leg): 14 March 1995 V Birmingham City (h) 2–3
Heald, Hendon, Austin, Bellamy, Purse, Bogie, Cockerill, Dempsey, McGleish, West (Warren), Read (Hague)
Scorers: Purse, McGleish
Att: 10,830

1995–96
First round: 17 October v Swansea City (a) 0–0
Caldwell, Warren, Stanislaus, Bellamy, Hendon, McCarthy (Baker), Chapman, Lakin, A. Kelly, Inglethorpe, Hanson
Att: 1,562
7 November v Shrewsbury Town (h) 1–3
Fearon, Hendon, Austin, Bellamy, McCarthy, Cockerill, Brooks (Baker), Chapman, A. Kelly, L. Williams, Hanson (Purse)
Scorer: Hendon
Att: 1,437

1996–97
First round: 10 December v Luton Town (a) 1–2
Weaver, Hendon, Naylor, Joseph, Warren, Arnott (Inglethorpe), Ling, Chapman, Channing, McGleish, West
Scorer: Ling
Att: 1,594

1997–98
First round: 9 December v Colchester United (h) 1–0
Mackenzie, Channing, Naylor, Warren, Clark, Smith, Ling, Inglethorpe, Griffiths (Simpson), Harris (Hanson), Baker
Scorer: Inglethorpe
Att: 933
Second round: 6 January v AFC Bournemouth (a) 0–2
Hyde, Channing, Naylor, Smith, R. Joseph, Bennett (Baker), Pitcher, Cooper, Richards (Hanson), Griffiths, Simpson (Harris)
Att: 1,732

1998–99
First round: 8 December v Peterborough United (a) 0–3
Mackenzie, Canham, Morrison (Curran), Warren, Martin, Downer, Brown, Inglethorpe, Baker, Maskell, Watts
Att: 1,801

1999–2000
First round: 8 December v Reading (a) 0–1
Bayes, Walschaerts, Ampadu, Hicks (Rowbotham), Downer, Clark, McGhee, Martin (M. Joseph), Brkovic (McLean), Richards, Christie.
Att: 1,561

LDV Vans Trophy

2000–01
First round: Bye
Second round: 9 January v Wycombe Wanderers (h) 0–2
Bayes, Joseph, Smith (Martin), McGhee, (Mansley), Lockwood, Walchaerts, McElholm, Brkovic, Houghton, Opara
Att: 946

2001–02
First round: 16 October v Dagenham & Redbridge (a) 2–3
The match ended 2–2 after extra-time. Dagenham gained victory on the golden-goal rule when Goodwin headed in from a corner on 102 minutes.
Morris, McElholm (Canham), Smith, McGhee, Herrera, Beall, Minton, Harris, Martin, Watts (Ibehre), McLean (Constantine)
Scorers: Smith, McLean
Att: 2,642

2002–03
First round: 23 October v Peterborough United (h) 3–2
Morris, Barnard, Lockwood, Smith, Iriekpen, Miller, Canham, Martin, Toner (Harris),Thorpe (Watts), Hatcher (Ibehre)
Scorers: Iriekpen, Barnard, Lockwood
Att: 953
Second round: 12 November v AFC Bournemouth (a) 0–1
Morris, Barnard, Lockwood, Smith, Iriekpen, Miller, Harris, Toner, Martin (Brazier), Hatcher (Watts), Nugent
Att: 2,724

2003–04
First round: 15 October v Dagenham & Redbridge (a) 1–4
Harrison, Hunt, Peters, McGhee, Lockwood, Purser, Ebdon, McCormack (Jones), Forbes (Thorpe), Ibehre, Tate (Alexander)
Scorer: Lockwood (pen)
Att: 1,857

2004–05
First round: 28 September v Woking (a) 3–0
Morris, D. Barnard, Lockwood, Simpson (Hunt), Carlisle (Duncan), Steele (Alexander), Miller, Ibehre, Peters, Newey, Saah
Scorers: Ibehre, Saah, Miller
Att: 1,166

Second round: 2 November v Cambridge United (a) 2–0
Morris, D. Barnard, Lockwood, Mackie, Zakuani, Hunt, Saah, Carlisle (Duncan), Newey, Scott, (Wardley), Ibehre
Scorers: Ibehre, Carlisle
Att: 1,812
Third round: 30 November v Walsall (h) 1–0
Morris, D. Barnard (Duncan), Lockwood, Mackie, White, Simpson, Saah, Newey, Carlisle, Barnard L, (Wardley), Ibehre (Scott)
Mark Wright (og)
Att: 1,452
Southern area semi-final: 25 January v Bristol Rovers (h) 1–2
Morris, D. Barnard, Lockwood, Miller, White, Mackie, Hunt, Simpson, Scott, Steele, Alexander
Att: 1,846

2005–06
South first round: 18 October v Yeovil Town (h) 2–0
Morris, Miller, Palmer, Zakuani, Hanson, Easton, McMahon, Carlisle (Demetriou), Alexander, Echanomi, Duncan (Saah)
Scorers: Hanson, Alexander
Att: 958
South second round: 28 November v Oxford United (a) 0–1
Morris (Garner), Barnard (Demetriou), Palmer, Hanson, Mackie, Easton, McMahon, Carlisle, Ibehre (Alexander), Steele, Duncan

Leading goalscorers

40 goals or more

Player	*Lge*	*FAC*	*FLC*	*Total*	*Total games played*
Tommy Johnston	121	2	0	123	123
Ken Facey	74	5	0	79	323
Ted Crawford	67	6	-	73	212
Kevin Godfrey	63	5	4	72	298(+33)
Mickey Bullock	65	1	3	69	297(+10)
Richard McFadden	66	2	-	68	142
Steve Castle	56	6	5	67	282(+24)
Billy Rees	58	8	-	66	198
Reg Tricker	60	3	-	63	137
Carl Griffiths	51	6	3	60	128(+9)
Peter Kitchen	49	9	2	60	127(+5)
Dave Dunmore	54	2	2	58	168
Dennis Pacey	46	12	-	58	135
Ian Juryeff	45	7	3	55	125(+5)
Mark Cooper *	48	4	2	54	135(+35)
Barrie Fairbrother	41	7	2	50	193(+18)
Alan Comfort	46	1	1	48	167(+6)
Colin West	43	2	2	47	145(+10)
Ronnie Heckman	38	6	-	44	92
Frank Neary	44	0	-	44	81
Matthew Lockwood	40	2	2	43	320(+9)
Gary Alexander	40	1	0	41	132(+9)
Joe Mayo	36	3	1	40	171(+6)

* Mark Cooper's record includes four appearances and three goals in promotion Play-off matches in 1988–89, and Matthew Lockwoods' record includes six appearances and one goal in Play-off matches in 1998–99 and 2000–01.

Most goals in a season: League, FA Cup and League Cup

Player	Season	Division	League	FA Cup	FL Cup	Total	Total apps made that season
Tommy Johnston	1957–58	2	35	1	-	36	32
Ron Heckman	1955–56	3 South	23	6	-	29	40
Peter Kitchen	1977–78	2	21	7	1	29	53
Tommy Johnston	1956–57	2	27	0	-	27	43
Edmund Crawford	1935–36	3 South	23	2	-	25	46
Frank Neary	1948–49	3 South	25	0	-	25	41
Ken Facey	1954–55	3 South	22	1	-	23	46
Johnny Hartburn	1955–56	3 South	20	3	-	23	44
Charlie Fletcher	1931–32	3 South	20	2	-	22	44
Carl Griffiths	1997–98	3	18	1	3	22	37 (+2)

Players who scored four or more goals in a game

Five goals in a game

Player	Opponent	Venue	Date
Ronnie Heckman	Lovells Athletic (FAC)	(h)	19 Nov 1955

Four goals in a game (All League)

Player	Opponent	Venue	Date
Walter Leigh	Bradford City	(h)	13 Apr 1906
Albert Pape	Oldham Athletic	(h)	1 Sep 1924
Dennis Pacey	Colchester United	(h)	30 Apr 1953
Stan Morgan	Exeter City	(h)	26 Mar 1955
Johnny Hartburn	QPR	(h)	3 Mar 1956
Len Julians	Middlesbrough	(h)	28 Sep 1957
Tommy Johnston	Rotherham United	(h)	25 Dec 1957
Joe Elwood	Bristol City	(h)	29 Nov 1958
Eddie Brown	Sunderland	(h)	30 Mar 1959
Peter Kitchen	Millwall	(h)	21 Apr 1984
Steve Castle	Rochdale	(a)	5 May 1986

Orient's hat-trick countdown

Football League

Player	Opponent	Venue	Date
I. Evenson	Chesterfield	(h)	23 Sep 1905
W. Martin	Wolves	(h)	22 Dec 1906
W. Martin	Stockport County	(h)	28 Dec 1907
G. Scott	Leicester Fosse	(h)	30 Sep 1911
R. Dalrymple	Bristol City	(h)	25 Dec 1913
C. Ives	South Shields	(h)	27 Sep 1919
J. Tonner	Rotherham	(h)	30 Dec 1922
T. Green	Nelson	(h)	1 Sep 1923
D. Cock	Stoke City	(h)	13 Mar 1926
R. Dennison	Bristol City	(h)	8 Oct 1927
R. Turnbull	Middlesbrough	(h)	24 Nov 1928
J. Campbell	Torquay United	(a)	18 Jan 1930
J. Fowler (1 pen)	Coventry City	(h)	6 Sep 1930
R. Tricker	Bristol Rovers	(h)	20 Dec 1930
D. Imrie	Northampton Town	(a)	21 Apr 1932
D. Morris	Cardiff City	(h)	18 Nov 1933
D. Halliday	Southend United	(h)	20 Jan 1934
D. Halliday	Aldershot	(h)	10 Feb 1934
D. Halliday	Exeter City	(h)	24 Mar 1934
D. Halliday	Bristol Rovers	(h)	15 Dec 1934
T. Foster	Brighton & Hove A	(h)	6 Apr 1935
E. Crawford	Luton Town	(h)	31 Aug 1935
E. Crawford	Northampton Town	(h)	5 Oct 1935
E. Crawford	Southend United	(h)	1 Feb 1936
V. Farrell	Brighton & Hove A	(h)	25 Apr 1936
J. Fletcher	Bournemouth	(h)	9 Sep 1937
R. Williams	Southend United	(h)	22 Oct 1938
W. Pullen	Bristol City	(h)	7 Dec 1946
F. Neary (1 pen)	Torquay United	(h)	1 May 1948
F. Neary	Notts County	(h)	6 Nov 1948
G. Sutherland	Ipswich Town	(h)	17 Sep 1949
G. Sutherland	Ipswich Town	(a)	21 Jan 1950
J. Blair	Torquay United	(h)	10 Mar 1951
W. Rees	Exeter City	(h)	1 Sep 1951
D. Pacey	Bournemouth	(h)	29 Aug 1953

Football League

Player	Opponent	Venue	Date
V. Groves	Exeter City	(a)	6 Nov 1954
V. Groves	Torquay United	(a)	18 Dec 1954
J. Hartburn	Shrewsbury Town	(h)	22 Jan 1955
W. Rees	Walsall	(a)	5 May 1955
V. Groves	Colchester United	(h)	8 Sep 1955
K. Facey	Swindon Town	(h)	15 Oct 1955
K. Facey	Crystal Palace	(h)	12 Nov 1955
R. Heckman	ShrewsburyTown	(a)	3 Dec 1955
R. Heckman	QPR	(h)	3 Mar 1956
T. Johnston	Aldershot	(h)	17 Mar 1956
T. Johnston	Swansea Town	(h)	26 Oct 1957
T. Johnston	Grimsby Town	(h)	21 Dec 1957
T. Johnston	Bristol City	(h)	11 Jan 1958
P. Woosnam	Barnsley	(h)	6 Sep 1958
L. Julians	Middlesbrough	(h)	15 Nov 1958
J. Elwood	Charlton Athletic	(h)	11 Apr 1959
E. Brown	Middlesbrough	(h)	31 Oct 1959
M. Graham	Walsall	(a)	2 Sep 1961
D. Dunmore	Swansea Town	(a)	30 Dec 1961
E. Phillips	Portsmouth	(h)	22 Aug 1964
M. Jones	Doncaster Rovers	(h)	14 Apr 1967
C. Holton (1 pen)	Mansfield Town	(h)	12 May 1967
I. Bowyer	Cardiff City	(h)	21 Aug 1971
P. Kitchen	Mansfield Town	(h)	3 Dec 1977
P. Kitchen (1 pen)	Sheffield United	(h)	27 Mar 1978
T. Cunningham	Exeter City	(a)	18 Feb 1984
K. Godfrey	Bolton Wanderers	(h)	9 Apr 1985
A. Hull	Colchester United	(h)	15 Oct 1988
M Cooper	Scunthorpe United	(h)	13 May 1989
G. Berry	Bury	(h)	24 Mar 1992
T. Howard (1 pen)	Mansfield Town	(h)	28 Nov 1992
R. Taylor	Exeter City	(h)	23 Jan 1993
R. Otto	Brighton & Hove A	(a)	6 Feb 1993
M. Warren	Peterborough United	(h)	4 Feb 1995
C. West (1 pen)	Cardiff City	(h)	10 Feb 1996
S. Clark	Doncaster Rovers	(a)	2 Sep 1997
C. Griffiths	Doncaster Rovers	(h)	28 Dec 1997
C. Griffiths (2 pens)	Chester City	(a)	28 Dec 1999
W Purser	Boston United	(h)	5 Apr 2003
L Steele	Lincoln City	(a)	23 Oct 2004

FA Cup

Player	Opponent	Venue	Date
D. Pacey	Gorleston	(a*)	3 Dec 1951
W. Rees	Wrexham	(h)	19 Dec 1951
D. Pacey	Tranmere Rovers	(h)	14 Jan 1954
T. Richards	Brighton & Hove A	(h)	14 Nov 1998

* played at Highbury

Football League Cup

Player	Opponent	Venue	Date
M. Graham	Chester City	(h)	17 Oct 1962
G. Waites	Chester City	(h)	17 Oct 1962

Auto Windscreens Shield

Player	Opponent	Venue	Date
C. West (1 pen)	Fulham	(h)	18 Oct 1994

Most hat-tricks in League and Cup

David Halliday	4
Tommy Johnston	4
Ted Crawford	3
Vic Groves	3
Dennis Pacey	3
Billy Rees	3

Wartime hat-tricks or better

Four Goals

Player	*Opponent*	*Venue*	*Season*
A. Layton	Brentford (friendly)	(h)	1917–18
G. Hewitt	Fulham	(h)	1943–44
Three Goals			
R. Turnbull	Croydon Common	(a)	1915–16
J. Blake	Portsmouth	(h)	1916–17
J. Thompson	Brentford (friendly)	(h)	1917–18
R. Shankly	Southend	(h)	1939–40
R. Shankly	Brighton	(h)	1939–40
H. Smith	QPR	(h)	1939–40
C. McNeil	Arsenal	(h)	1940–41
M. Armstrong	Watford	(a)	1942–43
G. Hewitt	Fulham	(h)	1942–43
T. Ford	Fulham	(a)	1943–44
J. Younger	QPR	(a)	1944–45
A. Robson	Walsall	(a)	1945–46

Note: Turnbull, Blake, Thompson, McNeil, Armstrong, Hewitt, Ford, Younger and Robson were all guest players. Both Turnbull and Thompson played for Orient in later years.
Layton, Shankly and Smith were on the O's books.

Most productive decade for hat-tricks

The most productive decade for hat-tricks was the 1950s when 24 were recorded in the League and FA Cup by Orient players, followed by 16 in the 1930s. In the 1990s (up to 1998–99) 10 League and Cup hat-tricks were scored.

Topping the hat-trick chart, along with David Halliday, Tommy Johnston scored three goals in a match four times for Orient.

Orient's Captains 1905–2006 (excluding the war years)

The following list is of O's players who were appointed captain of the team. Also listed are those players who took over as temporary captain while the usual skipper was injured and those who were made captain for a special game. Those known players are listed after the main list.

Player	*Seasons*
Ike Evenson	1905–1906
Dave Buchanan	1906–1907
William Henderson	1907–1908
Herbert Reason	1908–1910
Mark Bell	1909–1910
Walter Whittaker	1909–1910
Fred Bevan	1910–1913
Fred Parker	1913–1915
Joe Nicholls	1919–1921
Jimmy Hugall	1920–1921
Samuel Tonner	1921–1923
Arthur Wood	1924–1927
Bert Rosier	1926–1927
John Galbraith	1927–1929
Ernie Morley	1928–1929
Jack Fowler	1930–1932
David Jones	1932–1933
William Fellowes	1933–1935
Frank Searle	1935–1938
Doug Hunt	1946–1947
William Stroud	1947–1948
James Richardson	1948 only
Arthur Banner	1948–1950
Tommy Brown	1950–1951
William Rees	1951 only
Tommy Brown	1952 only
Stan Aldous	1952–1957
Ken Facey	1957–1958
Eddie Baily	1959 only
Ken Facey	1959–1961
Stan Charlton	1961–1964
Andy Nelson	1965 only
Jimmy Scott	1965 only
John Smith	1965–1966
Brian Whitehouse	1966–1967
Brian Wood	1967–1968
Terry Mancini	1968 only
Jimmy Bloomfield	1969 only
Terry Mancini	1969–1971
Peter Bennett	1971–1972
Peter Allen	1972–1973
Tom Walley	1972 1973
Peter Allen	1973–1975
Tom Walley	1975–1976
Phil Hoadley	1976–1977
Glenn Roeder	1977 only
Phil Hoadley	1977–1978

Player	*Seasons*
Tony Grealish	1978–1979
Tommy Taylor	1979–1982
Bobby Fisher	1981–1982
Mervyn Day	1981–1983
Tommy Cunningham	1983–1985
David Peach	1982–1983
Bill Roffey	1982–1983
John Sitton	1985–1987
Tommy Cunningham	1986–1987
Kevin Hales	1987–1990
Paul Ward	1988–1989
John Sitton	1988–1991
Steve Castle	1990–1992
Gary Bellamy	1992–1993
Adrian Whitbread	1992–1993
Trevor Putney	1993–1994
Colin West	1993–1994
Glenn Cockerill	1994–1995
Ian Hendon	1994–1995
Darren Purse	1994–1995
Glenn Cockerill	1995–1996
Alvin Martin	1996–1997
Dominic Naylor	1996–1998
Dean Smith	1998–2003
Andrew Harris	2003
David McGhee	2003–2004

This is a list of known players who took over when the captain was injured or for a special game:

Billy Hind	pre-World War One
George Scott	pre-World War One
Billy Broadbent	1920s
David Halliday	1930s
Harold Taylor	mid–late 1930s
Ledger Ritson	1940s
Phil McKnight	1950s
George Wright	late 1950s
Cliff Holton	late 1960s
Barry Dyson	1969–1970 plus early 1970s
Terry Howard	early 1990s
Keith Day	early 1990s
Simon Clark	late 1990s
Greg Heald	2003
Matthew Lockwood	2003 & 2004–05
Alan White	2004–05
Michael Simpson	2004–05
John Mackie	2005–06

O's Top League Appearances

200 plus League appearances

Peter Allen	424 (+8)
Arthur Wood	373
Stan Charlton	367
Fred Parker	336
Terry Howard *	327 (+5)
Bill Roffey	324 (+4)
Bobby Fisher	308 (+6)
Stan Aldous	302
Ken Facey	301
Sid Bishop	296
Kevin Hales *	289 (+15)
Matthew Lockwood	286 (+9)
Ray Goddard	278
John Galbraith	277
Mickey Bullock	267 (+10)
Pat Welton	263
Kevin Godfrey	255 (+30)
Phil Hoadley	255
John Townrow	253
Dean Smith *	245
Steve Castle *	244 (+19)
Tommy Dixon	234
Nigel Gray	233
Tommy Taylor	228 (+2)
John Jackson	226
Mick Jones	223 (+5)
Matthew Joseph	223 (+5)
Les Blizzard	222
Jim Johnston	218
Phil White	217
George Scott	205
Cyril Lea	205
Ted Crawford	200

Kevin Hales

Note:
Hales and Howard's totals include four Play-off matches, Castle's total includes six (+1) Play off-matches, Dean Smith's record includes six Play-off matches and Matthew Joseph's record includes four Play-off matches, Matthew Lockwood's total includes six Play-off games.

Only two players have appeared in more than 400 Football League, FA Cup and League Cup games for the O's.

Peter Allen	473 (+8)
Stan Charlton	408

Kevin Godfrey

Players to have played 10 or more seasons for the O's

Player	*Period*	*No of Seasons*	*Total Apps**
Peter Allen	1965–66 to 1977–78	13	473 (+8)
Sid Bishop	1953–54 to 1964–65	12	323
Fred Parker	1907–08 to 1921–22	11	350
Stan Charlton	1952–53 to 1955–56		
	1958–59 to 1964–65	11	408
Phil White	1953–54 to 1963–64	11	233
Bill Roffey	1973–74 to 1983–84	11	358 (+6)
Kevin Godfrey	1977–78 to 1987–88	11	298 (+33)
Billy Bower	1905–06 to 1914–15	10	176
Arthur Wood	1921–22 to 1930–31	10	395
John Galbraith	1921–22 to 1930–31	10	296
Ken Facey	1952–53 to 1961–62	10	323
Bobby Fisher	1973–74 to 1982–83	10	353 (+7)
Kevin Hales	1983–84 to 1992–93	10	337 (+16)
Lee Harvey	1983–84 to 1992–93	10	162 (+52)

** (League and major Cups only)*

The Players from 1939–40

All playing records (appearances and goals) were expunged from the record books for these three matches and previously the names of these players were never listed as having been Orientals. Below we list the team line-ups and profile those six 39ers, who never appeared in the Football League for the O's.

Team line ups 1939–40, Football League Division Three South

26 August 1939 (H) v Ipswich Town 2–2 Attendance: 11,018
Ellis, Rumbold, Bungay, Taylor, McNeil, Black, Gore, McFadyen, Williams, Hann, Willshaw
Scorers: Gore, Williams.

31 August 1939 (H) v Southend United 0–0 Attendance: 6,012
Ellis, Rumbold, Bungay, Taylor, McNeil, Black, Gore, McFadyen, Williams, Hann, Willshaw

2 September 1939 (A) v Watford 1–1 Attendance: 4,850
Ellis, Rumbold, Bungay, Allum, McNeil, Black, Gore, McFadyen, Williams, Smith, Willshaw.
Scorer: Williams

Division Three South League table as at 2 September 1939.

	P	W	D	L	F	A	Pts
Reading	3	2	1	0	8	2	5
Exeter City	3	2	1	0	5	3	5
Notts County	2	2	0	0	6	3	4
Ipswich Town	3	1	2	0	5	3	4
Brighton & HA	3	1	2	0	5	4	4
Cardiff City	3	2	0	1	5	5	4
Crystal Palace	3	2	0	1	3	3	4
Bournemouth & BA	3	1	1	1	14	4	3
Mansfield Town	3	1	1	1	8	8	3
Bristol City	3	1	1	1	5	5	3
Norwich City	3	1	1	1	4	4	3
Torquay United	3	0	3	0	4	4	3
CLAPTON ORIENT	3	0	3	0	3	3	3
Southend United	3	1	1	1	3	3	3
Walsall	3	1	1	1	3	3	3
Queen's Park Rangers	3	0	2	1	4	5	2
Watford	3	0	2	1	4	5	2
Northampton Town	3	1	0	2	2	12	2
Aldershot	3	0	1	2	3	5	2
Swindon Town	3	0	1	2	2	4	1
Port Vale	2	0	1	1	0	1	1
Bristol Rovers	3	0	1	2	2	7	1

The six players never profiled before are:

Leonard Hector ALLUM (1939–44)

Right wing-half Len Allum was born in Reading on 16 July 1907. He joined the O's from Chelsea and played in only the third match of the abandoned season. After spells as an amateur with Maidenhead United, Fulham and Reading, the 5ft 9in and 10st England Amateur international turned professional with Chelsea in May 1932, making a total of 102 senior appearances, scoring twice. Allum played 109 wartime matches for the O's between 1939–44. He died in Reading on 15 May 1980, aged 72.

Season	League		Total	
	Apps	Gls	Apps	Gls
1939–40	1	0	1	0
	1	0	1	0

Reginald Harold BUNGAY (1939–40)

Born in Reading on 5 February 1911, Reg Bungay, a 5ft 9in and 11st left-back, looked a solid defender who played in all three of the abandoned matches. He started off his career with the Huntley & Palmers Works team before moving to Oxford City and then on to Tottenham Hotspur in 1931, and while at White Hart Lane he played for Spurs' nursery team, Haywards Sports, who were based in Enfield. It was while with Plymouth Argyle, who he joined in 1934, that he made his League debut versus West Ham United in September 1933. After just three senior appearances, he moved to Bristol City in June 1935 but moved on after nine League matches, joining Mansfield Town in June 1936, and it was with the Stags that he came to the fore, playing in 99 senior matches and scoring six goals. Bungay made four wartime appearances for the O's in 1939–40. He died in Plymouth during October 1986, aged 75.

Season	League		Total	
	Apps	Gls	Apps	Gls
1939–40	3	0	3	0
	3	0	3	0

John ELLIS (1939–40)

Goalkeeper John Ellis, who stood at 6ft tall and weighed 12st 5lb, was born in Tyldesley, Lancs, on 25 January 1912, and he joined the O's from Hull City in July 1939 and appeared in all three abandoned matches in preference to Stan Hall. Ellis commenced his career with Winsford United in the Cheshire County League, and after a short spell as an amateur with West Bromwich Albion he joined Wolverhampton Wanderers in February 1931 and made 21 First Division appearances.

In July 1934 Ellis moved to Bristol Rovers, and he was the man between the sticks on 13 April 1936, when he conceded 12 (yes, 12) goals against Luton Town in a Division Three South fixture at Kenilworth Road, witnessed by an Easter Monday crowd of 14,296. It was Joe Payne who bagged 10 of the goals, with George Martin – later to become a Luton manager – and Fred Roberts who netting the other two goals. During the 1935–36 season, he conceded 96 goals for Bristol Rovers.

In May 1938 Ellis moved on to Hull City and made 34 senior appearances. During wartime, Ellis made three appearances for the O's in 1939–40 and two appearances in 1941–42. After the war, he joined Stalybridge Celtic and later played for Mossley. He later became manager with one of his previous clubs, Winsford United, and afterwards he was a scout with Leeds United. Ellis died in Tyldesley during January 1994, aged 86.

At his peak, John Ellis was a fine custodian but would be remembered by football historians only as the 'keeper that Joe Payne smashed 10 goals past.

Season	League		Total	
	Apps	Gls	Apps	Gls
1939–40	3	0	3	0
	3	0	3	0

Leslie HANN (1939–40)

Leslie Hann was born in Tynemouth, Northumberland, on 3 June 1911 and played in two of the expunged matches. He started off with the Windy Nook club, West Ham United, on trial, the Ashington, Blyth Spartans and Felling Red Star FC before joining Accrington Stanley in March 1937, making 29 League appearances and scoring once. The 5ft 8in and 10st 10lb inside-forward was described at the time of signing for the O's on 13 July 1939 as an industrious and workman-like player. Hann played in just two wartime matches before leaving the club. He guested for Walsall in August 1942 and died in Gateshead during August 1988, aged 77.

Season	League		Total	
	Apps	Gls	Apps	Gls
1939–40	2	0	2	0
	2	0	2	0

William McFADYEN (1939–40)

Without doubt, Willie McFadyen was the most famous of the players in the O's squad for the new 1939–40 season. A real hot shot, Scottish forward, McFadyen, who stood at just 5ft 9in and weighed 11st 7lb, played in all three matches at inside-right. Born at Overton, near Wishaw, in Scotland on 23 June 1904, he started as a junior with Wishaw YMCA before signing for Motherwell in 1921. After a short loan spell with Bo'ness FC in 1922–23, he joined Clyde in October 1924.

McFadyen returned to Motherwell in March 1924 and had a tremendous goalscoring record of 251 Scottish League goals from just 278 appearances, which included a remarkable 52 goals from 38 Scottish League appearances in 1931–32 in their Championship-winning side, which stood as a record in Scottish senior football for many years and is still a Motherwell record. He was capped for Scotland against Wales on 4 October 1933 and against Austria on 29 November 1933, scoring in both matches. He appeared in Motherwell's losing Scottish Cup Final teams of 1931 and 1933.

While with Motherwell, the Scottish side played a series of annual friendlies at the O's Lea Bridge Road ground, and in one of those matches he netted four goals for the Scottish side in their 6–4 win; veteran David Halliday hit a hat-trick for the Londoners.

McFadyen was transferred to Huddersfield Town for a large fee on 18 December 1936, where he netted 19 goals from 48 League matches. While with the Yorkshire club, he appeared in the 1938 FA Cup Final at Wembley, losing to a last-minute goal by Preston North End's Mutch.

Thirty-five-year-old McFadyen joined the O's on a free transfer on 17 May 1939. He made just three wartime appearances for them, before guesting for Blackpool, Huddersfield Town, Nottingham Forest and Rochdale, while serving with the RAF during the hostilities.

After the war, he held a managerial position with Arbroath. He was appointed as manager of Dundee United in October 1945 and spent almost nine years at Tannadice until resigning in August 1954, when the club found themselves second from bottom in the B Division. On leaving full-time football, he became a qualified physiotherapist and chiropodist until his death in his native Scotland during 1971, aged 73.

Season	League		Total	
	Apps	Gls	Apps	Gls
1939–40	3	0	3	0
	3	0	3	0

John Law McNEIL (1939–40)

Johnny McNeil, who could play either at centre-half or as a centre-forward, was born in Inverkeithing, Scotland, during 1906. He started with Scottish junior side Bo'ness and was then with Mussleburgh Bruntonians FC. After a spell with Heart of Midlothian, he moved south of the border with Portsmouth on 6 December 1928, making 14 senior appearances and scoring seven goals, his first against Manchester United in a 3–0 win on 22 December.

McNeil moved to Reading in January 1930, and in three years he played 42 senior matches, scoring five goals. He then drifted to Guildford City in September 1931 and later returned to Hearts and Inverness Caledonian before moving to Plymouth Argyle in September 1934. During his five-year stay at Home Park, he made 145 senior appearances, scoring 13 goals. He moved to Orient in June 1939 and played in all three matches for the O's in 1939–40 and a further five wartime matches. He scored four goals in two matches during 1940–41. Later, he guested for Plymouth and was appointed manager of Welsh side Merthyr Town before he was appointed as manager of Torquay United in June 1947, where he was in charge until March 1950, his managerial record being: P158 W44 D33 L81.

McNeil was appointed manager of Bury on 1 March 1950 before leaving in November 1953. His managerial record reads: P158 W44 D33 L81.

Season	League		Total	
	Apps	Gls	Apps	Gls
1939–40	3	0	3	0
	3	0	3	0

The World War Two results, goalscorers, tables and players

A special thank you to four gentlemen for the supply of most of the statistics, League tables and some of the player details for the sections of the O's in the war years, namely:
Ian Nannestad, editor of the *Soccer History Magazine.*
Peter Holme, researcher at the Football Museum in Preston.
Andy Porter, historian of Tottenham Hotspur Football Club.
Peter Kungler for the Rec. Sport Soccer Statistics Foundation.

Clapton Orient appearances and goals, wartime football, between 1939–40 and 1945–46
1939–40 (League and Cup)
The season was spilt into two sections: South 'A' Division and South 'D' Division between October 1939 and June 1940. During April the O's played in the League Cup.

Appearances: D. J. Astley* 11, S.C. Barnes 1, F.L. Bartlett 34, R.W. Black 29, R.H. Bungay 1, F.W. Chadwick* 1, H. Collier* 1, F.W. Dawes* 3, J.S. Devine* 4, D.W. Flack* 2, C.A. Fletcher* 30, J.L. Forder* 1, A. Gage* 1, L.F. Gore 3, S.A. Hall 30, S.G. Hobbins 2, A. Ingle* 1, J. Jobling* 19, W.H. Layton* 1, A. Mulraney* 1, E. Perry* 1, H. Pitts* 1, D. Pryde* 1, F.H. Rist* 31, G. Rumbold 31, C. Sargent* 1, R. Shankly 24, H.M. Smith 32, R. Swinfen* 1, S. Tanner* 2, H. Taylor 27, D.W.J. Thomas* 4, E.W. Toser* 1, F.A. Tully 32, E. Vaux* 2, W. Whittaker* 1, G. Willshaw 26, A. Wilson* 1, R.C.A. Wright* 2.
Goalscorers: 24 Shankly, 11 Willshaw, 10 Smith, 6 Fletcher, 5 Astley, 4 Thomas, 3 Tully, 2 Perry, 1 Devine.
*Played as a guest player

South Regional Championships 1939–40

Group 'A'

	P	W	D	L	F	A	Pts
Arsenal	18	13	4	1	62	22	30
West Ham United	18	12	1	5	57	33	25
Millwall	18	8	5	5	46	38	21
Watford	18	9	3	6	44	38	21
Norwich City	18	7	6	5	41	36	20
Charlton Athletic	18	8	1	9	61	58	17
Crystal Palace	18	5	3	10	39	56	13
CLAPTON ORIENT	18	5	3	10	28	60	13
Tottenham Hotspur	18	5	2	11	37	43	12
Southend United	18	4	0	14	30	61	9

Group 'D' 1939–40

	P	W	D	L	F	A	Pts
Crystal Palace	18	13	1	4	64	30	27
Queen's Park Rangers	18	10	3	5	38	28	23
Watford	18	7	7	4	41	29	21
Southend United	18	8	3	7	41	37	19
CLAPTON ORIENT	18	7	3	8	33	45	17
Aldershot	18	7	3	8	38	36	17
Norwich City	17	6	4	7	31	31	16
Bournemouth & BA	17	7	2	8	38	40	16
Reading	18	6	2	10	31	42	14
Brighton & HA	18	2	4	12	30	65	8

Those statistics for 1939–40 do not include the three League matches played before the commencement of World War Two, the records for these matches were expunged.

1940–41 (League and League War Cup)
Appearances: M. Armstrong* 1, D.J. Astley* 8, L. Baines* 1, A. Barraclough* 1, F.L. Bartlett 16, ? Bates* 1, R. Bell* 1, R.W. Black 11, J. Burnett* 1, F. Butterworth* 1, H. Collier* 2, H.H. Collin* 2, S.T. Cousins* 1, J. Davie* 1, S.J. Devine* 2, B. Diaper* 1, S. Fieldus* 1, A.N. Fisher* 2, A. Fletcher*2, C.A. Fletcher 12, T. Galley* 1, ? Ghost* 1, I.C. Gillespie* 1, G. Gregory* 1, S.A. Hall 4, ? Houston* 1, G. Hyatt* 1, J. Jobling* 1, L. Jones* 1, D. Levene* 10, F. Levey* 1, G. Lunn* 6, J. McNeil 1, S. Montgomery 2, E. Muttitt* 1, D. Nelson* 1, Payne* 1, J. Pemberton* 1, E. Perry* 1, E. Phypers* 2, J. Raven* 1, J. Rawlings* 6, K.E. Reeves* 1, F.H. Rist* 1, G. Rumbold, 2, C. Sargent* 5, R. Shankly 3, F. Sidness* 1, H. Silver* 4, C. Skeggs* 2, F. Smith 5, H.M. Smith 5, G. Spears 1, J. Sperrin* 1, F.A. Tully 15, R. Wade 2, E. Weightman* 2, R. Williams 1, G. Willshaw 7, W.P. Wright 13.
Goalscorers: League: 3 Shankly, H. Smith, 2 Astley, C. Fletcher, Houston, Willshaw; 1 Gillespie, Gregory, Muttitt, Rawlings, Tully. League War Cup: 1 Astley, Fisher, Fletcher. London Cup: 4 McNeil; 2 C. Fletcher, Rawlings; 1 Fisher.

South Regional Championship
For the 1940–41 season, as mentioned above, in the introduction of this section, the clubs that took part in the Football League were divided into two groups, North

Region and South Region. Clapton Orient were in the Southern group, which comprised of 34 clubs. Because of costs and travelling problems and the dangers of travelling around the country at this time for the clubs, it was not possible to play each team at home and away, so each club played a different number of fixtures.

It was decided by the authorities that the League tables would not be decided on League points but rather on goal average. Unfortunately, Orient ended bottom of the Southern Section with an average of 0.288. However, a number of the London-based clubs and Reading were generally dissatisfied with the way the League had handled matters and decided to breakaway and form their own competition called the London Cup. It was broken into two groups of six teams, and Clapton Orient fell into Group B. The teams played each other both at home and away.

The following are the rankings according to goal average: (not including the London Cup)

	P	W	D	L	F	A Pts
Crystal Palace	27	16	4	7	86	441.954
West Ham United	25	14	6	5	70	391.794
Coventry City	10	5	3	2	28	161.750
Arsenal	19	10	5	4	66	381.736
Cardiff City	24	12	5	7	75	501.500
Reading	26	14	5	7	73	511.431
Norwich City	19	9	2	8	73	551.327
Watford	35	15	6	14	96	731.315
Portsmouth	31	16	2	13	92	711.296
Tottenham Hotspur	23	9	5	9	53	411.293
Millwall	31	16	5	10	73	571.280

	P	W	D	L	F	A Pts
Walsall	32	14	7	11	100	801.250
West Bromwich Albion	28	13	5	10	83	691.202
Leicester City	33	17	5	11	87	731.191
Northampton Town	30	14	3	13	84	711.183
Bristol City	20	10	2	8	55	481.145
Mansfield Town	29	12	6	11	77	681.132
Charlton Athletic	19	7	4	8	37	341.088
Aldershot	24	14	2	8	73	681.073
Brentford	23	9	3	11	51	511.000
Chelsea	23	10	4	9	57	580.981
Birmingham City	16	7	1	8	38	430.883
Fulham	30	10	7	13	62	730.849
Luton Town	35	11	7	17	82	1000.820
Stoke City	36	9	9	18	76	960.791
Queen's Park Rangers	23	8	3	12	47	600.783
Brighton & HA	25	8	7	10	51	750.680
Nottingham Forest	25	7	3	15	50	770.649
Bournemouth & BA	27	9	3	15	59	920.641
Notts County	21	8	3	10	42	660.636
Southend United	29	12	4	13	64	1010.633
Southampton	31	4	4	23	53	1110.477
Swansea Town	10	2	1	7	12	330.364
CLAPTON ORIENT	15	1	3	11	19	660.287

London Cup 1940–41

	P	W	D	L	F	A	Pts
Reading	10	6	4	0	29	8	16
Tottenham Hotspur	10	5	3	2	32	14	13
West Ham United	10	6	1	3	23	19	12
Arsenal	10	5	2	3	38	18	12
Millwall	10	2	1	7	13	26	5
CLAPTON ORIENT	10	0	1	9	9	59	1

The O's only point in the breakaway London Cup was a 3–3 draw at Arsenal.

1941–42 (League and Cup)

Appearances: A.V. Aicken 14, L.H. Allum 18, M. Armstrong* 22, ? Austin* 1, ? Barford 1, S. Barnes 31, F.L. Bartlett 35, ? Beswick* 6, R. W. Black 17, C. E. Brooks 30, ? Brown 1, E. Crawford 34, G.F. Curtis* 1, J. Dryden 15, J. Ellis 2, A.N. Fisher* 1, C.A. Fletcher 28, A. Griffin 7, S.A. Hall 33, ? Hedges* 1, J. Jobling* 1, E.M. Jones* 1, L. Kelly* 6, D. Levene 1, E. Lucas 2, ? McDonald 1, ? Nicholls 1, W. R. O'Dell 21, O. Parry* 1, ? Phillips 1, ? Rankin 1, ? Reynolds 1, G. Rumbold 3, H. Silver 1,G. Summerbee* 1, W. Straus* 2, J. Thorogood* 9, F.A. Tully 24, G.J. Willshaw 16, L.C. Woodroffe 2, W. P. Wright 2.

Goalscorers: League: 9 Armstrong, Willshaw; 4 Crawford, Dryden, Fletcher, O'Dell Tully; 2 Barnes; 1 Bestwick, own-goal. League Cup: Nil. London Cup: 4 Armstrong; 2 Crawford, Fletcher; 1 Dryden, O'Dell.

London League 1941–42

	P	W	D	L	F	A	Pts
Arsenal	30	23	2	5	108	43	48
Portsmouth	30	20	2	8	105	59	42
West Ham U	30	17	5	8	81	44	39
Aldershot	30	17	5	8	85	56	39
Tottenham Hotspur	30	15	8	7	61	41	38
Crystal Palace	30	14	6	10	70	53	34
Reading	30	13	8	9	76	58	34
Charlton Athletic	30	14	5	11	72	64	33
Brentford	30	14	2	14	80	76	30
Queen's Park Rangers	30	11	3	16	52	59	25
Fulham	30	10	4	16	79	99	24
Brighton & HA	30	9	4	17	71	108	22
Chelsea	30	8	4	18	56	88	20
Millwall	30	7	5	18	53	82	19
CLAPTON ORIENT	30	6	4	20	42	94	17
Watford	30	6	4	20	47	114	16

1942–43 League South, League Cup South Group 2

Appearances: A.V. Aicken 1, L. Allum 34, M. Armstrong* 18, S. Barnes 20, F.L. Bartlett 33, R.W. Black 21, W. Boyes* 5, J. Campbell* 5, W. Chitty* 1, E. Crawford 15, G.F. Curtis* 6, W. Dodgin 26, J.G. Dryden* 11, S. Fieldus* 1, A. Fletcher 9, A. Gage* 3, S.A. Hall 16, J. Hewitt 28, J. Iceton 1, A. Irving 1, T.H. Jobson* 1, ? Juby* 1, L. Kelly* 22, E. Lucas 4, J.S. McLuckie* 5, W.R. O'Dell* 15, H. Rickett 13, G. Rumbold 2, ? Saul* 1, J. Scott* 1, R. Shankly* 1, F. Shufflebottom* 8, C. Smith* 1, H.M. Smith 4, D. Summersett 10, G.H. Swinden* 1, F.A. Tully 2, H.Waller* 2, J. Warnes* 1, R. Williams 1, J. Williamson* 2, G.J. Willshaw 20, C.R. Young* 1.

Goalscorers: League: 14 Armstrong; 12 Hewitt; 8 Willshaw; 4 Dryden; 3 Summersett; 2 Crawford, Dodgin, O'Dell; 1 Barnes, Black, Fletcher, Lucas, Saul, Tully, own-goal. League Cup: 2 Hewitt, Summersett; 1 McLuckie, O'Dell.

London League 1942–43

	P	W	D	L	F	A	Pts
Arsenal	28	21	1	6	102	40	43
Tottenham Hotspur	28	16	6	6	68	28	38
Queen's Park Rangers	28	18	2	8	64	49	38
Portsmouth	28	16	3	9	66	52	35
Southampton	28	14	5	9	86	58	33
West Ham U	28	14	5	9	80	66	33
Chelsea	28	14	4	10	52	45	32
Aldershot	28	14	2	12	87	77	30
Brentford	28	12	5	11	64	63	29
Charlton Athletic	28	13	3	12	68	75	29

	P	W	D	L	F	A	Pts
CLAPTON ORIENT	28	11	5	12	54	72	27
Brighton & HA	28	10	5	13	65	73	25
Reading	28	9	6	13	67	74	24
Fulham	28	10	2	16	69	78	22
Crystal Palace	28	7	5	16	49	75	19
Miilwall	28	6	5	17	66	88	17
Watford	28	7	2	19	51	88	16
Luton Town	28	4	6	18	43	100	14

1943–44 (League and Cup)

Appearances: A.V. Aicken 10, L. Allum 29, F. Andrews 3, H. Ayres 18, H. Baines 10. F.L. Bartlett 29, J.J. Blackman* 2, J.M. Boyd* 1, W. Boyes* 2, H. Brophy* 1, B.L. Bryant* 16, J. Campbell* 1, A.G. Chalkley* 1, R.L. Clarke* 2, H.T. Cothliff* 1, E. Crawford 2, G.F. Curtis* 1, J.Daniels* 3, G. Dreyer* 6, J. Dugnolle* 6, T. Ford* 9, J. Fullwood* 1, A. Gage 4, P. Gallacher* 2, I.C. Gillespie* 13, S.R. Hall 1, J. Hewitt 12, F. Jones* 1, G. Kelly* 4, L. Kelly* 30, R. Kirkham* 1, E.S.G.V. Lambert* 1, W. Lane* 1, J. Liddell* 19, A.R. Lowes* 1, E. Lucas 1, G. Ludford* 6, J.S. McLuckie* 18, P. Molloy* 2, E. Muttitt* 2, J. Oakes* 1, W.R. O'Dell* 15, O. Parry* 1, C. Perkins* 1, H. Rickett 31, P. Robinson* 1, A.P. Robson* 3, G. Rumbold 4, L. Salmon* 1, A.W. Saul 10, W. Saunders 1, A. Seddon* 1, H. Sharpe 5, F. Shufflebottom* 1, J. Simpson* 1, C. Smith* 30, J. Stewart* 1, D. Summersett 11, S. Weaver* 2, J. Wilkinson 3.

Goalscorers: League: 8 Bryant; 4 Smith; 3 O'Dell; 2 Ford, Saunders; 1 Ayres, Blackman, Clarke, Crawford, Gillespie, Liddell, Lowes, Lucas, Parry, Robson, Saul, Summersett, own-goal. League Cup: 3 Ford; 1 L. Kelly, Sharpe, Smith, own-goal.

London League 1943–44

	P	W	D	L	F	A	Pts
Tottenham Hotspur	30	19	8	3	71	36	46
West Ham United	30	17	7	6	74	39	41
Queen's Park Rangers	30	14	12	4	69	54	40
Arsenal	30	14	10	6	72	42	38
Crystal Palace	30	16	5	9	75	53	37
Portsmouth	30	16	5	9	68	59	37
Brentford	30	14	7	9	71	51	35
Chelsea	30	16	2	12	79	55	34
Fulham	30	11	9	10	80	73	31
Millwall	30	13	4	13	70	66	30
Aldershot	30	12	6	12	64	73	30
Reading	30	12	3	15	73	62	27
Southampton	30	10	7	13	67	88	27
Charlton Athletic	30	9	7	14	57	73	25
Watford	30	6	8	16	58	80	20
Brighton & HA	30	9	2	19	55	82	20
CLAPTON ORIENT	30	4	3	23	32	87	11
Luton Town	30	3	5	22	42	104	11

1944–45 (League and Cup)

Appearances: G.R. Antonio* 2, L.H. Allum 21, S. Barnes 1, F.L. Bartlett 26, A Beattie* 1, J.J. Blackman* 6, ? Boyd 1, J.H. Browne* 3, W. Bunyan 1, B.D. Colloff 15, F. Cross 3, J. Daniels* 23, A.G. Dawes* 1, J. Dugnolle* 27, T. Ford* 24, G.A. Foreman* 1, R.A. French 1, I.C. Gillespie* 14, S.A. Hall 17, A.B. Harrison 3, J. Jameson* 1, G. Kelly 5, L. Kelly* 3, F.J. Kurz* 1, G. Kitching 1, J. Liddell 24, E.S. Love 2, G.R. Lucas 4, F. Ludham* 1, F. Morrad* 13, J. Nairn* 1, F.R. Needham* 5, W.R. O'Dell* 19, W. Parry 32, H. Rickett 19, H. Rothery* 1, G. Rumbold 24, H.G. Sharpe 2, H.M. Smith 1, A Somerfield* 1, A. Stewart* 9, R.P. Walsh 1, H. Walters* 18, W. Whitfield* 1, W.P. Wright 1, A.Younger* 8.

Goalscorers: League: 6 Daniels, Ford; 5 O'Dell; 4 Younger; 2 Colloff, G. Kelly, Liddell, Parry, Pond; 1 Blackman, Browne, Cross, Dugnolle, Foreman, Morrad, Walters, own-goal. League Cup: 3 Ford; 1 Blackburn, Daniels.

London League 1944–45

	P	W	D	L	F	A	Pts
Tottenham Hotspur	30	23	6	1	81	30	52
West Ham U	30	22	3	5	96	47	47
Brentford	30	17	4	9	87	57	38
Chelsea	30	16	5	9	100	55	37
Southampton	30	17	3	10	96	69	37
Crystal Palace	30	15	5	10	74	70	35
Reading	30	14	6	10	78	68	34
Arsenal	30	13	3	13	77	67	31
Queen's Park Rangers	30	10	10	10	70	61	30
Watford	30	11	6	13	66	84	28
Fulham	30	11	4	15	79	83	26
Portsmouth	30	11	4	15	36	61	26
Charlton Athletic	30	12	2	16	72	81	26
Brighton & HA	30	10	2	18	66	95	22
Luton T	30	6	7	17	56	104	19
Aldershot	30	7	4	19	44	85	18
Millwall	30	5	7	18	50	84	17
CLAPTON ORIENT	30	5	7	18	39	86	17

1945–46 (League and Division 3 South Cup and FA Cup)

Appearances: L.H. Allum 6, D. J. Astley* 1, E.A. Ballard 5, C.H. Barnard* 1, S. Barnes 11, F.L. Bartlett 34, J. Baynham* 9, R. Beer 1, J. Blain* 4, P.S. Buchanan* 1, A. Calverley* 1, W. B. Campbell 3, J. T. Clark 12, W. Collins*

1, R. H. Cumner* 1, M. Dinnen 6, L. Dobson 1, J. H. Dugnolle* 5, A.Farley 11, H. Ferrier* 1, C.A. Fletcher 2, R.A. French 1, B. Froom 8, J.F.A. Fullbrook 5, ? Georgson 2, G.W. Goodyear* 1, L. Gore 20, G. Griffiths 1, S.A. Hall 27, D.A. Hunt 5, T. Howshall* 12, J. Jobling* 1, G. Kirby 1, H. Knott* 1, E. Lewis 7, J. Liddell 18, E. Love 1, G.R. Lucas 1, G. Marriott 6, A. McMurdo 2, L.D. Medley* 2, G. Merritt 6, A. Moss* 3, F.G. Morrad* 3, ? Oldham 1, J. Owen 9, L. Palmer 1, H. Parr 21, W.E. Pullen 20, W. A. Rawlinson* 1, A. Ringrose* 13, L. Ritson 5,A.P. Robson* 4, G. Rumbold 20, W. Saunders* 1, E. Slade 5, F. Smith* 2, J. Smith* 4, A. Somerfield* 2, A.W. A.Stock* 13, J. Taylor* 2, A. Tidswell 1, H. Walters* 12, G. Watley 2, C. Wilson* 1, D.A. Wrampling* 4, A.W. Young* 1.

Goalscorers: League: 5 Stock; 4 Gore, Parr, Pullen; 3 Dinnern, Robson; 2 Campbell; 1 Fletcher, Morrad, Somerfield. FA Cup: Gore, Parr. Division Three South Cup: 4 Parr; 2 Campbell, Medley, Pullen, Robson, Smith (J.); 1 Baynham, Froom, Gore, Howshall, Hunt, Merritt, Somerfield, Taylor.

Division Three South (North Region) – First Championship played over first half of season

	P	W	D	L	F	A	Pts
Queen's Park Rangers	20	14	4	2	50	15	32
Norwich City	20	11	4	5	54	31	26
Port Vale	20	9	6	5	34	25	24
Watford	20	10	2	8	42	47	22
Ipswich Town	20	8	4	8	33	36	20
Notts County	20	8	4	8	39	47	20
Northampton Town	20	8	3	9	37	34	19
CLAPTON ORIENT	20	5	6	9	28	42	16
Walsall	20	6	3	11	31	42	15
Southend United	20	5	5	10	33	49	15
Mansfield Town	20	3	5	12	29	42	11

Division Three South Cup – North Region Qualifying Competition played over second half of season

	P	W	D	L	F	A	Pts
Queen's Park Rangers	16	11	3	2	38	11	25
Walsall	16	10	4	2	34	18	24
Mansfield Town	16	8	4	4	24	15	20
Southend United	16	7	5	4	22	21	19
Norwich City	16	7	2	7	27	25	16
Ipswich Town	16	7	1	8	19	24	15
CLAPTON ORIENT	16	6	3	7	22	31	15
Port Vale	16	5	4	7	21	25	14
Northampton Town	16	5	2	9	27	29	12
Watford	16	5	1	10	23	35	11
Notts County	16	5	0	11	17	31	10

Note: Also refer to the season-by-season chapter for seasons 1939–40 to 1945–46

Orient's International players

When Glyn Garner gained his first full cap for Wales in the 2–1 defeat against Trinidad & Tobago in Graz, Austria on 27 May 2006, before an 8,000 crowd, he became only the O's 16th player to achieve this feat while with the club and the first for Northern Ireland. The first O's player to represent his country was Owen Williams for England on 22 October 1923 against Northern Ireland at West Bromwich. The first list includes only full caps while with Orient.

Home Countries

England

John Ernest Townrow: 2 caps v Scotland 1925, v Wales 1926.

Owen Williams: 2 caps v Northern Ireland 1923, v Wales 1923.

Northern Ireland

Ciaran Toner: 2 caps v Italy 2003, v Spain 2003.

Republic of Ireland (Eire)

Anthony Patrick Grealish: 7 caps v Norway 1976, v Poland 1976, v Norway 1978, v Denmark 1978, v Northern Ireland 1979, v England 1979, v West Germany 1979. Grealish gained a total of 45 full caps for his country during his playing career, scoring 8 goals.

Wales

Thomas John Evans: 3 caps v Scotland 1927, v England 1928, v Scotland 1928. Evans gained a total of 4 caps for his country during his playing career.

Glyn Garner: 1 cap v Trinidad & Tobago 2006.

Edward Lawrence: 1 cap v Northern Ireland 1930. Lawrence gained a total of 2 caps for his country during his playing career.

Peter Malcolm Lucas: 4 caps v Northern Ireland 1962, v Mexico 1962, v Scotland 1963, v England 1963.

Thomas James Mills: 2 caps v England 1934, v Northern Ireland 1934. Mills gained a total of 4 caps for his country during his playing career.

Ernest James Morley: 3 caps v England 1929, v Scotland 1929, v Northern Ireland 1929. Morley gained a total of 4 caps for his country during his playing career.

Philip Abraham Woosnam: 1 cap v Scotland 1958. Woosnam gained a total of 17 caps for his country during his playing career with 4 goals.

Other Countries

Barbados

Matthew Nathan Adolphus Joseph: 2 caps v Guatemala 2000, v USA 2000.

Congo, Democratic Republic

Gabriel Zakuani: 2005.

New Zealand

Christopher Vincent Zoricich: 3 caps v Fiji 1992, v Vanuatu 1992. Zoricich has gained a total of more than 60 caps for his county up to January 2005.

Nigeria

Tunji Babajide Banjo: 7 caps v Tunisia 1981, v Tanzania 1981, v Guinea 1981, v Algeria 1982.

John Okechukwu Chiedozie: 7 caps v Tunisia 1981, v Tanzania 1981, v Guinea 1981, v Algeria 1982. Chiedozie gained a total of 9 caps for his country during his playing career.

Leading internationally-capped Orient players

Tunji Banjo: 7 caps for Nigeria.

John Chiedozie: 7 caps for Nigeria.

Tony Grealish: 7 caps for Eire.

Other Representative Honours

This list is honours obtained by players while on Orient's books

England 'B'

Victor George Groves.

Glenn Victor Roeder.

Mervyn Richard Day (reserve).

Northern Ireland 'B'

Joseph Patrick Elwood.

Northern Ireland Under-23

Peter Malcolm Lucas (captain).

Republic of Ireland (Eire) Under-21

Henry Timothy Hughton.

Football League

John Thompson Johnston

John Ernest Townrow.

Frederick Walter Bevan (reserve).

FA touring team

Victor George Groves.

Charles William Hannaford.

Ronald Ernest Heckman (he was chosen to tour with the FA but an injury prevented him making the trip).

England XI

John Ernest Townrow.

England international trial

Richard McFadden.

Northern Ireland XI

Joseph Patrick Elwood.

South Professional XI

Arthur Wood.

South Representative XI

John Ernest Townrow.

London XI & London FA XI

Richard McFadden.

George Scott.

Frederick George Parker.

Arthur Banner.

Harold Frank Neary.
William Henry Naylor.
Victor George Groves.
Cryril Henry Trailor (reserve).
Ronald Edmund Foster (reserve).

London (Inter-Cities Fairs Cup)

Philip McKnight.
Philip Abraham Woosnam.
Victor George Groves.

Third Division South XI

Stanley Charlton.
Victor George Groves was chosen but injury prevented him appearing.

Army representative teams

Derek Healy.
Brian Harvill Jackson.
Philip Abraham Woosnam.

Amateur internationals

Great Britain: Michael John Pinner.
England: Herbert Montedan Garland-Wells, Victor George Groves, James Leonard Lewis, Lionel Arthur Louch, Michael John Pinner.
Northern Ireland: Patrick Joseph Hasty.
Wales: Trefor Owen, Philip Abraham Woosnam.

Youth internationals

England: James Bulmer, Wayne Burnett, Stephen John Bowtell, Alan Cheesewright, Thomas Dillon, Alan Durrant, Gordon Harold Gregory, Lee Derek Harvey, John George Lewis, Terence Edmund Price, Mark Stuart Smith, Thomas Frederick Taylor, Paul Frank Went, Ronald Wootten, Christopher Gerald Bart-Williams, Nathan Beckett.
Republic of Ireland (Eire): Kevin Patrick Nugent, George O'Hanlon, Mark O'Neill.
Wales: Andrew Stephenson.

O's player career records 1904–05 to 2005–06

There have been a total of 964 players since 1904–05, when the O's first enterered the FA Cup, who have worn the first-team colours. These totals do not include Play-off games or the expunged matches in 1939–40, totals for both of these appear at the end of the main list. (NC = Non Contract, tr = trial)

Player	Birth	Death if known	Pos	From	To	League Apps	League Sub	League Gls	FA Cup Apps	FA Cup Sub	FA Cup Gls	FL Cup Apps	FL Cup Sub	FL Cup Gls	Total Apps	Total Sub	Total Gls
Achampong, Kenneth	Kilburn 26/6/1966		M	Charlton A 1990	Marseilles 1993	64	19	7	7	1	0	5	2	0	76	22	7
Ackerman, Anthony Alan	Islington 20/2/1948		D	West Ham U 1966	Corby T 1968	4	0	0	0	0	0	0	0	0	4	0	0
Adams, George	Falkirk 16/10/1926		WH	Chelmsford C 1949	Bath C 1950	4	0	0	0	0	0	-	-	-	4	0	0
Affleck, David Roy	Coylton 26/7/1912	11/8/1984	D	Bristol C 1935	Southampton 1937	66	0	0	5	0	0	-	-	-	71	0	0
Akinfenwa, Saheed Adebayo	Walthamstow 10/5/1982		F	Boston U 2003	Doncaster R 2004	0	1	0	0	1	0	0	0	0	0	2	0
Aldous, Stanley Elvey R.	Northfleet 10/2/1923	17/10/1995	D	Gravesend & N 1950	Headington U 1958	302	0	3	25	0	0	-	-	-	327	0	3
Alexander, Gary George	Peckham 15/8/1979		F	Swindon Town 2003	Current	123	12	40	7	0	1	2	1	0	132	9	41
Allder, Douglas Stewart	Hammersmith 30/12/1951		F	Millwall 1975	Torquay U 1977	34	7	0	3	1	0	1	2	0	38	10	0
Allen, Albert Robert	Bromley-by-Bow 11/10/1916	Feb 1992	F	Spurs Junior 1933	Leytonstone 1934	1	0	0	0	0	0	-	-	-	1	0	0
Allen, James	Amble 18/8/1913	1979	WH	QPR 1937	Non-League 1938	5	0	0	3	0	0	-	-	-	8	0	0
Allen, Peter Charles **	Hove 1/11/1946		M	Tottenham H jun 1965	Millwall 1978	424	8	27	25	0	1	24	0	1	473	8	29
Ames. Leslie Ethelbert G.	Elham 3/12/1905	26/2/1990	F	Folkestone 1926	Gillingham 1931	14	0	0	0	0	0	-	-	-	14	0	0
Ampadu Patrick Kwame	Bradford 20/12/1970		M	Swansea C 1998	Exeter C 2000	69	3	2	4	1	1	8	0	0	82	4	3
Anderson, Thomas Cowan	Haddington 24/9/1934		F	Melbourne G 1967	Limerick 1968	8	1	0	0	0	0	1	0	0	9	1	0
Andrews, James Patrick	Invergordon 1/2/1927		F	West Ham U 1956	QPR 1959	36	0	8	0	0	0	-	-	-	36	0	8
Ansah, Andrew	Lewisham 19/3/1969		F	Hong Kong NC 1997	Hayes 1997	0	2	0	0	0	0	0	0	0	0	2	0
Arber, Robert Leonard	Poplar 13/1/1951		D	Arsenal youth 1968	Rangers (South Africa) 1974	31	0	0	2	0	1	1	0	0	34	0	1
Archell, Graham Leonard	Islington 8/2/1950		F	O's youth 1965	Folkestone T 1970	5	2	0	0	0	0	2	0	0	7	2	0
Archer, Jack	Hackney		D	Amateur 1895	Non-League 1905	-	-	-	6	0	0	-	-	-	6	0	0
Archibald, James Mitchell	Dunfermline 18/9/1892	25/1/1975	WH	Aberdare A 1923	Southend U 1926	49	0	1	3	0	0	-	-	-	52	0	1
Armitage, Kenneth	SEE UNDER FENTON																
Armstrong, James Harris	Lemington-upon-Spa 8/3/1904	13/4/1971	D	Easington Colliery 1926	QPR 1928	2	0	0	0	0	0	-	-	-	2	0	0
Arnott, Andrew John	Chatham 18/10/1973		D	Gillingham 1995	Fulham 1997	47	3	6	2	0	0	2	0	0	51	3	6
Ashton, Hubert	Calcutta, India 13/2/1898	17/6/1979	D	Bristol R 1926	Gillingham 1927	5	0	0	0	0	0	-	-	-	5	0	0
Atkin, Paul Anthony	Nottingham 3/9/1969		D	York C (loan) 1997	York C 1997	5	0	0	0	0	0	0	0	0	5	0	0
Austin, Kevin Levi	Hackney, 12/2/1973		D	Saffron Waldon T 1993	Lincoln C 1996	101	8	3	6	0	0	4	0	1	111	8	4
Ayorinde, Samuel Tayo	Lagos, Nigeria 20/10/1974		F	Sturm Graz (Austria) 1995	Dover A 1997	7	6	2	1	0	0	1	1	0	9	7	2
Bacon, Cyril William	Hammersmith 9/11/1919		WH	RAF Hayes 1946	Brentford (tr) 1950	118	0	3	3	0	0	-	-	-	121	0	3
Bailey, Daniel	East Ham 26/5/1893	3/4/1967	F	Charlton A 1922	Retired 1923	18	0	4	1	0	0	-	-	-	19	0	4
Baily, Edward Francis	Clapton 6/8/1925		M	Nottingham F 1958	O's Coach 1960	29	0	3	1	0	0	-	-	-	30	0	3
Baker, Joseph Philip	Kentish Town 19/4/1977		F	Charlton A 1995	Sutton U 1999	25	52	3	0	5	0	1	3	2	24	60	5
Baker, Stephen	Newcastle 16/6/1962		D	Southampton 1988	AFC Bournemouth 1991	105	7	6	4	2	0	13	1	0	122	10	6
Ballard, Edgar Albert	Brentford 16/6/1920		WH	Brentford 1946	Southampton 1947												
" " "				Southampton 1952	Snowdon Colliery 1953	26	0	1	1	0	0	-	-	-	27	0	1

Player	Birth	Death if known	Pos	From	To	League Apps	League Sub	League Gls	FA Cup Apps	FA Cup Sub	FA Cup Gls	FL Cup Apps	FL Cup Sub	FL Cup Gls	Total Apps	Total Sub	Total Gls
Banfied, Neil Anthony	Poplar 20/1/1962		D	Adelaide C (Aus) 1983	Dagenham & R 1985	30	1	0	3	0	0	2	0	0	35	1	0
Banjo, Tunji Babajide	Kensington 19/2/1960		M	O's youth 1976	AEL Limasol (Greece) 1982	20	7	1	0	2	0	2	0	0	22	9	1
Banner, Arthur	Sheffield 28/6/1918	30/4/1980	D	West Ham U 1948	Sittingbourne 1953	164	0	1	14	0	1	-	-	-	178	0	2
Barke, William	SEE UNDER NAYLOR																
Barnard, Donny	Forest Gate 1/7/1984		D	O's youth 2000	Current	81	40	1	3	3	0	0	2	0	84	45	1
Barnard, Lee James	Romford 18/7/1984		F	Tottenham H (loan) 2004	Tottenham H 2005	3	5	0	1	0	0	0	0	0	4	5	0
Barnett, Gary Lloyd	Stratford-u-Avon 11/3/1963		F	Huddersfield T 1993	Scunthorpe U 1995	47	16	7	4	0	0	3	0	0	54	16	7
Barr, John Victor	Medway 1902	1950	F	Folkestone T 1922	Chatham T 1923	8	0	0	0	0	0	-	-	-	8	0	0
Barrett, Scott	Illkeston 2/4/1963		G	Cambridge U 1998	Grays A 2003	99	0	0	6	1	0	2	0	0	107	1	0
Barry, George	Islington 19/9/1967		D	Fisher 1994	Fisher 1995	5	1	0	0	0	0	0	0	0	5	1	0
Bart-Williams, Christopher	Freetown, S Leone 16/6/1974		M	O's youth 1989	Sheffield W 1991	34	2	2	0	0	0	4	0	0	38	2	2
Bartlett, Frederick Leslie	Reading 5/3/1913	1968	D	QPR 1937	Gloucester C 1949	96	0	0	6	0	0	-	-	-	102	0	0
Batten, Herbert George	Bedminster 14/5/1898	15/5/1956	F	Reading 1927	Northfleet 1929	31	0	6	0	0	0	-	-	-	31	0	6
Bayes, Ashley John	Lincoln 19/4/1972		G	Torquay U 1999	Bohemians (Ireland) 2002	68	1	0	5	0	0	7	0	0	80	1	0
Baynham, John	Rhondda 21/4/1918	Feb 1995	F	Brentford 1946	Swindon T 1948	60	0	7	2	0	0	-	-	-	62	0	7
Beale, Peter Edward	London		F	Leyton 1908	New Brompton 1909	5	0	1	1	0	0	-	-	-	6	0	1
Beall, Matthew John	Enfield 4/12/1977		M	Cambridge U 1998	Cambridge C 2002	63	22	3	6	2	0	2	0	0	70	24	3
Beason, Malcolm Lloyd	Dulwich 1/12/1955		M	Crystal Palace 1975	Retired 1976	0	1	0	0	0	0	0	0	0	0	1	0
Beesley, Paul	Liverpool 21/7/1965		D	Wigan A 1989	Sheffield U 1990	32	0	1	1	0	0	0	0	0	33	0	1
Bell, Joseph	Shettleston, Scotland		F	Dumbarton 1924	Aberdare A 1926	2	0	0	0	0	0	-	-	-	2	0	0
Bell, Mark Dickson	Edinburgh 8/2/1881	26/10/1961	WH	Fulham 1907	Leyton 1910	88	0	4	7	0	2	-	-	-	95	0	6
Bellamy, Gary	Worksop 4/7/1962		D	Wolverhampton W 1992	Braintree T 1996	129	3	6	7	0	0	2	0	0	138	3	6
Bennett, Michael Richard	Camberwell 27//7/1969		M	Cambridge C 1997	Brighton & Hove A 1998	1	1	0	0	0	0	0	0	0	1	1	0
Bennett, Peter Leslie	Hillingdon 24/6/1946		D/M	West Ham U 1970	O's Coach 1980	195	4	13	18	0	0	8	0	1	221	4	14
Benson, Charles George	Sunderland		F	Sunderland College 1913	Bishop Auckland 1913	1	0	0	0	0	0	-	-	-	1	0	0
Benstock, Daniel	Hackney 10/7/1970		M	Barking 1992	Purfleet 1994	17	4	0	0	0	0	0	2	0	17	6	0
Berry, Claude	London		WH	Amateur 1900	Non-League 1905	-	-	-	6	0	0	-	-	-	6	0	0
Berry, Gregory	Linford 5//3/1971		F	East Thurrock U 1989	Wimbledon 1992												
" "				Millwall (loan) 1996	Millwall 1996	72	15	14	8	2	2	6	0	3	86	17	19
Best, Jeremiah	Mickley 23/1/1901	1975	F	Falls River (USA) 1931	Darlington 1933	51	0	17	4	0	0	-	-	-	55	0	17
Bevan, Frederick Walter	Poplar 27/2/1879	10/12/1935	F	Derby Co 1909	Chatham 1914	118	0	35	4	0	1	-	-	-	122	0	36
Biggs, Anthony	Greenford 17/4/1936		F	Arsenal 1958	Guildford 1961	4	0	1	0	0	0	-	-	-	4	0	1
Bishop, Sidney Harold R.	Tooting 8/4/1934		D	Chase of Chertsey 1952	Hastings U 1965	296	0	4	18	0	0	9	0	0	323	0	4
Black, Robert Watson	Washington, Co D'm 17/7/1915	1979	WH	West Ham 1938	Retired 1946	23	0	0	2	0	0	-	-	-	25	0	0
Blackhall, Mark Christopher	Upney 17/11/1960		F	O's youth 1975	Chelmsford C 1983	12	6	1	1	1	0	1	1	0	14	8	1
Blackwell, Clifford Harold	Wortley, Sheffield 1902		G	Aberdeen 1930	Preston North End 1932	15	0	0	1	0	0	-	-	-	16	0	0
Blair, James Alfred	Whiteinch 6/1/1918	12/7/1983	M	Bournemouth 1949	Ramsgate A 1953	104	0	26	4	0	0	-	-	-	108	0	26
Blatchford, Patrick John	Plymouth 28/12/1925	1981	F	Plymouth A 1951	Bideford T 1954	60	0	8	9	0	1	-	-	-	69	0	9
Bliss, Herbert	Willenhall 29/3/1890	14/6/1968	F	Tottenham H 1922	Bournemouth & B 1925	70	0	20	1	0	0	-	-	-	71	0	20
Blizzard, Leslie William	Acton 13/3/1923	1996	D	Yeovil T 1950	Headington U 1956	223	0	12	25	0	0	-	-	-	248	0	12

Player	Birth	Death if known	Pos	From	To	League			FA Cup			FL Cup			Total		
						Apps	Sub	Gls	Apps	Sub	Gls	Apps	Sub	Gls	Apps	Sub	Gls
Bloomfield, James Henry	Kensington 15/2/1934	3/4/1983	M	Plymouth A 1968	Leicester C (manager) 1971	43	2	3	2	0	1	2	0	0	47	2	4
Boden, James Arthur	Northwich 1881	1942	D	Glossop North E 1905	Aston Villa 1906	27	0	5	6	0	3	-	-	-	33	0	8
Bogie, Ian	Newcastle 6/12/1967		M	Millwall 1993	Port Vale 1995	62	3	5	2	0	0	2	0	0	66	3	5
Bolland, Gordon Edward	Boston, Lincs 12/8/1943		F	Chelsea 1962	Norwich C 1964	63	0	19	7	0	0	3	0	3	73	0	22
Bolton, James McFarlane	Clydebank 22/3/1906		WH	St Johnstone 1930	York C 1932	37	0	1	5	0	0	-	-	-	42	0	1
Bourne, Richard Arthur	Roundle Jan 1881	1944	F	Preston NE 1905	WBA 1907	56	0	2	6	0	1	-	-	-	62	0	3
Bow, James	Lochore, Fife 14/12/1910		F	St Barnards 1934	Gateshead 1936	0	0	0	1	0	0	-	-	-	1	0	0
Bower, William	Dalston 18/9/1887	Feb 1954	G	Peel Institute 1905	New Brompton 1915	171	0	0	5	0	0	-	-	-	176	0	0
Bowles, Stanley	Manchester 24/12/1948		M	Nottingham F 1980	Brentford 1981	46	0	7	1	0	0	3	0	0	50	0	7
Bowtell, Stephen John	Bethnal Green 2/12/1950		G	O's youth 1968	Margate 1973	8	0	0	0	0	0	0	0	0	8	0	0
Bowyer, Ian	Little Sutton 6/6/1951		F	Manchester C 1971	Nottingham F 1973	75	3	19	5	0	2	5	0	2	85	3	23
Bowyer, Thomas William	Wolverhampton 1895		F	Stoke C 1919	Gillingham 1920	21	0	6	0	0	0	-	-	-	21	0	6
Boyd, Hugh	Glasgow		WH	Portadown 1936	East Stirling 1937	2	0	0	0	0	0	-	-	-	2	0	0
Boyle, John	Motherwell 25/12/1946		M	Brighton & HA 1973	Tampa Bay R (USA) 1975	18	0	0	4	0	0	0	0	0	22	0	0
Boyle, Peter	Carlingford 1877	24/6/1939	D	Motherwell 1905	Wigan T 1906	11	0	0	2	0	0	-	-	-	13	0	0
Brabrook, Peter	Greenwich 8/11/1937		F	West Ham U 1968	Romford 1971	70	2	6	2	1	0	6	0	0	78	3	6
Bradbury, George	Matlock 26/4/1897	1974	D	Hartshay Colliery 1920	Sc'thorpe & Lindsay U 1922	32	0	2	1	0	0	-	-	-	33	0	2
Bradbury, Terence Eugene	Paddington 15/11/1939		WH	Southend U 1966	Wrexham 1967	25	2	0	3	0	0	1	0	0	29	2	0
Bradley, James Leslie	Lesmahagow 1892		F	Luton T 1920	Scottish amateur 1921	5	0	1	0	0	0	-	-	-	5	0	1
Brahan, Marcel Eric Louis	Stepney 3/12/1926	12/1995	D	Walthamstow A 1955	Walthamstow A 1956	1	0	0	0	0	0	-	-	-	1	0	0
Bratby, John Lewis	Belper 15/5/1895	12/12/1992	F	Matlock T 1920	Retired 1924	27	0	1	0	0	0	-	-	-	27	0	1
Brazier, Matthew Ronald	Whipps Cross 2/7/1976		M	Cardiff C 2002	Released, QPR (tr) 2004	46	0	2	0	1	0	3	0	0	49	1	2
Brinton, John Victor	Avonmouth 11/7/1916	22/2/1997	F	Stockport Co 1948	Streets FC 1949	4	0	1	0	0	0	-	-	-	4	0	1
Brisley, Terence William	Stepney 4/7/1950		M	O's youth 1963	Millwall 1975	133	9	9	7	1	0	9	0	0	149	10	9
Brissett, Jason Curtis	Redbridge 7/9/1974		F	Wallsall 2000	Stevenage B 2000	2	2	0	0	0	0	1	1	0	3	3	0
Brkovic, Ahmet	Dubrovnik, Croatia 23/9/1974		M	Varteks Varazdin (Cro) 1999	Luton T 2001	59	10	7	4	0	2	3	0	0	66	10	9
Broadbent, William Henry	Chaddleston 20/11/1901	14/2/1979	WH	Brentford 1925	Preston NE 1932	198	0	8	11	0	0	-	-	-	209	0	8
Brooks, Charles Edward	Kent		D	Folkestone T 1937	Crystal Palace 1939	4	0	0	1	0	0	-	-	-	5	0	0
Brooks, Shaun	south London 9/10/1962		M	Crystal Palace 1983	AFC Bournemouth 1987												
" "				AFC Bournemouth 1994	Poole T 1996	182	16	28	13	1	4	12	0	1	207	17	33
Brown, Charles George	Earlsford 7/12/1909		WH	Dartford 1936	Non-League 1937	1	0	0	0	0	0	-	-	-	1	0	0
Brown, Edwin	Preston 28/2/1926		F	Birmingham C 1959	Scarborough 1961	63	0	28	1	0	0	2	0	1	66	0	29
Brown, Thomas Law	Glenbuck 17/4/1921	10/5/1966	M	Charlton A 1950	Dartford coach 1953	99	0	5	10	0	2	-	-	-	109	0	7
Brown, William Charles	Canning Town 24/4/1920	1992	F	Romford 1946	Non-League 1947	2	0	1	0	0	0	-	-	-	2	0	1
Brown, William Ian	Silverton 6/9/1910	15/1/1993	D	Brentford 1947	Chingford T 1948	26	0	0	1	0	0	-	-	-	27	0	0
Bruce, John Jack	Trimdon Dec 1908	Dec 1998	G	Tunbridge Wells R 1932	Whitecrofts 1933	19	0	0	1	0	0	-	-	-	20	0	0
Bruce, Robert	Belfast 14/10/1928		F	Leicester C 1951	Ireland 1952	1	0	0	0	0	0	-	-	-	1	0	0
Bryant, Eric	Birmingham 18/11/1921	2/12/1995	F	Plymouth A 1951	Chelmsford C 1952	12	0	1	0	0	0	-	-	-	12	0	1
Buchanan, David	Bellshire 1873		WH	Plymouth A 1906	Leyton 1908	65	0	2	5	0	3	-	-	-	70	0	5
Bullock, Michael Edwin	Stoke 2/10/1946		F	Oxford U 1968	Halifax T 1976	267	10	65	16	0	1	14	0	3	297	10	69
Burgess, Michael Rupert	Montreal (Canada) 17//4/1932		F	Bradford C 1953	Newport Co 1956	31	0	12	5	0	2	-	-	-	36	0	14

Player	Birth	Death if known	Pos	From	To	League Apps	League Sub	League Gls	FA Cup Apps	FA Cup Sub	FA Cup Gls	FL Cup Apps	FL Cup Sub	FL Cup Gls	Total Apps	Total Sub	Total Gls
Burnett, Wayne	Lambeth 4/9/1971		M	O's youth 1987	Blackburn R 1992	34	6	1	3	1	0	3	1	0	40	8	2
Burridge, Peter John	Harlow 30/12/1933		F	Barnet 1958	Millwall 1961	6	0	2	1	0	0	-	-	-	7	0	2
Butler, Joseph	Lawleybank 1879	Aug 1941	G	Stockport Co 1905	Stockport Co 1906	20	0	0	4	0	0	-	-	-	24	0	0
Cadette, Richard Raymond	Hammersmith 21/3/1965		F	Wembley 1984	Southend U 1985	19	2	4	1	0	1	4	0	0	24	2	5
Cadiou, Frederick	Paris (France) 20/4/1969		F	BS Wasquehal (Fr) 2000 (tr)	BS Wasquehal 2000	0	3	0	0	0	0	0	0	0	0	3	0
Cairney, Charles	Blantyre (Scotland) 21/9/1926	25/3/1995	WH	Celtic 1950	Barry T 1951	4	0	0	0	0	0	-	-	-	4	0	0
Calderhead Jnr, David	Dumfries 1889		D	Motherwell 1919	Lincoln C 1921	1	0	0	0	0	0	-	-	-	1	0	0
Caldwell, James	London		F	Willsden 1907	Hastings & St Leonards 1908	12	0	0	0	0	0	-	-	-	12	0	0
Caldwell, Peter James	Dorchester 5/6/1972		G	QPR 1995	USA 1997	31	0	0	0	0	0	2	0	0	33	0	0
Caldwell, Thomas	London 1886		F	West Ham St Pauls 1907	Southend U 1908	7	0	0	0	0	0	-	-	-	7	0	0
Campbell, Alexander	Glasgow		D	Albion R 1926	Connah's Q & Shotton 1928	23	0	0	0	0	0	-	-	-	23	0	0
Campbell, Gary	Belfast 4/4/1966		F	Leyton-Wingate 1990	Bromley 1990	4	4	0	0	0	0	0	0	0	4	4	0
Campbell, Hugh	Glasgow 1916		F	Glasgow Rangers 1935	Cardiff C 1936	8	0	1	0	0	0	-	-	-	8	0	1
Campbell, John	South Shields 12/5/1901	Jan 1983	F	West Ham U 1929	Retired injury 1930	25	0	9	6	0	2	-	-	-	31	0	11
Campbell, Joseph	Glasgow 28/3/1925		M	Glasgow Celtic 1949	Gillingham 1950	5	0	1	0	0	0	-	-	-	5	0	1
Campbell, Kevin Joseph	Lambeth 4/2/1970		F	Arsenal (loan) 1989	Arsenal 1989	16	0	9	0	0	0	0	0	0	16	0	9
Campbell-Ryce, James J.	Waterloo 4/6/1983		F	Charlton A (loan) 2002	Charlton A 2002	16	1	2	0	0	0	2	0	1	18	1	3
Candy, George Walter	London 1886		F	Salisbury 1908	Non-League 1909	3	0	0	0	0	0	-	-	-	3	0	0
Canham, Scott	Newham 5/11/1974		M	Brentford 1998	Chesham U 2000												
" "				Chesham U 2001		35	14	6	3	0	1	0	1	0	38	15	7
Canvin, Cyril Edward	Hemel Hempstead 23/1/1924	3/11/1950	F	Aspley 1946	Aspley 1947	3	0	0	0	0	0	-	-	-	3	0	0
Capleton, Melvyn	Hackney 24/10/1973		G	Grays A 1998	Southend U 1998	0	0	0	0	0	0	1	0	0	1	0	0
Carey, Peter Richard	Barking 14/4/1933		D	Barking 1956	QPR 1960	34	0	2	2	0	0	-	-	-	36	0	2
Carey, William Anderson	Govan 14/8/1898	1944	WH	Peebles R 1926	Peebles R 1927	3	0	0	0	0	0	-	-	-	3	0	0
Carlisle, Wayne Thomas	Lisburn, N. Ireland 9/9/1979		F	Bristol R 2004	Exeter C 2006	27	13	3	2	3	1	1	0	0	30	16	4
Carrington, George Albert	Poplar 20/6/1888		G	Ford Sports 1919	Millwall (tr) 1920	1	0	0	0	0	0	-	-	-	1	0	0
Carter, Daniel Stephen	Hackney 29/6/1969		F	Billericay T 1988	Peterborough U 1995	168	20	22	10	0	3	13	3	2	191	23	27
Carter, Robert Hector A.	Stepney 23/4/1982		M	O's youth 1997	Released 2001	0	2	0	0	0	0	1	0	0	1	2	0
Carter, William John	Woking 11/9/1945		M	O's youth 1963	Hillingdon 1967	26	3	3	3	1	0	1	0	0	30	4	3
Cass, David William Royce	Forest Gate 27/3/1962		G	Billericay T 1987	Billericay T 1988	7	0	0	0	0	0	0	0	0	7	0	0
Castle, Stephen Charles	Barkingside 17/5/1966		M	O's youth 1983	Plymouth Argyle 1992												
" " "				Birmingham C (loan) 1997	Birmingham C 1997												
" " "				Peterbrough U 2000	Stevanage B 2001	238	19	56	23	2	6	15	2	5	276	23	67
Cater, Ronald	Fulham 2/2/1922		D	West Ham U 1951	Non-League 1952	13	0	0	1	0	0	-	-	-	14	0	0
Cavendish, Sidney William	Overseal Oct 1876	July 1954	F	Freemantle 1904	Salisbury C 1905	0	0	0	4	0	0	-	-	-	4	0	0
Channing, Justin Andrew	Reading 19/11/1968		F	Bristol R 1996	Purfleet 1998	69	5	5	4	0	1	3	1	0	76	6	6
Chapman, Daniel Graham	Greenwich 21/11/1974		D/M	Millwall 1995	Welling U 1997	69	9	4	2	1	0	2	1	0	73	11	4
Chapman, John	Islington 1895		F	Southall 1919	Excelsior 1920	9	0	2	0	0	0	-	-	-	9	0	2
Chapman, Vernon William	Leicester 9/5/1921		F	Leicester C 1947	Brush Sports 1949	31	0	7	0	0	0	-	-	-	31	0	7
Charlton, Stanley	Exeter 28/6/1929		D	Bromley 1952	Arsenal 1956												

Player	Birth	Death if known	Pos	From	To	League			FA Cup			FL Cup			Total		
						Apps	Sub	Gls	Apps	Sub	Gls	Apps	Sub	Gls	Apps	Sub	Gls
" "				Arsenal 1958	Weymouth 1965	367	0	2	28	0	0	13	0	0	408	0	2
Chiedozie, John Okechukwu	Owerri, Nigeria 18/4/1960		F	O's youth 1976	Notts Co 1981	131	14	20	7	0	2	8	0	1	146	14	23
Chillingworth, Daniel Thomas	Cambridge 13/9/1981		F	Cambridge U (loan) 2004	Cambridge U 2005	8	0	2	0	0	0	0	0	0	8	0	2
Chisem, Frank	Darlington 4/10/1907		D	Tunbridge Wells R 1932	Shildon Railway A 1935	1	0	0	0	0	0	-	-	-	1	0	0
Christie, Iyseden	Coventry 14/11/1976		F	Mansfield T 1999	Mansfield T 2002	32	26	12	1	2	1	4	1	1	37	29	14
Clapham, James Richard	Lincoln 7/12/1975		D	Tottenham H (loan) 1997	Tottenham H 1997	6	0	0	0	0	0	0	0	0	6	0	0
Clark, David George	Ilford 19/1/1938		D	Leyton 1961	Retired, O's trainer 1965	4	0	0	0	0	0	2	0	0	6	0	0
Clark, Joseph Thomas Henry	Bermondsey 2/3/1920		D	Gravesend & N'fleet 1946	Margate 1947	18	0	0	1	0	0	-	-	-	19	0	0
Clark, Simon	Boston, Lincs 12/3/1967		D	Peterborough U 1997	Colchester U 2000	98	0	10	8	0	0	7	0	0	113	0	10
Clark, William	Beith 16/9/1900		F	Beith 1924	Beith 1925	4	0	0	0	0	0	-	-	-	4	0	0
Clarke, Derek	Willenhall 19/2/1950		F	Oxford U 1976	Crewe Alexandra 1979	30	6	6	1	0	0	0	0	0	31	6	6
Clegg, John	Sheffield 1/1/1890		G	The Wednesday 1913	Bradford Park Ave 1914	8	0	0	1	0	0	-	-	-	9	0	0
Coates, Ralph	Hetton-le-Hole 26/4/1946		M/F	Tottenham H 1978	O's coach 1980	76	0	12	5	0	0	3	0	0	84	0	12
Cobb, Paul Mark	Tilbury 13/12/1972		F	Purfleet 1990	Enfield 1992	3	2	0	0	0	0	0	0	0	3	2	0
Cochran, Albert George	Ebbw Vale 26/11/1939		G	Plymouth A (junior)	Folkestone T 1963	1	0	0	0	0	0	0	0	0	1	0	0
Cock, Donald James	Hayle 8/7/1896	31/8/1974	F	Arsenal 1925	Wolverhampton W 1927	64	0	28	6	0	3	-	-	-	70	0	31
Cockerill, Glenn	Grimsby 25/8/1959		M	Southampton 1993	Fulham 1996	89	1	7	3	0	0	4	0	1	96	1	8
Cockle, Ernest Samuel	West Ham 12/9/1896	11/6/1966	F	Green & Siley Weir 1920	Margate 1921	20	0	4	2	0	0	-	-	-	22	0	4
Codling, Allan	Guisborough 24/2/1911	24/2/1991	WH	Folkestone T 1936	Darlington 1938	32	0	3	0	0	0	-	-	-	32	0	3
Codling, Rowland	Norton Tees 22/2/1880	1940	D	Stockport Co 1905	Aston Villa 1906	28	0	1	6	0	0	-	-	-	34	0	1
Colkin, Lee	Nuneaton 15/7/1974		D	North'ton T (loan) 1997	Northampton T 1997	5	6	0	0	0	0	0	1	0	5	7	0
Collins, William Charles Elvert	Rymney, Wales 16/10/1902	23/1/1977	F	Cardiff C 1927	Lovells A 1929	40	0	1	3	0	0	-	-	-	43	0	1
Comfort, Alan	Aldershot 8/12/1964		F	Cambridge U 1986	Middlesbrough 1989	144	5	46	9	1	1	9	0	1	163	6	48
Connelly, Edward John	Dumbarton 9/12/1916	16/2/1990	F	Luton T 1948	Brighton & HA 1949	32	0	5	2	0	1	-	-	-	34	0	6
Connor, Paul	Bishop Auckland 12/01/1979		F	Swansea C 2006	Current	15	1	5	0	0	0	0	0	0	15	1	5
Conroy, Michael George	Johnstone 31/7/1957		M	Wrexham 1987	Cork C 1988	2	1	0	0	0	0	0	0	0	2	1	0
Constantine, Leon	Hackney 24/2/1978		F	Millwall (loan) 2001	Millwall 2001	9	1	3	0	0	0	0	0	0	9	1	3
Cook, Reuben	Dunston-on-Tyne 9/3/1933		WH	Arsenal 1956	Tonbridge 1958	2	0	0	0	0	0	-	-	-	2	0	0
Cooper, Kenneth Herbert L.	Romford 20/2/1911	14/7/1971	F	Corinthians 1932	Corinthians 1933	4	0	0	0	0	0	-	-	-	4	0	0
Cooper, Mark David	Watford 5/4/1967		F	Gillingham 1989	Barnet 1994	117	33	45	8	2	4	6	0	2	131	35	51
Cooper, Mark Nicholas	Wakefield 18/12/1968		M	Hartlepool U 1997	Rushden & D 1998	0	1	0	0	0	0	0	0	0	0	1	0
Cooper, Shaun	Isle of Wight 5/10/1983		D	Portsmouth (loan) 2003	Portsmouth 2003												
" "				Porstmouth (loan) 2004	Portsmouth 2004	9	0	0	0	0	0	0	0	0	9	0	0
Corbett, Patrick Avalon	Hackney 12/2/1963		D	Tottenham H 1983	Elo Kuopio (Finland) 1986	77	0	2	2	0	0	9	0	0	88	0	2
Corden, Simon Wayne	Leek 1/11/1975		M	Scunthorpe U 2006	Current	8	2	0	0	0	0	0	0	0	8	0	2
Corkindale, William Joseph	Langley Green 9/5/1901	13/8/1972	F	Swansea T 1926	Millwall 1929	96	0	17	6	0	1	-	-	-	102	0	18
Corner, David Edward	Sunderland 15/5/1966		D	Sunderland 1988	Darlington 1889	4	0	0	0	0	0	2	0	0	6	0	0
Cornwell, John Anthony	Bethnal Green 13/10/1964		M	O's youth 1981	Newcastle U 1987	194	9	35	14	0	2	9	1	2	217	10	39
Cotton, Roy William	Fulham 14/11/1955		F	Brentford 1974	Aldershot 1976	0	3	0	0	0	0	1	0	0	1	3	0
Coull, Charles Dickson	Dundee 27/11/1912	7/5/1991	D	Glasgow Celtic 1934	Southport 1935												

Player	Birth	Death if known	Pos	From	To	League Apps	League Sub	League Gls	FA Cup Apps	FA Cup Sub	FA Cup Gls	FL Cup Apps	FL Cup Sub	FL Cup Gls	Total Apps	Total Sub	Total Gls
" " "				Southport 1936	Portadown 1937	4	0	0	0	0	0	-	-	-	4	0	0
Crawford, Edmund Charles	Filey 31/10/1906	1977	F	Liverpool 1933	Dagerfors (Sw) coach 1945	200	0	67	12	0	6	-	-	-	212	0	73
Crompton, Wynn	Cefn-y-Bedd 11/2/1907	28/5/1988	D	Tunbridge Wells Ra 1933	Crystal Palace 1935	79	0	0	6	0	0	-	-	-	85	0	0
Cropper, Arthur	Brimington 2/1/1906	25/10/1949	F	Norwich C 1930	Gillingham 1932	27	0	10	2	0	1	-	-	-	29	0	11
Cross, Roger George	East Ham 20/10/1948		F	West Ham U (loan) 1968	West Ham U 1968	4	2	2	0	0	0	0	0	0	4	2	2
Crossan, Errol Gilmour	Montreal (Can) 6/10/1930		F	Norwich C 1961	Toronto C (Canada) 1961	8	0	2	2	0	0	0	0	0	10	0	2
Cunningham, Laurence Paul	Archway 8/3/1956	15/7/1989	F	O's youth 1973	West Bromwich A 1977	72	3	15	5	1	0	5	0	1	82	4	16
Cunningham, Thomas Edward	Bethanl Green 7/12/1955		D	Wimbledon 1981	Fisher A 1987	162	0	17	12	0	0	7	1	2	181	1	19
Curran, Daniel Lee	Brentwood 13/6/1981		F	O's youth 1997	Purfleet 2000	0	1	0	0	1	0	0	1	0	0	3	0
Currie, Daniel	Hampstead 29/11/1995		M	West Ham U (loan) 1995	West Ham U 1996	9	1	0	0	0	0	0	0	0	9	1	0
Dale, Guy Paul	Barnsley 1894	14/12/1920	G	Barnsley 1920	Died car accident 1920	1	0	0	0	0	0	-	-	-	1	0	0
Dalrymple, Robert Rodie	Glasgow 2/1/1880	July 1970	F	Fulham 1911	Ton Pentre coach 1920	139	0	38	4	0	0	-	-	-	143	0	38
Davidson, David Blyth Logie	Lanark 25/3/1920	1954	D	Bradford Park Ave 1946	Headington U 1950	84	0	1	4	0	0	-	-	-	88	0	1
Davies, David Ivor	Bridgend 21/7/1932		F	Pyle 1952	Ramsgate A 1954	4	0	0	1	0	0	-	-	-	5	0	1
Davies, Dudley	Shoreham 27/12/1924		F	Charlton A 1950	Non-League 1952	17	0	2	1	0	0	-	-	-	18	0	2
Davies Reginald Walter	Tipton 10/10/1933		G	Millwall 1963	Port Vale 1964												
" " "				Port Vale 1965	Retired 1966	27	0	0	0	0	0	1	0	0	28	0	0
Davin, Martin	Dumbarton 9/9/1905	9/11/1957	F	Airdrieonians 1933	Ashford T 1934	15	0	2	0	0	0	-	-	-	15	0	2
Davis, Edwin	Bedminster Jan 1892	l 6/3/1954	G	Bristol C 1912	Porstmouth 1913	4	0	0	1	0	0	-	-	-	5	0	0
Davis, Frederick Robert	Hackney 1913		F	Walthamstow Ave 1936	Walthamstow Ave 1937	2	0	0	0	0	0	-	-	-	2	0	0
Dawson, Thomas	Springwell 15/12/1901	30/11/1977	D	Stoke C 1932	Gateshead 1933	19	0	0	1	0	0	-	-	-	20	0	0
Day, Keith David	Grays 29/11/1962		D	Colchester U 1987	Sittingbourne 1993	184	8	9	14	1	1	17	0	1	215	9	11
Day, Mervyn Richard	Chelmsford 26/6/1955		G	West Ham U 1979	Aston Villa 1983	170	0	0	10	0	0	8	0	0	188	0	0
Deeley, Norman Victor	Wednesbury 30/11/1933		F	Wolverhampton W 1962	Worcester C 1964	73	0	9	7	0	2	6	0	2	86	0	13
Demetriou, Jason	Newham 18/11/1987		D	O's youth 2004	Current	1	2	0	0	0	0	0	0	0	1	2	0
Dempsey, Mark Anthony	Dublin 10/12/1972		M	Gillingham 1994	Shrewsbury T 1995	43	0	1	1	1	0	2	0	0	46	1	1
Dennison, Robert	Arnold 16/10/1900	24/6/1973	F	Manchester C 1926	Chesterfield 1929	70	0	28	6	0	3	-	-	-	76	0	31
Denton, Frederick George	Barnet 7/5/1899	26/9/1969	F	Chatham T 1920	Chatham T 1921	3	0	0	0	0	0	-	-	-	3	0	0
Deverall, Harold Reginald	Petersfield 5/5/1916	11/6/1999	WH	Reading 1948	Retired 1953	114	0	2	13	0	1	-	-	-	127	0	3
Dickenson, Kevin James	Hackney 24/11/1962		D	Charlton A 1985	Retired 1992	190	2	3	18	0	0	17	0	0	225	2	3
Dimmock, James Henry	Edmonton, London 5/12/1900	23/12/1972	F	Tottenham H 1932	Ashford 1934	18	0	3	1	0	0	-	-	-	19	0	3
Dix, Joseph Charles	Geddington 1886		F	Portsmouth 1910	Retired after WWI	148	0	11	7	0	0	-	-	-	155	0	11
Dixon, Thomas Henry	Seaham 17/9/1899		WH	Murton Coll Welf 1919	Southend U 1927	234	0	15	10	0	0	-	-	-	244	0	15
Dodds, Leslie Smith	Patishead 20/9/1912	29/11/1967	F	Wellington T 1937	Hartlepools U 1939	53	0	4	4	0	0	-	-	-	57	0	4
Dodgin Snr, William	Gateshead 17/4/1909	16/10/1999	WH	Charlton A 1937	Southampton 1939	62	0	1	2	0	0	-	-	-	64	0	1
Dolan, Joseph Thomas	Harrow 27/5/1980		D	Millwall 2005	Canvey Island 2006	1	0	0	0	0	0	0	1	0	1	1	0
Dominy, Arthur Albert	South Stoneham 11/2/1893	23/9/1974	F	Gillingham 1929	Newport, I of W 1930	5	0	1	2	0	0	-	-	-	7	0	1
Donn, Nigel	Maidstone 2/3/1962		M	Karpalo (Finland) 1892	Maidstone U 1983	22	1	2	1	0	0	2	0	0	25	1	2
Donnellan, Leopold John	Willesdon 19/1/1965		M	Chelsea (loan) 1984	Chelsea 1985	6	0	0	2	0	0	0	0	0	8	0	0
Dorrian, Christopher	Harlow 3/4/1982		D	O's youth 1998	Chelmsford C 2002	4	1	0	2	0	0	1	0	0	7	1	0

Player	Birth	Death if known	Pos	From	To	League Apps	League Sub	League Gls	FA Cup Apps	FA Cup Sub	FA Cup Gls	FL Cup Apps	FL Cup Sub	FL Cup Gls	Total Apps	Total Sub	Total Gls
Dougal, David Wishart	Dundee 22/3/1882	5/3/1937	F	Grimsby T 1905	Reading 1907	50	0	3	5	0	3	-	-	-	55	0	6
Downer, Simon	Rush Green 19/10/1981		D	O's youth 1997	Aldershot T 2004	64	15	0	3	1	0	3	2	0	70	18	0
Downing, Derrick Graham	Doncaster 3/11/1945		F	Middlesbrough 1972	Hartlepool U 1977	100	4	12	4	2	0	8	0	2	112	6	14
Dryden, John George	Sunderland 16/9/1919	2004	F	Swindon T 1948	Tonbridge 1950	40	0	10	3	0	0	-	-	-	43	0	10
Dryden, William	Amble		F	Choppington 1912	Watford 1913	13	0	6	1	0	0	-	-	-	14	0	6
Dudley, Samuel	Dudley Port 26/11/1907	14/1/1985	WH	Coleraine 1930	Chelsea 1932	12	0	1	0	0	0	-	-	-	12	0	1
Duffus, John Murison	Aberdeen 10/5/1901	18/9/1975	F	Caerau (Wales) 1922	Tottenham H 1923	6	0	0	0	0	0	-	-	-	6	0	0
Duffus, Robert Morrice D.	Aberdeen 28/2/1891	19/3/1948	D	Millwall 1922	Accrington Stanley 1923	5	0	0	0	0	0	-	-	-	5	0	0
Duffy, Bernard	Uddingston 7/7/1900		WH	Chelsea 1927	Shelbourne 1929	70	0	1	4	0	0	-	-	-	74	0	1
Duncan, Derek Henry	Newham 23/4/1987		M	O's youth 2002	Current	6	11	0	0	2	0	0	0	0	6	13	0
Dunmore, David Gerald Ivor	Whitehaven 8/2/1934		F	West Ham U 1961	York C 1965	147	0	54	12	0	2	9	0	2	168	0	58
Dunn, Herbert Bertram	Carshalton 15/8/1895		F	Alloa A 1924	Non-League 1926	4	0	0	0	0	0	-	-	-	4	0	0
Dunne, Thomas Joseph	Glasgow 22/6/1946		M	St Anthony's 1964	Albion Rovers 1965	1	0	0	0	0	0	0	0	0	1	0	0
Dyson, John Barry	Oldham 6/9/1942	26/2/1995	M	Watford 1968	Colchester U 1973	154	6	28	9	0	3	6	0	0	169	6	31
Eadie, Douglas	Edinburgh 22/9/1946		F	West Ham U (loan) 1967	West Ham U 1967	2	0	0	0	0	0	0	0	0	2	0	0
Eagles, Alan James	Edgware 6/9/1933	6/11/1995	D	Carshalton A 1957	Colchester U 1961	75	0	0	3	0	0	2	0	0	80	0	0
Earl, Stanley James William	Alton 9/7/1929		D	Portsmouth 1953	Swindon T 1956	33	0	0	4	0	0	-	-	-	37	0	0
Earle,Stanley George James	Stratford 6//9/1897	26/9/1971	F	West Ham U 1932	Walthamstow A 1932	15	0	1	1	0	0	-	-	-	16	0	1
Eastman, George Frederick	Leyton 7//4/1903	15/3/1991	D	Chatham T 1928	Sachoux (France) 1931	13	0	0	5	0	1	-	-	-	18	0	1
Easton, Craig	Bellshill, Scotland 26/02/1979		M	Livingston 2005	Current	36	5	4	3	0	1	1	0	0	40	4	5
Ebden, Marcus	Pontypool 17/10/1970		M	Chesterfield 2003	Tamworth T 2003	10	4	0	0	0	0	0	1	0	10	5	0
Echanomi, Efe Anthony	Nigeria 27/9/1986		F	O's junior 2002	Current	4	30	8	0	1	0	1	0	0	5	31	8
Edley, William	Lancashire		WH	Stockport Co 1907	Non-League 1908	0	0	0	1	0	0	-	-	-	1	0	0
Edmonds, Alfred John	Brighton 16/10/1902	Mar 1942	D/F	Brighton & HA 1929	Bury 1932	89	0	18	4	0	0	-	-	-	93	0	18
Edwards, Edmund Clifford	Thurcroft 1912	Aug 1991	M	Bury 1935	Mossley 1936	1	0	0	0	0	0	-	-	-	1	0	0
Edwards, Evan Jenkins	Bedlinog 14/12/1896	1958	F	Darlington 1929	O's coach 1930	4	0	0	0	0	0	-	-	-	4	0	0
Edwards, Stanley Llewellyn	Dawdon 17/10/1926	14/1/1989	F	Colchester U 1953	Retired 1956	2	0	1	0	0	0	-	-	-	2	0	1
Elliott, Robert	Clapton		F	Local amateur 1905	Non-League 1906	0	0	0	1	0	0	-	-	-	1	0	0
Ellis, Frederick Charles	Isle of Sheppey 7/10/1900	1970	WH	Watford 1932	Ashford T 1933	27	0	0	0	0	0	-	-	-	27	0	0
Elwood, Joseph Patrick	Belfast 26/10/1939		F	Glenavon 1958	Ards 1966	101	2	25	8	0	4	0	0	0	109	2	29
Emery, Herbert John Charles	Bristol 18/2/1910	13/8/1995	G	Cardiff Corries 1928	Rotherham U 1929												
" " " "				Rotherham U 1931	Newport Co 1933	62	0	0	3	0	0	-	-	-	65	0	0
Evans, John Alwyn	Aberystwyth 22/10/1922	24/2/1956	D	Millwall 1950	Retired 1954	149	0	0	19	0	0	-	-	-	168	0	0
Evans, Nolan	Ashton-in-Makerfield	1948	D	Exeter C 1912	Retired after WWI	111	0	1	5	0	0	-	-	-	116	0	1
Evans, Rhys Karl	Swindon 27/1/1982		G	Chelsea (loan) 2002	Chelsea 2002	7	0	0	0	0	0	0	0	0	7	0	0
Evans, Thomas John	Maerdy 7/4/1903		D	Maerdy 1924	Newcastle U 1927												
" " "				Newcastle U 1930	Merthyr T 1932	79	0	1	8	0	0	-	-	-	87	0	1
Evenson, Isaac	Manchester 11/1882	1954	D/F	Leicester Fosse 1905	West Bromwich A 1907	63	0	8	4	0	2	-	-	-	67	0	10
Everitt, Michael Richard	Mile End 21/3/1958		F	Crystal Palace youth 1975	Hornchurch 1977	0	1	0	0	0	0	0	0	0	0	1	0
Facey, Kenneth William	Clapton 12/10/1927		F/WH	Leyton 1952	Retired, O's coach 1963	301	0	74	19	0	5	3	0	0	323	0	79

Player	Birth	Death if known	Pos	From	To	League Apps	League Sub	League Gls	FA Cup Apps	FA Cup Sub	FA Cup Gls	FL Cup Apps	FL Cup Sub	FL Cup Gls	Total Apps	Total Sub	Total Gls
Fairbrother, Barrie Edward	Hackney 30/12/1950		F	O's youth 1967	Millwall 1975	171	17	41	15	0	7	7	1	2	193	18	50
Farley, Alexander	Finchley 11/5/1925		D	Cromwell A 1945	Bournemouth 1948	15	0	0	3	0	0	-	-	-	18	0	0
Farrell, Francis	Wishaw 1916		M	Hibernian 1937	Hibernian 1939	2	0	0	0	0	0	-	-	-	2	0	0
Farrell, Vincent	Preston 11/9/1908	25/4/1987	F	Preston North E 1934	Exeter C 1937	79	0	21	3	0	0	-	-	-	82	0	21
Fashanu, Justinus Soni	Hackney 19/2/1961	2/5/1998	F	West Ham U 1990	Southall 1990	3	2	0	0	0	0	0	0	0	3	2	0
Fearon, Ronald Thomas	Romford 19/11/1960			Ipswich T (loan) 1995	Ipwsich T 1995												
" " "				Wichita W'gs (USA) 1995	Ashford T 1996	18	0	0	1	0	0	0	0	0	19	0	0
Fee, Gregory Paul	Halifax 24/6/1964		D	Sheffield W (loan) 1990	Sheff W 1996	4	1	0	0	0	0	0	0	0	4	1	0
Fellowes, William James	Bradford 15/3/1910	Nov 1987	D	Plymouth A 1933	Luton T 1935	78	0	1	6	0	0	-	-	-	84	0	1
Fenn, Neale Michael Charles	Edmonton, London 18/1/1977		F	Tottenham H (loan) 1998	Tottenham H 1998	3	0	0	0	0	0	0	0	0	3	0	0
Fenton, Kenneth James	Bramley 23/10/1920	1952	D	Gainsborough Trin 1946	Oldham A 1947	7	0	0	0	0	0	-	-	-	7	0	0
Ferry, Gordon	Sunderland 22/12/1943		D	Arsenal 1965	Atlanta Chiefs (USA) 1967	42	0	0	1	0	0	1	0	0	44	0	0
Findlay, William	Motherwell 1901		WH	Peebles R 1926	Peebles R 1927	2	0	0	0	0	0	-	-	-	2	0	0
Finlayson, John	Cowdenbeath 14/6/1912		D	Cowdenbeath 1933	Luton T 1935	11	0	0	0	0	0	-	-	-	11	0	0
Finlayson, William	Thornliebank 29/3/1899		F	Chelsea 1924	Brentford 1925	21	0	2	1	0	0	-	-	-	22	0	2
Finney, Stephen Kenneth	Hexham 31/10/1973		F	Carlisle U 1998	Gretna 1999	2	3	0	0	0	0	0	0	0	2	3	0
Fishenden, Paul	Hillingdon 2/8/1963		F	Wimbledon (loan) 1986	Wimbledon 1986	4	0	0	1	0	0	0	0	0	5	0	0
Fisher, Frederick	Hetton-le-Hole 28/11/1924	2004	F	Shrewsbury T 1954	Non-League 1956	2	0	1	0	0	0	-	-	-	2	0	1
Fisher, Frederick William	Hucknall 1910		F	Gillingham 1936	Newport I of W 1937	2	0	0	0	0	0	-	-	-	2	0	0
Fisher, Robert Paul	Wembley 3/8/1956		D	O's youth 1971	Cambridge U 1982	308	6	4	26	0	0	19	1	1	353	7	5
Fitzgerald, Scott Peter	Hillingdon 18/11/1979		F	Watford loan 2005	Watford 2005	1	0	0	0	0	0	0	0	0	1	0	0
Flatt, Colin Harold	Blyth 30/1/1940		F	Wisbech T 1965	Southend U 1966	32	1	8	1	0	0	0	0	0	33	1	8
Fletcher, Charles Alfred	Homerton 28/10/1905	22/8/1980	F	Non-League 1927	Crystal Palace 1928												
" " "				Merthyr T 1930	Brentford 1933	120	0	32	6	0	2	-	-	-	126	0	34
Fletcher, Gary	Widnes 4//6/1981		F	Northwich Victoria 2001	Lincoln C 2003	10	11	1	2	0	0	1	0	1	13	11	2
Fletcher, John Jack Robert	Tyne Dock 1910		F	Queen's Park R 1936	Southampton 1938	55	0	11	1	0	0	-	-	-	56	0	11
Flint, Kenneth	Selston 12/11/1923		F	Aldershot 1958	Bath C 1958	4	0	0	0	0	0	-	-	-	4	0	0
Fogg, William Henry	Birkenhead 9/3/1903	29/7/1966	D	Huddersfield T 1933	New Brighton 1936	81	0	2	5	0	0	-	-	-	86	0	2
Forbes, Alexander Rooney	Dundee 21/1/1925		WH	Arsenal 1956	Fulham 1957	8	0	0	0	0	0	-	-	-	8	0	0
Forbes, Boniek Manuel G.	Guinea Bissau 30/9/1983		F	O's youth 2000	Ford U (Redbridge) 2004	0	13	0	0	2	0	0	0	0	0	15	0
Forge, Nicolas	Roanne (France) 13/5/1971		D	Darlington 2001	ASOA Valenciennes 2001	1	0	0	0	0	0	0	0	0	1	0	0
Forrest, James Jack Henry	Shildon 1891		WH	Shildon 1913	Northampton T 1922	126	0	10	7	0	0	-	-	-	133	0	10
Forsyth, David	Falkirk 1945		D	Kirkintilloch Rob Roy 1964	Durban C (SA) 1967	32	0	0	0	4	0	1	0	0	37	0	0
Fortune-West, Leopold	Stratford 9/4/1971		F	Gillingham (loan) 1997	Gillingham 1997	1	4	0	0	0	0	0	0	0	1	4	0
Foster, Colin John	Chislehurst 16/7/1964		D	O's youth 1981	Nottingham Forest 1987	173	1	10	19	0	5	12	0	0	204	1	15
Foster, Ronald Edmund	Islington 22/11/1938		F	Clapton 1957	Grimsby T 1962	72	0	17	6	0	4	7	0	3	85	0	24
Foster, Thomas Curtis	Easington 30/6/1908	1982	F	Reading 1934	Swansea T 1936	19	0	11	5	0	2	-	-	-	24	0	13
Fowler, John Jack	Cardiff 3/12/1899	26/2/1975	D/F	Swansea T 1930	Retired 1932	75	0	15	5	0	0	-	-	-	80	0	15
Francis, George James	Poplar 18/6/1896	29/9/1923	D	Non-League 1919	Folkestone 1920	1	0	0	0	0	0	-	-	-	1	0	0
Francis, Keith Roy	Yeovil 22/7/1929		M	Yeovil T 1950	Yeovil T 1952	3	0	0	0	0	0	-	-	-	3	0	0

Player	Birth	Death if known	Pos	From	To	League Apps	League Sub	League Gls	FA Cup Apps	FA Cup Sub	FA Cup Gls	FL Cup Apps	FL Cup Sub	FL Cup Gls	Total Apps	Total Sub	Total Gls
French, James John B.	Tannochside 31/12/1907		F	Tunbridge Wells R 1933	Released 1934	4	0	1	0	0	0	-	-	-	4	0	1
Froom, Raymond	London		WH	Southall 1945	Southall 1946	0	0	0	2	0	0	-	-	-	2	0	0
Fry, Barry Francis	Bedford 7/4/1945		M	Gravesend & N 1966	Bedford T 1967												
" " "				Bedford T 1967	Romford 1968	7	6	0	0	0	0	1	0	0	8	6	0
Fullbrook, John Frederick	Grays 15/7/1918	Mar 1992	D	Plymouth A 1945	Dartford 1948	36	0	1	1	0	0	-	-	-	37	0	1
Fulton, Raymond Hamilton	Hendon 24/9/1953		D	West Ham U 1972	Folkestone T 1973	1	0	0	0	0	0	0	0	0	1	0	0
Galbraith, John McDonald	Renton		D	Shawfield 1921	Cardiff C 1931	277	0	9	19	0	1	-	-	-	296	0	10
Galloway, David Wilson	Kirkaldy 6/5/1910	Kent 1979	M	Carlisle U 1938	Tunbridge Wells R 1939	2	0	0	0	0	0	-	-	-	2	0	0
Gamble, Bradley David	Southwark 4/2/1975		F	O's youth 1991	Fisher A 1994	1	0	0	0	0	0	0	0	0	1	0	0
Garbutt, Henry Penty	Pontefract 12/11/1907	Feb 1986	WH	Tottenham H 1930	Accrington Stanley 1931	9	0	1	0	0	0	-	-	-	9	0	1
Garcia, Richard	Perth, Australia 4/9/1981		F	West Ham U (loan) 2000	West Ham U 2000	18	0	4	0	0	0	3	0	0	21	0	4
Gardner, James Robert	Felixstowe 29/7/1901		F	Bristol R 1926	Lovells A 1929	31	0	17	1	0	0	-	-	-	32	0	17
Garland, Peter John	Croydon 20/1/1971		M	Charlton A 1996	Crawley T 1997	13	8	0	2	0	0	1	0	0	16	8	0
Garland-Wells, Herbert M.	Brockley 14/11/1907	6/6/1993	G	Oxford Univ 1929	Fulham 1930	11	0	0	0	0	0	-	-	-	11	0	0
Gates, George John	Hammersmith		F	Brentford 1906	Grimsby T 1909	53	0	7	3	0	0	-	-	-	56	0	7
Gavigan, Peter	Gorbals 11/12/1897	2/3/1977	F	Fulham 1925	Bilston U 1926	62	0	4	6	0	0	-	-	-	68	0	4
Gay, James McLean	Perthshire 17/3/1897	31/8/1967	D	Coventry C 1928	Watford 1930	40	0	0	4	0	0	-	-	-	44	0	0
George, Frank Richard	Stepney 20/11/1933		G	Carshalton A 1957	Watford 1963	119	0	0	12	0	0	8	0	0	139	0	0
Gerula, Stanislaw Eugeniusz	Poland 21/2/1924	29/8/1979	G	Carpathians 1948	Walthamstow Ave 1950	30	0	0	1	0	0	-	-	-	31	0	0
Gibbs, Derek William	Fulham 22/12/1934		M	Chelsea 1960	QPR 1963	33	0	4	5	0	2	4	0	1	42	0	7
Gibson, Harold Thomas	Hoxton		WH	Hoxton Hall 1913	Retired after WWI	30	0	0	0	0	0	-	-	-	30	0	0
Gibson, Kenneth	Clapton		F	Saracens 1905	Saracens 1906	5	0	1	0	0	0	-	-	-	5	0	1
Gibson, Thomas Richard D.	Manchester 12/5/1929		WH	Sheffield W 1960	Buxton 1961	8	0	0	0	0	0	0	0	0	8	0	0
Giles, David Charles	Cardiff 21/9/1956		M	Swansea C (loan) 1981	Swansea C 1981	3	0	2	0	0	0	0	0	0	3	0	2
Gill, James Joshua Allison	Crook 21/7/1903	6/9/1985	G	Bradford C 1933	Accrington St 1934	19	0	0	3	0	0	-	-	-	22	0	0
Gillatt, Kenneth Ernest	Wensleydale 18/1/1900	1971	F	Matlock T 1920	Burnley (tr) 1923	61	0	6	2	0	0	-	-	-	63	0	6
Gilson, Thomas Aubrey	Lichfield 1/6/1879	2/3/1912	D	Bristol C 1905	Brentford 1906	2	0	0	0	0	0	-	-	-	2	0	0
Glidden, Gilbert Swinburne	Sunderland 15/12/1915	Oct 1988	D	Reading as coach 1950	PE teacher 1951	1	0	0	0	0	0	-	-	-	1	0	0
Glover, Allan Richard	Laleham 21/10/1950		M	West Bromwich A 1977	Brentford 1978	37	0	5	0	0	0	1	0	0	38	0	5
Glynn, Terence Robert	Hackney 17/12/1958		F	O's youth 1975	Brentford (tr) 1977	1	1	0	0	0	0	0	0	0	1	1	0
Goddard, Raymond	Fulham 13/2/1949		G	Fulham 1967	Millwall 1974	278	0	0	20	0	0	13	0	0	311	0	0
Godfrey, Kevin	Kennington 24/2/1960		F	O's youth 1976	Brentford 1988	255	30	63	28	1	5	15	2	4	298	33	72
Goffin, Richard Robert	Clapton 1886		F	Peel Institute 1907	New Brompton 1911	65	0	12	1	0	1	-	-	-	66	0	13
Goodgame, Anthony	Hammersmith 19/2/1946		D	Fulham 1966	Hillingdon Borough 1967	7	1	0	0	0	0	0	0	0	7	1	0
Goodman, Albert Abraham	Dalston 3/9/1890	7/12/1959	D	Gillingham 1925	Guildford C 1926	12	0	0	0	0	0	-	-	-	12	0	0
Gore, Frederick Leslie	Coventry 21/1/1914	22/01/1991	F	Bradford C 1939	Yeovil T 1946	0	0	0	2	0	1	-	-	-	2	0	1
Gough, Cecil William McKinley	Cirencester 17/10/1901	16/5/1963	WH	Bristol R 1925	QPR 1926												
" " " "				Torquay U 1928	Canterbury Waverly 1929	7	0	0	0	0	0	-	-	-	7	0	0
Gough, Neil	Harlow 1/9/1981		M	O's youth 1998	Hampton & Richmond 2002	2	13	1	0	0	0	0	1	0	2	14	1
Gould, Ronald Donald	Bethnal Green 27/9/1982		M	O's youth 1999	Hampton & Richmond 2002	0	2	0	0	0	0	0	0	0	0	2	0

Player	Birth	Death if known	Pos	From	To	League Apps	League Sub	League Gls	FA Cup Apps	FA Cup Sub	FA Cup Gls	FL Cup Apps	FL Cup Sub	FL Cup Gls	Total Apps	Total Sub	Total Gls
Graham, James Arthur	Corby 13/1/1911	28/11/1987	F	Southend U 1937	Yeovil & Petters U 1938	9	0	1	1	0	1	-	-	-	10	0	2
Graham, Malcolm	Wakefield 26/1/1934		F	Bristol C 1960	QPR 1963	75	0	29	4	0	0	5	0	5	84	0	34
Grant, George	Bonnyrigg		F	St Bernards 1938	Ballymena 1939	19	0	4	1	0	0	-	-	-	20	0	4
Grapes, Lionel Oliver	London		G	Shepherds B (loan) 1912	Shepherds B 1912	2	0	0	0	0	0	-	-	-	2	0	0
Gray, Andrew	Southampton 25/10/1973		F	Reading 1992	Slough T 1996	16	16	3	1	0	1	0	2	0	17	18	4
Gray, Mark Stuart	Tenby 24/11/1959		F	Fulham 1979	Swansea C (tr) 1981	1	1	0	0	0	0	0	0	0	1	1	0
Gray, Nigel Robert	Fulham 2/11/1956		D	O's youth 1973	Swindon T 1983	233	0	4	20	1	0	8	0	0	261	1	4
Gray, Thomas	Portsmouth 18/10/1891	12/3/1978	G	Portsmouth 1919	Guildford C 1921	12	0	0	1	0	0	-	-	-	13	0	0
Gray, Wayne	Camberwell 7/11/1980		F	Wimbledon (loan) 2001	Wimbledon 2002	13	2	5	2	0	1	0	0	0	15	2	6
Gray, William Patrick	Durham 24/5/1927		F	Dinnington Colliery 1947	Chelsea 1949	19	0	1	1	0	0	-	-	-	20	0	1
Grealish, Anthony Patrick	Paddington 21/9/1956		M	O's youth 1972	Luton T 1979	169	2	10	17	0	0	6	1	0	192	3	10
Greechan, James	Scotland		F	Brentford 1907	Stockport C 1909	30	0	8	3	0	3	-	-	-	33	0	11
Green, Thomas	Liverpool 25/11/1893	l/10/1975	F	Stockport Co 1923	Hearts 1924	24	0	10	3	0	0	-	-	-	27	0	10
Gregory, Gordon Harold	Hackney 24/10/1943		F	O's youth 1960	Charlton A 1966	79	0	12	3	0	0	5	0	3	87	0	15
Gregory, Jack Leslie	Southampton 25/1/1925		D	Southampton 1955	Bournemouth & BA 1959	91	0	0	4	0	0	-	-	-	95	0	0
Greygoose, Dean	Torquay 18/12/1964		G	Cambridge U 1985	Crystal Palace 1986	1	0	0	0	0	0	0	0	0	1	0	0
Griffiths, Carl Brian	Oswestry 16/7/1971		F	Peterb'gh U (loan) 1996	Peterborough U 1996												
" " "				Peterborough U 1997	Port Vale 1999												
" " "				Port Vale 1999	Luton T 2001	111	7	51	8	0	6	9	2	3	128	9	60
Griffiths, Thomas	Manchester		WH	Exeter C 1912	Llanelli 1914	12	0	0	1	0	0	-	-	-	13	0	0
Grimsdell, Arthur	Watford 23/3/1894	13/3/1963	WH	Tottenham H 1929	Retired 1930	11	0	0	6	0	2	-	-	-	17	0	2
Groombridge, David Henry	Norbury 13/4/1930		G	Hayes 1951	Retired 1960	133	0	0	9	0	0	-	-	-	142	0	0
Groves, Victor George	Stepney 5/11/1932		F	Walthamstow Ave 1954	Arsenal 1955	42	0	24	2	0	1	-	-	-	44	0	25
Hackett, Warren James	Plaistow 16/12/1971		D/M	Tottenham H 1990	Doncaster R 1994	74	2	3	8	0	2	4	0	0	86	2	5
Hadland, Phillip Jonathan	Warrington 20/10/1980		M	Rochdale 2001	Brighton & HA 2001	0	5	1	0	0	0	0	1	0	0	6	1
Hague, Paul	Consett 16/9/1972		D	Gillingham 1994	Gateshead 1996	17	1	1	0	0	0	0	0	0	17	0	1
Haig-Brown, Alan Roderick	Godalming 6/9/1877	25/3/1918	F	Brighton & HA 1906	Lacing College 1906	4	0	1	0	0	0	-	-	-	4	0	1
Hales, Kevin Peter	Dartford 13/1/1961		M	Chelsea 1983	Welling U 1993	285	15	23	25	1	0	23	0	2	333	16	25
Hales Snr, William	Walthamstow		D	Walthamstow Gr 1911	West Ham U (tr) 1911	1	0	0	0	0	0	-	-	-	1	0	0
Hales Jnr, William Alfred	Hackney 24/7/1910	15/2/1986	F	Thames Assoc 1931	Non-League 1933	13	0	3	0	0	0	-	-	-	13	0	3
Hall, Stanley Arthur	Southgate 18/2/1917	23/9/1999	G	Finchley 1938	Yeovil T 1947	26	0	0	2	0	0	-	-	-	28	0	0
Halliday, David	Dumfries 11/12/1897	5/1/1970	F	Manchester C 1933	Yeovil & Petters U 1935	53	0	33	3	0	3	-	-	-	56	0	36
Hallybone jnr, James M.	Leytonstone 15/5/1962		M	O's youth 1978	Halifax T 1982	5	3	0	3	0	0	0	0	0	8	3	0
Halom, Victor Lewis	Swadlincote 3/10/1948		F	Charlton A (loan) 1967	Charlton A 1967												
" " "				Charlton A 1967	Fulham 1968	53	0	12	5	0	3	4	0	4	62	0	19
Halse, Harold James	Stratford 1/1/1886	25/3/1949	F	Barking 1905	Southend U 1906	2	0	1	0	0	0	-	-	-	2	0	1
Hamberger, Stephen	Hackney 1959		D	Walthamstow A 1978	Maidstone U 1980	0	0	0	0	0	0	1	0	0	1	0	0
Hammond, Dean John	Hastings 7/3/1983		M	Brighton & HA (loan) 2003	Brighton & HA 2003	6	2	0	1	0	0	0	0	0	7	2	0
Hammond, George	Sunderland 1880		F	Lincoln C 1904	Gainsborough Trinity 1905												
" "				Gainsborough Trinity 1906	Croydon Common 1906	4	0	0	3	0	2	-	-	-	7	0	2

Player	Birth	Death if known	Pos	From	To	League Apps	League Sub	League Gls	FA Cup Apps	FA Cup Sub	FA Cup Gls	FL Cup Apps	FL Cup Sub	FL Cup Gls	Total Apps	Total Sub	Total Gls
Hannaford, Charles William	Finsbury Park 8/1/1896	7/1970	F	Charlton A 1924	Manchester U 1927												
" " "				Manchester U 1929	Retired 1929	67	0	10	1	0	0	-	-	-	68	0	10
Hanson, Christian	Middlesbrough 3/8/1981		D	Port Vale 2005	Grays A 2005	0	2	0	0	0	0	0	0	0	0	2	0
Hanson, David Paul	Huddersfield 19/11/1968		F	Hednesford T 1995	Halifax T 1998	26	22	5	1	1	0	1	1	0	28	24	5
Harnwell, Jamie Richard	Perth (Australia) 21/7/1977		D	Perth Glory (Aus) 2003	Welling U 2003	1	2	0	0	0	0	0	0	0	1	2	0
Harper, David	Peckham 29/9/1938		M	Swindon T 1967	Retired 1971	82	3	4	6	0	0	6	0	1	94	3	5
Harriott, Marvin Lee	Dulwich 20/4/1974		D	Barnsley (loan) 1993	Barnsley 1993	8	0	0	1	0	0	0	0	0	9	0	0
Harris, Andrew David D.	Springs (S.Africa) 26/2/1977		D/M	Southend U 1999	Chester C 2003	143	6	2	9	0	0	11	0	0	163	6	2
Harris, Jason Andre S.	Sutton 24/11/1976		F	Crystal Palace 1997	Preston NE 1998	22	15	7	2	0	0	1	0	0	25	15	7
Harris, Jeffrey Bruce	Stepney 11/6/1942		D	Hendon 1961	Hendon 1962												
" " "				Enfield 1964	Romford 1965	14	0	0	0	0	0	0	0	0	14	0	0
Harris, Paul Edwin	Hackney 19/5/1953		D	C's youth 1969	Swansea C 1975	96	0	4	7	0	0	7	2	0	110	2	4
Harris, Thomas Alfred	Chelsea 8/11/1924	11/10/2001	F	Fulham 1951	Colchester U 1953	31	0	11	5	0	2	-	-	-	36	0	13
Harrison, Lee David	Billericay 12/9/1971		G	Barnet 2003	Peterborough U 2005	59	1	0	3	1	0	1	0	0	63	2	0
Hartburn, John	Houghton-le-Sp'g 20/12/1920	21/1/2001	F	Millwall 1954	Yiewsley 1958	112	0	36	7	0	3	-	-	-	119	0	39
Harvey, Lee Derek	Harlow 21/12/1966		F	C's youth 1981	Nottingham Forest 1993	135	49	23	10	4	2	13	3	3	158	56	28
Haslam, Harold	Manchester 30/7/1921	11/9/1986	D	Brighton & HA 1948	Guildford C 1949	7	0	0	0	0	0	-	-	-	7	0	0
Hasty, Patrick Joseph	Belfast 17/3/1932	2000	F	Tooting & Mitcham 1958	QPR 1959	2	0	2	0	0	0	-	-	-	2	0	2
Hatcher, Daniel Ian	Newport, I of W 24/12/1983		F	C's youth 2000	Newport I of W 2003	3	13	0	1	2	0	0	0	0	4	15	0
Hawkins, Herbert Henry	Lambeth 15/7/1923	Mar 1982	F	Gravesend & N 1951	Non-League 1953	5	0	0	1	0	0	-	-	-	6	0	0
Hawley, John East	Partington 8/5/1954		F	Arsenal (loan) 1982	Arsenal 1982	4	0	1	1	0	0	0	0	0	4	0	1
Hayward, William Arthur	Blaina 16/11/1906	1976	WH	Newport Co 1926	Tottenham H 1927												
" " "				Tottenham H 1931	Non-League 1932	10	0	0	0	0	0	-	-	-	10	0	0
Heald, Gregory James	Enfield 26/9/1971		D	Barnet 2003	Rochdale 2004	9	0	1	0	0	0	0	0	0	9	0	1
Heald, Paul Andrew	Wath-on-Dearne 20/9/1968		G	Sheffield U 1988	Wimbledon 1995	176	0	0	9	0	0	13	0	0	198	0	0
Hearty, Hugh	Lesmahagow 22/3/1913	Apr 1992	D	Cardiff C 1936	Retired (policeman) 1939	98	0	2	6	0	0	-	-	-	104	0	2
Hebdon, John Jack Thomas	Castleford 12/11/1902	21/3/1956	D	Thames Assoc 1932	Halifax T 1932	4	0	0	0	0	0	-	-	-	4	0	0
Heckman, Ronald Ernest	Peckham 23/11/1929	26/11/1990	F	Bromley 1955	Millwall 1957	87	0	38	5	0	6	-	-	-	92	0	44
Hedman, Rudolph Gideon	Lambeth 16/11/1964		D	Crystal P (loan) 1989	Crystal Palace 1990	5	0	0	0	0	0	0	0	0	5	0	0
Heidenstrom, Bjorn Glav	Porsgrunn (Norway) 15/1/1968		M	Odd BK Grenland (tr) 1996	Odd BK Grenland 1997	3	1	0	0	0	0	0	0	0	3	1	0
Heinemann, George Henry	Stafford 17/12/1905	1970	WH	Crystal Palace 1935	Wellington T 1938	86	0	1	7	0	0	-	-	-	93	0	1
Henderson, Alastair Ian	Anderston 1911		WH	Liverpool 1933	Scottish Border Lge 1935	18	0	0	3	0	0	-	-	-	21	0	0
Henderson, James Thomas	Morpeth 1877		F	Preston NE 1909	Rochdale 1910	26	0	4	1	0	0	-	-	-	27	0	4
Henderson, William	Linlithgow 1878		D	Reading 1906	New Brompton 1909	47	0	0	4	0	0	-	-	-	51	0	0
Henderson, William	Morpeth		D	Morpeth T 1910	Morpeth T 1912	16	0	0	0	0	0	-	-	-	16	0	0
Henderson, William	Edinburgh 1898	1964	F	Preston NE 1925	Heart of Midlothian 1926	29	0	7	4	0	1	-	-	-	33	0	8
Hendon, Ian	Ilford 5/12/1971		D	Tottenham H (loan) 1992	Tottenham H 1992												
" "				Tottenham H 1993	Notts Co 1997	135	2	5	7	0	0	8	0	0	150	2	5
Heppolette, Richard A.W.	Bhusawal, India 8/4/1949		M	Preston NE 1972	Crystal Palace 1976	113	0	10	6	0	0	3	0	0	122	0	10
Herod, Edwin Redvers Baden	Ilford 16/5/1900	9/5/1973	D	Swindon T 1935	Retired 1937	53	0	0	7	0	0	-	-	-	60	0	0

Player	Birth	Death if known	Pos	From	To	League Apps	League Sub	League Gls	FA Cup Apps	FA Cup Sub	FA Cup Gls	FL Cup Apps	FL Cup Sub	FL Cup Gls	Total Apps	Total Sub	Total Gls
Herrera, Roberto	Torquay 12/6/1970		D	Torquay U 2001	Merthyr Tydfil 2001	2	0	0	0	1	0	-	-	-	2	1	0
Hibbs, Gary Thomas	Hammersmith 26/1/1957		M	O's youth 1972	Aldershot 1977	1	0	0	0	0	0	-		-	1	0	0
Hicks, Stuart Jason	Peterborough 30/5/1967		D	Scarborough 1997	Chester C 2000	77	1	0	6	0	0	9	0	0	92	1	0
Higginbotham, Henry	Sydney, Australia 27/7/1894	5/6/1950	WH	Luton T 1922	Nelson 1924	19	0	1	0	0	0	-	-	-	19	0	1
Higgins, Ronald Valentine	Silvertown 14/2/1923		F	Green & Siley Weir 1949	Tonbridge 1950	2	0	0	0	0	0	-	-	-	2	0	0
Hillam, Charles Emmanuel	Burnley 6/10/1908	Apr 1958	G	Manchester U 1934	Southend 1938	125	0	0	9	0	0	-	-	-	134	0	0
Hills, Jack	Hackney		F	Amateur football 1899	Amateur football 1906	2	0	0	7	0	0	-	-	-	9	0	0
Hind, William	Percy Main Apr 1885		WH	Fulham 1908	Ton Pentre (trainer) 1920	198	0	7	6	0	0	-	-	-	204	0	7
Hoadley, Philip Frederick W.	Battersea 6/1/1952		D	Crystal Palace 1971	Norwich C 1979	255	0	9	24	0	2	16	0	1	295	0	12
Hoar, Sidney Walter	Leagrave 28//11/1895	4/5/1969	F	Arsenal 1929	Retired 1930	26	0	3	5	0	0	-	-	-	31	0	3
Hobbins, Sidney George	Plumstead 16/5/ 1916	16/3/1984	G	Millwall 1949	Retired 1950	11	0	0	0	0	0	-	-	-	11	0	0
Hockton, Daniel	Barking 7/2/1979		F	Millwall (loan) 1999	Millwall 2000	1	4	0	0	0	0	1	0	0	2	4	0
Hoddle, Carl	Harlow 8/3/1967		M	Bishop Stortford 1989	Barnet 1991	19	9	2	0	0	0	1	0	0	20	9	2
Hodge, Stephen Brian	Nottingham 25/10/1962		M	Hong Kong 1997	Retired 1997	1	0	0	0	0	0	0	0	0	1	0	0
Hodges, Lee Leslie	Newham 2/3/1978		M	West Ham U (loan) 1997	West Ham U 1997	3	0	0	0	0	0	0	0	0	3	0	0
Holland, Jonathan Jack	Preston 23//4/1901	Apr 1999	F	Newport Co 1927	Carlisle U 1929	18	0	4	0	0	0	-	-	-	18	0	4
Holligan, Gavin Victor	Lambeth 5/8/1980		F	West Ham U (loan) 1999	West Ham U 1999	1	0	0	0	0	0	1	0	0	2	0	0
Hollow, Michael John	Nazeing 5/9/1943	2003	D	Bishop Stortford 1961	Peterborough U 1965	34	0	0	0	0	0	1	0	0	35	0	0
Holmes, Norman Darley	Hillside 1891		D	Leeds C 1910	Huddersfield T 1913	4	0	0	0	0	0	-	-	-	4	0	0
Holmes, William Marsden	Darley Hillside 1875	18/2/1922	D	Manchester C 1905	O's manager 1908	46	0	0	5	0	0	-	-	-	51	0	0
Holton, Clifford Charles	Oxford 29/4/1929	4/6/1996	F	Charlton A 1966	Retired 1967	47	0	17	3	0	0	2	0	1	52	0	18
Hope, Philip	Kimblesworth 24/4/1897	3/1/1969	D	Southend U 1927	Rochdale 1928	18	0	0	1	0	0	-	-	-	19	0	0
Houchen, Keith Morton	Middlesbrough 25/7/1960		F	Hartlepool U 1982	York C 1984	74	2	20	3	0	0	3	0	1	80	2	21
Houghton, Scott Arron	Hitchen 22/10/1971		F	Southend U 2000	Halifax T 2002	28	15	6	3	0	1	1	0	1	32	15	8
Howard, Terence	Stepney, 26/2/1966		M	Chelsea 1987	Wycombe W 1995	323	5	31	23	1	3	26	0	1	372	6	35
Howe, Albert Richard Henry	Greenwich 16/11/1938		D	Crystal Palace 1967	Colchester U 1969	91	0	0	5	0	0	5	0	0	101	0	0
Howes, Shaun Colin	Norwich 7/11/1977		D	Cambridge U 1996	Billericay T 1997	3	2	0	0	0	0	0	0	0	3	2	0
Howshall, Samuel	Salisbury		F	Salisbury T 1907	Salisbury T 1908	2	0	0	1	0	0	-	-	-	3	0	0
Hugall, James Cockburn	Whitburn 26/4/1889	23/9/1927	G	Whitburn FC 1910	Hamilton Aca 1922	140	0	0	3	0	0	-	-	-	143	0	0
Hughes, Robert Arthur	Holywell 13/12/1904	1973	F	Blackpool 1929	Altrincham 1931	6	0	1	0	0	0	-	-	-	6	0	1
Hughton, Henry Timothy	Stratford 18/11/1959		D/M	O's youth 1975	Crystal Palace 1892												
" " "				Brentford 1986	Sweden 1988	120	9	2	9	0	0	5	0	1	134	9	3
Hull, Alan Edward	Rochford 4/9/1962		F	Barking 1987	Enfield 1981	54	25	17	3	4	1	4	4	1	61	33	19
Hull, Archibald James	East Ham 8/8/1902	6/3/1978	D	West Ham U 1930	Ilford 1930	1	0	0	0	0	0	-	-	-	1	0	0
Hunt, David John	Dulwich 10/9/1982		D/M	Crystal Palace 2003	Northampton T 2005	57	8	1	3	0	1	2	0	0	62	8	2
Hunt, Douglas Arthur	Shipton Bellinger 19/5/1914	May 1989	F	Sheffield W 1946	Gloucester C 1948	61	0	16	2	0	1	-	-	-	63	0	17
Hunt, Harold	Hackney, London		F	Non-League 1905	Non-League 1906	1	0	0	0	0	0	-	-	-	1	0	0
Hunt, Warren	Portsmouth 2/3/1984		F	Portsmouth (loan) 2004	Portsmouth 2004	6	0	0	0	0	0	0	0	0	6	0	0
Hunter, William	Sunderland 1888		F	Manchester U 1913	Lincoln C 1914	9	0	1	1	0	0	-	-	-	10	0	1
Hurley, William Henry	Leytonstone 11/12/1959		F	O's youth 1975	Retired 1977	1	1	0	0	0	0	0	0	0	1	1	0

Player	Birth	Death if known	Pos	From	To	League Apps	League Sub	League Gls	FA Cup Apps	FA Cup Sub	FA Cup Gls	FL Cup Apps	FL Cup Sub	FL Cup Gls	Total Apps	Total Sub	Total Gls
Hurst, Aaron	Bolton 1/12/1912	3/1/1979	D	Blackpool 1935	Bury 1936	1	0	0	0	0	0	-	-	-	1	0	0
Hutchings, Carl Emil	Hammersmith 24/9/1974		M	Southend U 2000	Farnborough T 2003	30	8	2	0	0	0	2	0	0	32	8	2
Hyde, Paul David	Hayes 7/4/1963		G	Leicester C (loan) 1997	Leicester C 1997												
" " "				Leicester C 1997	Dover A 1999	41	0	0	2	0	0	4	0	0	47	0	0
Ibehre, Jabo Oshevire	Islington 28/1/1983		F	O's youth 1999	Current	82	66	25	9	3	1	2	3	2	93	72	28
Iceton, Jacob	West Auckland 22/10/1903	Apr 1981	G	Aldershot 1936	Worcester C 1939	40	0	0	3	0	0	-	-	-	43	0	0
Imrie, David	Scotland		F	Chicago Brickl'rs FC 1931	Scotland 1932	12	0	7	0	0	0	-	-	-	12	0	7
Ing, Joseph Charles	Walthamstow		WH	Clapton Warwick 1915	Northfleet 1920	17	0	0	1	0	0	-	-	-	18	0	0
Inglethorpe, Alexander M.	Epsom 14/11/1971		F	Watford 1995	Exeter C 2000	105	18	32	4	5	0	7	0	3	114	23	35
Iriekpen, Ezomo	London 14/5/1982		D	West Ham U (loan) 2002	West Ham U 2002	5	0	1	1	0	0	0	0	0	6	0	1
Ives, Charles Benjamin	Tottenham 1889	14/4/1962	F	QPR 1919	Ton Pentre 1920	17	0	4	0	0	0	-	-	-	17	0	4
Jack, Robert Rollo	Bolton 2/4/1902	Apr 1994	F	Bolton W 1929	Yeovil & Petters U 1932	79	0	22	4	0	0	-	-	-	83	0	22
Jackett, Frank	Ystalyfera, Wales 5/7/1927		M	Watford 1953	Ramsgate A 1954	4	0	0	0	0	0	-	-	-	4	0	0
Jackson, Brian Harvill	Walton-on-Thames 1/4/1933		F	Chase of Chertsey 1950	Liverpool 1951	38	0	2	0	0	0	-	-	-	38	0	2
Jackson, John Keith	Hammersmith 5/9/1942		G	Crystal Palace 1973	Millwall 1979	226	0	0	19	0	0	11	0	0	256	0	0
Jacques, Robin	London 1897	Aug 1923	F	West Norwood 1922	Fulham 1923	4	0	2	0	0	0	-	-	-	4	0	2
Jenkins, Thomas Ernest	Bethnal Green 2/12/1947		F	O's youth 1966	Margate 1968	1	0	0	0	0	0	0	0	0	1	0	0
Jennings, Percival	Consett 27/3/1907		D	Blackpool 1930	Annfields Plain 1933	19	0	0	0	0	0	-	-	-	19	0	0
Jennings, William John	Hackney 20/2/1952		F	West Ham U 1979	Luton T 1982	64	3	21	5	0	3	6	0	2	75	3	26
Jewhurst, Frederick Harold	Hoxton 30/9/1897	17/5/1949	WH	Southend U 1927	Dartford 1929	1	0	0	0	0	0	-	-	-	1	0	0
Jeyes, James	London		D	Non-League 1914	Non-League 1915	1	0	0	0	0	0	-	-	-	1	0	0
John, Stephen Paul	Brentwood 22/12/1966		D	O's youth 1982	Retired 1987	23	0	0	3	0	0	0	0	0	26	0	0
Johnson, Geoffrey Harold	Fulham		D	Southend U 1908	Chelsea 1912	82	0	4	2	0	0	-	-	-	84	0	4
Johnson, John Joseph	Rossendale 1882		F	Luton T 1912	Brentford 1913	3	0	0	0	0	0	-	-	-	3	0	0
Johnson, Peter James	Hackney 18/2/1954		F	Tottenham H (youth) 1972	Greece 1974	1	2	0	0	0	0	0	0	0	1	2	0
Johnson, Victor Ralph	Hethersett 15/4/1922		F	Norwich C 1947	Lowestoft T 1947	7	0	2	0	0	0	-	-	-	7	0	2
Johnston, John Thompson	Sunderland		D	Middlesbrough 1908	Retired after WWI 1916	218	0	1	6	0	0	-	-	-	224	0	1
Johnston, Thomas Bourhill *	Loanhead 18/8/1927		F	Newport Co 1956	Blackburn R 1958												
" " "				Blackburn R 1959	Gillingham 1961	180	0	121	7	0	2	3	0	0	190	0	123
Jonas, William	Blyth 1892	27/7/1916	F	Havanna R 1912	Died in WWI 1916	70	0	21	4	0	2	-	-	-	74	0	23
Jones, Andrew Mark	Wrexham 9/1/1963		F	AFC Bournemouth 1991	Retired 1993	44	15	13	4	2	1	2	0	0	50	17	14
Jones, Christopher Harry	Jersey 18/4/1956		F	Charlton A 1984	St Albans C 1987	106	1	19	11	0	2	5	0	1	122	1	22
Jones, David Owen	Cardiff 28/10/1910	20/5/ 1971	D	Ebbw Vale 1931	Leicester C 1933	55	0	0	4	0	0	-	-	-	59	0	0
Jones, Michael Keith	Berkhampstead 8/1/1945		D	Chelsea 1966	Charlton A 1971	223	5	16	15	0	0	10	0	0	248	5	16
Jones, Selwyn Thomas	Rhos 3/4/1929	Sep 1995	F	Sheffield W 1952	Non-League 1953	6	0	0	0	0	0	-	-	-	6	0	0
Jones, William Kenneth	Gillingham 26/6/1983		D	O's youth 1999	Kidderminster H 2005	68	4	0	3	1	0	2	0	0	73	5	0
Jones-Quartey, David	Harrow 3/7/1964		F	Barnet 1988	Burnley 1989	0	2	0	0	0	0	0	0	0	0	2	0
Joseph, Matthew Nathan A.	Bethnal Green 30/9/1972		D	Cambridge U 1998	Canvey Island 2004	219	5	2	15	1	0	9	1	0	243	7	2
Joseph, Roger Anthony	Paddington 24/12/1965		D	Wimbledon 1996	West Bromwich A 1997												
" " "				West Bromwich A 1998	Retired 2000												

Player	Birth	Death if known	Pos	From	To	League Apps	League Sub	League Gls	FA Cup Apps	FA Cup Sub	FA Cup Gls	FL Cup Apps	FL Cup Sub	FL Cup Gls	Total Apps	Total Sub	Total Gls
" " "				O's trial 2001	Kings Lynn 2001	41	23	0	1	2	0	3	2	0	45	27	0
Julians, Leonard Bruce	Tottenham 19/6/1933	17/12/1993	F	Walthamstow Ave 1950	Arsenal 1958	66	0	35	2	0	1	-	-	-	68	0	36
Juniper, Edward	Shadwell 3/12/1901	Apr 1990	F	Non-League 1920	Non-League 1922	9	0	1	0	0	0	-	-	-	9	0	1
Juryeff, Ian Martin	Gosport 24/11/1962		F	Southampton 1985	Halifax T 1989	106	5	45	10	0	7	9	0	3	125	5	55
Kane, John Peter	Hackney 15/12/1960		D	O's Junior 1976	Rainham T 1980	0	1	0	0	0	0	0	0	0	0	1	0
Kean, Archibald	Barrhead 30/9/1894		F	Croy Celtic 1921	Lincoln C 1922	11	0	0	0	0	0	-	-	-	11	0	0
Keen, Walter James	Loudwater Apr 1904	6/5/1968	D	Fulham 1932	London Transport team 1935	53	0	2	1	0	0	-	-	-	54	0	2
Keith, Joseph Richard	Plaistow 1/10/1978		M	Colchester U 2005	Current	41	1	2	5	0	1	0	1	0	46	2	3
Kelly, Nyree Anthony O.	Meridan 14/2/1966		F	Bury 1995	Colchester U 1996	38	5	4	1	0	0	2	0	0	41	5	4
Kelly, Russell	Ballymoney 10/8/1976		D/M	Chelsea 1996	Darlington 1996	5	1	0	0	0	0	0	0	0	5	1	0
Kerr, Robert Charles	Larkhall 1904		F	Wolverhampton W 1927	Worcester C 1929	31	0	8	0	0	0	-	-	-	31	0	8
Kerrins, Wayne Michael	Brentwood 5/8/1965		D	Fulham (loan) 1989	Fulham 1989	3	0	0	0	0	0	0	0	0	3	0	0
Ketteridge, Stephen Jack	Stevenage 7/11/1959		M	Crystal Palace 1987	Aylesbury U 1989	26	5	1	0	1	0	2	3	0	28	9	1
Key, John Peter	Chelsea 5/11/1937		F	Coventry C 1968	Retired (injury) 1969	9	1	0	0	0	0	0	2	0	9	3	0
Key, Richard Martin	Coventry 13/4/1956		G	Cambridge U 1983	Brentford 1984	42	0	0	1	0	0	2	0	0	45	0	0
King, Edward	Blyth 1890		D	Woolwich Arsenal 1914	Went to war 1915	17	0	0	0	0	0	-	-	-	17	0	0
King, Raymond	Warkworth 15/8/1924		G	Newcastle U 1946	Ashington 1947	1	0	0	0	0	0	-	-	-	1	0	0
Kingaby, Herbert Charles	Hackney Jan 1880	1957	F	West Hampstead 1904	Aston Villa 1906	26	0	4	10	0	3	-	-	-	36	0	7
Kitchen, David Edward S.	Rintein, Germany 11/6/1967		D	Frickley T 1992	Doncaster R 1994	35	8	1	4	0	0	2	0	0	41	8	1
Kitchen, Michael Peter	Mexborough 16/2/1952		F	Doncaster R 1977	Fulham 1979	110	4	49	12	0	9	5	1	2	127	5	60
Lakin, Barry	Dartford 19/9/1973		M/F	Gillingham (youth) 1991	Welling U 1996	41	13	2	2	2	1	4	0	0	47	15	3
Lamberton, George	Rossendale 24/12/1880	18/5/1954	F	Luton T 1905	Norwich C 1906	26	0	3	6	0	4	-	-	-	32	0	7
Lamberton, James	Haslingden 9/2/1877	1929	D	Stalybridge Celtic 1905	Norwich C 1906	33	0	0	6	0	0	-	-	-	39	0	0
Landells, Jack John	Gateshead 11/11/1904	1960	F	Walsall 1937	Chelmsford C 1938	2	0	0	0	0	0	-	-	-	2	0	0
Lane, William	Hackney		F	Non-League 1904	Non-League 1905	-	-	-	6	0	1	-	-	-	6	0	1
Lane, William Henry Charles	Tottenham 28/10/1903	10/11/1985	WH	Bristol C 1937	Retired manager Brentford	12	0	1	2	0	1	-	-	-	14	0	2
Lappin, Hubert Henry	Manchester Jan 1879	May 1925	F	Rossendale U 1906	Chester 1907	38	0	1	-	-	-	-	-	-	38	0	1
Lawrence, Edward	Cefn Mawr 24/8/1907	20/7/1989	D	Wrexham 1928	Notts Co 1931												
" "				B'mouth & BA 1937	Notts Co 1939	121	0	2	12	0	0	-	-	-	133	0	2
Layton, Arthur Richard	West Ham 1890	1962	F	Spittlefields A 1914	Northfleet 1920	26	0	4	2	0	0	-	-	-	28	0	4
Lazarus, Mark	Stepney 5/12/1938		F	Barking 1957	QPR 1960												
" "				Crystal Palace 1969	Folkestone T 1972	101	1	18	6	0	1	3	0	1	110	1	20
Lea, Cyril	Moss, Wrexham 5/8/1934		D	Bradley R 1957	Ipswich T 1964	205	0	0	14	0	0	9	0	0	228	0	0
Leather, John George	Bethnal Green 9/5/1901	9/1/1967	G	Non-League 1926	Non-League 1926	1	0	0	0	0	0	-	-	-	1	0	0
Lee, Christian	Aylesbury 8/10/1976		F	Gillingham (loan) 2001	Gillingham 2001	2	1	0	0	0	0	0	0	0	2	1	0
Lee, James	Rotherham 26/1/1926	2001	D	Chelsea 1954	Swindon T 1956	67	0	1	4	0	0	-	-	-	71	0	1
Lee, John Charles	Morpeth		F	Morpeth T 1910	Exeter C 1913	20	0	1	0	0	0	-	-	-	20	0	1
Lee, Trevor Carl	Lewisham 3/7/1954		F	Gillingham (loan) 1982	Gillingham 1982	5	0	0	0	0	0	0	0	0	5	0	0
Le Flem, Richard Peter	Bradford–on-Avon 12/7/1942		F	Middlesbrough 1966	Retired (injury)	11	0	2	0	0	0	0	0	0	11	0	2
Leggett, Sydney	Clapton 1897		F	Fulham 1914	Tunbridge Wells R 1921	1	0	0	0	0	0	-	-	-	1	0	0

Player	Birth	Death if known	Pos	From	To	League Apps	League Sub	League Gls	FA Cup Apps	FA Cup Sub	FA Cup Gls	FL Cup Apps	FL Cup Sub	FL Cup Gls	Total Apps	Total Sub	Total Gls
Leigertwood, Mikele B.	Enfield 12/1/1982		D	Wimbledon (loan) 2001	Wimbledon 2001	8	0	0	2	0	0	0	0	0	10	0	0
Leigh, Walter Herbert	Yardley 11/1874	1938	F	New Brompton 1905	Hastings U 1906												
" " "				Hastings U 1907	Kettering T 1908	40	0	11	7	0	4	-	-	-	47	0	15
Le May, Frederick John S.	Bethnal Green 2/2/1907	Sep 1988	F	Watford 1932	Margate 1933	10	0	0	0	0	0	-	-	-	10	0	0
Leonard, Anthony Michael	Ireland		F	Reading 1906	Plymouth Argyle 1907	37	0	7	-	-	-	-	-	-	37	0	7
Lewis, Edward	West Bromwich 21/6/1926		G	West Bromwich A 1946	Retired (injury) 1946	5	0	0	0	0	0	-	-	-	5	0	0
Lewis, Edward	Manchester 3/1/1935		D	West Ham U 1958	Folkestown T 1964	143	0	5	15	0	4	6	0	0	164	0	9
Lewis, James Leonard	Hackney 26/6/1927		F	Walthamstow Ave 1950	Walthamstow Ave 1951	4	0	0	0	0	0	-	-	-	4	0	0
Lewis, John George	Hackney 9/5/1954		M	O's youth 1971	Romford 1974	0	2	0	0	0	0	0	0	0	0	2	0
Liddell, Edward	Sunderland 27/5/1878	22/11/1968	D	Gainsborough Tr 1913	Southend U 1913	193	0	3	8	0	0	-	-	-	201	0	3
Liddell, John Gilbert Hay	Edinburgh 14/4/1915	Sussex 1986	F	Bolton W 1944	Bolton W 1946	-	-	-	2	0	0	-	-	-	2	0	0
Lillie, John	Newcastle-upon-Tyne		D	QPR 1925	Blyth Spartans 1926	5	0	0	0	0	0	-	-	-	5	0	0
Ling, Martin	West Ham 15/7/1966		M	Swindon T 1996	Brighton & HA 2000	143	5	8	9	1	0	13	0	0	165	6	8
Linger, Paul Hayden	Stepney 20/12/1974		M	Charlton A 1997	Brighton & HA 1997	1	2	0	0	1	0	0	0	0	1	3	0
Linton, Malcolm Wilton	Southend-on-Sea 13/2/1952		D	Southend U 1968	Tampa Bay R's (USA) 1975	14	5	0	3	0	0	0	1	0	17	6	0
Little, Walter James	Southall 10/11/1897	15/8/1976	D	Brighton & HA 1929	Retired injury 1930	24	0	0	1	0	0	-	-	-	25	0	0
Livett, Simon Robert	Newham 8/1/1969		M	West Ham U 1992	Cambridge U 1994	16	8	0	2	0	0	2	0	0	20	8	0
Livingstone, Allan McKenzie	Alexandria 2/12/1899	11/4/1970	D	New Brighton 1926	Merthyr T 1927	1	0	0	0	0	0	-	-	-	1	0	0
Lockwood, Matthew D.	Rochford 17/10/1976		D/M	Bristol R 1998	Current	280	9	40	22	0	2	14	0	2	315	9	44
Lomas, William	Pendalton 4/7/1885	17/6/1976	F	York C 1913	Tranmere R 1914	5	0	0	0	0	0	-	-	-	5	0	0
Louch, Lionel Arthur	Brentford 4/7/1888	Feb 1967	F	Portsmouth 1908	Southend U 1910	36	0	10	2	0	0	-	-	-	38	0	10
Low, Joshua David	Bristol 15/2/1979		F	Bristol R 1999	Cardiff C 1999	2	3	1	0	0	0	1	0	0	3	3	1
Lucas, George Richard	London		M	Walthamstow Ave 1942	Leyton 1946	-	-	-	1	0	0	-	-	-	1	0	0
Lucas, Oliver Henry	Paisley 14/1/1923		D	St Mirren 1948	Scotland 1950	2	0	0	0	0	0	-	-	-	2	0	0
Lucas, Peter Malcolm	Bradley 7/10/1938		D	Bradley R 1958	Norwich C 1964	157	0	6	11	0	0	8	0	0	176	0	6
Lucas, Thomas	St Helens 20/9/1895	11/12/1953	D	Liverpool 1933	Ashford T manager 1934	21	0	0	4	0	0	-	-	-	25	0	0
Ludden, Dominic James	Basildon 30/3/1974		D	O's youth 1991	Watford 1994	50	8	1	0	1	0	1	0	0	51	9	1
Lusted, Leslie Reginald	Reading 20/9/1931		F	O's youth 1949	Harwich & Parkeston 1951												
" " "				Harwich & P'son 1952	Aldershot 1954	23	0	6	0	0	0	-	-	-	23	0	6
Lyons, Albert Thomas	Hednesford 5/3/1902	10/5/1981	D	Army 1926	Tottenham H 1930	76	0	0	6	0	1	-	-	-	82	0	1
McAleer, Joseph	Blythswood 8/3/1910		F	Lincoln C 1935	Gillingham 1936	18	0	4	3	0	1	-	-	-	21	0	5
McCarthy, Alan James	Wandsworth 11/1/1972		M	QPR 1995	Boreham Wood 1997	43	4	0	0	0	0	2	0	0	45	4	0
McClellan, Sidney Benjamin	Dagenham 11/6/1925	15/12/1970	F	Portsmouth 1958	Romford 1959	12	0	4	1	0	0	-	-	-	13	0	4
McCombe, James	Bothwell 4/6/1915		F	Clyde 1936	Dartford 1939	45	0	8	2	0	0	-	-	-	47	0	8
McCormack, Alan	Dublin 10/1/1984		M	Preston NE (loan) 2003	Preston NE 2003	8	2	0	0	0	0	0	0	0	8	2	0
McCormick, Stephen	Dumbarton 14/8/1969		F	Dundee (loan) 1998	Dundee 1998	1	3	0	0	0	0	2	0	0	3	3	0
MacDonald, Robert James	Inverness 25/2/1895	1/4/1971	D	Heart of Midlothian 1927	Retired 1929	37	0	0	1	0	0	-	-	-	38	0	0
McDonald, Terence James	Stepney 12/11/1938		F	West Ham U 1959	Reading 1965	152	0	23	7	0	1	12	0	3	171	0	27
McDougald, David E. jnr	Big Springs (USA) 12/1/1975		F	Millwall 1998	Dagenham & Redb'e 1999	3	5	0	1	1	0	0	0	0	4	6	0
McElholm, Brendan Anthony	Omagh, N. Ireland 7/7/1982		D	Dunbreen Colts 1998	Omagh T 2002	6	11	0	0	0	0	1	2	0	7	13	0

Player	Birth	Death if known	Pos	From	To	League			FA Cup			FL Cup			Total		
						Apps	Sub	Gls	Apps	Sub	Gls	Apps	Sub	Gls	Apps	Sub	Gls
McEwan, William	Glasgow 29/8/1914	Dec 1991	F	QPR 1950	Gravesend & N'fleet 1951	21	0	3	0	0	0	-	-	-	21	0	3
McFadden, Richard	Cambuslang 1889	23/10/1916	F	Wallsend Park V 1911	Died WWI 1916	137	0	66	5	0	2	-	-	-	142	0	68
McGeachy, Joseph	Glasgow 21/4/1920	1985	F	Third Lanark 1948	Workington 1952	74	0	4	3	0	1	-	-	-	77	0	5
McGeorge, James Lumley	Sunderland 8/6/1945		F	Spennymore U 1965	Mansfield T 1966	16	0	0	0	0	0	1	0	0	17	0	0
McGeorge, Kenneth Robert	London		D/F	Finchley 1896	Finchley 1898												
" " "				West Ham U 1902	Finchley 1906	14	0	0	7	0	2	-	-	-	21	0	2
McGhee, David Christopher	Worthing 19/6/1976		D/M	Stevenage B 1999	Canvey Island 2004	108	7	7	9	0	0	5	0	0	122	7	7
McGleish, Scott	Barnet 10/2/1974		F	Charlton A (loan) 1995	Charlton A 1995												
" "				Peterborough U 1996	Barnet 1997	40	2	8	1	0	0	3	0	1	44	2	9
McGrea, Joseph Russell	Kirkdale 24/10/1903	19/11/1975	D	Bradford C 1930	Macclesfield T 1932	4	0	0	0	0	0	-	-	-	4	0	0
McKay, James Alexander	Custom House Apr 1901		F	Fulham 1924	Aldershot 1926	8	0	3	0	0	0	-	-	-	8	0	3
McKechnie, John James	Inverness		D	Stockport Co 1923	Crewe Alexandra 1926	47	0	0	3	0	0	-	-	-	50	0	0
McKeeman, Alexander	Port Glasgow 26/2/1924		F	Port Glasgow 1946	Port Glasgow 1947	1	0	0	0	0	0	-	-	-	1	0	0
MacKenzie, Christopher N.	Northampton 14/5/1972		G	Hereford U 1997	Nuneaton B 1999	30	0	0	5	0	0	3	0	0	38	0	0
Mackie, John	Enfield 5/7/1976		D	Reading 2004	Current	86	1	11	5	0	1	1	0	0	92	1	12
McKnight, Philip	Camlachie 15/6/1924		D	Chelsea 1954	O's coach 1960	161	0	2	8	0	0	-	-	-	169	0	2
McLaughlan, Robert	Kilwinning 1902		F	Kilwinning R'gers 1925	Scotland 1926	19	0	3	4	0	0	-	-	-	23	0	3
McLean, Aaron	Hammersmith 25/5/1983		F	O's youth 1999	Aldershot T 2003	5	35	2	0	3	0	0	0	0	5	38	2
McLean, Robert	Glasgow		F	Bo'ness 1908	Leyton 1910	39	0	2	0	0	0	-	-	-	39	0	2
McMahon, Daryl	Dublin, Ireland 10/10/1983		M	Port Vale 2004	Current	39	18	5	2	3	0	1	0	1	42	21	6
McMahon, Edward	Addleworth 1885		F	York C 1913	Boscombe 1914	3	0	0	0	0	0	-	-	-	3	0	0
McMahon, Peter John	Marylebone 30/4/1934		M	Chase of Chertsey 1951	Aldershot 1958	66	0	1	5	0	0	-	-	-	71	0	1
McMillan, Stuart Thomas	Leicester 17/9/1896	27/9/1963	F	Nottingham F 1928	Retired (injury) 1930	23	0	1	1	0	0	-	-	-	24	0	1
McNeil, Mark John	Bethnal Green 3/12/1962		F	O's youth 1979	Aldershot 1984	76	13	12	2	1	1	2	2	0	80	16	13
Mallett, Joseph	Dunstan-on-Tyne 8/1/1916	8/2/2004	D	Southampton 1953	O's coach 1955	27	0	1	3	0	0	-	-	-	30	0	1
Mancini, Michael Leonard	Hammersmith 8/6/1956		M	Fulham 1984	Retired 1984	2	0	0	0	0	0	0	0	0	2	0	0
Mancini, Terence John	Camden Town 4/10/1942		D	Port Elizabeth (SA) 1967	QPR 1971	167	0	16	12	0	1	9	0	0	188	0	17
Mankelow, James Anthony	Highams Park 4/9/1964		F	O's youth 1981	Walthamstow Ave 1983	1	1	0	0	0	0	0	0	0	1	1	0
Manns, Thomas	Eastwood 2/5/1908		D	Manchester U 1934	Carlisle U 1935	3	0	1	2	0	0	-	-	-	5	0	1
Mansley, Chad Andrew	Newcastle (Aus) 13/11/1980		F	Watford 2000	Newcastle U (Aus) 2001	0	1	0	0	1	0	0	0	0	0	2	0
Mansley, Vincent Clifford	Skipton 5/4/1921		M	Yeovil 1952	Street FC 1953	10	0	0	0	0	0	-	-	-	10	0	0
Margerrison, John William	Bushey 20/10/1955		M	Fulham 1979	Kansas CC (USA) 1982	77	3	6	6	0	0	5	0	1	88	3	7
Marks, Michael David	Waterloo 23/3/1968		F	Millwall 1988	Fisher A 1989	3	0	0	0	0	0	0	0	0	3	0	0
Martin, Alvin Edward	Bootle 29/7/1958		D	West Ham U 1996	Southend U manager 1997	16	1	0	0	0	0	2	0	0	18	1	0
Martin, David	East Ham 25/4/1963		M	Gillingham 1996	Northampton T 1996	8	0	0	0	0	0	2	0	0	10	0	0
Martin, Jae Andrew	Hampstead 5/2/1976		F	Southend U (loan) 1994	Southend U 1994	1	3	0	0	0	0	0	0	0	1	3	0
Martin, John	Bethnal Green 15/7/1981		M	O's youth 1995	Farnborough T 2003	74	18	5	5	1	1	5	2	0	84	21	6
Martin, William Thomas J.	Poplar 27/4/1883	11/12/1954	D/F	Hull C 1906	Stockport Co 1908	61	0	28	3	0	2	-	-	-	64	0	30
Maskell, Craig Dell	Aldershot 10/4/1968		F	Happy Valley (HK) 1998	Hampton & Richm'd B 1999	15	8	2	0	2	0	2	0	0	17	10	2
Mason, Robert Henry	Tipton 22/3/1936		F	Wolverhampton W 1963	Poole T 1964	23	0	0	0	0	0	1	0	0	24	0	0

Player	Birth	Death if known	Pos	From	To	League Apps	League Sub	League Gls	FA Cup Apps	FA Cup Sub	FA Cup Gls	FL Cup Apps	FL Cup Sub	FL Cup Gls	Total Apps	Total Sub	Total Gls
Massey, Roy	Mexborough 10/9/1943		F	Rotherham U 1967	Colchester U 1969	58	5	13	6	0	1	4	0	1	68	5	15
Mayo, Joseph	Tipton 25/5/1952		F	West Bromwich A 1977	Cambridge U 1981	150	5	36	13	0	3	8	1	1	171	6	40
Mayson, John Dunnett	Southport 24/10/1908	22/6/1991	F	Bolton W 1933	Hull C 1936	79	0	22	6	0	1	-	-	-	85	0	23
Menlove, Bertram	St Albans 8/12/1892	3/7/1970	F	Bangor C	Coleraine 1930	0	0	0	1	0	0	-	-	-	1	0	0
Merritt, Harold George	Ormskirk 22/9/1920	2004	F	Everton 1945	Non-League 1947	1	0	0	2	0	0	-	-	-	3	0	0
Metchick, David John	Bakewell 14/8/1943		M	Fulham 1964	Peterborough U 1967	75	0	15	5	0	2	2	0	0	82	0	17
Meynell, Thomas	Southwick-on-Wear		D	Goole T 1909	Rochdale 1910	16	0	2	0	0	0	-	-	-	16	0	2
Miles,Iidris	Neath 2/8/1908	Oct 1983	F	Leicester C 1934	Exeter C 1937	73	0	6	6	0	0	-	-	-	79	0	6
Miller, Justin	Johannesb'g (SA) 16/12/1980		D	Ipswich T (loan) 2002	Ipswich T 2002												
" "				Ipswich T 2003	Current	123	9	3	9	1	0	4	0	0	136	10	3
Millington, John	Leigh 1912		F	Bolton W 1934	Notts Co 1935	2	0	0	0	0	0	-	-	-	2	0	0
Mills, Thomas James	Ton Pentre 28/12/1911	15/5/1979	M	Trocadero Hotel XI 1929	Leicester C 1934	119	0	20	13	0	3	-	-	-	132	0	23
Minton, Jeffrey Simon T.	Hackney 28/12/1973		M	Rotherham U 2001	Grays A 2002	32	1	5	4	0	0	1	0	1	37	1	6
Mooney, Dean Francis	Paddington 24/7/1956		F	O's youth 1972	Dulwich Hamlet 1976	16	6	3	0	0	0	0	0	0	16	6	3
Mooney, John	Denniston, Glasgow 13/6/1897		M	Barrow 1926	Scottish Non-League 1927	0	0	0	1	0	0	-	-	-	1	0	0
Moores, Ian Richard	Newcastle 5/10/1998	12/1/1998	F	Tottenham H 1978	Bolton W 1982	110	7	26	12	0	3	2	1	2	124	8	31
Morgan, Alfred Stanley	Abergwynfi 10/10/1920	1971	M	Millwall 1953	Falmouth T 1956	96	0	24	9	0	2	-	-	-	105	0	26
Morley, Ernest James	Sketty 11/9/1901	26/1/1975	D	Swansea T 1928	Retired (injury) 1931	71	0	0	10	0	0	-	-	-	81	0	0
Morrad, Frank George	Brentford 28/2/1920		F	Notts Co 1944	Brighton & HA 1948	25	0	11	0	0	0	-	-	-	25	0	11
Morris, David Hyman	London 25/11/1897	20/12/1985	F	Swindon T 1933	Cheltenham T 1934	13	0	8	2	0	3	-	-	-	15	0	11
Morris, Glenn James	Woolwich 20/12/1983		G	O's youth 2000	Current	66	2	0	0	0	0	3	1	0	71	3	0
Morris, James	Bury		G	Bury 1914	Bury 1915	4	0	0	0	0	0	-	-	-	4	0	0
Morrison, David Ellison	Walthamstow 30/11/1974		M	Peterborough U 1997	Bohemians (Ireland) 2000	21	25	3	1	0	0	2	5	0	24	30	3
Morrison, Murdoch	Glasgow 9/10/1924	1975	G	Luton T 1947	Scottish Non-League 1948	10	0	0	0	0	0	-	-	-	10	0	0
Moss, Robert	Chigwell 13/2/1952		F	O's youth 1969	Colchester U 1972	2	3	1	0	0	0	0	0	0	2	3	1
Mountford, Peter	Stoke 13/4/1960		M	Charlton A 1985	Fisher A 1987	27	6	2	3	3	0	1	1	0	31	10	2
Murray, Jade Alan	Islington 23/9/1981		F	O's youth 1998	Barking & East H U 2002	0	2	0	0	0	0	0	1	0	0	3	0
Musgrove, Malcolm	Lynemouth 8/7/1933		F	West Ham U 1962	O's coach 1965	83	0	14	7	0	4	1	0	0	91	0	18
Naylor, Dominic John	Watford 12/8/1970		D	Gillingham 1996	Stevenage B 1998	87	0	4	4	0	0	6	0	0	97	0	4
Naylor, William Henry	Sheffield 23/11/1919	1989	F	Brentford 1947	Retired (injury) 1949	64	0	14	2	0	0	-	-	-	66	0	14
Neary, Harold Frank	Aldershot 6/3/1921	2003	F	West Ham U 1947	QPR 1949	78	0	44	3	0	0	-	-	-	81	0	44
Nelson, Andrew Nesbitt	Custom House 5/7/1935		D	Ipswich T 1964	Plymouth Argyle 1965	43	0	0	1	0	0	2	0	0	46	0	0
Newell, Paul Clayton	Greenwich 23/2/1969		G	Southend U 1990	Barnet 1994	61	0	0	3	0	0	3	0	0	67	0	0
Newey, Thomas	Sheffield 31/10/1982		F	Leeds U 2003	Cambridge U 2004	34	20	3	2	2	0	1	1	0	37	23	3
Newman, Ronald Vernon	Portsmouth 19/1/1934		F	Portsmouth 1961	Crystal Palace 1962	14	0	1	2	0	0	1	0	0	0	17	1
Newton, Adam	Ascot 4/12/1980		M	West Ham U (loan) 2002	West Ham U 2002	10	0	1	0	0	0	0	0	0	10	0	1
Newton, Reginald William	Limehouse 30/6/1926		G	Dagenham W'ks XI 1948	Brentford 1949	23	0	0	2	0	0	-	-	-	25	0	0
Nicholas, Anthony W.L.	West Ham 16/4/1938		F	Chelmsford C 1965	Dartford 1966	8	1	2	1	0	0	0	0	0	9	1	2
Nicholls, Joseph Edward	Bilston		D	Wolverhampton W 1919	Bilston U 1925	117	0	2	3	0	0	-	-	-	120	0	2
Nicholson, Derek	Harrow 8/4/1936		F	Chase of Chertsey 1953	QPR 1958	6	0	0	0	0	0	-	-	-	6	0	0

Player	Birth	Death if known	Pos	From	To	League Apps	League Sub	League Gls	FA Cup Apps	FA Cup Sub	FA Cup Gls	FL Cup Apps	FL Cup Sub	FL Cup Gls	Total Apps	Total Sub	Total Gls
Nicholson, George Harold	Wetherall 25/1/1932		G	Accrington St 1959	Bristol C 1961	4	0	0	0	0	0	-	-	-	4	0	0
Nicholson, Joseph Robinson	Ryhope 4/6/1898	1974	D	Ryhope 1919	Cardiff C 1924	145	0	4	2	0	0	-	-	-	147	0	4
Nicol, Allan William	Grays, Middlesex		F	Grays A 1904	Grays A 1905	-	-	-	6	0	3	-	-	-	6	0	3
Nugent, Kevin Patrick	Edmonton, London 10/4/1969		F	O's youth 1986	Plymouth Argyle 1992												
" " "				Cardiff C 2002	Swansea C 2003	103	19	23	11	0	3	10	3	7	124	22	33
Nunn, Alfred Sydney	Holborn 15/11/1899	20/2/1946	F	Non-League 1920	Folkestone 1924	19	0	0	0	0	0	-	-	-	19	0	0
Oakes, Scott John	Leicester 5/8/1972		M	Cambridge U 2001	Released (injury) 2001												
" " "				O's trial 2002	St Albans C 2002	11	0	0	0	0	0	1	0	0	12	0	0
O'Brien, George	Dunfermline 22/11/1935		F	Southampton 1966	Aldershot 1966	17	0	3	0	0	0	1	0	0	18	0	3
O'Gara, James	Maryhill, Glasgow 1888		M	Middlesborough 1907	Dundee Hibs 1909	1	0	0	0	0	0	-	-	-	1	0	0
Okai, Stephen Patrick	Ghana 3/12/1973		M	O's youth 1990	Barnet 1994	11	14	4	1	1	0	1	1	0	13	16	4
Oliver, Frank	Southampton		F	Everton 1906	Southport Central 1908												
" "				Southport Central 1912	Non-League 1913	39	0	10	1	0	0	-	-	-	40	0	10
Omoyinmi, Emmanuel	Nigeria 28/12/1977		F	West Ham U (loan) 1999	West Ham U 1999	3	1	1	0	0	0	0	0	0	3	1	1
Opara, Kelechi-Krisantos	Oweri, Nigeria 21/12/1981		F	Colchester U 2000	Billericay T 2001	3	3	0	1	0	0	0	0	0	4	3	0
Opinel, Sasha Fernand	Bourge-Saint-Maurice 9/4/1977		D	Bournemouth 2001	Nancy (France) 2001	9	2	1	0	0	0	0	0	0	9	2	1
Orton, Richard William	London		F	Non-League 1905	Non-League 1906	8	0	1	0	0	0	-	-	-	8	0	1
Osgood, Keith	Ealing 8/5/1955		D	Derby County 1981	Cambridge U 1984	36	0	0	5	0	0	1	0	1	42	0	1
O'Shaughnessy, Michael J.	Bow 15/4/1955		G	O's youth 1969	Harlow T 1975	1	0	0	0	0	0	0	0	0	1	0	0
O'Shea, Timothy James	Westminster 12/11/1966		M	Tottenham H 1988	Gillingham 1989	7	2	1	2	0	0	0	0	0	9	2	1
Osmond, Joseph Edward	Seaham Harbour 1897	1/6/1955	D	S'derland West End 1919	Hartlepool U 1923	50	0	0	2	0	0	-	-	-	52	0	0
Otto, Ricky	Hackney 9/11/1967		F	Dartford 1990	Southend U 1993	41	15	12	2	1	0	3	0	0	46	16	12
Owen, Jonathan	London		F	Non-League 1945	Non-League 1946	-	-	-	1	0	0	-	-	-	1	0	0
Owen, Trefor	Flint 20/2/1933	2001	D	Tooting & Mitcham 1958	Bath C 1961	15	0	0	1	0	0	1	0	0	17	0	0
Pacey, Dennis Frank	Feltham 22/9/1928		F	Walton & Hersham 1951	Millwall 1954	120	0	46	15	0	12	-	-	-	135	0	58
Palmer, Aiden Witting	Enfield 2/1/1987		D	O's youth 2003	Current	6	2	0	0	0	0	1	0	0	7	2	0
Pape, Albert Arthur	Elsecar 13/6/1897	18/11/1955	F	Notts Co 1924	Man U 1925	24	0	11	1	0	0	-	-	-	25	0	11
Parker, Frederick George	Weymouth 18/6/1886	1949	F	Salisbury 1907	Folkestone T (man'r) 1922	336	0	34	14	0	0	-	-	-	350	0	34
Parkinson, Alan	Dagenham 12/4/1948		G	Aveley 1967	Barking 1967	1	0	0	0	0	0	0	0	0	1	0	0
Parmenter, Terence Leslie	Romford 21/10/1947		F	Fulham 1969	Gillingham 1971	34	3	3	0	0	0	0	0	0	34	3	3
Parr, Henry Harold	Newark 23/10/1915	Lincoln 2004	F	Lincoln C 1945	Lincoln C 1946	-	-	-	2	0	1	-	-	-	2	0	1
Parsons, David	Greenwich 25/2/1982		M	O's youth 1999	Purfleet 2002	1	0	0	0	0	0	0	0	0	1	0	0
Parsons, Stephen Paul	Hammersmith 7/10/1957		M	Wimbledon 1980	Hayes 1981	36	0	6	1	0	0	2	0	0	39	0	6
Partridge, David	Westminster 26/11/1978		D	Dundee U (loan) 2002	Dundee U 2002	6	1	0	1	0	0	0	0	0	7	1	0
Pateman, George Edward	Chatham 18/5/1910	21/3/1973	F	Bradford C 1935	Reading 1935	9	0	1	0	0	0	-	-	-	9	0	1
Paterson, James	St Ninians 1908		F	Reading 1938	Retired 1939	5	0	0	0	0	0	-	-	-	5	0	0
Pattison, Frank	Middlesbrough 7/3/1889		F	Sunderland District 1913	Lincoln C 1914	7	0	0	0	0	0	-	-	-	7	0	0
Pattison, John Morris	Eastwood 19/12/1918		F	QPR 1950	Dover 1951	43	0	10	1	0	0	-	-	-	44	0	10
Payne, David Ronald	Croydon 25/4/1947		D	Crystal Palace 1973	Millwall 1978	88	5	0	8	1	0	8	0	0	104	6	0
Peach, David Sidney	Bedford 21/1/1951		D	Swindon T 1982	R.S. Southampton 1983	47	0	6	2	0	0	1	0	0	50	0	6

Player	Birth	Death if known	Pos	From	To	League Apps	League Sub	League Gls	FA Cup Apps	FA Cup Sub	FA Cup Gls	FL Cup Apps	FL Cup Sub	FL Cup Gls	Total Apps	Total Sub	Total Gls
Peacock, Joseph John	Wigan 15/3/1897	14/3/1979	F	Sheffied Wed 1931	Sliepner (Sweden) 1933	54	0	0	1	0	0	-	-	-	55	0	0
Pemberton, Frank	London		D	Non-League 1906	Non-League 1908	4	0	0	0	0	0	-	-	-	4	0	0
Penfold, Mark	Woolwich 9/12/1956		D	Charlton A 1979	Maidstone U 1981	3	0	1	0	0	0	0	0	0	3	0	1
Percy, Andrew	Ilford 1912		F	Ilford 1938	Plymouth Argyle 1939	4	0	0	0	0	0	-	-	-	4	0	0
Perifimou, Christopher	Enfield 27/11/1975		M	O's youth 1994	Barnet 1995	3	1	0	0	0	0	0	0	0	3	1	0
Peters, Mark	St Asaph (Wales) 6/7/1972		D	Rushden & Diam'ds 2003	Cambridge U 2005	39	2	2	2	0	0	0	0	0	41	2	2
Phillips, Edward John	Leiston 21/8/1933		F	Ipswich T 1964	Luton T 1965	36	0	17	0	0	0	2	0	2	38	0	19
Phillips, George Raymond	Tottenham 11/10/1912	13/3/1993	F	Northfleet U 1932	Millwall 1933	3	0	1	0	0	0	-	-	-	3	0	1
Phillips, Wilfred John	Brierley Hill 9/8/1895	25/2/1973	F	West Ham U 1932	Stourbridge 1933	24	0	4	0	0	0	-	-	-	24	0	4
Pickering, Wilfred Hunter	Murton Colliery 13/11/1906	8/2/1952	D	Southport 1932	Southport 1933	12	0	0	0	0	0	-	-	-	12	0	0
Pike, Geoffrey Alan	Clapton 28/9/1956		M	Notts County 1989	Retired, O's y'th coach 1991	36	8	1	5	0	2	6	0	1	47	8	4
Pinamonte, Lorenzo	Foggia, Italy 9/5/1978		F	Brentford (loan) 200	Brentford 2001	5	6	2	0	0	0	0	0	0	5	6	2
Pinner, Michael John	Boston, Lincs 16/2/1934		G	Hendon 1962	Distlllery 1965	77	0	0	4	0	0	2	0	0	83	0	0
Pitcher, Darren Edward J.	Stepney 12/10/1969		M	Crystal Palace (loan) 1998	Crystal Palace retired (inj) 1998	1	0	0	0	0	0	0	0	0	1	0	0
Plume, Richard William	Tottenham 9/6/1949		M	Millwall 1969	Barnet 1971	12	6	1	0	0	0	0	0	0	12	6	1
Pole, Harold Edward William	Kessingland 25/3/1922		D	Ipswich T 1951	Chelmsford C 1953	12	0	0	0	0	0	0	0	0	12	0	0
Possee, Derek James	Southwark 14/2/1946		F	Crystal Palace 1974	Vancouver Wh (Can) 1977	77	3	11	6	0	2	5	0	0	88	3	13
Poulton, George Henry	Holborn 23/4/1929		F	Gillingham 1952	Gravesend & N'fleet 1956	61	0	24	9	0	3	-	-	-	70	0	27
Poulton, Thomas	Hackney		D	Clapton Imperial 1904	Clapton Imperial 1906	0	0	0	1	0	0	-	-	-	1	0	0
Price, David James	Caterham 23/6/1955		M	Crystal Palace 1983	Wealdstone 1983	10	0	0	0	0	0	0	0	0	10	0	0
Price, Terence Edmund	Colchester 11/10/45		F	O's youth 1963	Colchester U 1967	86	1	18	5	0	1	4	0	0	95	1	19
Prior, Philip	Hackney 1890		F	Non-League 1909	Bury 1912	19	0	3	1	0	0	-	-	-	20	0	3
Pritchard, Andrew Smart	Airdrie 23/6/1912		D	Ards (Ireland) 1939	off to war 1939	1	0	0	0	0	0	-	-	-	1	0	0
Proudfoot, Peter	Wishaw 25/11/1880	4/3/1941	D	Millwall A 1905	Chelsea 1906	26	0	0	6	0	1	-	-	-	32	0	1
Pullen, Walter Ernest	Ripley 2/8/1919	1977	F	Army 1945	Gloucester C 1950	117	0	37	3	0	0	-	-	-	120	0	37
Purse, Darren John	Stepney 14/2/1977		D	O's youth 1993	Oxford U 1996	48	7	3	1	0	0	2	0	0	51	7	3
Purser, Wayne Montague	Basildon 13/4/1980		M/F	Barnet 2003	Hornchurch 2004	36	14	9	2	0	1	1	0	0	40	14	10
Putney, Trevor Anthony	Harold Hill 11/2/1961		M	Watford 1993	Colchester U 1994	20	2	2	0	0	0	2	0	0	22	2	2
Queen, Gerald	Paisley 15/1/1945		F	Crystal Palace 1972	Arcadia Shep'ds (SA) 1977	149	7	34	9	1	1	7	0	1	165	8	36
Rafter, Sean	Rochford 20/5/1957		G	Leicester C 1979	Non-League 1981	2	0	0	1	0	0	0	0	0	3	0	0
Ramage, George McIntosh	Newbattle 29/1/1937		G	Colchester U 1964	Luton T 1965	4	0	0	0	0	0	1	0	0	5	0	0
Rance, John	London		D	QPR 1904	Non-League 1905	-	-	-	6	0	0	-	-	-	6	0	0
Raynor, Paul James	Nottingham 29/4/1966		M	Guang Deong (China) 1998	Stevenage B 1998	6	9	0	0	0	0	1	1	0	7	10	0
Read, Paul Colin	Harlow 25/9/1973		F	Arsenal (loan) 1995	Arsenal 1995	11	0	0	0	0	0	0	0	0	11	0	0
Reason, Herbert	Wanstead		D	Woodford 1904	Retired after WWI 1915	91	0	4	4	0	0	-	-	-	95	0	4
Redding, Joseph	Amersham		G	Amersham 1904	Amerham 1906	7	0	0	9	0	0	-	-	-	16	0	0
Reed, Charles	Durham		D	Darlington 1909	Non-League 1910	2	0	0	0	0	0	-	-	-	2	0	0
Reed, George	Altofts 7/2/1904		D	Crystal Palace 1935	Plymouth A (coach) 1936	1	0	0	0	0	0	-	-	-	1	0	0
Rees, Melvyn John	Cardiff 25/1/1967	30/5/1993	G	Watford (loan) 1990	Watford 1990	9	0	0	0	0	0	0	0	0	9	0	0
Rees, William Derek	Blaengarw 10/3/1924	25/7/1996	F	Tottenham H 1950	Headington U 1955	184	0	58	14	0	8	-	-	-	198	0	66

Player	Birth	Death if known	Pos	From	To	League Apps	League Sub	League Gls	FA Cup Apps	FA Cup Sub	FA Cup Gls	FL Cup Apps	FL Cup Sub	FL Cup Gls	Total Apps	Total Sub	Total Gls
Regis, David	Paddington 3/3/1964		F	Barnsley 1997	Lincoln C 1997	4	0	0	0	0	0	0	0	0	4	0	0
Reid, Thomas	Calderbank 1901		F	Port Vale 1927	Northwich Victoria 1927	7	0	2	0	0	0	-	-	-	7	0	2
Reinelt, Robert Squire	Loughton 11/3/1974		M	Brighton & Hove A 1998	Stevenage B 1998	2	5	0	0	0	0	0	4	1	2	9	1
Rennie, John Forgan	Kirkcaldy 24/5/1911		D	Hibernian 1938	Selby T 1939	6	0	0	0	0	0	-	-	-	6	0	0
Rennox, Clatworthy	Shotts (Scotland) 25/2/1897		F	Wishaw 1921	Manchester U 1925	101	0	24	4	0	1	-	-	-	105	0	25
Reynolds, Jack William	Manchester 1878		F	Burton U 1904	Grimsby T 1905	-	-	-	6	0	3	-	-	-	6	0	3
Reynolds, Walter	Ecclesall 24/11/1906	4/8/1944	F	Leeds U 1931	Burnley 1932	2	0	0	0	0	0	-	-	-	2	0	0
Richards, Anthony	Newham 17/9/1973		F	Cambridge U 1997	Barnet 2000	47	16	11	2	0	3	3	3	1	52	19	15
Richardson, Craig Thomas	Newham 8/10/1979		D	O's youth 1997	Released (misconduct) 1997	1	0	0	0	0	0	0	1	0	1	1	0
Richardson, James Robert	Ashington 8/2/1911	28/8/1964	F	Millwall 1948	O's trainer 1951	15	0	0	0	0	0	-	-	-	15	0	0
Riches, Steven Alexander	Sydney, Australia 6/8/1976		F	Warringh Dolphins 1996	Raunds Town 1996	2	3	0	0	0	0	0	0	0	2	3	0
Richmond, William Crichton	Kirkcaldy 1/3/1900	1973	D	Walsall 1938	Guildford C 1939	1	0	0	0	0	0	-	-	-	1	0	0
Riddell, Norman	Morpeth 1886	1918	D	Rochdale 1911	Rossendale U 1912	11	0	0	1	0	0	-	-	-	12	0	0
Riddick, Gordon George	Langlebury 6/11/1943		F	Charlton A 1970	Northampton T 1972	13	8	3	0	0	0	0	0	0	13	8	3
Ridley, Robert	Sunderland		F	Sunderland Royal R 1915	Seaham Colliery 1915	17	0	1	0	0	0	-	-	-	17	0	1
Rigby, Arthur	Chorlton 7/6/1900	25/3/1960	F	Middlesbrough 1933	Crewe Alex 1935	69	0	18	4	0	1	-	-	-	73	0	19
Ritson, Ledger	Gateshead 28/4/192	1977	D	Army / Hitchen T 1946	Retired (injured) 1948	84	0	0	1	0	0	-	-	-	85	0	0
Roach, John	Dalston		D	Clapton W 1905	Non-League 1908	1	0	0	1	0	0	-	-	-	2	0	0
Robb, William Lawson	Cambuslang 23/12/1927	2002	D	Aberdeen 1950	Albion R1951	5	0	0	0	0	0	-	-	-	5	0	0
Roberts, Frederick	Rhyl 7//5/1916	Jun 1985	F	Bury 1946	Non-League 1947	18	0	2	1	0	0	-	-	-	19	0	2
Roberts, Joseph	Tranmere 2/9/1900	9/3/1984	F	Southport 1931	Luton T 1931	2	0	0	3	0	0	-	-	-	5	0	0
Robertson, Alfred Joseph	Sunderland 2/7/1908	May 1984	G	Bradford PA 1933	Bristol R 1935	50	0	0	3	0	0	-	-	-	53	0	0
Robertson, Robert	London		D	Non-League 1901	Non-League 1905	-	-	-	1	0	0	-	-	-	1	0	0
Robertson, William Gibb	Glasgow 13/11/1928	Jun 1973	G	Chelsea 1960	Dover A 1963	47	0	0	2	0	0	2	0	0	51	0	0
Robinson, Samuel Henry	Hucknall 15/12/1010		D	Mansfield T 1933	Guildford C 1934	2	0	0	0	0	0	-	-	-	2	0	0
Roeder, Glenn Victor	Woodford 13/12/1955		D	O's youth 1972	QPR 1978												
" " "				Millwall 1991	Purfleet 1992	113	10	4	14	0	0	8	0	0	135	10	4
Rofe, Dennis	Epping 1/6/1950		D	O's youth 1967	Leicester C 1972	170	1	6	11	0	0	7	0	0	188	1	6
Roffey, William Robert	Stepney 6/2/1954		D	Crystal Palace 1973	Millwall 1984	324	4	8	18	1	1	16	1	0	358	6	9
Rogers, William	Summerhill 1905	14/1/1936	D	Bristol Rovers 1933	Bangor C 1934	3	0	0	0	0	0	-	-	-	3	0	0
Rooney, Robert	Glasgow 26/10/1920	1992	D	Clyde 1948	Workington T 1951	66	0	2	1	0	0	-	-	-	67	0	2
Rose, Stephen Benjamin	London 10/1/1895		D	Arsenal 1922	Non-League 1923	3	0	0	0	0	0	-	-	-	3	0	0
Roseboom, Edward	Govan 24/11/1896	1980	F	Nelson 1924	Rochdale 1924	3	0	0	0	0	0	-	-	-	3	0	0
Rosier, Bertram Leonard	Hanwell 21/3/1893	18/2/1939	D	Brentford 1923	Southend U 1927	136	0	1	5	0	0	-	-	-	141	0	1
Rossiter, Ambrose	Ashford 24/11/1907	Sep 1993	D	Gillingham 1936	Retired 1937	7	0	2	0	0	0	-	-	-	7	0	2
Rossiter, Donald Paul	Strood 8/6/1935		F	Arsenal 1956	Dartford 1956	1	0	0	0	0	0	-	-	-	1	0	0
Roulson, Joseph	Sheffield 7/10/1891	7/12/1952	D	Swansea T 1924	Retired 1925	16	0	0	0	0	0	-	-	-	16	0	0
Rouse, Victor Raymond	Swansea 16/3/1936		G	Oxford U 1965	Atlanta Chiefs (US) 1966	40	0	0	1	0	0	1	0	0	42	0	0
Rowbotham, Darren	Cardiff 22/10/1966		F	Exeter C (loan) 1999	Exeter C 1999	4	2	0	0	0	0	0	0	0	4	2	0
Rufus, Marvin Marcel	Lewisham 11/9/1976		M	Charlton A 1995	Romford 1995	5	2	0	0	0	0	0	0	0	5	2	0

Player	Birth	Death if known	Pos	From	To	League Apps	League Sub	League Gls	FA Cup Apps	FA Cup Sub	FA Cup Gls	FL Cup Apps	FL Cup Sub	FL Cup Gls	Total Apps	Total Sub	Total Gls
Rumbold, George Arthur	Alton 10/7/1911	12/12/1995	D	Crystal Palace 1937	Ipswich T 1946	52	0	0	4	0	0	-	-	-	56	0	0
Rutherford, John	Percy Main 12/10/1897	21/4/1963	F	Arsenal 1926	Retired 1927	9	0	0	0	0	0	-	-	-	9	0	0
Ryan, Vaughan William	Westminster 2/9/1968		M	Wimbledon 1992	Dundee (tr) 1995	40	4	0	3	0	0	2	1	0	45	5	0
Saah, Brian Ebo	Rush Green 16/12/1986		M/D	O's youth 2002	Current	15	6	0	1	1	0	0	1	0	16	8	0
Sage, William	Edmonton, London 11/11/1893	21/6/1968	D	Tottenham H 1927	Dartford 1928	12	0	0	0	0	0	-	-	-	12	0	0
Sales, Ronald Duncan	South Shields 19/9/1920	Aug 1995	D	Newcastle U 1947	Hartlepool U 1950	46	0	3	2	0	0	-	-	-	48	0	3
Sam, Lloyd	Leeds 27/9/1984		F	Charlton A (loan) 2004	Charlton A 2004	5	5	0	0	0	0	0	0	0	5	5	0
Sanders, Arthur William	Edmonton, London 8/5/1901	26/9/1983	F	Tottenham H 1929	Retired 1933	53	0	5	3	0	1	-	-	-	56	0	6
Sayer, Andrew Clive	Park Royal 6/6/1966		F	Fulham 1990	Slough T 1992	23	7	6	0	0	0	4	0	1	27	7	7
Scott, Andrew	Epsom 2/8/1972		M/F	Oxford U 2004	Retired, O's youth coach 2005	45	2	10	2	0	0	1	0	0	48	2	10
Scott, George	West Stanley 29/9/1885	16/8/1916	F	S'derland West End 1908	Died WW1 1916	205	0	33	8	0	1	-	-	-	213	0	34
Scott, James Dennis	Dagenham 5/9/1945		M	Chelsea 1962	Durban C (S. Africa) 1966	22	1	6	0	0	0	0	0	0	22	1	6
Sealey, Alan William	Canning Town 22/4/1942	4/2/1996	F	O's youth 1959	West Ham U 1961	4	0	1	0	0	0	0	0	0	4	0	1
Sealey Leslie Jesse	Bethnal Green 29/9/1957	19/8/2001	G	West Ham U 1996	West Ham U 1996	12	0	0	0	0	0	2	0	0	14	0	0
Searle, Frank Burnett	Hednesford 30/1/1906	16/6/1977	D	Watford 1934	Retired 1938	122	0	1	8	0	0	-	-	-	130	0	1
Seigel, Arnold William	Islington 21/3/1919		F	Hendon 1949	Hendon 1949	9	0	0	0	0	0	-	-	-	9	0	0
Sewell, John David	Deptford 7/7/1939		D	Crystal Palace 1971	St Louis AS (US) 1972	5	2	0	0	0	0	0	1	0	5	3	0
Sexton, David James	Islington 6/4/1930		F	West Ham U 1956	Brighton &HA 1957	24	0	4	1	0	0	-	-	-	25	0	4
Shankly, Robert	Douglas 11/2/1909		F	Barrow 1937	Retired 1946	13	0	0	0	0	0	-	-	-	13	0	0
Shaw, Colin Michael	St Albans 19/6/1943		F	Norwich C 1965	Arcadia (S. Africa) 1966	7	0	0	0	0	0	0	0	0	7	0	0
Shaw, Jonathan Frederick	Wallsend		F	Wallsend Park V 1908	Non-League 1909	19	0	2	0	0	0	-	-	-	19	0	2
Shea, Daniel Harold	Wapping 6/11/1887	25/121960	F	Coventry C 1925	Sheppey U 1926	33	0	8	0	0	0	-	-	-	33	0	8
Shearer, James	Inverkeithling		F	Dundee Hibs 1921	Dundee Hibs 1921	4	0	0	0	0	0	-	-	-	4	0	0
Shearer, Lee Sean	Southend 23/10/1977		D	O's youth 1994	Dover A 1997	14	4	1	1	0	0	1	1	0	16	5	1
Shelley, Geoffrey	Fulham Apr 1885		D	Tunbridge Wells R 1907	Tunbridge Wells R 1909												
" "				Tunbridge Wells R 1910	Non-League 1912	9	0	0	0	0	0	-	-	-	9	0	0
Sherratt, James Aaron	Warrington 24/12/1921		D/F	Hartlepool U 1948	Workington T 1952	39	0	8	2	0	0	-	-	-	41	0	8
Shilton, Peter Leslie	Leicester 18/9/1949		G	West Ham U 1996	Hong Kong 1997	9	0	0	1	0	0	-	-	-	10	0	0
Shinners, Paul	Westminster 8/1/1959		F	Gillingham 1985	Barnet 1989	73	4	32	10	1	4	3	2	1	86	7	37
Shoemake, Kevin Paul	Wickford 28/1/1965		G	O's youth 1981	Welling U 1984	4	0	0	0	0	0	0	0	0	4	0	0
Shorey, Nicholas Robert	Romford 19/2/1981		D/M	O's youth 1999	Reading 2001	12	3	0	1	0	0	0	0	0	13	3	0
Silkman, Barry	Stepney, London 29/6/1952		M	QPR 1981	Southend U 1985	133	7	14	9	1	1	7	0	1	149	8	16
Silvester, Bertram Edward	Stratford		D	Non-League 1911	Non-League 1912	1	0	0	0	0	0	-	-	-	1	0	0
Simba, Amara Sylla	Dakar, Senegal 23/12/1961		F	FC Leon (Mexico) 1998	Kingstonian 2000	27	10	13	5	2	1	0	2	0	32	14	14
Simmonds, Christopher K.	Plymouth 5/8/1920	1992	F	Millwall 1950	Workington T 1951	15	0	1	1	0	0	-	-	-	16	0	1
Simons, Henry Thomas	Hackney 26/11/1887	26/8/1956	F	Peel Institute 1906	Leyton 1906	7	0	1	0	0	0	-	-	-	7	0	1
Simpson, Colin Robertson	Oxford 30/4/1976		F	Henden 1997	Sutton U 1999	9	5	3	0	0	0	0	0	0	9	5	3
Simpson, Michael	Nottingham 28/2/1974				Current	90	0	3	7	0	0	2	0	0	99	0	3
Simpson, Owen	Prudhoe 18/9/1943		D	Rotherham U 1967	Colchester U 1968	36	0	4	5	0	1	0	0	0	41	0	5
Sitton, John Edmund	Hackney 21/10/1959		D	Gillingham 1985	O's Sch of Exc (coach) 1991	166	4	7	13	1	0	19	1	0	198	6	7

Player	Birth	Death if known	Pos	From	To	League			FA Cup			FL Cup			Total		
						Apps	Sub	Gls	Apps	Sub	Gls	Apps	Sub	Gls	Apps	Sub	Gls
Skelton, George Alfred	Thurcroft 27/11/1919	9/1994	F	Huddersfield T 1947	Non-League 1948	3	0	0	0	0	0	-	-	-	3	0	0
Skivington, Michael Noel	Glasgow 24/12/1921		D	Dundalk 1949	Gillingham 1950	5	0	0	0	0	0	-	-	-	5	0	0
Slater, Malcolm Bruce	Buckie 22/10/1939		F	Southend U 1967	Inverness Caledonian 1967	111	0	4	7	0	1	7	0	0	125	0	5
Slater, Thomas Arthur W.	Chester-le-Street 25/2/1908	1976	G	Murton Coll Welf 1926	Port Vale 1930	20	0	0	2	0	0	-	-	-	22	0	0
Smalley, Mark Anthony	Newark-on-Trent 2/1/1965		D	Nottingham F 1987	Mansfield T 1990	59	5	4	4	0	0	2	0	0	65	5	4
Smeulders, John	Hackney 28/3/1957		G	O's youth 1972	AFC Bournemouth 1979	0	0	0	0	0	0	2	0	0	2	0	0
Smith, Alan	Newcastle 15/10/1921		F	Brentford 1949	Tonbridge 1950	6	0	1	0	0	0	-	-	-	6	0	1
Smith, Dean	West Bromwich 19/3/1971		D	Hereford U 1997	Sheffield Wed 2003												
" "				Port Vale 2005 (as player and youth coach)		239	0	32	19	0	4	18	0	0	276	0	36
Smith, George	Tottenham		G	Tottenham H (loan) 1914	Tottenham H 1914	2	0	0	0	0	0	-	-	-	2	0	0
Smith, George	Sunderland 20/11/1908		D	Easington Colliery 1932	Darlington 1932	2	0	0	0	0	0	-	-	-	2	0	0
Smith, Harold McPherson	Dundee 14/10/1911		F	Raith Rovers 1934	Retired 1946	149	0	34	14	0	3	-	-	-	163	0	37
Smith, Henry Harold	Walthamstow 14/10/1901		F	Non-League 1919	Royal London U 1925	167	0	9	5	0	1	-	-	-	172	0	10
Smith, James	Bolton 1/1/1920		F	Burnley 1946	Croydon Rovers 1948	22	0	3	0	0	0	-	-	-	22	0	3
Smith, James Harold	Sheffield 6/12/1930		F	Chelsea 1955	Retired (injured) 1957	37	0	3	2	0	0	-	-	-	39	0	3
Smith, John	Shoreditch 4/1/1939	1988	M	Coventry C 1965	Torquay U 1966	38	1	3	1	0	0	0	0	0	39	1	3
Smith John William	Whitburn 20/10/1898	19/1/1977	F	Bournemouth & BA 1936	O's Coach 1936	5	0	0	2	0	0	-	-	-	7	0	0
Smith, Keith Wilson	Woodville 15/9/1940		F	Darlington 1967	Notts Co 1967	3	0	0	0	0	0	0	0	0	3	0	0
Smith, Mark Stuart	Carlisle 4/4/1962		D	O's youth 1979	Tilbury 1981	3	0	0	0	0	0	0	0	0	3	0	0
Smith, Matthew	Grimsby		D	Watford 1937	Tunbridge Wells R 1939	5	0	0	0	0	0	-	-	-	5	0	0
Smith, Peter Alec	Islington 20/11/1964		D/M	O's youth 1981	Barking 1983	8	6	0	0	0	0	-	-	-	8	6	0
Smith, Stephen Charles	Hednesford 27/3/1896	16/12/1980	F	Southend U 1927	QPR 1928	6	0	1	1	0	0	0	0	0	7	0	1
Snedden, John Duncan	Bonnybridge 3/2/1942		D	Charlton A 1966	PE City (S. Africa) 1968	26	1	3	0	0	0	2	0	0	28	1	3
Sorrell, Dennis James	Lambeth 7/10/1940		M	O's youth 1964	Woodford T 1966												
" " "				Woodford T 1957	Chelsea 1962												
" " "				Chelsea 1964	Romford 1966	111	0	4	3	0	0	5	0	0	0	119	4
Spence, James Frederick V.	Uphall 19/1/1904	1968	D	Phumpherston R 1926	Thames Assoc 1930	30	0	3	1	0	0	-	-	-	31	0	3
Spencer, Alfred	London		F	Army 1913	Ret'd (wounded WWI) 1916	1	0	0	0	0	0	-	-	-	1	0	0
Spottiswood, Robert	Crewe		D	Crystal Palace 1919	Caerphilly T 1920	1	0	0	0	0	0	-	-	-	1	0	0
Stanislaus, Roger Edmund P.	Hammersmith 2/11/1968		M	Bury 1995	Banned drugs 1996	20	1	0	1	0	0	1	0	0	22	1	0
Steel, Daniel	New Mills 2/5/1884	29/4/1931	D	Third Lanark 1931	Retired WWI 1918	23	0	0	1	0	0	-	-	-	24	0	0
Steele, Lee Anthony James	Liverpool 7/12/1973		F	Oxford U 2004	Current	51	15	20	2	1	2	1	1	1	54	17	23
Stephens, Kevin Alexander	Enfield 28/7/1984		D	QPR 1999	Redbridge 2004	2	2	0	0	0	0	0	0	0	2	2	0
Stevens, George James	Hackney		F	Non-League 1914	Non-League 1915	1	0	0	0	0	0	-	-	-	1	0	0
Stewart, Thomas Worley	Sunderland 1881		D	Sunderland Royal R 1906	Brighton & HA 1908	50	0	0	4	0	0	-	-	-	54	0	0
Still, John Leonard	West Ham 24/4/1950		D	O's youth 1967	Charlton A (tr) 1967	1	0	0	0	0	0	0	0	0	1	0	0
Stimson, Mark Nicholas	Plaistow 27/12/1967		D	Tottenham H (loan) 1988	Tottenham H 1988												
" " "				Southend U 1999	Canvey Island 1999	12	0	0	0	0	0	0	0	0	12	0	0
Stonehouse, George	Wallsend		D	Wallsend Park V 1911	Wallsend PV 1913	3	0	0	0	0	0	-	-	-	3	0	0
Street, Terence Edward	Poplar 9/12/1948		M	O's youth 1965	Ashford T 1967	1	0	0	0	0	0	0	0	0	1	0	0

Player	Birth	Death if known	Pos	From	To	League Apps	League Sub	League Gls	FA Cup Apps	FA Cup Sub	FA Cup Gls	FL Cup Apps	FL Cup Sub	FL Cup Gls	Total Apps	Total Sub	Total Gls
Streets, Stanley Edward E.	Grantham 25/6/1901	29/1/1961	F	Blackpool 1926	Exeter C 1928	12	0	1	1	0	0	-	-	-	13	0	1
Stride, David Roy	Lymington 14/3/1958		D	Millwall 1984	Dallas (US) 1985	29	0	0	1	0	0	4	0	0	34	0	0
Stroud, William James A.	Hammersmith 7/7/1919		D	Southampton 1946	Newport Co 1950	65	0	1	1	0	0	-	-	-	66	0	1
Surtees, Albert Edward	Wellington Quay 1902	30/7/1963	F	Southend U 1927	Wellington T 1928	1	0	0	1	0	0	-	-	-	2	0	0
Sussex, Andrew Robert	Islington 23/11/1964		M	O's youth 1980	Crewe Alexandra 1988	126	18	17	8	0	1	7	1	2	141	19	20
Sutherland, George Burns	Bathgate 11/9/1923	1969	F	Partick Thistle 1949	Hereford U 1951	42	0	22	0	0	0	-	-	-	42	0	22
Tann, Adam John	Fakenham 12/5/1982		D	Notts Co 2006	Current	8	2	1	0	0	0	0	0	0	8	2	1
Tate, Christopher Douglas	York 27/12/1977		F	Scarborough 2000	Mansfield T 2004	34	41	10	1	2	1	0	1	0	35	44	11
Taylor, Archibald	Glasgow 4/10/1918	1976	F	Reading 1948	Bath C 1951	46	0	1	1	0	0	-	-	-	47	0	1
Taylor, Harold William	Boston, Lincs 20/12/1910	15/11/1970	M	Southport 1933	Retired 1946	174	0	13	16	0	3	-	-	-	190	0	16
Taylor, John Swinley	Cowdenbeath 17/8/1909	17/3/1964	D	Halifax T 1934	Bristol C 1936	30	0	0	2	0	0	-	-	-	32	0	0
Taylor, Peter John	Southend-on-Sea 3/1/1953		F	Tottenham H 1980	Maidstone U (pl-coach) 1982	49	7	11	2	0	0	4	0	0	55	7	11
Taylor, Robert	Norwich 30/4/1971		F	Norwich C (loan) 1991	Norwich C 1991												
" "				Norwich C 1991	Brentford 1994	54	22	21	2	1	0	1	1	0	57	24	21
Taylor, Thomas Frederick	Hornchurch 26/9/1951		D	O's youth 1966	West Ham U 1970												
" "				West Ham U 1979	Charlton A 1982	228	2	9	13	0	1	13	0	0	254	2	10
Taylor, William	Edinburgh 31/7/1939	1981	M/D	Bonnyrigg Rose 1959	Nottingham F 1963	23	0	0	0	0	0	4	0	0	27	0	0
Thacker, Francis William	Sheepbridge 1876	8/9/1949	D	Chesterfield T 1906	Rotherham Co 1907	34	0	1	3	0	0	-	-	-	37	0	1
Thomas, Edward	Newton-le-Willows 23/10/1933	12/11/2003	F	Derby Co 1967	Nuneaton B 1968	11	0	2	0	0	0	0	0	0	11	0	2
Thomas, Louis Llewellyn	Fulham 4/1884		F	Fulham 1906	Tunbridge Wells R 1906	6	0	1	0	0	0	-	-	-	6	0	1
Thomas, Martin Russell	Lymington 12/9/1973		M	Southampton (loan) 1994	Southampton 1994	5	0	2	0	0	0	0	0	0	5	0	2
Thompson, Andrew	Newc'e-u-Lyme 21/1/1899	1/1/1970	F	Chester C 1932	Ashford T 1934	18	0	5	1	0	0	-	-	-	19	0	5
Thompson, Benjamin S.	Southwick Jul 1882		F	Fulham 1908	West Hartlepool U 1909	6	0	0	0	0	0	-	-	-	6	0	0
Thompson, James William	Plaistow 19/4/1898	27/8/1984	F	Coventry C 1924	Luton T 1925	1	0	0	0	0	0	-	-	-	1	0	0
Thompson, Thomas	Norwich		G	Norwich C 1906	Non-League 1907	1	0	0	0	0	0	-	-	-	1	0	0
Thomson, Norman Shaw	Glasgow 20/2/1901	6/6/1984	F	Luton T 1927	Brighton & HA 1927	10	0	2	0	0	0	-	-	-	10	0	2
Thorne, Adrian Ernest	Hove 2/8/1937		F	Exeter C 1965	Cheltenham T 1966	2	0	0	0	0	0	0	0	0	2	0	0
Thorpe, Lee Anthony	Wolverhampton 14/12/1975		F	Lincoln C 2002	Bristol Rovers 2004	42	13	12	1	0	0	2	0	1	45	13	13
Tidman, Oliver Eustace	Margate 16/3/1911		D/M	Bristol Rovers 1937	Chelmsford C 1938	1	0	0	0	0	0	-	-	-	1	0	0
Tilley, Arthur William	West Calder		F	Fletton U 1912	Lincoln C (tr) 1914	1	0	0	0	0	0	-	-	-	1	0	0
Timons, Christopher Bryan	Old Langworth 8/12/1974		D	Chesterfield 1997	Gainsborough Trinity 1998	6	0	2	0	0	0	0	0	0	6	0	2
Tolliday, Stanley Albert	Hackney 6/8/1922	Walsall 1951	G	Non-League 1946	Walsall 1950	64	0	0	2	0	0	-	-	-	66	0	0
Tomlinson, Michael Lloyd	Lambeth 15/9/1972		F	O's youth 1989	Barnet 1994	7	7	1	1	0	0	4	0	1	12	7	2
Toner, Ciaran	Craigavon, N.I. 30/6/1981		M	Bristol Rovers 2002	Lincoln C 2004	41	11	2	1	0	0	2	0	1	44	11	2
Tonner, James Edward	Bridgetown 31/3/1896	1985	F	Dunfermline 1919	Lochgelly U 1920	12	0	0	1	0	0	-	-	-	13	0	0
Tonner, John Jack	Holytown 20/2/1898	1978	F	Dunfermline 1919	Fulham 1926	143	0	35	11	0	4	-	-	-	154	0	39
Tonner, Samuel	Dunfermline 9/8/1894	1976	D	East Fife 1919	Bristol C 1925	186	0	13	8	0	0	-	-	-	194	0	13
Townley, James Chadwick	Blackburn 2/5/1902	3/2/1983	F	Brighton & HA 1929	Switzerland 1931	19	0	2	0	0	0	-	-	-	19	0	2
Townrow, John Ernest	Stratford 28/3/1901	11/4/1969	D	Fairburn House 1919	Chelsea 1927	253	0	5	12	0	0	-	-	-	265	0	5
Trailor, Cyril Henry	Merthyr Tydfil 15/5/1919	28/8/1986	M	Tottenham H 1949	Bedford T 1951	39	0	0	1	0	0	-	-	-	40	0	0

Player	Birth	Death if known	Pos	From	To	League Apps	League Sub	League Gls	FA Cup Apps	FA Cup Sub	FA Cup Gls	FL Cup Apps	FL Cup Sub	FL Cup Gls	Total Apps	Total Sub	Total Gls
Tricker, Reginald William	Karachi, India 5/10/1904	9/6/1990	F	Arsenal 1929	Margate 1933	131	0	60	6	0	3	-	-	-	137	0	63
Tudor, Shane Anthony	Wolverhampton 10/2/1982		M	Cambridge U 2005	Current	29	4	4	5	0	1	1	0	0	35	4	5
Tully, Frederick Charles A.	St Pancras 4/7/1907	28/8/1973	F	Southampton 1937	Retired 1946	57	0	18	4	0	1	-	-	-	61	0	19
Tully, James Andrew	Newcastle-upon Tyne 1885		F	West Stanley 1909	Rochdale 1911	5	0	1	0	0	0	-	-	-	5	0	1
Turley, William Lee	Wolverhampton 15/7/1973		G	North'pton T (loan) 1998	Northampton T 1998	14	0	0	0	0	0	0	0	0	14	0	0
Turnbull, Robert Hamilton	Dumbarton 22/6/1894	Dec 1944	F	Chelsea 1928	Charlton A 1929	39	0	18	4	0	0	-	-	-	43	0	18
Turner, Christopher Robert	Sheffield 15/9/1958		G	Sheffield W 1991	O's asst manager 1995	58	0	0	6	0	0	4	0	0	68	0	0
Turner, Michael Thomas	Lewisham 9/11/1983		D	Charlton A (loan) 2003	Charlton A 2003	7	0	1	0	0	0	0	0	0	7	0	1
Underwood, Austin Toby	Street 1880	1967	F	Glossop North End 1909	Non-League 1910	37	0	1	1	0	0	-	-	-	38	0	1
Van Den Eyden, Ike	Belgium		D	Belgium 1914	Belgium 1914	12	0	0	0	0	0	-	-	-	12	0	0
Vango, Alfred James	Bethnal Green 23/12/1900	24/11/1977	D	QPR 1932	London Paper Co	23	0	0	0	0	0	-	-	-	23	0	0
Vanner, Richard Thomas	Farnham 14/11/1903	15/7/1978	F	Tottenham H 1929	Aldershot 1931	35	0	4	2	0	1	-	-	-	37	0	5
Vasseur, Emmanuel	Calais, France 3/9/1976		M	Calais 2001	Calais 2001	0	2	0	0	0	0	0	0	0	0	2	0
Vincent, Robert George	Newcastle 23/11/1962		M	Sunderland 1982	Brisbane Lions (Aus) 1983	8	1	0	0	0	0	2	0	0	10	1	0
Waite, George Henry	Bradford 1/3/1894	Apr 1972	F	Leicester C 1923	Hartlepool U 1926	62	0	9	3	0	0	-	-	-	65	0	9
Waites, George Edward	Stepney 12/3/1938	24/8/2000	F	Harwich & P 1958	Norwich C 1961												
" " "				Norwich C 1962	Brighton & HA 1962	45	0	9	0	0	0	2	0	3	47	0	12
Wall, Thomas Peter	Brockton 13/9/1944		D	Crystal P (loan) 1972	Crystal Palace 1972	10	0	0	0	0	0	0	0	0	10	0	0
Waller, Henry Harold	Ashington 20/8/1917	1984	D	Arsenal 1947	Ashington 1948	17	0	0	1	0	0	-	-	-	18	0	0
Walley, John Thomas	Caernarvon 27/2/1945		D	Watford 1971	Watford 1976	155	2	6	11	0	0	7	0	0	173	2	6
Wallis, Scott	Enfield 28/6/1988		M	O's youth 2004	Current	0	3	0	0	0	0	0	0	0	0	3	0
Walschaerts, Wim	Antwerp, Belgium 5/11/1972		M	KFC Tielen (Belg) 1998	Strombeek (Belg) 2001	120	5	9	10	0	2	9	1	0	139	6	11
Walters, Thomas Charles	Trealaw 15/6/1909	27/1/1968	F	Watford 1938	Dartford 1939	23	0	9	0	0	0	-	-	-	23	0	9
Walton, Richard	Hull 12/9/1924		D	Leicester C 1948	Exeter C 1951	63	0	4	0	0	0	-	-	-	63	0	4
Ward, Felix	Seaham Harbour 1886		F	Fulham 1908	Southend U 1909	33	0	1	0	0	0	-	-	-	33	0	1
Ward, Gerald	Stepney 5/10/1936	Jan 1994	M	Arsenal 1963	Cambridge C 1965	44	0	2	1	0	0	3	0	0	48	0	2
Ward, Paul Terence	Fishburn 15/9/1963		M	Darlington 1988	Scunthorpe U 1989	30	1	1	3	0	1	5	0	0	38	1	2
Wardley, Stuart James	Cambridge 10/9/1974		M	Torquay U 2002	Cambridge U 2005	4	2	0	0	1	0	0	0	0	4	3	0
Ware, Edward Alfrred G.	Chatham 17/9/1906	10/9/1976	F	Brentford 1933	Swindon T 1936	106	0	3	8	0	1	-	-	-	114	0	4
Warren, Mark Wayne	Hackney 12/11/1974		D/M	O's youth 1991	Notts County 1999	134	18	5	5	1	0	8	1	2	147	20	7
Waterall, Albert	Radford 1/3/1887	8/3/1963	D	QPR 1926	Grantham 1927	2	0	1	0	0	0	-	-	-	2	0	1
Watson, George Sutton	Milton Regis 10/4/1907	1/4/1974	F	Crystal Palace 1931	Nuneaton B 1932	2	0	0	0	0	0	-	-	-	2	0	0
Watson, Mark Leon	Birmingham 28/12/1973		F	West Ham U (loan) 1995	West Ham U 1995	0	1	1	0	0	0	0	0	0	0	1	1
Watts, Ernest Albert	Woolhampton 1874		D/G	Reading 1906	Reading 1907	2	0	0	0	0	0	-	-	-	2	0	0
Watts, Steven	Peckham 11/7/1976		F	Fisher A 1998	Shrewsbury T 2003	69	63	29	8	3	4	5	2	2	82	68	35
Weaver, Luke Dennis S.	Woolwich 26/6/1979		G	O's youth 1996	Sunderland 1998	9	0	0	1	0	0	10	0	0	10	0	0
Webb, David James	Stratford 9/4/1946		D	West Ham U youth 1963	Southampton 1966	63	0	3	1	0	0	3	0	0	66	0	3
Webb, Simon	Castle Bar, Ireland 19/1/1978		D/M	Tottenham H 1999	Bohemians (Ireland) 2000	3	1	0	0	0	0	0	0	0	3	1	0
Wedge, Roger	Prenton Park 6/3/1944		F	O's youth 1961	Tunbridge Wells 1963	0	0	0	0	0	0	1	0	0	1	0	0
Wells, Peter Alan	Nottingham 13/8/1956		G	Millwall 1985	Fisher A 1989	148	0	0	17	0	0	13	0	0	178	0	0

Player	Birth	Death if known	Pos	From	To	League Apps	League Sub	League Gls	FA Cup Apps	FA Cup Sub	FA Cup Gls	FL Cup Apps	FL Cup Sub	FL Cup Gls	Total Apps	Total Sub	Total Gls
Wells, Thomas Charles	Nunhead 21/9/1905	13/8/1971	F	Swindon T 1936	Retired 1937	4	0	1	0	0	0	-	-	-	4	0	1
Welton, Roy Patrick	Eltham 3/5/1928		G	Chislehurst 1949	QPR 1958	263	0	0	18	0	0	-	-	-	281	0	0
Went, Paul Frank	Bromley-by-Bow 12/10/1949		D	O's youth 1965	Charlton A 1967												
" " "				Cardiff C 1976	O's coach 1979	93	2	8	6	0	0	2	0	0	101	2	8
Werge, Edwin	Sidcup 9/9/1936		F	Arcadia Sh (S Africa) 1966	Bexley U 1968	30	3	0	1	1	0	1	0	0	32	4	0
West, Colin	Wallsend 13/11/1962		F	Swansea C 1993	Rushden & Diam'ds 1998	132	10	43	7	0	2	6	0	2	145	10	47
Westcott, Jonathan	Shoreditch		F	Non-League 1905	Non-League 1906	0	0	0	1	0	0	-	-	-	1	0	0
Whipp, Percival	Gorbals, Glasgow 28/6/1893		F	Ton Pentre 1921	Sunderland 1922												
" "				Leeds U 1927	Brentford 1929	88	0	25	6	0	1	-	-	-	94	0	26
Whitbread, Adrian Richard	Epping 22/10/1971		D	O's youth 1989	Swindon T 1993	125	0	2	11	0	1	10	1	0	146	1	3
White, Alan	Darlington 22/3/1976		D	Colchester U 2004	Boston U 2005	26	0	0	2	0	0	1	0	0	29	0	0
White, Philip George John	Fulham 29/12/1930	Jun 2000	F	Wealdstone 1953	Retired (injured) 1964	217	0	28	10	0	0	6	0	0	233	0	28
White, Thomas	London 1883		F	Non-League 1904	Non-League 1905	-	-	-	1	0	1	-	-	-	1	0	1
Whitehouse, Brian	West Bromwich 8/9/1935		F	Charlton A 1966	Luton T (coach) 1988	52	0	6	3	0	1	1	0	0	56	0	7
Whiteley, Albert	Sheffield 13/7/1932		F	Sheffield Wed 1952	Ramsgate A 1954	18	0	3	0	0	0	-	-	-	18	0	3
Whittaker, James Henry	Bolton		F	Manchester C 1907	Non-League 1908	17	0	1	5	0	2	-	-	-	22	0	3
Whittaker, Walter	Manchester 20/9/1878	2/6/1917	G	Reading 1907	Exeter C 1910	90	0	0	6	0	0	-	-	-	96	0	0
Whittle, Alan	Liverpool 10/3/1950		F	Sheffield U (tr) 1976	Persepolis (Iran) 1977												
" "				Persepolis (Iran) 1977	AFC Bournemouth 1980	47	3	6	3	0	2	2	3	0	52	6	8
Whyte, Christopher A.	Islington 2/9/1961		D	Detroit Neon (USA) 1997	Oxford U 1997	1	0	0	0	0	0	0	0	0	1	0	0
Whyte, Crawford	Ryhope 4/12/1907	11/8/1984	D	Hartlepool U 1938	Floriana (Malta) 1939	6	0	0	0	0	0	-	-	-	6	0	0
Wightman, Thomas	London		D	Non-League 1905	Non-League 1906	0	0	0	1	0	0	-	-	-	1	0	0
Wilder, Christopher John	Stocksbridge 23/9/1967		D	Sheffield U (loan) 1992	Sheffield U 1992	16	0	1	0	0	0	0	0	0	16	0	1
Wilkie, Glen Alan	Bethnal Green 22/1/1977		D/M	O's youth 1995	IFK Mariehamn 1997	10	1	0	0	0	0	0	0	0	10	1	0
Wilkins, Dean Mark	Hillingdon 12/7/1962		M	Brighton & HA (loan) 1984	Brighton & HA 1984	10	0	0	0	0	0	0	0	0	10	0	0
Wilkins, Raymond Colin	Hillingdon 14/9/1956		M	Millwall 1997	Fulham asst manager 1997	3	0	0	0	0	0	0	0	0	3	0	0
Willemse, Stanley Bernard	Hove 23/8/1924		D	Chelsea 1956	Retired 1958	59	0	2	1	0	0	-	-	-	60	0	2
Williams, Emlyn	Aberaman 1903		F	Aberdare T 1928	Hull C 1929	4	0	1	0	0	0	-	-	-	4	0	1
Williams, Ernest Harold	Rhyl		D	Rhyl 1907	Rhyl 1908	5	0	0	0	0	0	-	-	-	5	0	0
Williams, Jack Walter	Bury		F	Bury 1909	Leyton 1910	12	0	3	0	0	0	-	-	-	12	0	3
Williams, Jesse Thomas	Cefn-y-Bedd 24/6/1903	20/10/1972	F	Middlesbrough 1928	Rhyl 1929	31	0	3	1	0	0	-	-	-	32	0	3
Williams, Lee	Harold Hill 13/3/1977		M	O's youth 1995	Billericay T 1999	1	2	0	1	0	0	0	0	0	2	2	0
Williams, Michael John	Stepney 9/10/1978		M	O's youth 1997	Sligo Rovers (Ireland) 1998	0	1	0	0	0	0	0	0	0	0	1	0
Williams, Owen	Ryhope 23/9/1895	9/12/1960	F	Easington Colliery 1919	Middlesbrough 1924	162	0	33	8	0	2	-	-	-	170	0	35
Williams, Roderick	Newport 2/12/1909	Aug 1987	F	West Ham U 1938	Retired 1942	35	0	16	2	0	2	-	-	-	37	0	18
Williams, Thomas H.	Easington 23/5/1899	14/12/1960	F	Ryhope Colliery 1921	Charlton A 1923	26	0	6	0	0	0	-	-	-	26	0	6
Willingham, Alfred	London		F	Non-League 1910	Millwall (tr) 1911	1	0	0	0	0	0	-	-	-	1	0	0
Willis, Harold Herbert	Clapton		D	Clapton Warwick 1908	Maidstone U 1914	136	0	1	5	0	0	-	-	-	141	0	1
Wiilis, Ronald Ian	Romford, 27/12/1947		G	O's youth 1966	Charlton A 1967	45	0	0	3	0	0	2	0	0	50	0	0
Willshaw, George James	Hackney 18/10/1912	Sep 1993	F	Bristol C 1939	Retired 1947	12	0	2	0	0	0	-	-	-	12	0	2

Player	Birth	Death if known	Pos	From	To	League Apps	League Sub	League Gls	FA Cup Apps	FA Cup Sub	FA Cup Gls	FL Cup Apps	FL Cup Sub	FL Cup Gls	Total Apps	Total Sub	Total Gls
Wilmot, Rhys James	Rogiet, Newport 21/2/1962		G	Arsenal (loan) 1984	Arsenal 1985	46	0	0	4	0	0	4	0	0	54	0	0
Wingham, Harold Charles	Selsey 25/6/1895	24/2/1969	D	Bournemouth &BA 1924	Norwich C 1925	5	0	0	0	0	0	-	-	-	5	0	0
Winston, Samuel Anthony	Islington 6/8/1978		F	Tottenham H 1996	Yeovil T 1997	3	8	1	0	2	1	0	0	0	3	10	2
Witheridge, Thomas Henry	Amersham 25/5/1911	7/3/1985	F	Non-League 1931	Non-League 1932	1	0	0	0	0	0	-	-	-	1	0	0
Woan, Donald	Bootle 7/11/1927		F	Liverpool 1951	Bradford C 1952	25	0	5	9	0	0	-	-	-	34	0	5
Wood, Arthur	Walsall 14/1/1894	8/4/21941	G	Southampton 1921	Ryde Sports 1931	373	0	0	22	0	0	-	-	-	395	0	0
Wood, Brian Thomas	Hamworthy 8/12/1940		D	Crystal Palace 1966	Colchester U 1968	58	0	3	5	0	0	1	0	0	64	0	3
Wood, Edward John	West Ham 23/10/1919	Oct 1993	F	West Ham U 1949	Margate 1950	9	0	1	1	0	0	-	-	-	10	0	1
Woodward, Joseph Henry	Catford Feb 1904	1974	G	Southend U 1927	QPR 1928	1	0	0	0	0	0	-	-	-	1	0	0
Woodward, Kenneth Robert	Battersea 16/11/1947		F	Crystal Palace 1966	Non-League 1967	1	0	0	0	0	0	-	-	-	1	0	0
Woosnam, Philip Abraham	Caersws 22/12/1932		F	Sutton U 1954	West Ham U 1958	108	0	19	4	0	0	-	-	-	112	0	19
Wootten, James Thomas	Midlands		F	Leyton 1905	Leyton 1906	10	0	2	1	0	0	-	-	-	11	0	2
Worboys, Allen Albert A.	Barnet 7/11/1899	11/5/1980	D	Army 1919	Crawford U 1923	43	0	1	3	0	0	-	-	-	46	0	1
Worrell, Colin Harvey	Great Yarmouth 29/8/1943		D	Norwich C 1964	Charlton A 1966	51	0	0	1	0	0	1	0	0	53	0	0
Wright, George William	Ramsgate 19/3/1930	Sep 2000	D	West Ham U 1958	Gillingham 1962	87	0	1	1	0	0	0	0	0	88	0	1
Wright, William Peter	Sheffield 1903	Oct 1993	D	Non-League 1930	O's trainer 1935	1	0	0	0	0	0	-	-	-	1	0	0
Yardley, James	Wishaw 16/4/1903	24/9/1959	F	Bellhaven Oaks 1925	Third Lanark 1927	29	0	3	0	0	0	-	-	-	29	0	3
Yews, Thomas Pearce	Wingate 28/2/1902	19/8/1966	F	West Ham U 1933	Retired 1934	3	0	0	0	0	0	-	-	-	3	0	0
Youngs, Thomas Anthony J.	Bury St Edmunds 31/8/1979		M	Northampton T 2005	Bury 2005	6	4	1	0	0	0	0	0	0	6	4	1
Zakuani, Gabriel	Kinshasa, Zaire 31/5/1986		D	O's youth 2002	Fulham	84	3	3	7	0	0	2	0	0	93	3	3
Zoricich, Christopher Vincent	Henderson (NZ) 3/5/1969		D	Papatoetoe (NZ) 1990	Central U (NZ) 1993	53	9	1	2	2	0	4	1	0	59	12	1

** Peter Allen club appearance record holder.
* Tommy Johnston club goals record holder.

Play-off appearances and records

Leyton Orient have played in three promotional Play-offs – 1988–89, 1998–99 and 2000–01, they have made the Finals on each occasion winning one and losing two. The policy of the Football League is appearances in Play-offs are classed as 'other matches' and have never, as yet, been recorded in League totals. Therefore, players who have appeared in Play-off matches for O's are recorded below.

1988–89
Semi-final: 1
1st Leg: Leyton Orient 2 Scarborough 0, 2nd Leg: Scarborough 1 Leyton Orient 0
Final: 1st Leg Wrexham 0 Leyton Orient 0, 2nd Leg: Leyton Orient 2 (Harvey, Cooper) Wrexham 1

1998–99
Semi-final: 1st Leg: Leyton Orient 0 Rotherham United 0, 2nd Leg: Rotherham United 0 Leyton Orient 0 (Orient won 4–2 on penalties)
Final: Leyton Orient 0 Scunthorpe United 0 (At Wembley Stadium)

2000–01
Semi-final: 1st Leg: Hull City 1 Leyton Orient 0, 2nd Leg: Leyton Orient 2 (Watts, Lockwood) Hull City 0
Final: Blackpool 4 Leyton Orient 0 (At Millennium Stadium) (Tate, Houghton)

Player	*Season*	*Appearances*		*Goals*
		Apps	*Sub*	
Baker, Stephen	1988–89	4	0	0
Barrett, Scott	1998–99	3	0	0
Bayes, Ashley	2000–01	3	0	0
Beall, William	1998–99	3	0	0
Brkovic, Ahmet	2000–01	0	2	0
Carter, Daniel	1988–89	0	1	0
Castle, Stephen	1988–89 & 2000–01	6	1	0
Clark, Simon	1998–99	3	0	0
Comfort, Alan	1988–89	4	0	0
Cooper, Mark	1988–89	4	0	3
Day, Keith	1988–89	4	0	0
Dickenson, Kevin	1988–89	4	0	0
Downer, Simon	2000–01	3	0	0
Hales, Kevin	1988–89	4	0	0
Harris, Andrew	2000–01	1	1	0
Harvey, Lee	1988–89	4	0	1
Heald, Paul	1988–89	4	0	0
Hicks, Stuart	1998–99	1	1	0

Houghton, Scott	2000–01	3	0	1
Howard, Terence	1988–89	4	0	0
Ibehre, Jabo	2000–01	3	0	0
Inglethorpe, Alex	1998–99	0	2	0
Joseph, Matthew	1998–99 & 2000–01	4	0	0
Joseph, Roger	1998–99	3	0	0
Ling, Martin	1998–99	3	0	0
Lockwood, Matthew	1998–99 & 2000–01	6	0	1
McGhee, David	2000–01	3	0	0
Martin, John	2000–01	0	2	0
Maskell, Craig	1998–99	0	2	0
Morrison, David	1998–99	0	1	0
Richards, Anthony	1998–99	3	0	0
Simba, Amara	1998–99	3	0	0
Sitton, John	1988–89	4	0	0
Smith, Dean	1998–99 & 2000–01	6	0	0
Stimson, Mark	1998–99	1	1	0
Tate, Christopher	2000–01	1	2	1
Walschaerts, Wim	2000–01	3	0	0
Ward, Paul	1988–89	0	3	0
Watts, Steven	1998–99 & 2000–01	5	0	1

The 1939–40 expunged season

The season was ended after just three matches when World War Two started. The League was abandoned and all playing records were expunged. These are the players who played for the O's in those three matches.

Player	*Apps*	*Goals*
Allum, Leonard	1	0
Black, Robert	3	0
Bungay, Reginald	3	0
Ellis, John	3	0
Gore, Leslie	3	1
Hann, Leslie	2	0
McFadyen, William	3	0
McNeil, John	3	0
Rumbold, George	3	0
Smith, Harold	1	0
Taylor, Harold	2	0
Williams, Roderick	3	2
Willshaw, George	3	0

Roll of Honour

Adam Akers
Alan Akers
Ian Anders
Bill Appleby
Michael Ashdown
Bill Badger
Ted Baker
Mike Bakewell
Keith Bardoe
Dennis Barefield
Tom Baxter
Ted Bell
Adam Bickmore
Martin Bickmore
Matt 'The Hat' Bilby
Martin Bird
Michael Bird
William Bird
David Block
Helen Block
Paul Bonney
Michael Brangwyn
Les Bristow
Matt Bristow
Roy Jeffrey Brown
Chris Buckley
Robert Budd
Russell Burcham
Kevin Burdekin

Barry Burke
Paul Bushell
Trevor Bushell
Elliot Michael Byrne
Ryan Campen
Frank Cass
Steve Cedar
Alan J. Chandler
Alby Clark
Steve Clarke
Alex Clifford
James Clifford
Roy Clifford
Christopher Convey
David J. Cook
Phill Cook
Andrew Cornwall
Michael Cornwall
Michael J. Cornwall
Mick Counter
Andrew Cowell
Stuart Cracknell
Roy Cushway
Steve Daniels
Haydn Davies
Christopher Davis
Keith Davis
Keith Davis
Dennis Dawkins
Michael Defries
Nicholas Dixon
Michael Dockerty

David Dodd
Mark Dollemore
Chris Doulin
Ron Dullage
D. Edwards
Julian Jay Edwards
Kenneth John Edwards
Pam Edwards
Robert John Edwards
Terry Ellis
David J. Evans
Steve Fowell
Graham Frake
Kevin Frake
Fred Gammons
Henry J. Garratt
Denis Gibbard
Basil David Giddens
David Fredrick Giddens
Leslie John Giddens
Irving Gold
Vasco Gomes
Graham Goodall
Tim Goodworth
David Gould
David Graham
James Graham
David Grisdale
David Groves
Alan Harvey
Richard Hayden (Burgerman)
Bryan E. Herman

Colin B. Herman
Michael Higgins
Homerton College
C.J. Horsnell
Geoff Hotten
Steve Howlett
Ron Hudson
Terry D. Hurley
Daniel C. Hyde
Frederick Jackson
David James
David Jenkins
Stephen Jenkins
Jean Johnston
Tommy Johnston
Allan Jones
Richard Kavanagh
Chris Kennedy
Graham Kennedy
A.C. Kingston
Dave Knight
J. Lambert
Gary Lane
The Lay Family
Gary Lewis
Gary Lewis
Justin Lindy
Stephen Lord
Ronald Loveless
Albert Mansfield
Malcolm Mears
Gary Mellish

Jean-Louis Micallef
Steve Micallef
Walter Micallef
Gary Moore
Colin Murrell
Steve Neal
Alan Nicholls
David Nicholls
Janice Nichols
Linda Nichols
Ray Nichols
David R. Nolson
Taylor Northrop
Kevin Paul Nunn
Paul Nunn
Nigel Oattes
Jim O'Leary
Katie O'Leary
Gudrun Osborne
Tony Osborne
Patersons, Bexley
Michael Perdeaux
Grant Ian Perry
James Pettigrew
John Pettigrew
James Pope
David Randlesome
Suzanne Randlesome
Andrew Raybould
Philip Renew
James Restall
William Restall

Norman Reynolds
Brian Rigby
Graham Roast
Paul Roberts
Stan Robertson
John Rochford
Stephen Rooks
Clive H. Rosen
"Funky" Lol Ross
Michael J. Ryan
Geoff Salmon
John Samuels
Keith Saville
Martin Scott
Philip Shamplina
Barry Sherrick
Colin Sherrin
Simon Shipperlee
Terry Shuttleworth
Ed Silvester
Brian L. Smith
Martin P. Smith
Nigel Smith
Theodore Arthur Balfour Smith
Sonenfield Family
Gary Stevenson
Paul Stevenson
Martin Strong
Ken Sutton
Scott Tappin
J. Tarrant
John Taylor

Alan Thomas
Tommy Tomkins
Kieran Toms
Tony Ruffy
Sid Toole
Michael Toull
Alan Trollope
Alan G. Turner
Keith Underwood
John Veale
Lee Veale
Ian Waldron
Kevin Wallbank
Dave Watkins
John Watts
Roger Webber
William Welton
Kathy White
Michael Williams
David Emas-Willis
Paul Stephen Willis
Brad Wilson
Tony Wilson
Keith S. Winch
Jeff Wiseman
Mark Wiseman
Stephen Withers
David J. Wixley
Paul Wood
Rob Worthington
David H. York
Michael Young